THE CONCISE ENCYCLOPEDIA OF COMMUNICATION

The *International Communication Association* (ICA) is an academic association for scholars interested in the study, teaching, and application of all aspects of human and mediated communication. ICA began more than 50 years ago as a small association of US researchers and is now a truly international association, with more than 4,500 members in 80 countries. Since 2003, ICA has been officially associated with the United Nations as a non-governmental association. The ICA has partnered with Wiley Blackwell to publish the 12-volume *International Encyclopedia of Communication* (Donsbach 2008, www.communicationencyclopedia.com).

THE CONCISE ENCYCLOPEDIA OF
COMMUNICATION

EDITED BY
WOLFGANG DONSBACH

WILEY Blackwell

This edition first published 2015
© 2015 John Wiley & Sons, Inc.

Registered Office
John Wiley & Sons, Ltd., The Atrium, Southern Gate, Chichester, West Sussex, PO19 8SQ, UK

Editorial Offices
350 Main Street, Malden, MA 02148-5020, USA
9600 Garsington Road, Oxford, OX4 2DQ, UK
The Atrium, Southern Gate, Chichester, West Sussex, PO19 8SQ, UK

For details of our global editorial offices, for customer services, and for information about how to apply for permission to reuse the copyright material in this book please see our website at www.wiley.com/wiley-blackwell.

The right of Wolfgang Donsbach to be identified as the author of the editorial material in this work has been asserted in accordance with the UK Copyright, Designs and Patents Act 1988.

All rights reserved. No part of this publication may be reproduced, stored in a retrieval system, or transmitted, in any form or by any means, electronic, mechanical, photocopying, recording or otherwise, except as permitted by the UK Copyright, Designs and Patents Act 1988, without the prior permission of the publisher.

Wiley also publishes its books in a variety of electronic formats. Some content that appears in print may not be available in electronic books.

Designations used by companies to distinguish their products are often claimed as trademarks. All brand names and product names used in this book are trade names, service marks, trademarks or registered trademarks of their respective owners. The publisher is not associated with any product or vendor mentioned in this book.

Limit of Liability/Disclaimer of Warranty: While the publisher and authors have used their best efforts in preparing this book, they make no representations or warranties with respect to the accuracy or completeness of the contents of this book and specifically disclaim any implied warranties of merchantability or fitness for a particular purpose. It is sold on the understanding that the publisher is not engaged in rendering professional services and neither the publisher nor the author shall be liable for damages arising herefrom. If professional advice or other expert assistance is required, the services of a competent professional should be sought.

Library of Congress Cataloging-in-Publication Data

The concise encyclopedia of communication / edited by Wolfgang Donsbach.
    pages   cm
  Includes bibliographical references and index.
  ISBN 978-1-118-78930-8 (cloth) – ISBN 978-1-118-78932-2 (pbk.)   1. Communication–Encyclopedias.
 I. Donsbach, Wolfgang, 1949– editor.
  P87.5.C66 2015
  302′.03–dc23

2014029776

A catalogue record for this book is available from the British Library.

Cover image: © Zffoto /Shutterstock

Set in 9.5/11.5pt Minion by SPi Publisher Services, Pondicherry, India
Printed and bound in Malaysia by Vivar Printing Sdn Bhd

Contents

Contributors — vi

Introduction — xvii

Acknowledgments — xxi

Lexicon — xxiii

Communication A–Z — 1

Index — 660

Contributors

Walid A. Afifi, University of Iowa

Iftekhar Ahmed, University of North Texas

Sameer Ahmed, Wilmer Cutler Pickering Hale and Dorr LLP

Alan B. Albarran, University of North Texas

Stuart Allan, Cardiff University, UK

Tim Ambler, London Business School

Kay Amert, University of Iowa

Soontae An, Ewha Womans University

Robin Andersen, Fordham University

C. W. Anderson, College of Staten Island (CUNY)

James A. Anderson, University of Utah

Marc Andrejevic, University of Iowa

Charles Antaki, Loughborough University

Cristiano Antonelli, University of Turin

Osei Appiah, Ohio State University

Paul Arblaster, Zuyd University, Maastricht

Ronald C. Arnett, Duquesne University

Chris Atton, Edinburgh Napier University

Robert K. Avery, University of Utah

Ana Azurmendi, University of Navarra

Beth Babin-Gallagher, Arizona State University

Christine Bachen, Santa Clara University

Philip M. Backlund, Central Washington University

Jeremy N. Bailenson, Stanford University

Michael Bailey, University of Essex

Susan C. Baker, Cape Breton University

Sandra J. Ball-Rokeach, University of Southern California

Albert Bandura, Stanford University

Jo Bardoel, University of Amsterdam and Radboud University Nijmegen

Brooke Barnett, Elon University

Kevin G. Barnhurst, University of Leeds

Naomi S. Baron, American University

Benjamin J. Bates, University of Tennessee

Leslie A. Baxter, University of Iowa

Geoffrey Baym, University of North Carolina at Greensboro

Wayne A. Beach, San Diego State University

Bart Beaty, University of Calgary

Martin Becerra, National University of Quilmes

CONTRIBUTORS

Lee B. Becker, University of Georgia

Johannes W. J. Beentjes, University of Amsterdam

Jon Bekken, Albright College

George E. Belch, San Diego State University

Michael A. Belch, San Diego State University

William L. Benoit, Ohio University

Gary Bente, University of Cologne

Günter Bentele, University of Leipzig

Bethan Benwell, University of Stirling

Evangelia Berdou, Institute of Development Studies

Charles R. Berger, University of California, Davis

John Beynon, University of Glamorgan

Helena Bilandzic, University of Augsburg

Daniel Biltereyst, Ghent University

S. Elizabeth Bird, University of South Florida

Thomas Birkner, University of Münster

Jay David Bolter, Georgia Institute of Technology

Heinz Bonfadelli, University of Zurich

Melanie Booth-Butterfield, West Virginia University

Jérôme Bourdon, Tel Aviv University

Nicholas David Bowman, West Virginia University

Andy Boyan, Michigan State University

Oliver Boyd-Barrett, Bowling Green State University

Dale Brashers, University of Illinois at Urbana–Champaign

Peggy Simcic Brønn, Norwegian School of Management

Fred Bronner, University of Amsterdam

Hans-Bernd Brosius, Ludwig Maximilian University of Munich

Jennings Bryant, University of Alabama

Richard Buchanan, Case Western Reserve University

Warren Buckland, Oxford Brookes University

Moniek Buijzen, Radboud University Nijmegen

Roland Burkart, University of Vienna

Robert Burnett, Karlstad University

Brad Bushman, Ohio State University

Richard Buttny, Syracuse University

Carolyn M. Byerly, Howard University

Andrew Calabrese, University of Colorado at Boulder

John T. Caldwell, University of California, Los Angeles

Daniel J. Canary, Arizona State University

Joseph N. Cappella, University of Pennsylvania

Donal Carbaugh, University of Massachusetts-Amherst

Nico Carpentier, Free University of Brussels and Charles University in Prague

Craig E. Carroll, New York University

Cynthia Carter, Cardiff University

Lisa Cartwright, University of California, San Diego

Fred H. Cate, Indiana University

Young-Gil Chae, Hankuk University of Foreign Studies

Anita Chi-Kwan Lee, University of Hong Kong

Jay P. Childers, University of Kansas

Lars Thøger Christensen, Copenhagen Business School

Clifford G. Christians, University of Illinois Urbana–Champaign

Steven E. Clayman, University of California, Los Angeles

Richard Clément, University of Ottawa

Paul Cobley, Middlesex University

David L. Collinson, Lancaster University Management School

Martin Conboy, University of Sheffield

Caryn A. Conley, New York University

Mike Conway, Indiana University

W. Timothy Coombs, University of Central Florida

Ann Cooper-Chen, Ohio University

François Cooren, University of Montreal

Joep P. Cornelissen, VU University Amsterdam and University of Leeds

Robert L. Craig, University of St. Thomas

Robert T. Craig, University of Colorado at Boulder

Diana Crane-Hevre, University of Pennsylvania

Sean Cubitt, Goldsmiths, University of London

William R. Cupach, Illinois State University

Michael Curtin, University of California, Santa Barbara

John Daly, University of Texas at Austin

Gregor Daschmann, Johannes Gutenberg University of Mainz

Sandra Davidson, University of Missouri–Columbia

John Davies, Brigham Young University

James W. Dearing, Michigan State University

Marjan de Bruin, University of the West Indies, Jamaica

Patrick de Pelsmacker, University of Antwerp and Ghent University

Emmanuel Derieux, University of Paris II

Mark Deuze, Indiana University Bloomington

Sherry Devereaux Ferguson, University of Ottawa

Hazel Dicken-Garcia, University of Minnesota

James Price Dillard, Pennsylvania State University

Gail Dines, Wheelock College, Boston

Marya L. Doerfel, Rutgers University

David Domingo, Université Libre de Bruxelles

Wolfgang Donsbach, Dresden University of Technology

Johanna Dorer, University of Vienna

John D. H. Downing, Southern Illinois University

Rob Drew, Saginaw Valley State University

Sharon Dunwoody, University of Wisconsin–Madison

Timothy Edgar, Emerson College

Renee Edwards, Louisiana State University

Mara Einstein, Queens College, City University of New York

Martin Eisend, European University Viadrina in Frankfurt (Oder)

Paul Ekblom, University of the Arts London

Lyombe Eko, University of Iowa

C. Michael Elavsky, Pennsylvania State University

Donald G. Ellis, University of Hartford

Richard Leo Enos, Texas Christian University

Franz-Rudolf Esch, EBS Unversity of Business and Law

Frank Esser, University of Zurich

William P. Eveland, Jr., Ohio State University

David R. Ewoldsen, Ohio State University

Andreas Fahr, University of Fribourg

Anthony L. Fargo, Indiana University

Bob M. Fennis, University of Groningen

Shalom M. Fisch, MediaKidz Research & Consulting

Martin Fishbein, University of Pennsylvania

Carla L. Fisher, George Mason University

Wes Fondren, Coastal Carolina University

Kirsten Foot, University of Washington

John A. Fortunato, Fordham Graduate School of Business

Karen A. Foss, University of New Mexico

Jesse Fox, Stanford University

Lawrence R. Frey, University of Colorado Boulder

Ann Bainbridge Frymier, Miami University

Robert N. Gaines, University of Maryland

Cindy Gallois, University of Queensland

Shiv Ganesh, Massey University

Seeta Peña Gangadharan, Open Technology Institute

Cecilie Gaziano, Research Solutions, Inc., Minneapolis, MN, USA

Katja Gelbrich, Catholic University of Eichstaett-Ingolstadt

Cherian George, Hong Kong Baptist University

Eytan Gilboa, Bar-Ilan University

Howard Giles, University of California, Santa Barbara

Rosalind Gill, City University, London

Carroll J. Glynn, Ohio State University

Daena J. Goldsmith, Lewis & Clark College

Dennis S. Gouran, Pennsylvania State University

Karla K. Gower, University of Alabama

Doris A. Graber, University of Illinois at Chicago

John O. Greene, Purdue University

Kimberly Gregson, Ithaca College

Michael Griffin, Macalester College

Robert J. Griffin, Marquette University

Kristen Grimmer, University of Kansas

Bruce E. Gronbeck, University of Iowa

Jacob Groshek, Boston University

Lawrence Grossberg, University of North Carolina at Chapel Hill

Laura K. Guerrero, Arizona State University

Barrie Gunter, University of Leicester

Robert A. Hackett, Simon Fraser University

Nina Haferkamp, Independent Scholar

Michael L. Haley, International Communication Association

Jon Hall, University of Otago

Kirk Hallahan, Colorado State University

Martin Halstuk, Penn State University

Cees Hamelink, University of Amsterdam

Dale Hample, University of Maryland

Thomas Hanitzsch, Ludwig Maximilian University of Munich

Hans V. Hansen, University of Windsor

Joy L. Hart, University of Louisville

Maren Hartmann, Berlin University of the Arts

Tilo Hartmann, VU University Amsterdam

Jake Harwood, University of Arizona

Uwe Hasebrink, Hans Bredow Institute for Media Research at the University of Hamburg

Robert Hassan, University of Melbourne

Richard Hawkins, University of Calgary

Robert Hawkins, University of Wisconsin–Madison

Andrew F. Hayes, Ohio State University

Robert L. Heath, University of Houston

Lorna Heaton, University of Montreal

Radha S. Hegde, New York University

Don Heider, Loyola University Chicago

Heikki Heikkila, University of Tampere

Amanda R. Hemmesch, St. Cloud State University

Alfred Hermida, University of British Columbia

Susan C. Herring, Indiana University

Douglas Blanks Hindman, Washington State University

Lindsay H. Hoffman, University of Delaware

Christina Holtz-Bacha, University of Erlangen-Nuremberg

CONTRIBUTORS

Derina Holtzhausen, Oklahoma State University

Gregory G. Holyk, Langer Research Associates

James M. Honeycutt, Louisisana State University

Jan-Christopher Horak, University of California, Los Angeles

Edward Horowitz, Cleveland State University

Brant Houston, University of Illinois Urbana–Champaign

Chia-Fang (Sandy) Hsu, University of Wyoming

Heather E. Hudson, University of Alaska Anchorage

Robert Huesca, Trinity University

L. Rowell Huesmann, University of Michigan

Michael E. Huge, Ohio State University

Wendy Hui Kyong Chun, Brown University

Craig R. Hullett, University of Wisconsin–Madison

Mary Lee Hummert, University of Kansas

Myiah J. Hutchens, University of Arizona

Holly R. Hutchins, University of Houston (retired)

Cornelia Ilie, Zayed University, Abu Dhabi

Yasuhiro Inoue, Hiroshima City University

Youichi Ito, Akita International University

Shanto Iyengar, Stanford University

Matt Jackson, Pennsylvania State University

Thomas Jacobson, Temple University

Adam Jacobsson, Stockholm University

Eva-Maria Jacobsson, KTH Royal Institute of Technology

Sue Curry Jansen, Muhlenberg College

Sharon E. Jarvis, University of Texas at Austin

Per Jauert, Aarhus University

Leo W. Jeffres, Cleveland State University

Klaus Bruhn Jensen, University of Copenhagen

Robert Jensen, University of Texas at Austin

Kathryn Jenson White, University of Oklahoma

Suneel Jethani, University of Melbourne

Carey Jewitt, University of London

John Jirik, Lehigh University

Susanne M. Jones, University of Minnesota

Garth Jowett, University of Houston

Joo-Young Jung, International Christian University

Richard Kahn, University of North Dakota

Lynda Lee Kaid, University of Florida

Anja Kalch, University of Augsburg

Ali M. Kanso, University of Texas at San Antonio

Stuart Jay Kaplan, Lewis and Clark College

Tamar Katriel, University of Haifa

Patricia Kearney, California State University, Long Beach

Patrick Keating, Trinity University

William Keith, University of Wisconsin–Milwaukee

Kathy Kellermann, ComCon Kathy Kellermann Communication Consulting

Douglas Kellner, University of California, Los Angeles

Susan Kemper, University of Kansas

Hans Mathias Kepplinger, Johannes Gutenberg University of Mainz

Robert L. Kerr, University of Oklahoma

Joann Keyton, North Carolina State University

Do Kyun Kim, University of Louisiana Lafayette

Joohan Kim, Yonsei University

Young Yun Kim, University of Oklahoma

Paul E. King, Texas Christian University

Spiro Kiousis, University of Florida

Jenny Kitzinger, Cardiff University

Ullamaija Kivikuru, University of Helsinki

Jan Kleinnijenhuis, Free University Amsterdam

Wolfgang Kleinwächter, Aarhus University

Christoph Klimmt, Hanover University of Music, Drama, and Media

Thomas Knieper, University of Passau

Leanne K. Knobloch, University of Illinois

Silvia Knobloch-Westerwick, Ohio State University

Karlyn Kohrs Campbell, University of Minnesota

Elly A. Konijn, Vrije Universiteit Amsterdam

Emily Zobel Kontos, Harvard School of Public Health

Irene Koshick, University of Illinois at Urbana–Champaign

Marwan M. Kraidy, University of Pennsylvania

Klaus Krippendorff, University of Pennsylvania

Michael Kunczik, Johannes Gutenberg University of Mainz (Emeritus)

William M. Kunz, University of Washington Tacoma

Jacqueline Lambiase, Texas Christian University

Claudia Lampert, Hans-Bredow-Institut, Hamburg

Richard Leo Lanigan, Jr., Southern Illinois University

Thomas B. Lawrence, Simon Fraser University

Anahí Lazarte-Morales, Our Lady of Grace School

Eun-Ju Lee, Seoul National University

Kwan Min Lee, University of Southern California

Tien-Tsung Lee, University of Kansas

Dafna Lemish, Southern Illinois University Carbondale

Timothy R. Levine, Korea University

Han Z. Li, University of Northern British Columbia

Xiaoping Li, China Central Television

S. Robert Lichter, George Mason University

Tae-Seop Lim, University of Wisconsin–Milwaukee

Rebecca Ann Lind, University of Illinois at Chicago

Rich Ling, IT University of Copenhagen

Isaac M. Lipkus, Duke University School of Nursing

Sonia Livingstone, London School of Economics and Political Science

Wilson Lowrey, University of Alabama

Robert J. Lunn, FocalPoint Analytics, Oxnard, CA

Philippe J. Maarek, University of East Paris

Peter Mack, Warburg Institute, University of London

Winston Mano, University of Westminster

Robin Mansell, London School of Economics and Political Science

Frank Marcinkowski, University of Münster

Marie-Louise Mares, University of Wisconsin–Madison

Helen Margetts, University of Oxford

Drew Margolin, Cornell University

José Marques de Melo, Methodist University of São Paulo

Guillermo Mastrini, University of Buenos Aires

Dana Mastro, University of Arizona

Donald Matheson, University of Canterbury

Marcus Maurer, Johannes Gutenberg University of Mainz

Sharon R. Mazzarella, James Madison University

Gianpietro Mazzoleni, University of Milan

Matthew P. McAllister, Pennsylvania State University

Samuel McCormick, San Francisco State University

Liz McFall, Open University

Douglas M. McLeod, University of Wisconsin–Madison

Mark Lawrence McPhail, University of Wisconsin–Whitewater

Denis McQuail, University of Amsterdam

Mary M. Meares, University of Alabama

Jamie Medhurst, Aberystwyth University

Kaitlynn Mendes, De Montfort University

Debra Merskin, University of Oregon

Paul Messaris, University of Pennsylvania

Joshua Meyrowitz, University of New Hampshire

Frank E. Millar, University of Wyoming

Katherine I. Miller, Arizona State University

Peter V. Miller, Northwestern University

Toby Miller, University of Cardiff/Murdoch

Young Min, Korea University

Vijay Mishra, Murdoch University, Perth

Bella Mody, University of Colorado at Boulder

Wiebke Möhring, Hanover University of Applied Sciences and Arts

Peter Monge, University of Southern California

Michael Morgan, University of Massachusetts Amherst

Sherwyn P. Morreale, University of Colorado at Colorado Springs

Nancy Morris, Temple University

Vincent Mosco, Queen's University, Ontario

Patricia Moy, University of Washington

Marion G. Müller, Jacobs University Bremen

Megan Mullen, University of Wisconsin–Parkside

Dennis K. Mumby, University of North Carolina at Chapel Hill

Graham Murdock, Loughborough University

Andrew D. Murray, London School of Economics and Political Science

Scott A. Myers, West Virginia University

Graham Mytton, Freelance Consultant and Trainer in Market and Audience Research and Media Governance

Orayb Aref Najjar, Northern Illinois University

Philip M. Napoli, Fordham University

Amy I. Nathanson, Ohio State University

Ian Neath, Memorial University of Newfoundland

Richard Alan Nelson, Louisiana State University

Josef Nerb, Freiburg University of Education

John Nerone, University of Illinois at Urbana–Champaign

W. Russell Neuman, University of Michigan

Julianne H. Newton, University of Oregon

Sik Hung Ng, City University of Hong Kong

Jörg-Uwe Nieland, German Sport University Cologne /University of Duisburg

Matthew C. Nisbet, American University

Seth M. Noar, University of North Carolina at Chapel Hill

Hillel Nossek, College of Management, Academic Studies

Jon F. Nussbaum, Pennsylvania State University

Daniel O'Keefe, Northwestern University

Mary Beth Oliver, Pennsylvania State University

James Owens, University of Illinois at Chicago

Claudia Padovani, University of Padua

Zhongdang Pan, University of Wisconsin–Madison

Stylianos Papathanassopoulos, National and Kapodistrian University of Athens

Shawn J. Parry-Giles, University of Maryland

Chris Paterson, University of Leeds

Pier Paolo Patrucco, University of Turin

Miles L. Patterson, University of Missouri–St Louis

Wolfram Peiser, Ludwig Maximilian University of Munich

Richard M. Perloff, Cleveland State University

Laurent Pernot, University of Strasbourg

Elizabeth M. Perse, University of Delaware

Christina Peter, Ludwig Maximilian University of Munich

Jochen Peter, University of Amsterdam

John Durham Peters, University of Iowa

Thomas Petersen, Allensbach Institute

Gary Pettey, Cleveland State University

Barbara Pfetsch, Free University of Berlin

Dana Polan, New York University

John C. Pollock, College of New Jersey

Marshall Scott Poole, University of Illinois at Urbana–Champaign

Jonathan Potter, Loughborough University

Catherine Preston, University of Kansas

Frank Priess, Konrad Adenauer Foundation

Chris Priestman, Staffordshire University

Linda L. Putnam, University of California, Santa Barbara

Peter Putnis, University of Canberra

Thorsten Quandt, Westfälische Wilhelms-University Münster

Francesco Quatraro, University of Nice

Marc Raboy, McGill University

Lana F. Rakow, University of North Dakota

Shoba Ramanadhan, Dana-Farber Cancer Institute

Arthur A. Raney, Florida State University

Juliana Raupp, Free University of Berlin

Stephen D. Reese, University of Texas at Austin

Leonard Reinecke, Johannes Gutenberg University of Mainz

Carsten Reinemann, Ludwig Maximilian-University of Munich

Amy Reynolds, Louisiana State University

Nancy Rhodes, Ohio State University

Diana Rieger, University of Cologne

Andreea Deciu Ritivoi, Carnegie Mellon University

Patrick Rössler, University of Erfurt

Ulrike Röttger, University of Münster

Hernando Rojas, University of Wisconsin–Madison

Michael E. Roloff, Northwestern University

Holger Roschk, Catholic University of Eichstaett-Ingolstadt

David R. Roskos-Ewoldsen, Ohio State University

Karen Ross, Northumbria University

David Rowe, University of Western Sydney

Alan M. Rubin, Kent State University

Rebecca B. Rubin, Kent State University

Georg Ruhrmann, University of Jena

Betteke van Ruler, University of Amsterdam

Janet B. Ruscher, Tulane University

Joseph Russomanno, Arizona State University

Marie-Laure Ryan, Independent scholar

Roger L. Sadler, Western Illinois University

Alyssa A. Samek, Drake University

Jakub Samochowiec, University of Basel

Wendy Samter, Bryant University

Stephanie Lee Sargent Weaver, Northrop Grumman/Centers for Disease Control and Prevention

Amit M. Schejter, Ben-Gurion University of the Negev and Pennsylvania State University

Helmut Scherer, Hanover University of Music, Drama, and Media

Bertram Scheufele, University of Hohenheim

Dietram A. Scheufele, University of Wisconsin–Madison

Daniela Schlütz, Hanover University of Music, Drama and Media

Beate Schneider, Hanover University of Music, Drama and Media

Steve Schneider, State University of New York Institute of Technology

Armin Scholl, University of Münster

Barbara Schouten, University of Amsterdam

Holger Schramm, University of Würzburg

Winfried Schulz, University of Erlangen-Nuremberg

Wolfgang Schweiger, University of Hohenheim

Glenn Scott, Elon University

Chris Segrin, University of Arizona

David R. Seibold, University of California, Santa Barbara

Holli A. Semetko, Emory University

Gianluca Sergi, University of Nottingham

Jan Servaes, City University of Hong Kong

Masoud Shadnam, NEOMA Business School

Dhavan V. Shah, University of Wisconsin–Madison

Hemant Shah, University of Wisconsin–Madison

Donald L. Shaw, University of North Carolina at Chapel Hill

Kim Bartel Sheehan, University of Oregon

John L. Sherry, Michigan State University

Mark Shevy, Northern Michigan University

Dong Hee Shin, Sungkyunkwan University

K. M. Shrivastava, Indian Institute of Mass Communication

L. J. Shrum, HEC Paris

Nancy Signorielli, University of Delaware

Peter Simonson, University of Colorado at Boulder

John Sinclair, University of Melbourne

Jane B. Singer, City University London

Edith Smit, University of Amsterdam

Peter B. Smith, University of Sussex

Sandi W. Smith, Michigan State University

Matthew Soar, Concordia University

Braxton Soderman, University of California, Irvine

Lawrence Soley, Marquette University

Denise Haunani Solomon, Pennsylvania State University

Prasun Sonwalkar, University of the West of England

Glenn G. Sparks, Purdue University

Brian H. Spitzberg, San Diego State University

Lee Sproull, New York University

Annabelle Sreberny, University of London

Don W. Stacks, University of Miami

Linda Steiner, University of Maryland

Clay Steinman, Macalester College

Robert L. Stevenson, University of North Carolina at Chapel Hill

Charles J. Stewart, Purdue University

Rudolf Stöber, University of Bamberg

Cynthia Stohl, University of California, Santa Barbara

J. Douglas Storey, Johns Hopkins Bloomberg School of Public Health

Joseph Straubhaar, University of Texas at Austin

Kristina Strödter, Justus Liebig University

Jenny Sundén, Södertörn University

Richard F. Taflinger, Washington State University

Damian Tambini, London School of Economics and Political Science

Philip M. Taylor, University of Leeds

Hedwig te Molder, Wageningen University/ University of Twente

Gerard J. Tellis, University of Southern California

Daya Kishan Thussu, University of Westminster

Linda Tickle-Degnen, Tufts University

Stella Ting-Toomey, California State University, Fullerton

Karen Tracy, University of Colorado at Boulder

Sarah J. Tracy, Arizona State University

Michael W. Traugott, University of Michigan

Yariv Tsfati, University of Haifa

Kathleen J. Turner, Davidson College

Kyle James Tusing, University of Arizona

Dagmar C. Unz, University of Applied Sciences Würzburg-Schweinfurt

Patti M. Valkenburg, University of Amsterdam

Elizabeth Van Couvering, London School of Economics and Political Science

Bas van den Putte, University of Amsterdam

Margot van der Goot, University of Amsterdam

Shenja van der Graaf, iMinds-SMIT, Vrije Universiteit Brussel

Frans H. van Eemeren, University of Amsterdam & Leiden University

Theo van Leeuwen, University of Technology Sydney

Lyn Van Swol, University of Wisconsin–Madison

Elena Vartanova, Lomonosov Moscow State University

Dejan Verčič, University of Ljubljana

Paul Hendriks Vettehen, Radboud University Nijmegen

K. Viswanath, Harvard University

Susana N. Vittadini Andrés, University of Buenos Aires

Ingrid Volkmer, University of Melbourne

Peter Vorderer, University of Mannheim

Karin Wahl-Jorgensen, Cardiff University

Jennifer H. Waldeck, Chapman University

Kandi L. Walker, University of Louisville

Devin Wallace-Williams, Washington Hospitality Public Charter High School

Joseph B. Walther, Michigan State University

Michaela Wänke, University of Basel

Janet Wasko, University of Oregon

Bernadette Watson, University of Queensland

Ann Weatherall, Victoria University of Wellington

David H. Weaver, Indiana University

James B. Weaver, III, Centers for Disease Control and Prevention, Atlanta

René Weber, University of California, Santa Barbara

Frank Webster, City University London

James G. Webster, Northwestern University

Stefan Wehmeier, University of Greifswald

Gabriel Weimann, University of Haifa

Siegfried Weischenberg, University of Hamburg

Doreen Weisenhaus, University of Hong Kong

Hartmut Wessler, University of Mannheim

Jürgen Wilke, Johannes Gutenberg University of Mainz

Holley A. Wilkin, Georgia State University

Karin Gwinn Wilkins, University of Texas at Austin

Kenton T. Wilkinson, Texas Tech University

Lars Willnat, Indiana University

Steven R. Wilson, Purdue University

Brian Winston, University of Lincoln

Werner Wirth, University of Zurich

Russ Witcher, Tennessee Tech University

Kim Witte, Michigan State University

Holger Wormer, Dortmund University of Technology

Dominic Wring, Loughborough University

Jina H. Yoo, University of Missouri–St. Louis

Shuhua Zhou, University of Alabama

Dolf Zillmann, University of Alabama

Astrid Zipfel, Heinrich Heine University of Düsseldorf

Thomas Zittel, Goethe-University Frankfurt

Theodore E. Zorn, Massey University

Marvin Zuckermann, University of Delaware

Introduction

This *Concise Encyclopedia of Communication* presents an authoritative and up-to-date account of the evidence in the dynamic and interdisciplinary field of communication, written by the best scholars in the field and developed from the highly praised twelve-volume *International Encyclopedia of Communication*, first published in 2008.

Wikipedia or Communipedia? The Value of Authority

Even in academic circles one can often hear the argument that the time of encyclopedias is over. Wikipedia and the search results of Google or Yahoo have it all anyway – and they draw from different sources, thus operating in a more pluralistic way. Indeed, Wikipedia and search engines are exciting steps forward in the documentation and sometimes even the creation of our knowledge about the world. One can look up almost everything on the Internet, and many scholars, including myself, use these tools many times a day, e.g. for learning the meaning of a foreign term, the lifecourse of an important figure, or even the basic content of an unfamiliar theory.

But when it comes to topics that are more important, for one's life or one's work, topics that are crucial or even risky, we must address the question of which source we can rely on – be it with news about important issues or any other kind of knowledge. On the web things look pretty much alike, often fancy, and presumably 'authoritative'. There is no visual and haptic authority against which they can be judged as there was in the pre-digital world. The print version of *Encyclopedia Britannica*, now itself history, did convey such an aura of the ultimate and best knowledge about everything. But with websites it is often difficult to distinguish the pros from the amateurs, the experts from the activists, or the neutral sources from PR.

This often difficult distinction of sources according to their credibility is of particular relevance when it comes to scientific work. Students who write a thesis on a subject, scholars who want to explore the evidence in a field that is not their own specialty, or the general public looking for practical advice: they all need ascertained evidence, evidence that is the best possible in the respective field, evidence that is not biased by a lack of competence, ideology, or economic interests. In short, they need the evidence that the most knowledgeable people in this area can come up with.

From a systemic point of view it is the core function of science to supply to society this best possible, 'approved' knowledge about an area; in the words of the late German sociologist Niklas Luhmann to apply the code "true/false" to assertions about reality. These assessments enable other subsystems of society to make rational decisions. Looked at from the individual's point of view, scientific knowledge feeds our psychological control motivation: we want to understand things, explain what has happened and – even more important in practical life – know what *will* happen when we do certain things, make decisions, be it investments or allowing our children to use certain media. Scientific evidence can supply this knowledge, and this is why social systems have always supported professions who supply this knowledge – in earlier times based on narratives that shamans and priests provided, since the Enlightenment predominantly based on systematic evidence as proposed by great scholars like Francis Bacon in the sixteenth and seventeenth century and Auguste Comte in the nineteenth.

Of course, it may happen that what is "true" today can be "wrong" tomorrow. And on many topics there is no such approved, unanimously agreed-upon, evidence but only a provisional consensus, and sometimes not even that, but only a body of hotly debated evidence. But even the documentation of doubts and controversies represents scientific evidence. When scholars agree to disagree, be it on the role of man in climate change or on the effects of violent computer games – as they do in both cases – then at least we can say what we can about the phenomena to the best of our knowledge as of today. Knowledge needs the authority of the best experts in order to give orientation. And this is why an encyclopedia in an academic field like communication still makes sense. We sometimes call the different publications in this overall ICA/Wiley Blackwell project our "Communipedia" – rich and searchable like Wikipedia but with the authority of the scientific community in communication.

The Interplay of People and Organizations

To live up to this standard requires people and organizations. Let me start with the organizations: this encyclopedia is an ICA product. The International Communication Association, with its now almost 4,500 members from some 80 countries, constitutes the backbone of our scientific community. At its conferences and in its publications (many of the flagship journals in the field are ICA journals) it assembles the most up-to-date and relevant communication research worldwide. When we were working towards the completion of the twelve-volume IEC I started with the ICA divisions, used the expertise and the overview of the division heads to decide about the selection of headwords and of authors. Thus, the authority of ICA as our major scientific organization is transferred to and validates all our different encyclopedias – 2015 will see the start of our new series of about 15 multi-volume sub-disciplinary encyclopedias of communication – and, we hope, these publications will contribute to the authority of ICA.

As some people believe that we don't need reference works any more (see above) there are also some who think the business of academic publishing has had its day. Having worked now for more than ten years closely with Blackwell (since 2007 part of Wiley Blackwell) I have a clear view on the central functions that publishing companies fulfill even in a digitalized world. Only the professionals at a commercial but academically committed company such as Wiley Blackwell have an expert view of the market and thus of what is needed in a particular field, supply and control the necessary procedures for bringing a publication from idea to print (online and offline), and have the know-how and the resources for marketing, especially when it comes to international markets. This business competence is, though, worthless without a commitment to research and to the processes and standards of good academic work. Academic publishing companies would never be accepted by research community without this commitment. And here, Wiley Blackwell is certainly a special and extremely successful case. Wiley Blackwell publishes 1,400 peer-reviewed journals (and of course thousands of books) in cooperation with no less than 700 academic and professional societies – a clear indication of trust and an acknowledgement of the publisher's expertise *and* commitment.

If ICA and Wiley Blackwell are the organizational skeleton of this work, the authors and area editors are its flesh, its substance. An encyclopedia can only live up to the standards outlined above if the people who act as gatekeepers, judges of what is relevant to be covered, and who act as reporters on the state-of-the-art of a theory, concept, or problem have the best knowledge of this respective field and the highest academic standards. Indeed, many of those who have played the role of area editor have been presidents of ICA or regional and national associations, division heads, ICA Fellows, or carried out other functions for which having a bird's-eye view of the field is essential. And those who have contributed as authors are the people whose name the reader will find wherever he or she researches the current literature on the subject; the key people in their area, the scholars who have done major research in their field and often the authors of milestone publications.

It is this interplay of these organizational and individual actors that in the end produces the academic authority of the ICA/Wiley Blackwell encyclopedias, in this case the *Concise Encyclopedia of Communication*. Of course, it also needs a researcher/manager at the helm who knits this all together so that in the end a student anywhere in the world can open the volume or log in to the website through his or her library and be sure of finding the best possible approximation to "truth", i.e. an authoritative and up-to-date account of the evidence on the subject he or she is looking for.

The Difficult Field of Communication

Robert Craig starts the entry "Communication as a Field and Discipline" in this Encyclopedia with the sentence: "The modern field of communication is highly diverse in methods, theories, and objects of study." Several intellectual traditions from the humanities and social sciences inform our field, and as a consequence, communication is anything but clearly defined – within countries and even more so between countries. What one encounters when starting as a student in a bachelor's or master's program in "communication", or when investigating the research fields of a department with this name depends very much on the tradition and location of the department and on the people running it. Different objects, different epistemologies, different theories, and different methods – the field is still struggling with its identity and many from outside question that it ever had one in the first place. The fact that this problematic field has grown in the last half century like almost no other discipline is the best argument against its critics. Obviously, there is a strong demand for the evidence that it can supply.

We have sought to represent the diversity of the field in this encyclopedia. As there are, for some matters, contending camps challenging each other's methods and/or evidence, not every colleague will be happy about the selection of headwords and authors or the way a subject is covered. But this reference work does not exist to make scholars happy: rather it aims to give students and other interested readers the best possible, neutral account of research. The fact that reference works and handbooks have become popular in the field of communication shows that it has, despite its problematic identity and existing disputes, reached a certain maturity, something that was not there a few decades ago.

How We Have Proceeded

This single-volume *Concise Encyclopedia of Communication* (CEC) builds on the twelve-volume *International Encyclopedia of Communication* (IEC), published in 2008. The original printed version of the IEC had 1,339 entries ranging from less than 1,000 to more than 6,000 words. Converting the IEC into the CEC meant primarily three tasks: (1) selecting headwords, (2) abridging the corresponding entries, and (3) updating their content.

As a first step the editor went back to the area editors of the IEC and asked them to name the 50 percent of headwords they deemed the most important in their area and which, therefore, they would like to see printed in a concise reference work. Most area editors made this decision. In cases where they did not respond the editor stepped in. In addition, some fine-tuning was necessary in order to avoid overlap and give sufficient coherence to the headword system. This resulted in 577 subjects covered by more than 500 authors, about 43 percent of the subjects covered in the IEC.

As the publisher imposed a word limit for the overall volume, the next step required assigning a maximum word count to each entry. We have used three length categories for the CEC entries: 400, 800, and 1,300 words, adding up to close to 400,000 words of text for the entries for the whole volume. Again, these decisions had to be made against criteria of relevance and coherence.

We contacted all authors of the entries that we kept for the CEC and asked them to abridge their original text to the assigned length and to update. As it could be anticipated that not every author would have the time or motivation to do so, the editor also offered to do this for him or her. This happened in one out of four cases. Thus, what the reader finds here is another product of a major part of the international scientific community in the field of communication.

Wolfgang Donsbach, Editor

Acknowledgments

The editor of an academic reference work certainly needs a profound overview, more a generalist than a specialist perspective on the field, and I can only hope that my talents sufficed for this. But, at least as much, the editor needs managerial skills, because such a work is anything but a one-man show. As I have indicated in the Introduction, this book is the joint product of the whole scientific community of communication – and in this definition I explicitly include people whose job is not to do research themselves but who have, in very different functions, contributed to the content.

My first thanks go to the more than 500 *authors* who have already contributed to the *International Encyclopedia of Communication* (IEC), the great majority of whom volunteered to abridge and update their entries for this concise edition (CEC). We all know that contributing to reference works is not the prime publishing task of academics today, but the majority of our authors already had such a high reputation that they could afford to let the next peer-reviewed journal article wait a while…

Almost all of the authors and the headwords of the entries they contributed were picked by the 30 *area editors* who already were the editorial backbone of the IEC. And I should not forget to thank the two Advisory Editors of the IEC, *Jennings Bryant* and *Robert T. Craig*, for their continuous stewardship in this whole project of ICA–Wiley Blackwell encyclopedias.

Over the ten years that we have cooperated, *Elizabeth P. Swayze*, Senior Editor for Communication and Media Studies at Wiley, and I have developed not only a fruitful and effective working relationship but a deep personal friendship, both built on trust, reliability, and mutual appreciation of our competencies. For this project, two other people at the Wiley office in Malden, Massachusetts, kept us on track and always gave excellent advice: *Julia Kirk*, Senior Project Editor for our field, and *Tiffany Mok*, in charge of all major reference works. On a side-note: when we started the IEC many years ago, Tiffany was an intern – she has built a remarkable career since then.

My closest ally at the Dresden office has been *Anne Hennig*, a graduate student in communication, who has probably been the only person who has always had a complete overview of where we were in the editorial process, of which authors were lagging behind, or where the editor himself had dropped the ball. Six weeks after we had sent all entries to the publisher, Anne gave birth to twins, another pressure on the whole project that forced us to keep to the timeline. *Anja Obermüller*, a junior lecturer at our department, as well as *Isabelle Freiling*, *Johanna Haupt* and *Sonia Robak*, research assistants, helped with proof-reading.

What we had to proof-read had gone through the hands of *Felicity Marsh* in the UK who organized copy-editing and *Alec McAulay* who did most of this job – in an amazingly fast and thorough manner. Thus, the CEC is not only 'international' in terms of its authors but also its whole production team.

Last but not least I would like to express my gratitude to a handful of people who did not directly contribute but made my contribution possible. My secretary *Katrin Presberger* competently organized my professional life in critical periods, and all the other *colleagues at the Institute of Media and Communication* at Technische Universität Dresden had to make up for contributions that, at times, I could not give. My closest friend and estimable colleague *Thomas E. Patterson*, professor at Harvard University's Shorenstein Center has, as always, given a major intellectual input into everything I do, academically and in life in general.

Finally, I am deeply grateful to my wife Eva and our now teenage son Tom who both had, once again after the 'IEC times', to live with a diminished family life…

Wolfgang Donsbach
Dresden, October 2014

Lexicon

A

Accountability of the Media
Accounting Research
Acculturation Processes and Communication
Action Assembly Theory
Advertisement Campaign Management
Advertising
Advertising, Cross-Cultural
Advertising, Economics of
Advertising Effectiveness
Advertising Effectiveness, Measurement of
Advertising: Global Industry
Advertising, History of
Advertising Law and Regulations
Advertising as Persuasion
Advertising: Responses across the Life-Span
Advertising Strategies
Advocacy Journalism
Affective Disposition Theories
Affects and Media Exposure
Africa: Media Systems
Age Identity and Communication
Agenda Building
Agenda-Setting Effects
Aging and Message Production and Processing
Alternative Journalism
Anime
Applied Communication Research
Appraisal Theory
Arab Satellite TV News
Archiving of Internet Content
Art as Communication
Asia: Media Systems
Attending to the Mass Media
Attitude–Behavior Consistency
Attitudes
Audience Research
Audience Segmentation
Audiences, Female
Australia: Media System

B

Bad News in Medicine, Communicating
BBC
BBC World Service
Behavioral Norms: Perception through the Media
Bi- and Multilingualism
Bias in the News
Bollywood
Book
Branding
Brands
Broadcast Journalism
Broadcast Talk

C

Cable Television
Canada: Media System
Caricature
Censorship
Censorship, History of

Change Management and Communication
China Central Television, Foreign Language Program of
China: Media System
Cinema
Cinematography
Citizen Journalism
Classroom Student–Teacher Interaction
Climate of Opinion
CNN
Code
Code as Law
Cognitive Dissonance Theory
Cognitive Science
Commercialization: Impact on Media Content
Commodification of the Media
Communication Accommodation Theory
Communication Apprehension
Communication Apprehension: Intervention Techniques
Communication Apprehension and Social Anxiety
Communication: Definitions and Concepts
Communication as a Field and Discipline
Communication: History of the Idea
Communication Inequalities
Communication and Law
Communication Law and Policy: Africa
Communication Law and Policy: Asia
Communication Law and Policy: Europe
Communication Law and Policy: Middle East
Communication Law and Policy: North America
Communication Law and Policy: South America
Communication Management
Communication and Media Studies, History of
Communication Networks
Communication Skill Acquisition
Communication Skills across the Life-Span
Communication and Social Change: Research Methods
Communication Technology and Democracy
Communication Technology and Development
Communication Technology Standards
Communicology
Community Media
Compliance Gaining
Computer Games and Child Development
Computer–User Interaction
Concentration in Media Systems
Consensus-Oriented Public Relations
Construction of Reality through the News
Consumer Culture
Consumers in Media Markets
Content Analysis, Qualitative
Content Analysis, Quantitative
Conversation Analysis
Co-Orientation Model of Public Relations
Copyright
Corporate Communication
Corporate and Organizational Identity
Corporate Reputation
Correlation Analysis
Crime and Communication Technology
Crisis Communication
Critical Theory
Cross-Media Marketing
Cross-Media Production
Cultivation Effects
Cultural Imperialism Theories
Cultural Patterns and Communication
Cultural Products as Tradable Services
Cultural Studies
Culture and Communication, Ethnographic Perspectives on
Culture: Definitions and Concepts
Culture Industries
Cyberfeminism
Cybernetics

D

Deception Detection Accuracy
Decision-Making Processes in Organizations
Deliberativeness in Political Communication
Delphi Studies
Design
Determination Theory in Public Relations
Development Communication
Development Communication Campaigns
Development Discourse
Development Institutions
Development Journalism
Developmental Communication
Diffusion of Information and Innovation
Digital Divide
Digital Imagery
Digital Media, History of
Discourse
Discourse Analysis
Discourse Comprehension
Discursive Psychology
Disney

Diversification of Media Markets
Domestication of Technology

E

E-Democracy
Educational Communication
Educational Media
Educational Media Content
Educational Television, Children's Responses to
E-Government
Elaboration Likelihood Model
Election Campaign Communication
Election Surveys
Electronic Mail
Emotion and Communication in Organizations
Emotional Arousal Theory
Encoding–Decoding
Entertainment Content and Reality Perception
Environment and Social Interaction
Environmental Communication
Escapism
Ethics in Journalism
Ethnic Journalism
Ethnic Media and their Influence
Ethnicity and Exposure to Communication
Ethnography of Communication
European Union: Communication Law
Excitation and Arousal
Exemplification and Exemplars, Effects of
Expectancy Violation
Experiment, Field
Experiment, Laboratory
Exposure to Communication Content
Exposure to Print Media
Exposure to Radio
Exposure to Television
Exposure to the Internet
Extended Parallel Process Model
Extra-Media Data

F

Facebook
Fear Induction through Media Content
Federal Communications Commission (FCC)
Feminist and Gender Studies
Feminist Media
Feminist Media Studies, Transnational
Feminization of Media Content
Fiction
Field Research

Film Genres
Film Production
Film Theory
Financial Communication
Flow Theory
Framing Effects
Framing of the News
France: Media System
Freedom of Communication
Freedom of Information
Freedom of the Press, Concept of

G

Gay, Lesbian, Bisexual, and Transgender Media Studies
Gender and Discourse
Gender and Journalism
Gender: Representation in the Media
Genre
Germany: Media System
Girl Culture
Globalization of the Media
Globalization of Organizations
Globalization Theories
Goals, Cognitive Aspects of
Goals, Social Aspects of
Graphic Design
Grounded Theory
Group Communication
Group Decision-Making, Functional Theory of

H

Health Campaigns, Communication in
Health Communication
Health Communication and the Internet
Health Literacy
Hermeneutics
Historic Key Events and the Media
Hollywood

I

Iconography
Identities and Discourse
Image Restoration Theory
Imagined Interactions
India: Media System
Information
Information and Communication Technology, Economics of

Information Literacy
Information Processing
Information Processing: Self-Concept
Information Seeking
Information Society
Informational Utility
Infotainment
Ingratiation and Affinity Seeking
Institutional Theory
Instructional Television
Integrated Marketing Communications
Intellectual Property Law
Interaction
Interactivity, Concept of
Intercultural Conflict Styles and Facework
Intercultural and Intergroup Communication
Intergenerational Communication
Intergroup Accommodative Processes
Intergroup Communication and Discursive Psychology
Intergroup Contact and Communication
Intergroup Reconciliation, Processes of
Intermediality
International Association for Media and Communication Research (IAMCR)
International Communication
International Communication Agencies
International Communication Association (ICA)
International News Reporting
International Radio
International Television
Internet: International Regulation
Internet Law and Regulation
Internet News
Internet and Popular Culture
Interorganizational Communication
Interpersonal Attraction
Interpersonal Communication
Interpersonal Communication Competence and Social Skills
Interpersonal Communication, Sex and Gender Differences in
Interpersonal Conflict
Interpretive Journalism
Interview, Qualitative
Interview, Standardized
Involvement with Media Content
Issue Management
Issue Management in Politics

J

Japan: Media System
Journalism
Journalism Education
Journalism, History of
Journalism: Legal Situation
Journalists, Credibility of
Journalists' Role Perception

K

Knowledge Gap Effects
Knowledge Management

L

Language and the Internet
Language and Social Interaction
Latin America: Media Systems
Latitude of Acceptance
Leadership in Organizations
Learning and Communication
Linguistic Pragmatics
Linguistics
Listening
Longitudinal Analysis

M

Marital Communication
Marketing
Marketing: Communication Tools
Markets of the Media
Masculinity and Media
Meaning
Measurement Theory
Media
Media Conglomerates
Media Content and Social Networks
Media Diplomacy
Media Ecology
Media Economics
Media Effects
Media Effects: Direct and Indirect Effects
Media Effects, History of
Media Effects, Strength of
Media Equation Theory
Media Events and Pseudo-Events
Media and Group Representations
Media History

Media Literacy
Media Messages and Family Communication
Media and Perceptions of Reality
Media Performance
Media Planning
Media Production and Content
Media System Dependency Theory
Media Use and Child Development
Media Use, International Comparison of
Media Use across the Life-Span
Media Use by Social Variable
Mediated Populism
Mediated Social Interaction
Mediated Terrorism
Mediatization of Politics
Medium Theory
Memory
Message Discrimination
Message Production
Meta-Analysis
Metadiscourse
Metaphor
Mexico: Media System
Minority Journalism
Mobility, Technology for
Models of Communication
Modernity
Mood Management
Music Industry

N

Narrative News Story
Negotiation and Bargaining
Network Organizations through Communication Technology
Neutrality
New World Information and Communication Order (NWICO)
News
News Agencies, History of
News Corporation
News Cycles
News Factors
News Ideologies
News Processing across the Life-Span
News Routines
News Sources
News Story
News Values

Newspaper, History of
Newspaper, Visual Design of
Nonverbal Communication and Culture

O

Objectivity in Reporting
Observation
Online Journalism
Online Media
Online Research
Open Source
Operationalization
Opinion Leader
Organization–Public Relationships
Organizational Change Processes
Organizational Communication
Organizational Communication: Critical Approaches
Organizational Communication: Postmodern Approaches
Organizational Conflict
Organizational Culture
Organizational Image
Organizations, Cultural Diversity in

P

Parasocial Interactions and Relationships
Parental Mediation Strategies
Participatory Action Research
Participatory Communication
Pedagogy, Communication in
Perceived Reality as a Social Process
Perception
Personal Communication by CMC
Personality and Exposure to Communication
Persuasion
Phenomenology
Photography
Photojournalism
Physiological Measurement
Planned Behavior, Theory of
Planned Social Change through Communication
Pluralistic Ignorance
Pluralistic Ignorance and Ideological Biases
Politainment
Politeness Theory
Political Advertising
Political Cognitions
Political Communication

Political Communication Systems
Political Economy of the Media
Political Efficacy
Political Journalists
Political Knowledge
Political Language
Political Marketing
Political Media Use
Political Persuasion
Political Socialization through the Media
Popular Communication
Popular Communication and Social Class
Popular Music
Pornography, Feminist Debates on
Pornography Use across the Life-Span
Postfeminism
Postmodernism and Communication
Power in Intergroup Settings
Prejudiced and Discriminatory Communication
Presence
Prevention and Communication
Priming Theory
Printing, History of
Privacy
Privatization of the Media
Professionalization of Journalism
Propaganda
Propaganda, Visual Communication of
Propaganda in World War II
Public Affairs
Public Broadcasting, History of
Public Broadcasting Systems
Public Opinion
Public Opinion Polling
Public Relations
Public Relations Evaluation
Public Relations: Media Influence
Public Relations Planning
Public Sphere

Q

Qualitative Methodology
Quality of the News
Quantitative Methodology
Questions and Questioning

R

Radio for Development
Radio: Social History

Rapport
Realism in Film and Photography
Reality and Media Reality
Reality TV
Reasoned Action, Theory of
Reciprocal Effects
Regression Analysis
Relational Control
Relational Dialectics
Relational Uncertainty
Reliability
Remediation
Response Rates
Rhetoric, Argument, and Persuasion
Rhetoric and Dialectic
Rhetoric and Ethics
Rhetoric and Gender
Rhetoric, Greek
Rhetoric and History
Rhetoric and Language
Rhetoric and Logic
Rhetoric and Media Studies
Rhetoric and Politics
Rhetoric, Pre-Socratic
Rhetoric and Race
Rhetoric, Roman
Rhetoric and Social Protest
Rhetorical Criticism
Rhetorical Studies
Rhetorics: New Rhetorics
Risk Communication
Risk Perceptions
Russia: Media System

S

Sampling, Random
Satellite Communication, Global
Satellite Communication, Regulation of
Satellite Television
Schemas
Science Journalism
Scripts
Search Engines
Segmentation of the Advertising Audience
Selective Exposure
Selective Perception and Selective Retention
Self-Presentation
Self-Regulation of the Media
Semiotics
Sensation Seeking

Sensationalism
Sex Role Stereotypes in the Media
Sexism in the Media
Sexual Violence in the Media
Sign
Situation Comedies
Social Cognitive Theory
Social Comparison Theory
Social Conflict and Communication
Social Exchange
Social Marketing
Social Media
Social Perception
Social Stereotyping and Communication
Social Support in Interpersonal Communication
Sony Corporation
Source Protection
Special Effects
Speech Anxiety
Speech Communication, History of
Speech Fluency and Speech Errors
Spiral of Silence
Sports and the Media, History of
Standards of News
Stimulus–Response Model
Storytelling and Narration
Strategic Communication
Strategic Framing
Structuralism
Student Communication Competence
Survey

T

Tabloidization
Taste Culture
Teacher Communication Style
Teacher Influence and Persuasion
Technology and Communication
Televised Debates
Television Broadcasting, Regulation of
Television for Development
Television as Popular Culture
Television, Social History of
Television, Visual Characteristics of
Terrorism and Communication Technologies
Text and Intertextuality
Third-Person Effects
Time Warner Inc.
Transnational Civil Society
Trust of Publics
Truth and Media Content
Twitter
Two-Step Flow of Communication

U

Uncertainty and Communication
Uncertainty Management
Uncertainty Reduction Theory
UNESCO
United Kingdom: Media System
United Nations, Communication Policies of
United States of America: Media System
Uses and Gratifications

V

Validity
Video Games
Violence against Journalists
Violence as Media Content
Violence as Media Content, Effects of
Violence as Media Content, Effects on Children of
Visual Communication
Visual Culture
Visual Representation

W

War Propaganda
Watergate Scandal
Web 2.0 and the News
Women in the Media, Images of
Women's Communication and Language

Y

Youth Culture

A

Accountability of the Media

YOUNG MIN
Korea University

The accountability of the media is a normative notion that underlies the balance of freedom and social responsibility across media structure, performance, and product.

From the birth of the press, its freedom has been strongly connected with social expectations for the media to protect the public interest and to improve the quality of democracy (→ Freedom of the Press, Concept of). Fundamentally, it is a matter of *balancing freedom and responsibility*, and two measures have been used primarily for that purpose: the market and the law. Neither approach, however, has proven successful. The free market measures often fail to secure plurality in media ownership and diversity in media content. On the other hand, legal regulations, such as → censorship and other repressive measures legislated to protect the public good, often infringe freedom itself.

Many *alternatives* to these two approaches have been suggested. The theory of 'social responsibility' emphasizes the importance of media freedom to scrutinize power and to provide accurate information. It suggests that the media's obligations to society be fulfilled primarily by self-regulation, i.e., by the voluntary efforts of media owners and practitioners (→ Ethics in Journalism; Professionalization of Journalism). Although the theory contributed to the notion of media responsibility, it was not successful in detailing exactly how to hold the free market media socially responsible.

The concept of media accountability is a much wider concept than self-regulation, denoting both the media's legal obligation to prevent or reduce any negative consequences of its practices and its moral duty to provide quality service for the public. Accountability is also a process-oriented concept defining how the media answer, to whom, and for what.

There exist diverse *ways of achieving media accountability*, which include legal and legislative regulation, and involve the market, the civil society (or the public), and the media profession itself (McQuail 2003). To sum up: media accountability represents an effort to establish the rules by which the media perform socially expected functions in a democracy while preserving freedom and extending it to more people and incorporating more diverse voices.

See also: ▶ CENSORSHIP ▶ ETHICS IN JOURNALISM ▶ FREEDOM OF THE PRESS, CONCEPT OF ▶ PROFESSIONALIZATION OF JOURNALISM

REFERENCES AND SUGGESTED READINGS

Bertrand, C.-J. (2005). Introduction: Media accountability. *Pacific Journalism Review*, 11(2), 5–16.
McQuail, D. (2003). *Media accountability and freedom of publication*. Oxford: Oxford University Press.
Merritt, M. & McCombs, M. (2004). *The two w's of journalism: The why and what of public affairs reporting*. Mahwah, NJ: Lawrence Erlbaum.

Accounting Research

RICHARD BUTTNY
Syracuse University

Research on verbal accounting examines how language is used to explain or make sense of events. Citing one's motive or describing the context may serve to portray events in a different way – as understandable, excusable, or less culpable. An accounting can range from a lengthy → discourse (a narrative or courtroom cross-examination) to a single word or nonverbal substitute, e.g., a shoulder shrug. In routine circumstances accounts are not necessary; persons, actions, and events speak for themselves. The need for accounts arises when something problematic or out of the ordinary occurs. Another's question, challenge, or blame makes an account relevant from the actor (Goffman 1971).

Accounts 'for' actions arise in response to some troubles or blame; accounts attempt to remediate the incident or one's responsibility for it (Scott & Lyman 1968). Excuses are a paradigmatic kind of account. Accounts may serve as a reason for why one did what one did. Accounts 'of' action involve a person's sense-making for events such as relationships, personal crises, or changes of life course. A story-like account or narrative would be the paradigmatic form. Narratives can account by conveying a temporal sequence of events, the cast of characters, and the actor's part in portraying events in a particular way (→ Storytelling and Narration). This approach captures our need to interpret our lives, particularly in times of stress or trauma (Orbuch 1997).

Given that an accounting is offered to other(s), the recipient may honor the account or not. An account may not be addressed at all by the recipient. Alternatively the recipient may question the account, thereby prompting further accounts (→ Questions and Questioning). The larger the problematic event, the more likely it is that the actor's accounts will be questioned. Accounts are typically partial and selective, so it is difficult to tell the whole story in the initial accounting. Persons may be probed by recipients so that accounts get incrementally unpacked and expanded. Accountings are collaboratively achieved among interlocutors. Persons may alter their account as it is retold to different recipients.

See also: ▶ DISCOURSE ▶ LANGUAGE AND SOCIAL INTERACTION ▶ QUESTIONS AND QUESTIONING ▶ STORYTELLING AND NARRATION

REFERENCES AND SUGGESTED READING

Goffman, E. (1971). *Relations in public: Microstudies of the public order*. New York: Harper & Row.
Orbuch, T. L. (1997). People's accounts count: The sociology of accounts. *Annual Review of Sociology*, 23, 455–478.
Scott, M. L. & Lyman, S. M. (1968). Accounts. *American Sociological Review*, 33, 46–62.

Acculturation Processes and Communication

YOUNG YUN KIM
University of Oklahoma

From immigrants and refugees seeking to build a new life in a foreign land to temporary sojourners such as international students and employees of multinational companies, numerous people change homes each year crossing cultural boundaries. Although unique in circumstances, all cultural strangers embark on the common project of acculturation: the learning, practicing, and internalizing of the symbols and routinized behaviors prevalent in the new cultural environment (→ Intercultural and Intergroup Communication).

The acculturation phenomenon often accompanies the experience of 'deculturation,' that is, at least temporary unlearning or replacement of some of the original cultural habits. The interplay of acculturation and deculturation experiences facilitates 'cross-cultural adaptation,' the process of internal change in the individual leading to a relatively stable, reciprocal, and functional relationship with a given host environment. Given sufficient time, even those who interact with natives with the intention of confining themselves to only superficial relationships are likely to be at least minimally adapted to the host culture "in spite of themselves" (Taft 1977, 150).

Since the 1930s, research on immigrant acculturation has been extensive across social science disciplines, and has produced ample empirical evidence documenting the long-term, cumulative adaptive change in individuals, the direction of assimilation, a state of psychological, social, and cultural convergence to those of the natives. Kim's (2001) *integrative theory of cross-cultural adaptation*, for example, offers a multidimensional model, in which cultural strangers' intrapersonal, interpersonal, and mass communication activities drive the dynamic and interactive process of becoming increasingly 'fit' in their psychological and functional relationship with the host environment.

The traditional cumulative–progressive trajectory has been challenged in recent decades by some investigators who conceive the acculturation–adaptation phenomenon from a pluralistic perspective on intergroup relations. Among the widely utilized pluralistic approaches is Berry's (1980) *psychological theory of acculturation*. Focusing on individuals' conscious or unconscious identity orientations with respect to their original culture and the host society, Berry's theory identifies four "acculturation strategies": "assimilation," "integration," "separation," and "marginalization."

See also: ▶ CULTURE: DEFINITIONS AND CONCEPTS ▶ ETHNIC MEDIA AND THEIR INFLUENCE ▶ INTERCULTURAL AND INTERGROUP COMMUNICATION

REFERENCES AND SUGGESTED READINGS

Berry, J. (1980). Acculturation as varieties of adaptation. In A. Padilla (ed.), *Acculturation: theory: Models and some new findings*. Washington, DC: Westview, pp. 9–25.

Kim, Y. Y. (2001). *Becoming intercultural: An integrative theory of communication and cross-cultural adaptation*. Thousand Oaks, CA: Sage.

Taft, R. (1977). Coping with unfamiliar cultures. In N. Warren (ed.), *Studies in cross-cultural psychology*, vol. 1. London: Academic Press, pp. 121–153.

Action Assembly Theory

JOHN O. GREENE
Purdue University

Action assembly theory (AAT) seeks to explain message behavior (both verbal and nonverbal) by describing the system of mental structures and processes that give rise to those behaviors (→ Message Production). As such, AAT is a member of the broader class of cognitive theories of message production (→ Cognitive Science). AAT, in turn, is itself an umbrella category for any of a variety of actual and potential specific theories that share certain central features, most prominently the notion that actions are created by integrating (or assembling) elemental features represented in long-term memory (→ Memory) in code systems representing multiple levels of abstraction. Two distinct exemplars of this class are found in Greene (1984, 1997).

In the language of AAT, 'action features,' the fundamental building blocks of thought and overt action, are stored in memory in units called 'procedural records.' The theory then specifies two processes involved in making use of action features to produce messages: 'activation,' (the process by which features relevant to one's goals and ongoing activities are selected) and 'assembly' (the process of integrating activated features).

Because difficulties in assembly are held to be reflected in the time required to formulate and execute messages, a number of studies conducted within the AAT framework have examined speech fluency and speech rate (→ Speech Fluency and Speech Errors). These studies include investigations of the impact of attempting to design messages that address multiple goals and the effects of advance message planning on speech fluency. Another program of research has examined the impact of practice, or skill acquisition, on the speed of message production. AAT has also been applied in studies of the nature of the self, communication apprehension, and the behavioral correlates of deception. Yet another series of studies informed by AAT has focused on 'creative facility' – individual differences in the ability to formulate novel, socially appropriate messages. Most recently, AAT has been brought to bear in theorizing about 'transcendent interactions' – conversations characterized by a deep sense of absorption and connection with one's interlocutor.

See also: ▶ COGNITIVE SCIENCE ▶ COMMUNICATION APPREHENSION ▶ COMMUNICATION SKILL ACQUISITION ▶ GOALS, COGNITIVE ASPECTS OF ▶ INTERPERSONAL COMMUNICATION COMPETENCE AND SOCIAL SKILLS ▶ MEMORY ▶ MESSAGE PRODUCTION ▶ SCRIPTS ▶ SPEECH FLUENCY AND SPEECH ERRORS

REFERENCES AND SUGGESTED READINGS

Greene, J. O. (1984). A cognitive approach to human communication: An action assembly theory. *Communication Monographs*, 51, 289–306.

Greene, J. O. (1997). A second generation action assembly theory. In J. O. Greene (ed.), *Message production: Advances in communication theory*. Mahwah, NJ: Lawrence Erlbaum, pp. 51–85.

Greene, J. O. & Herbers, L. E. (2011). Conditions of interpersonal transcendence. *International Journal of Listening*, 25, 66–84.

Advertisement Campaign Management

ALI M. KANSO
University of Texas at San Antonio

The key to an effective advertising campaign is solid management. The process embodies a wide range of activities that may include brainstorming, consumer surveys, and media analysis. As a communication tool, advertising must consider the product type and factors affecting the sponsor's relationships with its publics. Managing the advertising campaign involves the following *eight steps* (→ Advertising Strategies):

Conducting a Situation Analysis: The purpose is to provide a research foundation that can be used to establish objectives, specify strategies, and articulate tactics. The analysis encompasses the company, consumer, market, product, and competition.

Identifying Problems and Opportunities: This step involves a close look at the firm's prior and current marketing processes, its financial and organizational competencies, its actual or potential areas of profitability, and forces that threaten its growth.

Establishing Short-term and Long-term Objectives: Once the advertiser identifies opportunities, the next step is to establish clear, specific, singular, realistic, measurable, and time-bound objectives.

Determining the Advertising Appropriation and Budgeting: Advertisers weigh the relative importance of price, product, or brand before deciding how and where to allocate expenditures.

Developing a Creative Strategy: Major components include: definition of the key problem, description of the product, identification of the persons who are most likely to purchase the product, clarification of the competition, specification of the consumer benefits, articulation of the reasons that support the benefit claim, determination of the message tone, and formulation of a call for action.

Creating Messages: The creation of effective messages requires the use of keywords and other qualities. Advertisers work meticulously to produce well-targeted, thought provoking, involving, and rewarding messages.

Selecting Appropriate Media: Several decisions have to be made to: identify the target audience(s), select the geographic area, determine the desirable level of reach within a time period, specify the frequency of advertising messages, decide the timing and continuity of the campaign, and choose the media that offer the best match with the intended market.

Outlining a Plan to Measure the Outcome: Measuring the campaign effectiveness is a dynamic process that involves all stages of the campaign but each stage may require different techniques.

In conclusion, managing an advertising campaign is a challenge that entails many interrelated decisions and requires strategic thinking. Advertisers must have a radar system to continuously forecast the consumers' wants and needs.

See also: ▶ ADVERTISING ▶ ADVERTISING EFFECTIVENESS ▶ ADVERTISING STRATEGIES ▶ STRATEGIC COMMUNICATION

SUGGESTED READING

Avery, J. (2010). *Advertising campaign planning: Developing an advertising campaign-based marketing plan,* 4th edn. Chicago: Copy Workshop.

Advertising

TIM AMBLER

London Business School

Advertising has been defined as "any paid form of non personal communication about an organization, product, service, or idea by an identified sponsor" (Alexander 1965, 9). Advertising intrudes into our lives and is not always welcome. Some scholars suspect that we are being manipulated by dark arts. Today, an estimated US$ 500 billion is spent worldwide on local, national, and international advertising.

History

Since the dawn of time, sellers have been seeking to attract attention and present their wares in ways that encourage sales. A contemporary classified ad for a second-hand bicycle is substantively the same as an ad for a Roman chariot 2,000 years ago. Media have changed, notably broadcast and digital, and our understanding of how ads work has changed, but advertising itself has changed much less. Advertising has always provided information, used emotional appeals to sell to us, and reminded us. But it used to be less pervasive than it is today because of the limited media and the limited number of goods then available for trading.

Advertising agencies have existed since at least the eighteenth century but their formal standing as experts dates from the mid-nineteenth century in developed markets and the late twentieth century in the late developers. The importance of small start-up agencies is as great as it ever was but globalization has also promoted mergers of the larger, more mature, agencies into perhaps half a dozen multinationals. This is significant because with classic packaged goods, or fast-moving consumer goods, advertisers have shifted budgets from advertising to promotions, but the slack has mostly been taken up by new advertisers such as financial services and government. As a share of world GDP, however, advertising appears to have grown (www.warc.com).

Measurement techniques have become more sophisticated partly in response to advertiser demands to see quantified results and partly as advertisers and their agencies have taken a more scientific approach to understanding how advertising works. Content has increased in variety with more entertainment and appeals to emotion but this has largely been driven by the wish to exploit new media. Perceptions of different advertising styles may be seen as evolutionary by those involved but the changes in style also reflect the fashion cycles that are necessary to maintain the appearance of novelty (McDonald & Scott 2007).

The Advertiser's Perspective

In recent years, the brief from client to agency setting out requirements has been increasingly formalized. The briefing itself is an interactive process as the agency brings its own experience and negotiating skills, typically, to making the goals easier to achieve and the budget bigger. What should emerge from the process is a clear identification of the target market and the changes the advertising should achieve. The brief should not describe the means, i.e., what the ad should contain, but the end, i.e., challenge the agency with what the campaign should achieve.

Ads work in two stages: they change brand equity (what is in consumer heads) and brand equity, at a later date, changes consumer behavior. That may imply that the goals for the ad campaign should be set by changes in brand equity (intermediate) metrics and the budget made available in those terms. In practice few advertisers formalize brand equity measurement in that way. Furthermore the correlation between intermediate and behavioral metrics can be poor so clients typically prefer the latter, e.g., sales or penetration or profit, where advertising can measurably deliver those goals.

Media neutral planning (MNP; Saunders 2004) as well as → integrated marketing communications (IMC; Schultz 1993) share the idea that communications should be planned from the consumer's perspective. The target market should ultimately determine the relevant media both in terms of readership and in providing the appropriate context for the copy. Thus, media considerations are less driven by reach (how many people see it), frequency, or the cost per 1,000 readers (or viewers) than the relevance of the media and whether, in that context, the message is likely to work.

This leads to the question of how the ads might be expected to work. For a new product or brand, the primary aim is, typically, achieving awareness. Thereafter, advertising works mostly through two approaches, broadly classified as either active or central processing, involving argument and logic, or passive peripheral processing, which relies on cues (→ Elaboration Likelihood Model).

Pre-testing is a contentious topic. Predictiveness is dubious and ads are rarely pre-tested against the particular goals for the campaign. Post-campaign assessment, on the other hand, is not contentious in principle although there are various competing approaches. Post-campaign assessment usually takes the form of 'tracking,' i.e., the key brand equity metrics are consistently monitored over time, for example, on a monthly basis (for a summary see White 2005).

The Consumer's Perspective

From as early as the first half of the nineteenth century, there has been public ambivalence toward advertising. It is seen as manipulative, intrusive, and seeking to persuade us to buy what we do not need (such as lottery tickets) or to buy what is bad for us (such as alcohol, tobacco, or fatty foods). Because brand leaders are typically more expensive than their private label equivalents, some argue that advertising causes us to pay more than we should.

On the other hand, advertising pays for the media we enjoy such as television, newspapers, and the Internet. Quite often we enjoy the ads themselves which enter into general parlance such as 'It does what it says on the tin'.

Finally we should note that the consumer's attitude towards advertising is driven by television advertising rather than all media (Jin & Lutz 2013).

The Social Perspective

Opponents of advertising claim that it commercializes culture, undermines values, and leads to less happiness as society is reminded of what it cannot afford (→ Commercialization: Impact on Media Content). Supporters argue that advertising merely mirrors society as it is. They see it as a necessary part of a healthy market and contend that it has contributed to the growth of GDP and widespread prosperity (O'Guinn & Faber 1991).

Advertising in itself is neither good nor bad, but it can be good or bad in the way it is used. Accordingly, most countries have developed regulation as a means to control 'bad,' or potentially harmful, advertising while allowing 'good' advertising a reasonably free rein. Regulation, much of it self-regulation, has grown rapidly since the 1960s to meet increasing cultural sensitivities but also to dissuade governments from interfering. Self-regulation is seen as being more flexible and responsive to consumer protection than legal rules, but governmental wish to control the industry has led to 'co-regulation,' i.e., government retaining the right to intervene when they deem it necessary.

See also: ▶ ADVERTISEMENT CAMPAIGN MANAGEMENT ▶ ADVERTISING EFFECTIVENESS ▶ ADVERTISING EFFECTIVENESS, MEASUREMENT OF ▶ ADVERTISING LAW AND REGULATION ▶ ADVERTISING STRATEGIES ▶ BRANDS ▶ COMMERCIALIZATION: IMPACT ON MEDIA CONTENT ▶ ELABORATION LIKELIHOOD MODEL ▶ INTEGRATED MARKETING COMMUNICATIONS

REFERENCES AND SUGGESTED READINGS

Alexander, R. S. (ed.) (1965). *Marketing definitions*. Chicago: American Marketing Organization.

Ambler, T. & Roberts, J. H. (2006). *Beware the silver metric: Marketing performance measurement has to be multidimensional*. Marketing Science Institute, Report 06–113. Cambridge, MA: Marketing Science Institute.

Jin, H. S. & Lutz, R. J. (2013). The Typicality and Accessibility of Consumer Attitudes Toward Television Advertising: Implications for the Measurement of Attitudes Toward Advertising in General. *Journal of Advertising* 42(4), 343-357.

McDonald, C. & Scott, J. (2007). Brief history of advertising. In G. J. Tellis & T. Ambler (eds.), *The Sage handbook of advertising*. Thousand Oaks, CA: Sage.

Nerlove, M. & Arrow, K. (1962). Optimal advertising policy under dynamic conditions. *Economica*, 29, May, 129–142.

O'Guinn, T. C. & Faber, R. J. (1991). Mass communication theory and research. In H. H. Kassarjian & T. S. Robertson (eds.), *Handbook of consumer behavior theory and research*. Englewood Cliffs, NJ: Prentice-Hall, pp. 349–400.

Saunders, J. (2004). *Communications challenge: A practical guide to media neutral planning*. London: Account Planning Group.

Schultz, D. E. (1993). Integrated marketing communications: Maybe definition is in the point of view. *Marketing News*, January 18, 17.

White, R. (2005). Tracking ads and communications. *Admap*, 460, 12–15.

Advertising, Cross-Cultural

HOLGER ROSCHK
Catholic University of Eichstaett-Ingolstadt

KATJA GELBRICH
Catholic University of Eichstaett-Ingolstadt

MARTIN EISEND
European University Viadrina in Frankfurt (Oder)

With the globalization of markets, advertising professionals are faced with the question whether to standardize their message internationally or to tailor it to each country's target culture. Culture can be seen as the values shared by the members of a society (→ Culture: Definitions and Concepts). Adapting the message to the target audience enables companies to conform with cultural values, while standardizing entails the risk of violation of cultural rules. Theories such as learning theories and related empirical findings suggest that advertising is most persuasive if it conforms to recipients' values (e.g., Teng & Laroche 2006). Further, results of a contemporary cross-cultural meta-analysis for gender stereotyping show that sex role portrayal in advertising reflects past gender-related value changes in society (Eisend 2010; → Sex Role Stereotypes in the Media). In other words, advertising is (or should be) a mirror of society and the culture it is directed toward. Culture interferes with advertising in various ways. It impacts advertising objectives, message appeals, sex role portrayal, and humor.

Advertising objectives such as attracting attention or increasing purchase intention need to be adapted to the culture-specific communication style. In high-context societies such as Japan, little is explicitly stated and communication relies more on contextual cues, whereas in low-context cultures like the US, direct communication is favored. Accordingly, advertising is less persuasive in Japan than in the US. It aims at anchoring a product in the recipient's mind rather than at direct trial.

The goal of *appealing* to values like adventure or freedom is to condition a product or service in such a way that the audience associates it with these values. Extensive content-analytic research on advertising campaigns across cultures indicates that the values stressed tend to correspond to the countries' societal values, although economic and political transitions may be responsible for some contradictory results. For instance, in cultures such as Russia or Mexico, where individuals accept that power is distributed unequally, advertising appeals to status symbols more often than in egalitarian cultures like the US. Advertisements reflect self-achievement more often in individualistic cultures like France, in which individuals see themselves as detached from others, compared to collectivistic cultures like China, in which individuals' identity is stronger linked to their social network. The opposite holds true for sociability.

Sex roles are learned during the socialization process and differ across cultures. In masculine societies like Japan, sex roles are distinct and stronger gender stereotyping in advertising can be observed compared to feminine cultures like Sweden, where sex roles overlap. However, these results are relative. For instance, even in feminine cultures, more men than women appear in professional situations, while women are more often portrayed in non-job activities. Thus, gender stereotyping is prevalent across cultures, though it has decreased over the years mainly due to developments in high-masculinity countries (Eisend 2010).

Humor plays a vital role in message creation. It is a subversive play with conventions, norms, or ideas of a society, which comes in forms such as puns, jokes, irony, or satire. Since nonmembers of the society usually do not know those conventions they cannot understand the advertisement. Hence, humor is unlikely to travel across cultures. Failed humor can even confuse or offend the audience.

Advertising may also *break with societal rules*. There is ample anecdotal evidence for campaigns, which on purpose or accidentally violate cultural values, for instance, by depicting unfavorable sex roles. The Italian clothing company Benetton is a prominent example for its offensive campaigns. Shock advertisements, depicting, for example, a black woman as a wet nurse, and an unwashed newborn baby with the umbilical cord still attached, gave rise not only to public criticism, but also to consumer movements boycotting the company's products.

However, when most advertisers stick to traditional values there are various motives for breaking with them. Nonconforming advertisements may be successful as they gain attention through originality, fulfill the need for novelty seeking, or appeal to transnational target groups, who want to distinguish themselves from their own culture. Further, these advertisements may target values which are desired by a society, but are not practiced. For instance, New Zealand and Sweden are rather individualistic countries with regard to the way that people act, but people in both countries seek more collectivism. Breaking with cultural rules also allows companies to intentionally position themselves as foreign.

See also: ▶ ADVERTISING ▶ ADVERTISING EFFECTIVENESS, MEASUREMENT OF ▶ ADVERTISING STRATEGIES ▶ CULTURE: DEFINITIONS AND CONCEPTS ▶ SEX ROLE STEREOTYPES IN THE MEDIA

REFERENCES AND SUGGESTED READINGS

De Mooij, M. K. (2013). *Global marketing and advertising: Understanding cultural paradoxes*, 4th edn. Thousand Oaks, CA: Sage.

Eisend, M. (2010). A meta-analysis of gender roles in advertising. *Journal of the Academy of Marketing Science*, 38(4), 418–440.

Müller, S. & Gelbrich, K. (2014). Interkulturelles marketing [Cross-cultural marketing], 2nd edn. Munich: Vahlen.

Teng, L. & Laroche, M. (2006). Interactive effects of appeals, arguments, and competition across North American and Chinese cultures. *Journal of International Marketing*, 14(4), 110–128.

Advertising, Economics of

MATTHEW P. MCALLISTER
Pennsylvania State University

The economics of → advertising shape the history, current state, and future of media. Advertising revenue influences media not just through the insertion of ads, but also its nonadvertising content and access.

By 1900 both the US newspaper and magazine industries generated most of their revenue from advertising. Readers went from being primarily revenue providers – the customer/market of media – to being the commodity sold to the media's larger customer, advertisers. For-profit broadcasting was nearly completely dependent upon advertising. Other media carry only advertising and promotional messages, including billboards, direct mail, and branded websites. The advertising industry involves three powerful groups: advertisers, advertising agencies, and media. The largest advertisers are multinational conglomerates such as Procter and Gamble, spending billions annually. The US receives the most advertising spending, with China a rapidly growing second. *Agencies* engage in creative, research, → media planning and buying. Large global holding companies such as Omnicom own multiple full-service agencies that integrate marketing, advertising, and public relations functions, and leverage their market share in negotiations with media companies.

Advocates contend that advertising encourages lower prices through economies of scale, economic growth, and 'free' media. Criticisms include the barrier to entry for new commodities, and incentives for the growth of large *media monopolies*. Advertising also suppresses criticism of the industry and encourages pro-consumption messages in media content. Some media audiences are more valuable than others: audiences with disposable income and a susceptibility to advertising may find many content options.

Changes in advertising spending affect media viability. Decreasing advertising revenue for newspapers triggered concern about the future of → journalism. Digital's interactivity and convergence have attracted advertising spending and facilitated behavioral measures such as 'cost-per-click.' The resulting emphasis on data mining has turned media companies into audience-information brokers that collect audiences' media use and consumption patterns (→ Exposure to Communication Content).

Branded entertainment, where advertisers involved in the production processes and integrate the selling function in traditionally autonomous genres, also changes the economic conventional wisdom of advertising.

See also: ▶ ADVERTISING ▶ ADVERTISING, HISTORY OF ▶ BRANDS ▶ COMMERCIALIZATION: IMPACT ON MEDIA CONTENT ▶ COMMODIFICATION OF THE MEDIA ▶ CONCENTRATION IN MEDIA SYSTEMS ▶ CONSUMER CULTURE ▶ CONSUMERS IN MEDIA MARKETS ▶ EXPOSURE TO COMMUNICATION CONTENT ▶ EXPOSURE TO THE INTERNET ▶ GLOBALIZATION OF THE MEDIA ▶ JOURNALISM ▶ MEDIA CONGLOMERATES ▶ MEDIA ECONOMICS ▶ MEDIA PLANNING

REFERENCES AND SUGGESTED READINGS

Baker, C. E. (1994). *Advertising and a democratic press.* Princeton, NJ: Princeton University Press.

Sinclair, J. (2012). *Advertising, the media, and globalization: A world in motion.* London: Routledge.

Turow, J. (2011). *The Daily You: How the new advertising industry is defining your identity and your worth.* New Haven, CT: Yale University Press.

Advertising Effectiveness

GERARD J. TELLIS

University of Southern California

By the term 'advertising effectiveness,' we mean what changes → advertising creates in markets. Beyond changes in markets, advertising also creates changes in consumers' awareness, → attitudes, beliefs, and intentions. In the interest of focus and parsimony, this entry concentrates on the effects of advertising *only on market behavior*. This topic has been the subject of research from the time firms began to advertise, over a hundred years ago. Scientific research has begun to accumulate especially in the last 50 years (Tellis 2004; Tellis & Ambler 2007). This research falls within one of two paradigms: behavioral research and econometric research. Behavioral research uses theater or laboratory experiments to address the effects of advertising on awareness, attitudes, beliefs, and intentions (→ Experiment, Laboratory). On the other hand, field research uses field experiments (→ Experiment, Field) and econometric models to assess the effects of advertising on market behavior. We can classify field research into three groups: contemporaneous effects of ad intensity, dynamic effects of ad intensity, and effects of ad content. These subjects are the focus of the next three sections.

Contemporaneous Effects of Ad Intensity

Weight studies examine the effect of differences in ad budget across time periods or regions on sales. The main focus of such studies is to determine whether an increase in budget translates into a proportional or profitable increase in sales of the advertised product. Research leads to the following four important and surprising findings. First, changes in weight alone do not cause dramatic or substantive changes in sales. Second, prolonged cessation of advertising sometimes leads to deleterious effects on sales. Third, if advertising is effective, its effects are visible early on in the life of a campaign. Fourth, changes in media used, content of the ad, product advertised, target segments, or scheduling of ads are more likely to cause changes in sales than are changes in weight alone. These results have three implications. First, firms could be over-advertising; as a result, cutbacks in advertising do not lead to a loss in sales. Second, advertising may have delayed or even permanent effects, so that continued advertising at the same level is not always necessary. Third, a firm's budget increase or original budget itself may be more fruitfully employed in changes in media, content, target segments, product, or schedule rather than in weight alone.

Research on *advertising elasticity*, i.e. the percentage change in sales for a 1 percent change in the level of advertising, leads to the following important findings. First, across all studies, the mean estimated advertising elasticity is about 0.1, i.e., about one-twentieth the corresponding price elasticity. Second, advertising elasticity has been declining over time. Third, advertising elasticity is higher in earlier than later stages of the product life cycle, and for durables than non-durables. Fourth, advertising elasticities are higher for aggregate data than for disaggregate data, probably due to data-aggregation bias. These results suggest that price discounting may lead to a greater increase in sales than does an advertising increase; however, whether that increase is profitable would depend on the level of price cut, which consumers use it, and how much of that gets to the ultimate consumer rather than being pocketed by distributors. They also suggest that advertising may be more profitable for new products, while price discounting may be more profitable for mature products.

Research on *advertising frequency* leads to the following five findings. First, the effects of advertising exposure are less prominent and immediate and more fragile than those of price or promotion on brand choice. Second, in general, increasing frequency of exposures increases probability of brand choice at a decreasing rate. Third, for mature, frequently purchased products, the optimum level of exposure may be relatively small, ranging from one to three exposures a week. Fourth, brand loyalty may moderate response to ad exposures, in that established brands have an earlier and lower peak response to ad exposures than newer brands. Fifth, brand choice *may* be more responsive to the number of consumers the ad reaches than to the frequency with which it is repeated. These results suggest, among other things, that advertisers need to target loyal and nonbuyers of their products with different levels of exposures.

Dynamic Effects of Ad Intensity

The *carryover effect of advertising* is that effect it has on sales beyond the moment or time of exposure. Econometric studies have typically estimated the size and duration of the carryover effect. Research leads to the following main findings. First, advertising typically has some carryover, so that all its effectiveness does not occur in the contemporaneous time period to its exposure to the consumer. Second, the estimated effect of advertising depends on the level of data aggregation. Estimated carryover effects tend to be longer with the use of more aggregate data. In general, the more disaggregate the time period of data, the less biased is the estimated effect of advertising carryover. Further, the effect of advertising may last for fairly short periods – hours, days, or weeks – rather than for long periods such as months or years. Third, advertising's effects vary by region, city, and time of the day. Fourth, the carryover effect of advertising is as large as its current or instantaneous effect. These findings suggest, first, that advertisers should neither assume their advertising has only contemporaneous effects nor assume that is has very long-term carryover; second, advertisers need to evaluate the carryover effect of their advertising and do so with as temporally disaggregate data as they can find or collect; third, advertisers need to analyze effects by region and time period rather than rely on simple generalizations.

Ad campaigns *wear out* if run long enough. Wear-out occurs more slowly for ad content that is complex, emotional, or ambiguous, for ads that are less rather than more effective, for infrequently rather than frequently purchased products, for exposures spread apart rather than clustered together, for light rather than heavy viewers of TV, and for campaigns with increasing variety of ads or ad content. A break in a campaign may lead to an increase in effectiveness of the ad; if that happens, the ad wears out even faster than it did the first time around. In rare cases, possibly for new products, advertising seems to have permanent effects. That is, the effect of advertising persists even after the advertising is withdrawn. One of the implications of these findings for advertisers is that an ad which is ineffective early on should be discontinued. Also, whenever resources and time permit, advertisers should test their ads for wear-in and wear-out and accordingly decide on the duration of the ad campaign.

Effects of Ad Content

Research on ad content seems to suggest the following preliminary findings. First, changes in the creative, medium, target segment, or product itself sometimes lead to changes in sales, even though increases in the level of advertising by itself does not. Second, informative appeals may be more important early rather than late in the product's life cycle. Conversely, emotional appeals may be more effective late rather than early in a product's life cycle. These findings have two important implications for advertisers. First, to increase effectiveness, advertisers should modify content more than increase weight or frequency. Second, advertisers need to test and typically vary the content of their advertising with the life stage of the product.

See also: ▶ ADVERTISEMENT CAMPAIGN MANAGEMENT ▶ ADVERTISING ▶ ADVERTISING EFFECTIVENESS, MEASUREMENT OF ▶ ADVERTISING STRATEGIES ▶ ATTITUDES ▶ BRANDS ▶ EXPERIMENT, FIELD ▶ EXPERIMENT, LABORATORY ▶ QUANTITATIVE METHODOLOGY

REFERENCES AND SUGGESTED READINGS

Eisend, M., Langner, T., & Okazaki, S. (2012). *Advances in advertising research*. vol. III: *Current insights and future trends*. Wiesbaden: Springer Verlag.

Rosengren, S., Dahlen, M., & Okazaki, S. (2013). *Advances in advertising research*. vol. IV: *The changing roles of advertising*. Wiesbaden: Springer Gabler.

Tellis, G. J. (2004). *Effective advertising: How, when, and why advertising works*. Thousand Oaks, CA: Sage.

Tellis, G. J. & Ambler, T. (eds.) (2007). *The Sage handbook of advertising*. Thousand Oaks, CA: Sage.

Advertising Effectiveness, Measurement of

FRED BRONNER
University of Amsterdam

Nowadays there is little argument in the commercial as well as academic world that campaigns should be monitored to manage them better in the marketplace (Advertisement Campaign Management). Which research design is adequate for measuring ad effect and which key performance indicators, divided into advertising response and brand response, have to be selected?

Answering questions about the effect of a campaign upon variables like brand awareness, brand sympathy, or brand usage, and isolating the net effect of an advertising campaign on changes requires an appropriate research design. When we combine two designs (pre-campaign/ post-campaign and exposed / non-exposed) we obtain a very powerful tool. The campaign effect score E equals $(a-b) - (c-d)$. The element $(a-b)$ can be considered as an indicator of the effect of developments taking place in the world that are not due to the campaign – the element $(c-d)$ represents the changes that take place separately from the campaign. Hence, we can separate campaign influence from other factors such as high levels of media attention (→ Experiment, Field; Experiment, Laboratory).

	Before	After
Exposed	b	a
Not Exposed	d	c

The most difficult challenge in this scheme is how to establish whether someone has been exposed to the campaign or not. The solution is the use of panels (→ Survey). In the *combined panel/ad hoc design* a pre-measurement is carried out on sample X. After the campaign this sample is subjected to a limited re-interview, exclusively to establish if they were exposed to the campaign or not. These exposure scores are added to the pre-measurement. An independent post-measurement is carried out on sample Y in which both exposure and effect variables are measured.

Daniel Starch wrote as long ago as 1923 that for an advertisement to be successful it must be seen, read, believed, remembered, and acted upon. In the Starch philosophy, and still today, an advertisement must first be seen. How can we measure accurately if a consumer has seen an ad (cognitive response)? In the research world there are two schools of thought on this: measure spontaneously, or show the TV commercial or print ad and ask if the consumer has seen it (recognition). Because visual prompts connect with memory traces more effectively than verbal prompts it is better to use recognition.

For *affective ad response* in a standardized approach, one set of beliefs about ads is used to compare strong and weak points of the ads over all beliefs. For *conative ad response* behavioral measures can be used. Nowadays, many print ads and TV commercials include in a lead to an Internet site. Post hoc qualitative research on site visitors can reveal much about the advertisement's role.

In nearly all effect studies, the *effect of advertising upon brand awareness* (cognitive brand response) is measured in three steps: top of mind ("Which beer brands do you know?" – first one mentioned), spontaneous ("Which beer brands do you know?" – all brands mentioned), and aided ("Here is a list of beer brands with their logos. Which ones do you know, at least by name?"). Familiarity can also be measured, and is a more nuanced scale ("just heard of / know just a little / know fair amount / know very well"; → Memory; Information Processing). For the measurement of *affective brand response* the brand that is the focus of the campaign and its main competitors are measured on a salient list of attributes (brand beliefs) relating to corporate-, product-, and user-profile facets. Finally, likely changes in behavior (conative brand response) are measured through the introduction of such measures as purchase consideration and intention. Advertising can influence future buying decisions even when subjects do not recollect ever having seen the ad. Neuro-marketing may shed more light on this phenomenon in future years.

Increasing *simultaneous media exposure* raises questions on how media advertising should be planned and measured in the near future. The use of multimedia and cross-media strategies will influence the measurement of advertising effectiveness.

See also: ▶ ADVERTISEMENT CAMPAIGN MANAGEMENT ▶ ADVERTISING EFFECTIVENESS ▶ ADVERTISING STRATEGIES ▶ EXPERIMENT, FIELD ▶ EXPERIMENT, LABORATORY ▶ INFORMATION PROCESSING ▶ MEMORY ▶ SURVEY

REFERENCES AND SUGGESTED READINGS

Bronner, A. E. & Neijens, P. (2006). Audience experiences of media context and embedded advertising: A comparison of eight media. *International Journal of Market Research*, 48(1), 81–100.

Eisend, M., Langner, T., & Okazaki, S. (2012). *Advances in Advertising Research (vol. III): current insights and future trends*. Wiesbaden: Springer Verlag.

Rosengren, S., Dahlen, M., & Okazaki, S. (2013). *Advances in advertising research (vol. IV): the changing roles of advertising*. Wiesbaden: Springer Gabler.

Starch, D. (1923). *Principles of advertising*. Chicago: A.W. Shaw.

Advertising: Global Industry

JOHN SINCLAIR
University of Melbourne

Advertising is the key link in the mutually sustained global expansion of consumer goods and services industries and the media of communication that carry their commercial messages (→ Advertising). It is the life-blood of the media, the motive force behind media industry development, and the publicly most visible dimension of → marketing.

The period since World War II has seen the internationalization of the advertising industry proceed in tandem with the emergence of the 'multinational,' now global, consumer goods corporation, as well as with the international expansion of new media, driven by their capacity to carry commercial messages to audiences (→ Globalization of the Media). The flow of advertising expenditure toward new media, notably subscription television and, more dramatically, the Internet, is undercutting the 'mass' media we have known in the past.

An accompanying drift to *nonadvertising forms of promotion* is tending to undermine the traditional business model on which the relationship between advertisers and the media has rested since the advent of commercial broadcasting. Instead of the media amassing audiences for sale to advertisers, the trend is propelling growth in new means of marketing delivery, particularly the mobile phone, the Internet, and interactive TV. This implies on the one hand a more fragmented society, but on the other, a more interactive relationship between producers and consumers (→ Audience Segmentation).

Recent theory and research have largely moved away from the study of advertising as such, and more toward consumer culture in general. In the process, there is also a useful fusion being achieved between the traditionally antagonistic camps of political economy and → cultural studies, under the rubric of "cultural economy" (McFall 2004), while some of the most innovative work in recent years has focused on brands and branding (Arvidsson 2006).

See also: ▶ ADVERTISING ▶ ADVERTISING, CROSS-CULTURAL ▶ ADVERTISING, ECONOMICS OF

▶ AUDIENCE SEGMENTATION ▶ BRANDING
▶ BRANDS ▶ CABLE TELEVISION ▶ CONSUMER
CULTURE ▶ CULTURAL STUDIES
▶ GLOBALIZATION OF THE MEDIA ▶ MARKETING
▶ POLITICAL ECONOMY OF THE MEDIA
▶ PUBLIC RELATIONS ▶ SATELLITE TELEVISION

REFERENCES AND SUGGESTED READINGS

Arvidsson, A. (2006). *Brands: Meaning and value in media culture*. London: Routledge.
McFall, L. (2004). *Advertising: A cultural economy*. London: Sage.
Sinclair, J. (2012). *Advertising, the media and globalisation*. London: Routledge.

Advertising, History of

LIZ MCFALL
Open University

The modern sense of → advertising can be traced to its origins in late-sixteenth century attempts to establish information bureaus. Theophraste Renaudot established the *Bureau d'adresse et de rencontre* in France in 1630 and published one of the first advertising newspapers. Similar offices and newspapers soon formed across Europe. By the 1750s, advertising newspapers proliferated in forms ranging from the state monopoly *Intelligenzblatt* in Prussia to the mixed economy of newspapers in England. The office function was superseded by the growing network of coffee houses (→ Public Opinion). Coffee houses played a role in the development of financial institutions acting as travel agents, insurance agents, hotels and 'conference centers.' Their main connection, however, was to the press and advertising. The earliest coffee houses distributed newspapers and acted as reading rooms (→ Newspaper, History of).

The *advertising agency system* developed from these early connections to coffee houses and newspapers. The first British advertising agency was Tayler and Newton, established in 1786, followed by Whites in 1800 and in 1812 by Reynells, Lawson and Barker, and Deacons. Archive material shows agencies involved in the distribution of news and newspapers, political parliamentary correspondence, and advising on advertisement design and placement. Some agencies combined advertising trade with services such as bookselling, insurance, dentistry, and undertaking. By the early twentieth century, advertising agencies in a recognizable form dominated the institutional field, with agencies increasingly offering a range of services to clients or 'accounts' under the 'full-service agency' model. *Full-service* was the term adopted by agencies which provided services including research and creative design, account management, and media space-buying. The full-service model competed with agencies providing minimal service and offering low rates by 'commission splitting' or farming bulk-bought space. By the middle of the twentieth century, the advertising industry had largely settled into the full-service model.

Historians differ over the precise dates of the *first printed advertisements*. The word 'advertisement' appears in print in the sixteenth century and over press announcements in the seventeenth century. These were not really advertisements in the contemporary sense. Rather, the term was interchangeable with 'announcement' or 'notice.' By the 1700s 'advertisement' was deployed in some newspapers to refer to particular types of advertisement while other newspapers completely refused paid content. Newspapers had a vested interest in accepting advertisements but this vied with reservations, best illustrated by the regulations imposed upon advertisers. The 'agate-only' rule, for example, stipulated that paid advertisements must use only small, classified typefaces. Advertisers used numerous techniques to circumvent these regulations for instance by using drop capitals, repetition, and acrostics to produce patterns. Instead of newspapers, broadsheets and posters were often used to create visual displays. Poetry, jokes, puzzles, rhythm, association, endorsement, and emotional blackmail were also used as persuasive devices. Samuel Johnson's comment "the improper disposition of advertisements," by which "the noblest objects may be so associated as to be made ridiculous," reveals the long historical disapproval of such rhetorical excesses.

Throughout its history, advertising has used a range of *media and technologies*. From the 1830s, gas lanterns were used to illuminate posters and shops, by the 1870s, magic lanterns displayed animated messages. Advertisements were placed on walls, windows, bridges, public transport, trees, barns, and cliff-faces. Poster sites were unregulated and competition was fierce. Placard-bearers were extensively used. Costumed men, women, and children carried boards or dressed up as the object advertised. There were also forgotten contraptions like 'advertising vans.' These mobile horse-drawn devices came in a variety of shapes: globes, pyramids and mosques, and were complemented by stationary advertising devices that stood in busy thoroughfares. The atmosphere was summed up in *The Times* in 1892 "advertisements are turning England into a sordid and disorderly spectacle from sea to sea … Fields and hillsides are being covered with unwonted crops of hoardings. The sky is defaced by unheavenly signs." Through such means nineteenth-century advertising messages pervaded both public and private, urban and rural environments.

See also: ▶ ADVERTISING ▶ MEDIA HISTORY ▶ NEWSPAPER, HISTORY OF ▶ PUBLIC OPINION

REFERENCES AND SUGGESTED READINGS

Lears, J. (1994). *Fables of abundance: A cultural history of advertising in America*. New York: Basic Books.
Leiss, W., Kline, S., Jhally, S., & Botterill, J. (2005). *Social communication in advertising*, 3rd edn. London: Routledge.
McFall, L. (2004). *Advertising: A cultural economy*. Thousand Oaks, CA: Sage.
Pope, D. (1983). *The making of modern advertising*. New York: Basic Books.
Presbrey, F. (1929). *The history and development of advertising*. New York: Greenwood.

Advertising Law and Regulations

SOONTAE AN
Ewha Womans University

The role of → advertising in society continues to expand around the world. In response, many societies face greater challenges in regulating advertising to protect the public from deceptive and unfair business conduct. Although the scope of advertising law and regulations varies from country to country, regulation is generally manifested as self-regulation by the industry and statutory regulation by various government bodies.

In many countries, *self-regulation* – voluntary, industry-wide control by advertisers – complements legal regulatory systems. Given that each self-regulatory system offers a different set of standards and codes, the International Chamber of Commerce (ICC) plays an important role in coordinating efforts to develop international guidelines and policies. The ICC publishes the International Code of Advertising Practice that is used and integrated into many self-regulatory systems around the world and handles complaints when the scope of a dispute spans multiple countries, or in cases where national self-regulatory systems do not exist. Other key international organizations include the International Advertising Association (IAA) and the World Federation of Advertisers.

With *statutory regulation*, a variety of judicial tools can be utilized to achieve prompt and efficient control of advertising practices. Depending on the nature and type of advertising, many different specialized government agencies oversee its regulation. For a long time, advertising was considered to be outside the *realm of freedom of expression*. When the US Supreme Court first considered the issue in 1942, it decided that "purely commercial advertising" was not the type of speech protected by the First Amendment. In 1976, that decision was explicitly overruled by the US Supreme Court, who reasoned that such advertisements conveyed vital information to the public and that a free enterprise economy depended upon a free flow of commercial information. Contrary to the US Supreme Court's categorical approach, the European courts have tended to apply the same principles to both commercial and non-commercial expression of speech.

Advertising of certain products or services has received closer regulatory scrutiny. For example, the issue of advertising toward children has prompted many restrictions. Furthermore, advertising of certain products is prohibited, especially on broadcast media. Direct-to-consumer prescription advertising is forbidden in all countries except in the US and New Zealand. In fact, advertising of cigarettes demonstrates a substantially different application of the commercial speech doctrine. Unlike the US and Canada, many European countries have imposed a comprehensive ban on tobacco advertising .

See also: ▶ ADVERTISING ▶ FREEDOM OF COMMUNICATION ▶ FREEDOM OF THE PRESS, CONCEPT OF ▶ SELF-REGULATION OF THE MEDIA

REFERENCES AND SUGGESTED READINGS

Boddewyn, J. J. (1992). *Global perspectives on advertising self-regulation: Principles and practices in thirty eight countries.* Westport, CT: Quorum Books.

Shaver, M. A. & An, S. (2013). The Global Advertising Regulation Handbook Armonk, NY: M.E. Sharpe.

Shiner, R. A. (2003). *Freedom of Commercial Expression.* Oxford: Oxford University Press.

Advertising as Persuasion

BOB M. FENNIS

University of Groningen

Advertising as → persuasion may be defined as intentional, commercial communication aimed at convincing consumers of the value of the product or brand advertised. It focuses on the impact of advertising stimuli on cognitive, affective, and behavioral consumer responses (Fennis & Stroebe 2010). As a classic approach, the so called "Yale studies" (Hovland, Janis, & Kelley 1953; → Media Effects, History of) produced the message-learning approach to persuasion stating that persuasion involves a four-stage process: attention, comprehension, yielding, and retention. Hence, persuasive ads are those that are attention-grabbing, easy to comprehend, convincing, and memorable (see Fennis & Stroebe 2010).

The → *elaboration likelihood model* (ELM; Petty & Cacioppo 1986) and the *heuristic systematic processing model* (HSM; Chaiken 1980) represent more contemporary approaches and assume that persuasion is a function of two distinct modes of processing that anchor a controlled–automatic continuum. When consumer motivation and/or ability are high, persuasion is the result of careful scrutiny of the true merits of the product that is advertised in the message. In contrast, when motivation and/or ability is low, persuasion comes about via less effortful means, with consumers basing their evaluations on message elements that offer shortcuts for inferring something about product quality.

While these frameworks rely on *conscious* information processing to understand persuasion effects, recent developments have centered on studying *unconscious* influences of advertising spurred, by work on automatic construct activation (i.e., 'priming'; Bargh 2002).

See also: ▶ ADVERTISING ▶ ADVERTISING EFFECTIVENESS, MEASUREMENT OF ▶ ATTENDING TO THE MASS MEDIA ▶ ATTITUDE–BEHAVIOR CONSISTENCY ▶ ELABORATION LIKELIHOOD MODEL ▶ INFORMATION PROCESSING ▶ MEDIA EFFECTS, HISTORY OF ▶ PERSUASION

REFERENCES AND SUGGESTED READINGS

Bargh, J. A. (2002). Losing consciousness: Automatic influences on consumer judgment, behavior, and motivation. *Journal of Consumer Research*, 29, 280–285.

Chaiken, S. (1980). Heuristic versus systematic information processing and the use of source versus message cues in persuasion. *Journal of Personality and Social Psychology*, 39, 752–766.

Fennis, B. M., & Stroebe, W. (2010). *The psychology of advertising.* Hove, UK: Psychology Press.

Hovland, C. I., Janis, I. L., & Kelley, H. H. (1953). *Communication and persuasion: Psychological studies of opinion change.* New Haven, CT: Yale University Press.

Petty, R. E. & Cacioppo, J. T. (1986). *Communication and persuasion: Central and peripheral routes to attitude change.* New York: Springer.

Advertising: Responses across the Life-Span

MONIEK BUIJZEN

Radboud University Nijmegen

Advertising responses are thoughts, emotions, and behaviors generated by exposure to commercial messages. Responses to → advertising can be divided into cognitive, affective, and behavioral responses. Cognitive responses include recall or recognition of advertisements and brands, affective responses include likes and dislikes of advertisements and brands, and behavioral responses involve purchasing and consuming the advertised brands (→ Advertising Effectiveness; Advertising Effectiveness, Measurement of).

Advertising research has shown that the way consumers respond to persuasive information varies greatly across different stages of life (John 1999). In particular, children are more receptive to persuasive information than adults, because they have less experience with it. Compared to adults, children are less able to come up with critical thoughts and counterarguments while being exposed to advertising.

During childhood and adolescence (→ Development Communication), children develop various advertising-related competencies, which are known as "advertising literacy" (Rozendaal et al. 2011; → Media Literacy). Seven *competencies* have been identified: (1) distinguishing commercials from programs, (2) recognition of advertising's source, (3) perception of the intended audience, (4) understanding advertising's selling intent, (5) understanding advertising's persuasive intent, (6) understanding of advertising tactics and appeals, (7) recognizing bias in advertising.

In addition to these conceptual advertising competencies, recent literature assumes that the development of advertising literacy is not only a matter of obtaining the necessary advertising knowledge, but also of acquiring the information-processing skills to apply that advertising knowledge while processing an advertisement (→ Information Processing). Due to the affect-based nature of contemporary advertising, in combination with children's immature cognitive abilities, children primarily process advertising under conditions of low elaboration (→ Elaboration Likelihood Model) and, consequently, are unlikely to apply conceptual advertising knowledge as a defense (Buijzen, Van Reijmersdal, & Owen 2010). Therefore, current conceptualizations of advertising literacy include three dimensions: *conceptual advertising literacy*, including the seven competencies, *advertising literacy performance*, involving the actual use of conceptual advertising knowledge, and *attitudinal advertising literacy*, including low-effort affective mechanisms, functioning as a defense under conditions of low elaboration.

As yet, advertising research has predominantly focused on the development of conceptual advertising literacy. Although it is assumed that advertising literacy performance and attitudinal advertising literacy emerge later in the developmental sequence, it is unclear at what stage. Moreover, there is a lack of knowledge on the differential impact of the three dimensions on the cognitive, affective, and behavioral responses to advertising.

To gain full understanding of advertising responses across the life-span, future research should recognize the conceptual complexity of both advertising responses and advertising literacy.

See also: ▶ ADVERTISING ▶ ADVERTISING EFFECTIVENESS ▶ ADVERTISING EFFECTIVENESS, MEASUREMENT OF ▶ ADVERTISING STRATEGIES ▶ DEVELOPMENT COMMUNICATION ▶ ELABORATION LIKELIHOOD MODEL ▶ INFORMATION PROCESSING ▶ MEDIA LITERACY

REFERENCES AND SUGGESTED READINGS

Buijzen, M., Van Reijmersdal, E. A., & Owen, L.H. (2010). Introducing the PCMC model: An investigative framework for young people's processing of commercial media content. *Communication Theory*, 20, 427–450.

John, D. R. (1999). Consumer socialization of children: A retrospective look at twenty-five years of research. *Journal of Consumer Research*, 26, 183–213.

Rozendaal, E., Lapierre, M., Buijzen, M., & Van Reijmersdal, E. A. (2011). Reconsidering advertising literacy as a defense against advertising effects. *Media Psychology*, 14, 333–354.

Advertising Strategies

BAS VAN DEN PUTTE
University of Amsterdam

Advertising strategy is the set of decisions an organization takes with respect to the employment of → advertising to reach one or more objectives among a specific target group. Each advertising strategy is based on the marketing strategy that encompasses the strategic decisions regarding all marketing activities, such as packaging, price, distribution, and promotion (→ Marketing). Within this set of marketing activities, advertising is part of the promotion strategy. Besides defining target group and communication objectives, main parts of the advertising strategy are message strategy and → media planning strategy. A further difference can be drawn between message strategy and creative execution strategy. The message strategy determines what communication objective is addressed by an advertisement; the creative execution defines how this objective is addressed. Though the ultimate goal of advertising is to maintain and increase the level of brand sales, most often advertising is employed to reach intermediate goals. Most important of these is communicating how a brand is positioned among its competitors. Other often-employed intermediate goals are brand awareness, generating a general positive feeling toward the brand, and purchase intention.

An important question is how the most effective message strategy can be selected. Generally it is advised, besides maintaining and increasing brand awareness, that the advertising strategy should match the main purchase motives of consumers. Many overviews of message strategies have been published and there is no generally agreed-upon typology. Nevertheless, a central element of most typologies is the difference between informational advertising that appeals to the rational mind and emotional advertising that appeals to the feelings of consumers (→ Cognitive Science).

An example is the well-known FCB grid which consists of four quadrants, defined by two dimensions: level of involvement and a thinking–feeling dimension. In the thinking dimension, often an important consumer motive is to solve a practical problem. In the high-involvement/thinking quadrant, the purchase is important to consumers and they make a rational decision based on functional information. Therefore, in this situation an informational message strategy should be used. In the low-involvement/thinking quadrant, buying behavior is habitual and consumers want to spend as little time and brain activity as possible on purchasing products, often fast-moving consumer goods. The primary aim of advertising is to remind consumers of the existence of the → brand. In the high-involvement/feeling quadrant, the consumer motive is ego gratification, that is, the need to defend, enhance, and express one's basic personality. The advice is to apply a message strategy that aims at relating the brand to the personality of the consumer. The low-involvement/feeling quadrant is reserved for products where involvement is low and the purchase decision is based on sensory gratification, that is, the desire to please one or more of the five senses. The message strategy should stress how the brand stimulates personal satisfaction, and advertising should induce product trial so people can experience the brand. Finally, social acceptance can be relevant in situations of both low and high involvement. The message strategy can address the need to be viewed favorably in the eyes of others.

Once the main message strategy is chosen, campaign developers can choose from a long list of creative execution strategies. How many product advantages should be mentioned, and should the best argument be mentioned first or last? Should the information be one- or two-sided? Should the conclusion be explicit or implicit? Should an endorser be employed and, if so, should this be a celebrity, expert, consumer, attractive or erotic model, or perhaps an animated character? Should the format be a testimonial, demonstration, product comparison, slice of life, or dramatization? Should humor be used, or fear? Unfortunately, there are no easy answers to these and many other questions. A particular executional factor may be highly effective in one advertising campaign, but may cause detrimental results in another campaign. The effectiveness of each executional factor is dependent on many variables, primarily the chosen advertising objective, the product category, and the motives and personal characteristics of the target group.

See also: ▶ ADVERTISEMENT CAMPAIGN MANAGEMENT ▶ ADVERTISING ▶ ADVERTISING EFFECTIVENESS ▶ ADVERTISING EFFECTIVENESS, MEASUREMENT OF ▶ ADVERTISING AS PERSUASION ▶ BRANDS ▶ COGNITIVE SCIENCE ▶ INFORMATION PROCESSING ▶ MARKETING ▶ MEDIA PLANNING ▶ PERSUASION ▶ SEGMENTATION OF THE ADVERTISING AUDIENCE ▶ VALIDITY

REFERENCES AND SUGGESTED READINGS

Armstrong, J. S. (2010). *Persuasive advertising: Evidence-based principles*. Basingstoke: Palgrave Macmillan.

Franzen, G. (1999). *Brands and advertising: How advertising effectiveness influences brand equity*. Henley-on-Thames: Admap.

Rossiter, J. R. & Percy, L. (1998). *Advertising communications and promotions management*. Boston: Irwin and McGraw-Hill.

Stewart, D. W. & Furse, D. H. (1986). *Effective television advertising: A study of 1000 commercials*. Lexington, MA: Lexington.

Van den Putte, B. (2002). An integrative framework for effective communication. In G. Bartels & W. Nelissen (eds.), *Marketing for sustainability: Towards transactional policy-making*. Amsterdam: IOS Press, pp. 83–95.

Advocacy Journalism

ROBERT JENSEN
University of Texas at Austin

The term 'advocacy journalism' describes the use of journalism techniques to promote a specific political or social cause. Other terms used for practice outside the mainstream include 'alternative,' 'gonzo,' or 'new journalism' (→ Alternative Journalism). The term is potentially meaningful only in opposition to a category of journalism that does not engage in advocacy, so-called *objective* journalism (→ Objectivity in Reporting).

This advocacy/objectivity dichotomy springs from political theory that asserts a special role for journalists in complex democratic societies. Journalists' claims to credibility are based in an assertion of neutrality. They argue for public trust by basing their report of facts, analysis, and opinion on rigorous information gathering. Professional self-monitoring produces what journalists consider an unbiased account of reality, rather than a selective account reflecting a guiding political agenda.

At one level, the term 'advocacy' might be useful in distinguishing, for example, journalistic efforts clearly serving a partisan agenda (such as a political party publication) from those officially serving nonpartisan ends (such as a commercial newspaper). But the distinction is not really between forms of journalism as much as between persuasion and journalism. Although so-called objective journalism assumes that, as a rule, disinterested observers tend to produce more reliable reports, a publication advocating a cause might have more accurate information and compelling analysis than a nonpartisan one. The intentions of those writing and editing the publication are the key distinguishing factor.

All reporters use a framework of analysis to understand the world and report on it. But reporting that contains open references to underlying political assumptions and conclusions seems to engage in advocacy, while the more conventional approach appears neutral. Both are independent in the sense of not being directed by a party or movement, but neither approach is in fact neutral. One explicitly endorses a political perspective critical of the powerful, while the other implicitly reinforces the political perspective of the elite (→ News Ideologies).

See also: ▶ ALTERNATIVE JOURNALISM ▶ JOURNALISTS' ROLE PERCEPTION ▶ NEWS IDEOLOGIES ▶ OBJECTIVITY IN REPORTING

REFERENCES AND SUGGESTED READINGS

Applegate, E. (2009). *Advocacy journalists: A biographical dictionary of writers and editors* Lanham, MD: Scarecrow Press.
Collings, A. (2001). *Words of fire: Independent journalists who challenge dictators, druglords, and other enemies of a free press*. New York: New York University Press.
Kessler, L. (1984). *The dissident press: Alternative journalism in American history*. Newbury Park, CA: Sage.
Mindich, D. T. Z. (1998). *Just the facts: How "objectivity" came to define American journalism*. New York: New York University Press.

Affective Disposition Theories

ARTHUR A. RANEY
Florida State University

Affective disposition theory (ADT) explains the process by which we enjoy different entertainment narratives. The theory conceptualizes media enjoyment – primarily thought of in hedonic terms – as the product of a viewer's emotional affiliations (i.e., affective dispositions) with characters and the outcomes experienced by those characters in the narrative (→ Parasocial Interactions and Relationships).

ADT contends that we form dispositions toward media characters in much the same way we do with people in the real world. First, we tend to like those whom we perceive to be similar to ourselves, with those perceptions being filtered through a moral lens. Thus, moral considerations govern the valence of the dispositions we form, with characters whose actions and motivations are judged to be morally correct liked more. Second, the intensity of those dispositions vary on a continuum from extremely positive through indifference to extremely negative, and may fluctuate as the narrative unfolds. Third, affective dispositions trigger empathy-based reactions toward things experienced by characters. As a result, with beloved protagonists, we hope for their success and fear for their failure; with hated villains, we desire the opposite. Finally, if the outcomes wished for by viewers are depicted in the narrative, then enjoyment increases in proportion to the strength of the affective dispositions held. If those hoped-for outcomes are not portrayed, then enjoyment suffers in proportion to the strength of the dispositions.

Despite subtle operational variations, the basic ADT formula has been demonstrated as stable across various genres, including humor, drama, frightening fare, → reality TV, sports, and digital games (→ Digital Imagery). Current ADT research further explores these cross-genre differences, as well as issues related to viewer and character morality, discrete emotional reactions toward characters, how expectations impact enjoyment, and non-hedonic/meaningful media experiences.

See also: ▶ DIGITAL IMAGERY ▶ FICTION ▶ MOOD MANAGEMENT ▶ PARASOCIAL INTERACTIONS AND RELATIONSHIPS ▶ REALITY TV ▶ SELECTIVE EXPOSURE ▶ USES AND GRATIFICATIONS

REFERENCES AND SUGGESTED READINGS

Raney, A. A. (2004). Expanding disposition theory: Reconsidering character liking, moral evaluations, and enjoyment. *Communication Theory*, 14(4), 348–369.

Zillmann, D. (2000). Basal morality in drama appreciation. In I. Bondebjerg (ed.), *Moving images, culture, and the mind*. Luton: University of Luton Press, pp. 53–63.

Zillmann, D. & Cantor, J. (1976). A disposition theory of humor and mirth. In T. Chapman & H. Foot (eds.), *Humor and laughter: Theory, research, and application*. London: Wiley, pp. 93–115.

Affects and Media Exposure

ELLY A. KONIJN
Vrije Universiteit Amsterdam

Affect covers various concepts, such as moods, feelings, and emotions and indicates either a positive or negative feeling state. *Mood* relates to an enduring affective state, no felt urgency, and not clearly elicited by an external event. Moods may also have a biochemical source, such as experimentally induced epinephrine effects. *Emotion* is clearly defined by a specific event, with a beginning and ending, has an object and relates to meaningful events. Emotions comprise the felt need to (not) act to serve one's goals or concerns. *Experiencing* (or felt) emotions should be differentiated from the *expression* of emotions (depicted).

Mood management theory states that people select particular media programming in order to avoid negative and restore pleasant feeling states (→ Mood Management). Through empathy with the sufferings of others, we feel empathic distress and fear for the fate of the sympathetic protagonist, whereas we hope for the devastation of his/her rivals (→ Affective Disposition Theories). Numerous related concepts have evolved such as → parasocial interactions and relationships or → presence. Scholars proposed using an umbrella concept (e.g., emotional involvement; appreciation) to be defined in terms of a tradeoff of parallel positive (e.g., empathy) and negative (e.g., detachment) affects (Konijn & Hoorn 2005).

Furthermore, uses and gratifications theory states that we seek media exposure for affective, informative, social, or dispersion-seeking motivations (→ Escapism; Uses and Gratifications). Social Comparison Theory adds that looking at others' sufferings may make us feel better (→ Social Comparison Theory). Aggressiveness from violent media exposure has largely been studied from a → social cognitive theory perspective (→ Violence as Media Content, Effects of). Emotion psychology further explains why we seek affective gratifications by media exposure just for the sake of being moved and the social sharing of emotions following basic human needs (Konijn 2012).

In the context of → persuasion, ads, and commercials, the study of affect, mood, and emotions has evolved as a field on its own, because (even negative) "emotions sell" (Williams & Aaker 2002; → Advertising Effectiveness). Mostly studied are fear appeals (→ Fear Induction through Media Content), humor, and attaching sexual affect to commercial content in creating a positive association with the product. The results of such affect-laden advertisements are mixed because consumers may remember the affect-arousing image (e.g., the joke) but not the message, the affect-laden images may not match with the advertised product, or be considered irrelevant by the consumer. In addition, social factors like watching with friends and relatives may further increase the affective response and the program's effectiveness.

Through the world-wide-web, much traditional media fare is readily available alongside interactive digital offerings, such as online gaming and → social media. As in real life, social and virtual lives are filled with affect and emotions. For example, boys play violent games to vent their anger, while others are engaged in cyberbullying, reviving the moral panic debate. Affective computing (Picard 1997) is an emerging research field focused on adding emotion to technology to make the interaction more human-like. Importantly, increased interaction with 'virtual others', such as virtual tutors, synthetic health coaches, and care robots is foreseen due to aging and limited resources.

Affect, moods, and emotions influence how the information derived from media exposure is processed (→ Information Processing). Emotional processing limits the capacity to cognitively process and store the information. Systematic (experimental) studies are scarce, especially on the role of emotions in acquiring real-world knowledge from fictional content. Research shows that emotionalized viewers are more inclined to take fiction for real than are non-emotional viewers. Based on neurobiological and developmental neuroscience, these scholars argued that because emotions are our 'life-vests,' they tell us what information to take seriously – mediated or not (Konijn 2012). Future research is warranted in detailing how affective processing of media fare impacts our knowledge structures, especially given our current 'mediated society' and the hybrid 'reality status' of many media messages, where affect and emotions may take the lead.

See also: ▶ ADVERTISING EFFECTIVENESS ▶ AFFECTIVE DISPOSITION THEORIES ▶ APPRAISAL THEORY ▶ ENTERTAINMENT CONTENT AND REALITY PERCEPTION ▶ ESCAPISM ▶ FEAR INDUCTION THROUGH MEDIA CONTENT ▶ INFORMATION PROCESSING ▶ INVOLVEMENT WITH MEDIA CONTENT ▶ INFORMATION PROCESSING ▶ MOOD MANAGEMENT ▶ PARASOCIAL INTERACTIONS AND RELATIONSHIPS ▶ PERSUASION ▶ PRESENCE ▶ SELECTIVE EXPOSURE ▶ SOCIAL COGNITIVE THEORY ▶ SOCIAL COMPARISON THEORY ▶ SOCIAL MEDIA ▶ USES AND GRATIFICATIONS ▶ VIOLENCE AS MEDIA CONTENT, EFFECTS OF

REFERENCES AND SUGGESTED READINGS

Döveling, K., Von Scheve, C., & Konijn, E. A. (eds.) (2010). *The Routledge handbook of emotions and mass media*. London: Routledge.

Frijda, N. H. (1986). *The emotions*. Cambridge: Cambridge University Press.

Konijn, E. A. (2012). The role of emotion in media use and effects. In: Dill, K. (ed.). *The Oxford handbook of media psychology*. Oxford: Oxford University Press, pp. 186–211.

Konijn, E. A. & Hoorn, J. F. (2005). Some like it bad. *Media Psychology*, 7(2), 107–144.

Picard, R. W. (1997). *Affective computing*. Cambridge, MA: MIT Press.

Williams, P. & Aaker, J. L. (2002). Can mixed emotions peacefully coexist? *Journal of Consumer Research*, 28, 636–649.

Africa: Media Systems

WINSTON MANO
University of Westminster

This entry concentrates on media systems in countries of Sub-Saharan Africa. The Sub-Saharan media system was born in the colonial era. The use of European languages, state-biased ownership systems, and limited media freedom are among colonial media attributes that continue in Sub-Saharan Africa, a 48-country region that is huge and diverse.

The spread and access to the mass media in Sub-Saharan Africa has been a highly uneven process. Among old media, radio has achieved the best penetration owing to its affordability and adaptability. Even the largely urban and elitist medium of television has shown remarkable growth in Africa. The figures for print media titles published in Sub-Saharan Africa also show a marked increase in titles and the total average circulation of dailies (World Association of Newspapers 2009). Today's rapid growth of the African media belies the fact that these mass media are recent and that they were mainly introduced during the colonial era.

Print and Radio

One of the most obvious features of Sub-Saharan African media is the way print media were introduced in different parts of the region. The press in English-speaking West Africa was the earliest in Sub-Saharan Africa. Missionaries also helped introduce newspapers in the region. By contrast to patterns in West Africa, in Anglophone *Southern and Central Africa*, the press was largely introduced by European settlers. The most notable newspapers at this time included the "Cape Argus," founded in 1857. The beginnings of the press in *East Africa* were not different from other parts of Africa. It was largely created for its settler population.

The *French colonial administration* in Africa actively discouraged the development of the press in the colonies. A heavy tax was placed on imported newsprint and printing machinery and in keeping with their policy of assimilation of Africans into French culture they preferred to freely circulate newspapers produced in the metropolis to their African colonies.

The introduction and organization of *radio* closely followed colonial political and administrative systems. The British deliberately promoted the use of local languages in an attempt to build an African audience. The French, unlike the British, who wanted to provide something of a public service to their colonies, pursued an entirely different policy and initially delayed the start of broadcasting in their colonial territories. French colonial policy of direct rule was mirrored in broadcasting, as all programming was initially French in orientation and in delivery. The Belgians left broadcasting to private individuals or religious groups. In both the French and the British colonies, radio was from the outset an arm for colonial policies (→ Radio for Development; Radio: Social History).

The Television Age

The television age came to Sub-Saharan Africa in the late 1950s, which was the period when colonial rule ended for many countries in the region. Elite and urban in character, television depended on foreign programming and was initially used mainly for entertainment purposes. Several Sub-Saharan African countries resisted television for many years. South Africa resisted television until 1976, because of what was seen by the apartheid government as its 'morally corruptive' influence and fears that it could provide information that would strengthen anti-apartheid forces (→ Cultural Imperialism Theories). However, for most countries in the region, the television age coincided with national independence, but the medium sadly remains a symbol of national status that hardly goes beyond the major African cities (→ Television for Development).

Independence and Democratization

Although colonial media were used to suppress and misinform Sub-Saharan Africans, alternative media also helped them achieve political independence in the 1960s. Post-independence media systems were close to one-party systems. In the processes of nation building, the ownership and control of broadcasting was more centralized than that of print media. On the whole, the legacy of western notions of media culture and practice is yet to be adequately reformed in order to address the expectations of the majority of Africans, especially those living in rural Africa.

In the 1990s, the changing African media became central to the new struggle for greater political and economic independence. By 2005, most countries had opened up their broadcasting sectors after many years of state monopoly of the sector. The 1990s ushered in a boom in private, local, community, and commercial radio stations across the regions (→ Community Media). In general, a wave of democracy in the 1990s brought with it multipartyism and a degree of media pluralism in many Sub-Saharan African countries (→ Communication Law and Policy: Africa).

The Twenty-First-Century African Media System

From 2000 to 2006 the number of Internet users in Africa grew by 625.8 percent. Such rapid growth was mainly driven by a rapid increase in mobile phone (cell phone) subscribers in the region, making Africa the first place where mobile subscribers outnumber fixed-line subscribers.

However, the overall picture in Sub-Saharan African countries seems to suggest that a very small group of privileged Africans have benefited. Regulatory and technological issues dominate the twenty-first-century African media system. State monopolies have been undermined by a *wave of deregulation*, commercialization, and privatization of broadcasting and telecommunications (→ Commercialization: Impact on Media Content).

A small but significant number of Africans is now able to receive popular radio and television content via terrestrial, satellite, cable, and Internet (→ Satellite Television). Most countries are taking advantage of the rapid development of new communications technologies and digitization. Sub-Saharan Africa has also seen a dramatic growth in the indigenous entertainment production industry such as the video film sector in Nigeria, now dubbed 'Nollywood.' Internet radio stations, online newspapers, and digital music libraries are set to continue revolutionizing the Sub-Saharan African media scene. To sum up, Sub-Saharan Africa's emerging media system is diverse and fast growing but to a large extent is heavily influenced by its colonial legacy.

See also: ▶ CENSORSHIP ▶ COMMERCIALIZATION: IMPACT ON MEDIA CONTENT ▶ COMMUNICATION LAW AND POLICY: AFRICA ▶ COMMUNITY MEDIA ▶ CULTURAL IMPERIALISM THEORIES ▶ DIGITAL MEDIA, HISTORY OF ▶ EDUCATIONAL COMMUNICATION ▶ POLITICAL COMMUNICATION ▶ RADIO FOR DEVELOPMENT ▶ RADIO: SOCIAL HISTORY ▶ SATELLITE TELEVISION ▶ TELEVISION FOR DEVELOPMENT

REFERENCES AND SUGGESTED READINGS

Bourgault, L. M. (1995). *Mass media in Sub-Saharan Africa.* Bloomington, IN: Indiana University Press.
Fardon, R. & Furniss, G. (eds.) (2000). *African broadcast cultures: Radio in transition.* Oxford: James Currey.
Honeyman, R. (2003). African regulation of satellite broadcasting in the era of convergent ICTS. In *Broadcasting policy and practice in Africa.* London: Article 19, pp. 71–113.
Internet World Stats (2014). Internet usage statistics for Africa. At http://www.internetworldstats.com/stats1.htm, accessed July 16, 2014.
Mudhai, O. F., Tettey, W., & Banda, F. (eds.) (2009). *African media and the digital public sphere.* Basingstoke: Palgrave Macmillan.
Mytton, G. (1983). *Mass communication in Africa.* London: Edward Arnold.
Mytton, G. (2000). Sub-Saharan surveys: From saucepan to dish-radio and TV in Africa. In R. Fardon & G. Furniss (eds.), *African broadcast cultures: Radio in transition.* Oxford: James Currey.
Nyamnjoh, F. (2005). *Africa's media: Democracy and the politics of belonging.* London: Zed Books.
World Association of Newspapers (2009). *Shaping the future of the news.* Paris. World Association of Newspapers and ZenithOptimedia.
World Bank (2006). *World Bank indicators 2006.* Washington, DC: World Bank.

Age Identity and Communication

JAKE HARWOOD
University of Arizona

Communication plays a substantial role in influencing understandings and self-presentations with regard to age. While increasing chronological age is at the heart of life-span development issues, our age group identifications and the age groups into which we are categorized are not deterministically organized by chronological age; they are malleable, and divisions between age groups are negotiated and open to socio-communicative construction (→ Discursive Psychology). Negative age stereotypes and prejudicial (ageist) attitudes are common (despite the fact that most of us will get old), which provides unique opportunities for identity scholars. A detailed overview of many of these processes is provided in Harwood (2007).

One approach to age identification and communication has been to examine *intergenerational processes* driven by age categorizations (→ Intergenerational Communication). Grounded in social identity theory and → communication accommodation theory, this work examines how age stereotypes lead to patronizing or baby-talk speech from young to old; this speech appears grounded in stereotypes of deafness or mental decline (→ Intergroup Accommodative Processes). This talk is often dissatisfying for older adults, and can yield negative outcomes, particularly as the older recipients of such speech are assumed to be incompetent by those overhearing it. Ryan et al. (1986) present core theory on this topic (the 'communication predicament of aging' model). Kemper and Harden (1999) describe disentangling the elements of this speech that are functional vs. counterproductive. Intergroup age stereotyping processes are closely related to age identities (→ Prejudiced and Discriminatory Communication). Other intergenerational processes are tied to life-span identifications: storytelling (→ Storytelling and Narration); attribution; reproaching; disclosing painful experiences, and intergenerational conflict. Much of this research is culturally limited and more work should examine cultural variability (e.g., laodao is a specifically Chinese pattern of repetitive complaining from old to young).

Age identities are raised, manipulated, avoided, and negotiated in naturalistic language use or discourse (Coupland & Coupland 1990 → Identities and Discourse). This includes work examining the disclosure of chronological age (DCA) in older adulthood (i.e., when and why older adults tell others exactly how old they are). Age categories are invoked in other ways too. An age-related role can be mentioned (widow, student, retiree), or descriptions of changes over time can be made (comparing past to present). Raising age in discourse serves particular discursive and identity purposes.

Age identities are *shaped by media*. Older people are underrepresented and devalued on television (Robinson et al. 2004), as are very young people (children and adolescents). Quantitative analyses also show that older people are often portrayed negatively (→ Social Stereotyping and Communication). Some qualitative work examines age representations in websites, skin care and tanning discourses, Internet chat rooms, and on specific television shows such as The Golden Girls. Further work should examine how aging is used in cosmetics advertising (e.g., anti-wrinkle creams), → news stories, extreme counter-stereotypical activities (sky diving), and → advertising.

Aging is often treated as synonymous with ill health and decline (Hummert & Nussbaum 2001; → Health Communication). Anti-ageist medical philosophies are sometimes invoked by physicians in dealing with older patients. These philosophies are well intentioned and may help some patients, however others may find comfort in attributing health problems to age.

See also: ▶ ADVERTISING ▶ AGING AND MESSAGE PRODUCTION AND PROCESSING ▶ COMMUNICATION ACCOMMODATION THEORY ▶ DISCURSIVE PSYCHOLOGY ▶ HEALTH COMMUNICATION ▶ IDENTITIES AND DISCOURSE ▶ INTERCULTURAL AND INTERGROUP COMMUNICATION ▶ INTERGENERATIONAL COMMUNICATION ▶ INTERGROUP ACCOMMODATIVE PROCESSES ▶ NEWS STORY ▶ PREJUDICED AND DISCRIMINATORY COMMUNICATION ▶ SOCIAL STEREOTYPING AND COMMUNICATION ▶ STORYTELLING AND NARRATION

REFERENCES AND SUGGESTED READINGS

Coupland, N. & Coupland, J. (1990). Language and later life: The diachrony and decrement predicament. In H. Giles & W.P. Robinson (eds.), *The handbook of language and social psychology*. Chichester: John Wiley, pp. 451–468.

Harwood, J. (2007). *Understanding communication and aging: Developing knowledge and awareness*. Thousand Oaks, CA: Sage.

Hummert, M. L. & Nussbaum, J. F. (2001). *Communication, aging, and health*. Mahwah, NJ: Lawrence Erlbaum.

Kemper, S. & Harden, T. (1999). Experimentally disentangling what's beneficial about elderspeak from what's not. *Psychology and Aging*, 14, 656–670.

Robinson, J. D., Skill, T., & Turner, J. W. (2004). Media usage patterns and portrayals of seniors. In J. F. Nussbaum & J. Coupland (eds.), *Handbook of communication and aging research*, 2nd edn. Mahwah, NJ: Erlbaum, pp. 423–450.

Ryan, E. B., Giles, H., Bartolucci, G., & Henwood, K. (1986). Psycholinguistic and social psychological components of communication by and with the elderly. *Language and Communication*, 6, 1–24.

Agenda Building

MATTHEW C. NISBET

American University

Agenda building refers to the process by which news organizations and journalists select certain events, issues, or sources to cover over others. The agenda-building literature is characterized by a diversity of theoretical and methodological approaches. However, a common thread is that news coverage is not a reflection of reality, but rather determined by a hierarchy of social influences (Shoemaker & Reese 1996; → Reality and Media Reality).

Research, for example, has explored the impact of ownership structure on the issues and plurality of perspectives considered newsworthy. Additionally, several scholars have examined how changes in technology and market forces have displaced coverage of policy-oriented hard news issues with coverage of soft news topics (→ Media Economics). Other research has focused on inter-media agenda setting, or the tendency for different types of news outlets to mirror closely the set of issues covered by just a few national news organizations.

Yet, most of the research on agenda building has focused on workplace and professional-level influences that shape news attention. This research investigates the unofficial set of ground rules that govern the interactions between journalists and their sources, privileging attention to certain issues, views, and societal actors over others.

Faced with financial and time pressures, journalists routinize their daily work by relying on → news values such as prominence, conflict, drama, proximity, timeliness, and objectivity (→ News Factors). They also rely heavily on storytelling themes and narrative to package complex events and issues and to make them appealing to specific audiences. In reporting the news, they often follow a common set of organizational rules, professionally derived standards of ethics and quality, shared judgments of authority and expertise and societal expectations relative to commonly held beliefs such as patriotism or religion (→ Ethics in Journalism). More recent work has examined how the cognitive and emotional needs of journalists can help explain common agenda-building phenomena, ranging from pack journalism to political bias (Donsbach 2004; → Bias in the News).

See also: ▶ BIAS IN THE NEWS ▶ ETHICS IN JOURNALISM ▶ MEDIA ECONOMICS ▶ NEWS FACTORS ▶ NEWS VALUES ▶ QUALITY OF THE NEWS ▶ REALITY AND MEDIA REALITY

REFERENCES AND SUGGESTED READINGS

Donsbach, W. (2004). Psychology of news decisions: Factors behind journalists' professional behavior. *Journalism*, 5, 131–157.

Shoemaker, P. J. & Reese, S. D. (1996). *Mediating the message: Theories of influence on mass media content.* White Plains, NY: Longman.

Agenda-Setting Effects

DAVID H. WEAVER
Indiana University

One of the most frequently cited approaches to studying media effects is known as the agenda-setting effect (or function) of mass media. First tested empirically in the 1968 US presidential election by North Carolina journalism professors Maxwell McCombs and Donald Shaw (McCombs & Shaw 1972), this approach originally focused on the ability of the mass media to tell the public what to think *about* rather than what to think. This was a sharp break from previous media effects studies that had focused on what people thought (their opinions and attitudes) and on behaviors such as voting (→ Media Effects, History of).

Since this initial study of media agenda setting, there have been hundreds of studies carried out by scholars in many countries (McCombs 2004) on *several aspects of agenda setting*. Most of these have focused on the relationship between news media ranking of issues (by amount and prominence of coverage) and public rankings of the perceived importance of these issues in various surveys, a type of research that Dearing and Rogers (1996) have called 'public' agenda setting, to distinguish it from studies that are concerned mainly with influences on the media agenda ('media' agenda setting) or on public policy agendas ('policy' agenda setting).

The *evidence* from scores of public agenda-setting studies is mixed, but on the whole it tends to support a positive correlation – and often a causal relationship – between media agendas and public agendas at the aggregate (or group) level, especially for relatively unobtrusive issues that do not directly impact the lives of the majority of the public, such as foreign policy and government scandal. At the individual level, the evidence is not as strong (Shehata & Strömbäck 2013). In the majority of studies to date, the unit of analysis on each agenda is an object, a public issue. But objects have attributes, or characteristics. Due to the limited capacity of the news agenda, however, journalists can only present a few aspects of any object in the news. Similarly, when people talk about and think about these objects – public issues, political candidates, etc. – the attributes ascribed to these objects also vary considerably in their salience. These agendas of attributes have been called 'the second level' of agenda setting to distinguish them from the first level, which has traditionally focused on issues (objects). The perspectives and frames that journalists employ draw attention to certain attributes of the objects of news coverage, as well as to the objects themselves (→ Framing Effects; Framing of the News).

Takeshita (2006) has identified *three critical problems* with agenda-setting research: process, identity, and environment. The 'process problem' focuses on the degree to which agenda setting is automatic and unthinking; the 'identity problem' is concerned with whether second-level or attribute agenda setting will become indistinguishable from framing or traditional persuasion research; and the 'environment problem' stems from the growth in the number of news outlets, and whether that will reduce and fragment the agenda-setting effect of media at the societal level.

Takeshita suggests that *future research* on agenda setting should focus on the factors that distinguish genuine or deliberative agenda setting from 'pseudo agenda setting' that is automatic and unthinking. He also suggests focusing on how the salience of certain attributes of a given object (be it an issue or a candidate) leads to the development of attitudes toward that object. In addition, it seems clear that more research is needed to clarify the similarities and differences between second-level agenda setting and framing, to specify the conditions under which media agendas are likely to influence not only public but also policymakers' agendas (Tan & Weaver 2010), and to study the influences on the media agenda.

See also: ▶ CONTENT ANALYSIS, QUANTITATIVE ▶ CORRELATION ANALYSIS ▶ FRAMING EFFECTS ▶ FRAMING OF THE NEWS ▶ INFORMATION PROCESSING ▶ MEDIA EFFECTS, HISTORY OF ▶ MEMORY ▶ PRIMING THEORY ▶ PUBLIC OPINION ▶ SURVEY

REFERENCES AND SUGGESTED READINGS

Dearing, J. W. & Rogers, E. M. (1996). *Agenda-setting*. Thousand Oaks, CA: Sage.

McCombs, M. (2004). *Setting the agenda: The mass media and public opinion*. Cambridge: Polity. (2nd edn in press.)

McCombs, M. E., & Shaw, D. L. (1972). The agenda-setting function of mass media. *Public Opinion Quarterly*, 36, 176–187.

Shehata, A. & Strömbäck, J. (2013). Not (yet) a new era of minimal effects: A study of agenda setting at the aggregate and individual levels. *Harvard International Journal of Press / Politics*, 18(2), 234–255.

Takeshita, T. (2006). Current critical problems in agenda-setting research. *International Journal of Public Opinion Research*, 18(3), 275–296.

Tan, Y. & Weaver, D. H. (2010). Media bias, public opinion, and policy liberalism from 1956 to 2004: A second-level agenda-setting study. *Mass Communication and Society*, 13(4), 412–434.

Aging and Message Production and Processing

SUSAN KEMPER
University of Kansas

Aging affects many aspects of message production and processing. The nature of conversation changes: older adults mix talk about the past with talk about the present, sharing by 'painful self-disclosures' of bereavement, ill health, and personal problems (→ Intergenerational Communication). Younger adults adopt elderspeak, a speech style characterized by exaggerated pitch and intonation, simplified grammar, limited vocabulary, a slow rate, 'we' pronouns, and diminutives like 'honey.' Elderspeak reinforces negative stereotypes of older adults as "child like", and expresses a sense of disrespect, limiting conversational interactions and contributing to older adults' social isolation and cognitive decline (→ Language and Social Interaction).

Older adults' conversational skills may be affected by the breakdown of inhibition, whereby irrelevant thoughts, personal preoccupations, and idiosyncratic associations intrude. Older adults' speech can be verbose and off-target. Older adults often experience the inability to recall a well-known word, name, or title when connections between the idea to words' phonology are broken. Such broken links become more numerous with aging, disrupting conversations, shifting the conversation from the topic under discussion to a focus on the older adults' memory problems (→ Speech Fluency and Speech Errors). Dementia accelerates and exaggerates age-related changes, especially the use of elderspeak, off-target verbosity, and word-finding problems, which contribute to caregiver burden, poor care, and poor quality of life for those with dementia.

A growing area of investigation concerns multitasking. The demands of even walking and talking at the same time may over-task older adults, detracting from their ability to process or produce messages and contributing to increased risk for falls or other accidents. New technologies offer the possibility of remediating for many age-related problems but also create new problems: How to optimize synthesized speech for older adults? Will older adults accept and trust health and medical recommendations administered by a 'nurse-bot'? How can websites be designed to facilitate older adults' search and retrieval of information?

See also: ▶ INTERGENERATIONAL COMMUNICATION ▶ LANGUAGE AND SOCIAL INTERACTION ▶ MEANING ▶ MESSAGE PRODUCTION ▶ SOCIAL STEREOTYPING AND COMMUNICATION ▶ SPEECH FLUENCY AND SPEECH ERRORS

SUGGESTED READINGS

Kemper, S. (2011). The effects of aging on language and communication. In R. Peach & L. Shapiro (eds.), *Cognition and acquired language disorders: A process-oriented approach*. San Diego: Elsevier.

Alternative Journalism

JON BEKKEN
Albright College

Alternative journalism is a fluid concept, often attributed to media practices unified only by their differing from mainstream → journalism. Recent scholarship focuses on practices that challenge the communicator/audience divide, including the range of voices presented, the privileging of marginalized news sources over traditional elites, a conscious identification with the audience being served, and a conception of journalism that promotes social action (Atton 2002; Downing 2001; → Citizen Journalism; Community Media; Development Journalism).

Dissidents have long contested the terrain of mass communications, from the underground printing presses used in eighteenth-century France to the anonymizers and remote hosting sites bloggers use to evade censors (→ Censorship). Throughout the nineteenth century, newspapers were central to Chartists' and socialists' efforts to build an oppositional working-class culture and campaign for their demands. Social media were widely credited with facilitating the Arab Spring that challenged regimes across the Middle East (→ Social Media).

Alternative journalism embraces advocacy, and does not so much serve its audience as constitute a process of cultural empowerment, creating and maintaining an alternative → public sphere that enables diverse publics to speak in their own voice (Rodríguez 2001; → Advocacy Journalism; Objectivity in Reporting; Journalists' Role Perception). Alternative journalism thus challenges the → professionalization of journalism. The labor press combined staff reports with articles written by readers, often describing their own working conditions and local struggles. These newspapers were often published by cooperatives that raised the necessary funds, elected editors, and convened regular meetings at which editors reported to their readers.

Today alternative journalists work in every medium, from clandestinely circulated news bulletins to the Free Speech Television Network. Although the so-called *marketplace of ideas* remains relentlessly inhospitable to alternative journalism, media activists continue to seize on new technologies and underserved audiences in their quest to forge a new kind of media practice.

See also: ▶ ADVOCACY JOURNALISM ▶ CENSORSHIP ▶ CITIZEN JOURNALISM ▶ COMMUNITY MEDIA ▶ DEVELOPMENT JOURNALISM ▶ ETHNIC JOURNALISM ▶ FEMINIST MEDIA ▶ JOURNALISM ▶ JOURNALISM, HISTORY OF ▶ JOURNALISTS' ROLE PERCEPTION ▶ MINORITY JOURNALISM ▶ OBJECTIVITY IN REPORTING ▶ PARTICIPATORY COMMUNICATION ▶ PROFESSIONALIZATION OF JOURNALISM ▶ PUBLIC SPHERE ▶ SOCIAL MEDIA

REFERENCES AND SUGGESTED READINGS

Atton, C. (2002). *Alternative media*. London: Sage.
Downing, J. (2001). *Radical media: Rebellious communication and social movements*. Thousand Oaks, CA: Sage.
Rodríguez, C. (2001). *Fissures in the mediascape: An international study of citizens' media*. Cresskill, NJ: Hampton.

Anime

ANNE COOPER-CHEN
Ohio University

The term anime is abbreviated from the Japanese word animēshon, which in turn is a direct transliteration of the English word animation. Comprising mainly Japanese TV series, anime features unique aesthetics, and range from action and drama to fantasy, horror, and comedy. The setting may be contemporary, futuristic, historic, or fantastical. Anime and related products – manga, toys, and → video games – challenge the worldwide dominance of US popular media. Starting as a major influence in about 1995 and abetted by the Internet, Japanese pop youth culture has spread not just to the US, but also to Europe (notably France), East Asia, and Latin America. In addition to half-hour TV episodes, the field of anime includes films, such as Hayao Mizaki's Spirited Away (winner of the US 2003 Animated Feature Oscar).

One can think of cartoons in Japan as a pyramid (→ Japan: Media System). At the bottom reside *manga*, thick periodicals printed on cheap newsprint that contain multiple storylines. At the next level are cartoon books of popular manga storylines. Moving up, one finds some of the books taking on life as Japanese-language TV anime or films. Of those, a few find their way overseas, either dubbed or subtitled. For example, a 1980 manga found new life as the 2011 movie From Up on Poppy Hill, directed by Hayao Miyazaki's son Goro (it grossed $61 million worldwide).

A noticeable anime (and manga) hallmark is characters' unnaturally large eyes, a legacy of the revered artist Osamu Tezuka (1928–1989) – not necessarily to achieve a foreign look, but because eyes could empathetically reflect emotions (→ Disney). Japan's first TV animation was broadcast in 1963, Tezuka's 30-minute series Tetsuwan Atom; it met with phenomenal success (a rating of 40.7 percent). As Astro Boy, the series was successfully exported. In the later 1960s, the dubbed Speed Racer became a children's TV series overseas. Japanese-ness was not evident in either anime.

The year 1995 marked a turning point for *exports*, when identifiably Japanese anime Dragon Ball and Sailor Moon appeared. Then in 1998 two blockbusters debuted: Pokemon for children and Dragon ball Z, which as Z became Cartoon Network's top-rated show. In 2013, 11 dubbed TV anime were running on that network. Overseas anime's status today ranks between a niche phenomenon and – especially in larger cities – a major cultural force.

See also: ▶ CINEMA ▶ DISNEY ▶ JAPAN: MEDIA SYSTEM ▶ VIDEO GAMES

REFERENCES AND SUGGESTED READINGS

Cooper-Chen, A. (2010). *Cartoon cultures: The globalization of Japanese popular media*. New York: Peter Lang.
Napier, S. J. (2007). *From impressionism to anime*. New York: Palgrave Macmillan.
Richmond, S. (2009). *The rough guide to anime*. New York: Rough Guides.

Applied Communication Research

DAVID R. SEIBOLD
University of California, Santa Barbara

Applied communication research refers to a type of communication scholarship as well as to a subfield of communication. In the first sense, applied communication scholarship emphasizes the creation of knowledge about communication in specific contexts, applicable to social issues, and often for the solution of societal problems. In the second, applied communication research references a sub-area of the discipline. Most evident in the United States, these sub-field structures serve as an umbrella for many professional practices and research foci.

While Eadie's (1982) "case for applied communication research" justified the area, disputes surrounding its legitimacy, the problematic dichotomy between 'basic' and 'applied' research, and the relationship between theory and practice have arisen and abated (Seibold 2000). Applied communication researchers acknowledge the recursivity of theory and practice, but do not agree on the extent to which they are equal aspects of applied communication research nor the extent to which they can/must be mutually informing (Seibold 2005). Applied communication researchers also differ on where to enter the circle for analytic or ameliorative purposes and how to insure both are retained in that process, including how to preserve scholarship in pursuit of service.

There are discernible trends in applied communication research. First, the range of research methods has broadened to include all of those in the communication discipline. Second, the evolving nature of the discipline has been mirrored in the evolution of applied communication research. Articles in the Journal of Applied Communication Research (JACR) reflect the scholarly foci of all divisions in the National Communication Association, the journal's sponsoring organization. Third, applied communication scholarship addresses a wider range of problems. Fourth, the number of scholars doing applied communication research has increased, as has their depth of engagement with problematic societal issues.

Finally, there has been an effort to delineate alternative forms of "engaged communication scholarship" (Dempsey & Barge, 2014). For example, Putnam (2009) distinguished applied communication research from other "faces" of engaged scholarship such as collaborative learning, activism and social justice, and practical theory. Applied communication research is problem-centered, and seeks to generate usable knowledge or to make extant theory and research findings applicable to real-world issues. Interventions usually follow the research process rather than occurring simultaneously. Applied communication research vocabularies include problem-orientation, relevance, and translation.

Cissna, Eadie, and Hickson (2009) identify four factors contributing to the development of the applied communication sub-field: (1) American communication scholars' struggle for disciplinary identity dating to 1914; (2) a drive over the next 60 years among members of what is now the National Communication Association (NCA) to build research-based knowledge of communication; (3) a desire to create knowledge that contributes to the solution to social problems; (4) a commitment to insuring that stakeholders are aware of and can utilize communication scholarship. As Cissna et al. chronicle, the institutionalization of applied communication research in America occurred through a number of concurrent applied projects in the 1970s, including a journal devoted entirely to scholarship on applied communication and with 'applied' in its title.

Over the past two decades, other structures evolved that further institutionalized applied communication research: divisions within professional associations and awards for scholarship; a dedicated journal and special issues of others; conferences and proceedings; edited volumes; graduate programs or emphases; curriculum tracks, individual courses, and textbooks. Examination of national communication association websites around the world reveals scant reference to the field, and only a few international universities offer applied communication degrees. While applied communication research is integral to communication scholarship worldwide, the term seems not to have entered the lexicon outside American scholarship and scholarly institutions.

See also: ▶ COMMUNICATION AS A FIELD AND DISCIPLINE

REFERENCES

Cissna, K. N., Eadie, W. F., & Hickson, M. III (2009). The development of applied communication research. In L. R. Frey & K. N. Cissna (eds.), *Handbook of applied communication*. Mahwah, NJ: Lawrence Erlbaum, pp. 3–25.

Dempsey, S. E. & Barge, J. K. (2014). Engaged scholarship and democracy. In L. L. Putnam & D. K. Mumby (eds.), *The SAGE handbook of organizational communication*. 3rd edn. Thousand Oaks, CA: Sage, pp. 665–688.

Eadie, W. F. (1982). The case for applied communication research. *Spectra*, 18(3), 1–2.

Putnam, L. L. (2009). *The four faces of engaged scholarship*. Keynote address presented at the 7th Aspen Conference on Engaged Scholarship, Aspen, Colorado, August.

Seibold, D. R. (2000). Applied communication scholarship: Less a matter of boundaries than of emphases. *Journal of Applied Communication Research*, 28, 183–187.

Seibold, D. R. (2005). Bridging theory and practice in organizational communication. In J. L. Simpson & P. Shockley-Zalabak (eds.), *Engaging communication, transforming organizations: Scholarship of engagement in action*. Cresskill, NJ: Hampton, pp. 13–44.

Appraisal Theory

JOSEF NERB

Freiburg University of Education

Appraisal theories of emotions offer a systematic linkage between cognitive evaluations of a situation and emotional reactions (see Moors et al. 2013). These theories link the cognitive appraisals of a situation to that person's emotional experiences (→ Cognitive Science). For example, the appraisal that a situation is positively relevant for a person is seen as determining positive emotions, whereas the appraisal of negative relevance for a person is regarded as determining negative emotions. Of course, there are additional appraisals and it is assumed that different patterns of appraisals further differentiate emotions. Within appraisal theories, emotions are seen as continuous processes, changing as appraisals are added or revised (→ Affective Disposition Theories; Affects and Media Exposure; Emotional Arousal Theory).

Some recent theorists postulate a reciprocal causation between cognitive appraisal and emotion. Adopting such a dynamic appraisal–emotion relationship has important implications for analyzing → media effects. Nerb and Spada (2001) developed the computational model ITERA for analyzing and predicting media effects including behavioral intentions of the audience assuming a *dynamic, bidirectional appraisal–emotion relationship*. Using fictitious but realistic newspaper reports about an environmental problem, the authors manipulated attributes determining the agent's responsibility for environmental damage (knowledge about the riskiness of an action; motive of the actor). Manipulating these appraisals of responsibility not only influenced participants' felt anger and sadness but also affected ratings on non-manipulated attributes of the negative event. The effects on those non-manipulated variables were coherent with the overall emotional reactions of the participants. Thus, participants' construals of the situation are consistent with the underlying appraisal pattern for anger.

Based on this research, Kepplinger, Geiss, & Siebert (2012) have proposed a comprehensive theory regarding the effects of media frames in scandals involving public figures model. Their model characterizes media coverage about damages and transgressions with regard to five aspects: (1) amount of damage caused and (2) agency; (3) involvement of selfish goals or altruistic/common goals (→ Goals, Cognitive Aspects of); (4) knowledge about the consequences of the causing behavior; (5) amount of control to act differently. Survey data showed that people either will develop anger and the consistent belief that the public figure is guilty with regard to all five frame components, or will feel sadness and arrive at the opposite conclusion and consistently excuse the public figure concerning all frame components.

See also: ▶ AFFECTIVE DISPOSITION THEORIES ▶ AFFECTS AND MEDIA EXPOSURE ▶ COGNITIVE SCIENCE ▶ EMOTIONAL AROUSAL THEORY ▶ GOALS, COGNITIVE ASPECTS OF ▶ INFORMATION PROCESSING ▶ MEDIA EFFECTS

REFERENCES AND SUGGESTED READINGS

Kepplinger, H., Geiss, S., & Siebert, S. (2012). Framing scandals: Cognitive and emotional media effects. *Journal Of Communication*, 62(4), 659–681.

Moors, A., Ellsworth, P. C., Scherer, K. R., & Frijda, N. H. (2013). Appraisal theories of emotion: State of the art and future development. *Emotion Review*, 5(2), 119–124.

Nerb, J. & Spada, H. (2001). Evaluation of environmental problems: A coherence model of cognition and emotion. *Cognition and Emotion*, 15, 521–551.

Arab Satellite TV News

MARWAN M. KRAIDY

University of Pennsylvania

Arab satellite television emerged in the context of the 1991 Gulf War. Since then, the evolution of the industry has evinced two changes of direction. First, in the 1990s, there was a shift from officially sanctioned national broadcasting systems to a process of regional media integration (→ Communication Law and Policy: Middle East). The second shift occurred around 2000, toward specialization and niche markets. The years 1991, 1996, and 2003 witnessed industry milestones. First, politically connected Saudi entrepreneurs launched the Middle East Broadcasting System (MBC) in London, and the Egyptian government launched the Egyptian Satellite Channel (ESC) in 1991. Then came the launch of Al Jazeera and the initiation of satellite operations by Lebanese broadcasters LBC and Future TV in 1996. In 2003, Al Arabiya went on the air as a Saudi-financed rival to Al Jazeera. As of 2007, there were more than 250 Arabic-language, transnational satellite television channels.

Though Arab satellite channels began broadcasting in the 1990s, the policy and technical infrastructure of Arab satellite television had *developed over three decades*. The Arab satellite organization ARABSAT was established in April 1976 as an organization affiliated with the Arab League. Oil-rich Saudi Arabia bankrolled ARABSAT, and the Saudi capital Riyadh housed ARABSAT's headquarters. First-generation satellites were launched in the 1980s, and several generations have been put into orbit since. In 1998, the Egyptian government, long a political rival of the Saudi royal family for pan-Arab leadership, launched the satellite NILESAT. Pan-Arab broadcasters could also use the European satellite HOTBIRD and still others. In the 1990s, Arab states either removed or stopped enforcing restrictions on satellite dish ownership, and some states developed 'media cities' with financial and labor incentives to national, Arab, and western companies. Dubai leads the way, with other less influential cities operating in Egypt and Jordan.

The combination of satellite technology, war, and economic considerations led to a *regionalization of Arab television*, aided by the presence of more than 200 million viewers living on a vast stretch of land from Morocco to Iraq and sharing the Arabic language. The new satellite channels attempted at first to replace terrestrial channels with a general format, mixing news and entertainment.

In → *news*, transnationalization led to the 'anywhere but here' news phenomenon, where each channel took the opportunity to criticize all countries and policies except the country in which that channel was based or that financed its operations. Al Jazeera is credited with creating a pan-Arab → public sphere, and criticized for neglecting local issues specific to countries or communities. The channel occasionally featured dissidents discussing sensitive political topics, but because of the need to retain a transnational audience, a small number of 'big' issues such as the Arab–Israeli conflict and the US occupation of Iraq took the lion's share of news attention, at the expense of local issues.

The most significant genre on Arab news channels was the *political talk show* (→ Broadcast Talk). The most famous is Al Jazeera's 'Al-Ittijah Al-Mu'akiss' (The Opposite Direction), a spin-off from → CNN's now defunct "Crossfire." Other shows have featured feminists debating clerics, dissidents arguing with regime representatives, and controversial artists defending their work. These talk shows were a dramatic illustration of the variety of opinions aired in Arab public discourse. Specialized satellite channels also attempted to lure niche audiences. This was especially the case with economically oriented channels.

Arab satellite television presents a unique case of a regional media industry developing rapidly both qualitatively and quantitatively, and creating a vibrant and complex regional sphere of information and culture. Relying on a transient and transnational workforce working increasingly on format-based productions destined for the pan-Arab market, and concentrated in Beirut, Cairo, and Dubai, Arab satellite television has established a strong regional, and even global, presence.

See also: ▶ BROADCAST TALK ▶ CNN ▶ COMMUNICATION LAW AND POLICY: MIDDLE EAST ▶ INTERNATIONAL TELEVISION ▶ NEWS ▶ PUBLIC SPHERE ▶ REALITY TV ▶ SATELLITE COMMUNICATION, GLOBAL ▶ SATELLITE TELEVISION

REFERENCES AND SUGGESTED READINGS

Ayish, M. I. (1997). Arab television goes commercial: A case study of the Middle East Broadcasting Center. *Gazette*, 59(6), 473–494.

Boyd, D. A. (1999). *Broadcasting in the Arab world: A survey of the electronic media in the Middle East.* Ames, IA: Iowa State University Press.

El-Nawawy, M. & Iskandar, A. (2003). *Al-Jazeera: Inside the Arab news network that rattles governments and*

redefines modern journalism. Boulder, CO: Westview Press.
Hafez, K. (2001). *Mass media, politics and society in the Middle East.* Cresskill, NJ: Hampton Press.
Kraidy, M. M. (2002). Arab satellite television between regionalization and globalization. *Global Media Journal*, 1(1). At http://repository.upenn.edu/asc_papers/186/, accessed July 16, 2014.
Lahlali, M. (2011). *Contemporary Arab broadcast media.* Edinburgh: Edinburgh University Press.
Rugh, W. (2004). *The Arab mass media: Newspapers, radio and television in Arab politics.* Westport, CT: Greenwood.

Archiving of Internet Content

STEVE SCHNEIDER
State University of New York Institute of Technology

KIRSTEN FOOT
University of Washington

Communication scholars interested in new media are increasingly archiving content of the Internet to examine retrospectively content produced and distributed on the web, and the behavior of those producing, sharing, and using the world wide web. New media scholars have begun to find web archives helpful as they seek to understand developments related to the web in a variety of ways. These may involve adapting traditional methods of social research such as content analysis, → ethnography, focus groups, → surveys, and experiments or developing methods (such as network analysis), hyperlink analysis, and other approaches to structural or phenomenological analyses of the web.

The *impetus for web archiving*, for both scholarly and historical purposes, dates from the 1980s, as institutions increasingly shifted their records from paper to electronic form. By 1995, *web harvesting programs* or 'crawlers' were developed, i.e. applications that traverse the web following links to pages, initially from a set of pre-defined seed URLs.

The *construction of a web archive* and accompanying infrastructure to facilitate scholarly analysis includes four distinct processes. First, the archive creators identify web pages and/or websites to be collected and specify rules for archiving page requisites, such as images, and for following links on archived pages. Next, crawling software is employed to collect the desired web objects. Finally, a system for displaying archived impressions is developed and an interface created to provide access to the archive.

Once objects have been archived, archivists need to address the task of *generating and storing metadata* at a level of analysis appropriate to the anticipated research. In terms of representativeness, there is growing concern that substantial archives of web content may exclude significant portions of the web – specifically, websites produced outside of North America, Europe, and Asia.

See also: ▶ CONTENT ANALYSIS, QUALITATIVE ▶ CONTENT ANALYSIS, QUANTITATIVE ▶ COPYRIGHT ▶ DIGITAL MEDIA, HISTORY OF ▶ ETHNOGRAPHY OF COMMUNICATION ▶ ONLINE RESEARCH ▶ SURVEY

REFERENCES AND SUGGESTED READINGS

Brugger, N. (2013). Web historiography and internet studies: Challenges and perspectives. *New Media & Society* 15, 752–764.
Schneider, S. & Foot, K. (2005). Web sphere analysis: An approach to studying online action. In C. Hine (ed.), *Virtual methods: Issues in social science research on the Internet.* Oxford: Berg.
Toyoda, M. & Kitsuregawa, M. (2012). The history of web archiving. *Proceedings of the IEEE*, 100, Special Centennial Issue, 1441, 1443, May 13 2012 doi: 10.1109/JPROC.2012.2189920. At http://ieeexplore.ieee.org/stamp/stamp.jsp?tp=&arnumber=6182575&isnumber=6259910, accessed July 15, 2014.

Art as Communication

MICHAEL GRIFFIN
Macalester College

In modern Western culture, art has increasingly been defined as an elite sphere of activity distinct from broader notions of social communication. Since Kant and Hume, discriminations of sensory beauty and 'delicacy of taste' have been invoked in judgments of aesthetic value that separate those forms of communication that qualify as art from those that do not. Yet in most cultures for most of human history, the creation of art has been socially organized, central to the communication of shared religious beliefs, mythic understandings of the world, and social relations. Indeed, the rise of technologies of mass communication were theorized in the twentieth century in terms of their relationship to the traditional arts, and media content often characterized the product of newly emerging → 'culture industries' (→ Printing, History of) as 'popular arts.'

Modernist definitions of art as non-utilitarian and honorific have tended to separate art activity from religion, education, craft, and other forms of functional communication in favor of an emphasis on individual self-expression, formalism, emotional evocation, or representations of the mysterious, the subconscious, or the ineffable. This has involved a movement away from the reaffirmation of common cultural knowledge and shared community values toward the marking of elite knowledge and memberships. Thus, the main recent sense of the word 'art' has referred to 'original' or 'unique' expression, and its communicative effect has shifted from the conscious articulation of social knowledge and cultural heritage to the idea of innovative individual creativity. Modern art has even been described as a "project of negation," that is, the progressive breaking free from established cultural practices, generating "a growing canon of prohibitions: representation, figuration, narration, harmony, unity" (Bernstein 2001, 21).

However, beyond the parameters of modern history and modernist aesthetic philosophy, the term art is more likely to be applied to a wide range of creative production that reflects and projects social relations, political power, and cultural beliefs and practices. As such, it encompasses ancient architectural structures, statues, obelisks, bas-reliefs, pottery, masks, and funerary arts, as well as the conventional fine arts of poetry, literature, drama, music, painting, and prints. These and other forms of artistic creativity have functioned as powerful social communication in virtually all cultures, reproducing established cultural heritage and the ideological assumptions of those social, economic, and political formations that support, or require, their creation (→ Culture: Definitions and Concepts; Cultural Studies). Studies in the sociology and social history of art identify such artistic production as the communication of prevalent ideas in a particular culture at a specific point in history – the result of the institutional and organizational contexts in which art production occurs.

Berger (1972), building from Benjamin (1968), makes a similar argument about the transformation of art made to fulfill a particular role in a specific place and time, to industrial objects reproduced and proliferated in multiple forms and contexts. The communicational function of paintings shifts when they are lifted from their original context and reproduced in advertising or on T-shirts (→ Visual Culture).

Art's function as communication is highly dependent upon its specific social use within particular institutional and organizational networks. For European and American sociologists in the twentieth century, the fragmentation of art forms and the rise of mass-mediated popular culture effaced distinctions between art and craft at the same time as it reinforced the notion of 'fine art' as a symbolic indicator of social status. Sociologists of art foregrounded the collective nature of artistic production, consumption, and valuation, pointing to the meaning of artistic activity for the social communication of groups (Becker 1982). The cooperative creation of artworks (in art studios, camera clubs, or by film crews), the viewing, reception, and purchase of artistic products by audiences and networks of fans or connoisseurs, and the definition and evaluation of art itself by educational institutions, galleries, and museums, all involve the sharing and exercise of cultural assumptions and communication practices within social groups.

At the same time, the capacity of figural and pictorial art to provide literal mappings and reflections of the world facilitated the descriptive power of visual media, and by extension its persuasive and manipulative potential (→ Photojournalism; Propaganda, Visual Communication of).

See also: ▶ CINEMA ▶ CULTURAL STUDIES ▶ CULTURE: DEFINITIONS AND CONCEPTS ▶ CULTURE INDUSTRIES ▶ DESIGN ▶ DIGITAL IMAGERY ▶ ICONOGRAPHY ▶ PHOTOGRAPHY ▶ PHOTOJOURNALISM ▶ PRINTING, HISTORY OF ▶ PROPAGANDA, VISUAL COMMUNICATION OF ▶ REALISM IN FILM AND PHOTOGRAPHY ▶ SIGN

▶ TASTE CULTURE ▶ VISUAL COMMUNICATION
▶ VISUAL CULTURE ▶ VISUAL REPRESENTATION

REFERENCES AND SUGGESTED READINGS

Baxandall, M. (1972). *Painting and experience in fifteenth-century Italy: A primer in the history of pictorial style*. Oxford: Clarendon Press.
Becker, H. S. (1982). *Art worlds*. Berkeley, CA: University of California Press.
Benjamin, W. (1968). The work of art in the age of mechanical reproduction. In W. Benjamin, *Illuminations* (ed. and intro. H. Arendt, trans. H. Zohn). New York: Schocken Books.
Berger, J. (1972). *Ways of seeing*. London: Penguin.
Bernstein, J. (ed.) (2001). *The culture industry: Selected essays on mass culture*. London: Routledge.
Wolff, J. (1993). *The social production of art*, 2nd edn. London: Palgrave Macmillan.

Asia: Media Systems

CHERIAN GEORGE
Hong Kong Baptist University

The 25-plus countries of south, east, and southeast Asia possess media systems that are extremely diverse. In political terms, the region comprises some of the world's largest multi-party democracies (India, Indonesia), but also most of its remaining one-party communist states (China, Vietnam, Laos) as well as a couple of hereditary absolutist systems (North Korea, Brunei). Market conditions are equally varied. While newspapers have been in dramatic decline in much of the developed West, the industry is lucrative and still growing in many of Asia's booming cities. However, there are also several smaller and poorer Asian markets (Bhutan, Cambodia, and Timor Leste, for example) where media sustainability is a major challenge even in their main cities, let alone the rural hinterland (→ Media Economics).

Communalities and Differences

Any analysis of Asian media should take into account the profound social and political divisions within countries. Most countries have a cosmopolitan elite with consumption habits similar to the cities of the advanced industrial world, but also communities struggling with poverty, low literacy and lack of communications connectivity. In many authoritarian systems, government control is usually not total, creating a bifurcated media space with strict regulation of print and broadcast media but relative freedom online. Mainstream commercial newspapers – typically the focus of the literature on media systems – are, in many Asian countries, confined to world of the urban elites and middle classes. Government broadcasters and community radio are still the main media in rural hinterlands. In countries with severe restrictions on press freedom (China, Vietnam, Malaysia, and Singapore), the Internet has emerged as a qualitatively distinct ecosystem.

The most influential suggestion of *commonality* across this vast region came in the 1990s, when analysts flirted with the notion of an 'Asian way' – referring to an approach to democracy supposedly informed by 'Asian' values of harmony, community, consensus, and respect for authority. Some Asian governments suggested to journalists that these values were rooted in Asian cultural norms; and that urgent development challenges were better addressed by cooperating with a nation's leaders than through a Western-style adversarial press (→ Journalists' Role Perception). The thesis was criticized for its selective and self-serving reading of the cultures and traditions of a continent with several millennia's worth of practical and philosophical grappling with questions of power, communication and the good society. At best, the Asian way was seen as a normative vision of some Asian leaders, not necessarily shared by most Asian journalists and bearing little connection with the actual dynamics of media-state contestation on the ground.

While Asian journalists operate in a very wide diversity of political, economic, cultural and organizational contexts, recent studies suggest that there is considerable normative agreement around what can be described as universal principles of professional journalism (→ Professionalization of Journalism). The notion that journalists should help ordinary citizens by giving them reliable information and keeping an eye on those in power appears to be widely shared. Even in China, frustration with rampant corruption has given the watchdog role greater moral legitimacy than the official communist precept of media as propaganda mouthpieces of the Party.

Communication Freedom in Asia

Over the decades, there have been advances in media freedom, driven by various forces (→ Freedom of Communication). Some countries liberalized their media regimes as part of major democratic reforms (South Korea since 1988, Indonesia since 1998, Myanmar since 2012). In line with international human rights norms, several countries have decriminalized defamation and introduced freedom of information laws or regulations. Even in states where there has been no great appetite for media liberalization, technological and economic transformations have widened people's choices. In the 1990s, → cable and → satellite television broke the stranglehold that government broadcasters used to exercise. This was followed by the Internet, which has allowed → news and opinion to circulate more freely.

Despite these positive changes, Asia remains a laggard in media freedom. Freedom House rates half the territories in the region as having 'not free' media, with only two (Japan and Taiwan) placed in the 'free' category. Violence against media workers and the impunity enjoyed by its perpetrators are a special problem, with Afghanistan, Pakistan and the Philippines rated among the least safe places in the world for journalists (→ Violence against Journalists).

Asian media dynamics cannot be fully understood without also attending to non-state actors. Mob action has been an increasingly important factor. Intolerant groups who are prepared to harass and physically attack news media professionals and premises are a greater threat to media freedom than government restrictions in several countries. This can be thought of as the dark side of 'people power' and shows that the growing role of → public opinion, when untempered by civic norms, need not have a liberal or progressive effect. These forces include the religious right (in Bangladesh, India, Indonesia, Malaysia, Pakistan) and hypernationalism (in China). Such mob action, although seemingly spontaneous, is usually instigated and supported by factions within the political elite.

Media Markets in Asia

Perhaps the single most important trend in Asian media systems has been the rise of the market as the dominant mechanism that shapes who gets to say what to whom. In societies where the media used to be little more than government mouthpieces, the entry of commercial considerations has been welcomed. In China, for example, newspapers mandated to pursue profits have had to be more responsive to public wants and needs. However, as predicted by critical perspectives in media studies, the market has not always served the public interest. The main wave of commercialization occurred in the 1990s, with the arrival of cable and satellite television technologies. This coincided with a global ideological climate of neoliberalism, which encouraged untrammeled profit-making facilitated by strong pro-business governments, while negating any role for independent public institutions in safeguarding the public interest (→ Markets of the Media; Diversification of Media Markets).

Accordingly, Asian media systems are strikingly devoid of independent public service broadcasting. Japan's NHK comes closest to fulfilling that role. Even in relatively democratic states such as India and Indonesia, governments retain control over their respective national broadcasters (→ Public Broadcasting Systems). As for the private sector, the region lacks independent regulators able to ensure that licenses are allocated according to transparent public-interest criteria. Instead, free-to-air and pay-TV licenses are in several countries (Bangladesh, Cambodia, Malaysia) given to proxies and cronies of ruling party politicians. In several other countries (Indonesia, Mongolia, the Philippines), TV channels have been acquired by owners who use them to further their business or political ambitions.

In Asia's newspaper industry, commercialization is associated with an erosion of editorial integrity, as professional journalistic considerations lose ground to the priorities of marketing departments or owners' private agendas. While journalism in Asia has a rich history – playing a heroic part in the independence struggles and democratic revolutions of several nations – the profession is generally ill-equipped to stand up to market pressures. In many countries, wages are too low to support a family, pressuring journalists to take on second jobs. In several countries, some reporters engage in 'envelope' journalism – receiving cash from newsmakers. This practice of paid news has been institutionalized by some Indian newspaper managements, who have taken to selling news space to election candidates (→ Commercialization: Impact on Media Content).

See also: ▶ CABLE TELEVISION
▶ COMMERCIALIZATION: IMPACT ON MEDIA CONTENT ▶ DIVERSIFICATION OF MEDIA MARKETS ▶ FREEDOM OF COMMUNICATION
▶ JOURNALISTS' ROLE PERCEPTION ▶ MARKETS OF THE MEDIA ▶ MEDIA ECONOMICS ▶ NEWS
▶ PROFESSIONALIZATION OF JOURNALISM
▶ PUBLIC BROADCASTING SYSTEMS ▶ PUBLIC OPINION ▶ SATELLITE TELEVISION
▶ VIOLENCE AGAINST JOURNALISTS

REFERENCES AND SUGGESTED READINGS

Bromley, M. & Romano, A. (eds.) (2005). *Journalism and democracy in Asia*. London: Routledge.
Freedom House (2013). *Freedom of the Press 2013*. At http://www.freedomhouse.org/report/freedom-press/freedom-press-2013, accessed July 25, 2014.
International Federation of Journalists. *Asia Pacific*. At http://asiapacific.ifj.org/en, accessed July 25, 2014.
Open Society Foundations. *Mapping Digital Media* reports. At http://www.opensocietyfoundations.org/projects/mapping-digital-media, accessed July 25, 2014.
WAN-IFRA (2012). *World Press Trends Report 2012*. Darmstadt: World Association of Newspapers and News Publishers.
Weaver, D. H. & Willnat, L. (eds.) (2012). *The global journalist in the 21st century*. London: Routledge.

Attending to the Mass Media

MARK SHEVY
Northern Michigan University

ROBERT HAWKINS
University of Wisconsin–Madison

Mass communication's impact has been shown at an individual level and in society at large, yet all mass communication must pass through the same narrow gateway before having these varied effects (→ Media Effects). Unless people receive mass communication through their eyes and ears (or sometimes touch), and cognitively process it, it is powerless. Attention is a central factor in understanding what it means to watch television and videos, use the Internet, listen to the radio, or read the newspaper. Although attention is a part of receiving and processing messages from all types of media, much of what we know comes from research on attending television and video.

In studies of mass communication and cognition (→ Cognitive Science), *attention* refers to a state of cognitive focus on a particular stimulus. As such, it is the first step in prominent media psychology models and theories (→ Information Processing; Learning and Communication; Social Cognitive Theory). Looking and listening are external manifestations of attention, not the attention itself. Attention thus involves directing sensory organs toward the acquisition of messages and other stimuli and allocating cognitive resources toward processing them. A television viewer must first focus on a character before information about that character can be cognitively decoded, comprehended, stored, and remembered.

Although attention as cognitive focus sounds like a singular construct, there are in fact *two separate aspects*: (1) where cognitive focus is directed (an either/or matter) and (2) the amount of effort directed to it. For the most part, questions about where one focuses and the amount of cognitive resources applied are different, despite carrying the same label of 'attention.' Researchers cannot directly observe the focus of a person's cognition, so attention is operationalized through indirect measures such as when and how long viewers look at a screen, what part of the screen they look at, cardiac deceleration, depressed alpha power in electroencephalogram (EEG) monitoring, and memory of message information (→ Operationalization; Physiological Measurement).

Attention can be *initiated in two ways*. The first is an involuntary response to some feature of the message. An automatic biological drive to attend to new or changing stimuli results in an orienting response (OR) that focuses cognitive resources on the stimuli without conscious control. For example, if a radio playing in the background at a workplace suddenly emits a loud noise, people may automatically shift their attention from their work to the radio for a moment. The *Limited Capacity Model of Motivated Mediated Message Processing* (LC4MP; Lang 2009) states that formal features and content that activate motivational systems (basic responses to positive stimuli such as food or unpleasant stimuli such as danger) may also elicit involuntary attention.

The second way is initiation by the viewer/listener as a *controlled and strategic process* (though perhaps overlearned and automatic). People can consciously try to attend to a stimulus, and they can learn strategies to allocate more attention to a medium when the most useful information is presented. For example, children's looks at the screen are often based upon comprehensibility. By the age of 2, toddlers learn which formal features (certain sounds, motions, edits) are associated with comprehensible content, and they use those features as attention cues (Anderson & Kirkorian 2006). Over time, attentional responses based on this learning can become essentially automatic (Lorch et al. 1979).

The theorized *purpose for attentional processes* is to avoid overloading the brain with information overload. The brain has a limited capacity for processing information, and attention determines which information will receive preference for cognitive resources.

Special *research topics* in attending to media investigate the development of attention strategies in infants and children, how cognitive resources are allocated, attentional inertia (the phenomenon in which the longer a look has lasted, the more likely it will continue), types of look lengths (40 percent of looks at television are 1.5 seconds or less), and effects of attention such as comprehension and learning. Some research also considers how various media (television, web pages, radio, newspapers, etc.) may have similar or different influences on attentional strategies and processes.

See also: ▶ COGNITIVE SCIENCE ▶ INFORMATION ▶ INFORMATION PROCESSING ▶ LEARNING AND COMMUNICATION ▶ LISTENING ▶ MEDIA EFFECTS ▶ MEMORY ▶ OPERATIONALIZATION ▶ PHYSIOLOGICAL MEASUREMENT ▶ SELECTIVE EXPOSURE ▶ SOCIAL COGNITIVE THEORY

REFERENCES AND SUGGESTED READINGS

Anderson, D. R. & Kirkorian, H. L. (2006). Attention and television. In J. Bryant & P. Vorderer (eds.), *Psychology of entertainment*. Mahwah, NJ: Lawrence Erlbaum, pp. 35–54.

Lang, A. (2009). The limited capacity model of motivated mediated message processing. In R.L. Nabi & M.B. Oliver (eds.), *The sage handbook of media processes and effects*. Thousand Oaks, CA: Sage, pp. 193–204.

Lorch, E. P., Anderson, D. R., & Levin, S. R. (1979). The relationship of visual attention to children's comprehension of television. *Child Development*, 50, pp. 722–727.

Attitude–Behavior Consistency

NANCY RHODES
Ohio State University

Does knowing a person's → attitude allow one to predict that person's behavior? Historically, attitudes were thought to be an important topic to study because early researchers assumed that attitudes are strongly related to behavior. However, work questioning the assumption that attitudes guide behavior began to accumulate. An influential paper published by Allan Wicker in 1969 found only a weak relationship. The resulting controversy fostered a somewhat contentious climate that nonetheless produced an abundance of creative ideas about the relationship of attitudes to behavior.

One *response to the concern* that attitudes were not predictive of behavior was the observation that behaviors and attitudes are often *measured at different levels of specificity* (→ Measurement Theory). Attitudes are typically measured as general assessments of attitude objects, whereas behavioral measurement is typically an observation or report of a single opportunity to engage in an action. Attempting to correlate one very specific construct with another construct that is vague usually will tend to reduce the observed correlations. Fishbein and Ajzen (1974) suggested measuring the attitude toward performing the behavior at a particular point in time. Asking the attitude question with that level of specificity improved the ability to predict behavior. Fishbein & Ajzen later went on to refine their ideas into models known as the → 'theory of reasoned action' and the → 'theory of planned behavior'.

Strongly held attitudes are more predictive of behavior than attitudes that are held more weakly. One way to think about strong attitudes is to consider how quickly an attitude judgment comes to mind upon encountering an attitude object. Russell Fazio (1990) and his colleagues were primarily concerned with *attitude accessibility*, or how easily attitudes are activated from → memory. According to this research, when attitudes are highly accessible, they are quickly activated in memory, and thus are more likely to be acted upon than less accessible attitudes. These accessible attitudes are activated immediately upon encountering an attitude object without conscious effort and thus more predictive of behavior than less accessible attitudes.

An additional aspect of attitude strength is the *confidence in the correctness of one's attitudes*. Attitude confidence has recently been investigated in an extension of the → Elaboration Likelihood Model. This meta-cognitive model has been used in investigations of persuasion (Petty, Briñol, & Tormala 2002) and the attitude–behavior relationship (Bergkvist 2009). Findings generally show that when people are more confident in their attitudes and in the thoughts they have in reaction to a persuasive message, their attitudes are more predictive of their behavior. Finally, an additional moderator of the attitude–behavior relationship is the *strength of the situation* in which the behavior might occur. Just as attitudes can be described as being strong or weak, situations also vary in strength. A strong situation is one in which the range of acceptable behaviors is very narrow, whereas a weak situation has a wider range of potential behaviors. Research indicates that attitudes are more predictive of behaviors when the situation is weak than when the situation is strong: Strong situations constrain behavior to the extent that all people behave similarly regardless of their attitudes, whereas in a weak situation, where the prescribed behavior is not clear, attitudes are far more likely to guide one's choice of action.

The attitude–behavior relation can also occur in the *reverse direction*: behavior can affect attitudes. Decades of research investigating → cognitive dissonance theory and self-perception theory demonstrated that engaging in counter-attitudinal behavior is likely to change one's attitudes to be consistent with the behavior.

See also: ▶ ATTITUDES ▶ COGNITIVE DISSONANCE THEORY ▶ ELABORATION LIKELIHOOD MODEL ▶ INFORMATION PROCESSING ▶ MEASUREMENT THEORY ▶ MEMORY ▶ PERSUASION ▶ PLANNED BEHAVIOR, THEORY OF ▶ REASONED ACTION, THEORY OF

REFERENCES AND SUGGESTED READINGS

Bergkvist, L. (2009). The role of confidence in attitude–intention and beliefs–attitude relationships. *International Journal of Advertising: The Quarterly Review of Marketing Communications*, 28(5), 863–880, doi:10.2501/S026504870920093X .

Fazio, R. H. (1990). Multiple processes by which attitudes guide behaviour: The MODE model as an integrative framework. In M. P. Zanna (ed.), *Advances in Experimental Social Psychology*, 23, 74–109.

Fishbein, M. & Ajzen, I. (1974). Attitudes toward objects as predictors of single and multiple behavioral criteria. *Psychological Review*, 81, 59–74.

Petty, R. E., Briñol, P., & Tormala, Z. L. (2002). Thought confidence as a determinant of persuasion: The self-validation hypothesis. *Journal of Personality and Social Psychology*, 82(5), 722–741, doi:10.1037/0022-3514.82.5.722.

Wicker, A. W. (1969). Attitude versus actions: The relationship of verbal and overt behavioral responses to attitude objects. *Journal of Social Issues*, 25(4), 41–78.

Attitudes

DAVID R. ROSKOS-EWOLDSEN

Ohio State University

Attitudes are defined as a *hypothetical construct involving the evaluation of some object*. They are hypothetical constructs because they cannot be directly observed but are measured indirectly. Attitudes also involve evaluations of how positively or negatively a person judges something. They are directed toward some object or thing such as Diet Coke, ideas such as democracy, individuals, groups of people, and so forth. People can have *ambivalent attitudes*. Attitude ambivalence refers to situations where people simultaneously have both positive and negative evaluations of an object. Another development in thinking about attitudes involved the functions that attitudes serve for people.

The early and extremely influential *tripartite model of attitudes* held that attitudes comprised three elements: affective, behavioral, and cognitive. The *affective component* of an attitude is the emotional or visceral reaction to the attitude object. The 'yuck' reaction to a cockroach involves the affective component of the attitude. The *behavioral component* of an attitude, historically considered the most important one, refers to the actions taken in regard to the attitude object. Research has shown that people's behavior influences their attitudes. Dissonance theory predicts that if people engage in behavior that is inconsistent with their attitudes, they may change their attitudes to be consistent with the behavior (→ Attitude–Behavior Consistency; Cognitive Dissonance Theory). The *cognitive component* encompasses people's thoughts and beliefs related to the attitude object. The beliefs about an object will influence what a person's attitude is toward the attitude object. Likewise, attitudes can influence the beliefs that people develop by biasing how information is processed.

An important distinction emerging in the study of attitudes involves *explicitly versus implicitly measured* attitudes. This distinction arose from research demonstrating that people's explicitly measured attitudes may reflect their motivation not to express an undesirable attitude such as a racist attitude. Implicit measures of attitudes involve measuring a person's attitude without the person being aware that the attitude is being measured so that the person is not motivated to "hide" the undesirable attitude.

See also: ▶ ADVERTISING AS PERSUASION
▶ ATTITUDE–BEHAVIOR CONSISTENCY
▶ COGNITIVE DISSONANCE THEORY
▶ ELABORATION LIKELIHOOD MODEL
▶ EXTENDED PARALLEL PROCESS MODEL
▶ INTERPERSONAL ATTRACTION ▶ MEMORY
▶ PERCEPTION ▶ PERSUASION ▶ POLITICAL PERSUASION

REFERENCES AND SUGGESTED READINGS

Albarracin, D., Johnson, B. T., & Zanna, M. P. (eds.) (2005). *The handbook of attitudes*. Mahwah, NJ: Lawrence Erlbaum.

Dillard, J. P. & Shen, L. (eds.) (2013). *The Sage handbook of persuasion: Development in theory and practice*. Los Angeles: Sage.

Eagly, A. H. & Chaiken, S. (1993). *The psychology of attitudes*. Fort Worth, TX: Harcourt Brace Jovanovich.

Audience Research

JAMES G. WEBSTER
Northwestern University

Audience research denotes the systematic study of any audience for any purpose. In practice, it usually means describing and analyzing patterns of media use, often for some commercial or administrative purpose. Such research became commonplace in the early twentieth century as new forms of advertiser-supported media, like radio, were introduced. Contemporary audience research uses a wide range of theories and methods, which can be organized using the familiar labels of theoretical vs applied, quantitative vs qualitative, and, somewhat less conventionally, custom vs syndicated research (→ Exposure to Communication Content).

Theoretical audience research operates on two conceptual levels: micro and macro. The former tends to look at audiences from the 'inside out,' adopting the perspective of an individual audience member. Of theoretical interest are the motivations behind media use, the stimuli that command attention (→ Attending to the Mass Media), and how media are used in everyday life. This perspective is common in psychology and → cultural studies. Macro-level research tends to look at audiences from the 'outside in,' attempting to understand their characteristics and behaviors in the aggregate. This perspective sees audiences as markets, publics, and/or networks and often draws on theories in sociology and → marketing (→ Markets of the Media).

Applied audience research provides information that can be acted upon by institutions. Since the early days of radio, advertisers have demanded surveys to authenticate the size and composition of audiences. This gave rise to audience "ratings" research, which has become essential to the operation of advertiser-supported media throughout much of the world, e.g. the Nielsen Ratings. Newer platforms, like the web and social media, now collect enormous amounts of data which are used for many applied purposes, such as monitoring visitors, assessing engagement, and making recommendations.

Quantitative research methods are common (→ Quantitative Methodology). Audience ratings companies use probability sampling (→ Sampling,

Random) and → surveys to estimate the audiences for an ever-growing number of media (e.g., radio, television, movies; → video games, mobile, Internet, etc.). Very large, nonrandom samples or panels are also used. For example, digital technologies that produce a record of their use (e.g., servers or digital set-top boxes) offer the prospect of survey-like behavioral data based on a census rather than a sample. Theorists and practitioners also assess the effectiveness of media with physiological measures like eye-movements, and experimental designs executed on the web, called "2A/B testing" (→ Media Effects). *Qualitative methods* (→ Qualitative Methodology), sometimes called audience ethnographies, include focus groups, unstructured interviews, and participant observation.

Custom research is tailor-made to serve a particular purpose. Much academic audience research intended for scholarly journals is, in that sense, 'customized.' Media organizations also do research for their own internal consumption. TV studios will, for example, conduct focus groups to assess audience reactions to new programs. Industry-commissioned studies designed to serve client interests can be quite useful internally, but for outsiders they often lack the apparent objectivity of syndicated research.

Syndicated audience research is a standardized research product that is sold to multiple subscribers. It plays an important role in media industries because its costs can be distributed across many buyers and it provides a credible, 'third–party' accounting of audiences independent of the media or advertisers. Measurement companies in the US and much of the world record audience behaviors using a variety of techniques, including diaries, servers, and 'people-meters.' These data are processed and packaged into different reports that constitute a "currency" used to buy and sell audiences.

Because of its pivotal role in the operation of media industries, syndicated research has been the target of critics, who generally voice one of three concerns. The first questions the accuracy of the data in the face of continued audience fragmentation. The second argues for measuring things other than exposure. The third poses more existential questions about the ability of media measurement to reshape audiences and commercial culture.

See also: ▶ ADVERTISING ▶ ATTENDING TO THE MASS MEDIA ▶ CULTURAL STUDIES ▶ EXPOSURE TO COMMUNICATION CONTENT ▶ MARKETING ▶ MARKETS OF THE MEDIA ▶ MEDIA EFFECTS ▶ OBSERVATION ▶ PUBLIC OPINION ▶ PUBLIC OPINION POLLING ▶ QUALITATIVE METHODOLOGY ▶ QUANTITATIVE METHODOLOGY ▶ SAMPLING, RANDOM ▶ SURVEY ▶ VIDEO GAMES

REFERENCES AND SUGGESTED READINGS

Gunter, B. (1999). *Media research methods: Measuring audiences, reactions and impact.* London: Sage.

Hartmann, T. (2009). *Media choice: A theoretical and empirical overview.* New York: Routledge.

Napoli, P. M. (2011). *Audience evolution: New technologies and the transformation of media audiences.* New York: Columbia University Press.

Turow, J. (2012). *The Daily You: How the new advertising industry is defining your identity and your worth.* New Haven, CT: Yale University Press.

Webster, J. G. (2014). *The marketplace of attention: How audiences take shape in an age of digital media.* Cambridge, MA: MIT Press.

Webster, J. G., Phalen, P. F., & Lichty, L. W. (2014). *Ratings analysis: Audience measurement and analytics,* 4th edn. New York: Routledge.

Audience Segmentation

RENÉ WEBER

University of California, Santa Barbara

Audience segmentation describes the process of partitioning mass audiences into smaller and smaller segments. It is considered as an inevitable outcome of competition in media markets (→ Audience Research; Consumers in Media Markets; Diversification of Media Markets; Markets of the Media). Hence, audience segmentation is expected to be stronger in high-competition media environments.

The concept has been introduced to describe changes in the concept of an audience through the transition from old to new media environments. McQuail (1997) summarizes the concept of audience segmentation by means of *four models* that represent different stages in the transition: (1) The unitary model (in the 1950s), when TV viewers had no ability to select a program, because there was only one channel available

(→ Exposure to Television); (2) the pluralism model (in the 1970s and 80s) with a status of 'limited diversification' of TV channels; (3) the core–periphery model (in the 1980s and 90s) where the multiplication of channels in many television markets made it possible that specific (special interest) channels had specific audiences; (4) the breakup model in which no core audience exists any more.

McQuail's four stages can be easily transferred to other traditional mass media such as radio and print. However, applying McQuail's models to new, interactive media, like the Internet or → video games, is more difficult (→ Exposure to the Internet). In these media environments users generate their own content and audience segmentation addresses both the free selection of specific media platforms and the generation of, and response to, individualized content. Hence, one might add a fifth model: the 'individualization model', which defines the highest possible degree of audience segmentation.

A closely related concept to audience segmentation is that of *audience polarization* (Webster & Phalen 1997). Audience polarization is defined as the tendency of individuals to move to the extremes of either consuming or avoiding some class of media content. There is also empirical evidence for a modest audience polarization. This tendency, however, is still mainly driven by the fact that many TV channels are still not available to all audiences.

See also: ▶ AUDIENCE RESEARCH ▶ CONSUMERS IN MEDIA MARKETS ▶ DIVERSIFICATION OF MEDIA MARKETS ▶ EXPOSURE TO TELEVISION ▶ EXPOSURE TO THE INTERNET ▶ MARKETS OF THE MEDIA ▶ SEGMENTATION OF THE ADVERTISING AUDIENCE ▶ VIDEO GAMES

REFERENCES AND SUGGESTED READINGS

McQuail, D. (1997). *Audience analysis*. Thousand Oaks, CA: Sage.
Webster, J. G. (2005). Beneath the veneer of segmentation: Television audience polarization in a multichannel world. *Journal of Communication*, 55(2), 366–382.
Webster, J. G. & Phalen, P. F. (1997). *The mass audience: Rediscovering the dominant model*. Mahwah, NJ: Lawrence Erlbaum.

Audiences, Female

KAREN ROSS
Northumbria University

Notions of 'the audience' have changed significantly over the past decades, but issues of gender continue to have relevance. Early studies of audiences in the 1930s suggested that in general terms, audiences were regarded as 'mass' and passive, forever in thrall to the propagandist tendencies of governments and big business (→ Propaganda). Decades later, audiences were understood as active 'users' of media for their own 'gratifications' (→ Uses and Gratifications). Some contemporary thinking shifted again so that the very notion of audience was dismissed in favor of seeing media consumers as atomized individuals, no longer sharing anything as communities of viewers or listeners. Instead, individuals were now to be seen to be both using and producing media ('produsage') as active agents of their own media behavior.

Although research on the female audience spans more than half a century, it was, arguably, the interest of (women) researchers who wanted to explore women's viewing behaviors as specifically gendered acts which marked a turning point during the late 1970s and early 1980s. Three studies of significance in this period were those of Dorothy Hobson (1982), Janice Radway (1984), and Ien Ang (1985), all of which showed the complex relationships which women have to genres such as soaps and romantic fiction. Current researchers have been keen to credit audiences with sophisticated deconstructive and interpretive skills, understanding their viewing behaviors and pleasures as forms of active engagement rather than passive dislocation. Some scholars have suggested that → genres such as soaps are themselves subversive genres, since the staple ingredients – infidelity, casual sex, unintended pregnancies, divorce, domestic violence, petty crime, and, more recently, storylines about sexuality – are directly antithetical to both the socially acceptable norms of romantic love contained within the domesticated and heterosexual marriage contract, but also the acceptable norms of feminine behavior.

Historically, the principal focus for much academic study of *women and film* has been textual analysis, and this strand of representation studies has been complemented, in more recent times, by a focus on films made by women directors. Work in the 1980s and 1990s mostly focused on women as audiences for film, demonstrating, as with soap audiences, the multiplicity of readings that audiences could bring to a single cultural product, as well as to an entire genre such as the 'woman's film,' identifying the importance of historical specificity as well as ethnic background in understanding different responses to texts (→ Ethnicity and Exposure to Communication). Jacqueline Bobo's (1995) study of African-American women showed the ways in which the practice of reading, both novels and films, could be empowering by placing the female spectator at the center of the analysis in ways which give her importance in her own right, as possessing agency, rather than being simply 'positioned' by the text.

The ways in which → advertising influences girls' and women's sense of self-worth through the representation of women and women's bodies in magazines have received considerable and enduring scrutiny over the past few decades (→ Advertising Effectiveness). Most of this work suggests that magazines work to the detriment of their readers by perpetuating heterosexist norms about appropriate forms of femininity, causing dissatisfaction among women (readers). While much audience research is situated within a white western paradigm, a number of important studies look beyond the Anglophone world, often showing that irrespective of the traditional norms of 'sanctioned' femininity associated with a particular country, young women may still aspire to the version of white bodily perfection promoted by global (fashion) advertising.

The rapid developments in information and communication technologies (ICTs) mean that we have to rethink what it means to be an audience, including a gendered audience, and consider the (potential, at least) shifts in power between the audience and the artifact (→ Technology and Communication). Although the initial take-up of the Internet was decidedly male, a number of studies now suggest that women are the fastest-growing group of Internet users, especially in relation to → social media and fan sites (→ Exposure to the Internet).

See also: ▶ ADVERTISING ▶ ADVERTISING EFFECTIVENESS ▶ AUDIENCE RESEARCH ▶ CULTURAL STUDIES ▶ ESCAPISM ▶ ETHNICITY AND EXPOSURE TO COMMUNICATION ▶ ETHNOGRAPHY OF COMMUNICATION ▶ EXPOSURE TO THE INTERNET ▶ FEMINIST MEDIA ▶ GENRE ▶ MASCULINITY AND MEDIA ▶ PARASOCIAL INTERACTIONS AND RELATIONSHIPS ▶ PROPAGANDA ▶ SOCIAL MEDIA ▶ TECHNOLOGY AND COMMUNICATION ▶ USES AND GRATIFICATIONS

REFERENCES AND SUGGESTED READINGS

Ang, I. (1985). *Watching Dallas: Soap opera and the melodramatic imagination*. London: Methuen.
Bobo, J. (1995). *Black women as cultural readers*. New York: Columbia University Press.
Hobson, D. (1982). *Crossroads: The drama of a soap opera*. London: Methuen.
Mulvey, L. (1975). Visual pleasure and narrative cinema. *Screen*, 16(3), 6–19.
Radway, J. (1984). *Reading the romance: Women, patriarchy and popular literature*. Chapel Hill, NC: University of North Carolina Press.
Ross, K. (ed.) (2012). *The handbook of gender, sex and media*. Oxford: Wiley-Blackwell.
Thornham, S. (2012). *What if I had been the hero? Investigating women's cinema*. London: British Film Institute.

Australia: Media System

PETER PUTNIS
University of Canberra

The Australian Constitution gives the federal government responsibility for the regulation of "postal, telegraphic, and other like services." Under this provision it also has responsibility for the regulation of all broadcasting and telecommunications in Australia. There are no press laws requiring newspaper licensing. The federal government's power over the press is limited to its general corporate affairs responsibilities and foreign investment. There is also no constitutional provision that explicitly guarantees freedom of the press. Australia has maintained the English tradition that freedom of speech is adequately protected by common law (→ Freedom of Communication; Freedom of the Press, Concept of).

Australia's first *newspaper*, the *Sydney Gazette*, which commenced publication in 1803, was published by the authority of the Governor of the British colony of New South Wales. However, by the 1830s controls had been largely lifted and seven papers had been established in the colony. As settlement spread to inland areas, the printing presses followed. In the 1890s it was observed that it was not unusual for towns of around 10,000 inhabitants to have four newspapers. Since the 1920s the trend has been toward a reduction in the number of titles and a concentration of ownership. In 1923 there were 26 dailies in Australia's six capital cities with 21 independent owners. By 1950 this had fallen to 15 dailies with ten owners. In 2014 Melbourne and Sydney have two daily newspapers, while all other capitals have one (→ Concentration in Media Systems). The Australian newspaper industry is one of the most highly concentrated in the world. Rupert Murdoch's → News Corporation accounts for 70 percent of the total circulation of major papers in Australia. The other major players are John Fairfax Limited, with 21 percent of the circulation, and WA Newspapers, with 9 percent. The Internet has spawned a deep structural adjustment process in the industry. With print editions facing rapidly reduced circulations and advertising revenues, newspaper groups have focused on building up digital formats. While digital subscriptions are growing, advertising revenue is anticipated to continue shrinking in the period 2014–17.

There is a dual system of *radio and television broadcasting* with two state-owned networks operating side by side with government-licensed commercial operators. Regular radio broadcasting began in 1923. In 1932 twelve existing radio stations were nationalized and formed the basis of the Australian Broadcasting Commission (ABC), modeled on the → BBC. The ABC now operates four national radio networks. A second publicly funded network, the Special Broadcasting Service (SBS), was established in 1978 and currently broadcasts in 68 languages to all major centers in Australia (→ Public Broadcasting Systems; Television Broadcasting, Regulation of). In 2010 there were about 270 commercial radio stations and 350 community radio licenses (→ Community Media). Regular commercial and public service television broadcasting began in 1956. There is a strong tradition of public service television through the ABC and SBS. As well as its general programming, the latter operates a National Indigenous Television channel (→ Ethnic Journalism; Ethnic Media and their Influence).

Commercial radio and television broadcasters are regulated by a licensing system administered by the Australian Communications and Media Authority (ACMA). The principle that has underpinned television regulation has been that, as spectrum allocation involves leasing a scarce and powerful resource to private interests, it is appropriate to attach conditions to licenses which reflect the public interest. These conditions cover programming (e.g., requirements for Australian content) and codes of practice. Australia's *commercial free-to-air television system* is dominated by three networks, Channels Seven, Nine, and Ten. Subscription television was introduced in 1995, utilizing both cable and satellite delivery systems (→ Cable Television; Satellite Television). The most powerful player in the Australian subscription television landscape is Foxtel, which had about 2.5 million subscribers in 2013.

The first decade of the twenty-first century saw major changes to the *structure and regulation of the Australian media* arising from the switch from analog to digital broadcasting, and the increasing number of available media distribution platforms, especially the Internet. The government is furthering growth in the digital economy through its rollout of a new national broadband network at a cost of over $A40 billion.

See also: ▶ BBC ▶ CABLE TELEVISION ▶ COMMUNICATION AND LAW ▶ COMMUNITY MEDIA ▶ CONCENTRATION IN MEDIA SYSTEMS ▶ ETHNIC JOURNALISM ▶ ETHNIC MEDIA AND THEIR INFLUENCE ▶ FREEDOM OF COMMUNICATION ▶ FREEDOM OF THE PRESS, CONCEPT OF ▶ NEWS CORPORATION ▶ PUBLIC BROADCASTING SYSTEMS ▶ RADIO: SOCIAL HISTORY ▶ SATELLITE TELEVISION ▶ TELEVISION BROADCASTING, REGULATION OF ▶ TELEVISION: SOCIAL HISTORY

REFERENCES AND SUGGESTED READINGS

Commonwealth of Australia (Australian Communication and Media Authority) (2013). Communications report 2012–13. At www.acma.gov.au/commsreport, accessed July 15, 2014.

Griffen-Foley, B. (2010). Radio. In S. Cunningham & G. Turner (eds.), *The media and communication in Australia*, 3rd edn. Sydney: Allen and Unwin, 113–131.

Tiffen, R. (2010). The press. In S. Cunningham & G. Turner (eds.), *The media and communication in Australia*, 3rd edn. Sydney: Allen and Unwin, 81–95.

Bad News in Medicine, Communicating

BARBARA SCHOUTEN,
University of Amsterdam

Communicating bad news is defined as any information that produces a negative alteration to a person's expectations about the future. Notwithstanding that there are instances in which information is probably universally appraised as bad, such as the sudden diagnosis of a fatal disease, interpreting information as bad news is regarded as subjective and depending on individual differences in personality, personal resources, cognitive appraisals, and expectations. Medical information, then, is defined as bad news only when a patient appraises it as such after its disclosure.

The dominant research questions in the field include how to successfully break bad news and how physicians and patients experience the delivery of bad news. Results indicate that patients and physicians agree on three main dimensions of the successful delivery of bad news: content of the message (what and how much information is given); facilitation (where and when information is conveyed); and support (emotional support during the interaction).

Crucial aspects of successfully delivering a bad-news message are maintaining a balance between honesty and sensitivity, ensuring that the information is communicated at a convenient time for the patient, and acknowledging the patient's emotional distress. Adequate information provision during bad-news consultations is related to greater patient satisfaction, fewer depressive and anxiety disorders, and better coping strategies.

However, many patients report a gap between the amount of received information and the amount of desired information. This finding may partly stem from physicians underestimating the extent to which patients want to be informed and partly from their reluctance to transmit bad news, the so-called *MUM effect*. There are several explanations for the occurrence of the *MUM effect*: the physicians' difficulties in handling their own emotions, the communicators' concern with undesirable emotional reactions on the side of the patient, and the communicators' concern with social norms, such as the norm to help. Another concern mentioned by physicians is their lack of training in delivering bad news.

See also: ▶ HEALTH COMMUNICATION
▶ INTERPERSONAL COMMUNICATION
▶ INTERPERSONAL COMMUNICATION

COMPETENCE AND SOCIAL SKILLS
▶ SOCIAL SUPPORT IN INTERPERSONAL COMMUNICATION

REFERENCES AND SUGGESTED READINGS

Eggly, S., Penner, L., Albrecht, T. L., Cline, R. J. W., Foster, T., Naughton, M., Peterson, A., & Ruckdeschel, J. C. (2006). Discussing bad news in the outpatient oncology clinic: Rethinking current communication guidelines. *Journal of Clinical Oncology*, 24(4), 716–719.

Harrison, M. E. & Walling, A. (2010). What do we know about giving bad news? A review. *Clinical Pediatrics*, 49(7), 619–626.

Paul, C. L., Clinton-McHarg, T., Sanson-Fisher, R. W., Douglas, H., & Webb, G. (2009). Are we there yet? The state of the evidence base for guidelines on breaking bad news to cancer patients. *European Journal of Cancer*, 45, 2290–2966.

BBC

MICHAEL BAILEY
University of Essex

The British Broadcasting Corporation (BBC) started life not as a public corporation but as a private company. Formed in 1922, the early BBC operated as a cartel, consisting of several wireless manufacturers, including the Marconi Wireless Telegraph Company. In 1927 the Crawford Parliamentary Committee recommended that "broadcasting be conducted by a public corporation acting as a Trustee for the national interest, and that its status and duties should correspond with those of a public service." On January 1, 1927, the BBC was effectively nationalized under Royal Charter, and as such became one of the earliest examples of a national public utility (→ Public Broadcasting Systems).

The institutional influence of the BBC and the public service legacy upon which it was founded only really abated with the 1980s and 1990s, a period that witnessed what was then the most significant overhaul to the ecology of British broadcasting, particularly the infrastructure of the BBC, which was made to adapt to the cultural hegemony of neoliberalism. In response to renewed attacks from the commercial broadcasting lobby demanding it become more publicly accountable, the BBC has reinvigorated the discourse of public service with its newly pledged commitment to "building public value," a managerial discourse aimed at costcutting and efficiency drives, all of which has impacted on the quality and creativity of its program-making. While some of the reforms within the BBC and its programming are to be commended, others are potentially detrimental to the BBC's public service ethos and its unique relationship with the public as citizens.

Notwithstanding the continuing shift toward populist broadcasting and renewed demands that the license fee be top-sliced and distributed between other public service broadcasters, the BBC remains one of the world's most influential and celebrated cultural institutions, widely revered as an authoritative source of information, trusted worldwide as a keeper of truth and the public interest.

See also: ▶ BBC WORLD SERVICE ▶ OBJECTIVITY IN REPORTING ▶ PUBLIC BROADCASTING, HISTORY OF ▶ PUBLIC BROADCASTING SYSTEMS ▶ UNITED KINGDOM: MEDIA SYSTEM

REFERENCES AND SUGGESTED READINGS

Crissell, A. (1997). *An introductory history of British broadcasting*. London: Routledge.

North, R. D. (2007). *"Scrap the BBC!" Ten years to set broadcasters free*. London: Social Affairs Unit.

Peacock, A. (2004). *Public service broadcasting without the BBC?* London: Institute of Economic Affairs.

BBC World Service

GRAHAM MYTTON
Freelance Consultant and Trainer in Market and Audience Research and Media Governance

The best-known international radio service and that with the largest audience is the BBC World Service (WS), which reaches a weekly global audience of 192 million. Until recently most of its listeners used shortwave, but following cuts to transmissions and investment in new media platforms an increasing proportion use the Internet, mobile phones, and local rebroadcasts. The largest of the BBC's 32 language services aside from

English is the Arabic service. It is now available both on radio and television, the latter launched in 1995 and relaunched in 2008. Funds for this new service were partly found by closing down 10 other language radio services.

The largest audiences have always been in countries where local freedom of media is restricted by poverty or political controls. Audiences in Africa are among the largest, and especially so in such strife-torn areas as Darfur, South Sudan, and Somalia, all examples of a recurring feature of the success of the BBC World Service – the strongest demand for it is where free and independent information is in short supply (→ Freedom of Communication; Freedom of Information). It was this feature of the World Service that prompted Kofi Annan, then secretary-general of the United Nations, to describe it in 1998 as "perhaps Britain's greatest gift to the world this century." The importance of the BBC in meeting information needs in areas of crisis and human deprivation led during the 1990s to the establishment of the World Service Trust, which later became BBC Media Action, an educational and development agency that had as its mission to "inform, connect and empower people around the world."

The vigorous independence of the BBC in its domestic services is a great strength to WS. Journalistic principles and practices are the same for both. From 2014 both BBC domestic and international broadcasting will be funded from the TV licence fee paid by nearly all households in the UK. This change has been welcomed by many as it should end suspicions of FCO involvement in WS. In 2011 the British Foreign and Commonwealth Office (FCO), which funded the BBC until 2014, cut funding by 16 percent. This led to the closure of broadcasts in five languages and severe cuts to seven others. Crucially, much shortwave broadcasting also ended.

See also: ▶ FREEDOM OF COMMUNICATION ▶ FREEDOM OF INFORMATION ▶ INTERNATIONAL RADIO ▶ INTERNATIONAL TELEVISION

REFERENCES AND SUGGESTED READINGS

North, R. D. (2007). *"Scrap the BBC!" Ten years to set broadcasters free*. London: Social Affairs Unit.

Walker, A. (1992). *A skyful of freedom: 60 years of the BBC World Service*. London: Broadside Books.

Behavioral Norms: Perception through the Media

DHAVAN V. SHAH
University of Wisconsin–Madison

HERNANDO ROJAS
University of Wisconsin-Madison

Social norms entail learned expectations of behavior or categorization that are deemed desirable, or at least appear as unproblematic for a specific social group in a given situation. Mass media have been found to help shape → perceptions of behavioral norms (→ Media and Perceptions of Reality). These perceptions are consequential for health behaviors, social and sexual practices, democratic participation, and a range of other outcomes.

To a certain extent all communication research traditions provide evidence of the importance of mass media in the *perception of behavioral norms*. From → agenda-setting effects and its focus on the relative importance of social problems that is provided by media attention, to cultivations of social reality by the disproportionate and continuous presentation of exemplars (→ Cultivation Effects), to more critical accounts in which elites secure consent for a given political order through the production and diffusion of meaning and values through mass media, the notion that media transmit behavioral norms is implied. The case for a direct relationship between exposure to mass media and differential perception of social reality is probably exemplified best by the cultivation tradition, according to which sustained exposure to mediated messages, particularly television, cultivates a common outlook on the world in which mediated reality becomes more important than real-world experiences.

There is also a long tradition of interventions in the form of communication campaigns that seek to *alter certain social behaviors* by providing cognitive or emotional appeals intended to influence what is considered "normal" (→ Communication and Social Change: Research Methods).

See also: ▶ AGENDA-SETTING EFFECTS
▶ CLIMATE OF OPINION ▶ COMMUNICATION
AND SOCIAL CHANGE: RESEARCH METHODS
▶ CULTIVATION EFFECTS ▶ MEDIA EFFECTS:
DIRECT AND INDIRECT EFFECTS ▶ MEDIA AND
PERCEPTIONS OF REALITY ▶ PERCEPTION
▶ PLURALISTIC IGNORANCE AND IDEOLOGICAL
BIASES ▶ POLITICAL SOCIALIZATION THROUGH
THE MEDIA ▶ SPIRAL OF SILENCE

REFERENCES AND SUGGESTED READINGS

Gunther, A. C., Bolt, D., Borzekowski, D. L. G., Liebhart, J. L., & Dillard, J. P. (2006). Presumed influence on peer norms: How mass media indirectly affect adolescent smoking. *Journal of Communication*, 56, 52–68.
Mutz, D. C. (1998). *Impersonal influence: How perceptions of mass collectives affect political attitudes.* Cambridge: Cambridge University Press.
Price, V., Nir, L., & Cappella, J. N. (2006). Normative and informational influences in online political discussion. *Communication Theory*, 16, 47–74.
Riddle, K. (2010). Always on my mind: Exploring how frequent, recent, and vivid television portrayals are used in the formation of social reality judgments. *Media Psychology*, 13, 155–179.
Yanovitzky, I. & Rimal, R. N. (2006). Communication and normative influence: An introduction to the special issue. *Communication Theory*, 16, 1–6.

Bi- and Multilingualism

RICHARD CLÉMENT
University of Ottawa

Merriam-Webster's online thesaurus defines *bilingualism* as "the ability to speak two languages: the frequent oral use of two languages," and *multilingualism* as "using or able to use several languages." Achieving a state of balanced bi/multilingualism is subject to the existence of contextual factors such as the equal status of the languages and the availability of a language community for each language, as well as individual factors such as positive attitudes toward bi/multilingualism and the languages. Besides intergroup attitudes, the more recent literature has supported the importance of *L2 confidence* as a determinant of L2 behavior and competence (Clément 1980).

Lambert (1978) first proposed that language learning outcomes could be very different for members of majority and minority groups. Notably, subtractive bilingualism would refer to a situation where members of a minority group would come to lose their first language as a result of learning the second one. Additive bilingualism, on the other hand, refers to situations where members of a majority group acquire L2 without losing L1. These aspects find an echo in Kim's (2005) *contextual theory of interethnic communication*.

Positive benefits from L2 acquisition and usage will be achieved only to the extent that the first language and culture are well established. This presupposes a social context that allows the development and transmission of the first language and culture. Although such conditions may be present for majority group members, they may not characterize the situation of minority group members, immigrants, refugees, and sojourners. The relative status of the first- and second-language speaking groups is a key determinant of the linguistic and cultural outcomes of bi/multilingualism.

See also: ▶ ACCULTURATION PROCESSES AND
COMMUNICATION ▶ COMMUNICATION
NETWORKS ▶ INTERCULTURAL AND INTERGROUP
COMMUNICATION ▶ INTERGROUP CONTACT
AND COMMUNICATION ▶ LANGUAGE AND
SOCIAL INTERACTION ▶ POWER IN
INTERGROUP SETTINGS

REFERENCES AND SUGGESTED READINGS

Clément, R. (1980). Ethnicity, contact and communicative competence in a second language. In H. Giles, W. P. Robinson, & P. M. Smith (eds.), *Language: Social psychological perspectives*. Oxford: Pergamon, pp. 147–154.
Kim, Y. Y. (2005). Association and dissociation: A contextual theory of interethnic communication. In W. B. Gudykunst (ed.), *Theorizing about intercultural communication*. Thousand Oaks, CA: Sage, pp. 323–350.
Lambert, W. E. (1978). Cognitive and socio-cultural consequences of bilingualism. *Canadian Modern Language Review*, 34, 537–547.

Bias in the News

TIEN-TSUNG LEE
University of Kansas

KIRSTEN GRIMMER
University of Kansas

A media bias, the opposite of objectivity (→ Objectivity in Reporting) is differential treatment of a particular side of an issue, which can be measured quantitatively or qualitatively. If one side receives proportionally less news coverage, or apparently more negative, inaccurate, or unbalanced coverage, a bias is shown (Simon et al. 1989; → News).

McQuail (1992) identifies four *types of bias*: open versus hidden and intended versus unintended. A *partisan* bias is open and intended (e.g., an editorial endorsement). *Propaganda* is intentional yet hidden (e.g., results of a firm's public relations efforts; → Propaganda). An *unwitting* bias is open and unintended (e.g., news events receiving coverage unequally). *Ideology* is unintended and hidden, and therefore difficult to define or detect as it is embedded in text. The manifestation of a media bias consists of three aspects: the ideologies and party affiliations of journalists, actual media content, and media organizations' structure.

Some authors believe mainstream media in industrialized western countries have a *conservative bias*, partially due to corporate owners supporting a capitalist and two-party-system status quo. Others argue that alternative political views are often considered un-newsworthy and ignored. Additionally, the media have been accused of having *racial, gender, religious, and class biases* (Wilson, Gutierrez, & Chao 2013). Others have claimed that a liberal and pro-Democratic bias exists in US mainstream media, which is unsupported.

"*Hostile media*" *studies* offer an explanation for the perception of a media bias and suggest supporters of an issue or a group might believe the media favor their opponents. The perception of a media bias is likely caused by an observer's own partisanship bias.

Another explanation for perceived media biases is that audiences likely seek political information they agree with, and process information in a way that *matches their existing view* (→ Selective Exposure; Selective Perception and Selective Retention). If they see a differing viewpoint in the news, they likely perceive a bias. Also, consumers may categorically assume all information from a certain source is completely biased and ignore it. If citizens are not exposed to, or are not open-minded about, perspectives they do not necessarily agree with, there can be negative consequences in a participatory democracy.

See also: ▶ ADVOCACY JOURNALISM ▶ JOURNALISTS' ROLE PERCEPTION ▶ MEDIA PRODUCTION AND CONTENT ▶ NEWS ▶ NEWS VALUES ▶ OBJECTIVITY IN REPORTING ▶ PROPAGANDA ▶ SELECTIVE EXPOSURE ▶ SELECTIVE PERCEPTION AND SELECTIVE RETENTION

REFERENCES AND SUGGESTED READINGS

McQuail, D. (1992). *Media performance*. London: Sage.
Niven, D. (2002). *Tilt? The search for media bias*. Westport, CT: Praeger.
Simon, T. F., Fico, F., & Lacy, S. (1989). Covering conflict and controversy: Measuring balance, fairness, defamation. *Journalism Quarterly*, 66, 427–434.
Wilson II, C. C., Gutierrez F. G., & Chao, L. M. (2013). *Racism, sexism, and the media*. Los Angeles, CA: Sage.

Bollywood

VIJAY MISHRA
Murdoch University, Perth

According to the *Oxford English Dictionary* (2005), Bollywood is a name of the Indian popular film industry, based in Bombay. Origin 1970s. "Blend of Bombay and Hollywood" (→ Hollywood). The *OED* definition acknowledges the strength of a film industry which, although a subset of the burgeoning Indian film industry (Bollywood's annual output of some 130 films is less than a fifth of the total), is now seen as India's transnational and transcultural popular art form.

The numbers in all respects for Bollywood are quite staggering, especially for an industry which was given 'industry status' only on May 10, 1998: a $3.5-billion-dollar-per-year industry which employs some 2.5 million people, ticket sales close to 4 billion every year and a growing international market. For example, Dabangg (2010) grossed $36 million at the box office, and 3 Idiots – the highest-grossing Bollywood film ever – $65 million (→ India: Media System).

Rendered through melodrama which, ever since the first Indian film, Phalke's Raja Harischchandra (1913), drew on the sentimental European novel, the Indian epic tradition, Persian narrative, a fair bit of Shakespeare and the influential Parsi theatre, Bollywood cinema has dealt with big issues – the idea of the nation-state, communal harmony, and justice. The highest-grossing hits of Bollywood from 1943 to 1994 – Kismet (1943), Barsaat (1949), Awara (1951), Aan (1952), Shree 420 (1955), Mother India (1957), Mughal-e-Azam (1960), Sholay (1975), and Hum Aapke Hain Koun (1994) – show the persistence of these themes and the durability of the melodramatic genre.

Then there was a sudden redefinition, not because of any significant change to the → genre itself but through a shift in the mode of production, consumption, and circulation. We now find a postmodern Bollywood, where instead of the old depth of language and dialogue (hallmarks of classic Bollywood cinema as seen, for example, in the 1953 Parineeta or the 1955 Devdas), techno-realism in production (seen in the remake of Parineeta (2006) and Devdas (2003)) and cosmopolitanism of theme have become the markers of Indian Bollywood modernity.

See also: ▶ GENRE ▶ HOLLYWOOD ▶ INDIA: MEDIA SYSTEM

REFERENCES

Gopal, S. (2011). *Conjugations: Marriage and form in new Bollywood cinema*. Chicago: University of Chicago Press.

Mishra, V. (2002). *Bollywood cinema: Temples of desire*. New York and London: Routledge.

Rajadhyaksha, A. (2003). 'The "Bollywoodization" of the Indian cinema: Cultural nationalism in a global arena.' *Inter-Asia Cultural Studies* 4 (1), 25–39.

Book

KAY AMERT
University of Iowa

The book is a durable vehicle for words and images and often is a central artifact in cultures with the written word. Those produced in the era before the advent of printing are unique 'manuscript' books that were made by hand (→ Printing, History of). The book became the first mass medium, and conventions for its presentation shaped those of later media. It can be distinguished from other printed and electronic media by the substantial length of its texts and by the diversity of its content, which ranges from the worldly and practical to the poetic and sublime.

While most books are edited, designed, produced, promoted, and distributed, the field of book publishing is diverse and includes small presses, specialty publishers, government publishing, the private press, and artists' books, inspiring many variant practices. *Materials* used in the construction of books must be light enough to be amassed in quantity and flexible enough to be rolled or folded. Papyrus, parchment, and paper all meet these requirements, with machine-made paper predominant in modern times. For economy, the sizes and shapes in which such materials originally are produced often act as determinants of the formats of books. By design or of necessity, book formats sometimes break out of these norms: 'elephant' folios and miniature books are two examples (→ Design). Comprehension of the content of most books requires a specific sequence of pages to accumulate meaning. Imposition (the placement of pages) and binding determine and enforce that order.

Producing the book has almost always required the use of teams of people and specialized equipment, in the modern era in an industrial setting to accomplish typesetting, proofreading, printing, and binding. The introduction of computers into this process from the 1960s changed the process of typesetting and revised writing and editing practices, eliminating steps in production and altering relations among personnel.

The computerization of *book ordering and shipping*, begun in the late twentieth century, reduced diversity among bookstores, encouraging centralization and the development of uniform chains. Online sale and the electronic ordering of books further unified bookselling.

See also: ▶ DESIGN ▶ GRAPHIC DESIGN ▶ PHOTOGRAPHY ▶ PRINTING, HISTORY OF

REFERENCES AND SUGGESTED READINGS

Coulmas, F. (1996). *The Blackwell encyclopedia of writing systems*. Cambridge, MA: Blackwell.
Steinberg, S. H. (1996). *Five hundred years of printing*. New Castle, DE: Oak Knoll.
Thompson, J. (2005). *Books in the digital age: The transformation of academic and higher education publishing in Britain and the United States*. Cambridge: Polity.

Branding

KATJA GELBRICH
Catholic University of Eichstaett-Ingolstadt

The term 'branding' is used for the identification of offers (products and services). Etymologically, the origin of the word can be found in the branding of cattle. Initially, the spectrum of meanings was closely restricted to the pure act of naming. In the course of time, a more tailored definition was suggested: integrated and harmonized use of all marketing-mix instruments with the aim of creating a concise, comprehensive, and positively discriminating brand image within the relevant competitive environment (→ Marketing).

However, this all-embracing concept is not clearly distinguishable from brand management. Hence, another definition situated between these two extremes has become widely accepted: the so-called *magic triangle of branding*. The triangle has the following three sides: brand name, trademark (for example, a logo), and product design and packaging. It is the task of branding to balance these three sides so that they position a brand uniquely (→ Brands).

Faced with the increasing globalization of many markets, the issue of the creation of global *brand names* has recently received much attention. The criteria mentioned in this context (e.g., short, simple brand names that release positive associations and are easily understandable and easily remembered) are of course also important for the branding of *national brands*. In a global context, however, such criteria as 'short, simple, easily remembered' have to be more strictly observed or differentiated.

Brand logos play a decisive role because visual impulses are more memorable than verbal ones and take a direct path to stored associations in the brain. For this reason, image logos are used more often than script logos. The images may in turn be abstract icons or tangible pictures.

The → *design and packaging* have to contribute to the high-quality, unique positioning of a brand. This can be obtained by a characteristic form and color as well as other features (e.g., materials).

See also: ▶ ADVERTISEMENT CAMPAIGN MANAGEMENT ▶ BRANDS ▶ CORPORATE REPUTATION ▶ DESIGN ▶ ICONOGRAPHY ▶ MARKETING ▶ ORGANIZATIONAL IMAGE ▶ VISUAL COMMUNICATION

REFERENCES AND SUGGESTED READINGS

Aaker, D. A. & Joachimsthaler, E. (2000). *Brand leadership*. New York: Free Press.
Coomber, S. (2007). *Branding*. Chichester: Capstone.
Shamoon, S. & Tehseen, S. (2011). Brand management: What next? *Interdisciplinary Journal of Contemporary Research in Business*, 2(12), 435–441.

Brands

KIM BARTEL SHEEHAN
University of Oregon

In the late 1800s, a brand was a tool used to identify ownership. As manufacturing processes improved throughout the Industrial Revolution, brands became a way for parity products to differentiate themselves. Today, a brand is a symbol that embodies a range of information connected with a company, a product, or a service. Elements of a brand include a name, a logo, and other visual elements such as images, colors, or typefaces (→ Branding).

Every year, Interbrand calculates the *brand value* of the world's top brands, i.e., the net present value of the earnings the brand is expected to generate and secure in the future for a specified one-year time period. The world's most valuable brand is Apple. In 2013 it had a brand value of US$98 trillion (www.interbrand.com). Only two non-US brands (Samsung and Toyota) made it into the top ten brands.

Brands have certain *advantages for the consumer*. They indicate value and quality. Consumers can use brand information to defend their own purchase decisions, which minimizes post-decisional dissonance (→ Cognitive Dissonance Theory). Consumers also use some brands to indicate to other consumers who they are, or who they would like to be.

Brands *are valuable for companies* as well. When consumers purchase a brand that they like, the brand is contributing to the commercial success of the company. If a consumer associates a brand with quality, the brand can command higher prices than a weaker brand. Strong brands allow for reduction in advertising expenditures. The brand accounts for more than a third of shareholder value in the average company, and in many cases for more than 70 percent of shareholder value.

Even *nonprofit organizations* have started embracing the brand as a key asset for obtaining donations, sponsorships, and volunteers. This represents a movement to have brands represent a company's key values in order to connect with consumers on a deeper, more emotive level.

See also: ▶ ADVERTISING ▶ ADVERTISING EFFECTIVENESS ▶ ADVERTISING STRATEGIES ▶ BRANDING ▶ COGNITIVE DISSONANCE THEORY ▶ INTEGRATED MARKETING COMMUNICATIONS ▶ MARKETING

REFERENCES AND SUGGESTED READINGS

Bedbury, S. (2002). *A new brand world*. New York: Viking.
Gyrd-Jones, R., Merrilees, B., & Miller, D. (2013). Revisiting the complexities of corporate branding: Issues, paradoxes, solutions. *Journal of Brand Management*, 20, 571–589.
Ries, A. & Ries, L. (2004). *The origin of brands: How product evolution creates endless possibilities for new brands*. New York: Collins.

Broadcast Journalism

MIKE CONWAY
Indiana University

Broadcast journalism took news off the page and extended it to radio and television in the mid-twentieth century. The first broadcast journalists came from other media including newspapers, news and photo magazines, theater newsreels, motion pictures, and documentary films.

In the United States, radio news found its purpose and audience during World War II. Concerning television, CBS, NBC, and a few local stations offered news programs before World War II (Conway 2009), but television news became an important platform after the war, as television diffused to a larger audience, becoming a true mass medium. In Britain, Japan, the Netherlands, and other nations that employed a user fee to pay for radio and television news, broadcast journalism tended to focus more on public affairs issues. In countries such as France the government kept parts of the broadcasting system under close watch, turning broadcast journalism into more of an official service (→ France: Media System; Public Broadcasting Systems).

In Asia, Taiwan has distinctly western news, with local versions of popular US programs such as "60 Minutes" and "Meet the Press," despite the mostly eastern influences on other television programming. In China, the government determined the direction of most news programming through the 1980s, when it began loosening some restrictions (→ China: Media System). Al Jazeera, based in Qatar, has adopted US news practices such as heated political debate, dramatic visuals, live coverage, and criticism of government decisions, altering the news landscape in Middle Eastern nations that previously stifled dissent (→ Arab Satellite TV News).

In the twenty-first century, broadcast news across the globe ranges from stark public affairs programming, through 24-hour live coverage, to sensational tabloid shows. The move to online and mobile platforms for news is presenting new challenges for traditional radio and television journalism.

See also: ▶ ARAB SATELLITE TV NEWS ▶ CHINA: MEDIA SYSTEM ▶ COMMODIFICATION OF THE

MEDIA ▶ FRANCE: MEDIA SYSTEM ▶ GERMANY: MEDIA SYSTEM ▶ INFOTAINMENT ▶ PUBLIC BROADCASTING SYSTEMS ▶ TELEVISION BROADCASTING, REGULATION OF

REFERENCES AND SUGGESTED READINGS

Conway, M. (2009). *The origins of television news in America: The visualizers of CBS in the 1940s.* New York: Peter Lang.

Pew Research Center (2011). How people learn about their local community. Project for Excellence in Journalism, September 26. At http://pewresearch.org/pubs/2105/local-news-television-internet-radio-newspapers, accessed July 18, 2014.

Zhang, W. (2004). Staging unity, celebrating Chineseness: Textual analysis of 2002 CCTV Spring Festival Eve Gala. *Asian Communication Research*, 1(2), 67–83.

Broadcast Talk

STEVEN E. CLAYMAN
University of California, Los Angeles

Most radio and television programming involves talk in some form, but the term *broadcast talk* is usually reserved for a type of content that differs from both fictional entertainment and news stories. It refers to programs that are informational, relatively unscripted, and organized around processes of interaction (→ Narrative News Story). Broadcast talk includes ad hoc events held at the initiative of public figures (e.g., news conferences, campaign debates, town meetings), as well as regularly scheduled programs (e.g., news interviews, celebrity talk shows, radio call-in shows). A range of journalistic and "infotainment" → genres fall into the category, each involving some combination of public figures, media professionals, and ordinary people as participants.

Broadcast talk programming has grown substantially in recent decades due to a confluence of factors. First, *technological changes* such as the rise of cable, satellite feeds, and more portable video equipment have enabled live encounters between program hosts and guests from around the world (→ Cable Television; Satellite Television). Second, economic conditions have encouraged broadcasters to exploit these opportunities, with marketplace volatility and internet competition fostering a willingness to experiment with new formats (→ Commodification of the Media). Third, such experimentation has taken place within an occupational culture that places a high value on "live" programming as the distinctive province of broadcasting.

Research so far has focused on the interactional forms and practices associated with various talk genres, e.g., "Conversational" talks (e.g., celebrity talk shows) vs more formal and specialized talks (e.g., campaign debates, news interviews). Other research considers what the form and content of broadcast talk reveals about, for instance, the professional norms of journalists or the evolving relations between them and public figures. Finally, researchers have also examined the impact of broadcast talk on subsequent news coverage, and on political knowledge, attitudes, and behavior.

See also: ▶ CABLE TELEVISION ▶ COMMODIFICATION OF THE MEDIA ▶ GENRE ▶ INFOTAINMENT ▶ LANGUAGE AND SOCIAL INTERACTION ▶ NARRATIVE NEWS STORY ▶ QUESTIONS AND QUESTIONING ▶ SATELLITE TELEVISION

REFERENCES AND SUGGESTED READINGS

Baum, M. A. & Jamison, A. (2011). "Soft news and the four Oprah effects." In R. Y. Shapiro and L. R. Jacobs (eds.), *The Oxford handbook of American public opinion and the media.* Oxford: Oxford University Press, pp. 121–137.

Clayman, S. E. & Heritage, J. (2002). *The news interview: Journalists and public figures on the air.* Cambridge: Cambridge University Press.

Hutchby, I. (2006). *Media talk: Conversation analysis and the study of broadcasting.* New York: Open University Press.

C

Cable Television

MEGAN MULLEN,
University of Wisconsin-Parkside

Cable television is subscription-based multichannel television program delivery relying on wires. Cable originated to extend broadcast signals, but during its mature years has delivered additional programming.

Cable began mainly in North America. Broadcast television had expanded following World War II, yet huge disparities existed among areas covered. Entrepreneurs in underserved regions constructed tall receiving antennas (headends) to capture and retransmit nearby signals for a fee. Thus began community antenna television (CATV; → Television, Social History of).

CATV expanded during the 1960s, but faced a fickle policy climate. Early in the decade, the US Federal Communications Commission (FCC) developed regulations, ostensibly to protect broadcast television, that prevented CATV from growing much. Later, CATV became the focus of 'Blue Sky' discourses, about reforming television. By the 1970s, US cable policy was more lenient, reflected in new rules of the → Federal Communications Commission (FCC) and revised copyright law (→ Copyright; United States of America: Media System). *Canada* saw increased regulation of cable following the 1968 creation of the Canadian Radio-television and Telecommunications Commission (CRTC), charged with protecting Canadian media sovereignty (→ Canada: Media System). *Mexico*'s cable industry began in the 1960s, to extend coverage of Telesistemo Mexicano (TSM; → Mexico: Media System).

Adoption of satellites during the 1970s was key in transforming CATV into modern cable (→ Satellite Television). In 1975, regional US pay-television service Home Box Office enlisted satellite to distribute programming nationwide. More networks launched; these included premium networks, charging subscribers directly, and basic networks, 'bundled' in a package for a flat monthly fee.

Cable began seeing competition from direct satellite delivery systems—C-band systems and later Ku-band DBS (direct broadcast satellite). By the late 1990s the Internet also competed with cable. The US 1996 Telecommunications Act attempted to address this emerging scenario. Popularity of multichannel television expanded worldwide starting in the 1990s. Countries with longstanding public television service now face competition from private broadcasters and cable/satellite services (→ Public Broadcasting Systems).

Recently, cable has faced challenges from Internet protocol television (IPTV), provided by telephone companies. To compete, operators have been offering high-speed Internet and cable telephone service. In programming, competition has come from streaming video websites including YouTube, Hulu, and Netflix.

See also: ▶ CANADA: MEDIA SYSTEM ▶ COPYRIGHT ▶ FEDERAL COMMUNICATIONS COMMISSION (FCC) ▶ MEXICO: MEDIA SYSTEM ▶ PUBLIC BROADCASTING SYSTEMS ▶ SATELLITE TELEVISION ▶ TELEVISION, SOCIAL HISTORY OF ▶ UNITED STATES OF AMERICA: MEDIA SYSTEM

REFERENCES AND SUGGESTED READINGS

Parsons, P. (2008). *Blue skies: A history of cable television*. Philadelphia: Temple University Press.

Canada: Media System

BART BEATY
University of Calgary

Canada's communication sector has been particularized by three factors: the country's close and often ambivalent relationship to the United States, its policy of official bilingualism, and its avowed dedication to the principle of multiculturalism. Of these differences, it is Canada's bilingual status that most clearly separates it from the American model (→ United States of America: Media System). Although some French-language radio and television services are available across the nation, they have limited audience outside the province of Quebec, and French-language daily newspapers have almost no circulation outside of that province. Concerns over the linguistic divisions among Canadians, as well as the perceived threat of American culture to English-Canadian identity formation, have characterized many governmental interventions into the media system (→ Bi- and Multilingualism).

Canadian *newspapers* originated in the eighteenth century and derived their origins from the influence of the New England colonies. Newspaper circulation doubled as Canada's population exploded between 1901 and 1911, and by 1938 there were 138 daily newspapers in the country. In 1917, Canadian newspapers formed the Canadian Press, a cooperative news agency, which allowed for a greater level of integration of news reporting across the geographically vast nation (→ News Agencies: History of). Since the 1960s, Canada's newspaper industry has been dominated by a shrinking number of increasingly large chains.

Canada's *magazine industry* differs significantly from the newspaper industry insofar as it is largely dominated by American publications. In 1961 the Royal Commission on Publications, the O'Leary Commission, recommended the imposition of a tariff on 'split-run' editions, or foreign-owned magazines that print a second edition in Canada in order to benefit from Canadian advertising revenues (→ Advertising). This recommendation became law in 1965. Challenged by the United States it was replaced by a compromise legislated in the Foreign Publishers Advertising Services Act of 1999.

Canada's national *broadcasting system* was initiated as a response to the Royal Commission on Radio Broadcasting (1928–1929), also known as the Aird Commission. The Aird Commission reported a widespread concern about the Americanization of Canadian airwaves, recommended that broadcasting be publicly owned, and advocated the establishment of a national public radio network. In 1932, this network, known as the Canadian Radio Broadcasting Commission (CRBC), was established. Four years later the passage of the Canadian Broadcasting Act changed the CRBC into a full-fledged crown corporation and altered its name to the Canadian Broadcasting Corporation (CBC; → Public Broadcasting Systems). The 1958 Broadcasting Act stripped the CBC of its regulatory powers and opened the door for the creation of national private broadcasting networks. The Canadian Radio-television and Telecommunications Commission (CRTC) was created in 1968, charged with granting and renewing broadcasting licenses, maintaining programming quotas, and ensuring the ongoing Canadian ownership of the broadcasting system. Cable television was introduced to Canada in 1952, subscriber specialty channels in 1983, significantly expanded in 1996, and again in 2000 when the CRTC approved the licenses of 283 new digital television channels (→ Cable Television).

Canada's *current television landscape* is comprised of six types of channels: (1) basic service analog stations comprising local over-the-air affiliates; (2) basic tier specialty channels; (3) tier-two digital specialty channels; foreign channels from (4) the United States and (5) other nations; and (6) premium movie services. Consistently, the most popular programs in English Canada mirror the most popular programs in the United States. By contrast, almost all of the most popular programs in French-speaking Canada are produced in Quebec and feature local celebrities.

Despite the creation of two Canadian digital networks in 2005 (Sirius Canada and XM Radio Canada), *radio* remains a predominantly local phenomenon in Canada. Unlike television and radio, the CRTC has largely left the Internet unregulated, allowing it to be developed by the private sector and academic communities. Canada is a world leader in broadband access. Increasingly, the Internet has become an important domestic communications technology, with almost two-thirds of users who access it from home doing so daily. Nonetheless, a notable gap has arisen between cities and rural areas, with urban Canadians significantly more likely to access the Internet (→ Communication Law and Policy: North America; Internet Law and Regulation).

See also: ▶ ADVERTISING ▶ BI- AND MULTILINGUALISM ▶ CABLE TELEVISION ▶ COMMUNICATION LAW AND POLICY: NORTH AMERICA ▶ INTERNET LAW AND REGULATION ▶ MEDIA CONGLOMERATES ▶ NEWS AGENCIES, HISTORY OF ▶ PUBLIC BROADCASTING SYSTEMS ▶ TELEVISION BROADCASTING, REGULATION OF ▶ UNITED STATES OF AMERICA: MEDIA SYSTEM

REFERENCES AND SUGGESTED READINGS

Attallah, P. & Shade, L. R. (2002). *Mediascapes: New patterns in Canadian communication*. Toronto, ON: Thomson Nelson.

Hildebrandt, K. (2005). *Canadian newspaper ownership in the era of convergence: Rediscovering social responsibility*. Edmonton, AL: University of Alberta Press.

Raboy, M. (1990). *Missed opportunities: The story of Canada's broadcasting policy*. Montreal, QC: McGill-Queen's University Press.

Vipond, M. (1992). *The mass media in Canada*. Toronto, ON: Lorimer.

Caricature

THOMAS KNIEPER
University of Passau

A caricature is an exaggerated and distorted image of a person or thing, which is characterized by visual likeness, immediate recognizability, and pictorial wit, irony, or satire. This visual burlesque can be insulting or complimentary. It is not uncommon that a caricature offends the sensibilities of a depicted person. Caricatures can serve editorial, illustrative, entertainment, or commercial purposes, as part of political cartoons, illustrations for books and articles, or standalone artwork. Caricatures can be standalone drawings or well-integrated depictions in a broader context. For example, caricatures of politicians can be one part of an editorial cartoon that comments on a political issue.

Etymologically the word 'caricature' originates from the Italian verb 'caricare', which means 'loaded' or 'overloaded', and the Italian noun 'carictura'. The word 'caricare' first appears in Italy around 1600, at the time of the rise of the artistic genre 'ritrattini carichi' (exaggerated pictures). In a preface to the 1646 published collection of etchings of the drawings of Annibale Carracci (1560–1609), it was pointed out that Carracci had employed 'caricare' for sketchy, satirical, and exaggerated portrait drawings.

The art of caricatura was further developed by Gianlorenzo Bernini (1598–1680). Aside from the external appearance of a depicted person, it was important for him to expose internal characteristics of personality or temperament. The intention behind this approach was not only to exaggerate unusual or unattractive features but to make the depicted person seem ridiculous. During his occupation at the court of Louis XIV in 1665, Bernini introduced the term 'caricature' to France. At the time, there was no conceptual equivalent for this term, which was translated into the French as portrait chargé. In the middle of the eighteenth century, the term *caricature* became popular in French.

In England the first definition of 'caricature' appears in the Bibliotheca abscondita in 1686.

Here, caricature was described as portraits of human faces using animal heads. In the middle of the eighteenth century there was a dispute over whether or not caricature satisfies artistic demands and quality criteria. William Hogarth (1697–1764) described caricature as "scrawniness." In 1743 Hogarth published his famous print 3 Characters – 4 Caricaturas to illustrate the difference between proper portraits and "scribbling." This dispute seemed to fade with the publication in 1813 of J. P. Malcom's An historical sketch of the art of caricaturing, a compilation of caricatures that defined the nature of the art. From this point caricature is a term used widely for all depictions of persons employing exaggeration or deformation. In the second half of the eighteenth century caricature became the generic term for political, curious, emblematic, and comic prints.

The evolution of the term caricature has followed a circuitous route. For Carracci, caricature was an exaggerated depiction of individual physiognomic characteristics. For Hogarth caricature was a flawed rendering of a grotesque illusion. For both, caricature was the selective depiction of isolated individual physiognomic guises and features, normally limited to the face and head. They were drawings that exaggerated the unique mental, physical, and other discernible characteristics or features of a person (Unverfehrt 1984).

Caricatures gained popularity among the upper class with broadsheets circulated for distraction and enjoyment among aristocratic circles in France and Italy. It was a kind of honor to be depicted. And it was considered a pleasant pastime to view the exaggerated drawings. In Britain this kind of amusement also became popular around the middle of the eighteenth century. The German emigrant Thomas Nast (1840–1902) carried the tradition of caricature and political commentary to the United States. By the twentieth century, caricature had come to be associated most often with political or editorial cartoons. Any editorial cartoon will show an issue from a particular point of view, which may shift the balance of debate and provoke thoughts that range from anger to whims. Editorial cartoons not only have the right but also the liability to be painful, cynical, and provocative.

However, caricature and 'cartoon' are not the same. A caricature is an exaggerated depiction of a particular person, characteristic, or thing and so can be a component of any cartoon. As such, caricature is a potential but not essential part of any cartoon.

See also: ▶ JOURNALISM, HISTORY OF ▶ MEDIA HISTORY ▶ POLITICAL COMMUNICATION ▶ PROPAGANDA, VISUAL COMMUNICATION OF ▶ VISUAL COMMUNICATION ▶ VISUAL REPRESENTATION

REFERENCES AND SUGGESTED READINGS

Bryant, M. & Heneage, S. (1994). *Dictionary of British cartoonists and caricaturists 1730–1980*. Aldershot: Scolar Press.
Knieper, T. (2002). *Die politische Karikatur: Eine journalistische Darstellungsform und deren Produzenten* [The political cartoon: A journalistic format and its authors]. Cologne: Herbert von Halem.
Lucie-Smith, E. (1981). *The art of caricature*. Ithaca, NY: Cornell University Press.
Unverfehrt, G. (1984). Karikatur: Zur Geschichte eines Begriffs [Caricature: History of a term]. In G. Langemeyer, G. Unverfehrt, H. Guratzsch, & C. Stölzl (eds.), *Bild als Waffe: Mittel und Motive der Karikatur in fünf Jahrhunderten* [Picture as weapon: Instruments and motives of caricature during five centuries]. Munich: Prestel, pp. 345–354.

Censorship

SAMEER AHMED
Wilmer Cutler Pickering Hale and Dorr LLP

Censorship is the control of speech and other forms of human expression. Bodies that partake in censorship attempt to provide stability for and strengthen their control over certain individuals and groups under their authority. Censorship commonly takes place in the following areas: morally questionable material like pornography, military intelligence, corporate secrets (→ Corporate Communication), government actions, and religiously objectionable material. Legally speaking, censorship involves the attempts of government agencies to restrict public forms of communication, such as holding public meetings and protests, publishing books and other written materials, and providing viewpoints and information in periodicals, or on the radio, television, and Internet

(→ Freedom of Communication; Freedom of Information; Freedom of the Press, Concept of). The two primary ways of censorship are through prior restraint or subsequent punishment. *Prior restraint* refers to a government's attempts to prevent material from being released to the public. Prior restraints include legislation requiring a person to seek permission before publishing information as well as orders barring the public release of material. *Subsequent punishment* attempts to censor material after it has been published. Types of subsequent punishment include lawsuits for defamation and criminal statutes for publishing offensive material.

A major question regarding prior restraint, as practiced by western democratic governments, is whether judicial injunctions should be viewed as objectionable as administrative censorship. Most forms of *administrative censorship* – when an administrative body rejects certain material prior to publication – are condemned universally by western democratic governments. However, they differ as to whether *judicial orders* to stop the issue of certain publications should be treated more tolerantly. Regarding *confidential government information*, European courts have been more accepting of prior restraints than their American counterparts.

See also: ▶ CENSORSHIP, HISTORY OF
▶ CHINA: MEDIA SYSTEM ▶ COMMUNICATION LAW AND POLICY: ASIA ▶ COMMUNICATION LAW AND POLICY: EUROPE ▶ COMMUNICATION LAW AND POLICY: MIDDLE EAST ▶ COMMUNICATION LAW AND POLICY: NORTH AMERICA
▶ CORPORATE COMMUNICATION ▶ FREEDOM OF COMMUNICATION ▶ FREEDOM OF INFORMATION
▶ FREEDOM OF THE PRESS, CONCEPT OF
▶ INTERNET LAW AND REGULATION
▶ JOURNALISM: LEGAL SITUATION ▶ PRINTING, HISTORY OF ▶ PUBLIC OPINION

REFERENCES AND SUGGESTED READINGS

Barendt, E. (2005). *Freedom of speech*. Oxford: Oxford University Press.
Blasi, V. (1981). Toward a theory of prior restraint: The central linkage. *Minnesota Law Review*, 66, 11–93.
Kalathil, S. & Boas, T. (2003). *Opened networks, closed regimes: The impact of the Internet on authoritarian rule*. Washington, DC: Carnegie Endowment for International Peace.

Censorship, History of

SUE CURRY JANSEN
Muhlenberg College

The English word 'censorship' is derived from the root 'cense' from the Latin 'censure': to estimate, rate, assess, judge. Censor was a title given to two magistrates in ancient Rome who were responsible for administering the census, and supervising public morals. When the Roman Empire became the Holy Roman Empire, the church assumed primary responsibility for → censorship.

The early *church* used its censorial authority to establish orthodoxy and condemn heresy. Written scripture codified the tenets of the Christian faith and secured the church's earthly authority, but the clergy possessed a monopoly over interpretation of the sacred text. The church began cataloguing forbidden texts as early as the second century; however the development of the Gutenberg press in the fifteenth century posed a profound challenge to church authority. Print facilitated the spread of heterodox ideas, especially Protestant reform (→ Printing, History of). The church responded by establishing an elaborate administrative system of prior censorship, requiring a license to publish (an imprimatur), and certification that a book had been inspected by a local Ordinary, usually the bishop. The church published its first index of forbidden books, known as the Pauline index, in 1559. The Index Librorum Prohibitorum went through 42 editions before it ceased publication in 1966.

State censorship bureaucracies adapted the administrative model pioneered by the church, with its central authority and local enforcement. Where the church publicly condemned objectionable ideas, however, state censorships routinely operate covertly as well as overtly. National security, often a contentious construct with expansive boundaries, provides the justification for covert state censorship (secrecy), especially in wartime, when all nation-states practice censorship.

Censorship in the west frequently involved *church and state collaborations*. In France, under the Ancien Régime, the Faculty of Theology at the University of Paris was responsible for censorship; later the king played a more prominent role; and then in the period prior to the revolution, the police served as censors. England followed the ecclesiastical model, publishing its first list of forbidden books in 1529. After 1557, the Stationers' Company, made up of printers and manuscript merchants, was granted a monopoly over the production and distribution of print by the crown; the Stationers' Company had the responsibility of suppressing all work that posed a danger to authority.

Throughout most of human history, censorship has been considered a legitimate prerogative of power: a means that authorities use to authorize normative systems. In condemning the evil and erroneous, censorship also defines and clarifies the meaning of the good, true, just, or at least the harmless. State censorship uses law and administrative procedures to enact and enforce censorship. The most comprehensive and longest lasting form of state censorship in recent history was put into place in *Russia* as an emergency measure by Lenin immediately following the victory of his forces in the Russian Revolution in 1917. State censorship remained formally in force until 1989, when the Supreme Soviet eliminated newspaper censorship. Lenin was acutely aware of the power of the press and arts as 'collective organizers' of propaganda, and mobilized them for socialist re-education. Technology posed special challenges to Soviet censors. Under Stalin, the typeface of every typewriter had to be registered so that illicit manuscripts could be traced. Administering these controls proved onerous; and in order to function at all, work routines were developed that gave higher level employees access to the "not allowed but possible."

China is expected to be the primary site of struggles for intellectual freedom (→ China: Media System). Its imposition of controls on the Internet, with the compliance of US-based software companies has become a *cause celebre* among Internet freedom advocacy groups (→ Advocacy Journalism).

See also: ▶ ADVOCACY JOURNALISM ▶ CENSORSHIP ▶ CHINA: MEDIA SYSTEM ▶ FREEDOM OF COMMUNICATION ▶ FREEDOM OF THE PRESS, CONCEPT OF ▶ INFORMATION AND COMMUNICATION TECHNOLOGY, ECONOMICS OF ▶ PRINTING, HISTORY OF ▶ SATELLITE TELEVISION ▶ SEARCH ENGINES

REFERENCES AND SUGGESTED READINGS

Coetzee, J. M. (1997). *Giving offense: Essays on censorship*. Chicago: University of Chicago Press.

Coliver, S., Hoffmann, P., Fitzpatrick, J., & Bowen, P. (eds.) (1999). *Secrecy and liberty: National security, freedom of expression and access to information*. The Hague: Kluwer.

Jansen, S. C. (1991). *Censorship: The knot that binds power and knowledge*. Oxford: Oxford University Press.

Levmore, S. & Nussbaum, M. C. (eds.) (2010). *The offensive internet: speech, privacy and reputation*. Cambridge, MA: Harvard University Press.

Petley, J. (2007). *Censoring the word*. London: Seagull Books.

Change Management and Communication

THEODORE E. ZORN
Massey University

Change management in the context of organizations is the process of planning, directing, and controlling a transition from one set of organizational conditions to another. Change management has been studied for many years in organization studies. It has not traditionally been considered a communication process, although models of change management typically include communication implicitly as a component of effective change management (→ Organizational Communication; Strategic Communication; Organizational Change Processes).

Several *trends* have led to change management and communication becoming more closely interrelated. First, the rate of organizational change has increased, as has the perceived importance of changing organizations; thus, organizational reputation is enhanced by the appearance of keeping up with the latest trends. Second, scholars have argued that change itself is constructed and co-constructed in → discourse. Finally, as strategic communication has become more prominent in organizational strategy, communication with stakeholders is seen as more central to change initiatives.

Much of the research on this topic is applied or 'managerialist' in orientation, although the body of interpretive and critical literature has been increasing rapidly. *Application-oriented research* has focused particularly on strategic means of announcing or initiating change, principles for communicating effectively with stakeholders, methods of stakeholder involvement, and means for managing resistance (e.g., Lewis 2011; → Applied Communication Research).

Interpretive and critical studies of communication in change management have focused on how change is symbolically enacted and socially constructed, the tensions and contradictions underlying change processes, and the political processes through which participants employ power (e.g., Bisel & Barge 2011). Both agents and stakeholders draw on prominent discourses in interpreting and framing change initiatives. For example, managers are influenced by hype surrounding new management trends and subsequently draw on this discourse in selling initiatives to stakeholders. Through resonance with these discourses – often framed in terms such as 'best practice,' – change communication campaigns take on legitimacy.

See also: ▶ APPLIED COMMUNICATION RESEARCH ▶ DISCOURSE ▶ ORGANIZATIONAL CHANGE PROCESSES ▶ ORGANIZATIONAL COMMUNICATION ▶ ORGANIZATIONAL COMMUNICATION: CRITICAL APPROACHES ▶ STRATEGIC COMMUNICATION

REFERENCES AND SUGGESTED READINGS

Bisel, R. S. & Barge, J. K. (2011). Discursive positioning and planned change in organizations. *Human Relations*, 64 (2), 257–283.

Lewis, L. K. (2011). *Organizational change: Creating change through strategic communication*. Chichester, UK: John Wiley.

China Central Television, Foreign Language Program of

JOHN JIRIK
Lehigh University

XIAOPING LI
China Central Television

China Central Television (CCTV) is the national broadcaster of the People's Republic of China (PRC) (→ China: Media System). The foreign language program of CCTV broadcasts globally to target markets via satellite and cable in Arabic, Chinese (Mandarin), English, French, Russian, and Spanish. CCTV's non-English and non-Chinese foreign language services are closely related to each other and to the original foreign language service in English. CCTV launched a joint French and Spanish service on October 1, 2004. The broadcaster split that service into separate French and Spanish channels on October 1, 2007. CCTV added an Arabic channel on July 25, 2009, and launched its Russian service on September 10, 2009.

In July 2009, CCTV restructured the news divisions of its domestic channels, combining them into a single 'super' department called the 'News Center.' CCTV-9 was renamed CCTV-News with the further development of the channel as a rolling news service. Apart from the rolling news service, CCTV-News, each of the other foreign language services offered almost the same block of programming four times a day.

The drive to bolster the PRC's image abroad through international TV programs is known as the "going out" project. It was launched in 2001 by the State Administration of Radio, Film and Television (SARFT) following the 15th Party Congress in 1997. High-level party and government officials repeatedly called for a global news channel with "Chinese characteristics" that could compete with the → CNN and → BBC and later Al Jazeera (→ Arab Satellite TV News). The "going out" project was designed to strengthen the PRC's 'soft power.' The concept of 'soft power' in Joseph Nye's (2004) sense of cultural influence is unavoidable in any current discussion of the PRC's overseas broadcasting.

Regardless of the scope of its reach, however, the real challenge for CCTV's foreign language programming is to overcome the perception that the emphasis on bolstering the PRC's 'soft power' means that the foreign language services are primarily propaganda channels. However, despite top-down editorial control, the reporters, producers, and editors at CCTV have consistently shown a willingness to push the boundaries of permissible reporting (Dong & Shi 2007).

See also: ▶ ARAB SATELLITE TV NEWS ▶ BBC ▶ CABLE TELEVISION ▶ CHINA: MEDIA SYSTEM ▶ CNN ▶ SATELLITE TELEVISION

REFERENCES AND SUGGESTED READINGS

Dong, S. G. & Shi, A. (2007). Chinese news in transition: Facing the challenge of global competition. In D. K. Thussu (ed.), *Media on the move: Global flow and contra-flow*. London: Routledge, pp. 182–197.

Nye, J. S. (2004). *Soft power: The means to success in world politics*. New York: Public Affairs.

China: Media System

SHUHUA ZHOU
University of Alabama

China is a leading civilization in the world. It occupies a total of 9,360,000 square kilometers of land in Asia, with a total population of approximately 1.3 billion. The General Administration of Press and Publication (GAPP) is the government's administrative agency responsible for drafting and enforcing China's press regulations. The GAPP has the legal authority to screen, censor, and ban any print, electronic, or Internet publication in China (→ Censorship).

China's State Administration of Radio, Film, and Television (SARFT) controls the content of all radio, television, satellite (→ Satellite Television), and Internet broadcasts in China. The Ministry for Information Industry is responsible for regulating China's telecommunications and software industries. It also controls the licensing and registration of all Internet information services (→ Internet Law and Regulation).

The Central Propaganda Department (CPD) is the Communist Party's counterpart to the government's GAPP and SARFT. Whereas the GAPP and SARFT exercise their powers through their authority to license publishers, the CPD is the organization primarily responsible for promoting and monitoring content to insure that China's publishers, in particular its news publishers, disseminate information consistent with the Communist Party's policies and agendas.

China was among the first nations to have printed newspapers. The country's earliest newspaper, Di Bao (Court Gazette), debuted in the Tang Dynasty, during the first half of the eighth century (→ Newspaper, History of). The number of Chinese newspapers increased more than tenfold from 1950 to 2012. According to the GAPP (GAPP 2012), China had a total of 1,918 newspaper titles as of July 2012. There were only a limited number of magazine and periodical titles until the 1970s in China. However, 9,867 magazine and periodical titles were published in 2012 (ibid.).

The nation's official *radio station* is the Central People's Broadcasting Station (CPBS). Every province and autonomous region has local broadcasting stations. China Radio International (CRI), the only national overseas broadcasting station, is aired to all parts of the world. The *television* era did not begin in China until 1958, when the Beijing TV Station began servicing the capital city with one channel. In 1965, there were 12 television and 93 radio stations in China. Now there are 2,185 television broadcast stations in China. CCTV is the largest and most powerful national television station in the country. In recent years, cable and digital television has witnessed rapid growth. Penetration rate of digital television reached 66.5% in 2013 (CNNIC, 2013; → China Central Television, Foreign Language Program of).

The first computer network in China was the China Academic Network (CANET), set up in 1987. It provided email exchange services with the global *Internet* via a gateway at Karlsruhe University in Germany. In spite of political and social concerns, the Internet has seen rapid growth in the last decade. Today, there are 564 million Internet users (CNNIC 2013), 42 percent of the country's total population. China also has 422 million mobile Internet users, which is 75 percent of all cell phone users (ibid.). By 2013, the number of domain names in China had reached 13.41 million (ibid.). Blogging has also become a new way of communication for scholars, researchers, novelists, and social activists.

Xinhua is the nation's official news agency, headquartered in Beijing. It was established in 1931 and is known as one of the major international news agencies in the world. China's membership of the World Trade Organization began in 2001, which also ushered in an age when the Chinese government organized state conglomerates by establishing *transregional multimedia news groups*. These include the China Radio, Film, and Television Group, the Guangzhou Daily Newspaper Group, the Beijing Daily Newspaper Group, the Wenhui Xinmin Associated Newspaper Group, the Liberation Daily Newspaper Group, the Zhejiang Daily Newspaper Group, the Hunan

Radio, TV, and Film Group, the Shanghai Radio, TV, and Film Group, and the China Radio, Film and Television Group (→ Media Conglomerates).

See also: ▶ CENSORSHIP ▶ CENSORSHIP, HISTORY OF ▶ CHINA CENTRAL TELEVISION, FOREIGN LANGUAGE PROGRAM OF ▶ COMMUNICATION LAW AND POLICY: ASIA ▶ INTERNET LAW AND REGULATION ▶ MEDIA CONGLOMERATES ▶ MEDIA ECONOMICS ▶ MEDIA HISTORY ▶ NEWSPAPER, HISTORY OF ▶ SATELLITE TELEVISION ▶ TELEVISION BROADCASTING, REGULATION OF

REFERENCES AND SUGGESTED READINGS

CNNIC (China Internet Network Information Center) (2013). *Statistical report on Internet development in China*. Beijing: CNNIC.
GAPP (General Administration of Press and Publication of the People's Republic of China) (2013). National Publication Statistics in 2012. At http://www.gapp.gov.cn/govpublic/80/684_2.shtml, accessed August 8, 2014.

Cinema

DANA POLAN
New York University

For at least the first half of the twentieth century (after which it confronted challenges for audiences' attention from television) the cinema dominated modern, mass-mediated → visual culture, and it continues to exert great impact on both leisure activities and the visual education of publics worldwide into the twenty-first century.

Cinema emerged out of nineteenth century visual culture as an art that gave motion to photographic still images (→ Cinematography). Soon, creative filmmakers used editing to construct increasingly complex narrative fictions. For the public, movies came to be identified with entertainment stories geared for mass consumption around the globe. Clearly, the hegemonic form of cinema through the twentieth century was the narrative, fiction film, with the US film industry in particular assuming domination of the world market (→ Film Production). Hollywood's fictions could be so strong as to cast their spell even over cinematic forms that promised alternatives to sheer entertainment and → escapism. Throughout its history, for instance, the documentary film may set out to educate but it also frequently intends to seduce, and here the rhetorical devices of Hollywood storytelling are frequently an evident resource.

Hollywood's hegemony over publicly shared image culture throughout the globe has raised concerns by censorship organizations, moral custodians, and even governments. For instance, in the domestic market of the US itself, worry over the movie content's potentially deleterious effects led to the imposition of a code of permissible content that achieved refinement at the beginning of the period of the sound film (the late 1920s and early 1930s) and then lasted for decades. At the same historical moment, some conservative religious figures who worried over the movies' impact on morals turned to social scientists for experiments that, they hoped, would 'prove' the cinema's negative effects on behavior, conduct, and even health and well-being: funded by a private foundation, the Payne Fund, the scientists produced over 10 volumes of studies (→ Media Effects, History of).

The history of cinema is simultaneously the history of a dominant *Hollywood industry* and of the diversity of alternatives that have arisen elsewhere over time. Globally, national film industries often seek identity in the production of films that they assume counter Hollywood escapism. For instance, in the 1960s and 1970s, a number of filmmakers in so-called "third world" countries set out, often with government support, to challenge their own media industries' risk of dependency on US hegemony in the cultural realm (→ Globalization of the Media).

From the second half of the twentieth century on, convergences ensued between cinema and other forms of moving-image culture. Today, theatrical projection of a film is often only the first step as films move across multiple media platforms – theater to DVD, to → cable television to computer screen, to hand-held device, etc. Without a doubt, digital exhibition will soon supplant most projection from film stock, and this rendering virtual of film images will no doubt further the convergence of cinema with other digital media such as television shows and → video games and will lead to new debate about just what cinema 'is'.

See also: ▶ ART AS COMMUNICATION
▶ CABLE TELEVISION ▶ CENSORSHIP
▶ CINEMATOGRAPHY ▶ DIGITAL IMAGERY
▶ ESCAPISM ▶ FILM GENRES ▶ FILM PRODUCTION
▶ FILM THEORY ▶ GLOBALIZATION OF
THE MEDIA ▶ HOLLYWOOD ▶ MEDIA EFFECTS,
HISTORY OF ▶ PROPAGANDA IN WORLD WAR II
▶ VIDEO GAMES ▶ VISUAL CULTURE

REFERENCES AND SUGGESTED READINGS

Bordwell, D., Thompson, K., & Staiger, J. (1985). *The classical Hollywood cinema: Film style and mode of production to 1960*. New York: Columbia University Press.

Casetti, F. (1999). *Theories of cinema, 1945–1990* (trans. F. Chiostri & E. G. Bartolini-Salimbeni). Austin, TX: University of Texas Press. (Original work published 1993).

Cook, D. (2004). *A history of narrative film*, 4th edn. New York: W. W. Norton.

Kahana, J. (2008). *Intelligence work: The state of American documentary*. New York: Oxford University Press.

Le Grice, M. (1977). *Abstract film and beyond*. Cambridge, MA: MIT Press.

Musser, C. (1990). *The emergence of cinema: The American screen to 1907*. Berkeley, CA: University of California Press.

Cinematography

PATRICK KEATING
Trinity University

Cinematography is the technique of photographing motion pictures (→ Film Production). Along with editing and staging, cinematography is one of the major components of a film's visual style.

Working with the director, the cinematographer can shape the appearance of an image by manipulating *three sets of tools*: the camera, film, and lighting. The *camera* presents the cinematographer with a number of possible variables, including the focal length of the lens, which determines the angle of view and the resulting sense of space; the size of the aperture, which can be opened or closed to allow more or less light into the camera; and the composition, which may be moving or static, viewing the subject from any possible angle. The choice of *film stock* can produce variations in contrast, color, and grain. Working with the laboratory, the cinematographer can adjust those values further through developing and printing. Recently, digital post-production tools have given filmmakers even greater ability to manipulate the image, albeit in ways that blur the boundaries between cinematography and special effects. Finally, *lighting* offers several variables, including direction, intensity, and contrast ratio. The most common arrangement in Hollywood is three-point lighting (→ Hollywood). In this system, a key light provides the primary illumination on the subject, a fill light brightens the shadows created by the key, and a back light separates the subject from the background. With subtle variations, this arrangement can produce the glamorous images of the romantic drama or the somber tonalities of the 'film noir.'

Perhaps the most celebrated analysis of *cinematographic style* is found in the work of André Bazin (1967). Linking cinema to photography, Bazin argues that photography is distinct from painting because of its ability to capture reality in all its ambiguity (→ Photography). Bazin criticizes editing-based styles because they fragment space and time in the interest of imposing meaning on the spectator. By contrast, deep-focus photography, in which the foreground and background are both in focus, encourages spectators to scan the frame; the result is closer to the relationship that the spectator has with the real world (→ Realism in Film and Photography). Later film theorists draw on → semiotics and psychoanalysis to launch a sharp critique of the realist style. According to Jean-Louis Comolli (1990), a deep-focus film is likely to sustain the dominant bourgeois ideology by reproducing the techniques of Renaissance perspective, thereby relying on dubious assumptions about a universally valid individual observer (→ Film Theory). Fabrice Revault d'Allonnes (1991) has produced a surprising mixture of semiotics and Bazinian realism, proposing a distinction between classic lighting, which reinforces the mood of the scene, and modern lighting, which does not. Like Comolli, d'Allonnes studies the ways that images signify. Like Bazin, he admires films that honor the ambiguity of reality.

Methodologically, historians of cinematography have adopted both quantitative and qualitative approaches. Salt (2009) has examined thousands of films looking for patterns in variables of cinematography, such as shot scale, as well as in variables of editing, such as cutting rates, tracking their changes over a century of cinema. This statistical method provides a background for more evaluative claims about the originality and influence of individual filmmakers (→ Quantitative Methodology). Some scholars have criticized Salt's approach, on the grounds that he pays too little attention to questions of ideology. Richard Dyer (1997) argues that Hollywood's three-point lighting system produced a particular standard of beauty – a standard that cannot be understood without considering the ideologically charged concept of 'whiteness.' This is particularly true for female stars, who often appear to be aglow (→ Women in the Media, Images of).

As *digital tools* have come to dominate filmmaking, the techniques of cinematography continue to change (→ Digital Imagery). The changes are obvious for cameras and film stock, but digital technology has even altered the way filmmakers approach lighting, which can now be modified in post-production. Some filmmakers lament the loss of traditional film; others hope to use the new tools to reproduce the established styles more efficiently; and still others predict that digital tools will produce distinctive new cinematographic styles.

See also: ▶ CINEMA ▶ DIGITAL IMAGERY ▶ FILM PRODUCTION ▶ FILM THEORY ▶ HOLLYWOOD ▶ PHOTOGRAPHY ▶ QUALITATIVE METHODOLOGY ▶ QUANTITATIVE METHODOLOGY ▶ REALISM IN FILM AND PHOTOGRAPHY ▶ SEMIOTICS ▶ TELEVISION, VISUAL CHARACTERISTICS OF ▶ WOMEN IN THE MEDIA, IMAGES OF

REFERENCES AND SUGGESTED READINGS

Bazin, A. (1967). *What is cinema?*, vol. I (trans. H. Gray). Berkeley, CA: University of California Press.
Comolli, J.-L. (1990). Technique and ideology: Camera, perspective, depth of field (trans. D. Matias). In N. Browne (ed.), *Cahiers du cinéma, 1969–1972: The politics of representation*. Cambridge, MA: Harvard University Press, pp. 213–247.
Dyer, R. (1997). *White*. London: Routledge.
Revault d'Allonnes, F. (1991). *La lumière au cinéma [Light in the cinema]*. Paris: Cahiers du cinéma.

Salt, B. (2009). *Film style and technology: History and analysis*, 3rd edn. London: Starword.

Citizen Journalism

CHRIS ATTON
Edinburgh Napier University

Citizen journalism refers to journalism produced not by professionals but by those outside mainstream media organizations. Citizen journalists typically have little or no training or professional qualifications, but write and report as citizens, members of communities, activists, and fans. The two broad types of citizen journalism are political and cultural.

The term 'citizen journalism' dates from the 2000s, but its practice is not new. The radical reformist newspapers that flourished in England from the late eighteenth to the mid nineteenth centuries had characteristics similar to recent citizen journalism: the so-called 'pauper management,' the stance as activists, and a close relationship with the audience. Citizen journalists practice across a range of media, from homeless-produced newspapers to community-based local radio and television stations. Print media offer scope for full participation. Broadcast media require technical competence and training. The Internet has permitted citizen journalism to expand. Despite barriers to access in many places, software allows users to set up websites and discussion groups with minimal expertise.

In *political practice*, citizen journalism adopts social responsibility but replaces an ideology of objectivity with oppositional practices (→ Objectivity in Reporting; Advocacy Journalism; Alternative Journalism). The practices emphasize first-person, eyewitness accounts by participants. They rework the populism of tabloid newspapers to recover a radical popular style of reporting. Their collective and anti-hierarchical forms of organization eschew demarcation and specialization.

Citizen journalism focuses less on the report as a commodity or on journalists as experts, not because of the novelty of knowledge they produce (a focus on uncovering hidden stories) but because of their new ways of thinking about and producing journalism (a focus on what kinds of knowledge they produce and how readers and writers may come together to make sense of the result). The nonprofessional status of citizen journalists tends to restrict the range of their reporting.

See also: ▶ ADVOCACY JOURNALISM ▶ ALTERNATIVE JOURNALISM ▶ CITIZEN JOURNALISM ▶ COMMUNITY MEDIA ▶ FEMINIST MEDIA ▶ GENDER AND JOURNALISM ▶ NEWS SOURCES ▶ OBJECTIVITY IN REPORTING ▶ PARTICIPATORY COMMUNICATION

REFERENCES AND SUGGESTED READINGS

Allan, S. (2013). *Citizen witnessing: Revisioning journalism in times of crisis.* Cambridge: Polity Press, 2013.

Allan, S. & Thorsen, E. (2010). *Citizen journalism: Global perspectives.* New York: Peter Lang.

Vujnovic, M., Singer, J. B., Paulussen, S., et al. (2010). Exploring the political-economic factors of participatory journalism: Views of online journalists in 10 countries. *Journalism Practice,* 4, 285–296.

Classroom Student–Teacher Interaction

SCOTT A. MYERS
West Virginia University

Within the instructional communication discipline, student–teacher instruction can be viewed from two perspectives: the rhetorical perspective and the relational perspective (Mottet & Beebe 2006). Teachers whose student–teacher interaction is governed by the rhetorical perspective communicate with their students as a means to influence or persuade them, whereas teachers whose student–teacher interaction is governed by the relational perspective communicate with their students as a means of developing a relationship. Teachers who teach from both these perspectives have students who are motivated to communicate with them, will participate in class, and will engage in out of-class communication with them (→ Teacher Communication Style; Teacher Influence and Persuasion).

When teaching from the *rhetorical perspective*, teachers must strive to be clear, make the content relevant, and be humorous. 'Clear' teachers are concerned with not only the clarity of course content, but the clarity of course procedures, course policies, and course expectations. Teachers who are 'relevant' are concerned with making the connection between course material and students' career goals, personal goals, and personal needs. Teachers who use humor do so by relaying humorous stories, telling anecdotes and jokes, and using exaggeration. When teaching from the *relational perspective*, teachers should attempt to engage in immediacy, which is the use of verbal and nonverbal behaviors (→ Nonverbal Communication and Culture) to decrease the physical and relational distance that exists between themselves and their students. Immediate teachers know and address their students by their names, ask students to share their feelings and thoughts, smile and use a friendly facial expression, and walk around the classroom.

Student communication motives refer to the primary reasons for students to communicate with their teachers (Martin, Mottet, & Myers 2000). Students who communicate with teachers for *relational reasons* do so to learn more about the teacher on a personal level. Students who communicate with teachers for *functional reasons* do so to acquire needed information about the course. Students who communicate with teachers for *participatory reasons* do so to demonstrate their involvement in the course. Students who communicate with teachers for *excuse-making reasons* do so to provide a reason for why their academic performance is suffering. Students who communicate with teachers for *sycophantic reasons* do so to make a favorable impression on teachers.

Participation is defined as the comments offered and questions asked by students during class time (Fassinger 2000), encapsulates the questions students ask and the clarification tactics and the information-seeking strategies they use. By asking questions, students can request help, request additional information, and check a point of view. *Clarification tactics* are the questions asked or statements made by students through which they indicate they need additional information in order to enhance their understanding of the subject matter. *Information seeking* allows students to acquire feedback and is used when they are unsure of how their performance is being evaluated. Students can seek information by asking the instructor directly or by paying attention to how teachers communicate with other students.

Out-of-class communication (OCC) refers to instances when students interact with their teachers outside of regularly, scheduled class time, including scheduled or impromptu office visits, email messages and telephone calls, and scheduled advising sessions. Many students who engage in OCC do so to inquire about course-related information, seek advice, share intellectual ideas, and discuss future career plans.

See also: ▶ NONVERBAL COMMUNICATION AND CULTURE ▶ PEDAGOGY, COMMUNICATION IN ▶ TEACHER COMMUNICATION STYLE ▶ TEACHER INFLUENCE AND PERSUASION

REFERENCES AND SUGGESTED READINGS

Fassinger, P. A. (2000). How classes influence students' participation in college classrooms. *Journal of Classroom Interaction*, 35(2), 38–47.
Martin, M. M., Mottet, T. P., & Myers, S. A. (2000). Students' motives for communicating with their instructors and affective and cognitive learning. *Psychological Reports*, 87, 830–834.
Mottet, T. P. & Beebe, S. A. (2006). Foundations of instructional communication. In T. P. Mottet, V. P. Richmond, & J. C. McCroskey (eds.), *Handbook of instructional communication: Rhetorical and relational perspectives*. Boston: Allyn and Bacon, pp. 3–32.
Myers, S. A. & Knox, R. L. (2001). The relationship between college student information-seeking behaviors and perceived verbal behaviors. *Communication Education*, 50, 343–356.
Terenzini, P. T., Pascarella, E. T., & Blimling, G. S. (1996). Students' out-of-class experiences and their influence in learning and cognitive development: A literature review. *Journal of College Student Development*, 37, 149–162.
Theophilides, C. & Terenzini, P. T. (1981). The relation between nonclassroom contact with faculty and students' perceptions of instructional quality. *Research in Higher Education*, 15, 255–269.

Climate of Opinion

LEO W. JEFFRES
Cleveland State University

'Climate of opinion' is a metaphor borrowed from the physical world to describe the 'perceived popularity' of opinions. Communication scholars often differentiate between → public opinion and popular opinion, between organized community and mass or crowd, between opinions based on consensus and those based on fleeting views. Policymakers generally respond to public opinion rather than popular opinions reported in media polls (→ Public Opinion Polling). Scholars have examined how the climate of opinion affects political discourse (Wyatt et al. 2000).

The importance of the media lies in its ability to affect public opinion and report popular opinion. When the issue is clear, e.g. whom voters support in an election, the public is generally quite accurate but not when the referent opinion is ambiguous (→ Pluralistic Ignorance; Pluralistic Ignorance and Ideological Biases).

Significance of the climate of opinion as a concept increased with introduction of the → *spiral of silence*, which said that what people learn from media reports of the climate affects interpersonal discussions. When people believe their opinions are in the majority or becoming more popular, they express their convictions openly, but if they think their opinions are in the minority, or losing favor, they fear disapproval and are less likely to discuss their opinions. Research shows support in numerous countries with diverse publics. The evidence so far also raises questions about its applicability based on how people process media messages conveying the climate of opinion, whether the media present a consonant portrayal of the climate of opinion, and how other factors like demographic characteristics or the nature of the issue affect the willingness to express an opinion besides a fear of social isolation. Another issue asks whether there is one climate of opinion or multiple climates. People live in various circumstances, so a national climate of opinion may be important for some topics, but individuals may respond to local climates for other issues. These distinctions may vary not only by geography but also by social groups (diverse versus homogeneous communities).

See also: ▶ PLURALISTIC IGNORANCE
▶ PLURALISTIC IGNORANCE AND IDEOLOGICAL
BIASES ▶ PUBLIC OPINION ▶ PUBLIC OPINION
POLLING ▶ SPIRAL OF SILENCE

REFERENCES AND SUGGESTED READINGS

Donsbach, W., Salmon, C. T., & Tsfati, Y (eds.) (2014). *The spiral of silence. New perspectives on communication and public opinion.* London: Routledge.
Jeffres, L. W., Neuendorf, K., & Atkin, D. (1999). Spirals of silence: Experiencing opinions when the climate of opinion is unambiguous. *Political Communication,* 16, 115–131.
Wyatt, R. O., Kim, J., & Katz, E. (2000). How feeling free to talk affects ordinary political conversation, purposeful argumentation, and civic participation. *Journalism and Mass Communication Quarterly,* 77, 99–114.

CNN

INGRID VOLKMER
University of Melbourne

Cable News Network (CNN) was launched in Atlanta, Georgia (USA), in 1980 and has become an icon of the globalized news world (→ News). CNN's rise as one of the most prominent global news organizations is based on a successful strategic integration of three key spheres of → journalism: (1) an innovative approach to internationalization (→ International News Reporting); (2) the invention of unique presentation styles, such as 'breaking news;' and (3) a continuous implementation of state-of-the-art technologies in order to reach clearly defined target audience segments.

As early as the 1980s, CNN began to establish a news exchange system with international broadcasters, and in the 1990s CNN International (CNNI) began to produce news programs for an international market. It was specifically the increasingly powerful role of CNN as the transnational journalistic gatekeeper during the Gulf War (1990–1991) that led to the launch of other international 24/7 news channels. Euronews, part of the European Broadcasting Union, was established in 1993, BBC World in 1995 (→ BBC World Service), Al Jazeera (in Arabic) in 1996 (→ Arab Satellite TV News), Channel News Asia (English and Chinese) in 1999, Al Arabiya in 2003, Russia Today in 2005, Al Jazeera English in 2006 and France 24 in 2006, all attempting to challenge not only CNN but the 'Anglo-Saxon view of the world.'

CNN's influence began to further fade not only internationally but also in the USA due to the network character of digital technologies, such as satellite (→ Satellite Communication, Global) and Internet. Today, CNN finds itself competing not only with other transnational organizations, but local channels and citizen journalism delivered instantaneously through websites, blogs, and mobile devices. CNN is increasingly partnering with → social media, such as YouTube, to create the online-video channel CNN BuzzFeed in 2013. Although the network had lost its once-dominant role in the global news sphere, CNN still constitutes a powerful model for 24/7 news journalism.

See also: ▶ ARAB SATELLITE TV NEWS ▶ BBC WORLD SERVICE ▶ INTERNATIONAL NEWS REPORTING ▶ JOURNALISM ▶ NEWS ▶ SATELLITE COMMUNICATION, GLOBAL ▶ SOCIAL MEDIA

REFERENCES AND SUGGESTED READINGS

Cushion, S. (2010). 'Three Phases of 24-Hour Television News.' In S. Cushion & J. Lewis (eds.) *The Rise of 24-Hour News Television.* New York: Peter Lang. pp. 15–30.
Robinson, P. (2002). *The CNN effect: The myth of news foreign policy and intervention.* London: Routledge.
Volkmer, I. (1999). *News in the global sphere: A study of CNN and its impact on global communication.* Luton: University of Luton Press.

Code

ROBERT L. CRAIG
University of St. Thomas

In → semiotics *code* designates a set of related → signs or signifying practices that correspond to a system of → meaning. What a sign signifies is generally understood as a marker of difference within this larger group or classification. For instance, the number sign '2' has no meaning without the number system as a whole; when listeners hear the word 'two' they understand that it represents a quantity different from 3, 4, and 5, etc., which were not uttered.

In media practice, communicators select from multiple codes hoping to communicate a preferred meaning. Thus, codes are also rules or norms that guide professional practice and interpretation. The degree to which communication takes place between an encoder and a decoder is based on their shared understanding of codes (→ Encoding–Decoding).

Media codes operate at technical/production, formal/aesthetic, social, professional, and ideological levels. For instance, taking photographs involves multiple selections from *technical codes,* such as different shutter speeds, lens types, aperture settings, lighting setups, etc. These choices affect a photograph's look and meaning; for instance, grainy photographs and their associated meanings result from technical selections (→ Photography).

Formal codes refer to stylistic choices journalists make. Technical writers write in a terse condensed style while reporters use the inverted pyramid (→ News). In photographic composition, formal codes include considerations such as camera angles, framing and balance. *Social codes* refer to broader sets of signs. Thus, readers employ their existing social and cultural knowledge and experience to infer meaning from an advertisement's model, her dress, make-up and jewelry, and the ad's design style.

Professional codes frame editors' expectations for journalists, helping them to deliver appropriate content and style; reporters covering → news would not write a feature or editorial. A professional photographer's blurry photo of a political candidate caught in a compromising situation would be lauded by editors, but a blurry food photograph rejected. Likewise, professional *ethical codes* prescribe different behavior for different message-making contexts. *Ideological codes* result from the fact that adhering to technical, formal, social, and professional codes creates patterns of representation that repeat narratives, which shape and reify people's expectations and social norms.

See also: ▶ ART AS COMMUNICATION
▶ ENCODING–DECODING ▶ FRAMING EFFECTS
▶ GRAPHIC DESIGN ▶ MEANING ▶ NARRATIVE
NEWS STORY ▶ NEWS ▶ NEWS FACTORS ▶ NEWS
VALUES ▶ NEWSPAPER, VISUAL DESIGN OF
▶ PHOTOGRAPHY ▶ PHOTOJOURNALISM
▶ SEMIOTICS ▶ SIGN ▶ STRUCTURALISM
▶ VISUAL COMMUNICATION ▶ VISUAL
REPRESENTATION

REFERENCES AND SUGGESTED READINGS

Barthes, R. (1972). *Mythologies.* New York: Hill and Wang. (Original work published 1957).
Fiske, J. (1987). *Television culture.* London: Methuen.
Hall, S. (1980). Encoding/decoding. In S. Hall, D. Hobson, A. Love, & P. Willis (eds.), *Culture, media and language.* London: Hutchison.

Code as Law

ANDREW D. MURRAY
London School of Economics and Political Science

In 1999 Professor Lawrence Lessig opened his book, Code and other laws of cyberspace, with a chapter entitled "Code is law." This short but complex phrase has, since then, found itself at the heart of a thorough interdisciplinary debate on how new media technologies have altered the configuration of centers of regulatory power and the application of regulatory control mechanisms. "Code is law" is, as a result, one of the most deceptively complex and debated phrases in contemporary regulatory theory (→ Internet Law and Regulation).

Lessig demonstrated that code in cyberspace represented control through architecture, one of four modalities of regulation along with law, markets, and norms. Each modality is described in terms of constraints on action. He demonstrated that design-based regulatory modalities are particularly effective in cyberspace. As he notes: "we can build, or architect, or code cyberspace to protect values that we believe are fundamental" (Lessig 1999, 6). This is an application of 'environmental plasticity' (Murray 2006), that attribute of cyberspace encountered when one ventures into the higher network layers. In its higher layers, cyberspace is an entirely virtual environment where code-writers have complete control over the environment.

This creates both a challenge and an opportunity for regulators. The opportunity is that, as environmental controls are self-executing, the designer/implementer of an architectural or code-based regulatory system need not invest in costly ex-post monitoring or enforcement agencies. The challenge is that this represents a shift in regulatory power from hierarchical, to private regulators such as software companies and network providers. This shift is stylized by Lessig as a move from East Coast Code (the code of Washington, DC) to West Coast Code (the code of Silicon Valley). The result is a migration of the regulatory center. East Coast code-makers increasingly seek to develop controls in cyberspace, not through the application of laws, but through mandating changes in the environmental code of the place (cyberspace): Code is thereby used as a substitute for law; or, to put it another way, with East Coast code-makers employing software code to bring about regulatory outcomes. "Code is Law."

See also: ▶ COMMUNICATION TECHNOLOGY AND DEMOCRACY ▶ E-GOVERNMENT ▶ INFORMATION SOCIETY ▶ INTERNET LAW AND REGULATION ▶ OPEN SOURCE

REFERENCES AND SUGGESTED READINGS

Lessig, L. (1999). *Code and other laws of cyberspace.* New York: Basic Books.
Mayer-Schönberger, V. (2008). Demystifying Lessig. *Wisconsin Law Review,* 713–746.
Murray, A. (2006). *The regulation of cyberspace: Control in the online environment.* Oxford: Routledge-Cavendish.

Cognitive Dissonance Theory

WOLFGANG DONSBACH
Dresden University of Technology

Cognitive dissonance is a theory developed in the late 1950s by psychologist Leon Festinger. It claims that people tend to avoid information and situations that are likely to increase a dissonance with their existing cognitions, such as beliefs, attitudes, or other value judgments. Together with the findings on → selective exposure in the seminal study The People's Choice it paved the way for the paradigm of weak media effects: when people selectively expose themselves to media content according to their already existing predispositions, persuasion through media content is almost impossible. This paradigm dominated the notions about media effects for three decades (→ Media Effects, History of).

Like several other consistency theories, Festinger's theory was based on the 'law of good gestalt,' suggesting that individuals will try to avoid dissonance and pursue a harmonious consonance between their many cognitions or even social relations. For instance, if a person perceived an argument against a political leader whom he or she otherwise admired, this person would try to resolve the tension between the two conflicting cognitions. Because of its compliance with day-to-day experience on the one hand and its contradiction to the normative image of a tolerant individual on the other, the theory immediately triggered numerous studies. Their results, however, remained all in all inconsistent. Also, Festinger's theory takes an already existing dissonance as the starting point for predictions about subsequent behaviour which might not be the normal situation when an individual is confronted with media messages.

Today, cognitive dissonance theory faces a revival in communication research because of the new communication environment created by the Internet. Many researchers assume that the increased number of often partisan sources on the Internet will increase the likelihood that people remain in so-called 'echo-chambers' of specific blogs or → social media, where they meet people who think alike.

See also: ▶ EXPOSURE TO COMMUNICATION CONTENT ▶ MEDIA EFFECTS, HISTORY OF ▶ SELECTIVE EXPOSURE ▶ SELECTIVE PERCEPTION AND SELECTIVE RETENTION ▶ SOCIAL MEDIA

REFERENCES AND SUGGESTED READINGS

Donsbach, W. & Mothes, C. (2012). The dissonant self. Contributions from dissonance theory to a new agenda for studying political communication. In Salmon, C. T. (ed.), *Communication Yearbook* 36. London: Routledge, pp. 3–44.
Festinger, L. (1957). *A theory of cognitive dissonance.* Stanford, CA: Stanford University Press.
Knobloch-Westerwick, S. (2012). Selective exposure and reinforcement of attitudes and partisanship before a presidential election. *Journal of Communication,* 62, 628–642.

Cognitive Science

JEREMY N. BAILENSON
Stanford University

JESSE FOX
Stanford University

Cognitive science is the study of mind and an interdisciplinary field that encompasses psychology, philosophy, computer science, education

(→ Learning and Communication), neuroscience, anthropology, and linguistics. The intellectual origins of the field can be traced back to the 1950s, when researchers first began to use formal mathematical representations and computational structures to model theories of mind.

What binds researchers across the various *contributing disciplines* is the notion that the processes that occur during cognition can be represented abstractly by some type of predictive representation. The nature of that specific representation depends on the discipline. For example, philosophers rely on formal logic, artificial intelligence researchers employ computer code, neuroscientists are guided by biological structure, and cognitive psychologists often use statistical analyses to fit data resulting from experimentation. By building theoretically driven, empirically tested structures of cognitive processes, cognitive scientists seek to increase understanding of the mind, as well as to build systems that are able to understand, predict, and generate human thought and action (→ Information Processing).

The *methods* employed by cognitive scientists vary greatly. For instance, linguists (→ Linguistics) are most concerned with developing formal systems of syntax, semantics, phonetics, and pragmatics. Psychologists rely primarily on laboratory experiments, aiming to understand how people form categories, reason, perceive stimuli, and encode, store, and retrieve memories (→ Experiment, Laboratory). Computer scientists most often build algorithms to simulate artificial intelligence, creating programs that can comprehend or generate language, exhibit creativity, or solve problems.

The fields of *communication and cognitive science* share many characteristics. One of the most fruitful ways of comparing the two fields may be to think of communication as a macro-version of cognitive science. Cognitive scientists create models of human behavior to gain insight into the underlying structure of the mind. In order to do so, they often study how a person interacts with some set of information or stimuli. Similarly, communication scholars examine the exchange of information among people to provide an understanding of the structure of human interaction. In communication, scholars study how people interact with others face to face as well as through media technologies and cultural artifacts.

See also: ▶ COMMUNICATION AS A FIELD AND DISCIPLINE ▶ CYBERNETICS ▶ EXPERIMENT, LABORATORY ▶ INFORMATION PROCESSING ▶ LEARNING AND COMMUNICATION ▶ LINGUISTICS ▶ MESSAGE PRODUCTION ▶ PRIMING THEORY ▶ SCHEMAS ▶ SCRIPTS ▶ SOCIAL COGNITIVE THEORY

REFERENCES AND SUGGESTED READINGS

Anderson, J. (2010). *Cognitive Psychology and its Implications*, 7th edn. New York: Worth.
Thagard, P. (2010). *The Brain and the Meaning of Life*. Princeton, NJ: Princeton University Press.
Newell, A. (1990). *Unified Theories of Cognition*. Cambridge, MA: Harvard University Press.

Commercialization: Impact on Media Content

JOHN A. FORTUNATO
Fordham Graduate School of Business

The primary business of the mass media is to produce content – fill the broadcast hours, the print pages, or the Internet site. Because of limits of time and space, selection of content is a necessary function. Many internal and external factors influence the mass media content selection decision-making process. Primary among those factors is the economics of the industry (→ Media Production and Content).

There is particularly concern about the extent of advertisers' influence dominating the content decision-making process (→ Advertising). Scholars argue that as a result of trying to deliver a mass audience to advertisers and not emphasize content that might lead to a reduction in audiences or advertisers, journalistic quality suffers (→ Quality of the News; Tabloidization). Scholars emphasize that because the news media play a prominent role in providing information in a democratic society their operating in only the advertisers' economic interests has negative consequences.

Other scholars contend that the advertisers' influence on media content is not significant. In evaluating the impact of commercialization, the question of what advertisers desire emerges. Advertisers pay large amounts of money because their investment guarantees them placement in the media outlet at the time and location desired, giving them access to the audience that participates in that mass media organization's content. It seems what the advertiser most desires is not necessarily to influence content, but simply to reach the largest possible numbers of its desired target audience that might buy their product as often as possible. In this philosophy, control or influence of media content is not a necessary condition to reaching an audience.

To support this idea, in a survey of network news correspondents from ABC, CBS, CNN, NBC, and PBS Price (2003) found that only 7 percent reported some advertiser pressure and 93.1 percent had never felt pressure from advertisers to report or not to report a story. No correspondents responded they were frequently pressured by advertisers to report or not to report a story, and only one respondent reported an occasional pressure of this sort from advertisers. With the purchase of advertising time well in advance, it is impossible for the advertisers who have bought time to know the exact topical content of a particular program or periodical.

See also: ▶ ADVERTISING ▶ MEDIA PRODUCTION AND CONTENT ▶ QUALITY OF THE NEWS ▶ SEGMENTATION OF THE ADVERTISING AUDIENCE ▶ STANDARDS OF NEWS ▶ TABLOIDIZATION

REFERENCES AND SUGGESTED READINGS

Price, C. J. (2003). Interfering owners or meddling advertisers: How network television news correspondents feel about ownership and advertiser influence on news stories. *Journal of Media Economics*, 16(3), 175–188.

Commodification of the Media

GRAHAM MURDOCK
Loughborough University

Commodification, the process of converting cultural experiences into saleable goods, has been a central dynamic of modern communication from the outset. The popular media that emerged at the end of eighteenth century had a double relation to the commodity system. Some, like books and theatre tickets, were simple commodities in their own right. Others, led by the popular press, also provided spaces where general consumer commodities could be advertised and promoted (→ Media History).

This commercialized organization of media has been *criticized on two grounds*. Linking access to cultural goods to ability to pay reinforces social inequalities. Reliance on advertising finance fills media space with promotional speech, privileges a consumerist world view, constructs audience attention as the primary commodity that media organizations sell to advertisers, and in the search to maximize audiences militates against aesthetic experiment and diversity by favoring cultural forms that are already popular (→ Cultural Products as Tradable Services).

In some countries these perceived limits of commercialized culture have been *countered by regulations* on advertising (→ Advertising Law and Regulation) and by public investment in cultural institutions free at the point of use and designed to cultivate citizenship rather than consumerism. Access to public libraries, museums, and galleries, was limited by location however. Broadcasting allowed the ethos of public service to be generalized (→ Public Broadcasting Systems). Over the last three decades however, the balance struck between commodities and public goods has been challenged by the global shift towards markets. Budgets for public cultural institutions have been squeezed and cut. Private enterprise has spearheaded new developments with lighter regulation. Advertising has proliferated and become increasingly integrated into cultural forms through sponsorship and product placement (→ Commercialization: Impact on Media Content).

Commodification also characterizes the *Internet* where popular uses are increasingly organized by a handful of companies who generate revenues by extending the principle of the audience as commodity, selling user data to advertisers and capitalizing on the on-line contributions produced by their voluntary labor on social networks and other sites. At the same time, the Internet has hosted new gift economies grounded in an ethos of reciprocity, as people collaborate to produce shared resources openly available to all, typified by Wikipedia. The future of social communication will be determined by the balance that is struck between them.

See also: ▶ ADVERTISING LAW AND REGULATION ▶ COMMERCIALIZATION: IMPACT ON MEDIA CONTENT ▶ CULTURAL PRODUCTS AS TRADABLE SERVICES ▶ MEDIA HISTORY ▶ PUBLIC BROADCASTING SYSTEMS

REFERENCES

McGuigan, L. & Mazerolle, V. (eds.) (2014). *The audience commodity in a digital age: Revisiting a critical theory of commercial media.* London: Peter Lang.

Murdock, G. (2011). Political economies as moral economies: Commodities, gifts and public goods. In J. Wasko, G. Murdock, & H. Sousa (eds.), *The handbook of political economy of communications.* Oxford: Wiley Blackwell, pp. 13–40.

Young, J. R. (1997). *An investigation of the theory of the commodity and its application to critical media studies.* Dissertation.com.

Communication Accommodation Theory

SUSAN C. BAKER
Cape Breton University

HOWARD GILES
University of California, Santa Barbara

In interpersonal situations, language can be used to convey information about a speaker's personality, social status, or group belonging. We do not interact the same way with every person we encounter. It is often desirable, or necessary to adjust our language patterns to our conversational partners. Sometimes we encode various forms of accommodation and non-accommodation deliberately and consciously, whereas at other times it emerges automatically and may not be decoded overtly (Giles & Gasiorek 2013).

Communication accommodation theory (CAT, initially speech accommodation theory), was first developed by Giles in the early 1970s to explain how we manage certain facets of interpersonal communication. Over the years, Giles and colleagues have elaborated and revised the theory (McGlone & Giles 2011) and it has assumed the status of a major socio-psychological theory of → language and social interaction (Tracy & Haspel 2004). It has embraced a wide range of communicative behaviors and has been applied in a rich array of contexts (Dragojevic, Gasiorek, & Giles in press; Giles & Soliz in press).

Accommodation refers to the way interactants adjust their communication behaviors to either diminish or enhance their social and communicative differences. *Convergence* occurs when interactants' communication styles become more similar to another. Upward convergence occurs when an individual approximates another's more formal communicative style, while downward convergence refers to matching another's more colloquial, or informal, style. Convergence is a means of signaling attraction to, respect for, and/or seeking approval of the other person. Social power is an important component of CAT(→ Power in Intergroup Settings). Those in socially inferior roles will converge more respectively to those in socially dominant roles than vice versa. People can also converge to underscore common social identities and to develop bonds with others.

CAT describes how individuals alter their communicative behavior to accommodate where they *believe* others to be (e.g. using an ethnic dialect with a known immigrant who has actually linguistically assimilated). In such cases, subjective convergence is translated into, and can be measured by, objective divergence. Additionally, people can accommodate to where others expect or wish them to be. In romantic situations, males take on more macho stances, while females might incline toward sounding more feminine – tactics called "speech complementarity." Such subjective moves are often based on social → stereotypes and therefore can be problematic when people "over-accommodate" to certain others.

Accommodation is not limited to converging behaviors. CAT has explained why interactants may choose to accentuate *communicative differences*. For instance, in "speech maintenance" people deliberately avoid using another's communicative style and, instead, retain their or their social group's idiosyncratic stance (e.g. not switching languages when they could easily do so). Furthermore, people can *diverge* from others by adopting a contrasting language, dialect, jargon, or speech rate.

Drawing upon social identity theory (e.g. Tajfel & Turner 1979), CAT argues that, when an ingroup is particularly valued, people will more likely want accentuate that positive identity by communicatively divergent means. Generally, recipients who perceive divergence directed at them tend to see the speaker in a negative light, despite extenuating circumstances.

CAT appeals to and captures the evolving histories, politics, and changing demographics of the cultures in which interactions that draw on accommodative moves are embedded. Although CAT has its limitations, it is supported by empirical research from diverse cultures and languages (Soliz & Giles in press), is invoked across disciplines and different methodologies, and has inspired satellite models in diverse areas.

See also: ▶ INTERCULTURAL CONFLICT STYLES AND FACEWORK ▶ INTERGROUP ACCOMMODATIVE PROCESSES ▶ LANGUAGE AND SOCIAL INTERACTION ▶ POWER IN INTERGROUP SETTINGS ▶ STEREOTYPES

REFERENCES AND SUGGESTED READINGS

Dragojevic, M., Gasiorek, J., & Giles, H. (in press). Communication accommodation. In C. R. Berger & M. L. Roloff (eds.), *Encyclopedia of interpersonal communication*. Oxford: Wiley Blackwell.

Giles, H. & Gasiorek, J. (2013). Parameters of non-accommodation: Refining and elaborating communication accommodation theory. In J. Forgas, J. László, & V. Orsolya Vincze (eds.), *Social cognition and communication*. New York: Psychology Press, pp. 155–172.

Giles, H. & Soliz, J. (in press). Communication accommodation theory. In D. Braithewaite & P. Schrodt (eds.), *Engaging interpersonal theories*, 2nd edn. Thousand Oaks, CA: Sage.

Soliz, J. & Giles, H. (in press). Relational and identity processes in communication: A contextual and meta-analytical review of Communication Accommodation Theory. In E. Cohen (ed.), *Communication yearbook 38*. Thousand Oaks, CA: Sage.

Tajfel, H. & Turner, J. C. (1979). An integrative theory of intergroup conflict. In W. C. Austin & S. Worchel (eds.), *The social psychology of intergroup relations*. Monterey: Brooks/Cole, pp. 35–53.

Tracy, K. & Haspel, K. (2004). Language and social interaction: Its institutional identity, intellectual landscape, and discipline-shifting agenda. *Journal of Communication*, 54, 788–816.

Communication Apprehension

JOOHAN KIM
Yonsei University

Communication apprehension refers to anxious feelings about one's own communication behaviors. McCroskey defines communication apprehension as "an individual's level of fear or anxiety associated with real or anticipated communication with another person or persons" (1977). It is closely associated with the imagination about the audience's negative feelings toward, and evaluations of, one's own communication behaviors.

The *main causes* are: (1) Desire to garner positive feedback from others and (2) lack of confidence in getting positive evaluations from others. Communication apprehension usually accompanies biophysical symptoms such as rapid and irregular heartbeat, increased blood pressure, perspiration, disturbed breathing, flushing, and so on. Desensitization training has been known as an *effective treatment*, because the excessive sensitivity to others' evaluations of oneself is one of most common cause.

Communication apprehension has been one of the most studied individual differences in the field of → interpersonal communication, under a variety of labels such as social anxiety, reticence, shyness, unwillingness to communicate, and social-communicative anxiety (Daly & McCroskey 1984; → Communication Apprehension and Social Anxiety). The scope of subjects includes dating anxiety, receiver apprehension or informational reception apprehension, singing apprehension, writing apprehension, and intercultural communication apprehension. More recent studies show that communicatively apprehensive or shy people tend to prefer online communication to face-to-face communication, and get higher gratification from it (Sheldon 2013).

It is not surprising that many types and versions of *communication apprehension measures* have been developed, including the Personal Report of Communication Apprehension, Writing Apprehension Test, and Test of Singing Apprehension. Most communication apprehension measures, however, are self-report scales. For future studies, communication scholars should consider using more objective measures, or biofeedback systems, reflecting emotional arousals such as heart rate variability and cortisol levels.

See also: ▶ COMMUNICATION APPREHENSION AND SOCIAL ANXIETY ▶ INTERPERSONAL COMMUNICATION

REFERENCES AND SUGGESTED READINGS

Daly, J. A., & McCroskey, J. C. (eds.) (1984). *Avoiding communication: Shyness, reticence, and communication apprehension*. Beverly Hills, CA: Sage.

McCroskey, J. C. (1977). Oral communication apprehension: A summary of recent theory and research. *Human Communication Research*, 4, 78–96.

Sheldon, P. (2013). Voices that cannot be heard: Can shyness explain how we communicate on Facebook versus face-to-face? *Computers in Human Behavior*, 29(4), 1402–1407.

Communication Apprehension: Intervention Techniques

CHIA-FANG (SANDY) HSU
University of Wyoming

Communication apprehension (CA) intervention techniques are empirically grounded methods to reduce communication anxiety, most commonly in public speaking contexts (→ Communication Apprehension; Communication Apprehension and Social Anxiety; Speech Anxiety). Treatments are typically categorized as cognitive, affective, or behavioral in nature, and instructors and counselors employ either one or a combination of the treatments outlined below.

Visualization (VIS), developed by Ayres & Hopf (1993) requires participants to listen to a script, vividly imagining positive, upbeat images of a successful speech. *Performance Visualization*, a variation of VIS, includes a behavioral practice component. The treatment involves viewing a video of an outstanding professional speaker, repeatedly imprinting the linked mental images of the video-taped speaker, and eventually replacing the vivid images with oneself as the speaker.

Ellis developed Rational Emotive Behavior Therapy (REBT), formerly rational emotive therapy (RET) to identify and address the dysfunctional thought processes and/or belief systems that lead to anxiety (see Ayres & Hopf 1993). Similar to REBT, *Cognitive Restructuring* (CR), developed by Meichenbaum, teaches people to identify maladaptive thoughts and develop coping statements to counteract them.

Communication Orientation Motivation (COM), developed by Motley, emphasizes teaching people to focus on the message of a speech and how it is understood by the audience, rather than the speech as an anxiety-provoking performance. In *Systematic Desensitization* (SD), developed by Wolpe, people are trained in relaxation techniques and instructed to create a relevant, personally tailored 'anxiety hierarchy', comprised of a set of imagined 'fear' situations arranged to be increasingly anxiety-provoking. People visualize these images until they can remain relaxed through the entire hierarchy (see Daly et al. 2009).

Finally, *Rhetoritherapy*, refined by Kelly, focuses primarily on behavioral skills related to composing and delivering a speech. The method includes instruction, goal setting, practice, in vivo assignments, and instructor feedback (see Daly et al. 2009).

See also: ▶ COMMUNICATION APPREHENSION ▶ COMMUNICATION APPREHENSION AND SOCIAL ANXIETY ▶ SPEECH ANXIETY

REFERENCES

Ayres, J. & Hopf, T. S. (1993). *Coping with speech anxiety*. Norwood, NJ: Ablex.

Daly, J., McCroskey, J. C., Ayres, J., Hopf, T., Ayres, D. M., & Wongprasert, T. K (eds.) (2009). *Avoiding communication: Shyness, reticence, and communication apprehension*, 3rd edn. Cresskill, NJ: Hampton Press.

Communication Apprehension and Social Anxiety

MELANIE BOOTH-BUTTERFIELD
West Virginia University

Communication apprehension (CA) is "the fear or anxiety associated with real or anticipated communication with others" (McCroskey 1984;

→ Communication Apprehension). CA is problematic when anxiety reaches levels that interfere with goal attainment. CA is emotionally based, although it does involve attitudinal and behavioral components (→ Attitudes). Low levels of anxiety may be perceived as excitement. But as anxiety increases it becomes aversive and interferes with communication demands.

Trait communication apprehension is an enduring orientation toward communication predisposing someone to respond to many kinds of communication with anxiety. Trait-apprehensive people will be fearful across time, and circumstance. *Audience-based CA* is consistent anxiety toward communication with a specific person or group.

State or situational CA is a transitory response to communication. It fluctuates across contexts, and when the situation terminates, the arousal dissipates. Certain settings have demands which may create *context-based CA*. Four primary contexts are: public speaking, meeting, groups, and dyads. *Public speaking* remains the most widely studied and feared communicative context. *Meeting or group* contexts may be less anxiety-provoking because participants share communicative responsibility. The *dyadic interpersonal* context tends to be the least anxiety-provoking, perhaps because rules are looser and subject to negotiation.

The most used *measure of trait CA* is the Personal Report of Communication Apprehension (PRCA-24). This 24-item scale measures four contexts of CA which are either summed or used individually to measure anxiety in specific contexts. The effects of high CA include: avoidance of communication; withdrawal or minimization of communication when interactions cannot be avoided; cognitive interference which distorts information processing; and behavioral disruption. Anxious people have lower self-perceptions and perceptions from others. They report self-focused negative thoughts, lower self-esteem, and need more structure. Higher CA is related to lower satisfaction with many types of communicative interactions. Others tend to view apprehensive individuals as more withdrawn, lonely, unattractive, low on immediacy and interaction involvement.

Overt behaviors reflect the need to avoid or minimize communication. The most consistent observable effects are less talking, minimal eye contact, neutral face, more pausing, either 'fidgety' movement or rigidity, and more disfluency. When assessing CA via behavioral output, it is best to observe clusters of behaviors.

See also: ▶ ATTITUDES ▶ COMMUNICATION APPREHENSION ▶ COMMUNICATION APPREHENSION: INTERVENTION TECHNIQUES

SUGGESTED READING

McCroskey, J. (1984). The communication apprehension perspective. In J. A. Daly & J. C. McCroskey (eds.), *Avoiding communication: Shyness, reticence, and communication apprehension*. Beverly Hills, CA: Sage, pp. 13–38.

Communication: Definitions and Concepts

PAUL COBLEY
Middlesex University

The Latin root of 'communication' – 'communicare' – means 'to share' or 'to be in relation with.' Through Indo-European etymological roots, it further relates to the words 'common,' 'commune,' and 'community,' suggesting an act of 'bringing together' (see Cobley and Schulz 2013; → Communication: History of the Idea). In the west, classic works of Greek philosophy set much of the agenda for understanding communication (Peters 1999, 36–50). Like many societies, early Greece was characterized by orality: communication by means of the voice, without the technology of writing. Oral communication, because it could not store information in the same ways and amounts as writing, evolved mnemonic, often poetic, devices to pass on traditions and cultural practices. Communication, in this formulation, was necessarily a locally situated process (→ Rhetoric, Greek).

Social Uses of Communication

The development of literate societies involved communication resulting in a *product* to be stored, distributed, and used as a reference for scientific analysis, critique, and political organization. Furthermore, written communication was also to be used for the reification of cultural and religious traditions. Writing brought a transformation in the experience of space and time: in contrast to oral messages, a communication in writing could be accessed at a later date than its composition; it could also be consumed in private.

Communication can be understood as a *repository of tradition*. In pre-print Europe, the protection of religious tradition was partnered by the preservation of writing, enshrining the 'Original Word' for the purposes of instruction. Before Gutenberg's invention of the printing press, writing was the preserve of monasteries, the locations in which scriptures were copied out longhand (→ Printing, History of). Following the introduction of print, communication became a key *symbolic resource* for social change.

In the centuries after 1450, Europe experienced major transformations of social life in which communication played a central role. Print facilitated widespread communication of messages that might be deemed educational or seditious, ultimately enabling confrontation (as in the Reformation) as well as specialization (sciences building on the Renaissance). Print promoted a more private, individual communication centered on the self. Yet, through its reach to a large audience, it also allowed public life in Europe to prosper, developing into what Habermas (1989) calls the (bourgeois) → public sphere. As Habermas shows, European coffee-house talk in the eighteenth century was driven by the content of printed periodicals and mainly oriented toward questions of literature and culture, even above politics.

Development of Communication Theory

A full-fledged 'communication theory' emerged in the twentieth century (→ Communication and Media Studies, History of). New technologies of communication during the period – photography, film, radio, television – stimulated the broadening of the understanding of communication. The understanding of communication in this period generally proceeded from the flow of Sender ==> Message ==> Receiver. The message requires *encoding and decoding* (→ Encoding–Decoding), indicating that it is not a perfect, transparent vehicle for → 'meaning': it mediates meaning as a result of being in a channel, even if the concept of mediation is given a variety of definitions across the human, social, and technical sciences (→ Media; Medium Theory).

On the other side, Lasswell (1948) represented a 'scientific,' *de-personalized understanding of communication*, which was taken further in an 'objective' account of communication by researchers in → cybernetics from the late 1940s. Producing models of communication, their work exemplifies the concept of communication as both product and process.

In the second half of the twentieth century, *medium theorists*, observing advances in the technology of communication, stressed that media are, in the phrase made famous by the Canadian communication theorist Marshall McLuhan, 'extensions' of humans. Like tools, media extend the capabilities of humans to reach out into a broader world of communication and interaction. However, as a corollary of this, the media transform humans' apprehension of the world and produce a consciousness that is tied to particular modes of communication, for example, orality and literacy. For medium theorists Innis, McLuhan, Havelock, Ong, Meyrowitz, Postman, Levinson, et al., all the major media of communication have entailed "paradigm shift[s] in cultural evolution" (Danesi 2002, 15).

In a parallel development, Lazarsfeld and colleagues put forward the idea of a → *two-step flow of communication*. This replaced the image of the audience as a set of unconnected individuals with, instead, a theory of → opinion leaders who, having been exposed to media, will circulate messages from the media and, hence, disseminate influence on a local basis. This idea replayed the concept of communication as a symbolic resource. In a summary assessment of contemporary → audience research, sociologist Joseph Klapper (1960) stressed the minimal effects of mass communication, conceptualizing communication instead, in a weak sense, as a common denominator of public life (→ Media Effects, History of).

Active Audience and Digitization

By the early 1980s, communication research emphasized 'the active audience,' recapitulating lessons from the → uses-and-gratifications approaches of Lazarsfeld et al., although often in a more critical perspective. The audience was found to be the locus of attitudes, values, experiences – ideological baggage that is brought to the act of decoding. As a result, audience members could be seen to actively and immediately reshape the communications they received, thoroughly transforming them in a manner that tended to invalidate the idea of an encoded message that is decoded by a receiver. Audiences do not simply decode, but 'make' or, at least, 'remake' communication.

From the 1990s onwards, computers entailed a *digitizing of communication* despite the persistence of naturalized, analogue graphic user interfaces remediating previous media forms. The use of computers for Internet access, along with the implementation of hypertext links, created the potential for nonlinear as well as many-to-many communication, summed up as *interactivity* (→ Interactivity, Concept of). Some traditional aspects of face-to-face communication were revamped through the 'time-space compression' which allowed global communication to take place instantaneously (email, video conferencing, mobile telephony, and so forth).

Other Forms of Communication

In addition to the theorizing of communication as taking place between individual humans, the nonverbal signs that are exchanged between *animals* can be said to actually communicate, as do the *verbal and nonverbal signs* passed between humans. The nonverbal signs that occur in components of organisms or plants also communicate. The concept of intrahuman and interspecies – as well as interhuman – message transfer amounts to a major reorientation of the understanding of communication, one in which human affairs constitute only a small part of communication in general.

Similarly, *noncommunication* (or miscommunication) in understanding what communication is should not be underestimated. This includes ambiguity, misunderstanding, lying, cheating, deception, and unconscious and willful self-deception (→ Interpersonal Communication; Language and Social Interaction). Indeed, the reliance of communication on signs to substitute for something else that "does not necessarily have to exist or to actually be somewhere at the moment that a sign stands in for it" (Eco 1976, 7) suggests the fraternity of communication with lying.

See also: ▶ AUDIENCE RESEARCH ▶ COMMUNICATION: HISTORY OF THE IDEA ▶ COMMUNICATION AND MEDIA STUDIES, HISTORY OF ▶ CYBERNETICS ▶ ENCODING–DECODING ▶ INTERACTIVITY, CONCEPT OF ▶ INTERPERSONAL COMMUNICATION ▶ LANGUAGE AND SOCIAL INTERACTION ▶ MEANING ▶ MEDIA ▶ MEDIA EFFECTS, HISTORY OF ▶ MEDIUM THEORY ▶ MODELS OF COMMUNICATION ▶ OPINION LEADER ▶ PRINTING; HISTORY OF ▶ PUBLIC SPHERE ▶ RHETORIK; GREEK ▶ SEMIOTICS ▶ TWO-STEP FLOW OF COMMUNICATION ▶ USES AND GRATIFICATIONS

REFERENCES AND SUGGESTED READINGS

Castells, M. (2009). *The rise of the network society*. 2nd edn. Oxford: Wiley Blackwell.

Cobley, P. (2006). *Communication theories*, 4 vols. London: Routledge.

Cobley, P. & Schulz, P. J. (2013). Introduction. In Cobley and Schulz (eds.), *Theories and Models of Communication*, Berlin: de Gruyter.

Danesi, M. (2002). *Understanding media semiotics*. London: Arnold.

Eco, U. (1976). *A theory of semiotics*. Bloomington, IN: Indiana University Press.

Habermas, J. (1989). *Structural transformation of the public sphere: An inquiry into a category of bourgeois society* (trans. T. Burger & F. Lawrence). Cambridge, MA: MIT Press.

Kim, M.-S. (2002). *Non-western perspectives on communication: Implications for theory and practice*. Thousand Oaks, CA: Sage.

Klapper, J. T. (1960). *The effects of mass communication*. New York: Free Press.

Lasswell, H. (1948). The structure and function of communication in society. In L. Bryson (ed.), *The communication of ideas*. New York: Institute for Religious and Social Studies, pp. 37–51.

Peters, J. D. (1999). *Speaking into the air: A history of the idea of communication*. Chicago and London: University of Chicago Press.

Shannon, C. E. & Weaver, W. (1949). *The mathematical theory of communication*. Urbana, IL: University of Illinois Press.

Communication as a Field and Discipline

ROBERT T. CRAIG
University of Colorado at Boulder

Academic studies of communication began to appear in the late nineteenth century on scattered topics such as transportation systems, crowd behavior, community, and newspapers, with important work being done in Germany, France, and the US. Communication research began to be recognized as a distinct academic field in the post-World War II period and underwent rapid growth and institutional consolidation as an academic discipline in the second half of the twentieth century (→ Communication and Media Studies, History of).

Academic Roots

The modern field of communication is highly diverse in methods, theories, and objects of study. The intellectual traditions that have informed this field have come primarily from two streams: the humanities and the social sciences. Antecedents of the *humanities* most relevant to communication go back to the ancient Greek arts of rhetoric, dialectic, and poetics (→ Rhetoric and Dialectic; Rhetoric, Greek; Rhetorical Studies). The humanistic disciplines of aesthetics, hermeneutics, historiography, and → linguistics are also among the intellectual traditions important to communication.

The second main stream that informs the modern field of communication emerged in the late nineteenth and early twentieth centuries with *experimental psychology and the social sciences*. The system of social science disciplines that crystallized in that period included anthropology, economics, political science, and sociology but not communication (Abbott 2001). However, communication became a topic of interest across disciplines and a stimulus to interdisciplinary work that eventually gave rise to the institutionalization of the communication field.

As the field was institutionalized, communication scholars constructed an eclectic theoretical core by collecting ideas relevant to communication from across the social sciences, humanities, and even engineering and the natural sciences. Craig (1999) identified *seven main traditions of communication* theory distinguished by different practical concepts of communication that underlie them: rhetoric, → semiotics, → cybernetics, → phenomenology, social psychology, sociocultural theory, and → critical theory. However, the field has been described in various other ways and continues to have no universally accepted overall structure.

Structure of the Discipline

The current state of communication research and education varies considerably within and among countries but can nevertheless be summarized with regard to some common themes. One theme certainly is *growth*: academic communication study is flourishing in many parts of the world, wherever political and economic conditions and academic institutions have allowed it to take root. Where growth has been stimulated to a great extent by demand for trained employees in burgeoning media and communication-related industries, which is often the case, growth is also associated with certain problems: strain on resources, an overemphasis on practical training of undergraduates that can stifle the development of a strong research discipline, and the threat of co-optation by commercial interests that are not necessarily aligned with academic and intellectual priorities.

Although always with much borrowing from Europe, communication research and education matured first in the US and spread from there. Overdependence on American and European concepts and practices and the need to develop locally based, culturally relevant knowledge of communication are common themes in other regions (e.g. Wang 2011). Yet, as that very emphasis on local development suggests, the field is increasingly internationalized, with global influences now flowing from many places.

The field of communication as a whole is served by two international *academic associations* of worldwide scope: the → International Communication Association (ICA) and the → International Association for Media and Communication Research (IAMCR). Several other international societies represent particular regions and sub-fields.

The Identity of the Field

Communication's status as a discipline and/or an interdisciplinary field has been debated internationally at least since the 1980s. The "ferment in the field" was addressed by a special issue of the Journal of Communication in 1983 (Gerbner 1983), a central theme of which, although not endorsed with equal enthusiasm by all contributors, was that the field of communication is a distinct academic discipline. Discussions of this theme foreshadowed elements of the 'communication science' model of communication as a social science discipline that was articulated in a series of prestigious publications over the following decade (e.g. Berger and Chaffee 1987). While the communication science model acknowledged a broader field of communication extending across a diverse array of academic disciplines and methodological approaches, it asserted the existence of, or at least the potential for, a coherent science of communication marked by characteristic methods, lines of research, and scientific theories. Others argued, however, that communication research would thrive intellectually only if studied as an interdisciplinary field, not as an isolated discipline (e.g. Beniger 1988).

The ferment in the field was taken up in a different way in ICA's 1985 annual conference on the theme "Beyond polemics: Paradigm dialogues" and a subsequent two-volume edited collection of essays (Dervin et al. 1989). In contrast to the communication science model, the framing vision of 'paradigm dialogues' emphasized epistemological pluralism, interdisciplinary openness, and critical reflexivity in communication studies. In 1993, the Journal of Communication revisited the question of disciplinary status in two successive special issues on "The future of the field" (Levy & Gurevitch 1993). The 48 articles in these issues expressed a variety of views and revealed no emerging consensus. Nor did any of these views clearly dominate the field by the early twenty-first century. The disconnection between interpersonal and mass communication research was still regarded as a problem, as was the continued institutional growth of the field without any consensus on a theoretical core and a rigorous scientific epistemology (Donsbach 2006).

By one relatively straightforward definition, an academic field becomes a discipline when it forms a faculty job market in which PhD-granting departments at different universities regularly hire each other's graduates (Abbott 2001). Communication does appear to meet this structural criterion. For example, a survey of ICA members conducted in 2005 found that two-thirds (rising to three-quarters of younger members) had received academic degrees in communication (Donsbach 2006). Studies have found that the network structure of the communication field increasingly resembles that of a unified discipline.

Applied Emphasis of the Communication Discipline

Communication as a discipline has a distinctly applied emphasis (→ Applied Communication Research). As Donsbach (2006) noted, growth of the communication field has been stimulated by the high demand for communication expertise in modern societies. The field's practical relevance to important policy concerns draws communication scholars into policy debates. Also driving the field toward an applied emphasis is its incorporation of, or close association with, a series of professional/occupational areas such as → journalism, → public relations, and intercultural training. Many areas of communication research also continue to be highly interdisciplinary. Contextually focused areas like → health communication and → political communication inherently straddle disciplinary boundaries. Study of the media as social institutions is unavoidably a multidisciplinary endeavor.

The open question is not whether communication will continue to be an interdisciplinary field, as it certainly will do, but is whether communication may also have a theoretical core that enables communication scholars to approach interdisciplinary topics from a distinct disciplinary viewpoint that adds real value to the interdisciplinary enterprise.

See also: ▶ APPLIED COMMUNICATION RESEARCH ▶ COMMUNICATION: DEFINITIONS AND CONCEPTS ▶ COMMUNICATION: HISTORY OF THE IDEA ▶ COMMUNICATION AND MEDIA STUDIES, HISTORY OF ▶ CRITICAL THEORY ▶ CULTURAL STUDIES ▶ CYBERNETICS ▶ HEALTH COMMUNICATION

▶ HERMENEUTICS ▶ INTERNATIONAL ASSOCIATION FOR MEDIA AND COMMUNICATION RESEARCH (IAMCR) ▶ INTERNATIONAL COMMUNICATION ASSOCIATION (ICA) ▶ JOURNALISM ▶ JOURNALISM EDUCATION ▶ LINGUISTICS ▶ PHENOMENOLOGY ▶ POLITICAL COMMUNICATION ▶ PUBLIC RELATIONS ▶ RHETORIC AND DIALECTIC ▶ RHETORIC, GREEK ▶ RHETORICAL STUDIES ▶ SEMIOTICS ▶ SPEECH COMMUNICATION, HISTORY OF ▶ UNESCO

REFERENCES AND SUGGESTED READINGS

Abbott, A. (2001). *Chaos of disciplines.* Chicago: University of Chicago Press.
Beniger, J. R. (1988). Information and communication. *Communication Research,* 15, 198–218.
Berger, C. R., & Chaffee, S. H. (eds.) (1987). *Handbook of communication science.* Newbury Park, CA: Sage.
Craig, R. T. (1999). Communication theory as a field. *Communication Theory,* 9, 119–161.
Deetz, S. A. (1994). Future of the discipline: The challenges, the research, and the social contribution. In S. A. Deetz (ed.), *Communication yearbook 17.* Thousand Oaks, CA: Sage, pp. 565–600.
Dervin, B., Grossberg, L., O'Keefe, B. J., & Wartella, E. (eds.) (1989). *Rethinking communication,* 2 vols. Newbury Park, CA: Sage.
Donsbach, W. (2006). The identity of communication research. *Journal of Communication,* 56(3), 437–448.
Gerbner, G. (ed.) (1983). Ferment in the field [special issue]. *Journal of Communication,* 33(3).
Levy, M. R. & Gurevitch, M. (eds.) (1993). The future of the field: Between fragmentation and cohesion [special issues]. *Journal of Communication,* 43(3/4).
Wang, G. (ed.) (2011). *De-westernizing communication research: Altering questions and changing frameworks.* London: Routledge.

Communication: History of the Idea

JOHN DURHAM PETERS
University of Iowa

Communication is not only a practice; it is also a concept with a long history (Chang 1996, Peters 1999). The term descends from the Latin 'communicatio', which meant a sharing or imparting. Since then it has taken on several not always consistent shades of → meaning. Communicatio comes from the root 'communis' (common, public) and has no relation to terms such as union or unity, but rather is linked to the Latin 'munus' (duty, gift), and thus is related to such terms as common, immune, mad, mean, meaning, municipal, and mutual.

Three lasting *strands of meaning* are already visible in Latin. The first is communication as a mutual exchange in language, found for instance in rhetorical theory (→ Rhetorical Studies). Second, in the 'Vulgate', the Latin translation of the Bible, communicatio can mean both tangible and intangible imparting, spanning both material and metaphysical senses. A third sense is communication as pollution or contamination. All three senses – rhetorical, spiritualist, and purist, respectively – persist into the modern Romance languages (French 'communication', Spanish 'comunicación', Italian 'comunicazione'), and especially English, which launched the concept of communication into the modern world. In both the King James Bible and Shakespeare, 'communication' can refer to both speech and sharing of tangible materials, but its decisive shaping took place in John Locke's enormously influential Essay Concerning Human Understanding (1690). Here 'communication' was the means by which two or more minds shared 'ideas' via language, a convention-based bridge between private meaning and public understanding, and thus both fallible and prone to abuse (→ Public Opinion). Though his concept of language was that of reasonable intercourse, he left the door open to later thinkers to see language as a private prison or a public tyrant.

Modern revolutions in transportation and distant signaling brought *new senses*. The term 'lines of communication' still describes military networks for moving troops, supplies, and intelligence. The American sociologist Charles Horton Cooley (1894) announced the key rupture: "transportation is physical, communication is psychical." This dematerialization of communication took its immediate inspiration from electricity – a potent medium and metaphor for human connection. By putting distant points into instantaneous contact, the electrical telegraph reanimated an older spiritualist sense of 'communication.' By the early twentieth century, 'communication' was an omnibus term for the varieties of human contacts.

A long line of critics in the nineteenth and twentieth centuries have lamented the ways in which communication made prized things common (ordinary, vulgar). Others saw authentic communication as a form of protest against a false world. For many modern thinkers, communication was both cure and disease, an ambiguity that goes back to 'communicatio' as sharing and as pollution. Some lamented the impossibility of communication between people while others feared the all-too-easy influence of → propaganda on others – variations on Locke's themes. Some psychiatrists and psychologists saw communication as therapeutic, a practice useful not only for treating individual psychopathologies but also for resolving global conflicts as well. Despite obvious and abundant contraindications, the notion that communication makes people better or happier does not seem to have lost its hold. Other thinkers of a more technical bent understood communication in terms of mathematics or cybernetics (Gleick 2011).

Over the course of the twentieth century almost every intellectual found something to say about 'communication' (Beniger 1990). The concept was an index of the age, and left a rich and sometimes confusing legacy for the academic field of communication studies (Craig 1999; → Communication as a Field and Discipline).

The history of the idea of communication reveals diverse semantic strands: rhetorical, spiritualist, purist, transportational, existentialist, communitarian, therapeutic, and technical. These lines of meaning give the term power and resonance. Some might consider it ironic that 'communication' as a term fails to live up to the ideal that it is often expected to fulfill – indisputable transmission of meaning. Rather, we might learn something profound about communication itself from the fact that even its name is full of competing meanings and visions. Plurality and difference seem to be our lot in both the theory and the practice of communication.

See also: ▶ COMMUNICATION: DEFINITIONS AND CONCEPTS ▶ COMMUNICATION AS A FIELD AND DISCIPLINE ▶ MEANING ▶ PROPAGANDA ▶ PUBLIC OPINION ▶ RHETORICAL STUDIES

REFERENCES AND SUGGESTED READINGS

Beniger, J. (1990). Who are the most important theorists of communication? *Communication Research*, 17, 698–715.

Chang, B. (1996). *Deconstructing communication: Representation, subject, and economies of exchange.* Minneapolis: University of Minnesota Press.

Cooley, C. H. (1894). *The theory of transportation.* Baltimore: American Economic Association.

Craig, R. T. (1999). Communication theory as a field. *Communication Theory*, 9, 119–161.

Gleick, J. (2011). *The Information: A history, a theory, a flood.* New York: Vintage.

Peters, J. D. (1999). *Speaking into the air: A history of the idea of communication.* Chicago: University of Chicago Press.

Communication Inequalities

SHOBA RAMANADHAN
Dana-Farber Cancer Institute

K. VISWANATH
Harvard University

Communication inequalities are differences among social groups in the generation, manipulation, and distribution of information at the group level and differences in access to and ability to take advantage of information at the individual level (Viswanath 2006).

Communication inequalities have been documented along *five broad dimensions*: (1) access to and use of communication technologies and media, (2) attention to health information, (3) active seeking of information, (4) information processing, and (5) communication effects on health outcomes.

It is hypothesized that inequalities in communication mediate the relationship between social determinants and health outcomes, thus serving as one potential explanation for health disparities (→ Health Communication; Health Literacy). In this way, one can explain health outcomes and health disparities by understanding how (1) structural determinants such as socio-economic status and (2) mediating mechanisms such as gender, age, and social networks (→ Communication Networks), lead to (3) differential communication outcomes, such as access to and use of information channels, attention to health content, recall of information, knowledge and comprehension, and capacity to act on relevant information.

In an era of rapid advances in healthcare, information flows are triggered frequently, yet the benefits from the flows accrue unequally among different social groups, as predicted by the knowledge gap hypothesis (Tichenor et al. 1970; → Knowledge Gap Effects). Given the proliferation of delivery platforms and the deluge of data, it becomes increasingly important to consider the inequalities present in the context in which new technologies are deployed (Viswanath et al. 2012). This raises important questions for communication research, policy, and practice to avoid creation or exacerbation of inequalities.

See also: ▶ COMMUNICATION NETWORKS ▶ DIFFUSION OF INFORMATION AND INNOVATION ▶ DIGITAL DIVIDE ▶ EXPOSURE TO COMMUNICATION CONTENT ▶ HEALTH COMMUNICATION ▶ HEALTH COMMUNICATION AND THE INTERNET ▶ HEALTH LITERACY ▶ KNOWLEDGE GAP EFFECTS ▶ MEDIA USE BY SOCIAL VARIABLE ▶ TECHNOLOGY AND COMMUNICATION

REFERENCES AND SUGGESTED READINGS

Tichenor, P. J., Donohue, G. A., & Olien C. N. (1970). Mass media and the differential growth in knowledge. *Public Opinion Quarterly*, 34(2), 158–170.

Viswanath, K. (2006). Public communication and its role in reducing and eliminating health disparities. In G. E. Thomson, F. Mitchell, & M. B. WIlliams (eds.), *Examining the health disparities research plan of the National Institutes of Health: Unfinished business*. Washington, DC: Institute of Medicine, pp. 215–253.

Viswanath, K., Nagler, R. H., Bigman-Galimore , C.A., McCauley, M. P., Jung, M., & Ramanadhan S. (2012). The communications revolution and health inequalities in the 21st century: implications for cancer control. *Cancer Epidemiology, Biomarkers and Prevention*, 21(10), 1701–1708.

Communication and Law

AMY REYNOLDS
Louisiana State University

The study of communication and law has traditionally been nation-specific, with a few exceptions, i.e., "those areas where particular technologies or common goals mandated a degree of international cooperation" (Huffman & Trauth 2002, 73). Perhaps the best examples of contemporary areas where technology and a common goal has allowed for substantially greater global cooperation are in the areas of intellectual property (→ Intellectual Property Law) and → Internet law and regulation.

Freedom of Expression

There is no such thing as absolute freedom of speech and the press. For freedom of expression is subject to various social, political, economic, or legal controls of its society. This is also true more broadly about freedom of expression, a term which many people use to refer to both free speech and free press (→ Freedom of the Press, Concept of). As Article 19 of the Universal Declaration of Human Rights states, "Everyone has the right to freedom of opinion and expression; this right includes freedom to hold opinions without interference and to seek, receive, and impart information and ideas through any media and regardless of frontiers" (Universal Declaration of Human Rights 1948).

In a democratic society, free press is considered equally important as *free speech*. The First Amendment to the US Constitution offers separate guarantees for speech and press, but in the US the two concepts are intertwined by well-established case law. The basic idea behind libertarianism is credited to English poet and philosopher John Milton. He had put forward the "marketplace of ideas" metaphor as early as 1644 in his Areopagitica. All democratic countries adopted the libertarian theories and embodied them in their constitutions or fundamental laws. Generally speaking, press and speech freedoms under the libertarian model are 'negative freedoms.' That is, they are freedom *from* governmental restraint.

Another model of press freedom exists in the *positive form*, which would focus on "the capacity to do or achieve certain ends" (Youm 2001, 5775). An example of an international positive model of press freedom came in 1978, when → UNESCO adopted a declaration containing not only demands for press freedom but also expectations towards a specific press coverage. The declaration, together with discussions on the → New World Information and Communication Order (NWICO) sparked heated debate about free press and the intention of the document. Licensing of the press is another dimension of positive law. Since the end of the Cold War in the late 1980s, the positive concept of press freedom, i.e. its absence, more often than not, has defined the standard for quality journalism around the world.

Contemporary Issues

Several freedom of expression issues have received a good amount of international and comparative law attention in recent years. Among them are defamation, → privacy, and hate speech, which is not surprising, given that these three areas showcase important contemporary legal issues that have international dimensions worthy of comparative study. *Defamation law* is a good illustration for the fact that communication law is more global than ever. Transnational media, along with the Internet, defy the traditional state-nation sovereignty of geography-bound communication. Where does the publication of defamation as a civil wrong take place when any statement is increasingly accessible via the Internet around the world?

American courts have invariably refused to enforce foreign *libel judgments* if the judgments were based on libel law incompatible with the First Amendment standards. It is still largely true that American libel law is more speech-friendly than the rest of the world. Nonetheless, an increasing number of countries are more willing to protect political expression – such as criticism of the government and government officials – than ever before. So, the actual or perceived gap between the US and other nations has narrowed. The European Convention on Human Rights' preference for political speech is clear-cut. The ECHR's rejection of criticism of the government as a crime reflects the functional value of freedom of expression as crucial to an effective political democracy.

Privacy as a basic human right is acknowledged in most international human rights declarations (→ Privacy). For example, Article 12 of the Universal Declaration of Human Rights and Article 17 of the International Covenant on Civil and Political Rights (ICCPR) both say that "no one shall be subjected to arbitrary or unlawful interference with his privacy . . . everyone has the right to the protection of the law against such interference or attacks." One of the issues in contemporary privacy law has to do with the balance of the privacy right against the rights of the media to pursue information. A case in Germany, centered on a series of photographs of Princess Caroline of Monaco that were published in a German magazine, used ad hoc balancing to determine whether privacy or press rights prevailed but, overall, strengthened the rights of the person in the news. With the increased use of the Internet, and increasing access to still and video cameras and technologies (for example, cameras in cell phones), privacy will become an increasingly important international communication law issue.

International law allows regulations on *hate speech*, and there are two human rights instruments – the International Covenant on Civil and Political Rights and the International Convention on the Elimination of All Forms of Racial Discrimination – that require governments to prohibit hate speech. The contrast in handling the speech in the US and France was highlighted in 2001, when Yahoo!, an Internet service provider in the US, was ordered by a French court to ban the display of Nazi insignia on its sites. The US court, however, held that "it is preferable to permit the nonviolent expression of offensive viewpoints rather than to impose viewpoint-based governmental regulation upon speech."

In addition to considering issues of race, some more recent laws have begun to address *religious hatred*. The tension between religious feelings and freedom of expression became an issue of communication law in 2005 when a Danish newspaper published several Muhammad caricatures.

Multidisciplinary Approaches to Communication Law Research

Which framework should prevail – law or communication? And are the disciplines of legal studies and communication, as a field grounded in social science, compatible? Despite the vastly different theoretical and methodological approaches of research in communication and law occurs, Reynolds and Barnett (2011) argue for more interdisciplinary work and a better integration of theory and methods that come from communication and law, despite law's heavily doctrinal approach. For scholars who want to understand communication and law, and freedom of expression, the contemporary trends that include multidisciplinary study as well as global comparative analyses provide a number of challenges sufficient to attract attention for many years to come.

See also: ▶ CENSORSHIP ▶ COMMUNICATION AS A FIELD AND DISCIPLINE ▶ COMMUNICATION AND MEDIA STUDIES, HISTORY OF ▶ FREEDOM OF THE PRESS, CONCEPT OF ▶ INTELLECTUAL PROPERTY LAW ▶ INTERNET LAW AND REGULATION ▶ JOURNALISM: LEGAL SITUATION ▶ MEDIA EFFECTS ▶ NEW WORLD INFORMATION AND COMMUNICATION ORDER (NWICO) ▶ PRIVACY ▶ SOURCE PROTECTION ▶ UNESCO ▶ UNITED NATIONS, COMMUNICATION POLICIES OF

REFERENCES AND SUGGESTED READINGS

Barendt, E. (2005). *Freedom of speech*, 2nd edn. Oxford: Oxford University Press.
Couprie, E. & Olsson, H. (1987). *Freedom of communication under the law: Case studies in nine countries*. Manchester: European Institute for the Media.
Fenwick, H. & Phillipson, G. (2006). *Media freedom under the Human Rights Act*. Oxford: Oxford University Press.
Huffman, J. L. & Trauth, D. M. (2002). Global communication law. In Y. R. Kamalipour (ed.), *Global communication*. Belmont, CA: Wadsworth/Thomson Learning, pp. 73–96.
Lomicky, C. S. & de Goede, T. C. (2005). *Handbook for research in media law*. Oxford: Blackwell.
Milton, J. (1925). *Areopagitica (and other tracts)*. London: J. M. Dent.
Pasadeos, Y., Bunker, M. D., & Kim, K. S. (2006). Influences on the media law literature: A divergence of mass communication scholars and legal scholars? *Communication Law and Policy*, 11, 179–206.
Reynolds, A. & Barnett, B. (2011). *Communication and law: Multidisciplinary approaches to research*. London: Routledge.
Stevenson, R. L. (2004). Freedom of the press around the world. In A. S. de Beer & J. C. Merrill (eds.), *Global journalism, topical issues, and media systems*, 4th edn. Harlow: Pearson, pp. 66–83.
Trager, R., Russomanno, J., Ross, S. D. & Reynolds, A. L. (eds.) (2014). *The law of journalism and mass communication*. 4th edn. Thousand Oaks, CA: Sage.
Ugland, E., Dennis, E. E., & Gillmor, D. M. (2003). Legal research in mass communication. In G. H. Stempel, III, D. H. Weaver, & G. C. Wilhoit (eds.), *Mass communication research and theory*. Boston, MA: Allyn and Bacon, pp. 386–405.
Youm, K. H. (2001). Freedom of the press. In N. J. Smelser & P. B. Baltes (eds.), *International encyclopedia of the social and behavioral sciences*. Oxford: Elsevier Science, pp. 5774–5779.

Communication Law and Policy: Africa

LYOMBE EKO
University of Iowa

The media law regimes in Africa are the result of three historical and political factors: the authoritarian colonial systems inherited at independence, international communication policy transfers from the UN and its specialized agencies, and the post-Cold War liberalization of the 1990s. The 54 countries on the African continent can be classified into *four major media law traditions*: (1) the English-speaking tradition, (2) the French-speaking tradition; (3) the systems of the Portuguese-speaking countries; and (4) the evolving media law regimes of North Africa.

The modern press was introduced in Freetown, Sierra Leone, in 1801 by former slaves from the US. The returnees brought with them some of the printing technology and press traditions of the American Republic (→ Printing, History of). Pockets of returning Africans also started newspapers in Liberia, Ghana, and Nigeria. Under British colonial rule, the press was modeled on British newspapers. The first press laws were 'sedition' laws passed to counter the scathing attacks of the African press against slavery and European colonialism.

Things were similar in Southern Africa, where the first newspaper, the government-owned Cape Town Gazette and African Advertiser, had been started in 1800. Conflicts between the governor and the press led the British government to issue a press ordinance in 1829. This law extended the freedom enjoyed by the British press to South African newspapers. In 1948, the National Party introduced the policy of apartheid, or strict racial segregation, and draconian press → censorship laws. In broadcasting, British colonial administrations introduced public broadcasting corporations modeled on the British Broadcasting Corporation in all British colonies (→ BBC). These localized versions of the BBC were aimed at serving British settlers in Africa.

French colonial policy was aimed at assimilating, 'civilizing,' and transforming Africans in French colonies into black Frenchmen and women. Though colonial law granted French colonies the right to publish newspapers, all publications were systematically censored. Radio was introduced in the French African colonies in the 1930s by a French government agency, 'La Société de Radiophonie de la France d'Outremer (SORAFOM)' the Radio Corporation of Overseas France.

From 1960 to 1990, *media law regimes* in Africa were a function of communication policies advanced by the United Nations Educational, Scientific, and Cultural Organization (→ UNESCO), the International Telecommunications Union (ITU), and the press laws inherited from the colonial era. Communication policy transfers from the international community to Africa started in 1958, when the General Assembly of the United Nations passed a resolution calling for the building of mass media facilities in the 'Non-Self-Governing Territories' in Africa and elsewhere. During the post independence period, all African countries ratified the Universal Declaration of Human Rights, which was translated into the 70 major languages spoken on the continent. Additionally, the majority of African countries ratified the African Charter on Human and Peoples' Rights of 1981, which also guarantees freedom of speech and of the press.

The fall of the Berlin Wall in 1989 and the collapse of the Soviet Union in 1991 triggered popular uprisings and *demands for political freedom* across the African continent (→ Freedom of Communication). In response, authoritarian regimes legalized opposition parties, and at least 50 African countries implicitly or explicitly granted constitutional protection to freedom of speech and freedom of the press. Nevertheless, newspapers and journalists in Gabon, Cameroon, Sierra Leone, Ethiopia, Eritrea, Liberia, Zimbabwe and other countries were either persecuted or prosecuted for their publications (→ Violence against Journalists). The media law environment in contemporary Africa is characterized by a system of law and disorder, a model of governance based on the triumph of arbitrary legalism over individual rights.

One of the major tasks of the African Union (founded in 2000) is to create a framework in respect of the Universal Declaration of Human Rights and the African Charter on Human and Peoples' Rights. Though virtually all African countries are signatories to these treaties, freedom of speech, freedom of the press, freedom of opinion, and freedom of religion have not always been respected across the continent (→ Freedom of the Press, Concept of). The African Union has created the African Union Commission on International Law, whose task is to begin the process of legal harmonization and creation of a culture of respect for international human rights norms, including freedom of speech and of the press, on the African continent.

See also: ▶ BBC ▶ CENSORSHIP ▶ FREEDOM OF COMMUNICATION ▶ FREEDOM OF THE PRESS, CONCEPT OF ▶ PRINTING, HISTORY OF ▶ UNESCO ▶ VIOLENCE AGAINST JOURNALISTS

REFERENCES AND SUGGESTED READINGS

Eko, L. (2001). Many spiders, one world wide web: Towards a typology of Internet regulation. *Communication Law and Policy*, 6, 448–460.

Eko, L. (2007). It's a political jungle out there: How four African newspaper cartoons dehumanized and "deterritorialized" African political leaders in the post-Cold War era. *International Communication Gazette*, 69(3), 219–238.

Nelken, D. (2003). Comparatists and transferability. In P. Legrand & R. Munday (eds.), *Comparative legal studies: Traditions and transitions*. Cambridge: Cambridge University Press, pp. 437–466.

Communication Law and Policy: Asia

DOREEN WEISENHAUS
University of Hong Kong

Communication law and policy in Asia covers a spectrum of issues involving widely varying political, cultural, and legal contexts across dozens of countries in the world's largest and most populous continent. While it can be difficult to generalize legal trends in the region because of a lack of conformity of interests and laws, or of agreement on what even constitutes Asia, several observations about the more significant developments at both the public level of media–government conflict and the private level involving civil litigation can be made. The rise in emerging democracies, burgeoning media markets, anti-terrorism efforts, and new media technologies, including the increasingly popular use of → social media, have been among the major factors affecting communication law and policy in Asia in the latter part of the twentieth and early twenty-first centuries. The manner in which individual countries have responded to these changes has resulted in part from the unique historical traditions in the region.

For many of the more than thirty jurisdictions in Southeast, East, and South Asia and Oceania, the region's long history of *European colonization* continues to have a major impact on media law and policy and the type of legal system the jurisdictions inherited. The *common law system*, imposed in territories under British rule, remains in such former colonies as India, Malaysia, Singapore, Brunei, Australia, New Zealand, Fiji, and Hong Kong. The French, Dutch, and Portuguese introduced *civil law systems* in their Asian colonies, including Vietnam, Cambodia, Laos, Indonesia, and Macau. Even without colonization, several jurisdictions – Japan, South Korea, China, Taiwan, and Thailand – adopted European-style civil codes. The significance of these systems extends to media law. Control by Spain and the United States over the Philippines left a legal system based on a combination of civil and common law. In fact, this blending of influences, including customary and religious law, in a common law or civil law system is a distinctive characteristic of many Asian nations. *Islamic law* or laws protecting Islamic interests are featured in Afghanistan, Bangladesh, Brunei, Indonesia, Malaysia, Pakistan, and Timor-Leste, which have sizable Muslim communities. Nepal's legal system is based on *Hindu legal concepts* and English common law.

As religion plays a larger role politically throughout the world, *nonsecular restrictions* figure prominently in press freedom issues in Asia (→ Freedom of the Press, Concept of). In 2010, Indonesia's Constitutional Court upheld a blasphemy law as valid, stating that Indonesia was a compromise between a secular state and an Islamic state. After the ruling, blasphemy prosecutions increased, including a prosecution against an atheist who wrote on → Facebook that "God did not exist." In Afghanistan an editor was sentenced to two years in prison for articles criticizing stoning and other Islamic punishments. In 1990, Pakistan's Federal Shariat Court held that "the penalty for contempt of the Holy Prophet … is death and nothing else."

As one of several communist countries in Asia, the *People's Republic of China* continues to loom large with its unusual form of media regulation. In late 2008, authorities made permanent a relaxation of reporting rules for foreign press put in place two years earlier in the run-up to the Beijing Olympics, although foreign journalists covering sensitive stories still often face temporary detention or other obstacles to their reporting. Rules governing foreign press are not applicable to mainland journalists, who are subjected to a much more restrictive regulatory scheme.

Nevertheless, the dramatic increase in the number of democracies in Asia, particularly since the 1980s, has generally resulted in *more legal protections for press freedoms* and, for some nations, the repeal of harsh laws from earlier, more restrictive eras. Countries such as Taiwan, South Korea, and the Philippines best typify this phenomenon. Most Asian countries have ensured *access to government records*, also known as right to information (RTI) laws.

The technical know-how and determination of *Internet users* in some Asian countries have created a fast-changing game of regulatory chess between the technically empowered citizens and governments struggling to contain what they view as harmful content. This has led to varied attempts to monitor and control the Internet, including shutting down sites, filtering, enacting new regulatory regimes, and applying more traditional criminal and civil laws (→ Internet Law and Regulation). The use of → Twitter, → Facebook, and YouTube in the 'Arab Spring' protests prompted China, India, and other countries to increase online censorship and other controls, including suspending Internet and cell phone access in troubled areas. Furthermore, China has been especially innovative and aggressive in Internet filtering, imposing regulations, and prosecuting online writers for violation of laws on state secrets, subversion, sedition and other criminal offences.

See also: ▶ COMMUNICATION AND LAW ▶ COPYRIGHT ▶ FACEBOOK ▶ FREEDOM OF INFORMATION ▶ FREEDOM OF THE PRESS, CONCEPT OF ▶ INTELLECTUAL PROPERTY LAW ▶ INTERNET LAW AND REGULATION ▶ JOURNALISM: LEGAL SITUATION ▶ PRIVACY ▶ SATELLITE COMMUNICATION, REGULATION OF ▶ SOCIAL MEDIA ▶ TELEVISION BROADCASTING, REGULATION OF ▶ TWITTER

REFERENCES AND SUGGESTED READINGS

Freedom House (2013). Freedom on the net 2013. At http://freedomhouse.org/report-types/freedom-net#.U9gHraPGCPQ, accessed July 30, 2014.

Glasser, C. J., Jr. (2013). *International libel and privacy handbook: A global reference for journalists, publishers, webmasters and lawyers*, 3rd edn. New York: Bloomberg.

Pearson, M. & Polden, M. (2011). *The journalist's guide to media law*, 4th edn. Sydney: Allen and Unwin.

Peerenboom, R., Peterson, C. J., & Chen, A. (eds.) (2006). *Human rights in Asia: A comparative legal study of twelve Asian jurisdictions, France and the USA*. London: Routledge.

OpenNet Initiative (2014). Asia. At https://opennet.net/research/regions/asia, accessed July 30, 2014.

Seneviratne, K. & Singarayar, S. (2006). *Asia's march toward freedom of expression and development*. Singapore: AMIC.

Weisenhaus, D. (2014). *Hong Kong media law: A guide for journalists and media professionals*, 2nd edn. Hong Kong: Hong Kong University Press.

Communication Law and Policy: Europe

ANA AZURMENDI
University of Navarra

The present media law of Europe has been shaped by two historical events, the *French Revolution* and the Russian Revolution. The Declaration of the Rights of Man and of the Citizen was proclaimed in Paris in August 1789. Article 11 states: "The free communication of thoughts and of opinions is one of the most precious rights of man: any citizen thus may speak, write, print freely, save [if it is necessary] to respond to the abuse of this liberty, in the cases determined by the law." It exerted a strong influence on all liberal constitutions and their provision of freedom of expression in Europe (→ Freedom of Communication). The English philosophers John Stuart Mill and John Locke prepared the basis for a liberal conception of the press (→ Freedom of the Press, Concept of). In Law of Libel and Liberty of the Press, Mill spoke about the essential role of freedom of expression in a democracy.

The *Russian Communist Revolution* created a system of censorship and control over the media, which rejected personal freedom of speech. The Decree on the Press of October 1917 included "temporary and extraordinary measures to stop the flow of dirt and slander." In the 1950s, the eastern and central European countries under Soviet domination adopted the Soviet system of media censorship and control.

At the end of World War II came the entity now known as the European Union. The definitive objective of the European Union has been to build strong cultural and political links among the member states. So the European Convention on Human Rights provides for freedom of expression as a right. The majority of the post-communist countries in eastern and central Europe have begun on their own paths to democracy. Their new constitutions guarantee freedom of expression, the right to information, and the right of privacy, as do those of many western European countries.

The Council of Europe has been a watchdog on human rights around the continent since 1950. The European Court of Human Rights has promoted freedom of expression over the years, especially since the mid 1970s. Its jurisdiction affects European countries that have signed the European Convention on Human Rights. As of December 2010, the Court had ruled in more than 500 cases on freedom of expression.

The European Union adopted its own Charter of Fundamental Rights of the European Union in January 2001. Article 11 of the EU Charter is similar to Article 10 of the European Convention on Human Rights: "Everyone has the right to freedom of expression. This right shall include freedom to hold opinions and to receive and impart information and ideas without interference by public authority and regardless of frontiers . . . The freedom and pluralism of the media shall be respected."

The EU views *audiovisual media* as essential to building a European identity among Europe's multi-citizenship. The promotion of inter-European delivery of audiovisual contents throughout the 'European audiovisual space' is the best support of the European multicultural identity. This started with the Television without Frontiers Directive of 1989, updated by the Audiovisual Media Services Directive of 2007, taking into account the technological developments of the Internet, mobile networks, and on-demand services. The main issues of the 1989 Directive are still relevant. Among them are advertising limits, the protection of minors and human dignity, cultural diversity, fair competition, and access to information (→ European Union: Communication Law). The EU audiovisual policy is related to public broadcasting in particular (→ Public Broadcasting Systems). The EU pays close attention to various controversies arising from public broadcasting services.

EU concern about *media concentration* issues has been addressed by the EU Parliament and Commission Resolutions, which are aware of decreased pluralism and the Commission's executive actions (→ Concentration in Media Systems). The EU's focus is to preclude one particular communication enterprise from dominating the European market (→ Media Conglomerates). But the necessity of being competitive in the global market has pressured the European Commission to compromise on its media concentration policy.

See also: ▶ CENSORSHIP ▶ CONCENTRATION IN MEDIA SYSTEMS ▶ EUROPEAN UNION: COMMUNICATION LAW ▶ FREEDOM OF COMMUNICATION ▶ FREEDOM OF THE PRESS, CONCEPT OF ▶ MEDIA CONGLOMERATES ▶ MEDIA HISTORY ▶ NEWSPAPER, HISTORY OF ▶ PROPAGANDA ▶ PUBLIC BROADCASTING SYSTEMS ▶ TELEVISION BROADCASTING, REGULATION OF

REFERENCES AND SUGGESTED READINGS

Bron, C. M. (2010). Financing and supervision of public service broadcasting. *IRIS Plus*, 4, 1–25.
Czepek, A., Hellwig, M., & Nowak, E., (2009). *Press freedom and pluralism in Europe: Concepts and conditions*, Chicago: University of Chicago Press–ECREA.
Derieux, E. (2010). *Droit des medias: Droit français, européen et international* [European and international media law]. Paris: LGDE.
Eko, S.L. (2012). *New media, old regimes: Case studies in comparative communication law and policy* Lanham, MD: Lexington Books.
Pauwels, C., Kalimo, H., Donders, K., & Van Rompuy B. (eds.) (2009). *Rethinking European media and communications policy*. Brussels: Institute for European Studies.
Valentini, C. & Nesti, G. (2010). *Public communication in the European Union: History, perspectives and challenges*. Newcastle-upon-Tyne: Cambridge Scholars.
Trappel, J., Meier, W. A., d'Haenens, L., Steemers, J., & Thomass, B.(2011). *Media in Europe today*. Chicago: Intellect.

Communication Law and Policy: Middle East

ORAYB AREF NAJJAR
Northern Illinois University

Twenty-two countries belong to the Arab League, established in 1945. Most of those countries were ruled by the Ottomans, British, French, or Italians. Thus, Arab countries have largely adopted legislation based mostly on the legal systems of their former colonial rulers. Egypt, however, has a longer and more established legal tradition that dates back to the Egyptian constitution of 1923, while some Gulf nations that were British 'protectorates' until 1971 have a less tested or developed legal tradition. The normative sources regulating speech rights in Israel consist of a number of British mandatory statutes incorporated into Israeli law in 1948 from the Law and Administration Ordinance, as well as Israeli legislation enacted by the Knesset after the establishment of the state. All Arab countries with the exception of Iraq still require licensing before publication. In almost all countries, minimum capitalization is required. Sometimes, licensing involves obtaining a certificate of good conduct from the ministry of interior or the intelligence services.

Israel enacted a → *freedom of information* law in 1998. The law allows any citizen or resident to access records held by government offices, local councils, and government-owned corporations. *Insult laws* have their origin in the concept of 'lèse-majesté' in the 1881 French law. The *right of reply* is found in the press laws of Bahrain, Egypt, Jordan, Lebanon, Libya, Morocco, Palestine, Syria, Tunisia, and Yemen among others. Israeli defamation law does not distinguish between defamation of private individuals and public officials or figures. The 9/11 attacks led Jordan, Egypt, Tunisia, and Bahrain to promulgate new press laws to fight terrorism.

As a result of the level of secularism vs Islamic observance, Arab countries use Sharia law sparingly or extensively. The Syrian constitution is the most secular. In contrast, Saudi Arabia's Article 1 in the Constitution states that Islam is its religion; God's Book and the Sunnah of His Prophet are its constitution.

In the mid-1990s, when Internet use was reserved for the well-to-do, most Arab governments did not attempt to censor it. As Internet use became common, some governments set up surveillance units.

See also: ▶ CENSORSHIP ▶ FREEDOM OF INFORMATION ▶ INTERNET LAW AND REGULATION ▶ JOURNALISM: LEGAL SITUATION ▶ VIOLENCE AGAINST JOURNALISTS

REFERENCES AND SUGGESTED READINGS

Meraz, S. & Papacharissi, Z. (2013). Networked Gatekeeping and Networked Framing on Egypt. *International Journal of the Press and Politics* 18(2), 1–29.
Reporters Without Borders (2014). Press Freedom Index. At http://en.rsf.org/press-freedom-index-2013,1054.html, accessed August 8, 2014.
Shukkier, Y. (2008). Freedom of the media in the Arab countries. Amman Center for Human Rights Studies, Amman, Jordan. At http://www.achrs.org/english/index.php/center-news-mainmenu-79/data-and-reports-mainmenu-37/148-summary-of-the-report-on-qfreedom-of-the-media-in-the-arab-countriesq-2008.html, accessed August 8, 2014.

Communication Law and Policy: North America

KARLA K. GOWER
University of Alabama

North America consists of 23 countries. The United States dominates the region in the area of communication law and policy, followed by Canada. Except for Cuba, the countries are democracies, with most of the legal systems based on American law, English common law, or French civil law. All have constitutions that protect the right of freedom of expression, but the extent of the right in practice varies (→ Freedom of Communication; Freedom of the Press, Concept of). According to the 2013 Freedom House report on freedom of the press, 13 of the countries are free (56.5 percent), seven are partly free (30.5 percent), and three, Cuba, Honduras, and Mexico, are not free.

The United States has the oldest constitution on the continent. The First Amendment prohibits any law from abridging *freedom of speech* or of the press (→ United States of America: Media System). Despite the First Amendment's absolute language, the courts allow restrictions on freedom of expression to protect a compelling government interest. The other countries have built the balancing mechanism into their constitutions. Freedom of expression in Canada, for example, is subject to "reasonable limits" as justified in a democracy (→ Canada: Media System; Mexico: Media System). *Cuba* has the most restrictive constitutional provisions, although it does allow free speech that conforms "to the aims of a Socialist society".

Constitutional protections for freedom of expression can be meaningless without *access to information* (→ Freedom of Information). The United States and Canada have had federal acts that permit access to certain government records since 1966 and 1983 respectively. Mexico, Jamaica, the Dominican Republic, Antigua and Barbuda, Honduras, and Guatemala have all passed access to information laws since 2002. Procedural hurdles, however, hamper the law's use in each of the countries. Barbados, El Salvador and Costa Rica have no freedom of information legislation.

Broadcasting is a mixture of private and public ownership with varying levels of regulation, except for Cuba, where the government owns all of the electronic media outlets. In the United States, despite being under private ownership, broadcasters are licensed by the → Federal Communications Commission (FCC) and are obliged to operate in the public interest. Canada has a similar system, but it also has the public, government-funded Canadian Broadcasting Corporation (→ Public Broadcasting Systems).

Most of the countries have no government restrictions on *Internet access* and content. The United States government's attempts at online censorship have been ruled unconstitutional. Commercial websites are restricted in the amount of information they can collect from minors, however. The Canadian government does not regulate Internet content, although some provincial legislation affects e-commerce, and several individuals have been fined for online hate messages. Cuba is the only country that strictly regulates Internet content and access.

Many countries have laws, such as criminal *defamation laws* and desacato (insult) laws, that make the constitutional provisions for free expression meaningless. The United States has the strongest protections for those criticizing the government (→ Journalism: Legal Situation). Defamation is still a criminal offense in some states, although rarely used. Public officials in libel suits are required to prove fault. And hate speech is generally protected. State shield laws protect journalists from subpoenas compelling them to reveal confidential sources, but no federal law exists (→ Source Protection). In *Canada*, journalists can be held in contempt for failing to reveal a source. And libel is still a criminal offense. Individuals can be fined for speech that exposes persons or groups to hatred. Defamation remains a criminal offense in many of the countries, although Costa Rica, Honduras and Guatemala have removed descacato laws from their criminal codes. As of 2003, individuals publishing false news that harms the public good in St Lucia are subject to a jail term. In Cuba, laws criminalizing "enemy propaganda" and the dissemination of "unauthorized news" effectively restrict freedom of speech.

See also: ▶ CANADA: MEDIA SYSTEM ▶ CENSORSHIP ▶ FEDERAL COMMUNICATIONS COMMISSION (FCC) ▶ FREEDOM OF COMMUNICATION ▶ FREEDOM OF INFORMATION ▶ FREEDOM OF THE PRESS, CONCEPT OF ▶ JOURNALISM: LEGAL SITUATION ▶ MEXICO: MEDIA SYSTEM ▶ PUBLIC BROADCASTING SYSTEMS ▶ SOURCE PROTECTION ▶ TELEVISION BROADCASTING, REGULATION OF ▶ UNITED STATES OF AMERICA: MEDIA SYSTEM

REFERENCES AND SUGGESTED READINGS

American Convention on Human Rights, O.A.S. (1992). Treaty Series No. 36, 1144 U.N.T.S. 123, entered into force July 18, 1978, reprinted in *Basic Documents Pertaining to Human Rights in the Inter-American System*, OEA/Ser. L.V/II.82 doc.6 rev.1 at 25.

Claude Reyes et al. v. Chile (2006). Judgment of September 19, 2006, *Inter-Am Ct. H.R.* (Ser. C) No. 151.

Freedom House (2013). Freedom of the press. At www.freedomhouse.org/report-types/freedom-press, accessed July 30, 2014.

Greene, M. (2007). *It's a crime: How insult laws stifle press freedom.* Reston, VA: World Press Freedom Committee.

Inter-American Commission on Human Rights (n.d.). Declaration of Principles on Freedom of Expression, approved by the Inter-American Commission. At http://www.oas.org/en/iachr/expression/showarticle.asp?artID=26, accessed July 30, 2014.

Pasqualucci, J. M. (2006). Criminal defamation and the evolution of the doctrine of freedom of expression in international law: Comparative jurisprudence of the Inter-American Court of Human Rights. *Vanderbilt Journal of Transnational Law*, 39, 379–433.

Communication Law and Policy: South America

SUSANA N. VITTADINI ANDRÉS
University of Buenos Aires

South America comprises 13 countries with a vast array of cultural backgrounds. Its cultural diversity stems from Spanish, French, Dutch, Portuguese, and a myriad of indigenous languages (→ Culture: Definition and Concepts; Cultural Patterns and Communication), which is reflected in South American communication law and policy.

In South American political culture, *caudillos*, or charismatic leaders, were a vital element in the "delegative democracies" (O'Donnell 1994), as they considered themselves the voice of the people. They often monopolized political decision-making processes. The Inter-American Commission on Human Rights (IACHR) and the Inter-American Court of Human Rights have protected, promoted, and defended human rights since the 1980s. Thus, many South American countries had to amend their constitutions to expand freedom of expression, → freedom of information, and other related rights (→ Freedom of Communication; Freedom of the Press, Concept of). Venezuela turned out to be an exception as on September 10, 2013 it withdrew from the American Convention on Human Rights and the Inter-American Court of Human Rights (IACHR). From then on complaints against this country could not be brought before the IACHR.

Several South American countries, including Peru, Argentina, and Bolivia, adopted *freedom of information* laws. In Bolivia, the Supreme Decree about Transparency and Access to Information exempts disclosure of information that affects territorial integrity and the existence of the democratic system, such as military strategic plans, financial information, and foreign relations. In Argentina, access to public information is expressly guaranteed by the constitution, and the Personal Data Protection Act governs access to personal data. Similar freedom of information laws have been enacted in Chile, Paraguay, and Brazil. But to implement the underlying principles of the freedom of information laws is no easy task, for various administrative and political reasons. Suriname, French Guiana, and Venezuela have yet to put freedom of information laws in place.

At present, *freedom of speech* in many South American countries is often limited extrajudicially, although it is constitutionally and statutorily guaranteed. Freedom of the press is brutally suppressed by some ruling authorities and those connected with drug trafficking. They kill, kidnap, or threaten journalists (→ Violence against Journalists). For example, Colombian guerrilla organizations and paramilitary groups threaten journalists whenever their activities are reported. In other countries, such as Peru and Paraguay, journalists are attacked and threatened so often that the organization Reporters Without Borders has officially denounced those governments. Physical suppression of journalists continues in South America because (1) there are still restrictive laws and political decisions standing in the way of free speech principles and (2) the absence of internal security and widespread corruption make it impossible to put into effect constitutional and regional human rights principles and norms. Importantly, however, the crime of contempt or *desacato* was abolished in Argentina in the 1990s due to people's pressure for democratic ways. It still remains on the books in Brazil, Peru, Uruguay and Venezuela.

In South America, Brazil is the country with the most *Internet* users, while Chile and Argentina have the highest penetration rates. ADSL is the leading broadband technology, although cable modems have a strong presence. Most countries have regulations about Internet service providers (ISPs), domains, and spam. Not everyone has access to the Internet due to economic constraints.

See also: ▶ CENSORSHIP ▶ COMMUNICATION AND LAW ▶ CULTURAL PATTERNS AND COMMUNICATION ▶ CULTURE: DEFINITIONS AND CONCEPTS ▶ DIGITAL DIVIDE ▶ FREEDOM OF COMMUNICATION ▶ FREEDOM OF INFORMATION ▶ FREEDOM OF THE PRESS, CONCEPT OF ▶ INTERNET LAW AND REGULATION ▶ JOURNALISM: LEGAL SITUATION ▶ POLITICAL MEDIA USE ▶ VIOLENCE AGAINST JOURNALISTS

REFERENCES AND SUGGESTED READINGS

Amnesty International (2013). Venezuela withdrawal from regional human rights instrument is a serious setback, 6 September 2013. At http://www.refworld.org/docid/522ee58b4.html, accessed July 30, 2014.

Hughes, S. & Lawson, C. (2005). The Barriers to media opening in Latin America. *Political Communication*, 22(1), 9.

O'Donnell, G. (1994). Delegative democracy. *Journal of Democracy*, 5(1), 6–59.

Reporters Without Borders (2013). Journalist's murder highlights threat from organized crime, political tension. At http://en.rsf.org/paraguay-journalist-s-murder-highlights-26-04-2013,44433.html, accessed July 30, 2014.

Reporters Without Borders (2014). *Annual report: Americas*. At www.rsf.org/IMG/pdf/rapport_en-3.pdf, accessed July 30, 2014.

Communication Management

PEGGY SIMCIC BRØNN
Norwegian School of Management

Communication management has several meanings: (1) a special way of managing; (2) the steering of all communications in the context of the organization; (3) a synonym for → public relations (PR). This entry focuses on the second approach.

An integrated approach to communication management, calling for increased cooperation and interaction between communication functions, has gained popularity in recent years. A primary reason for this is the need for consistency in communication. The marketing department that creates ad slogans (→ Advertising) that are inconsistent with an organization's stated identity of ethics, trust, etc., can damage an organization's reputation.

Grant (1996) argues that there are *four mechanisms* within an organization that integrate specialist knowledge (such as communication knowledge). These are: (1) rules and instructions consisting of procedures, standardized information, and communication systems; (2) the organization of the primary process in a sequential manner; (3) application of professional action in a relatively automatic manner, with the use of implicit protocols; and (4) group problem solving to be implemented when the complexity increases, a more personal and communication-intensive form of integration.

The ability to orchestrate (manage) communication is dependent on, among other things, organizational structure. Brønn, van Ruler, & Vercic (2005) provide a review of organization theory and communication. Broadly speaking, organizational research has attempted to describe and to understand the influence of organizational structure on communication.

A more extreme and thought-provoking group of theories that have emerged in recent years are those that see organizational structure as a communicative phenomenon (McPhee & Poole 2001, 529). An example of this form is the "formal structural communication" (FSC) model and various textual models of the organization. The FSC model is intended to highlight the "distinctive features of organizational communication that help to explain the proliferation of the complex organization as a social form" (McPhee & Poole 2001, 529).

See also: ▶ ADVERTISING ▶ CORPORATE COMMUNICATION ▶ INTEGRATED MARKETING COMMUNICATIONS ▶ MARKETING ▶ MARKETING: COMMUNICATION TOOLS ▶ ORGANIZATIONAL COMMUNICATION ▶ PUBLIC RELATIONS

REFERENCES AND SUGGESTED READINGS

Brønn, C., van Ruler, B., & Vercic, D. (2005). Organizations, communication and management. In P. S. Brønn & R. Wiig Berg (eds.), *Corporate communication: A strategic approach to building reputation.* Oslo: Gyldendal, pp. 59–92.

Grant, R. M. (1996). Toward a knowledge-based theory of the firm. *Strategic Management Journal,* 17, 109–122.

McPhee, R. D. & Poole, M. S. (2001). Organizational structures and configurations. In F. M. Jablin & L. L. Putnam (eds.), *The new handbook of organizational communications.* Thousand Oaks, CA: Sage, pp. 503–543.

Communication and Media Studies, History of

PETER SIMONSON
University of Colorado at Boulder

The international history of communication and media studies has yet to be written. To this point, most histories have been national, with disproportionate attention paid to North America and western Europe. These emphases are not unwarranted, for the field established itself first on either side of the North Atlantic and remains best-established in those regions today. By necessity, this entry follows some of the traditional historiographical lines while sketching more global developments from the field's intellectual prehistory through its institutionalization and international growth (→ Communication as a Field and Discipline).

The Prehistory of a Field

Though it has deep roots, 'communication' as a social concept emerged in the eighteenth century as part of European philosophical discourses of enlightenment and speculative histories of the growth of civilization from oral to literate societies (→ Communication: History of the Idea). In the late nineteenth century, communication became an object of sustained scholarly inquiry in political economy and sociology, with society cast as an organism whose transportation and communication systems functioned as nerves. From the 1890s forward, American, French, and German sociologists wrote treatises on communication in relation to publics, crowds, and the press. Newspapers also garnered attention, first by historians and then in the professionalizing academic fields of journalism and Zeitungswissenschaft (newspaper science; → Printing, History of). Journalism programs were also established in Latin America, South and East Asia, and the Arab Middle East in the interwar years. In the US, teachers of speech broke off from English departments in 1915, providing one locus for humanistic communication study thereafter (→ Speech Communication, History of).

From the 1920s forward, literary studies provided another humanistic home for journalism and media study, first in England and then many other countries. Interdisciplinary → *propaganda* research proliferated after World War I, blending critical analysis and media-literacy style citizen training (→ War Propaganda; Propaganda in World War II). Empirical social research on *film* also emerged in the interwar years (→ Film Theory). In Germany, 'Publizistik' was coined in 1926 to name a field concerned with publicity, media, and the formation of publics. Radio, marketing, and audience research effectively began in the 1930s, with Viennese émigré Paul Lazarsfeld playing a major role in establishing those fields in the US. In contrast to Lazarsfeld's positivist social science, another set of émigré scholars, associated with the Frankfurt School, critiqued mass communication by means of → Critical Theory.

Institutionalization, 1940s–1960s

Communication research institutionalized itself after World War II through institutes, departments, and professional associations. As a field organized under the name 'communication', its geographical center lay in the US through the 1960s. It was dominated by objectivist social science operating within a functionalist framework. Wilbur Schramm was a key figure, establishing research institutes at the University of Illinois (1948) and Stanford (1956) and exercising international influence through his work on → development communication. The National Society for the Study of Communication (an early version of the → International Communication Association) was founded in 1950 and launched the Journal of Communication. The idea of communication also garnered significant attention outside the new field in the immediate postwar period, indexing hopes for intergroup understanding and progress.

Often organized around other names, communication and media study also developed outside the US after the war. Some efforts were strongly international, like those coordinated by → UNESCO, which sponsored studies of mass communication systems around the world, funded research institutes (e.g. CIESPAL, the International Center for Advanced Study of Journalism in Latin America (1959), and established the → International Association of Mass Communication Research (IAMCR, 1957). Others developed more within national contexts, though with lines of influence crossing borders. In Europe, native traditions of Zeitungswissenschaft and Publizistik were re-established and journals were founded, (e.g. Gazette [1955]). In France, the field known as 'information' grew out of press studies. Press science was also established across the Soviet bloc, developed through Marxist-Leninist theories of journalism. New technologies also drove the field, with television studies appearing in Europe and North America by 1950 (→ Technology and Communication). In Asia, American foreign policy helped spread communications research – as part of the liberal democratic reconstruction of Japan in the late 1940s and development efforts in South Asia in the 1960s.

Other models for communication study also developed in the 1950s and 1960s. At the University of Toronto, where the political economist and historian Harold Lasswell taught, literary scholar Marshall McLuhan headed an interdisciplinary group that published the journal Explorations (1953–1959), providing a home for a distinctive blend of cultural, literary, and historical analysis that fed McLuhan's famous media theory of the 1960s (→ Medium Theory). In Paris, another interdisciplinary group that included Roland Barthes founded the Centre d'Études des Communications de Masse (CECMAS; 1960). It started the journal Communications (1962), which became the leading outlet for semiology late in the decade (→ Semiotics). In Britain the professor of English, Richard Hoggart, established the Centre for Contemporary Cultural Studies (CCCS) at Birmingham University (1964), the organizational birthplace of British → Cultural

Studies. By 1968, operating though a number of paradigms and traditions, communication study had gained at least basic institutional footholds around much of the world.

Globalization, 1970s–Present

In the 1970s, critical and interpretive scholars challenged dominant, US-centered paradigms based on functional analysis, limited media effects, positivist methodologies, and the politics of development communication. Left-leaning scholars in Latin America, Europe, the US, and the Arab world all offered critiques of American cultural imperialism and ways that development efforts cultivated dependency. The IAMCR provided an important institutional space for critical and political economic analyses of media industries and American power. British Cultural Studies interrogated the politics of media representations and turned toward subcultures and audiences. Sociologists threw light on the institutional and ideological construction of the → news (→ News Ideologies). Feminist studies of communication began to appear, as did social and cultural histories of communication. These all fed into the much-noted special issue of the Journal of Communication, "Ferment in the Field" (1983) and established lines of research that are well developed today. They have been counterbalanced by competing efforts to consolidate a discipline of communication as an empirical social science.

Institutionally, the field accelerated its internationalization. Growth has been differential, tied to specificities of national political and media systems and scholarly initiatives. Latin America organized regional communication associations in the late 1970s and 1980s. The end of dictatorships in Spain and Portugal made room for the growth of communication since the 1980s. The fall of Eastern Bloc communism in 1989 created similar space for the field to grow there. In China, the field has developed significantly since the mid-1990s following political liberalization a decade before. In India, the liberalization of the economy and growth of media industries fueled expansion of the field since the 1990s. Growth has been slower in Africa owing to a colonial legacy that limited widespread education. In sum, the global history of the field is multi-faceted, still awaiting historians to tell it more fully.

See also: ▶ COMMUNICATION AS A FIELD AND DISCIPLINE ▶ COMMUNICATION: HISTORY OF THE IDEA ▶ CRITICAL THEORY ▶ CULTURAL STUDIES ▶ DEVELOPMENT COMMUNICATION ▶ FILM THEORY ▶ INTERNATIONAL ASSOCIATION FOR MEDIA AND COMMUNICATION RESEARCH (IAMCR) ▶ INTERNATIONAL COMMUNICATION ASSOCIATION (ICA) ▶ MEDIA EFFECTS, HISTORY OF ▶ MEDIUM THEORY ▶ NEWS ▶ NEWS IDEOLOGIES ▶ PRINTING, HISTORY OF ▶ PROPAGANDA ▶ PROPAGANDA IN WORLD WAR II ▶ SEMIOTICS ▶ SPEECH COMMUNICATION, HISTORY OF ▶ TECHNOLOGY AND COMMUNICATION ▶ UNESCO ▶ WAR PROPAGANDA

REFERENCES AND SUGGESTED READINGS

Communication in Latin American Contexts (2010). Special Issue of *Communication Research Trends*, 29(2).
Delia, J. G. (1987). Communication research: A history. In C. R. Berger & S. H. Chaffee (eds.), *Handbook of communication science*. Newbury Park, CA: Sage, pp. 20–98.
Hardt, H. (2001). *Social theories of the press: Constituents of communication research, 1840s–1920s*. Lanham, MD: Rowman and Littlefield.
History of Communication Research Bibliography (n.d.). At www.historyofcommunicationresearch.org, accessed July 30, 2014.
Nerone, J., ed. (2013). *Media history and the foundations of media studies*. Oxford: Wiley Blackwell.
Park, D. W. & Pooley, J. (2008). *The History of media and communication research: Contested memories*. New York: Peter Lang.
Simonson, P., Peck, J., Craig, R.T., & Jackson, J.P., eds. (2013). *Handbook of communication history*. London: Routledge.

Communication Networks

PETER MONGE
University of Southern California

DREW MARGOLIN
Cornell University

Networks are structural configurations that emerge when sets of relations are applied to sets of entities. Entities are typically called 'nodes,' 'vertices,' or 'elements,' and relations are called 'links,' 'ties' or 'edges.' Communication networks reflect patterns based on signal, message and information flow relations among the elements of the network. The past two decades have produced unprecedented growth in network theorizing and research. Interest in communication and information networks now spans both the social sciences and the physical and life sciences. The study of communication networks tends to pursue one of two general research questions: (1) why are particular networks configured as they are? (2) What are the effects of different network configurations on the people, organizations, and institutions that comprise them (→ Organizational Communication).

Network Concepts and Measures

Nodes and ties can be studied in a variety of ways. Many relations can be applied to create communication networks such as "provides information to," "innovates with," or "is friends with." Networks can be created by applying one relation to the nodes, forming a 'uniplex network,' or by applying two or more relations to the nodes, forming a 'multiplex network.'

Typically, *relations are defined* on one set of nodes, such as people, called 'one-mode networks,' but can also be defined between two or more different sets of entities, such as people and documents or people and organizations. These are called '*n*-mode networks.' Two-mode networks that relate people through common participation in organizations (e.g., professional associations) or events (e.g., meetings) are often called 'affiliation networks.'

One important aspect of networks is their suitability for *multilevel analysis*, which compares different parts and wholes. For example, analysis can be at the level of nodes, dyads (a pair of nodes), triads (three nodes), cliques, or the entire network. 'Degree' is the total number of links a node has to others in the network. Various centrality measures capture how close each node is to the other nodes. Dyadic network properties include reciprocity, the degree to which a link from A to B is mirrored by a link from B to A. For triads, transitivity implies that if A communicates to B and B communicates to C, then A also communicates to C. 'Cliques' or 'clusters' are composed of members who relate more to each other than to others in the network.

Metrics also exist for networks as a whole. A 'component' is the largest subset of connected people. 'Connectivity' is the extent to which people are linked to one another. 'Density' is the ratio of the number of actual links to the possible number of links. 'Centralization' measures the variation in nodal centrality over the entire network. 'Clustering' is the extent to which nodes form links in neighborhoods where neighbors connect more to each other than nodes outside. Because networks describe relationships between entities that are not statistically independent, statistical tests of network properties require a special set of statistical methods.

Theories of Network Structure

The *evolution of a network* can be explained by four major factors: (1) endogenous factors internal to the network, (2) attributes of the nodes, (3) other networks and (4) network externalities. Primary endogenous factors in person–person and organization–organization networks are the tendency for reciprocity and transitivity. Recently, a new science of networks has identified several growth and decay principles that apply to networks across different contexts. One is 'preferential attachment,' which states that new entrants to a network will link to the nodes that have the greatest number of existing links. Another principle is the evolution of 'small world networks,' in which nodes are embedded in local clusters of transitive ties yet connect occasionally outside these clusters, bridging communities and allowing information to flow quickly through the network. An important *decay principle* is called the liability of newness, where new links tend to die off faster than older links. Research also suggests that networks have a carrying capacity – a total number of links that the network can support (Monge, Heiss, & Margolin, 2008).

Attributes are characteristics of the nodes that influence how they relate to each other. Typical variables include age, gender, religious and political affiliations, and physical proximity.' Other networks' reflect other sets of relations that might impact the focal network. For example, a work network might be highly influenced by a friendship network (among the same people). Other networks also include the same networks at earlier points in time. Finally, 'network externalities' refers to those factors outside of the network itself, including market forces, regulatory regimes, major environmental events, etc. Because several theoretical mechanisms might be operating on any specific focal network, Monge and Contractor (2003) recommend combining multiple theories to provide more comprehensive explanations.

The Effects of Networks

Network scholars have always been curious about the effects that information and other flows can have on various entities. Considerable network research has concentrated on the *network members* and considered how people and organizations are influenced by and make use of networks. For example the types of extended networks that exist in different local communities have been documented to better understand how people rely on family and friends to meet their needs. Nodes that fill particular network positions called structural holes tend to thrive and outperform other nodes. People are also influenced by communication through networks in ways they may not realize. Bond et al. (2012) show, for example, that people are more likely to vote if their friends report on Facebook that they voted.

Another research focus has been the *institutional performance* of networks. Castells (2000) describes how companies, industries, and national economies have all been challenged by the emergence of network organizations that are more flexible than hierarchies yet more stable than markets. Because networks are inherently relational, small effects at the node level can have larger or opposite effects at the network level. For example, Eagle et al. (2010) find an association between the diversity of communication networks and the economic performance of the region in which communication occurs. The achievement of a dominant position by one organization can lead to organizational stagnation for other organizations (Padgett & Powell, 2012).

New Areas of Network Research

Research is increasingly focusing on the *new networks* that have emerged with the development of new communication technologies. For example, the online collaboration of social resistance organizers or of players in online role-playing games (MMORPGs) have both been studied (→ Social Media). Researchers have also begun to consider the implications of the participation of *nonhuman actors* in these networks, particularly the mediating effects of cyber-infrastructure. Members of online communities may create both person-to-person and avatar-to-avatar networks as they communicate in different contexts (→ Network Organizations through Communication Technology). Network scholars are also increasingly studying *multiplex rather than single relations*. For example, Powell et al. (2005) examined four separate relations in their study of all the organizations involved in the evolution of the biotechnology industry: research and development, finance, sales and marketing, and licensing.

See also: ▶ MEDIA CONTENT AND SOCIAL NETWORKS ▶ NETWORK ORGANIZATIONS THROUGH COMMUNICATION TECHNOLOGY ▶ ORGANIZATIONAL COMMUNICATION ▶ SOCIAL MEDIA

REFERENCES AND SUGGESTED READINGS

Bond, R. M., Fariss, C. J., Jones, J. J., Kramer, A. D. I., Marlow, C., Settle, J. E., & Fowler, J. H. (2012). A 61-million-person experiment in social influence and political mobilization. *Nature*, 489(7415), 295–298. doi:10.1038/nature11421.

Castells, M. (2000). *The rise of the network society, vol. 1: The information age: Economy, society and culture*, 2nd edn. Oxford: Blackwell.

Eagle, N., Macy, M., & Claxton, R. (2010). Network diversity and economic development. *Science*, 328(5981), 1029–1031. doi:10.1126/science.1186605.

Monge, P. & Contractor, N. (2003). *Theories of communication networks*. New York: Oxford University Press.

Monge, P., Heiss, B. M., & Margolin, D. B. (2008). Communication network evolution in organizational communities: Network evolution. *Communication Theory*, 18(4), 449–477. doi:10.1111/j.1468-2885.2008.00330.x

Padgett, J. F. & Powell, W. W. (2012). *The emergence of organizations and markets*. Princeton, NJ: Princeton University Press.

Powell, W. W., White, D. R., Koput, K. W., & Owen-Smith, J. (2005). Network dynamics and field evolution: The growth of interorganizational collaboration in the life sciences. *American Journal of Sociology*, 110(4), 1132–1205.

Communication Skill Acquisition

JOHN O. GREENE
Purdue University

A large literature emphasizes the importance of communication skills for occupational success and personal well-being. Moreover, it is generally recognized that → message production and processing skills are developed and refined over time through instruction and practice.

A widely accepted model of skill acquisition holds that changes in performance quality reflect a person's progression through *three stages*: (1) a 'cognitive stage' in which skill-relevant information is held in long-term memory in declarative form (i.e., a set of facts about how to carry out the activity), (2) an 'associative stage' in which procedural memory representations are formed such that it is no longer necessary to keep rules and instructions in mind as one carries out the skill, and (3) an 'autonomous' stage in which procedural memory representations are strengthened such that behavior becomes increasingly rapid and automatic.

Considerable attention has been given to describing the functions that relate practice to improvements in performance quality. For *measures of performance quality* where values decrease with practice (e.g., time, error rate), the general equation is a power function:

$$P = BN^{-\alpha}$$

where P represents performance quality, B is the y-intercept representing performance quality with practice equal to zero, N is the number of practice trials, and α is the slope of the learning curve. One of the key implications of the fact that the course of skill acquisition is described by a power function is that skill development requires considerably more practice than one might suppose. Studies indicate that achieving expert performance in a variety of skill domains requires 10 years of concerted preparation.

While practice appears to be essential to enhanced performance, it is also the case that repetition may lead to no performance improvements at all. The most effective programs for improving communication skills incorporate three key elements: (1) instruction/observation, i.e. presentation of behavioral ideals; (2) implementation/practice; and (3) feedback. Maximum performance improvements come when practice involves deliberate focus on the details of one's activities, and feedback is most effective when it quickly follows performance trials.

See also: ▶ COMMUNICATION APPREHENSION AND SOCIAL ANXIETY ▶ COMMUNICATION SKILLS ACROSS THE LIFE-SPAN ▶ INTERPERSONAL COMMUNICATION ▶ INTERPERSONAL COMMUNICATION COMPETENCE AND SOCIAL SKILLS ▶ LEARNING AND COMMUNICATION ▶ MEMORY ▶ MESSAGE PRODUCTION

SUGGESTED READING

Greene, J. O. (2003). Models of adult communication skill acquisition: Practice and the course of performance improvement. In J.O. Greene & B.R. Burleson (eds.), *Handbook of communication and social interaction skills*. Mahwah, NJ: Lawrence Erlbaum, pp. 51–91.

Communication Skills across the Life-Span

WENDY SAMTER
Bryant University

This entry focuses on communication skills associated with same-sex friendship across the lifespan. One promising approach to this area of study involves analysis of friends' conceptions and expectations of the relationship, as well as the daily activities in which they engage. Understanding what people think of and do with their friends tells us something about the duties of being a friend, and the kinds of skills through which such duties are met. Unfortunately, space precludes discussion of gender differences. However, such differences are most pronounced in childhood and attenuate with age (→ Interpersonal Communication; Interpersonal Communication Competence and Social Skills).

In *early childhood*, friends are conceived of as 'nonspecific' others who share activities, time, and/or materials. Youngsters become friends because they play together; when this activity is absent, friendship ceases to exist. Play remains an important feature of friendship throughout middle childhood, but becomes more organized. Children begin to understand others have thoughts and feelings that differ from their own – and that some of these may center on evaluations of one another as 'friend'. Children also regard physical help as an indication of friendship and liking (Selman 1981). Throughout this time, several important interaction competencies reflect the idea that friendship revolves around play. Youngsters must be able to recognize and respond appropriately to others' emotional displays during play. Skills that foster coherent discourse are also associated with friendship success, as is the ability to enter games by integrating behavior with the ongoing activities of the group.

As individuals move into *middle childhood*, possessing a sense of humor, engaging in playful teasing, and having interesting gossip discriminates children who possess friends from those who do not. The nature of conflict also changes. Among young children, fights typically involve issues of social or object control. The most common responses to conflict are to vent angry feelings and to resist the other in nonaggressive ways. With development, children believe that conflict is common to all relationships, and distinguish between major and minor skirmishes. Conflicts often center on rules associated with social groups and activities (→ Intercultural and Intergroup Communication). Although negotiation becomes increasingly common with age, disengagement may be even more important (cf. Samter 2003).

Adolescents and young adults define friends as others who possess unique psychological dispositions. Friends are expected to share their innermost thoughts and feelings, thus providing each other with opportunities for intimacy and growth. Friendship is perceived as the most important source of emotional support in the adolescent's life, and loyalty is highly prized. Young adult friends report that they purposefully use self-disclosure to maintain their relationships, but note that much of it is about mundane topics. Task sharing, positivity, and routine contact have also been found to contribute to relational maintenance among friends (McEwan & Guerrero 2012). Emotional support is a prominent activity among adolescent and adult friends. Support strategies that acknowledge, elaborate, and legitimize another's feelings and perspective are regarded as the most sensitive and effective. Finally, conflict among adolescent and adult friends centers on violation of friendship rules. Individuals who are well liked avoid minor conflicts and employ integrative strategies to manage major ones (cf. Samter 2003).

Recent studies show that relatively few young adults (about 14 percent) report developing a close *online friendship*. Moreover, they tend to view real-world friendships as more likely than online friendships to possess interaction patterns promoting intimacy (Bane, Cornish, Erspamer, & Kampman 2010).

There is strong continuity in friendship conceptualizations across much of *adulthood*. However, the 'old-old,' alter the criteria they use to define friendship. *First*, face-to-face contact is not seen as essential for maintaining friendship. *Second*, friends do not have to be equal in status. *Third*, friends are identified as fun companions versus sources of support and esteem. Emotional support and self-disclosure thus become less important to friendship as people reach the last stage of life. In fact, people aged 85 and older report it is "inappropriate to bother others with problems" (Johnson & Troll 1994, 85).

Because most studies focus on the serious pursuits of friends, little is known about what makes someone enjoyable to be around. Further study of the nature and functions of online friendship is warranted. Finally, little attention has been directed toward understanding the relationship between specific communication skills and friendship success among the oldest old.

See also: ▶ INTERCULTURAL AND INTERGROUP COMMUNICATION
▶ INTERPERSONAL COMMUNICATION
▶ INTERPERSONAL COMMUNICATION COMPETENCE AND SOCIAL SKILLS

REFERENCES AND SUGGESTED READINGS

Bane, C. M., Cornish, M., Erspamer, N., & Kampman, L. (2010). Self-disclosure through weblogs and perceptions of online and "real-life" friendships among female bloggers. *Cyberpsychology, Behavior, and Social Networking*, 13, 131–139.

Johnson, C. L. & Troll, L. E. (1994). Constraints and facilitators to friendships in later life. *Gerontologist*, 34, 79–87.

McEwan, B. & Guerrero, L. K. (2012). Maintenance behavior and relationship quality as predictors of perceived availability of resources in newly formed college friendship networks. *Communication Studies*, 63, 421–440.

Samter, W. (2003). Friendship interaction skills across the lifespan. In J. O. Greene & B. R. Burleson (eds.), *Handbook of communication and social interaction skills*. Mahwah, NJ: Lawrence Erlbaum, pp. 637–684.

Selman, R. L. (1981). The child as a friendship philosopher. In S. R. Asher & J. M. Gottman (eds.), *The development of children's friendships*. Cambridge: Cambridge University Press, pp. 242–272.

Communication and Social Change: Research Methods

JOHN C. POLLOCK
College of New Jersey

Modern research methods for social/behavioral change reflect a tension between collecting data at the individual level while making inferences at macro-levels such as health-care systems, communities, and nations. This tension becomes more palpable when measuring the concerns of historically underserved, difficult-to-reach populations, those suffering the greatest inequalities in access to information, civic participation, and, in particular, health-care. Research questions are explored by focusing on multiple levels of analysis, 'participatory' and multidisciplinary approaches, and flexible measures of 'community.'

Communication studies often rely on national samples of self-reports on personal attitudes and values, drawing conclusions at the individual level (→ Quantitative Methodology). Despite the risk of 'ecological' or 'atomistic' fallacies, creative *comparisons of different levels of analysis*, especially at the city level, can illuminate previously unconfirmed connections between communication and social change. For example, differences in community-level demographics or social structure have been linked to variations in major newspaper coverage of critical issues, often called a 'community structure' approach, sometimes revealing a 'guard dog' relationship, in which media perpetuate existing social and political arrangements, and more recently revealing the opposite "vulnerability pattern" (Pollock 2013), in which media mirror the interests of more vulnerable populations.

Three research methodologies deserve attention: system-/multi-level, participatory, and multidisciplinary options. *System-level analyses* range from broad comparative/cross-national perspectives to neighborhood, city, county and metropolitan areas. Recent scholarship (Pollock and Storey 2012) outlines a broad social ecology of "comparative building blocks" for cross-national analysis, comparing the way different groups use universal resources (such as water) or regard universal threshold experiences in the life cycle (such as seeking prenatal and neonatal care for a first child), or promote health competence. Innovative media system categories can compare coverage of diseases/conditions in countries with different traditions of press freedom. Compared to reporting in 'repressive autocratic' countries, media in 'contained democratic' media systems in four sub-Saharan Anglophone countries are more likely to emphasize government efficacy fighting HIV/AIDS (D'Angelo, Pollock, Kiernicki, & Shaw 2013; → Health Communication; Health Campaigns, Communication in).

Participatory/interactive research designs invite deeper commitment than simply receiving information, especially in health communication. For instance, the "Entertainment-Education" (EE) activities of Tomaselli and associates in South Africa elaborate health promotion messages through traditional media such as television and radio and also community-level drama, song, dance, comic books, '911' call-in systems, etc., using creative community-level engagement to address gender-based violence, poverty, and HIV/AIDS (Tomaselli & Chasi 2011). Digital games via cell phones move health promotion campaigns closer to the interpersonal interaction that historically has complemented mass communication to spur shifts toward less risky behavior.

Multidisciplinary approaches illuminate audience or population information inequalities. Dependent variables community participation, civic engagement, collective action, and social capital – community interaction and solidarity – derive from political science and sociology. Framing, drawn from sociology and psychology, describes the way journalists organize news stories providing meaning to related events, indicating the advocacy of certain ideas (→ Framing Effects). Diverse approaches call for broadening the scope of research designs beyond traditional random samples of individuals to a variety of research designs and data collection tools. The effects of health disparities, communication inequalities, and the role of 'social contextual' factors like social class also warrant attention (Viswanath 2006).

To reduce health knowledge gaps, the 'community' unit of analysis is becoming elastic in seeking hard-to-reach and high-risk populations less through traditional telephone or residential interviews, more through community contexts and venues they inhabit – the workplace, meeting places, grocery stores, recreational locations or Internet sites of all kinds: blogs, bulletin boards, chatrooms, or websites themselves. To mitigate inequalities and health disparities, scholars use multiple levels of analysis, imaginative methodologies, and innovative measures and definitions of community.

See also: ▶ FRAMING EFFECTS ▶ HEALTH CAMPAIGNS, COMMUNICATION IN ▶ HEALTH COMMUNICATION ▶ PARTICIPATORY ACTION RESEARCH ▶ QUANTITATIVE METHODOLOGY

REFERENCES AND SUGGESTED READINGS

D'Angelo, P., Pollock, J. C., Kiernicki, K., & Shaw, D. (2013). Framing of AIDS in Africa: Press–state relations, HIV/AIDS news, and journalistic advocacy in four sub-Saharan Anglophone newspapers. *Politics and the Life Sciences*, 33(2), 90–146.
Pollock, J. C. (ed.). (2013). *Media and social inequality: Innovations in community structure research*. London: Routledge.
Pollock, J. C. & Storey, D. (2012). Comparative health communication. In F. Esser & T. Hanitzsch (eds.), *Handbook of comparative communication research*. London: Routledge, pp. 161–184.
Tomaselli, K. & Chasi, C. (eds.). (2011). *Development and public health communication*. Cape Town: Pearson Publishing.
Viswanath, K. (2006). Public communications and its role in reducing and eliminating health disparities. In G. E. Thomson, F. Mitchell, & M. B. Williams (eds.), *Examining the health disparities research plan of the National Institutes of Health: Unfinished business*. Washington, DC: Institute of Medicine, pp. 215–253.

Communication Technology and Democracy

NICO CARPENTIER

Free University of Brussels and Charles University in Prague

The role of communication technologies in democracy cannot be separated from the political-ideological nature (and limits) of democracy itself, and the different democratic models this generates, ranging from more centralized and elitist forms to more decentralized forms of societal decision-making and problem-solving. Communication technologies play a significant role, but they are not necessary neutral instruments in the service of enlightenment. They are always embedded in ideological constellations and various models of (non-)democracy. Moreover, communication technologies are not exclusive driving forces of society, but always part of a broader societal context.

For the more traditional approaches towards the communication technology–democracy relationship, the label of 'normative theories' is used, with the "Four Theories of the Press" (Siebert, Peterson, & Schramm 1956) as its starting point. In particular, the liberal/libertarian and the social responsibility models are relevant here, as they both combine an emphasis on information, control (the role of watchdog) and debate (as a market place of ideas). The social responsibility model adds the need for truthfulness, accuracy and comprehensiveness.

Critiques of these particular models, and later alternative models, emphasize the role of media to facilitate participation and civic agency. These approaches deal with participation in the media and through the media. Participation *through* the media focuses on the opportunities for participation in public debate, in what some call the

→ public sphere, following a consensus-oriented approach (in Habermas's concept), or what others call public spaces, following a more Mouffian, conflict-based model. In some cases, state actors have themselves deployed communication technologies to enhance citizen participation (→ E-Democracy).

Participation *in* the media focuses on the participation of nonprofessionals in the production of media output (content-related participation) and in media decision-making (structural participation), where they are exercising their right to communicate. Different types of media organizations articulate these roles differently, although community and alternative media have been particularly successful in offering more intense forms of citizen participation in and through the media (→ Community Media; Citizen Journalism). More recently, the use of online technologies has been lauded for further deepening the range of participatory possibilities. In both cases care needs to be taken not to overestimate this capacity.

See also: ▶ CITIZEN JOURNALISM ▶ COMMUNITY MEDIA ▶ E-DEMOCRACY ▶ PUBLIC SPHERE

REFERENCES AND SUGGESTED READINGS

Carpentier, N. (2011) *Media and Participation.* Chicago: Intellect.
Dahlgren, P. (2013) *The Political Web.* Basingstoke: Palgrave Macmillan.
Siebert, F., Peterson, T., & Schramm, W. (1956). *Four theories of the press.* Urbana, IL: University of Illinois Press.

Communication Technology and Development

HEATHER E. HUDSON
University of Alaska Anchorage

Information is critical to social and economic development (→ Development Communication; Technology and Communication). The ability to access and share information through telecommunications can contribute to the development process by improving several dimensions.

Contribution of Technology to Development

First, communication technology can enhance *efficiency*, or the ratio of output to cost. This can happen, for example, through use of just-in-time manufacturing and inventory systems and of information on weather and soil content to improve agricultural yields. (2) It can affect *effectiveness*, or the quality of products and services such as improving health-care through telemedicine (→ Health Communication). (3) It can improve *equity*, or the distribution of development benefits throughout society such as to rural and remote areas, or to minorities and disabled populations. (4) It can enhance *reach*, i.e. the ability to contact new customers or clients, for example, craftspeople reaching global markets online, or educators reaching students at work or at home.

Key technological trends driving the proliferation of new information and telecommunications services include capacity, digitization, ubiquity, and convergence. Advances in wireless technology such as mobile cellular networks and fixed wireless systems offer affordable means of reaching rural customers and urban areas without infrastructure in developing countries (→ Mobility, Technology for).

Implications of Technologies

There are several significant implications of these technological trends, particularly for developing regions. Costs of providing services are declining. The potential for competition is increasing. Lower costs make rural/remote areas more attractive. In addition, the sector has largely been restructured through privatization of formerly government-owned networks and liberalization to allow competition among services and across technologies (→ Privatization of the Media). All of these changes are taking place within a context of globalization, as international trade in goods and services expands and national economies become increasingly interdependent.

Of course, these new technologies and services are not yet available everywhere, and in developing regions where they do exist, many people cannot afford to use them (→ Digital Divide).

However, voice communication is now almost universally available through mobile telephony. There were more than 6 billion mobile subcriptions worldwide in 2012, of which nearly 5 billion were in developing countries. Subscribers, most of whom use prepaid phone cards, can not only make voice calls and send text messages, but in many countries, can transfer funds such as overseas remittances via mobile phone.

With the proliferation of portable devices (phones, tablets, notebook computers, etc.), mobile networks may be the means of increasing access to broadband in many developing regions. Telecentres and Internet cafes as well as libraries, schools, and post offices offer opportunities to access broadband.

Research Areas

Recent research grew out of numerous studies on the *role of telecommunications* in socio-economic development beginning in the late 1970s (see Hudson 2006). A study by Waverman, Meschi, and Fuss (2005) concluded that differences in the penetration and diffusion of mobile telephony appear to explain some differences in growth rates between developing countries. Also a World Bank (2009) econometric analysis of 120 countries showed that for every 10-percentage-point increase in the penetration of broadband services, there is a 1.2 percentage point increase in per capita GDP growth in high-income economies, and 1.38 percentage increase in developing countries. Field research from developing countries cites examples of rural residents using telecommunications to keeping in touch with family members who have left the village to seek work; families contacting scattered relatives; and rural staff such as nurses and teachers keeping in touch with colleagues and family members. Social media are greatly increasing these connections.

Other factors are necessary to contribute to socio-economic development. First, the cultural, economic, and political context; for example, if women are 'invisible' in public or in commerce, they are not likely to learn to use communication technologies without specific outreach activities. If there is no reliable transportation, producers may be forced to sell to a local middleman, even if they learn that prices are higher in the city. If there is no source of credit available, farmers may not be able to buy better seeds or pesticides, even if they learn that these inputs would improve their crop yield. Next, content matters. 'Infomediaries' can help to find and interpret useful content, but communication technologies' true potential will be realized only if more *relevant content in local languages* is produced. Finally, user capacity is important; users may require some training if they are to take advantage of access to communication technologies.

Communication technologies play an important role in *health services* in many developing countries for telemedicine or telehealth (→ Health Campaigns, Communication in), including emergency care, consultation, remote diagnosis, patient monitoring, training and continuing education, public health education, administration, data collection, and research and information sharing.

In Africa, radio in combination with mobile phones allows farmers to call in to *agricultural radio programs* to ask questions and provide feedback. Text messages alert farmers to upcoming radio programs. Recent research has shown that radio plus such forms of interactivity can result not only in greater awareness of new farming practices, but actual adoption by the participating farmers. (Sullivan and Hudson 2011).

Where teachers lack sufficient training to teach certain subjects, communication technologies can reach *students* directly, with the local teacher serving as an aide or tutor. Alternatively, communication technologies can improve the teachers' knowledge and skills by offering in-service courses for teachers using correspondence materials, radio, television, and the Internet.

Today, extension agents, health workers, and other working adults may *study online* at their workplaces or local training centers, or instructors may supplement traditional correspondence courses with online materials and assignments, and email interaction with other students. Universities are experimenting with MOOCs (massive open online courses) that offer another promising opportunity for motivated learners in developing countries to access to higher education. *Women* are using communication technologies to share information relevant to their work as teachers, community development workers, artisans, or entrepreneurs. Women entrepreneurs resell mobile phone services in African and Asia.

Some women in Latin America offer Spanish language tutoring via Skype.

See also: ▶ DEVELOPMENT COMMUNICATION ▶ DIGITAL DIVIDE ▶ HEALTH CAMPAIGNS, COMMUNICATION IN ▶ HEALTH COMMUNICATION ▶ MEDIA ECONOMICS ▶ MOBILITY, TECHNOLOGY FOR ▶ PRIVATIZATION OF THE MEDIA ▶ RADIO FOR DEVELOPMENT ▶ TECHNOLOGY AND COMMUNICATION

REFERENCES AND SUGGESTED READINGS

Benkler, Y. (2010). *Next generation connectivity: A review of broadband internet transitions and policy from around the world.* Berkman Centre for Internet and Society, Harvard University. At http://cyber.law.harvard.edu/pubrelease/broadband/, accessed July 31, 2014.

Cronin, F. J., Parker, E. B., Colleran, E. K., & Gold, M. A. (1991). Telecommunications infrastructure and economic growth: An analysis of causality. *Telecommunications Policy*, 15(6), 529.

Hudson, H. E. (1984). *When telephones reach the village: The role of telecommunications in rural development.* Norwood, NJ: Ablex.

Hudson, H. E. (2006). *From rural village to global village: Telecommunications for development in the information age.* Mahwah, NJ: Lawrence Erlbaum.

International Telecommunication Union (2012). *The State of broadband 2012: achieving digital inclusion for all.* A Report of the UN Broadband Commission. Geneva: ITU. At http://www.broadbandcommission.org/Documents/bb-annualreport2012.pdf, accessed July 31, 2014.

Mas, I. & Radcliffe, D. (2010). Mobile payments go viral: M-PESA in Kenya. Washington, DC: World Bank. At: http://siteresources.worldbank.org/AFRICAEXT/Resources/258643-1271798012256/M-PESA_Kenya.pdf, accessed July 31, 2014.

Sullivan, B. & Hudson, H. E. (2011). The new age of radio How ICTs are changing rural radio in Africa. Ottawa: Farm Radio International. At http://farmradio.wpengine.netdna-cdn.com/wp-content/uploads/farmradioictreport20111.pdf, accessed July 31, 2014.

Waverman, L., Meschi, M., & Fuss, M. (2005). The impact of telecoms on economic growth in developing countries. In *Africa: The impact of mobile phones.* Vodafone Policy Paper Series, March, 2005. At http://info.worldbank.org/etools/docs/library/152872/Vodafone%20Survey.pdf, accessed July 31, 2014.

World Bank (2009). *Information and communications for development 2009: Extending Reach and Increasing Impact.* Washington, DC: World Bank. At http://issuu.com/world.bank.publications/docs/9780821376058, accessed July 31, 2014.

World Bank (2012). *Information and communications for development 2012: Maximizing Mobile.* Washington, DC: World Bank. At http://siteresources.worldbank.org/EXTINFORMATIONANDCOMMUNICATIONANDTECHNOLOGIES/Resources/IC4D-2012-Report.pdf, accessed July 31, 2014.

Communication Technology Standards

RICHARD HAWKINS
University of Calgary

Communication technology standards are technical specifications that enable technological components from different suppliers to work together within a given communication system. Some standards refer to the physical interfaces between network and terminal equipment. Others refer to logical elements expressed in algorithms and embodied in software. In digital systems, many standards involve both physical and logical elements: a standardized physical interface is supported by standardized software elements. Standards are essential to telecommunication, broadcasting, and computer networks. More recently they have become crucial elements in the integration of digital networking and services environments.

Generally, it is understood that standards have strong collective characteristics; that they are applied across entire product or service segments or otherwise on an industry-wide basis. Thus, standards are considered to reflect a consensus among stakeholders to adopt common solutions to shared problems. One can distinguish between de facto (or 'market') standards and de jure standards as negotiated under the auspices of a standards development organization (SDO). In principle, standards are distinguished from regulations in that compliance with standards nominally is voluntary. Nevertheless, standards and regulations often are linked – a regulation may reference a technical standard or vice versa.

Standards reduce variety. By adopting a uniform solution to a problem that is common to many stakeholders, any loss in the value of discarded solutions will be regained and amplified for all stakeholders in the form of *production efficiencies* and overall reduction in the unit cost of standardized items. Reduction in variety is reckoned also to lead to *information efficiencies* between producers and users of technology. Thus, if we find a standardized connector on a computer keyboard or printer, we know that it will operate with any computer equipped with the appropriate standardized receptor. Understanding the relationship between standards and innovation is one of the most challenging theoretical and empirical issues. In the mid-1980s social scientists became interested in the role of standards in generating network effects – commonly expressed in terms of 'increasing returns to adoption' or 'positive externalities.' The Internet has the potential to enable virtually complete convergence of these environments.

See also: ▶ DIFFUSION OF INFORMATION AND INNOVATION ▶ OPEN SOURCE ▶ TELEVISION BROADCASTING, REGULATION OF

REFERENCES AND SUGGESTED READINGS

Blind, K. (2004). *The economics of standards*. Cheltenham: Edward Elgar.
Blind, K., Gaucha, S., & Hawkins, R. (2010). How stakeholders view the impacts of international ICT standards. *Telecommunications Policy*, 34(3), 162–174.
Jakobs, K. (ed.) (2000). *Information technology standards and standardization: A global perspective*. Hershey, PA: Idea Group.
Jakobs, K. (2007). ICT standards development – Finding the best platform. In G. Doumeingts, J. Müller, G. Morel, & B. Vallespir (eds.), *Enterprise interoperability: New challenges and approaches*. Heidelberg: Springer, pp. 543–552.
Greenstein, S. & Stango V. (eds.) (2007). *Standards and public policy*. Cambridge: Cambridge University Press.

Communicology

RICHARD LEO LANIGAN, JR
Southern Illinois University

Communicology is the critical study of → discourse and practice, especially the expressive body as mediated by the perception of cultural signs and → codes. It uses the qualitative methodology of *semiotic phenomenology* in which the expressive body discloses cultural codes, and cultural codes shape the perceptive body constituting the reflectivity, reversibility, and reflexivity of consciousness and experience. Communicology engages in the description, reduction, and interpretation of cultural phenomena as part of a transdisciplinary understanding. The scientific result is description (rather than prediction) in which → validity and → reliability are logical constructs based in the necessary and sufficient conditions of discovered systems (codes) based in consciousness and experience. The methodology is heuristic (semiotic) and recursive (phenomenological), being a logic in the tradition of Cassirer, Peirce, and Husserl (→ Qualitative Methodology; Semiotics).

Since the foundational work during the 1950s by Ruesch and Bateson in their book 'Communication' (1968), a widely accepted understanding of the networks of human discourse includes: (1) the intrapersonal level (or psychiatric/aesthetic domain), (2) the interpersonal level (or social domain), (3) the group level (or cultural domain), and (4) the intergroup level (or transcultural domain; → Intergroup Communication and Discursive Psychology). These interconnected network levels contain the discourse process outlined by Roman Jakobson's theory of human communication (Holenstein 1976).

In homage to the phenomenological work in → semiotics and normative logics by Charles S. Peirce and Edmund Husserl, Jakobson explicated the relationship between an Addresser who expresses (emotive function) and an Addressee who perceives (conative function) a commonly shared Message (poetic function), Code (metalinguistic function), Contact (phatic function), and Context (referential function) (→ Models of Communication). Operating on at least one of the four levels of discourse, these functions jointly constitute a semiotic world of phenomenological experience, what Yuri M. Lotman termed the "semiosphere".

'Communicology' is now widely used as an appropriate translation for the French 'communicologie' and the German 'Kommunikologie.' The institutionalization of the terms 'communicology' took place in 2000 with the founding of the International Communicology Institute.

See also: ▶ CODE ▶ DISCOURSE ▶ INTERGROUP COMMUNICATION AND DISCURSIVE PSYCHOLOGY ▶ MODELS OF COMMUNICATION ▶ PHENOMENOLOGY ▶ QUALITATIVE METHODOLOGY ▶ RELIABILITY ▶ SEMIOTICS ▶ VALIDITY

REFERENCES AND SUGGESTED READINGS

Holenstein, E. (1976). *Roman Jakobson's approach to language: Phenomenological structuralism* (trans. C. Schelbert & T. Schelbert). Bloomington, IN: Indiana University Press.

International Communicology Institute (2000). At http://communicology.org, accessed July 31, 2014.

Ruesch, J. & Bateson, G. (1968; 2008). *Communication: The social matrix of psychiatry*. New Brunswick, NJ: Transaction Publishers.

Community Media

ULLAMAIJA KIVIKURU
University of Helsinki

The concept of community media is understood as referring to small media institutions, often specifically to radio stations established in the so-called developing countries. The objective is to create local affinity, and through it, development. The aim is to 'give voice to the voiceless.'

Community media are established and run by local people, most often by local nongovernmental organizations (NGOs) or development projects. However, locality as a component for mediated communication does not belong to the southern media alone. In Europe in the 1970s and 1980s, a movement to re-establish local radio stations emerged, based on ideals similar to the community media movement. In this context 'local' means either geographical 'proximity' (people living close to each other) or 'locality' (more abstractly referring to people sharing a joint interest in politics, culture, or a hobby). The mode of addressing the public should be participatory. For instance, in Mozambique, there are roughly 80 community media centers, and in South Africa, more than 120 community radio stations. In Mozambique and Sri Lanka, community media have grown into multimedia centers or telecenters, including also other forms of mediated communication.

Most community media have an *educational policy line*. They reserve broadcasting time for campaign and project promotion as well as for talks with educational experts (→ Educational Media). In an ideal case, the community media activity is based on volunteer work. For example, during election campaigns, community media have supplied the community with markedly different material than national media. They have been found especially powerful in raising the status of women in communities.

Being off air and again on air is usual for community stations. Some critics have raised the question of whether donated equipment also brings with it regulative ties. The enormous demand for programs has also become obvious. In general, structural policies promoting local communication have been achieved fairly easily although some governmental organs have remained suspicious of the oppositional potential embedded in local media. However, a far more difficult issue is keeping the content focus on the local level.

See also: ▶ AFRICA: MEDIA SYSTEMS ▶ CITIZEN JOURNALISM ▶ DEVELOPMENT COMMUNICATION ▶ EDUCATIONAL MEDIA ▶ INDIA: MEDIA SYSTEM ▶ PARTICIPATORY COMMUNICATION ▶ PUBLIC BROADCASTING SYSTEMS ▶ RADIO FOR DEVELOPMENT ▶ UNESCO

SUGGESTED READINGS

Buckley, S. (2011): *Community media: A good practice handbook*. Paris: UNESCO.

Howley. K. (2012): *Understanding community media*. Los Angeles, CA: Sage.

Compliance Gaining

STEVEN R. WILSON
Purdue University

Compliance gaining occurs when one person attempts to convince a second to perform some desired behavior that the second otherwise might not perform. People seek compliance to accomplish tasks, yet how they do so affects levels of closeness and trust in their relationships.

Miller et al. (1977) conducted the *pioneering investigation* of compliance gaining. Participants read hypothetical scenarios that varied in whether their relationship with the other was interpersonal (e.g. romantic partner) or non-interpersonal (e.g. acquaintance) and whether their request had short- or long-term consequences. They then rated how likely they were to use 16 compliance-seeking strategies in each scenario. Participants reported being willing to use a larger variety of strategies within non-interpersonal as compared to interpersonal relationships. Although this study spurred a large body of research on how people select compliance-seeking strategies, few reliable predictors were identified.

Three *criticisms of such studies* emerged (Wilson 2002). First, studies were using ad hoc lists of strategies, making it difficult to discern whether ratings were based on message explicitness, reasoning, politeness, or some other quality. Second, researchers were implicitly adopting implausible models of how individuals produce messages during conversation. Third, researchers debated the validity of people rating their likelihood of using strategies in hypothetical scenarios.

Contemporary compliance-gaining research shares four assumptions. First, newer research is *meaning-centered,* given that it explores how participants conceive of their actions (→ Meaning). Rather than thinking globally about 'seeking compliance,' individuals report pursuing specific influence goals such as asking favors or giving advice. Second, contemporary research recognizes that people typically pursue multiple, conflicting goals and messages will vary in the degree to which they address multiple goals (Goldsmith 2004). Third, research emphasizes the *incremental, interactive nature of seeking compliance.* Finally, this research recognizes that meanings arise within relationships, institutions and cultures (Goldsmith 2004).

See also: ▶ INTERPERSONAL COMMUNICATION
▶ MEANING ▶ MESSAGE PRODUCTION
▶ PERSUASION

REFERENCES AND SUGGESTED READINGS

Goldsmith, D. G. (2004). *Communicating social support.* Cambridge: Cambridge University Press.
Miller, G. R., Boster, F. J., Roloff, M. E., & Seibold, D. (1977). Compliance-gaining message strategies: A typology and some findings concerning effects of situational differences. *Communication Monographs,* 44, 37–41.

Wilson, S. R. (2002). *Seeking and resisting compliance: Why people say what they do when trying to influence others.* Thousand Oaks, CA: Sage.

Computer Games and Child Development

JOHN L. SHERRY
Michigan State University

NICHOLAS DAVID BOWMAN
West Virginia University

Video games have been found to have both positive and negative effects on children, from increased academic test scores to increased aggression levels, but the results are mixed (→ Video Games). It is estimated that in the US 75 percent of children under the age of 18 are video game players and the amount of time they spend gaming daily is increasing. A Kaiser Family Foundation study found that the average time children play games daily in the US more than doubled between 1999 and 2009. Worldwide, the trend is similar, with the video game industry expected to grow to over US$68 billion in the year 2012.

In the most recent study of media use among the very young (age 0–6), video game play was found to be the least common recreational activity, with several studies reporting that young children play video games for less than six minutes per day. As children get older, their game play increases until it peaks in the preteen and early teen years. A 2010 study of US schoolchildren reports that children aged 8–10 play an average of 1 hour per day, children aged 11–14 1.42 hours per day, and children aged 15–18 1.13 hours daily (Rideout, Foehr, & Roberts 2010). Patterns of *gender differences* in video game play appear fairly early in development. One study found that US boys averaged 1.5 hours more game play per day than girls across all ages. In a meta-analysis of 90 media use studies, Marshall, Gorely, & Biddle (2006) estimated that US girls aged 7–10 spend around 30 minutes per day playing video games, while boys of the same age spend nearly 71 minutes per day playing video games. Clear differences in genre preferences between boys and girls exist as well. Boys prefer action, fighting, shooting, adventure, and sports games, while girls prefer platform, puzzle, and educational games. These gender differences in game preference are observed as early as 10 years of age (→ Media Use by Social Variable).

Part of the reason we see differences in amount of game use by age may be because → *uses and gratifications derived from game* play also vary by age. It appears that games begin as an intellectual challenge and as an expression of power fantasy, but become more of a social event as children progress through adolescence and into young adulthood. Data suggest that gamers of all ages (including children as young as 11) seek out social interaction in online virtual environments, taking advantage of the variety of players as well as the anonymity afforded in these games.

Scholars have found evidence of positive and negative *effects on childhood development* associated with video game play. One longitudinal study found that the young children (aged 4 and 5) who were exposed to developmentally appropriate software had increased intelligence scores, nonverbal skills, dexterity, and long-term memory compared with children who were exposed to less developmentally appropriate software. Research on 7- and 8-year-olds found that children who played video games had better hand–eye coordination and reaction time than children who did not. Another study found that video game play can significantly increase spatial skills in 10-year-olds. Playing newer-generation active video game systems, such as the Nintendo Wii, has been found to significantly increase physical activity in children aged 10–13, which might promote active lifestyles later in life.

Areas of concern include game play addiction, poor academic performance and violence in games. One study found that 14 percent of adolescents showed signs of game addiction, with males reporting more addictive usage than females. One study of 14 year-olds found that the poorest-performing students were typically the heaviest users of video games, while another study found no effect of game play on classroom performance. Finally, while there have been very few studies of children's violent game play, a recent meta-analysis found a weak link ($r = .07$) between game play and aggression in child samples (→ Violence as Media Content, Effects of; Violence as Media Content, Effects on Children of).

See also: ▶ MEDIA EFFECTS ▶ MEDIA USE BY SOCIAL VARIABLE ▶ USES AND GRATIFICATIONS ▶ VIDEO GAMES ▶ VIOLENCE AS MEDIA CONTENT, EFFECTS OF ▶ VIOLENCE AS MEDIA CONTENT, EFFECTS ON CHILDREN OF

REFERENCES AND SUGGESTED READINGS

Entertainment Software Association (2011). ESA facts and research. At www.theesa.com/facts/gamer_data.php, accessed July 31, 2014.

Marshall, S. J., Gorely, T., & Biddle, S. J. H. (2006). A descriptive epidemiology of screen-based media use in youth: A review and critique. *Journal of Adolescence*, 29(3), 333–349.

Rideout, V. J., Foehr, U. G., & Roberts, D. F., (2010). *Generation M²: Media in the lives of 8- to 18-year-olds*. Menlo Park, CA: Kaiser Family Foundation. At http://www.kff.org/entmedia/mh012010pkg.cfm, accessed July 29, 2014.

Subrahmanyam, K. & Greenfield, P. M. (1994). Effect of video game practice on spatial skills in girls and boys. *Journal of Applied Developmental Psychology*, 15, 13–32.

Vorderer, P. & Bryant, J. (eds.) (2006). *Playing video games: Motives, responses, and consequences*. Mahwah, NJ: Lawrence Erlbaum.

Computer–User Interaction

DAVID R. EWOLDSEN
Ohio State University

The world wide web has revolutionized the ways people communicate (→ Exposure to the Internet). People can have simultaneous online chats with colleagues across the world. Yet, people often communicate with a single individual so the communication is in many ways like → interpersonal communication (→ Mediated Social Interaction; Presence). Chatrooms have been created for many reasons, ranging from social interaction with liked others to sharing information about highly specific topics (→ Personal Communication by CMC). Massively multiplayer online games (MMOGs) have online communities within the games, such as the guilds that exist in 'World of Warcraft,' and online communities that exist outside of the game to discuss the game. Research on computer–user interaction has focused on how changes in the audience – mediated vs face-to-face – influence how people communicate with each other and the consequences of these differences (→ Exposure to Communication Content).

Early speculations concerning communication in online communities were stereotypic. The expectation was that chatrooms devoted to medical topics would focus on providing information to the users (Pena & Hancock 2006; → Information Seeking) or that communication concerning online games would be primarily focused on task-oriented issues because people were communicating to achieve goals within the game. However, research found that people often went to the online community on medical topics seeking empathy and support – not just factual information. Likewise, a study of communication in an online gaming community found that substantially more socio-emotional statements were produced than task-oriented statements (Pena & Hancock 2006).

Research on communication in online communities is in its infancy. But the existing research suggests interesting *insights into communication processes*. For example, people tend to do a poorer job of taking the perspective of the other people they are communicating with online (Jarvela & Hakkinen 2003). On the other hand, research also suggests that the longer a person spends on the web communicating with other people, the more sophisticated they become at online communication (Pena & Hancock 2006). Communication in online communities provides unique opportunities for studying basic interpersonal communication processes.

See also: ▶ EXPOSURE TO COMMUNICATION CONTENT ▶ EXPOSURE TO THE INTERNET ▶ GOALS, SOCIAL ASPECTS OF ▶ INFORMATION SEEKING ▶ INTERPERSONAL COMMUNICATION ▶ LANGUAGE AND THE INTERNET ▶ MEDIATED SOCIAL INTERACTION ▶ PERSONAL COMMUNICATION BY CMC ▶ PRESENCE ▶ VIDEO GAMES

REFERENCES AND SUGGESTED READINGS

Jarvela, S. & Hakkinen, P. (2003). The levels of web-based discussions: Using perspective taking theory as an analytical tool. In H. van Oostendorp (ed.), *Cognition in a digital world*. Mahwah, NJ: Lawrence Erlbaum, pp. 77–95.

Jenkins, H., Ford, S., & Green, J. (2013). *Spreadable media: Creating value and meaning in a networked culture*. New York: New York University Press.

Pena, J. & Hancock, J. T. (2006). An analysis of socioemotional and task communication in online multiplayer video games. *Communication Research*, 33, 92–109.

Concentration in Media Systems

GUILLERMO MASTRINI
University of Buenos Aires

MARTIN BECERRA
National University of Quilmes

Concentration in media systems can be analyzed from the market viewpoint or from the perspective of the companies involved. In the first case, concentration increases when the position of dominance or influence of the main companies becomes stronger, the public's power of choice is reduced and when some 'independent voices' disappear. From the business point of view, concentration implies industrial growth of the communications groups.

From a critical perspective, the main danger with concentration is the trend toward oligopoly (i.e., when the market is dominated by a small number of companies) and monopoly (when the market is dominated by a single firm, instead of a large number of companies). Less critical theories are more tolerant of concentration. Scholars of these theories argue that a certain amount of concentration stimulates innovation and economic development, so long as this dominant position does not entail abuse over long periods of time.

Three *forms of concentration* can be distinguished which are also found in other industries. First, 'horizontal integration' or monomedia expansion occurs when a company produces various final products within the same type of business. Monomedia expansion takes place within the same business, with the objective of increasing market share, eliminating idle capacity of the company, and allowing the formation of economies of scale. This type of concentration developed early in the history of the press, with the consolidation of press groups (→ Newspaper, History of). 'Vertical integration' or expansion takes place when companies that operate in different stages of the value or supply chain are added. In this case, the companies expand with the objective of embracing different phases of production, from raw materials to the finished product, in order to obtain a reduction of costs and better supply. 'Diagonal concentration' or lateral growth of conglomerates represents diversification outside the original business, with the objective of reducing risks by developing synergies. This is a long-term strategy with the objective of securing safer investments, to counteract the slightly lowering trend of decreasing profit rates.

Measuring concentration poses a problem. There are several recognized methods and indicators, such as the index of relative entropy, the GINI index, which can be represented by a Lorenz curve, the four-firm concentration ratio (CR4), and the Herfindahl–Hirschman (HH) index. Although concentration can be measured, it is much more complex to quantify its effects on pluralism and diversity.

There are three *dominant positions* on concentration: first, a liberal perspective that does not question concentration processes except for the case of monopoly; second, the critical school, which identifies concentration of ownership as one of the main capitalist mechanisms for its legitimacy; and, third, an eclectic position that does not share the critical view, but is concerned about the risks of concentration and argues for state interventionism to limit it. From a critical school perspective any concentration in the media has to be denounced because it creates an uneven distribution of power in the market as well as in the → culture industries.

Several works have approached the difficult task of *studying empirically* the processes of concentration of media ownership. Europe is the region with the greatest work on the subject. In Latin America, Mastrini and Becerra (2006) have carried out research that takes into account the structure of the cultural industries' markets and their levels of concentration. The research does not typically include a methodology to relate concentration of ownership with media content. All of these cases highlight the high level of concentration reached in the different markets, the presence of media and communication groups that have dominant positions in several media markets, and the need to have regulations that protect content diversity and media pluralism.

See also: ▶ COMMUNICATION LAW AND POLICY: EUROPE ▶ CROSS-MEDIA MARKETING ▶ CROSS-MEDIA PRODUCTION ▶ CULTURE INDUSTRIES ▶ GLOBALIZATION OF THE MEDIA ▶ MEDIA CONGLOMERATES ▶ MEDIA ECONOMICS ▶ NEWSPAPER, HISTORY OF

REFERENCES AND SUGGESTED READINGS

Bagdikian, B. (2004). *The new media monopoly.* Boston, MA: Beacon Press.

Baker, C. E. (2007). *Media concentration and democracy.* Cambridge: Cambridge University Press.

Compaine, B. (2005). *The media monopoly myth: How new competition is expanding our sources of information and entertainment.* Washington, DC: New Millennium Research Council.

Mastrini, G. & Becerra, M. (2006). *Periodistas y magnates: Estructura y concentración de las industrias culturales en América Latina.* [Journalists and press barons: Structure and concentration of the cultural industries in Latin America]. Buenos Aires: Prometeo.

Noam, E. M. (2009). *Media ownership and concentration in America.* Oxford: Oxford University Press.

Wasko, J., Murdoch, G., & Sousa, H. (eds.) (2011). *The handbook of political economy of communications.* Oxford: Wiley Blackwell.

Consensus-Oriented Public Relations

ROLAND BURKART

University of Vienna

Consensus-oriented public relations (COPR) is a concept for planning and evaluating → public relations (PR). In conflict-situations organizations are forced to present good arguments for communicating their interests and ideas (→ Corporate Communication; Crisis Communication). Therefore, understanding plays an important role within the PR management process (Burkart 2004, 2009).

The COPR model ties up with Jürgen Habermas' theory of "communicative action" (1984): communication partners must mutually trust that they fulfill four validity claims: intelligibility, truth, trustworthiness, and legitimacy. In cases of doubt there is a certain "repair mechanism," which is called → discourse. The process of 'understanding' is not an end in itself. Understanding becomes the mean for the coordination of actions, as the participants involved in this process aim at synchronizing their goals on the basis of common definitions of a situation.

The main impact of creating the COPR model was the possibility of differentiating communicative claims, so that this process of questioning can now be analyzed more systematically. PR managers have to be aware that their messages might be questioned: critical recipients will offer their doubts about the truth of PR information and the trustworthiness of the company, as well as the legitimacy of the company's interests (→ Trust of Publics). Only if it is possible to eliminate such doubts, or, even better, if doubts are prevented from the very beginning, the flow of communication will not be disturbed (→ Corporate Reputation). A case-study in the 1990s showed that the acceptance of a planned project correlated convincingly with the degree of understanding.

See also: ▶ ADVOCACY JOURNALISM ▶ CORPORATE COMMUNICATION ▶ CORPORATE REPUTATION ▶ CRISIS COMMUNICATION ▶ DISCOURSE ▶ ORGANIZATION–PUBLIC RELATIONSHIPS ▶ PUBLIC RELATIONS ▶ TRUST OF PUBLICS

REFERENCES AND SUGGESTED READINGS

Burkart, R. (2004). Consensus-oriented public relations (COPR): A conception for planning and evaluation of public relations. In B. van Ruler & D. Vercic (eds.), *Public relations in Europe: A nation-by-nation introduction to public relations theory and practice*. Berlin: Mouton De Gruyter, pp. 446–452.

Burkart, R. (2009). On Habermas: Understanding and public relations. In Ø. Ihlen, V. van Ruler, & M. Fredriksson (eds.), *Public relations and social theory: Key figures and concepts*. London: Routledge, pp. 141–165. At http://www.routledgecommunication.com/books/Public-Relations-and-Social-Theory-isbn9780415997867, accessed July 31, 2014.

Habermas, J. (1984). *The theory of communicative action: Vol. 1. Reason and the rationalization of society*. Boston: Beacon Press.

Construction of Reality through the News

DON HEIDER
Loyola University Chicago

Between the local newspaper, radio updates, the evening television newscasts, and now updates via the Internet, a PDA or cell phone, → news seems ubiquitous. But where does news come from? Fundamentally, news is a construction, and the nature of that construction is important to how we shape our view of the symbolic and mediated reality of the world (→ Reality and Media Reality).

News gathering may seem a simple process. An event happens, reporters go and gather facts, they write the stories, and we read or hear the stories (→ Objectivity in Reporting). On occasion it may happen just like that. But what remains invisible are the dozens and sometimes hundreds of decisions that went on behind the scenes, invisible to news consumers, before that story was covered, reported, written, or edited. There are some fairly simple considerations such as what → news factors were involved in the event, where did it happen, what else happened on the same day, or had there been similar events before? Furthermore, does the news organization have a policy about reporting events of this kind, and what is the individual journalist's subjective position towards the event and its actors?

In the 1970s and 1980s many scholars were concerned with the organizational structures surrounding the → news routines in a news organization. They saw news as a socially constructed product of a social process, partly institutional culture, partly human dynamics. Later studies represented a shift away from looking at structures to a stronger look at meaning-making in news (→ Meaning). This represents a shift from analyzing structural concerns to analyzing the texts and discourses themselves that are presented in news products (→ Discourse; Text and Intertextuality). Such studies concentrated on the news products, what journalists produced, to make their case that the political elite control ideas delivered through news media. Taking a less political-economic perspective, James Carey proposed the ritual model of communication, writing about how news can be seen as a means by which people survey the world each day to reinforce what they already believe.

See also: ▶ BIAS IN THE NEWS ▶ DISCOURSE ▶ MEANING ▶ NEUTRALITY ▶ NEWS ▶ NEWS FACTORS ▶ NEWS VALUES ▶ OBJECTIVITY IN REPORTING ▶ REALITY AND MEDIA REALITY ▶ STANDARDS OF NEWS ▶ TEXT AND INTERTEXTUALITY

REFERENCES AND SUGGESTED READINGS

Carey, J. W. (1989). *Communication as culture.* Boston, MA: Unwin Hyman.
Heider, D. (ed.) (2004). *Class and news.* Lanham, MD: Rowman and Littlefield.
Lippmann, W. (1922). *Public opinion.* New York: Free Press.
Shoemaker, P. & Reese, S. (2014). *Mediating the message in the 21st century: A media sociology perspective.* London: Routledge.

Consumer Culture

MATTHEW P. MCALLISTER
Pennsylvania State University

Consumer culture, the creation and cultivation of social → meaning from the → marketing, purchase, and display of branded commodities (→ Branding; Brands), is a central characteristic of modern and postmodern society. Elements include mass-produced goods, brand logos, product packaging, advertising campaigns, retail spaces, shopping activities, and consumption-centered media content.

In the 1800s, mass manufacturing incentivized marketing outside of companies' home communities, developing the idea of branding as a sales technique to generate symbolic trustworthiness. The expansion of national magazines facilitated the use of → advertising to create universally known brands and symbolic linkages to these brands. Advertising was key in inculcating people as consumers. Early consumer culture was profoundly hegemonic, encouraging mass consumption and placating alienated works, but also perhaps helped ease the great social changes of the early twentieth century.

Broadcasting expanded brand displays and was more dependent upon advertising revenue than print. Early television advertising may have rejuvenated consumerism after years of thrift from the Depression and World War II. Globalization cultivated transnational brands and a sharp distinction between sites of exploitative production and privileged consumption (→ Globalization of the Media). Sophisticated marketing research refined demographics, psychographics, and lifestyles to facilitate purchasing. Much modern media content – such as niche cable networks – are brand- and consumption-oriented even in their nonadvertising messages (→ Commercialization: Impact on Media Content; Cable Television). E-commerce, mobile convergence, and data mining have added to the tools of modern consumerism.

Commodity fetishism, conspicuous consumption, pseudo-individualism, and spectacle are critical concepts applied to consumer culture; feminist and environmental critiques are prominent. Alternatively, consumer symbols may be used to create unique cultural identities and cohesion. Digital consumerism creates the potential for user agency but also exploits free labor and further inculcates consumerist values.

See also: ▶ ADVERTISING ▶ ADVERTISING, HISTORY OF ▶ BRANDING ▶ BRANDS ▶ CABLE TELEVISION ▶ COMMERCIALIZATION: IMPACT ON MEDIA CONTENT ▶ COMMODIFICATION OF THE MEDIA ▶ CONSUMERS IN MEDIA MARKETS ▶ CRITICAL THEORY ▶ CULTURAL STUDIES ▶ GLOBALIZATION OF THE MEDIA ▶ MEANING ▶ MARKETING ▶ YOUTH CULTURE

REFERENCES AND SUGGESTED READINGS

Cross, G. (2000). *An all-consuming century: Why commercialism won in modern America.* New York: Columbia University Press.
Leiss, W., Kline, S., Jhally, S., & Botterill, J. (2005). *Social communication in advertising: Consumption in the mediated marketplace,* 3rd edn. London: Routledge.
Paterson, M. (2006). *Consumption and everyday life.* London: Routledge.

Consumers in Media Markets

PHILIP M. NAPOLI
Fordham University

Communication researchers have devoted a substantial amount of attention to understanding consumers in media markets. The processes by which audiences select between the various content options available, as well as the mechanisms by which media organizations seek to understand, anticipate, and respond to these choices have traditionally resided at the core of research focusing on media consumers. The study of media consumers fits within the somewhat broader framework of → audience research and is distinguished by its attention primarily to the economic dimensions of media consumption and the processes by which audiences select media products – as is reflected in the use of the term 'consumers' (→ Media Economics; Exposure to Communication Content). It is important to emphasize that to speak of media 'consumers' reflects the adoption of a certain perspective on the interaction between media organizations and individuals; one that is, by connotation, primarily commercial or economic in nature.

Studying the behavior of media consumers requires a focus on the allocation of two scarce resources: attention and money. The time spent consuming media has continued to expand, according to many measures – most likely due to increased multitasking on the part of consumers (→ Exposure to Print Media). Nonetheless, the attention of media consumers itself remains a scarce resource (Lanham 2006), particularly in an increasingly fragmented and cluttered media environment, in which available content options are growing exponentially, all of which compete aggressively for consumer attention. Similarly, there is a limit to what consumers can spend on media.

While early research on media consumers examined issues such as consumer satisfaction with various media products, over time the study of media consumers has come increasingly to focus on understanding how consumers choose to expose themselves to various media products. Empirical work has delved into a wide range of factors that impact consumers' choices in regards to individual media products. This work has considered both audience factors (i.e., the characteristics of the media consumers, such as tastes, preferences, and awareness of various content options) and media factors (i.e., the quantity of content options, the range of media consumption technologies available) in an effort to account for both the structural-level and individual-level factors that impact consumers' choices in the media marketplace. Research on 'one-way flows' has illustrated enduring patterns in media consumer behavior involving (as the name suggests) the tendency for the consumption of media products to flow from large markets to small markets (both nationally and internationally), but seldom vice versa.

Research on the behavior of media consumers does, however, face an increasingly difficult task in terms of identifying and predicting consumer behavioral patterns in increasingly fragmented media environments (→ Audience Segmentation). The much greater channel capacity of many media technologies, the rise of alternative distribution technologies, and the increased interactivity of the new media environment (→ Interactivity, Concept of) all contribute to a media landscape that is vastly different from the one in which early researchers could, for example, in the television context demonstrate with great consistency predictable patterns of 'audience flow' from one program to the next.

Research has shown fairly predictable patterns across the aggregate of content options. In contrast, however, perhaps one of the most enduring themes of the literature on media consumers is the tremendous uncertainty that inevitably revolves around the process by which consumers select individual content options.

To the extent that an understanding of media audiences as consumers is typically a perspective characteristic of the media organizations providing consumers with content, research on media consumers has also frequently addressed the related subject of how these organizations perceive their consumers, as well as the subject of how these organizations cope with the many distinctive and unpredictable characteristics of media consumer behavior (Napoli 2003).

The study of media consumers today faces its greatest challenges in terms of effectively accounting for the ever-growing array of media choices that are available, and in terms of effectively accounting for the various ways in which the interaction between content provider and consumer is changing. In a highly fragmented media environment, questions regarding the mechanisms by which media consumers become aware of the content options available to them become increasingly important – particularly in terms of developing an understanding of how consumers utilize the wide range of new search and navigation tools available to them in the new media environment.

See also: ▶ ADVERTISING, ECONOMICS OF ▶ AUDIENCE RESEARCH ▶ AUDIENCE SEGMENTATION ▶ EXPOSURE TO COMMUNICATION CONTENT ▶ EXPOSURE TO PRINT MEDIA ▶ GENRE ▶ INTERACTIVITY, CONCEPT OF ▶ MEDIA ECONOMICS ▶ SELECTIVE EXPOSURE ▶ USES AND GRATIFICATIONS

REFERENCES AND SUGGESTED READINGS

Dimmick, J. W. (2002). *Market competition and coexistence: The theory of the niche.* Mahwah, NJ: Lawrence Erlbaum.
Hindman, M. (2007). A mile wide and an inch deep: Measuring media diversity online and offline. In P. M. Napoli (ed.), *Media diversity and localism: Meaning and metrics.* Mahwah, NJ: Lawrence Erlbaum, pp. 327–347.
Lanham, R. (2006). *The economics of attention: Style and substance in the age of information.* Chicago: University of Chicago Press.
Napoli, P. M. (2003). *Audience economics: Media institutions and the audience marketplace.* New York: Columbia University Press.
Neuman, W. R. (1991). *The future of the mass audience.* Cambridge: Cambridge University Press.

Content Analysis, Qualitative

BERTRAM SCHEUFELE
University of Hohenheim

Like quantitative content analysis, qualitative content analysis is an empirical method of social sciences for analyzing live or recorded human communication such as newspaper articles, protocols of television → news or programs, transcripts of interviews, or protocols from → observations (→ Content Analysis, Quantitative). This written or transcribed material is called 'text material' in this context (→ Text and Intertextuality).

From a general perspective, there are two main *differences between quantitative and qualitative content analysis*. First, quantitative content analysis works deductively and measures quantitatively. In this respect, quantitative content analysis decomposes the text material into different parts and assigns numeric codes to these elements or parts. By contrast, qualitative content analysis works inductively by summarizing and classifying elements or parts of the text material and assigning labels or categories to them. In this respect, qualitative content analysis searches rather for 'coherent' meaning structures in the text material. Second, quantitative content analysis can deal with a large quantity of text material while qualitative content analysis is limited to a few pieces of text material. In practical respects, one can say that quantitative content analysis applies category schemas for the purpose of measuring quantitatively, whereas qualitative content analysis develops categories in a qualitative, rather inductive, or → hermeneutic, way. Further differences that are emphasized by advocates of → qualitative methodology or the qualitative paradigm will be discussed later.

In a wider sense, the term 'qualitative content analysis' subsumes quite different and various methods and techniques of analyzing text material qualitatively or hermeneutically. Examples are → grounded theory or → discourse analysis. In a more narrow sense, qualitative content analysis is a label for a specific type of qualitative text analysis that was developed by Philipp Mayring (2002). This type of qualitative content analysis tries to close the gap between the so-called quantitative and qualitative paradigm. From a more affirmative point of view, Mayring's content analysis has the advantage of being a systematic and more transparent research method, when compared, e.g., to grounded theory.

Qualitative content analysis is in fact different in its core features and in its methodological background. The first feature is *openness*. In terms of qualitative content analysis, researchers should be open enough to social reality by avoiding theoretically deduced and completely standardized coding schemas. Thus, qualitative content analysis mostly affords analyzing text material without pre-defined coding units, dimensions, or categories. The second feature is *communicativity*: social reality is established by and in interaction or communication. Thus, we can assume that all subjects interacting or communicating have a common meaning ground. This means that subjects share some knowledge about the motives and structures of interaction and communication, i.e., about how and why people act and communicate this and not that way, what they mean by certain concepts, and so on. Text material – e.g., the protocols of observing interactions or the transcripts of interviews – should therefore not be decomposed into different separate dimensions or categories as in quantitative content analysis.

The third feature is *naturalistics*. This standard is especially important for collecting or generating text material. If researchers interview a subject or a group of persons, they should keep the situation in which they collect information about subjects' interaction or communication as natural as possible. Finally, the fourth feature is *interpretativity*. It comprises two aspects: (1) qualitative content analysis aims at understanding everyday interpretations and attributions of meaning, and (2) it aims at typifying, i.e., at constructing patterns of meaning by analyzing the text material, and does not aim at representative statements about communication or interaction in the sense of a qualitative methodology.

See also: ▶ CONTENT ANALYSIS, QUANTITATIVE ▶ DISCOURSE ▶ DISCOURSE ANALYSIS ▶ GROUNDED THEORY ▶ HERMENEUTICS ▶ INTERVIEW, QUALITATIVE ▶ MEANING ▶ NEWS ▶ OBSERVATION ▶ QUALITATIVE METHODOLOGY ▶ QUANTITATIVE METHODOLOGY ▶ TEXT AND INTERTEXTUALITY

REFERENCES AND SUGGESTED READINGS

Cresswell, J. W. (2013). *Qualitative inquiry and research design: Choosing among five approaches*, 3rd edn. Thousand Oaks, CA: Sage.

Denzin, N. K. & Lincoln, Y. S. (eds.) (2011). *The Sage handbook of qualitative research*, 4th edn. Thousand Oaks, CA: Sage.

Kuckartz, U. (2014). *Qualitative text analysis: A guide to methods, practice and using software*. Thousand Oaks, CA: Sage.

Mayring, P. (2002). *Qualitative Inhaltsanalyse: Grundlagen und Techniken* [Qualitative content analysis: Foundations and techniques], 8th edn. Weinheim: Beltz.

Titscher, S., Meyer, M., Wodak, R., & Vetter, E. (2000). *Methods of text and discourse analysis*. Thousand Oaks, CA: Sage.

Content Analysis, Quantitative

BERTRAM SCHEUFELE
University of Hohenheim

Quantitative content analysis is an empirical method used in the social sciences primarily for analyzing recorded human communication in a quantitative, systematic, and intersubjective way. A quantitative content analysis can be applied to verbal material and to visual material such as the evening news or television entertainment. Besides → surveys and → observations quantitative content analysis belongs to the main methods of data collection in empirical communication research, with quantitative content analysis being the most prominent in the field (→ Survey).

Bernhard Berelson (1952) defined content analysis as "a research technique for the objective, systematic and quantitative description of the manifest content of communication." There has been much debate on what the word 'manifest' means: is it possible to analyze latent structures of human communication beyond the surface of the manifest text, i.e., the 'black marks on white'? In a more practical sense, the word 'manifest' should be interpreted in terms of 'making it manifest' through methodology.

In a quantitative content analysis the person charged with coding assigns numeric codes (taken from a category system) to certain elements of the text (e.g., issues or politicans mentioned in articles) by following a fixed plan (written down in a codebook). Quantitative content analysis differs from qualitative content analysis by not analyzing only a few but many units of analysis (→ Content Analysis, Qualitative). While qualitative content analysis works rather inductively by summarizing and classifying elements and by assigning labels or categories to them, quantitative content analysis works deductively and measures quantitatively by assigning numeric codes to parts of the material to be coded.

There are three major *purposes of quantitative content analysis*: (1) making inferences about the antecedents of communication, e.g., comparing the coverage of a liberal and a conservative newspaper; (2) merely describing features of the text; and (3) drawing inferences about the effects of communication. Strictly speaking, such an inference is not possible when nothing but the message is examined.

A technique that meets the semantic and syntactical structures of communication is the Semantic Structure and Content Analysis developed by Werner Früh. The technique considers various elements of communication as well as the relations between them. For instance, it analyzes persons and roles mentioned in newspaper articles.

Most quantitative content analyses examine text or verbal material, i.e., transcribed or recorded human communication. Studies analyzing *visual material* like films, television advertisements, or televised debates between presidential candidates are comparably rare because visual material is more difficult to code than verbal or text material.

A more or less recent development in quantitative content analysis is *computer-assisted content analysis*, where a computer program counts keywords and searches for related words in the same paragraph, for example. Before the coding process begins, all the relevant keywords or phrases in a so-called coding dictionary – an equivalent of the codebook of a conventional content analysis – have to be listed. While there has been recent progress by applying machine-learning techniques (e.g., Scharkow 2013), human coders are still not redundant.

Current challenges for quantitative content analysis stem from the *Internet*, where the content of a private weblog, arguments in an online chat, or the pictures in an online gallery can be subject to analysis. On the internet, the population from which a sample is taken for analysis may not be fixed but can change over time. It is therefore important to store all relevant communication for a specific study. Thus most studies analyze online communication work with samples that are more or less clearly defined (→ Online Research). More recently 'web crawlers' have been applied which browse the internet for content that is in the researcher's focus.

Like any other method in the social sciences, quantitative content analysis has to meet certain *standards* of quantitative empirical research like intersubjectivity, systematic (i.e., that coding rules and sampling criteria are invariantly applied to all material), → reliability, and → validity. The criterion of reliability calls for the codebook to be dependable. In general, codebooks have to be tested for inter-coder-reliability (test of the similarity of coding of the same material between different coders) before the coding process itself starts.

See also: ▶ AGENDA-SETTING EFFECTS
▶ CONTENT ANALYSIS, QUALITATIVE
▶ CULTIVATION EFFECTS ▶ OBSERVATION
▶ ONLINE RESEARCH ▶ QUANTITATIVE METHODOLOGY ▶ RELIABILITY ▶ SURVEY
▶ VALIDITY

REFERENCES AND SUGGESTED READINGS

Berelson, B. (1952). *Content analysis in communication research*. Glencoe, IL: The Free Press.
Früh, W. (2011). *Inhaltsanalyse: Theorie und Praxis*, 7th edn [Content analysis: Theory and practice]. Constance: UVK.
Krippendorff, K. (2013). *Content analysis: An introduction to its methodology*, 3rd edn. Thousand Oaks, CA: Sage.
Neuendorf, K. A. (2002). *The content analysis guidebook*. Thousand Oaks, CA: Sage.
Riffe, D., Lacy, S., & Fico, F. G. (2014). *Analyzing media messages: Using quantitative content analysis in research*, 3rd edn. London: Routledge.
Scharkow, M. (2013). Thematic content analysis using supervised machine learning: An empirical evaluation using German online news. *Quality & Quantity*, 47(2), 761–773.

Conversation Analysis

WAYNE A. BEACH
San Diego State University

Conversation Analysis (CA) is a primary mode of inquiry for closely examining how speakers organize everyday → interactions. The practices and patterns of ordinary communication are revealed as speakers make available their understandings moment-by-moment and collaborate in producing distinct courses of unfolding action. Research materials are naturally occurring audio and video recordings, and carefully produced transcriptions, of a broad range of interactions comprising the social worlds of diverse speakers, relationships, activities, and events (→ Qualitative Methodology).

A *defining feature of CA* is the descriptive rigor and explanatory force brought to recordings and transcriptions, a proof-by-exemplar methodology of analytic induction. What speakers display and demonstrate in real time, in the first instance by and for them, become resources for analysts to warrant claims, progressively advance evidence about the organization of social interaction, and seek to establish consensus about the most compelling depictions of interactional conduct. By giving priority to recordings and transcriptions, it is also recognized that detailed features and contingencies of interactional events cannot be intuited, nor adequately reconstructed, through field notes, interviews, or other forms of self-reported information. Attention is thus not drawn to individuals' interpretive or perceptual experiences, but to the turn-by-turn and embodied coordination of local actions within an 'architecture of intersubjectivity' – an organization in which "a context of publicly displayed and continuously up-dated intersubjective understandings is systematically sustained" (Heritage 1984, 259).

While CA has historically given primary attention to the ongoing orderliness of talk within single cases and collections of social interaction, the interplay of vocal and visible orientations to gesture, gaze, related body movements, objects (e.g., instruments or medical records), and spatial environments are basic and enduring concerns (e.g., Goodwin, LeBaron, & Streeck 2011).

The *analytic dimensions of CA* investigations are broad and vibrant, revealing the organization of frequently recognized yet taken-for-granted features of language and action. The empirical rigor and theoretical implications arising from CA have proven invaluable for scholars researching → language and social interaction/LSI (e.g., Fitch & Sanders 2004). Empirical attention is given to an array of ordinary conversations during phone calls and face-to-face interactions, including family members, friends, acquaintances, young children, parents, and daycare providers.

Topics range from activities such as laughter in interaction, to delivering and receiving good and bad news. Analysis also focuses on more specialized institutional settings involving diverse encounters between lay persons and bureaucratic representatives, including interactions between patients and providers during visits to medical clinics, counseling and therapy sessions, or journalists and public figures participating in → news and broadcast interviews (→ Broadcast Talk). Emerging studies such as how family members talk through cancer on the telephone, applying basic CA findings to improve talk in institutions, and emotions as socially constructed actions continue to expand the horizons and relevance of CA investigations.

See also: ▶ BROADCAST TALK ▶ INTERACTION
▶ LANGUAGE AND SOCIAL INTERACTION
▶ NEWS ▶ QUALITATIVE METHODOLOGY
▶ QUESTIONS AND QUESTIONING

REFERENCES AND SUGGESTED READINGS

Antaki, C. (ed). (2011). *Applied conversation analysis: Intervention and change in institutional talk.* Basingstoke: Palgrave Macmillan.

Beach, W. A. (ed.) (2013). *Handbook of patient-provider interactions: Raising and responding to concerns about life, illness, and disease.* New York: Hampton Press.

Fitch, K. & Sanders, R. E. (eds.) (2004). *Handbook of language and social interaction.* Mahwah, NJ: Lawrence Erlbaum.

Goodwin, C., LeBaron, C., & Streeck, J. (2011). *Embodied interaction: Language and the body in the material world.* Cambridge: Cambridge University Press.

Heritage, J. (1984). *Garfinkel and ethnomethodology.* Cambridge: Polity Press.

Sidnell, J. & T. Stivers (eds.) (2013). *Handbook of conversation analysis.* Oxford: Wiley Blackwell.

Co-Orientation Model of Public Relations

DEJAN VERČIČ
University of Ljubljana

Public relations (PR) is a strategic management function responsible for cultivation of good relations between an organization and its strategic constituencies (→ Public Relations). The ultimate goal of PR is social harmony. The co-orientation model of PR assumes that organizations prefer harmony to conflict and that they can use communication for that purpose (→ Organization–Public Relationships; Consensus-Oriented Public Relations).

The co-orientation model of PR originates in psychological balance theory, which is a motivational theory of attitude change. People use communication as a tool to resolve an imbalance: friends who like each other should be able to communicate their differences in perception of the third person and, in that process of communication, find a compromise, or perhaps one of them might change their opinion. This is a symmetry theory where communication leads to more interpersonal similarity (→ Interpersonal Communication).

Co-orientation entered PR via the interpersonal model to elicit key ideas on how organizations and constituencies relate to each other (→ Social Perception; Organizational Communication). The co-orientation model enables us to answer questions such as: how does an organization view something of common interest with a strategic constituency? How does that constituency perceive that area of common interest? How does the organization perceive the constituency's views? And how does the constituency perceive the organization's views? This type of questioning is known in PR practice as a 'gap analysis,' a method where practitioners audit organizations and selected constituencies and describe their perceptions as being more or less distant. Where discrepancies are the greatest, intervention is proposed and communication is used to increase accuracy of perceptions. The co-orientation model has been recently used also for developing PR ethics and international public relations.

See also: ▶ CHANGE MANAGEMENT AND COMMUNICATION ▶ CONSENSUS-ORIENTED PUBLIC RELATIONS ▶ INTERPERSONAL COMMUNICATION ▶ ORGANIZATIONAL COMMUNICATION ▶ ORGANIZATION–PUBLIC RELATIONSHIPS ▶ PUBLIC RELATIONS ▶ PUBLIC RELATIONS EVALUATION ▶ SOCIAL PERCEPTION

REFERENCES AND SUGGESTED READINGS

Broom, G. M. (2013). Co-orientation theory. In R. L. Heath (ed.), *Encyclopedia of public relations*, 2nd ed., vol. 1. Thousand Oaks, CA: Sage, pp. 195–198.

Broom, G. M. (2005). Co-orientation theory. In R. L. Heath (ed.), *Encyclopedia of public relations*, vol. 1. Thousand Oaks, CA: Sage, pp. 197–200.

Copyright

MATT JACKSON
Pennsylvania State University

Copyright is a legal concept that creates property rights in expression. Protection begins the moment the expression is fixed (stored) in a tangible medium. The copyright owner is granted control over the reproduction, distribution, public performance, public communication, and public display of the work as well as any derivative works based on the work (→ Intellectual Property Law). The origin of copyright can be traced to the printing privileges granted to encourage the development of presses and movable type in the fifteenth century (→ Printing, History of). In 1710, England passed the first copyright statute granting rights to the author rather than the printer.

The *economic rationale* for copyright law is based on two related concepts, 'public goods,' and 'economies of scale.' A public good refers to a resource that can be consumed simultaneously by multiple users without depleting the resource and it is difficult to exclude individuals who do not pay for the use. Economies of scale is when the average cost to produce a product decreases as production increases. Without copyright protection, a competitor can acquire a copy of a work and then make and sell copies more cheaply than the producer who had to pay for the initial production costs (→ Media Economics). Copyright law creates a legal right to exclude nonpayers and competitors to encourage investment in new expression. Society benefits because more works are produced. However, copyright increases the price of those works, limiting society's access.

In addition to the economic rationale for copyright, many nations' laws are influenced by the *concept of moral rights*. An author's expression is seen as an extension of her personality and therefore personal to her. Moreover, the author invests time and labor in creating the expression. Many commentators argue the author has a natural right to control how her expression is used. While the economic rationale for copyright is based on a public policy objective of encouraging creation for the benefit of society, the moral rationale is based on the author's private right to control her expression.

Copyright is the subject of multiple international treaties, beginning with the Berne Convention for the Protection of Literary and Artistic Works, established in 1886. Other major copyright treaties include the Agreement on Trade-Related Aspects of Intellectual Property Rights (TRIPS Agreement) and the World Intellectual Property Organization's (WIPO) Copyright Treaty and Performances and *Phonograms Treaty*. Because each nation's copyright law only applies within its borders, there is increasing pressure for harmonization to create uniform protection worldwide. Attempts to increase protection are controversial since copyright often is seen as favoring developed nations at the expense of developing nations.

The primary safeguard against the restrictive nature of copyright is the *idea/expression dichotomy*. Copyright only protects expression, not the facts or ideas being expressed. However, many commentators argue there are situations where copying expression serves important free-speech interests. Most nations include exceptions and limitations to insure that copyright does not limit public debate or the advancement of knowledge. The United States has one of the broadest exceptions, 'fair use,' which allows limited copying for news reporting, research, comment, criticism, and other purposes.

Copyright law has changed dramatically as *new technologies* are invented to create, store, and distribute copyrighted expression (→ Technology and Communication). Expression contained in a digital file can be copied effortlessly and distributed globally via the Internet. The content industries seek stricter domestic and international laws that would grant copyright owners more power and increase the penalties for infringement. Copyright owners have begun to use technological protection measures (TPMs) and other forms of digital rights management (DRM) to prevent users from copying and distributing content without authorization. The WIPO treaties mandate that each member country provide legal protection for TPMs to prevent users from circumventing the protection measures (→ Internet Law and Regulation).

See also: ▶ CENSORSHIP, HISTORY OF ▶ FREEDOM OF COMMUNICATION ▶ INTELLECTUAL PROPERTY LAW ▶ INTERNET LAW AND REGULATION ▶ MEDIA ECONOMICS ▶ OPEN SOURCE ▶ PRINTING, HISTORY OF ▶ SATELLITE TELEVISION ▶ TECHNOLOGY AND COMMUNICATION

REFERENCES AND SUGGESTED READINGS

Goldstein, P. (2001). *International copyright: Principles, law, and practice.* Oxford: Oxford University Press.
Goldstein, P. (2003). *Copyright's highway: From Gutenberg to the celestial jukebox,* rev. edn. Stanford, CA: Stanford University Press.
Landes, W. M. & Posner, R. A. (1989). An economic analysis of copyright law. *Journal of Legal Studies*, 18, 325–363.
Litman, J. (2001). *Digital copyright.* New York: Prometheus.
Patterson, L. R. (1968). *Copyright in historical perspective.* Nashville, TN: Vanderbilt University Press.
Vaidhyanathan, S. (2001). *Copyrights and copywrongs: The rise of intellectual property and how it threatens creativity.* New York: New York University Press.

Corporate Communication

JOEP P. CORNELISSEN

VU University Amsterdam and University of Leeds

Perhaps the best way to define corporate communication is to look at the way in which the function developed in companies. Until the 1980s, professionals responsible for communication within their organizations had used the term → 'public relations' to describe communication with stakeholders (a term still used in academic circles across the world). This public relations (PR) function, which was tactical in most companies, largely consisted of communication to the press.

Definition

From the 1990s, professionals started to use the term corporate communication, which they defined as a broader function that consolidates a range of communication disciplines and expertise into a single corporate communication or corporate affairs department. This broad focus is also reflected in the word 'corporate' in corporate communication. The word of course refers to the *business setting* in which corporate communication became established as a separate function (alongside other functions such as human resources and finance).

There is also an important second sense in which the word is being used. 'Corporate' originally stems from the Latin expressions for 'body' ('corpus') and for 'forming into a body ('corporare'), which emphasizes a unified way of looking at internal and external communication disciplines. That is, instead of looking at specialized disciplines or stakeholder groups separately, the corporate communication function starts from the perspective of the *bodily organization as a whole* when communicating to all internal and external stakeholders.

The definition of corporate communication and the conceptual terrain that it covers has evolved as a result of its incorporation into undergraduate and postgraduate degrees at business schools. Whereas communication courses have traditionally been part of degree programs in schools of communication and journalism (→ Communication as a Field and Discipline), the business equivalent of the subject was refashioned in terms of management theory and education. This development echoed the sentiments expressed above about the need for a redefinition of *communication as a management function*. Argenti, one of the first professors in corporate communication at a US business school, puts it this way: "business schools are the most appropriate home for the discipline, because like other functional areas within the corporation (such as marketing, finance, production, and human resource management), corporate communication exists as a real and important part of most organizations. As such, it should rightfully be housed in that branch of the academy that deals with business administration or graduate schools of business."

Shelby (1993, 255) defined corporate communication as "an umbrella for a variety of communication forms and formats" that "includes public relations (speech writing, press/community relations), public affairs (including lobbying activities), and employee, customer, and stockholder communication." All of these forms of communication in Shelby's view share a focus on communicating about the organization to "collectivities [i.e., stakeholders] that exist inside and outside organizations" (1993, 255).

Van Riel (1995) added to Shelby's early definition the idea that all these forms of communication need to be actively managed and coordinated to present a consistent image of the organization to all stakeholders. He defined corporate communication as "an instrument of management by means of which all consciously used forms of internal and external communication are harmonized as effectively and efficiently as possible," with the overall objective of creating "a favorable basis for relationships with groups upon which the company is dependent" (1995, 26). More recently, Cornelissen (2011, 5) provided a slight alteration to this definition when he described corporate communication as "a management function that offers a framework for the effective coordination of all internal and external communication with the overall purpose of establishing and maintaining favourable reputations with stakeholder groups upon which the organization is dependent."

Orchestration, Integration, Transparency

All three definitions characterize corporate communication as a management function within organizations that involves communication professionals engaging in different forms of communication (e.g., → public affairs) with internal and external stakeholders. In line with these early definitions, Van Riel (1995) stressed the importance of 'orchestration' of all forms of communication, whilst Christensen and Cornelissen (2011) document the emphasis on integration in many corporate communication texts.

Orchestration and integration refer to the coordination of all forms of communication so that its contents convey the same corporate image or 'corporate identity' of the organization and leave a consistent impression or 'reputation' with stakeholders (→ Corporate Reputation; Corporate and Organizational Identity; Organizational Image). Much theory-building and research have since focused on these concepts of corporate identity and corporate reputation and have argued that it is strategically important for organizations to achieve 'alignment' or 'transparency' (e.g., Fombrun & Rindova 2000; Hatch & Schultz 2001).

According to Fombrun and Rindova (2000, 94), *transparency* is "a state in which the internal identity of the firm reflects positively the expectations of key stakeholders and the beliefs of these stakeholders about the firm reflect accurately the internally held identity." Along these lines, researchers stress the particular importance of consonance between (1) the organizational culture as articulated by senior managers and as experienced by employees; (2) corporate identity (i.e., the image projected by the organization); (3) corporate image (i.e., the immediate impression of an organization in relation to a specific message or image); and (4) corporate reputation (i.e., an individual's collective representation of past images of an organization, induced through either communication or past experiences).

Importantly too, where these elements are nonaligned (so that, e.g., the rhetoric of corporate identity does not match the experienced reality), a range of sub-optimal outcomes is anticipated, including employee disengagement, customer dissatisfaction, and general organizational atrophy (e.g., Christensen & Cornelissen 2011; Hatch & Schultz 2001).

See also: ▶ COMMUNICATION AS A FIELD AND DISCIPLINE ▶ COMMUNICATION MANAGEMENT ▶ CORPORATE AND ORGANIZATIONAL IDENTITY ▶ CORPORATE REPUTATION ▶ CRISIS COMMUNICATION ▶ ISSUE MANAGEMENT ▶ ORGANIZATION–PUBLIC RELATIONSHIPS ▶ ORGANIZATIONAL COMMUNICATION ▶ ORGANIZATIONAL IMAGE ▶ PUBLIC AFFAIRS ▶ PUBLIC RELATIONS ▶ PUBLIC RELATIONS: MEDIA INFLUENCE ▶ STRATEGIC COMMUNICATION

REFERENCES AND SUGGESTED READINGS

Christensen, L. T. & Cornelissen, J. P. (2011). Bridging corporate and organizational communication: Review, development and a look to the future. *Management Communication Quarterly*, 25(3), 383–414.

Cornelissen, J. (2011). *Corporate communication: Theory and practice*, 3rd edn. Thousand Oaks, CA: Sage.

Fombrun, C. & Rindova, V. (2000). The road to transparency: Reputation management at Royal Dutch/Shell. In M. Schultz, M. J. Hatch, & M. H. Larsen (eds.), *The expressive organization*. Oxford: Oxford University Press, pp. 77–96.

Hatch, M. J. & Schultz, M. (2001). Are the strategic stars aligned for your corporate brand? *Harvard Business Review*, 79(2), 128–135.

Shelby, A. N. (1993). Organizational, business, management, and corporate communication: An analysis of boundaries and relationships. *Journal of Business Communication*, 30, 241–267.

Van Riel, C. B. M. (1995). *Principles of corporate communication*. Englewood Cliffs, NJ: Prentice Hall.

Corporate and Organizational Identity

LARS THØGER CHRISTENSEN
Copenhagen Business School

Identity is a salient issue in modern society and one of the most prominent concerns of contemporary organizations. Like individuals, organizations increasingly talk about 'having' identities, seeking identities, expressing identities, and even changing identities. Identity-related activities, consequently, consume a growing amount of resources in contemporary organizations and involve communication practices at many different levels. Still, the question of what identity means in the context of an organization is far from settled (→ Organizational Communication).

On the one hand, the notion of identity is used to describe the special or unique features that characterize a social entity and set it apart from its surroundings. In this sense, identity is something solid, reliable, and continuous, in other words, something deeply rooted in the 'personality' of the social entity. On the other hand, the notion of shaping and changing identities leaves the impression that identity is an ongoing project that can and should be planned, manufactured, and communicated into existence.

This equivocality is reflected in the literature on *organizational* identity where descriptions of identity as essence and continuity coexist with discussions of identity as projects of communication. With their now classical definition of organizational identity as the "central, distinct, and enduring dimensions of an organization," management scholars Stuart Albert and David Whetten represent the former perspective (Whetten 2006). By contrast, management scholars Blake Ashforth and Fred Mael regard organizational identity as more fluid and malleable and define it as "unfolding and stylized narratives about the 'soul' or essence of the organization" (Ashforth & Mael 1996, 21). From this perspective, organizations enact their identities through the stories they, directly or indirectly, tell about themselves, their past, their ambitions, and their perceptions of the environment.

In the hope of circumscribing conceptual confusion, some writings try to establish a clear distinction between 'corporate identity' and 'organizational identity,' reducing the former to the sum of symbols that organizations seek to manipulate in order to shape their identity (e.g., logos, uniforms, → design, advertisements, stories, etc.), and reserving the latter for the 'deeper' layers of identity, i.e., the organization's 'intrinsic' traits or characteristics. From a communication perspective, however, such a definitional solution is problematic because it implies a clear dividing line between the world of communication and the organizational reality 'behind,' excluding the possibility that corporate symbols and messages are significant forces in the transformation of organizational identities (Christensen & Askegaard 2001).

Because different audiences refer to different aspects when they describe an organization (e.g., its products, logos, stories, behaviors, reputations, etc.), it is evident that the identity of an organization is not a given feature, but a reference point or a theme that we activate whenever we try to express what we believe an organization 'is.' While some versions of this theme seem more powerful than others, backed up, for example, by corporate advertising campaigns or managerial decisions, such official readings of organizational identity are frequently challenged by alternative interpretations provided, e.g., by inquisitive journalists or critical interest groups who claim that their description of the organization is more true or realistic than the official version (Alvesson & Willmott 2002).

Similar conceptual complexity characterizes the related notion of *image* (→ Organizational Image). While some writings seek to reserve 'identity' for the sender side and 'image' for the receiver side of the communication process, the picture becomes fuzzier when we acknowledge, along with social psychologists, that organizational identities are shaped through the perceptions of significant others (Dutton & Dukerich 1991). To influence such perceptions, contemporary organizations carefully manage their messages, including *corporate design* (logos, uniforms, architecture, etc.) and *corporate communications* (commercials, manuals, publications, etc.). Acknowledging that they are important sources of identity for the modern individual, organizations seek to stimulate feelings of identification and belonging among consumers and employees. Organizational identification refers to situations where people define themselves in terms of an organization, including its products, its missions, its slogans, and its values (e.g., Cheney, Christensen, & Dailey 2013).

See also: ▶ ADVERTISING ▶ BRANDING ▶ BRANDS ▶ COMMUNICATION MANAGEMENT ▶ CORPORATE COMMUNICATION ▶ DESIGN ▶ ORGANIZATIONAL COMMUNICATION ▶ ORGANIZATIONAL CULTURE ▶ ORGANIZATIONAL IMAGE

REFERENCES AND SUGGESTED READINGS

Alvesson, M., & Willmott, H. (2002). Identity regulation as organizational control: Producing the appropriate individual. *Journal of Management Studies*, 39(5), 619–644.

Ashforth, B. E. & Mael, F. A. (1996). Organizational identity and strategy as a context for the individual. *Advances in Strategic Management*, 13, 19–64.

Cheney, G., Christensen, L. T., & Dailey, S. L. (2013). Communicating identity and identification in and around organizations. In L. L. Putnam & D. Mumby (eds.), *The Sage Handbook of Organizational Communication*. Thousand Oaks, CA: Sage, pp. 695–716.

Christensen, L. T. & Askegaard, S. (2001). Corporate identity and corporate image revisited: A semiotic perspective. *European Journal of Marketing*, 35(4), 292–315.

Dutton, J. E., & Dukerich, J. M. (1991). Keeping an eye on the mirror: Image and identity in organizational adaptation. *Academy of Management Journal*, 34, 517–554.

Whetten, D. A. (2006). Albert and Whetten revisited: Strengthening the concept of organizational identity. *Journal of Management Inquiry*, 15(3), 219–234.

Corporate Reputation

CRAIG E. CARROLL
New York University

Corporate reputation refers to what is generally said about an organization. Thus, reputations are messages. As messages, reputations are also noise or feedback. Both sources and listeners of reputation messages must decide. A corporate reputation gains credence when people believe it is widely held. A reputation does not necessarily correspond to the truth. Instead, it is sufficient that it is supposed to be true. Once people accept reputation as a social fact, additional information-seeking behavior about the organization, including whether even to become involved with the organization, is reduced (→ Corporate Communication; Organizational Communication).

Reputation has *four dimensions*: awareness, esteem, attributes, and associations. Before an organization has a reputation, people must be aware of its presence. Public esteem concerns the public's liking, trust, admiration, and respect for an organization (→ Organization–Public Relationships). Organizations usually have a reputation for something, but not always. Topics usually involved are attributes or traits. The most common attributes are leadership, workplace culture, social (including environmental) responsibility, governance, and financial performance. Technical efficiency attributes include ethics, quality, innovation, safety, security, and sustainability. Traits are tied to the existence of an organization, and cannot easily be changed without changing the character of the organization. Corporate associations are linkages to attributes, issues, ideas, individuals, or organizations.

Organizations can improve their reputations by managing their behavior, messages, relationships, and impact. Scholars contend that organizations find adjusting their symbolic environment is easier than adjusting their behavior.

Carroll, Greyser, and Schreiber (2012) identify *different types of reputation*, including actual ("what we really are"), conceived reputation ("what we are seen to be"), construed reputation ("what we think others see"), communicated reputation ("what we say we are"), covenanted reputation ("what the brand stands for"), ideal ("what we ought to be"), and desired reputation ("what we wish to be").

See also: ▶ CORPORATE COMMUNICATION
▶ ORGANIZATION–PUBLIC RELATIONSHIPS
▶ ORGANIZATIONAL COMMUNICATION
▶ PUBLIC RELATIONS

REFERENCES AND SUGGESTED READINGS

Bromley, D. B. (1993). *Reputation, image, and impression management*. Chichester: John Wiley.

Carroll, C. E. (2013). *The handbook of communication and corporate reputation*, 1st edn. Oxford: Wiley Blackwell.

Carroll, C. E., Greyser, S. A., & Schreiber, E. (2011). Building and maintaining reputation through communications. In C. Caywood (ed.), *The international handbook of strategic public relations and integrated communications*. New York: McGraw-Hill, pp. 457–476.

Correlation Analysis

RENÉ WEBER
University of California, Santa Barbara

A correlation analysis is a statistical procedure that evaluates the association between two sets of variables. The association between variables can be linear or nonlinear. In communication research, however, correlation analyses are mostly used to evaluate linear relationships. Sets of variables may include one or many variables. Associations between two variables (two sets of one variable) can be analyzed with a *bivariate correlation analysis*. Associations between one (dependent) variable and a set of two or more (independent) variables can be studied using *multiple correlation (regression) analysis*. Relationships between sets of many (independent and dependent) variables can be investigated using *canonical correlation analysis*.

Among the quantitative research methodologies, correlation analyses are recognized as one of the most important and influential data analysis procedures for communication research and for social science research in general (→ Quantitative Methodology). Explanation and prediction are generally considered the quintessence of any scientific inquiry. One can use variables to explain and predict other variables only if there is an association between them. The *Product–Moment Correlation Coefficient* (also known as Pearson's r) is a widely applied measure for the bivariate linear correlation between two variables. A detailed demonstration of all necessary calculations, including the statistical test procedure, can be found in Weber and Fuller (2013).

The product–moment correlation coefficient will be a value between −1 and +1. A value of

0 indicates that the two variables are linearly independent, i.e., have nothing in common. A value of +1 or −1 would be interpreted as a perfect linear positive or negative relationship ('the more of variable X the less of variable Y', or vice versa). The squared correlation coefficient indicates the proportion of common variance between the two variables and is called the 'coefficient of determination.' Many authors have suggested guidelines for the practical interpretation of a correlation coefficient's size. The question is whether a given correlation coefficient indicates a small, medium, or strong association between variables. Weber and Popova (2012), for example, have analyzed thousands of correlations across various areas in communication research. Overall, they found that correlation coefficients in communication research fall close to Cohen's (1988) definition of small, medium, and large effects ($r = .1, .3, .5$, respectively).

See also: ▶ QUANTITATIVE METHODOLOGY

REFERENCES AND SUGGESTED READINGS

Cohen, J. (1988). *Statistical power analysis for the behavioral sciences*. Hillsdale, NJ: Lawrence Erlbaum.
Weber, R. & Fuller, R. (2013). *Statistical methods for communication researchers and professionals*. Dubuque, IA: Kendall Hunt.
Weber, R. & Popova, L. (2012). Testing equivalence in communication research: Theory and applications. *Communication Methods and Measures*, 6(3), 190–213.

Crime and Communication Technology

PAUL EKBLOM
University of the Arts London

Crime has a complex, evolving relationship with the communications *function* and communication *technology*. Crime control involves conventional law enforcement and 'scientific' approaches. Crime varies in target from property to persons, organizations, and systems; in motive from materialism to sex, revenge, and ideology; in complexity from vandalism to people-trafficking. *Fear of crime* independently reduces quality of life, implicating the Media (→ Risk Perception). The *trust* supporting transactions, customarily generated face-to-face, is unavailable from remote communications.

Communications can be *misappropriated* (hardware stolen, service fraudulently obtained); or *mistreated*, including damage via hacking. *Mishandling* includes improperly obtaining/altering messages. *Misjustification* occurs when pedophiles, through self-selecting newsgroups, assume their activities are widespread (→ Network Organizations through Communication Technology). *Misbehavior* includes 'trolling' (aggressive social media messages). Communications *misused* for crime include deception (phishing), selling stolen goods, coordinating riots, and detonating bombs.

Law enforcement has significant limitations. Preventive approaches promising greater capacity and cost-effectiveness and fewer side-effects include situational crime prevention. This changes immediate environments via perceived risk, effort, and reward to influence opportunity and criminals' decisions to offend.

The Conjunction of Criminal Opportunity framework combines situational and offender-based perspectives on causation and prevention. For Collins and Mansell (2004), who apply it to cyberspace, it describes causation of criminal events via offenders predisposed, motivated, and equipped for crime, encountering or engineering crime situations with vulnerable targets in conducive environments. Situations may lack crime-preventers and contain 'crime promoters': careless users, say, or those knowingly supplying illicit passwords.

Designers face tradeoffs between security vs cost, convenience, privacy, and safety. Making systems simultaneously user-friendly whilst abuser-unfriendly demands informed creativity, subtlety, and competence in technology and human factors. Designers of new applications/systems rarely 'think thief': marketing vulnerable products/services generates 'crime harvests,' then awkward retrofitted security. Preventive methods are perishable: crime-preventers, in an arms race, must out-innovate criminals; and anticipate, researching offender capabilities, horizon-scanning, building in future-proofing, and generating varied security measures.

See also: ▶ INTERNET LAW AND REGULATION ▶ MEDIA USE AND CHILD DEVELOPMENT ▶ NETWORK ORGANIZATIONS THROUGH COMMUNICATION TECHNOLOGY ▶ RISK PERCEPTIONS ▶ TERRORISM AND COMMUNICATION TECHNOLOGIES

REFERENCES AND SUGGESTED READINGS

Collins, B. & Mansell, R. (2004). *Cyber trust and crime prevention: A synthesis of the state-of-the-art science reviews.* London: Department for Business, Innovation and Science.

Ekblom, P. (2012) (ed.). *Design against crime: Crime proofing everyday objects.* Boulder, CO: Lynne Rienner.

Home Office (2013). *Cyber crime: A review of the evidence.* London: Home Office.

Crisis Communication

W. TIMOTHY COOMBS
University of Central Florida

A 'crisis' is the perception of an unpredictable event that threatens important stakeholder expectations, significantly impacts the organization's performance, and/or creates negative outcomes. The topic of crisis communication has attracted a great deal of attention from researchers in → public relations, → corporate communication, → marketing, and management. The emphasis of crisis communication is usually about what the organization says and does in response to the crisis, the public statements and actions by management (Benoit 1995; Coombs 2007; → Organizational Communication). The belief is that how an organization communicates during a crisis has important ramifications for how stakeholders will (1) perceive the organization in crisis, such as its reputation and (2) interact with the organization in the future.

Crisis communication can be divided into two broad categories: public crisis communication and private crisis communication. *Public crisis communication* is composed of the messages (words and actions) directed toward stakeholders outside of the crisis team (customers, communities, investors, suppliers, government agencies, news media, and employees). *Private crisis communication* is composed of messages between crisis team members and private messages sent to employees. The public statements made during a crisis are a function of the private discussions and deliberations by the crisis team.

The public crisis communication research has two broad traditions: (1) rhetorical and (2) social-psychological. The *rhetorical tradition* is rooted in apologia (→ Rhetorical Studies). Apologia is a genre that examines how people respond to character attacks, or self-defense. Keith Hearit (1994) adopted apologia to crisis communication. William Benoit (1995) created the image restoration theory (→ Organizational Image) which assumes that communication is goal-directed, and that maintaining a positive image (reputation) is a central goal of communication.

The *social–psychological tradition* is rooted in attribution theory. Attribution theory posits that people search for the cause of events, especially events that are unexpected and negative. People will attribute a cause either to the person involved in the event or to external factors. The causal attributions people make influence their feelings and behaviors toward the actor (Weiner 2006). It is logical to connect crises and attribution theory. Stakeholders will make attributions about the cause of a crisis (a negative event) by assessing crisis responsibility. Stakeholder attributions of responsibility for a crisis to an organization have perceptual and behavioral consequences for the organization (Coombs & Holladay 2005). If the organization is deemed responsible, the reputation (a key perception of an organization) will suffer.

Situational crisis communication theory (SCCT) offers one framework for predicting stakeholder attributions of crisis responsibility and reactions to crises. SCCT argues that by understanding the threat presented by a crisis situation, crisis managers can determine which crisis response strategy or strategies will maximize reputational protection and reduce the likelihood of negative behaviors. SCCT fuses the rhetorical and social–psychological traditions. Situational awareness is the focal point of *private crisis* communication. In general, situational awareness is when the crisis team feels it has enough information and knowledge to make a decision (Kolfschoten et al., 2006). Knowledge is the end result of processing information. Information is the raw material and knowledge is the output (→ Knowledge Management). For the crisis team, situational awareness indicates that there is a perception and understanding of the crisis situation, and the ability to predict its effects and to determine what actions to address.

See also: ▶ CHANGE MANAGEMENT AND COMMUNICATION ▶ CORPORATE COMMUNICATION ▶ IMAGE RESTORATION THEORY ▶ INFORMATION ▶ KNOWLEDGE MANAGEMENT ▶ MARKETING ▶ ORGANIZATIONAL CHANGE PROCESSES ▶ ORGANIZATIONAL COMMUNICATION ▶ ORGANIZATIONAL IMAGE ▶ ORGANIZATION–PUBLIC RELATIONSHIPS ▶ PUBLIC RELATIONS ▶ RHETORICAL STUDIES ▶ TRUST OF PUBLICS

REFERENCES AND SUGGESTED READINGS

Benoit, W. L. (1995). *Accounts, excuses, and apologies: A theory of image restoration*. Albany, NY: SUNY Press.
Coombs, W. T. (2007). Protecting organization reputations during a crisis: The development and application of situational crisis communication theory. *Corporate Reputation Review*, 10(3), 163–176.
Coombs, W. T. & Holladay, S. J. (2005). Exploratory study of stakeholder emotions: Affect and crisis. In N. M. Ashkanasy, W. J. Zerbe, & C. E. J. Hartel (eds.), *Research on emotion in organizations, vol. 1: The effect of affect in organizational settings*. New York: Elsevier, pp. 271–288.
Hearit, K. M. (1994). Apologies and public relations crises at Chrysler, Toshiba, and Volvo. *Public Relations Review*, 20(2), 113–125.
Kolfschoten, G. L., Briggs, R. O., De Vreede, G. J., Jacobs, P. H., & Appelman, J. H. (2006). A conceptual foundation of the thinkLet concept for Collaboration Engineering. *International Journal of Human-Computer Studies*, 64(7), 611–621.
Weiner, B. (2006). *Social motivation, justice, and the moral emotions: An attributional approach*. Mahwah, NJ: Lawrence Erlbaum.

Critical Theory

GRAHAM MURDOCK
Loughborough University

The phrase 'critical theory' was coined by the German philosopher and sociologist Max Horkheimer in his 1937 essay, Critical and Traditional Theory – a manifesto for the approach that he and his colleagues had been developing at the pioneering interdisciplinary Institute for Social Research in Frankfurt. Following Marx, the group, later known as the 'Frankfurt School', set out to reveal the structural processes that blocked the realization and reconciliation of the Enlightenment values of liberty, equality, and solidarity. Witnessing Hitler's spectacular rise to power, they paid particular attention to the role of culture and ideology (→ Culture: Definitions and Concepts).

As Jewish intellectuals their situation became untenable and the Institute moved to Paris and later the United States. Some members worked for the US government's war effort. Others explored the fragility of democratic values and the pressures to conform in American culture. In the group's best-known work, The Dialectic of Enlightenment, Horkheimer and his closest collaborator, Theodore W. Adorno, argued that the most effective conduit of ideology was not overt → propaganda but the 'culture industry' promoted by commercial entertainment (→ Culture Industries; Consumer Culture; Taste Culture). They saw its reliance on standardized cultural forms with proven market reach endlessly reproducing a set repertoire of ideas and images, squeezing out alternatives. For Adorno, an accomplished musician, this betrayed art's true mission of cultivating critical perception by challenging and overturning established expectations.

When World War II ended the Frankfurt group dispersed. Some remained in the United States but Horkheimer and Adorno returned to Germany to re-establish the Institute. The young scholars they attracted, led by Jürgen Habermas, responded to the challenge of rebuilding democracy by stressing the need for a vigorous → public sphere promoting rational deliberation on key issues (→ Deliberativeness in Political Communication). Habermas saw the media system's increasing orientation to entertainment rather than enlightenment posing problems for this project, but offered no general analysis of the tensions between democracy and commercialization. This task was taken up by European and North American scholars, who set out to develop a critical political economy of the contemporary culture industries, with books like Herbert Schiller's Culture, Inc. (1989) and Nicholas Garnham's Capitalism and Communication (1990) establishing a now central tradition of research.

See also: ▶ COMMODIFICATION OF THE MEDIA
▶ CONSUMER CULTURE ▶ CULTURE: DEFINITIONS AND CONCEPTS ▶ CULTURE INDUSTRIES
▶ DELIBERATIVENESS IN POLITICAL COMMUNICATION
▶ POLITICAL ECONOMY OF THE MEDIA
▶ PROPAGANDA ▶ PUBLIC SPHERE ▶ TASTE CULTURE

REFERENCES AND SUGGESTED READINGS

Adorno, T. (1991). *The culture industry: Selected essays on mass culture.* London: Routledge.
Horkheimer, M. & Adorno, T. (1973). *Dialectic of enlightenment.* London: Allen Lane.
Steinert, Heinz (2003). *Culture industry.* Cambridge: Polity.

Cross-Media Marketing

BENJAMIN J. BATES
University of Tennessee

Marketing refers to activities that promote and organize the distribution and sales of products to consumers (→ Marketing). Specifying 'cross-media' focuses on those activities that involve multiple media. As such, the term 'cross-media marketing' can be used to describe two somewhat related phenomena: general marketing and promotion activities that cross media boundaries (→ Advertising Strategies; Markets of the Media); and efforts to increase sales of content by distributing them in a variety of media forms and devices.

Increasing competition and the rise of new media forms have fragmented audiences and markets (→ Audience Segmentation; Consumers in Media Markets), making cross-media marketing more critical to comprehensive marketing strategies. The changing production and distribution cost structures brought about by technological developments have made repurposing and revisioning content in multiple formats and media more viable (→ Information and Communication Technology, Economics of; Media Economics).

Several trends favor increased cross-media marketing. Increased *horizontal integration* among media conglomerates (→ Media Conglomerates) has facilitated cross-media promotions and marketing of content 'in-house,' making such strategies even more cost-efficient. The rise of → Integrated Marketing Communications stresses the value of combining increasingly fragmented audiences over general audiences, while utilizing particular advantages of specific media. The rising emphasis on → branding facilitates interest in expanding content delivery options while recognizing its ability to promote brand value. The rise of the Internet and mobile communication has enabled new forms of interactive and → social marketing and online advertising.

Currently, prospects for both aspects (advertising across media, and distributing content across media) look promising. Industry research is showing increased use of online and mobile media (see reports from Ooyala and Nielsen, among others), while also working on defining better cross media audience metrics. Cross-media marketing is joining online, social, and mobile as mainstream marketing strategies.

See also: ▶ ADVERTISING, ECONOMICS OF
▶ ADVERTISING STRATEGIES ▶ AUDIENCE SEGMENTATION ▶ BRANDING ▶ CONSUMERS IN MEDIA MARKETS ▶ INFORMATION AND COMMUNICATION TECHNOLOGY, ECONOMICS OF
▶ INTEGRATED MARKETING COMMUNICATIONS
▶ MARKETING ▶ MARKETS OF THE MEDIA ▶ MEDIA CONGLOMERATES ▶ MEDIA ECONOMICS ▶ SOCIAL MARKETING ▶ TECHNOLOGY AND COMMUNICATION

REFERENCES AND SUGGESTED READINGS

Feldman, V. (2005). *Leveraging mobile media: Cross-media strategy and innovation policy for mobile media communication.* New York: Physica.
Spinellis, D. (ed.) (2003). *Cross-media service delivery.* Norwell, MA: Kluwer.
Vizjak, A. & Ringlstetter, M. (eds.) (2003). *Media management: Leveraging content for profitable growth.* Berlin: Springer.

Cross-Media Production

DAVID DOMINGO
Université Libre de Bruxelles

Mainly used to refer to → news, cross-media production is the coordinated reporting of events in several media outlets (press, radio, television, websites, mobile apps, Internet). The concept can also apply to other media products systematically designed for and delivered in different media formats. Practitioners and scholars use the term convergence to refer to the process of developing cross-media strategies in newsrooms.

Three *theoretical models* (Garcia Avilés et al. 2013) attempt to capture the sheer diversity of cross-media strategies adopted by media organizations: coordination of isolated platforms, where each outlet retains an autonomous newsroom; integrated newsrooms, where a single team produces stories for any medium; and cross-media, where an effort is made to plan the production of news across outlets, often in the form of a multimedia desk with members of each separate newsroom. In integrated newsrooms, journalists usually gather information using multiple tools and skills and adapt the materials to different outlets. Multi-skill roles may give reporters more control over the final products of their work, but may also overload them with technical procedures, leaving less room for journalistic interpretation.

Empirical research has concentrated on the perceptions of professionals involved in cross-media production. General attitudes toward convergence are positive, but journalists perceive a lack of training, time pressure, and business-driven strategies – namely the reduction of production costs – as the main barriers to success and quality in cross-media production (Singer 2004). Other constraints detected include differences in journalistic culture in the converging newsrooms, media regulations, resistance from unions, and lack of management leadership (Paulussen, Geens, & Vandenbrande 2011).

See also: ▶ MEDIA PRODUCTION AND CONTENT ▶ NEWS ▶ ONLINE JOURNALISM ▶ QUALITY OF THE NEWS

REFERENCES AND SUGGESTED READINGS

García-Avilés, J. A., Kaltenbrunner, A., & Meier, K. (2013). Media convergence revisited: Lessons learned on newsroom integration in Austria, Germany and Spain. Paper presented at the Future of Journalism Conference, University of Cardiff.

Paulussen, S., Geens, D., & Vandenbrande, K. (2011). Fostering a culture of collaboration: Organizational challenges of newsroom innovation. In D. Domingo & C. Paterson (eds.), *Making online news: Newsroom ethnography in the second decade of Internet journalism*. New York: Peter Lang, pp. 3–14.

Singer, J. B. (2004). Strange bedfellows? The diffusion of convergence in four news organizations. *Journalism Studies*, 5(1), 3–18.

Cultivation Effects

NANCY SIGNORIELLI

University of Delaware

Television is the world's storyteller, telling most of the stories to most of the people, most of the time whether viewed on a traditional set, computer, smart phone, or other device. It is unique because it provides a common set of images to virtually all members of society and because people spend more time with television than other media. Cultivation theory is one approach to understanding television's role in society.

Methodologically, cultivation studies begin with identifying the most recurrent and stable patterns in television content. These findings are used to generate questions designed to uncover people's conceptions about social reality (→ Media and Perceptions of Reality). These questions are then presented to samples of the audience. Respondents are divided into light, medium, or heavy viewers on a sample-by-sample basis. The questions about social reality do not mention television but provide answers that reflect images seen on television or those found in reality. The resulting relationships between the amount of viewing and the tendency to respond in terms of what is seen on television reflects television's contribution to viewers' conceptions of social reality, i.e., cultivation effects.

Cultivation analysis assumes that those who watch less television are exposed to more diverse information (from both mediated and interpersonal sources) compared to those who watch more television. Consequently, cultivation theory predicts that the more time a person spends watching television, the more likely it is that their views about reality will reflect what they have seen on television.

Cultivation is a *continual, dynamic, ongoing process*, not a unidirectional flow of influence from television to viewers. Scholars have found two processes that reflect differences in how cultivation may work, 'resonance' and 'mainstreaming.'

First, direct experience may be important for some viewers, and the phenomenon called *resonance* illustrates how a person's everyday reality and patterns of television viewing may provide a double dose of messages that 'resonate' and amplify cultivation. For example, those who live in high-crime urban areas often show stronger relationships between the amount of viewing and stated fear of crime.

Second, television provides a shared daily ritual of highly compelling and informative content for diversified viewers. Television programs typically eliminate boundaries of age, class, and region. Consequently the *mainstream* is a relative commonality of outlooks and values cultivated by consistent and heavy exposure to the world of television. The phenomenon of mainstreaming means that attitudes or behaviors that would ordinarily be attributed to different social or political characteristics may be diminished or absent in groups of heavy television viewers. For example, for some topics, the beliefs of those who designate themselves as liberal or conservative are often very different when they are light television viewers. But, when heavy television viewers who call themselves liberal or conservative are asked about these same topics, those classified as liberals may give responses that are somewhat more conservative and the conservatives may give responses that are somewhat more liberal. The result is that both groups reflect beliefs that are more moderate or middle-of-the-road.

Cultivation analysis is most often associated with concerns about *television violence*. Studies of television content have consistently found that US television's prime-time world has had a consistent and fairly high level of violence for more than 40 years. Approximately six out of ten programs have violence that occurs at the rate of four to five acts of violence per program (Morgan et al. 2009). As a result, cultivation studies have predicted and found that those who watch more television tend to see the world as a more violent place. Those who watch more television are more fearful and believe that they are living in a mean and dangerous world (→ Violence as Media Content; Violence as Media Content, Effects of; Violence as Media Content, Effects on Children of).

Evidence of cultivation is not, however, limited to studies of fear and violence. For example, television programs consistently underrepresent women and women's roles, and analyses have found that those who watch more television tend to give more gender-stereotyped answers to questions about the roles of men and women in society (→ Sex Role Stereotypes in the Media). Scholars are currently looking at the conceptual and methodological implications of cultivation on numerous levels. Cross-cultural studies are helping us to understand the generalizability of cultivation on a worldwide basis. New technologies also are increasingly relevant for cultivation effects research.

See also: *Exposure* to Television ▶ Media and Perceptions of Reality ▶ Media Effects ▶ Media Effects: Direct and Indirect Effects ▶ Sex Role Stereotypes in the Media ▶ Television: Social History of ▶ Violence as Media Content ▶ Violence as Media Content, Effects of ▶ Violence as Media Content, Effects on Children of ▶ Women in the Media, Images of

REFERENCES AND SUGGESTED READINGS

Morgan, M., Shanahan, J., & Signorielli, N. (2009). Growing up with television: Cultivation processes. In J. Bryant & M. B. Oliver (eds.), *Media effects: Advances in theory and research*, 3rd edn. Hillsdale, NJ: Lawrence Erlbaum, pp. 34–49.

Morgan, M., Shanahan, J., & Signorielli, N. (2012). *Living with television now: Advances in cultivation theory and research*. New York: Peter Lang.

Weimann, G. (2000). *Communicating unreality: Mass media and reconstruction of realities*. Thousand Oaks, CA: Sage.

Cultural Imperialism Theories

NANCY MORRIS
Temple University

The cultural imperialism thesis states, broadly, that a powerful country uses cultural means to achieve or support the political and economic ends of imperialism that were historically attained through military force and occupation. In this view, the tools of culture can smooth the way for domination by exposing people to lifestyles to aspire to, products to desire, and even new sources of allegiance (→ Culture: Definitions and Concepts).

The notion of cultural imperialism appears embedded in critiques of the US export of media programming to other countries. Those lodging the charge of cultural imperialism have asserted that Western films, TV shows, and commodities serve as → propaganda for a consumerism-based capitalist model of society (→ Consumer Culture). Gaining adherents for this model, the argument goes, would create overseas markets and political environments favorable to western – particularly US – interests. In the process, the autonomy of receiving countries, as well as their cultures, values, and identities, would be weakened or destroyed.

The intellectual roots of the cultural imperialism thesis lie in world systems theory (Wallerstein 1974), which categorizes the countries of the world by their degree of development and trade domination. Dependency theory, a 1960s and 1970s Latin American outgrowth of world systems theory, elaborated the notion that underdevelopment was not simply a matter of countries' differential progress, but rather conferred structural advantages on developed countries. Therefore it was in the interest of powerful countries to maintain their domination. During the same period, analyses of the global trade in film and television programs confirmed that the US was the world's principal exporter of audiovisual material, while importing very little (Nordenstreng & Varis 1974). Together, these concepts – of the advantage to industrialized countries of domination and of the 'one-way flow' of audiovisual material internationally – contributed to the charge that in their search for worldwide markets and ideologically sympathetic populations, states and transnational corporations were practicing cultural imperialism.

The name most associated with the cultural imperialism thesis is Herbert Schiller. In Mass Communication and American Empire he stated: "Directly by economic control, indirectly by trade and a foreign emulation effect, communications have become a decisive element in the extension of United States world power" (1969, 163). In Schiller's view, US government and business sectors were attempting to mold developing countries' values and institutions to benefit US objectives. Another approach to this issue focused on media content. How to Read Donald Duck, a seminal study by Latin American author Ariel Dorfman and European scholar Armand Mattelart, was first published in Chile in 1971. This book parsed Disney comic books distributed in Latin America and found messages of native inferiority that the authors maintained were designed to induce readers to discard their own cultural identities and accept US superiority.

These analyses both paralleled and intersected debates about the regulation of media imports in the interest of national development (→ Development Communication). This controversy pitted the US/UK conception of the 'free flow of information,' which promoted unregulated markets in news and entertainment against other countries' insistence on the need for balance in media exchanges, particularly of → news. This position was expressed in the → UNESCO-based call for a new world information and communication order (NWICO), which centered on concerns recognizably related to cultural imperialism claims.

There exist few explicit formulations of cultural imperialism as a theory. John Tomlinson notes that cultural imperialism is a "generic concept" that covers various propositions that, while related, do not share a precise meaning (1991, 9). Critics have argued that the concept lacks a clear definition, overlooks the complexities of culture, and disregards the role of audiences in interpreting media texts. Overall, the specific claims of proponents of the cultural imperialism thesis have not been supported by empirical research. As a → critical theory, however, cultural imperialism has provided a framework for thinking about global media flows and the power of state and commerce.

In the twenty-first century, the term has been eclipsed. Digital media, channel proliferation, and the resultant growing capacity for audience members to be content producers have dented the monolithic power of large media corporations. As ways of conceptualizing and analyzing multidirectional cultural interactions, the concepts of cultural hybridity and globalization have largely supplanted cultural imperialism in discussions of international media flows.

See also: ▶ CONSUMER CULTURE ▶ CRITICAL THEORY ▶ CULTURE: DEFINITIONS AND CONCEPTS ▶ DEVELOPMENT COMMUNICATION

▶ GLOBALIZATION THEORIES
▶ INTERNATIONAL COMMUNICATION
▶ NEWS ▶ PROPAGANDA ▶ UNESCO

REFERENCES AND SUGGESTED READINGS

Dorfman, A., & Mattelart, A. (1983[1971]). *How to read Donald Duck: Imperialist ideology and the Disney comic.* New York: Bagnolet/International General.

Nordenstreng, K. & Varis, T. (1974). *Television traffic: A one-way street?* Paris: UNESCO.

Schiller, H. I. (1969). *Mass communications and American empire.* New York: Beacon Press.

Tomlinson, J. (1991). *Cultural imperialism.* Baltimore, MD Johns Hopkins University Press.

Wallerstein, I. (1974). *The modern world system.* New York: Academic Press.

Cultural Patterns and Communication

PETER B. SMITH
University of Sussex

A culture exists when a number of persons interpret the events around them in relatively similar ways. These shared interpretations typically include the → meanings of both the behaviors of others and the physical entities around them. Culture is a concept applicable to marriages, teams, tribes, organizations, and nations. There is less consensus within nations than within smaller groupings, but cross-cultural psychologists have found value in studying nations as cultures (→ Culture: Definitions and Concepts).

By comparing survey responses from over 50 nations, Hofstede (2001) identified dimensions describing cultural differences between nations. These dimensions predict how communication varies between nations. His contrast between *individualism and collectivism* has proved especially fruitful. Within more (mostly western) individualistic nations persons emphasize their personal attributes and see their linkages with others as based on individual choice, which may be terminated if they do not meet one's life goals.

Within more collectivistic nations, persons see their identity more in terms of long-term commitment to family, tribe, or organization. Nations cannot simply be categorized as individualistic or collectivistic, but vary between these extremes.

In individualistic settings, the priority is to establish oneself as attractive, coherent, competent, and trustworthy. In collectivist cultures, communication among one's ingroup emphasizes face and harmony. However, outside one's group, communication may be as direct as is found in individualist cultures, so as to preserve the integrity and honor of one's group. Research (Smith et al. 2013) shows that individualism-collectivism predicts directness of communication, nonverbal aspects of communication (→ Nonverbal Communication and Culture), emotional expression, politeness, concern with face (→ Intercultural Conflict Styles and Facework), embarrassability, receptiveness to types of feedback, styles of negotiation, and response to different advertisements (→ Advertising, Cross-Cultural).

Communication is best understood as an interaction between individuals' dispositions and their broader context. To become effective, individuals must learn how to convey desired meanings within the interpretive system in which they are located. This becomes problematic for those who move from one culture to another (→ Acculturation Processes and Communication).

See also: ▶ ACCULTURATION PROCESSES AND COMMUNICATION ▶ ADVERTISING, CROSS-CULTURAL ▶ CULTURE: DEFINITIONS AND CONCEPTS ▶ GROUP COMMUNICATION ▶ INTERCULTURAL CONFLICT STYLES AND FACEWORK ▶ MEANING ▶ NONVERBAL COMMUNICATION AND CULTURE

REFERENCES AND SUGGESTED READINGS

Hofstede, G. (2001). *Culture's consequences: Comparing values, behaviors, institutions and organizations across nations.* Thousand Oaks, CA: Sage.

Smith, P. B., Fischer, R., Vignoles, V.L., & Bond, M.H. (2013). *Understanding social psychology across cultures.* Thousand Oaks, CA: Sage.

Cultural Products as Tradable Services

KENTON T. WILKINSON
Texas Tech University

The term 'cultural product' refers to media artifacts such as books, newspapers, recorded music, films, television programs, and related audiovisual materials. The international trade in cultural products is often sensitive because they express cultural values of the societies that produce them, yet are also economic goods created, distributed, then interpreted by audiences under market conditions. Thus cultural products' power to influence a society's aesthetic, ideological, and economic environments have led to disagreements over their exchange across political, cultural, and linguistic boundaries. Historically, more developed nations have used cultural products as vehicles for asserting soft power while less developed nations favored restricting products' importation as they endeavored to increase their domestic cultural production capabilities.

During the nineteenth century, as cultural products began to occupy a more central position in cultural and economic relations among nations and social groups, national governments elaborated and began to enforce cultural policies. In the mid-twentieth century, critical scholars combined analyses of mass-media ownership and control with critiques of cultural products' content to assess their economic, ideological, and aesthetic impacts (Horkheimer & Adorno 1996[1944]); → Critical Theory). These themes were later taken up in debates at → UNESCO over a New World Information and Communication Order (MacBride Commission 2004[1980]).

Concerns about undue influence applied through media were articulated in the → cultural imperialism theories which, in the 1960s–1980s, asserted that western culture displaced local culture in less developed nations where imported cultural products overshadowed locally produced media content. The subsequent push toward globalization shifted the focus on cultural products to the effects of free trade (Galperin 1999; → Globalization Theories). With the advent of digital communication in the 1990s–2000s, defining cultural products, analyzing their exchange, and distinguishing among producers and consumers became a challenge (→ Digital Media, History of).

See also: ▶ BOOK ▶ CRITICAL THEORY ▶ CULTURE: DEFINITIONS AND CONCEPTS ▶ CULTURAL IMPERIALISM THEORIES ▶ CULTURE INDUSTRIES ▶ DIGITAL MEDIA, HISTORY OF ▶ GLOBALIZATION THEORIES ▶ MARKETS OF THE MEDIA ▶ POLITICAL ECONOMY OF THE MEDIA ▶ PRINTING, HISTORY OF ▶ UNESCO

REFERENCES AND SUGGESTED READINGS

Galperin, H. (1999). Cultural industries policy in regional trade agreements: The cases of NAFTA, the European Union and MERCOSUR. *Media, Culture and Society*, 21(5), 627–648.

Horkheimer, M. & Adorno, T. W. (1996[1944]). *Dialectic of Enlightenment* (trans. J. Cumming). New York: Continuum.

MacBride Commission (2004[1980]). *Many voices, one world: Towards a new, more just and more efficient world information and communication order* [Twenty-fifth anniversary edition of the 'MacBride Report']. Lanham, MD: Rowman and Littlefield.

Cultural Studies

LAWRENCE GROSSBERG
University of North Carolina at Chapel Hill

Cultural Studies is an interdisciplinary project with a significant presence in the field of communication as well as in other humanities and social sciences. Many formations of Cultural Studies emerged in different geographical and disciplinary locations after World War II – the most well-known being the Birmingham Centre for Contemporary Cultural Studies in the 1960s and 1970s. Unlike the disciplines and many interdisciplinary fields, Cultural Studies is not defined by a singular object, place, or method, but by a focus on the context as a field of struggles to construct, deconstruct, and reconstruct particular sets of relationships. The questions and resources defining any particular formation of Cultural Studies are always a response to the challenges posed by the context understood as a 'problem space.' The theoretical tools, methodological practices, empirical 'objects', and political stakes involved in any analysis are always contextually specific.

While some of these traditions of the project emerged as a result of encounters and conversations with English-language work in Cultural Studies, others, especially in Asia and Latin America, emerged out of their own traditions of cultural and political analysis following World War II. For example, the founding work of Néstor García Canclini and Jesús Martín-Barbero has made Cultural Studies an important political–intellectual project in Latin America. In the English-language literature in communication, the most important and influential figures have been Raymond Williams, Stuart Hall, and James Carey.

Key Concepts

Four key concepts ground the project of Cultural Studies: culture, context, or relationality; power, and the popular. *Culture* has several meanings, which cultural studies holds together productively: (1) symbolic or discursive mediation or meaning-making; (2) a particular set of activities and texts, including art and popular culture; and (3) the whole way of life of a group of people. Hence, every aspect of human life is both partly (but never only) cultural and is part of a larger cultural totality (→ Culture: Definitions and Concepts).

Cultural Studies sees every element or aspect of human life relationally; what something is, is constituted by its relations; taken together, the sum of these relations constitutes a particular lived context. But context defines not only its object but also its research practice. If much academic work moves from the complex to the simple, from the concrete to the typical, Cultural Studies embraces the complexity and singularity of contexts. Culture has to be related to – it is constituted by – everything that is not culture, including, e.g., economics, the state, and various social institutions. This radical contextuality is expressed in the key notion of 'articulation,' which defines the historical and analytic practice of making, unmaking, and remaking relations according to a logic of contingency, 'without guarantees.' Cultural Studies operates in the space between two assumptions: on the one hand, that the structure of lived social reality is inevitable, fixed, and determined, and on the other hand, that social relations have no reality or stability whatsoever.

For Cultural Studies, contexts exist as material *configurations of power*, or better as fields of struggles over power. Here, power is understood as the ongoing production of structures of inequality. One dimension of power (e.g., class) does not necessarily explain another (e.g., gender), nor will changing one necessarily change the other; power operates at different levels, including the state, civil institutions, social differences and modes of belonging, discourses, everyday life, emotions, and the body. Much work has focused on the relations of social, cultural, and political identities and differences – as well as the intersections among them: class, race, ethnicity, gender, sexuality, indiginity, differentially abled, etc. (→ Ethnicity and Exposure to Communication; Popular Communication and Social Class; Feminist and Gender Studies).

In these struggles, culture is a crucial agency for configuring, consolidating, and resisting power. Exhibiting fissures and fault lines that may become active sites of struggle and transformation, power can be seen as always contradictory and incomplete. Cultural Studies examines how power infiltrates, contaminates, and limits the possibilities that people have of living their lives in humane, dignified, and secure ways; it also explores the possibilities for change through an analysis of the existing fields of power. Cultural studies, then, investigates how people are empowered and disempowered by the particular discursive practices through which their everyday lives are articulated in relation to the wider structures of social, economic, and political power.

Finally, Cultural Studies is concerned with the lived realities of power, and thus with an understanding of the popular, not merely as popular culture, but as the full set of maps, logics, and languages within which people understand their lives, calculate values and commitments, and decide on the where and how they belong in the world, and where and how they are willing to accept what is or demand and even produce change. Cultural Studies refuses to assume that people are cultural dopes, passively manipulated by dominant power. Cultural Studies examines how people attempt to assert themselves in the face of power, the determinations that constrain and empower them, and the possibilities available to them. Therefore, Cultural Studies has no single politics. While it puts knowledge in the service of a popular politics, it also attempts to make politics listen to the authority of knowledge.

Research Models and Problematics

Cultural Studies takes many different forms, but the two major presentations can be described as 'the circuit of culture' and conjunctural analysis. In communication, cultural studies is most commonly concerned with the former, describing and intervening in the ways in which texts, → discourses, and other cultural practices are produced within, circulate through, and operate on the everyday life of human beings and the institutions of society. It is often (too simply) presented in terms of the complex relationship among texts, context, and audiences, or among production, circulation, reception, and consumption. Because of its focus on the popular as the everyday lives of 'ordinary' people, such work commonly focuses on popular and media cultures.

Conjunctural analysis has an even broader scope, looking at the struggle to organize the social formation according to the interests of particular groups and the alliances among them. Here the focus is generally on various dimensions, technologies, and social organizations' power – including questions of ideology, hegemony (as consensus, common sense, and/or winning consent to leadership), biopolitics, sovereignty, otherness, capitalism, etc. Generally, the social formation is understood as a field of competing and allied forces battling to win control of the various social spaces and institutions. Society itself is constructed as a field of forces in which temporary and unequal balances are forged at the intersection of economic, political, and cultural struggles and strategies.

See also: ▶ COMMUNICATION AND MEDIA STUDIES, HISTORY ▶ CRITICAL THEORY ▶ CULTURE: DEFINITIONS AND CONCEPTS ▶ DISCOURSE ▶ DISCOURSE ANALYSIS ▶ ETHNICITY AND EXPOSURE TO COMMUNICATION ▶ FEMINIST AND GENDER STUDIES ▶ POPULAR COMMUNICATION AND SOCIAL CLASS ▶ POSTMODERNISM AND COMMUNICATION ▶ POWER IN INTERGROUP SETTINGS

REFERENCES AND SUGGESTED READINGS

Abbas, A. & Nguyet, J. (eds.) (2005). *Internationalizing cultural studies*. Oxford: Blackwell.
Carey, J. W. (1989). *Communication as culture: Essays on media and society*. Boston, MA: Unwin Hyman.
Chen, K-H. (ed.) (1998). *Trajectories: Inter-Asia cultural studies*. London: Routledge.
del Sarta, A., Ríos, A., & Trigo, A. (eds.) (2004). *The Latin American cultural studies reader*. Durham, NC: Duke University Press.
Grossberg, L. (1997). *Cultural studies in the future tense*. Durham, NC: Duke University Press.
Grossberg, L., Nelson, C., & Treichler, P. (eds.) (1992). *Cultural studies*. New York: Routledge.
Miller, T. (ed.) (2001). *A companion to cultural studies*. Oxford: Blackwell.
Morley, D. & Chen, K-H. (eds.) (1996). *Stuart Hall: Critical dialogues in cultural studies*. London: Routledge.

Culture and Communication, Ethnographic Perspectives on

DONAL CARBAUGH
University of Massachusetts-Amherst

Studies of communication and culture have been conducted in a variety of productive ways in several academic fields. Studies with an ethnographic perspective are a subset of these as they highlight cultural variability and do so with ethnographic methodology (→ Cultural Patterns and Communication; Culture: Definitions and Concepts; Ethnography of Communication).

It is assumed that communication and culture are inextricably tied and that their relationship can be studied through ethnographic theory and methodology. This brings several assumptions with it: (1) communication is a situated practice, and process, that is formative of social life; (2) communication is in some sense distinctive in its cultural scenes and communities; and that (3) ethnographic study of the social situations and communities in which communication occurs can indeed unveil the cultural features in communication conduct. In this way, ethnography provides a general way of studying communication that is not simply the implementation of a set of specific methods (such as interviewing and participant observation), but also a theoretical orientation to communication and culture.

Ethnographic studies of communication and culture involve systematic observations of socially situated practices. For example, Carbaugh (2005) has explored how communication among people from different regional and national communities is coded differently. Studies of this kind are conducted ethnographically through four basic modes of inquiry: by describing the communication of concern in exacting and detailed ways; by interpreting the meaningfulness of that communication to those who have produced it; by comparatively analysing the practices so described and interpreted; and occasionally, by critically assessing the resulting intergroup, or intercultural dynamics at play in these interactions. When put together, the set creates robust ethnographic accounts of communication and culture.

See also: ▶ COMMUNICATION: DEFINITIONS AND CONCEPTS ▶ CONVERSATION ANALYSIS ▶ CULTURAL PATTERNS AND COMMUNICATION ▶ CULTURAL STUDIES ▶ CULTURE: DEFINITIONS AND CONCEPTS ▶ DISCOURSE ANALYSIS ▶ ETHNOGRAPHY OF COMMUNICATION ▶ INTERCULTURAL CONFLICT STYLES AND FACEWORK

REFERENCES AND SUGGESTED READINGS

Boromisza-Habashi, D. (2000). *Speaking hatefully: Culture, communication, and political action in Hungary.* University Park, PA: Pennsylvania State University Press.

Carbaugh, D. (2005). *Cultures in conversation.* Mahwah, NJ: Lawrence Erlbaum.

Wilkins, R. (2005). The optimal form: Inadequacies and excessiveness within the "asiallinen" [matter-of-fact] nonverbal style in public and civic settings in Finland. *Journal of Communication,* 55, 383–401.

Culture: Definitions and Concepts

PAUL COBLEY
Middlesex University

The term 'culture' has roots in the Latin verb 'colere,' among whose associated meanings is 'to cultivate.' Commonly, culture has come to be understood as consisting of all the structures and processes of → meaning in which communication takes place. If culture resides in communication, societies with mass communication will have increasingly diverse and diffuse cultures, and no common cultural core.

Summarizing elements of prevalent conceptions of culture across the humanities and social sciences, Jenks (2003, 8–9) offered a *fourfold typology.* First, culture is a cerebral or cognitive *capacity.* This notion considers culture the product of a uniquely human consciousness, an exemplification of the status of humans as 'chosen.' Second, culture is *embodied and collective.* Culture can be seen as evidence of moral development, indeed, an evolutionary feature of humans as a group and species. However, this understanding of culture also informed the civilizing process that was foisted on to 'savage' or 'primitive' societies as part of imperialism and colonialism. Third, culture is a *descriptive category*: it refers to a body of work, "the best which has been thought and said in the world" (Arnold 1869) – special knowledge, training, and socialization whose products are commemorated in museums and archives. Yet, any account of which insights are special or best is not just descriptive, but normative. Fourth, culture has been understood as a *social category.* This is the idea, widespread in contemporary research, that culture constitutes the whole way of life of humans generally and of specific social groups and peoples.

The breadth of such a typology re-emphasizes the open-ended status of culture in modernity. Mass communication has produced a proliferation in the number and types of texts and other cultural artifacts; it has also, in extending their availability, resulted in a blurring of the boundaries between texts intended for the elite and those for the 'masses.' Still, despite reports and debates concerning a collapse of the high-culture/low-culture distinction, it remains important to assess cultural practices in the context of other social structures.

Culture often seems, in this way, to have a consensual core meaning; but it also harbors a *series of connotations* that give rise to continuous scientific as well as social debate. One key connotation of culture is civilization, the idea that participation in a culture qualifies the individual for membership and, even, status within a community. Further, at the community level, culture as ongoing cultivation suggests dynamism, emergence, and potential change, partly in opposition to the static implications of 'tradition,' especially in a modern context. As such, culture generally connotes process and movement: a process of educating and socializing people within specific webs of meaning, and a movement of meanings within and, perhaps, beyond a given community. In the last case, culture may amount to a colonizing process, complementing political and economic imperialism, or extending a national monoculture, e.g., through elite adoption and transformation of popular culture.

The *boundaries of culture* are frequently challenged from both within and without. In the second half of the twentieth century, it became increasingly clear that western culture was producing a number of distinctive 'subcultures' internally. These are generally thought to consist of communities of people who come together to pursue practices and observe customs that are somehow divorced from or in opposition to 'mainstream culture.' Facilitated and amplified by the mass media, subcultures form within as well as across national boundaries. The relation of subcultures to culture in general, however, remains ambiguous. On the one hand, mainstream culture may integrate and co-opt subculture in an ultimately elitist fashion; on the other hand, sub-cultures may transform mainstream culture in an egalitarian direction as sub-cultural vocabularies and styles become naturalized forms of communication in the culture.

Mass communication, globalization (→ Globalization of the Media), and intensified commerce have meant that different cultures are increasingly exposed to diverse communicative practices and traditions – both verbal and nonverbal – far beyond translation in any traditional sense. The idea of monocultures is being challenged by notions of *cultural hybridity*. For example, postcolonial theory has suggested that only mental and physical repression have enabled particular cultures to maintain a mythical monocultural status. Similarly, research on imperialism has noted that western cultures, in addition to imposing themselves on those being colonized, were changed in the interaction (Bhabha 1985; → Cultural Imperialism Theories). In the case of commercial exchanges, cultures can be seen, over time, to enter into a more consensual process of hybridization of culture.

See also: ▶ CULTURAL IMPERIALISM THEORIES ▶ CULTURAL PATTERNS AND COMMUNICATION ▶ CULTURAL PRODUCTS AS TRADABLE SERVICES ▶ CULTURAL STUDIES ▶ CULTURE AND COMMUNICATION, ETHNOGRAPHIC PERSPECTIVES ON ▶ CULTURE INDUSTRIES ▶ GLOBALIZATION OF THE MEDIA ▶ MEANING

REFERENCES AND SUGGESTED READINGS

Arnold, M. (1869). *Culture and anarchy: An essay in political and social criticism*. London: Smith, Elder.
Bhabha, H. K. (1985). Signs taken for wonders: Questions of ambivalence and authority under a tree outside Delhi, May 1817. *Critical Inquiry*, 12(1), 144–165.
Jenks, C. (2003). General introduction. In *Culture: Critical concepts in sociology*, 4 vols. London: Routledge, vol. 1, pp. 1–19.

Culture Industries

C. MICHAEL ELAVSKY
Pennsylvania State University

The study of the culture industries has grown increasingly more complex in the field of communications in light of how expanding research into their organization, activities, and logics connects with evolving arguments related to culture, commercialism, and social control. Largely originating in Adorno and Horkheimer's The Dialectic of Enlightenment (1944), the term 'culture industry' was initially utilized to criticize the proliferation of commercial mass culture and what the authors perceived as the increasingly routinized and dehumanizing techniques employed in the processes of cultural production (→ Critical Theory).

In light of a growing recognition of the greater complexity surrounding cultural production, the term 'cultural industries' emerged as a way of speaking about the varied investigations into institutions that produce symbolic objects/commercial products related to the construction of social meaning, illustrating the dynamic variation among these institutions invested in integrating cultural objects/ideas into the realm of capital.

Interdisciplinary scholarship in the 1970s and 1980s further illuminated how media institutions and products have political and cultural implications beyond their economic relations of production. In turn, several terms – i.e., cultural industries, media industries, production of culture, creative industries, cultural work, cultural economy – have arisen to provide different lenses for examining cultural production from different perspectives. Nonetheless, a consensus has generally emerged which recognizes "the complex, ambivalent, and contested" nature of the cultural industries, the texts they produce, and the social relations of symbolic creativity that constitutes activities within them, while simultaneously acknowledging the very real power they wield as networks of logics and forces (Hesmondhalgh 2012, 3).

Consequently, many of Adorno and Horkheimer's original charges still resonate and remain relevant and pressing concerns today for scholars examining the operations of the cultural industries and their relationship with society. Future research will most certainly continue to explore the links between institutional organization and praxis, technological innovation, culture, power, and the role of agency as they relate to the processes of cultural production and questions of social justice within the expanding realm of global capitalism.

See also: ▶ CRITICAL THEORY ▶ CULTURE: DEFINITIONS AND CONCEPTS

REFERENCES AND SUGGESTED READINGS

Adorno, T., & Horkheimer, M. (1977[1944]). The culture industry: Enlightenment as mass deception. In J. Curran, M. Gurevitch, & J. Wollacott (eds.), *Mass communication and society*. London: Edward Arnold, pp. 349–383.

Hesmondhalgh, D. (2012). *The cultural industries*, 3rd edn. Thousand Oaks, CA: Sage.

Holt, J. & Perren, A. (eds.) (2009). *Media industries: History, theory, and method*. Oxford: Wiley Blackwell.

Cyberfeminism

JENNY SUNDÉN

Södertörn University

Cyberfeminism as feminist theory and practice is a historically specific concept of the 1990s which grew out of feminist uses of the early world wide web. The concept of cyberfeminism was used for the first time by Australian artists' group VNS Matrix in their Cyberfeminist Manifesto for the 21st Century (1991), and soon after by British cultural theorist Sadie Plant. Cyberfeminism refers to a wide range of feminist practices, ranging from high theory to political techno-art, science-fiction writing, game design, and activism.

The work of VNS Matrix shuttled between art, politics, and theory through strategies of irony and parody common to third-wave feminism. Sentences like "The clitoris is a direct line to the matrix," from their manifesto, have not only been interpreted as bad girls talking dirty, but can also be seen as female appropriation of computer technologies that traditionally have been viewed as belonging to a masculine domain.

Theoretically oriented cyberfeminism operates primarily in the intersection of feminist theory and technoscience studies, in relation to which feminist historian of science Donna Haraway's (1991) cyborg is an emblematic figure (→ Cybernetics). Thinkers such as Sandy Stone and Sadie Plant envisioned the Internet as a space in which a feminist utopia could be realized. Stone used her transsexual body as an argument in the area of political transgressions, and imagined cyberspace as a place in which the unexpected compositions of the cross-dressed or transgender body are the norm (→ Gay, Lesbian, Bisexual, and Transgender Media Studies).

Feminist philosopher Rosi Braidotti (1996) argued for a "cyberfeminism with a difference" and pointed at the risks for women in buying into the notion of cyberspace as a place for subversive identity performances, freed from the limitations of the physical body. According to Braidotti, rather than liberating women, this repeats the Cartesian fallacy of separating mind from body. The dream of getting rid of the body reflects an understanding of masculinity as abstraction and of men as physically disconnected and independent, which, she argued, is being remapped onto cyberspace discourses.

See also: ▶ CYBERNETICS ▶ FEMINIST AND GENDER STUDIES ▶ FEMINIST MEDIA ▶ FEMINIST MEDIA STUDIES, TRANSNATIONAL ▶ GAY, LESBIAN, BISEXUAL, AND TRANSGENDER MEDIA STUDIES ▶ POSTFEMINISM

REFERENCES AND SUGGESTED READINGS

Braidotti, R. (1996). Cyberfeminism with a difference. At www.let.ruu.nl/womens_studies/rosi/ braidot1.htm, accessed July 30, 2014.

Haraway, D. J. (1991). A cyborg manifesto: Science, technology, and socialist-feminism in the late twentieth century. In D. J. Haraway (ed.), *Simians, Cyborgs and Women: The Reinvention of Nature*. New York: Routledge, pp. 149–181.

VNS Matrix (1991). Cyberfeminist manifesto for the 21st century. At www.obn.org/reading_room/manifestos/html/cyberfeminist.html, accessed July 30, 2014.

Cybernetics

KLAUS KRIPPENDORFF
University of Pennsylvania

Cybernetics is a transdisciplinary discourse that reflexively addresses circularly organized systems in any form or discipline. Its name was derived by Norbert Wiener (1948) from the Greek 'kybernētēs' for 'steersman,' known for the ability to maintain a course under adverse environmental conditions. Wiener recognized that systems capable of pursuing own goals, including of maintaining themselves, are circularly organized.

Heron of Alexandria (about 400 BC), probably the earliest chronicler of engineering accomplishments, described an unusual mechanism that kept the flame of oil lamps steady. The idea of automata, from mechanical clocks to the golem of Prague, has fueled human imagination for centuries. Situations in which A causes B, B causes C, and C causes A have been chided as inconsistent, tautological, or paradoxical. Yet, Watts's eighteenth-century steam engine, which literally powered the Industrial Revolution, included a regulator embodying that circularity to assure constant performance despite varying loads. During Wiener's tenure at MIT, industrial servo- or feedback mechanisms were being developed. Wiener recognized the generality of circularity and envisioned a science of communication and control within technological, biological, and social systems.

Cybernetics brought together some of the most important postwar intellectuals, including Erving Goffman and Talcott Parsons. Cybernetics quickly expanded its conceptions to embrace neural networks (McCulloch), communication structures in groups (Bavelas), cultural patterns of interaction (Mead), mind (Ashby, Bateson), management (Stafford Beer), and political systems (Karl Deutsch). These scholars shared the fascination for the *abilities of biological and social systems to preserve their integrity* in the face of disturbances from their environments. But when exploring where such systems 'failed,' it became apparent that circular causalities also accounted for predictable escalations, even breakdowns of the very circular organization that constituted them. Explosions, cancer, fights, revolutions, ecological imbalances, and economic growths came to be characterized as morphogenetic, as distinct from homeostatic systems.

Starting with Shannon's mathematical theory of communication, commonly known as → *information theory*, digital conceptions decisively influenced the development of information and mediated communication technologies. Today's digitalization of nearly all media from CDs to the Internet attests to the richer vocabularies provided by digital as opposed to analog conceptions. 'Recursion', the repeated application of a function to its results, turned out to be another productive circularity. Networks and recursions defined two *alternative paths in the development of computers*. Network conceptions gave rise to parallel computers, capable of learning, recursions to state-determined sequential machines, in need of programming. Mathematical conceptions of computation maintained a distinction between data and the operations that transformed them. Von Neumann proposed a way to store programs in the same memory as the data to which they were applied. This enabled programming computers so that programs could call on other programs, including on themselves. It accounted for the exponential growth of computing power.

Cybernetics theorized *other circularities* such as self-references in language (→ Language and Social Interaction), self-fulfilling prophecies in sociology, and autopoiesis in biology. It developed theories of feedback, games, complexity, computation, intelligence amplification, perceptual control, self-replication, emergence, enactment, viable (social) systems, and learning organizations.

The epistemology of cybernetics deviates from the traditional scientific preoccupation with describing the universe by detached observers in at least three ways. First, interactive involvement renders cyberneticians integral parts of the systems of their attention (thus, cyberneticians are reflexive participants, not mere observers). Second, cybernetics encourages building, modeling, or simulating the systems of interest within the constraints of their material affordances.

Third, it does not commit cybernetics to causal explanations. Rather, it locates cybernetic objects in spaces of possibilities, constructed in language, not observable without it. Bateson (1972) recognized the evolutionary nature of cybernetics, suggesting that its theories offer accounts of why something cannot exist while leaving open what could evolve.

Cybernetic epistemology encouraged *two developments*. First, von Foerster's (1996) second-order cybernetics. It celebrates 'the observer' as the key to understanding. The second recognizes cybernetics as a → discourse that constructs realities (not merely describing it). It recognizes cybernetics' double *reflexivity*: As communications, cybernetic theories become validated by what their stakeholders do with them and therefore must account for their consequences. Therefore, cyberneticians need to attend to the increasingly cybernetic nature of the social realities that their work continues to inform or construct and the spaces provided for the discourse to grow responsibly.

Cybernetics did not establish itself as a discipline with its own academic institutions. It remains an enormously productive *transdiscipline*. It gave birth to several disciplines: computer science, artificial intelligence, family systems theory, constructivism, and information science. The prefix 'cyber-' in popular literature about intelligent artefacts is evidence of how the fruits of cybernetics are growing in contemporary culture, fueling a sense of liberation from traditional authorities, geographical and social distances, informational limitations, and technological determinisms.

See also: ▶ COMMUNICATION: HISTORY OF THE IDEA ▶ DISCOURSE ▶ INFORMATION ▶ INTERACTION ▶ INTERPERSONAL COMMUNICATION ▶ LANGUAGE AND SOCIAL INTERACTION

REFERENCES AND SUGGESTED READINGS

Ashby, W. R. (1956). *An introduction to cybernetics.* London: Chapman and Hall.
Bateson, G. (1972). *Steps to an ecology of mind.* New York: Ballantine.
Foerster, H. von (ed.) (1996[1974]). *Cybernetics of cybernetics*, 2nd edn. Minneapolis, MN: Future Systems..
Heims, S. J. (1991). *The cybernetics group.* Cambridge, MA: MIT Press.
Mead, M. (1968). The cybernetics of cybernetics. In H. von Foerster, J. D. White, L. J. Peterson, & J. K. Russell (eds.), *Purposive systems: First annual symposium of the American Society for Cybernetics.* New York: Spartan, pp. 1–11.
Wiener, N. (1948). *Cybernetics, or control and communication in the animal and machine.* New York: John Wiley.

Deception Detection Accuracy

TIMOTHY R. LEVINE
Korea University

Deception detection refers to the extent to which people can correctly distinguish truths and lies. Social scientists have been studying accuracy in deception detection for several decades and this research leads to several well documented conclusions. In general, people are statistically better than chance at correctly distinguishing deceptive and honest messages, but not by much. In experiments where people could obtain 50 percent by mere chance, accuracy averages between 53 percent and 54 percent.

Besides near-chance accuracy, research also finds that most people tend to be truth-biased. That is, most people tend to believe messages more often than they infer lies. Because people guess honesty in deception detection experiments more often than they guess lie, accuracy on truths is typically higher than accuracy for lies. The finding that truth accuracy is higher than lie accuracy is known as the 'veracity effect.'

Slightly-better-than-chance accuracy extends to research using student and non-student samples, motivated and unmotivated lies, lies involving interaction between people and non-interactive lies, spontaneous and planned lies, and is regardless of media. Studies involving face-to-face interaction, videotaped truths and lies, audio-only communication (e.g., telephone), and text-based media all yield accuracy levels slightly above chance.

Although it is commonly believed that liars can be caught by attention to nonverbal deception cues, research does not support nonverbal lie detection. The reason for this is that nonverbal behaviors are simply not very diagnostic (→ Nonverbal Communication and Culture). For example, although many people believe that liars won't look a person in the eye while lying, research shows no difference in gaze between truthful and deceptive communicators. Even cues that have some validity like vocal pitch are only weakly associated with honesty. Instead, most lies are detected either by comparing what is said to some evidence or by getting a lie to confess to a deception.

See also: ▶ NONVERBAL COMMUNICATION AND CULTURE

SUGGESTED READINGS

Bond, C. F., Jr. & DePaulo, B. M. (2006). Accuracy of deception judgments. *Personality and Social Psychology Review*, 10, 214–234.

Hartwig, M., Granhag, P. A., Stromwall, L. A., & Vrij, A. (2005). Detecting deception via strategic disclosure of evidence. *Law and Human Behavior*, 29, 469–484.

Levine, T. R., Serota, K. B. Shulman, H., Clare, D. D., Park, H. S., Shaw, A. S., Shim, J. C., & Lee, J. H.(2011). Sender demeanor: Individual differences in sender believability have a powerful impact on deception detection judgments. *Human Communication Research*, 37, 377–403.

Park, H. S., Levine, T. R., McCornack, S. A., Morrison, K., & Ferrara, M. (2002). How people really detect lies. *Communication Monographs*, 69, 144–157.

Decision-Making Processes in Organizations

MARSHALL SCOTT POOLE
University of Illinois at Urbana-Champaign

IFTEKHAR AHMED
University of North Texas

Organizational decision-making is a primary process in organizations. Three perspectives on decision-making can be distinguished in communication scholarship: (1) as unitary actions taken by a single individual – a manager or leader – or by a group; (2) as driven by the organizational context; and (3) as socially constructed (→ Organizational Communication).

The *rational decision model* aspires to systematize analysis and maximize the returns a decision will yield for the organization. A rational decision-maker gathers complete information about the situation and choices, generates all feasible decision options, evaluates each option thoroughly using an array of criteria that represent the various benefits and costs that the options might yield, and chooses the option that maximizes return. Herbert Simon (1976) and others criticized the classical rational model on the grounds that that decision-makers can rarely obtain complete information, that criteria are often fuzzy and changeable, that it requires too much cognitive capacity to estimate realization of benefits and costs, and that the cognitive load involved in managing all the information that the rational model requires is far beyond the capacity of human and organizational information processing (→ Knowledge Management).

The alternative model of *bounded rationality* better captured the process by which decision-makers operate. Here, decision-makers operate according to the principle of satisficing. In making decisions based on satisficing, decision-makers acquire an understanding of the situation that is sufficient to enable them to proceed and search through available alternatives until they find one that satisfies the criteria that are most important to them in the situation at hand. Studies show that decision-makers with deep experience and expertise in an area make decisions that are as good or better than those by organizations employing the classic rational model (Conrad & Poole 2012, 286–293).

This perspective argues that a decision is not just an isolated action, but is part of a stream of past decisions that provide context for the decision at hand and of future decisions.

According to this perspective, organizational decisions vary widely, from routine, immediate operating decisions, to longer-term decisions by middle managers and staff, to very long-term strategic decisions by top management. The organizational decision process can be described as a set of 'flows' involving a mix of the decision types that move through the organization among departments and parties (Mintzberg 1979). For instance, a problem detected at the operational level and given an immediate 'fix' may then become an object of an exception decision if the fix does not work, and then involve a coordinative decision to handle future cases. If the problem is important enough it may be involved in a strategic decision, which is then implemented through coordinative and operational decisions (Conrad & Poole 2012).

Karl Weick (1995) exemplifies the *social constructionist position* in his argument that people and organizations often act before they think. Many organizational 'decisions' are rationalizations post hoc of actions that members have taken. Decision-making serves a symbolic purpose as a justification and cover for organizational members so that they can appear rational. Narratives serve as an important tool for constructing and rationalizing decisions. Narratives may present an integrative view of the decision consistent with the unitary decision model, different viewpoints suggesting that the decision did not reflect the views of all participants, or a fragmented view of the decision that stresses substantially different viewpoints and interpretations of the same decision (→ Storytelling and Narration).

Conrad (1993) highlights the role of *values in organizational decision-making processes* that are often treated as neutral by the scholars in the three perspectives. Deetz (2003) critiques the larger governance schemes that frame organizational decision-making. He argues that these schemes incorporate a narrow set of values that reflect the interests of stockholders, top management, and elites (→ Schemas; Strategic Framing). For organizational decision-making to be truly responsive to stakeholder concerns, it is important that all stakeholders participate in the decision process without the presumption that some are superior to others, and that all premises be open to consideration.

See also: ▶ KNOWLEDGE MANAGEMENT ▶ ORGANIZATIONAL COMMUNICATION ▶ SCHEMAS ▶ STORYTELLING AND NARRATION ▶ STRATEGIC FRAMING

REFERENCES AND SUGGESTED READINGS

Conrad, C. (ed.) (1993). *The ethical nexus*. Norwood, NJ: Ablex.
Conrad, C., & Poole, M. S. (2012). *Strategic organizational communication*, 7th edn. Malden, MA: Wiley Blackwell.
Deetz, S. (2003). Corporate governance, communication, and getting social values into the decisional chain. *Management Communication Quarterly*, 16(4), 606–611.
Mintzberg, H. (1979). *The structuring of organizations*. Englewood Cliffs, NJ: Prentice Hall.
Simon, H. A. (1976). *Administrative behavior: A study of decision-making processes in administrative organizations*, 3rd edn. New York: Free Press.
Weick, K. (1995). *Sensemaking in organizations*. Thousand Oaks, CA: Sage.

Deliberativeness in Political Communication

HARTMUT WESSLER
University of Mannheim

Deliberativeness denotes a quality of → political communication that centers around argumentative exchange in a climate of mutual respect and civility. Normatively, the standard of deliberativeness is used to evaluate political communication processes and settings, and to suggest possible ways to improve them. Empirically, deliberativeness has been studied in parliamentary debate, in → news media content and television talk shows (→ Broadcast Talk), in online discussion forums and → social media as well as in civil society organizations and everyday political talk among citizens.

Standards of deliberativeness are central to normative theories of deliberative democracy (Gastil 2008), which hold that deliberation fosters both the cognitive quality of political judgment and mutual respect and social cohesion between deliberators. On the *input* side of mediated deliberation deliberativeness is measured by the inclusiveness of political debate, particularly with respect to weakly organized civil society actors. Concerning the *throughput*, research has ascertained the level of substantive engagement between contrasting positions as well as of justifications offered for political positions. On the *output* side demands for substantive consensus as a result of public deliberation have been abandoned in favor of a standard of "reasoned dissent" (Wessler 2008).

In citizen deliberation, the degree of deliberativeness is measured by citizens' argument repertoires, i.e., their awareness of rationales for their own positions as well as for possible counterpositions. Both elements of argument repertoire have been shown to increase with increased exposure to political disagreement in citizens' personal networks. Nondeliberative media content such as, for example, confrontational talk shows tend to reduce tolerance for opposing positions among citizens and thus have detrimental effects on democratic virtues. Empirical research has produced support for some core tenets of deliberative theory although many specific claims still need to be investigated (Mutz 2008).

See also: ▶ BROADCAST TALK ▶ DISCOURSE ▶ NEWS ▶ POLITICAL COMMUNICATION ▶ POLITICAL MEDIA USE ▶ PUBLIC OPINION ▶ SOCIAL MEDIA

REFERENCES AND SUGGESTED READINGS

Gastil, J. (2008). *Political communication and deliberation*. Thousand Oaks, CA: Sage.

Mutz, D. C. (2008). Is deliberative democracy a falsifiable theory? *Annual Review of Political Science*, 11, 521–538. doi:10.1146/annurev.polisci.11.081306.070308

Wessler, H. (2008). Investigating deliberativeness comparatively. *Political Communication*, 25(1), 1–22 doi:10.1080/10584600701807752.

Delphi Studies

STEFAN WEHMEIER
University of Greifswald

Delphi studies are a method to obtain knowledge for decision-making in future tasks. In Delphi studies experts' ideas and opinions are systematically surveyed. The data are gathered through a series of questionnaires interspersed with controlled and anonymous feedback. The goal of most Delphi studies is to create a group consensus. Although the method is named after the Greek oracle at Delphi, it is a young research method: a spin-off from defense research in the beginning of the Cold War.

The principle of Delphi studies is based on panel → surveys; however, in contrast to such surveys, participants in Delphi studies are confronted with feedback from all participants. Two main assumptions are central: first, the judgment of a group is claimed as superior to judgments of individuals, and, second, the multilevel process of opinion forming is preferred as more valid than the single-level process (Häder 2002). The classic design uses formalized questionnaires that are submitted to experts in the fields analyzed. The experts are anonymous; the feedback is sent in an averaged form and the questionnaire is repeated at least once. One main aim of the anonymous answering is to bypass the disadvantages of conventional group questionnaires where social orientation through the identification of communicative or rhetoric leaders has an impact on the result.

The research design differs as the number of questionnaires varies between two and four and the number of participants varies between a dozen and more than 3,000. The main criticisms are that participants feel pressured to find a consensus and that it simplifies the complex tasks of forecasting. In mass communication, Delphi is applied in different fields such as new communication technologies (Beck, Glotz, & Vogelsang 2000) and → public relations (Wehmeier 2009).

See also: ▶ ELECTION SURVEYS ▶ PUBLIC RELATIONS ▶ QUALITATIVE METHODOLOGY ▶ QUANTITATIVE METHODOLOGY ▶ SURVEY

REFERENCES AND SUGGESTED READINGS

Beck, K., Glotz, P., & Vogelsang, G. (2000). *Die Zukunft des Internet: Internationale Delphi-Befragung zur Entwicklung der Online-Kommunikation* [The future of the Internet: An international Delphi study on the development of online communication]. Konstanz: UVK.

Häder, M. (2002). *Delphi-Befragungen* [Delphi questionnaires]. Wiesbaden: Westdeutscher Verlag.

Wehmeier, S. (2009). Out of the fog and into the future. Directions of public relations theory building, research, and practice – a Delphi study. *Canadian Journal of Communication*, 34, 265–282.

Design

RICHARD BUCHANAN
Case Western Reserve University

Design is the human power to conceive, plan, and make all of the products that serve human beings in the accomplishment of their individual and collective purposes. It is both a cultural and practical art, providing a high degree of forethought for communications, artifacts, actions, and organizations (→ Art as Communication). The disciplines of design emerged in a variety of places in Europe and the United States, but the Bauhaus (1918–1933), a school established in Germany during the Weimar period, is widely regarded as the place where these disciplines emerged around a single coherent vision.

Designers and design theorists often recognize four broad classes of products, sometimes called the 'four orders of design,' representing different kinds of design problems. The first area, *mass communication*, focuses on symbols and images, yielding a class of products whose explicit purpose is communication. The evolution of the term 'graphic design' into → 'visual communication' and, most recently, 'communication design' indicates the field that emerged. It is a field of communication and demonstration, presenting information and arguments for audiences in all areas of culture.

The second area of design problems, *mass production*, focuses on physical artifacts, yielding the class of tangible goods, objects, buildings, and technological marvels that are often regarded as the most visible sign of modern technological culture. Communication in this class of products begins with the interface between the product and the person who uses or operates it but also includes the subtle, indirect communication that comes from forms and materials (→ Cultural Patterns and Communication). The third area of problems focuses on *actions and interactions*. This involves the design of activities for living, working, playing, and learning (e.g. interaction design or game design). The fourth class of design problems focuses on the *creation of environments, organizations, and systems*, e.g. "public sector" design.

Many people regard design as an art of styling and aesthetics, concerned primarily with the visual appearance of products. However, designers create products to solve problems, and the central feature of their work is the discovery of the ideas and arguments upon which products are based.

See also: ▶ ART AS COMMUNICATION
▶ CULTURAL PATTERNS AND COMMUNICATION
▶ TECHNOLOGY AND COMMUNICATION
▶ VISUAL COMMUNICATION

REFERENCES AND SUGGESTED READINGS

Buchanan, R. & Margolin, V. (1995). *Discovering design: Explorations in design studies*. Chicago, IL: University of Chicago Press.
Meggs, P. B. (1992). *A history of graphic design*. Hoboken, NJ: John Wiley.
Moholy-Nagy, L. (1947). *Vision in motion*. Chicago, IL: P. Theobald.

Determination Theory in Public Relations

JULIANA RAUPP
Free University of Berlin

Studies under the heading of determination theory focus on the question of how media content is produced. In German-language → public relations research, the term 'determination theory' was coined after an initial study by Baerns (1991, 1st pub. 1985). By conducting an extensive content analysis (→ Content Analysis, Quantitative), Baerns demonstrated that more than two-thirds of all news items appeared to be based on information provided by information subsidies. Based on these results, Baerns argued that public relations activities apparently control the issues and timing of media content. The term 'determination hypotheses' was coined with regard to this statement, and communication scholars in German-speaking countries began for the first time to take PR seriously as a possible determining factor in media content (→ News; Quality of the News).

The main assumption of determination theory is that public relations and → journalism are opponents which both aim at influencing media content. Empirically, determination studies are typically based on input-output analyses: press releases and other information subsidies as well as the media coverage on a certain issue are examined in order to find out the proportion of news articles which rely on identifiable PR sources, on other sources, or on journalists' own investigations. In Baerns' initial study, she calculated that on average 63 percent of the media coverage is based on information subsidies. However, later studies found much lower determination ratios.

Determination theory is criticized for taking into account only one direction of influence, for conceiving the relationship between PR and journalism solely as an adversarial one, and for methodological reasons. Nevertheless, determination theory provides empirical evidence of PR's ability to set the news agenda, and is compatible to research on news values, news bias, and gatekeeping as it focuses on the question of how extra-media information enters the news media and thereby becomes news itself.

See also: ▶ CONTENT ANALYSIS, QUANTITATIVE
▶ JOURNALISM ▶ NEWS ▶ QUALITY OF THE NEWS ▶ PUBLIC RELATIONS

REFERENCES AND SUGGESTED READINGS

Baerns, B. (1987). Journalism versus public relations in the Federal Republic of Germany. In D. L. Paletz (ed.), *Political communication research*. Norwood, NJ: Ablex, pp. 88–107.

Baerns, B. (1991). *Öffentlichkeitsarbeit oder Journalismus? Zum Einfluss im Mediensystem*, 2nd edn [*Public relations or journalism? On influence in the media system*]. Cologne: Wissenschaft und Politik. (Original study published 1985).

Raupp, J. (2008). Determinationsthese [Thesis of Determination]. In G. Bentele; R. Fröhlich, & P. Szyszka (eds.), *Handbuch der Public Relations: Wissenschaftliche Grundlagen und berufliches Handeln*, 2nd edn, (192–208). [*Handbook of Public Relations: Scientific foundations and professional behavior*]. Wiesbaden: VS Verlag.

Development Communication

KARIN GWINN WILKINS
University of Texas at Austin

Development communication refers to strategic communication toward and about social change. Development encompasses intentional strategies designed to benefit the public good, whether in terms of material, political, or social needs. Communication engages mediation by communities, movements, and organizations within these institutional and social structures to promote beneficial dialogic action. This subject is considered in terms of its historical context, academic approaches, and research agendas.

Historical Context

Historically, development strategies have targeted developing countries, meaning those with fewer resources than the wealthier countries supporting bilateral and multilateral development institutions. More recently, development goals have been incorporated into social and political protests, through transnational movements actively engaged in promoting economic, political, social, or cultural progress. Social change may be occurring as a result of a variety of factors, such as long-term shifts in policies and political leadership, economic circumstances, demographic characteristics, normative conditions, and ideological values: development communication intersects with social change at the point of intentional, strategic, organized interventions (→ Planned Social Change through Communication).

Following World War II, development communication emerged as a foreign aid strategy, designed by northern and western institutions to promote modernization among less wealthy countries. Early approaches articulated by Daniel Lerner, Wilbur Schramm, and others advocated the promotion of media toward national modernization. Critics raised concerns with hierarchical communication transmissions devoid of historical, structural, or geopolitical context, with some arguing for more participatory processes (→ International Communication).

Justifications for participatory development have varied greatly (→ Participatory Communication). Development institutions interested in creating efficient and effective projects understand participation as a necessary tool for achieving defined ends. Other → development institutions concerned with the ethical aspects of participation are more likely to conceive of participation as an end in itself, regardless of project outcomes. Some participatory approaches build on more resistant strategies to fight oppressive conditions, inspired through Freire's work in liberation theology. These concerns resonate with recent attention in development to the importance of social and political movements in the broader context of social change.

Although the focus of development communication has changed over time from concerns with modernity, to dependency, cultural imperialism, globalization, participation, and resistance, these shifts have not evolved in a linear fashion (→ Globalization Theories; Cultural Imperialism Theories). Many underlying concerns with power, whether conceived within political-economic structures or within community contexts, or whether posited as hegemonic or pluralist processes, remain. Highlighting experiences of oppression and dominance, a reframing of the 'geometry of development' shifts the landscape of development from nation-states in north/south orientations toward a more fluid sense of transnational collectivities and agencies.

Academic attention to development communication typically addresses programs designed to communicate for social change, or what can be called "communicating for development." More recent critical approaches of development concern "communicating about development," questioning the way that social change projects articulate assumptions about problems, solutions, and communities. These are not mutually exclusive endeavors: ongoing critique and research engaged through communicating about development should contribute to improving strategies for communicating for social change.

Communicating for Development

Communicating for development engages intentional strategies to promote socially beneficial goals. Development problems often addressed through these projects can be found in health, agriculture, governance, population, nutrition, sustainable development, and other subjects. These programs address a variety of themes, such as stimulating economic growth, promoting transparent governance, asserting cultural identities, and creating social spaces for community dialogue, through project implementation.

Communication interventions may help to mobilize support, create awareness, foster norms, encourage behavior change, influence policymakers, or even shift frames of social issues. The goals themselves vary with the underlying approach taken to development, such as social change frameworks based in social marketing, entertainment education, or media advocacy. What unites these approaches is having an intentional, organized strategy toward a specific, noncommercial goal. These types of projects differ, however, in terms of the types of groups they address and the nature of the social change process assumed. Some projects integrate more than one of these types of interventions in broader programmatic efforts. They also may incorporate a variety of mediated technologies as part of their strategic intervention. Communications technologies and processes contribute to these strategic approaches to directed social change.

Communicating about Development

A complementary approach within the broader field of development communication addresses the topic of communication about development. Critical of a development industry that appears to channel resources yet has worsening rather than improving consequences, some scholars position development as a particular → discourse that communicates problematic assumptions about the nature of the problems addressed, appropriate solutions, and communities at risk.

The ideological assumptions of development are deconstructed and criticized in this approach. The underlying issue questions how development communicates particular ideological assumptions, and, moreover, what the implications are in terms of understanding power. Power can be understood as a negotiated and fluid process through which some agencies have the economic, cultural, and other resources to dominate and advance their agendas, whereas other groups have the potential to subvert and resist. Some development strategies explicitly take on the goal of empowerment, advocating the rights and responsibilities of particular communities.

Recent attention to postdevelopment posits social movements as radical alternatives to dominant development structures and ideologies. In this regard, social movements are seen not as a way to transform or improve mainstream development, but as potential channels for resistance. Opening our gaze to the possibilities of more resistant strategies means advocating a more inclusive conceptualization of development and social change.

Research Agendas

Development communication requires research as integral to the dialogic implementation and assessment of programs. Individual projects need to be analyzed not only in terms of their defined objectives, but also as they relate to broader programmatic strategies and underlying social problems. Monitoring and evaluation research allows an assessment of the program consequences, in order to contribute to improving future projects.

Although quite different in strategies implemented and theories engaged, these approaches are united in their attempts to build on communication toward and about social change. Sharing a profound concern with devastating conditions worldwide, critical scholars and advocates broaden their vision of development communication to include concerns with inequities and to advocate for social justice. Development communication continues to offer an increasingly holistic and far-reaching framework for engaging in dialogue and action toward social change. Future research can inform development communication to improve its contribution toward resolving global concerns.

See also: ▶ COMMUNICATION AND SOCIAL CHANGE: RESEARCH METHODS ▶ CULTURAL IMPERIALISM THEORIES ▶ DEVELOPMENT COMMUNICATION CAMPAIGNS ▶ DEVELOPMENT DISCOURSE ▶ DEVELOPMENT INSTITUTIONS ▶ DISCOURSE ▶ GLOBALIZATION THEORIES ▶ INTERNATIONAL COMMUNICATION ▶ PARTICIPATORY COMMUNICATION ▶ PLANNED SOCIAL CHANGE THROUGH COMMUNICATION

REFERENCES AND SUGGESTED READINGS

Dutta, M. (2011). *Communicating social change: Structure, culture, agency.* London: Routledge.
Enghel, F. & Wilkins, K. (eds.) (2012). Communication, media and development: Problems and perspectives. *Nordicom,* Special Issue, 31.
Escobar, A. (1995). *Encountering development: The making and unmaking of the third world.* Princeton, NJ: Princeton University Press.
Gumucio-Dagron, A. & Tufte, T. (2006). *Communication for social change anthology: Historical and contemporary readings.* South Orange, NJ: Communication for Social Change Consortium.
McAnany, E. (2012). *Saving the world: A brief history of communication for development and social change.* Urbana, IL: University of Illinois Press.
Melkote. S. (ed.) (2012). *Development communication in directed social change: A reappraisal of theory and practice.* Singapore: AMIC.
Nedervee Pieterse, J. (2001). *Development theory: Deconstructions/reconstructions.* Thousand Oaks, CA: Sage.
Sparks, C. (2007). *Globalization, development and the mass media.* Thousand Oaks, CA: Sage.
Wilkins, K. & Mody, B. (eds.) (2001). Communication, development, social change, and global disparity *Communication Theory,* Special issue, 11(4).
Wilkins, K., Tufte, T., & Obregon, R. (eds.) (2014). *Handbook of development communication and social change.* Oxford: Wiley Blackwell.

Development Communication Campaigns

J. DOUGLAS STOREY

Johns Hopkins Bloomberg School of Public Health

Contemporary communication campaign theory and practice owe much to public health movements (→ Health Campaigns, Communication in) and to the abolition of slavery movement in America and Britain beginning in the late eighteenth century, both of which are early examples of large-scale organized attempts to influence mass publics through the use of communication.

Beginning in the 1950s, post-World War II reconstruction efforts took full advantage of national broadcasting media to encourage such things as agricultural innovation, childhood immunization, and contraception; and national independence movements used national and local media to create or renew identities based on new political boundaries and mobilize populations to support political agendas. Mixed success with these large national communication campaigns drew attention to structural, political, and economic factors – particularly inequities in access to resources and control over them – that constrain or facilitate access to and use of campaign information. Beginning in the 1970s, these concerns pushed campaigns to re-assess the relationship between campaign designers and their audiences, resulting in more participation by beneficiaries in the design, implementation, and evaluation of campaigns and more integrated, multilevel campaigns that address individual, as well as structural, change (Rogers & Storey 1987).

So-called *social marketing campaigns* (Kotler, Lee, & Roberto 2002) redefine behaviors, such as recycling glass or plastic, or condom use to prevent HIV transmission, as 'products' and apply the principles of marketing to the promotion of behaviors that have personal or social but little or no commercial value for the adopter (→ Social Marketing). Worldwide, commercially oriented campaigns draw inspiration from popular culture and build on social and political structures and trends in order to make their products appealing and relevant to consumers.

Although there are many variations, Rogers and Storey (1987) identify *four attributes that characterize communication campaigns.* (1) Campaigns are purposive; the desired outcomes of campaigns can range from individual cognitive changes in knowledge, attitudes, or behaviors to societal-level structural changes in political systems or the distribution of resources. (2) Campaigns typically target large audiences. (3) Because campaigns are results-oriented, they often specify a time period within which those results should be achieved. (4) Campaigns consist of *an organized set of communication activities*: Communication activities refer not just to the dissemination or exchange of information, but also to the other support functions that make campaigns run smoothly and effectively. The P-Process (Piotrow et al. 1997) describes one such set of activities ranging from systematic audience research, needs assessment and situation analysis, through strategic design, message development and pre-testing, implementation, and monitoring of campaign activities, to campaign evaluation and replanning.

Variations in the ways campaigns are organized and conducted can be described in terms of three broad dimensions: the level of objectives, the locus of desired change, and the locus of benefit (Rogers & Storey 1987). *Level of objectives* refers to the type of effect sought, ranging from relatively simple awareness or knowledge gain to relatively complex mobilization and maintenance of behavior. *Locus of change* refers to whether changes are sought at higher or lower levels of social aggregation from the individual level to the group, community, institutional, or societal level. *Locus of benefit* refers to whether successful achievement of campaign objectives primarily benefits the campaign designers or the campaign audience.

Given the enormous variety of campaigns and campaign objectives, it is difficult to generalize the *effectiveness of campaigns*. For example, Snyder and Hamilton (2002) analyzed 48 health campaigns conducted in the US for which impact evaluation data could be found in the published literature. Overall, they found that health communication campaigns using mass media achieved on average an eight percentage point change in behavior among members of the targeted population, with greater effect sizes achieved by campaigns that targeted larger audiences. The size of the effect varied by type of behavior, with seat belt use, oral health, and alcohol abuse reduction campaigns being the most successful. Greater effects were found for campaigns focused on adoption of new behaviors compared with prevention or cessation of problem behaviors (→ Advertising Effectiveness; Advertising Effectiveness, Measurement of).

See also: ▶ ADVERTISING ▶ ADVERTISING EFFECTIVENESS ▶ ADVERTISING EFFECTIVENESS, MEASUREMENT OF ▶ ADVERTISING STRATEGIES ▶ APPLIED COMMUNICATION RESEARCH ▶ AUDIENCE RESEARCH ▶ AUDIENCE SEGMENTATION ▶ HEALTH CAMPAIGNS, COMMUNICATION IN ▶ MARKETING ▶ META-ANALYSIS ▶ PERSUASION ▶ SEGMENTATION OF THE ADVERTISING AUDIENCE ▶ SOCIAL MARKETING ▶ STRATEGIC COMMUNICATION

REFERENCES AND SUGGESTED READINGS

Kotler, P., Lee, N. R., & Roberto, N. L. (2002). *Social marketing: Improving the quality of life.* Thousand Oaks, CA: Sage.

Piotrow, P. T., Kincaid, D. L., Rimon, J. G., III, & Rinehart, W. E. (1997). *Health communication: Lessons from family planning and reproductive health.* Westport, CT: Praeger.

Rogers, E. M. & Storey, J. D. (1987). Communication campaigns. In C. Berger & S. Chaffee (eds.), *Handbook of communication science.* Thousand Oaks, CA: Sage, pp. 817–849.

Snyder, L. B. & Hamilton, M. A. (2002). A meta-analysis of US health campaign effects on behavior: Emphasize enforcement, exposure, and new information and beware the secular trend. In R. C. Hornik (ed.), *Public health communication: Evidence for behavior change.* Mahwah, NJ: Lawrence Erlbaum, pp. 357–383.

Development Discourse

YOUNG-GIL CHAE
Hankuk University of Foreign Studies

Development discourse refers to the process of articulating knowledge and power through which particular concepts, theories, and practices for social change are created and reproduced (Escobar 1995; Crush 1996). Historically, the approach to development in terms of discourse has evolved out of debates on modernization and Marxist dependency theory rooted in social evolutionism. Departing from the linear models of social progress, this approach to development seeks to articulate the processes and meanings of more nuanced social control and challenges. Epistemological premises are grounded in poststructuralist concepts asserting language and → discourse of development as systematically organizing power through the subjectivity of social actors and their actions.

Attention to development discourse emerged in the 1990s, building upon critical approaches to → development communication studies. Development discourse studies tend to view dominant models of development as a highly contested domain in which dominant groups attempt to assert control over marginalized groups of people (→ Power in Intergroup Settings). Studies of development discourse tend to examine strategic communicative intervention of → development institutions for social change in terms of the constructed problems and solutions designated toward concerned communities (→ Strategic Communication).

Discussions of development discourse often parallel the concept of postdevelopment (Escobar 1995), because they attempt to shift the analytical frame of → discourse analysis to envision the popular resistance of local communities. Instead of reinscribing dominant development projects, they intend to criticize the logics and devices constructed by and for development industries. Thus, they value the knowledge and experiences of local, self-reliant participatory and collective actions as the fundamental sources for alternative social change, both at local and global levels (→ Participatory Communication). Some critics question the feasibility of dominant development discourse to envision an alternative approach to social change (Pieterse 2001). Dominant development discourse fails to offer a venue for restructuring processes of social change, instead providing an 'ideological platform' that benefits the work of the development industry and the logic of the global capitalist system.

See also: ▶ COMMUNITY MEDIA ▶ DEVELOPMENT COMMUNICATION ▶ DEVELOPMENT INSTITUTIONS ▶ DISCOURSE ▶ DISCOURSE ANALYSIS ▶ PARTICIPATORY COMMUNICATION ▶ POWER IN INTERGROUP SETTINGS ▶ STRATEGIC COMMUNICATION

REFERENCES AND SUGGESTED READINGS

Crush, J. (1996). Introduction: Imaging development. In J. Crush (ed.), *The power of development*. London: Routledge.

Escobar, A. (1995). *Encountering development: The making and unmaking of the third world*. Princeton, NJ: Princeton University Press.

Pieterse, J. N. (2001). *Development theory: Deconstructions/reconstructions*. Thousand Oaks, CA: Sage.

Development Institutions

JACOB GROSHEK
Boston University

Development institutions are organizational bodies whose primary goals are to improve conditions in regions that have historically lacked basic levels of physical services and socio-political rights. Many of these bodies engage communication for development strategies (→ Development Communication). At present, there are over 70,000 international organizations with a total budget in the hundreds of billions of dollars devoted to improving social, economic, political, and health conditions around the world, specifically in less developed countries (→ International Communication Agencies). The current status of modern international development organizations can be traced back to the end of World War II and the official launch of the United Nations that helped catalyze international modernization efforts.

In addition to the UN, the US Agency for International Development assists developing countries and employs a wide range of communication strategies to support its programs of disaster relief, poverty eradication, and democratic reform (Melkote & Steeves 2001). In Europe, the Organization for Economic Cooperation and Development (OECD) offers assistance to more than 70 developing countries. One of its major programs promotes information and communication technologies in sustainable economic growth and social welfare. Nongovernmental organizations include trade unions, faith-based organizations, community groups, indigenous peoples' organizations, and foundations under the umbrella title of civil society organizations (e.g. private foundations such as the Bill and Melinda Gates Foundation; Mody 2003; → Transnational Civil Society).

Development organizations operate at the international, regional, national, and community levels. Principal missions among many include developing media organizations, augmenting journalists' rights (Wilson 2004; → Development Journalism), access to Internet and mobile communication networks (Carpentier & Servaes 2006; → United Nations, Communication Policies of), health-care practices, reduction of poverty, or support of migrants (→ Health Campaigns, Communication in).

See also: ▶ DEVELOPMENT COMMUNICATION ▶ DEVELOPMENT JOURNALISM ▶ HEALTH CAMPAIGNS, COMMUNICATION IN ▶ HEALTH COMMUNICATION ▶ INTERNATIONAL COMMUNICATION AGENCIES ▶ TRANSNATIONAL CIVIL SOCIETY ▶ UNESCO ▶ UNITED NATIONS, COMMUNICATION POLICIES OF

REFERENCES AND SUGGESTED READINGS

Carpentier, N. & Servaes, J. (2006). *Towards a sustainable information society: Deconstructing WSIS*. Portland, OR: Intellect.
Directory of Development Organizations (2011). Resource guide to development organizations and the Internet. At www.devdir.org/index.html, accessed August 1, 2014.
Melkote, S. R., & Steeves, H. L. (2001). *Communication for development in the third world: Theory and practice for empowerment*. Thousand Oaks, CA: Sage.
Mody, B. (2003). *International and development communication: A twenty-first-century perspective*. Thousand Oaks, CA: Sage.
Servaes, J. (1999). *Communication for development: One world, multiple cultures*. Cresskill, NJ: Hampton Press.
Wilson, E. (2004). *The information revolution and developing countries*. Cambridge, MA: Massachusetts Institute of Technology Press.

Development Journalism

HEMANT SHAH
University of Wisconsin-Madison

During the 1970s and 1980s, the United Nations Educational, Scientific, and Cultural Organization (→ UNESCO) was the site of vociferous debate about global communication (→ New World Information and Communication Order). Among the most contentious issues in the debate was 'development journalism' – a term referring to the role of the press in the process of socio-economic development, primarily in countries of the south (→ Development Communication).

Development journalism implied an adversarial relationship between independent news media and the government in which reporters offer critical evaluation and interpretation of development plans and their implementation. Development journalism challenges traditional → news values, gives priority to the needs of ordinary people, and recognizes that objectivity is a myth (→ Objectivity in Reporting). It results in news that provides constructive criticism of government and its agencies, informs readers how the development process affects them, and highlights local self-help projects. Critics proclaimed the failure of development journalism despite recognizing the vast differences between how development journalism was originally conceptualized and how the term was appropriated to serve as a rationale for state control of national media.

Shah (1996) has summarized development journalism as comprising the following *five principles*: (1) concerned with social, cultural and political aspects of development, not just the economic; (2) democratic and emphasizing communication from the 'bottom up;' (3) pragmatic and unconventional in its approach to reporting; (4) taking on the role of professional intellectuals, providing energy for social movements and helping create awareness about the need for action; (5) encouraging the production of development journalism at multiple sites, both geographically and within the overall structure of the news industry.

Development journalism is similar to the public journalism approaches to reporting developed in the United States in the 1990s by academics and journalists concerned with a crisis of media and democracy.

See also: ▶ ADVOCACY JOURNALISM ▶ CITIZEN JOURNALISM ▶ DEVELOPMENT COMMUNICATION ▶ FREEDOM OF THE PRESS, CONCEPT OF ▶ JOURNALISM ▶ JOURNALISTS' ROLE PERCEPTION ▶ NEWS VALUES ▶ NEW WORLD INFORMATION AND COMMUNICATION ORDER (NWICO) ▶ OBJECTIVITY IN REPORTING ▶ UNESCO

REFERENCES AND SUGGESTED READINGS

Golding, P. (1974). Media role in national development: Critique of a theoretical orthodoxy. *Journal of Communication*, 24, 39–53.
Shah, H. (1996). Modernization, marginalization, and emancipation: Toward a normative model for journalism and national development. *Communication Theory*, 6, 143–166.
Sussman, L. (1978). Developmental journalism: The ideological factor. In P. C. Horton (ed.), *The third world and press freedom*. New York: Praeger, pp. 74–92.

Skjerdal, T. (2011). Development Journalism Revived: The Case of Ethiopia. *Equid Novi: African Journalism Studies*, 32, 58–74.

Developmental Communication

JON F. NUSSBAUM
Pennsylvania State University

CARLA L. FISHER
George Mason University

Developmental communication is an area of study grounded in psychological as well as sociological research. Pecchioni et al. (2005) in their text "Life-span Communication", which was published to update Nussbaum's (1989) book "Life-span Communication: Normative Processes" define life-span developmental communication as a perspective that "deals with description, explanation, and modification of the communication process across the life span" (p. 10). They also outlined five propositions exemplifying the need for this approach to answer many communication-related inquiries.

Significance of Developmental Communication Research

First, they note that it is important to recognize that communication is, by nature, developmental. In other words, communication is a process over time rather than a single event. Second, they advocate acknowledging multiple influences in order to obtain a comprehensive understanding of interactive behavior. Their third proposition asserts that when scholars examine communication change over the life-span, they must appreciate both quantitative and qualitative change because quantitative changes are useful in depicting "a difference in degree," whereas qualitative changes display a "fundamental departure in the meaning of an event or a relationship" (Pecchioni et al. 2005).

In their final two propositions, they address theory and method. The fourth proposition advocates including all theories that are testable. Most communication theories lack any consideration of development, yet life-span scholars fully appreciate that any theory may be useful in expanding knowledge of communication behavior. Moreover, this perspective does not exclude any theory of behavior or development. As a result, developmental communication studies have been firmly grounded in communication theory (Nussbaum & Friedrich 2005; → Communication Skills across the Life-Span).

Incorporating Communication Theory

Developmental communication studies can incorporate theory from all paradigms of thought (Pecchioni et al. 2005). Pecchioni and colleagues note that, at one end of the spectrum, interpretive and → critical theories are useful in attributing → meaning to social interaction as well as in unveiling factors that influence these experiences (→ Mediated Social Interaction). For instance, an interpretive perspective is useful in examining how we communicatively make sense of our social experiences across time through the use of stories. Similarly, critical approaches, such as power and language studies, aid in illuminating factors, like power, that impact communication over the life-span (→ Power in Intergroup Settings). At the other end of the spectrum, scientific theories enable scholars to examine more universal communicative patterns by using scientific methods to control variables in order to reach more generalizable conclusions from multiple data sets (Pecchioni et al. 2005). The latter approach is more common in the communication discipline as communication theory has typically been generated from this approach (→ Quantitative Methodology).

In addition to the above-mentioned scientific theories, → communication accommodation theory (CAT) has greatly contributed to developmental communication research as well as to the communication discipline as a whole (Ryan et al. 1986; → Intergenerational Communication). Like many life-span studies, CAT views age as a marker related to change. In this case, age is a group identifier that influences behavior leading to generational differences in attitude and behavior. CAT posits that younger adults influenced by negative age stereotypes will over-accommodate their speech with elderly adults. As a result, older adults may encounter negative social experiences with younger generations, which may lead to their avoidance of future interactions. Scholars have also used CAT to advance various models of communication and aging stereotypes. Ryan et al. (1986) introduced the communication predicament of aging model (CPA) to demonstrate that in social interactions, age-related cues (i.e., physical appearance, age, behavior, and socio-cultural signs) activate age-related stereotypes that negatively affect intergenerational interactions, leading for example to over- or under-accommodation results (Coupland et al. 1988). Hummert, Wiemann, & Nussbaum (1994), on the other side, discovered that some stereotypes are positive (→ Social Stereotyping and Communication).

Capturing Communication Development over Time

While developmental communication scholars should be attuned to integrating theory in their investigations, they must also choose methodologies that enable them to capture change over time (Nussbaum et al. 2002; Nussbaum & Friedrich 2005; Pecchioni et al. 2005). A critical area of concern is the issue of capturing intra- versus interindividual change. To date, most life-span communication research has examined interindividual change. These researchers typically utilize cross-sectional designs to compare communicative behavior between age groups. By doing so, scholars can only suggest behavioral change over the life-span. Consequently, cross-sectional studies often produce findings that lead to misinterpretations of intra- versus interindividual changes over time (Schaie & Hofer 2001; Nussbaum et al. 2002; Pecchioni et al. 2005), illustrating the point that in order to fully appreciate, examine, and interpret communication change, designs and methodologies need to capture developmental change utilizing longitudinal methods (→ Longitudinal Analysis).

See also: ▶ ADVERTISING: RESPONSES ACROSS THE LIFE-SPAN ▶ COMMUNICATION ACCOMMODATION THEORY ▶ COMMUNICATION SKILLS ACROSS THE LIFE-SPAN ▶ CRITICAL THEORY ▶ INTERGENERATIONAL COMMUNICATION ▶ INTERPERSONAL COMMUNICATION COMPETENCE AND SOCIAL SKILLS ▶ LONGITUDINAL ANALYSIS ▶ MEANING ▶ MEDIA USE ACROSS THE LIFE-SPAN ▶ MEDIATED SOCIAL INTERACTION ▶ PARENTAL MEDIATION STRATEGIES ▶ POWER IN INTERGROUP SETTINGS ▶ QUANTITATIVE METHODOLOGY ▶ SOCIAL STEREOTYPING AND COMMUNICATION ▶ SOCIAL SUPPORT IN INTERPERSONAL COMMUNICATION

REFERENCES AND SUGGESTED READINGS

Baltes, P. B. (1987). Theoretical propositions of life-span developmental psychology: On the dynamics between growth and decline. *Developmental Psychology*, 23, 611–626.

Baltes, P. B. & Nesselroade, J. R. (1979). The developmental analysis of individual differences on multiple measures. In J. R. Nesselroade & H. W. Reese (eds.), *Life-span developmental psychology: Methodological issues*. New York: Academic Press, pp. 1–40.

Baltes, P. B., Reese, H. W., & Nesselroade, J. R. (1988). *Life-span developmental psychology: Introduction to research methods*. Hillsdale, NJ: Lawrence Erlbaum.

Coupland, J., Coupland, N., Giles, H., Henwood, K., & Wiemann, J. (1988). Elderly self disclosure: Interactional and intergroup issues. *Language and Communication*, 8, 109–133.

Hummert, M. L. (1994). Stereotypes of the elderly and patronizing speech. In M. L. Hummert, J. M. Wiemann, & J. F. Nussbaum (eds.), *Interpersonal communication in older adulthood: Interdisciplinary theory and research*. Thousand Oaks, CA: Sage, pp. 162–184.

Hummert, M. L., Wiemann, M., & Nussbaum, J. F. (eds.), *Interpersonal communication in older adulthood: Interdisciplinary theory and research*. Thousand Oaks, CA: Sage.

Nussbaum, J. F. & Friedrich, G. (2005). Instruction/developmental communication: Current theory, research, and future trends. *Journal of Communication*, 55, 578–593.

Nussbaum, J. F., Pecchioni, L., Robinson, J. D., & Thompson, T. (2000). *Communication and aging*, 2nd edn. Mahwah, NJ: Lawrence Erlbaum.

Nussbaum, J. F., Pecchioni, L., Baringer, D., & Kundrat, A. L. (2002). Lifespan communication. In W. B. Gudykunst (ed.), *Communication yearbook 26*. Mahwah, NJ: Lawrence Erlbaum, pp. 366–389.

Pecchioni, L. L., Wright, K., & Nussbaum, J. F. (2005). *Life-span communication*. Mahwah, NJ: Lawrence Erlbaum.

Ryan, E. B., Giles, H., Bartolucci, G., & Henwood, K. (1986). Psycholinguistics and social psychological components of communication by and with the elderly. *Language and Communication*, 6, 1–24.

Schaie, K. W. & Hofer, S. M. (2001). Longitudinal studies in research on aging. In J. E. Birren & K. W. Schaie (eds.), *Handbook of the psychology of aging*, 5th edn. San Diego, CA: Academic Press, pp. 55–77.

Williams, A. & Nussbaum, J. F. (2001). *Intergenerational communication across the life span.* Mahwah, NJ: Lawrence Erlbaum.

Diffusion of information and innovation

JAMES W. DEARING
Michigan State University

DO KYUN KIM
University of Louisiana Lafayette

'Diffusion' is a multifaceted perspective about social change in which individuals, innovations, and the mediated environment affect how rapidly change occurs. Scholars dating back to the German social philosopher Georg Simmel and the French sociologist Gabriel Tarde theorized about imitative behavior at the level of small groups and within communities, and the relation between these micro-level processes to macro-level social change. In the 100 years since, researchers have conceptualized diffusion at the macro sociological level of sector, system, national or state change (Dearing et al. 2006), the social psychological or communicative level of local relationships and how those linkages affect adoption patterns (Katz & Lazarsfeld 1955), or the psychological level of how individuals perceive innovations (Manning et al. 1995).

Diffusion concepts have been *operationalized and used* to purposively spread pro-social innovations through → development communication in Colombia, Pakistan, Brazil, Nigeria, India, Finland, Korea, Tanzania, Bolivia, Vietnam and other countries. Since 2000, diffusion studies have traced and explained the spread of kindergartens across cultures throughout the world, the spread of schools of choice policies among the 50 states in America, the diffusion of tobacco control policies back and forth between Canadian and US political jurisdictions, the adoption of participatory approaches in community health system planning, the spread of e-commerce, and the online spread of social norms among adolescents. Studies such as these form the basis of the generalized codification of key concepts and the general over-time pattern of diffusion from a literature of thousands of publications as synthesized by the communication scholar Everett M. Rogers in his five editions of Diffusion of Innovations. Diffusion concepts have also contributed importantly to theoretical and conceptual development of social learning theory, social network theory, entertainment education, and dissemination and implementation science in health (Brownson et al. 2012).

Rogers has laid out the *terminology for diffusion theory*. He defines diffusion as "the process in which an innovation is communicated through certain channels over time among the members of a social system" (Rogers 2003, 5). An innovation is anything that potential adopters perceive to be new, inclusive of new ideas and beliefs, explicit and tacit knowledge, processes and protocols, tools and technologies, even value belief systems. The first 2.5 percent of adopters he called "innovators;" the next 13.5 percent "early adopters" (a category that includes the subset of → opinion leaders); followed by the "early majority" (34 percent), "late majority" (34 percent), and "laggards" (16 percent). Diffusion conceptualizes individuals as progressing through stages of change as they first confront, make sense of, and then routinize that which was new to them.

The *underlying causality* is as follows: The perception of newness creates uncertainty in the mind of potential adopters about what they should do or how they should respond to the opportunity presented to them about an innovation. Uncertainty leads to a feeling of discomfort or cognitive dissonance (→ Cognitive Dissonance Theory), which propels the individual to seek out first descriptive information about the innovation (typically through mediated mass and specialty channels) and then evaluative information (through non-mediated and mediated interpersonal channels). Then perception of innovation attributes becomes important. Simplicity, low cost, effectiveness, compatibility, how observable the results of an innovation are, and how trialable an innovation is, are positively related to individual-level adoption and hence system-wide diffusion.

Many diffusionists take a *macro structural perspective* on diffusion, especially those in population planning, demography, economics, international relations, anthropology, and → linguistics. Such scholars conceptualize waves of innovations washing over societies, and serving as the means by which social change occurs, as in → agenda building or → agenda-setting effects. Their units of adoption are countries or cultures. Other scholars, including many in communication studies, conceptualize diffusion at a *micro level* of analysis of focusing on the predictors of positive adoption decisions of individuals or organizations, or interpersonal relations and how they mediate the effects of information exposure about innovations, or local social networks and how network position is related to adoption decisions.

See also: ▶ AGENDA BUILDING ▶ AGENDA SETTING EFFECTS ▶ COGNITIVE DISSONANCE THEORY ▶ DEVELOPMENT COMMUNICATION ▶ LINGUISTICS ▶ OPINION LEADER ▶ TWO-STEP FLOW OF COMMUNICATION

REFERENCES AND SUGGESTED READINGS

Brownson, R., Colditz, G., & Proctor, E. (eds.) (2012). *Dissemination and implementation research in health: Translating science to practice.* Oxford: Oxford University Press.

Dearing, J. W., Maibach, E., & Buller, D. (2006). A convergent diffusion and social marketing approach for disseminating proven approaches to physical activity promotion. *American Journal of Preventive Medicine,* 31(4S), S11–S23.

Katz, E. & Lazarsfeld, P. F. (1955). *Personal influence: The part played by people in the flow of mass communications.* New York: Free Press.

Manning, K. C., Bearden, W. O., & Madden, T. J. (1995). Consumer innovativeness and the adoption process. *Journal of Consumer Psychology,* 4(4), 329–345.

Rogers, E. M. (2003). *Diffusion of innovations,* 5th edn. New York: Free Press.

Digital Divide

SANDRA J. BALL-ROKEACH
University of Southern California

JOO-YOUNG JUNG
International Christian University

'The digital divide' terminology is often used in policy discourse to refer simply to access to information and communication technologies (ICTs). It is a misnomer in at least two ways. First, it suggests that there is something new and different about the particular information and communication inequalities that surround digital technologies, whereas it is just the most recent case of inequality spawned by the advent of new ICTs. Hence, we should include a historical perspective in our examination of communication technologies and inequality. Second, it is the definite article 'the' in 'the digital divide' that falsely suggests a single dimension dividing people into haves and have-nots when it comes to ICTs. Digital divides are better conceived as occurring at multiple levels of analysis and as a multidimensional phenomenon (Norris 2001).

One of the first things that researchers do when a new technology emerges is to track its diffusion through the population to note differences between the people who have early access and those who do not (→ Diffusion of Information and Innovation). The idea of a divide comes with the belief that access privileges people in some way; for example, people with access can communicate farther, more quickly, more easily, and less expensively than people without access. With respect to ICTs, there are continuing large-scale survey research efforts to track patterns of access and utilization (→ Survey). These studies, generally conducted at the *individual or household level of analysis,* uncover familiar patterns. Those with relatively early access to ICTs tend to be well educated, at higher income levels, younger, and members of a majority race or ethnicity (→ Exposure to the Internet).

While the majority of studies are done at the individual or household level, ICT inequalities are also meaningfully analyzed at the *level of community* or residential area. There are, in other words, *divides between communities* that are or are not able to take advantage of resources that are available in digital form; for example, resources offered by institutions that concern quality of everyday-life dimensions such as health, transportation, leisure, education, and political representation. In addition to the individual/household (micro) and community (meso) levels of analysis, there are studies of *digital divides between nation-states* (macro). In this instance the haves are generally the developed world and the have-nots are the developing nations. In addition to the vertical dimension of ICT access (haves/have-nots, haveless) that are of primary concern in the early diffusion of digital technologies, horizontal dimensions of digital divides emerge as people go beyond access to consider *qualitative dimensions* of how ICTs are employed in daily life. For example, the technological quality of connection is likely to affect people's Internet use. Hargittai (2002) speaks of a 'skills divide' or a 'second-level digital divide.' Among those with relatively good ICT access, there are profound differences in the skills people develop when they engage ICTs. Generally, the people who develop higher-level Internet skills are wealthier and better educated.

As with any other communication technology, there are wide variations in what people do with ICTs in the course of seeking to achieve everyday-life personal and social goals. *What people do on the Internet*, for example, may reflect individual differences (e.g., skill level or personal goals), but often these differences are grounded in their socio-cultural and ethnic orientations (Kim, Jung, & Ball-Rokeach 2007). Other important sources of variation include age and gender. There are, furthermore, substantial divides or differences in how people go online (e.g. at home, at work, using a personal computer or a mobile device).

Future research will continue to be focused on the many dimensions of these divides, on the reasons that this language maintains its currency in national and international policy debates, and on the social, political, and economic consequences of failures to adequately address the complexity of the issues in this area.

See also: ▶ COMMUNICATION INEQUALITIES ▶ DIFFUSION OF INFORMATION AND INNOVATION ▶ DIGITAL MEDIA, HISTORY OF ▶ EXPOSURE TO THE INTERNET ▶ ONLINE MEDIA ▶ SURVEY

REFERENCES AND SUGGESTED READINGS

Hargittai, E. (2002). Second-level digital divide: Differences in people's online skills. *First Monday: Peer-reviewed Journal of the Internet*, 7(4). At http://firstmonday.org/ojs/index.php/fm/article/view/942, accessed August 1, 2014.

Huang, J. & Russell, S. (2006). The digital divide and academic achievement. *Electronic Library*, 24(2), 160–173.

Kim, Y.-C., Jung, J.-Y., & Ball-Rokeach, S. J. (2007). Ethnicity, place, and communication technology: Effects of ethnicity on multi-dimensional Internet connectedness. *Information Technology and People*, 20(3), 282–303.

Matei, S. & Ball-Rokeach, S. J. (2003). The Internet in the communication infrastructure of ethnically-marked neighborhoods: Meso or macro-linkage? *Journal of Communication*, 53(4), 642–657.

Norris, P. (2001). *Digital divide: Civic engagement, information poverty, and the Internet worldwide*. Cambridge: Cambridge University Press.

Digital Imagery

PAUL MESSARIS
University of Pennsylvania

In a digital image, patterns of light and color are represented by a rectangular grid of pictorial elements, known as pixels. Variations in brightness or color from one pixel to another occur in terms of discrete, fixed units – hence, 'digitally' – instead of the continuous gradations employed by analog media. These properties of digital images have substantial technological consequences. Digital images can be copied repeatedly with no significant loss of information. Likewise, they can be transmitted without significant loss across computer networks. Perhaps most notably, from a communications perspective, digital images that started out as photographs can be manipulated and altered by computer (→ Photography).

Software for the manipulation of photographs has been widely available since the early 1990s. This development has facilitated the following *types of photo-manipulation*: (1) detaching an object in the image from its background more precisely and more efficiently than was typically the case through traditional cut-and-paste methods; (2) selectively resizing portions of an image relative to the rest of the image; (3) cloning parts of an image and pasting the cloned patterns, colors, or textures elsewhere in the image; and (4) changing an image's brightness, contrast, and/or color values in a much less cumbersome manner than that entailed in traditional photographic darkroom work. In one combination or another, these four types of operations have been responsible for most of the instances of photo-manipulation that have periodically raised public concerns about the social implications of digital imaging.

Two somewhat contradictory tendencies recur in *scholarly analyses* of this aspect of digital imaging. On the one side are those writers who are concerned about the erosion of the evidentiary value of photography. As Mitchell (1992) has argued, during a century and a half of traditional photography, the chemical basis of image creation had underwritten public belief in a causal link between photographs and reality. According to Mitchell, the advent of digital imaging has severed that link and ushered in a new, 'post-photographic era,' in which photographs are now no closer to reality than handmade pictures or other non-photographic images are. In seeming opposition to such views, though, other writers have argued that the 'idea of photographic truth' has always been an illusion and that photographs that were recorded on celluloid and printed on paper have always been subject to alteration through cutting and pasting (Kember 2003). Moreover, since every photograph is the product of an inevitable act of selection as to where and when to record an image, there is a sense in which no photograph can avoid manipulating reality. Accordingly, writers such as Newton (2001) have argued that, far from representing a radical departure from earlier photographic culture, what digital images have brought about is a heightened appreciation of the complex nature of photographic truth and falsehood.

Although issues of photo-manipulation have received the lion's share of attention there are also other important ways in which digital images have affected the nature of visual communication. The other characteristics of digital imaging – their replicability and ease of distribution – are significant in themselves, even when an image has not been manipulated in any significant way. These characteristics are often the focus of studies of nonprofessional users of digital imaging technology (e.g., Griffin 2008). Because the market for digital media has experienced the same trend toward lower prices that has occurred in other sectors of the computer-related economy, the development of digital imaging has led to unprecedented levels of public access to the technologies of visual production, post-production, and distribution. These developments, in turn, have nourished a widespread belief that digital technologies may loosen the grip that large corporate media have historically exercised over the flow of public communication.

See also: ▶ ETHICS IN JOURNALISM ▶ FILM PRODUCTION ▶ MEDIA HISTORY ▶ PHOTOGRAPHY ▶ SPECIAL EFFECTS ▶ VISUAL COMMUNICATION

REFERENCES AND SUGGESTED READINGS

Griffin, M. (2008). Visual competence and media literacy: Can one exist without the other? *Visual Studies*, 23(2), 113–129.

Kember, S. (2003). The shadow of the object: Photography and realism. In L. Wells, (ed.), *The photography reader*. London: Routledge, pp. 202–217.

Messaris, P. (2012). Visual "literacy" in the digital age. *Review of Communication,* 12(2), 101–117.

Mitchell, W. J. (1992). *The reconfigured eye: Visual truth in the post-photographic era.* Cambridge, MA: MIT Press.

Newton, J. (2001). *The burden of visual truth: The role of photojournalism in mediating reality.* Mahwah, NJ: Lawrence Erlbaum.

Ritchin, F. (2009). *After photography.* New York: W.W. Norton & Co., Inc.

Digital Media, History of

WENDY HUI KYONG CHUN
Brown University

BRAXTON SODERMAN
University of California, Irvine

Digital media comprise content created, disseminated, and/or stored using digital computers (digital cinema, websites, etc.; → video games), as well as their physical embodiment (hard drives, DVDs, smartphones, etc.). Digital media are often defined in contrast to 'analog media.' Whereas analog transcription records continuous signals of information in their original form (e.g., a strip of celluloid film that chemically captures actual waves of light), digital systems of encoding break this continuous signal into discrete units and represent this information as binary code, i.e., a series of 1s and 0s stored on and manipulated by a computer (→ Encoding–Decoding). The history of digital media documents the development of computers from glorified calculators to devices that are radically transforming human communications, entertainment, and economic production.

While the history of discrete and digital media can be traced back to the nineteenth century – for example, Joseph Jacquard's weaving loom which used punch card codes to automate complex weaving patterns – the first digital computers where produced during World War II: Konrad Zuse's Z3 calculator, the Colossus machines, and ENIAC. In the decades after the war, improvements in digital hardware inaugurated by these machines gave rise to the fundamental components of digital media.

Higher-level *programming languages*, which enable language-based exchange between man and machine, first appeared with Short Code developed for the UNIVAC system (1950). Interacting with and programming early machines often meant providing them with input in the form of punch cards. The development of real-time interfaces allowed the user to input information into the computer system through various devices and receive output in real time. For example, the WHIRLWIND, a project initiated by the US Navy and MIT to produce a universal cockpit simulator eventually evolved into a continent-wide missile detection system known as SAGE. This system employed a 'light pen' interface which allowed the user to provide the computer with simple commands by touching its display (Edwards 1996). Real-time interfaces were the first step toward developing graphic user interfaces (GUIs) in which computers respond in real time to user input framed as an intervention on a graphical display. Modern GUIs – such as Microsoft Windows or the Mac OS – have made the computer a more accessible vehicle of empowerment for the wider public by hiding the inner workings of the digital machine from the user.

The Internet has provided a means of circulation that makes digital media mass media. The Internet stems from ARPANET, a US military-funded network designed to link together several research sites which transmitted its first message in 1969. In 1983, with the formal adoption of TCP/IP, the Internet proper emerged based on an open protocol to link differently configured local area networks. Commercial transactions were prohibited on the Internet until 1991, and before 1991 popular forms of communications were email (→ Electronic Mail), newsgroups (1979), and Internet Relay Chat (IRC, 1988), as well as multi-user text-based games and public forums (1978). With the arival of visual Internet browsers such as Netscape Navigator in the 1990s the Internet became a mass communications technology and a popular form of digital media with the spread of homepages, search engines, and new businesses such as Amazon.com.

While the history of digital media encompasses the technological structures of digital computation, it also implies the study of digitized media forms such as digital video and sound, video games, and newer forms such as mobile and → social media. Thus, the current landscape for studying the history of digital media is multiple – from the study of the growing importance of the video game to the rise of digital cinema and the history of computer graphics, from the study of new forms of media distribution such as Netflix, YouTube and Tumblr to the history of digital networks that have spurred the growth of cloud computing and powerful social networks such as → Facebook and → Twitter.

One of the most important contributions of the study of the history of digital media as a whole has been the displacement of the idea that the digital inaugurates a radically new culture, divorced from historical change and media transition.

See also: ▶ DIGITAL DIVIDE ▶ ELECTRONIC MAIL ▶ ENCODING–DECODING ▶ FACEBOOK ▶ INFORMATION AND COMMUNICATION ▶ INTERACTIVITY, CONCEPT OF ▶ INTERNET AND POPULAR CULTURE ▶ MEDIA HISTORY ▶ OPEN SOURCE ▶ SOCIAL MEDIA ▶ TWITTER ▶ VIDEO GAMES

REFERENCES AND SUGGESTED READINGS

Campbell-Kelly, M. & Aspray, W. (1996). *Computer: A history of the information machine*. New York: Basic Books.
Edwards, P. (1996). *The closed world: Computers and the politics of discourse in Cold War America*. Cambridge, MA: MIT Press.
Wardrip-Fruin, N. & Montfort, N. (eds.) (2003). *The new media reader*. Cambridge, MA: MIT Press.

Discourse

PAUL COBLEY
Middlesex University

As a common term in English, discourse means any extended verbal communication, such as Jesus's discourse with the people (John 6: 22–71)

or, "The Disinherited Knight then addressed his discourse to Baldwin" (Scott, Ivanhoe). Discourse is lengthy but targeted speech between individuals or between an individual and a group.

As a theoretical term, discourse gained in importance during the twentieth century, both in the relatively new discipline of → linguistics and in the newer discipline of communication study, taking on *two distinct meanings*. First, it refers to stretches of communication beyond the small units that are examined with the traditional methods of linguistic analysis. Second, discourse directs attention to the social origins and consequences of communications.

The first meaning of discourse – units of communication larger than sentences – tends to imply the second meaning – communication as embedded in society – which requires more than a descriptive account of language. As a rhetorical form and a social practice, the concept of discourse further relates to two other conceptions of communication beyond the sentence level. 'Text' is a theoretically neutral concept that refers to a string of verbal or nonverbal signs – written paragraphs, paintings, films, dance performances, gestures, etc. (→ Text and Intertextuality). *Genre* denotes a group of texts that share particular features, and which have been shaped for specific audiences and purposes (→ Genre). As such, genres, in addition to being discourses in themselves, may frame specific social discourses – drama, debate, → journalism, → advertising, etc.

As social discourses, texts and genres ultimately entail the exercise of power. While implicit in earlier understandings of discourse, power was defined as its key constituent following the works of Foucault, providing a reference point for the social understanding of discourse, the second meaning above. Foucault (1980) suggested that a particular manifestation of communication leads to an embodiment of power in discourse. Because the state cannot be omnipotent, power is often exercised (in an apparently nonstate fashion) through discourses. Although discourses open up possibilities for what may be said or thought, their very organization also delimits what can in fact be said or thought in a particular social sphere (→ Spiral of Silence). Such discourses include those addressing the body, education, gender, public health, etc.

See also: ▶ ADVERTISING ▶ GENRE ▶ JOURNALISM ▶ LINGUISTICS ▶ POLITICAL DISCOURSE ▶ SPIRAL OF SILENCE ▶ TEXT AND INTERTEXTUALITY

REFERENCES AND SUGGESTED READINGS

Foucault, M. (1980). Truth and power. In C. Gordon (ed.), *Power/Knowledge: Selected interviews and other writings, 1972–1977*. Hassocks, UK: Harvester, pp. 109–133.

Discourse Analysis

BERTRAM SCHEUFELE
University of Hohenheim

Like qualitative content analysis and → Grounded Theory, discourse analysis can be conceived as a qualitative empirical method of analyzing mostly recorded human communication (→ Content Analysis, Qualitative). In general terms, discourse analysis serves for analyzing written or spoken language use within a society or in public. Discourse analysis quite often implies a normative element. For instance, the critical discourse approach (e. g., Wodak & Meyer 2009) asks about social hierarchies by studying language as a form of social practice. This approach is thus convinced that social and political domination is reproduced by speech, talk, and discourse.

There are different *approaches of discourse analysis* in several scientific disciplines. Some forms refer to poststructuralism (e.g., Michel Foucault), some are based on socio- or psycholinguistics (e.g., Ruth Wodak, Teun A. van Dijk) and some more or less belong to communication research (e.g., William A. Gamson). The historical or critical discourse analysis combines sociological aspects and linguistic elements, as well as aspects of cognitive psychology in a coherent research program. While qualitative content analysis or Grounded Theory can be applied to different text material from different theoretical perspectives, discourse analysis is tied to the theoretical core construct of discourse.

Despite all their differences, most definitions of discourse analysis *share four crucial aspects*: (1) Discourses refer to political or social issues which are relevant for society or at least for a major group of people. (2) The elements of discourses can be arguments, speech acts, neologisms, words, rhetorical strategies, etc. (3) Discourses can be analyzed by studying text corpora like party political programs, official documents, transcripts of parliamentary debates, or historical sources. (4) Discourses are processes of collectively constructing social reality.

See also: ▶ CONTENT ANALYSIS, QUALITATIVE ▶ CONTENT ANALYSIS, QUANTITATIVE ▶ DISCOURSE ▶ GROUNDED THEORY ▶ LANGUAGE AND SOCIAL INTERACTION ▶ LINGUISTICS

REFERENCES AND SUGGESTED READINGS

Bell, A. & Garrett, P. (eds.) (1998). *Approaches to media discourse.* Oxford: Blackwell.
Dijk, T. A. van (ed.) (1985). *Discourse and communication: New approaches to the analysis of mass media discourse and communication.* Berlin: Walter de Gruyter.
Keller, R., Hirsefeld, A., Schneider, W., & Viehöver, W. (ed.) (2006). *Handbuch sozialwissenschaftliche Diskursanalyse.* Bd. 1: *Theorie und Methoden [Handbook of social scientific discourse analysis.* Vol. 1: *Theory and methods],* 2nd edn. Wiesbaden: VS.
Keller, R., Hirsefeld, A., Schneider, W., & Viehöver, W. (ed.) (2010). *Handbuch sozialwissenschaftliche Diskursanalyse.* Bd. 2: *Forschungspraxis [Handbook of social scientific discourse analysis.* Vol. 2: *Research practice].* 4th edn. Wiesbaden: VS.
Titscher, S., Meyer, M., Wodak, R., & Vetter, E. (2000). *Methods of text and discourse analysis.* Thousand Oaks, CA: Sage.
Wodak, R. & Meyer, M. (ed.) (2009). *Methods for critical discourse analysis.* 2nd edn. Thousand Oaks: CA: Sage.

Discourse Comprehension

DONALD G. ELLIS
University of Hartford

Discourse comprehension is the act of interpreting a written or spoken message by integrating the incoming information into the memory or knowledge structures of the interpreter. As such it involves social and pragmatic knowledge as well as grammatical and logical knowledge. People are able to arrive at the correct meaning for a word because they rely on prior knowledge structures such as → scripts (Schank and Abelson, 1977).

Functionality is a first principle of discourse comprehension. Functionality means that all language accomplishes something. Its expression performs some 'work.'

Functionality is contrasted with structural approaches, which are more concerned with language as a formal autonomous system. The main discourse comprehension processes are (a) speech act assignment, (b) the coherence mechanisms that assist with tracking information, and (c) the interpretive codes used by communicators (→ Language and Social Interaction).

A 'speech act' is the performative aspect of an utterance that produces action so the utterance (e.g., "I am sorry for missing the meeting") is the genuine accomplishment of certain action (to apologize). 'Coherence' is concerned with making sequences of messages sensible or coherent. It is concerned with the general organizational patterns that lend order to discourse. Coherence is either local or global (see Ellis 1999) meaning it is concerned with the internal organization of text or larger macro frameworks that manage interpretations. 'Interpretive codes' are at the highest level of generality and account for the subjective and cultural experiences of language users and how these inform the comprehension process. For instance, Katriel (1986) has shown how Israeli Jews and Arabs have ways of speaking that emerge from their respective cultures and how these are sometimes responsible for misunderstandings (→ Intercultural and Intergroup Communication).

Randy: "What are you up to tonight?" Sue: "I've got an exam tomorrow." In this example a speech act would be assigned (question–answer) followed by more general cultural knowledge about the patterns of interaction and history of the relationship to determine speaker intent (Is Randy asking Sue for a date or is it just a general inquiry?). Recent work in communication directs attention to situated cultural context and the practical rules of communicators.

See also: ▶ DISCOURSE ▶ DISCOURSE ANALYSIS ▶ INTERCULTURAL AND INTERGROUP COMMUNICATION ▶ LANGUAGE AND SOCIAL INTERACTION ▶ SCRIPTS ▶ WOMEN'S COMMUNICATION AND LANGUAGE

REFERENCES AND SUGGESTED READINGS

Ellis, D. G. (1999). *From language to communication.* Mahwah, NJ: Lawrence Erlbaum.
Katriel, T. (1986). *Talking straight: Dugri speech in Israeli sabra culture.* Cambridge: Cambridge University Press.
Schank, R. C. & Abelson, R. P. (1977). *Scripts, plans, goals, and understanding.* Hillsdale, NJ: Lawrence Erlbaum.

Discursive Psychology

HEDWIG TE MOLDER

Wageningen University/University of Twente

Discursive psychology examines how psychological issues are made relevant and put to use in everyday talk. The step from assuming that talk reflects to looking at what talk does is paramount. Rather than determining the truth value of what people report, discursive psychologists analyze how direct and indirect appeals to mental states *do* things in the interaction, such as accusing, complaining, and complimenting.

Early work on 'interpretative repertoires' (Potter & Wetherell 1987) is rooted in diverse disciplines such as Wittgensteinian philosophy, ethnomethodology, poststructuralism and social studies of science. Derek Edwards and Jonathan Potter are the founders of what is currently associated with the term discursive psychology. Like conversation analysts (→ Conversation Analysis), discursive psychologists are interested in close empirical investigation of naturally occurring data. They work from detailed transcripts of audio or video recordings, derived from a variety of natural settings such as phone calls between friends and police interrogations.

Discursive psychology shares the *conversation analytic focus* on 'activity sequences' as the core concept for understanding what people do in interaction. The emphasis on turns and sequences rather than isolated spates of talk is both a theoretical and a methodological starting point. Publicly displayed understandings of what is being said are an important 'proof procedure' for the analyst. A sequential focus can be supplemented with a rhetorical analysis by inspecting the discourse for actual or potential alternative versions of what is being said (Edwards 1997).

Edwards and Potter distinguish *three major strands* in discursive psychology. (1) The reworking of traditional psychological topics such as attitude, memory, and → scripts into discursive practices. (2) Studies of how psychological terms are deployed in everyday talk (intent, motive, remembering, seeing, etc.). (3) A strand focusing on psychological themes as they are drawn upon in less overt ways. Recent work in discursive psychology bears a strong resemblance to conversation analytic research, for example with regard to their shared interest in epistemics. Some differences remain, for example concerning the status of cognition (te Molder & Potter 2005).

See also: ▶ CONVERSATION ANALYSIS ▶ IDENTITIES AND DISCOURSE ▶ SCRIPTS

REFERENCES AND SUGGESTED READINGS

Edwards, D. (1997). *Discourse and cognition.* Thousand Oaks, CA: Sage.
Potter, J. & Wetherell, M. (1987). *Discourse and social psychology: Beyond attitudes and behaviour.* Thousand Oaks, CA: Sage.
te Molder, H. & Potter, J. (eds.) (2005). *Conversation and cognition.* Cambridge: Cambridge University Press.

Disney

JANET WASKO

University of Oregon

Though the Walt Disney Company began as an independent production company producing cartoons distributed by other companies, the company developed into one of the largest entertainment conglomerates in the world (→ Media Conglomerates). The Walt Disney Studio was opened in → Hollywood in 1927, introduced Mickey Mouse, the character who came to symbolize the company, and developed short films featuring sound and animation innovations. Disney also developed merchandising connected to its cartoon characters. The company expanded into feature-length animation with Snow White and the Seven Dwarfs (1937) and diversified into television and theme parks in the 1950s. By the 1960s, the Disney → brand was firmly established in live action, animation, television, theme parks, and merchandise. A new management team took over in the mid-1980s and cut costs, implemented new diversification strategies, and further developed corporate synergy. In 1995, the company bought Capital Cities/ABC and for a short while became the world's largest media company. The company purchased the animated studio Pixar in 2006, the comic books company Marvel in 2009, and Lucas Film in 2012. The company reported total revenues of over $42 billion in 2012.

At the end of 2013, the Walt Disney Company included five divisions. The Studio Entertainment division produces and distributes motion pictures, musical recordings, and live stage productions. Consumer Products oversees the merchandising activities of the company, which claims to be the world's largest licensor of intellectual property and the largest publisher of children's books and magazines (→ Intellectual Property Law). The Parks and Resorts division oversees parks and resorts on three continents, a cruise line, a vacation-ownership program, and guided family tours. Media Networks oversees television, cable (→ Cable Television), and radio holdings. Disney's cable activities are highlighted by ESPN, a diversified franchise that includes domestic and international cable networks, regional syndication. The Interactive Media Group creates and distributes Disney content across interactive media platforms, especially games and online services (→ Interactivity, Concept of).

See also: ▶ BRAND ▶ CABLE TELEVISION ▶ HOLLYWOOD ▶ INTELLECTUAL PROPERTY LAW ▶ INTERACTIVITY, CONCEPT OF ▶ MEDIA CONGLOMERATES ▶ SPORTS AND THE MEDIA, HISTORY OF

REFERENCES AND SUGGESTED READINGS

Schickel, R. (1997). *The Disney version: The life, times, art, and commerce of Walt Disney*, 3rd edn. New York: Simon & Schuster.
Wasko, J. (2001). *Understanding Disney: The manufacture of fantasy*. Cambridge: Polity.
Watts, S. (1997). *The Magic Kingdom: Walt Disney and the American way of life*. Boston: Houghton Mifflin.

Diversification of Media Markets

WILLIAM M. KUNZ
University of Washington Tacoma

Diversification is a defining characteristic of modern → media conglomerates. It can be divided into two broad groups: Product diversification involves the expansion of firms into different lines of business or industries; market diversification entails the adaptation of a given product to reach additional customers or users. Product diversification is the most common and can be further classified as either unrelated diversification, also known as corporate or conglomerate diversification, or related diversification, also known as concentric diversification.

There was a time when true product diversification, or corporate diversification, was in vogue, but related or concentric diversification is now far more common. *Concentric diversification* involves the acquisition of firms that are related to the core business in critical areas. This allows firms to improve their strengths and reduce their weaknesses through the investment in logical adjacencies. The News Corp acquisition of Twentieth Century-Fox in 1985 can be used as a line of demarcation, as the Fox deal represents the related diversification that has been dominant since the mid-1980s. In 1986, Rupert Murdoch purchased seven broadcast television stations from Metromedia and launched the Fox Television Network. In short order, Twentieth Century-Fox became the content producer for a string of media outlets around the world (→ News Corporation).

Market diversification is also quite significant in the examination of media firms and markets and has become even more critical with the introduction of new delivery platforms. The most basic form of market diversification is geographic or international diversification (→ Globalization of the Media). One of the defining characteristics of most media products is that almost the entire cost of production is incurred in the creation of the master unit, known as the 'first print' cost in films, with duplicates produced at little additional cost. The motion picture business provides a prime example of the benefits of such diversification. Avatar generated over $750 million at the box office in the United States after its release in

December 2009, but it grossed far more overseas, in excess of $2 billion (→ Cinema; Film Production). The adaptation of products represents another aspect of media diversisification. The evolution of new digital technologies (DVD, pads, smartphones) has created additional distribution channels for media products.

See also: ▶ CINEMA ▶ FILM PRODUCTION ▶ GLOBALIZATION OF THE MEDIA ▶ MEDIA CONGLOMERATES ▶ NEWS CORPORATION

REFERENCES AND SUGGESTED READINGS

Chan-Olmsted, S. M. & Chang, B.-H. (2003). Diversification strategy of global media conglomerates: Examining its patterns and determinants. *Journal of Media Economics*, 16(4), 213–233.

Piscitello, L. (2004). Corporate diversification, coherence, and economic performance. *Industrial and Corporate Change*, 13(5), 757–787.

Rijamampianina, R., Abratt, R., & February, Y. (2003). A framework for concentric diversification through sustainable competitive advantage. *Management Decision*, 41(4), 362–371.

Domestication of Technology

MAREN HARTMANN
Berlin University of the Arts

The domestication of technology is an approach within the area of media appropriation studies. It describes the process of media (technology) adoption in everyday life, and especially within households. Two major strands of the domestication approach have originally been developed, only one of which is clearly within the field of media and communication studies. The other is located in the field of social studies of technology. Other fields have come to forefront in recent years (e.g. → Design; Technology and Communication). The domestication idea was first developed at the beginning of the 1990s, primarily in the UK, but has spread widely since. The research methods similarly moved from ethnographic methods in the beginning to a range of qualitative and quantitative methods since (→ Ethnography of Communication; Quantitative Methodology; Qualitative Methodology). Equally, the original emphasis on the household context has long disappeared to now include a range of environments or social settings.

The original emphasis of the concept on the media's materiality represented a move away from a concentration on the media text to the media itself (→ Medium Theory). The emphasis on the context of media use underlines the close relation to → cultural studies as well as to feminist engagements with media use (→ Feminist and Gender Studies). Other references include technology studies and the diffusion of innovations approach (→ Diffusion of Information and Innovation), but domestication emphasizes the meaning-making via media use (→ Meaning).

In this approach the concept of 'media appropriation' suggests that media are first made, then adopted and integrated as objects that find a place in daily routines, i.e. commodification, imagination, appropriation, objectification, incorporation, and conversion (→ Commodification of the Media). The combination of the media as material objects and content providers is reflected in the idea of 'double articulation.' The challenge for the further development of the domestication concept lies in its open character and its (seemingly contradictory) lack of openness for, the new'.

See also: ▶ COMMODIFICATION OF THE MEDIA ▶ CULTURAL STUDIES ▶ DESIGN ▶ DIFFUSION OF INFORMATION AND INNOVATION ▶ ETHNOGRAPHY OF COMMUNICATION ▶ FEMINIST AND GENDER STUDIES ▶ MEANING ▶ MEDIUM THEORY ▶ QUALITATIVE METHODOLOGY ▶ QUANTITATIVE METHODOLOGY ▶ TECHNOLOGY AND COMMUNICATION

REFERENCES AND SUGGESTED READINGS

Berker, T., Hartmann, M., Punie, Y., & Ward, K. (2006). *Domestication of media and technology*. Maidenhead: Open University Press.

Morley, D. (2003). What's "home" got to do with it? Contradictory dynamics in the domestication of technology and the dislocation of domesticity. *European Journal of Cultural Studies*, 6(4), 435–458.

Silverstone, R. & Hirsch, E. (eds.) (1992). *Consuming technologies: Media and information in domestic spaces*. London: Routledge.

E-Democracy

THOMAS ZITTEL
Goethe-University Frankfurt

The concept of electronic democracy implies the use of electronic media of communication to facilitate political participation and thus to enhance democracy (→ Participatory Communication). It should be kept distinct from 'electronic participation.' The latter focuses on the communication strategies of individual citizens while the former emphasizes the media choices of political authorities and related governmental policies. Research on electronic democracy is built upon a number of core research questions asking about the specific uses of electronic media in democratic contexts, their prerequisites, and their larger ramifications for the democratic process (Coleman & Blumler 2008; Chadwick & Howard 2010).

Research on the specific uses of electronic media stresses *three basic models of electronic democracy*. A first model perceives new electronic media as a cost-effective *means for direct decision-making* via electronic voting. From this perspective, electronic media provide citizens with the necessary information on the issues at stake. Individual choices could then be taken via a simple push of a button in private homes, could be electronically transferred, and could be aggregated in a central computer controlled by voting authorities. A second model portrays electronic media primarily as a means to better *link representatives with their constituents* and to reform the electoral process. According to this view, electronic media enable political representatives to augment the transparency of the parliamentary process, to solicit public opinion on particular policy issues, to implement new forms of citizen consultations, and to allow citizens to elect their representatives via electronic media.

A third model pictures electronic media primarily as a means to *strengthen public dialogue* prior to political decision-making. From this perspective, the functioning of the formal decision-making process – be it representative or direct – is dependent upon informed and enlightened citizens and their opinions. According to proponents of this model of electronic democracy, horizontal electronically mediated communication could serve as a means to organize reasoned public dialogues prior to governmental decisions.

Dramatic changes in media technology are considered a crucial *prerequisite for electronic democracy* (→ Communication Technology and

The Concise Encyclopedia of Communication, First Edition. Edited by Wolfgang Donsbach.
© 2015 John Wiley & Sons, Inc. Published 2015 by John Wiley & Sons, Inc.

Democracy). Generally, this concerns a process that spans a long period of time, encompassing a multitude of technological developments from the first telegraph wire connecting both sides of the Atlantic Ocean in 1862 through to the diffusion of the Internet in the 1990s. However, with regard to electronic democracy, digital media and especially the Internet are considered to be of key importance. The Internet opens up new opportunities for mass communication and also decreases the costs of mass communication. Most importantly, from this perspective, the Internet determines new cultural contexts and related demands that put pressures on governments to adapt and to take advantage of new technological opportunities to communicate and to interact with citizens (Castells 2001).

A fair number of students of electronic democracy contradict notions of crude technological determinism. Instead, they emphasize particular *social or institutional factors* serving as necessary prerequisites for electronic democracy. For example, levels of economic development and social changes in established democracies such as the 'cognitive' and 'postmaterialist' revolutions are considered to spur new participatory needs and thus frame and influence developments in electronic communication and technology (Norris 2001; → Digital Divide). Also, political institutions such as electoral systems or the types of government are considered to constrain political authorities in their strategic media choices and thus their approaches towards electronic democracy (Margolis & Resnick 2000).

The *larger ramifications* of electronic democracy for the democratic process is a last major issue in academic and public debate. Cyber-optimists perceive electronic democracy as a magic bullet that will right all wrongs in current democracies by solving , e.g., current crises in political participation, by allowing for more political pluralism, and by facilitating more reasoned political debate. In contrast, Cyber-skeptics emphasize technological risks and malfunctions and especially the risk of political authorities abusing electronic media to jeopardize civil liberties (Mozorov 2012).

See also: ▶ COMMUNICATION TECHNOLOGY AND DEMOCRACY ▶ DIGITAL DIVIDE ▶ INFORMATION SOCIETY ▶ PARTICIPATORY COMMUNICATION

REFERENCES AND SUGGESTED READINGS

Castells, M. (2001). *The Internet galaxy: Reflections on the Internet, business, and society*. Oxford: Oxford University Press.
Chadwick, A. & Howard, P. N. (eds.) (2010). *Routledge handbook of Internet politics*. London: Routledge.
Coleman, S. & Blumler, J. G. (2008). *The Internet and democratic citizenship: Theory, practice, and policy*. Cambridge: Cambridge University Press.
Margolis, M. & Resnick, D. (2000). *Politics as usual: The cyberspace "revolution."* Thousand Oaks, CA: Sage.
Mozorov, E. (2012). *The Net delusion: The dark side of Internet freedom*. New York: Public Affairs.

Educational Communication

REBECCA B. RUBIN
Kent State University

Educational communication is an umbrella term that encompasses all speaking, listening, and relational constructs and concepts that relate to learning. In the past, researchers have been interested in characteristics of teachers that enhance or hinder learning; student characteristics that increase or inhibit learning; teaching strategies that augment learning; how best to give criticism of student writing and speeches; how best to evaluate student work; how public speaking is best taught; and what should be taught in speech communication and media curricula. More recent work has expanded to the effects of media on children, child development processes, and the use of pedagogical methods and newer technologies to facilitate classroom or distance education.

Historical Development

The speech communication discipline began as a group of teachers interested in how best to instruct students in the basics of public speaking. Interest in how to teach new and different facets of the field emerged on a regular basis in the academic journals as interest grew in public speaking, rhetoric, persuasion, and debate, and later in group, interpersonal, nonverbal, intercultural, health, organizational, and family communication. Scholarly concern about K-12, undergraduate, and graduate curricula, as well as the effectiveness of the basic college communication course and speech across the curriculum, also abounded.

Likewise, early interest in journalism education later extended to radio, television, electronic media, → advertising, → public relations, and new technologies. This latter area expanded over the past few decades into using television as an instructional device and the effects of media content on children (→ Educational Media; Educational Media Content; Instructional Television). More recent interest has been in the use of new technology in the classroom or in place of a classroom. Paralleling these interests were studies focused on how teachers can communicate better in the classroom and contribute scholarship in the education area (→ Pedagogy, Communication in).

Current Research Interests

Most undergraduate and graduate programs offer classes in how best to teach various communication classes in K-12, college undergraduate, graduate, speaking across the curriculum, and basic course settings. Recent *advances in technology* have seen past interest in the use of television in instruction move to interests in distance learning and computer-assisted instructional technology in the classroom. Although lectures enhanced by visual technology have consistently produced greater learning, results are mixed for the superiority of traditional vs web-based vs web-assisted instruction.

Whereas 'communication education' focused on how to teach speech and related communication classes, 'instructional communication,' a broader term, concentrated on how teachers can better communicate with students in the classroom, no matter what the subject.

Research in the *rhetorical approach* found, for instance, that teachers who are clear, make their content relevant, and structure their messages achieve greater understanding. Several different types of questions asked by teachers lead to different types of assessments. For instance, recall questions assess memory, whereas summary questions assess ability to synthesize. Teachers can punish students (i.e., use coercive strategies) for misbehaving, reward them for behaving in acceptable ways, enact legitimate power in classroom management, use referent power to enhance student identification with them, and increase expert power through increased credibility and authority. Teachers use various classroom-management techniques to take charge of the learning environment, and reward-based techniques tend to work far better than punishment-based ones.

Research in the *relational tradition* found that teacher verbal (e.g., use of 'we,' more self-disclosure, informal names, etc.) and nonverbal (e.g., use of smiling, head nods, eye contact, touch, etc.) immediacy tends to result in greater student motivation and liking for the teacher and subject taught. Recent research has even examined effects of teacher self-disclosure on → Facebook on student learning. Teacher humor must also be seen as appropriate in order to be effective at motivating students to learn. These and other teacher behaviors can lead to feelings of significance, value, and confirmation in students, by which students feel empowered to learn just through teacher–student interaction.

As mentioned earlier, one of the main goals of communication education has been to increase *communication skills*. Educators have attempted to identify important skills – message construction, persuading, informing, relating – that can be enhanced through instruction and that can be reliably assessed (→ Student Communication Competence). Through this feedback, students can later reflect upon and critique their own communication outside the classroom.

Two major lines of research have examined the *impact of educational media on learning*. First, interest in all forms of educational media has led to examination of the programs shown and how learning occurs from this content (e.g., Sesame Street; → Educational Media Content). In addition, media literacy programs have been created in school systems to teach children (K-12) and college students how best to critique media messages and understand the commercial nature of the media (→ Media Literacy). The second line of research has examined the use of media in education. Today, PowerPoint, interactive whiteboards, LCD projectors, and other software and hardware technologies are commonplace in instruction, and concern focuses on whether the technology enhances or diverts learning efforts. Often, social networking sites substitute for face-to-face interpersonal interaction.

Future Research

Computer technology at all levels of education has changed the nature of the communication classroom. Journalism students no longer pound out news stories on manual typewriters, and speech students are expected to enhance their presentations with electronic media products. Furthermore, when teachers move from the role of information presenter to that of guide, coach, motivator, or facilitator, the nature of communication will change, especially when highly evolved interactive multimedia technology is involved. Effectiveness of distance education most likely will emerge as a related topic, again as the variety of interactive channels increases for interaction with students.

Other trends have been to examine the *interactive teaching/learning environment* and the use of teams in the classroom (Shelton, et al. 1999). Much of the research in the past 20–25 years has actually examined the teacher–student communication environment, identifying communication behaviors that can enhance learning. This interaction has become more mediated through use of email, bulletin boards, chatrooms, blogs, Facebook, Skype, tweets, and other out-of-class opportunities for interaction.

See also: ▶ ADVERTISING ▶ CLASSROOM STUDENT–TEACHER INTERACTION ▶ COMMUNICATION APPREHENSION: INTERVENTION TECHNIQUES ▶ EDUCATIONAL MEDIA ▶ EDUCATIONAL MEDIA CONTENT ▶ FACEBOOK ▶ INSTRUCTIONAL TELEVISION ▶ MEDIA LITERACY ▶ PEDAGOGY, COMMUNICATION IN ▶ PUBLIC RELATIONS ▶ STUDENT COMMUNICATION COMPETENCE ▶ TEACHER COMMUNICATION STYLE ▶ TEACHER INFLUENCE AND PERSUASION

REFERENCES AND SUGGESTED READINGS

Allen, M., Mabry, E., Mattrey, M., Bourhis, J., Titsworth, S., & Burrell, N. (2004). Evaluating the effectiveness of distance learning: A comparison using meta-analysis. *Journal of Communication*, 54, 402–420.

Gayle, B. M., Preiss, R. W., Burrell, N., & Allen, M. (eds.) (2006). *Classroom communication and instructional processes: Advances through meta-analysis.* Mahwah, NJ: Lawrence Erlbaum.

Mills, C. B. & Carwile, A. M. (2009). The good, the bad, and the borderline: Separating teasing from bullying. *Communication Education*, 58, 276–301.

Morreale, S., Backlund, P., Hay, E., & Moore, M. (2011). Assessment of oral communication: A major review of the historical development and trends in the movement from 1975 to 2009. *Communication Education*, 60(2), 255–278.

Morreale, S. P. & Pearson, J. C. (2008). Why communication education is important: The centrality of the discipline in the 21st century. *Communication Education*, 57, 224–240.

Mottet, T. P., Richmond, V. P., & McCroskey, J. C. (eds.) (2006). *Handbook of instructional communication: Rhetorical and relational perspectives.* Boston, MA: Allyn and Bacon.

Rubin, R. B. (2009). Measurement in instructional communication. In R. B. Rubin, A. M. Rubin, E. E. Graham, E. M. Perse, & D. R. Seibold (eds.), *Communication research measures II: A sourcebook.* New York: Routledge, pp. 43–56.

Shelton, M. W., Lane, D. R., & Waldhart, E. S. (1999). A review and assessment of national educational trends in communication instruction. *Communication Education*, 48, 228–237.

Spector, J. M., Merrill, M. D., Elen, J. & Bishop, M. J. (2013) (eds.). *Handbook of research for educational communications and technology*, 4th edn. New York: Springer.

Vangelisti, A. L., Daly, J. A., & Friedrich, G. W. (eds.) (1999). *Teaching communication: Theory, research, and methods*, 2nd edn. Mahwah, NJ: Lawrence Erlbaum.

Educational Media

SHALOM M. FISCH
MediaKidz Research & Consulting

The idea of using mass media for educational purposes is by no means a new one. Books, songs, games: all of these are forms of media that have served as effective educational tools for centuries. There is a tremendous range of processes through which educational media are *produced*. At one end of the spectrum, some producers create media based entirely on their own creative instincts. At the other end of the spectrum lies the model used by production companies such as Sesame Workshop (formerly Children's Television Workshop) where production staff, educational content experts, and researchers collaborate closely at all stages of production (→ Educational Media Content).

Perhaps the most prominent – and certainly the most extensively researched – example of an educationally effective television series is Sesame Street. Studies demonstrate that extended viewing of this series produces significant immediate effects on a wide range of academic skills among preschool children (e.g., knowledge of the alphabet, vocabulary size, letter–word knowledge, math skills, sorting and classification). Comparable effects have been found for international co-productions of Sesame Street in countries such as Mexico, Turkey, Portugal, and Russia. In addition, several *longitudinal studies* have found long-term effects of the series as well. In the longest-term study to date, even high-school students who had watched more educational television – and Sesame Street in particular – as preschoolers had significantly higher grades in English, mathematics, and science in junior high or high school. They also used books more often, showed higher academic self-esteem, and placed a higher value on academic performance (→ Educational Television, Children's Responses to).

Because *interactive media* are newer than educational television, less research is currently available to evaluate their impact on children's learning. Students' use of the Internet as an informational resource opens the opportunity for unprecedented access to material on a tremendous range of topics. Yet students' reliance on online information is also a matter of some concern, because much of the information posted on the Internet is not subject to the same sort of review or validation as material published in a book or newspaper. As a result, information found online may be subject to blatant inaccuracy or bias that children fail to recognize. Although the area has not yet been researched extensively, several empirical studies have shown that well-designed *computer games* and applications can serve as useful tools for both formal and informal education (→ Computer Games and Child Development).

In contrast to the extensive empirical research literature, there have been far fewer attempts to construct *theoretical models* of the cognitive processing responsible for such effects. Fisch's (2004) *capacity model* predicts that comprehension of educational content will be stronger, not only when the resource demands for processing the educational content are low, but when the resource demands for processing the narrative content are low as well. Mayer and Moreno's (2003) cognitive theory of learning from media (CTLM) approach to high-tech multimedia is also grounded in the integration of information and the limitations of working memory. According to this model, users learning from multimedia must attend to and acquire information from multiple sensory modalities (visual, auditory, tactile, etc.), and their ability to do so is constrained by the limitations of working memory.

Today, it is increasingly common for projects to span more than one media platform, so that (for example) an educational television series might be accompanied by a related website, hands-on outreach materials, or even a museum exhibit or live show. This raises questions as to how learning from combined use of related, multiple-media platforms (known as *cross-platform learning*) compares to learning from a single medium. Perhaps the most important impact of research lies in its ability to inform the production of new programming. By identifying what 'works' research can help producers build on the most effective techniques as they create new material.

See also: ▶ COMPUTER GAMES AND CHILD DEVELOPMENT ▶ EDUCATIONAL MEDIA CONTENT ▶ EDUCATIONAL TELEVISION, CHILDREN'S RESPONSES TO ▶ INFORMATION LITERACY ▶ INFORMATION PROCESSING ▶ INFOTAINMENT ▶ INSTRUCTIONAL TELEVISION

REFERENCES AND SUGGESTED READINGS

Anderson, D. R., Huston, A. C., Schmitt, K. L., Linebarger, D. L., & Wright, J. C. (2001). Early childhood television viewing and adolescent behavior. *Monographs of the Society for Research in Child Development*, 66(1).

Fisch, S. M. (2004). *Children's learning from educational television: Sesame Street and beyond*. Mahwah, NJ: Lawrence Erlbaum.

Huston, A. C., Anderson, D. R., Wright, J. C., Linebarger, D. L., & Schmitt, K. L. (2001). Sesame Street viewers as adolescents: The recontact study. In S. M. Fisch & R. T. Truglio (eds.), *"G" is for "growing": Thirty years of research on children and Sesame Street*. Mahwah, NJ: Lawrence Erlbaum, pp. 131–144.

Mayer, R. E. & Moreno, R. (2003). Nine ways to reduce cognitive load in multimedia learning. *Educational Psychologist*, 38, 43–52.

Metzger, M. J. (2007). Making sense of credibility on the web: Models for evaluating online information and recommendations for future research. *Journal of* the American Society for Information Science and Technology, 58(13), 2078–2091.

Parka, S. & Burforda, S. (2013). A longitudinal study on the uses of mobile tablet devices and changes in digital media literacy of young adults. *Educational Media International*, 50(4), 266–280.

Educational Media Content

JENNINGS BRYANT
University of Alabama

Educational media content refers to mediated messages designed to teach or provide opportunities for learning. The nature of mediated education varies greatly, ranging from formal curriculum-based message systems designed for classroom consumption to informal or pro-social media messages with the potential for producing incidental learning or pro-social change (→ Educational Media).

In *historical perspective,* education has been an important goal and function of print media from their earliest formulations. Whether the words and other significant instructional symbols were carved into clay or written on papyrus or vellum, many of the earliest extant media message systems were educational in nature, with contents ranging from an ancient Egyptian pharaoh's instructional manual on effective communication to canons of early religious communities (e.g., Bible, Torah, Koran), which were employed both to help convert unbelievers and to instruct the converted. Even today, print media are an invaluable portion of the lesson plans for teachers from primary school through postgraduate education. The story is similar for the place of education and instruction in the history of film, although the transition from the celluloid medium to diverse forms of electronic educational media is more complete than for its print cousins. Educational radio began when, in 1922, the British Broadcasting Company (later the British Broadcasting Corporation; i.e., the → BBC) was to enable independent British broadcasters to utilize wireless communication to educate, inform, and entertain all British citizens, free from political interference and commercial pressure. The concept of educational television programming was mainly developed in the middle of the twentieth century in the US.

Major developments in both computing and telecommunications fused to inaugurate the information age by *digital media* that was to truly revolutionize the role and form of educational media (→ Digital Media, History of). The introduction of educational videos and DVDs, the maturing of distance education, and the explosion of video and computer games, as well as the remarkable diffusion and adoption of the Internet as a vehicle for teaching/learning, have created an educational media landscape that is undergoing remarkably rapid evolution and reformulation.

It is difficult to examine educational television, especially children's educational programming, without focusing on the US. The programming of the Children's Television Workshop (CTW, now Sesame Workshop) revolutionized children's educational television, in part because CTW developed an innovative program-development model that brought together producers, educational advisors, and researchers to create innovative and effective educational programming. The CTW team programmed for the developmental level of their programs' targeted audiences, and they harnessed the formal features of the television medium to meet specific instructional goals, while also addressing critical societal needs. Such needs encompassed getting young children reading for school (e.g., Sesame Street), improving the reading skills of school-age children (e.g., The Electric Company), and guiding girls toward career interests in science (e.g., 3–2–1 Contact).

Many of the most popular children's educational programs in other countries are co-productions with US agencies and corporations like PBS Kids, Sesame Workshop, Nickelodeon, and Disney. Moreover, other successful educational television-program production and distribution houses with a worldwide reach, such as the Discovery Channel and National Geographic Television, are based in the US. Given these caveats, most countries with any sort of public-service broadcasting initiative have developed educational television programs (→ Public Broadcasting Systems). More general examples of advancements in children's educational television abound worldwide. For example, in 1997 the German public broadcasting stations founded the KinderKanal (or KiKa – the children's channel), a channel devoted exclusively to programs for children, including educational programs.

The twenty-first century has witnessed an explosion in *electronic educational media*, including media with quality production values that target preschoolers and are designed for home use. The use of such products by young children typically countervails the American Academy of Pediatrics' recommendations that babies under age 2 have no screen time whatsoever, and that other preschoolers have no more than two hours per day of screen time. As the twenty-first century unfolds, rarely is it valid to consider one educational medium in isolation, because convergence has produced an amalgamation of educational media message systems of all types, typically anchored on the backbone of the Internet.

See also: ▶ BBC ▶ DIGITAL MEDIA, HISTORY OF ▶ EDUCATIONAL COMMUNICATION ▶ EDUCATIONAL MEDIA ▶ EDUCATIONAL TELEVISION, CHILDREN'S RESPONSES TO ▶ FEDERAL COMMUNICATIONS COMMISSION (FCC) ▶ LEARNING AND COMMUNICATION ▶ MEDIA USE AND CHILD DEVELOPMENT ▶ PUBLIC BROADCASTING SYSTEM ▶ VIDEO GAMES

REFERENCES AND SUGGESTED READINGS

Garrison, M. M. & Christakis, D. A. (2005). *A teacher in the living room? Educational media for babies, toddlers and preschoolers.* Menlo Park, CA: Kaiser Family Foundation.

Jordan, A. B. (2000). *Is the three-hour rule living up to its potential? An analysis of educational television for children in the 1999/2000 broadcast season.* Philadelphia, PA: Annenberg Public Policy Center of the University of Pennsylvania.

Kleeman, D. W. (2001). Prix Jeunesse as a force for cultural diversity. In D. G. Singer & J. L. Singer (eds.), *Handbook of children and the media.* Thousand Oaks, CA: Sage, pp. 521–531.

Educational Television, Children's Responses to

JENNINGS BRYANT
University of Alabama

WES FONDREN
Coastal Carolina University

One of the most immediate ways children can respond to educational programming is simply by choosing to watch a particular program rather than all others available. A question that has arisen is to what degree children are deliberately selecting what they are attending to when watching television. *Attention* to progamming is another research stream. Not surprisingly, the levels of activity and passivity appear to be dependent on the age of the child and developmental status. Young children, such as preschoolers, tend to focus their attention on shows that contain frequent changes in visual and auditory stimuli in brief segments presented at a rapid pace. As children age, they attend to slower-paced programming that is more plot driven than stimulus driven. This shift is believed to reflect the increasing cognitive sophistication of older children, which allows for more goal-oriented viewing (→ Attending to the Mass Media).

A key factor in *comprehension* is the level of prior salient knowledge the child brings to the content. Comprehension is not solely a function of age, but also of environmental factors that impact development (e.g., educational emphasis in the home, school curricula). Similarly, as children develop cognitively there is an *increased ability to make inferences*. This ability can help children make sense of situations where necessary information may not be explicit. Further, over time learned behavior becomes automatic, requiring less conscious effort, and allowing more mental energy and attention to be spent on → information processing and assimilation (automaticity).

Numerous studies of children who view educational television have revealed that they show increased abilities in reading, writing, mathematics, science, and knowing current events (Fisch 2002). Frequent goals of educational programs have been to present positive social lessons and *promote prosocial attitudes and behavior* in children. Research has shown that pro-social benefits for children often increased when educational messages were accompanied by similar activities separate from television viewing. A related goal often is to *reduce antisocial attitudes and behaviors*.

See also: ▶ ATTENDING TO THE MASS MEDIA ▶ EDUCATIONAL COMMUNICATION ▶ EDUCATIONAL MEDIA ▶ EDUCATIONAL MEDIA CONTENT ▶ INFORMATION PROCESSING ▶ MEDIA USE AND CHILD DEVELOPMENT ▶ PARENTAL MEDIATION STRATEGIES ▶ SELECTIVE PERCEPTION AND SELECTIVE RETENTION ▶ SELECTIVE EXPOSURE

REFERENCES AND SUGGESTED READINGS

Fisch, S. M. (2002). Vast wasteland or vast opportunity? Effects of educational television on children's academic knowledge, skills, and attitudes. In J. Bryant & D. Zillmann (eds.), *Media effects: Advances in theory and research*, 2nd edn. Mahwah, NJ: Lawrence Erlbaum, pp. 397–426.

Singer, D. G. & Singer, J. L. (2001). *Handbook of children and the media*. Thousand Oaks, CA: Sage.

Strasburger, V. C., Wilson, B. J. & Jordan, A. (2009). *Children, adolescents, and the media*. Thousand Oaks: Sage.

Van Evra, J. P. (2004). *Television and child development*, 3rd edn. Mahwah, NJ: Lawrence Erlbaum.

E-Government

HELEN MARGETTS
University of Oxford

E-government may be defined as the use by government of information and communication technologies, internally and to interact with citizens, firms, nongovernmental organizations, and other governments. E-government in practice, therefore, consists of both complex networks of information systems within government organizations and a huge range of websites with which citizens can communicate, interact, and transact. The term 'e-government' only came into common usage in the 1990s as societal use of the Internet became widespread. While earlier technologies were largely internally facing, the Internet for the first time provided government with the possibility to interact electronically with individuals and organizations outside government (→ E-Democracy). With the Internet, the possibilities for cost reduction increased. They also create new possibilities for new policy 'windows' in terms of innovation. Digital technologies open up potential for innovation in the use of all four of the 'tools' of government policy: nodality (the capacity to collect and disseminate information), authority, treasure (money, or other exchangeable benefits), and organizational capacity.

Until the 2000s, academic *visions of e-government* tended to range from the highly utopian to the severely dystopian, with a lack of sustained empirical research filling the middle of the spectrum. 'Hyper-modernists' have argued that as the Internet and associated technologies become ubiquitous, government will become more and more efficient and therefore smaller, until eventually governmental organizations themselves will become increasingly irrelevant. Toffler (1990) argued that the decentralization afforded by information technology would inevitably lead to political decentralization as well, so that eventually bureaucracy itself would become irrelevant. While also believing in transformation for government through technology, 'anti-modernists' concentrated on the negative effects, believing that e-government would be more powerful, and more intrusive in the lives of citizens, than traditional bureaucracy and lead to a 'computer state' or a 'control state.'

Only in the 2000s did a sustained body of *research* begin to develop; however, the minority of it in communications. The study of e-government has become heavily populated by management consultancies, IT corporations, and international organizations, which have produced a number of reports and rankings of countries in terms of their e-government development (United Nations, 2012). Neither the wildest dreams of the hyper-modernists, nor the worst nightmares of the anti-modernists appear to have materialized. The use of the Internet varies widely across societies and also across governments, but use of information and communication technologies has not in any deterministic way caused liberal democratic governments to become less liberal or less democratic. Neither have authoritarian governments necessarily become more authoritarian, although the nature of their authoritarian techniques has changed. But in all these countries the new capacity for their subjects to develop social networks outside their country and to be aware of developments in the rest of the world can outweigh the increased control that technologies internal to government permit (→ China: Media System).

As for the hyper-modernists, their visions are challenged by the trend for governments in most countries to lag behind commercial organizations, and indeed society in general, in capitalizing on the potential benefits of Internet technologies. Others have identified a number of cultural barriers to e-government development, both from the supply side (in terms of civil servants being resistant to new electronic channels) and the demand side (in terms of citizens being willing to interact with government in new ways). However, the *potential for e-government* to look different from traditional notions of government remains, with the opening up of a wide range of new options for policymakers. Most of these potential applications of e-government have a key distinguishing feature: Governments can identify and treat groups of citizens differently according to their circumstances and need. For nodality, information can be targeted at specific groups, through websites used by specific age groups or group-targeted emails. Treasure, in terms of social welfare benefits or tax credits, for example, can be easily means-tested according to other financial information held by government. Authority can also be targeted, through 'fast-track' border control systems, for example. Even physical organization can be group-targeted, e.g., through barriers that respond to transponders fitted to police and emergency vehicles but not to normal cars, as used in city centers in several parts of the world. Furthermore, as Internet-based technologies themselves developed toward Web 2.0 applications, where users generate content through recommender and reputational systems, blog, wikipedias, social networking sites, and user feedback systems, governments too have to innovate if they want to take advantage of applications like these.

See also: ▶ CENSORSHIP ▶ CHINA: MEDIA SYSTEM ▶ E-DEMOCRACY ▶ EXPOSURE TO THE INTERNET ▶ INFORMATION SOCIETY ▶ SOCIAL MEDIA

REFERENCES AND SUGGESTED READINGS

Chadwick, A. (2011). Explaining the failure of an online citizen engagement initiative: The role of internal institutional variables. *Journal of Information Technology & Politics*, 8(1), 21–40.

Hood, C. & Margetts, H. (2007). *The tools of government in the digital age*. Basingstoke: Palgrave Macmillan.

Millard, J. (2010). e-Government 1.5: Is the Bottle Half Full or Half Empty? *European Journal of ePractice*, 9, 1–16.

Ozkan, S. & Kanat, I. E. (2011). e-Government adoption model based on theory of planned behavior: Empirical validation. *Government Information Quarterly*, 28(4), 503–513, doi:10.1016/j.giq.2010.10.007.

Taipale, S. (2013). The use of e-government services and the Internet: The role of socio-demographic, economic and geographical predictors. *Telecommunications Policy*, 37 (4/5), 413–422.

Toffler, A. (1990). *Power shift*. New York: Bantam.

United Nations. (2012). *E-government survey 2012: E-government for the people*. New York: Department of Economic and Social Affairs, United Nations.

Elaboration Likelihood Model

DANIEL O'KEEFE
Northwestern University

The elaboration likelihood model (ELM) of → persuasion suggests that important variations in the nature of persuasion are a function of the likelihood that receivers will engage in elaboration of (that is, thinking about) information relevant to the persuasive issue. Depending on the degree of elaboration, two different kinds of persuasion process can be engaged. These two persuasion processes are called the "central route" and the "peripheral route" (Petty & Cacioppo 1986; → Media Effects).

The *central route* represents the persuasion processes involved when elaboration is relatively high. Where persuasion is achieved through the central route, it commonly comes about through extensive issue-relevant thinking: careful examination of the information contained in the message, close scrutiny of the message's arguments, and so on. The *peripheral route* represents the persuasion processes involved when elaboration is relatively low. Where persuasion is achieved through peripheral routes, it commonly comes about because the receiver employs some simple decision rule (some heuristic principle) to evaluate the advocated position. For example, receivers might be guided by whether they find the communicator credible (→ Information Processing).

The amount of elaboration in a given situation (and hence which route is activated) is influenced by a number of factors, which can be classified broadly as influencing either elaboration motivation or elaboration ability. Elaboration motivation can be influenced by the relevance of the topic (greater personal relevance leads to greater elaboration motivation) and by the receiver's level of 'need for cognition,' a personality characteristic reflecting the tendency to enjoy thinking

(→ Personality and Exposure to Communication). Elaboration ability can be influenced by the presence of distraction in the persuasive setting or the amount of relevant background knowledge.

Because central-route and peripheral-route persuasion have different *underlying processes*, the factors determining persuasive success correspondingly differ. In *central-route persuasion*, persuasive effects depend upon the predominant valence (positive or negative) of the receiver's issue-relevant thoughts. To the extent that the receiver is led to have predominantly favorable thoughts about the advocated position, the message will presumably be relatively successful. The predominant valence of elaboration is influenced by whether the message's advocated position is pro-attitudinal or counter-attitudinal for the receiver (everything else being equal, pro-attitudinal messages will likely evoke predominantly favorable thoughts, counter-attitudinal messages predominantly unfavorable thoughts) and by the strength of the message's arguments (better-quality arguments lead to more positive thoughts).

By contrast, in *peripheral-route persuasion*, receivers use heuristic principles, simple decision procedures activated by peripheral cues. For example, in the credibility heuristic, rather than carefully considering the message's arguments, receivers simply rely on the communicator's apparent expertise as a guide to what to believe. Other heuristics are based on the receiver's liking for the communicator and on the reactions of others to the message. As elaboration increases, the influence of such heuristics diminishes – but where receivers are unable or unmotivated to engage in message scrutiny, these shortcuts are relied upon.

The ELM emphasizes that any given variable can *influence persuasion in three ways*. It might affect the degree of elaboration (and thus influence the degree to which central-route or peripheral-route processes are engaged), it might serve as a peripheral cue (and so influence persuasive outcomes when peripheral-route persuasion is occurring), or it might influence the valence of elaboration (and so influence persuasive outcomes when central-route persuasion is occurring). For example, credibility might activate the credibility heuristic or it might influence the amount of elaboration (as when receivers decide that the communicator's expertise makes the message worth attending to closely). Because variables can play different roles in persuasion, a variable might have very different effects on persuasion from one situation to the next.

See also: ▶ ATTITUDE–BEHAVIOR CONSISTENCY ▶ ATTITUDES ▶ INFORMATION PROCESSING ▶ INVOLVEMENT WITH MEDIA CONTENT ▶ MEDIA EFFECTS ▶ PERSONALITY AND EXPOSURE TO COMMUNICATION ▶ PERSUASION

REFERENCES AND SUGGESTED READINGS

Petty, R. E. & Cacioppo, J. T. (1986). *Communication and persuasion: Central and peripheral routes to attitude change.* New York: Springer.

Petty, R. E., Cacioppo, J. T., Strathman, A. J., & Priester, J. R. (2005). To think or not to think: Exploring two routes to persuasion. In T. C. Brock & M. C. Green (eds.), *Persuasion: Psychological insights and perspectives*, 2nd edn. Thousand Oaks, CA: Sage, pp. 81–116.

Petty, R. E. & Wegener, D. T. (1999). The elaboration likelihood model: Current status and controversies. In S. Chaiken & Y. Trope (eds.), *Dual-process models in social psychology.* New York: Guilford, pp. 41–72.

Slater, M. (2002). Involvement as goal-directed strategic processing: Extending the elaboration likelihood model. In J. P. Dillard & M. Pfau (eds.), *The persuasion handbook: Developments in theory and practice.* Thousand Oaks, CA: Sage, pp. 175–194.

Tormala, Z. L., Briñol, P., & Petty, R. E. (2007). Multiple roles for source credibility under high elaboration: It's all in the timing. *Social Cognition*, 25, 536–552, doi: 10.1521/soco.2007.25.4.536.

Election Campaign Communication

HOLLI A. SEMETKO
Emory University

Election campaigns are among the most important events in the lives of democracies and societies in transition. Campaigns often constitute the high points in public debate about political issues (→ Political Communication). Election campaign communication is shaped by different national, cultural, and regional contexts, party and media systems, candidate characteristics, and regulatory environments

(→ Political Communication Systems). The balance of party and media forces in shaping the news agenda has been forever changed by the increasing role played by citizens and interest groups in generating messages and news about parties, leaders, and issues through a variety of traditional and new online media, and the latest popular social media platforms.

As parties and candidates focus on staying 'on message' in the increasingly complicated campaign environment, venues for → strategic communication abound (Norris et al. 1999). The transformation of campaign communication in the traditional news media over the past few decades reveals a greater tendency toward personalized reporting on the top party leaders or candidates, greater emphasis on campaign rhetoric as opposed to information about party policies, and increasingly negative as opposed to neutral or favorable reporting on the candidates in the campaign (→ Political Persuasion). Published → election surveys and forecasts, often commissioned by the media, have given high prominence to the question of who is ahead and who is trailing behind. While negative news may diminish turnout in some elections in the US (Patterson 2002), in other national contexts voters have been found to be both "cynical and engaged" (de Vreese & Semetko 2006; → Political Efficacy).

Election campaigns often serve as a 'laboratory' for developing and testing media effects models (→ Media Effects). Several key concepts of media effects research, such as the selectivity principle and the opinion leader concept, originate from election campaign research (→ Selective Exposure; Selective Perception and Selective Retention; Opinion Leader; Two-Step Flow of Communication; Media Effects, History of). The concept of agenda-setting, which is one of the most widely used in contemporary communication research, has been advanced in election campaign studies (→ Agenda-Setting Effects). Framing refers to the context in which an issue or a problem is discussed, that provides a certain evaluation or interpretation (→ Framing of the News). Framing effects refer to when the important attributes of a message lead us to make judgments about a problem or issue (→ Framing Effects). This is particularly relevant during election campaigns when parties and candidates are trying to frame the issue in their favor (→ Strategic Framing; Issue Management in Politics).

Candidates and parties have more to gain and more to lose in the *new media environment*. Politically interested citizens can have a potentially greater voice and impact on the day-to-day campaign agenda simply by consistently offering their opinions and developing a reputation online (→ E-Democracy; Twitter). A key characteristic of media convergence is an emphasis on visuals. As television and the Internet become more graphic and visual and less text-driven, there will be new forms of political learning (→ Political Knowledge; Visual Communication; Television, Visual Characteristics of).

Technology and the new communication platforms created in the past decade have taken campaigning to a new level in countries around the world. Soon after the first internet elections emerged, in which candidates and parties designed effective online campaigns using new social media, the shift to mobile occurred. Campaign advertising and news now operate in "hybrid media systems" (Chadwick 2013), in which traditional and new media, and popular social media, together orchestrate campaign agendas.

See also: ▶ AGENDA-SETTING EFFECTS ▶ E-DEMOCRACY ▶ ELECTION SURVEYS ▶ FRAMING EFFECTS ▶ FRAMING OF THE NEWS ▶ ISSUE MANAGEMENT IN POLITICS ▶ MEDIA EFFECTS ▶ MEDIA EFFECTS, HISTORY OF ▶ OPINION LEADER ▶ POLITICAL ADVERTISING ▶ POLITICAL COGNITIONS ▶ POLITICAL COMMUNICATION ▶ POLITICAL COMMUNICATION SYSTEMS ▶ POLITICAL EFFICACY ▶ POLITICAL KNOWLEDGE ▶ POLITICAL MARKETING ▶ POLITICAL MEDIA USE ▶ POLITICAL PERSUASION ▶ SELECTIVE EXPOSURE ▶ SELECTIVE PERCEPTION AND SELECTIVE RETENTION ▶ STRATEGIC COMMUNICATION ▶ STRATEGIC FRAMING ▶ TELEVISED DEBATES ▶ TELEVISION, VISUAL CHARACTERISTICS OF ▶ TWITTER ▶ TWO-STEP FLOW OF COMMUNICATION ▶ VISUAL COMMUNICATION

REFERENCES AND SUGGESTED READINGS

Baum, M. (2002). Sex, lies, and war: How soft news brings foreign policy to the inattentive public. *American Political Science Review*, 96, 91–109.

de Vreese, C. H., & Semetko, H. A. (2006). *Political campaigning in referendums: Framing the referendum issue*. London: Routledge.

Chadwick, A. (2013). *The Hybrid Media System: Politics and Power*. Oxford: Oxford University Press.

Graber, D. A. (2001). *Processing politics: Learning from television in the Internet age*. Chicago, IL: University of Chicago Press.

Norris, P., Curtice, J., Sanders, D., Scammell, M., & Semetko, H. A. (1999). *On message: Communicating the campaign*. Thousand Oaks, CA: Sage.

Patterson, T. (2002). *The vanishing voter: Public involvement in an age of uncertainty*. New York: Knopf.

Vergeer, M. & Hermans, L. (2013). Campaigning on Twitter: Microblogging and online social networking as campaign tools in the 2010 General Elections in the Netherlands. *Journal of Computer-Mediated Communication*, 18(4), 399–419.

Election Surveys

THOMAS PETERSEN
Allensbach Institute

Election research has played a decisive part in the development of the methods of survey research from the beginning. More than market and media research, election research has awoken, in a special way, the curiosity and the ambition of researchers, and thus strongly affected empirical social research. It is significant that the breakthroughs of both the modern method of the representative survey and the empirical methods in communication research are connected with studies in electoral choice (→ Public Opinion Polling; Quantitative Methodology).

The first attempts at analyzing elections using statistical methods can be traced back to the early twentieth century. In 1905, the German researcher R. Blank published a detailed social science analysis of the social democratic party's electorate. A decade later, attempts began to predict future electoral behavior on the basis of pre-election polls. In 1936, George Gallup, Elmo Roper, and Archibald Crossley first applied face-to-face surveys based on representative population samples to the prediction of election results in the US presidential election. They correctly predicted Franklin D. Roosevelt's victory, whereas other political analysts had expected a victory of the Republican candidate Alf Landon.

Very soon after George Gallup's success in 1936, election surveys became a fixed quantity in the media's election coverage, at first in the US and after World War II in Western Europe. Today, election surveys are conducted in almost all democratic states. From the start, the institutes conducting election surveys were confronted with the allegation that the publication of their results *might affect the democratic process* and thus interfere with the voters' free decision. Studies, however, have clearly shown that the effect of published election survey results is in fact weak (Hardmeier 2008). For this reason, and because of fundamental judicial considerations, repeated attempts to ban the publication of election survey results before elections have failed in several countries (Donsbach 2001).

There are two basically different *types of election surveys*: exit polls and pre-election surveys, with the former usually dominating media coverage on election day, while the latter are more important for in-depth analyses of the background of elections. In 'exit polls' a representative sample of voters is interviewed immediately upon leaving the polling station. Results are published before the first returns come in on election night. They mostly allow a very precise estimate of the election result. In countries where it is doubtful whether the vote count is conducted correctly, exit polls are also a good control on the official electoral process, provided they can be conducted independently (Frankovic 2008). In contrast, 'pre-election surveys' use the same methods as surveys on other subjects. Pre-election polls offer a much more detailed analytical potential than exit polls.

Spectacular errors in election forecasts, such as in the US presidential elections in 1948, have always produced, aside from intensive scientific research of the causes of the failure, a public discussion of the uses of survey research as a political information medium and its quality. Partly, these discussions are based on a misunderstanding of the *possibilities and limits of survey research*. There are several ways *to measure the deviation of election forecasts* from election outcomes. Most of these use either the difference between survey and vote shares of individual parties or candidates in percentage points or the gap between the two leading candidates as the basis of their computation. The latter are especially suited to the US political system, in which elections are almost always dominated by two parties or candidates

(Traugott 2005). More complex modern computation models, which try to connect the various advantages of traditional methods, also assume an electoral or party system that is at least similar to the US system (e.g., Martin et al. 2005). In countries with a more complex party system, the average deviation of prognosis from actual outcome across all parties, multiplied by the largest deviation for any single party, usually provides a practical basis for analysis.

See also: ▶ PUBLIC OPINION POLLING
▶ QUANTITATIVE METHODOLOGY

REFERENCES AND SUGGESTED READINGS

Best, S. J. & Krueger, B. S. (eds.) (2012). *Exit polls: surveying the American electorate, 1927–2010*. Los Angeles, CA: CQ Press.

Donsbach, W. (2001). *Who's afraid of election polls? Normative and empirical arguments for the freedom of pre-election surveys*. Amsterdam: Foundation for Information.

Frankovic, K. (2008). Exit polls and pre-election polls. In W. Donsbach & M. W. Traugott (eds.), *The Sage handbook of public opinion research*. Los Angeles, CA: Sage, pp. 570–579.

Hardmeier, S. (2008). The effects of published polls on citizens. In W. Donsbach & M. W. Traugott (eds.), *Handbook of public opinion research*. Los Angeles, CA: Sage, pp. 504–515.

Martin, E. A., Traugott, M., & Kennedy, C. (2005). A review and proposal for a new measure of poll accuracy. *Public Opinion Quarterly*, 69, 342–369.

Traugott, M. W. (2005). The accuracy of the national preelection polls in the 2004 presidential election. *Public Opinion Quarterly* 69(5), 642–654.

Electronic Mail

ROBERT HASSAN
University of Melbourne

SUNEEL JETHANI
University of Melbourne

Electronic mail ('email') is a primarily text-based form of communication exchanged between computing devices that incorporates hyperlinks, or file attachments. Originally developed and used by the military, computer scientists, and other specialists, email has grown into one of the most common forms of human communication (→ Digital Media, History of). An estimated 150 billion emails are generated each day, and this figure grows exponentially.

The *popularity* of email has been hailed as contributing to the creation of a "virtual community" (Rheingold 2000). It has also been argued that email is a creative medium where self-expression has taken new forms, such as the use of 'emoticons,' where emotions may be expressed in text by arranging printable characters into icons, such as :-) to symbolize happiness, and acronyms such as 'LOL' (laugh out loud; → Self-Presentation). In the workplace, email communication can link an organization with its customers and increase productivity to allow workers in multiple locations to communicate, share documents, and work collaboratively without the need for face-to-face or telephone communication.

From a *negative perspective*, an estimated 88 percent of total daily email volume occurs in the form of junk email or 'spam.' Another related concern is identity theft through practices such as 'phishing,' where individuals posing as representatives of institutions such as banks make fraudulent attempts to gain passwords and credit card details. Some argue that email also degrades the 'art of conversation.' A perennial issue facing people today is 'email overload' (Bellotti et al. 2005). This trend has led to the development of a range of email management techniques such as 'Inbox Zero' (Mann 2007). Most commentators see the growth of email continuing as a central feature of networked communications (→ Network Organizations through Communication Technology). However, in some countries younger people use email less and SMS and IM more and view email as an 'older' and more 'formal' mode (Lee 2005).

Future developments in email are likely to bring more functional user interfaces, new ways of automatically sorting and prioritizing emails, better ways to handle attached files, more advanced methods for filtering and assessing the credibility of emails received, and new ways to integrate email with other forms of online social communication.

See also: ▶ DIGITAL MEDIA, HISTORY OF
▶ FACEBOOK ▶ NETWORK ORGANIZATIONS THROUGH COMMUNICATION TECHNOLOGY
▶ SELF-PRESENTATION

REFERENCES AND SUGGESTED READINGS

Bellotti, V., Ducheneaut, N., Howard, M., Smith, I., & Grinter, R. E. (2005). Quality versus quantity: E-mail centric task management and its relation with overload. *Human–Computer Interaction*, 20(1–2), 89–138.

Lee, O. (2005). Analysis of new generation learner characteristics: College students' use of cyber communication. *Journal of Korean Computer Education*, 8(4), 25–36.

Mann, M. (2007). Inbox Zero: Action-based email. At http://www.43folders.com/izero, accessed August 3, 2014.

Rheingold, H. (2000). *The virtual community.* Cambridge, MA: MIT Press.

Emotion and Communication in Organizations

SARAH J. TRACY
Arizona State University

Emotions and feelings are important components of organizational communication. 'Emotions' refer to the external display of the affected state, the meaning of which is negotiated and constructed through organizational norms. 'Feelings,' in contrast, are considered subjective experiences that reside in individuals.

Burnout research has examined emotional exhaustion at work, depersonalization or a negative shift toward others, and a decreased sense of personal accomplishment. Communication researchers have differentiated between healthy empathic concern and counterproductive emotional contagion that leads to burnout. Workplace bullying is a toxic combination of unrelenting emotional abuse, social ostracism, interactional terrorizing, and other destructive communication that erodes organizational health and damages employee well-being (Lutgen-Sandvik & Tracy 2012). Studies of 'emotional labor' examine employees who create emotion – in the form of smiling, caring, or disciplining others – as part of the organizational product.

In contrast to early views of emotion as either pathology or something to be managed, the concept of 'bounded emotionality' suggests an alternative approach toward organizing which highlights nurturance, caring, community, and supportiveness (Mumby & Putnam 1992). Compassion is an emerging emotion concept in → organizational communication. Conceptualized as a three-part process of recognizing, responding, and (re)acting to another's pain (Way & Tracy, 2012), research has found that caring interactions at work dramatically improve people's workplace experience. The connection of positive moods and organizational effectiveness has spurred research on humor, laughter, and joking in the workplace. These final two areas of research reflect a trend toward positive organizational scholarship. Scholars in positive psychology argue that research has spent too much time studying emotion's dark side (e.g., bullying, emotive dissonance, burnout) and that attention should be turned to positive emotions (well-being, happiness, compassion, love, and humor).

See also: ▶ APPRAISAL THEORY ▶ ORGANIZATIONAL COMMUNICATION ▶ ORGANIZATIONAL COMMUNICATION: CRITICAL APPROACHES ▶ ORGANIZATIONAL COMMUNICATION: POSTMODERN APPROACHES ▶ ORGANIZATIONAL CONFLICT ▶ ORGANIZATIONAL CULTURE ▶ SOCIAL SUPPORT IN INTERPERSONAL COMMUNICATION

REFERENCES AND SUGGESTED READINGS

Lutgen-Sandvik, P. & Tracy, S. J. (2012). Answering five key questions about workplace bullying: How communication scholarship provides thought leadership for transforming abuse at work. *Management Communication Quarterly*, 26, 3–47.

Mumby, D. K. & Putnam, L. L. (1992). The politics of emotion: A feminist reading of bounded rationality. *Academy of Management Review*, 17, 465–486.

Way, D. & Tracy, S. J. (2012). Conceptualizing compassion as recognizing, relating and (re)acting: An ethnographic study of compassionate communication at hospice. *Communication Monographs*, 79, 292–315.

Emotional Arousal Theory

DOLF ZILLMANN
University of Alabama

Arousal is commonly construed as the experience of restlessness, excitation, and agitation. It manifests itself in heightened overt and covert bodily activities that create a readiness for action. Acute states of such arousal characterize all vital emotions, and the subjective experience of these acute states is part and parcel of all strong feelings. Emotional arousal is consequently seen as an essential component of such experiences as pleasure and displeasure, sadness and happiness, love and hate, despair and elation, gaiety and dejection, rage and exultation, exhilaration and grief, frustration and triumph, merriment and fear, anger and joy, and so on.

Based on Schachter's (1964) two-factor theory of emotion Zillmann (1996) proposed a *three-factor theory of emotion* that retains the distinction between energization by arousal and guidance by cognition. A dispositional factor integrates ontogenetically fixed and acquired dispositions in accounting for the autonomic mediation of excitatory reactivity and the guidance of immediate, deliberate, overt behaviors. An experiential factor entails the cognitive evaluation of prevailing circumstances, including the appraisal of bodily feedback (→ Sensation Seeking).

As both the evocation of emotions and the modification of moods are essential factors in the appeal and effects of media presentations, and as the intensity of both emotions and moods is largely determined by excitatory reactivity, it is imperative to consider *arousal in the context of media influence*. Intense excitement is sought via exposure to the communication media as much as through overt individual or social actions. The fact that the evocation of diverse emotions can be compacted in media presentations or in interactive media formats, such as games, actually provides optimal conditions for the creation of arousal escalations and, ultimately, for intense experiences of joyous excitement (Zillmann 2006; → Excitation and Arousal; Media Effects).

Arousal influences permeate numerous other effects of media exposure too. It has been shown, for instance, that exposure to highly arousing pleasant erotica can facilitate social aggression more than can somewhat less arousing exposure to violence (→ Violence as Media Content, Effects of; Media Effects; Fear Induction through Media Content).

See also: ▶ APPRAISAL THEORY ▶ EXCITATION AND AROUSAL ▶ FEAR INDUCTION THROUGH MEDIA CONTENT ▶ INFORMATION PROCESSING ▶ MEDIA EFFECTS ▶ MOOD MANAGEMENT ▶ SENSATION SEEKING ▶ VIOLENCE AS MEDIA CONTENT, EFFECTS OF

REFERENCES AND SUGGESTED READINGS

Ekman, P. (1999). Basic emotions. In T. Dalgleish & M. J. Power (eds.), *Handbook of cognition and emotion*. Chichester: John Wiley, pp. 45–60.

Frijda, N. H. (2005). Emotional experience. *Cognition and Emotion*, 19 (4), 473–497.

Schachter, S. (1964). The interaction of cognitive and physiological determinants of emotional state. In L. Berkowitz (ed.), *Advances in experimental social psychology*, vol. 1. New York: Academic Press, pp. 49–80.

Zillmann, D. (2006). Dramaturgy for emotions from fictional narration. In J. Bryant & P. Vorderer (eds.), *Psychology of entertainment*. Mahwah, NJ: Lawrence Erlbaum, pp. 215–238.

Encoding-Decoding

TOBY MILLER
University of Cardiff/Murdoch

Encoding and decoding have been key concepts in communication for over fifty years, in keeping with the idea that language is a → code, and how it is received is as significant as how it is conceived. Its most prominent place, however, is in media and → cultural studies, where it has been used to integrate the analysis of texts, producers, technologies, and audiences by thinking of them as coeval participants in the making of → meaning.

Encoding-decoding within media and cultural studies *derives* from the rejection of psychological models of → media effects. In the 1960s, the ethnomethodologist Harold Garfinkel coined the notion of a "cultural dope," a mythic figure who supposedly "produces the stable features of the society by acting in compliance with pre-established and legitimate alternatives of action that the common culture provides" (Garfinkel 1992, 68). In the mid-1960s, Umberto Eco developed the notion of encoding-decoding, open texts, and aberrant readings by audiences (Eco 1972). Eco looked at the ways that meanings were put into Italian TV programs by producers and deciphered by viewers, and the differences between these practices. His insights were picked up by the political sociologist Frank Parkin (1971), then by cultural studies theorist Stuart Hall (1980).

There have been *two principal methodological iterations* of the encoding-decoding approach: → uses and gratifications (U&G) and ethnography/cultural studies. Uses and gratifications operates from a psychological model of needs and pleasures; cultural studies from a political one of needs and pleasures. U&G focuses on what are regarded as fundamental psychological drives that define how people use the media to gratify themselves. Conversely, cultural studies' ethnographic work has shown some of the limitations to claims that viewers are stitched into certain perspectives by the interplay of narrative, dialogue, and image. Together, they have brought into question the notion that audiences are blank slates ready to be written on by media messages.

See also: ▶ AUDIENCE RESEARCH ▶ CODE ▶ CULTURAL STUDIES ▶ ETHNOGRAPHY OF COMMUNICATION ▶ MEANING ▶ MEDIA EFFECTS ▶ TEXT AND INTERTEXTUALITY ▶ USES AND GRATIFICATIONS

REFERENCES AND SUGGESTED READINGS

Eco, U. (1972). Towards a semiotic inquiry into the television message (trans. P. Splendore). *Working Papers in Cultural Studies*, 3, 103–21.

Garfinkel, H. (1992). *Studies in ethnomethodology*. Cambridge: Polity.

Hall, S. (1980). Encoding/decoding. In S. Hall, D. Hobson, A. Lowe, & P. Willis (eds.), *Culture, media, language*. London: Hutchinson, pp. 128–139.

Parkin, F. (1971). *Class inequality and political order*. London: McGibbon and Kee.

Entertainment Content and Reality Perception

GABRIEL WEIMANN
University of Haifa

A common focus of communication research has been the public's perceptions of reality as based on mass-mediated contents and images (→ Media and Perceptions of Reality). Social reality perceptions are best defined as individuals' conceptions of the world. They include perceptions of others' opinions and behavior, social indicators such as crime, wealth, careers, professions, sex roles, and more (→ Reality and Media Reality).

An important element of the modern mass-mediated world is the *integration of news and entertainment*, facts and fiction, events, and stories into a symbolic environment in which reality and fiction are almost inseparable. Thus, the news becomes storytelling while soap operas become news. They present to us realities from other cultures, other social strata – and despite their fictional nature – are seen and interpreted as realities. The so-called → 'infotainment' narrative of the modern media affects us all. How can one make the distinction between fictional representation and factual 'real-world' information when both are so well integrated into our mediated environments?

Living in a mass-mediated world is the result of several processes: our reliance on media sources to know and interpret the 'world out there,' the distorting effect of the selection process in the media and the practice of writing news as 'storytelling,' and the mixture of information and fiction where real and fictional worlds become a homogeneous, synthetic reality.

The most important work on the impact of mass-mediated realities on audiences' perceptions has been done within the tradition of George Gerbner's *cultivation theory*. Essentially, the theory states that heavy exposure to mass media, namely television, creates and cultivates perceptions of reality more consistent with a media-conjured version of reality than with what actual reality is. It began with the "Cultural Indicators" research project in the mid-1960s, aiming to study whether and how watching television may influence viewers' ideas of what the everyday world is like. Cultivation theorists argue that television has long-term effects which are small, gradual, indirect, but cumulative and significant (→ Cultivation Effects).

One of the major constructs of cultivation theory is 'mainstreaming,' the homogenization of people's divergent perceptions of social reality into a convergent mainstream. This apparently happens through a process of construction, whereby viewers learn 'facts' about the real world from observing the world of television.

Several researchers have attempted to *refine the notion of cultivation* by examining closely the cognitive processes involved. A key distinction suggested by these studies is that there are two stages of the cognitive process: 'first-order' effects (general beliefs about the everyday world, such as about the prevalence of violence) and 'second-order' effects (the resulting specific attitudes, such as fear of strangers or of walking alone). Other studies revealed the psychological processes involved in cultivation of reality perceptions. Thus, some argued that 'source confusion' (the tendency of individuals to confuse events from news stories with those from fictional contents) is promoting stronger cultivation effects while others explained the cognitive mechanism of cultivation in terms of accessing information in the memory.

The important assets of *computer-mediated communication* (CMC) are its 'vividness' and speed; easy access to everywhere in cyberspace with no time or distance limits. What happens when virtual reality becomes more appealing than 'real' reality? Will large numbers of us abandon socially relevant pursuits for virtual travel in the media world? As computers' capabilities to develop increasingly complex and realistic images advance, the illusion of reality will become even more convincing. When virtual realities in computer-mediated entertainment are the only source of information people can use to experience places, situations, and actions, one can expect a powerful impact. Williams (2006) found that participants in an online game changed their perceptions of real-world dangers. However, these dangers only corresponded to events and situations found in the game world and not to real-world crimes. Computer-mediated communication is giving new meaning to the idea of 'mediated realities' and should be related to cultivation theory. Although the cultivation paradigm highlighted the role of television, the basic argument seems even more valid in the case of CMC.

See also: ▶ CONSTRUCTION OF REALITY THROUGH THE NEWS ▶ CULTIVATION EFFECTS ▶ INFOTAINMENT ▶ MEDIA AND PERCEPTIONS OF REALITY ▶ MEDIA SYSTEM DEPENDENCY THEORY ▶ REALITY AND MEDIA REALITY

REFERENCES AND SUGGESTED READINGS

Cohen, J. & Weimann, G. (2000). Cultivation revisited: Some genres have some effects on some viewers. *Communication Reports*, 13, 1–17.

Eveland, W. P. (2002). The impact of news and entertainment media on perceptions of social reality. In J. P. Dillard & M. Pfau (eds.), *The persuasion handbook: Developments in theory and practice*. Newbury Park, CA: Sage, pp. 691–727.

Lippmann, W. (1922). *Public opinion*. New York: Macmillan.

Weimann, G. (2000). *Communicating unreality: Mass media and reconstruction of realities*. Los Angeles, CA: Sage.

Williams, D. (2006). Virtual cultivation: Online worlds, offline perceptions. *Journal of Communication*, 56, 69–87.

Environment and Social Interaction

MILES L. PATTERSON
University of Missouri–St Louis

Every face-to-face → interaction occurs in a specific location. For example, where people live affects social behavior. Urban dwellers typically initiate less eye contact with strangers and help them less than suburbanites or small-town residents do. This decreased sensitivity to others may be the product of "social overload," leading automatically to filtering out less important events (Milgram 1970).

Advances in the technological environment over the last 75 years have changed patterns of interaction. Prior to the common availability of television and air conditioning, people spent more time outside, interacting with their neighbors. Although technological advances, such as the Internet and mobile phones, permit convenient remote communication, increased dependence on these technologies adversely affects the frequency and quality of face-to-face communication (Bugeja 2005; → Interpersonal Communication). People select settings, but settings also select the people who use them. For example, a church service or a school board meeting each attract people with relatively similar interests and expectations into a setting. The combination of these influences in any setting promotes relatively homogeneous behavior across people. The *physical characteristics* of settings also affect interactions. In the business world, higher-status individuals have larger, better-furnished offices. These features reinforce the office holders' power in interacting with subordinates. In home settings, the furniture in most living rooms is usually arranged to accommodate the easy viewing of a television, not to facilitate more comfortable facing positions for conversations.

In conclusion, the physical environment not only constrains our behavioral options, but also primes specific actions and social judgments about others, often automatically and outside of awareness (Loersch & Payne 2011).

See also: ▶ INTERACTION ▶ INTERPERSONAL COMMUNICATION

REFERENCES AND SUGGESTED READINGS

Bugeja, M. (2005). *Interpersonal divide*. Oxford: Oxford University Press.

Loersch, C. & Payne, B. K. (2011). The situated inference model: An integrative account of the effects of primes on perception, behavior, and motivation. *Perspectives on Psychological Science*, 6, 234–252.

Milgram, S. (1970). The experience of living in cities. *Science*, 167, 1461–1468.

Environmental Communication

ROBERT J. GRIFFIN
Marquette University

SHARON DUNWOODY
University of Wisconsin–Madison

'Environmental communication' refers to communication about the natural environment and ecosystem, commonly focusing on the relationships that human beings and their institutions have with the nonhuman natural environment. Much of this communication, historically, has been generated by concern about various environmental problems and issues (e.g., global warming, energy, smog, extinction of species, land uses, population growth, water quality).

Environmental communication can take many forms and can occur through a diverse set of communication channels. Thus, communication scholars of various stripes might readily find environmental communication applicable to their interests in various media. Most *content analyses* on environmental issues examine print – not broadcast or Internet – outlets and most offer descriptions of patterns of coverage across media or over time (→ Content Analysis, Quantitative). Although there exists no meta-analysis of these studies, we isolate a few of the more common patterns below. Coverage of a single environmental issue will be erratic, not sustained, over time. Journalism tackles individual topics in relatively brief, discrete bits and does so only when events or processes coincide with news values such as timeliness or magnitude (→ News Routines; News Values).

Journalistic norms may be prominent drivers of coverage strategies (→ Journalists' Role Perception; Ethics in Journalism). For example, since journalists cannot be arbiters of scientific truth when that truth is contested (a common situation in science), they instead aim to include in stories a variety of truth claims, often 'balancing' these viewpoints in an effort to convey to audiences a sense of the range of views (→ Objectivity in Reporting). Stories, by definition, are dominated by interpretive frameworks, and scholars argue that these frameworks can be important predictors of the 'take-home message' that a reader or viewer will derive from a journalistic piece.

Studies of *frames* employed in stories about risks to the environment suggest that they can stem from a complex welter of factors, including a journalist's a priori knowledge of an issue, a willingness to buy into the first frame that is offered as an issue comes to light, and even the social structure of the community in which the media organization operates (Campbell 2014; Lakoff 2010).

Kahlor et al. (2006) investigated some of the factors that could increase the likelihood that people would seek and process information about impersonal risks, that is, risks not to oneself but to others or to the environment. Specifically, they used elements of the *risk information seeking and processing (RISP) model* (see Griffin et al. 2013) to examine how residents of two cities dealt with information about risks to an ecological issue. The RISP model proposes that more active seeking and processing of risk information is facilitated, directly or indirectly, by combinations of some key variables, including (1) information insufficiency; (2) a person's capacity to seek and process the risk information; (3) a person's beliefs about communication channels that carry the information; (4) informational subjective norms (felt social pressures to be informed about the risk); and (5) affective responses to the risk (→ Affective Disposition Theories).

Today, much environmental communication can be discovered on the Internet, such as bloggers' opinions on global warming, local environmental groups' interactive websites mapping hazardous chemicals stored in the community, etc. Among the challenges to environmental communicators, and among the key topics of interest to those who study environmental communication, are the communication of risk and uncertainty to lay audiences, the interpretation of the attendant technical and scientific information for non-experts, differences in orientation to the environment based on various cultural, structural, and social factors, and issues related to public concern about the 'impersonal' environment.

See also: ▶ AFFECTIVE DISPOSITION THEORIES ▶ ATTITUDES ▶ CONTENT ANALYSIS, QUANTITATIVE ▶ ETHICS IN JOURNALISM ▶ FRAMING EFFECTS ▶ FRAMING OF THE NEWS ▶ INFORMATION PROCESSING ▶ INFORMATION SEEKING ▶ JOURNALISTS' ROLE PERCEPTION ▶ NEWS ROUTINES ▶ NEWS VALUES ▶ OBJECTIVITY IN REPORTING ▶ PLANNED BEHAVIOR, THEORY OF ▶ REASONED ACTION, THEORY OF ▶ RISK COMMUNICATION ▶ RISK PERCEPTIONS ▶ SOCIAL CONFLICT AND COMMUNICATION ▶ UNCERTAINTY AND COMMUNICATION

REFERENCES AND SUGGESTED READINGS

Campbell, V. (2014). Framing environmental risks and natural disasters in factual entertainment television. *Environmental Communication*, 8(1), 58–74.
Cox, J. R. (2010). *Environmental Communication and the Public Sphere*. Thousand Oaks, CA: Sage.
Dunwoody, S. & Griffin, R. J. (1993). Journalistic strategies for reporting long-term environmental issues: A case study of three superfund sites. In A. Hansen (ed.), *The mass media and environmental issues*. London: Leicester University Press, pp. 22–50.
Griffin, R.J., Dunwoody, S., & Yang, Z. J. (2013). Linking risk messages to information seeking and processing. In C. Salmon (ed.), *Communication Yearbook 36*. London: Routledge, pp. 323–362.
Kahlor, L., Dunwoody, S., Griffin, R. J., & Neuwirth, K. (2006). Seeking and processing information about impersonal risk. *Science Communication*, 28, 163–194.

Lakoff, G. (2010). Why it matters how we frame the environment. *Environmental Communication* 4(1), 70–81.

Escapism

CHRISTOPH KLIMMT
Hanover University of Music, Drama, and Media

Escapism was introduced as an explanation for people's use of entertainment media in the 1950s. The original understanding of escapism was rooted in the assumption that many working-class people in western mass societies were 'alienated' and suffered from poor life satisfaction (→ Media Use by Social Variable). Alienation was assumed to breed the desire to evade everyday sorrows and troubles by involving oneself in fantasy worlds that offer relief and distraction.

As the typical content of 1950s and 1960s entertainment programming indicated a sharp contrast to the stipulated social reality of 'the masses' (e.g., radio soap operas), involvement with such programming was theorized to serve the function of making people forget temporarily about their troublesome life circumstances by 'diving' into mediated worlds of (more) happiness and luck (→ Involvement with Media Content). In addition to the motivational dimension of escapism, the notion was also discussed in terms of the effects of escapist media use on people's life and performance in social roles (→ Media Effects; Entertainment Content and Reality Perception).

While the notion of escapism has not been addressed by much research since the public debate in the 1950s and 1960s, its *motivational component* (i.e., a diversion and relief motivation as driver of media use) has been picked up in various lines of research. For instance, Henning and Vorderer (2001) elaborated a specific escape motivation, namely the desire to avoid thinking about oneself.

In terms of *communication theory*, elements of escapism are reflected in most approaches to media selection, for instance → mood management theory and contemporary accounts of → uses and gratifications. The assumptions about a dysfunctional impact of escapism on people's life performance has been counterbalanced by the fact that some scholars consider the use of media entertainment and the accompanying 'escape' from real-life stressors as a benign contribution to well-being (i.e., as 'vacation' instead of 'flight' from real-life circumstances).

See also: ▶ ENTERTAINMENT CONTENT AND REALITY PERCEPTION ▶ EXPOSURE TO PRINT MEDIA ▶ EXPOSURE TO THE INTERNET ▶ EXPOSURE TO RADIO ▶ EXPOSURE TO TELEVISION ▶ INVOLVEMENT WITH MEDIA CONTENT ▶ MEDIA EFFECTS ▶ MEDIA USE BY SOCIAL VARIABLE ▶ MOOD MANAGEMENT ▶ SELECTIVE EXPOSURE ▶ USES AND GRATIFICATIONS

REFERENCES AND SUGGESTED READINGS

Bryant, J. & Vorderer, P. (eds.) (2006). *Psychology of entertainment*. Mahwah, NJ: Lawrence Erlbaum.

Henning, B. & Vorderer, P. (2001). Psychological escapism: Predicting the amount of television viewing by need for cognition. *Journal of Communication,* 51, 100–120.

Katz, E. & Foulkes, D. (1962). On the use of the mass media as "escape": Clarification of a concept. *Public Opinion Quarterly,* 26, 377–388.

Ethics in Journalism

CLIFFORD G. CHRISTIANS
University of Illinois Urbana–Champaign

Journalism ethics is a branch of applied philosophy. Beginning with moral issues in medicine, the field expanded from the mid-twentieth century to include such professions as law, business, journalism, and engineering. Applied ethics has developed over the decades from merely describing actual moral behavior to establishing principles that guide decision-making. Journalism ethics retains an interest in the concrete, everyday challenges of professional practice, but considers it crucial to integrate those principles as well.

In its ideal forms, news serves the public interest, that is, the interests not of readers and viewers but of citizens (→ Quality of the News). From this perspective, social responsibility theory has become the most common form of journalism ethics in democratic societies around the world (→ Journalists' Role Perception). With the same core ideas but different nuances in countries across the globe, for social responsibility ethics the major issue facing journalism today is the principle of truth.

In the US, the Commission on Freedom of the Press published its report A Free and Responsible Press in 1947. Named for the commission chairman, Robert Hutchins of the University of Chicago, the report insisted that the news media have an obligation to society, instead of promoting the interests of government or pursuing private prerogatives to publish and make a profit. In 1980, the MacBride report, Many Voices, One World, put social responsibility in explicitly international terms (→ UNESCO; International Communication; Development Communication; Development Journalism). Most of Europe takes social responsibility for granted as the dominant policy in journalism practices and media structures, including public service broadcasting (→ Public Broadcasting Systems). Since the 1990s, civic or community journalism has been restyling the press toward greater citizen involvement and a healthier public life (→ Participatory Communication; Citizen Journalism). In Latin America, for example, more public journalism projects have been carried out than on any other continent.

Ethics is not a question of personal choices but a matter of social and cultural duties. Humans have a moral obligation to one another; therefore journalism ought to appeal to listeners and readers about human values and conceptions of the good. The press's obligation to truth is standard in journalism ethics. Truth-telling is the generally accepted norm of the media professions, and credible language is pivotal to the very existence of journalism. But living up to this ideal has been virtually impossible. Budget constraints, deadlines, and self-serving sources complicate the production of truth in news writing. Sophisticated technology accommodates almost unlimited news copy and requires choices without the opportunity to sift through the intricacies of truth-telling (→ Truth and Media Content).

There are different *notions of 'truth'*. The mainstream press has defined itself overall as objectivist, so that the facts seem to mirror reality and genuine knowledge is scientific. Here, news corresponds to accurate representation and precise data, and professionalism stands for impartiality. Journalistic morality is equivalent to unbiased reporting of neutral data (→ Bias in the News; Neutrality; Objectivity in Reporting; Reality and Media Reality). Another concept of truth is disclosure, getting to the heart of the matter. Reporters seek what might be called interpretive sufficiency. The best journalists understand from the inside the attitudes, culture, language, and definitions of the persons and events that enter news reporting. In addition, ethical diversity offers a challenge to journalism ethics. Only specific social situations that nurture human identity can determine what is worth preserving. In the era of cultural diversity, when the truth principle is honored in journalism, particular cultures, ethnicities, and religions will flourish (→ Ethnic Journalism; Minority Journalism).

Social responsibility is explicitly cross-cultural in character. The canon of journalism ethics has been largely western, gender-biased, and monocultural. To succeed under current conditions, professional ethics must instead be international, gender-inclusive, and multicultural. The global reach of communication systems and institutions requires an ethics commensurate in scope. Thus the current efforts toward a diversified ethics of social responsibility journalism build on a level playing field that respects all cultures equally. Because every culture has something important to say to all human beings, a journalism ethics in the interactive, transnational mode is the greatest challenge today worldwide.

See also: ▶ BIAS IN THE NEWS ▶ CITIZEN JOURNALISM ▶ DEVELOPMENT COMMUNICATION ▶ DEVELOPMENT JOURNALISM ▶ ETHNIC JOURNALISM ▶ INTERNATIONAL COMMUNICATION ▶ JOURNALISTS' ROLE PERCEPTION ▶ MINORITY JOURNALISM ▶ NEUTRALITY; OBJECTIVITY IN REPORTING ▶ PARTICIPATORY COMMUNICATION ▶ PUBLIC BROADCASTING SYSTEMS ▶ QUALITY OF THE NEWS ▶ REALITY AND MEDIA REALITY ▶ TRUTH AND MEDIA CONTENT ▶ UNESCO

REFERENCES AND SUGGESTED READINGS

Christians, C., Fackler, M., & Ferré, J. (2012). *Ethics for Public Communications: Defining Moments in Media History*. Oxford: Oxford University Press.
Christians, C. & Nordenstreng, K. (2004). Social responsibility worldwide. *Journal of Mass Media Ethics*, 19(1), 3–28.
Fortner, R. & Fackler, M. (2011). *The handbook of global communication and media ethics*. Oxford: Wiley Blackwell.
Plaisance, P. (2013). *Media ethics: Key principles for responsible practice*. 2nd ed. Thousand Oaks, CA: Sage.
Ward, S. (2011). *Ethics and the Media: An Introduction*. Cambridge: Cambridge University Press.

Ethnic Journalism
ANAHÍ LAZARTE-MORALES
Our Lady of Grace School

Ethnic journalism is the practice of journalism by, for, and about ethnic groups. Ethnic journalism involves ethnically differentiated groups living within a dominant culture. These groups are often disenfranchised and have limited access to media production. Ethnic journalism ideally constructs representations in harmony with how the group sees itself, as a strategy for political advocacy and cultural preservation (→ Advocacy Journalism). Ethnic media and journalism emerge during times of political and economic stress, to denounce discrimination and energize mobilization. In some cases, they link to movements for political autonomy. Catalan and Basque news media in Spain, for instance, are part of the historical struggles for political independence.

Audiences use ethnic news media to help them navigate and engage mainstream society, find resources and services, understand the larger political events that affect them, and maintain a connection to their ethnic group and identity. Noncommercial ethnic media struggle to operate with limited resources, e.g., through competition from mainstream media companies targeting ethnic minorities. A profit-driven logic may suppress diversity within the ethnic group to reach the largest portion of the audience (→ Media Economics).

Research on ethnic journalism emerged with the growth of the foreign-language press during times of increased immigration in the first half of the twentieth century. In a context of cultural globalization, studying ethnic journalism is a way to explore cultural identity as a resource for political mobilization (→ Globalization Theories). Ethnic news media production is also relevant to research about groups historically at the political and economic margins. The institutional histories of ethnic media, which often apply political pressure to make communication policies and media production more inclusive, receive considerable attention. Researchers are shifting their focus to the levels of production, content, and consumption.

See also: ▶ ADVOCACY JOURNALISM ▶ GLOBALIZATION THEORIES ▶ MEDIA ECONOMICS ▶ MINORITY JOURNALISM ▶ SOCIAL STEREOTYPING AND COMMUNICATION

REFERENCES AND SUGGESTED READINGS

Matsaganis, M. D., Katz, S. V., & Ball-Rokeach, S. J. (2011). *Understanding ethnic media, consumers, and societies.* Thousand Oaks, CA: Sage.

Park, R. E. (1922). *Immigrant press and its control.* New York: Harper.

Riggins, S. H. (1992). *Ethnic minority media: An international perspective.* Newbury Park, CA: Sage.

Ethnic Media and their Influence

OSEI APPIAH
Ohio State University

Ethnic media are media vehicles (e.g., specific programs, publications, promotional pieces) that carry culturally relevant messages designed for and targeted to a particular ethnic group. Studies have demonstrated the rapid growth and success of ethnic media in North America and throughout the world. Studies found that culturally relevant media reach the greater portion of ethnic minorities like blacks, Hispanics, and Asian-Americans in the US. Also, a majority says that they prefer ethnic media to mainstream media, particularly for news information.

Concerning underlying *theoretical foundations* persuasion literature suggests that audiences are more likely to be influenced by a message if they perceive it as coming from a source similar, rather than dissimilar, to themselves. Identification theory states that individuals automatically assess their level of similarity with a source which drives them to choose a source based on perceived similarities between themselves and the source. This notion is supported by distinctiveness theory, which states that a person's own distinctive traits (e.g., black, red-headed) will be more salient to him or her than more prevalent traits (e.g., white, brunette) possessed by other people in his or her environment.

In general, the use of ethnic media results in a stronger perceived similarity with the group and a greater identification with characters in ethnic media (Appiah 2004).

There is also a growing body of work that has investigated *how white audiences respond to ethnic-specific media and characters.* Studies clearly show that these media and characters have succeeded in attracting and persuading mainstream audiences. White respondents' more favorable responses to culturally relevant media and characters have been explained, in part, by the term 'cultural voyeurism' that is conceptualized as the process by which a viewer seeks knowledge about and gratification from ethnic minority characters by viewing them using a specific medium. This notion implies that white audiences may seek, observe, and emulate ethnic minority characters in ads, in music, and on television to gain general information about their dress, music, and vernacular primarily because these characters are perceived to possess certain socially desirable traits.

See also: ▶ ADVERTISING ▶ AUDIENCE SEGMENTATION ▶ ETHNICITY AND EXPOSURE TO COMMUNICATION

REFERENCES AND SUGGESTED READINGS

Appiah, O. (2004). Effects of ethnic identification on web browsers' attitudes toward, and navigational patterns on, race-targeted sites. *Communication Research,* 31, 312–337.

Deuze, M. (2006). Ethnic media, community media and participatory culture. *Journalism,* 7, 262–280.

Matsaganis, M. D., Katz, V. S. & Ball-Rokeach, S. (2011). *Understanding ethnic media: Producers, consumers, and societies.* Thousand Oaks, CA: Sage.

Ethnicity and Exposure to Communication

HOLLEY A. WILKIN
Georgia State University

Ethnicity is socially constructed. Aspects deemed as important (e.g. religion, race) in defining ethnic groups vary between countries and research studies. Ethnicity is often a co-variate in message exposure and/or effects studies (→ Exposure to Communication Content; Audience Research; Media Effects). It is often implicated in → Knowledge Gap Effects and → digital divide research.

Early media use research concentrated on → Exposure to television. In the US, the consensus was that blacks and Latinos watch more television than whites. Ethnic minorities in the UK – e.g., Indian, Pakistani, Bangladeshi, Black Caribbean, Black African, and Chinese – often watch less television (OfCom 2007). Recent research has compared new immigrant groups (e.g., Chinese vs Korean Americans) and 'geo-ethnic' groups (interaction of ethnicity and geographical space). Acculturation plays a role in whether immigrants of various ethnic backgrounds prefer media in their native language to that of their host country.

Several researchers have stressed the value-added of examining media in context (→ Media Ecology). People construct different communication ecologies – the web of interpersonal and media (new and old or mainstream, and local and/or ethnic) connections—in order to achieve their everyday goals. There is no question that ethnic differences exist in exposure to communication, and these differences can have implications for disparities between groups. With increasing diversity of communication resource options, ethnic and intra-ethnic exposure studies need to take place within an ecological framework.

See also: ▶ AUDIENCE RESEARCH ▶ DIGITAL DIVIDE ▶ EXPOSURE TO COMMUNICATION CONTENT ▶ EXPOSURE TO TELEVISION ▶ KNOWLEDGE GAP EFFECTS ▶ MEDIA ECOLOGY ▶ MEDIA EFFECTS

REFERENCES AND SUGGESTED READINGS

Greenberg, B. S., Mastro, D., & Brand, J. E. (2002). Minorities and the mass media: Television into the 21st century. In J. Bryant & D. Zillmann (eds.), *Media effects: Advances in theory and research*, 2nd ed. Mahwah, NJ: Lawrence Erlbaum, pp. 333–351.

Matsaganis, M. D., Katz, V. K., & Ball-Rokeach, S. J. (2011). *Understanding ethnic media: Producers, consumers, and societies.* Thousand Oaks, CA: Sage.

OfCom (Office of Communications) (2007). Communications market special report: Ethnic minority groups and communications services. At www.ofcom.org.uk/research/cm/ethnic_minority/ethnic_grps.pdf, accessed September 2, 2014.

Ethnography of Communication

DONAL CARBAUGH
University of Massachusetts Amherst

What are the means of communication used by people when they conduct their everyday lives; and what → meanings does this communication have for them? These are central questions guiding the ethnography of communication (EC), which is an approach to the study of culturally distinctive means and meanings of communication. EC has been used to produce hundreds of research reports about locally patterned practices of communication, and has focused attention primarily on the situated uses of language (→ Language and Social Interaction). It has also explored various other means and media of communication including traditional media, the Internet and → social media, oral and printed literature, writing systems, sign languages, various gestural dynamics, silence, or visual signs (→ Sign).

Research topics of ethnography of communication include (1) the linguistic resources people use in context, not just grammar in the traditional sense, but the socially situated uses and meanings of words and their relations, including sequential forms of expression; (2) the various media used when communicating, and their comparative analysis, such as online 'messaging' and how it compares to face-to-face messaging; (3) the way verbal and nonverbal signs create and reveal social codes of identity, relationships, emotions, place, and communication itself (→ Nonverbal Communication and Culture). Reports about these and other dynamics focus on particular ways a medium of communication is used (e.g., how Saudis use online communication, or how the Amish use computers), on particular ways of speaking (e.g., arranged by national, ethnic, and/or gendered styles), on the analysis of particular communication events (e.g., political elections, oratory, deliberations), on specific acts of communication (e.g., directives, apologizing, campaigning), and on the role of communication in specific institutions of social life (e.g., medicine, politics, law, education, religion).

In addition, the ethnography of communication is a theoretical as well as a methodological approach to communication. *As a theoretical perspective*, it offers a system of concepts that can be used to conceptualize the basic phenomena of study, and a set of components for detailed analyses of those phenomena. The phenomena of study are communication event, communication act, communication situation, and speech community. The components of each are the setting or scene, the participants, act sequence, key, instruments, norms for interaction and interpretation, and genre. *As a methodology*, it offers procedures for analyzing communication practices as formative of social life. The methodology typically involves various procedures for empirical analysis, including participant observation in the contexts of everyday, social life, as well as interviewing participants about communication in those contexts (→ Qualitative Methodology).

Collections of research reports were published in the 1970s that helped move such study from the periphery of some disciplinary concerns in linguistics, anthropology, sociology, and rhetoric (→ Rhetorical Studies) to more central concerns in the study of communication and culture (→ Culture: Definition and Concepts). These studies explored aspects of communication that were often overlooked, such as gender role enactment, the social processes of litigation, marginalized styles, social uses of verbal play, and culturally distinctive styles of speaking. By the late 1980s and 1990s, a bibliography of over 250 research papers in the ethnography of communication had been published. Recent ethnographies of communication have examined mass-media texts in various societies, political processes at the grassroots and at national levels, interpersonal communication in many cultural settings, → organizational communication in various contexts from medicine to education, intercultural

communication around the globe, processes of power, advantaged and disadvantaged practices, and so on (→ Health Communication; Educational Communication; Intercultural and Intergroup Communication). Ethnographers of communication thus demonstrate how communication is formative of social and cultural lives, comparatively analyzing both the cultural features and the cross-cultural properties of communication.

See also: ▶ CULTURE: DEFINITION AND CONCEPTS ▶ DISCOURSE COMPREHENSION ▶ EDUCATIONAL COMMUNICATION ▶ HEALTH COMMUNICATION ▶ INTERCULTURAL AND INTERGROUP COMMUNICATION ▶ INTERGROUP CONTACT AND COMMUNICATION ▶ LANGUAGE AND SOCIAL INTERACTION ▶ MEANING ▶ NONVERBAL COMMUNICATION AND CULTURE ▶ ORGANIZATIONAL COMMUNICATION ▶ QUALITATIVE METHODOLOGY ▶ RHETORICAL STUDIES ▶ SIGN ▶ SOCIAL MEDIA

REFERENCES AND SUGGESTED READINGS

Basso, K. (1996). *Wisdom sits in places.* Albuquerque, NM: University of New Mexico Press.
Carbaugh, D. (2005). *Cultures in conversation.* Mahwah, NJ: Lawrence Erlbaum.
Fitch, K. L. (1998). *Speaking relationally: Culture, communication, and interpersonal connection.* New York: Guilford Press.
Gumperz, J. & Hymes, D. (eds.) (1972). *Directions in sociolinguistics: The ethnography of communication.* New York: Holt, Rinehart and Winston.
Katriel, T. (2004). *Dialogic moments: From soul talks to talk radio in Israeli culture.* Detroit, MI: Wayne State University Press.
Philipsen, G. (2002). Cultural communication. In W. Gudykunst & B. Mody (eds.), *Handbook of international and intercultural communication.* Thousand Oaks, CA: Sage, pp. 51–67.

European Union: Communication Law

AMIT M. SCHEJTER

Ben-Gurion University of the Negev and Pennsylvania State University

As of 2014 the European Union (EU) consists of 28 countries (http://europa.eu/about-eu/countries/index_en.htm). It resembles a conventional federal state (Tsebelis & Garrett 2001), although it allows each of its member states to maintain its national sovereignty. The Council of Ministers, which directly represents the member states, and the European Parliament, which is elected directly by the citizens of these states, both resemble a traditional bi-cameral legislature. The Commission of the European Communities, the EU's administrative branch, is in charge of drafting bills and enforcing legislation. The European Court of Justice (ECJ) functions as the judicial branch of the EU. Among the binding legal instruments of the Union are: (1) regulations, which apply to all EU citizens; (2) directives, which apply to the member states and aim to harmonize the goals of national laws across the Union, while leaving individual member states with the means of achieving these goals at the national level; and (3) decisions, which apply to specific situations.

The *basic assumptions* underlying each European nation's communications law and policy were historically quite similar, believing that broadcasting was too important to be left to the whims of the free market (Levy 1999), and creating national public service broadcasters (→ Public Broadcasting Systems). Because they considered telecommunications a natural monopoly and a public utility as well, they maintained control over telecommunications through state-owned post, telegraph, and telephone monopolies, governed by the public service principles (Sandholz 1998). The first and most significant initiative of the EU in its audiovisual policy was the 1989 "Television without Frontiers" directive (TVWF; Hirsch & Petersen 1998), which was substantially revised in 1997 and in 2007, in response to the changing political and technological realities of Europe. The TVWF aimed not only to harmonize legislation across member states, but, more importantly, to unify the rules for television broadcasts across national borders, as "without frontiers" was seen as a basic element of European unity (Wheeler 2004; → Television Broadcasting, Regulation of).

In December 2008, the *Audiovisual Media Services Directive* (AVMSD) came into force, replacing the TVWF. The new directive additionally distinguishes "linear audiovisual media services" (analog and digital television, live streaming, webcasting, and near-video-on-demand) from "nonlinear audiovisual media services" (on-demand services). Because "nonlinear services" are distinct from "linear services" in the user's choice and control, and in their impact on society, the directive imposes lighter restrictions on them. The new directive eases some of the restrictions on advertising at the same time as requiring more regulation of food advertising in children's programming and for 'product placement' (Schejter 2006).

A major effort of European Union policy has been to insure *public service broadcasting's independence* and to secure its appropriate funding framework, which enables it to fulfill its mission. The legal dispute between commercial and public broadcasters centered on the articles of the treaty that called for fair competition in the Common Market and the meaning of "state aid," under Article 87 of the Treaty, which prohibits it if competition is undermined or is likely to be so. The commercial television companies argued that the license fees collected by the states to support PSBs constituted such aid. The Commission and the ECJ adopted a balanced approach to this issue, limiting the allocation of "state aid" to television programming that fulfilled the public service remit of the PSBs and served the "democratic, social, and cultural needs of each society."

In the area of *telecommunications* a new regulatory framework of 2003 allows rejection of the legacy regulation that created different legal arrangements for different technologies, in favor of a new framework that first identifies what services are provided by the technologies and then harmonizes the rules regarding those services, regardless of the technologies involved ('technological neutrality'; → Technology and Communication). The EU's option for competition law limits specific communications law provisions (ex ante regulations) only to those product markets that are deemed uncompetitive. In November 2009, the Union agreed on a package of reforms in the telecommunications sector. A new European telecommunications regulator called the Body of European Regulators of Electronic Communications (BEREC) was set up. See all legal documents under: http://europa.eu.int/eur-lex.

See also: ▶ COMMUNICATION LAW AND POLICY: EUROPE ▶ PUBLIC BROADCASTING SYSTEMS ▶ TELEVISION BROADCASTING, REGULATION OF ▶ TECHNOLOGY AND COMMUNICATION

REFERENCES AND SUGGESTED READINGS

Hirsch, M. & Petersen, V. (1998). European policy initiatives. In D. McQuail & K. Siune (eds.), *Media policy: Convergence, concentration, and commerce.* Euromedia Research Group. London: Sage, pp. 207–217.

Levy, D. (1999). *Europe's digital revolution: Broadcasting regulation, the EU and the nation state.* London: Routledge.

Sandholtz, W. (1998). The emergence of a supranational telecommunications regime. In W. Sandholtz & A. Stone-Sweet (eds.), *European integration and supranational governance.* Oxford: Oxford University Press, pp. 134–163.

Schejter, A. (2006). "Art thou for us, or for our adversaries?" Communicative action and the regulation of product placement: A comparative study and a tool for analysis. *Tulane Journal of International and Comparative Law*, 15(1), 89–119.

Tsebelis, G. & Garrett, G. (2001). The institutional foundations of intergovernmentalism and supranationalism in the European Union. *International Organization*, 55, 357–390.

Wheeler, M. (2004). Supranational regulation: Television and the European Union. *European Journal of Communication*, 19, 349–369.

Excitation and Arousal

GARY BENTE
University of Cologne

DIANA RIEGER
University of Cologne

A thrilling movie well describes the type of media stimuli that come to our mind when we use the terms excitation and arousal in everyday language. In scientific terms arousal can be defined as a state of alertness and physiological activation elicited by external or internal stimuli, which demand an adaptive response of the organism. Although vigorous actions like 'fight' or 'flight' might be dysfunctional or inappropriate in the daily life of civilized humans, evolution has preserved basic physiological alarm mechanisms, leaving the organism with a new type of adaptive task: to cope with arousal and excitation without launching behavioral programs.

A broadly accepted multidimensional *definition of arousal* was introduced by Lacey (1967), differentiating between cortical, autonomous, and behavioral arousal. *Cortical arousal* is associated with the ascending reticular activating system (ARAS) located in the brainstem. It receives input from the sensory receptors and projects nonspecifically into the cerebral cortex, producing a general cortical activation. The ARAS is responsible for tonic activation (i.e., being awake, drowsy, or sleepy) as well as for phasic activation (momentary alertness). *Autonomous arousal* is associated with the activity of the autonomous nervous system (ANS). The ANS consists of two antagonistic parts: the sympathetic and the parasympathetic parts. Arousal is associated with the activation of the sympathetic subsystem, while the parasympathetic part mainly serves inhibitory functions. *Behavioral arousal* describes the activation of the motor system, which can be observed as agitation or measured as muscular innervation using electromyography (EMG).

Schachter and Singer (1962) formulated the influential two-factor theory of emotion, in which arousal represents the unspecific intensity component of emotions, while the specific hedonic quality of an emotion depends on the cognitive appraisal of the situation. Based on this assumption, Zillmann (1983) formulated the *excitation transfer theory.* It holds that due to slower physiological processes, the unspecific arousal part of emotions has a longer decay time than the cognitive appraisal of the situation. Thus, arousal stemming from a thrilling scene can pertain and affect the intensity of joy experienced during the happy ending. The model has also been applied to effects of media violence, suggesting that it is not necessarily the content, but the transfer of excitation effects which contributes to aggressive behavior after media exposure (→ Violence as Media Content, Effects of).

Both hedonic quality and arousal can be moderated by cognitive processes. Lazarus and Alfert (1964) could show that intellectualizing commentaries accompanying or preceding most unpleasant images (a film of genital surgery), could significantly reduce autonomous arousal (sympathetic activation) during stimulus exposure. The prominent role of cognitive processes in the genesis and perception of emotions has been stated in so-called appraisal theories of emotion (→ Affects and Media Exposure; Emotional Arousal Theory).

In many cases communication content aims at providing information and thus primarily addresses the *cognitive system of the recipient*. Arousal can be an important determinant of → information processing, including attention, comprehension, learning, and → memory. There are two mechanisms thought to determine how attention is allocated to media stimuli. One is the *orienting response* (OR), which occurs whenever the organism is confronted with a new, unexpected, or salient stimulus and which is accompanied by the allocation of cognitive resources.

A second mechanism is Lang's (2009) *Limited Capacity Model of Motivated Mediated Message Processing* which assumes two basic motivational systems responsible for resource allocation: the *appetitive* system is activated through positive media messages in order to approach those contents and facilitate information intake. In contrast, the aversive system responds to negative media stimuli and prepares the organism to defend against potential harm and threat. In neutral environments with rather low levels of arousal the appetitive system is more active which is referred to as the *positivity offset*.

From an evolutionary perspective, the positivity offset enables the individual to explore the environment and be creative. Whenever the environment provides negative cues, the aversive system is activated more quickly, called the *negativity bias*. This bias is considered to enable vigilance and prevent harm and loss for the individual.

An important motivation for media use is mood regulation and in particular recovery from stress and work strain. *Mood Management Theory* posits that mood repair can be achieved through the media's excitatory potential; i.e., their impact on arousal. Assuming a homeostatic principle, the theory predicts that bored individuals choose arousing media content whereas stressed individuals prefer calm, relaxing content (→ Mood Management).

See also: ▶ AFFECTS AND MEDIA EXPOSURE ▶ EDUCATIONAL MEDIA CONTENT ▶ EMOTIONAL AROUSAL THEORY ▶ EXPOSURE TO COMMUNICATION CONTENT ▶ INFORMATION PROCESSING ▶ LEARNING AND COMMUNICATION ▶ MEMORY ▶ MOOD MANAGEMENT ▶ PHYSIOLOGICAL MEASUREMENT ▶ SENSATION SEEKING ▶ VIOLENCE AS MEDIA CONTENT, EFFECTS OF

REFERENCES AND SUGGESTED READINGS

Lacey, J. I. (1967). Somatic response patterning and stress: Some revisions of activation theory. In M. Appley & R. Trumbull (eds.), *Psychological stress: Issues in research*. New York: Appleton-Century-Crofts.

Lang, A. (2009). The limited capacity model of motivated mediated message processing. In R. Nabi & M. B. Oliver (eds.), *The SageHandbook of Mass Media Processes and Effects*. Thousand Oaks, CA: Sage, pp. 193–204.

Lazarus, R. S. & Alfert, E. (1964). Short-circuiting of threat by experimentally altering cognitive appraisal. *Journal of Abnormal and Social Psychology*, 69(2), 195–205.

Schachter, S. & Singer, J. (1962). Cognitive, social, and physiological determinants of emotional state. *Psychological Review*, 69(5), 379–399.

Zillmann, D. (1983). Transfer of excitation in emotional behavior. In J. T. Cacioppo & R. E. Petty (eds.), *Social psychophysiology: A sourcebook*. New York: Guilford, pp. 215–240.

Exemplification and Exemplars, Effects of

GREGOR DASCHMANN
Johannes Gutenberg University of Mainz

The term 'exemplification effect' describes the influence of illustrating case descriptions in media presentations on the recipients' perceptions of issues. General claims (e.g., 'growing poverty in society') often are illustrated by presenting single-case information describing individual experiences or testimonials (e.g., testimonials of the homeless). The single cases serve as examples that illustrate (i.e., 'exemplify') the general claim. In the news media, the use of examples is on the increase because journalists have to make their contributions vivid and comprehensive. A biased selection of examples in the media is a particular problem (→ Bias in the News). However, as a rule, the recipients' conceptions are strongly influenced by the number and type of the exemplars, whereas the general information often is ignored.

Most studies on the *impact of exemplification* have investigated their effect on → social perception and → climate of opinion. The more dramatic, extreme, and emotional the displayed cases are, the stronger are the effects. Presentation features such as personalization, vividness, or direct speech increase these effects, too. Exemplification effects are reproduced in different kinds of media and for different types of issues. Recent research shows that statements in → social media may also trigger this effect (Peter et al. 2014). There are no systematic relationships with age, gender, and education, or with several psychological traits or states, e.g., empathy, involvement, or knowledge.

Findings in social psychology can help to *explain the effects*. It is assumed that the exemplification effect is rooted in a basic cognitive mechanism of inductive learning ("episodic affinity") from episodic case information (Daschmann 2001). The mechanism increases the ability to draw general conclusions based on everyday experiences. The 'heuristic' may be seen as a product of evolutionary development which is reasonably correct when general conclusions are drawn from typical cases (→ Elaboration Likelihood Model). However, if applied to untypical cases as they occur in media coverage, misperceptions are the rule.

See also: ▶ BIAS IN THE NEWS ▶ CLIMATE OF OPINION ▶ ELABORATION LIKELIHOOD MODEL ▶ FRAMING EFFECTS ▶ INFORMATION PROCESSING ▶ SOCIAL MEDIA ▶ SOCIAL PERCEPTION

REFERENCES AND SUGGESTED READINGS

Daschmann, G. (2001). *Der Einfluss von Fallbeispielen auf Leserurteile: Experimentelle Untersuchungen zur Medienwirkung* [The impact of examples on readers' judgments: Experiments in media effects research]. Constance: UVK.
Peter, C., Rossmann, C., & Keyling, T. (2014). Exemplification 2.0. Roles of direct and indirect social information in conveying health messages through social network sites. *Journal of Media Psychology*, 26, 19–28.
Zillmann, D. & Brosius, H.-B. (2000). *Exemplification theory*. Mahwah, NJ: Lawrence Erlbaum.

Expectancy Violation

LAURA K. GUERRERO
Arizona State University

According to Expectancy Violations Theory (EVT; Burgoon & Hale 1988), people have expectations about how others will act in a given situation, based on social and cultural norms as well as personal experiences. When receivers perceive that a sender has violated these expectations, an expectancy violation occurred. Behavior that confirms people's expectations generally goes unnoticed, whereas unexpected behavior captures people's attention and heightens arousal. Sometimes arousal change is aversive, leading to a fight-or-flight response. At other times arousal takes the form of an orientation response that leads people to scan the environment for information to help them interpret and evaluate the unexpected behaviour (→ Interpersonal Communication).

Evaluations are largely made based on valence and reward value. *Valence* refers to how positive or negative an expectancy violation is compared to the expected behavior. Negative expectancy violations occur when the unexpected behavior is worse than the expected behavior, whereas positive expectancy violations occur when the unexpected behavior is better than the expected behavior. Some expectancy violations are clearly positive or negative. For example, receiving extra affection from a loved one is almost always valenced positively; being ignored by a loved one is almost always valenced negatively.

Reward value refers to the level of regard a person has for someone based on characteristics such as physical attractiveness, social attractiveness, and status. When the meaning of an expectancy violation is ambiguous, reward value helps determine whether the behavior is valenced positively or negatively. For instance, receiving an unexpected hug from an acquaintance could be valenced positively or negatively depending on the degree to which the acquaintance is attractive, popular, or has high status (→ Interpersonal Attraction).

Valence and reward value work together to predict responses to expectancy violations, including reciprocity and compensation. *Reciprocity* occurs when a person responds to an unexpected behavior with a similar behavior (e.g., a hug is met with a smile). *Compensation* occurs when a person responds to an unexpected behavior with a dissimilar behavior (e.g., a person pulls back when hugged). Intimacy levels are also connected to reciprocity and compensation. People engage in reciprocity when they welcome the change in intimacy that an expected behaviour represents. When the unexpected behavior is perceived as representing more or less intimacy than wanted, compensation usually follows.

See also: ▶ INTERPERSONAL ATTRACTION ▶ INTERPERSONAL COMMUNICATION ▶ UNCERTAINTY REDUCTION THEORY

REFERENCES AND SELECTED READINGS

Burgoon, J. K. & Hale, J. L. (1988). Nonverbal expectancy violations: Model elaboration and application to immediacy behaviors. *Communication Monographs*, 55, 58–79.

Experiment, Field

JAMES B. WEAVER, III
Centers for Disease Control and Prevention, Atlanta

Research utilizing experimentation is increasingly being conducted in venues outside the research laboratory (→ Experiment, Laboratory). Such projects, when they involve the manipulation of an independent variable in realistic circumstances, are called 'field experiments.'

Conceptually, the differences between the laboratory experiment and the field experiment are slight; ideally, both are structured on one of the true experimental designs and consequently incorporate randomization and manipulable experimental treatments or interventions (i.e., independent variables) as fundamental components (→ Sampling, Random). However, field experiments, because they are undertaken in circumstances not radically different from everyday life, can afford the researcher greater *external* → *validity*. Following the initial experimental treatment, for example, research participants in field experiments typically continue functioning in their everyday social settings with little investigator interaction until outcomes assessment (i.e., dependent measures). This can significantly reduce the reactive or interactive influence on subsequent outcomes resulting from participants' awareness of the research procedure and enhance external validity.

At the same time, however, undertaking experimentation in the field can involve *complications* rarely seen in laboratory experiments. Field experiments, for instance, typically entail a significantly longer time frame (e.g., weeks and months rather than hours and days) and often engage a substantially larger number of research participants. The process of identifying eligible research participants in field experiments can be difficult, and the failure to retain research participants for follow-up (i.e., outcomes assessment) can be a serious threat to the generalizability of research results. Additionally, field experimentation commonly occurs in settings permeated with systematic and random noise where achieving an adequate degree of measurement precision or accuracy can be difficult (→ Measurement Theory). Some threats to internal validity (e.g., compensatory rivalry and the Hawthorne effect) can be particularly problematic in field experiments.

Generally, field experiments appear most commonly in → health communication research, with such projects typically operationalized as randomized controlled trials. Guidelines and practices incorporated in the randomized controlled trial, which is a refinement of the basic pre-test/post-test control group design, assist the researcher in overcoming many of the common limitations encountered in field experiments. Consequently, the randomized controlled trial, if effectively implemented, can yield the strongest evidence of causality of all research undertaken in realistic environmental and situational circumstances.

See also: ▶ COMMUNICATION SKILLS ACROSS THE LIFE-SPAN ▶ EXPERIMENT, LABORATORY ▶ HEALTH COMMUNICATION ▶ MEASUREMENT THEORY ▶ MEDIA EFFECTS ▶ SAMPLING, RANDOM ▶ VALIDITY

REFERENCES AND SUGGESTED READINGS

Jensen, K. B. (2012). *The handbook of media and communication research: qualitative and quantitative methodologies*, 2nd edn. London: Routledge.
Kerlinger, F. N. (1986). *Foundations of behavioral research*, 3rd edn. New York: Holt, Rinehart and Winston.
Wimmer, R. D. & Dominick, J. R. (2011). *Mass media research: An introduction*, 9th edn. Belmont, CA: Wadsworth/Thomson Learning.

Experiment, Laboratory

JAMES B. WEAVER, III
Centers for Disease Control and Prevention, Atlanta

Research utilizing experimentation is undertaken in a variety of contexts and settings. Overwhelmingly, the most common setting for experimentation in communication is the laboratory experiment. Laboratory experiments, when effectively operationalized (→ Operationalization) and carried out, afford strict experimental control by allowing for isolation of the research situation from the variety of extraneous influences that can impact both experimental treatment or intervention (i.e., independent variable) and the subsequent outcome (i.e., dependent variable). Accordingly, laboratory experiments are typically structured on the more rigorous 'true experimental designs' and, consequently, yield the strongest evidence of causality (Wimmer & Dominick 2011).

An array of *locales* can be utilized in staging laboratory experiments, ranging from general purpose accommodations such as conference rooms, classrooms, lecture halls, and theatres to facilities specifically designed for experimentation. It is the researcher's ability to structure and manipulate the experimental environment (e.g., lighting, temperature, soundproofing, seating arrangement of research participants), not the specific locale, that is the defining characteristic of experiments in the laboratory setting.

Beyond situational and environment control, the laboratory setting allows *substantial control* over all aspects of the research process. Working in a laboratory setting, for example, significantly enhances the researcher's ability to accurately identify eligible research participants, insure their random assignment to treatment conditions, and extensively observe their progression through the research activity. The level of specificity achievable in the operationalization of independent variables – or, in other words, the extent and certainty with which treatment manipulations can be accomplished – and the consistency of their re-enactment are both extremely high in laboratory experiments. Equally important, the degree of precision possible in outcomes (i.e., dependent variables) assessment, which promotes measurement reliability, is a key aspect of experimentation in laboratory settings (Kerlinger 1986).

Experiments in laboratory settings can also involve potential *disadvantages*. Perhaps the most obvious shortcoming is operational and environmental *artificiality*. Laboratory experiments facilitate the precise and systematic observation of human reactions under controlled conditions; but sometimes the experimental situation and/or experimental procedure is rather sterile and unnatural. Some behavioral and perceptual outcomes observed under such circumstances can have little direct application to those occurring in natural surroundings.

Because laboratory experiments typically involve extensive interaction between the researcher and research participants, the potential is great that *researcher biases* can emerge as threats to internal and external validity. 'Experimenter bias' is introduced into the experimental process when the researcher subtly communicates expectations about outcomes to the research participants. 'Observer bias' occurs during outcome measurement when the researcher overemphasizes expected behaviors and ignores unanticipated ones. Blinding methods are frequently incorporated into experimental procedures to avoid such distorting influences.

Laboratory experiments have proven instrumental in almost all areas of communication research, enlightening both our understanding of basic communication phenomena and informing theory construction. Examples of such research areas are the theories of deceptive message production, interaction adaptation theory, → selective exposure to communication, attitude accessibility, excitation transfer theory, and many other fields of → media effects. For instance, Bryant and Zillmann (1984) put their subjects in the two experimental groups in mood stages of either boredom or stress (by having them calculate mathematical tasks of different demands). Subsequently, they measured the time subjects in both groups spent with either exciting or calming video material. The study revealed the (subconscious) motivation to use media content for moderating one's mood stages.

See also: ▶ ATTITUDES ▶ EMOTIONAL AROUSAL THEORY ▶ EXPERIMENT, FIELD ▶ MEDIA EFFECTS ▶ MOOD MANAGEMENT ▶ OPERATIONALIZATION ▶ SELECTIVE EXPOSURE ▶ VALIDITY

REFERENCES AND SUGGESTED READINGS

Bryant, J. & Zillmann, D. (1984). Using television to alleviate boredom and stress: Selective exposure as a function of induced excitational states. *Journal of Broadcasting*, 28(1), 1–20.

Jensen, K. B. (2012). *The handbook of media and communication research: qualitative and quantitative methodologies*, 2nd edn. London: Routledge.

Kerlinger, F. N. (1986). *Foundations of behavioral research*, 3rd edn. New York: Holt, Rinehart and Winston.

Miller, D. C. & Salkind, N. J. (2002). *Handbook of research design and social measurement*, 6th edn. Thousand Oaks, CA: Sage.

Myers, A. & Hansen, C. H. (2005). *Experimental psychology*, 6th edn. Belmont, CA: Wadsworth/Thomson Learning.

Wimmer, R. D. & Dominick, J. R. (2011). *Mass media research: An introduction*, 9th edn. Belmont, CA: Wadsworth/Thomson Learning.

Exposure to Communication Content

PETER VORDERER
University of Mannheim

LEONARD REINECKE
Johannes Gutenberg University of Mainz

'Exposure to communication content' describes one of the most recent areas of specialization within the communication discipline. It is located at the intersection of → media effects research and → audience research. This new perspective is primarily, but not exclusively, 'psychological' in its theorizing; it focuses on micro-level analyses but also describes macro-structures in explaining what happens during exposure. It looks at new technology as much as it looks at more traditional media, but most importantly, it studies what happens before people become exposed to media content, what happens while they are exposed, and finally what happens right after exposure, i.e., as immediate consequence of it, thereby reaching into the realm of media effects research.

Development and Mapping of the Research Field

In an attempt to not only describe and explain the final effects of communication but also to include the processes involved during and even before exposure, scholars have defined new concepts, models (→ Models of Communication), and even theories from different disciplines and academic backgrounds, such as psychology and sociology but also from the humanities. Scholars in psychology primarily have formed a more differentiated understanding of how and why different (groups of) individuals approach specific media contents, whereas those with a humanistic background primarily have examined the media content itself and its (often social, socio-economic) context. In doing so, humanist scholars complicated what social scientists have often oversimplified. Thus, the overall picture of what is believed to happen during exposure to media content has become rather complex.

Most of the theoretical constructs that researchers have developed to describe the specific processes that *precede exposure* to communication and have an impact on it concern individual processes that lead to exposure (see Hartmann 2009 for an overview), such as personality (→ Personality and Exposure to Communication) or the specific individual motives and interests guiding media exposure, such as → escapism, → information seeking, or → sensation seeking. The main differences between these concepts lie in their theoretical complexity, and their specificity. Constructs like → mood management reduce the complexity of a media user's decision process to a single dimension (i.e., the maximization of positive mood). The more inclusive concept 'behind' mood management, → selective exposure, claims that the selection of specific media content follows some psychological regularity, mood management being the most important one.

Examining what has been thought to occur *during exposure*, ethnicity and → media use by social variables are considered to affect how the audience deals with content. In addition to this, research has also addressed how individuals relate cognitively and affectively to characters on the screen by engaging in so-called → parasocial interactions and relationships with them. Due to many new technologies emerging recently, researchers have applied additional constructs such as → presence and → involvement with media content, → computer–user interaction, and physiological processes like → excitation and arousal. Some of these constructs are defined on the basis of what we know from psychology and from cognitive science about → perception (see Lang 2009), while others refer to the affective quality of such experiences (see Bryant & Vorderer 2006).

Compared to the many processes and constructs studied during and before exposure, only a few that occur *after exposure* were addressed – probably because they have most often been linked to the area of media effects (see Zillmann & Oliver 2009). One example of such processes is addiction and exposure, which does not limit itself to any step in the process, but refers to an effect of exposure that leads someone to constantly reinitiate the process again and again and without much awareness of its coercive nature.

The majority of available *theories and models* have tried to analyze exposure by referring to what precedes it, i.e., by linking exposure to the reasons media users may have for acting in a particular way. Those theories focus on either cognitive or affective processes. According to → cognitive dissonance theory, exposure to communication content is a function of whether a message is consistent with the users' attitudes. Affective disposition theories suggest that media users are primarily interested in witnessing protagonists succeed and antagonists fail, having developed affective dispositions toward them – which explains exposure to entertainment content (→ Affective Disposition Theories). More generally, the → uses and gratifications perspective asserts that media users choose content that promises to gratify their interests and needs. Looking at the immediate consequences of exposure to communication content, → social cognitive theory is arguably the most influential attempt to describe and explain why exposure to a specific content may lead to certain consequences.

Another way of systematizing the field of exposure to communication content is to distinguish between various *types of content*. In that respect, research on exposure to print media, television, and radio follows a theoretical tradition that is well embedded in the discipline of communication (→ Exposure to Print Media; Exposure to Radio; Exposure to Television). In contrast, more recent lines of research, such as those that study → exposure to the Internet, are more interdisciplinary in nature.

The final perspective that is taken here to systematize the various contributions to the field of exposure to communication content is one that distinguishes between the *different audiences*.

Over recent years, empirical research on the audience has grown in size but also diversified itself to address not only the general public but also the audiences of specific media offerings. While being studied, the audience itself has changed, thus, → audience segmentation has attracted a lot of interest within the discipline.

Outlook

Where will this development lead, and what may we expect? In a situation like this, scholars often suggest the integration of loose ends, i.e., a synergistic approach to integrate various perspectives. However, this expectation is probably unrealistic, at least for the near future, given the variety of theoretical approaches within this research context. In addition to the presence of competing theoretical paradigms, research in the field of exposure to communication content has also been characterized by numerous changes in the concept of the individual (or user) throughout its development (e.g., the concept of a weak audience in early communication research vs. the idea of a strong and active audience in the uses and gratifications tradition; cf. Potter 2009).

In sum, it thus can be suggested that the area of exposure to communication content is expanding in different directions and differentiating its view on the media user and the processes involved in media exposure. As a consequence, increased theoretical coherence and integration in the area may be a rather long way off.

See also: ▶ AFFECTIVE DISPOSITION THEORIES ▶ AFFECTS AND MEDIA EXPOSURE ▶ AUDIENCE RESEARCH ▶ AUDIENCE SEGMENTATION ▶ COGNITIVE DISSONANCE THEORY ▶ COMPUTER–USER INTERACTION ▶ ESCAPISM ▶ ETHNICITY AND EXPOSURE TO COMMUNICATION ▶ EXCITATION AND AROUSAL ▶ EXPOSURE TO PRINT MEDIA ▶ EXPOSURE TO RADIO ▶ EXPOSURE TO TELEVISION ▶ EXPOSURE TO THE INTERNET ▶ INFORMATION SEEKING ▶ INVOLVEMENT WITH MEDIA CONTENT ▶ MEDIA EFFECTS ▶ MEDIA EFFECTS, HISTORY OF ▶ MEDIA EQUATION THEORY ▶ MEDIA USE, INTERNATIONAL COMPARISON OF ▶ MEDIA USE BY SOCIAL VARIABLE ▶ MODELS OF

COMMUNICATION ▶ MOOD MANAGEMENT
▶ PARASOCIAL INTERACTIONS AND RELATIONSHIPS
▶ PERCEPTION ▶ PERSONALITY AND EXPOSURE
TO COMMUNICATION ▶ PRESENCE ▶ SELECTIVE
EXPOSURE ▶ SELECTIVE PERCEPTION AND
SELECTIVE RETENTION ▶ SENSATION SEEKING
▶ SOCIAL COGNITIVE THEORY ▶ SOCIAL
COMPARISON THEORY ▶ USES AND GRATIFICATIONS

REFERENCES AND SUGGESTED READINGS

Bryant, J. & Vorderer, P. (eds.) (2006). *Psychology of entertainment*. Mahwah, NJ: Lawrence Erlbaum.

Hartmann, T. (ed.) (2009). *Media choice: A theoretical and empirical overview*. New York: Routledge.

Lang, A. (2009). The limited capacity model of motivated mediated message processing. In R. L. Nabi & M. B. Oliver (eds.), *The Sage handbook of media processes and effects*. Thousand Oaks, CA: Sage, pp. 193–204.

Potter, W. J. (2009). Conceptualizing the audience. In R. L. Nabi & M. B. Oliver (eds.), *The Sage handbook of media processes and effects*. Thousand Oaks, CA: Sage, pp. 19–34.

Vorderer, P. (2008). Exposure to communication content. In W. Donsbach (ed.), *International encyclopedia of communication*. Oxford: Blackwell.

Zillmann, D. & Oliver, M. B. (eds.). (2009). *Media effects: Advances in theory and research*, 3rd edn. London: Routledge.

Exposure to Print Media

WIEBKE MÖHRING
Hanover University of Applied Sciences and Arts

BEATE SCHNEIDER
Hanover University of Music, Drama and Media

People use periodically published printed mass media in many different ways. Print media serve as sources of orientation and → information, provide models of behavior, and serve as frames of reference for possible dissociation and identification, differentiation, and participation. Additionally, they provide content for personal communication (→ Interpersonal Communication), relaxation, and emotional relief. International comparative research on the use of print media has to take into account that motivation for using print media, as well as their circulation and availability, is embedded in the cultural, political, and societal structures of the national systems in question, and that it is also dependent on economic conditions (→ Media Use, International Comparison of).

Level of education and literacy are significant socio-cultural *indicators for print media use* in a given country (→ Media Use by Social Variable). Reading skills and motivation, both essential conditions for reading, are complexly interrelated. Reading is a cognitive process (→ Cognitive Science). The reader actively and constructively incorporates the content of the text into pre-existing knowledge structures, based on the reader's familiarity with language, the used media, and knowledge of the world (→ Information Processing). In addition, the reader's motivation and interests play a pivotal role. Compared to electronic media, reading print media requires complete attention and focus, excluding all other activities (→ Attending to the Mass Media). On the other hand, the *mode of exposure* allows to use print media irrespective of place and time and thus offers higher accessibility and flexibility to be interrupted and to resume reading at the user's discretion. A number of factors influence newspaper use: income, age, sex, level of education, race, length of residence in a community, mobility, number of children in a household, marital status, housing condition, and interest in politics. Respondents name lack of time, lack of interest, preference for a different medium, and cost as reasons for not reading newspapers.

Generally speaking, we can identify three *subject areas* that stimulate the use of print media: 'hard news' (e.g., politics and business; → News), 'soft news' (e.g., people or society), and sports (→ Sports and the Media, History of), while local interest topics cut across these three subject areas. Notwithstanding the continuing strength of the newspaper market in many countries, a downward trend in newspaper reading can be observed worldwide. Consequently circulation and coverage of dailies have been decreasing for years. Online distribution can hardly absorb the losses (→ Internet News; Online Media; van der Wurff & Lauf 2005; Mögerle 2009).

In contrast to newspapers, magazines in their very special variety are particularly sensitive to trends and fashions, both national and global. *Magazines* have to adapt quickly and strongly to the altered needs of their readership. Consequently, fluctuation in the magazine market is high. This trend is reinforced by the readers' behavior. Nowadays, readers use a broader range of titles, and traditional target groups are losing validity (→ Audience Segmentation). Reader motivation and the functions of magazines vary widely and cover the whole spectrum, from specific information to distraction or entertainment. At the same time, magazines represent certain images and thus can also take over functions of social identification for the user.

Measuring print media use and impact presents a methodological challenge. Readers often use different sources of information, talk about content, and understand reports differently. The general problem in readership research is the respondents' recall of sources and the given fact that sources of information are usually more easily forgotten than the information itself (→ Audience Research).

See also: ▶ ATTENDING TO THE MASS MEDIA ▶ AUDIENCE RESEARCH ▶ AUDIENCE SEGMENTATION ▶ COGNITIVE SCIENCE ▶ INFORMATION ▶ INFORMATION PROCESSING ▶ INTERNET NEWS ▶ INTERPERSONAL COMMUNICATION ▶ LONGITUDINAL ANALYSIS ▶ MEANING ▶ MEDIA ECONOMICS ▶ MEDIA USE, INTERNATIONAL COMPARISON OF ▶ MEDIA USE BY SOCIAL VARIABLE ▶ NEWS ▶ ONLINE MEDIA ▶ SPORTS AND THE MEDIA, HISTORY OF

REFERENCES AND SUGGESTED READINGS

Hasebrink, U. (2012). Comparing media use and reception. In F. Esser & M. Hanitzsch (eds.) *The handbook of comparative communication research*. London: Routledge, pp. 382–399.

Mögerle, U. (2009). *Substitution oder Komplementarität? Die Nutzung von Online- und Print-Zeitungen im Wandel.* [Substitute or complement? The changing use of online and print newspapers]. Constance: UVK.

Waal, E. de, Schönbach, K., & Lauf, E. (2005). Online newspapers: A substitute or complement for print newspapers and other information channels? *Communications*, 30, 55–72.

World Association of Newspapers (2012). *World press trends 2012*. Paris: WAN.

van der Wurff, R. & Lauf, E. (eds.) (2005). *Print and online newspapers in Europe: A comparative analysis in 16 countries*. Amsterdam: Het Spinhuis.

Exposure to Radio

HOLGER SCHRAMM
University of Würzburg

Radio is the medium with the highest relevance for media users in daily life – at least with respect to the amount of exposure time (→ Radio: Social History). People in western industrialized countries listen to radio for about three hours each day, with about 80 percent of daily reach. Radio consumption has decreased massively since the beginning of the twenty-first century, especially among people under the age of 40, due to the increasing use of mobile music media like MP3 players (Schramm 2006). About 90 percent of radio consumption occurs while people pursue other activities at the same time, such as eating, working at home (e.g., cleaning, cooking, ironing), working outside home (e.g., gardening, office work), or car driving (MacFarland 1997).

People use radio for several *motives*. Its central function is accompanying other activities in order to ease workload, to abridge time, and to compensate monotony. Further, several emotional motives can be identified in radio use: stimulation of excitation, activation versus damping/catalyzing of excitation, abreaction, relaxation (→ Excitation and Arousal), wallowing in memories, distraction, day dreaming (→ Escapism), social belonging, affiliation (→ Social Identity Theory), distinction, social comparison (→ Social Comparison Theory), → parasocial interactions and relationships, social alternative, and → information seeking and life assistance (MacFarland 1997; Schramm 2006; → Audience Research; Affects and Media Exposure; Mood Management). The primary *content* of most radio programs is music with a music portion, on average, of about 70 percent. In order to create music programs compatible with large groups of people, the degree of complexity of radio music must remain rather low (Ahlkvist & Fisher 2000).

See also: ▶ AFFECTS AND MEDIA EXPOSURE ▶ AUDIENCE RESEARCH ▶ AUDIENCE SEGMENTATION ▶ ESCAPISM ▶ EXCITATION AND AROUSAL ▶ INFORMATION SEEKING ▶ MOOD MANAGEMENT ▶ PARASOCIAL INTERACTIONS AND

RELATIONSHIPS ▶ RADIO: SOCIAL HISTORY ▶ SOCIAL COMPARISON THEORY ▶ SOCIAL IDENTITY THEORY

REFERENCES AND SUGGESTED READINGS

Ahlkvist, J. A. & Fisher, G. (2000). And the hits just keep on coming: Music programming standardization in commercial radio. *Poetics*, 27, 301–325.

MacFarland, D. T. (1997). *Future radio programming strategies: Cultivating listenership in the digital age.* Mahwah, NJ: Lawrence Erlbaum.

Schramm, H. (2006). Consumption and effects of music in the media. *Communication Research Trends*, 25(4), 3–29.

Exposure to Television

UWE HASEBRINK

Hans Bredow Institute for Media Research at the University of Hamburg

Research on exposure to television deals with the question, what do people do with television? The television industry has an existential interest in finding out how many people watch its programs, in order to sell these data to the advertising industry (→ Media Economics). Beyond this, information on exposure to television is a necessary condition for statements on the role of television in people's everyday lives and its social and individual consequences (→ Exposure to Communication Content).

The dominant line of research aims to describe and explain the *viewing behavior of aggregate audiences*. The industry has developed sophisticated mechanisms to construct the "mass audience" as the dominant model of research (Webster & Phalen 1997). In most countries this research relies on electronic meter systems that register any screen-related activity (→ Audience Research). The most common indicator for TV exposure is 'reach,' the percentage of the population that had at least one contact with the particular television offer of interest. Over the last years in most developed countries the reach of television on an average day has been stable on a high level (75 to 85 percent of the population; IP Networks 2013). The viewing time indicator reflects the average duration of use; recent figures for industrialized countries are between three and five hours per day for every person (IP Networks 2013). Particular attention is paid to channel-related indicators. The share of a channel or program expresses the percentage of viewing time devoted to this channel or program compared to the total viewing time. In recent years the average share of channels has been decreasing substantially, a finding that is interpreted as → audience segmentation (Webster 2005, 367).

Another practically interesting line of research is called *audience duplication research*, because it is empirically based on the percentage of viewers of a certain program who also watch a certain other program at another time (Cooper 1996). The concept of 'channel loyalty' means that viewers tend to select programs on a particular channel. More specifically, the 'inheritance effect' means that viewers of a program are likely to watch the next program on the same channel. 'Repeat viewing' is defined as the degree to which viewers are likely to watch two different episodes of the same program.

Some other lines of research, mainly in the academic area, examine *exposure to television as individual behavior*. This kind of research is more interested in the psychological processes linked to the selection, interpretation, and appropriation of televised content, in interindividual differences between viewer groups, and in intraindividual differences between situations. With regard to interindividual differences between (groups of) viewers, a general finding is that elderly people watch substantially more television than younger people (→ Media Use across the Life-Span), and people with less formal education more than better-educated people (→ Media Use by Social Variable). Another explanation for stable interindividual differences in exposure to television refers to traits. In particular; → sensation seeking is one factor that explains differences in the extent to which people watch exciting action and violence-oriented programs.The broad research on → selective exposure to television has provided strong evidence of how viewers, based on their individual needs and interests, selectively compose their personal television repertoire. Finally, affects and moods have been shown to be important determinants of viewing behavior (→ Affects and Media Exposure; Mood Management).

One of the *future conceptual challenges* of research on television exposure will be how to identify and classify the increasing number of audiovisual services that are similar to television but not (yet) regarded as television. Due to these challenges of new media environments Napoli (2011, 149ff) even questions the role of exposure as the former key concept of audience research, and points to the increasing importance of alternative audience conceptualizations, e.g., interest, appreciation, and engagement.

See also: ▶ ADVERTISING ▶ AFFECTS AND MEDIA EXPOSURE ▶ AUDIENCE RESEARCH ▶ AUDIENCE SEGMENTATION ▶ EXPOSURE TO COMMUNICATION CONTENT ▶ MEDIA ECONOMICS ▶ MEDIA USE ACROSS THE LIFE-SPAN ▶ MEDIA USE BY SOCIAL VARIABLE ▶ MOOD MANAGEMENT ▶ SELECTIVE EXPOSURE ▶ SENSATION SEEKING

REFERENCES AND SUGGESTED READINGS

Cooper, R. (1996). The status and future of audience duplication research: An assessment of ratings-based theories of audience behavior. *Journal of Broadcasting and Electronic Media*, 40, 96–111.

IP Networks (2013). *Television: International key facts.* Paris: IP Networks.

Napoli, P. M. (2011). *Audience evolution. New technologies and the transformation of media audiences.* New York: Columbia University Press.

Webster, J. G. (2005). Beneath the veneer of fragmentation: Television audience polarization in a multichannel world. *Journal of Communication*, 56(2), 366–382.

Webster, J. G. & Phalen, P. F. (1997). *The mass audience: Rediscovering the dominant model.* Mahwah, NJ: Lawrence Erlbaum.

Exposure to the Internet

ROBERT J. LUNN

FocalPoint Analytics, Oxnard, CA

This entry refrains from presenting rapidly changing descriptive data on the use of the Internet (for international data see Internet World Stats 2014; Pew Research 2014), but with the factors explaining growth of and differences in exposure to the Internet between countries.

Numerous studies have established that the diffusion of Internet access follows an S-shaped curve. What is not well understood are the factors responsible for different levels of Internet access among different countries (→ Digital Divide; Media Use, International Comparison of). Many theories of the diffusion of innovations, such as the Bass model, focus on individual factors, such as perceived need (Bass 1969; → Diffusion of Information and Innovation; Media Use by Social Variable). The inadequacy of this theoretical stance becomes readily apparent when we consider that cultures exhibiting low levels of gender empowerment deny Internet access to half of their populations. This example of the influence of culture (→ Culture: Definitions and Concepts) also illustrates that adoption of the Internet is affected by factors beyond simple exposure to the technology.

A common misconception, termed the '*pro-innovation bias*,' occurs when researchers assume that innovations, such as the Internet, will eventually be adopted by all members of a social system. In reality, the degree to which innovations diffuse through a population is a complex function of many different factors, some of which act to impede the diffusion process. Pro-innovation bias is inadvertently created when researchers plot percent adoption of an innovation at a single time point, using multiple countries. The resultant curve is indeed often S-shaped but it carries with it the implicit assumption that all of the plotted countries will follow a universal diffusion trajectory, and that, in time, countries at the lower left of the curve will eventually 'catch up' with the countries on the top right of the curve.

Several researchers have suggested that the primary reason for cross-national inequalities in Internet access resides in *differential economic development* (e.g., Norris 2001). In this regard, findings that implicate public investment in human capital and infrastructure are important because they associate aspects of economic influence beyond the concept of GDP per capita with a country's degree of Internet access. Increases in life expectancy and literacy require long-term investments in large-scale public services and facilities, such as public health, telecommunications, or schools. Aspects of wealth such as education and infrastructure take a considerable amount of time to develop, and consequently policies designed to enhance Internet access through interventions of short-term economic aid are questionable.

Norris (2001) considers individuals who prescribe an economic interventionist policy as "cyber-optimists." In conjunction with short-term economic aid, a cyber-optimist would expect Internet access to eventually diffuse throughout a country's entire population. This diffusion pattern (the "normalization" pattern) might typically be expected to occur in wealthy countries with cultures that value and reward innovative behavior. Alternatively, "cyber-pessimists" would expect that, regardless of economic aid, digital technology would more likely amplify existing inequalities of power, wealth, and education, creating deeper divisions between the advantaged and disadvantaged (→ Technology and Communication). This *stratification pattern of Internet diffusion* suggests that individuals who do adopt are subject to country-specific cultural and economic restrictions rather than the simple fulfillment of individual needs and exposure to the technology through mass media. Both adoption patterns yield S-shaped curves that can be fitted by mathematical formulations such as the Bass model. However, results following a stratification pattern are difficult to explain in terms of social contagion theory or Bass model coefficients.

Given the normalization and stratification diffusion patterns, it is natural to ask whether the factors responsible for the diffusion of Internet access are amenable to 'quick-fix' treatments, such as the insertion of technology or short-term economic aid, or whether the degree of Internet access is shaped by more *deep-seated forces, such as culture*. Norris reports that affluent Middle Eastern countries have relatively low Internet access levels, which challenges the assertion that economic factors are solely responsible for degree of Internet access. Notably, the culture of these countries acts to inhibit Internet access for half of their population, i.e., females (→ Feminist and Gender Studies). This is decidedly not a small effect and points to the danger of making generalizations when predictive factors are causally entangled.

A second point of consideration is that explanations, based on *social contagion theory,* should work best in countries that support a normalization pattern of Internet adoption (e.g., the US and western European countries). In these countries, we would expect the adoption decision to be largely under an individual's control moderated by their exposure to mass media. However, social contagion models should fail when attempting to predict Internet diffusion in countries that follow the stratification pattern of diffusion. When examined from this perspective, social contagion explanations for the diffusion of innovations and the use of classical Bass model coefficients appear to be an artifact of early diffusion research that predominantly focused on the US and western European countries. These are countries where the individual-oriented normalization diffusion pattern is found and inhibiting factors such as fear, diminished gender empowerment, and low levels of long-term economic development are minimized.

The implication of the existing explanations for cross-country differences in Internet exposure is that models need to utilize a mixed-level hierarchical modeling approach, where one level defines the moderating influence of country-specific factors and another level deals with individual needs and communication channels.

See also: ▶ AFFECTS AND MEDIA EXPOSURE ▶ CULTURE: DEFINITIONS AND CONCEPTS ▶ DIFFUSION OF INFORMATION AND INNOVATION ▶ DIGITAL DIVIDE ▶ ETHNICITY AND EXPOSURE TO COMMUNICATION ▶ EXPOSURE TO COMMUNICATION CONTENT ▶ FEMINIST AND GENDER STUDIES ▶ INTERPERSONAL COMMUNICATION ▶ INVOLVEMENT WITH MEDIA CONTENT ▶ LONGITUDINAL ANALYSIS ▶ MEDIA USE BY SOCIAL VARIABLE ▶ MEDIA USE, INTERNATIONAL COMPARISON OF ▶ REGRESSION ANALYSIS ▶ SAMPLING, RANDOM ▶ TECHNOLOGY AND COMMUNICATION ▶ TWO-STEP FLOW OF COMMUNICATION ▶ USES AND GRATIFICATIONS ▶ VALIDITY

REFERENCES AND SUGGESTED READINGS

Bass, F. (1969). A new product growth model for consumer durables. *Management Science*, 15, 215–227.

Blank, G. & Groselj, D. (2014). Dimensions of Internet use: amount, variety, and types. *Information, Communication & Society*, 17(4), 417–435.

Hargittai E. (2010). Digital na(t)ives? Variation in internet skills and uses among members of the Net Generation. *Sociological Inquiry*, 80, 92–113.
Internet World Stats (2014). At http://www.internetworldstats.com/stats.htm, accessed August 4, 2014.
Norris, P. (2001). *Digital divide: Civic engagement, information poverty, and the Internet worldwide.* Cambridge: Cambridge University Press.
Pew Research (2014). Pew Research Internet Project. At http://www.pewinternet.org/, accessed August 4, 2014.
Rogers, E. (1995). *Diffusion of innovations*, 4th edn. New York: Free Press.

Extended Parallel Process Model

KIM WITTE
Michigan State University

According to the Extended Parallel Process Model (EPPM), when people are faced with a threat they either control the danger or control their fear about the threat. The variables that cause individuals to either control the danger or control their fear are defined as follows.

Perceived threat, or the degree to which we feel susceptible to a serious threat, is composed of two dimensions. The first refers to the perceived seriousness of a threat or the magnitude of harm we think we might experience if the threat occurred (e.g., injury, loss, death, disgrace, etc.). The second dimension, susceptibility to threat, is the perceived likelihood of experiencing a threat. *Perceived efficacy*, or the degree to which we believe we can feasibly carry out a recommended response to avert a threat, is also composed of two dimensions: our beliefs about whether or not a recommended response works in averting a threat (response efficacy) and beliefs about our ability to perform the recommended response (self-efficacy).

Overall, the EPPM suggests that when people feel at-risk for a significant threat they become scared and are motivated to act. Perceptions of self-efficacy and response efficacy determine whether people are motivated to control the danger or control their fear. When people feel able to perform an action that they think effectively averts a threat (strong perceptions of self-efficacy and response efficacy), then they are motivated to control the danger and engage in self-protective health behaviors. In contrast, when people either feel unable to perform a recommended response and/or they believe the response to be ineffective, they give up trying to control the danger. Instead they control the fear by denying their risk, defensively avoiding the issue, adopting a fatalistic attitude, or perceiving manipulation.

The EPPM has been used to guide education entertainment radio dramas, worker notification programs for beryllium exposure. The EPPM can be used to tailor messages to promote danger control responses via interpersonal channels (as in counselor–client, doctor–patient, or peer educator encounters), mass media channels, or → social media.

See also: ▶ APPLIED COMMUNICATION RESEARCH ▶ HEALTH CAMPAIGNS, COMMUNICATION IN ▶ HEALTH COMMUNICATION ▶ INFORMATION PROCESSING ▶ PERSUASION ▶ RISK COMMUNICATION ▶ RISK PERCEPTIONS ▶ SOCIAL MEDIA

REFERENCES AND SUGGESTED READINGS

Cho H., Witte K. (2005). Managing fear in public health campaigns: A theory-based formative evaluation process. *Health Promotion Practice*, 6(4), 482–90.
Witte, K. (1992). Putting the fear back into fear appeals: The extended parallel process model. *Communication Monographs*, 59, 329–349.
Witte, K. & Roberto, A. (2009). Fear appeals and public health: Managing fear and creating hope. In L. Frey and K. Cissna (eds.), *Handbook of applied communication research*. London: Routledge, pp. 584–610.

Extra-Media Data

WOLFGANG DONSBACH
Dresden University of Technology

The term "extra-media data" describes a methodological approach to assessing the quality of media content. The phrase was coined in the early 1970s by Swedish scholar Karl Erik Rosengren (1970) during a controversy about the criteria needed to assess → bias in the news. Rosengren suggested that researchers should evaluate the performance of news media, for instance the influence of → news factors on → news value, by comparing media coverage to external, primarily statistical indicators. In communication research today we can find at least *three different approaches* to assessing the quality of media content by sources from outside.

Funkhouser (1973) used *statistical data* and compared the number of news articles on several political issues in the USA in the 1960s with statistical indicators for their real salience, for instance the number of US soldiers fighting in Vietnam. In their seminal "McArthur-Day study" Lang and Lang (1953) compared the impressions of an event when seen on television with the *impression of the same event when participating* in it. The authors attributed the discrepancy between these impressions to a → reciprocal effect created by the presence of the television camera itself. Many years later Donsbach et al. (1993) applied the same approach in an experimental study on a campaign speech. Lichter et al. (1986) *surveyed experts* on nuclear energy about the potential risks of this technology and compared the result to the opinions expressed by experts cited or interviewed in the media.

These examples show that the use of such reality indicators for an assessment of media coverage by extra-media data is problematic. In most cases the concrete indicators used either represent only a certain aspect of the issue or event they are supposed to indicate, or may be biased themselves. Further, there are many areas where no such extra-media data exist. Nevertheless, if one assumes that some scientific measure of the quality of reality representation in the media is important, the comparison of media content with extra-media data is probably the strongest tool.

See also: ▶ BIAS IN THE NEWS ▶ MEDIA EFFECTS: DIRECT AND INDIRECT EFFECTS ▶ NEWS FACTORS ▶ NEWS VALUES ▶ OBJECTIVITY IN REPORTING ▶ RECIPROCAL EFFECTS

REFERENCES AND SUGGESTED READINGS

Donsbach, W., Brosius, H.-B., & Mattenklott, A. (1993). How unique is the perspective of television? A field experiment on the perception of a campaign event by participants and television viewers. *Political Communication*, 10(1), 41–57.

Funkhouser, R. (1973). The issues of the sixties: An exploratory study in the dynamics of public opinion. *Public Opinion Quarterly*, 37(1), 62–75.

Lang, K. & Lang, G. E. (1953). The unique perspective of television and its effect. *American Sociological Review*, 18(1), 3–12.

Lichter, S. R. Rothman, S., & Lichter, L. (1986). *The Media Elite: America's New Power-brokers*. Bethesda, MD: Adler & Adler.

Rosengren, K. E. (1970). International news: Intra and extra media data. *Acta Sociologica*, 13, 96–109.

F

Facebook

DONALD MATHESON
University of Canterbury

Facebook is the world's largest social networking service (SNS; → Social Media). Launched in 2004, it has quickly extended beyond Harvard University to become intertwined with many aspects of social life, from friendships to playing games to commerce and politics. How Facebook is used – and why it has become so successful – are central questions of much research.

Facebook is best *understood as a social environment*. That is, it is used by different people for many different purposes. There is wide agreement among researchers that people tend to use Facebook more to deepen existing social relations than to make new connections, although the ease with which temporary and distant relationships can be entered into is also central to its appeal (→ Communication Networks; Network Organizations through Communication Technology). Some US-based research suggests Facebook operates by a logic or culture favoring honesty about identity and that its users tend to be more socially engaged than the wider population or have a stronger desire to connect with others. However, these early generalizations are being revised as other cultures are studied – see, e.g., Miller's ethnography (2011) on Trinidadian uses of Facebook for scandal, gossip and sexual display.

Much research focuses on Facebook's wider impact on social and political life, e.g., its role in protests during the 2011 Arab Spring revolts (→ Communication Technology and Democracy). Concerns over Facebook's privacy standards and mining of personal data have fed the critique that the company accelerates a culture of 'participatory surveillance.' It is the central example of the emergence of marketing focused on selling interpersonal relationships to which the platform has contributed (→ Marketing: Communication Tools).

See also: ▶ COMMUNICATION NETWORKS ▶ MARKETING: COMMUNICATION TOOLS ▶ NETWORK ORGANIZATIONS THROUGH COMMUNICATION TECHNOLOGY ▶ ONLINE MEDIA ▶ SOCIAL MEDIA ▶ TECHNOLOGY AND COMMUNICATION ▶ COMMUNICATION TECHNOLOGY AND DEMOCRACY

REFERENCES AND SUGGESTED READINGS

Joinson, A. (2008). "Looking at," "looking up" or "keeping up with" people? Motives and uses of Facebook. *CHI 2008 Proceedings*, April 5–10, Florence, pp. 1027–1036.

Miller, D. (2011). *Tales from Facebook*. Cambridge: Polity.

Wilson, R. E., Gosling, S. D. & Graham, L. T. (2012). A review of Facebook research in the social sciences. *Perspectives on Psychological Science*, 7(3), 203–220.

Fear Induction through Media Content

GLENN G. SPARKS
Purdue University

The capacity for media messages to induce fear has been the object of scholarly inquiry since at least the 1930s, when the Payne Fund Studies launched the first systematic effort to study the impact of media on children and adolescents. As part of that effort, Herbert Blumer (1933) found that 93 percent of the children who participated in his study reported that they had been scared by something seen in a motion picture. Despite the prevalence of fright reactions to media indicated by Blumer's finding, there was little research on this topic for nearly 50 years (→ Media Effects, History of). The fact that media presentations induced fear became apparent in sporadic scholarly reports about media impact or in news reports such as those that followed the 1938 broadcast of the radio play by Orson Welles, The War of the Worlds. A few scholarly reports in the 1950s and 1960s devoted attention to the media's capacity to induce fear in audiences but, for the most part, the topic received little attention until the 1980s.

In the 1980s, research initiated by US researcher Joanne Cantor developed the research on media-induced fear in a theoretical and systematic fashion (Cantor 1994). The first studies in this program of research were designed in order to identify the types of movies and TV programs that were most likely to cause fright reactions in children at different points in their cognitive development. A second emphasis in this research was to identify the coping behaviors that parents could employ to successfully reduce media-induced fears in their children (→ Violence as Media Content, Effects on Children of). Building upon the developmental psychology of Jean Piaget, Cantor made sense of children's fright reactions to media by emphasizing a child's level of cognitive functioning at either the pre-operational (2–7 years) or concrete operational (7–11 years) stage of development. For example, in the younger age group, children's fright reactions to media are far more likely to be determined by visual appearances. In the simplest terms, if something looks scary, then younger children are likely to be scared. In contrast, children in the older age group are able to integrate conceptual information into their perceptions such that they can discount visual appearances in favor of other facts that help to override any fear (Sparks & Cantor 1986).

In 1983, the broadcast of a movie about nuclear holocaust (The Day After) inspired research that helped to document the potential of media to induce fear in audiences. The broadcast was noteworthy in that it inspired an entire article in American Psychologist (Schofield & Pavelchak 1983). Studies of the emotional fallout from the movie by other research teams (e.g., Palmer et al. 1983) served to galvanize an interest in children's fear reactions to media that had begun earlier in the decade.

One phenomenon that is likely to attract the attention of future researchers is the tendency for some individuals to suffer lingering emotional reactions to frightening media that may endure for days, weeks, months, and even years after initial exposure to the media stimulus. The fact that some people suffer such disturbances is well documented (Bozzuto 1975). Research by Hoekstra, Harris, and Helmick (1999) explored autobiographical memories of movie-induced fear and found strong evidence that media fear induced in childhood is easily recalled by college students years after the precipitating media event. Cantor has drawn upon the work of LeDoux (1996) in suggesting that the amygdala may play a pivotal role in preserving fright responses that arise from media.

Several recent studies show a growing interest in the capacity of particular types of news reports to induce fear and other negative emotions in viewers. Unz, Schwab, and Winterhoff-Spurk (2008) studied exposure to different kinds of violence in news reports and found that fear was one of the typical emotional reactions that viewers experienced. More recently, Nellis and

Savage (2012) completed a telephone survey of over 500 respondents and discovered a positive relationship between exposure to news reports about terrorism and fear for the safety of others as a result of a terror attack.

See also: ▶ EMOTIONAL AROUSAL THEORY ▶ EXCITATION AND AROUSAL ▶ MEDIA EFFECTS, HISTORY OF ▶ VIOLENCE AS MEDIA CONTENT, EFFECTS ON CHILDREN OF ▶ PHYSIOLOGICAL MEASUREMENT ▶ SENSATION SEEKING ▶ VIOLENCE AS MEDIA CONTENT ▶ VIOLENCE AS MEDIA CONTENT, EFFECTS OF ▶ VIOLENCE AS MEDIA CONTENT, EFFECTS ON CHILDREN OF

REFERENCES AND SUGGESTED READINGS

Blumer, H. (1933). *Movies and conduct*. London: Macmillan.

Bozzuto, J. C. (1975). Cinematic neurosis following "The Exorcist." *Journal of Nervous and Mental Disease*, 161, 43–48.

Cantor, J. (1994). Fright reactions to mass media. In J. Bryant & D. Zillmann (eds.), *Media effects: Advances in theory and research*. Hillsdale, NJ: Lawrence Erlbaum, pp. 213–245.

Hoekstra, S. J., Harris, R. J., & Helmick, A. L. (1999). Autobiographical memories about the experience of seeing frightening movies in childhood. *Media Psychology*, 1(2), 117–140.

LeDoux, J. (1996). *The emotional brain: The mysterious underpinnings of emotional life*. New York: Simon and Schuster.

Nellis, A. M. & Savage, J. (2012). Does watching the news affect fear of terrorism?: The importance of media exposure on terrorism fear. *Crime & Delinquency*, 58(5): 748–768.

Palmer, E., Hockett, A., & Dean, W. (1983). The television family and children's fright reactions. *Journal of Family Issues*, 4(2), 279–292.

Schofield, J. & Pavelchak, M. (1983). The Day After: The impact of a media event. *American Psychologist*, 40(5), 542–548.

Sparks, G. & Cantor, J. (1986). Developmental differences in fright responses to a television program depicting a character transformation. *Journal of Broadcasting and Electronic Media*, 30, 309–323.

Unz, D., Schwab, F., & Winterhoff-Spurk, P. (2008). TV news – the daily horror: Emotional effects of violent television news. *Journal of Media Psychology*, 20(4), 141–155.

Federal Communications Commission (FCC)

CHRIS PATERSON
University of Leeds

SEETA PEÑA GANGADHARAN
Open Technology Institute

The Federal Communications Commission (FCC) is the regulatory agency in the United States charged with oversight of electronic communications (→ Television Broadcasting, Regulation of; United States of America: Media System). Since the 1980s, it has taken much of the blame for the lack of diversity and the concentration of ownership in US broadcasting, the rise of media conglomerates, and pro-market regulation of Internet-related industries.

The agency was *created in 1934*, when Congress passed the Communications Act. Since its creation, the commission has been controversial. It was meant to uphold the decision of Congress following World War I that broadcasting should be mostly commercial and free of government control; but also to insure that access to the airwaves was allocated responsibly and that those granted access put the public's interest before their own. With three of the five appointed commissioners representing the president's party, the agency tends to keep broadcast policy aligned with ruling party ideology.

The Communications Act has been amended many times and still dictates most US communications policy. With jurisdiction over the use of radio spectrum, the FCC is most well known for licensing broadcast stations and using its authority to enforce basic regulations. Broadcasters have wide leeway in what they can and cannot do, and despite public protest, fines for breaching regulations are rare, and revocations of licenses or denials of license renewal even rarer.

The FCC also regulates *Internet-based communications* but with greater leniency than broadcasting (→ Internet Law and Regulation). The Telecommunications Act of 1996 distinguished information services from telecommunication services, limiting the agency's power over broadband providers. Debate over network neutrality questions whether the FCC has the authority to prevent Internet service providers from discriminating in the types of data that travel over its networks. As broadband services become the mainstay of the modern communications landscape, the FCC's limited authority over information services may coincide with a decline of its power and influence.

See also: ▶ COMMUNICATION LAW AND POLICY: NORTH AMERICA ▶ INTERNET LAW AND REGULATION ▶ PUBLIC BROADCASTING SYSTEMS ▶ TELEVISION BROADCASTING, REGULATION OF ▶ UNITED STATES OF AMERICA: MEDIA SYSTEM

REFERENCES AND SUGGESTED READINGS

McChesney, R. (2004). *The problem of the media: US communication politics in the 21st century*. New York: Monthly Review Press.

Wu, T. (2003). Network neutrality, broadband discrimination. *Colorado Journal of Telecommunications and High Technology Law*, 2, 11–12, 20–21.

Feminist and Gender Studies

CYNTHIA CARTER
Cardiff University

KAITLYNN MENDES
De Montfort University

Feminist and gender studies represent key fields of research within communication studies today. It is difficult to discuss their emergence and developments as two separate entities, as the two often overlap. However, it can be noted that mainstream forms of gender studies research tend to differ from feminist studies politically, theoretically, and methodologically. As Dow and Condit (2005, 449) argue, "The field of communication has come too far to categorize all research on women, or even gender, as feminist in its orientation. Rather, the moniker of 'feminist' is reserved for research that studies communication theories and practices from a perspective that ultimately is oriented toward the achievement of 'gender justice,' a goal that takes into account the ways that gender always already intersects with race, ethnicity, sexuality, and class."

As a *political movement* for gender justice, feminist communication scholarship always has at its core a goal of examining how gender relations are represented (→ Gender: Representation in the Media; Media and Perceptions of Reality), the ways in which audiences make sense of them, or how media practitioners contribute to perpetuating gender injustice. At the center of this is the view that hierarchical gender relations (re)produce social inequalities across time and cultures, thereby making it difficult for men and women to be equal partners in democratic society. Feminist communication research is tied to a political movement for structural social change rather than individual change. As such, feminist scholarly research is inseparable from activist forms of feminism. On the other hand, gender studies are not implicitly political in the sense of having an agenda for social change on the basis of gender equality. Instead, the principal aim has been one of raising public awareness about the ways in which gender affects the individual's life choices and chances, and thus women's and men's relative opportunities for personal and career success.

Gender Studies in Communication

Communication scholarship examining gender issues has a longer history than that of feminist scholarship. 'Gender studies' usually refers to the social constructions of masculinity and femininity. However, studies on sex roles – or the belief that women and men are innately different – are often included in this definition. Until the 1980s, it was generally assumed that gender research would focus on women, but this soon extended to the ways in which men and masculinity were portrayed and (re)constructed (→ Masculinity and the Media).

As noted above, gender and communication studies have largely been grounded in assumptions about the individual's acquisition of gendered attitudes and behaviors, and the ways in which socially constructed gender roles can negatively impact on the individual's life chances, especially in terms of sense of self-worth, → social perceptions of women, and their career prospects.

Feminist Studies in Communication

Feminist thought, political activity, and scholarship come in a myriad of different forms, from western constructions such as liberal, radical, socialist, and postmodern feminism (→ Postmodernism and Communication), as well as the more recent phenomenon of → postfeminism, to the development of postcolonial and transnational feminist theory (→ Feminist Media Studies, Transnational). Globally, we have also seen the development of Latina, black, Islamic, and Asian feminist theory. The range of conceptual and methodological approaches within feminism has led to different forms and practices of communication research and feminisms that are increasingly sensitive to cultural, social, and economic differences (as well as points of connection locally and internationally).

One of the most notable interventions second-wave feminist communication scholars have made over the past few decades centers on the analysis of the ways in which women are *portrayed in the media* (→ Content Analysis, Qualitative; Content Analysis, Quantitative). Numerous studies found that the most recurrent media images of women were those of submissive wives and mothers located within domestic settings (→ Women in the Media, Images of). Additionally, research on female journalists confirmed that they were typically relegated to covering 'soft' or human-interest news and that those who read the news on television were often judged by appearance over their journalistic experience (→ Gender: Representation in the Media). Here, the argument was that taken together these things led to an undervaluation of women's contributions to society and their status as citizens.

Some researchers, however, came to the view that such content analyses were problematic because they were only able to comment on the manifest media content of specific images rather than wider structures of → meaning. Out of this developed, particularly in Europe, critical forms of analysis, such as the semiotic and ideological analyses of British → cultural studies (→ Semiotics).

New Developments

From the 1980s onward, *more complex approaches* to the analysis of gender in the media emerged. New theories were advanced by poststructuralism and postmodernism, for instance, which provided feminist communication scholars with conceptual frameworks that went beyond calls for the media to reflect more realistic images of women, to instead embrace the argument that the media play an important role in constructing certain gendered realities.

This research eventually led the way to an interest in understanding how the media help to *construct gender identity and subjectivity*, which are seen to be partial and fragmented, rather than unified and rational, assumptions underpinning previous notions of gender subjectivity. This development allowed feminist communication scholars to see gender as fluid and open to change, rather than immutable and ahistorical. In opening up gender to this sort of theoretical scrutiny, it also followed that feminism itself was re-examined with a view to exploring the ways in which mainstream forms of feminism could be used to advance the position of certain women (particularly white, middle-class, heterosexual women), while at the same time doing little to raise awareness or improve the position of women of color, working-class women, lesbians, women with disabilities, etc. It was at this point that there began to develop postcolonial and transnational forms of feminism, as well as black feminism, Latina feminism, Islamic feminism, cyberfeminism, and third-wave feminism, among others, highlighting the extent to which western political thought, including that of some forms of feminism, had tended to silence the voices of those who were not included in the dominant discourses of western feminism.

See also: ▶ CONTENT ANALYSIS, QUALITATIVE ▶ CONTENT ANALYSIS, QUANTITATIVE ▶ CULTURAL STUDIES ▶ ETHNOGRAPHY OF COMMUNICATION ▶ FEMINIST MEDIA STUDIES, TRANSNATIONAL ▶ FILM GENRES ▶ GENDER AND DISCOURSE ▶ GENDER AND JOURNALISM ▶ GENDER: REPRESENTATION IN THE MEDIA ▶ IDENTITIES AND DISCOURSE ▶ INTERPERSONAL COMMUNICATION, SEX AND GENDER DIFFERENCES IN ▶ JOURNALISM ▶ LANGUAGE AND SOCIAL INTERACTION ▶ MASCULINITY AND THE MEDIA ▶ MEANING ▶ MEDIA AND PERCEPTIONS OF REALITY ▶ PORNOGRAPHY, FEMINIST DEBATES ON

▶ POSTFEMINISM ▶ POSTMODERNISM AND COMMUNICATION ▶ SEMIOTICS ▶ SEX ROLE STEREOTYPES IN THE MEDIA ▶ SEXISM IN THE MEDIA ▶ SEXUAL VIOLENCE IN THE MEDIA ▶ SOCIAL PERCEPTION ▶ SOCIAL STEREOTYPING AND COMMUNICATION ▶ WOMEN IN THE MEDIA, IMAGES OF ▶ WOMEN'S COMMUNICATION AND LANGUAGE

REFERENCES AND SUGGESTED READINGS

Byerly, C.M. (ed.) (2013). *The Palgrave international handbook of women and journalism.* Basingstoke: Palgrave Macmillan.
Carter, C., Steiner, L., & McLaughlin, L. (eds.) (2014). *The Routledge companion to media and gender.* London: Routledge.
Dow, B. & Condit, C. M. (2005). The state of the art in feminist scholarship in communication. *Journal of Communication*, 55(3), 448–478.
Gill, R. (2007). *Gender and the media.* Cambridge: Polity.
Watson, E. and Shaw, M. E. (eds.) (2011). *Performing American masculinities: The 21st-century man in popular culture.* Indianapolis, IN: Indiana University Press.

Feminist Media

LINDA STEINER
University of Maryland

'Feminist media' describes media that advocate expanded political, social, and cultural roles for women and expose gender oppression – interstructured with oppression by sexual orientation, class, race, ethnicity, and religion, or other bases of invidious distinction. Advocates can thereby redefine news, share information unavailable in mainstream media, challenge conventional (typically gendered) power hierarchies, and sustain a feminist community (→ Advocacy Journalism). Participants experiment with alternative ways of organizing their work, articulate their own ethical standards, and develop their media skills. Feminist journalism originally emerged from efforts on behalf of other causes, such as the abolition of slavery, as well as ones specifically for women, such as health and dress reform, and especially voting rights.

Notably, both mainstream media and periodicals of the radical countercultural movements of the 1960s were seen to marginalize – or altogether ignore – feminist issues and the newly emerging feminist movement (→ Women in the Media, Images of). So, literally hundreds of feminist periodicals emerged in the 1970s. Some lasted only for a year or less, given the economic, physical, and time burdens of production. Feminist magazines were specifically designed for and by different races, ethnicities, religions, professions, sexualities, and political persuasions. The larger magazines usually tried to reach women outside the liberation movement, or at least to unite disparate factions within feminism.

Arguably, the Internet more easily accommodates feminists. Low costs (of entry production and distribution), design plasticity, and potential for online feedback and interactivity allow 'cyberfeminists' (→ Cyberfeminism) to experiment in the name of individuality, self-expression, and choice. Beginning in the late 1980s, a new feminism emerged that emphasized multiculturalism, everyday domestic politics, and individual freedoms; its advocates continue to exploit the affordances of the Internet. Many use blogs and related social networking sites, including YouTube.

See also: ▶ ADVOCACY JOURNALISM
▶ CYBERFEMINISM ▶ FEMINIST MEDIA STUDIES, TRANSNATIONAL ▶ GAY, LESBIAN, BISEXUAL, AND TRANSGENDER MEDIA STUDIES ▶ GENDER: REPRESENTATION IN THE MEDIA ▶ POSTFEMINISM ▶ SEX ROLE STEREOTYPES IN THE MEDIA ▶ SEXISM IN THE MEDIA ▶ WOMEN IN THE MEDIA, IMAGES OF

REFERENCES AND SUGGESTED READINGS

"Feminist Media Production in Europe." (n.d.). Grassroots feminism. At http://www.grassrootsfeminism.net/cms/node/760, accessed July 25, 2014.
Zobl, E. & Drüeke, R. (eds.) (2012). *Feminist media: Participatory spaces, networks and cultural citizenship.* Bielefeld: transcript.

Feminist Media Studies, Transnational

RADHA S. HEGDE
New York University

Transnational feminist media studies responds to the challenges posed by globalization (→ Globalization Theories). Scholars representing this approach assume that the cross-border movement of capital, commodities, images, and people has led to interconnected lines of power and forms of gendered inequities. New technologies, systems of media representation, and digital networks would serve as crucial nodes in the transport and circulation of these modalities of power. Enmeshed in these changes are regulatory regimes that remain classed, raced, and gendered. Transnational analysis enables alternate feminist mappings of globalization which deconstruct and critique universalist assumptions, the essentialization of cultures, and the circulatory power of Euro modernity (→ Modernity), while maintaining that cultural politics exceeds national boundaries (→ Culture: Definitions and Concepts).

Transnational feminist media scholarship, greatly influenced by postcolonial theory, begins from the premise that we decenter the singular perspective of the west while considering the political particularities of ethnicity, gender, and sexuality. While globalization has necessitated new forms of labor and migration, new global actors typically fall outside the frame of dominant accounts of global processes. The mediated production of culture has to be situated against the backdrop of larger flows, and a pervasive neo-liberal worldview. The term 'transnational' offers conceptual pliability and provides an analytical rubric for feminist scholars to move beyond modes of liberal multiculturalism and produce politically and intellectually incisive scholarship.

The focus on the transnational forces a rethinking of categories such as nation, tradition, modernity, and culture in pliable terms. Transnational feminist scholarship does not claim allegiance to a particular method or approach that privileges political economy over cultural approaches. Instead, the transnational directs our scholarly response to the cross-cutting issues of race, class, and gender that intersect and travel across geographic and political landscapes (→ Gender: Representation in the Media).

See also: ▶ CULTURE: DEFINITIONS AND CONCEPTS ▶ FEMINIST AND GENDER STUDIES ▶ GENDER: REPRESENTATION IN THE MEDIA ▶ GLOBALIZATION THEORIES ▶ MODERNITY ▶ POPULAR COMMUNICATION AND SOCIAL CLASS

REFERENCES AND SUGGESTED READINGS

Grewal, I. & Kaplan, C. (eds.) (1994). *Scattered hegemonies: Postmodernity and transnational feminist practices*. Minneapolis, MN: University of Minnesota Press.

Hegde, R. (ed.) (2011). *Circuits of visibility: Gender and transnational media cultures*. New York: New York University Press.

Sassen, S. (1998). *Globalization and its discontents*. New York: New Press.

Feminization of Media Content

JOHANNA DORER
University of Vienna

The term 'feminization' tends to be used in communication studies in two basic ways. On the one hand, it describes any increases in the proportion of women working in a particular media profession. On the other, it refers to a process in which communication norms, values, and behaviors coded as 'masculine' are becoming gradually modified, if not replaced, by others associated with the 'feminine.'

Well-known *gendered binary hierarchies*, read as chains of equivalents for masculinity versus femininity, include, among others: public vs commercial broadcasting, serious papers vs tabloids (→ Tabloidization), national and international politics vs local interest and gossip, public vs private or personal issues, public vs aesthetic interest, information vs entertainment, facts vs opinion, or objective vs emotional style (→ Objectivity in Reporting). In all of these, the dimension coded as masculine is regarded as the norm, conferring prestige and professional status, whereas the dimension coded as feminine carries low prestige and is equated with a lack of professionalism.

Initially, it was hoped that as more female journalists were hired, the underrepresentation and discriminatory portrayal of women in media content would change as a result (→ Sex Role Stereotypes in the Media; Women in the Media, Images of). This claim has not yet been substantiated; however, it does appear that, similar to other counter-hegemonic discourses, the gradual emergence of feminist public spheres, and feminist publications catering to them, is influencing and challenging sexism in the mainstream media.

It may well have been changes in media genres and content – produced in part by increasing commercialization and a growing market orientation, with its emphasis on human interest and soft, emotional, or sensational news – that has paved the way for more women entering the field of journalism (→ Commercialization: Impact on Media Content). As in other professions, it has been the emancipation of women generally that has led to more women gaining admission to journalism and related fields. This has been reinforced by a growing media differentiation, such as public and commercial broadcasting, local and transnational coverage, and new formats in the print media, public relations, and online journalism (→ Diversification of Media Markets).

See also: ▶ COMMERCIALISATION: IMPACT ON MEDIA CONTENT ▶ DIVERSIFICATION OF MEDIA MARKETS ▶ GENDER AND JOURNALISM ▶ GENDER: REPRESENTATION IN THE MEDIA ▶ GENRE ▶ JOURNALISM ▶ OBJECTIVITY IN REPORTING ▶ POPULAR CULTURE ▶ SEX ROLE STEREOTYPES IN THE MEDIA ▶ SEXISM IN THE MEDIA ▶ TABLOIDIZATION ▶ WOMEN IN THE MEDIA, IMAGES OF

REFERENCES AND SUGGESTED READINGS

Chambers, D., Steiner, L., & Fleming, C. (2005). *Women and journalism*. London: Routledge.
Dorer, J. (2005). The gendered relationship between journalism and public relations in Austria and Germany. *Communications*, 30(2), 183–200.
Mayer, V. (2014). To communicate is human; to chat is female. The feminization of US media work. In C. Carter, L. Steiner, & L. McLaughlin (eds.), *The Routledge companion to media and gender*. London: Routledge, pp. 51–60.

Fiction

MARIE-LAURE RYAN
Independent scholar

The term 'fiction' refers to a representation not committed to the truth. The overwhelming majority of fictions are narratives, but not all narratives are fictional (e.g., → news or biographies). The fictionality of a text is a pragmatic issue, i.e., not a matter of what the text is about, but a matter of how it is used in social interaction. Even though literary critics have detected stylistic features that betray fictional status, these features are not mandatory. The fictional status of a text is usually suggested to users through a so-called paratextual device, such as the labels 'novel,' 'short story,' or 'drama.' These labels instruct the user how to process the information of the text (→ Text and Intertextuality).

Fictionality is a relevant *analytical category for all media* and art forms that involve a language track: literature, film, drama, opera (→ Art as Communication). For philosophers such as John Searle (1975) and Kendall Walton (1990), the nature of fiction lies in pretense and make-believe. While Searle regards fictionality as "pretending to make assertions," Walton defines fiction as a "prop in a game of make-believe", that is, as an object that inspires imagining rather than belief. In novels, authors pretend to be narrators who describe actual states of affairs, while in drama and film (→ Film Genres), actors pretend to be characters. The relevance of the concept of fiction for media without a language track is more controversial.

The concept is better *applicable* to the images of film and → photography than to painting because these images are obtained through a mechanical recording device that gives them documentary value. They become fictional when this value is playfully subverted through pretense. As a man-made artifact, painting has a much more limited documentary potential, and rather than developing a fictionality of its own, it can only be considered fictional when it illustrates a fictional story. The necessary condition for the use of a type of → signs (→ Semiotics) to be regarded as fiction is that these signs can also be used to make truth claims.

See also: ▶ ART AS COMMUNICATION ▶ FILM GENRES ▶ METAPHOR ▶ NEWS ▶ PHOTOGRAPHY ▶ SEMIOTICS ▶ SIGNS ▶ STORYTELLING AND NARRATION ▶ TEXT AND INTERTEXTUALITY

REFERENCES AND SUGGESTED READINGS

Lewis, D. (1978). Truth in fiction. *American Philosophical Quarterly*, 15, 37–46.

Searle, J. (1975). The logical status of fictional discourse. *New Literary History*, 6, 319–32.
Walton. K. (1990). *Mimesis as make-believe: On the foundations of the representational arts*. Cambridge, MA: Harvard University Press.

Field Research

JAMES A. ANDERSON
University of Utah

Field research is a somewhat dated term that is used to describe research conducted under the naturally occurring contingencies of unmanipulated or naturally manipulated contexts. In this usage it is contrasted with laboratory research, which is to be conducted under highly controlled circumstances and fully manipulated contexts (→ Experiment, Laboratory). Field researchers catalog objects, places, and spaces, do content analysis, perform → surveys, do case studies, hold interviews, conduct focus groups, perform non-participative observation of naturally occurring behavior, or use similar research methodologies (→ Experiment, Field; Content Analysis, Quantitative). The cataloging of objects, places, and spaces generally has to do with their role in some activity. Objects might be a tool, a ceremonial element, or ritual implement; a place might be a geographical or architectural configuration that facilitates an enactment or set of beliefs.

The significant components in all of these methods are (a) the targeted object, place, space, or text is considered an actuality whose existence does not depend on the research; (b) the respondent retains a high level of autonomy of action; (c) the researcher is considered a neutral element and not a stakeholder in the object/place/text/action; (d) the relationship between the researcher and the respondent is not part of the results; (e) the respondent's behavior is considered to be naturally occurring; and (f) the responses given are (therefore) ingenuously true. The data are descriptors of the respondent and/or the action, and the findings are considered descriptive rather than causal in character.

Field research is generally not considered part of the 'interpretive turn' of qualitative methods, ethnography, or social action perspectives (→ Qualitative Methodology; Ethnography of Communication). The principal difference between interpretive field methods and objective field methods is the former's commitment to member understandings and the latter's dependence on some form of literal meaning. Interpretivists hold that nothing reads itself; the meaning of things is rarely obvious; and what can be understood through impersonal observation is merely a surface reading.

See also: ▶ CONTENT ANALYSIS, QUANTITATIVE ▶ ETHNOGRAPHY OF COMMUNICATION ▶ EXPERIMENT, FIELD ▶ EXPERIMENT, LABORATORY ▶ QUALITATIVE METHODOLOGY ▶ SURVEY

REFERENCES AND SUGGESTED READINGS

Atkinson, P. (1990). *The ethnographic imagination: Textual constructions of reality*. London: Routledge.
Diesing, P. (1971). *Patterns of discovery in the social sciences*. New York: Aldine.
Presser, C. A. & Dasilva, P. B. (1996). *Sociology and interpretation: From Weber to Habermas*. Albany, NY: SUNY Press.

Film Genres

CATHERINE PRESTON
University of Kansas

Film genre refers to specific structure or thematic content as organized by the narrative and stylistic or formal aspects, setting or mise-en-scène, costume, character, and → cinematography. Fiction film genres have their origin in literary genres: comedy, tragedy, and melodrama. Others are based more specifically on cinematic capabilities such as documentary, experimental, and animation (Stam 2000, 14). The development of genre criticism can be divided into three areas: text, industry, and audience. Film scholarship has conceived → 'meaning' as a discursive construction that occurs within a particular historical context and is related to other social, political, and aesthetic formations. In reference to the study of film genres, this has meant an ongoing conceptual broadening of the relations between genre aesthetics, industry, and audience expectations.

Early *genre criticism* focused on the → Hollywood film text, specifically on narrative, → iconography, themes and motifs (→ Film Theory). Critics argued that, through iconography, Western and Gangster genres communicated cultural myths (Stam 2000). In the early 1980s this approach was found to be problematic as it ignored other film genres that lacked the iconography of the Western. Contemporary theoretical frameworks, such as psychoanalysis, postmodernism, and postcolonialism, have had a significant impact on genre analysis (→ Postmodernism and Communication). In an effort to move beyond use of myth as a primary operation of genre, critics argued that identity of genres depends on the specific relations established between a range of elements rather than on the selective representation of particular motifs (Gledhill 2000, 224). For example, the postmodern genre is characterized by irony, parody, hybridity, bricolage, and pastiche. Staiger (1997) criticizes American film industry as a form of "inbreeding" because of its lack of cinematic creativity as production becomes increasingly cannibalistic through seemingly endless sequels, prequels, and remakes.

An *audience studies perspective* examines genres as provisional and malleable conceptual environments, in which viewers participate in construction of meaning as well as modify frameworks. An implicit communication between producers and consumers, it allows the audience to approach any given film from a range of expectations in which issues of texts and aesthetic overlap with those of "industry and institution, history and society, culture and audiences" (Gledhill 2000, 221).

An *industry approach* analyzes genre as an economic method of production, marketing, and distribution of film which attempts to control the ongoing uncertainties of the business (→ Political Economy of the Media). For example, diminishing domestic ticket sales has led to the increased production of the action film specifically for export to a global audience. The most profitable genre on a global scale, these films become identifiable in part by their lack of dependence on dialogue for narrative progression.

In the new media environment of digital production many scholars assert that previous nomenclature used to refer to film types is not as operative (→ Digital Media, History of; Digital Imagery). Much genre criticism emerged from analysis of the Hollywood classical period and cannot easily be transposed to the contemporary situation. Not intended to reference the industry's aesthetic deficiencies, 'mode' is a more adequate reference to contemporary production trends that fall outside the traditional generic method of organization. 'Serial mode' refers to Hollywood's tendency toward sequels, prequels, series, follow-ups, and franchises as well as 'blockbuster,' 'event cinema,' 'summer movies,' and 'special effects movies.'

Andrew Darley argues that in a postmodern culture of intertextuality and radical eclecticism brought about by new technological developments "genre has a far more limited structural role to play," referring perhaps to nothing more than "the general level of a form itself – narrative cinema" (Darley 2000, 144). Nonetheless, it remains a useful conceptual tool both for audiences and those studying the relationship between American film, international film, and global culture.

See also: ▶ BOLLYWOOD ▶ CINEMA ▶ CINEMATOGRAPHY ▶ DIGITAL IMAGERY ▶ DIGITAL MEDIA, HISTORY OF ▶ FILM PRODUCTION ▶ FILM THEORY ▶ GENRE ▶ HOLLYWOOD ▶ ICONOGRAPHY ▶ MEANING ▶ POLITICAL ECONOMY OF THE MEDIA ▶ POPULAR CULTURE ▶ POSTMODERNISM AND COMMUNICATION ▶ TEXT AND INTERTEXTUALITY ▶ VISUAL COMMUNICATION

REFERENCES AND SUGGESTED READINGS

Darley, A. (2000). *Visual digital culture: Surface play and spectacle in new media genres.* London: Routledge.
Gledhill, C. (2000). Rethinking genre. In C. Gledhill & L. Williams (eds.), *Reinventing film studies.* London: Arnold, pp. 221–243.
Moine, R. (2008). *Cinema Genres* (trans. Alistair Fox and Hilary Radner). Oxford: Blackwell.
Staiger, J. (1997). Hybrid or inbred: The purity hypothesis and Hollywood genre history. *Film Criticism*, 22(1), 5–20.
Stam, R. (2000). *Film theory: An introduction.* Oxford: Blackwell.

Film Production

GIANLUCA SERGI
University of Nottingham

The term 'film production' routinely indicates the stage in the making of a movie where actual filming takes place. While this usage is shared by both the public and filmmakers, it is somewhat misleading in that it draws attention to just one aspect of filmmaking at the expense of a fuller understanding of the different stages of production and of the key relationships at the heart of the filmmaking process.

Pre-production, the earliest stage of production, involves a handful of people who are in a position to shape a film project. Traditionally an original idea is developed or developed from existing material. Producers, writers, actors, and directors may all have a share in this process, though the relative contribution of each will vary substantially from case to case. This stage is extremely complex: Despite lengthy negotiations involving a number of professionals, many projects never get past this first hurdle. Indeed, it is not uncommon for directors to be replaced at this stage, and for projects to change hands within a studio or even go to a different studio altogether. This instability can become problematic since financial backing needs to be secured: the popular belief that → Hollywood operates according to a 'cookie-cutting' approach does not adequately account for the complexities and vagaries of this development stage.

The director and the producer are usually in charge of the project at this stage. The distinction between financial and administrative duties (the domain of the producer) and creative tasks (understood as the domain of the director) that is traditionally understood as regulating this key relationship is also somewhat artificial: time, budget, and individual personalities come together in a number of potential combinations. Despite substantial variations in practices, filmmakers and studios alike will see the producer as perhaps the only figure who can ensure that all those involved in the production of a film work to the same brief, acting also as liaison between the director and studios. Engendering a common sense of purpose (something that filmmakers often refer to as 'vision') of what the film would ideally ultimately feel, look, and sound like would appear to be a basic requirement at this stage (→ Cinema). For a fuller account of the key individual roles in filmmaking, see Goldman (1985).

Once the production team has been assembled, locations have been selected, and a draft version of the script is available, the project moves into the *production* or *filming* stage. Interestingly, many directors indicate this stage as the least enjoyable phase of the filmmaking process. This view is mostly due to the huge pressure that is placed on filmmakers to make a great deal of decisions in a very short amount of time. Indeed, many see the cumulative effect of the inevitable mistakes that are made along the way as a direct threat to the ultimate success of the project, especially during principal photography (i.e., when all key personnel are involved in shooting).

Once filming has been completed, the film moves into *post-production*. In the majority of projects editors put together a rough edit of the film (using a temporary soundtrack), to which both the composer and the sound team will work. Often working to accelerated schedules due to a combination of pre-arranged release dates and filming delays and reshoots, the editorial teams face a constant race against time. It is also not rare at this stage of the project for the director and other members of the original crew to have begun work on a different project. This, in effect, means that a considerable amount of delegation of responsibilities may have to take place from the director to the film editor and the supervising sound editor. This is one of the key reasons why so many directors prefer to work with the same crew wherever possible: the relationship they develop over the years ensures that working to the same brief does not require their constant presence at every stage of the production.

See also: ▶ CINEMA ▶ CINEMATOGRAPHY ▶ FILM THEORY ▶ HOLLYWOOD

REFERENCES AND SUGGESTED READINGS

Breskin, D. (1997). *Inner views: Filmmakers in conversation*. New York: Da Capo.
Goldman, W. (1985). *Adventures in the screen trade*. London: Futura.
Heisner, B. (1997). *Production design in contemporary American film: A critical study of 23 American films and their designers*. London: McFarland.
Obst, L. (1996). *Hello, he lied: And other truths from the Hollywood trenches*. New York: Broadway.
Oldham, G. (1995). *First cut: Conversations with film editors*. Berkeley, CA: University of California Press.
Schaefer, D. & Salvato, L. (1984). *Masters of light: Conversations with contemporary cinematographers*. Berkeley, CA: University of California Press.

Schanzer, K. & Wright, T. L. (1993). *American screenwriters: The insiders look at the craft and the business of writing movies*. New York: Avon.

Thom, R. (1999). Designing a movie for sound. At www.filmsound.org/articles/designing_for_sound.htm, accessed July 26, 2014.

Film Theory

WARREN BUCKLAND
Oxford Brookes University

Film theory is a form of speculative thought that aims to make visible the underlying structures and absent causes that confer order and intelligibility upon films. These structures and causes, while not observable in themselves, are made visible by theory. The ultimate objective of film theory is to construct models of film's nonobservable underlying structures. A particular theory enables the analyst to identify specific aspects of a film's structure, and to look at and listen to the film from the perspective of its own values. The aim of 'theory' is to construct different conceptual perspectives on a film.

Classical film theory, which dominated from the 1920s to the early 1960s, tried to define film as an art and attempted to achieve this from an idealist perspective by focusing on film's ontology, or 'essence.' Different classical film theorists located film's essence in two incommensurate, diametrically opposed qualities of cinema: its photographic recording capacity (e.g., 'Realists' such as André Bazin and Siegfried Kracauer) and its unique formal techniques that offer a new way of seeing (e.g., 'Formalists' such as Rudolf Arnheim [1957] and Sergei Eisenstein).

In the 1960s, *film semioticians* such as Christian Metz did not conceive 'film' to be a pre-given, unproblematic entity, nor did they try to define its essence. Instead, they aimed to define film's specificity by constructing a general model of its underlying system of → codes. Metz's first semiotic model was the "grande syntagmatique" (1974a), which outlined the different spatiotemporal codes underlying and lending structure to all narrative films. Metz's second semiotic model, developed in Language and Cinema (1974b), defined filmic specificity in terms of a specific combination of five overlapping codes – iconicity, mechanical duplication, multiplicity, movement, and mechanically produced multiple moving images.

Out of semiotics emerged *modern film theory* of the 1970s (sometimes called 'contemporary film theory') of (again) Metz, Jean-Louis Baudry, theorists centered around the journal Screen (Stephen Heath, Colin MacCabe) and feminist film scholars (Laura Mulvey) (see Rosen 1986). They combined the Marxism of Louis Althusser with the psychoanalysis of Jacques Lacan to examine the underlying ideological, social, and psychical absent causes that structure mainstream films and create the illusion of spectators as free, coherent subjects. They then mapped out the space for an oppositional avant-garde cinema that would break the ideological hold over mainstream film (→ Structuralism).

Cognitive film theory emerged in the 1980s as an alternative to modern film theory. Cognitivists share with the modernists a focus on the specific nature of the interface between film and spectator. But whereas the modernists examined the way a film addresses the spectator's irrational/unconscious desires and fantasies, the cognitivists analyzed the knowledge and competence spectators employ to comprehend films and engage them on rational and emotional levels (Bordwell 1985; Branigan 1992; Tan 1996; → Cognitive Science).

The *New Lacanians* (most notably Slavoj Žižek) are united by a new concern with what has been called the 'ethics' of psychoanalysis and its contemporary political ramifications, which revolve around democracy, totalitarianism, universality, and multiculturalism. Instead of concentrating on the imaginary and the symbolic when assessing the film experience in relation to a spectator, the New Lacanians focus on the imaginary and the real.

Film scholars not persuaded by psychoanalytic or Marxist film theory, but equally dissatisfied with the cognitivists' analysis of rational and emotional reactions to films, have turned to the French philosopher Gilles Deleuze. Deleuze's two books on cinema (The Movement Image [1986] and The Time Image [1989]), offer an alternative conceptualization of the film experience as an embodied, spatio-temporal event. Deleuze is not a film theorist in the commonly accepted sense, for he theorizes with rather than about the cinema. What seems to have drawn him to the cinema is the relation of bodies, matter, and perception, seen as a traditional philosophical problem, and in the twentieth century most vigorously explored by phenomenology.

See also: ▶ CODE ▶ COGNITIVE SCIENCE ▶ FILM GENRES ▶ FILM PRODUCTION ▶ STRUCTURALISM ▶ VISUAL COMMUNICATION ▶ VISUAL CULTURE ▶ VISUAL REPRESENTATION

REFERENCES AND SUGGESTED READINGS

Arnheim, R. (1957). *Film as art*. Berkeley, CA: University of California Press.
Bordwell, D. (1985). *Narration in the fiction film*. London: Routledge.
Branigan, E. (1992). *Narrative comprehension and film*. London: Routledge.
Deleuze, G. (1986). *Cinema 1: The movement image* (trans. H. Tomlinson and B. Habberjam). London: Athlone.
Deleuze, G. (1989). *Cinema 2: The time image* (trans. H. Tomlinson and R. Galeta). London: Athlone.
Metz, C. (1974a). *Film language: A semiotics of the cinema*(trans. M. Taylor). Oxford: Oxford University Press.
Metz, C. (1974b). *Language and cinema* (trans. D.-J. Umiker-Sebeok). The Hague: Mouton de Gruyter.
Rosen, P. (ed.) (1986). *Narrative, apparatus, ideology: A film theory reader*. New York: Columbia University Press.
Tan, E. S. (1996). *Emotion and the structure of narrative film: Film as an emotional machine* (trans. B. Fasting). Mahwah, NJ: Lawrence Erlbaum.

Financial Communication

HOLLY R. HUTCHINS
University of Houston (retired)

Financial communication entails all of the strategies, tactics, and tools used to share financial data and recommendations with investors and other interested parties. Around the world, companies need strong, proactive financial communication competencies to successfully help shape the evolution of capital markets for themselves and their industries. In return, companies likely will see the benefits in stock price and operating performance. Thompson (2002, 1) defines 'investor relations' (IR) as "a strategic management responsibility that integrates finance, communication, marketing and securities laws compliance to enable the most effective two-way communication between a company, the financial community, and other constituencies, which ultimately contributes to a company's securities achieving fair valuation."

Financial communication *evolved* during the 1960s and 1970s with a promotional flair. Annual reports became costly showpieces. 'Dog and pony shows,' the euphemism for multimedia presentations at analyst and stockholder meetings, became the trademark of full-service → public relations (PR) departments. Financial communicators were technicians, leveraging their communication skills to create the necessary tools, such as reports, speeches, and multimedia presentations, to inform the investment community.

The *bull market* throughout the 1990s and into the twenty-first century led to two developments that dramatically altered the financial communication landscape. First, the competition for capital and for market visibility became intense. Second, the boom rudely forced aside the notion of investing for long-term value and replaced it with a very short-term focused approach that worried about satisfying capital markets quarter to quarter.

Financial scandals at Enron, Global Crossing, WorldCom, Tyco International, Adelphia Communications, and other blue-chip companies argued for *new standards of financial communication*. Multiple issues were blamed, among them aggressive accounting practices to meet quarterly earnings expectations, conflicts of interest between research and investment banking, weaknesses in board oversight, or conflicts of interest between auditing and consulting in major accounting firms.

Five developments are singled out for fueling the future growth of IR: (1) a greater need to satisfy more stringent disclosure requirements; (2) a broader communications role in the company; (3) a more proactive attitude by corporate managements toward IR; (4) more involvement in the strategic planning process; and (5) greater information needs from institutions and portfolio managers.

See also: ▶ CORPORATE COMMUNICATION ▶ ORGANIZATIONAL COMMUNICATION ▶ ORGANIZATION–PUBLIC RELATIONSHIPS ▶ PUBLIC RELATIONS ▶ PUBLIC RELATIONS PLANNING ▶ STRATEGIC COMMUNICATION

REFERENCES AND SUGGESTED READINGS

Berstein, L. (2003). Strategic communication: Defining a concept. *National Investor Relations Institute Investor Relations Update*, January, 1-6.

Driscoll, E. (2006). Sarbanes-Oxley not NYSE For New York. At http://eddriscoll.com/archives/009133.php, accessed 26 July 2014.

Thompson, L. M., Jr. (2002). Major developments affecting IR in 2002. National Investor Relations Institute Executive Alert, December 20, 1-13.

Flow Theory

ANJA KALCH
University of Augsburg

HELENA BILANDZIC
University of Augsburg

Flow is a state sustained by intrinsic motivation that describes the desirable experience of being completely immersed in an activity (→ Involvement with Media Content), during which other stimuli present in the surroundings are not attended to. The concept was originally proposed by Mihaly Csikszentmihalyi in the 1970s (Csikszentmihalyi 1988) as an explanation for the pleasurable feelings elicited by everyday creative activities like painting, playing musical instruments, or dancing, and the motivation to engage in them.

In a state of optimal experience a person feels cognitively effective and wishes to maintain this enjoyable feeling. Csikszentmihalyi specified the concept by defining *nine dimensions*: someone who experiences flow is (1) fully concentrated on the specific task and experiences a (2) sense of control over the action. This is accompanied by (3) losing both awareness of oneself and one's surroundings and (4) track of time; as a consequence, (5) action and awareness appear to be merged. Whether flow occurs or not depends on the relationship between an individual's skill in carrying out a task and the challenges of the task. To experience flow, (6) skill level and challenge level must match. In this case, executing the task is (7) intrinsically rewarding and becomes autotelic. Activities that provide a clear goal-structure (8) and direct feedback (9) are most likely to create flow.

In the context of media uses and effects research flow is very similar to concepts such as absorption, → presence or transportation. Flow has been integrated into theories of narrative engagement and enjoyment, especially in the context of → video games. In media contexts, too, flow experiences are a result of a balanced relationship between skills of media users, e.g., abilities to interpret messages or play video games, and the challenges imposed by the text or game (Sherry 2004). Watching television or listening to the radio are typically not associated with difficulty; however, Sherry (2004) argues that demands for cognitive abilities of media users depend on the complexity of the media content.

See also: ▶ INVOLVEMENT WITH MEDIA CONTENT ▶ PERSUASION ▶ PRESENCE ▶ VIDEO GAMES

REFERENCES AND SUGGESTED READINGS

Csikszentmihalyi, M. (1988). The flow experience and its significance for human psychology. In M. Csikszentmihalyi & I. S. Csikszentmihalyi (eds.), *Optimal experience: Psychological studies of flow in consciousness*. Cambridge: Cambridge University Press, pp. 15-35.

Sherry, J. L. (2004). Flow and media enjoyment. *Communication Theory*, 14(4), 328-347.

Weber, R., Tamborini, R., Westcott-Baker, A., & Kantor, B. (2009). Theorizing flow and media enjoyment as cognitive synchronization of attentional and reward networks. *Communication Theory*, 19, 397-422.

Framing Effects

DIETRAM A. SCHEUFELE
University of Wisconsin-Madison

There is no single commonly accepted definition of framing in the field of communication. In fact, political communication scholars have offered a variety of conceptual and operational approaches to framing that all differ with respect to their underlying assumptions, the way they define frames and framing, their operational definitions, and very often also the outcomes of framing. Previous research can be classified based on its level of analysis and the specific process of framing that various studies have focused on. Scheufele (1999) differentiated *media frames* and *audience frames*. Based on these two broader concepts, he distinguished four processes that classify areas of framing research and outline the links among them: frame building, frame setting, individual-level effects of framing, and journalists as audiences for frames.

Types of Frames and Framing Processes

Media frames are defined as "a central organizing idea or story line that provides meaning to an unfolding strip of events" (Gamson & Modigliani 1987, 143). Media frames are important tools for journalists to reduce complexity and convey issues, such as welfare reform or stem cell research, in a way that allows audiences to make sense of them with limited amounts of prior information. For journalists, framing is therefore a means of presenting information in a format that fits the modalities and constraints of the medium they are writing or producing news content for (→ Framing of the News; News Routines).

Media frames work as organizing themes or ideas because they play to individual-level interpretive schemas among audiences (*audience frames*). These schemas are tools for information processing that allow people to categorize new information quickly and efficiently, based on how that information is framed or described by journalists. Audience frames can be defined as "mentally stored clusters of ideas that guide individuals' processing of information" (Entman 1993, 53). Two *types of frame of reference* can be used to interpret and process information: global and long-term political views on the one hand, and short-term, issue-related frames of reference on the other hand. Goffman's (1974) idea of frames of reference refers to more long-term, socialized schemas that are often socialized and shared in societies or at least within certain groups in societies. But in addition to these more long-term and broadly shared schemas, there are also short-term, issue-related frames of reference that are learned from mass media and that can have a significant impact on perceiving, organizing, and interpreting incoming information and on drawing inferences from that information (Pan & Kosicki 1993).

The Price, Tewksbury, and Powers (1997) applicability model of framing offers a theoretical explanation of *how media frames and audience frames interact* to influence individual perceptions and attitudes. They argue that frames work only if they are applicable to a specific interpretive schema. These interpretive schemas can be pre-existing ones that are acquired through socialization processes (→ Political Socialization through the Media) or other types of learning. But they can also be part of the message itself. Price et al.'s applicability model does imply that when audience members do not have an interpretive schema available to them in → memory, or the schema is not provided in a news story, a frame that applies the construct in a message will not be effective. Framing effects therefore vary in strength as a partial function of the fit between the schemas that a frame suggests should be applied to an issue, and either the presence of those frames in audience members' existing knowledge or the content of the message (Scheufele & Tewksbury 2007).

Theoretical Explanations of Framing

Psychological approaches to framing research are often traced back to Daniel Kahneman and Amos Tversky's (1979) notions of bounded rationality, more broadly, and prospect theory, in particular. The basic idea assumes that a given piece of information will be interpreted differently depending on which interpretive schema an individual applies. More importantly, however, different interpretive schemas can be invoked by framing the same message differently.

Sociological approaches to framing are often traced back to Erving Goffman's (1974) notion of frames or primary frameworks. Goffman assumes that individuals cannot understand the world fully and therefore actively classify and interpret their life experiences to make sense of the world around them. An individual's reaction to new information therefore depends on interpretive schemas Goffman calls "primary frameworks" (Goffman 1974, 21).

Framing is a *multi-level construct*. The term has been used almost interchangeably to describe individual-level media effects, macro-level influences on news content, and other related processes. At least four interrelated processes involving framing at different levels of analysis have been identified. *Frame building* refers to the linkages between various intrinsic and extrinsic influences on news coverage and the frames used in news coverage. These influences include the personal predispositions of journalists, organizational routines and pressures, the efforts by outside groups to promote certain frames, the impact of other parallel issues or events, and the type of policy arena where decision-making or conflict might take place. *Frame setting* refers to the process of frame transfer from media outlets to audiences. Most communication research has focused on a third process: *individual-level effects of framing*. These individual-level outcomes include attributions of responsibility, support for various policy proposals, or citizen competence. The last process related to framing that political communication scholars have explored is the idea of *journalists themselves as audiences for frames*.

Unresolved Issues in Framing Research

Framing research continues to struggle with at least three unresolved issues related to how the concept has been defined or measured. First, some scholars have argued that framing is just a *conceptual extension of agenda setting*. Like agenda setting, they argue, framing increases the salience of certain 'aspects' of an issue and therefore can be labeled "second-level agenda setting." A number of scholars, however, have rejected that notion (for an overview, see Price et al. 1997; Scheufele & Tewksbury 2007). Rather, agenda setting is based on the notion of attitude accessibility. Framing is based on the concept of context-based perception, that is, on the assumption that subtle changes in the wording of the description of a situation might affect how audience members interpret this situation. In other words, framing influences *how* audiences think about issues, not by making aspects of the issue more salient, but by invoking interpretive schemas that influence the interpretation of incoming information.

The second unresolved area of framing research concerns the different *types of frames* identified in previous research. Scholars have operationalized media frames along dichotomies, such as episodic vs thematic frames or issue vs conflict frames or game schema coverage. As a result, communication researchers continue to

have only a limited understanding of the specific frames that can trigger certain underlying interpretive schemas among audiences and therefore lead to various behavioral or cognitive outcomes. The final challenge for communication researchers is the *inherent conflict between the different approaches* to framing research that originated from the psychological and sociological foundations of the concept outlined earlier.

See also: ▶ AGENDA-SETTING EFFECTS ▶ EXEMPLIFICATION AND EXEMPLARS, EFFECTS OF ▶ FRAMING OF THE NEWS ▶ INFORMATION PROCESSING ▶ MEDIA EFFECTS ▶ MEDIA PRODUCTION AND CONTENT ▶ MEMORY ▶ NEWS ROUTINES ▶ OBSERVATION ▶ PERSUASION ▶ POLITICAL SOCIALIZATION THROUGH THE MEDIA ▶ PRIMING THEORY ▶ STRATEGIC FRAMING

REFERENCES AND SUGGESTED READINGS

Entman, R. M. (1993). Framing: Towards clarification of a fractured paradigm. *Journal of Communication*, 43, 51–58.

Gamson, W. A. & Modigliani, A. (1987). The changing culture of affirmative action. In R. G. Braungart & M. M. Braungart (eds.), *Research in political sociology*, vol. 3. Greenwich, CT: JAI Press, pp. 137–177.

Goffman, E. (1974). *Frame analysis: An essay on the organization of experience*. New York: Harper and Row.

Iyengar, S. (1991). *Is anyone responsible? How television frames political issues*. Chicago: University of Chicago Press.

Kahneman, D. & Tversky, A. (1979). Prospect theory: Analysis of decision under risk. *Econometrica*, 47(2), 263–291.

Lim, J. & Jones, L. (2010). A baseline summary of framing research in public relations from 1990 to 2009. *Public Relations Review*, 36(3), 292–297.

Pan, Z. & Kosicki, G. M. (1993). Framing analysis: An approach to news discourse. *Political Communication*, 10, 55–75.

Price, V., Tewksbury, D., & Powers, E. (1997). Switching trains of thought: The impact of news frames on readers' cognitive responses. *Communication Research*, 24, 481–506.

Scheufele, D. A. (1999). Framing as a theory of media effects. *Journal of Communication*, 49(1), 103–122.

Scheufele, D. A. & Tewksbury, D. (2007). Framing, agenda-setting, and priming: The evolution of three media effects models. *Journal of Communication*, 57(1), 9–20.

Framing of the News

ZHONGDANG PAN
University of Wisconsin–Madison

Among various definitions of framing, the most widely circulated comes from Robert Entman: "To frame is to *select some aspects of a perceived reality and make them more salient in a communicating text, in such a way as to promote a particular problem definition, causal interpretation, moral evaluation, and/or treatment recommendation* for the item described" (Entman 1993, 52; original emphasis). Focusing on the cognitive underpinnings associated with salience, this definition describes how varying salience is accomplished (via selection), where a frame resides (in text), and how such a text produces real political consequences (proving certain problem definition and policy prescription). In essence, frames are templates (ideas and principles) embedded in news texts; they are used to organize, and are also signified by, various symbolic elements like catchphrases or images.

Framing of news is a *joint operation* of journalists and various other social actors. These social actors operate as sources that supply journalists with not only information but also the primary definitions and vocabularies concerning an issue or event that is to be represented in news stories. In a pluralistic society, these social actors are not monolithic.

News framing research to date can be roughly grouped into *two broad categories*. In the first category, researchers have analyzed *news texts* in order to examine how an issue is framed in the news or how the framing of an issue in the media has evolved over time. In the second category, researchers have examined *effects* of news frames and how they cognitively evolve.

Six different *systems of frame classification* can be identified in the research literature: (1) gain vs loss frames; (2) thematic vs episodic frames (also individual vs societal frames); (3) strategy vs issue frames in media coverage of election campaigns and policy debates; (4) value frames (i.e., some enduring values functioning as 'central organizing ideas' in news texts); (5) news values as frames (such as human interest, conflict); and (6) mental templates based on familiar social institutions being used metaphorically in representing unfamiliar or more complex issues.

See also: ▶ AGENDA BUILDING ▶ AGENDA-SETTING EFFECTS ▶ DISCOURSE ▶ FRAMING EFFECTS ▶ MEDIA EFFECTS ▶ NEWS IDEOLOGIES ▶ NEWS ROUTINES ▶ NEWS VALUES ▶ POLITICAL COMMUNICATION ▶ PRIMING THEORY ▶ PUBLIC OPINION

REFERENCES AND SUGGESTED READINGS

Entman, R. M. (1993). Framing: Toward clarification of a fractured paradigm. *Journal of Communication*, 43, 51–58.

Lecheler, Sophie & Vresse, Claes H. de (2012). News framing and public opinion: A mediation analysis of framing effects on political attitudes. *Journalism & Mass Communication Quarterly*, 89(2), 185–204.

Pan, Z. & Kosicki, G. M. (1993). Framing analysis: An approach to news discourse. *Political Communication*, 10, 55–75.

Scheufele, D. A. & Tewksbury, D. (2007). Framing, agenda-setting, and priming: The evolution of three media effects models. *Journal of Communication*, 57(1), 9–20.

France: Media System

PHILIPPE J. MAAREK
University of East Paris

The French media was bound by law as early as 1789, when freedom of speech was one of the main demands of the French Revolution. Print media are now governed by regulations based on the law of July 29, 1881, which established freedom of the press and printed material as a principle (→ Freedom of the Press, Concept of).

Where audiovisual media are concerned, things have been rather different. Television and radio were a state monopoly for most of the twentieth century until socialist politician François Mitterrand became president in 1981 (→ Television Broadcasting, Regulation of). The law of September 30, 1986 on freedom of communication established a strong, fully independent regulating body for the audiovisual media, the Conseil Supérieur de l'Audiovisuel (CSA). But French audiovisual media law currently faces three problems. First, the independent authority which regulates the Internet, the Autorité de Régulation des Communications Électroniques et des Postes (ARCEP), has a clear conflict of legal competence which is yet to be resolved with the CSA because of the increasing use of broadband Internet to convey 'classic' television channels as well as new ones carried, for instance, by YouTube or Dailymotion. The second problem is the discrepancies between the French and EU legal systems. The EU 'Television without Borders' Directive has thrown the French legal system into disarray, since under this law any channel authorized in any EU country is automatically authorized in the rest of the Union, outside CSA control. The third problem arises from a recurrent instability caused by political attempts to modify the system as soon as election results change the political balance. In 2013, for instance, the authority which oversees the fight against Internet piracy, the Haute Autorité pour la diffusion des oeuvres et la protection des droits sur Internet (HADOPI), was stripped of most of its powers – and of 25 percent of its funding – by the new socialist government.

The print press is split into two main areas, which are quite different: daily newspapers and magazines and other non-dailies. National and regional daily newspapers do not do particularly well, with a very small circulation compared with that in similar countries (about 2.5 million copies). The three main national dailies, Le Monde, Le Figaro and Libération, have recently been bought by wealthy investors seeking influence and ready to take on the newspapers' debts. Ouest France, prevalent in the western part of the country, is the most important regional daily, selling about 750,000 copies a day. Among magazines – generally in better health – TV magazines have had the highest circulation for decades, though they are under threat from the free TV program guides included as supplements with some national and regional dailies. The leading magazine publisher used to be the Lagardère group, with its internationally known titles like Elle or Première, but its owner, Arnaud Lagardère, is progressively dismantling the group to fund his other activities. The German-origin Prisma group and the French part of the Italian Mondadori Press are important players in the sector.

Radio economics in France are still a consequence of radio's longstanding situation as a state monopoly. Three of the biggest radio groups are just as they were before 1980: state-owned multichannel Radio France and two private radio groups created in the 1950s, RTL and the Lagardère-owned Europe 1. Recent entrants to the field are the NRJ Group (music) and BFM Radio (news). Most of the hundreds of so-called 'free radio' stations authorized in 1981 did not survive or remained local.

The *structure of French television* has changed considerably since the mid 1980s. State-owned France Television is still a major player, but is hindered by financial difficulties. The TF1 group remains dominant, but with the appearance of new cable and digital channels its audience market share has gone down to only around 25 percent. The other major players are M6, initially dedicated to music but now a strong generalist channel, and Canal Plus, the first and dominant pay-TV channel, part of the Vivendi Group. The rise of independent group BFM, with its two TV channels, has been surprising, since it very quickly became the leading 24-hour news network.

As for the *Internet* and *mobile phone network*, the leader is still Orange, the former telecommunications monopoly France Telecom, now privatized. An independent player, Free, is a vigorous challenger: it has an efficient Internet terminal, the 'Freebox,' and made a strong entry in 2012 on the mobile phone market with a monthly subscription of only 2 euros. This has destabilized Orange, but more seriously damaged the two other smaller mobile phone players, Bouygues and SFR. About 70 percent of homes have broadband access.

See also: ▶ FREEDOM OF THE PRESS, CONCEPT OF ▶ INTERNET LAW AND REGULATION ▶ MEDIA ECONOMICS ▶ TELEVISION BROADCASTING, REGULATION OF

REFERENCES AND SUGGESTED READINGS

Balle, F. (2011). *Médias et sociétés* [Media and societies], 15th edn. Paris: Montchrestien.

Derieux, E. & Granchet, A. (2013). *Droit des médias* [Media law], 5th edn. Paris: Dalloz.

Franceschini, L. & de Bellescize, D. (2003). *Droit de la communication* [Communication law]. Paris: Presses Universitaires de France.

Statistical sources: ARCEP at www.arcep.fr; CSA at www.csa.fr; OJD (Office de Justification de la diffusion) at www.ojd.com.

Freedom of Communication

BRIAN WINSTON
University of Lincoln

The struggle for the practice of free 'mass' communication begins with the emergence of newspapers in the seventeenth century, but the press freedoms gained over the next 300 years have been limited to print (→ Newspaper, History of; Freedom of the Press, Concept of). Even in the west a media-blind right of free expression has never been established, and newer media from film through broadcasting and beyond have been subject to the imposition, or the attempted imposition, of specific controls.

Freedom of expression as a right was *born in western Europe* as a consequence of a desire to practice religion, within the bounds of Christianity, according to the dictates of one's own conscience. Printing allowed for uncorrupted religious texts and enabled authority more efficiently to communicate with its subjects; but dissidents of all persuasions from heretics to astronomers could also use printing from type to promulgate their alternative views (→ Printing, History of). Authority attempted to control the press to its own advantage with licensing systems, but these censorship regimes were, as often as not, very leaky.

In 1644, during the English Civil War, the poet John Milton published, deliberately unlicensed: "The Areopagitica: A speech of Mr. John Milton for the Liberty of UNLICENS'D PRINTING, to the PARLIAMENT OF ENGLAND." "Give me the liberty to know," he wrote, "to utter, and to argue freely according to conscience above all liberties" (Milton 1951). The Areopagitica was, however, no plea for unbridled free expression. Milton did not envisage, nor did the majority of those who succeeded him in holding free expression dear, a libertarian free-for-all. Necessary constraints upon expression would remain in place. The liberty was only from what came to be known as 'prior restraint.' In 1720, the London journalists John Trenchard and Thomas Gordon, writing together under the pen-name 'Cato,' argued for a more general right of free expression (Trenchard & Gordon 1995, letter 15). Still this freedom only applied to print; the British stage, remained censored by a court official until 1968.

Despite the failure to establish a media-blind right of free expression, by the end of the eighteenth century the principle was established in law. Article XI of the Rights of Man and of the Citizen, passed in August 1789 at the outset of the French Revolution, finally makes the rhetoric of 'Cato' law. It did not last; but it did in the United States. The First Amendment, adopted in 1791, stated: "Congress shall make no law respecting an establishment of religion, or prohibiting the free exercise thereof; or of abridging the freedom of speech or of the press." This is still in force.

With the coming of the *new media of the twentieth century* – → cinema, radio, and television – the tendency was to follow the model of the stage rather than of the press. With cinema, licensing controls were imposed. For radio the state needed to allocate wavebands to prevent interference. The interference in content this encouraged was carried over into television (→ Radio: Social History; Television, Social History of).

The contradiction between a fundamental right of expression and the control of specific media remains unaddressed. Article 10 of the European Convention on Human Rights (1950), for example, states in a fashion to be found widely repeated in both international declarations and national laws since World War II: "Everyone has the right to freedom of expression. This right shall include freedom to hold opinions and to receive and impart information and ideas without interference by public authority and regardless of frontiers." Yet this article goes on in overtly contradictory language to allow a state to require "the licensing of broadcasting, television or cinema entertainments" without specifically excluding content regulation by prior constraint (Directorate of Human Rights 1992).

Up to the present the concept of free media expression has seen *constraints* by general laws and the principle that expression shall cause no legally measurable harm; by the nature of the medium involved; and by the changing social determinants of what constitutes expression sanctioned by community standards.

See also: ▶ ACCOUNTABILITY OF THE MEDIA ▶ CENSORSHIP ▶ CENSORSHIP, HISTORY OF ▶ CINEMA ▶ COMMUNICATION AND LAW ▶ FREEDOM OF THE PRESS, CONCEPT OF ▶ INTERNET LAW AND REGULATION

▶ JOURNALISM, HISTORY OF ▶ MEDIA HISTORY
▶ NEWSPAPER, HISTORY OF ▶ PRINTING,
HISTORY OF ▶ RADIO: SOCIAL HISTORY
▶ TELEVISION BROADCASTING, REGULATION OF
▶ TELEVISION, SOCIAL HISTORY OF ▶ TRUTH
AND MEDIA CONTENT

REFERENCES AND SUGGESTED READINGS

Braudel, F. (1993[1987]). *A history of civilizations* (trans. R. Mayne). Harmondsworth: Penguin.
Directorate of Human Rights. (1992). *Human rights in international law*. Strasbourg: Council of Europe Press.
Galilei, G. (1980). *Selected works*, trans. S. Drake. Oxford: Oxford University Press.
Milton, J. (1951[1644]). *"Areopagitica" and "Of education."* Northbrook, IL: AHM.
Trenchard, J. & Gordon, T. (1995[1720]). *Cato's letters: Essays on liberty*. 2 vols (ed. R. Hamowy). Indianapolis: Liberty Fund.
Winston, B. (2005). *Messages: Free expression media and the west from Gutenberg to Google*. London: Routledge.
Wyatt, Robert O. (1991). *Free expression and the American public: A survey commemorating the 200th anniversary of the First Amendment*. Washington, DC: American Society of Newspaper Editors.

Freedom of Information

MARTIN HALSTUK
Penn State University

More than 80 nations around the world have adopted some form of a Freedom of Information (FOI) Law. Typically, FOI laws pertain to a right of public access to government-held records. The United States Freedom of Information Act (FOIA), which was approved by Congress in 1965, has been a model for a majority of the international open-records laws. Before the FOIA was enacted about a dozen nations had some kind of open-records law, though these were typically weak and created for commercial purposes (→ Communication Law and Policy: North America).

The rise of transparent governance is grounded in the accountability principle of a representative democracy – namely that in an open and democratic society citizens must have a right of access to government-held information so they can hold the government responsible for its actions, and make informed decisions pertaining to self-rule.

Current laws vary in strength and weaknesses. China, for instance, recently marked the fifth anniversary of its version of an open-records statute called the Open Government Information law. It is a relatively weak law in terms of which government agencies are subject to the law, and heavily laden with exemptions to disclosure (→ Communication Law and Policy: Asia). All open-records laws have exemptions and vary in substantial ways. Typically, there are several exemptions common to all transparency of records laws: These categories include national defense and intelligence information, personal → privacy, law enforcement, commercial and business proprietary information, and executive privilege (e.g., records of deliberative processes that precede enactment of a law).

Most FOIA laws make information available to the general public and do not require that the requester provide a reason for acquiring the information. The legal bases for FOI laws can also vary widely from nation to nation. In some countries, freedom of information is embodied in laws that protect freedom of expression and freedom of the press. In other nations, it is a separate and distinct right.

See also: ▶ CHINA: MEDIA SYSTEM
▶ COMMUNICATION LAW AND POLICY: AFRICA
▶ COMMUNICATION LAW AND POLICY: ASIA
▶ COMMUNICATION LAW AND POLICY: EUROPE
▶ COMMUNICATION LAW AND POLICY: MIDDLE EAST ▶ COMMUNICATION LAW AND POLICY: NORTH AMERICA ▶ COMMUNICATION LAW AND POLICY: SOUTH AMERICA ▶ FREEDOM OF INFORMATION ▶ FREEDOM OF THE PRESS, CONCEPT OF ▶ PRIVACY

REFERENCES AND SUGGESTED READINGS

Banisar, D. (2006). Freedom of information around the world 2006: A global survey of access to government information laws. At www.privacyinternational.org/foi/foisurvey2006.pdf, accessed July 26, 2014.
Cuillier, D. & Davis, C. (2011). *The art of access: Strategies for acquiring public records*. Washington, DC: CQ Press.
Shrivastava, K. M. (2009). *The right to information: A global perspective*. New Delhi: Lancer.

Freedom of the Press, Concept of

JOSEPH RUSSOMANNO
Arizona State University

Freedom of the press generally refers to the concept that media operate absent externally-imposed control or influence regarding the content they choose to publish and distribute. Historically, there has been an impulse by those who hold power to repress expression – spoken and written – particularly statements or opinions contrary to the policies of those in power (→ Censorship). The beginning of serious reasoning against repressive institutions – e.g., governments – and their inclination to proscribe expression is often credited to John Milton's *Areopagitica* (1644). Published during the Enlightenment, *Areopagitica* not only ridiculed England's licensing of the press, but also advocated for all ideas and opinions to be expressed and then fully considered, thereby allowing truth – or at least a close approximation of it – to be realized. This is the notion of an open marketplace of ideas (→ Freedom of Communication; Freedom of Information).

Among those influenced by the Enlightenment was James Madison, the primary author of the US Constitution's First Amendment. Madison was also instrumental in structuring the US government, one premised on three branches checking one another. Press freedom was viewed as crucial in a self-governing democracy. This role of a free press in a democratic society is highlighted by the label the 'fourth estate' – an unofficial fourth government branch that holds officials in the other branches accountable. Historically, a rebellion against authoritarian control contributed to the development of democratic governments and, in turn, libertarian press systems (→ Media History). These are in place today in many nations, including throughout western Europe, much of the Americas, and in several Pacific Rim nations. Even these liberal-minded countries, however, have histories of not only struggling with the interpretation and implementation of freedom of expression, but also histories of speech and press suppression. For instance, in the US law struggled with the issue of how far to extend press freedom beyond merely prohibiting prior restraint – censorship imposed before publication.

See also: ▶ CENSORSHIP ▶ CENSORSHIP, HISTORY OF ▶ COMMUNICATION AND LAW ▶ FREEDOM OF COMMUNICATION ▶ FREEDOM OF INFORMATION ▶ INTERNET LAW AND REGULATION ▶ MEDIA HISTORY

REFERENCES AND SUGGESTED READINGS

Altschull, J. H. (1990). *From Milton to McLuhan: The ideas behind American journalism*. Harlow: Longman.
Levy, L. W. (1985). *Emergence of a free press*. Oxford: Oxford University Press.
Trager, R. & Dickerson, D. L. (1999). *Freedom of expression in the 21st century*. Thousand Oaks, CA: Pine Forge.

Gay, Lesbian, Bisexual, and Transgender Media Studies

ANITA CHI-KWAN LEE
University of Hong Kong

Gay, lesbian, bisexual, and transgender (GLBT) media studies investigate the ideological functions of GLBT and queer media representations by employing critical and theoretical methods from gender, psychoanalytic, semiotic, and → film theories to interpret meaning in these representations. GLBT media studies examine how the sexual identity categories of 'gay,' 'lesbian,' 'bisexual,' 'transgender,' 'queer,' and 'straight' are constructed in the media; how minority sexualities are represented; and why they are so represented. 'Queer media,' 'queer representation,' 'queer media representation,' and 'queer cultural production' are terms frequently used in the field.

It is argued that the use of GLBT and its variants (e.g., 'LGB' and 'LGBT') serves to reinforce a common concept based on the binary opposition of 'straight' as the norm against the rest as 'the other,' ignoring their innate differences and the different issues faced by each group. Meanwhile, the term 'queer' has been reappropriated since the late 1980s as an umbrella term for the marginalized sexual minorities, from an expression of homophobic abuse in the past. Teresa de Lauretis was the first theorist to use the phrase 'queer theory' in print in her 1991 essay of that title.

Both controversial terms, 'GLBT' and 'queer' underline different concerns. GLBT studies are occupied with whether nature or nurture is the cause of homosexuality, while the latter is less interested in this. Queer theory looks at how the construction of the different categories of alternative sexualities functions in culture (→ Cultural Studies), while GLBT studies are more concerned with identity affirmation of the different sexual minority groups for the advancement of the GLBT political movement. Queer theory has emerged to challenge essentialist notions of homosexuality and heterosexuality, questioning cultural assumptions that are often immersed in heterosexist presumptions.

Many media scholars have argued for the rarity of queer representation on television in the last century. Before the 1960s, there were very few representations of homosexuality in American films, because of the Production Code (the Hays Code, 1934–1967), a set of industry guidelines about what was and was not considered morally acceptable in the production of motion pictures

---

The Concise Encyclopedia of Communication, First Edition. Edited by Wolfgang Donsbach.
© 2015 John Wiley & Sons, Inc. Published 2015 by John Wiley & Sons, Inc.

for a public audience. In early 1960s, only a few daring British films were released in America which offered commentary about homophobia. Then, GLBT media studies flourished with GLBT representation appearing in the American cinema. The oldest lesbian and gay film festival in the world, the San Francisco International Lesbian and Gay Film Festival, was first launched in 1977. Theorist B. Ruby Rich coined the term "New Queer Cinema" in the early 1990s to denote the collection of critically acclaimed queer films. There is now a profusion of mainstream, alternative, and 'in-between' sources of GLBT and queer media representation found in television, radio, popular music, advertising, magazines, and newspapers. Same-sex erotic passions are often referenced in popular music to symbolize transgression. The public's fascination with sexual ambiguity has rendered the chameleon-like androgynous fashion models, such as 'femiman' Andrej Pejic and transsexual male Lea T, and popular music icons, like Lady Gaga, ever more appealing and popular, the latter expanding her fan base to much of the world as a result of her campaigning for important GLBT issues.

The increasing number of gay and lesbian characters in the different English-language contemporary media questions whether their visibility represents a certain kind of political victory. Despite the trend to promote gayness as a lifestyle, and gay personalities as fashionable, stylish, and having cultured tastes, some have contended that the subversive potential in the images are now undermined and weakened by the mainstreaming of these images.

See also: ▶ AFFECTS AND MEDIA EXPOSURE ▶ AUDIENCE RESEARCH ▶ CRITICAL THEORY ▶ CULTURAL STUDIES ▶ CULTURE INDUSTRIES ▶ DISCOURSE ▶ FILM THEORY ▶ GLOBALIZATION OF THE MEDIA ▶ HOLLYWOOD ▶ SOCIAL STEREOTYPING AND COMMUNICATION

REFERENCES AND SUGGESTED READINGS

Aaron, M. (ed.) (2004). *New queer cinema: A critical reader*. Edinburgh: Edinburgh University Press.
Daniel, L. & Jackson, C. (eds.) (2003). *The bent lens: A world guide to gay and lesbian film*, 2nd edn. Singapore: Alyson.
Doty, A. & Gove, B. (1997). Queer representation in the mass media. In A. Medhurst & S. R. Munt (eds.), *Lesbian and gay studies: A critical introduction*. London: Cassell, pp. 84–98.
Dyer, R. (ed.) (1977). *Gays and film*. London: British Film Institute.
Porter, D. & Prince, D. (2010). *Fifty years of queer cinema: 500 of the best GLBTQ films ever made*. New York: Blood Moon Productions.
Russo, V. (1981). *The celluloid closet: Homosexuality in the movies*. New York: Harper and Row.

Gender and Discourse

ANN WEATHERALL
Victoria University of Wellington

The topic of gender and discourse emerged and further developed gender and language studies which arose out of the women's movement in the 1970s. Feminists documented how language, in both structure and patterns of use, encoded dominant beliefs about women's inferiority. A landmark publication was Robin Lakoff's (1975) Language and Woman's Place. She argued that women's social place was reflected in their speech, which she described as ingratiating, hesitant, and weak. Women's secondary status was also revealed in reference terms, which were more frequently negative and sexual than were terms for men. An important and ongoing debate has been whether language merely reflected gender inequality or whether it also maintained and reproduced sex-based discrimination.

Over time there has been a *diversification of subject matter* in this area (e.g., Holmes & Meyerhoff 2003). For instance, women's talk has been studied not just comparatively but for what it reveals about women's lives (→ Women's Communication and Language). The study of gender in language has also broadened. There is a general consensus that women are no longer as invisible as they once were. Less encouraging is that representations of women and men continue to be overwhelmingly consistent with sex stereotypes (→ Sexism in the Media; Sex Role Stereotypes in the Media). Vital new areas of research are computer-mediated communication and sexuality.

An important new way of thinking about gender and language is part of a broader movement across the social sciences that has been referred to as the 'discursive turn.' Here, → discourse alludes to a rejection of ideas regarding language as a simple system of representation. Instead, language as discourse powerfully produces → meaning and knowledge. The discursive turn brings with it a landmark change in the way gender is conceptualized. While gender essentialism posits that relatively stable biological and/or social factors cause differences between women and men, constructionism views gender differences as a product of cultural meaning systems.

See also: ▶ DISCOURSE ▶ DISCURSIVE PSYCHOLOGY ▶ IDENTITIES AND DISCOURSE ▶ MEANING ▶ SEXISM IN THE MEDIA ▶ SEX ROLE STEREOTYPES IN THE MEDIA ▶ WOMEN'S COMMUNICATION AND LANGUAGE

REFERENCES AND SUGGESTED READINGS

Holmes, J. & Meyerhoff, M. (eds.) (2003). *Blackwell handbook for language and gender*. Oxford: Blackwell.
Lakoff, R. (1975). *Language and woman's place*. New York: Harper and Row.
Weatherall, A. (2002). *Gender, language and discourse*. London: Routledge.

Gender and Journalism

MARJAN DE BRUIN
University of the West Indies, Jamaica

Gender and journalism became a popular area of study in the mid-1990s when gender gained recognition as a powerful variable defining feminine and masculine professional roles and behavior. It started from the premise that gender notions color what journalists consider appropriate professional behavior for women and for men (→ Journalists' Role Perception).

The initial research, in the 1970s, assumed that a greater presence of women in the media would influence the media agenda (→ Agenda Building), which, in turn, would stimulate the inclusion of more women's issues in public debate. Research on gender patterns in media employment concentrated on male and female *presence in organizations*. These studies showed that in the media workforce of many countries women formed a minority, and occupied a small fraction of middle management and an even smaller one in senior management.

In the late 1990s studies attempted to correlate women's presence in media organizations with *qualities of content*. However, the assumption that a greater presence of women in the media workforce would lead to changes in their portrayal ignored the influence of the media organization – on content as well as on content producers (→ Media Production and Content; Social Stereotyping and Communication; Sex Role Stereotypes in the Media).

Debates in the first decade of the twenty-first century broke away from the idea of organizations as gender-neutral entities and recognized that the behavior of employees is the outcome of much more complex processes, in which gender was only one of the major determinants (→ Organizational Culture).

Gender identities, professional identities, and organizational identities play an important and useful role in the current debates on gender and journalism. However, new information and communication technologies force researchers to think on a wider scale. In recent debates on gender and journalism authors point out that the web discourse, in which the agency of men and women takes on a new meaning, may still need to be interrogated with the familiar questions in mind, if it replicates the same power relations that have been surfacing in research over some decades.

See also: ▶ AGENDA BUILDING ▶ JOURNALISTS ROLE PERCEPTION ▶ MEDIA PRODUCTION AND CONTENT ▶ ORGANIZATIONAL CULTURE ▶ QUALITY OF THE NEWS ▶ SEX ROLE STEREOTYPES IN THE MEDIA ▶ SOCIAL STEREOTYPING AND COMMUNICATION

REFERENCES AND SUGGESTED READINGS

Carter, C., Branston, G., & Allan, S. (eds.) (1998). *News, gender and power*. London: Routledge.
De Bruin, M., & Ross, K. (eds.) (2004). *Gender and newsroom cultures: Identities at work*. Cresskill, NJ: Hampton Press.
Van Zoonen, L. (1994). *Feminist media studies*. London: Sage.

Gender: Representation in the Media

DAFNA LEMISH
Southern Illinois University Carbondale

The study of representations of gender in the media understands gender to be socially constructed – an ongoing process of learned sets of behaviors, expectations, perceptions, and subjectivities that define what it means to be a woman or a man. The main assumption of these studies is that a cultural ordering that presents gender differences as biologically determined and 'natural' conceals the working of patriarchal ideology. "One is not born a woman, but becomes one" is Simone de Beauvoir's formative statement that captured the essence of this process (1989[1949]). Representations are grounded in contemporary ideological assumptions and discourses that are produced, reproduced, and circulated in the media as part of a shared culture. They have been blamed for reaffirming and supporting gender hierarchies existing worldwide, maintaining the general subordination of women by reproducing social perceptions that legitimize dominant ideologies of patriarchy and colonialism (→ Media and Perceptions of Reality).

Feminist theorizing also recognizes that gender is an unstable and *highly contested social category*, and that gender experiences and identities are heterogeneous, fluid, ambiguous, incoherent, and ever changing. Gender is always situated in a particular cultural context and historicity, and is conflated with other social categories such as race, class, ethnicity, religion, and sexuality (→ Culture: Definitions and Concepts). As a result, the process of gender representation is strongly linked to other socially constructed systems of difference and exclusion and their analysis is thus part of the feminist project of problematizing and critiquing our ways of knowing.

Gender representations in the media have *two complementary meanings* (Ganguly 1992). One meaning refers to representations as 'portraits,' or the 'making present' of women and men in the media. This meaning of representation calls attention to those ideologies, interests, life circumstances, and privileges (be they class, race, sexuality, or others) that influence the way gender is constructed. The second meaning relates to 'proxy,' or 'speaking out for" women and men. We ask: Who gets a voice in the media? Who speaks on behalf of whom? And who gets to represent themselves?

Femininity Versus Masculinity

A central critique of gender representations is the well-entrenched, historical construction of femininity and masculinity as binary as well as hierarchical oppositions. While men have been mostly presented as the 'normal,' representing the majority of society, women have been presented as the minority 'other,' the 'second sex' – the exception, the incomplete, the damaged, the marginal, and sometimes even the bizarre. Such a dichotomization can be tied to other forms of dualistic thought rooted in the Enlightenment worldview, including such divisions as those constructed between rational/emotional, spirit/body, culture/nature, public/private, subject/object, west/east, and modern/traditional. Systematically, men and women have been constructed as inhibiting the opposing sides of the dualities, with the masculine associated with the highly valued rational-spirit-culture-public-subject-west-modern, and the feminine with the devalued emotional-body-nature-private-object-east-traditional.

Critical examinations of *media representations* around the world found systematically the relegating of the feminine to the private sphere, restricting presentation of women to the bodily functions of sex and reproduction, and locating women within the world of emotions where rational thought is lacking and behavior uncultivated. Women have been represented as less logical, ambitious, active, independent, heroic, and dominant; and at the same time also as more romantic, sensitive, dependent, emotional, and vulnerable (→ Sex Role Stereotypes in the Media). The popular 'beauty myth' (Wolf 1991) perpetuated in the media has been accused of sending women on an endless quest for an appearance that is unattainable and guarantees a life of frustration, feelings of inadequacy, and a wasteful exploitation of emotional, intellectual, and material resources, as women's happiness and self-fulfillment become dependent on beautification through consumption. Such representations perpetuate the female dichotomy of the 'Madonna' on one hand and the 'whore' on the other. As 'Madonna,' women are cast in the role of mother who gives birth, nurtures, raises, sacrifices herself, and finally mourns her loved ones. As 'whore,' they are pressed into the mold of sexual object, the essence of whose existence is tantalizing and threatening to the male, and whose ultimate fate is to be punished as a victim of violence and exploitation. Such media representations, claim critics, legitimize the dehumanization of women and relate to them as objects lacking consciousness, individuality, or sexual agency (→ Women in the Media, Images of).

Hegemonic masculinity, too, has been constructed as a 'natural' state of being, commonly conceived and framed within several normative expectations: physical domination and subordination of others (humans and nature alike); occupational achievements and a purposeful and rational attitude; familial patriarchy, the man being the protector and provider; daring and staying outside the domestic sphere; sexual lust with heterosexuality as the dominant model (Hanke 1998). Men have been largely portrayed as more rational, individual, independent, exercising self-restraint, technologically oriented, having difficulty with expressing emotion or displaying weakness. They demonstrate the bonding of 'men in arms' through expressions of solidarity, loyalty, determination, and a sense of purpose. In contrast to the emphasis on women's appearance, men are defined by their action: women 'appear' and men 'do' (→ Masculinity and the Media).

Difference and Diversity

The contributions of postcolonial theorizing that challenge the representation of marginalized others (Hegde 1998) and the influence of commercial forces in search of audiences have resulted in growing diversity of gender representations and array of opinions and contradictions (Meyers 1999). Attributes of such 'postfeminist' media representations include portrayals of females who are complex and distinct from one another on a variety of variables (such as race, ethnicity, sexuality, class, religion, education, age, marital status, motherhood, personal abilities and disabilities (Gill 2007; → Postfeminism). Some female characters 'want it all' rather than making a choice between family and career; between feminism and femininity. Representations of 'power feminism,' that celebrate women's abilities and achievements, are becoming more commonplace in popular media. These include images of super-women and 'action chicks' (Inness 2004), who are allowed to demonstrate masculine qualities of toughness and power as long as they also conform to the ideal sexual appearance. Deconstructing binary categories of gender and sexuality, in particular, allows the growing experimentation with representations of gay, transgender, transsexual, and bisexual lives.

Despite such developments, some scholars suggest that older stereotypes have been replaced by new ones, creating a form of 'enlightened sexism' that conveys "the seductive message that feminism's work is done" (Douglas 2010). Feminist analysis of gender representations thus needs to go beyond reflexive critique of representations and the institutions that produce them and call for action research that also advances gender equity in society (Lemish 2010).

See also: ▶ CULTURE: DEFINITIONS AND CONCEPTS ▶ GAY, LESBIAN, BISEXUAL, AND TRANSGENDER MEDIA STUDIES ▶ MASCULINITY AND THE MEDIA ▶ MEDIA AND PERCEPTION OF REALITY ▶ PORNOGRAPHY, FEMINIST DEBATES ON ▶ POSTFEMINISM ▶ SEX ROLE STEREOTYPES IN THE MEDIA ▶ WOMEN IN THE MEDIA, IMAGES OF

REFERENCES AND SUGGESTED READINGS

de Beauvoir, S. (1989[1949]). *The second sex*. New York: Vintage Books.
Douglas, S. J. (2010). *Enlightened sexism: The seductive message that feminism's work is done*. New York: Times Books.
Ganguly, K. (1992). Accounting for others: Feminism and representation. In L. F. Rakow (ed.), *Women making meaning: New feminist directions in communication*. London: Routledge, pp. 60–79.
Gill, R. (2007). *Gender and the media*. Cambridge: Polity.
Hanke, R. (1998). Theorizing masculinity with/in the media. *Communication Theory*, 8, 193–203.

Hegde, R. S. (1998). A view from elsewhere: Locating difference and the politics of representation from a transnational feminist perspective. *Communication Theory*, 8(3), 271–297.

Inness, S. A. (ed.) (2004). *Action chicks: New images of tough women in popular culture*. Basingstoke: Palgrave Macmillan.

Lemish, D. (2010). *Screening gender on children's television: The views of producers around the world*. London: Routledge.

Meyers, M. (ed.) (1999). *Mediated women: Representations in popular culture*. Cresskill, NJ: Hampton Press.

Wolf, N. (1991). *The beauty myth: How images of beauty are used against women*. New York: Doubleday/Anchor Books.

Genre

PAUL COBLEY
Middlesex University

The English term 'genre' derives – via French – from the same Latin root as 'general.' The concept of genre is important to communication research because it designates not only specific kinds of messages, but also their characteristic social uses by audiences. In ancient Greece, tragedy and comedy were recognized as specific genres, being constituents of the wider genre, drama. In such narrow and wide conceptions of the term, genre refers to a set of basic textual patterns that generate many and varied concrete texts (→ Text and Intertextuality).

The most *common understanding of genre* in the contemporary world focuses on the many popular genres that are consumed in quantities not previously witnessed in history (→ Popular Communication). Such genres include romances, thrillers, science fiction, soap opera, and fantasy in the realm of → fiction, but also → news, → advertising and documentary. Furthermore, all these genres are distributed across a range of interrelated media: print, radio, television, film, the Internet. However, genre is now also extended to the understanding of everyday communication, e.g., speeches, technical instructions, or debates (Martin & Rose 2006).

The idea that a genre is a formula has been paired, traditionally, with a view of genres as self-contained. Yet, clearly, many modern popular genres are *hybrid in nature*. As a result, in the multimedia environment of the present, it has become important to promote audiences' awareness of genres and their hybrids as a crucial component of → media literacy. In addition, theories of readership tended to assume that markedly generic texts were somehow exempt from polysemy. Whereas a genre was previously defined by its 'formula,' so that an analysis of a generic text could be carried out as an immanent and neutral undertaking, genre now is understood more as an idea or expectation, implemented by readers through readings that are interested and contextual (Cobley 2005).

See also: ▶ ADVERTISING ▶ CINEMA ▶ FICTION ▶ FILM THEORY ▶ INTERMEDIALITY ▶ MEDIA LITERACY ▶ NEWS ▶ POPULAR COMMUNICATION ▶ STRUCTURALISM ▶ TEXT AND INTERTEXTUALITY

REFERENCES AND SUGGESTED READINGS

Altman, R. (1999). *Film/Genre*. London: British Film Institute.

Cobley, P. (2005). Objectivity and immanence in genre theory. In G. Dowd, L. Stevenson, & J. Strong (eds.), *Genre Matters: Interdisciplinary Perspectives*. London: Intellect, pp. 41–54.

Martin, J. R. & Rose, D. (2006). *Genre relations: Mapping culture*. London: Equinox.

Germany: Media System

JÜRGEN WILKE
Johannes Gutenberg University of Mainz

Germany is the most populous country in Europe, with 81 million inhabitants, consisting of 16 federal states (since reunification in 1990). It is a parliamentary democracy with a multiparty system. The administrative authorities are divided between the federal government and the federal state governments. This division of power is also of great importance for the German media system. According to the typology of Hallin and Mancini (2004), Germany is located in the area of the "north European or democratic corporatist model" characterized by high newspaper circulations, external pluralism of the press, a great level of professionalization among journalists, and state regulation particularly with regard to the public broadcasting system.

Germany is regarded as the birthplace of the modern mass media. Johannes Gutenberg invented the printing press in Mainz around 1450 (→ Printing, History of). The first periodical papers were developed at the beginning of the seventeenth century (*Relation* in 1605, and *Aviso* in 1609; → Newspaper, History of). As early as the sixteenth century, → censorship had been introduced as a means of controlling the printing profession. In Germany, the implementation of freedom of press took longer than in England or the United States (→ Freedom of the Press, Concept of; Censorship, History of). Only in 1874, after the German Reich had been founded as a nation-state, was the freedom of press legally guaranteed. When the Nazis seized power in 1933 and erected a totalitarian regime, the press (together with all other media) was subjugated to a strict controlling system.

The very first radio program in Germany was broadcast on October 29, 1923, in Berlin. After 1933 the Nazis centralized broadcasting and put it under the control of the propaganda ministry (→ Propaganda; Propaganda in World War II). In 1945, a completely new period in the history of the German media system began. The fundamental decisions were made by the Allied victors. The constitution of the Federal Republic of Germany, founded on May 23, 1949, guarantees in Article 5 freedom of opinion as well as the freedom of the press, the freedom of broadcasting, and the freedom of film. Also guaranteed is → freedom of information; censorship is forbidden.

Germany still has a well-developed *press system* which nonetheless is suffering from concentration. Most prevalent are regional newspapers. They are predominantly delivered on subscription. There are only a few newspapers with a nationwide circulation (such as *Frankfurter Allgemeine Zeitung* and *Süddeutsche Zeitung*). Also, the number of tabloid papers is limited. The biggest of them is *Bild*, at 2.9 million copies it is the newspaper with the largest circulation in Germany. In 2011, 133 independent 'editorial units', i.e. independent daily newspapers that produce local, national, and international news independently in all editorial areas, were published in Germany. The total circulation of the daily press amounted to 21.8 million copies. The number of readers per 1,000 is about 315.

For decades, an exclusively public broadcasting system existed in Germany (ARD and ZDF). New technologies gave the starting signal for the dual broadcasting system. Today it consists of two pillars: the still powerful public broadcasting organizations and the numerous private program providers, with RTL and the Sat.1/ProSieben groups as the biggest. Their licenses are issued by telecommunication agencies of the federal states (→ Television Broadcasting, Regulation of). Today, all in all, more than 200 radio programs and 250 TV channels can be received. Due to the sheer size of the free TV market, pay TV has not managed to become widely accepted.

In the mid-1990s, the Internet was introduced in Germany for general use, and it expanded quickly. In 2012, 76 percent of the population used the Internet at least occasionally. Differences do still exist according to age. Today, almost all German daily newspapers and numerous magazines are present on the Internet with their own websites (→ Online Media).

See also: ▶ CENSORSHIP, HISTORY OF ▶ CONCENTRATION IN MEDIA SYSTEMS ▶ EUROPEAN UNION: COMMUNICATION LAW ▶ FREEDOM OF INFORMATION ▶ FREEDOM OF THE PRESS, CONCEPT OF ▶ MEDIA CONGLOMERATES ▶ NEWSPAPER, HISTORY OF ▶ ONLINE MEDIA ▶ PROPAGANDA ▶ PROPAGANDA IN WORLD WAR II ▶ PRINTING, HISTORY OF ▶ TELEVISION BROADCASTING, REGULATION OF

REFERENCES AND SUGGESTED READINGS

Beck, K. (2012). *Das Mediensystem Deutschlands. Strukturen, Märkte, Regulierung [Germany's Media System. Structures, Markets, Regulation]*. Wiesbaden: Springer.

Dussel, K. (2010). Deutsche Rundfunkgeschichte: Eine Einführung *[History of German broadcasting: An introduction]*, 3rd edn. Constance: UVK Medien.

Hallin, D. C. & Mancini, P. (2004). *Comparing media systems: Three models of media and politics*. Cambridge: Cambridge University Press.

Kleinsteuber, H. J. (2004). Germany. In M. Kelly, G. Mazzoleni, & D. McQuail (eds.), *The media in Europe: The Euromedia handbook.*, Thousand Oaks, CA: Sage, pp. 78–90.

Schütz, W. J. (2005). *Zeitungen in Deutschland: Verlage und ihr publizistisches Angebot 1949–2004* [Newspapers in Germany: Publishers and their newspaper supply], 2 vols. Berlin: Vistas.

Wilke, J. (1999). Mediengeschichte der Bundesrepublik Deutschland [*Media history in the Federal Republic of Germany*]. Cologne: Böhlau.

Girl Culture

SHARON R. MAZZARELLA
James Madison University

While mainstream cultural artifacts (e.g., films, books, fashion, etc.) produced specifically for and about girls have been popular since the early years of the twentieth century, academic research on girls and their complex relationship with girl culture is still fairly new to the communication discipline. Early research on this topic tended to focus on girls as audiences (rather than producers) and as vulnerable (to the effects of mass culture). Communication scholars examining girl culture today have been greatly influenced by girls' (or girlhood) studies (→ Feminist and Gender Studies) as they examine a range of mass-produced girl culture artifacts, including teen magazines, young, female pop musicians, Teen-girl television, fashion trends, and international girl culture franchises (→ Audiences, Female).

Scholars now engage in nuanced and theoretically grounded deconstructions of such cultural texts (→ Text and Intertextuality). This leads to the fastest-growing area of girl culture scholarship – studies that listen to the voices of girls themselves in order to (1) hear how girls actively negotiate and even resist these cultural artifacts; and (2) listen to, see, and read their voices through the cultural products they themselves create. Technological innovations such as digital video/filmmaking and the Internet have enabled young people to produce their own media messages – a phenomenon that is particularly prevalent in girl culture. For example, communication scholars have examined the Internet as a space fostering girls' self-expression, community building, identity play, and expressions of girl power (→ Cyberfeminism).

Nearly a decade ago, Mary Celeste Kearney (1998, 285) labeled the "emergence of girls as cultural producers" as "one of the most interesting transformations to have occurred in youth culture in the last two decades."

See also: ▶ AUDIENCES, FEMALE ▶ CYBERFEMINISM ▶ FEMINIST AND GENDER STUDIES ▶ FEMINIST MEDIA ▶ GENDER: REPRESENTATION IN THE MEDIA ▶ TEXT AND INTERTEXTUALITY ▶ YOUTH CULTURE

REFERENCES AND SUGGESTED READINGS

Kearney, M. C. (1998). Producing girls. In S. A. Inness (ed.), *Delinquents and debutantes: Twentieth-century American girls' cultures*. New York: New York University Press, pp. 285–310.

Globalization of the Media

DAYA KISHAN THUSSU
University of Westminster

Like many other spheres of contemporary life, the media have been profoundly affected by the processes of globalization (→ Globalization Theories). During the 1990s, the global media landscape was transformed as a result of the deregulation and privatization of broadcasting and telecommunication, enabling a quantum leap in the production and distribution of media products across continents and in real time. In the era of real-time communications, people all over the world can watch live as events unfold, be it political upheavals and civil wars like in Syria or major sports events like the soccer world cup or Olympics. With the convergence of television and the Internet, and the growing availability of broadband, media consumers today can also share information and entertainment programs and, with digital devices, even generate and distribute their own media. The globalization of the media has enabled the creation of a thriving international market, which now encompasses the globe (Thussu 2007; Waisbord 2013).

Opening Up the Media Market

It has been pointed out that the globalization of the media is not entirely new: during the nineteenth century the world was connected by cable and wireless telegraphy, and news agencies such as Reuters were early examples of global media (→ News Agencies, History of). However, in almost every country, the media, historically, were considered a national institution. The state played an important role in the development of the private press (through subsidies) and especially in the growth of radio and television, key media for national integration and a sense of cultural identity, with a remit to inform and educate as well as entertain. In the communist world, the mass media were even considered part of the legitimate state → propaganda machinery. In many developing countries, too, the mass media were used by ruling elites to retain their hold on power (→ Development Communication). Globalization has brought dynamic media, challenging state → censorship and widening the → public sphere, while at the same time also leading to the concentration of media power in a few, unelected, transnational corporations (Baker 2007; → Concentration in Media Systems).

Benefiting from globalization, *transnational media corporations*, such as → Disney, → Time Warner Inc., and → News Corporation, came to dominate the global media industry by virtue of their ownership of multiple networks and production facilities and the huge increase in transnational traffic in media products. The USA leads the field in the export of audiovisual products. Its media are available across the globe in English or in dubbed or indigenized versions. CNN, with its availability in 270 million households outside the US, or search engine Google, with an average of 6 billion searches per day, being prime examples (→ CNN; Search Engines). Hollywood films dominate market in films share in most countries (→ Hollywood; Film Production). The globalization of the media has been made possible by digital technologies and the growing availability of affordable communication satellites (→ Digital Media, History of; Satellite Television).

Global Media: Flow and Contraflow

The resulting growth of multichannel networks has made the global media landscape more complex: it is now multicultural, multilingual, and multinational. Digital communication technologies in broadcasting and now broadband have given viewers in many countries the ability to access simultaneously a vast array of local, national, regional, and international media. A whole range of television networks is now available to viewers around the world: → news (e.g. CNN, BBC World, Al Jazeera), documentary (Discovery, National Geographic), sports (ESPN), and entertainment (Cartoon Network, Disney, HBO), to name the most prominent genres (→ International Television).

Though the media flow from the west (mainly the US) to other parts of the world has increased, there is a small but significant flow in the other direction. Countries like China, Japan, South Korea, Brazil, and India have become increasingly important in the circulation of cultural products. Japan is a major exporter in animation films, South Korea of entertainment (including → video games), and Mexico of soap operas ('telenovelas;' Martinez 2005). Another major non-western presence in the global media market is the growing visibility of India's Hindi film industry, which, in terms of production and viewership, is the world's largest (→ Bollywood). In the arena of news and current affairs, international news channels such as Al Jazeera, Russia Today, or the foreign-language network of China Central Television compete with western players (→ Arab Satellite TV News; China Central Television, Foreign Language Program of).

Al Jazeera English is an interesting example of media 'glocalization,' drawing on the professionalism of the BBC's public service ethos but aiming to privilege a southern perspective on global issues (→ BBC World Service). Such hybridization is not uncommon and helps in a better understanding of strategies being adopted by the major western media corporations to maximize their entry into emerging markets around the globe. Also, major Hollywood studios are increasingly using local production facilities in Europe, Asia, and Latin America.

Challenging Dominance?

The prominent examples of media flows from and to the nonwestern world may give the impression that global media have become more diverse and even democratic. However, despite the growing trend toward contraflow, the revenues of nonwestern media organizations, with a few exceptions, are relatively small, and their global impact is restricted to geocultural markets or at best to small pockets of regional transnational consumers. Critical theorists have argued that the transnational corporations, with the support of their respective governments, exert indirect control over the developing countries, dominating markets, resources, production, and labor (→ Critical Theory; Political Economy of the Media; Media System Dependency Theory).

While some have argued that the global–national–local interaction is producing "heterogeneous disjunctures" rather than a globally homogenized culture (Appadurai 1990), others have championed the cause of cultural hybridity, formed out of an adaptation of western media genres to suit local cultural conventions (Kraidy 2005; → Culture: Definitions and Concepts). Such hybridization of the media takes shape within a broader new-liberal ideological framework. It could be argued that glocalized media are contributing to a culture that celebrates the supremacy of the market and liberal democracy, as defined by the west. That the message is in local languages may in fact be a more effective way of legitimizing the ideological imperatives of a free market system: one that privileges the private and undermines the public media.

See also: ▶ ARAB SATELLITE TV NEWS ▶ BBC WORLD SERVICE ▶ BOLLYWOOD ▶ CABLE TELEVISION ▶ CENSORSHIP ▶ CHINA CENTRAL TELEVISION, FOREIGN LANGUAGE PROGRAM OF ▶ CNN ▶ CONCENTRATION IN MEDIA SYSTEMS ▶ CRITICAL THEORY ▶ CULTURE: DEFINITIONS AND CONCEPTS ▶ DEVELOPMENT COMMUNICATION ▶ DIGITAL MEDIA, HISTORY OF ▶ DISNEY ▶ FILM PRODUCTION ▶ GLOBALIZATION THEORIES ▶ HOLLYWOOD ▶ INTERNATIONAL TELEVISION ▶ MEDIA CONGLOMERATES ▶ MEDIA SYSTEM DEPENDENCY THEORY ▶ NEW WORLD INFORMATION AND COMMUNICATION ORDER (NWICO) ▶ NEWS ▶ NEWS AGENCIES, HISTORY OF ▶ NEWS CORPORATION ▶ POLITICAL ECONOMY OF THE MEDIA ▶ PROPAGANDA ▶ PUBLIC SPHERE ▶ SATELLITE TELEVISION ▶ SEARCH ENGINES ▶ TIME WARNER INC. ▶ UNESCO ▶ VIDEO GAMES

REFERENCES AND SUGGESTED READINGS

Appadurai, A. (1990). Disjuncture and difference in the global cultural economy. *Public Culture*, 2(2), 1–24.

Baker, C. E. (2007). *Media concentration and democracy: Why ownership matters*. Cambridge: Cambridge University Press.

Boyd-Barrett, O. (2006). Cyberspace, globalization and empire. *Global Media and Communication*, 2(1), 21–41.

Chalaby, J. (ed.) (2005). *Transnational television worldwide: Towards a new media order*. London: I. B. Tauris.

Curtin, M. (2012). Chinese media and globalization. *Chinese Journal of Communication*, 5(1), 1–9.

Kraidy, M. (2005). *Hybridity, or, the cultural logic of globalization*. Philadelphia, PA: Temple University Press.

Martinez, I. (2005). Romancing the globe. *Foreign Policy*, November.

Thussu, D. K. (ed.) (2007). *Media on the move: Global flow and contra-flow*. London: Routledge.

Thussu, D. K. (2013). De-Americanising media studies and the rise of "Chindia". *Javnost – The Public*, 20(4), 31–44.

Waisbord, S. (2013). A metatheory of mediatization and globalization? *Journal of Multicultural Discourses*, 8(3), 182–189.

Globalization of Organizations

CYNTHIA STOHL

University of California, Santa Barbara

Globalization embodies the rapid, deepening, and widening connectedness associated with the many political, social, economic, and cultural changes taking place around the world. *Three dynamic processes* constitute globalization and each strongly influences and is influenced by communication: compression of time and space; disembedding of events and institutions, permitting new realignments and restructuring of social interaction across time and space; and increases in global consciousness through processes of reflexivity (Giddens 1990).

Although the word 'globalization' first appeared in Webster's dictionary in 1961, it was not until the mid-1990s that globalization became a noteworthy *concept in organizational studies*. Until that time, organizational communication scholars primarily addressed issues of structural convergence (exploring how organizations were becoming more similar) or organizational divergence (focusing on the organizing effects of cultural variability). Little work addressed the dynamic tensions associated with increasing global interdependence and volatility. Today scholars recognize that the free flow of goods, services, money, and ideas impact and are impacted by organizational communication practices. No longer circumscribed by socio-geographic borders, organizations of all types must address the complexities of operating within a multicultural communicative, legal, moral, technological, and social context (→ Globalization Theories).

Four major questions undergird the research. The *first* asks what types of organizational and interorganizational forms can achieve the flexibility, responsiveness, speed, and efficient knowledge storage, retrieval, and dissemination needed to address the complexity of contemporary production and distribution as well as global problems such as climate change and terrorism. Research suggests emergent networks are today's quintessential organizational form (Monge & Fulk 1999).

The *second* fundamental question addresses how organizations adapt to the tensions associated with the simultaneous competitive pressures for global convergence and the cultural imperative to maintain national, regional, and group identities. Studies indicate that a central communication challenge for global organizations is the management of paradoxes of identity within and across work groups and organizations (Stohl 2005). *Third* are questions related to the ways in which individuals and organizations leverage the entrepreneurial and insitutional capacities for collective action embedded in the new technological environment. The enhanced mass collaborations made possible by the decentralized and aggregating capabilities of social media have changed the nature of global organizing, decision making, and the individual–organizational relationship (Bennett & Segerberg 2013). The *fourth question* explores the ethical responsibilities and implications of the emerging world order. There are vigorous ethical debates relating to issues of relativism versus universalism, coporate social responsibility, cultural imperialism, and possibilities for voice (Stohl & Ganesh 2013).

To answer these questions scholars operate from *several theoretical perspectives*. Intercultural and intergroup theorists examine the changing internal and external dynamics of organizations and study, for example, what factors facilitate interactions among dispersed multicultural workforces as well as the ways in which cultural differences affect mergers and acquistions (→ Intercultural and Intergroup Communication). Network scholars explore the increasing number and types of contemporary collaborations by examining the emerging structures among organizational sectors (→ Communication Networks). Critical scholars address the enactment of and resistance to inequality in the new global order, the changing nature of corporate social responsibility, and the exploration of postcolonial forms of organizing (→ Critical Theory). Researchers who view communication as an interpretive symbolic process approach globalization as intersubjectively constructed. Globalization contributes to new formations of work/personal identities that challenge traditional definitions of who we are and what we do.

Organizational communication scholarship and globalization theory require an understanding of past and present economic, socio-cultural, political, and organizational practices and a sensitivity to ethical and social consequences of organizational action. Theoretical advancements in collection action theory, contingency theory, and institutional theory are gaining momentum (Stohl & Ganesh 2013). The complexity of the phenomenon also calls for studies utilizing qualitative, ethnographic, historical, survey, network, as well as parametric and non parametirc statistical approaches. A critical challenge to organizational researchers is to make sure that theories, methods, and data are comparable and appropriate across contexts and language groups.

See also: ▶ COMMUNICATION NETWORKS ▶ CRITICAL THEORY ▶ GLOBALIZATION THEORIES ▶ INTERCULTURAL AND INTERGROUP COMMUNICATION ▶ ORGANIZATIONAL COMMUNICATION

REFERENCES AND SUGGESTED READINGS

Bennett, L. & Segerberg, A. (2013). *The logic of connective action.* Cambridge: Cambridge University Press.
Ganesh, S., Zoller, H. M., & Cheney, G. (2005). Transforming resistance, broadening our boundaries: Critical organizational communication studies

meets globalization from below. *Communication Monographs*, 72(2), 169–191.

Giddens, A. (1990). *The consequences of modernity*. Stanford, CA: Stanford University Press.

Monge, P. & Fulk, J. (1999). Communication technologies for global network organizations. In G. DeSanctis & J. Fulk (eds.), *Communication technologies and organizational forms*. Thousand Oaks, CA: Sage, pp. 71–100.

Stohl, C. (2005). Globalization theory. In S. May & D. Mumby (eds.), *Engaging organizational communication: Theory and research*. Thousand Oaks: CA: Sage, pp. 223–262.

Stohl, C. & Ganesh S. (2013). Generating globalization. In D. Mumby & L. Purnam (eds), *The Sage handbook of organizational communication*. Thousand Oaks, CA: Sage, pp. 717–742.

Globalization Theories

ANNABELLE SREBERNY

University of London

An interconnected set of terms – globalization, global, globality – dominated analytic discourse toward the end of the twentieth century. There are several discourses about globalization. Social theorists agree that 'globalization' is best thought of as a skein of interlocking processes but not on what those processes might be. Held et al. (1999) suggested that four comparative spatio-temporal dimensions marked out the contemporary period: the extensity of global networks; the intensity of global interconnectedness; the velocity of global flows; and the impact propensity of global interconnectedness. Thus, globalization processes are argued to stretch political, social, and economic relations beyond clear territorial principles of organization, challenging the deeply embedded notion in the social sciences of the national society as the central unit of analysis. Yet the analytic issue remains: what is the *key* driver producing such effects?

Many analysts see globalization as the expansion of transnational practices, especially practices that originate with nonstate actors and cross-state borders, or simply the development of global social relations. Some theorists consider the complex skeins of economic and cultural connectivity that tie different parts of the world together now constitute a new post-societal era. Some fear a homogenization of culture as western, materialist values and desires spread around the world, while others suggested hybridization to be a key process. Historicized argument recognizes that all cultures have been hybridized through time and questions the natio-centric definition of 'culture' that often pertains in such arguments (→ Culture: Definitions and Concepts).

A closely allied term is 'globality,' coined and defined by Robertson (1991) as the increasing awareness that the world is, indeed, a single place. He argued that the consequences for new claims to identity formation were among the key issues facing the twenty-first century, so that an analysis was needed of new forms of collectivity and the individual. Thus, contemporary issues such as global warming and nuclear power are seen as problems that no single state could solve but which require coordinated action across the system of states, with involvement of the global citizenry.

Media and communications play an important role in globalization. First, communications technologies of various kinds provide the visible and invisible skeins of connectivity on which other processes of globalization rely. Second, press and broadcasting remain key carriers of news, and are thus powerful socializing agents of the new globality. Yet there are also many rapidly developing media industries in the global south (Brazil, India, China, Egypt). A third argument regarding cultural globalization focuses on media formats, especially in entertainment, where a western show transmutes to suit a different cultural location. A fourth and final argument focuses on technological convergence through digitization, whereby the dividing lines between the media industries, telecommunications, and computerization blur and offer novel spaces for participation. Social network sites such as YouTube, MySpace, and → Facebook (→ Social Media) have become showcases for global creativity, involving millions of nonprofessional content items, as well as platforms for political commentary and satire that could evade national censorship practices. Diasporas and home populations could actually share virtual spaces for engagement and dialogue, with unknown potential for reshaping national politics, while citizen journalists and bloggers challenge mainstream media content from their own countries and beyond.

While the economic logic of capital is a central driving force of globalization, as Marx and Engels recognized a century and a half ago, giving the term a hostile usage, its unfolding has produced contradictory impacts and responses, not least because of the increased visibility of global processes via communications. Further analysis of grounded real-world processes of globalization should produce more refined theorization and the repudiation of simplistic totalizations.

See also: ▶ ARAB SATELLITE TV NEWS ▶ CHINA CENTRAL TELEVISION, FOREIGN PROGRAM ▶ CULTURAL IMPERIALISM THEORIES ▶ CULTURE: DEFINITIONS AND CONCEPTS ▶ DIFFUSION OF INFORMATION AND INNOVATION ▶ FACEBOOK ▶ INTERNATIONAL COMMUNICATION ▶ INTERNET LAW AND REGULATION ▶ MEDIA CONGLOMERATES ▶ POLITICAL ECONOMY OF THE MEDIA ▶ SOCIAL MEDIA

REFERENCES AND SUGGESTED READINGS

Giddens, A. (1990). *The consequences of modernity*. Cambridge: Polity.
Held, D., McGrew, A., Goldblatt, D., & Perraton, J. (eds.) (1999). *Global transformations*. Cambridge: Polity.
Hirst, P. & Thompson, G. (2009). *Globalization in question*, 3rd edn. Cambridge: Polity.
Kraidy, M. (2005). *Hybridity or the cultural logic of globalization*. Philadelphia, PA: Temple University Press.
Mann, M. (2013). *The sources of social power: Volume 4, Globalizations, 1945–2011*. Cambridge: Cambridge University Press.
Robertson, R. (1991). Social theory, cultural relativity and the problem of globality. In A. D. King (ed.), *Culture, globalization and the world-system*. London: Macmillan.

Goals, Cognitive Aspects of

JAMES PRICE DILLARD
Pennsylvania State University

A goal is a future state of affairs that a person wishes to attain or maintain. Most research posits a theoretical sequence in which goals prompt planning which, in turn, results in message output (→ Goals, Social Aspects of).

Two complementary explanations have been offered for the *origin of goals*. One is that interaction goals derive from *abstract, long-term objectives* that are similar to values (Dillard 1990). For instance, a person who possesses the high-level goal of maintaining good health might approach another person to become 'work-out buddies' (a mid-level goal). When she says, "Having that kind of commitment would help us both get some regular exercise," it suggests micro-level goals such as showing respect and affinity in this particular interaction.

The second type of explanation calls on the theoretical machinery of → *cognitive science*. Cognitive models of → message production assume that individuals possess knowledge of interaction goals and circumstances that might facilitate or threaten goal achievement. Information is stored in → memory, where memory is modeled as an associative network. Cognitive rules are activated by a match between the situational features associated with the rule and the perceived features of the situation in which the actors finds themselves. For example, a message source is likely to form the goal of 'enforcing an obligation' when (1) an individual of lesser status (2) fails to perform a promised behavior that (3) has consequences for the source (Wilson 2002, 169).

Cognitive representations of goals may change over time, especially during the course of interaction. Keck & Samp (2007) found that 66 percent of the intervals in their investigation showed goal shift during a conflict interaction. Just as goal-based theories of message production predict, interlocutors adapt their goals and behavior to one another during conversation.

See also: ▶ COMPLIANCE GAINING ▶ COGNITIVE SCIENCE ▶ GOALS, SOCIAL ASPECTS OF ▶ MEMORY ▶ MESSAGE PRODUCTION

REFERENCES AND SUGGESTED READINGS

Dillard, J. P. (1990). A goal-driven model of interpersonal influence. In J. P. Dillard (ed.), *Seeking compliance: The production of interpersonal influence messages*. Scottsdale, AZ: Gorsuch-Scarisbrick, pp. 41–56.
Keck, K. L. & Samp, J. A. (2007). The dynamic nature of goals and message production as revealed in a

sequential analysis of conflict interactions. *Human Communication Research*, 33, 27–47.

Wilson, S. R. (2002). *Seeking and resisting compliance: What people say, what they do when trying to influence others*. Thousand Oaks, CA: Sage.

Goals, Social Aspects of

JAMES PRICE DILLARD
Pennsylvania State University

A goal-oriented perspective on communication entails the assumption that social interaction is an instrument for achieving objectives. Communication is the means by which something gets done. This does not mean that all goals are self-interested. Indeed, many actions are undertaken to benefit the well-being of the other interactant or of the collective (→ Interpersonal Communication).

A distinction is drawn between primary and secondary goals (Dillard et al. 1989). The *primary goal* provides the explanation for the social episode. It is the answer to the question: what are the interactants doing? Secondary goals are all of the concerns that follow from consideration of the primary goal. For example, if one individual wishes to give advice to another person, the message source may be concerned about appearing overbearing and thereby giving offense. Primary goals serve two social functions. One is motivational. They are primary in the sense that they initiate the process that results in message production. Primary goals also serve a social → meaning function. They give meaning to the social episode by offering a culturally viable explanation for the communicative transaction. In so doing, they also enable individuals to identify the beginning and ending points of the social episode. Segmentation is valuable for making sense of what might otherwise be viewed as an undifferentiated outpouring of behavior.

Secondary goals are concerns that follow from the consideration of a primary goal. One such concern is face. When a speaker wishes to know the time, she may use various linguistic constructions to lessen the threat to the hearer. "I'm sorry to bother you, but . . ." recognizes that individuals have a right to be left alone and that a request for information intrudes upon that right. By including the phrase, the speaker has crafted a message request that will not only obtain the desired information, but also will achieve the goal of respecting the other social actor. Different writers have produced different sets of secondary goals.

See also: ▶ GOALS, COGNITIVE ASPECTS OF
▶ INTERPERSONAL COMMUNICATION
▶ MEANING ▶ MESSAGE PRODUCTION

REFERENCES AND SUGGESTED READINGS

Dillard, J. P., Segrin, C., & Harden, J. M. (1989). Primary and secondary goals in the interpersonal influence process. *Communication Monographs*, 56, 19–38.

Graphic Design

MATTHEW SOAR
Concordia University

'Graphic design' refers, in essence, to the artful arrangement of images and text on a variety of surfaces and in a range of forms. Typical pieces of graphic design include: posters; books; CD, DVD, and book covers; brochures and flyers; magazines and newspapers; logos, trademarks, → branding and corporate identity systems; product packaging; annual reports; T-shirts; signage and way-finding systems; websites; and motion graphics (e.g., film title sequences, TV station identifiers, and promos). Related and sometimes overlapping activities include product design, exhibition and information design, type design and typography, and design for interactivity (websites, kiosks, DVD-ROMs; → Design; Interactivity, Concept of).

Graphic designers might work individually, or in small-to-medium-sized studio partnerships, or in service-oriented departments within larger organizations, in sectors such as book publishing, the music industry, highways departments, computer software, or pharmaceuticals. Apart from their applied creative role, designers may have other duties such as commissioning and overseeing printing, liaising with clients, or developing strategic plans for business, branding, or marketing. Graphic design is an increasingly professionalized practice. The International Council of Graphic Design Associations (ICOGRADA) currently represents the interests of nearly 100 such entities in nearly 50 countries around the world. These associations cover only a fraction of those involved in the panoply of professional, trade, and artisanal practices that together constitute graphic design.

The terms 'graphic design' and 'graphic designer' are widely believed to have first appeared in print in the US as recently as 1922, in an article titled "New kind of printing calls for new design" (Dwiggins 1999). Regardless, the *roots of graphic design* are both broad and complex. Influences and precursors in Europe and North America include: the creation of → propaganda posters during two world wars; commercial art; and various art movements and schools, including Futurism, Constructivism, Arts and Crafts, the Secessionists, DADA, Bauhaus, and De Stijl (Hollis 1994; Meggs 1998; Drucker & McVarish 2012). The 'ukiyo-e' movement was singularly influential in the development of graphic design practice in Japan, given that country's extended cultural isolation until the nineteenth century (Meggs 1998).

In spite of the ubiquity of its work, graphic design has been addressed only fleetingly, and often anonymously, in the communication literature, for instance in *The Medium is the Massage*, a collaboration between Marshall McLuhan and the designer Quentin Fiore (1967). Formal encounters between graphic design and communication theory have been rare. An early exemplar was the appearance of C. Wright Mills at the International Design Conference in Aspen (IDCA), where he gave a talk titled "Man in the middle: The designer" (Mills 1963). Mills's essay brought an early, and much-needed *sociological eye* to the activities of designers, and also anticipated Pierre Bourdieu's notion of the cultural intermediary: an individual whose function is to provide a bridge, or liaison, between the two distinct worlds of production and consumption (Bourdieu 1984).

The *discourse of graphic design practice* is overwhelmingly celebratory, promotional, and technique-oriented; the trade literature far outweighs the available avenues for more reflective, critical perspectives. Key in this respect have been long-standing arguments about what graphic design should be used for. In the 1930s, Otto Neurath introduced ISOTYPE (International System of Typographic Picture Education), a highly formalized graphic method for presenting complex statistical information using only pictorial icons. This approach has been highly influential in the development of information graphics, international signage systems, and computer icons. While graphic design is also intrinsically about information and persuasion, it has long been used as a form of personal and political expression, for example, the protest posters of John Heartfield, Grapus, and Gran Fury, and the recent rise of culture jamming.

See also: ▶ ART AS COMMUNICATION ▶ BRANDING ▶ CULTURE INDUSTRIES ▶ DESIGN ▶ DIGITAL IMAGERY ▶ DIGITAL MEDIA, HISTORY OF ▶ INTERACTIVITY, CONCEPT OF ▶ NEWSPAPER, VISUAL DESIGN OF ▶ PRINTING, HISTORY OF ▶ PROPAGANDA ▶ VISUAL COMMUNICATION ▶ VISUAL CULTURE ▶ VISUAL REPRESENTATION

REFERENCES AND SUGGESTED READINGS

Bourdieu, P. (1984). *Distinction: A social critique of the judgment of taste* (trans. R. Nice). London: Routledge and Kegan Paul.

Drucker, J. & McVarish, E. (2012). *Graphic design history: A critical guide*, 2nd edn. Upper Saddle River, NJ: Pearson Prentice Hall.

Dwiggins, W. A. (1999). New kind of printing calls for new design. In M. Bierut, J. Helfand, S. Heller, & R. Poynor (eds.), *Looking closer 3: Classic writings on graphic design*. New York: Allworth Press, pp. 14–18.

Hollis, R. (1994). *Graphic design: A concise history*. London: Thames and Hudson.

McLuhan, M. & Fiore, Q. (1967). *The medium is the massage: An inventory of effects*. New York: Bantam Books.

Meggs, P. (1998). *A history of graphic design*, 3rd edn. New York: John Wiley.

Mills, C. W. (1963). Man in the middle: The designer. In I. L. Horowitz (ed.), *Power, politics and people: The collected essays of C. Wright Mills*. New York: Oxford University Press, pp. 374–386.

Grounded Theory

BERTRAM SCHEUFELE
University of Hohenheim

In its original sense 'grounded theory' stands for a methodology, research program, and method of qualitative research. In a narrower but also more practical sense the term describes a qualitative technique of text analysis comparable to qualitative content analysis (→ Content Analysis, Qualitative) and → discourse analysis. Barney Glaser and Anselm Strauss (1967/2008) introduced grounded theory as a general research program for developing substantial (specific) or formal (general) theory by starting without (too) many assumptions and working immediately with the 'data' (mostly text material) – this is what the term 'grounded' refers to (→ Qualitative Methodology).

The crucial procedure of the approach is called 'coding.' One usually starts with 'open coding,' i.e., with conceptualizing transcripts line by line. In this stage of theory emergence, one conceptualizes a lot of phrases and obtains many codes, which are compared to other material, merged, renamed, and modified. The second technique is called 'axial or substantive coding.' Here one searches for phrases in the transcripts helping to explain the behavior mentioned by the interviewee. In doing so, one generates links between concepts and tries to establish hypotheses. In the third technique, called 'selective coding,' one looks only at those parts of the interview transcripts relevant from the perspective of the core variable. In addition, category lists and memos are ordered theoretically, concepts are related to the core variable(s), and links between concepts as well as vague concepts are finally specified.

'Theoretical sampling,' in contrast to random sampling (→ Sampling, Random), means continuous sampling and transforming of sampling criteria during the whole research process. Whether to take this or that part of an interview transcript, for instance, depends on the stage of theory development: with open coding in the beginning all material is important at first. But when a core category has been found, new material is chosen with this category in mind.

Strauss and Glaser have developed the basic idea into different directions. While Strauss has established a more systematic and at least partly deductive research technique, Glaser has emphasized more the inductive aspects of grounded theory and demands that researchers avoid research literature before starting to generate the theory.

See also: ▶ CONTENT ANALYSIS, QUALITATIVE ▶ DISCOURSE ANALYSIS ▶ INTERVIEW, QUALITATIVE ▶ QUALITATIVE METHODOLOGY ▶ SAMPLING, RANDOM ▶ TEXT AND INTERTEXTUALITY

REFERENCES AND SUGGESTED READINGS

Birks, M. & Mills, J. (2011). *Grounded theory. A practical guide*. Thousand Oaks, CA: Sage.
Cresswell, J. W. (2013). *Qualitative inquiry and research design: Choosing among five approaches*, 3rd edn. Thousands Oaks, CA: Sage.
Glaser, B. G. & Strauss, A. L. (1967/2008). *The discovery of grounded theory: Strategies for qualitative research*. 3rd paperback edn. New Brunswick, NJ: Aldine.
Titscher, S., Meyer, M., Wodak, R., & Vetter, E. (2000). *Methods of text and discourse analysis*. Thousands Oaks, CA: Sage.

Group Communication

LAWRENCE R. FREY
University of Colorado Boulder

Group communication scholarship focuses on (1) symbol use in small collectivities (three people minimum), called a 'symbolic-management focus'; and (2) how groups and group processes are products of collective symbolic activity, called a 'symbolic-constitutive focus' (Frey & Sunwolf 2004). Both perspectives view a group as a significant communication site; indeed, because it is the minimum unit for the confluence of influence from both individuals and social contexts, the group is the fundamental unit of communication research (Poole 1998).

Theories of group communication include systems, functional, symbolic convergence, structuration, and the symbolic-interpretive perspective. Systems theory views groups as comprised of inputs (preceding variables), throughputs (interaction processes), and outputs. In that symbolic-management perspective, communication is a throughput influenced by inputs (e.g., members' characteristics) and affecting outputs (e.g., decisions made). According to functional theory, effective group work requires satisfaction of functional prerequisites (e.g., identifying a range of solutions to problems), with communication being the means of satisfying those requirements.

Symbolic-constitutive theories include: (1) symbolic convergence theory, which describes how group members come to share a common social reality through recurring communication forms (e.g., fantasy themes); (2) structuration theory, which explores how members' enactment of structures (rules and resources) (re)produces the group system; and (3) the symbolic-interpretive perspective, with groups constituted through recursive relationships among symbolic predispositions (e.g., members' communication preferences), practices (e.g., sharing stories), and processes and products (e.g., developing group culture).

Scholars study both task and relational communication, and laboratory and natural groups, employing both quantitative and qualitative methods. Historically, researchers studied whether groups or individuals solved tasks better, investigating relationships between communication and decision-making in task groups. 'Process scholars' studied communication processes by which decisions developed, focusing, for instance, on group communication developmental stages; 'outcome scholars' studied how communication (e.g., → information processing, discussion procedures, and, later, new communication technologies) affects group decision-making (→ Technology and Communication).

Scholars, however, also soon studied relational communication in groups. Whereas early research explored how communication in laboratory task groups affected relational outcomes (e.g., members' satisfaction), contemporary research examines relational messages (e.g., social support), processes (e.g., relationship development), and positive (e.g., cohesiveness) and negative (e.g., groupthink) outcomes (see Barker et al. 2000) in various natural groups.

Because of the task emphasis, initially, group communication was studied in laboratories. External validity critiques of that research, however, led to studying natural groups. In addition to natural task groups (e.g., organizational teams), researchers investigated relational groups, including families and support groups, as well as gangs and other 'dark-side' groups. Those studies led to the 'bona fide group perspective,' which challenged the 'container model' of groups as closed entities with fixed boundaries, and that focused solely on internal group processes, by identifying two interrelated characteristics examined in subsequent research: stable yet permeable group boundaries and groups' interdependence with relevant contexts.

In addition to quantitative experiments (→ Experiment, Field; Experiment, Laboratory; Quantitative Methodology) and → surveys, group communication scholars have led the way in using interaction analysis, quantitative observation of → discourse (→ Interaction; Imagined Interactions; Discourse Analysis). Recently, qualitative methods, including ethnography, discourse analysis, and rhetorical analysis, as well as mixed methods, are employed to study natural, bona fide groups (→ Qualitative Methodology; Ethnography of Communication). Studying group communication, however, poses challenges: (1) whether to focus on individuals, members' relationships, or the group entity; (2) accounting for fluidity and permeability of group boundaries; (3) the interaction unit to code (e.g., speech acts, combinations, or entire discussions); and (4) group variable designation (e.g., cohesiveness can be an input, throughput, and/or output variable). Scholars also employ quantitative and qualitative methods to assess group communication facilitation effects.

Studies reveal that groups engaged in naturally occurring discussion can flounder and perform ineffectively; consequently, facilitation meeting procedures are often needed to structure group communication. Meeting procedures have been shown to facilitate group creation, conflict management, task and relational communication, and team communication (see Sunwolf & Frey 2005).

See also: ▶ DISCOURSE ▶ DISCOURSE ANALYSIS ▶ ETHNOGRAPHY OF COMMUNICATION ▶ EXPERIMENT, FIELD ▶ EXPERIMENT, LABORATORY ▶ GROUP DECISION-MAKING, FUNCTIONAL THEORY OF ▶ IMAGINED INTERACTIONS ▶ INFORMATION PROCESSING ▶ INTERACTIONS ▶ QUALITATIVE METHODOLOGY ▶ QUANTITATIVE METHODOLOGY ▶ SURVEY ▶ TECHNOLOGY AND COMMUNICATION

REFERENCES AND SUGGESTED READINGS

Barker, V. E., Abrams, J. R., Tiyaamornwong, V., Seibold, D. R., Duggan, A., Park, H. S., & Sebastian, M. (2000). New contexts for relational communication in groups. *Small Group Research*, 31(4), 470–503.

Frey, L. R. & Sunwolf (2004). The symbolic–interpretive perspective on group dynamics. *Small Group Research*, 35(3), 277–306.

Frey, L. R. (ed.), Gouran, D. S., & Poole, M. S. (assoc. eds.) (1999). *The handbook of group theory and research*. Thousand Oaks, CA: Sage.

Poole, M. S. (1998). The small group should be *the* fundamental unit of communication research. In J. S. Trent (ed.), *Communication: Views from the helm for the twenty-first century*. Needham Heights, MA: Allyn and Bacon, pp. 94–97.

Sunwolf & Frey, L. R. (2005). Facilitating group communication. In S. A. Wheelan (ed.), *The handbook of group research and practice*. Thousand Oaks, CA: Sage, pp. 485–509.

Group Decision-Making, Functional Theory of

DENNIS S. GOURAN

Pennsylvania State University

The functional theory of group decision-making, while relatively recent as a formal structure, has grounding in earlier scholarly work by John Dewey (the method of reflective thinking), Robert F. Bales (equilibrium theory), and Irving L. Janis (the groupthink hypothesis and model of vigilance) (see Gouran & Hirokawa 2003). The theory is predicated on a single premise: effective decision-making (the referent for which is 'choosing appropriately') is proportionate to the extent that communication serves to insure that the members have adequately satisfied the requirements posed by their tasks (→ Decision-Making Processes in Organizations). Not only does communication serve directly to address specific task requirements but also indirectly in group members' overcoming constraints, both internal and external, on how they are performing (Gouran 2010).

The theory rests on ten assumptions and comprises eight general propositions, one of which has five components (see Gouran & Hirokawa 1996). The propositions all relate to the functions that communication should or does serve to heighten the probability that a decision-making or problem-solving group will choose appropriately. (Gouran and Hirokawa 2003 have also published a highly abridged version of the theory consisting of the four most vital assumptions and three most central propositions.) To the extent that communication fails to serve the functions the two versions of the theory specify under the conditions assumed, in general, it is less likely that a group will, or even can, perform effectively in the sense noted.

See also: ▶ DECISION-MAKING PROCESSES IN ORGANIZATIONS ▶ GROUP COMMUNICATION ▶ SPEECH COMMUNICATION, HISTORY OF

REFERENCES AND SUGGESTED READINGS

Gouran, D. S. (2010). Overcoming sources of irrationality that complicate working in decision-making groups. In S. Schuman (ed.), *The handbook of working with difficult groups: How they are difficult, why they are difficult, and what you can do about it*. San Francisco: Jossey-Bass, pp. 137–152, 379–381.

Gouran, D. S. & Hirokawa, R. Y. (1996). Functional theory and communication in decision-making and problem-solving groups: An expanded view. In R. Y. Hirokawa & M. S. Poole (eds.), *Communication and group decision-making*, 2nd edn. Thousand Oaks, CA: Sage, pp. 55–80.

Gouran, D. S. & Hirokawa, R. Y. (2003). Effective decision making and problem solving in groups: A functional perspective. In R. Y. Hirokawa, R. S. Cathcart, L. A. Samovar, & L. D. Henman (eds.), *Small group communication*, 8th edn. New York: Oxford University Press, pp. 27–38.

H

Health Campaigns, Communication in

SETH M. NOAR

University of North Carolina at Chapel Hill

Health communication campaigns have long been a tool used to influence the health of the public in countries around the world. Campaigns are an organized set of communication activities to produce health effects or outcomes in a relatively large number of individuals, typically within a specified period of time. Traditionally, campaigns were thought to only be capable of raising awareness and perhaps improving the attitudes and social norms of a particular audience. More recent work, however, has provided evidence that properly designed and implemented campaigns can impact health behaviors (e.g., Hornik 2002; Snyder et al. 2004; Noar 2006; → Health Communication).

Principles of Campaign Design

Perhaps the most valuable lessons being learned in the campaign literature are the conditions under which campaigns tend to be most effective. These can be referred to as principles of effective campaign design (Noar 2006; Rogers & Storey 1987). Formative research involves *two phases*. The first phase focuses on gathering data regarding audience characteristics, the behavior at issue, and message channels (→ Audience Research). The second phase is focused on testing initial campaign messages with target audience members in order to gain feedback on the appropriateness and persuasive impact of those messages. No matter what the topic, formative research is thought to be crucial to truly understanding the target audience.

Theory is indispensable in campaigns and it serves as an important conceptual foundation for any health communication campaign. In fact, theories serve a number of important roles, including suggesting: (1) important behavioral determinants that campaign messages might focus on; (2) variables for → audience segmentation; and (3) variables to apply in evaluating campaigns. In the health communication campaigns area, a broad range of theories have been used, including theories of health behavior, exemplification, and agenda setting (→ Agenda-Setting Effects; Media Effects). A key consideration in any campaign has to do with defining the audience. This is accomplished by dividing the population of interest into smaller, more homogeneous groups. The ultimate purpose of segmentation is to create

---

The Concise Encyclopedia of Communication, First Edition. Edited by Wolfgang Donsbach.
© 2015 John Wiley & Sons, Inc. Published 2015 by John Wiley & Sons, Inc.

groups that have similar message and channel preferences, and can thus be targeted with persuasive messages specifically designed for those segments.

Once a clear audience segment (or segments) has been defined, messages can be developed and then pre-tested. There are a *variety of approaches* that can be used, such as: (1) fear appeals – these messages should increase levels of both fear and self-efficacy (building individuals' confidence that they can carry out the recommended behavior; → Fear Induction through Media Content); (2) message framing – positive (gain-framed) messages are most effective in impacting preventive behaviors, while negative (loss-framed) messages are most effective in impacting screening behaviors (→ Framing Effects; Framing of the News); and (3) narrative approach –often used within entertainment education, this approach suggests that storylines that provide positive role models and reduce counterarguments are most effective (→ Storytelling and Narration).

Campaigns utilize a number of *channels and strategies* to reach their intended audience. These include mass communication channels such as television, radio, and print media, as well as small media such as posters, billboards, bus → signs, and other materials and outlets. Some campaigns include community-wide components such as community events, workshops, → public relations activities, and coordination with school-based programs. Campaigns are also now taking advantage of the Internet and social media as campaign channels (→ Health Communication and the Internet).

Evaluating Campaigns

Process evaluation refers to the monitoring and collection of data on fidelity and implementation of campaign activities, and it answers several questions, such as: Did campaign messages air in the channels (and specific placements within those channels) in which they were intended to air? Was a significant proportion of the target audience exposed to the campaign messages? Are there any mid-course corrections that can be made to elements of the campaign to improve reach and/or frequency of exposure to the campaign?

Outcome evaluation is concerned with assessing whether a campaign had its intended impact, and this is one of the most challenging aspects of campaigns. Unlike other kinds of health interventions, campaigns are conducted in the field and do not lend themselves to controlled evaluation designs (→ Experiment, Field). Consequently, most of the evidence for the effects of campaigns comes from research studies that leave open many threats to internal → validity (Valente 2001; Hornik 2002). Indeed, popular designs used to evaluate health communication campaigns include post-test-only designs, where a campaign is followed by a post-only → survey assessing campaign exposure and campaign-relevant variables, and pre-test–post-test designs, where a pre-test survey is given, the campaign takes place, and is followed by a post-test survey. Some campaigns use designs that are more rigorous and thus decrease threats to internal validity, such as pre-test–post-test control group designs, which include a control community for comparison purposes, and time-series designs, where multiple surveys are given both before and after a campaign is executed.

Directions for Campaign Research

Perhaps the most compelling current issue is the changing media environment and the implications of this for health communication campaigns. Recent work by media and health communication scholars has described the transformation of the world wide web from a technology to deliver one-way, simple communications to a technology that engages participants as active agents in the creation and dissemination of information and messages, or Web 2.0 (Thackeray et al. 2008). This has profound implications for campaigns, as it has the potential to change campaign audiences from passive recipients of messages to active agents in the campaign itself (→ Interactivity, Concept of). Practitioners are also increasingly using such new media in attempts to extend both the reach and impact of their campaigns, and researchers are studying how such technologies can be best harnessed for effective health communication (→ Communication Networks).

See also: ▶ AGENDA-SETTING EFFECTS
▶ AUDIENCE RESEARCH ▶ AUDIENCE SEGMENTATION
▶ COMMUNICATION NETWORKS ▶ DIFFUSION OF
INFORMATION AND INNOVATION ▶ EXPERIMENT,
FIELD ▶ FEAR INDUCTION THROUGH MEDIA
CONTENT ▶ FRAMING EFFECTS ▶ FRAMING
OF THE NEWS ▶ HEALTH COMMUNICATION
▶ HEALTH COMMUNICATION AND THE INTERNET
▶ HEALTH LITERACY ▶ INTERACTIVITY, CONCEPT
OF ▶ KNOWLEDGE GAP EFFECTS ▶ MEDIA
EFFECTS ▶ PERSUASION ▶ PUBLIC RELATIONS
▶ REASONED ACTION, THEORY OF ▶ SIGN
▶ SOCIAL COGNITIVE THEORY ▶ SOCIAL
MARKETING ▶ STORYTELLING AND NARRATION
▶ STRATEGIC FRAMING ▶ SURVEY ▶ VALIDITY

REFERENCES AND SUGGESTED READINGS

Hornik, R. C. (ed.) (2002). *Public health communication: Evidence for behavior change.* Mahwah, NJ: Lawrence Erlbaum.

Noar, S. M. (2006). A 10-year retrospective of research in health mass media campaigns: Where do we go from here? *Journal of Health Communication*, 11, 21–42.

Rogers, E. M. & Storey, J. D. (1987). Communication campaigns. In C. R. Berger & S. H. Chafee (eds.), *Handbook of communication science.* Thousand Oaks, CA: Sage, pp. 817–846.

Snyder, L. B., Hamilton, M. A., Mitchell, E. W., Kiwanuka-Tondo, J., Fleming-Milici, F., & Proctor, D. (2004). A meta-analysis of the effect of mediated health communication campaigns on behavior change in the United States. *Journal of Health Communication*, 9(1), 71–96.

Thackeray, R., Neiger, B. L., Hanson, C. L., & McKenzie, J. F. (2008). Enhancing promotional strategies within social marketing programs: Use of Web 2.0 social media. *Health Promotion Practice*, 9(4), 338–343.

Valente, T. W. (2001). Evaluating communication campaigns. In R. E. Rice & C. K. Atkin (eds.), *Public communication campaigns*, 3rd edn. Thousand Oaks, CA: Sage, pp. 105–124.

Health Communication

K. VISWANATH
Harvard University

Health communication is the study and application of the generation, creation, and dissemination of health-related information, health-related interactions among individual social actors and institutions, and their effects on different publics including individuals, community groups, and institutions. The challenges inherent in disease prevention and health promotion warrant a multidisciplinary and multilevel approach that examines the role of distal factors such as social and economic policies and health policies, near-proximal factors such as neighborhoods and health-care organizations, and proximal factors such as individual lifestyles to explain individual and population health. Some have argued that communication is one thread that could connect the distal and proximal factors to explain individual and population health. Given this charge, health communication, though primarily a derivative field, draws from and contributes to such fields as mass communication, journalism, communication studies, epidemiology, public health, health behavior and health education, medicine, sociology, and psychology, among others.

Organization of the Field

There is no simple or complete way to organize the field of health communication, though several sub-fields have existed depending on one's research interests, as well as adventitious and historical circumstances. At the *individual level*, the focus is twofold: (1) how health cognitions affect, and behaviors influence and are influenced by, health communications; and (2) how interpersonal interactions between patients, family members, and providers, and with members of their social network, influence health outcomes. At the *organizational level*, some have studied the role of communication within health-care systems and how organization of the media and the practices of media professionals may influence population and individual health.

Finally, at the *societal level*, the focus is on large-scale social changes and the role of communication with such changes. For example, one might examine how → strategic communications as well as natural diffusion of information impact individual and population health; or how communication mediates and is influenced by social determinants such as social class, neighborhood, social cohesion and conflict, social and economic policies, and how that impacts individual and population health.

Even as these levels provide a useful organizing framework, *two caveats* are warranted. First, policymaking and research related to health may affect more than one level. Second, interest in a level of analysis and pursuit of work at one level is not inconsequential. Locating a problem at one level, and studying it at that level, have implications for the kind of policy or practice that is likely to emerge from that research.

Interpersonal Communication

Extensive attention has been given to understanding the consequences of *communication between physicians and patients* on patient satisfaction, adherence, and quality of life. One theme is who controls the interaction between providers and patients, known as 'relational control.' A second theme focuses on the outcomes of patient–provider interactions. Extensive research has documented that patient–provider communication influences patient satisfaction which, in turn, is related to patient adherence and compliance to treatment regimens, ease of distress, physiological response, length of stay in the hospital, quality of life, and health status, among others. Third, researchers have documented stark differences in patient preparation and access, and in care received and health outcomes, between social classes as well as racial and ethnic groups.

The implications of *interpersonal interaction in the context of families, friends, co-workers, and voluntary associations* on health outcomes have become one of the most dynamic areas of research in health communication. This topic has been pursued from diverse theoretical viewpoints by researchers focusing on social networks, social support, family communications, and social capital based on the researcher's disciplinary origins and research interests. In addition to social support, social networks can accelerate or decelerate diffusion of new information, and also influence how it is interpreted (Himelboim & Han 2014). Members within networks can serve as role models for lifestyle behaviors such as smoking and obesity. The emergence and spread of the Internet have broadened the scope of interpersonal interaction and its influence in health communication by moderating the limits of geography.

Mass Media and Health

The *incidental and routine use of media* for → news and entertainment serves four functions in health. (1) The *informational function* is served when casual use of media for news or other purposes may expose the audience to developments on new treatments or new drugs, alert them to risk factors, or warn them of impending threats such as avian flu; (2) media serve an *instrumental function* by providing information that facilitates action; e.g., in times of natural disasters the audience may learn about places where they should take shelter, and information of this kind allows for practical action; (3) media defines what is acceptable and legitimate, performing a *social control* function; (4) the *communal function* is served when media provide social support, generate social capital, and connect people to social institutions and groups.

Information seeking, as a construct, has gained greater currency in recent times as more information on health has become routinely available because of greater coverage of health in the media, the spread of health-related content on the world wide web, or the consumerist movement in health that promotes informed or shared decision-making (→ Information Seeking). It is widely assumed that under certain conditions some people actively look for health information to seek a second opinion, make a more informed choice on treatments, and learn in greater depth about a health problem that afflicts them or their friends or family members.

The most visible and popular means of strategic communications is through *health campaigns* which have become a critical arsenal in health promotion. A typical health campaign attempts to promote change by increasing the amount of information on the health topic, and by defining the issue of interest in such a way as to promote health or prevent disease. Recent reviews of the vast literature on health campaigns have identified conditions under which health campaigns can be successful (e.g. Noar 2006; Randolph & Viswanath 2004).

Emerging Challenges/Dimensions

First, the combined impact of computers and telecommunications on society has been transformative, impinging on almost every facet of human life including art, culture, science, and education.

Consumer informatics integrates consumer information needs and preferences with clinical systems to empower patients to take charge of their healthcare, bring down costs, and improve quality of care. For example, the integration of electronic medical records with communications should facilitate communications between patients and providers, send automatic reminders to patients to stay on schedule, and help patients navigate the health-care system (→ Mobility, Technology for). Second, technological developments are coinciding with the *consumerist movement* in health-care. The paternalistic model that characterized the physician–patient relationship is slowly being complemented by alternative models such as shared/informed decision-making models (SDM/IDM) or patient-centered communication (PCC). Third, the significant investments in biomedical research enterprise in the developing world, and movement toward more evidence-based medicine, have led to calls for translation of the knowledge from the laboratory to the clinic and the community. Lastly, an urgent and a moral imperative in health is addressing the profound inequities in access to health-care and the disproportionate burden of disease faced by certain groups.

See also: ▶ ADVERTISING ▶ ATTITUDES ▶ COMMUNICATION INEQUALITIES ▶ CULTIVATION EFFECTS ▶ DEVELOPMENT COMMUNICATION CAMPAIGNS ▶ ENVIRONMENTAL COMMUNICATION ▶ FEAR INDUCTION THROUGH MEDIA CONTENT ▶ FRAMING EFFECTS ▶ HEALTH CAMPAIGNS, COMMUNICATION IN ▶ HEALTH COMMUNICATION AND THE INTERNET ▶ HEALTH LITERACY ▶ INFORMATION PROCESSING ▶ INFORMATION SEEKING ▶ INTERPERSONAL COMMUNICATION ▶ KNOWLEDGE GAP EFFECTS ▶ MEDIA EFFECTS ▶ MOBILITY, TECHNOLOGY FOR ▶ NEWS ▶ PERSUASION ▶ PLANNED BEHAVIOR, THEORY OF ▶ REASONED ACTION, THEORY OF ▶ RISK COMMUNICATION ▶ RISK PERCEPTIONS ▶ SOCIAL MARKETING ▶ STRATEGIC COMMUNICATION

REFERENCES AND SUGGESTED READINGS

Epstein, R. M. & Street, R. L., Jr. (2007). *Patient-centered communication in cancer care: Promoting healing and reducing suffering*. NIH Publication no. 07-6225. Bethesda, MD: National Cancer Institute.

Glanz, K., Rimer, B., & Viswanath, K. (eds.) (2008). *Health behavior and health education: Theory, research, and practice*. 4th ed. San Francisco, CA: Jossey-Bass.

Himelboim, I. & Han, J. Y. (2014). Cancer talk on twitter: Community structure and information sources in breast and prostate cancer social networks. *Journal of Health Communication: International Perspectives*, 19(2), 210–225.

Hornik, R. (ed.) (2002). *Public health communication: Evidence for behavior change*. Mahwah, NJ: Lawrence Erlbaum.

McCauley, M., Blake, K., Meissner, H., & Viswanath, K. (2013). The social group influences of U.S. health journalists and their impact on the newsmaking process. *Health Education Research*, 28(20), 339–51.

Noar, S. M. (2006). A 10-year retrospective of research in health mass media campaigns: Where do we go from here? *Journal of Health Communication*, 11, 21–42.

Obregon, R. & Waisbord, S. (eds.) (2012). *The handbook of global health communication*. Oxford: Wiley Blackwell.

Parker, J. C. & Thorson, E. (2008). *Health communication in the new media landscape*. New York: Springer.

Randolph, W. & Viswanath, K. (2004). Lessons learned from public health mass media campaigns: Marketing health in a crowded media world. *Annual Review of Public Health*, 25, 419–37.

Snyder, L. B. & Hamilton, M. A. (2002). A meta-analysis of U.S. health campaign effects on behavior: Emphasize enforcement, exposure, and new information, and beware of secular trend. In R. Hornik (ed.), *Public health communication: Evidence for behavior change*. Mahwah, NJ: Lawrence Erlbaum, pp. 357–383.

Viswanath, K. (2005). The communications revolution and cancer control. *Nature Reviews Cancer*, 5(10), 828–835.

Health Communication and the Internet

HEINZ BONFADELLI
University of Zurich

'E-Health' is a relatively new term used to describe a heterogeneous set of phenomena associated with health applications (health informatics) and provision of health care or health communication in general via the Internet and Web 2.0 and also via mobile phones. For Eysenbach (2001), "the term characterizes not only a technical development, but also a state-of-mind, a way of thinking, an attitude, and a commitment for networked, global thinking, to improve health care locally, regionally, and worldwide by using information and communication technology."

The Internet offers several *advantages* but also some challenges to health communication. Its possibility for interactive communications similar to interpersonal communication can be used to target and customize the information to the user's needs, to foster motivation, and to strengthen impact (→ Health Literacy). Internet-based health services have the capacity to economically reach unlimited and geographically widespread audiences, thereby increasing efficiency and decreasing costs. Furthermore, the Internet can be used flexibly anywhere and at any time. In contrast to traditional mass media, the quantitative capacity of the Internet in terms of information abundance, as well as the depth and specialization of health information provided, is almost unlimited.

Besides these opportunities and strengths, there are *limitations and threats* as well. First, the fact that people need to be motivated to actively search for information may limit its reach, as it is usually the more educated and more active who access the Internet (→ Digital Divide). Second, the reliability and trustworthiness of health messages offered on the Internet can become an issue because information providers or sources behind the information are not clear. As a consequence, it is not easy for users to estimate the credibility of a source. Another concern is privacy issues regarding E-Health users and patient records.

There are an enormous and ever-growing number of *public and private providers of* health information on the Internet at local, state, and international level. The range of health content provided by them includes news (e.g., outbreaks of disease), statistics, lifestyle advice and health tips, health promotion, and disease prevention. Besides, there are even more health providers in the private area, such as insurance companies, health advisory services, and pharmaceutical firms. Last, a large number of health communities in form of discussion groups and forums exist where many different health-related topics are discussed and personal health experiences are exchanged. The use of the Internet supports traditional health services and applications, but new services have also been created in recent years in the areas of e-content (e.g., health information and orientation, medical databases), e-commerce (e.g., online pharmaceutical providers), e-connectivity (intranets of hospitals), e-computer applications, and e-care (e.g., telehealth monitoring, telesurgery).

Eysenbach et al. (2002) provide a meta-analysis of empirical studies assessing the quality of the health information provided online. Most frequently valuated criteria are: accuracy, completeness, readability, design, disclosure, and references provided. Most of the studies included found significant quality problems, and criticized, among other things, the lack of completeness or accuracy and difficulty in finding high-quality sites.

It is difficult to estimate the number of *users of E-Health* but a survey conducted in the US (Pew Internet 2011) estimates that 80 percent of internet users and 59 percent of the total population look for health information online, and looking for health information is the third most popular online activity. A study by Andreassen et al. (2007) reports slightly lower levels in seven countries in Europe. In general, younger people between the ages of 18 and 49, women, whites, and adults with college education and/or living in higher-income households are using E-Health more. It seems that most of the users of online health information are satisfied with the content they are looking for, and rate the searched information as helpful, giving new insights, and even believe it (Ayantunde et al. 2007). Besides usage research, there are a growing number of studies analysing the *effectiveness of purposeful internet interventions* (Webb et al. 2010). But up to now, there is only limited evidence concerning the far-reaching consequences of the Internet as a new information source and service provider in the field of health communication.

See also: ▶ DIGITAL DIVIDE ▶ HEALTH COMMUNICATION ▶ HEALTH LITERACY

REFERENCES AND SUGGESTED READINGS

Andreassen, H. K., Bujnowska-Fedak, M. M., Chronaki, C. E., Dumitru, R.C., Pudule, I., Santana, S.,Voss, H., & Wynn, R. (2007). European citizens' use of E-health services: A study of seven countries. *BMC Public Health*, 7(53). At http://www.biomedcentral.com/content/pdf/1471-2458-7-53.pdf, accessed September 2, 2014.

Ayantunde, A. A., Welch, N. T., & Parsons, S. (2007). A survey of patient satisfaction and use of the internet for health information. *Journal of Clinical Practice*, 61(3), 458–462.

Eysenbach, G. (2001): What is e-health? *Journal of Medical Internet Research*, 3(2), e20.

Eysenbach, G., Powell, J., Kuss, O., & Sa, E.-R. (2002). Empirical studies assessing the quality of health information for consumers on the world wide web: A systematic review. *Journal of the American Medical Association*, 287(20), 2691–2700.

Pew Internet. (2011). Health Topics. 80% of internet users look for health information online. At http://www.pewinternet.org/Reports/2011/HealthTopics.aspx, accessed August 6, 2014.

Webb, Th., Joseph, J., Yardley, L., & Michie, S. (2010). Using the internet to promote health behavior change: A systematic review and meta-analysis of the impact of theoretical basis, use of behavior change techniques, and mode of delivery on efficacy. *Journal of Medical Internet Research*, at www.jmir.org/2010/1/e4/, accessed August 6, 2014.

Health Literacy

EMILY ZOBEL KONTOS
Harvard School of Public Health

Health literacy can be defined as the degree to which individuals have the capacity to obtain, process, and understand basic health information and services needed to make appropriate health decisions. Health literacy focuses on the *interaction* between individual-level skills and structural factors such as health-sector demands.

In one of the earliest attempts to examine *health-related literacy tasks* (HALS), researchers identified 191 health-related tasks among the National Adult Literacy Survey (NALS) and International Adult Literacy Surveys (IALS) (→ survey) and analyzed the health literacy of US adults (Rudd et al. 2004). They found that some 12 percent (23 million of US adults) are estimated to have skills in the lowest level on the HALS, while an additional 7 percent (13.4 million) are not able to perform even simple health-literacy tasks such as locate dosage information on a medicine label.

A variety of health-related materials have been assessed over the years and researchers report that an overwhelming majority of the materials score at reading-grade levels that far exceed the reading ability of the average adult. International assessments of health materials, focused mainly on informed consent documents, echo these findings.

Researchers also investigated the association between health literacy and health outcomes. For instance, with the development of *health-specific reading assessment tools* such as the Rapid Estimate of Adult Literacy in Medicine (REALM), they were able to assess patients' health-related reading skills and then correlate the readability/literacy levels with health outcomes in a clinical setting. Both correlated strongly. In addition to the ill effects on the individual patient, limited health literacy places a burden on health-care systems which in turn impacts the overall economic consequences to society.

As the field of health literacy evolves more research is required to rigorously examine the full breadth of the construct as illustrated in its definition: the degree to which individuals have the capacity to obtain, process, and understand basic health information and services needed to make appropriate health decisions.

See also: ▶ COMMUNICATION INEQUALITIES ▶ HEALTH COMMUNICATION ▶ INFORMATION LITERACY ▶ KNOWLEDGE GAP EFFECTS ▶ MEDIA LITERACY ▶ SURVEY

REFERENCES AND SUGGESTED READINGS

Jordan, J. E., Buchbinder, R., Briggs, A. M., Elsworth, G. R., Busija, L., Batterham, R., & Osborne, R. H. (2014). The Health Literacy Management Scale (HeLMS): A measure of an individual's capacity to seek, understand and use health information within the healthcare setting. *Patient Education and Counseling*, 91(2), 228–235.

Kutner, M., Greenberg, E., & Baer, J. (2005) *National assessment of adult literacy: A first look at the literacy of America's adults in the twenty-first century*. Washington, DC: US Department of Education.

Nielsen-Bohlman, L., Panzer, A. M., & Kindig, D. A. (eds.) (2004). *Health literacy: A prescription to end confusion*. Washington, DC: Institute of Medicine.

Rudd, R, Kirsch, I., & Yamamoto, K. (2004). *Literacy and Health in America: Policy Information Report*. Princeton, NJ: Educational Testing Service.

Hermeneutics

JOHN DURHAM PETERS
University of Iowa

SAMUEL MCCORMICK
San Francisco State University

'Hermeneutics' comes from the name of the Greek messenger-god, Hermes – the patron of travelers, rogues, liars, and thieves. As the carrier of messages between gods and mortals, Hermes had to be fluent in both of their idioms. It was his task to build and maintain an interpretive bridge between alien worlds. Since he was also a trickster who could deliver messages in garbled form, the Greek verb hermeneuō meant to decipher cryptic or obscure meanings, and, more generally, to explain, translate, and express (Gadamer 1971). The term hermeneutics descends from this root, via the Latin hermeneutica, and has been used in English and German since the late seventeenth century.

Today hermeneutics has *two main senses*: the art of reading texts, and the philosophy of textual interpretation and human understanding (→ Text and Intertextuality). Wherever there is unintelligibility, there is a hermeneutic problem. Hermeneutics, like communication, is the general theory of dealing with problematic → meanings. It aims to decipher lost sense with an almost therapeutic mission of liberating meanings that have been frozen into muteness or madness by the passage of time or culture.

Hermeneutics has enjoyed some recognition in the field of communication studies (→ Communication as a Field and Discipline). It received a particularly warm welcome in the 1970s, due in large part to the philosophical support it lent to → qualitative methodology. With a greater interest in power since the 1980s, communication scholars tended to turn to critical and poststructuralist theories (→ Critical Theory), though interest in hermeneutics persists as a key to understanding the curiously distanced communicative situation of broadcasting, and abiding questions in rhetorical theory (Hyde 2001; → Rhetorical Studies). If communication is fundamentally a matter of distance and its bridging, and human existence is fundamentally interpretive, then hermeneutics holds a key to understanding communication in general. Whether taken strictly or broadly, hermeneutics still has much to say about basic communication problems.

See also: ▶ COMMUNICATION AS A FIELD AND DISCIPLINE ▶ CRITICAL THEORY ▶ MEANING ▶ POSTMODERNISM AND COMMUNICATION ▶ QUALITATIVE METHODOLOGY ▶ RHETORICAL STUDIES ▶ TEXT AND INTERTEXTUALITY

REFERENCES AND SUGGESTED READINGS

Gadamer, H.-G. (1971). Hermeneutik [Hermeneutics]. In J. Ritter (ed.), *Historisches Wörterbuch der Philosophie* [Historical dictionary of philosophy]. Basle: Schwabe, pp. 1061–1073.
Hyde, M. (2001). Hermeneutics. In T. Sloane (ed.), *Encyclopedia of rhetoric*. Oxford: Oxford University Press, pp. 329–337.

Historic Key Events and the Media

RUDOLF STÖBER
University of Bamberg

Historic key events are genuine events with historical importance. Four factors are important to consider in this regard: (1) historic key events have a short and distinct duration; (2) historic key events have a significant impact on later times; (3) historic key events are not primarily created for media attention; (4) historic key events are ambiguous and subjective in many ways. On the one hand, the mass media cover key events; on the other hand, media routines can be used for political or other purposes. The ambiguous status of a key event is due to the point of view.

Historic key events have to be distinguished clearly from media events or 'pseudo-events' that exist only in anticipation of the news media's coverage (Boorstin 1962; → Media Events and Pseudo-Events). In historical perspective, some key events, when they happened, did not receive media coverage at all. However, under normal circumstances, the coverage of historic key events by the media is one indicator of the importance of the event in itself and leads to follow-up coverage of minor similar events (Kepplinger &

Habermeier 1995), for example, even small incidents involving airplanes attracted greater media attention after 9/11. The status of an event as 'historic' and 'key' depends on its specific importance, which is relative, not absolute. For instance, many historic key events are only important for a particular nation. The status of a key event also is related to the bias of the significant effects of the event in history. Many key events have positive effects for one interest group but create negative effects for others. The bias of the media coverage depends on the varying points of view (→ Bias in the News).

Historic key events become emblematic by way of the attribution of importance to them, which may be biased, and media coverage plays an important part in forging the symbolism. The concentration of the distinct event in a short historic moment at a given place makes both media coverage and forging the symbol easy. The assassination of Archduke Franz Ferdinand in 1914, which led to World War I, was the symbolic end of the nineteenth and the beginning of the twentieth century. The murder of John F. Kennedy marked the end of the American dream of 'Camelot' in 1963. The raising and tearing down of the Berlin Wall marked the climax and the end of the Cold War in 1961 and 1989, respectively. The terrorist attacks of 9/11 upon symbols of America's strength started the worldwide 'war on terror' in 2001.

Media coverage does overload some historic key events with *symbolic significance*. The landing on the moon in 1969 serves as an example: Its significance for improving life on earth or men's relationship to the universe is still unclear. The most impressive key event of recent years, the terrorist attacks of September 11, confounds the rule that every historic key event is a 'genuine' and not a 'mediated'. The symbolic nature of the attacks underlines its character as a media event: the Twin Towers as a symbol of US high finance, the Pentagon of its military strength, and the Capitol or White House of its political system indicate that 9/11 was arranged for the media. The attacks on America's symbols may not have been so choreographed in former times, when there were no TV networks or video cameras (→ Mediated Terrorism; Propaganda). In history media coverage of key events has followed some general trends: (1) the time delay between event and media coverage has been reduced dramatically; (2) media involvement in historic key event coverage has expanded; (3) the impact of the news media's coverage of key events on the audience has increased; (4) key events are illustrated with the most impressive material. All these trends are related to changes in the media system itself.

At present the principal methodology employed in research in historic key event coverage is content analysis, which has been used to study isolated events (→ Content Analysis, Qualitative; Content Analysis, Quantitative). Future research should take into account a combination of content analysis, reception research, media structure analysis, and historical criticism.

See also: ▶ BIAS IN THE NEWS ▶ CONTENT ANALYSIS, QUALITATIVE ▶ CONTENT ANALYSIS, QUANTITATIVE ▶ JOURNALISM, HISTORY OF ▶ MEDIA EVENTS AND PSEUDO-EVENTS ▶ MEDIA HISTORY ▶ MEDIATED TERRORISM ▶ NEWS FACTORS ▶ NEWS ROUTINES ▶ NEWS VALUES ▶ NEWSPAPER, HISTORY OF ▶ POLITICAL COMMUNICATION ▶ PROPAGANDA

REFERENCES AND SUGGESTED READINGS

Boorstin, D. J. (1962). *The image; or, what happened to the American dream*. New York: Atheneum. Couldry, N. (2003). *Media rituals: A critical approach*. London: Routledge.

Emery, M., Emery, E., & Roberts, N. L. (2000). *The press and America: An interpretative history of the mass media*, 9th edn. Harlow: Pearson Education.

Kepplinger, H. M. & Habermeier, J. (1995). The impact of key events on the presentation of reality. *European Journal of Communication*, 10(3), 371–390.

Hollywood

JAN-CHRISTOPHER HORAK
University of California, Los Angeles

Hollywood is the metaphoric, if not exactly the geographic, center of the American film, television, cable, music, and digital media industry. Ripe with symbolic meaning for media consumers across the globe, Hollywood exists almost purely in the collective imagination, since it is neither incorporated as a city, nor definable by strict borders as a geographic location within the city of Los Angeles. Even in terms of its real geography, Hollywood was only one of several industry centers, and of the major film studios, only Paramount, RKO, and Columbia maintained production facilities directly in Hollywood. Nevertheless, millions of tourists flock each year to 'Hollywood,' which has also had its ups and downs as a piece of real estate.

It was merely sunshine and the diversity of topographies that *lured filmmakers* from New York and New Jersey to southern California. In the early days of the film industry, producers shot on outdoor stages in natural light, rather than utilizing electric light, so that dependable sunshine was a must. Southern California's mixture of seascapes, mountains, desert, and other topographies in a relatively limited area was thus a plus. The *first permanent film studio* in Hollywood was established by David Horsely's Nestor Film Company in 1911. Within months, 15 other film production companies had established production facilities in Hollywood. By 1913, then, Hollywood had over 8,000 inhabitants, many of them working in the budding movie industry.

The 1920s saw Hollywood and the American film industry dominate the world market by structuring itself as a vertically and horizontally integrated industry. Since the huge American market allowed companies to amortize their product domestically, they could undersell the foreign competition abroad. 'Hollywood' became a worldwide → brand name. In 1927 the first Oscars were staged at the Roosevelt Hotel. In its classical phase from the 1920s to the 1950s, Hollywood was a monolithic economic system, a multinational monopoly of corporations, whose structure of film production, distribution, and exhibition was based on laws of scientific management, an intense division of labor, the pioneering use of modern advertising techniques, and complete control of the market (→ Concentration in Media Systems).

Hollywood's → *discourse* always supported a romantic mythology, because the very commodity this industry produced was fantasy and fictional narratives (→ Fiction). Film images sought to transport an audience from the real world into a universe of myth, where audience desires could find at least partial satisfaction (→ Uses and Gratifications). In terms of *film technique*, this meant utilizing a system of 'invisible editing' that would hide the breaks between individual shots, creating a seamless visual flow. Dramatically, films had to traverse an arch from exposition to the building of conflict to a resolution through a happy ending, with heterosexual union being the driving narrative force of practically every film story. The *star system* had evolved in the decade 1911–1920, just as Hollywood was ascending. It soon became apparent that selling 'stars' was the most efficient means of selling films.

In 1916, landmark Supreme Court decision held that the production and distribution of movies was a business, rather than a matter of communication, and therefore, unlike the theatre or newspapers, not subject to First Amendment guarantees of free speech. This ruling was not overturned until the 1970s, leading to a period of liberalization in sexual and social content, yet even today a rating system, enforced by the Motion Picture Producers and Distributors Association, restricts access to the commercial media market (→ Censorship, History of; Freedom of Communication).

It took a few decades, but Hollywood eventually reinvented itself as a group of transnational, *multimedia conglomerates* that dominate all forms of media: Walt Disney Company (→ Disney), Paramount Pictures (Viacom), Sony Pictures, Universal Studios (General Electric), and Warner Brothers (AOL/Time Warner) control film, television networks, cable channels and providers, digital media, Internet portals, recorded music, billboards, newspapers, and radio stations.

By the first decade of the twenty-first century, income from *digital media* far outstripped that of the box office, so that the industry once again evolved structurally. The big companies dominate virtually all public communications media (→ Culture Industries; Media Conglomerates). At the same time, the rise of digital media delivery to cinemas and the Internet and those media's infinite reproducibility have led to significant loss of ability to control content (→ Internet Law and Regulation). It remains a central question and issue of communications research to ascertain whether and, if it does so, just how the democratic process can or does survive, given the massive domination of virtually all communications media by a handful of gatekeepers.

See also: ▶ BRANDS ▶ CENSORSHIP ▶ CENSORSHIP, HISTORY OF ▶ CINEMA ▶ CONCENTRATION IN MEDIA SYSTEMS ▶ CULTURE INDUSTRIES ▶ DISCOURSE ▶ DISNEY ▶ ENTERTAINMENT CONTENT AND REALITY PERCEPTION ▶ FICTION ▶ FILM GENRES ▶ FILM PRODUCTION ▶ FILM THEORY ▶ FREEDOM OF COMMUNICATION ▶ INTERNET LAW AND REGULATION ▶ MEDIA CONGLOMERATES ▶ STORYTELLING AND NARRATION ▶ USES AND GRATIFICATIONS ▶ VISUAL REPRESENTATION

REFERENCES AND SUGGESTED READINGS

Biskind, P. (1998). *Easy riders, raging bulls: How the sex-drugs-and-rock-'n'-roll generation saved Hollywood.* New York: Simon and Schuster.

Friedrich, O. (1997). *City of nets: A portrait of Hollywood in the 1940s.* Berkeley, CA: University of California Press.

Powdermaker, H. (1979[1950]). *Hollywood, the dream factory.* New York: Arno Press.

Schatz, T. (1996). *The genius of the system: Hollywood filmmaking in the studio era.* New York: Henry Holt.

I

Iconography

MARION G. MÜLLER
Jacobs University Bremen

Iconography is both a method and an approach to studying the content and meanings of visuals. In its colloquial use, the term 'iconography' describes the motif of a particular picture or a specific group of artworks. A general distinction can be made between religious, mainly Christian iconography and secular or political iconography. In its modern connotation it was framed by the German art historian Aby M. Warburg (1866–1929) at the beginning of the twentieth century.

Iconography can best be described as a qualitative method of visual content analysis and interpretation, influenced by cultural traditions and guided by research interests originating in both the humanities and the social sciences (→ Content Analysis, Qualitative). In its Warburgian sense, iconography/iconology is an interdisciplinary comparative method, focused on the 'visual interval,' both temporal and spatial.

Pre-iconographical description focuses on the primary or natural subject matter, which is usually the 'world of artistic motifs.' *Iconographical analysis* is concerned with 'conventional subject matter' – culturally shared visual → signs and connotations – and thus the world of images, stories, and allegories. *Iconological interpretation* aims to unravel the "intrinsic meaning or content constituting the world of 'symbolical' values" (Panofsky 1982[1955], 40; → Semiotics). Warburg himself enlarged the scope of art history by including "any visual image," regardless of its artistic quality. This meant that press photographs and other forms of mass-mediated imagery could be considered appropriate objects of study for art history (→ Art as Communication; Photojournalism; Visual Communication).

At the beginning of the twenty-first century, the combination of visual interpretation as a method and political pictures as a topic appears to be experiencing a revival, reflecting the need for explanation of visual phenomena like the terrorist instrumentalization of visuals (→ Mediated Terrorism), the publication of torture images at the Abu Ghraib prison in Iraq, or the controversy about the publication of Muhammad cartoons (Müller & Özcan 2007; → Caricature).

See also: ▶ ART AS COMMUNICATION ▶ CARICATURE ▶ CODE ▶ CONTENT ANALYSIS, QUALITATIVE ▶ CULTURE: DEFINITIONS AND CONCEPTS ▶ MEDIATED TERRORISM

The Concise Encyclopedia of Communication, First Edition. Edited by Wolfgang Donsbach.
© 2015 John Wiley & Sons, Inc. Published 2015 by John Wiley & Sons, Inc.

▶ PHOTOJOURNALISM ▶ SEMIOTICS ▶ SIGN
▶ VISUAL COMMUNICATION ▶ VISUAL
REPRESENTATION

REFERENCES AND SUGGESTED READINGS

Büttner, F. & Gottdang, A. (2006). *Einführung in die Ikonographie: Wege zur Deutung von Bildinhalten* [Introduction to iconography: Paths to interpreting the content of images]. Munich: C. H. Beck.

Müller, M. G. & Özcan, E. (2007). The political iconography of Muhammad cartoons: Understanding cultural conflict and political action. *PS: Political Science and Politics*, 40, 287–291.

Panofsky, E. (1982[1955]). Iconography and iconology: An introduction to the study of Renaissance art. In E. Panofsky, *Meaning in the visual arts*. Chicago, IL: University of Chicago Press, pp. 26–54.

Identities and Discourse

CHARLES ANTAKI
Loughborough University

Discourse analysts are interested in identity in the sense of the category that an individual belongs to (or is made to belong to). The way that society classifies people, the laws it draws up, the visual images it promotes, the jokes it finds funny – all these are discursive ways of allocating persons to categorical identities.

Discourse analysis is a varied set of analytic practices (→ Discourse Analysis). Its *five core features*, applied to the study of identity, are these: (1) identities are to be understood not as essential and unchanging, but as subject to active construction, and liable to be imposed and resisted; (2) they appear in talk or text that is naturally found (in the sense of not invented or imagined by the researcher); (3) the identity words are to be understood in their co-text at least, and their more distant context if doing so can be defended; (4) the analyst is to be sensitive to the words' non-literal meaning or force; (5) the analyst is to reveal the consequences achieved by the identities conjured by the words' use – as enjoyed by those responsible for the words, and suffered by their addressees, or the world at large.

Interviews are still probably the method of choice for most qualitative researchers in the social sciences, on the proposition that they give respondents the freedom to express themselves, while at the same time allowing the researcher to probe specific questions that interest them. In analyzing identity, a respondent's account of themselves and their experiences might be subjected to a thematic analysis, a narrative analysis, an interpretive phenomenological analysis, or to methods of free association borrowed from psychoanalysis. All these analyses differ among themselves, but they all look to find something between the lines of the respondent's account (→ Interview, Qualitative).

Away from interviews, the ethnographically minded discourse researcher will locate people's words in their context and culture. Interviews may form part of the ethnographic researcher's toolkit, but principally as a way of informing the researcher of local meanings and → codes; the analysis will be done on recordings of language as it is actually used, and identities as they come into play. Researchers in an ethnomethodological tradition will eschew interviews entirely, in favor of analyzing the ways that people publicly identify themselves, or allude to their or others' identities, as they go about their everyday business (→ Ethnography of Communication). They may use methods that pay close attention to the precise sequence of talk (e.g., → conversation analysis) to see how identities are brought into active service in the particular moment of the interaction, for particular interactional effects, whether casual or institutional.

Some discourse analysts prefer to approach their data from a given perspective on power and ideology in society, arguing that one must understand the social conditions of the production of a text before one can start reasonably to analyze it. The umbrella term 'critical discourse analysis' shelters a broad family of analysts, but all are concerned to identify the operation of power and ideology in discourse. Identities, their argument runs, are not always innocent, nor always under the control of the person identified; they can be oppressive, and the burden can be resisted (→ Critical Theory).

See also: ▶ CODE ▶ CONVERSATION ANALYSIS
▶ CRITICAL THEORY ▶ DISCOURSE ANALYSIS
▶ DISCURSIVE PSYCHOLOGY ▶ ETHNOGRAPHY
OF COMMUNICATION ▶ INTERVIEW, QUALITATIVE

REFERENCES AND SUGGESTED READINGS

Bamberg, M., De Fina, A., & Schiffrin, D. (2011). Discourse and identity construction. In S. Schwartz, K. Luyckx, & V. Vignoles (eds.), *Handbook of identity theory and research*. New York: Springer, pp. 177–199.

Benwell, B. M. & Stokoe, E. (2006). *Discourse and identity*. Edinburgh: Edinburgh University Press.

Edwards, D. (1991). Categories are for talking: On the cognitive and discursive bases of categorization. *Theory and Psychology*, 1, 515–542.

Sacks, H. (1992). *Lectures on conversation*, vols. 1 and 2. Oxford: Blackwell.

Tracy, K. (2002). *Everyday talk: Building and reflecting identities*. New York: Guilford.

Wodak, R., De Cillia, R., Reisigl, M., Liebhart, K., & Hirsch, A.; trans. Mitten, R. & Unger, J. W. (2009). *The discursive construction of national identity*, 2nd edn. Edinburgh: Edinburgh University Press.

Image Restoration Theory

WILLIAM L. BENOIT
Ohio University

Image restoration (image repair) theory concerns what to say when we are accused or suspected of wrongdoing. Reputation influences how others will treat us. People, organizations, and countries use image repair (→ Organizational Image).

Accusations have two components: responsibility and offensiveness. An image is at risk only when one is believed to be responsible for an offensive act (→ Crisis Communication). Image repair includes five general options: (1) 'denial' argues that the accused is not responsible for the offensive act; (2) one may try to 'evade responsibility' with several strategies; (3) one can try to 'reduce offensiveness' of the offensive act; (4) 'corrective action' attempts to fix or prevent recurrence of the problem; and (5) 'mortification' confesses and asks for forgiveness. Fourteen total strategies, explained in Benoit (1995), exist.

Persuaders select image repair strategies with the accusations, the target audience, and the facts of the case in mind. Using more strategies is not necessarily better. Some strategies go together well, but some strategies do not work well together, for example, 'I did not steal' (denial) and 'I stole for my starving family' (justification, or transcendence). The facts are important in image repair. One who is innocent probably should use denial (although not all genuine denials are believed). One who is guilty probably should confess. Telling the truth is, of course, the right thing to do; however, some must worry about avoiding lawsuits. One must implement the selected strategies in a message using arguments and evidence that are likely to be persuasive to the audience.

In general, people do not like to admit wrongdoing. On the other hand, audiences usually want wrongdoers to admit their mistakes. So, the option that is often most likely to persuade audiences – mortification – tends to be shunned by those accused of wrongdoing. However, a false denial is often found out, at which point the offender will have committed two wrongs: the original offensive act and then the lie.

See also: ▶ CRISIS COMMUNICATION ▶ ORGANIZATIONAL IMAGE ▶ PUBLIC RELATIONS

REFERENCES AND SUGGESTED READINGS

Benoit, W. L. (1995). *Accounts, excuses, and apologies: A theory of image restoration discourse*. Albany, NY: SUNY Press.

Benoit, W. L. (1997). Image restoration discourse and crisis communication. *Public Relations Review*, 23, 177–186.

Coombs, W. T. (1999). *Ongoing crisis communication: Planning, managing, and responding*. Thousand Oaks, CA: Sage.

Imagined Interactions

JAMES M. HONEYCUTT
Louisiana State University

Imagined interactions are a type of social cognition and mental imagery (→ Information Processing; Cognitive Science), theoretically grounded in symbolic interactionism and cognitive script theory (→ Scripts), in which individuals imagine conversations with significant others for a variety of purposes (Honeycutt 2003). The imagined interaction construct has provided a beneficial mechanism for studying intrapersonal and interpersonal communication (→ Interpersonal Communication). Imagined interactions are a type of daydreaming that has definitive attributes and serves a number of functions including rehearsal, self-understanding, relational maintenance, managing conflict, catharsis, and compensation.

There are six *functions of imagined interactions*. First, they maintain relationships, as intrusive thinking occurs in which the partner is thought about outside of his or her physical presence. It has been found that they occur with friends, family members, intimate partners, roommates, and co-workers (Honeycutt 2003). They also occur among geographically separated couples. A second function of imagined interactions is rehearsing and planning messages (→ Strategic Communication). Individuals report how they prepare for important encounters and even think of various messages depending on their interaction partner's responses. A third function of imagined interactions is self-understanding, as imagined interactions allow people to clarify their own thoughts and promote understanding of their own views. The fourth function, catharsis, allows people to release emotions and vent feelings of frustration or joy. There is tension relief and anxiety reduction. This often occurs in conjunction with the fifth, compensation, function, in which individuals compensate for the lack of actual conversations. The final function is conflict management, which has resulted in a sub-theory in itself. The conflict management function of imagined interactions explains recurring conflict in personal relationships.

Honeycutt (2003) has presented three *axioms* and nine *theorems* for managing conflict, with numerous studies supporting them. Some therapists lament that counseling and intervention may not result in longitudinal benefits in getting couples to communicate constructively. Conflict may be maintained through retroactive and proactive imagined interactions that link a series of interactions. People may experience negative emotions as they 'replay' such encounters. The conflict management function of imagined interactions helps explain why instructions on rational models for conflict resolution often fail, as people regress to old ways for resolving conflict (e.g., 'I win; you lose'). Old interaction scripts that are nonproductive may be mindlessly retrieved from long-term memory. Thus, conflict episodes may pick up where they last left off, despite a period of physical separation. In the meantime, conflict is maintained in the mind using the retroactive and proactive (rehearsal) features of imagined interactions. In this regard, imagined interaction conflict management theory explains why popular 'time-out' strategies advocated by educational interventionists may fail regularly.

The Survey of Imagined Interactions has proved to be a reliable *measure of imagined interactions* (Honeycutt 2003). An alternative measure, "Talk-out-loud" procedures, in which individuals role-play what they would say to a relational partner about an important relational issue (e.g., financial management, sexual relations) that they have chosen as problematic in their relationship, have been used in imagined interaction research. A third method is using interviews as a means of studying marital couples and their use of imagined interactions. A fourth method is journal accounts.

There are numerous *personality, relational, individual, and physiological differences* that are reviewed by Honeycutt (2003; 2010). Studies of couples who imagine discussing pleasing and displeasing topics reveal that heart-rate variability accompanies imagined interactions and actual discussions. Physiological linkage is the matching of heart rate, blood pressure, skin conductance, sweating, or other physiological variables that distinguish happy from unhappy couples in which the display of negative emotions (e.g., anger begets anger) is accompanied by both a reciprocity in physiology among unhappy couples when they argue. The strongest sign of physiological linkage occurred when partners were discussing their pleasing topic (partial $r = \cdot 25$). Correlations around $\cdot 30$ reflect a moderate association. Conversely, when discussing displeasing topics, the correlation was only $\cdot 10$. When comparing his heart rate in the Imagined Interaction induction with his heart rate while actually discussing a pleasing topic resulted in a cross-correlation of $\cdot 10$, while it was $\cdot 17$ when compared to her discussing her pleasing topic. Other research has revealed that an increase in diastolic pressure while viewing escalating conflict is associated with taking conflict personally as well as ruminating about arguing.

See also: ▶ COGNITIVE SCIENCE ▶ INFORMATION PROCESSING ▶ INTERPERSONAL COMMUNICATION ▶ SCHEMAS ▶ SCRIPTS ▶ STRATEGIC COMMUNICATION

REFERENCES AND SUGGESTED READINGS

Gottman, J. M. (1994). *What predicts divorce?* Hillsdale, NJ: Lawrence Erlbaum.

Honeycutt, J. M. (2003). *Imagined interactions: Daydreaming about communication.* Cresskill, NJ: Hampton Press.

Honeycutt, James M. (2010). Forgive but don't forget: Correlates of rumination about conflict. In J. M. Honeycutt (ed.), *Imagine that: Studies in imagined interaction.* Cresskill, NJ: Hampton Press, pp. 17–29.

India: Media System

K. M. SHRIVASTAVA

Indian Institute of Mass Communication

India, with a population of more than 1.3 billion, is a multiethnic, multilingual, multi-religious, pluralistic society. Politically it is a union of states (28 states and 7 union territories) and a sovereign, secular, democratic republic with a bicameral, multiparty, parliamentary system of government. It has a written constitution, adopted by the Constituent Assembly on November 26, 1949, which came into force on January 26, 1950. India is an ancient civilization. There is evidence of human activity in India at least from 20,000 BCE (Bhimbetka rock paintings); of farming from 7000 BCE; and of city life from 2700 BCE (Harappa).

As public writings, India had the Rock Edicts of Emperor Asoka (*c.*273–236 BCE), writings on leaves and bark mentioned by the Uzbek scholar Al-Biruni (973–1049 CE) in his book Kitabu'l Hind (1030 CE), and newsletters (akhbar) mentioned by Emperor Zahiruddin Muhammad Babur in 1527, before the modern printing press landed in India on September 6, 1556. The first *modern newspaper* was the Bengal Gazette *or* Calcutta General Advertiser founded by James Augustus Hicky on January 29, 1780. In 2014, the Indian press, with over 80,000 registered newspapers serving a multilingual, diverse society, is independent and competitive, with various forms of ownership ranging from individuals, firms, and joint-stock companies to trusts. The 2012 Indian Readership Survey (IRS) from the Media Research and Users Council (MRUC) found that among the top 20 Indian dailies there is only one English-language daily, the Times of India, ranking sixth. The top three are the Hindi dailies Dainik Jagran, Dainik Bhaskar, and Hindustan. Though under discussion, there are as yet no cross-media ownership restrictions, and foreign investment has been allowed to differing degrees according to the nature of the media product (→ Newspaper, History of).

Radio came to India in 1921 and was initially in private hands. The government bowed to public pressure by starting the Indian State Broadcasting Service, which was rechristened All India Radio (AIR) in 1935. At the time of independence, after the creation of Pakistan, AIR had a network of 6 stations and 18 transmitters, and covered 2.5 percent of the area and 11 percent of the population. AIR, the public radio network run by Prasar Bharti Corporation, now has 406 broadcasting centers, including 194 FM relay centers, with 577 transmitters (144 medium-frequency (MW), 48 high-frequency (SW), and 385 frequency modulation (FM)) covering 99 percent of the area and 99.5 percent of the population of the country. AIR is going digital and will end analog by 2015. AIR remained a monopoly until May 2000, when the government opened it up to private FM broadcasters, 245 of which were operational in 2013. Community radio stations (→ Community Media) have been allowed to be run by educational institutions and nongovernmental organizations (NGOs). In 2013 a total of 151 community radio stations were operational (→ Radio: Social History).

Television came to India in September 1959 as an educational experiment involving → UNESCO. Doordarshan, the public TV network run by Prasar Bharti, has a monopoly of terrestrial broadcasting, with 67 studio centers and 1,415 transmitters, and operates 35 channels: 7 national channels, 11 regional language satellite channels, 12 state networks, and 1 international channel. The flagship DD1 channel reaches some 400 million viewers. In 2013, there were 795 private satelite TV channels in India. FICCI-KPMG (2012) estimates a 17 percent CAGR (compounded annual growth rate) of the television industry during 2011–2016 (→ Television: Social History; Exposure to Television).

In 2012 Internet users were estimated at 121 million. Mobile phone companies have also introduced the Internet, and broadband connectivity is expanding. India has the third largest number of Internet users after China and the US and, with an estimated 919 million mobile phones in 2012, it is second only to China (→ Exposure to the Internet).

India's entertainment and media sector is expected to grow steadily over the next five years. The industry is expected to grow at 18 percent annually from 2012 to 2017. Indian media companies are also expanding in foreign markets. For example, Zee claims to serve more than 500 million viewers in more than 120 countries across the globe in seven different languages.

Article 19(1)(a) of the Constitution of India provides that all citizens shall have the right to "freedom of speech and expression," and the courts have interpreted this as including freedom of the press. With the exception of the Internal Emergency of June 26, 1975, to March 21, 1977, there has been no censorship. Thus, in the typology developed by Hallin and Mancini (2004), the Indian media system is close to a "liberal model," as there is a relative dominance of market mechanisms and of commercial media.

See also: ▶ COMMUNITY MEDIA ▶ EXPOSURE TO TELEVISION ▶ EXPOSURE TO THE INTERNET ▶ NEWSPAPER, HISTORY OF ▶ RADIO: SOCIAL HISTORY ▶ TELEVISION, SOCIAL HISTORY ▶ UNESCO

REFERENCES AND SUGGESTED READINGS

FICCI-KPMG (2012). *FICCI-KPMG Media and Entertainment Industry Report 2012*. Mumbai: KPMG.
Hallin, D. & Mancini, P. (2004). *Comparing media systems: Three models of media and politics*. Cambridge: Cambridge University Press.
Shrivastava, K. M. (2005). *Broadcast journalism in the 21st century*. New Delhi: New Dawn.

Information

KLAUS KRIPPENDORFF

University of Pennsylvania

A widely used metaphor locates information as the content of messages or inherent in data – as if it were an entity that could be carried from one place to another, purchased, or owned. This metaphor is seriously misleading. Gregory Bateson (1972, 381) characterized communication as the circulation of differences in society. The acknowledgement that differences do not reside in nature but result from acts of drawing distinctions leads to *defining information* as the difference that drawing distinctions in one empirical domain makes in another. Information theories quantify these differences in terms of 'bits,' a short of 'binary digits,' or the number of binary distinctions needed to gain certainty within and across such domains.

The *logical theory of information* (Krippendorff, 1986, 13 ff.) quantifies the difference between two uncertainties U, before and after a message was received, in terms of the binary logarithm of the number N of possibilities in each situation:

$$I_{message} = U_{before} - U_{after} = \log_2 N_{before} - \log_2 N_{after}$$
$$= -\log_2 \frac{N_{after}}{N_{before}} \text{ (bits)}$$

Inasmuch as yes or no answers to questions distinguish between two possibilities, bits can be equated with the number of binary questions whose answers select among a set of possibilities. For example, the well-known party game Twenty Questions can exhaust up to $2^{20} = 1,048,576$, i.e., over a million conceptual alternatives. Each answer to well-chosen questions reduces that number by half (→ Uncertainty Reduction Theory).

Information is always *relative to an observer*. For example, the graphical, distributional, linguistic, or authorial properties of texts afford a reader numerous distinctions. Psychological, linguistic, and situational contingencies tend to render only some of them relevant, which keeps the amount of information to be processed within tolerable limits (→ Language and Social Interaction; Text and Intertextuality). Information is not tied to materiality. Receiving the same message a second time does not add information to the first. The relation between texts and the uncertainties they reduce is one of abduction. Abduction is informative; logical deductions do not say anything new.

The *statistical theory of information* was pioneered by Claude E. Shannon. For him, "the fundamental problem of communication is that of reproducing at one point, either exactly or approximately a message selected at another point" (Shannon & Weaver, 1949, 3). He called the statistical analogue to the uncertainty U

entropy and defined entropy in terms of observed probabilities p_a, rather than the number N of logical possibilities in a variable, say A:

$$H(A) = -\sum_{a \in A} p_a \log_2 p_a$$

Shannon's theory provides a calculus that partitions the entropies in variables into various conceptually meaningful quantities. The simplest expression for the amount of information transmitted $T(S:R)$ between a source S and a receiver R is defined as the difference between the entropy at the receiver $H(R)$ without knowledge of the source and the entropy remaining at that receiver $H_S(R)$, or noise, after the source is known.

$$T(S:R) = H(R) - H_S(R) \leq \min[H(S), H(R)]$$

The amount of information transmitted is upwardly limited by the entropies $H(S)$ or $H(R)$ and the difference between what could be transmitted and what actually is transmitted is a measure of redundancy. Shannon's theorems concern how much redundancy is needed to counter noise – without redundancy one would not be able to correct typographical errors or understand slurred speech – deciphering encrypted messages and developing unbreakable codes. Above all, he theorized limits that generalize the second law of thermodynamics.

The *algorithmic theory of information* is due to the Russian statistician Andrei Nikolaevich Kolmogorov (1965). He sought to quantify the complexity of any object, text, analytical protocol, or computer program in terms of the computational resources needed to reproduce it. The latter used a minimal algorithmic language consisting of strings of 0 s and 1 s. Because binary characters represent one bit each, the length of such descriptions equals the $\log_2$ of the number of possible sequences of that length. Here, redundancy is the difference between the lengths of a description and the shortest possible one. Redundancy makes it possible to compress files into more efficient forms and to optimize the efficiency of computer code.

Historically, information theory was eagerly embraced by early theoreticians of human communication. Wilbur Schramm, Charles Osgood, Collin Cherry, and Gregory Bateson, for example, embraced it for it provided a scientifically sound vocabulary and measures of a novel concept that seemed to be the essence of communication (→ Communication as a Field and Discipline). Critics who argue that mathematical theories are too rigid to address uncertainties in human communication may have a point. Information theory is a theory of observable variation. It does not speculate what happens inside individual minds, treating cognition as a medium of communication.

See also: ▶ COMMUNICATION AS A FIELD AND DISCIPLINE ▶ CYBERNETICS ▶ LANGUAGE AND SOCIAL INTERACTION ▶ MEANING ▶ MODELS OF COMMUNICATION ▶ TEXT AND INTERTEXTUALITY ▶ UNCERTAINTY REDUCTION THEORY

REFERENCES AND SUGGESTED READINGS

Bateson, G. (1972). *Steps to an ecology of mind*. New York: Ballantine Books.

Kolmogorov, A. N. (1965). Three approaches to the quantitative definition of information. *Problemy Peredachi Informatsii*, 1(1), 3–11.

Krippendorff, K. (1986). *Information theory; Structural models for qualitative data*. Beverly Hills, CA: Sage.

Shannon, C. E. & Weaver, W. (1949). *The mathematical theory of communication*. Urbana, IL: University of Illinois Press.

Information and Communication Technology, Economics of

CRISTIANO ANTONELLI
University of Turin

PIER PAOLO PATRUCCO
University of Turin

FRANCESCO QUATRARO
University of Nice

Information and communication technology or technologies (ICT, ICTs) may be considered as a clear exemplar of the salient features and ingredients of a path-dependent and complex process based upon an array of complementary localized technological changes. Indeed, the path leading to the generation and adoption of ICT emerged out of a collective and interactive process induced by relevant changes in the economic environment. This stimulated the creative reaction of an array of learning agents based in a fertile context characterized by effective knowledge-governance mechanisms and positive feedback magnified by local externalities.

Beginning in the late 1960s the US experienced a progressive erosion of its economic and technological leadership. This decline in performance induced a myriad of interdependent, sequential, and creative efforts directed toward the introduction of complementary technological innovations. These were based upon the exploitation of locally abundant production factors, favorable conditions of use, and access to a large knowledge commons and localized learning processes. The main result of these developments has been the creation of a new technological system with a strong skill bias.

In the decades following their introduction, ICTs have improved considerably, and have slowly acquired the features of a general-purpose technology (GPT). These technologies have a high degree of fungibility, that is, usability in many different contexts, strong complementarities, and considerable spillover effects. Along with the improvements, the diffusion of ICT across US firms stemmed from a process of sequential, creative adoption (Lipsey et al. 2005).

The integration of the array of interdependent, localized, and sequential innovations, characterized by substantial indivisibility, has been *shaped by the implementation* of: (1) economies of localized learning due to the increasing specialization in specific technological areas, the advantages of the growth in the number of users (network externalities), and the gains from the accumulation of know-how in complementary technologies (knowledge externalities); (2) qualified user–producer and business–academic interactions; and (3) organizational innovations, such as standardization committees (→ Communication Technology Standards), technological platforms, and technological clubs and alliances, to improve the dynamic coordination of the wide range of actors, products, and technologies into a single working system. This has resulted in the complementarity, compatibility, and interoperability of a variety of new localized technologies.

The *effects of the introduction* of ICT have been powerful. The US economy has been enjoying a new surge in productivity since 1995. The ICT industry has played a key role in this as a result of the rapid technological developments in the semiconductor industry. Strong US technological leadership encouraged a new international division of labor, which reversed the situation that prevailed in the 1980s. The US quickly became the main producer and user of ICTs, while the rest of the advanced countries engaged in creative adoption, involving adapting the technology to the idiosyncratic conditions of their markets and industrial structures.

Because of the strong directional skill bias of ICTs, a → *digital divide* is emerging between countries that have the 'right' amount of human capital and access to the knowledge commons. These countries are able to participate in the process of cumulative technological change and creative adoption. Other countries can, at best, adopt ICTs passively and enjoy fewer chances to take advantage of the new opportunities for productivity growth. Nevertheless, ICTs are global in character because they bring about increases in productivity and efficiency, such that their adoption is profitable across a great array of products and processes, and regions (Antonelli 2011).

The complex nature of ICT, and the complementarity among different physical devices and platforms, have led to the identification of *two notions*. First, the notion of 'essential facility' defines telecommunication networks as essential resources that are fundamental to economic development and thus need to be freed up and accessed by the largest possible share of firms and citizens. Second, according to the notion of 'economies of density,' production and distribution costs of telecommunication services decline with an increase in the number of users, leading to a steep reduction in the price of telecommunication services for both firms and citizens' evaluation.

ICTs represent a clear case of a *path-dependent complex process* based upon the complementarity of a myriad of localized technological changes. At any point in time the structure of the existing endowments, industries, and regions, and the networks of communication flows in place among innovative agents, exert strong effects on their creative efforts so as to shape the direction and the rate of technological change. When effective knowledge-governance mechanisms are in place, the result may be a sweeping gale of innovations.

See also: ▶ COMMUNICATION TECHNOLOGY STANDARDS ▶ DIFFUSION OF INFORMATION AND INNOVATION ▶ DIGITAL DIVIDE ▶ KNOWLEDGE MANAGEMENT ▶ NETWORK ORGANIZATIONS THROUGH COMMUNICATION TECHNOLOGY

REFERENCES AND SUGGESTED READINGS

Antonelli, C. (2008). *Localized technological change: Ingredients, governance and processes*. London: Routledge.
Antonelli, C. (ed.) (2011). *Handbook on the economic complexity of technological change*. Cheltenham: Edward Elgar.
Fransman, M. (2010). *The new ICT ecosystem: Implications for policy and regulation*. Cambridge: Cambridge University Press.
Lipsey, R. G., Carlaw, K. I., & Bekar, C. T. (2005). *Economic transformations: General purpose technologies and long term economic growth*. Oxford: Oxford University Press.
Von Hippel, E. (2005). *Democratizing innovation*. Cambridge, MA: MIT Press.

Information Literacy

SONIA LIVINGSTONE
London School of Economics and Political Science

ELIZABETH VAN COUVERING
London School of Economics and Political Science

New → information and communication technologies (ICTs) pose significant challenges for their users. They require the rapid development and continual updating of diverse skills, competences, and knowledge, from the most familiar to the brand-new, and from the most basic to the highly sophisticated. In academic research, these skills and knowledge requirements are increasingly brought together under the rubric of information literacy. By using the term 'literacy,' the skills needed to operate ICTs are related to the ability to read and write, although the concept is still being developed.

The expectation is that the information-literate person is able to participate fully in the world of work, for example, by being an 'information worker' or a 'knowledge worker.' However, the specific nature of key information literacy skills is still under debate. At a minimum these skills include the abilities to access, navigate, critique, and create the content and services available via ICTs. The conceptual foundations of information literacy lie in → information processing, the study of how symbols become information, and how information, in turn, becomes knowledge. Drawing on this approach, which is based in cognitive psychology, a range of experimental studies has been conducted in which tasks are performed and user reactions are tested and tracked. Information literacy is linked historically to computer skills, and so research also examines people's (generally, adults') ability to manipulate hardware and software in order to find information efficiently and effectively.

Researchers in the fields of education and library studies have been instrumental in distinguishing technical skills (e.g., the ability to open a web browser on a computer) from information skills (e.g., the ability to assess whether the information on a web page is reliable). These researchers have focused on motivation and the appropriateness of content as key barriers to use, rather than attributing poor usage to deficient technical skills. The study of information literacy has developed separately from the study of → media literacy, but the two traditions are beginning to converge, with some researchers referring to the notion of digital literacy (Livingstone et al., 2008).

See also: ▶ MEDIA LITERACY ▶ INFORMATION AND COMMUNICATION TECHNOLOGY; ECONOMICS OF ▶ INFORMATION PROCESSING

REFERENCES AND SUGGESTED READINGS

Gasser, U., Cortesi, S., Malik, M., & Lee, A. (2012). *Youth and digital media: From credibility to information quality*. Cambridge, MA: Berkman Center for Internet & Society at Harvard University. At http://cyber.law.harvard.edu/node/7486, accessed August 6, 2014.
Livingstone, S., Van Couvering, E., & Thumim, N. (2008). Converging traditions of research on media and information literacies: Disciplinary, critical and methodological issues. In D. J. Leu, J. Coiro, M. Knobel, & C. Lankshear (eds.), *Handbook of research on new literacies*. Mahwah, NJ: Lawrence Erlbaum. At http://eprints.lse.ac.uk/23564/, accessed August 6, 2014.

UNESCO (2013). *Overview of information literacy resources worldwide*. At http://www.unesco.org/new/fileadmin/MULTIMEDIA/HQ/CI/CI/pdf/news/overview_info_lit_resources.pdf, accessed August 6, 2014.

Information Processing

JOHN O. GREENE
Purdue University

Information processing is an approach to the study of behavior that seeks to explain what people think, say, and do by describing the mental systems that give rise to those phenomena. At the heart of the information-processing perspective is the conception of the mind as a representational system. That is, the mind is viewed as a system that (1) holds information in some form; and (2) processes (i.e., utilizes, transforms, manipulates) that information in some way in carrying out its input-processing and behavioral-production activities. The mind is viewed not as a single representational system, but as a collection of subsystems, each coding information in its own way, and each carrying out its own particular operations on that information. The basic idea, then, is to describe how information is held in one or more subsystems, and how that information is processed in those subsystems, in order to explain the perceptual, mental, and behavioral phenomena of interest. The information-processing perspective has proven to be enormously important in advancing our understanding of a wide range of phenomena of interest to communication scholars (→ Cognitive Science; Memory).

Intellectual Foundations and Basic Approaches

Philosophers have concerned themselves with the nature of knowledge and thought since ancient times, and systematic, empirical investigations of mental processes date as far back as the late 1800s. Beginning in the period 1915–1925, experimental psychology came to be dominated by *behaviorism*, a stance most closely identified with the American psychologist John Watson. The desire to pursue a purely objective science of behavior led Watson to argue that appeals to mentalistic concepts had no place in psychology. A successive generation of scholars, the *radical behaviorists*, including most notably, B. F. Skinner, were willing to admit mental states and processes, but deemed such internal events tangential and ultimately unnecessary for understanding human behavior.

The period between 1950 and 1970 witnessed the emergence of a new experimental psychology, one that, in contrast to behaviorism, accorded central prominence to mentalistic structures and processes. This *cognitive psychology* drew from an array of disciplines in advancing a view of the mind as an information-processing system, i.e., one in which stimulus inputs were subjected to a series of processing stages, culminating in overt responses.

The domain of information processing and cognition is enormously heterogeneous, reflecting a wide array of both general conceptual approaches and specific characterizations of theoretical mechanisms, aimed at explicating a near-limitless list of behavioral and mental phenomena, and drawing upon a variety of sources and types of data. No single overarching conceptual framework is likely to encompass the breadth of the domain, but, at least with respect to conceptual approaches and theoretical mechanisms, it may be possible to develop a rudimentary organizational framework that can accommodate many of the most important contributions by drawing on the work of Daniel Dennett (e.g., 1987).

Dennett distinguished three *approaches for apprehending and predicting the behavior of complex systems* like chess-playing computers, or human beings. The *physical stance* seeks to understand the behavior of such systems by recourse to their physical constitution, i.e., the solid-state electronics of the computer or, for people, their neurophysiology. A second approach, the *design stance*, seeks to apprehend a system's behavior in terms of functional (rather than physical) mechanisms. That is, in order to behave as it does, the system must carry out various functions, and the task is one of characterizing the nature of the mechanisms by which those functions are executed. Importantly, the same function can be carried out in two systems with very different physical constitution, a fact that makes the physical character of a system of secondary concern to theorists pursuing design-stance accounts.

Finally, the *intentional stance* seeks to understand and predict a system's behavior by ascribing to that system various beliefs, goals, expectations, and so on. Thus, the system's behavior is seen to reflect choices made in order to accomplish goals in light of the information at the system's disposal.

The Intentional Stance

As noted, the intentional stance seeks to apprehend a system's behavior in terms of its goals and beliefs. Fundamental to this approach is an assumption of rationality, i.e., goals and beliefs are useful in explaining and predicting behavior only as long as the system does what it should, given its objectives and knowledge. Intentional-stance accounts of human behavior typically reflect a corollary assumption of self-awareness: The individual is assumed to be aware of his or her own mental states and activities.

Intentional accounts, then, make ready use of ordinary mental concepts, or "folk psychology" – concepts and terms afforded by everyday language and central to people's lay understanding of their own behavior and that of others (Churchland 1988; Flanagan 1991). Examples of ordinary mental concepts that have found widespread application in theorizing about communication behavior include "attitudes," "plans," and "goals."

Design and Hybrid Intentional/Design-Stance Approaches

The aim of design-stance approaches is to explain behavior by recourse to the functional design of a system. Importantly, on the design stance, explanation and prediction do not depend upon an assumption of rationality, nor are the mental processes of interest necessarily consciously available to the individual. The fundamental method of the design stance has been characterized as that of "transcendental deduction" (Flanagan 1991). This simply means that the theorist observes some input–output regularity and posits the nature of the system that would produce such a regularity.

Examples of design-stance concepts commonly employed in the field of communication include → 'scripts,' → 'schemas,' and 'associative networks.' Moreover, it is not uncommon to see hybrid intentional/design theories in which the nature and dynamics of intentional-stance concepts are explicated by recourse to 'deeper' design-stance mechanisms, as for example in the case of treatments of 'self-concept' (→ Information Processing: Self-Concept) and associative network conceptions of 'attitudes.'

The Physical Stance

Physical-stance theories and models pursue explanations cast at the level of neuroanatomical systems and processes. In contrast to intentional- and design-stance approaches, then, physical-stance explanations are cast at the level of brain rather than mind. Research in this tradition has very often been conducted in fields other than communication, but does bear on topics of central interest to communication scholars. As examples, there are studies of brain activity while viewing media violence (e.g., Anderson & Murray 2006), processing facial expressions of emotion (e.g., Phelps 2006), and when engaged in acts of deception (e.g., Ganis 2013). Finally, just as there are hybrid intentional/design stance theories, the emerging field of *cognitive neuroscience* (Gazzaniga 1995) seeks to bridge the gap between design and physical-stance approaches by examining the way in which brain gives rise to mind.

See also: ▶ ACTION ASSEMBLY THEORY ▶ ATTENDING TO THE MASS MEDIA ▶ ATTITUDE–BEHAVIOR CONSISTENCY ▶ COGNITIVE SCIENCE ▶ DISCOURSE COMPREHENSION ▶ EXPERIMENT, LABORATORY ▶ GOALS, COGNITIVE ASPECTS OF ▶ GOALS, SOCIAL ASPECTS OF ▶ INFORMATION PROCESSING: SELF-CONCEPT ▶ LINGUISTICS ▶ LISTENING ▶ MEMORY ▶ MESSAGE PRODUCTION ▶ NEWS PROCESSING ACROSS THE LIFE-SPAN ▶ SCHEMAS ▶ SCRIPTS ▶ SPEECH FLUENCY AND SPEECH ERRORS ▶ UNCERTAINTY REDUCTION THEORY

REFERENCES AND SUGGESTED READINGS

Anderson, D. R. & Murray, J. P. (eds.) (2006). Special issue: fMRI in media psychology research. *Media Psychology*, 8(1).

Churchland, P. M. (1988). *Matter and consciousness*, rev. edn. Cambridge, MA: Bradford.

Dennett, D. (1987). *The intentional stance*. Cambridge, MA: Bradford.

Flanagan, O. J., Jr. (1991). *The science of the mind*, 2nd edn. Cambridge, MA: MIT Press.

Ganis, G. (2013). *The cognitive neuroscience of deception*. Paper presented at CogSci, Berlin, July.

Gazzaniga, M. S. (ed.) (1995). *The cognitive neurosciences*. Cambridge, MA: Bradford.

Greene, J. O. & Dorrance Hall, E. (2013). Cognitive theories of communication. In P. Cobley & P. J. Schulz (eds.), *Theories and models of communication*. Berlin: De Gruyter, pp. 181–197.

Phelps, E. A. (2006). Emotion and cognition: Insights from studies of the human amygdala. *Annual Review of Psychology*, 57, 27–53.

Information Processing: Self-Concept

RENEE EDWARDS
Louisiana State University

Self-concept refers to personal identity or the body of knowledge that an individual holds about the self, including self-esteem. The self and self-concept influence → information processing in several specific ways. First, information that is relevant to the self-concept is retrieved more rapidly and successfully than other information (→ Memory). Second, the self-concept is a frame in person → perception. Traits important to the self are used in judging others. Third, individuals actively seek situations and relational partners who provide feedback consistent with their self-concepts (→ Cognitive Dissonance Theory). Finally, individuals interpret information in a way that is consistent with their self-concepts and personalities.

Concern with self-concept is generally traced to the symbolic interactionists. George Herbert Mead (1934) argued that each interaction partner calls forth a different "self" as a result of the unique responses that are communicated by the other (→ Self-Presentation). McCall and Simmons (1966) distinguished between personal and social identities. Social identity is a conventional dimension tied to generic expectations of social roles, whereas personal identity is the actor's unique interpretation of the role. In the 1970s and 1980s, communication theorists investigated self-concept and self-esteem in public-speaking situations, ethnic identities, technology, and the role of speech. Recently, researchers have investigated how self-concept is affected by aging or a health condition.

The self is central to understanding the world. Individuals use a combination of behaviors and cognitions in self-verification processes (Swann & Brooks 2012). Social actors maintain their sense of self by seeking out interaction partners who perceive them the way they perceive themselves. For example, individuals with negative self-views prefer partners who give them negative feedback. When interaction partners do not confirm their sense of self, individuals attempt to shape perceptions held by the partners to make them consistent with the social actor's own view of self. If social actors are unsuccessful at conveying their self-concepts to their interaction partners, they may withdraw from the relationship. College students, for example, are more likely to leave roommates who do not validate their self-conceptions.

Self-esteem is an individual's evaluation of the self as positive (high self-esteem) or negative (low self-esteem) (Baumeister et al. 2003). Self-esteem is relatively stable (a trait dimension), but fluctuates around a baseline in response to success and failure (a state dimension). Self-esteem is positively related to self-reported communication competence, happiness, and life-satisfaction. Individuals with high self-esteem report better interpersonal relationships than individuals with low self-esteem, but objective measures do not provide evidence for their assessments. Self-esteem is positively related to academic success; it appears to be a consequence of success rather than a cause of it. Individuals seek out relational partners and contexts consistent with their self-evaluations.

High self-esteem can have negative consequences, such as higher levels of prejudice and derogation of out-group members. The category of individuals with high self-esteem includes narcissists and individuals with defensive self-esteem as well as those who genuinely accept their shortcomings. Communication research examining self-esteem has not investigated negative consequences or explored the complex nature of self-esteem.

Two *competing views of self-concept* are self-schemas and self-categorizations. A *self-schema* is a stable knowledge structure about the self that allows individuals to understand their social experiences. Individuals are 'schematic' with respect to a trait (e.g., competitiveness) if they perceive the characteristic to be true of them and it is important to their self-definition. In contrast, the *self-categorization approach* (Turner 1987) draws a distinction between personal identity and social identity. Personal identity defines an individual in comparison to other members of the same group (a woman perceives herself as competitive compared to other women). Social identity refers to the characteristics that define an individual when compared to members of a relevant outgroup (as a woman, she sees herself as less competitive than men). Self-concept is the identity that is salient at any given time; it is dependent on situational cues rather than being a function of a stable knowledge structure.

See also: ▶ COGNITIVE DISSONANCE THEORY ▶ INFORMATION PROCESSING ▶ MEMORY ▶ PERCEPTION ▶ PERSONALITY AND EXPOSURE TO COMMUNICATION ▶ SCHEMAS ▶ SELF-PRESENTATION

REFERENCES AND SUGGESTED READINGS

Baumeister, R. F., Campbell, J. D., Krueger, J. I., & Vohs, K. D. (2003). Does high self-esteem cause better performance, interpersonal success, happiness, or healthier lifestyles? *Psychological Science in the Public Interest*, 4, 1–44.

McCall, G. J. & Simmons, J. L. (1966). *Identities and interactions*. New York: Free Press.

Mead, G. H. (1934). *Mind, self, and society*. Chicago, IL: Chicago University Press.

Swann, W. B. & Brooks, M. (2012). Why threats trigger compensatory reactions: The need for coherence and quest for self-verification. *Social Cognition*, 30, 758–777.

Turner, J. C. (1987). *Rediscovering the social group: A self-categorization theory*. Oxford: Basil Blackwell.

Information Seeking

SILVIA KNOBLOCH-WESTERWICK
Ohio State University

Scholars in communication research have employed the term 'information seeking' in a variety of contexts. In the interpersonal communication context 'information seeking' has been categorized into using passive, active, and interactive strategies to gain information about others, in particular in episodes of initial interaction between strangers (Berger 2002). Predictors and effectiveness of information seeking in organizational settings have also been studied because, obviously, newcomers who have just entered an organization need to acquire a lot of information to perform adequately. Seeking health information is generally viewed as a highly desirable behavior. The informed patient should be in a better position to understand diagnosis and to decide on and support treatments, as well as to prevent health problems.

A key research question is, however, why people attend to certain kinds of *media information* while avoiding others, and furthermore what factors produce situational and interpersonal differences in information-seeking processes. Information seeking includes a great variety of media-use behaviors, which can be categorized in *two broad types*: information receptivity and information search. The former is an openness to a question resulting from encountering cues during habitual information scanning of media messages; the latter characterizes deliberate, intentional seeking of information that is potentially capable of reducing uncertainty, of satisfying curiosity, and of problem-solving (→ Information Processing). Uncertainty is construed as a lack of knowledge about events, situations, and issues (→ Uncertainty and Communication). Such a lack of knowledge is assumed to impede formation of the → attitudes needed for appropriate behavior (→ Attitude–Behavior Consistency).

Early dissonance research produced results that showed → informational utility to foster selective exposure despite the dissonance-evoking capacity of messages. Later research explicated the construct of informational utility by suggesting the sub-dimensions of magnitude, likelihood, immediacy, and efficacy, which foster more information exposure the more the aspect applies.

See also: ▶ ATTITUDES ▶ ATTIUDE-BEHAVIOR CONSISTENCY ▶ COGNITIVE DISSONANCE THEORY ▶ EXPOSURE TO THE INTERNET ▶ HEALTH COMMUNICATION ▶ INFORMATION ▶ INFORMATION PROCESSING ▶ INFORMATIONAL

UTILITY ▶ INTERPERSONAL COMMUNICATION
▶ KNOWLEDGE MANAGEMENT ▶ MEDIA CONTENT
AND SOCIAL NETWORKS ▶ ORGANIZATIONAL
COMMUNICATION ▶ POLITICAL COMMUNICATION
▶ SELECTIVE EXPOSURE ▶ TWO-STEP FLOW OF
COMMUNICATION ▶ MEDIA CONTENT AND SOCIAL
NETWORKS ▶ UNCERTAINTY AND COMMUNICATION
▶ UNCERTAINTY REDUCTION THEORY

REFERENCES AND SUGGESTED READINGS

Atkin, C. K. (1973). Instrumental utilities and information seeking. In P. Clark (ed.), *New models of communication research*. Newbury Park, CA: Sage, pp. 205–242.

Berger, C. R. (2002). Strategic and nonstrategic information acquisition. *Human Communication Research*, 28(2), 287–297.

Westerwick, A., Kleinman, S., & Knobloch-Westerwick, S. (2013). Turn a blind eye if you care: Impacts of attitude consistency, importance, and credibility on seeking of political information and implications for attitudes. *Journal of Communication*, 63, 432–453.

Information Society

FRANK WEBSTER

City University London

The designation 'information society' presupposes that information plays a defining role in the way we live today. There is a great deal more information than ever before. However, quantitative increases do not necessarily indicate the qualitative change that is conjured in designating a new type of society. Most commentators adopt a quantitative measure when considering the information society. This implies that a qualitative change follows from the quantitative increase in information, an argument that is not necessarily valid. In fact, it is possible to argue that relatively small quantitative changes can lead to major social transformations. For instance, it can be argued that expert knowledge has become central to the functioning of the modern world, that only a small minority of such experts is required because they command the axes of change, while the vast majority of people are surplus to requirements (→ Political Knowledge).

The most common form of *definition of an information society* is the one that takes *technologies as the marker* of informational increase. Recently it has been information and communications technologies (ICTs), the Internet especially, that are taken to identify the coming of the information society (→ Mobility, Technology for). But prior to the Internet an information society had already been heralded on the basis of different technologies, e.g. the PC and the microchip. A second problem is the lack of analysis of the actual relation between technology and the coming information society. A third problem is the challenge of 'technological determinism' that is evident in such accounts and which is criticized for its linear causal logic (→ Technology and Communication). The *economic definition* involves analysts calculating the worth of information businesses such as education, entertainment, and publishing and comparing them over time: as steel and engineering decline in comparison to, say, finance services, then so there develops a case for suggesting that an information society is being brought into being as the relative value of the latter increases.

Third, there is an *occupational definition* which suggests that, as jobs in information increase while those in industry and agriculture decline, then so emerges an information society. We have seen a transition from male-dominated manual occupations to feminized and information-saturated occupations. The expansion of white-collar occupations and the diminishment of manual labor means that we are witnessing the dominance of jobs that function with information as their key resource (Bell 1973). In this sense we have an information society because information work predominates. A fourth definition focuses on *networks* to emphasize the flows of information between people and places. A core notion here is that networks enable the transformation of time and space, allow the acceleration of activities, and mean that processes of globalization are encouraged (→ Globalization Theories). It is an approach closely associated with the work of Manuel Castells (1942–), whose trilogy (1996–1998) detailed the heightened significance of networks and ways in which they transform business, politics, and culture (→ Network Organizations through Communication Technology; Communication Networks).

A fifth definition involves the *increase in culture* (→ Culture: Definitions and Concepts). This centers on the increase in symbols, from fashion to media, to emphasize that we inhabit nowadays a world in which we are saturated in → signs – from the architecture of cities to the decoration of the body, from round-the-clock television to always-on broadband Internet services (→ Popular Communication; Visual Culture). It is asserted that the expansion of culture signals that we now inhabit a new world. Why this should be so is not demonstrated.

Whether it is a technological, economic, occupational, spatial, or cultural conception, we are left with problematical notions of what constitutes, and how to distinguish, an information society, in spite of the fact that large numbers of commentators offer the concept as a means of understanding the world today.

It is important that we remain aware of these difficulties of definition. Though as a heuristic device the term 'information society' has value in helping us to explore features of the contemporary world, it is far too inexact to be acceptable as a definitive term.

See also: ▶ COMMUNICATION NETWORKS ▶ CULTURE: DEFINITIONS AND CONCEPTS ▶ GLOBALIZATION THEORIES ▶ INFORMATION ▶ MOBILITY, TECHNOLOGY FOR ▶ NETWORK ORGANIZATIONS THROUGH COMMUNICATION TECHNOLOGY ▶ POLITICAL KNOWLEDGE ▶ POPULAR COMMUNICATION ▶ SIGN ▶ TECHNOLOGY AND COMMUNICATION ▶ VISUAL CULTURE

REFERENCES AND SUGGESTED READINGS

Bell, D. (1973). *The coming of post-industrial society: A venture in social forecasting*. Harmondsworth: Peregrine.

Castells, M. (1996–1998). *The information age: Economy, society and culture*, 3 vols. Oxford: Blackwell.

Webster, F. (2014). *Theories of the information society*, 4th edn. London: Routledge.

Informational Utility

SILVIA KNOBLOCH-WESTERWICK
Ohio State University

In the context of → information seeking through the use of mass media, the concept of informational utility has been developed to predict which information items an individual will attend to and which will be ignored. Atkin (1973) suggested four domains of informational utility and conceptualized information to potentially meet four needs resulting from uncertainties in how to respond to everyday environmental requirements. In his theory, information is needed for adaptation to the environment, cognitive adaptation (surveillance), behavioral adaptation (performance), affective adaptation (guidance), and sometimes defensive adaptation (reinforcement). Cognitive adaptation (surveillance) has attracted most attention in subsequent research.

On surveillance as an informational utility facet, Atkin stated that the individual "maintains surveillance over potential changes that may require adaptive adjustments, monitoring threats or opportunities and forming cognitive orientations such as comprehension, expectations, and beliefs" (Atkin 1973, 212). More specific predictions on surveillance needs, as they may guide selective exposure to information, can be derived from a more *detailed model of informational utility* developed by the author. This model projects that information relating to individuals' immediate and prospective encounter of threats or opportunities will have a varying utility for these individuals. The degree of this utilty will increase with (1) the perceived magnitude of challenges or gratifications; (2) the perceived likelihood of their materialization; (3) their perceived proximity in time or immediacy; and (4) their perceived efficacy to influence the suggested events or consequences.

Depending on the extent to which these dimensions characterize reported events, the news report carries utility for the recipient. The increased utility of messages, in turn, fosters longer exposure to information. Hence, it is the perceived utility of information that motivates exposure; low-utility material is passed over in favor of attention to material of higher utility. Drawing on the classic approach/avoidance dichotomy, these impacts are suggested for both negative and positive news reports, as information on both threats and opportunities should carry utility.

See also: ▶ ATTENDING TO THE MASS MEDIA ▶ COGNITIVE DISSONANCE THEORY ▶ ELABORATION LIKELIHOOD MODEL ▶ EXPOSURE TO COMMUNICATION CONTENT ▶ EXTENDED PARALLEL

▶ PROCESS MODEL ▶ INFORMATION SEEKING
▶ PERSUASION ▶ SELECTIVE EXPOSURE
▶ SELECTIVE PERCEPTION AND SELECTIVE RETENTION

REFERENCES AND SUGGESTED READINGS

Atkin, C. K. (1973). Instrumental utilities and information seeking. In P. Clark (ed.), *New models of communication research*. Newbury Park, CA: Sage, pp. 205–242.

Knobloch-Westerwick, S., Dillman Carpentier, F., Blumhoff, A., & Nickel, N. (2005). Informational utility effects on selective exposure to good and bad news: A cross-cultural investigation. *Journalism and Mass Communication Quarterly*, 82, 181–195.

Knobloch-Westerwick, S. & Meng, J. (2011). Reinforcement of the political self through selective exposure to political messages. *Journal of Communication*, 61(2), 349–368.

Infotainment

GEOFFREY BAYM
University of North Carolina at Greensboro

The term 'infotainment' refers to a cluster of program types that blur traditional distinctions between information-oriented and entertainment-based genres of television programming. Primarily a pejorative term, infotainment is often used to denote the decline of hard news and public affairs discussion programs and the corresponding development of a variety of entertainment shows that mimic the style of news. At the same time, however, the early years of the twenty-first century have seen a complex spectrum of hybrid programming with a potentially wide range of implications for public information, political communication, and democratic discourse.

The *emergence of infotainment* has been enabled by a confluence of technological, economic, and cultural changes that have created a media landscape structured by the competing forces of fragmentation and integration. Advances in personal computer-based technologies of media production have significantly lowered barriers to entry, in terms of both the capital and expertise required to create and distribute informational content.

Much scholarly concern with the phenomenon has focused on the encroachment of entertainment on the domain of news. The conflation of news with entertainment is indicated, for instance, by news producers' frequent use of music, fast-paced editing, and a variety of visual and aural effects to build a sense of drama in the news story; a disproportionate interest in celebrity, sports, and lifestyle topics; and a celebration of individual newscasters as marketable personalities. Recently, scholarly attention has turned to the other side of infotainment: the increasing penetration of news form and content into entertainment programming.

Scholarly approaches to infotainment investigate the negative effects of the phenomenon for public information, political communication, the democratic process, and political culture. An expanding body of scholarship, however, is developing the counterargument: that infotainment is not just good for democracy, but perhaps necessary because it is democratizing political discourse by legitimizing narrative and affective forms of reasoning, acknowledging the irreversible interconnection between politics and popular culture, and drawing linkages between politics and the audience's everyday lives.

See also: ▶ COMMERCIALIZATION: IMPACT ON MEDIA CONTENT ▶ EXPOSURE TO COMMUNICATION CONTENT ▶ GENRE ▶ POLITAINMENT ▶ PUBLIC SPHERE ▶ TABLOIDIZATION

REFERENCES AND SUGGESTED READINGS

Baym, G. (2010). *From Cronkite to Colbert: The evolution of broadcast news*. Oxford: Oxford University Press.

Jones, J. P. (2010). *Entertaining politics: Satiric television and political engagement*, 2nd edn. Lanham, MD: Rowman and Littlefield.

Thussu, D. (2009). *News as entertainment: The rise of global infotainment*. Thousand Oaks, CA: Sage.

Ingratiation and Affinity Seeking

JOHN DALY
University of Texas at Austin

People often try to get others to like them when initiating and intensifying romances, friendships, and even brief encounters. When they do this they are engaging in 'affinity seeking' (→ Interpersonal Communication). The affinity-seeking construct (Bell & Daly 1984) highlights the dynamic and strategic notion suggesting that people intentionally engage in certain behaviors in hopes of engendering liking. For instance, people might systematically highlight their similarity on some attitudes with someone to make the other person see them positively. Or, they might dress up, fix their hair, and even exercise, hoping to get another person's attention. The key move made in the affinity-seeking construct was emphasizing the strategic intentionality of behaviors that people use to ingratiate themselves to others.

Affinity seeking falls under the broader rubric of impression management (→ Self-Presentation). In their early research Bell and Daly found seven more general clusters in the *major strategies* people typically use when they engage in ingratiation: (1) control and visibility (e.g., presenting an interesting self, being dynamic); (2) mutual trust (e.g., being open, appearing trustworthy); (3) politeness (e.g., following conversational rules); (4) concern and caring (e.g., listening); (5) other involvement (e.g., engaging in nonverbal immediacy); (6) self-involvement (e.g., influencing perceptions of closeness); and (7) commonalities (e.g., highlighting similarities). These seven clusters fall along *three dimensions*: (1) activity: active/passive; (2) aggressiveness; and (3) orientation. A person's affinity-seeking skills and competency are assessed via observation, peer ratings, and self-ratings.

Using a number of different measures and methods, researchers have found that successful affinity seeking typically has positive *consequences in relationships* and interactions. Affinity seeking is positively and significantly associated with variables such as extroversion, assertiveness, and interaction involvement, and inversely and significantly related to constructs such as communication apprehension, loneliness, and neuroticism. Soon after the affinity-seeking concept was introduced, Bell et al. (1987) proffered the related concept of *affinity maintenance*. Affinity maintenance behaviors are strategies people actively use to maintain, as opposed to establish, positive relationships with others.

See also: ▶ INTERPERSONAL ATTRACTION
▶ INTERPERSONAL COMMUNICATION
▶ SELF-PRESENTATION

REFERENCES AND SUGGESTED READINGS

Bell, R. A. & Daly, J. A. (1984). The affinity-seeking function of communication. *Communication Monographs*, 51, 91–115.
Bell, R. A., Daly, J. A., & Gonzalez, M. C. (1987). Affinity maintenance and its relationship to women's marital satisfaction. *Journal of Marriage and the Family*, 49, 445–454.
Stafford, L., Dainton, M., & Haas, S. (2000). Measuring routine and strategic relational maintenance: Scale revision, sex versus gender roles, and the prediction of relational characteristics. *Communication Monographs*, 67, 306–323.

Institutional Theory

THOMAS B. LAWRENCE
Simon Fraser University

MASOUD SHADNAM
NEOMA Business School

Institutional theory is a theoretical framework for analyzing social (particularly organizational) phenomena, which views the social world as significantly comprising institutions – enduring rules, practices, and structures that set conditions on action. Institutions are fundamental in explaining the social world because they are built into the social order, and direct the flow of social life. Institutions condition action because departures from them are automatically counteracted by social controls that make deviation from the social order costly. These controls associate nonconformity with increased costs, through an increase in risk, greater cognitive demands, or a reduction in legitimacy and the resources that accompany it (→ Organizational Communication).

The new wave of academic interest and attention to what became known as *neo-institutional theory* started with two seminal works in the area of organization theory. First, Meyer and Rowan (1977) argued that, in modern societies, organizations are in a highly institutionalized context of various professions, policies, and programs, which serve as powerful myths. Many organizations ceremonially incorporate these products, services, techniques, policies, and programs, because they are understood to produce rationality. In this way, organizations do not necessarily make their structures more efficient in terms of task-performing functions. Rather, organizations align their structures with the institutional context, and in so doing gain legitimacy, resources, stability, and better survival chances. The second key work that established neo-institutional theory was DiMaggio and Powell's (1983) analysis of the institutional processes by means of which the institutional context forces organizations to be *isomorphic* – similar to each other, in form and practice.

More recent institutional research has focused on the question of how social actors may purposively influence their institutional context. This line of research was initiated by the introduction of the concept of *institutional entrepreneurship* and has attracted a great deal of attention in recent years. This issue has been developed as the more general concept of *institutional work* – purposive action aimed at creating, maintaining, or disrupting institutions (Lawrence & Suddaby 2006).

See also: ▶ LANGUAGE AND SOCIAL INTERACTION
▶ MEANING ▶ ORGANIZATIONAL COMMUNICATION
▶ ORGANIZATIONAL COMMUNICATION: POSTMODERN APPROACHES ▶ PHENOMENOLOGY

REFERENCES AND SUGGESTED READINGS

DiMaggio, P. J. & Powell, W. W. (1983). The iron cage revisited: Institutional isomorphism and collective rationality in organizational fields. *American Sociological Review*, 48, 147–160.
Lawrence, T. B. & Suddaby, R. (2006). Institutions and institutional work. In S. R. Clegg, C. Hardy, T. B. Lawrence, & W. R. Nord (eds.), *Handbook of organization studies*, 2nd edn. Thousand Oaks, CA: Sage, pp. 215–254.
Meyer, J. W. & Rowan, B. (1977). Institutionalized organizations: Formal structure as myth and ceremony. *American Journal of Sociology*, 83, 340–363.

Instructional Television

ROBERT K. AVERY
University of Utah

The term 'instructional television' (ITV) is multidimensional, with definitions varying widely, depending on context, time period examined, and other factors. The term is frequently related or used interchangeably with other terms in this encyclopedia, including Classroom Instructional Technology and → Educational Media, among others. At the most basic level, ITV refers to the use of the medium of television to deliver instructional content to one or more viewers, but the multiple interpretations of the term are tied directly to delivery/reception variables, content variables, and viewer variables.

ITV has existed as long as the medium of television itself, since some of the earliest experimental demonstrations of the medium in both Great Britain and the United States were for the purpose of instruction. When the → Federal Communications Commission (FCC) in the US (→ United States of America: Media System) authorized noncommercial educational television in 1952, a number of the licenses subsequently awarded were assigned to boards of education, school districts, and other instructional agencies that developed the medium of television for direct formal instruction in the classroom setting.

Although some functions have been taken over by computer-mediated forms of communication, ITV in one form or another is an important part of the curricular offerings of virtually every modern school, college, and university in the world today. Research established early on that television was an effective means of delivering information to students, and that when content was properly designed, viewers could learn as much from ITV as from a classroom teacher. The classroom of the twenty-first century is rich in media resources, regardless of the grade level or subject area. The fundamental production principles developed by ITV pioneers continue to be utilized today, as visual and auditory content or videos pervade the seemingly countless delivery and reception platforms of our mediated instructional environment.

See also: ▶ EDUCATIONAL MEDIA ▶ EDUCATIONAL MEDIA CONTENT ▶ FEDERAL COMMUNICATIONS COMMISSION (FCC) ▶ MEDIA PRODUCTION AND CONTENT ▶ UNITED STATES OF AMERICA: MEDIA SYSTEM

REFERENCES AND SUGGESTED READINGS

Center for Children and Technology (2004). *Television goes to school: The impact of video on student learning in formal education*. Washington, DC: Corporation for Public Broadcasting.

Ely, D. P. (ed.) (1996). *Classic writings in instructional technology*. New York: Libraries Unlimited.

Integrated Marketing Communications

MICHAEL A. BELCH
San Diego State University

GEORGE E. BELCH
San Diego State University

Integrated Marketing Communications (IMC) is "A concept of marketing communications planning that recognizes the added value of a comprehensive plan that evaluates the strategic roles of a variety of communications disciplines – for example, general advertising, direct response, sales promotion, and public relations – and combines these disciplines to provide clarity, consistency, and maximum communications impact" (Belch & Belch 2012). As consumers' needs and media habits have changed, media continue to proliferate and evolve, and clients continue to demand accountability, the need for an integrated approach has become obvious.

The changing media landscape requires marketers to rethink their communications strategies (→ Marketing; Marketing: Communication Tools). Besides watching less TV, younger demographic groups subscribe to fewer magazines (most of which are specialty magazines as opposed to general news), rarely read the newspapers (and almost always online), shop online, and are seemingly addicted to their smart phones and → social media. Mobile media are changing all aspects of shopping and communicating. Technological changes have enabled receivers to obtain information when they want it, not when the marketer sends it, and to interact, not just passively accept messages (→ Advertising; Advertising Strategies).

To adopt an IMC orientation, companies must (1) recognize that consumer perceptions of a company and its brands are a synthesis of all the messages consumers receive or contacts they have with the company; (2) identify all of the contacts that a consumer has with the company, including advertisements, → public relations, word of mouth, sponsorships and/or events, and social media postings – among others; (3) consider the strengths and weakness of the various communication channels that form an effective IMC program; (4) create a consistent unified message to current and potential customers; (5) focus attention on the achievement of communications objectives, which will lead to the attainment of marketing goals; (6) develop new metrics and keep traditional measures to evaluate the effectiveness of IMC programs. Finally, companies have to (7) reorganize the department or agency responsible for communications. Eliminating communications silos is critical.

See also: ▶ ADVERTISING ▶ ADVERTISING STRATEGIES ▶ MARKETING ▶ MARKETING: COMMUNICATION TOOLS ▶ PUBLIC RELATIONS ▶ SOCIAL MEDIA

REFERENCES AND SUGGESTED READINGS

Belch, G. E. & Belch, M. A. (2012). *Advertising and promotion: An Integrated Marketing Communications perspective*, 9th edn. New York: McGraw Hill-Irwin.

Intellectual Property Law

ROBERT L. KERR
University of Oklahoma

The law of intellectual property encompasses legal concerns represented by → copyrights, trademarks, patents, design rights, trade secrets, and related concerns. It focuses on protecting the rights of the owners of intellectual property to control when and if a work is reproduced, related adaptations, and distribution and performance.

Intellectual property law is in a more dynamic state of tension than ever before, driven by two historic and interrelated phenomena of the late twentieth and early twenty-first centuries: The fact that most intellectual property has been both internationalized and digitized. Protected works can be digitally copied and distributed anywhere in the world, in unlimited numbers, and virtually instantly via the Internet, satellite transmission, and other media (→ Digital Media, History of). Intellectual property law today races to keep pace in a struggle between what rights creators shall have in relation to their works and the direction in which intellectual property law should evolve in response to revolutionary technological changes.

Multinational efforts to more greatly protect intellectual property began more than a century ago and have been vastly advanced in recent years. The Berne Convention for the Protection of Literary and Artistic Works, first instituted in 1886, is the oldest and most important international copyright treaty. The Agreement on Trade-Related Aspects of Intellectual Property Rights (TRIPS) is considered the most significant strengthening of international norms in intellectual property law to date. Such legislative efforts have generated considerable criticism that corporate commercial interests are locking away too much of the world's creative capital. Although it was once relatively common for creative works to fall into the public domain over time, lengthened copyright terms and other protections have slowed that process, arguably undermining the traditional balance between encouraging creators to produce by protecting their work in limited ways and encouraging further creativity through sharing of common cultural stock. Owners of protected works, however, argue that the value of their intellectual property rights can be dramatically diminished by technologies that make possible virtually unlimited copying and distribution of their works without permission or compensation.

See also: ▶ ADVERTISING LAW AND REGULATION ▶ COMMUNICATION AND LAW ▶ COMMUNICATION TECHNOLOGY AND DEVELOPMENT ▶ COPYRIGHT ▶ DIGITAL MEDIA, HISTORY OF ▶ FREEDOM OF COMMUNICATION ▶ INTERNET LAW AND REGULATION ▶ OPEN SOURCE

REFERENCES AND SUGGESTED READINGS

Lessig, L. (2004). *Free culture: How big media uses technology and the law to lock down culture and control creativity.* Harmondsworth: Penguin.

Masterson, J. T., Jr. (ed.) (2004). *International trademarks and copyrights: Enforcement and management.* Chicago, IL: American Bar Association.

Stim, R. (2006). *Patent, copyright, and trademark*, 8th edn. Berkeley, CA: Nolo.

Interaction

W. RUSSELL NEUMAN
University of Michigan

The term 'interaction' is used to identify a pattern of reciprocal influence or exchange among two or more entities. While the core idea of interaction is very close to the concept of communication, a terminology of interaction tends to suggest a particular set of preferred epistemologies, methodologies, and analytical objects in communication research.

Interaction in communication scholarship most often signals a counterpoint to what is still widely perceived as a dominant one-way transmission model of communication effects, typically associated with the early researchers. In comparison, → cultural studies scholars, for instance, frequently emphasize the way in which audience members interact with – actively interpret and appropriate – the symbols and ideas that are prevalent in popular culture, rather than simply being influenced by them (→ Media Effects, History of).

The idea of interaction has also influenced communication research at a *social-systemic level*. Because interaction is critical to the frameworks of some of the most distinguished social and cultural theorists, especially those with an interest in the cultural reproduction of inequality, several of these have developed neologisms to capture the specific role of interaction processes in their theory-building. In each case, however, the motivation has been to reject a simple one-way causality and to acknowledge a multidirectional behavioral phenomenon. Anthony Giddens (1984), for one, with his influential notion of "structuration", emphasized what he calls a duality of structure (→ Group Communication). Society and culture, accordingly, do not simplistically determine individual → perception or behavior. But, if cultural traditions resonate with a freely initiated human agency, they function to reproduce the social structure, which survives and evolves in interaction with successive generations of human actors.

When communication scholars do refer to interaction, it is frequently in the tradition studying → interpersonal communication, i.e., the *micro-analysis* of routinized, contextualized, and usually dyadic exchanges between individuals.

A specific position, in the study of communication as well as other research fields, is the symbolic interactionist perspective as coined by Herbert Blumer.

The term 'interaction' appears only irregularly in current communication scholarship. That seems likely to change in the decades ahead, as new interactive technologies of mediated communication, including the Internet, digital information retrieval and control systems, and → video games, grow and spread (→ Communication Networks; Network Organizations through Communication Technology).

See also: ▶ COMMUNICATION NETWORKS ▶ CULTURAL STUDIES ▶ GROUP COMMUNICATION ▶ INTERPERSONAL COMMUNICATION ▶ MEDIA EFFECTS, HISTORY OF ▶ NETWORK ORGANIZATIONS THROUGH COMMUNICATION TECHNOLOGY ▶ PERCEPTION ▶ VIDEO GAMES

REFERENCES AND SUGGESTED READINGS

Blumer, H. (1969). *Symbolic interactionism: Perspective and method.* Berkeley, CA: University of California Press.

Giddens, A. (ed.) (1984). *The constitution of society.* Berkeley, CA: University of California Press.

Interactivity, Concept of

W. RUSSELL NEUMAN
University of Michigan

Interactivity refers to the phenomenon of mutual adaptation, usually between a communication medium such as the Internet or a → video game and a human user of that medium. The key element is *responsiveness* – what one says or does depends on another – a notion clearly rooted in human face-to-face conversation (→ Interpersonal Communication).

From several typologies of interactivity one can derive *four common themes* even as terminologies vary. The first and perhaps most straightforward criterion is the *directionality* of communication. Advanced digital systems and the Internet changed conditions, compared to traditional media, fundamentally, as every audience member was empowered to send as well as receive data, text, audio, and video (→ Digital Media, History of). The second criterion is *selectivity* – the breadth of choice that is available to the user in terms of both types and formats of information and entertainment. The third criterion is responsiveness – the rapidity with which and extent to which a medium responds to user input. The fourth criterion is *awareness*, defined as the degree of reciprocal awareness of system states and user reactions.

Bucy (2004), among others, made the case that interactivity should be *conceptualized* exclusively as a *perceptual variable*, arguing that the perceived reality of participating is more important than the technical reality of users' actual input or control. Others argue that it is at least necessary analytically to separate user inclinations and skills from the technical capacities of systems. Perhaps, in time, communication research will acknowledge several components of interactivity in a multilayered model: (1) the technical affordance of interactivity (or components thereof), (2) the user's perception of an interactive potential, (3) the actual use of the affordance, and (4) behavioral outcomes resulting from either perception or use.

The literature on interactivity has been more utopian than dystopian, tending to celebrate the benefits of presumed higher levels of attention, engagement, learning, and satisfaction. In historical perspective, however, this might be akin to arguing that if there are more books in libraries, the populace will be better informed. The interactive affordances of new media systems may indeed contribute significantly to positive outcomes, but only under certain conditions of expectation and motivation, with appropriate designs, and for certain types of users.

See also: ▶ AFFECTIVE DISPOSITION THEORIES ▶ COMPUTER–USER INTERACTION ▶ DIGITAL MEDIA, HISTORY OF ▶ INFORMATION SEEKING ▶ INTERACTION ▶ INTERPERSONAL COMMUNICATION ▶ MEDIA EQUATION THEORY ▶ PARASOCIAL INTERACTIONS AND RELATIONSHIPS ▶ VIDEO GAMES

REFERENCES AND SUGGESTED READINGS

Bucy, E. R. (2004). Interactivity in society: Locating an elusive concept. *The Information Society*, 20, 373–383.

McMillan, S. J. (2005). Exploring models of interactivity from multiple research traditions. In L. A. Lievrouw & S. Livingstone (eds.), *Handbook of new media*. Thousand Oaks, CA: Sage, pp. 162–182.

Reinhard, Carrie Lynn D. (2011). Studying the interpretive and physical aspects of interactivity: Revisiting interactivity as a situated interplay of structure and agencies. *Communications: The European Journal of Communication Research*, 36(3), 353–374

Sundar, S. S. (2004). Theorizing interactivity's effects. *The Information Society*, 20, 385–389.

Intercultural Conflict Styles and Facework

STELLA TING-TOOMEY
California State University, Fullerton

Competent intercultural conflict management depends on many factors. One of the key factors is to increase our awareness and knowledge concerning diverse conflict styles and facework issues. Intercultural conflict can be defined as any implicit or explicit antagonistic struggle between persons of different cultures due, in part, to cultural or ethnic group membership differences. Beyond cultural group membership differences and intergroup historical grievances, differences in situational expectations, goal orientations, conflict styles, facework tendencies, and perceived scarce resources (e.g., time, power currencies) may further complicate an already complex conflict situation.

Some prominent sources of intercultural conflict include cultural/ethnic value clashes, communication decoding problems, and identity inattention issues (→ Encoding–Decoding). Cultural value clash issues can involve the clash of individualistic 'I-identity' values with collectivistic 'we-identity' values with one party emphasizing 'self-face-saving' and the other party valuing 'relational-face-compromising' (→ Intercultural and Intergroup Communication). In connecting national cultures with face concerns, for example, research reveals that while 'individualists' (e.g., US respondents) tend to use more direct, self-face concern conflict behaviors (e.g., dominating/competing style), 'collectivists' (e.g., Taiwanese and Chinese respondents) tend to use more indirect, other-face concern conflict behaviors (e.g., avoiding and obliging styles). In addition, self-face concern has been associated positively with dominating and emotionally expressive conflict styles.

Self-face concern is the protective concern for one's own identity image when one's own face is threatened in the conflict episode. Other-face concern is the concern for accommodating the other conflict party's identity image. Mutual-face concern is the concern for both parties' images and for the image of the relationship. A new addition, communal-face concern (e.g., extended family or close-knit network circle) is the concern for upholding ingroup-based face sensibility and sensitivity (Ting-Toomey & Oetzel, 2013).

Conflict style is defined as the broad-based verbal and nonverbal responses to conflict in a variety of frustrating conflict situations. Whether we choose to engage in or disengage from a conflict process often depends on our ingrained cultural conflict habits and how we negotiate various face concerns. Face is really about identity respect and other-identity consideration issues within and beyond the actual conflict encounter. It is tied to the emotional significance and estimated appraisals that we attach to our own social self-worth and the social self-worth of others (Ting-Toomey & Kurogi 1998).

In a nutshell, Ting-Toomey's (2005) *conflict face-negotiation theory* assumes that: (1) people in all cultures try to maintain and negotiate face in all communication situations; (2) the concept of face is especially problematic in emotionally threatening or identity vulnerable situations when the situated identities of the communicators are called into question; (3) the cultural value spectrums of individualism–collectivism and small/large power distance shape facework concerns and styles; (4) individualist and collectivist value patterns shape members' preferences for self-oriented facework versus other-oriented facework; (5) small and large power-distance value patterns shape members' preferences for horizontal-based facework versus vertical-based facework; (6) the value dimensions, in conjunction with individual, relational, and situational factors, influence the use of particular facework behaviors in particular cultural scenes; and (7) intercultural facework competence refers to the optimal integration of knowledge, mindfulness, and communication skills in managing vulnerable identity-based conflict situations appropriately, effectively, and adaptively (→ Interpersonal Communication). In a direct empirical test of the theory (Oetzel & Ting-Toomey 2003), the research program uncovered that self-face concern was associated positively with dominating style and other-face concern was associated positively with avoiding and integrating styles. The research also found significant differences between subjects from different countries (→ International Communication).

Current face-negotiation theory effort has been directed to testing the intricate relationship among face, emotional facets, and conflict styles in different cultures. Further effort has also extended the face-negotiation theory to the realm of intergroup (i.e., different social identity membership issues such as intergenerational family conflicts) face-threatening and face-honoring situations, and examining the shifting values of face in diaspora communities.

See also: ▶ ENCODING–DECODING ▶ INTERCULTURAL AND INTERGROUP COMMUNICATION
▶ INTERNATIONAL COMMUNICATION
▶ INTERPERSONAL COMMUNICATION
▶ LANGUAGE AND SOCIAL INTERACTION

REFERENCES AND SUGGESTED READINGS

Oetzel, J., Garcia, A., & Ting-Toomey, S. (2008). An analysis of the relationships among face concerns and facework behaviors in perceived conflict situations: A four-culture investigation. *International Journal of Conflict Management*, 19, 382–403.

Oetzel, J. G. & Ting-Toomey, S. (2003). Face concerns in interpersonal conflict: A cross-cultural empirical test of the face-negotiation theory. *Communication Research*, 30, 599–624.

Ting-Toomey, S. (2005). The matrix of face: An updated face-negotiation theory. In W. B. Gudykunst (ed.), *Theorizing about intercultural communication*. Thousand Oaks, CA: Sage, pp. 71–92.

Ting-Toomey, S. & Kurogi, A. (1998). Facework competence in intercultural conflict. *International Journal of Intercultural Relations*, 22, 187–225.

Ting-Toomey, S. & Oetzel, J. G. (2013). Culture-based situational conflict model: An update and expansion. In J. G. Oetzel & S. Ting-Toomey (eds.), *The Sage Handbook of Conflict Communication*, 2nd edn. Thousand Oaks, CA: Sage, pp. 763–789.

Zhang, R., Ting-Toomey, S., Dorjee, T., & Lee, P. (2012). Culture and self-construal as predictors of relational responses to emotional infidelity: China and the United States. *Chinese Journal of Communication*, 5, 137–159.

Intercultural and Intergroup Communication

BERNADETTE WATSON
University of Queensland

HOWARD GILES
University of California, Santa Barbara

Social groups, such as adolescents and ethnic groups, very often have their own distinctive cultures that include specialized foods, customs and rituals, literature, music, while other intergroup situations (e.g., artificially constructed laboratory groups) constitute social categories that cannot claim such cultural artifacts. This entry compares two parallel traditions of theorizing communication between such groups: Intercultural communication (ICC; Gudykunst 2002) and Intergroup communication (IGC; Giles 2012).

Origins of the Theories

ICC has been studied for over 50 years (see Leeds-Hurwitz 1990) and developed to focus on how different cultures are distinguished from one another through their management of behaviors such as personal space and gestures. Particular attention has been devoted to understanding the cultural values that underpin different cultures' communicative practices, including individualism–collectivism, high–low contexts, and so forth (Watson 2012). From the ICC perspective, when an individual recognizes that he is engaged in an intercultural interaction, the focus remains on competent interpersonal communication (→ Intercultural Conflict Styles and Facework)

In contrast to ICC, the IGC approach came out of social identity theory (SIT: Tajfel 1978) which states that individuals categorize themselves and others into social groups and have a need to compare themselves with others, as a way of attaining a positive self-concept. We seek to favor our own groups (ingroups) compared to groups to which we do not belong (outgroups) and, communicatively act in accord with these social identities (Giles & Giles 2012). To join an outgroup, as, for instance, with immigrants wishing to acculturate into a host community, we communicate with members in ways akin to them so that we may gain membership to that group (Giles et al. 2012). SIT is not a communication theory but, rather, represents a theory of intergroup behavior and cognitions. Communication theories such as → communication accommodation theory explain how and why individuals engage in specific communication strategies when they interact with representatives of salient ingroups and outgroups.

Applications

Wiseman (2002) detailed the applications of ICC competence to assist individuals from differing cultures to communicate effectively with one another (→ Culture: Definition and Concepts). The ICC literature embraces a skills training approach, the premises of which are that individuals must have knowledge of the culture with which they engage, the motivation to effectively communicate (including intercultural sensitivity and empathy), and appropriate communication skills. Interactions are viewed as activities that occur at the interpersonal level.

In contrast, the main focus in IGC is on interactants implicitly (and sometimes explicitly) taking on the role of being representatives of their respective cultures. This explicit acknowledgment that at times our intergroup identities take precedence has important implications for any interaction. Individuals who perceive that their personal identity is salient may engage in different communications strategies from those who believe they are representative of a particular group. Whether individual or group identities, or both, are made salient will shape the communication process in different ways which, in turn, can reconstruct the very nature of those identities (Dragojevic & Giles in press).

The way a group or culture expresses its unique identity through a dialect, specialized jargon, or nonverbal demeanor (→ Nonverbal Communication and Culture), is fundamental to a healthy social identity, and to one (under differing conditions) that group members can vigorously and creatively sustain and proliferate. Intercultural communication is not subsumed under, or even a special case of, intergroup communication, but rather the two are parallel traditions capable of significant coalescence (Gudykunst 2002).

Assumptions of Both Theories

There are assumptions within ICC theories that are not held in IGC (Brabant et al. 2007). These are: that strangers to a new culture will take on an ethno-relativist position; they need to be educated in the new culture's values and norms; and when strangers possess knowledge of the culture and use expedient communication skills, effective communication will prevail. However, there is no extension within ICC theories to predict and explain when misunderstanding could in some cases be inevitable, despite any one individual's excellent skills and cultural knowledge. Sociopsychological theories that emphasize the intergroup nature of intercultural communication, rather than only its interpersonal aspects, directly address miscommunication and related issues of prejudice and intercultural tensions.

IGC is highly cognizant of how *status and power differentials* impact communication behavior. Power is, arguably, not a key consideration in ICC and the implicit overarching assumption is that competent communication is the main communication goal (→ Power in Intergroup Settings). However, when two individuals from different cultures with a history of power differentials and consequent perceived injustices come together, effective and competent communication may not be their mutual goal. A training and skills focus on achieving effective communication does not take account of the fact that culturally-salient power differentials may dictate what is appropriate communication for any particular encounter.

ICC as well as IGC – beyond the study of national and ethnic groups – can truly embrace an array of different categories including older people, homosexuals, bisexuals, or academicians from different disciplines, as well as those embedded in for example, religious, or organizational cultures (Giles 2012). Importantly, their members may view themselves as belonging to a group that owns specific characteristics and traits that set them apart from others. IGC theories distinguish between "me" in an interaction as an individual and "us" as a virtual representative of a group. While intercultural as well as intergroup perspectives have sometimes been infused into studies in such contexts, there is much more room for invoking each other's positions. The challenge is to move toward bringing these two theoretical viewpoints together in order to explain and predict the variables that determine effective and ineffective interactions (Kim, forthcoming).

See also: ▶ COMMUNICATION ACCOMMODATION THEORY ▶ CULTURAL PATTERNS AND COMMUNICATION ▶ CULTURE: DEFINITIONS AND CONCEPTS ▶ CULTURE AND COMMUNICATION, ETHNOGRAPHIC PERSPECTIVES ON ▶ INTERCULTURAL CONFLICT STYLES AND FACEWORK ▶ INTERGROUP COMMUNICATION AND DISCURSIVE PSYCHOLOGY ▶ INTERGROUP CONTACT AND COMMUNICATION ▶ MEDIA AND GROUP REPRESENTATIONS ▶ NONVERBAL COMMUNICATION AND CULTURE ▶ POWER IN INTERGROUP SETTINGS ▶ PREJUDICED AND DISCRIMINATORY COMMUNICATION ▶ SOCIAL STEREOTYPING AND COMMUNICATION

REFERENCES AND SUGGESTED READINGS

Brabant, M., Watson, B. M., & Gallois, C. (2007). Psychological perspectives: Social psychology, language and intercultural communication. In H. Kotthoff & H. Spencer-Oatey (eds.), *Handbook of intercultural communication*. Berlin: Mouton de Gruyter, pp. 55–75.

Dragojevic, M. & Giles, H. (in press). Language and interpersonal communication: Their intergroup dynamics. In C. R. Berger (ed.), *Handbook of interpersonal communication*. Berlin: De Gruyter Mouton.

Giles, H. (ed.) (2012). *The handbook of intergroup communication*. London: Routledge.

Giles, H., Bonilla, D., & Speer, R. (2012). Acculturating intergroup vitalities, accommodation and contact. In J. Jackson (ed.), *Routledge handbook of intercultural communication*. London: Routledge, pp. 244–259.

Giles, H. & Giles, J. L. (2012). Ingroups and outgroups communicating. In A. Kuyulo (ed.), *Inter/cultural communication: Representation and construction of culture in everyday interaction*. Thousand Oaks, CA: Sage, pp. 141–162.

Gudykunst, W. B. (2002). Intercultural communication theories. In W. B. Gudykunst & B. Mody (eds.), *Handbook of international and intercultural communication*, 2nd edn. Thousand Oaks, CA: Sage, pp. 183–205.

Kim, Y. Y. (ed.) (forthcoming). *The international encyclopedia of intercultural communication*. New York: Wiley Blackwell.

Leeds-Hurwitz, W. (1990). Notes on the history of intercultural communication: The Foreign Service Institute and the mandate for intercultural training. *Quarterly Journal of Speech*, 76, 262–281.

Tajfel, H. (ed.) (1978). *Differentiation between social groups: Studies in the social psychology of intergroup relations*. New York: Academic Press.

Watson, B. M. (2012). Intercultural and cross-cultural communication. In A. Kurylo (ed.), *Inter/cultural communication*. Thousand Oaks, CA: Sage, pp. 25–46.

Wiseman, R. L. (2002). Intercultural communication competence In W. B. Gudykunst & B. Mody (eds.), *Handbook of international and intercultural communication*, 2nd edn. Thousand Oaks, CA: Sage, pp. 207–224.

Intergenerational Communication

MARY LEE HUMMERT
University of Kansas

The term 'intergenerational communication' applies to interactions involving individuals who are from different age cohorts or age groups. Families provide ready examples of individuals whose communication would be classified as intergenerational: parent and child or grandparent and grandchild. These interactions stand in contrast to intragenerational communication or communication between individuals from the same generation or age cohort, such as siblings. Intergenerational communication occurs outside the family context as well. Any interaction between a child and an adult, a young person and one who is middle-aged or older, or a middle-aged person and an older person fits the definition of intergenerational communication. As a result, much communication in daily life – in the workplace, social settings, and the home – is intergenerational in nature.

Although common, intergenerational communication carries a strong *potential for miscommunication* and unsatisfying interpersonal interactions. This occurs not only because people from different age cohorts vary in their life experiences, but also because people at different points in the life-span vary in their communication goals, needs, and behaviors. Other challenges to satisfying intergenerational communication come from age stereotypes and social role expectations, which can also vary across cultures (→ Social Stereotyping and Communication). Some intergenerational communication problems, even conflicts, can be tied to the participants' being from different age cohorts. Examples include the divergent life experiences reflected in the differing value placed on thriftiness by members of the 'greatest generation' (which came of age during the Great Depression and World War II) and 'baby-boomers,' or the importance placed on careers by baby-boomers versus 'generation Xers' emphasis on work–life balance (Myers & Davis 2012).

Several *theoretical approaches* can be distinguished. The 'cohort approach' to understanding intergenerational communication presumes that individuals are, to an extent, prisoners of their history, and therefore does not consider the role of individual development across the life-span as an influence on intergenerational communication. The 'life-span developmental approach' recognizes that communication needs, goals, and skills change as individuals move through the various age groups from childhood to older adulthood (Williams & Nussbaum 2001; → Developmental Communication). 'Socio-emotional selectivity theory' illustrates how communication needs and goals differ for those early and late in the life-span (English & Carstensen, 2014). According to this theory, young adults face life tasks (e.g., choosing a career, finding a mate) that make new experiences and new communication partners their primary communication goals. They seek variety and novelty in communication, which increases their risk of experiencing some encounters with negative emotional consequences. Older individuals, in contrast, seek to maximize their positive emotional experiences through an emphasis on interactions with a few well-known communication partners. These differing communication goals of young and older persons can also lead to misunderstanding and intergenerational conflict, especially within families as they negotiate the amount of time spent together, topics of conversation, etc. Two *communication behaviors* have been especially associated with advancing age: reminiscence and painful self-disclosures. Both may reflect developmental processes. Reminiscence and painful self-disclosures involve revealing personal information about a problem or negative life event in conversation with a relative stranger.

Because age groups are social groups, intergenerational communication can also be examined from an *intergroup perspective* (Hummert 2012). Communication accommodation theory provides a framework for understanding how stereotypes about members of other age groups lead to expectations about appropriate communication behaviors in intergenerational interactions (→ Communication Accommodation Theory). Just as stereotypes can affect intergenerational communication, so can communication expectations for *social roles*. Social role expectations may conflict with age role expectations (e.g. age and rank or parent–child relationships) and long-term role relationships may evolve over the life-span. Both can contribute to problematic intergenerational communication. The parent–child relationship illustrates the second case. The nominal familial roles stay the same across the life-span. That is, the parent is always the parent and the child is always the child, whether the parent is 40 and the child is 10 or the parent is 80 and the child is 50.

The majority of the research on intergenerational communication has focused on western cultures such as those in the United States and Western Europe (Giles & Gasiorek 2011). To the extent that cultures differ in their values, they can also have different age stereotypes, norms for social roles, and standards for acceptable intergenerational communication behaviors (→ Culture: Definitions and Concepts).

See also: ▶ AGE IDENTITY AND COMMUNICATION
▶ COMMUNICATION ACCOMMODATION THEORY
▶ COMMUNICATION SKILLS ACROSS THE LIFE-SPAN
▶ CULTURE: DEFINITIONS AND CONCEPTS
▶ DEVELOPMENTAL COMMUNICATION
▶ INTERCULTURAL AND INTERGROUP COMMUNICATION
▶ INTERGROUP ACCOMMODATIVE PROCESSES
▶ POWER IN INTERGROUP SETTINGS ▶ SOCIAL STEREOTYPING AND COMMUNICATION

REFERENCES AND SUGGESTED READINGS

English, T. & Carstensen, L. L. (2014). Selective narrowing of social networks across adulthood is associated with improved emotional experience in daily life. *International Journal of Behavioral Development*, 38, 195–202.

Giles, H. & Gasiorek, J. (2011). Intergenerational communication practices. In K. W. Schaie & S. L. Willis (eds.), *Handbook of the psychology of aging*, 7th edn. San Diego, CA: Academic Press, pp. 233–247.

Hummert, M. L. (2012). Challenges and opportunities for communication between age groups. In H. Giles (ed.), *The handbook of intergroup communication*. London: Routledge, pp. 223–236.

Myers, K. K. & Davis, C. W. (2012). Communication between the generations. In H. Giles (ed.), *The handbook of intergroup communication*. London: Routledge, pp. 237–249.

Williams, A. & Nussbaum, J. F. (2001). *Intergenerational communication across the life span*. Mahwah, NJ: Lawrence Erlbaum.

Intergroup Accommodative Processes

CINDY GALLOIS
University of Queensland

We constantly interact with people from different social groups: cultures, ethnic groups, genders, ages, occupations, organizations, even clubs (→ Intercultural and Intergroup Communication; Culture: Definitions and Concepts). Intergroup accommodation focuses on the ways in which we modify language and communication as a function of our and others' group memberships in context. The main theory describing and explaining them is → Communication Accommodation Theory (CAT: see Gallois et al. 2005).

Language and style change to signal important group memberships. A French–English bilingual in Canada may switch from English to French to signal the importance of being French Canadian, and may even refuse to speak English to an English Canadian. Other choices include changing accent, formality of style, jargon or slang use, or particular nonverbal behavior. This idea is linked to language attitudes. Intergroup processes are closely tied to social identity, or a person's sense of self as a group member. Social identity is most salient whenever groups are in conflict or rivalry, whereas personal identity and interpersonal processes are more salient in friendly contexts.

Accommodative processes describe the ways we reflect our attitude and identity through language and communication. We may use expressive language and communication to show identification or solidarity, and thus to bring another person psychologically closer to us (accommodation). Alternatively, we may communicate hostility or rivalry (counter-accommodation), reflect a (perhaps unintentional) patronizing or ingratiating attitude (over-accommodation), or mark our own social identity distinctly from another's (under-accommodation); these all indicate 'nonaccommodation.' We may change our communicative behavior to be more like that of the conversational partner (convergence) or less like it (divergence). Often, however communication as viewed by outsiders does not reflect communicators' own perceptions. For example, in mixed-gender conversations, people may adopt exaggerated versions of their own gender's behavior, but believe they are converging to the other gender. Sometimes, people lack the linguistic or communicative skills to converge (Giles et al. 1991; → Gender and Discourse).

Accommodation can be across any group boundary, and signaled by a wide array of linguistic, nonverbal, and discursive moves (→ Intergroup Communication and Discursive Psychology; Nonverbal Communication and Culture). Accommodative strategies, in addition to the above, include 'nonapproximation strategies.' Accommodation in intergroup contexts begins with socio-historical context, including history and societal norms. At the individual level, it is reflected in initial orientation, including strength and salience of social identity. These lead to one's accommodative stance, or motivation to accommodate (or not). Accommodative stance is expressed in accommodative strategies employed by speakers. These include approximation – changing communication to be more like the other person or emphasizing one's own group markers); interpretability – communicative behaviors intended to make the encounter easier or harder for the other person to participate in; discourse management – whether each person communicates to share the conversation; interpersonal control – whether each person treats the other as an individual of equal status; and relational expression – intended to maintain or threaten the relationship or another's status and face. Overall, stance is aimed toward a more or less intergroup interaction. Strategies are translated into behavior and tactics, which change across the interaction. There is no one-to-one correspondence between strategies and tactics, or between them and specific behaviors. In interaction, behavior is perceived and labeled by other interactants, and people make attributions about each other's motives and goals. Finally, these attributions result in intentions about whether and how to interact with the other person or the person's group in the future.

The study of accommodative intergroup processes now emphasizes close examination of encounters, particularly organizational behavior. A key new finding is that accommodation by police to citizens is the strongest predictor of attitudes toward police across cultures and social classes (Giles et al. 2007). Increasingly, there are links to qualitative approaches to intergroup relations (→ Discourse Analysis).

See also: ▶ COMMUNICATION ACCOMMODATION THEORY ▶ CULTURE: DEFINITIONS AND CONCEPTS ▶ DISCOURSE ANALYSIS ▶ GENDER AND DISCOURSE ▶ INTERCULTURAL AND INTERGROUP COMMUNICATION ▶ INTERGROUP COMMUNICATION AND DISCURSIVE PSYCHOLOGY ▶ NONVERBAL COMMUNICATION AND CULTURE

REFERENCES AND SUGGESTED READINGS

Gallois, C., Ogay, T., & Giles, H. (2005). Communication accommodation theory: A look back and a look ahead. In W. Gudykunst (ed.), *Theorizing about intercultural communication*. Thousand Oaks, CA: Sage, pp. 121–148.

Giles, H., Coupland, N., & Coupland, J. (1991). Accommodation theory: Communication, context, and consequence. In H. Giles, J. Coupland, & N. Coupland (eds.), *Contexts of accommodation*. Cambridge: Cambridge University Press, pp. 1–68.

Giles, H., Hajek, C., Barker, V., Lin, M.-C., Zhang, Y. B., Hummert, M. L., & Anderson, M. C. (2007). Accommodation and institutional talk: Communicative dimensions of police–civilian encounters. In A. Weatherall, B. M. Watson, & C. Gallois (eds.), *The social psychology of language and discourse*. Basingstoke: Palgrave Macmillan, pp. 131–159.

Intergroup Communication and Discursive Psychology

JONATHAN POTTER
Loughborough University

Discursive psychology studies intergroup relations through analyzing the way discourse works in the practical settings in which intergroup issues become live: for example, major public events such as parliamentary debates on migration and asylum; institutional interaction such as where the police interview a suspect who has been accused of racist violence, and everyday talk, such as conversations about political positions and nationality over a family meal (→ Intercultural and Intergroup Communication).

The key point is that social groups become live entities as they are invoked in practical settings through the telling of stories and building descriptions in talk and texts (→ Text and Intertextuality). A full understanding of conflict and racism will need to explicate these discourse processes. It must describe the building blocks which people draw on to assemble their talk and texts as well as the practices through which the building is done in specific settings. These building blocks can be as simple as words such as "asylum seeker" or as complex as organized explanatory units such as "interpretative repertoires".

Key studies have considered discourse and racism. Wetherell & Potter (1992) showed how the discourse of professional, white majority group New Zealanders constructed a version of intergroup relations that stifled social change and yet managed the relevance of noxious categories such as bigot. Intergroup relations was built using a range of maxims, commonplaces ("everyone should be treated equally") and repertoires of culture that Billig has called the "kaleidoscope of common sense". Durrheim & Dixon (2005) found that in post-apartheid South Africa strong support for the principle of desegregation was combined with racist stereotyping and a weave of 'practical' arguments that justified segregation (→ Social Stereotyping and Communication).

A common feature of discursive research has been its highlighting of the heterogeneity of the discourse resources that people have available to them and the subtle ways in which they can assemble versions of events, cultures and politics to support specific courses of action. Any understanding of social change and its failure must understand the role of this web of resources.

See also: ▶ ACCOUNTING RESEARCH ▶ CONVERSATION ANALYSIS ▶ DISCURSIVE PSYCHOLOGY ▶ IDENTITIES AND DISCOURSE ▶ INTERCULTURAL AND INTERGROUP COMMUNICATION ▶ PREJUDICED AND DISCRIMINATORY COMMUNICATION ▶ SOCIAL COGNITIVE THEORY ▶ SOCIAL STEREOTYPING AND COMMUNICATION ▶ TEXT AND INTERTEXTUALITY

REFERENCES AND SUGGESTED READINGS

Condor, S. (2006). Temporality and collectivity: Diversity, history and the rhetorical construction of national entitativity. *British Journal of Social Psychology*, 45, 657–682.
Durrheim, K. & Dixon, J. A. (2005). *Racial encounter: The social psychology of contact and desegregation*. London: Psychology Press.
Wetherell, M. & Potter, J. (1992). *Mapping the language of racism: Discourse and the legitimation of exploitation*. Hemel Hempstead: Harvester Wheatsheaf.

Intergroup Contact and Communication

JAKE HARWOOD
University of Arizona

Intergroup contact occurs when members of different social groups come into contact with one another. Research has focused on whether/when such contact influences attitudes and prejudices about the respective groups (→ Intercultural and Intergroup Communication). Intergroup contact requires at least minimal awareness of group difference among the participants. "Ingroups" are the groups into which individuals categorize themselves, or into which they might be categorized by others. "Outgroups" are those to which the individual does not belong (e.g., for Muslim men, outgroups include Hindus, women, or children).

Intergroup contact theory (Allport 1954; Brown & Hewstone 2005) claims that contact improves intergroup attitudes, but that facilitating conditions have to be present: equal status, cooperative contact, and the support of relevant authorities. Recent meta-analysis confirms that contact can improve attitudes, and the facilitating conditions help but are not essential (Pettigrew & Tropp 2006). In contact theory, some researchers focus on whether dealing with others as individuals (rather than group members) facilitates contact. Others focus on the role of superordinate identification (moving to a higher level of categorization) in overcoming intergroup hostilities (e.g., "we're all humans"). This same effect can be achieved with "cross-cutting" categorizations: reframing an intergroup situation as int*ra*group (e.g., Muslim and Christian men focusing on their shared gender).

Communication processes have received little attention in contact research even though intergroup contact is by definition a communicative event. *Self-disclosure* is an important communication variable that has been studied. Intergroup relationships high in self-disclosure involve less intergroup prejudice than more superficial intergroup relationships. Self-disclosure develops depth in relationships, and reveals more detailed information about the outgroup member, presumably making it unlikely that straightforward negative perceptions of the outgroup can be maintained (→ Social Stereotyping and Communication). Self-disclosure is also associated with increased perceptions of outgroup heterogeneity. Social support, direct expressions of affection, and accommodation processes seem ripe for examination as determinants of attitudinal change (→ Intergroup Accommodative Processes), providing insight on the process by which contact influences attitudes. These communication behaviors characterize friendships; contact within friendships is a fruitful contact context.

Awareness of group memberships is a defining feature of intergroup contact, but important questions surround the extent and nature of that awareness. Some perspectives argue that group awareness must be high (and that outgroup members must be 'typical' of their group) for attitudes about one individual to generalize to attitudes about the entire outgroup (Brown & Hewstone, 2005). Atypical outgroup members are treated as exceptions, and do not influence prejudice. Group salience/typicality is associated with more negative contact, perhaps because of the anxiety engendered in intergroup situations. Thus, contact that is most likely to generalize is not likely to yield positive outcomes: negative contact may generalize more easily than positive (Paolini et al. 2006).

Indirect *contact* covers multiple diverse areas of research. Extended contact addresses situations in which knowledge of an ingroup friend's intergroup relationships causes positive intergroup attitudes. Media (or parasocial; → Parasocial Interactions and Relationships) contact operates when exposure to media portrayals of outgroup members affects attitudes (Joyce & Harwood, 2012) – an effect typically explained via social learning/modeling processes (→ Media and Group Representations; Social Cognitive Theory). Broader cultural contact also has effects. For example, bilingual education reduces prejudice independent of other contact experience (→ Prejudiced and Discriminatory Communication). Imagined contact operates when people imagine intergroup contact rather than actually experiencing it. Indirect contact is important because it circumvents many logistical and affective barriers to actual contact (see Harwood, 2010, for an integrative model of indirect and direct contact).

See also: ▶ INTERCULTURAL AND INTERGROUP COMMUNICATION ▶ INTERGROUP ACCOMMODATIVE PROCESSES ▶ MEDIA AND GROUP REPRESENTATIONS ▶ PARASOCIAL INTERACTIONS AND RELATIONSHIPS ▶ PREJUDICED AND DISCRIMINATORY COMMUNICATION ▶ SOCIAL COGNITIVE THEORY ▶ SOCIAL STEREOTYPING AND COMMUNICATION

REFERENCES AND SUGGESTED READINGS

Allport, G. W. (1954). *The nature of prejudice*. Reading, MA: Addison-Wesley.

Brown, R. & Hewstone, M. (2005). An integrative theory of intergroup contact. In M. Zanna (ed.), *Advances in experimental social psychology*, vol. 37. San Diego, CA: Academic Press, pp. 255–343.

Harwood, J. (2010). The contact space: A novel framework for intergroup contact research. *Journal of Language and Social Psychology*, 29, 147–177. doi: 10.1177/0261927X09359520.

Joyce, N. & Harwood, J. (online first, 2012). Improving intergroup attitudes through televised vicarious intergroup contact: Social cognitive processing of ingroup and outgroup information. *Communication Research*. doi:10.1177/0093650212447944.

Paolini, S., Harwood, J., & Rubin, M. (2010). Negative intergroup contact makes group memberships salient: Explaining why intergroup conflict endures. *Personality and Social Psychology Bulletin*, 36, 1723–1738. doi:10.1177/0146167210388667.

Pettigrew, T. F. & Tropp, L. R. (2006). A meta-analytic test of intergroup contact theory. *Journal of Personality and Social Psychology*, 90, 751–783.

Intergroup Reconciliation, Processes of

HOWARD GILES
University of California, Santa Barbara

Intergroup reconciliation refers to the process of establishing or restoring harmonious (and even friendly) relations between conflicting groups in contact, and has been studied with respect to the roles of apologies, forgiveness, and deliberative communication (amongst other mediating variables).

History has recorded the stark reluctance of some groups to apologize for past transgressions (e.g., Japanese brutalities in World War II) while, at other times, a group's public apology for past intergroup harm has received considerable media attention, as in the Irish Republic Army's apology for bringing about many civilian deaths. Philpot & Hornsey (2008) underscored the limitations of the (albeit perhaps necessary) enactment of a full-blown apology. In their study, Japanese government officials were purported to have apologized for causing the deaths of Australian prisoners of war. While it did have a positive effect in conveying remorse and was more effective than no apology, it failed to promote forgiveness (an important element enabling reconciliation) among Australian respondents. Indeed, they also argued that *unforgiveness* is a powerful social advantage an ingroup may often be reluctant to squander. Studies have also found that when trust is low, apologetic stances can regarded as devious or worse than no such expressions at all. However, the means to achieving intergroup trust is elusive.

In studying intractable conflicts, Ellis (e.g., 2012) went beyond current theorizing about the values and complexities of intergroup contact (→ Intergroup Contact and Communication) to the critical *communication dynamics* that can come into play. Besides a readiness for compromise, Ellis discussed the need for both groups to be empathic, take responsibility for past humiliations and injustices, de-escalate threats to the other's identity and existence, and be ingroup-critical. He proposed not only the need for de- and re-categorizing the involved intergroup parties into a viable superordinate entity, but also for competing groups jointly to redefine and rewrite their intergroup histories *together*, thereby empowering both entities. Ellis argued also that problem-solving in the form such so-called "deliberative communication" can assist the construction of superordinate identities that facilitate the acceptance of different points of view and tolerance for diversity, both central to the reconciliation process.

Further work on the interrelationships between apologies, forgiveness, and trust (as well as shame, guilt, and reparations) provides a solid foundation from which to pursue theoretically-guided applied communication research across a plethora of intergroup conflict settings on this enormously significant societal topic.

See also: ▶ INTERCULTURAL AND INTERGROUP COMMUNICATION ▶ INTERGROUP CONTACT AND COMMUNICATION ▶ TRUST OF PUBLICS

REFERENCES AND SUGGESTED READINGS

Ellis, D. G. (2012). *Deliberative communication and ethnopolitical conflict*. New York: Peter Lang.

Nadler, A., Malloy, T., & Fisher, J. D. (eds.) (2008). *Social psychology of intergroup reconciliation*. Oxford: Oxford University Press.

Philpot, C. R. & Hornsey, M. J. (2008). What happens when groups say sorry: The effect of intergroup apologies on their recipients. *Personality and Social Psychology Bulletin*, 34, 474–487.

Intermediality

KLAUS BRUHN JENSEN
University of Copenhagen

Intermediality refers to the interconnectedness of modern media of communication – as means of expression and exchange; as components of particular communicative strategies; and as constituents of a wider cultural environment.

Three *conceptions of intermediality* derive from three notions of what is a medium (→ Medium Theory). First, intermediality is the combination of separate material vehicles of representation and reproduction, as exemplified by the audio and video channels of television. Second, the term denotes communication through several sensory modalities at once, for instance, music and moving images. Third, intermediality concerns the interrelations between media as institutions in society, as addressed by technological and economic terms such as convergence and conglomeration.

As a term and a *theoretical concept*, intermediality has been most widely used in reference to multiple modalities of experience, as examined in aesthetic and humanistic traditions of communication research. Crediting an 1812 use of "intermedium" by the poet Samuel Taylor Coleridge, in 1965 Dick Higgins reintroduced "intermedia" to art theory in the context of the Fluxus movement (Higgins 2001; → Art as Communication). In media studies, the aesthetic focus on intermedia relations has been placed in historical perspective by research on how a given medium 'remediates' other media (Bolter & Grusin 1999; → Remediation). The general differences, similarities, and complementarities between historically shifting media have also been the focus of so-called medium theory since the foundational work by Harold Innis and Marshall McLuhan.

The various 'inter' structures of media – including hypertext and hypermedia – are currently being reshaped as part of an open-ended process of digitization. What used to be understood as separate media might, in the future, be produced, distributed, and consumed as one (inter)medium. At the institutional level, however, the jury is still out on the wider tendencies towards a convergence or divergence of media in terms of their technological developments and social applications (Jensen 2010).

See also: ▶ ART AS COMMUNICATION ▶ MEDIA HISTORY ▶ MEDIUM THEORY ▶ REMEDIATION ▶ TEXT AND INTERTEXTUALITY

REFERENCES AND SUGGESTED READINGS

Bolter, J. D. & Grusin, R. (1999). *Remediation: Understanding new media*. Cambridge, MA: MIT Press.

Higgins, D. (2001). Intermedia. *Leonardo*, 34(1), 49-54.
Jensen, K. B. (2010). *Media convergence: The three degrees of network, mass, and interpersonal communication*. London: Routledge.

International Association for Media and Communication Research (IAMCR)

CEES HAMELINK
University of Amsterdam

The International Association for Media and Communication Research (IAMCR) is an international professional organization in the field of media and communication research (www.iamcr.org). Its aims are to promote global inclusiveness and excellence in research, to stimulate interest in media and communication research, to disseminate information about research results, and to provide a forum where researchers can meet to exchange information about their work.

The history of the IAMCR is closely linked to the development of a proposal first initiated by the → UNESCO Committee on Technical Needs in the Mass Media in 1946. This committee drafted a constitution for an "International Institute of the Press and Information, designed to promote the training of journalists and the study of press problems throughout the world." In December 1956 an international conference took place at Strasbourg, where a committee was formed that prepared the constituent assembly of what was to become the IAMCR. This constituent assembly took place on December 18 and 19, 1957, at UNESCO headquarters.

The identifying characteristics of the association can be summed up as its ecumenical nature (in the sense of interdisciplinary and multi-method approaches to research topics), its global inclusiveness, which is reflected in its use of three official languages (English, French, and Spanish), and the active encouragement of the participation of young scholars, women, and researchers from economically disadvantaged regions of the world.

See also ▶ INTERNATIONAL COMMUNICATION ASSOCIATION ▶ UNESCO

REFERENCES AND SUGGESTED READINGS

Halloran, J. D. (ed.) (1979). *International Association for Mass Communication Research: Past, present and future*. Leicester: Centre for Mass Communication Research.
United Nations (1948). *Proceedings of the Freedom of Information Conference*, Geneva.
Wells, C. (1987). *The UN, UNESCO and the politics of knowledge*. London: Macmillan.

International Communication

JOHN D. H. DOWNING
Southern Illinois University

The → propaganda operations of the great powers in the twentieth century – today often reframed as 'soft power' – mostly initiated interest in the field of international communication. Lasswell first addressed the propaganda issue early in the 1920s. The long Cold War entrenched this issue in government-funded research priorities. Then the preferred term was 'psychological warfare,' not 'propaganda' (→ War Propaganda).

Four Theories of the Press, by Siebert, Petersen and Schramm (1956), was the first major comparative media study. The theories in question were normative, the official views of media goals in four contrasting polities: authoritarian, libertarian, Soviet, and "social responsibility." Comparative news studies have substantially revived recently (→ Political Communication Systems).

Another major stimulus to research was 'third world' development, often framed (→ Framing Effects) at the time by the modernization' schema which held that unless the west's → modernity spread, global raw materials and markets risked Soviet/Chinese takeover. Lerner's book, The Passing of Traditional Society (1958) and Rogers' Diffusion of Innovations (1962) were key texts (→ Development Communication).

Schiller's series of studies of global media from 1969 onwards (e.g. Schiller 1991) challenged this schema. From the 1980s onwards, he argued emerging ICTs were being used to intensify transnational corporate hegemony. A second challenge came from Armand Mattelart (2000), who wrote on international advertising, international communication history, and multicultural policies, but paid more attention to cultural dynamics than Schiller.

Three Theories of International Communication

'Cultural imperialism' (Schiller, Mattelart) covered education, religion, business practice, consumerism, law, governmentality, dress, as well as media. The term framed the US as a global superpower pursuing cultural domination overseas. Tomlinson (1991) argued that cultural imperialism presumed that third world media users could not interpret western media fare in their own ways, and that the term's popularity canalized discontent at modernity's juggernaut. China's (→ China: Media System) and India's global media industries (→ India: Media System), and Nigeria's video-movie industry (Nollywood), considerably complicated these issues.

The 'hybridization' metaphor focused on how global audiences refract cultural imports (Kraidy 2005). Some Latin American scholars argued that Latin America's history of Indigenous, European, and African exchange, and Mexican–US cultural exchanges, made the metaphor more compelling. The notion of 'cultural proximity', although critiqued for cultural essentialism, claimed that regional or linguistic resonances often rivaled foreign cultural imports' attractiveness. The emergence of 'Hallyu', the 'Korean Wave' of media exports, complicated the picture further.

'Globalization' could mean cultural imperialism, modernity, postmodernity, or even the ascendancy of free-market dogma. The roles of computer networks, satellites (→ Satellite Communication, Global), and global media firms were plainly central, as were key world cities. Some found the term over-stated for the media and information sectors (→ Globalization of the Media; Globalization Theories).

Global Media Firms

Global media players such as Apple, Google, Microsoft, Amazon, Bertelsmann, → News Corp., Samsung, → Sony and Time Warner Inc. (Fitzgerald 2012) usually have varied media interests (e.g., cinema, publishing, music, video games, theme parks). Advertising (→ Advertising: Global Industry), → public relations and → marketing firms also play significant roles internationally (Sinclair 2012). The recorded music industry has three key global players (Warner Music, Universal Music and Sony Music).

This scenario marks a sea change from some decades earlier, when cultural policies were often run by government ministries. All these companies are considerably smaller in financial terms than General Motors or ExxonMobil. Nonetheless, although media products are tradable commodities (→ Cultural Products as Tradable Services), their cultural impact cannot be assessed simply by the money spent on them.

Global Media Policies

In the years before and since World War II, the US government worked in a sustained manner to promote the 'free flow of information policy' (→ Freedom of Communication). This challenged British domination of ocean cable traffic and its Reuters news agency. Attempts to forge partly noncommercial global policies emerged in the 1970s NWICO debates (Many Voices, One World, 1980/2004, the MacBride Report), and the 2003 and 2005 World Summits on the Information Society (WSIS). The international Internet Governance Forum has emphasized 'multi-stake-holderism', i.e. the public, not just states and corporations, has a compelling interest in framing Internet policies (→ Internet: International Regulation).

Certain trade regimes and international agencies influence transnational communication policies: the World Trade Organization, the North American Free Trade Agreement (NAFTA), the European Union, → UNESCO, the World Intellectual Property Organization (WIPO), the International Telecommunication Union (ITU), and the Internet Corporation for Assigned Names and Numbers (ICANN).

Within the EU, France has actively supported exempting cultural products trade from WTO rules (the so-called 'cultural exception'), while the UK has militantly supported the US. Canada and South Korea, amongst others, have supported France's stance. Global media and information policy has been marked by clashing agendas.

Global News Flows

The 1980 MacBride Report noted how most western news coverage (as now) emanated within the global north and reported on its doings. International news about the global south, when available at all, focused on disasters, natural or political (→ International News Reporting). This made for a gravely under-informed planetary citizenry.

However, the turn of the millennium witnessed new international news interventions. Established stalwarts, such as the BBC World Service, Voice of America, → CNN International, Deutsche Welle, Radio France Internationale, and Vatican Radio, were joined by → Arab satelliteTV news and entertainment channels, and China's English-language global TV channel CCTV-9 (→ China Central Television, Foreign Language Program of). Britain's *The Guardian* newspaper could claim 16 million Internet readers worldwide.

Nonhegemonic International Communication Flows

Given the increasing activity of global social movements of many kinds, it appears likely that nonhegemonic transnational media may become a growing force. The emergence of the Qatar-based news broadcaster Al-Jazeera is an example. It has challenged the deferential state broadcast news of the Arabic-speaking world, and influential US government definitions of Middle Eastern affairs.

Perhaps the successful anti-apartheid movement (1948–94), challenging the white-minority regime which ran South Africa during those decades, could be defined as the first major transnational media campaign. In a series of countries, independent media, campaigning mainstream journalists, ongoing demonstrations, university teach-ins, media smuggled into and out of South Africa, the African National Congress's Zambia radio station, very effectively combined together over time.

See also: ▶ ADVERTISING: GLOBAL INDUSTRY ▶ ARAB SATELLITE TV NEWS ▶ BBC ▶ CHINA CENTRAL TELEVISION; FOREIGN LANGUAGE PROGRAM OF ▶ CHINA: MEDIA SYSTEM ▶ CNN ▶ CULTURAL IMPERIALISM THEORIES ▶ CULTURAL PRODUCTS AS TRADABLE SERVICES ▶ CULTURAL STUDIES ▶ DEVELOPMENT COMMUNICATION ▶ DIFFUSION OF INFORMATION AND INNOVATION ▶ FRAMING EFFECTS ▶ FREEDOM OF COMMUNICATION ▶ GLOBALIZATION OF THE MEDIA ▶ GLOBALIZATION THEORIES ▶ INDIA: MEDIA SYSTEM ▶ INTERCULTURAL AND INTERGROUP COMMUNICATION ▶ INTERNATIONAL COMMUNICATION AGENCIES ▶ INTERNATIONAL NEWS REPORTING ▶ INTERNATIONAL RADIO ▶ INTERNATIONAL TELEVISION ▶ INTERNET: INTERNATIONAL REGULATION ▶ MARKETING ▶ MODERNITY ▶ NEW WORLD INFORMATION AND COMMUNICATION ORDER (NWICO) ▶ NEWS CORPORATION ▶ POLITICAL COMMUNICATION SYSTEMS ▶ POSTMODERNISM AND COMMUNICATION ▶ PROPAGANDA ▶ PUBLIC RELATIONS ▶ SATELLITE COMMUNICATION, GLOBAL ▶ SONY CORPORATION ▶ TRANSNATIONAL CIVIL SOCIETY ▶ UNESCO ▶ WAR PROPAGANDA

REFERENCES AND SUGGESTED READINGS

Curtin, M. & Shah, H. (eds.) (2010). *Reorienting global communication: Indian and Chinese media beyond borders.* Urbana, IL: University of Illinois Press.

Fitzgerald, S. (2012) *Corporations and cultural industries.* New York: Lexington.

Kraidy, M. (2005). *Hybridity, or the cultural logic of globalization.* Philadelphia, PA: Temple University Press.

Lerner, D. (1958). *The passing of traditional society.* Glencoe, IL: Free Press.

Mattelart, A. (2000). *Networking the world: 1794–2000.* Minneapolis, MN: University of Minnesota Press.

Rogers, E. (2003). *Diffusion of innovations,* 5th edn. Glencoe, NY: Free Press. (Original work published 1962).

Schiller, H. (1991). Not yet a post-imperialist order. *Critical Studies in Mass Communication,* 8(1), 13–28.

Siebert, F., Peterson, T., & Schramm, W. (1956). *Four theories of the press.* Urbana, IL: University of Illinois Press.

Sinclair, J. (2012). *Advertising, the media and globalization.* London: Routledge.

Tomlinson, J. (1991). *Cultural imperialism.* Baltimore, MD: Johns Hopkins University Press.

International Communication Agencies

MARC RABOY
McGill University

International communication agencies play a significant role in the global media governance environment. Whether under the aegis of the

United Nations (UN), or as independent authorities (→ United Nations, Communication Policies of), they spearhead multilateral and multistakeholder collaboration on issues like intellectual property (→ Intellectual Property Law; Copyright), Internet governance (→ Internet Law and Regulation; Internet: International Regulation), media ownership (→ Concentration in Media Systems), network infrastructure, cultural diversity, → privacy and surveillance, as well as promoting communication for human rights and development objectives. (Ó Siochrú & Girard 2002; Raboy 2002). These agencies bring together governments, the private sector and civil society, to influence, inform, and direct decision-making for relevant policy matters.

International efforts for the regulation of cross-border communication date to the 1860s, and dealt, first, with postal services and, soon after, with the new technology of telegraphy. The first intergovernmental organization, the International Telegraph Union (ITU, now International Telecommunication Union), was set up in 1865 to provide a framework for international telegraphy. The Treaty of Berne (1875) created the General Postal Union (now the Universal Postal Union, UPU), and an international convention on copyright was also adopted in Berne in 1886. With the emergence of wireless communication (radio), new issues arose that required international agreement. International conferences in 1927 and 1932 drafted international regulations on radio that remain essentially in effect today.

The United Nations Education, Scientific and Cultural Organization (→ UNESCO) was established in 1945. The 1948 Universal Declaration of Human Rights established freedom of expression as a fundamental human right. In the commercial sphere, the 1947 General Agreement on Tariffs and Trade (GATT, managed since 1995 by the World Trade Organization) accepted the legitimacy of foreign film import quotas. The *United Nations* communication agencies each provide leadership on a specific aspect of international communication (→ Development Communication). International agencies in the field of communication have also emerged outside the UN system. The Internet Corporation for Assigned Names and Numbers (ICANN), an international, nonprofit corporation, is responsible for various functions of domain name system management.

See also: ▶ CONCENTRATION IN MEDIA SYSTEMS ▶ COPYRIGHT ▶ CULTURAL PRODUCTS AS TRADABLE SERVICES ▶ CULTURE: DEFINITIONS AND CONCEPTS ▶ DEVELOPMENT COMMUNICATION ▶ DIGITAL DIVIDE ▶ GLOBALIZATION THEORIES ▶ INTELLECTUAL PROPERTY LAW ▶ INTERNATIONAL COMMUNICATION ▶ INTERNET LAW AND REGULATION ▶ INTERNET: INTERNATIONAL REGULATION ▶ MEDIA CONGLOMERATES ▶ NEW WORLD INFORMATION AND COMMUNICATION ORDER (NWICO) ▶ PRIVACY ▶ UNESCO ▶ UNITED NATIONS, COMMUNICATION POLICIES OF

REFERENCES AND SUGGESTED READINGS

Ó Siochrú, S. & Girard, B. (2002). *Global media governance: A beginner's guide.* Lanham, MD: Rowman & Littlefield.
Raboy, M. (ed.) (2002). *Global media policy in the new millennium.* Luton: University of Luton Press.
WSIS (2012). Basic information: About WSIS. At http://www.itu.int/wsis/basic/background.html, accessed August 8, 2014.

International Communication Association (ICA)

MICHAEL L. HALEY
International Communication Association

The International Communication Association (ICA) began in 1950 as a small association of US researchers and is now a truly international association with more than 4,500 members in 85 countries. With its headquarters in Washington, DC, the ICA publishes five refereed journals, a yearbook, and a monthly online newsletter; sponsors a book series; and holds regional conferences and an annual conference. The annual conference meets around the world on a geographical rotation in the Americas, Asia, and Europe. The ICA's diverse structure of 25 divisions and special interest groups represents sub-fields of communication research (→ Communication as a Field and Discipline). Since 2003, the ICA has been officially associated with the United Nations as a nongovernmental association (NGO).

The overall *purposes* of the ICA are to advance the scholarly study of human communication and to facilitate the implementation of such study in order to be of maximum benefit to humankind by (1) encouraging the systematic study of theories, processes, and skills of human communication; and (2) facilitating the dissemination of research through an organizational structure responsive to communication study areas, a program of organizational affiliates, regular sponsorship of international meetings, and a commitment to a program of scholarly publication.

The *international identity* of the ICA has been a key issue with several debates about what it means to be 'international.' The most significant change began in the late 1990s when the ICA purposefully set about to change itself from a US-based organization that happened to have international members to a truly international organization that happened to be based in the US.

ICA is an organization of continuous change that highlights the fluid nature, improvisation, and cyclical process of organizations and organizational change without any seeming end state. At the same time, it continues to engage in the clearly purposeful, infrequent, and divergent behavior that is symptomatic of episodic change. The two processes have served the organization in complementary fashion.

See also: ▶ COMMUNICATION AS A FIELD AND DISCIPLINE ▶ INTERNATIONAL ASSOCIATION FOR MEDIA AND COMMUNICATION RESEARCH (IAMCR) ▶ INTERNATIONAL COMMUNICATION ▶ SPEECH COMMUNICATION, HISTORY OF

International News Reporting

CHRIS PATERSON
University of Leeds

International news reporting evolved with the advent of the telegraph in the mid-1800s. The explosion of foreign news that followed largely supported the colonial empires; it also focused on international conflicts involving them (while all but ignoring others).

Only a relatively small number of large media organizations routinely engage in international reporting. These include the global news services such as the → BBC, → CNN, and news agencies (Reuters, Associated Press, Agence France-Presse), and large newspapers and broadcasters from the world's wealthiest countries, such as the New York Times, Le Monde, NHK in Japan, or the Canadian Broadcasting Corporation. Foreign coverage is most often provided, if at all, through news agency subscriptions or the purchase of syndicated stories from larger organizations. Only the rare international journey is undertaken, usually to find a 'local angle' on a massive story receiving saturation coverage by the global press.

A classic critique of international reporting bore the label 'parachute journalism,' signifying the practice of jetting correspondents to breaking stories around the world, where they would spend just hours or days before moving on to the next. As international coverage increasingly became conflict reporting parachute journalism evolved into 'rooftop' journalism, where inaccessible military action a great distance away was described to international television audiences by correspondents on the roofs of luxury hotels.

Numerous journalists have been expelled from countries by having their visas or work permits revoked, but given the high numbers of journalists killed in recent years, this is now regarded as a mild penalty – if not a badge of honor (→ Violence against Journalists).

Crucial *technological change* in international reporting has come about since the mid-1990s, driven mostly by the ability to compress, and therefore transmit more cheaply, streams of digital information, including high-quality television pictures. Smaller and better cameras, satellite video-telephones, video transmission via Internet and laptop computers, enabling the writing of stories and editing of pictures in the field, have revolutionized the logistics of news gathering, and allowed journalists to distribute their content by television, radio, newspaper, Internet, and, increasingly, mobile phone from nearly anywhere on earth.

See also: ▶ ARAB SATELLITE TV NEWS ▶ BBC ▶ CNN ▶ CULTURAL IMPERIALISM THEORIES ▶ INTERNATIONAL COMMUNICATION ▶ INTERNATIONAL TELEVISION ▶ INTERNET ▶ JOURNALISM ▶ NEWS ▶ NEWS AGENCIES,

HISTORY OF ▶ TELEVISION NEWS ▶ VIOLENCE AGAINST JOURNALISTS

REFERENCES AND SUGGESTED READINGS

Carruthers, S. (2011) *The media at war*, 2nd edn. Basingstoke: Palgrave Macmillan.
Hamilton, J. (2004). Redefining foreign correspondence. *Journalism*, 5(3), 301–322.
Paterson, C. (2011) *The international television news agencies: The world from London*. New York: Peter Lang.
Williams, K. (2011) *International journalism*. Thousand Oaks, CA: Sage.

International Radio

PER JAUERT
Aarhus University

Since radio broadcasting was launched shortly after World War I, it has served two culturally different functions. On the one hand it was an effective instrument in the nation-building process, and on the other it was from its initial years distributed on a global scale. Over the past century, radio in large part shaped a national sense of shared imaginations and frames of reference, and at the same time also maintained its position as an international medium.

During the 1930s radio was perceived as one of the most powerful media to influence → public opinion. The Nazis described and used it as an efficient → propaganda instrument (Hendy 2000). American, British, and other European broadcasters – public, state, and private – shared the assessment of radio as an instrument of strong political influence. Apart from the interventionist use of radio as a political instrument, one also finds services related to the export and dissemination of cultural values and commodities. From the mid-1960s, the → BBC World Service, Deutsche Welle, and Radio France Internationale mainly served these functions.

With the introduction of the FM band from around 1960, radio became a more clearly defined national medium. The FM band is limited to a range of 50 miles, but has a better hi-fi sound quality than AM, and thus was an excellent vehicle for the expanding popular music industry (→ Music Industry; Popular Music). During the late 1990s three major platforms for radio distribution were adopted: analog broadcast radio, digital audio broadcasting (specialized channel formats), and radio on the Internet/web radio, where the user is able to compose different media elements from the website, often parallel streaming of the analog channels, streaming audio, and supplementary written information, video clips, downloading of programs (podcasting), and other features.

See also: ▶ BBC WORLD SERVICE ▶ DIGITAL MEDIA, HISTORY OF ▶ EXPOSURE TO RADIO ▶ INTERNATIONAL COMMUNICATION ▶ MUSIC INDUSTRY ▶ POPULAR MUSIC ▶ PROPAGANDA ▶ PUBLIC OPINION ▶ RADIO: SOCIAL HISTORY

REFERENCES

Hendy, D. (2000). *Radio in the global age*. Cambridge: Polity.
Scannell, P. (1996). *Radio, television and modern life*. Oxford: Blackwell.
Milan, S. (2013). *Social Movements and Their Technologies*. Basingstoke: Palgrave Macmillan.

International Television

MICHAEL CURTIN
University of California, Santa Barbara

During the latter half of the twentieth century, most discussions about international television tended to focus on national media systems and relations of exchange among those systems. Since the 1990s, however, television has increasingly been studied as a global phenomenon. Although national systems still figure prominently, research and policy debates now explore the ways in which television participates in broader processes of globalization (→ Globalization of the Media; Globalization Theories).

The crisis of legitimacy of many national broadcast media in Europe in the 1980s was exacerbated by a growing competition from transnational satellite services that fell outside the domain of national broadcast regulation (→ Satellite Communication, Global; Satellite Television). Businesses supported these new technologies since they promised to expand the availability of television advertising time and diminish government control over the airwaves. Cable and satellite channels initially targeted two groups: transnational niche viewers, e.g., business executives, sports enthusiasts, and music video fans, and sub-national niche groups, e.g., regional, local, or ethnic audiences (→ Cable Television). These trends soon spread beyond Europe to countries such as India, Australia, and Indonesia. Meanwhile, in countries where national commercial systems had long prevailed, existing broadcasters likewise found themselves challenged by a growing number of niche competitors.

Changes in television were further stimulated by a new generation of *corporate moguls* – such as Rupert Murdoch (→ News Corporation), Ted Turner (→ CNN), and Akio Morita (→ Sony Corporation) – who aspired to build global media empires that integrated television, music, motion picture, → video games, and other media enterprises. This 'neo-network era' of multiple channels and flexible corporate structures has also fostered the growth of commercial media conglomerates outside the west, such as Zee TV in India and Phoenix TV in China. And it has forced western corporations, such as Viacom, to adapt their content to local and regional markets around the globe.

Many scholars took a *critical perspective* on international television. Television's changing character worldwide was seen part of a broader process of globalization that has been unfolding for at least 500 years and was facilitated already over the past 150 years by electronic communication technologies like the telegraph, telephone, radio, cinema, television, and computer. Throughout the twentieth century, preserving and promoting national culture over the airwaves was characterized as a key element of national sovereignty. Critics warned that the huge flood of media messages exported from the core industrialized countries served the interests of a western ruling class by squeezing out authentic local voices and promoting a culture of consumption. This "media imperialism" thesis emerged in the 1960s and enjoyed widespread acceptance into the 1980s (→ Cultural Imperialism Theories).

Others began to notice the erosion of → Hollywood's dominance as the productivity of local TV industries increased. One indication of these new patterns of TV flow can be gleaned from the *emergence of global media capitals*, such as Bombay (now Mumbai), Cairo, and Hong Kong, each of them now competing for growing shares of the global media market (→ Bollywood). Such locales have developed transnational logics of production and distribution, ones that do not necessarily correspond to the geography, interests, or policies of particular nation-states. Finally, even in countries where the presence of US programs is pervasive, the impact on viewers remains a matter of speculation. Cultural studies researchers have shown how audiences make unanticipated uses of television programming, often reworking the meanings of transnational television texts to accommodate the circumstances of their local social context. Consequently, the homogenizing effect of transnational television flows has been called into question.

These challenges to the media imperialism thesis have formed the foundation of globalization studies of television and they have opened the door to new critical perspectives. By fostering a web of complex connectivity, television participates in the production of new opportunities as well as new anxieties. Our increasingly 'glocal' popular culture may, in fact, lay the foundations for nascent transnational political movements around issues such as labor, ecology, and human rights.

The study of international television today examines programming, audiences, and institutions, but it also encourages us to consider the role that electronic media have played for almost two centuries in the longer trajectory of globalization. Writing shortly before the first television satellite launch in 1962, Marshall McLuhan hyperbolically heralded the arrival of a "global village." Perhaps more modestly today, we might suggest that television facilitates processes whereby villages around the world increasingly perceive their circumstances in relation to global issues, forces, and institutions, as well as local and national ones.

See also: ▶ BOLLYWOOD ▶ CABLE TELEVISION ▶ CNN ▶ CULTURAL IMPERIALISM THEORIES ▶ CULTURAL PRODUCTS AS TRADABLE SERVICES ▶ GLOBALIZATION OF THE MEDIA ▶ GLOBALIZATION THEORIES ▶ HOLLYWOOD ▶ MEDIA CONGLOMERATES ▶ NEWS CORPORATION

▶ POLITICAL ECONOMY OF THE MEDIA ▶ SATELLITE COMMUNICATION, GLOBAL ▶ SATELLITE TELEVISION ▶ SONY CORPORATION ▶ TELEVISION BROADCASTING, REGULATION OF ▶ VIDEO GAMES

REFERENCES AND SUGGESTED READINGS

Ang, I. (1996). *Living room wars: Rethinking media audiences for a postmodern world.* London: Routledge.

Curtin, M. (2007). *Playing to the world's biggest audience: The globalization of Chinese film and TV.* Berkeley, CA: University of California Press.

Morley, D. (2000). *Home territories: Media, mobility, and identity.* London: Routledge.

Paterson, C. (2011). *The International Television News Agencies. The World from London.* New York: Peter Lang.

Tomlinson, J. (1999). *Globalization and culture.* Chicago, IL: University of Chicago Press.

Internet: International Regulation

WOLFGANG KLEINWÄCHTER
Aarhus University

The first Internet governance institutions reflected the layered, decentralized and denationalized technical architecture of the Internet. For different issues, different nongovernmental and global institutions were established as, inter alia, the Internet Engineering Task Force, the Internet Architecture Board, the Internet Assigned Numbers Authority for domain names and numbers, and the Internet Society for social and economic issues. This network of organizations was further enhanced in the 1990s by the establishment of the World Wide Web Consortium (W3C) for web protocols, Regional Internet Registries for the IP addresses and others. The *Internet Assigned Numbers Authority (IANA)* was established by the father of the domain name system Jon Postel (University of Southern California). In 1988 his institute entered into an agreement with the US Department of Commerce including some funding mechanisms and a shared responsibility which gave the National Information and Telecommunication Authority (NTIA) of the DoC an oversight role.

In July 1997 the Clinton Administration announced that it would transfer some of its oversight functions to a new corporation with the aim of privatizing and globalizing the emerging domain name market based on the principles of security, stability, competition and bottom up multi-stakeholder policy development. In 1998 the *Internet Corporation for Assigned Names and Numbers (ICANN)* was established. ICANN got a mandate to coordinate policies for domain names, IP addresses, protocols and root servers. The US Department of Commerce entered into a Memorandum of Understanding with ICANN, but separated the so-called IANA functions – the oversight over the root server plus some elements for allocation of IP address blocks and Internet Protocol parameters assignments – in a special contract and put this again under the oversight of the National Telecommunication and Information Administration (NTIA) of the US Department of Commerce (DoC).

In 2009, the Obama administration gave ICANN its formal independence via a so-called *Affirmation of Commitments (AoC)*, which liberated it from its duties to report to the US government. The AoC introduced an issue based decentralized Review Mechanism where multi-stakeholder review teams oversee ICANN's performance in various fields such as accountability and transparency, security and stability, competition and database management. The AoC also fixes ICANN's legal seat and headquarters in Marina del Rey, California, but does not forbid ICANN continuing to globalize itself. ICANN is a private corporation which operates under not-for-profit public law. It is managed by a board which is composed of 16 voting members (eight come from a Nominating Committee, six from Supporting Organizations, one from the At-Large Advisory Committee, plus the elected CEO. Five non-voting liaisons, representing the technical community and the governments, complete the Board.

The main *policy-development bodies of ICANN* are the Generic Domain Name Supporting Organization, the Country Code Supporting Organization and the Address Supporting Organization. Each of these is managed by a council which is elected by the constituencies of the supporting organizations. Constituencies are, inter alia, Internet registries, registrars, the business community, the noncommercial user constituency, not-for-profit organizations, and the trademark community. A special role is played by the Governmental Advisory Committee (GAC), which has a membership of 134 governments (as at 2014). As the name suggests, governments have only an advisory role within ICANN.

At the *governmental level*, discussed within the United Nations (→ United Nations, Communication Policies of) and the International Telecommunication Union, there are differing viewpoints on the role of governments in Internet regulation, with the United States opting for the liberal approach, as practiced in ICANN, and China opting for more leadership by governments. A UN working group came to a compromise definition declaring that all stakeholders have to be involved. This multi-stakeholder model is based on the concept of sharing policy development and decision-making. Furthermore, it differentiates between the evolution and the use of the Internet. This broad definition made clear that Internet governance is much more than merely Internet names and numbers and goes far beyond the ICANN vs. ITU conflict.

Additionally, the *UN Working Group on Internet Governance* recommended the establishment of an Internet Governance Forum (IGF) as a discussion platform to discuss public policy related Internet issues. The IGF was designed as a non-decision-making body, convened by the UN Secretary General but distanced from the UN bureaucracy with its own lightweight Secretariat in Geneva. Over the years the IGF transformed itself into a high-level annual meeting-place of more than 2,000 participants from all over the world for the discussion of all related public policy Internet issues. Its annual meetings became something like the 'Davos of the Internet.' However the fact that the IGF has no decision-making capacity remains a cause of criticism, in particular by developing countries.

The process of enhanced cooperation remains an *issue of controversy*. The two different interpretations of Internet regulation deadlock any progress. In the meantime, Internet governance is becoming a focus of more and more governmental and nongovernmental policy activities at other levels including the G8 summits and OECD.

See also: ▶ UNITED NATIONS, COMMUNICATION POLICIES OF

REFERENCES AND FURTHER READING

Hamm, I. & Machill, M. (2001). *Who Controls the Internet? ICANN as a Case Study in Global Internet Governance*. Gütersloh: Verlag Bertelsmann Stiftung. At: http://www.bertelsmann-stiftung.de/cps/rde/xbcr/SID-80708384-1F7BFF70/bst/xcms_bst_dms_15627_15628_2.pdf, accessed August 8, 2014.

Noman, H. (2011). *In the Name of God: Faith-Based Internet Censorship in Majority Muslim Countries*. At: https://opennet.net/sites/opennet.net/files/ONI_NameofGod_1_08_2011.pdf, accessed August 8, 2014.

Van Eeten, M. J. G. & Mueller, M. (2012). Where is the governance in Internet governance? *New Media & Society*, 15 (5), 720–736.

Mueller, M. & Kuerbis, B. (2014). Internet Governance Project. Roadmap for globalizing IANA: Four principles and a proposal for reform. A submission to the Global Multistakeholder Meeting on the Future of Internet Governance. At http://www.internetgovernance.org/wordpress/wp-content/uploads/ICANNreformglobalizingIANAfinal.pdf, accessed August 8, 2014.

ICANN (2014). Governmental Advisory Committee. At http://www.icann.org/en/news/correspondence/gac-to-board-27mar14-en.pdf, accessed August 8, 2014.

Internet Law and Regulation

LYOMBE EKO
University of Iowa

The Internet is a global network of computer networks. It is regulated by all countries within the framework of their political, economic, social, and cultural regimes. This multiplicity of regulatory approaches has transformed cyberspace into a series of interconnected jurisdictions. (→ Communication and Law).

Since the Internet is a global multi-communication space, its regulation is multilayered. The basic unit of Internet regulation is code, the programming software or logic that makes the Internet function. In his highly acclaimed book, *Code and Other Laws of Cyberspace*, Lawrence Lessig (1999) conceptualized Internet regulation as space dominated by corporate commercial technologies and the logic of their underlying computer codes, operating within the framework of the rule of law. Additionally, through code, information and communication technologies are used to regulate the behavior of Internet users on a global scale, in accordance with the values, ideals, and ethics of manufacturers, controllers, and hardware and software designers.

Multilateral or International Regulations

International regulation of the Internet consists of a basket of conventions, United Nations resolutions, declarations, and plans of action that cover electronic commerce and electronic signatures, child pornography, and intellectual property. The legal basis for the suppression of *child pornography* on the Internet is the United Nations Convention on the Rights of the Child. As child pornography became prevalent on the Internet, the UN General Assembly adopted the Optional Protocol to the Convention on the Rights of the Child on the Sale of Children, Child Prostitution and Child Pornography. The United Nations called for worldwide criminalization of the production, distribution, exportation, transmission, importation, and intentional possession and advertising of child pornography.

One of the most significant multilateral Internet agreements on *intellectual property* was carried out within the framework of the World Intellectual Property Organization (WIPO). WIPO's Internet Domain Name Process involves making recommendations on the management of Internet domain names and addresses worldwide. The WIPO process also involves the settlement of disputes arising from intellectual property issues associated with domain names.

The Neo-Mercantilist Model

The American political and economic system is premised on the notion that the United States is a marketplace of ideas (→ Freedom of Communication; Freedom of the Press, Concept of). As such, except in the narrowest of circumstances, the government may not regulate speech on the basis of its content. These principles are the foundation of the country's neo-mercantilist Internet law regime. In 1997, the Clinton–Gore administration offered the world a framework for the expansion and regulation of electronic commerce. The administration conceptualized the Internet as a global capitalist marketplace. The Clinton–Gore framework essentially globalized America's libertarian principles (→ Globalization of the Media): the marketplace of ideas, laissez-faire economics, free trade, and the free flow of information, goods, and services.

One of the most contentious issues of the Internet age is unauthorized online peer-to-peer exchange of copyrighted material. The first free music exchange company, Napster, was shut down when federal courts in the United States found that users who participated in the peer-to-peer music exchange promoted by the company infringed on the exclusive reproduction and distribution rights of musicians and record companies. In 2005, the Supreme Court of the United States held in MGM v. Grokster that companies whose free software allowed peer-to-peer distribution of lawful and unlawful copyrighted material on the Internet by third parties were liable for acts of infringement facilitated by the software.

Other Models of Regulation

Under its ideology of 'exception culturelle' (*cultural exception*), France has classified the French language, and the French media and telecommunications infrastructure, as part of its cultural heritage that should be jealously protected against Anglo-American domination. This culturalist perspective has also been applied to the Internet. In order to protect French national identity, language, and culture on the Internet, new terminology spawned by Internet technology is systematically replaced with French neologisms (→ Cultural Products as Tradable Services; Communication Law and Policy: Europe; France: Media System).

The Internet has, over the years, been increasingly impacted by 'Euro-governmentality,' the hierarchical relationship between the European Union (and to a lesser extent, the Council of Europe) and European nation-states. The *Euro-communitarian Internet regulatory system* is a market-based system of governance characterized by the formulation and transfer of directives, in specific issue areas of Internet communication, from the European Union to its member countries. The system is based on the transposition and uniform application of EU Directives on the Information Society for purposes of harmonization.

In the '*gateway model*' a governmental agency serves as the gateway to the Internet. Usually, the government creates a national intranet that insulates and isolates the country domain from the rest of the Internet. Access to the Internet is thus granted or denied in the name of national security, culture, morality, or some other governmental interest. The gateway model of Internet regulation is most evident in Russia, China, Burma, Cuba, North Korea, and other countries (→ China: Media System; Communication Law and Policy: Asia; Russia: Media System).

Geert Hofstede (2005) advanced a typology of cultural dimensions that includes a "*Confucian-Asian cluster*" of countries ranging from China and Japan, through South Korea and Vietnam. Tu Wei-ming and other scholars assert that Confucianism has enjoyed a resurgence in Asia since the 1980s, where its cultural values have been reinvented and reasserted as a defense mechanism against cultural globalization. These countries have a Confucianist model of Internet regulation that reflects culture-specific appropriations of the governmentality, worldview, and social hierarchies that originated in China.

The postures of *Arab-Islamic countries* toward the Internet have evolved over time. They have gone from active resistance – the Internet was viewed as a conduit for western decadence that would infect Arab Islamic culture – to allowing controlled access to government-approved content on national intranets that insulate and isolate country domains from the live, uncensored Internet. During the Arab uprisings that started in 2010, many governments shut down the Internet to prevent social media from being used to rally anti-government demonstrators.

With the diffusion of the Internet around the world in the 1990s, the World Bank and the International Monetary Fund (IMF), United Nations agencies, and international aid agencies conceptualized the Internet as a catalyst for economic and social development in the third world. The main shortcoming of this rather deterministic '*developmentalist model*' of the international community is that it focuses almost exclusively on Internet connectivity and pays little or no attention to infrastructural and content issues.

(→ Africa: Media Systems; Communication Law and Policy: Africa).

See also: ▶ AFRICA: MEDIA SYSTEMS ▶ CHINA: MEDIA SYSTEM ▶ COMMUNICATION AND LAW ▶ COMMUNICATION LAW AND POLICY: AFRICA ▶ COMMUNICATION LAW AND POLICY: ASIA ▶ COMMUNICATION LAW AND POLICY: EUROPE ▶ CULTURAL PRODUCTS AS TRADABLE SERVICES ▶ FRANCE: MEDIA SYSTEM ▶ FREEDOM OF COMMUNICATION ▶ FREEDOM OF THE PRESS, CONCEPT OF ▶ GLOBALIZATION OF THE MEDIA ▶ INTELLECTUAL PROPERTY LAW ▶ INTERNATIONAL COMMUNICATION ▶ INTERNET: INTERNATIONAL REGULATION ▶ PRIVACY ▶ RUSSIA: MEDIA SYSTEM

REFERENCES AND SUGGESTED READINGS

Clinton, W. & Gore, A. (1997). *A framework for electronic commerce*. Washington, DC: United States Printing Office.

Eko, L. (2001). Many spiders, one world wide web: Towards a typology of Internet regulation. *Communication Law and Policy*, 6, 448–460.

Eko, L. (2006). New medium: Old free speech regimes: The historical and ideological foundations of French and American regulation of bias-motivated speech and symbolic expression on the Internet. *Loyola of Los Angeles International and Comparative Law Review*, 28(1), 69–127.

Hofstede, Geert H. (2005). *Cultures and organizations: Software of the mind*. New York: McGraw-Hill.

Lessig, L. (1999). *Code and other laws of cyberspace*. New York: Basic Books.

Mattelart, A. (2002). *La mondialisation de la communication* [Globalization of communication]. Paris: Presses Universitaires de France.

Tu Wei-ming (ed.) (1996). *Confucian traditions in East Asian modernity*. Cambridge, MA: Harvard University Press.

Internet News

MARK DEUZE
Indiana University Bloomington

THORSTEN QUANDT
Westfälische Wilhelms-University Münster

Between the release of the world wide web standard in 1991, the start of the first online news publications worldwide in the mid-1990s, the 'Kidon

Media-Link' international database of 18,318 online news media in 2006, and the emergence of 70 million or more weblogs and podcasts, of which about one-tenth focus on news, one could say the web has become a widely accepted and used platform for the production and dissemination of news – by both professional reporters and amateurs (→ Citizen Journalism). Not only have thousands of professional news media started websites, but millions of individual users and special interest groups have used the web as an outlet for their news as well.

Research on internet news has addressed several topics. As journalists are now using the Internet regularly in their daily work several scholars have studied the effects of this adoption process, including the practices of computer-assisted reporting (CAR). Another aspect related to CAR is how to deal with online communication such as email, posts in newsgroups and discussion forums, weblogs, and instant or chat messages (including SMS and MMS via cell phones) in an environment where the verification of information is extremely difficult due to the often anonymous, fast-paced (or instantaneous) communication involved. With the integration of user-generated content (UGC) into mainstream media (e.g. via user-produced pictures or eyewitness accounts), the filtering, checking, and reworking of material supplied by lay people becomes an important aspect of editorial work (→ Web 2.0 and the News). In parallel with this development, questions of authorship, quality, and process control – and essentially the meaning of journalism in an open system – gain significance (Singer et al. 2011). Several studies also signal the worrying fact that the Internet sometimes even causes journalists to spend more time at their computer instead of going 'out on the street.'

Online journalism should be seen as journalism produced more or less exclusively for the web (the graphic user interface of the Internet; → Online Journalism). It has been functionally differentiated from other kinds of journalism by using its technological component as a determining factor in terms of an operational definition – just like the fields of print, radio, and television journalism before it. The online journalist has to make decisions on which media format or formats best tell a certain story (multimediality), has to consider options for the public to respond, interact, or even customize certain stories (interactivity), and thinks about ways to connect the story to other stories, archives, resources, and so on through hyperlinks.

How online journalists in their daily work articulate the characteristics of the new medium can be considered across *two dimensions*. First, online journalists are more likely than their offline colleagues to consider interactivity-related issues (such as providing a forum for public debate) among the most important aspects of their job. Internet news thus exists somewhere on a continuum between professionally produced content and the provision of public connectivity (→ Interactivity, Concept of). The second dimension represents the level of participatory communication offered through a news site. A site can be considered to be 'open' when it allows users to share comments and posts, and upload files without moderating or filtering intervention, or 'closed' when users may participate but their communicative acts are subject to strict editorial moderation and control (Domingo et al. 2008).

It is possible to map four more or less distinct *categories of Internet news*. The most widespread form of Internet news is the 'mainstream news site,' generally offering a selection of (aggregated) editorial content and a minimal, usually filtered or moderated, form of participatory communication. 'Index and category sites' are generally operated by net-based companies such as certain search engines, marketing firms, Internet service providers, or enterprising individuals. 'Meta- and comment sites' contain numerous examples of Internet news that either serve as a platform to exchange and discuss news published elsewhere online, or offer an outlet for so-called 'alternative', non-mainstream, or nonprofit news (→ Alternative Journalism). 'Share and discussion sites,' finally, are places where any meaningful distinction between the producer and the user, between the news professional and the amateur reporter, or between opinion and fact, for that matter, is lost.

See also: ▶ ALTERNATIVE JOURNALISM ▶ CITIZEN JOURNALISM ▶ INTERACTIVITY, CONCEPT OF ▶ JOURNALISM ▶ NEWS ▶ NEWS PRODUCTION AND TECHNOLOGY ▶ ONLINE JOURNALISM ▶ WEB 2.0 AND THE NEWS

REFERENCES AND SUGGESTED READINGS

Deuze, M. (2003). The web and its journalisms: Considering the consequences of different types of news media online. *New Media and Society*, 5(2), 203–230.

Domingo, D., Quandt, T., Heinonen, A., Paulussen, S., Singer, J., & Vujnovic, M. (2008). Participatory journalism practices in the media and beyond: An international comparative study of initiatives in online newspapers. *Journalism Practice*, 2(3), 326–342.

Paterson, C. & Domingo, D. (2008). *Making online news: The ethnography of new media production*. New York: Peter Lang.

Quinn, S. (2006). *Convergent journalism*. New York: Peter Lang.

Singer, J., Hermida, A., Domingo, D. et al. (2011). *Participatory journalism: Guarding open gates at online newspapers*. New York: Wiley Blackwell.

Internet and Popular Culture

JACQUELINE LAMBIASE
Texas Christian University

Communication created and shared through the Internet has proliferated since 1990, with nearly 4 billion people worldwide adapting to the web's creative spaces through easy-to-use technology on computers, mobile phones, smart phones, and tablets (→ Exposure to the Internet). The Internet not only provides access to web spaces where people view or listen to professional and amateur digital video, photographs, music, and stories, but also allows people to produce and disseminate their creative materials to mass audiences (→ Photography; Popular Music). In this respect, the Internet serves as a literal 'circuit of culture,' a theory explaining human identity, production, consumption, regulation, and representation of the cultural objects of everyday life (→ Information Society).

The most common *popular communication applications* for the Internet include social networking (→ Social Media), blogging, instant messaging, and → electronic mail messages. With rising use of email in the mid-1990s, attachments containing *computer-generated images* began to be exchanged among private individuals, with some attachments achieving incredible popularity. Weblogging sites provide templates to make reverse chronology journal postings easy for users. Other social networking sites such as → Twitter.com or → Facebook.com, started in 2004 and now serving more over one billion users, also provide templates for users who create personal web pages linked to networks of real-world friends and new online acquaintances. All of these social media sites allow users to share opinions, links, and media with communities of interest through an RSS (Really Simple Syndication) feed, which updates material across the web in real time, causing some messages or images to 'go viral,' reaching thousands of people within hours (→ Network Organizations through Communication Technology).

Personal and collaborative websites – where users are encouraged to upload their own digital art, music, photography, video, and written text through peer-to-peer file sharing – serve a variety of interests including mass media, religion, politics, education, and celebrity fandom. Online literary efforts include hypertextual novels, websites that allow people to upload stories about favorite characters or to share fan-written television scripts.

See also: ▶ COMMUNICATION TECHNOLOGY AND DEMOCRACY ▶ COPYRIGHT ▶ ELECTRONIC MAIL ▶ EXPOSURE TO THE INTERNET ▶ FACEBOOK ▶ INFORMATION AND COMMUNICATION TECHNOLOGY, DEVELOPMENT OF ▶ INFORMATION SOCIETY ▶ INTELLECTUAL PROPERTY LAW ▶ INTERACTIVITY, CONCEPT OF ▶ INTERNATIONAL COMMUNICATION ▶ NETWORK ORGANIZATIONS THROUGH COMMUNICATION TECHNOLOGY ▶ PHOTOGRAPHY ▶ POPULAR MUSIC ▶ SOCIAL MEDIA ▶ TWITTER

REFERENCES AND SUGGESTED READINGS

Fishwick, M. (2004). *Probing popular culture: On and off the Internet*. Binghamton, NY: Haworth.

Hermes, J. (2005). *Re-reading popular culture*. Malden, MA: Blackwell.

Hills, M. (2002). *Fan cultures*. London: Routledge.

Johnson, S. (2006). *Everything bad is good for you: How today's popular culture is actually making us smarter*. New York: Riverhead.

Interorganizational Communication

MARYA L. DOERFEL
Rutgers University

Interorganizational communication (IOC) emphasizes relationships organizations have with external constituents as opposed to relationships that occur internally. IOC considers issues like information flows, information sharing, reputation, cooperation, competition, coalition building, and power (→ Organizational Communication).

Scholarship considers organizational roles within social structures and how structures influence and are influenced by organizational power, reputation, dependency on others, market share, and social influence. A substantial component involves understanding relationships from a social networks perspective (→ Communication Networks).

Macro-level theory involves analysis of the greater interorganizational contexts in the pursuit of uncovering idealized structures, understanding dynamics of interorganizational systems, and investigating how collective systems are formed and maintained. Communication scholarship typically identifies individual organizational actions and their subsequent contribution to a greater context of relationships. Theory development is in areas of reputation, social influence, cooperative/competitive relationships, and evolutionary dynamics. Overall, interorganizational structures are assessed with a variety of *methodological approaches,* and theory development is tightly coupled with such methodologies. For example, dense networks of local organizations indicate social capital; macro structures of communication flows indicate distribution of power.

On the *micro-level* 'alliance theories' suggest that organizations network with others in order to manage uncertainty and relationships. Extending information sharing to seemingly altruistic intentions, 'public goods theory' attempts to unravel the nature of organizational activities that contribute to overall collective benefits without necessarily offering instantly observable advantages to contributors. Early developments reflect the underlying principle that IOC is marked by the simultaneous existence of cooperative–competitive relationships. Such studies showed the evolution of communication activities that facilitated sharing resources without realizing instant reward for such behavior (e.g., Browning et al. 1995).

Monge et al. (1998) integrated communication technologies as a resource for supporting information sharing and collective action. Ongoing collaborative activities create a neutral 'space' for information sharing, and that information sharing begins with small contributions with transformation toward more collective, cooperative ventures. Future research is directed toward understanding the IOC processes that facilitate collaborative endeavors and result in collective advantages.

'Resource dependency theory' explains the influence of organizations' roles in their environment relative to the extent to which they are wielders or needy of resources. More reliant organizations are more likely to cooperate, comply with external demands, and engage in activities that support obtaining resources. Meanwhile, resource-wielding organizations reap benefits including improved reputation, power, and social influence. Doerfel & Taylor (2005) showed that the extent to which an organization is seen as cooperative relates to the extent to which the organization needs more key resources. Flanagin et al. (2001) demonstrated advantages associated with early entrants to cooperative ventures-founding members experienced greater reputational benefits and more social influence than later system entrants.

IOC also involves stakeholders, which can include other organizations and also those who care about ("have a stake in") the focal organization such as volunteers and employees. Lewis et al. (2003) integrated stakeholder theory and resource dependency theory in understanding communication strategies used by organizations during planned change (→ Organizational Change Processes). IOC research demonstrates that 'history matters.' Cooperation-competition, reputation and social influence related to and emerge from past relationships. New directions promote models that advance psychological, social, and communication theory (multi-theoretical models) with individuals', groups', and organizations' interactions (multilevel models).

See also: ▶ COMMUNICATION NETWORKS ▶ GLOBALIZATION OF ORGANIZATIONS ▶ INSTITUTIONAL THEORY ▶ KNOWLEDGE MANAGEMENT ▶ ORGANIZATIONAL CHANGE PROCESSES ▶ ORGANIZATIONAL COMMUNICATION

REFERENCES AND SUGGESTED READINGS

Browning, L. D., Beyer, J. M., & Shetler, J. C. (1995). Building cooperation in a competitive industry: SEMATECH and the semiconductor industry. *Academy of Management Journal*, 38, 113–151.

Doerfel, M. L. & Taylor, M. (2005). Network dynamics of interorganizational communication: The Croatian civil society movement. *Communication Monographs*, 71, 373–394.

Flanagin, A. J., Monge, P., & Fulk, J. (2001). The value of formative investment in organizational federations. *Human Communication Research*, 27, 69–93.

Lewis, L. K., Richardson, B. K., & Hamel, S. A. (2003). When the "stakes" are communicative: The lamb's and the lion's share during nonprofit planned change. *Human Communication Research*, 29, 400–430.

Monge, P. & Contractor, N. S. (2003). *Theories of communication networks*. Oxford: Oxford University Press.

Monge, P., Fulk, J., Kalman, M. E., Flanagin, A. J., Parnassa, C., & Rumsey, S. (1998). Production of collective action in alliance-based interorganizational communication and information systems. *Organization Science*, 9, 411–433.

Stohl, M. & Stohl, C. (2005). Human rights, nation states, and NGOs: Structural holes and the emergence of global regimes. *Communication Monographs*, 72, 442–467.

Interpersonal Attraction

SUSANNE M. JONES
University of Minnesota

Interpersonal attraction was conceptualized initially as a relatively stable attitude that leads to positive sentiments for another person and that serves as the catalyst for initiating interpersonal interaction. It is now viewed as a dynamic, affective force that draws people together and permeates all stages of interpersonal relationships (→ Ingratiation and Affinity Seeking).

McCroskey & McCain (1974) identified *three types of interpersonal attraction*. Task attraction refers to our desire to work with someone, whereas physical attraction occurs when we are drawn to a person's physical appearance. Social attraction reflects our desire to develop a friendship with that person. Their interpersonal attraction scale (IAS) measures these three types of attraction. Judgments of physical attractiveness are one of the top predictors of interpersonal attraction. Both sexes are biased toward beauty and tend to perceive physically attractive people as more rewarding than physically unattractive people. A second factor that influences interpersonal attraction is similarity. Similar others are attractive because they serve as universal reinforcers of our worldview. Several communication qualities seem also to play a crucial role in interpersonal attraction; among them are warmth, sociability, and competent communication (→ Interpersonal Communication Competence and Social Skills). Proximity and familiarity are two final predictors of attractiveness.

Integral to the vast majority of interpersonal attraction studies is the assumption that we find others attractive if we perceive them to be rewarding, an idea that has been drawn from → social exchange theories. Berger and Calabrese's → Uncertainty Reduction Theory (URT) contends that it is not perceived reward value per se that causes attraction; rather it is the extent to which we are able to reduce our initial uncertainty about others that attracts us to others. A second theoretical approach that explains the causes and outcomes of attraction is *social evolutionary theory* (Buss 1994). Humans, like all mammalian species, are driven to advance the species by mating with those who are most genetically fit. Genetic fitness is manifested in phenotypic features such as physical attractiveness and other personality characteristics. Consequently, people are drawn to those who possess advantageous phenotypic features because these features suggest strong genes and thus provide a survival advantage.

See also: ▶ INGRATIATION AND AFFINITY SEEKING ▶ INTERPERSONAL COMMUNICATION COMPETENCE AND SOCIAL SKILLS ▶ SOCIAL EXCHANGE ▶ UNCERTAINTY REDUCTION THEORY

REFERENCES AND SUGGESTED READINGS

Berscheid, E. & Walster, E. H. (1969). *Interpersonal attraction*. Reading, MA: Addison Wesley.

Buss, D. M. (1994). *The evolution of desire: Strategies of human mating*. New York: Basic Books.

McCroskey, J. C. & McCain, T. A. (1974). The measurement of interpersonal attraction. *Speech Monographs*, 41, 261–266.

Interpersonal Communication

CHARLES R. BERGER
University of California, Davis

Interpersonal communication concerns the study of social interaction between people. Interpersonal communication theory and research seek to understand how individuals use discourse and nonverbal actions to achieve a variety of instrumental and communication goals. Interpersonal communication has been traditionally viewed as a process that occurs between people encountering each other face to face. Increasingly, however, social interaction is being accomplished through the use of interactive media. As a sub-field of the communication discipline, interpersonal communication can be divided into the six unique but related areas of study described below.

Uncertainty in Interpersonal Communication

When individuals engage in social interaction with each other, they cannot be completely certain of their conversational partners' current goals, emotional states, beliefs, attitudes, and future actions. Individuals also harbor uncertainties about how they should act toward their partners. These uncertainties are maximal when strangers meet, but uncertainties can also arise in close relationships of long duration. → Uncertainty Reduction Theory (URT; Berger & Calabrese 1975) proposes that individuals must reduce their uncertainties to some degree in order to be able to fashion verbal discourse and actions that will allow them to achieve their interaction goals.

URT has found purchase in explaining social interaction in intercultural (Gudykunst 1995) and organizational (Kramer 2004) communication contexts (→ Organizational Communication; Intercultural and Intergroup Communication). Individuals may experience uncertainty with respect to their relationships with each other (→ Relational Uncertainty), and individuals may not necessarily be motivated to reduce their uncertainty when they anticipate experiencing negative outcomes by so doing (→ Uncertainty Management).

Interpersonal Adaption

When individuals converse, they show strong proclivities to reciprocate each other's verbal and nonverbal behaviors. Although the forces for reciprocity in social interaction are highly pervasive, there are conditions under which interacting individuals will show compensation in response to each other's behaviors. Compensation occurs when a behavior displayed by one person is not matched in some way by another. A number of alternative theories have been devised to illuminate the conditions under which reciprocity and compensation are likely to occur, especially with respect to nonverbal behaviors. Although these theories differ in terms of their explanations for reciprocity/compensation, they share a common assumption that when expectations for nonverbal behavior are violated, individuals tend to experience arousal. Research comparing these theories has been inconclusive and has prompted the development of Interaction Adaptation Theory (Burgoon et al. 2010).

Message Production

Just as language is a tool for attaining everyday goals, social interaction is an instrument for goal achievement. Consistent with this proposition, constructivist researchers have endeavored to determine the characteristics of messages deemed to be effective for achieving a variety of goals, most of them concerned with → persuasion. A more comprehensive and abstract message production theory labeled → Action Assembly Theory (Greene 1997) has been developed to explain how individuals produce actions and discourse. Theories featuring such knowledge structures as scripts and plans have also been devised (Berger 1997). According to these Goal-Plan-Action (GPA) theories (Dillard et al. 2002), scripts and plans are hierarchically organized knowledge structures representing action sequences that will bring about the achievement of goals. Once goals are activated, these knowledge structures guide actions toward goal attainment.

Relationship Development

Interpersonal communication plays a critical role in the development, maintenance, and deterioration of social and personal relationships. A central question researchers have sought to answer is why some relationships become closer over time while others grow distant and perhaps end. Social exchange theories have frequently been invoked to explain why relationship growth and deterioration occur (Roloff 1981; → Social Exchange). These theories suggest that individuals experience both rewards for and costs of being in relationships with each other. Favorable relative reward/cost ratios fuel relationship growth, whereas unfavorable ratios are associated with relationship deterioration. Relational dialectics researchers contend that the development of relationships is fraught with dialectical tensions that may serve to pull individuals in opposite directions simultaneously (Baxter & Montgomery 1996; → Relational Dialectics). Because tensions between these polarities shift over time, relationships are in a constant state of flux.

Deceptive Communication

Many interpersonal communication researchers recognize that deception is an integral part of social interaction. Many times 'white lies' are told to help co-interlocutors save face when potentially embarrassing circumstances arise in social situations (→ Politeness Theory). Two enduring questions concerning deceptive communication have attracted considerable research attention. One of these concerns the degree to which engaging in deception alters nonverbal behaviors; i.e. do truth tellers' nonverbal behaviors differ systematically from those of individuals who are telling lies? Specific behaviors may be diagnostic of deceptive communication in specific individuals; however, no universal nonverbal indicator of deceptive communication has yet been identified (→ Deception Detection Accuracy).The second enduring question is the degree to which individuals are skilled at detecting deception. Research has shown that most individuals, including law-enforcement professionals, are not very adept at detecting deception.

Mediated Social Interaction

Increasingly, social interaction is being accomplished through various communication technologies. These developments have prompted a concomitant increase in research aimed at understanding their potential individual and social effects (→ Mediated Social Interaction). Research has sought to determine how computer-mediated communication (CMC) and face-to-face (FtF) interaction differ with respect the outcomes associated with their use (Walther 2010). Because text-based CMC filters out many nonverbal cues available to people engaged in FtF interactions, it is presumed that communication via text-based CMC is more task focused than is FtF communication. Although relatively cue-deprived, text-based CMC venues may be useful for initially encountering and screening potential friends and romantic partners, they apparently do not afford sufficient information for developing close relationships. Individuals who initially meet in the text-based CMC world usually elect to communicate with each other through other channels, e.g., phone and FtF encounters.

See also: ▶ ACTION ASSEMBLY THEORY ▶ DECEPTION DETECTION ACCURACY ▶ IMAGINED INTERACTIONS ▶ INGRATIATION AND AFFINITY SEEKING ▶ INTERCULTURAL AND INTERGROUP COMMUNICATION ▶ INTERPERSONAL COMMUNICATION COMPETENCE AND SOCIAL SKILLS ▶ INTERPERSONAL CONFLICT ▶ MARITAL COMMUNICATION ▶ MEDIATED SOCIAL INTERACTION ▶ ORGANIZATIONAL COMMUNICATION ▶ PERSUASION ▶ POLITENESS THEORY ▶ RELATIONAL CONTROL ▶ RELATIONAL DIALECTICS ▶ RELATIONAL UNCERTAINTY ▶ SOCIAL EXCHANGE ▶ SOCIAL SUPPORT IN INTERPERSONAL COMMUNICATION ▶ UNCERTAINTY MANAGEMENT ▶ UNCERTAINTY REDUCTION THEORY

REFERENCES AND SUGGESTED READINGS

Baxter, L. A. & Montgomery, B. M. (1996). *Relating: Dialogues and dialectics.* New York: Guilford.

Berger, C. R. (1997). *Planning strategic interaction: Attaining goals through communicative action.* Mahwah, NJ: Lawrence Erlbaum.

Berger, C. R. & Calabrese, R. J. (1975). Some explorations in initial interaction and beyond: Toward a developmental theory of interpersonal communication. *Human Communication Research,* 1, 99–112.

Burgoon, J. K., Floyd, K., & Guerrero, L. K. (2010). Nonverbal communication theories of interaction adaptation. In C. R. Berger, M. E. Roloff, & D. R. Roskos-Ewoldsen (eds.), *Handbook of communication science,* 2nd edn. Thousand Oaks, CA: Sage, pp. 93–108.

Dillard, J. P., Anderson, J. W., & Knobloch, L. K. (2002). Interpersonal influence. In M. L. Knapp & J. A. Daly (eds.), *Handbook of interpersonal communication,* 3rd edn. Thousand Oaks, CA: Sage, pp. 425–474.

Greene, J. O. (1997). A second generation action assembly theory. In J. O. Greene (ed.), *Message production: Advances in communication theory.* Mahwah, NJ: Lawrence Erlbaum, pp. 151–170.

Gudykunst, W. B. (1995). Anxiety/uncertainty management (AUM) theory. In R. L. Wiseman (ed.), *Intercultural communication theory.* Thousand Oaks, CA: Sage, pp. 8–58.

Kramer, M. W. (2004). *Managing uncertainty in organizational communication.* Mahwah, NJ: Lawrence Erlbaum.

Roloff, M. E. (1981). *Interpersonal communication: The social exchange approach.* Beverly Hills, CA: Sage.

Walther, J. B. (2010). Computer-mediated communication. In C. R. Berger, M. E. Roloff, & D. R. Roskos-Ewoldsen (eds.), *Handbook of communication science,* 2nd edn. Thousand Oaks, CA: Sage, pp. 489–505.

Interpersonal Communication Competence and Social Skills

BRIAN H. SPITZBERG
San Diego State University

Interpersonal communication competence and social skills are concerned with both the performance of communication and the evaluation of its quality. 'Interpersonal communication competence' is typically defined either as the ability to enact message behavior that fulfills requirements of a given situation, or as the subjective evaluation of the quality of message behavior. The first conception views competence as a set of skills or abilities that enable repeated, goal-directed behaviors that fulfill task demands of a particular communication context. The second conception, i.e. the judgment of what constitutes a 'good' message behavior brings with it a perceptual dimension that necessarily connects the ability perspective to the subjective evaluation perspective. 'Social skills' are similarly defined as either the ability to perform various requisite behaviors in everyday interpersonal encounters, or the evaluation of the quality of performance in such encounters.

A variety of communication dispositions have revealed substantial *genetic components* in social intelligence. To the extent that social skills are genetically enabled, a set of neurological and physiological processes associated with social skills would be likely. For example, research has demonstrated connections between affectionate skills and stress hormones and conflict skill deficits and immune function. One particular development has been the discovery of 'mirror neurons' and their relationship to empathic skills. Mirror neurons are identified by the fact that the same neurons discharge signals for actions that are enacted as well as observed. This discovery suggested a capacity to decode the actions of others in the process of encoding actions by self, a fundamental component of social perception and empathy (Nagy et al., 2010). Further research has begun to examine audiovisual and communicative mirror neurons, as well as neural correlates of emotion recognition (Lee & Siegle 2012). The interpretation is that over time, from early attunement and attachment interactions throughout life, genetic capacities and opportunities for observation of social actions populate neuron coding in action contexts, and such coding facilitates attribution of intentions and social comprehension in interaction contexts.

Most approaches to interpersonal communication competence vary in the extent to which they attend to some combination of affect (motivation), cognition (knowledge), behaviors, outcomes, and evaluations (Spitzberg 2009). *Motivational approaches* tend to focus on social anxiety (→ Communication Apprehension and Social Anxiety) or goals (→ Goals, Social Aspects of). *Knowledge approaches* tend to focus on the mental processes by which communicative action is produced (→ Action Assembly Theory). *Skills approaches* tend to focus on the behavioral abilities that represent quality performance. Finally, *outcomes approaches* tend to focus on the extent to which communication fulfills or violates expectancies (→ Expectancy Violation), or the subjective dimensions by which communication quality is evaluated or achieves objective outcomes (e.g., recounts information content of a message accurately as a measure of listening).

Exemplary research on interpersonal communication competence examines its role in phenomena such as depression, loneliness, and drug abuse. Other research examines its role in the intercultural adaptation of sojourners, adapting to interpersonal or group differences, or adapting face-to-face skills to a computer-mediated context. Over 100 *measures* have been identified, and depending on the particular purpose of research, there are approximately a dozen measures available with sufficient research traditions to recommend their use. Examination of the measures of interpersonal communication competence and social skills produces a list of well over 100 potentially distinct skills attributed to competence.

There are five persistent *challenges to assessment* of interpersonal communication competence: (1) identifying the appropriate domain of skills; (2) the problem that skills exist at different levels of abstraction, at the level of molecular skills (e.g., eye contact) or more molar skills (e.g., assertiveness); (3) whether to measure competence as a trait or state; (4) identifying the most appropriate judge of interpersonal communication competence (a person evaluating self, a person judging a conversational partner, a person being evaluated by an uninvolved third party, or a person being evaluated by an expert judge); and the differentiation between objective and subjective evaluations.

Future research may show promise from advances in theory development or from application of the analysis of expert communicators in certain targeted interpersonal contexts (e.g., managers, negotiators, etc.).

See also: ▶ ACTION ASSEMBLY THEORY ▶ COMMUNICATION APPREHENSION AND SOCIAL ANXIETY ▶ COMMUNICATION SKILLS ACROSS THE LIFE-SPAN ▶ EXPECTANCY VIOLATION ▶ GOALS, SOCIAL ASPECTS OF ▶ LISTENING ▶ STUDENT COMMUNICATION COMPETENCE

REFERENCES AND SUGGESTED READINGS

Lee, K. H. & Siegle, G. J. (2012). Common and distinct brain networks underlying explicit emotional evaluation: A meta-analytic study. *Social Cognitive and Affective Neuroscience*, 7, 521–534.

Nagy, E., Liotti, M., Brown, S., Waiter, G., Bromiley, A. et al. (2010). The neural mechanisms of reciprocal communication. *Brain Research*, 1353, 159–167.

Shah, D. V., McLeod, J. M., & Lee, N. (2009). Communication competence as a foundation for civic competence: Processes of socialization into citizenship. *Political Communication*, 26(1), 102–117.

Spitzberg, B. H. (2009). Axioms for a theory of intercultural communication competence. *Annual Review of English Learning and Teaching*, 14, 69–81.

Spitzberg, B. H. & Cupach, W. R. (2011). Interpersonal skills. In M. L. Knapp & J. A. Daly (eds.), *Handbook of interpersonal communication*, 4th edn. Thousand Oaks, CA: Sage, pp. 481–524.

Interpersonal Communication, Sex and Gender Differences in

DANIEL J. CANARY
Arizona State University

BETH BABIN-GALLAGHER
Arizona State University

Sex differences refer to behavioral variations between men and women based on biological differences; gender differences refer to behavioral variations between people due to cultural, sociological, and/or psychological differences. This entry focuses on the manner in which sex differences affect interpersonal communication behavior (→ Gender and Discourse; Interpersonal Communication).

Self-disclosure refers to information about oneself that is shared with others. Much research suggests that women self-disclose more than do men to friends, parents, spouses, and strangers. For example, women self-disclose more intimately and discuss more topics than do men in their friendships, and men and women differ in their expectations for intimacy in romantic relationships. Although sex differences in self-disclosure appear to be consistent, the significance of those differences is debatable since the effect sizes reported in studies are generally small.

Relational maintenance behaviors refer to ongoing actions and activities undertaken to keep one's personal relationships as one wants them to be. Several studies have found that women use more openness and sharing tasks to maintain their close involvements than do men, and some research indicates that men are more likely to rely on positivity and assurances (Canary & Wahba 2006). Overall, however, a slight tendency exists for women to engage in maintenance actions more than do men.

In contexts of *conflict communication*, where they have familiar footing, women appear to be equally or more assertive and confronting than are men. Assertive behaviors include such tactics as attempts to discuss the problem, identifying causes for the conflict, self-disclosure, and so forth. Confronting, assertive behaviors include showing anger, blaming the partner, and putting down the partner. Men tend to engage in more avoidance tactics, including withdrawing from the situation and denying the problem. One explanation for these differences focuses on how boys and girls tend to segregate into groups in the playground, with boys involved in team sports that rely on clearly defined rules of the game and girls engaged in less structured games that focus on relational interaction in lieu of scoring points. Because, on this view, girls develop their conflict negotiation skills whereas boys do not, women tend to want to discuss relational issues and details and men prefer to avoid them. An alternative explanation is that because women are less benefited in conjugal relationships with men, women have more to complain about. A third explanation resides in how men tend to be very sensitive to their own physiological reactions to conflict and withdraw as the result of trying to retain self-control. Women, however, tend to ignore physiological reactions in their focus on attempts to solve relational problems.

Although men and women are more similar than different regarding *supportive communication* research has revealed that women are more likely than men to seek and provide emotional support (e.g., expressions of sympathy), attend to the other's feelings, and engage in more highly person-centered (HPC) comforting messages.

Performing a meta-analysis of *nonverbal behavior*, Hall (2006) found that women display more nonverbal sensitivity and smiling than do men. That is, women tend to be more capable than men at reading cognitive and affective meanings conveyed nonverbally. This effect is largely due to women's superior reading of facial expressions but not vocal or postural variations. On the other side, Andersen (2006) found that men can decipher spatial nonverbal behaviors and mapping better than women can. Social role theory proposes that the division of labor has led to differences in how men and women relate to other people. An alternative theoretic explanation derives from evolutionary theory, which posits that men's larger size required them to hunt and to battle competitors. Due to their ability to breastfeed and to their smaller size, women remained at home and took care of children as well as injured warriors, which involved learning how to ascertain the meaning of nonverbal messages.

See also: ▶ GENDER AND DISCOURSE ▶ INTERPERSONAL COMMUNICATION ▶ INTERPERSONAL CONFLICT ▶ SOCIAL EXCHANGE ▶ SOCIAL SUPPORT IN INTERPERSONAL COMMUNICATION

REFERENCES AND SUGGESTED READINGS

Canary, D. J. & Wahba, J. (2006). Do women work harder than men at maintaining relationships? In K. Dindia & D. J. Canary (eds.), *Sex differences and similarities in communication*, 2nd edn. Mahwah, NJ: Lawrence Erlbaum, pp. 359–377.

Dindia, K. & Canary, D. J. (eds.) (2006). *Sex differences and similarities in communication*, 2nd edn. Mahwah, NJ: Lawrence Erlbaum.

Hall, J. A. (2006). How big are nonverbal sex differences? The case of smiling and nonverbal sensitivity. In K. Dindia & D. J. Canary (eds.), *Sex differences and similarities in communication*, 2nd edn. Mahwah, NJ: Lawrence Erlbaum, pp. 59–82.

Reis, H. T. & Sprecher, S. (eds.). (2009). *Encyclopedia of human relationships*. Thousand Oaks, CA: Sage.

Siegman, A.W. & Feldstein, S. (2009). *Nonverbal behavior and communication*. New York: Psychology Press.

Interpersonal Conflict

WILLIAM R. CUPACH
Illinois State University

Interpersonal conflict occurs when individuals perceive their own self-interest to be incompatible with another person's interest, and the other person's actions undermine the achievement of self-interest. Such incompatibilities are commonplace in all kinds of interpersonal relationships, including those among friends, romantic partners, family members, and co-workers. The opportunities for conflict are greatest in relationships characterized by interdependency and intimate exchange, such as marriage. It is through communication that conflicts are recognized, expressed, and managed.

Numerous *sources of perceived incompatibility* can trigger interpersonal conflict. Sometimes one person's goal clashes with another's (→ Goals, Social Aspects of). Other times, parties disagree about the means to achieve a common goal, or they mistakenly perceive incompatibility due to miscommunication or lack of communication. Conflicts often emerge when behavior violates expectations (→ Expectancy Violation) or runs contrary to social or relational rules. Under such circumstances, one person perceives another's behavior as annoying, inappropriate, interfering, offensive, or otherwise dispreferred. Conflicts can also reflect broader relationship issues such as power, intimacy, privacy, respect, trust, and commitment. Conflicts about relationship issues and personality tend to be more serious and more difficult to resolve than conflicts about particular behaviors.

Occasionally the source of conflict is not about the incompatibility that is expressed. In such cases the confrontational person creates a conflict to vent latent (and perhaps subconscious) dissatisfaction unrelated to the expressed conflict. For instance, a friend may criticize a companion's behavior, but the real source of discontent is a bad mood due to a stressful day at work.

One common distinction used to characterize conflict behavior is its constructive versus destructive nature. *Constructive conflict* conveys neutral or positive affect, assumes a collaborative orientation, and tends to be relationship-preserving. Constructive conflict is reflected in behaviors that focus on problem solving, show respect, save face, share information, and validate each person's worth. *Destructive conflict*, on the other hand, conveys negative affect, assumes a competitive orientation, and tends to be relationship-undermining. Behaviors that demean, ridicule, attack, and coerce are typically destructive.

When individuals perceive a conflict, they can choose either to *confront the issue or avoid it*. People withhold their dissatisfactions when the issue is relatively trivial, when they see little hope of resolving the conflict, or when they feel that confrontation will yield irreparable damage to the relationship. Neither confrontation nor avoidance of conflict is always constructive or destructive. Effective confrontation can yield positive consequences, such as promoting desired change, finding creative solutions to problems, defusing negative arousal, and developing relational solidarity. When confrontation goes awry, it can lead to polarization, stalemate, relationship damage, and physical violence. Thus, strategic avoidance of some conflicts is necessary for interpersonal relationships to develop and be maintained. However, systematically withholding complaints is damaging to relationships when the avoided issues are important, recurring, and foster growing feelings of resentment.

The *attributions* one makes about another's conflict behaviors influence how one responds to that behavior. Individuals in distressed relationships are more likely to view their partner's conflict behavior as global rather than confined to a single issue, stable rather than fleeting, and personality-driven rather than context-driven. Moreover, they perceive their partner's conflict behavior as intentional, blameworthy, and selfishly motivated. These interpretations foster defensive, hostile, and otherwise destructive responses, which further erode relationship stability.

See also: ▶ EXPECTANCY VIOLATION ▶ GOALS, SOCIAL ASPECTS OF ▶ INTERCULTURAL CONFLICT STYLES AND FACEWORK ▶ MARITAL COMMUNICATION ▶ NEGOTIATION AND BARGAINING

REFERENCES AND SUGGESTED READINGS

Canary, D. J., Lakey, S. G., & Sillars, A. (2013). Managing conflict in a competent manner: A mindful look at events that matter. In J. G. Oetzel & S. Ting-Toomey (eds.), *The Sage handbook of conflict communication: Integrating theory, research, and practice*, 2nd edn. Thousand Oaks, CA: Sage, pp. 263–289.

Caughlin, J. P., Vangelisti, A. L., & Mikucki-Enyart, S. (2013). Conflict in dating and marital relationships. In J. G. Oetzel & S. Ting-Toomey (eds.), *The Sage handbook of conflict communication: Integrating theory, research, and practice*, 2nd edn. Thousand Oaks, CA: Sage, pp. 161–186.

Gottman, J. M. (1994). *What predicts divorce: The relationship between marital processes and marital outcomes*. Hillsdale, NJ: Lawrence Erlbaum.

Roloff, M. E. & Chiles, B. W. (2011). Interpersonal conflict: Recent trends. In M. L. Knapp & J. A. Daly (eds.), *The Sage handbook of conflict communication: Integrating theory, research, and practice*, 2nd edn. Thousand Oaks, CA: Sage, pp. 423–442.

Interpretive Journalism

BRANT HOUSTON
University of Illinois Urbana–Champaign

Interpretive journalism goes beyond the basic facts of an event or topic to provide context, analysis, and possible consequences. Interpretive journalists are expected to have expertise about a subject and to look for motives and influences that explain what they are reporting. Interpretive journalism also overlaps with other forms of reporting (→ Advocacy Journalism) in which journalists identify who committed wrong or what caused failure.

The levels of interpretation have generally risen since the beginning of the twentieth century in the US (Barnhurst & Mutz 1997; → Journalism, History of) while in Africa, Europe and Latin America interpretation has been at the forefront of reporting. For example, journalist Walter Lippmann in 1920 urged reporters to base their work on facts and analysis. Journalism professor Curtis D. MacDougall encapsulated those concepts in his 1937 textbook Interpretative Reporting (1987). Critics say interpretive journalism permits baseless comment and bias (→ Bias in the News). Yet, journalists in African countries routinely intersperse opinion in articles and in western Europe, objectivity was seldom a central professional value (Donsbach & Klett 1993; → Objectivity in Reporting; Journalists' Role Perception).

Leading journalists now say the public will need more interpretive journalism because the Internet offers complex information and unsupported opinion (→ Internet News; Citizen Journalism). But some media observers say objectivity and impartiality will become more important as journalism globalizes (→ Globalization of the Media).

See also: ▶ ADVOCACY JOURNALISM ▶ BIAS IN THE NEWS ▶ CITIZEN JOURNALISM ▶ GLOBALIZATION OF THE MEDIA ▶ INTERNET NEWS ▶ JOURNALISM, HISTORY OF ▶ JOURNALISTS, CREDIBILITY OF ▶ JOURNALISTS' ROLE PERCEPTION ▶ NARRATIVE NEWS STORY ▶ NEUTRALITY ▶ NEWS ▶ OBJECTIVITY IN REPORTING ▶ WATERGATE SCANDAL

REFERENCES AND SUGGESTED READINGS

Barnhurst, K. & Mutz, D. (1997). American journalism and the decline of event-centered reporting. *Journal of Communication*, 47(4), 27–53.

Donsbach, W. & Klett, B. (1993). Subjective objectivity: How journalists in four countries determine the key term of their profession. *Gazette*, 51, 53–83.

MacDougall, C. D. (1987). *Interpretative reporting*, 9th edn. New York: Macmillan.

Interview, Qualitative

DANIELA SCHLÜTZ
Hanover University of Music, Drama and Media

WIEBKE MÖHRING
Hanover University of Applied Sciences and Arts

In a qualitative interview, trained interviewers, often the researcher him- or herself, embark on a question and answer exchange. In contrast to quantitative interviews (→ Interview, Standardized) the interviewer asks open-ended questions and has more flexibility in adjusting the question wording to the individual respondent and the situation. At first sight, a qualitative interview resembles a common conversation. Unlike any day-to-day conversation, however, this method of collecting empirical data follows specific rules and aims at a predefined goal.

An open-ended interview can be conducted for two different reasons. It may be explorative, i.e., aiming at a first understanding of a topic and a deeper insight into the relevant dimensions. An explorative interview is only the first in a series of other, usually standardized research steps. A qualitative interview, on the other hand, is a method of inquiry in its own right. It is theoretically rooted in Mead's symbolic interactionism (Carreira da Silva 2007). The high value of open-ended interviews lies in the fact that respondents reveal their individual understanding of the topic in question in the context of and from their social position. Qualitative interviewing cannot and does not seek to produce statistical evidence but provides an insight in individual sense-making processes.

Qualitative interviews can be conducted individually or in a group situation. *Individual interviews* can be differentiated by two dimensions: their degree of standardization (open vs. semi-structured) on the one hand and the kind of knowledge they elicit (narrative-episodic vs. semantic-analytic) on the other hand. More structured types make use of an interview guideline with pre-selected dimensions (but without strict order or specific wording). Completely open-ended interviews (also called in-depth interviews) reconstruct social events as first-hand experience via storytelling. The underlying notion is that stories are less influenced by ex post rationalizations.

Group interviews (or 'focus groups') bring together a group of subjects to discuss an issue in the presence of a moderator. He or she stimulates a dialogue, ensures that the topic of discussion stays in focus while eliciting a wide range of opinions. It is important to note that a group interview is not just an easy way to obtain a range of opinions from different people at the same time in order to speed up social research. Group dynamics will interfere with every single opinion. Group interviews should, therefore, only be conducted if the research topic in question is linked to social interaction (like notions of → public opinion).

Two *basic approaches* can be distinguished. Focus groups are used to generate hypotheses and research questions in a group situation by utilizing a focus to concentrate the respondents' attention on a particular subject. They allow for identifying the salient dimensions of a complex topic to complement further quantitative research (explorative approach). The group discussion approach, on the other hand, is based on the notion that meaning is created socially. The interactive nature of a group discussion makes this process both visible and understandable. The groups are representatives of real social entities such as classes and thus share common interpretative codes that are disclosed within the discussions.

The interviews, be they individual or group discussions, are audio- or video-taped in an unobtrusive way and later transcribed. The *transcripts* are analyzed manually or, more frequently, by using qualitative data analysis (QDA) software. The aim is to reduce complexity and to expose underlying structures. Two basic ways of analyzing can be distinguished: theoretical and thematic coding (→ Content Analysis, Qualitative). The latter uses a priori categories; the former works on the material at hand for building categories ('open coding;' Glaser & Strauss, 1967; → Grounded Theory). In both cases, the guiding principle is the interaction between the material and the (emerging) theory (hermeneutic circle). The main focus varies between interpretative sensitivity and systematic coding.

Qualitative studies usually search for the special or the typical rather than the general, they seek to generate variance instead of explaining it. Therefore, sampling does not strive for representativeness. More relevant sampling criteria are typicality and accessibility. Two sampling methods are used in qualitative studies: classic and theoretical sampling. The former applies an a priori matrix based on specific characteristics to choose the subjects. The latter evolves during the research progress based on the collected findings and their theoretical saturation.

See also: ▶ CONTENT ANALYSIS, QUALITATIVE
▶ GROUNDED THEORY ▶ INTERVIEW, STANDARDIZED ▶ PUBLIC OPINION
▶ QUALITATIVE METHODOLOGY

REFERENCES AND SUGGESTED READINGS

Carreira da Silva, F. (2007). *G. H. Mead: A critical introduction*. Cambridge: Polity Press.
Denzin, N. K. & Lincoln, Y. S. (eds.) (2000). *Handbook of qualitative research*, 2nd edn. Thousand Oaks, CA: Sage.
Denzin, N. K. & Lincoln, Y. S. (eds.) (2011). *Handbook of qualitative research*, 4th edn. Thousand Oaks, CA: Sage.
Flick, U. (2009). *An introduction to qualitative research*, 4th edn. Thousand Oaks, CA: Sage.
Glaser, B. G. & Strauss, A. (1967). *The discovery of grounded theory. Strategies for qualitative research*. Chicago, IL: Aldine.
Merton, R. K. (1987). The focussed interview and focus groups: Continuities and discontinuities. *Public Opinion Quarterly*, 51, 550–566.

Interview, Standardized

WIEBKE MÖHRING
Hanover University of Applied Sciences and Arts

DANIELA SCHLÜTZ
Hanover University of Music, Drama and Media

Quantitative surveys usually comprise standardized interviews conducted by using a questionnaire. The term 'standardization' reflects the pre-determination of the course of the interview. In a fully standardized questionnaire each respondent is presented with the same stimulus, i.e., an identical question wording. Therefore, the response (i.e., the answer) is, in theory, statistically comparable to that of another respondent which allows for generalization. Furthermore, the sequence of the questions is exactly specified and the social situation should be constant in every interview.

Standardization aims at the comparability of results as an important prerequisite for generalization and *representativeness* of the whole → survey. Apart from using a specific sampling technique, this is achieved by a high degree of standardization and by complying with specific criteria regarding selection, training, and control of the interviewers. In media and communication research, quantitative interviews are frequently employed because researchers strive for representative results, e.g. in audience research or studies of → public opinion.

There are several methods of conduct or 'modes'. Quantitative interviews can be conducted orally, either in person (face-to-face interview) or via telephone. They can also be carried out in writing (self-administered questionnaire). All three forms may be supported by use of the computer. The interview situation will change significantly according to the applied mode.

In standardized interviews the *interviewer* has a different role than in qualitative interviews (→ Interview, Qualitative). Their task is to set the stimulus interviewers in an invariant way without knowing too much about the purpose of the study. The question then directly activates a multi-level *cognitive process* consisting of at least five steps (Schwarz & Oyserman 2001, 129). The interviewee has to (1) understand the question, (2) recall the relevant behavior, (3) make inferences and estimations concerning this behavior, (4) adapt his or her answer to fit the response format, and (5) edit the answer for reasons of social desirability. This process implies that respondents are able and willing to report their behavior properly.

A quantitative survey is normally based on a particular research question. The relevant theoretical constructs are translated into appropriate indicators which then become the content of respective questions (→ *Operationalization*). The final version of the questionnaire is subject to a pre-test and afterwards submitted to the selected sample. Subsequently, the data are transferred into a data processing program and statistically analyzed.

Each of these steps is prone to *possible error* and has to be conducted meticulously to guarantee methodological quality. The operationalization of the research question, i.e. the wording of the questionnaire, is a particularly important step. First, this requires the pre-definition of the indicators that have to be collected. Second, they have to be phrased in a wording comprehensible to all respondents. In a good questionnaire, the researcher's frame of reference is transferred into questions that are adequate to the respondents' frame of reference. In methodological research, this aspect is the subject of many studies because the survey's → reliability and → validity depend on the quality of the questions and the respondents' understanding of them. Thus, survey questions have to be clear and concrete, explicit, and nonsuggestive.

Generally, there are two *types of questions*: open-ended (without alternative answers) and closed ones (including all alternative answers). Because research has shown that open-ended questions are more prone to error (due to different memory and verbalization capabilities on the side of the respondent) closed questions are mostly used in standardized interviews. Closed questions enable the researcher to compare respondents as the answers define the frame of reference. These categories guide the respondents more strongly and constrain them at the same time. Therefore, they are regarded as more valid and reliable than open-ended questions. There are various forms of closed questions. They may be simple alternative questions, multi-choice questions with a range of possible answers, ranking scales to measure order, or rating scales to measure intensity. The scale types can be classified as nominal, ordinal, or interval according to the data level they produce.

See also: ▶ ELECTION SURVEYS ▶ INTERVIEW, QUALITATIVE ▶ OPERATIONALIZATION ▶ PUBLIC OPINION ▶ PUBLIC OPINION POLLING ▶ RELIABILITY ▶ SURVEY ▶ VALIDITY

REFERENCES AND SUGGESTED READINGS

Bradburn, N., Sudman, S., & Wansink, B. (2004). *Asking questions: the definitive guide to questionnaire design.* San Francisco, CA: Jossey-Bass.

Möhring, W. & Schlütz, D. (2010). *Die Befragung in der Kommunikationswissenschaft* [Standardized interviewing in communication research]. Wiesbaden: VS.

Schwarz, N. & Oyserman, D. (2001). Asking questions about behavior: Cognition, communication, and questionnaire construction. *American Journal of Evaluation*, 22, 127–160.

Sudman, S., Bradburn, N. M., & Schwarz, N. (1996). *Thinking about answers: The application of cognitive processes to survey methodology.* San Francisco, CA: Jossey-Bass.

Involvement with Media Content

WERNER WIRTH
University of Zurich

In modern communication research, involvement is included in numerous theories and empirical studies of → information processing, → persuasion, → advertising, knowledge acquisition, and other → media effects. It is mainly linked with or defined as more elaborative, self-determined, active, and in-depth processing of media content. However, conceptualizations of involvement are multifaceted. In general, one can distinguish between a broader and a more confined concept of involvement.

Involvement as a meta-concept or a general research perspective encompasses a family of related though distinct concepts that inform us of how users are occupied with the media and their content in diverse ways, and how they engage with them in a cognitive, affective, conative, and motivational way (Salmon 1986). These concepts include cognitive responses, felt emotions, attention, recall, → information seeking, and discussions about a topic. More confined, a process-oriented definition of involvement directly refers to the phase of media usage and encompasses the intensity of an individual's cognitive, emotional, or conative engagement with the media message (Cameron 1983, Wirth, 2006).

In origin, involvement is rooted in *three major research traditions*. (1) Within the social judgment theory, ego-involvement is the relatedness of an issue to a person's self-picture and self-identity (Salmon 1986). In contrast, task-involvement results from the experimental manipulation performed by the researcher (→ Experiment, Laboratory). (2) In the framework of the dual process theories on persuasion, involvement is conceptualized as personal relevance of an issue (→ Elaboration Likelihood Model). (3) In (early) consumer research, involvement is conceptualized as conscious bridging experiences between the life of a media user and a media stimulus.

Audience and effects research sometimes differentiates between the often high-involved usage of print media and the frequently low-involved usage of electronic media (→ Exposure to Radio; Exposure to Television). Alternatively, within the → Uses-and-Gratifications approach, involvement is part of the concept of audience activity. Further, we can distinguish between different references or 'targets of involvement' (e.g. the message, a product, a protagonist), long-term/persistent versus short-term/situational involvement, the 'components of involvement' (cognitive, affective, conative/motivational), the 'valence of involvement' (negative versus positive), and the 'intensity of involvement' (Salmon, 1986; Wirth 2006).

See also: ▶ ADVERTISING ▶ ELABORATION LIKELIHOOD MODEL ▶ EXPERIMENTAL DESIGN ▶ EXPERIMENT; LABORATORY ▶ EXPOSURE TO COMMUNICATION CONTENT ▶ EXPOSURE TO RADIO ▶ EXPOSURE TO TELEVISION ▶ INFORMATION PROCESSING ▶ INFORMATION SEEKING ▶ MEDIA EFFECTS ▶ PARASOCIAL INTERACTIONS AND RELATIONSHIPS ▶ PERSUASION ▶ SOCIAL IDENTITY THEORY ▶ USES AND GRATIFICATIONS

REFERENCES AND SUGGESTED READINGS

Cameron, G. L. (1993). Spreading activation and involvement: An experimental test of a cognitive model of involvement. *Journalism Quarterly*, 70, 854–867.

Salmon, C. T. (1986). Perspectives on involvement in consumer and communication research. In B. Dervin & M. J. Voigt (eds.), *Progress in communication sciences*. Beverly Hills, CA: Sage, pp. 243–268.

Wirth, W. (2006). Involvement. In J. Bryant & P. Vorderer (eds.), *Psychology of entertainment*. Mahwah, NJ: Lawrence Erlbaum, pp. 199–213.

Issue Management

ULRIKE RÖTTGER
University of Münster

Issue management is a systematic procedure that helps organizations to identify, analyze, and respond to external or internal concerns that can significantly affect them. On this note, strategic issues management is a managerial function, which creates the information bases for a proactive examination of (potentially) critical themes that can limit strategic scope (→ Strategic Communication). It has to be accentuated that issues management does not solely relate to the effects of a crisis or a conflict. It also considers the positive and negative repercussions concerning promotional themes in regard to a → brand or a company image.

Issues are debatable topics of public interest that are connected with controversial opinions, expectations, or problem solutions by an organization and its stakeholders. Issues have actual or potential effects on the organization. An issue is an immediate problem requiring a solution (Heath 2006, 82–83; → Crisis Communication).

There is a wide variety of models for the issues management process mostly differentiating between five or six *key stages* (see in particular Chase 1984; Dutton & Jackson 1987). *Issue identification*: It is important to observe the environment systematically, continually, and comprehensively, in order to identify weak signals that point to a conflict topic or a chance as early as possible. Scanning is the inductive observation of the environment. In a second step, potential issues as well as known issues are observed more closely (monitoring).

Analysis and interpretation: Issues must be prioritized with respect to their relevance, exigency, and consideration of the amount of resources dedicated to deal with the issues. Furthermore, the future trend of the issue will be forecast on the basis of its current and past development.

Selection and prioritizing of key issues: The organization must develop action decisions and issue positions to its key issues. The key issues need to be further researched and observed. *Development of the strategy and program implementation*: The results of the analysis are the basis for the development of the strategy which can be reactive, adaptive, proactive, initiative, and interactive. *Program evaluation*: The evaluation of the output and outcome is a great challenge, since successful issues management shows up finally in the fact that an issue is not escalated or has not become public.

See also: ▶ CRISIS COMMUNICATION ▶ ISSUES MANAGEMENT IN POLITICS ▶ ORGANIZATIONAL COMMUNICATION ▶ PUBLIC RELATIONS ▶ STRATEGIC COMMUNICATION

REFERENCES AND SUGGESTED READINGS

Chase, W. H. (1984). *Issue management: Origins of the future*. Stamford, CT: Issue Action.

Dutton, J. E. & Jackson, S. E. (1987). Categorizing strategic issues: Links to organizational action. *Academy of Management Review*, 12, 76–90.

Heath, R. L. (2006). A rhetorical theory approach to issues management. In C. H. Botan & V. Hazleton (eds.), *Public relations theory II*. Mahwah, NJ: Lawrence Erlbaum, pp. 63–99.

Issue Management in Politics

SPIRO KIOUSIS
University of Florida

Issue management in politics refers to the process by which politicians, campaigns, parties, and other political groups identify, prioritize, develop, and convey positions on key issues (→ Issue Management). A step in effective political issue management involves formative and evaluative research where groups investigate the perceptions, attitudes, and behaviors of target audiences concerning policy preferences and problems.

From a theoretical standpoint, the concepts of → agenda building and agenda setting (→ Agenda-Setting Effects) are germane for understanding the process of political issue management. The core proposition of agenda-setting theory is that the issues made salient in news media often become the issues that are considered important in public opinion (McCombs & Shaw 1972). Agenda building suggests that issue salience is determined by several groups in addition to media and voters, such as politicians, organizations, and activists, and involves reciprocal influence. Thus, an integral part of successful issue management entails developing strategies for dealing with these diverse sets of stakeholders and constituencies.

A vital factor impacting the issue-management process involves meaningfully classifying different types of issues, including obtrusive vs. unobtrusive issues and concrete vs. abstract issues. The tone and frames associated with issues are also relevant for issue-management purposes (→ Framing Effects). The use of information subsidies by political groups or organizations to exert influence on news media, voters, and other stakeholders represents a pervasive approach for effective issue management (news releases, interviews, political advertising, social media messages (→ Facebook; Twitter), 'op-ed pieces').

Much of the scholarly and applied interest in political issue management is based on the premise that issue perceptions and opinions sway elections. The concept of priming provides insight into how this influence transpires (→ Priming Theory). As a consequence, political campaigns and groups aim to influence the news media agenda by highlighting issues with which their organizations or candidates perform well. Issue-ownership theory indicates that certain political parties are thought to handle some issues more competently than other parties.

See also: ▶ AGENDA BUILDING
▶ AGENDA-SETTING EFFECTS ▶ ELECTION CAMPAIGN COMMUNICATION ▶ FACEBOOK
▶ FRAMING EFFECTS ▶ ISSUE MANAGEMENT
▶ MEDIA EVENTS AND PSEUDO-EVENTS
▶ POLITICAL ADVERTISING ▶ POLITICAL COMMUNICATION ▶ PRIMING THEORY
▶ TWITTER

REFERENCES AND SUGGESTED READINGS

Kiousis, S., Mitrook, M., Wu, X., & Seltzer, T. (2006). First- and second-level agenda-building and agenda-setting effects: Exploring the linkages among candidate news releases, media coverage, and public opinion during the 2002 Florida gubernatorial election. *Journal of Public Relations Research*, 18, 265–285.

McCombs, M. E. & Shaw, D. L. (1972). Agenda-setting function of mass media. *Public Opinion Quarterly*, 36, 176–184.

Japan: Media System

YASUHIRO INOUE
Hiroshima City University

YOUICHI ITO
Akita International University

Japan is unique in terms of its media structure. Most major newspaper companies in Japan hold their shares internally. Japan's corporate law allows this internal stock holding in order to prevent external editorial influence and acquisition. Partly because of this, no large media conglomerates are owned primarily by non-media corporations, unlike the case in other industrialized countries (→ Concentration in Media Systems; Media Conglomerates). Another reason for the difficulty in taking over any Japanese media company is that there exist several media 'keiretsu' or groups that are closely intertwined in terms of both stock holdings and personal relationships.

The key actors in the keiretsu are the five *national newspapers*, each of which has close financial and personal ties to one of the five commercial television networks. Regional and local newspapers also own one of the regional and local television stations in their circulation areas. About 70 million copies are published each day by 108 newspaper companies in Japan, which is second to China (96 million, → China: Media System). In terms of per-capita circulation, Japan ranks the highest in the world (633 copies per thousand): more than twice that of the US (→ United States of America: Media System) and six times that of China.

General newspapers in Japan can be categorized into three kinds: national, regional (called 'block'), and local. There are five nationals (the Yomiuri Shimbun, the Asahi Shimbun, the Mainichi Shimbun, the Nihon Keizai Shimbun, and the Sankei Shimbun). Each has a circulation of more than 2 million and is regarded as a 'quality paper.' The Yomiuri publishes 10 million morning and 4 million evening papers. The second largest, the Asahi, publishes a total of 12 million copies a day. The Nihon Keizai (Nikkei), which publishes 4.5 million copies daily, has the largest circulation of any economics paper in the world. Most newspapers, including blocks and local newspapers, publish morning and evening editions, which is one of the particular characteristics of Japanese newspapers. Another characteristic is a heavy reliance on a home-delivery system. In total, 94 percent of all general newspapers are delivered to homes every day by exclusive distributors. Four national newspapers (all but Nikkei)

The Concise Encyclopedia of Communication, First Edition. Edited by Wolfgang Donsbach.
© 2015 John Wiley & Sons, Inc. Published 2015 by John Wiley & Sons, Inc.

and all three block newspapers publish sports newspapers, which are sports- and entertainment-oriented and fall into the category of tabloid press. Nikkei, in turn, publishes three trade papers. All the nationals have publishing divisions and issue weekly or monthly magazines as well as books. In addition, the Yomiuri and the Asahi own two of the top ten advertising agencies in Japan.

Television service is provided by a dual broadcasting system consisting of the public broadcasting corporation and commercial broadcasters. The public television service Nihon Hoso Kyokai (NHK) is the second largest broadcasting corporation in the world after the → BBC (→ Public Broadcasting Systems). Supported by viewers' fees, NHK broadcasts two channels nationwide through a network of 54 stations. It also conducts satellite broadcasting with two channels. Although NHK is not state-run, its annual budget and executive personnel proposals must be approved by the Diet, the Japanese parliament. The five commercial broadcasters based in Tokyo, who are all affiliated with major national newspapers, are Nihon TV (NTV, affiliated with the Yomiuri), TV Asahi (affiliated with the Asahi), Tokyo Broadcasting Systems (TBS, affiliated with the Mainichi), Fuji TV (affiliated with the Sankei), and TV Tokyo (affiliated with the Nikkei). These broadcasters are network stations (key stations) affiliated with regional and local stations. The key stations provide their affiliated stations not only with news, but also with programs that account for 80 to 90 percent of local broadcasting time.

In terms of *online news media*, Japan's mainstream media are reluctant to be fully committed to Internet service. Major newspapers and NHK have started and keep developing their own news sites. But the information provided on their websites is very limited, both in terms of amount and in terms of depth, because they are not sure whether they can maintain their existing business scale by switching from paper subscription to web subscription.

Major national newspapers and television networks are relatively homogeneous in agendas, or news items (in straight news), but diverse in opinions (in editorials). The contents of major national newspapers and television networks tend to be similar because of the organizations' deep commitment to impartiality and neutrality stipulated in their code of ethics. One of the reasons for so much conformity in the news agenda has to do with the 'kisha' (reporters) club system, which is unique to the Japanese news media industry. Kisha clubs are attached to nearly every government office and major organization all over Japan. Until the mid-1990s, foreign-media reporters were not allowed to join most major clubs, and Japanese magazine reporters and freelance journalists are still generally excluded.

See also: ▶ BBC ▶ CHINA: MEDIA SYSTEM ▶ CONCENTRATION IN MEDIA SYSTEMS ▶ MEDIA CONGLOMERATES ▶ NEUTRALITY ▶ NEWS ROUTINES ▶ OBJECTIVITY IN REPORTING ▶ PUBLIC BROADCASTING SYSTEMS ▶ UNITED STATES OF AMERICA: MEDIA SYSTEM

REFERENCES AND SUGGESTED READINGS

Inoue, Y. (2004). Media literasi [*Media literacy*]. Tokyo: Nihon Hyoron Sha.

Ito, Y. (2006). Some trends in communication research and education in Japan. In K. W. Y. Leung, J. Kenny, & P. S. N. Lee (eds.), *Global trends in communication education and research*. Cresskill, NJ: Hampton Press, pp. 115–131.

Pharr, S. J. & Krauss, E. S. (eds.) (1996). Media and politics in Japan. Honolulu, HI: University of Hawaii Press.

Journalism

KEVIN G. BARNHURST
University of Leeds

JAMES OWENS
University of Illinois at Chicago

Journalism is a constellation of practices that have acquired special status within the larger domain of communication through a long history that separated out news sharing from its origins in → interpersonal communication. Telling others about events in one's social and physical surroundings is a common, everyday activity in human cultures, and news as a genre of the interactions has the primary characteristic of being new to the listener. A main difficulty for sharing intelligence is ascertaining truth, or, put the other way round, distinguishing intelligence from gossip (→ Truth and Media Content). Telling about events, supplying novelty, and discerning factual truth from the process are the main rudiments that came to define journalism as a cultural practice.

History

Journalism is a modern-era phenomenon (→ Journalism, History of) that began its *separation from ordinary communication* first with correspondence in the form of newsletters sent out in multiple copies to existing social networks (→ Media Content and Social Networks).

Newsletter authors also required some facility to produce more than one copy and to distribute the result, as well as sufficient social status to make their activity appear to have value for recipients. With the advent of the printing press some early newssheets imitated hand-made newsletters, but the primary model for all printing was the book as printer-editors incorporated the sharing of new intelligences into their line of business.

The main claim to distinction for journalism has come through a close alliance with political life. Politics impinged on printing from the beginning in the form of government controls, and printing itself quickly became a political act of either cooperation with or defiance of the powerful, or the state. Journalism developed at the nexus of negotiating boundaries to demarcate private life, civil society (or the market), and the state from each other, and in some perspectives that zone became a special or sacred space (→ Privacy; Public Sphere). It was a short step then for the emerging press to become enmeshed in politics, an alliance of two initially and perhaps continually unsavory activities, an irony often lost on practitioners and scholars. The nineteenth century turned newspapers into the central node of news as an economic activity.

Differentiation among Journalists

Although fiction writing occasionally imitates news, journalism differs fundamentally in practice.

Separating the occupation of journalist from author is one marker of a project under way by the early twentieth century to make journalism into a particular kind of profession (→ Professionalization of Journalism). Other markers include the emergence of acceptable practices, training programs, associations, and codes of ethics (→ Ethics in Journalism). In many parts of the world, journalism remained part of and firmly aligned with literary work, and even in nations where the professional project predominated, such as the United States, movements of long-form and literary journalism arose.

From its birth in the industrialized newsroom, journalism developed customary patterns for all aspects of work (→ News Routines). The best-known example is the 'beat,' combining location and process so that a reporter goes through a set of routines to gather information from predictable and reliable places. As an occupational category, journalism in the nineteenth century merged several tasks: principally those of the 'editor,' who managed some aspect of content from a central office, the 'correspondent,' who ventured out as a worldly traveler and (perhaps imperial) observer of affairs, and various forms of 'news hound,' who did piecework as local scavengers to fill the editorial hole by the inch, pursuing a particular topic or venue such as crime or the docks. As journalism emerged as a professional project, *specialization* produced new bundles of tasks.

The production of news content has become more portable across traditional print and broadcast media as the tasks journalists perform *converge on digital technology* (→ Cross-Media Production). The changes might point to multimedia journalism or instead to a de-skilling of practice as the tools shift from professionals' into others' hands. In many countries, citizens can now tell each other their own news by writing and distributing it electronically from home, a community center, library, or mobile device (→ Citizen Journalism). During political crises in Africa and the Arab uprisings of 2011, citizen journalists appear to have contributed to movements against established political power.

Scholarly Study and Prospects

Alignments between industry and the academy for the purposes of job training helped shape journalism research (→ Journalism Education). The first university journalism programs grew from the organized efforts of publishers and press associations to harness academic work to the project of making journalism respectable.

By the late 1940s, social science became the dominant paradigm for academic inquiry into journalism, organized generally around the concept of 'mass communication.' Humanities approaches fell behind, and studies employing quantitative methodology published in the journal of news media research, Journalism Quarterly, rose from 10 to 48 percent between 1937 and 1957. Earlier paradigms treated journalism as a powerful force in defining social problems, propagating government ideas, and fomenting public support, but the functionalist thinking among scholars at mid-century saw journalism as limited in its effects (→ Media Effects).

By the 1960s intellectual currents such as → semiotics influenced thinking about journalism. Social scientists studied journalists' autonomy from surrounding forces. By the 1970s fault lines emerged in the dominant social scientific paradigm after research found that greater effects could occur among distinct social groups than among general audiences, and that journalism had influence in setting priorities among political elites (→ Agenda-Setting Effects). In Britain → cultural studies scholars analyzed journalism texts, and social critics described how capitalist ownership and shared values among media professionals helped support class domination. US sociologists examined news and conducted fieldwork among journalists.

In the early 1980s the communication discipline underwent a period of ferment, and journalism study moved along new vectors. Particularly in relation to political life, → framing effects developed as a research approach (→ Framing of the News). Under the emerging conditions of postmodernism, attention to news was declining among youth, and journalism as a professional project entered a conscious period of crisis (→ Postmodernism and Communication). Industrial changes liberalized state-controlled media in some countries; cable, talk radio, and other alternatives to traditional news outlets proliferated in countries with commercial systems; and new populist media arose as tabloid journalism spread globally. Scholars of journalism engaged in *political and economic critiques* that examined the relationship of media organizations to centers of social control.

The 'new journalism studies' incorporated concepts of narrative, myth, ideology, and hegemony and engaged in professional critique, political and economic analysis, and sociological observation. The paradigm took institutional form in anthologies, new journals, and in the creation and rapid growth of a Journalism Studies Division in the → International Communication Association (ICA).

See also: ▶ ADVOCACY JOURNALISM ▶ AGENDA-SETTING EFFECTS ▶ ALTERNATIVE JOURNALISM ▶ BROADCAST JOURNALISM ▶ CENSORSHIP ▶ CITIZEN JOURNALISM ▶ COMMUNICATION AS A FIELD AND DISCIPLINE ▶ CROSS-MEDIA PRODUCTION ▶ CULTURAL STUDIES ▶ ETHICS IN JOURNALISM ▶ ETHNIC JOURNALISM ▶ FEMINIST MEDIA ▶ FRAMING EFFECTS ▶ FRAMING OF THE NEWS ▶ GENDER AND JOURNALISM ▶ INTERNATIONAL COMMUNICATION ASSOCIATION (ICA) ▶ INTERPERSONAL COMMUNICATION ▶ JOURNALISM EDUCATION ▶ JOURNALISM, HISTORY OF ▶ JOURNALISTS, CREDIBILITY OF ▶ JOURNALISTS' ROLE PERCEPTION ▶ MEDIA CONTENT AND SOCIAL NETWORKS ▶ MEDIA ECONOMICS ▶ MEDIA EFFECTS ▶ NARRATIVE NEWS STORY ▶ NEWS CYCLES ▶ NEWS IDEOLOGIES ▶ NEWS ROUTINES ▶ NEWS SOURCES ▶ NEWS STORY ▶ NEWS VALUES ▶ OBJECTIVITY IN REPORTING ▶ ONLINE JOURNALISM ▶ PHOTOJOURNALISM ▶ POLITICAL ECONOMY OF THE MEDIA ▶ POLITICAL JOURNALISTS ▶ POSTMODERNISM AND COMMUNICATION ▶ PRIVACY ▶ PROFESSIONALIZATION OF JOURNALISM ▶ PROPAGANDA ▶ PUBLIC SPHERE ▶ SCIENCE JOURNALISM ▶ SEMIOTICS ▶ SENSATIONALISM ▶ STANDARDS OF NEWS ▶ TRUTH AND MEDIA CONTENT ▶ VIOLENCE AGAINST JOURNALISTS ▶ VIOLENCE AS MEDIA CONTENT ▶ VISUAL COMMUNICATION

REFERENCES AND SUGGESTED READINGS

Allan, S. (ed.) (2010). *The Routledge companion to news and journalism*. London: Routledge. Anderson, P. J., Williams, M., & Ogola, G. (2013). *The future of quality news journalism. A cross-continental analysis.* London: Routledge.

Aouragh, M. & Alexander, A. (2011). The Egyptian experience: Sense and nonsense of the internet revolution, *International Journal of Communication*, 5, 1344–1358.

Barnhurst, K. G. (2011). The problem of modern time in American journalism. *KronoScope*, 11(1–2), 98–123.

Barnhurst, K. G. & Nerone, J. (2001). *The form of news: A history*. New York: Guilford.

Chouliaraki, L. (2013). Re-mediation, inter-mediation, trans-mediation: The cosmopolitan trajectories of convergent journalism. *Journalism Studies*, 14(2), 267–283.

Deuze, M. (2010). Journalism and convergence culture. In S. Allan (ed.), *The Routledge companion to news and journalism*. London: Routledge, pp. 267–276.

Donsbach, W. (2010). Journalists and their professional identities. In S. Allan (ed), *The Routledge companion to news and journalism*. London: Routledge, pp. 38–48.

Etling, B., Kelly, J., Faris, R., & Palfrey, J. (2010). Mapping the Arabic blogosphere: Politics and dissent online. *New Media and Society*, 12(8), 1225–1243.

Franklin, B. & Mensing, D. (eds.) (2011). *Journalism education, training and employment*. London: Routledge.

Lewis, Seth C. (2012). The tension between professional control and open participation: Journalism and its boundaries. *Information, Communication & Society*, 15(6), 836–866.

Vujnovic, M., Singer, J. B., Paulussen, S., Heinonen, A., Reich, Z., Quandt, T., Hermida, A., & Domingo, D. (2010). Exploring the political-economic factors of participatory journalism: Views of online journalists in 10 countries. *Journalism Practice*, 4, 285–296.

Zelizer, B. (2004). *Taking journalism seriously*. Thousand Oaks, CA: Sage.

Journalism Education

LEE B. BECKER
University of Georgia

Journalism education historically has been instruction for work in the news departments of media organizations, both print and electronic. Journalistic instruction can take place before journalists enter the workforce, during early employment, and at later career stages. It can involve practical training in the skills of the journalist and broader education about the context of that work (→ Professionalization of Journalism). The training can cover skills in reporting (information gathering and evaluation), writing (language use and storytelling techniques, including photography, videography, and graphics), and editing (including story presentation and integration into the news format). Education about the context of journalism can include topics such as the social setting and impact of news, journalism history and law, and news ethics.

Education for entry-level journalism has followed *three main traditions*. The earliest journalists learned their skills *on the job*, usually beside a journeyman. That tradition has persisted until now, most notably in the United Kingdom. A tradition usually associated with the US centers on *university instruction* before entering the workforce. A tradition associated with continental Europe houses journalism instruction in *training institutions* other than the university and separate from the industry. Variants of these traditions exist in nearly every country even today.

Proponents view journalism education as important because it gives journalists skills and values that affect what they do, e.g., expertise to be better gatherers and interpreters of information, and writing and video-shooting skills to fashion better reports, which audiences will more likely attend to and understand. The outcome should be a better-informed citizenry. Although the evidence for that assumption is largely anecdotal, news media companies support it in their habits. Larger organizations employ specialized journalists to cover medicine, transportation, legal affairs, defense, and the like, because they believe that specialized knowledge, acquired through training or on the job, makes for better reporters and editors, to the benefit of citizens.

The organizations that employ the graduates believe that journalism training supplies more productive members of the workforce. A journalist who knows which sources to approach, how to conduct an interview, how to write in news style (→ News), and how to work under deadlines will likely produce the news product quickly and cost-effectively. A journalist trained in libel and other legal constraints on news will likely help the employing organization avoid legal problems. From education, the employer gets a type of certification of a journalist's basic skills.

Journalism education can be used as a means of *political control*. In eastern European countries under communism, for example, journalists generally could not hold the top news leadership positions unless they had trained at one of a few university journalism programs. The training guaranteed that journalists followed the techniques and values of the state information system. The values of the host society always influence journalism, and journalism education is necessarily one means to exert social control over journalism practice.

Post-employment training for working journalists has become common in many countries. In some countries, union contracts guarantee training opportunities for journalists. As part of media assistance, donor countries around the world commonly include training for working journalists. The employer, an educational institution, or an independent organization may offer mid-career training. The programs, running from a few hours to several months of intensive study, may take place at work or at another institution. Specialized journalism training organizations offer some programs, and universities offer others, as extensions of existing journalism curricula. Programs may focus on specific skills, such as software use or government databases, or on general knowledge, such as health research methods. Web resources increasingly supplement the programs, and some training takes place exclusively online. Working journalists may know about and regard the programs highly, but little systematic information exists about the effectiveness of the training. Promoters say that participants have more motivation and advance in their careers. Sharing experiences may improve individual performance and journalism in general. Research does suggest that long programs give journalists a respite, a time to gain new enthusiasm for work and for subsequent stages of their careers.

The competencies of journalists, acquired through education before and after employment, may affect the news construction process, but research has not yet documented to what extent. More important, research has not examined how variants in journalism education affect news work. Do university- and industry-based programs produce reporters with different value systems? Do journalists educated in the humanities produce a different version of news than those educated in the social science tradition?

See also: ▶ BROADCAST JOURNALISM ▶ NEWS ▶ PROFESSIONALIZATION OF JOURNALISM ▶ STANDARDS OF NEWS

REFERENCES AND SUGGESTED READINGS

Becker, L. B., Vlad, T., & Kalpen, K. (2012). 2011 Annual survey of journalism and mass communication enrollments. *Journalism & Mass Communication Educator*, 67(4), 333–361.

Donsbach, W. (2013). Journalism as the new knowledge profession and consequences for journalism education. *Journalism*, 15(6), 661–677.

Josephi, B. (ed.) (2010). *Journalism education in countries with limited media freedom*. New York: Peter Lang.

Journalism, History of

JOHN NERONE
University of Illinois at Urbana–Champaign

The history of → journalism, inclusively defined, encompasses the history of news and news media, including, among other things, the history of print, broadcast, and computer technology; of news work, news routines, and news workers; and of news organizations, including newspapers and other media outlets as well as wire services and feature syndicates. Defined more narrowly, the history of journalism refers to the emergence of a set of values and explanations that discipline, regulate, and justify news practices. Journalisms are socially constructed, and appear in different guises at different times in different national cultures in reference to different media.

Journalism as Historical Construct

Commentators began to apply the term 'journalism' to some of the content of newspapers in the early nineteenth century. By the end of the century, journalism came to refer to a specific kind of reportage in the modern west. The word 'journalist' appears first describing the opinionated, politicized newspaper writers of post-revolutionary France. The word then appeared in English news reports but continued to refer to French essayists. It was subsequently applied to English and US essayists, but continued to refer to opinion writing until the second half of the century. Then it began to be applied to news-gathering practices, which were becoming increasingly routinized (→ Newspaper, History of; News Routines).

Early newspapers responded to religious and economic concerns. Most governments, anxious to keep public affairs out of the hands of ordinary people, created systems of censorship and tried to suppress political news (→ Censorship; Censorship, History of). But practicalities made this difficult. Recurring periods of intra-elite conflict produced breakdowns in censorship systems.

As censorship systems failed, the various nations of western Europe and North America developed what Jürgen Habermas (1989) has described as a bourgeois → public sphere. In this formulation, such a public sphere appeared as a space between civil society and the state and worked both as a buffer zone, preventing state interference in private life, and as a steering mechanism, allowing citizens to deliberate in an uncoerced manner to form → public opinion. The newspaper became a key part of a system for representing public opinion. Shortly into the nineteenth century, a frankly partisan model of newspaper politics prevailed in western Europe and North America. It was this style of newspapering that occasioned the first use of the word 'journalism.'

International Patterns

Journalism seems to have a shared history in the modern west. In most national histories, there was first a transition from opinion to factual observation, followed by a split between correspondence and reporting, followed by the emergence of a professional journalism centered on objective expert reportage (→ Objectivity in Reporting). And, in most countries, this history was complicated by the emergence of pictorial journalism (→ Photojournalism), followed by broadcasting. What distinguishes these national histories, however, is the different experiences with censorship and other forms of media regulation, as well as the differing states of political development. In the late nineteenth and the twentieth centuries, the west exported its models of journalism to other regions of the world.

The shift from opinion to fact followed the emergence of a mass daily press. This shift centered on Britain and North America. By the 1820s, the United States had a partisan press system with a high popular readership. In the 1830s, cheap daily newspapers, or 'penny papers,' began to circulate in urban centers; the content of all newspapers shifted toward event-oriented news. In Britain the growth of a popular press was delayed by stamp taxes on newspapers, which were finally repealed in 1851. Printing presses adopted first steam power, then rotary cylinder plates, followed by stereotyping, and finally linotype typesetting. The telegraph enhanced the commoditization of news and the growth of wire services and press agencies.

As newspapers became more commoditized, they began to hire reporters (Baldasty 1991). Unlike correspondents, who had a personal voice, reporters were meant to faithfully record facts: to transcribe speeches, to present minutes of meetings, to compile shipping lists and current prices, to relate police court proceedings. Reporters were the information workers of industrializing newspapers. Industrializing newspapers adopted a set of norms that distinguished between their high-value or sacred mission and their more profane work of earning success in a competitive marketplace. The sacred mission was to create an informed self-governing public. The profane work of the news seemed to produce a misinformed public whose tastes and intellect had been affected by → sensationalism. And the competitive marketplace seemed to favor greedy and increasingly monopolistic industrialists with a political agenda of their own.

Modern Constructions

The modern notion of journalism mediates between the sacred and profane and merges the work of the correspondent and the reporter. In Anglo-American history, the key term in this journalism has been objectivity. Objective journalists are always aware of their own subjectivity, but police it, separating their own values from impersonal reports. Michael Schudson (1978) has described this form of objectivity as arising from a dialectic of naïve empiricism and radical subjectivism. A similar dialectic is evident in the rise of pictorial journalism, which took raw material from photography and sketch artistry to make engravings that promised fidelity to an objective reality.

A tribe of indicators can trace the *rise of professional journalism* in the west. Canons of journalism ethics (→ Ethics in Journalism), professional associations and schools of journalism (→ Journalism Education), the byline, the inverted pyramid form and summary lead (which, counterintuitively, tells stories from end to beginning), and the habit of balancing and sourcing all became familiar around the same time. The excesses of World War I intensified the drive for → professionalization of journalism.

By the 1920s an *alternative model of professionalism* had appeared, first in the Soviet Union, then in other anti-capitalist states. Soviet and Chinese journalism adopted some notions of bourgeois professionalism, wedded them to vanguardism, and institutionalized the resulting construct in state monopoly institutions. Elsewhere, alternative forms of journalism appeared (→ Advocacy Journalism; Alternative Journalism; Minority Journalism). Usually, alternative journalisms were tied to a group within the larger society, whether based on some aspect of identity (gender, race, ethnicity, class) or on the advocacy of a particular position. Globally, the twentieth century saw the rise of broadcast journalism. In some countries, broadcast media were privately owned; in others, there were monopolistic national broadcast authorities. In either case, broadcasting seemed to intensify the process of professionalization.

Prospective

Forms of news considered distinctive to the Anglo-American tradition continued to spread in the late twentieth century. Investigative journalism spread to Latin America, for instance (Waisbord 2000). The retreat of state-supported broadcast authorities in Europe brought the introduction of more commercial television news programming. The collapse of the Soviet bloc sparked a wave of commercial media ventures and partisan journalism.

Meanwhile, within the west, the end of the twentieth century saw the erosion of what Dan Hallin (1994) has called the "high modernism of journalism." The rise of the 24-hour television news service, of new, so-called personal, media like talk radio and the blogosphere, of the tabloid form (→ Tabloidization) and a hybrid journalism, especially in the Scandinavian countries, and of a new form of partisan media power associated with broadcast entrepreneurs like Silvio Berlusconi and Rupert Murdoch eroded journalism's institutional authority.

See also: ▶ ADVOCACY JOURNALISM ▶ ALTERNATIVE JOURNALISM ▶ CENSORSHIP ▶ CENSORSHIP, HISTORY OF ▶ CITIZEN JOURNALISM ▶ ETHICS IN JOURNALISM ▶ FREEDOM OF INFORMATION ▶ FREEDOM OF THE PRESS, CONCEPT OF ▶ JOURNALISM ▶ JOURNALISM EDUCATION ▶ MEDIA HISTORY ▶ MINORITY JOURNALISM ▶ NEWS AGENCIES, HISTORY OF ▶ NEWS ROUTINES ▶ NEWSPAPER, HISTORY OF ▶ OBJECTIVITY IN REPORTING ▶ PHOTOJOURNALISM ▶ PRINTING, HISTORY OF ▶ PROFESSIONALIZATION OF JOURNALISM ▶ PUBLIC JOURNALISM ▶ PUBLIC OPINION ▶ PUBLIC SPHERE ▶ SENSATIONALISM ▶ STANDARDS OF NEWS ▶ TABLOIDIZATION

REFERENCES AND SUGGESTED READINGS

Baldasty, G. J. (1991). *The commercialization of news in the nineteenth century*. Madison, WI: University of Wisconsin Press.
Barnhurst, K. G. & Nerone, J. (2001). *The form of news: A history*. New York: Guilford.
Chalaby, J. (2001). *The invention of journalism*. Basingstoke: Palgrave Macmillan.
Habermas, J. (1989). *Structural transformation of the public sphere*. Cambridge, MA: MIT Press.
Hallin, D. (1994). *We keep America on top of the world: Television journalism and the public sphere*. London: Routledge.
Hallin, D. & Mancini, P. (2004). *Comparing media systems*. Cambridge: Cambridge University Press.
Schudson, M. (1978). *Discovering the news: A social history of the American newspaper*. New York: Basic Books.
Waisbord, S. (2000). *Watchdog journalism in South America*. New York: Columbia University Press.

Journalism: Legal Situation

SANDRA DAVIDSON
University of Missouri-Columbia

Knowledge is power, said Englishman Francis Bacon (1561–1626). But sometimes journalists have knowledge while government has power. This can lead to clashes and even imprisonment or death for journalists (→ Violence against Journalists). Dissident writer Alexander Solzhenitsyn languished in the Gulag Archipelago before the Soviet Union fell. Azerbaijani newspaper editor Eynulla Fatullayev was released in May

2011 after four years imprisonment for criminal libel. Hong Kong journalist Ching Cheong, sentenced on charges of spying for Taiwan, was freed in February 2008 after 1,000 days in a Chinese prison.

In September 2013 alone, the New York-based *Committee to Protect Journalists* reported these among many other cases: Uzbek authorities' arrest for "hooliganism" of Sergei Naumov, a freelance journalist who reports on human rights abuses; Nairobi's restrictions on visitors to jailed journalist Reeyot Alemu. The journalist jailed longest is Uzbek editor Muhammad Bekjanov, imprisoned since 1999 and sentenced in 2012 to another five years. In December 2012, the Committee reported the highest number of jailings worldwide: 232. Turkey led with 49 jailed journalists. These nations rounded out the top ten: Iran, China, Eritrea, Syria, Vietnam, Azerbaijan, Ethiopia, Uzbekistan and Saudi Arabia. Paris-based *Reporters Without Borders* also closely follows arrests. For example, it condemned the arrest of eight journalists, with one beaten by police, during post-election protests in March 2012 in Moscow and Saint Petersburg. It denounced a court's September 2013 decision in Murmansk to place Russian freelance photographer Denis Sinyakov in two months of preventive detention after authorities intercepted the Greenpeace vessel he was aboard in Russian waters.

In the United States, journalists who refuse to reveal sources risk jail time. The Supreme Court ruled 5–4 in Branzburg v. Hayes (1972) that the First Amendment does not protect journalists ordered to reveal confidential sources to grand juries (→ Source Protection). The record US imprisonment is 226 days, spent by videographer Josh Wolf, who refused to testify before a federal grand jury or hand over his raw videotape of a G8 Summit protest that resulted in injury to a police officer in San Francisco, California, in July 2005. As part of an agreement for his release, he gave up the videotape. There is no US federal shield law, but 40 of 50 states and the District of Columbia had shield laws in 2013.

Threat of jail for refusal to reveal sources can occur in any country lacking *shield protection*. In 2005, two Australian journalists from the Herald Sun faced that threat. This helped prompt calls for shield laws in Australia which is now passed. The first test of such a law occurred in Western Australia in August 2013, when a court refused to order journalist Steve Pennels to reveal his sources to billionaire Gina Rinehart. In October 2006, Japan's Supreme Court protected a reporter from the Japan Broadcasting Company, ruling that a reporter's protection of confidential sources is a form of protecting one's occupation. The media law passed in Iceland in 2011 offers shield protection. In Sweden, journalist's privilege is a constitutional right under the Freedom of the Press Act, which was adopted in 1766 and is part of the Swedish Constitution. Strengthened in 1949, the Act protects → news sources, making illegal the investigation of identities of anonymous sources. Its shield law authorizes criminal prosecution of journalists if a confidential source's identity is revealed without the source's authorization. It forbids public officials to inquire about journalistic sources. If public officials violate the law, they face fines or up to one year in jail. Belgium also has a strong law protecting journalists' sources. WikiLeaks routes its submissions through Belgium and Sweden because of their strong protection of sources.

International law on journalist's privilege is media-friendly. Two international courts have accepted claims that the confidentiality of journalistic sources is part of a right to freedom of expression. The European Court of Human Rights declared in 1996 that journalists have a right not to disclose their sources unless an overriding, countervailing interest outweighs the confidentiality of news sources. The International Criminal Tribunal for the former Yugoslavia held in 2002 that war correspondents cannot be compelled to testify about their sources, except under extraordinary circumstances. Still, going to jail remains an occupational hazard for journalists in many countries.

See also: ▶ COMMUNICATION AND LAW ▶ COMMUNICATION LAW AND POLICY: AFRICA ▶ COMMUNICATION LAW AND POLICY: ASIA ▶ COMMUNICATION LAW AND POLICY: EUROPE ▶ COMMUNICATION LAW AND POLICY: MIDDLE EAST ▶ COMMUNICATION LAW AND POLICY: NORTH AMERICA ▶ COMMUNICATION LAW AND POLICY: SOUTH AMERICA ▶ EUROPEAN UNION: COMMUNICATION LAW ▶ JOURNALISM ▶ NEWS SOURCES ▶ SOURCE PROTECTION ▶ VIOLENCE AGAINST JOURNALISTS

REFERENCES AND SUGGESTED READINGS

Committee to Protect Journalists (2012). 2012 prison census; 232 journalists jailed worldwide. At http://cpj.org/imprisoned/2012.php, accessed August 2, 2014.

Committee to Protect Journalists (2013). 2013 prison census; 211 journalists jailed worldwide. At http://cpj.org/imprisoned/2013.php, accessed August 2, 2014.

Committee to Protect Journalists (2012). Special Reports: Number of jailed journalists sets global record. At http://www.cpj.org/reports/2012/12/imprisoned-journalists-world-record.php, accessed August 2, 2014.

Davidson, S. & Herrera, D. (2012). Needed: More Than a Paper Shield. *William & Mary Bill of Rights Law Journal*, 20(May), 1277–1394.

Reporters Without Borders (2012). Press Barometers. At http://en.rsf.org/press-freedom-barometer-journalists-imprisoned.html?annee=2012, accessed August 2, 2014.

Journalists, Credibility of

YARIV TSFATI
University of Haifa

Credibility is a central professional value for journalists. Scholars and journalists disagree about what constitutes credibility, but agree that it relates primarily to the truthfulness, believablity and accuracy of the facts journalists report. However, scholars argue that credibility goes beyond believability (Metzger et al. 2003), and demonstrate that it encompasses fairness, lack of bias, accuracy, completeness, and trustworthiness (Meyer 1988; → Bias in the News; Quality of the News). Additional definitions of credibility connote broader expectations of audiences from journalism which depend on norms of professionalism and vary across contexts (→ Professionalization of Journalism). In the US, for example, crediblity spans over a wide variety of professional values, whereas in Europe professional culture puts somewhat less emphasis on objectivity and → neutrality.

Surveys of journalists worldwide have documented the importance of credibility as a norm. Journalists' codes of ethics make credibility a central tenet and view it as the rationale for many journalistic dictates. The centrality of credibility for journalists could also be inferred from journalists' rhetoric following professional scandals that potentially jeopardize audience trust (→ Ethics in Journalism).

Much empirical work has been dedicated to deciphering the reasons behind a dramatic decline in audience perceptions of media credibility in the US starting in the 1970s. Recently it has been suggested (Ladd, 2012) that the main causes include economic pressures on media (that lower the level of journalistic professionalism), political polarization (that increases elite criticism on media) and media → tabloidization (→ Commercialization: Impact on Media Content). Research on the consequences of audience perceptions of media credibility demonstrate that those who rate journalists low on credibility tend to diversify their news diets and attend to more alternative news. Perceived news credibility was also found to moderate an array of → media effects (Ladd, 2012).

See also: ▶ BIAS IN THE NEWS ▶ COMMERCIALIZATION: IMPACT ON MEDIA CONTENT ▶ ETHICS IN JOURNALISM ▶ MEDIA EFFECTS ▶ NEUTRALITY ▶ PROFESSIONALIZATION OF JOURNALISM ▶ QUALITY OF THE NEWS ▶ STANDARDS OF NEWS ▶ TABLOIDIZATION ▶ TRUST OF PUBLICS

REFERENCES AND SUGGESTED READINGS

Ladd, J. M. (2012). *Why Americans hate the media and how it matters.* Princeton, NJ: Princeton University Press.

Metzger, M. J., Flangin, A. J., Eyal, K., Lemus, D. R., & McCann, R. M. (2003). Credibility for the 21st century: Integrating perspectives on source, message and media credibility in the information age. *Communication Yearbook*, 27, 293–335.

Meyer, P. (1988). Defining and measuring credibility of newspapers: Developing an index. *Journalism Quarterly*, 65, 567–588.

Journalists' Role Perception

WOLFGANG DONSBACH
Dresden University of Technology

'Journalists' role perceptions' can be defined as generalized expectations of society towards their profession, and as actions and beliefs that the professionals see as normatively acceptable – that will influence their behavior on the job. The concept is important for describing how journalists in different cultures and media systems understand their work and its social function. Journalists' role perceptions have been studied primarily for news workers covering politics and current affairs.

The most widely used *ideal types* for role perceptions were identified by Morris Janowitz (1975), who distinguished between the 'gatekeeper' and the 'advocate.' These types differ in their picture of the audience (self-dependent vs dependent), and their criteria for news selection (according to news factors vs according to instrumentality). Normative typologies serve a heuristic purpose in research. For instance, Patterson (1995) distinguished between the roles of 'signaler,' 'common carrier,' 'watchdog,' and 'public representative.' Finally, role perceptions have emerged from surveys of journalists and subsequent *data analyses* – like the distinctions 'information dissemination,' 'interpretative–investigative,' and 'adversary.' Some normative proposals for journalistic role models like the 'politically constructive' expectations towards journalists in developing countries (→ Development Journalism) or the proposal of the new, more politically active role in form of 'public journalism' (→ Citizen Journalism) triggered debates in academia and the profession.

For democratic countries, the existing theoretical role models can be collapsed into *three dimensions*, all of them interrelated. On the 'participant–observational' dimension, journalists can choose between actively seeking to influence the political process and trying to function as impartial conduits for political reporting. On the 'advocacy–neutral' dimension the alternatives are expressing subjective values and beliefs or maintaining strict neutrality and fairness to all sides. On the 'commercial–educational dimension,' journalists can strive either to reach the widest audience by serving its tastes and patterns of media exposure or to make news decisions based on what is good for democracy and public discourse. Journalists in all countries acquire elements of all three dimensions from the available.

A country's history is the most decisive factor for *differences in journalism between countries*. For instance, economic and social changes in the US population in the first half of the nineteenth century, as well as the commercial motivation of publishers to reach the widest possible audience, together drove US newspapers to adopt a less partisan position and to develop basic professional standards such as the norm of objectivity (→ Objectivity in Reporting). Aside from these intercultural differences, the role perception of journalists within a given media system can also differ according to their individual training, socialization, institutional demands, or personal job motivations.

The changes brought to social communication through the → *Internet* have again raised discussions about journalists' role perceptions. Several authors argue that the function of public communication is no longer restricted to professional journalists working for large media institutions, because today anybody can be a journalist, for example through blogging or in the → social media. Authors differ, though, in their view of what makes an activity "journalistic." Besides personal competencies and resources it might well be that the role perception, motivation, and ethical foundation of those who cover public issues make the difference – in whatever technical and institutional framework it happens (Donsbach, 2009; → Online Journalism; Web 2.0 and the News).

Communication researchers have applied a variety of *methods and empirical indicators* to assess journalists' role perceptions, surveys being the most frequently used methods, in addition to content analyses and participant observations. Comparative investigations are particularly valuable because they allow benchmarking with other professional cultures and can help interpret and evaluate the role perceptions measured in one country or in one professional sector. A questionnaire first used for US journalists in the 1980s was later applied in 20 other countries (Weaver 1997). In the early 1990s a survey conducted almost simultaneously in five countries measured the role perceptions and professional norms of journalists involved in daily news decisions (Donsbach & Patterson 2004), and between 2007 and 2011 the 'Worlds of Journalism' project was in the field.

Empirical evidence shows that western news systems are more alike than different, although their differences are important and consequential for journalists' performance. Besides differences on the aggregate between countries, role perceptions can differ considerably among individual journalists and media organizations (Hanitzsch & Donsbach 2012). Role perceptions within the countries can also change, sometimes through key events as the → Watergate scandal in the USA. Several studies have brought evidence that the general role model of journalism changed in the 1960s from the ideology of paternalism to the ideology of criticism.

See also: ▶ ADVOCACY JOURNALISM ▶ CITIZEN JOURNALISM ▶ DEVELOPMENT JOURNALISM ▶ JOURNALISM, HISTORY OF ▶ INTERNET JOURNALISM ▶ OBJECTIVITY IN REPORTING ▶ ONLINE JOURNALISM ▶ PROFESSIONALIZATION OF JOURNALISM ▶ SOCIAL MEDIA ▶ WATERGATE SCANDAL ▶ WEB 2.0 AND THE NEWS

REFERENCES AND SUGGESTED READINGS

Donsbach, W. (2009). Journalists and their professional identities. In S. Allen (ed.), *The Routledge Companion to news and journalism*. London: Routledge, pp. 38–48.

Hanitzsch, T. & Donsbach, W. (2012). Comparing journalism cultures. In F. Esser & T. Hanitzsch (eds.), *The handbook of comparative communication research*. London: Routledge, pp. 262–275.

Janowitz, M. (1975). Professional models in journalism: The gatekeeper and the advocate. *Journalism Quarterly*, 52, 618–626.

Patterson, T. E. (1995). *The American democracy*, 7th edn. New York: McGraw-Hill.

Weaver, D. H. (ed.) (1997). *The global journalist: News people around the world*. Cresskill, NJ: Philip Seib.

K

Knowledge Gap Effects

CECILIE GAZIANO
Research Solutions, Inc., Minneapolis, MN, USA

The knowledge gap hypothesis proposes that as levels of information increase in a community or a society, people with lower socioeconomic status (SES) get that information at a slower rate than people with higher SES, so disparity between 'haves' and 'have-nots' tends to increase, rather than decrease (Tichenor et al. 1970).

The gap is studied at one time or over time and on the levels of individuals or collectivities (Gaziano & Gaziano 2009; → Political Knowledge; Health Campaigns, Communication in; Media Use by Social Variable). The most frequent indicator of SES studied is formal education. 'Knowledge' means information acquired through learning processes. 'Gap' means the relation between SES and knowledge. Types of information transmission, such as media use, people's attention to information sources, or publicity circulating in collectivities, should vary because the prediction concerns differing levels of information diffusion.

Reasons for decreased differentials have included high conflict associated with issues; high media coverage; high discussion about topics; relatively smaller and homogeneous communities, as opposed to larger, heterogeneous communities; basic concern of issues to all; and forgetting occurring over time among all groups (→ Memory). Sometimes knowledge gaps narrow or close (see, e.g., Hwang & Jeong 2009).

See also: ▶ COMMUNICATION INEQUALITIES ▶ DIFFUSION OF INFORMATION AND INNOVATION ▶ DIGITAL DIVIDE ▶ HEALTH CAMPAIGNS, COMMUNICATION IN ▶ INFORMATION PROCESSING ▶ MEDIA USE BY SOCIAL VARIABLE ▶ MEMORY ▶ POLITICAL KNOWLEDGE

REFERENCES AND SUGGESTED READINGS

Gaziano, C. & Gaziano, E. (2009). Theories and methods in knowledge gap research. In D. W. Stacks & M. Salwen (eds.), *An integrated approach to communication theory and research*, 2nd edn. New York: Taylor and Francis, pp. 122–136.

Hwang, Y. & Jeong, S.-H. (2009). Revisiting the knowledge gap hypothesis: A meta-analysis of thirty-five years of research. *Journalism and Mass Communication Quarterly*, 86(3), 513–532.

Tichenor, P. J., Donohue, G. A., & Olien, C. N. (1970). Mass media flow and differential growth in knowledge. *Public Opinion Quarterly*, 34(2), 159–170.

Knowledge Management

LORNA HEATON
University of Montreal

In the business world, knowledge management (KM) commonly refers to the preservation, sharing, and development of knowledge that is deemed critical, strategic, or important. Knowledge management projects range from setting up intranets, to using collaborative or workflow software, mentoring, or sharing information on best practices. Typically tied to organizational objectives, these practices are attempts to identify, create, represent, and distribute knowledge throughout the organization (→ Organizational Communication).

KM provides a framework that builds on past experiences and creates new mechanisms for exchanging and creating knowledge. Implicit is the recognition that knowledge, and not simply information, is the primary source of an organization's innovative potential. Generally, information appears to become knowledge when it is interpreted in context.

We can identify three general perspectives on KM. In the dominant, *cognitive perspective* knowledge is a commodity and an asset, something that can be accounted for and managed. Typically, there are a number of processes involved: knowledge identification; capture or acquisition; generation; validation; diffusion; storage; retrieval; and use or re-use. In this perspective, Nonaka's spiral model of knowledge creation and management (Nonaka & Takeuchi 1995) has been most influential. The "SECI process" is a sequence of interaction between tacit and explicit knowledge through four modes of knowledge conversion: from socialization (tacit-to-tacit), to externalization (tacit-to-explicit), to combination (explicit-to-explicit), to internalization (explicit-to-tacit). The result is a dynamic spiral, which widens as it moves from individual to group to organization levels, explaining how individual knowledge is transformed into organizational knowledge and vice versa.

Networking perspectives on KM acknowledge that individuals have social as well as economic motives, and that their actions are influenced by networks of relationships in which they are embedded. Information technologies are important as facilitating tools for maintaining and building knowledge networks that integrate collaboration patterns in order to control the flow of information and forge strategic alliances both within and across organizations.

Both the cognitive and network models of KM suppose a high degree of planning and formalization. In contrast, the *community perspective* builds on the notion that knowledge and practice are inseparable. Community members work together to re-create and apply transferred information in locally situated, appropriate ways. Knowledge is generated locally and collectively, through the social construction of new meanings and understandings (Orlikowski 2002). The challenge for organizations approaching KM from this perspective is to encourage enabling organizational practices, such as providing spaces for exchange and a nurturing environment.

Information technology is a key enabler of KM programs. Project management systems that incorporate workflow and status tracking, as well as document sharing, increasingly in the 'cloud,' have extended the scope of KM. As technologies gain in sophistication, they are progressively more capable of providing meaningful support for knowledge sharing in organizations. For example, intelligent information filtering and extraction (such as recommender systems) have become commonplace. More recently, social computing tools (such as bookmarks, blogs, and wikis) have allowed more unstructured approaches to the transfer, capture, and creation of knowledge, including the development of new forms of communities, networks, or matrixed organizations. Developments in visualization techniques such as concept mapping and image indexing, semantic technologies for search and retrieval and content management (Web 3.0), and data mining, may hold promise for KM initiatives.

Advanced technologies cannot solve all knowledge management problems, however. IT tends to reduce the complexity or richness of knowledge in order to be able to code it. Database entries in knowledge repositories are only valuable if they correspond with users' sense-giving processes (→ Meaning). Constructing an information technology infrastructure for knowledge does not, in itself, guarantee that organization members will use the system. The literature on best practices in KM suggests that fostering an environment conducive to knowledge sharing and open communication is vital in any KM strategy. A final consideration is a strong, shared vision and a strong link to business priorities.

See also: ▶ MEANING ▶ NETWORK ORGANIZATIONS THROUGH COMMUNICATION TECHNOLOGY ▶ ORGANIZATIONAL COMMUNICATION ▶ STORYTELLING AND NARRATION

REFERENCES AND SUGGESTED READINGS

Cook, S. D. & Brown, J. S. (1999). Bridging epistemologies: The generative dance between organizational knowledge and organizational knowing. *Organization Science*, 10(4), 381–400.

Nonaka, I. & Takeuchi, H. (1995). *The knowledge-creating company*. Oxford: Oxford University Press.

Orlikowski, W. (2002). Knowing in practice: Enacting a collective capability in distributed organizing. *Organization Science*, 13(3), 249–273.

Styhre, A. (2003). *Understanding knowledge management: Critical and postmodern perspectives*. Copenhagen: Copenhagen Business School Press.

Zorn, T. & May, S. K. (eds.) (2002). Forum on knowledge management and/as organizational communication. *Management Communication Quarterly*, 16(2), 237–291.

L

Language and the Internet

SUSAN C. HERRING
Indiana University

Language and (or 'on') the Internet refers to human language produced and displayed through computer-mediated communication (CMC) systems that are mostly text-based, such as email, chat, text messaging, web forums, blogs, microblogs, and wikis. Increasingly, 'Internet language' is mediated by mobile technologies.

Research on language and the Internet may be grouped into *five major areas*. 'Classification research' characterizes computer-mediated language in relation to the traditional modalities of writing and speech; as modes or genres (→ Genre); or in terms of features, such as synchronicity, that cut across modes. Research on the structural features of Internet language focuses mainly on typography, orthography, and new word formations. The use of abbreviations (e.g., 'ms' for 'message'), acronyms (e.g., 'LOL' for 'laughing out loud'), number homophones (e.g., 'l8r' for 'later'), and emoticons (combinations of keyboard symbols that represent facial expressions) have been claimed to characterize Internet language.

A third area of research, discourse patterns, addresses pragmatic phenomena such as politeness (and rudeness, including 'flaming'), relevance, and speech acts (→ Linguistic Pragmatics); interactional phenomena such as turn-taking, repairs, topic establishment, maintenance, and drift (→ Conversation Analysis); and register phenomena such as gender styles, regional dialects, and ingroup language practices (→ Intercultural and Intergroup Communication). Some scholars study Internet language as a 'lens through which to understand human behavior' more generally, rather than to describe language for its own sake. Concepts that have been addressed include collaboration, community, identity, influence, power, and reputation, all of which are instantiated online through typed discourse. Finally, languages and language ecologies have increasingly attracted attention as the Internet expands its global scope. The Internet has been claimed to accelerate the spread of English and other large regional languages such as Spanish and Chinese, although scholars disagree on whether this is occurring at the expense of smaller languages.

See also: ▶ CONVERSATION ANALYSIS ▶ DISCOURSE ▶ ELECTRONIC MAIL ▶ GENRE ▶ INTERCULTURAL AND INTERGROUP COMMUNICATION ▶ LINGUISTIC PRAGMATICS ▶ LINGUISTICS ▶ PERSONAL COMMUNICATION BY CMC

REFERENCES AND SUGGESTED READINGS

Androutsopoulos, J. (2006). Introduction: Sociolinguistics and computer-mediated communication. *Journal of Sociolinguistics*, 10(4), 419–438.

Danet, B. & Herring, S. C. (eds.) (2007). *The multilingual Internet: Language, culture, and communication online*. Oxford: Oxford University Press.

Herring, S. C. (2012). Grammar and electronic communication. In C. Chapelle (ed.), *Encyclopedia of applied linguistics*. Oxford: Wiley Blackwell.

Language and Social Interaction

KAREN TRACY
University of Colorado at Boulder

Language and social interaction (LSI) studies how language, gesture, voice, and other features of talk and written texts shape meaning-making. LSI defines itself by *how* it investigates questions about communication. It is the commitment to study of social life in its culturally inflected, complex, and context-sensitive particularity that makes LSI work distinctive. To understand LSI as an area of communication research, one needs to proceed in bottom-up and top-down directions. Handbooks of LSI research (e.g., Fitch & Sanders 2005) usually adopt a top-down approach, but the distinctive character of LSI work would be obscured if explication were restricted to prominent theoretical approaches. Bottom-up research includes a focus on understanding basic units of language and interaction, explicating functions that talk serves, and identification of strategies of important sites of interaction.

Approaches to LSI

Approaches to LSI come in flavors. The three most prominent are: (1) → *Conversation Analysis* (CA): Developed by sociologist Harvey Sacks (1992), CA is committed to building an observational science of social life. CA's first step is to collect tapes of ordinary talk and create detailed transcripts that capture as many features of talk as possible. Then CA seeks to identify interaction patterns. (2) → *Ethnography of Communication* (EOC): Extending the anthropological work of Dell Hymes, EOC shows how a community of people speak, interpret others' actions, and, more broadly, understand what it means to be a person and have relationships. Gerry Philipsen's (1975) study of ways to "speak like a man" in a working-class Chicago community was key in bringing the EOC tradition to communication.

(3) The third tradition, → *Discourse Analysis* (DA), is actually better thought of as an umbrella for multiple LSI approaches that are neither conversation analysis nor EOC. DA includes → Discursive Psychology, an approach initially developed by Jonathan Potter and colleagues that explores how everyday psychological terms are used and how psychological matters are managed rhetorically. Two DA approaches developed by communication scholars are "Action-implicative Discourse Analysis," developed by Karen Tracy, which focuses on explicating the problems of a practice, the conversational strategies of key participants, and participants' normative beliefs about good conduct; and "Design Theory," developed by Mark Aakhus and Sally Jackson, which integrates linguistic pragmatic ideas and ideas from argument theory to consider how participation and conduct in a range of communicative practices ought to be designed.

In addition to the above most prominent approaches LSI research is informed by *ideas from communities of practice*, a tradition developed by Jean Lave and Etienne Wenger that studies how people pursue a common activity; "speech acts theory" developed by philosopher John Austin to dispute other philosophers who treated the purpose of language as making representational statements about the world; "politeness theories," which explains why communicators deviate from maximally efficient communication, of which Brown and Levinson's version is the most well known; and "Critical Discourse Analysis" (Tracy et al. 2011), which studies texts, usually written ones, with the goal of exposing how power gets naturalized and how discourse practices are marshaled to suggest objectivity while all the time systematically advantaging those who have power. Finally, the ideas of Mikhail Bakhtin, who wrote in the early years of the twentieth century, have been influential, especially his notion of the utterance as the basic unit of interaction. LSI work has primarily been interested in what happens in interaction among people – not what goes on in their minds, but this scholarly tendency has been changing in recent years.

Basic Concepts and Findings

LSI examines people talking with others in a range of social occasions to accomplish complementary and antagonistic purposes. LSI studies typically accomplish three things: (1) they identify distinctive features of language and/or interaction; (2) they describe the interpersonal, organizational, or political functions that talk is serving; and (3) they show how the particulars of (1) and (2) come together to create interactional sites that are communicatively distinctive.

(1) Among the *features of language* dialect has received particular attention from researchers. When people speak a language, they always speak a particular dialect or variety of it whether the language be Korean or English. Features of pronunciation and grammar, for instance, are used differently by communicators of different geographic regions. Another small bit of talk that is ubiquitous, likely to appear at interactionally sensitive moments, is the metadiscursive comment (→ Metadiscourse). Metadiscourse labels communicative acts (e.g., 'an argument') and makes visible speakers' beliefs about how communication is working. If one were to tally what aspects of talk have been studied particularly extensively, the most researched unit would undoubtedly be questions (Freed & Ehrlich 2010). Besides the rather obvious goal of gaining information, questions are how speakers claim status for self or give deference to the conversational partner. Another interesting, multipurpose unit of talk is the narrative. Narratives are extended talk units and they are often used to do sensitive actions such as disagreeing, giving advice, or advancing an argument.

(2) By and large LSI researchers have been especially interested in understanding *how people design and vary speech acts* that are sensitive. Studied acts have included directives, apologies, and accounts. Although information giving is recognized as an important function of talk, it is the less visible functions that have been given the most attention. Less obvious functions include the way talk in workplace settings strengthens bonds of connection among people or gives support for managing difficult moments. 'Supportive talk,' for example, is designed to avoid offending, and LSI scholars have been interested in design features of this kind of talk. Another function of talk is identity-work (Tracy & Robles 2013). A speaker's talk inevitably presents the kind of person the speaker is and altercasts the other as well.

Of all the kinds of *identity* that have been examined, none has received as much attention as what it means to talk like a woman or a man. Much recent work shows how the performance of gender is strongly shaped by a speaker's social class, race, and national culture. LSI scholars also see it as important to problematize generalizations about power. Among the vast number of talk features that could be attributed to power differences, they might also be accomplishing different functions. When we attend to discourse functions at societal and institutional levels, we notice a range of different aims served by talk, with one being the enactment of democracy; it is through talk that democracy touches down and becomes a concrete practice.

(3) *Interaction* has a distinctive shape and set of problems in each institutional setting. Healthcare settings have been studied extensively, as have courtroom discourse, broadcast talk, and political exchange. Ilie (2010), for instance, examined the discourse strategies of speakers in European parliaments. Language and social interaction is a distinctive area of communication study. Its trademark is the use of excerpts of talk to make claims about important units of interaction, the structure of social action, how identities and institutions are constructed, how culture is displayed discursively, and so on.

See also: ▶ CONVERSATION ANALYSIS ▶ DISCOURSE ANALYSIS ▶ ETHNOGRAPHY OF COMMUNICATION ▶ IDENTITIES AND DISCOURSE ▶ LINGUISTIC PRAGMATICS ▶ METADISCOURSE

REFERENCES AND SUGGESTED READINGS

Fitch, K. & Sanders, R. E. (eds.) (2005). *Handbook of language and social interaction*. Mahwah, NJ: Lawrence Erlbaum.

Freed, A. F. & Ehrlich, S. (eds.) (2010). *"Why do you ask?" The functions of questions in institutional discourse*. Oxford: Oxford University Press.

Ilie, C. (2010). *European parliaments under scrutiny: Discourse strategies and interaction practices*. Amsterdam: John Benjamins.

Philipsen, G. (1975). Speaking "like a man" in Teamsterville: Cultural patterns of role enactment in an urban neighborhood. *Quarterly Journal of Speech*, 61, 13–22.

Sacks, H. (1992). *Lectures on conversation*. Oxford: Blackwell.

Tracy, K., Martinez-Guillem, S., Robles, J. S., & Casteline, K. E. (2011). Critical discourse analysis and (US) communication scholarship: Recovering old connections, envisioning new ones. In C. Salmon (ed.), *Communication yearbook 35*. Los Angeles, CA: Sage, pp. 239–286.

Tracy, K, and Robles, J. S. (2013). *Everyday talk: Building and reflecting identities*, 2nd edn. New York: Guilford.

Latin America: Media Systems

JOSÉ MARQUES DE MELO
Methodist University of São Paulo

Latin America is a geopolitical region composed of historic nations and immigrant communities, shaped by the old colonial order and reinforced by cultural traditions such as Catholicism as the official religion, and the Spanish and Portuguese languages as the communication tools adopted by the majority of its population. From an economic perspective the important media markets in the region are 12 in number: the giant Brazilian market, followed by the large Mexican market, and then the four medium-sized countries: Argentina, Chile, Colombia and Venezuela, and finally small nations like Ecuador, Peru and Uruguay.

All of these countries have media systems consisting of a mixture of commercial mass media (as industrial products) and folk media (as artisanal goods), generating an asymmetrical configuration. The intellectual backwardness and cognitive sluggishness of the colonial era delayed the civilizing process in the independent nations. The majority of the population in Latin American countries was made up of native American people and African slaves (illiterate, oppressed, and impoverished). In all these societies, the marginalized communities created rudimentary communication flows. Relying on popular cultural manifestations that are reminiscent of rural traditions, they are still struggling to adapt to city life, as they encounter experiences produced by mass media flows (→ cinema; music industry).

At the beginning of the twenty-first century, Latin America's communication industry is dominated by audiovisual media, mainly television, followed by radio. TV and radio are present in almost all households. The role of print media is small. Advertising expenditure in Latin America reached a total of 40 billion US$ in 2012. Most of it, as much as 65 percent, was spent on television, 20 percent on newspapers, 5 percent each on radio, magazines, and other media.

The Media Market

Restricted to privileged segments of Latin American society, newspapers help shape → public opinion. Their readers are members of the country's power elite in government, civil society, and the media industry. The main source of education, information, and entertainment for the lower classes, *radio*, was historically a local or regional medium, but satellite communication has enabled the development of national networks (→ Satellite Communication, Global). The system is composed of two rival sectors: a powerful commercial sector controlled by entrepreneurs and politicians, and a popular, not always 'legal' but well managed social movements sector, involving religious communities, ethnic groups, and radical societies (→ Community Media). With the beginning of the digital era, television in Latin American countries increased its audience and now has the greatest socio-cultural impact on society.

The region's leading TV network for several years, Rede Globo (Brazil) and Televisa (Mexico), hold the loyalty of majority audiences. Most programs are nationally produced, with an audience preference for entertainment (fiction, sports, and comedy, Telenovelas take up much airtime), followed by information (→ News). Latin America's television industry has gradually reduced its dependence on imports. In fact, it became a global exporter of television content in the final two decades of the twentieth century, selling telenovelas, music shows, and sports programs to other countries.

Society, Religion, and the Media

Since the early 1950s, when the first television channels started to operate in Brazil and Mexico, the relationship between institutional religion and commercial television has been ambiguous, reflecting the hegemonic policy of the Catholic

Church, despite the plurality of religions throughout the continent, including Afro-Latin American groups. At first, an attitude of suspicion prevailed, characteristic of the era before the Second Vatican Concilium. Representatives of the Catholic Church rejected the spirit of the new technologies. But they soon learned that telecommunication could play an important role in evangelical work, especially in rapidly urbanizing societies, where people were experiencing massive processes of migration, replacing traditional cultural values with modern social behavior. The ambiguity is also reflected by actors inside the cultural industries. They struggle between two tendencies: the owners' 'profit obsession' and the unions' 'political correctness.' There is very little attention paid to the public interest, citizenship and morality.

It is important to understand that Latin America is still a region where democracy, social justice and economic equality have become stronger only in recent years. Mass communication has been a tool in the hands of state and private oligarchies. Television was originally a way to transmit and impose elite visions, the majority generated abroad. But as it converted to a system obliged to follow the rules of the mass market, many signs of national popular culture began to be incorporated in almost all countries. This mechanism is called 'mestizaje' (melting point), where tradition and modernity, national and transnational, cultivated and rustic, are creatively mixed.

Because of this change, TV is now acting as an alternative school for large sections of Latin American populations, mainly illiterate people or young citizens early excluded from formal schooling. This increases the responsibility of universities to educate more effectively the professionals who will take on the tasks of collective education in the new century. It also means there is a need for an ethical revolution in the mass media business: the acceptance of an understanding that broadcasters' main job is to help the people to overcome poverty, to help them become consumers of goods and services that today are enjoyed by a small contingent of the privileged. In this struggle for survival, spiritual messages delivered through television in Latin America do not avoid the daily problems of real existence. Entertainment programs, such as serial fiction, present a space to dream and to cultivate fantasies but also enable many viewers to recognize their cultural identities. This socializing process offers psychological compensations for human beings marginalized from 'western consumerism.'

The Role of the Internet and Folk Media

The Internet has grown enormously in the region. It is estimated that the Internet now has about 90 million users in Brazil alone, making it the fifth largest market in the world, surpassed only by China, the USA, India, and Japan. What do Latin Americans search for on the Internet? Most of them log on to the web for practical reasons, although a significant number of them admit to a preference for entertainment.

The folk-media subsystem remains autonomous in relation to the mass-media subsystem, but it also addresses its counterpart dialectically. Sometimes it serves as a mediator that filters and transmits meanings generated elsewhere. At other times, it fills in the gaps left open by the mass media. The interactive tension between folk media and mass media adds strength and vitality to Latin America's transitional status in the early twenty-first century.

See also: ▶ CINEMA ▶ COMMUNITY MEDIA ▶ MEXICO: MEDIA SYSTEM ▶ MUSIC INDUSTRY ▶ NEWS ▶ PUBLIC OPINION ▶ SATELLITE COMMUNICATION, GLOBAL

REFERENCES AND SUGGESTED READINGS

Grupo de Mídia (2013). *Mídia Dados*. São Paulo: Grupo de Mídia SP.
IPEA. (2013). *Panorama da Comunicação e das Telecomunicações no Brasil*. São Paulo: IPEA.
US Media Consulting (2013). *Latin America's media market 2013*. At http://usmediaconsulting.com/img/uploads/pdf/Latam-and-Brazil-Media-Market-2013.pdf, accessed August 15, 2014.

Latitude of Acceptance

MICHAEL KUNCZIK
Johannes Gutenberg University of Mainz (Emeritus)

'Latitude of acceptance' describes the position on an attitude scale that is most acceptable to a person on a given topic plus other positions which are considered acceptable. Social-judgment theorists assume that → attitudes concerning important topics are bipolar and people have an internal reference scale. The initial attitude on an issue with high ego-involvement influences the reaction to a communication representing a different view.

The *discrepancy of a communication* from one's own position is decisive for the amount of change achieved by a source because message discrepancy affects the perception of the quality of a message. More discrepant messages are perceived as being more unfair, more illogical, more boring, etc. In order to explain whether a person will change toward or away from a position advocated by a source, Sherif and Hovland (1961) developed their "assimilation-contrast theory."

Within the *latitude of acceptance* a source's opinion is distorted perceptually as being more similar to one's own opinion than it really is ("assimilation effect"). Because the source's point of view is perceived as being similar to one's own, the mere reinforcement of one's already existing attitude will be the most likely effect. The width of the latitude of acceptance is dependent on the importance of the issue: the more important an issue, the smaller the latitude of acceptance. Within the *latitude of rejection* (the positions one finds objectionable), a source's opinion is perceived as further removed from one's own stand than it really is ("contrast effect"). The changing of attitudes in the direction of the source's position is extremely unlikely.

The *zone of indifference* (latitude of non-commitment) allows an individual to remain neutral (moderate) regarding certain positions. With opinions neither accepted nor rejected, perceptual distortions are least likely to happen. In this zone of indifference, attitudes are most likely to be changed in the direction advocated. A large latitude of non-commitment is typical of an individual who is not deeply involved. The size of the latitude of non-commitment also proves to be an index of susceptibility to change.

See also: ▶ ATTITUDES ▶ INVOLVEMENT WITH MEDIA CONTENT ▶ MEDIA EFFECTS ▶ MEDIA EFFECTS, STRENGTH OF ▶ PROPAGANDA

REFERENCES AND SUGGESTED READINGS

Hovland, C., Harvey, O. J., & Sherif, M. (1957). Assimilation and contrast effects in reactions to communication and attitude change. *Journal of Abnormal and Social Psychology*, 55(3), 244–252.

Johnson, B. T., Lin, H.-Y., Symons, C., Campbell, L. A., & Ekstein, G. (1995). Initial beliefs and attitudinal latitudes as factors in persuasion. *Personal and Social Psychology Bulletin*, 21, 502–511.

Sherif, M. & Hovland, C. I. (1961). *Social judgement: Assimilation and contrast effects in communication and attitude change.* New Haven, CT: Yale University Press.

Leadership in Organizations

DAVID L. COLLINSON
Lancaster University Management School

Communication processes are central to leadership dynamics. Within organizations, communication and leadership frequently interact in complex, mutually reinforcing and sometimes contradictory and paradoxical ways. Leadership researchers have developed many theories, most of which concentrate on the qualities and behaviors necessary to be an 'effective leader' (e.g., transformational leadership, emotional intelligence). Although these theories have produced useful insights about leaders' behaviors and skills, many have tended to rely on heroic images of the 'great man,' and to romanticize leaders by developing overly exaggerated views of what they are able to achieve (→ Organizational Communication).

There is a growing recognition that leadership in organizations is better understood as an inherently *relational, collaborative, and interdependent process*. These post-heroic insights are suggestive of new forms of organizational communication. Rather than the traditional top-down model of 'command and control,' there is a growing view that communication in leadership dynamics is dispersed through team-based interdependencies and fluid, multidirectional social interactions and networks of influence, especially in high performance organizations.

More *critical perspectives* suggest that communication between leaders and followers is usually embedded in asymmetrical power relations, and typically shaped by situated control practices that are historically specific. Critical writers recognize that leaders' power can take multiple economic, political, discursive, and ideological forms. They show how control is a deeply embedded and inescapable feature of leadership structures, cultures, and communication practices. Leaders in organizations can exercise control by 'managing meaning' and defining situations in ways that suit their purposes through, for example, constructing corporate visions, shaping structures and cultures, intensifying and monitoring work, and by making key HR decisions.

'Toxic leaders' may exercise power in coercive, dictatorial, and narcissistic ways. Alternatively, the excessive positivity of 'Prozac leaders' can silence followers and leave organizations ill-prepared to deal with unanticipated events. Critical perspectives also highlight how forms of leader control (particularly coercive practices) can produce resistance and dissent. It is likely that future critical research on leadership communication will extend these insights into the dilemmas, paradoxes, and dialectics of leadership.

See also: ▶ DECISION-MAKING PROCESSES IN ORGANIZATIONS ▶ ORGANIZATIONAL CULTURE ▶ ORGANIZATIONS, CULTURAL DIVERSITY IN

REFERENCES AND SUGGESTED READINGS

Collinson, D. L. (2006). Rethinking followership: A post-structuralist analysis of follower identities. *Leadership Quarterly*, 17(2), 179–189.

Grint, K. (2005). *Leadership: Limits and possibilities*. Basingstoke: Palgrave Macmillan.

Sinclair, A. (2007). *Leadership for the disillusioned*. London: Allen and Unwin.

Learning and Communication

ANN BAINBRIDGE FRYMIER
Miami University

Learning has been studied since the beginning of the twentieth century and has been heavily influenced by psychology. Learning is generally defined as a persistent change in either behavior, cognitions, or, more recently, neural pathways. Instructional communication examines the role of communication in learning environments. In this scholarship, learning has been measured with content tests and with self-report measures. Because of the emphasis on generalizing across disciplines, instructional communication research has heavily relied on self-report measures of learning. The self-report measures most frequently used are the learning indicators scale, the cognitive learning measure, and the affective learning measure. The use of self-reported learning is based on the assumption that adult students are aware of their learning and can self-report the general quantity they have learned from a class. Instructional communication research has focused on how teacher-communication behavior impacts student learning.

Teacher immediacy has received the most research attention and is defined as a perception of physical and/or psychological closeness between people. The correlation between nonverbal immediacy and affective learning has typically been moderate and positive. Immediacy has consistently been positively related to self-reported cognitive learning, and has also been associated with a higher rate of recall in a handful of experimental studies. Immediacy appears to impact primarily students' attitudes and motivation, which, in turn, has some impact on cognitive learning.

A second teacher variable, *affinity seeking*, refers to the active process by which individuals attempt to get others to like them, with 25 strategies having been identified (→ Ingratiation and Affinity Seeking). Multiple studies have concluded that both K-12 and college teachers use affinity seeking to gain student liking, and that some affinity-seeking strategies are associated with student affect and motivation. The following strategies have consistently been identified as useful for teachers: facilitate enjoyment, optimism, assume equality, conversational rule-keeping, comfortable self, dynamism, elicit other's disclosure, altruism, listening, and sensitivity (→ Teacher Communication Style).

Influencing students to do specific tasks is referred to as compliance gaining, which is a concept rooted in power. Teacher enactment of power has primarily been in terms of 22 compliance-gaining strategies referred to as behavioral alteration techniques (BATs). Most of the BATs can be classified as enacting one of the five power bases (reward, coercive, legitimate, referent, and expert). The BATs based in referent, expert, and reward power are associated with affective learning, and those based in coercive and legitimate power are negatively associated with affective learning. An extension of teacher power is student perceptions of teacher credibility, which consists of students' perceptions of the teacher's caring, competence, and trustworthiness. Teacher behaviors such as immediacy, affinity seeking, clarity, and confirmation positively influence perceptions of teacher credibility.

Content structure and presentation also influences student learning. *Clarity* refers to teacher behaviors that contribute to the fidelity of instructional messages. When teachers are clear they do things such as use examples, stress important points, use organizational cues to facilitate student note-taking, and have clear assignments. Clarity accounts for more variance than nonverbal immediacy. When students perceive the instructor's message as *relevant*, they see the content as satisfying personal needs, personal goals, and/or career goals. Research also reveals that the use of *humor* is associated with learning and that teachers use a variety of humorous messages (some of which are inappropriate). How students behave in the classroom also impacts the learning environment. The student characteristic of → communication apprehension (CA) is the fear or anxiety associated with real or anticipated communication, and has consistently been negatively associated with student learning and other student outcomes. Highly apprehensive students learn less, receive lower grades, and have lower ACT scores.

Since the 1970s, communication scholars have examined the role of communication variables in learning environments on the premise that teaching is communicating and to be an effective teacher, one must be an effective communicator. Scholars have purposely avoided studying the presentation of specific content. Rather they have focused on identifying effective communication behaviors that go across disciplines. Verbal and nonverbal communication behaviors that communicate approach, liking, caring, and interest in students have consistently been found to be positively associated with affective learning and motivation and, to a lesser degree, with cognitive learning.

See also: ▶ COMMUNICATION APPREHENSION ▶ COMMUNICATION APPREHENSION: INTERVENTION TECHNIQUES ▶ INGRATIATION AND AFFINITY SEEKING ▶ ORGANIZATIONAL CULTURE ▶ PEDAGOGY, COMMUNICATION IN ▶ TEACHER COMMUNICATION STYLE

REFERENCES AND SELECTED READINGS

Bloom, B. S. (1956). *Taxonomy of educational objectives, handbook I: Cognitive domain.* New York: David McKay.

Chesebro, J. L. & Wanzer, M. B. (2006). Instructional message variables. In T. P. Mottet, V. P. Richmond, & J. C. McCroskey (eds.), *Handbook of instructional communication.* Boston, MA: Allyn and Bacon, pp. 89–116.

Mottet, T. P. & Richmond, V. P. (1998). Newer is not necessarily better: A reexamination of the affective learning instrument. *Communication Research Reports*, 15, 370–378.

Plax, T. G., Kearney, P., McCroskey, J. C., & Richmond, V. P. (1986). Power in the classroom VI: Verbal control strategies, nonverbal immediacy and affective learning. *Communication Education*, 35, 43–55.

Richmond, V. P., Gorham, J., & McCroskey, J. C. (1987). The relationship between selected immediacy behaviors and cognitive learning. *Communication Yearbook*, 10, 574–590.

Linguistic Pragmatics

FRANÇOIS COOREN
University of Montreal

Linguistic pragmatics is "the study of language usage" (Levinson, 1983, 5). At least five phenomena tend to qualify as typical objects of this field of study: speech acts, presuppositions, conversational implicatures, politeness, and indexical expressions. We will focus on two of them: speech act theory and conversational implicatures (→ Linguistics).

According to Austin (1962), the founder of "speech act theory," three types of action can be identified when someone communicates verbally: A "locutionary act," which consists of saying something; an "illocutionary act," which is what is done *in* saying something (for instance, 'This painting is beautiful' consists of asserting something about a painting); and a "perlocutionary act" which refers to the consequences of a given illocutionary act (for instance, making B look more carefully at the painting). Searle (1979) proposed a *typology of five speech acts*: assertives (i.e., holding something to be true, as in 'This painting is beautiful'), commissives (i.e., committing oneself, as in 'I will come'), directives (i.e., getting someone to do something, as in 'Give me a hand!'), expressives (i.e., expressing a psychological state vis-à-vis something previously performed, as in 'I apologize for calling so late'), and declarations (i.e., transforming the world by making it conform to what is declared, as in 'I hereby declare you husband and wife').

H. Paul Grice (1975) first introduced the topic of conversational implicatures by identifying what he called the cooperative principle, which is phrased as follows: "Make your conversational contribution such as is required, at the stage at which it occurs, by the accepted purpose or direction of the talk exchange in which you are engaged." There is a general presumption that when people interact with each other, they intend to abide by this principle. Thus, if the literal content of what an interlocutor says appears to deviate from this principle, there is then an inference that this person might mean something else; hence the idea of implicature.

Grice presented *four specific maxims* to specify the cooperative principle: quantity ("Make your contribution as informative as it is required"), quality ("Try to make your contribution one that is true"), relation ("Be relevant"), and manner ("Be perspicuous"). Each time an interactant appears to breach one of these maxims in communicating, this can be interpreted as implicating something else. In other words, implicatures function because it is presupposed that people cooperate to convey meaning.

See also: ▶ LINGUISTICS ▶ POLITENESS THEORY ▶ SEMIOTICS

REFERENCES AND SUGGESTED READINGS

Austin, J. L. (1962). *How to do things with words*. Cambridge, MA: Harvard University Press.
Grice, H. P. (1975). Logic and conversation. In P. Cole & J. L. Morgan (eds.), *Syntax and Semantics*, Vol. 3. New York: Academic Press, pp. 41–58.
Levinson, S. C. (1983). *Pragmatics*. Cambridge: Cambridge University Press.
Searle, J. R. (1979). *Expression and meaning: Studies in the theory of speech acts*. Cambridge: Cambridge University Press.

Linguistics

NAOMI S. BARON
American University

Linguistics is the study of language. However, linguists disagree on the scope of 'language.' Debates continue over whether linguistics examines just human speech or also encompasses areas such as animal communication, written language, artificial languages, or electronically mediated communication (e.g., email, text messaging, and online social networking).

Modern linguistics began in the late nineteenth century as a search for relationships between languages such as Sanskrit and German, leading to creation of the field of historical linguistics, with a focus on Indo-European languages. By the early twentieth century, interest shifted to linguistic diversity among native populations, first in the Americas and subsequently in Africa. This new approach (known as American Descriptivism or American Structuralism) emphasized empirical observation of living language users. Beginning in the mid-1950s, Noam Chomsky argued that instead of approaching language empirically, linguistics should be based on rationalist principles. The ultimate object of study was the core of human linguistic abilities ("universal grammar") with which all people were innately endowed. Followers of Chomsky strove to characterize what native speakers know about their language in principle (linguistic competence), not how they actually use language (linguistic performance). Chomsky's theories have been increasingly challenged, including criticism for excluding semantics from his model, objections to his dismissing language use as not relevant, and rejection of his transformational model.

Regardless of theoretical bent, linguists generally divide their inquiry with respect to several *conceptual parameters*. One distinction is between examining language at a specific moment in time (synchronically) versus tracing language change (diachronically). A second parameter decomposes language into multiple levels for analysis: phonology (sounds), morphology (units of meaning that combine to form words), and syntax (how words are combined to form sentences). Other levels include semantics (word and sentence meaning), discourse analysis (connected speech), and pragmatics (language structure and meaning in nonlinguistic context).

By the end of the twentieth century, linguists were actively working in such areas as language in social context, first and second language acquisition, → bi- and multilingualism, neurological bases for language, and examination of large corpora of spoken or written text. Linguists are also increasingly interested in cultural and political dimensions of language. Considerable efforts are being spent on recording and rejuvenating engendered languages. A related area of concern is the status of English as an international lingua franca, including the legitimacy of a variety of world 'Englishes.'

See also: ▶ BI- AND MULTILINGUALISM ▶ COGNITIVE SCIENCE ▶ DISCOURSE ▶ LANGUAGE AND SOCIAL INTERACTION ▶ LANGUAGE AND THE INTERNET ▶ LINGUISTIC PRAGMATICS

REFERENCES AND SUGGESTED READINGS

Austin, P. & Sallabank, J. (eds.) (2011). *The Cambridge handbook of endangered languages.* Cambridge: Cambridge University Press.
Bloomfield, L. (1933). *Language.* New York: Henry Holt.
Chomsky, N. (1957). *Syntactic structures.* The Hague: Mouton.

Listening

PAUL E. KING
Texas Christian University

As scholars adopted the transmission metaphor of communication popularized by Shannon and Weaver, listening was conceived as the act of receiving and understanding messages (Nichols & Stevens 1957). More recently, as communication scholars have favored a transactional perspective of communication involving the social construction of → meaning, views of listening have evolved to reflect a multidimensional orientation.

For example, *popular tests of listening* acuity such as the Kentucky Comprehensive Listening Test, the Watson–Barker Listening Test, and the Communication Competency Assessment Instrument assess several types, or aspects, of listening: following instructions, remembering information presented in short talks, recognizing central ideas, correctly inferring the meaning of statements from both verbal context and nonverbal cues, resisting distractions, and differentiating facts from opinions. On a more practical, everyday level, listening is understood to mean the communication activities associated with effective message interpretation. This orientation toward applied communication is heavily reflected in published materials related to listening and in listening improvement programs (→ Message Production; Message Discrimination).

In addition to the information-processing perspective, scholars also maintain an important *humanistic perspective* of the construct. An effective listener not only processes information effectively, but also demonstrates interest in and empathy with the speaker. While this approach has frequently been the subject of scholarly inquiry and reflection, it is most often seen in clinical and instructional materials in areas such as counseling, interviewing, mentoring, mediation, and general → interpersonal communication. An excellent example of this applied, humanistic approach to listening is Carl Rogers's "active listening" (Rogers & Farson 1973). Also widely known as "nondirective therapy," active listening has met with widespread acclaim for a variety of reasons, not the least of which is its sensitivity to the maxim 'First, do no harm.' Today, it has become pervasive in the field of clinical psychology.

The topic of listening, however defined, has become enormously popular. Proficiency in listening is a major concern in business and industry. Additionally, the International Listening Association supports the professional activities of members from a variety of countries, sponsors a scholarly journal, the International Journal of Listening, and holds an annual convention.

See also: ▶ DISCOURSE COMPREHENSION
▶ INFORMATION PROCESSING ▶ INTERPERSONAL COMMUNICATION ▶ MEANING ▶ MESSAGE DISCRIMINATION ▶C MESSAGE PRODUCTION

REFERENCES AND SUGGESTED READINGS

Nichols, R. G. & Stevens, L. A. (1957). *Are you listening?* New York: McGraw-Hill.
Rogers, C. R. & Farson, R. E. (1973). Active listening. In R. Huseman, C. M. Logue, & D. I. Freshley (eds.), *Readings in interpersonal and organizational communication*. Boston, MA: Holbrooks.

Longitudinal Analysis

HELMUT SCHERER
Hanover University of Music, Drama, and Media

Longitudinal studies conduct the same survey several times. They allow for a dynamic approach, a longitudinal analysis. We may distinguish between trend studies and panel studies. A trend study employs different respondents for each survey, while a panel study requires the use of the same respondents each time for a multiple survey. *Trend studies* can be conducted in relatively quick succession. A large number of data measured at regularly spaced intervals allows for the application of time-series analysis. Trend studies do not permit the analysis of changes at an individual level.

Panel studies allow for the collection of more data on the individual respondent. They have a greater reliability in the assessment of changes, because when comparing two individual samples, the sampling error always has to be taken into account (→ Sampling, Random). The sampling error can have a different effect on each of the samples. Panel studies can reveal hidden trends. A marketing campaign, for example, may lead to a better assessment of the product in question in one sector of the population while causing negative reactions in another sector. If we compared two independent samples, we would underestimate the actual change caused by the marketing campaign. Only a panel can provide a clear picture. Panels are generally considered to be a useful method for the analysis of causal relationships. Cross-lagged panel-correlation analysis (CLPC) can be considered to be the standard method in causal analysis in panel studies.

On the other hand, panel studies require a greater willingness to cooperate on the part of the respondents. They have to be available for repeated questioning and allow the collection of private information. It is often the case that respondents do not take part in all surveys, so that the sample size decreases progressively. This phenomenon is called 'panel mortality.' The 'panel effect' is the assumed phenomenon that respondents might change their answers due to being repeatedly contacted in the course of the research project.

See also: ▶ EXPERIMENT, LABORATORY
▶ INTERVIEW, STANDARDIZED ▶ SAMPLING, RANDOM ▶ SURVEY

REFERENCES AND SUGGESTED READINGS

Campbell, D. T. & Stanley, J. C. (1963). *Experimental and quasi-experimental designs for research*. Chicago, IL: Rand McNally.
Lazarsfeld, P. F. (1940). "Panel" studies. *Public Opinion Quarterly*, 4, 122–128.
McCullough, C. B. (1978). Effect of variables using panel data: A review of techniques. *Public Opinion Quarterly*, 42, 199–220.

Marital Communication

CHRIS SEGRIN
University of Arizona

Marital communication refers to the communication that transpires between spouses. Many people feel that communication is the key to marital success, and therefore interest in marital communication is often undertaken to discover why some marriages fail and to help couples maintain a successful marriage.

Researchers have identified distinct *types of marriages* on the basis of couples' communication behaviours. Fitzpatrick's (1988) couple typology describes three types of marriages. "Traditional couples" hold conventional values toward their marriage, are interdependent, and are willing to engage in conflict when serious issues emerge. "Independent couples" are unconventional in their marital ideology, somewhat interdependent, and generally unrestrained in their conflict engagement. Finally, "separate couples" are the most autonomous and least likely to engage in conflict, while also holding somewhat conventional values. Gottman (1994) presented findings on a comparable typology of marriages, based on the nature of couples' conflicts. 'Validators' tend to be mostly positive during their conflicts, showing mutual respect and validation of their partner's emotions and perspective. 'Volatile couples' tend to be more explosive and argumentative, while also expressing substantial positivity. In contrast, 'avoiders' prefer to minimize their disagreements and avoid discussing them altogether. Gottman observed obvious connections between his marital typology and that of Fitzpatrick (i.e., traditionals = validators, independents = volatiles, and separates = avoiders).

The *study of conflict* has a privileged status among marital communication researchers because of the belief that effective conflict management is vital to marital success and that excessive conflict is destructive to marriage (→ Interpersonal conflict). It is not conflict per se that is harmful to marital satisfaction, but how conflict is handled. Particularly destructive marital conflict behaviours include demand–withdrawal (one spouse presents a complaint or criticism and the other becomes defensive and avoids discussion), negative affect reciprocity (the negative emotional expression of one spouse is met with a comparable expression of negative affect from the other), complaining/criticizing (the commingling of a complaint with criticism of the partner), defensiveness (protecting the self by denying any responsibility

The Concise Encyclopedia of Communication, First Edition. Edited by Wolfgang Donsbach.
© 2015 John Wiley & Sons, Inc. Published 2015 by John Wiley & Sons, Inc.

for wrongdoing), contempt (mocking or insulting the partner), and stonewalling (showing no signs of listening to the partner).

See also: ▶ INTERPERSONAL CONFLICT

REFERENCES AND SUGGESTED READINGS

Fitzpatrick, M. A. (1988). *Between husbands and wives.* Newbury Park, CA: Sage.

Gottman, J. M. (1994). *What predicts divorce: The relationship between marital processes and marital outcomes.* Mahwah, NJ: Lawrence Erlbaum.

Marketing

FRANZ-RUDOLF ESCH
EBS University of Business and Law

KRISTINA STRÖDTER
Justus Liebig University

Marketing can be defined in the sense of market-oriented business leadership. This market orientation is characterized by all relevant activities and processes of the company that focus on consumers' needs and wants (Esch 2012). To focus on consumers and the market, it is one of the basic tasks of marketing to find out about relevant consumers' needs and wants. Therefore, it is important to thoroughly analyze consumers. Once marketers know consumers' needs, the next step is to develop products and services that satisfy them.

In the twenty-first century, companies face changing customer values, which are observably getting more diverse. Even one and the same person can have different needs in different situations. The phenomenon of 'hybrid consumption' is rapidly emerging. Firms try to react to these specific needs by offering customized products. Another challenge is increased global competition. This trend is intensified by new information and communication technologies like the Internet, which make it easier to sell products worldwide. But also for consumers the world has become more complex because they are bombarded by too much information. This trend is accompanied by products becoming outdated sooner (Lim & Tang 2006). In this environment, launching new products successfully is a real challenge.

Designing Marketing Strategies

A marketing plan, as the core of marketing management, is the central instrument for directing, synchronizing, and coordinating all marketing activities. First, it is important for marketers to develop an understanding of their customers. Based on this knowledge, goals and strategies must be determined. In this context, there are three levels that need to be planned systematically: (1) the marketing goal, which represents the situation strived for; (2) marketing strategies, i.e., the roads leading to that goal; and (3) marketing instruments necessary to 'walk the road' (Esch et al. 2013). The classic set of marketing activities is summarized by the '4Ps' (product, price, placement, promotion).

The 4Ps are the pillars of marketing, while → branding is its base, on which all marketing activities are built. Therefore, it is crucial to base marketing strategies on a thoroughly planned branding strategy. To ensure that the implemented activities help the company to achieve its goals, it is important to control activities, strategies, and goals regularly. In this context, progress in the achievement of the company's objectives has to be measured. Besides controlling the effectiveness of strategies and activities, marketers should revise whether the marketing goals are still worth striving for or whether they are outdated.

The Brand As the Base for Marketing Activities

A brand can be defined as a mental image in the minds of the target group that leads to identification and differentiation and affects people's choices (Esch 2012; → Brand). Brand identity and brand positioning together serve as the essential basis for all brand decisions. In contrast to brand image, which refers to the perception of the brand, brand identity and positioning are in the company's sphere of action.

Principally, companies face three basic options to lead their brands: (1) product brands; (2) family brands; and (3) corporate brands. Using a *product brand* strategy, every product of a company forms an own-brand; this means 'one brand = one product = one brand promise' (e.g.,

Procter & Gamble, with brands like Pringles, Ariel, and Pampers). A *family brand* comprises several products under one brand, e.g., Maggi or Nivea. The advantage of this strategy is that all offerings of a brand profit from its existing brand image. *Corporate brands* are used for all products of a company. The primary aim of this strategy is to establish a clear profile of the company and its competencies.

Raising Consumers' Brand Awareness and Brand Image with Communication

Communication is an effective instrument to build unique brand images in consumers' minds. Integrated communication is understood as the integration of form and content of all communication activities, which unifies and reinforces the impressions made. In integrated communication, verbal as well as nonverbal elements can be used. These either transfer distinctive image associations (BMW is sporty and dynamic) or form an anchor to enhance brand awareness, e.g., by using a particular color code or symbols (→ Integrated Marketing Communications; Marketing: Communication Tools).

As a basic principle, communication instruments can be divided into *personal and mass communication*. Personal communication distinguishes itself by greater credibility of the communicator, the possibility to respond to the listener's needs, and the information conveyed by nonverbal communication. Moreover, personal communication offers higher flexibility.

A *customer's buying cycle* can be broken down into four different stages. (1) The buying cycle starts when a consumer gets in touch with a product. This first contact happens through mass communication, e.g., through TV commercials. (2) In the second stage, the consumer starts gathering more information. In this stage, personal communication is very important. (3) When a customer is finally buying a product, personal communication is essential. The assistant should give advice about special features and different models of the product. (4) While the customer is using the product, a company should stay in touch with the customer. Brochures, events, or telephone calls by the company help the company to get feedback about its product and services.

Price Elasticity and Differentiation

To find out what price leads to maximal profits, managers should estimate the demand and costs associated with the alternative prices and choose that price which leads to the highest estimated profits. There are many factors that affect a company's cost and turnover functions; e.g., pricing has an effect on further variables, like competitors and their reactions, the product's and brand's image as well as consumers' reactions. To assess the change in demand due to changes in prices, marketers need to know about consumers' price sensitivity and price elasticity, which describe changes in demand due to a 1 percent rise in price.

Price differentiation refers to selling principally the same products to different consumers or groups of consumers at different prices. The aim of this strategy is to skim as much as possible of the *consumer surplus*, which can be defined as the difference in consumers' willingness to pay and the price actually paid. One can distinguish between three *different forms of price differentiation*. According to first-order differentiation, prices are set individually for each customer to perfectly skim his or her willingness to pay. According to second-order differentiation, consumers decide independently to which price category they belong. By contrast, third-order differentiation does not enable consumers to choose their category themselves. Segments and the respective prices are pre-arranged by the company.

Developing an Optimal Distribution Strategy

Distribution is more than getting products to potential customers. When planning their distribution strategy, marketers must decide on whether to sell their product directly or indirectly to the end consumers, and whether their product should be distributed universally or selectively. Companies that *distribute their goods directly* sell their products to the end consumer without interposing any external distributors.

The *indirect distribution* strategy can be sub-categorized based on the number of intermediaries involved. Supermarkets are often one-tier distribution systems, whereas pharmacies and florists are two-tier systems, consisting of retail and wholesale. A special form of indirect distribution is franchising, where a company's products are distributed by legally and economically independent firms whose relationship to the producing firm is regulated by contract (e.g., McDonald's). One of the major disadvantages of intermediaries is the producer's loss of control, i.e., how the products are presented in the stores.

See also: ▶ ADVERTISING ▶ ADVERTISING EFFECTIVENESS ▶ ADVERTISING EFFECTIVENESS, MEASUREMENT OF ▶ ADVERTISING STRATEGIES ▶ BRANDING ▶ BRANDS ▶ CORPORATE AND ORGANIZATIONAL IDENTITY ▶ GLOBALIZATION OF ORGANIZATIONS ▶ INTEGRATED MARKETING COMMUNICATIONS ▶ MARKETING: COMMUNICATION TOOLS ▶ PUBLIC RELATIONS ▶ SEGMENTATION OF THE ADVERTISING AUDIENCE ▶ VISUAL COMMUNICATION

REFERENCES AND SUGGESTED READINGS

Boone, L. E. & Kurtz, D. L. (2013). *Contemporary marketing*, 15th edn. Cincinnati, OH: South Western Educational Publishing.

Coughlan, A. T., Anderson, E., Stern, L. W., & El-Ansary, A. I. (2006). *Marketing channels*. 7th edition. Upper Saddle River, NJ: Prentice Hall.

Drucker, P. F. (1954). *The practice of management*. London: HarperCollins.

Eagle, L. Dahl, S. & Czarnecka, B. (2014). *Marketing communications*. London: Routledge.

Esch, F.-R. (2012). *Strategie und Technik der Markenführung* [Strategy and techniques of brand management], 7th edn. Wiesbaden: Gabler.

Esch, F.-R., Hermann, A., & Sattler, H. (2013). *Marketing. Eine managementorientierte Einführung* [Marketing: A management-oriented introduction]. 4th edn. Munich: Vahlen.

Keller, K. L. (2012). *Strategic brand management: Building, measuring, and managing brand equity*, 4th edn. Upper Saddle River, NJ: Prentice Hall.

Kotler, P. & Armstrong, G. (2012). *Marketing: An introduction*, 11th edn. New York: Prentice Hall.

Lim, W. S. & Tang, C. S. (2006). Optimal product rollover strategies. *European Journal of Operational Research*, 174(2), 905–922.

Mooji, M. K. (2014). *Global marketing and advertising: Understanding cultural paradoxes*, 4th edn. Thousand Oaks, CA: Sage.

Marketing: Communication Tools

RICHARD ALAN NELSON
Louisiana State University

Marketing communication involves the ongoing process of relationship building with target audiences on all matters that affect marketing and business performance. Targeted are those groups of people an organization needs to communicate with in order to meet goals and objectives.

A number of marketing communications options are available that help companies build and maintain audience, increase market share and market awareness, acquire new business, and build more fruitful relationships with existing clients. *Advertising* is a planned communication activity that utilizes controlled messages carried by the media to persuade audiences. Any form of nonpersonal one-way communication about products, ideas, goods, or services paid for by an identified sponsor can be grouped under the advertising umbrella. Research indicates that consumers tend to perceive advertised goods as more legitimate. Another key advantage is that advertising typically reaches large, geographically dispersed audiences, often with high frequency (→ Advertising; Segmentation of the Advertising Audience).

Public relations is most associated with maintaining good relationships with the company's various publics by promoting a good 'corporate image.' Since public relations appears in many forms (as news reports, sponsored events, etc.), it tends to be highly credible with audiences and reaches many prospects missed via other forms of promotion. Despite being cost-effective, public relations is often the most underused element in the promotional mix (→ Public Relations). *Publicity messages* are conveyed to the public through the mass media and are a component of public relations linked to press agentry.

Any communication to carefully targeted individual consumers designed to generate an immediate commercial response is *direct marketing* (i.e., an order, request for information, or sales visit). All direct-response advertising is structured around three basic elements: (1) the message communicates a definite offer; (2) the recipient is given the information necessary to make a decision; and (3) the ad makes it easy to say 'yes' immediately by including one or more response devices (e.g., a coupon). *Sponsorships* are defined as payment (in fees, goods, or services) in return for the rights to a public association with another organization and/or event (naming rights, onsite banners, cross-advertising, etc.).

Most businesses have a sales force whose members make *personal presentations* to persuade a prospective customer to commit to buying a good, a service, or even an idea. The seller generally interprets brand features in terms of buyer benefits, and the salesperson can be critical when the number of potential customers is limited and the product is technical and/or expensive. *Promotional products* comprise an advertising, sales-promotion, publicity, and motivational communication medium that displays the sponsoring organization's name, logo, or message on useful articles of merchandise.

Sales promotions are defined as those activities other than personal selling, advertising, and publicity that stimulate consumer purchasing. Sales promotions are typically short-term field marketing and merchandising incentives to encourage purchase or sale of a product or service. Examples of point-of-sale and business sales promotion vehicles include contests, coupons, rebates, refund offers, and sweepstakes.

The potentially huge number of viewers who can take action ('word-of-mouth marketing') is one attraction of *Internet campaigning*. A well-placed link on a popular website, or passed from friend to friend, may generate millions of page hits very quickly. The impact of → Facebook, YouTube, and other → social media has caught the attention of major marketers. By tapping into these 'virtual communities,' i.e., individuals who share common identification, companies are finding they can mobilize interest through 'viral-marketing' techniques. By identifying opinion leaders in a market segment and providing them with special incentives, sponsors are also creating 'buzz' within target groups. Also, rich *email* (graphically designed email that is forwardable and trackable) is among the new Internet-based technologies for e-commerce.

The accelerating changes we see in communication technologies are evidence of a fundamental shift in society as a whole. Many commentators argue that we are at a historical turning point similar to that which marked the introduction of movable type in Europe and the rise of industrialism. No one is yet sure what 'globalism' really means in terms of the way we live or how we conduct business. Shifts that give consumers greater control over messages they pay attention to are definitely changing the notion of the marketplace. Combined with the erosion of older models of how media deliver audiences, these developments are temporarily causing consternation among many marketers who are still groping to find what works. Given past performance, they are likely to be successful.

See also: ▶ ADVERTISING ▶ ADVERTISING AS PERSUASION ▶ ADVERTISEMENT CAMPAIGN MANAGEMENT ▶ ADVERTISING EFFECTIVENESS ▶ ADVERTISING EFFECTIVENESS, MEASUREMENT MARKETING ▶ ADVERTISING, HISTORY OF ▶ ADVERTISING STRATEGIES ▶ BRANDING ▶ BRANDS ▶ CENSORSHIP ▶ CONSUMER CULTURE ▶ CORPORATE COMMUNICATION ▶ CROSS-MEDIA MARKETING ▶ FACEBOOK ▶ INTEGRATED MARKETING COMMUNICATIONS ▶ MEDIA EFFECTS ▶ MEDIA PLANNING ▶ ORGANIZATIONAL COMMUNICATION ▶ PERSUASION ▶ PROPAGANDA ▶ PUBLIC RELATIONS ▶ PUBLIC RELATIONS: MEDIA INFLUENCE ▶ PUBLIC RELATIONS PLANNING ▶ SEGMENTATION OF THE ADVERTISING AUDIENCE ▶ SOCIAL MARKETING ▶ SOCIAL MEDIA ▶ STRATEGIC COMMUNICATION

REFERENCES AND SUGGESTED READINGS

Blythe, J. (2012). *Essentials of marketing communications*, 5th edn. Harlow: Pearson Education.
Dahlén, M., Lange, F., & Smith, T. (2008). *Marketing communications*. Chichester: John Wiley.
De Pelsmacker, P., Geuens, M., & Van den Bergh, J. (2013). *Marketing communications. A European perspective*. Harlow: Pearson Education.
Donaldson, B., & O'Toole, T. (2007). *Strategic market relationships: From strategy to implementation*, 2nd edn. Chichester: John Wiley.
Eagle, L. Dahl, S., & Czarnecka, B. (2014). *Marketing communications*. London: Routledge.
Kirby, J., & Marsden, P. (2006). *Connected marketing: The viral, buzz and word of mouth revolution*. Oxford: Butterworth-Heinemann.

Markets of the Media

BENJAMIN J. BATES
University of Tennessee

The essence of the concept 'markets of the media' is the identification and understanding of the context where producers supply, and audiences consume, media content – with the inevitable economic, social, and political ramifications that result from their behaviors. Defining a market is the primary step; as that identifies who is involved in supply and demand and facilitates understanding of market behaviors; allowing prediction of outcomes, even under changing conditions.

Markets in Economics

Markets exist as the contexts where those seeking to supply goods and services interact with those seeking to acquire them (demand). Three factors *define a market*: the determination of the good (or service), identifying those who seek to provide the good, and identifying those who are capable of acquiring the good. Generally, the more specific the identification of the good, the easier it is to determine and understand remaining market characteristics and structure, and market behaviors.

Several *aspects of market structure* impact market operations: presence of market power, barriers to entry, and externalities. Market power happens when supply or demand is dominated by a few market participants whose market share is enough that it can impact pricing. Normally this happens when there are few participants (monopoly, oligopoly), perhaps facilitated by barriers to entry (constraints on who participates resulting from technological, economic, or regulatory limits), and product differentiation (monopolistic competition – where product differences are enough that they can split markets into segments). Externalities refers to impacts that market behaviors have outside the market (social benefits from information use), or impacts that outside factors have within markets (such as taxes or subsidies).

Information goods and services, including media content, share some other distinctive features. There are public goods attributes: 'nonrivalrous consumption,' which means that consumption by some does not materially affect consumption by others, and 'nonexcludability,' which refers to the difficulty of preventing access to the good by those who have not purchased it. Information markets also suffer from 'imperfect information'; information goods tend to have a high degree of originality, and gaining full knowledge of the good typically requires its consumption; thus, potential consumers (and suppliers) typically base their decisions on incomplete or imperfect information about the product and market. Imperfect information is a major contributor to the variability and uncertainty in value perceptions among consumers (as is variation in consumer tastes and preferences), which also impacts consumption decisions. These lead to some distinctive marketing behaviors – differentiated content and close substitutes, the use of bundling (combining multiple pieces of content within a single packaged product) to aggregate value and reduce uncertainty, and an emphasis on branding and consistency across content offerings to establish norms for expected value.

Media Markets and Market Failures

Historically, media markets were defined by medium, with content form and distribution range tied to technical attributes of the particular medium. Newspapers, → books, movies, music, radio, television – all focused on providing content that took advantage of distinctive characteristics of their distribution medium and network. Both producers and consumers coupled content and medium in their conceptualization of media products and markets. Media markets were clear and distinct, and largely independent of one another.

However, few media markets fit the norms for 'typical' or perfectly competitive markets; entry barriers, public goods attributes, and imperfect information result in market power, resulting in markets that didn't achieve what was considered to be socially or economically optimal outcomes. They meet the economic definition of 'market failure,' i.e., not perfectly competitive; this was used to justify regulatory intrusions into the market to 'fix' the 'failure.' To be effective, these efforts need to be based on an accurate understanding of market forces and behaviors. To illustrate, → copyright and intellectual property policy is a legal response to one set of market failures (the public good characteristics; → Intellectual Property Law). The solution, though, is the creation of monopoly rights and the granting of monopoly power to the owner of those rights, which happen to create a different kind of market failure, one of possibly greater consequence (Lessig 2004).

Additionally, most media and audiences operate in multiple *interlinked markets* rather than single independent markets. Media firms, for example, may bundle content with advertising in their products; in the content market, audiences need to provide their time and attention in order to consume the content. Audience attention and content are complements, and media operate in content markets trading content for attention, and then operate in advertising markets to sell that attention to advertisers.

Still, the greatest driver of *market transformation* is the rise of the digital network economy. Digital technologies have dramatically lowered production costs for virtually all content forms, and enabled content to be provided across media formats. One result has been an explosion in available content. Digital networks have radically reduced content storage and distribution costs, expanding the scope and reach of markets, in the process removing many of the old barriers to entry and encouraging market convergence. With the introductions of new devices for accessing and consuming media content (mobile), opportunities for producing, accessing, and consuming media content have vastly expanded, transforming both markets and the market behaviors that determine supply and demand curves within media markets (→ Digital Media, History of). These transformations are helping to decouple content and media. 'Media' consumption is increasingly driven by active interest in content, with the means of distribution and display of secondary interest. This is a radical shift in the basis of audience behavior that drives demand and media use and will contribute to further market transformation.

Emerging Market Issues

The confluence of technological innovations, policy shifts, → globalization of the media, and evolving audience demand is radically transforming media markets. The inherent cost advantages of the digital network economy (Benkler 2006) – an advantage that increases with continued innovation – are driving most traditional media into the digital marketplace while triggering rapid market expansion toward globalization. There are fundamental changes occurring in how supply and demand are determined, and how media markets are defined ("fuzzy markets"; Lacey 2004). A major concern for media outlets is over which definition of market should it base their business models; should they stick with the old or seek to take advantage of the opportunities market transformation present?

Media regulators and policymakers face the same issue when addressing 'failure' of media markets. For example, current copyright law emphasizes restricting and controlling access to (and consumption of) content, with fees based on the more limited consumption patterns of traditional media marketplaces and set on a national basis. This is limiting the ability to expand markets globally, as well as limiting development of new markets and distribution strategies.

See also: ▶ ADVERTISING, ECONOMICS OF ▶ AUDIENCE RESEARCH ▶ AUDIENCE SEGMENTATION ▶ BOOK ▶ CABLE TELEVISION ▶ CONCENTRATION IN MEDIA SYSTEMS ▶ CONSUMERS IN MEDIA MARKETS ▶ COPYRIGHT ▶ CROSS-MEDIA MARKETING ▶ DIGITAL DIVIDE ▶ DIGITAL MEDIA, HISTORY OF ▶ DIVERSIFICATION OF MEDIA MARKETS ▶ GLOBALIZATION OF THE MEDIA ▶ INTELLECTUAL PROPERTY LAW ▶ MEDIA CONGLOMERATES ▶ MEDIA ECONOMICS ▶ POLITICAL ECONOMY OF THE MEDIA ▶ PRIVATIZATION OF THE MEDIA ▶ RADIO BROADCASTING, REGULATION OF ▶ TECHNOLOGY AND COMMUNICATION ▶ TELEVISION BROADCASTING, REGULATION OF

REFERENCES AND SUGGESTED READINGS

Albarran, A. B. (2002). *Media economics: Understanding markets, industries, and concepts*, 2nd edn. Ames, IA: Iowa State University Press.

Albarran, A. B., Chan-Olmstead, S., & Wirth, M. O. (eds.) (2005). *Handbook of media management and economics*. Mahwah, NJ: Lawrence Erlbaum.

Baker, C. E. (2002). *Media, markets, and democracy*. Cambridge: Cambridge University Press.

Bates, B. J. & Albright, K. (2006). Network and distribution economics. In A. Albarran et al. (eds.), *Handbook of Media Management and Economics*. Hillsdale, NJ: Lawrence Erlbaum, pp. 417–443.

Benkler, Y. (2006). *The wealth of networks: How social production transforms markets and freedom*. New Haven, CT: Yale University Press.

Hoskins, S., McFadyen, S. M., & Finn, A. (2004). *Media economics: Applying economics to new and traditional media*. Thousand Oaks, CA: Sage.

Kops, M. (2006). Globalizing media markets: Benefits and costs, winners and losers. Working Paper No. 211e. Cologne: Institute for Broadcasting Economics, University of Cologne.

Lacey, S. (2004). Fuzzy market structure and differentiation. In R. G. Picard (ed.), *Strategic responses to media market changes*. Jonkoping: Jonkoping International Business School, pp. 83–95.

Lessig, L. (2004). *Free culture: The nature and future of creativity*. Harmondsworth: Penguin.

Napoli, P. M. (2003). *Audience economics: Media institutions and the audience marketplace*. New York: Columbia University Press.

Picard, R. G. & Wildman, S. (eds.), (2014). *International handbook on the economics of media*. Cheltenham: Edward Elgar.

Zerdick, A., Picot, A., Schrape, K., Burgelman, J-C., Silverstone, R., Feldmann, V., Wernick, C. & Wolff, C. (eds.) (2005). *E-merging media: Communication and the media economy of the future*. New York: Springer.

Masculinity and the Media

JOHN BEYNON
University of Glamorgan

BETHAN BENWELL
University of Stirling

The focus of this entry is upon televisual masculinities in the western world while making it evident that the approach adopted could also be applied to other media genres (→ Television as Popular Culture). From the mid-1950s to the late 1970s, the depiction of gender on television was highly stereotypical and critiqued by second-wave feminists (→ Sexism in the Media). Throughout the 1970s and 1980s, narrow gender stereotypes were challenged. Male leads increasingly combined toughness with a degree of vulnerability (Inspector Morse). Men, too, were becoming increasingly fashion-conscious (Miami Vice), without any real diminution of masculine power. During the 1990s, gender stereotypes were further eroded, or sometimes knowingly explored and referenced (Buffy the Vampire Slayer, Friends, Frasier, and Sex and the City), and male intimacy and homosocial bonding became common forms of representation (Feasey 2008, 24).

In the contemporary, postmodern era, TV shows (fiction and nonfiction), have further deconstructed gender binaries by their normative portrayal of alternative and marginal masculinities, among them gay masculinity (Six Feet Under, The Wire, and True Blood), transgendered identities (Hayley Cropper in the UK soap Coronation Street), and female masculinity (Felicia 'Snoop' Pearson in The Wire). Whilst representations of gender on television have changed considerably since the early 1960s (→ Gender: Representation in the Media), it might be argued that traditional gender stereotypes continue to be regenerated. Reality, sporting, and magazine-format TV have seen a resurgence of hypermasculine, often dangerous pursuits (e.g., Deadliest Catch, Top Gear, Jackass) imbued with 'laddish' values, and popular reality shows continue to represent gender as essentially polarized and heterosexual. Whilst gender-literate television writers and directors are prepared to experiment with nontraditional and subversive representations of masculinity. others might conclude that television continues to reflect, rather than instigate, meaningful and enduring social change.

See also: ▶ GAY, LESBIAN, BISEXUAL, AND TRANSGENDER MEDIA STUDIES ▶ GENDER: REPRESENTATION IN THE MEDIA ▶ POSTMODERNISM AND COMMUNICATION ▶ SEX ROLE STEREOTYPES IN THE MEDIA ▶ SEXISM IN THE MEDIA ▶ TELEVISION AS POPULAR CULTURE

REFERENCES AND SUGGESTED READINGS

Bignell, J. & Lacey, S. (eds.) (2005). *Popular television drama: Critical perspectives*. Manchester: Manchester University Press.

Feasey, R. (2008). *Masculinity and popular television*. Edinburgh: Edinburgh University Press.

Hermes, J. (2005). *Re-reading popular culture: Rethinking gender, television, and popular media audiences.* Oxford: Wiley Blackwell.

Meaning

KLAUS BRUHN JENSEN
University of Copenhagen

The concept of meaning is most commonly associated with humanistic perspectives on the texts of communication and their interpretation by culturally situated audiences. In comparison, → information denotes a social scientific conception of the differences that communication makes in later events and contexts.

Three *notions of meaning* have entered into communication research. First, meaning implies a saturated sense of self: an identity and an orientation toward others. Second, meaning is the outcome of innumerable communicative exchanges, accumulating as tradition (→ Culture: Definitions and Concepts). Third, meaning is an emphatically contested terrain – an object of reflexivity. The terminology of 'meaning production' suggests that people literally produce meanings and identities for themselves, and, in communication, they jointly accomplish meaningful social realities.

As an analytical object, meaning can be operationalized in four *ideal-typical models* (Jensen 2012, 11) where the constituents may, or may not, make up a pre-defined inventory and the structure a fixed matrix. This leads to four types: 'deterministic', 'generative', 'stochastic', and 'indeterministic.' Communication is rarely an entirely deterministic or indeterministic process. Thus, the two main models of meaning in media and communication research are the stochastic and generative types. The stochastic type is witnessed in the prototypical social scientific survey, experimental, or content-analytical study. Given a pre-defined range of content or response units, the question is which of these, and in which configurations, are manifest, as measured by an appropriate statistical technique. The generative type is associated with humanistic media studies, typically qualitative analyses of how meanings are generated in and through media texts and audience reception (→ Qualitative Methodology).

See also: ▶ COGNITIVE SCIENCE ▶ CULTURAL STUDIES ▶ CULTURE: DEFINITIONS AND CONCEPTS ▶ INFORMATION ▶ MODERNITY ▶ PHENOMENOLOGY ▶ POSTMODERNISM AND COMMUNICATION ▶ QUALITATIVE METHODOLGY ▶ STRUCTURALISM

REFERENCES AND SUGGESTED READINGS

Jensen, K. B. (ed.) (2012). *A handbook of media and communication research: Qualitative and quantitative methodologies,* 2nd edn. London: Routledge.

Ogden, C. K. & Richards, I. A. (1989). *The meaning of meaning: A study of the influence of language upon thought and of the science of symbolism.* New York: Harcourt Brace Jovanovich.

Measurement Theory

STEPHANIE SARGENT WEAVER
Northrop Grumman/Centers for Disease Control and Prevention

Measurement theory is a sub-field of methodology that deals with the relationship between theoretical constructs and their measurement in the research process.

Generally scientists make a deliberate decision to observe, are equally deliberate about what they will observe, take precautions against erroneous observations, and record their observations carefully as measurements. Ultimately, measurement is the process whereby a thing, concept, or object measured is compared against a point of limitation (→ Quantitative Methodology; Qualitative Methodology).

In measurement, there are *three central concepts*: numerals, assignment, and rules (e.g. Wimmer & Dominick 2014). *Numerals* are symbols such as S, 5, 10, or 100, and have no explicit quantitative meaning. *Assignment* is the designation of numerals or numbers to certain objects or events. For example, we assign numbers to classify people by how they get their news. *Rules* specify the way that numerals or numbers are to be assigned. Rules are the foundation of any measurement system, so if the rules are faulty the measurement system will be faulty, too. For some research studies, the rules can be obvious (i.e., measuring reading speed with a stopwatch) or not so obvious (i.e., measuring 'enjoyment of televised sports').

In addition, measurement systems also strive to be isomorphic to reality. Basically, isomorphism means identity or similarity of form or structure. To strive for isomorphism, researchers must define the sets of objects being measured and the numerical sets from which they assign numerals to those objects, and check that the rules of assignment or correspondence are tied to 'reality.' To assess isomorphism to reality, researchers ask the question, 'Is this set of objects isomorphic to that set of objects?' In the social sciences, researchers must ask the question, "Do the measurement procedures being used have some rational and empirical correspondence with 'reality'?" (Kerlinger & Lee 1999). The ultimate question that must be asked is 'Is the measurement procedure isomorphic to reality?'

In 1946, Stevens suggested *four levels, or types, of measurement*. *Nominal measurement* is the weakest form of measurement and identifies variables whose values have no mathematical interpretation. In addition, they must be mutually exclusive and exhaustive. Examples are gender, ethnicity, occupation, religious affiliation, and social security number. In the *ordinal scale* of measurement, we think in terms of the symbols > (greater than) or < (less than). The ordinal scale implies that the entity being measured is quantified in terms of being of a higher or lower or a greater or lesser order than a comparative entity. In measuring on the ordinal scale, the relationship is always asymmetrical. Examples are a student's academic level and socio-economic status.

The *interval scale* of measurement is characterized by two features: it has (1) equal units of measurement; and (2) an arbitrarily established zero point. It includes the characteristics of the nominal and ordinal scales, plus the numbers indicating the values of a variable represent fixed measurement units, and there is no absolute or fixed zero point. The most familiar examples of interval-level measurement are in both the Fahrenheit (F) and Celsius (C) scales as well as rating scales employed to assess opinions on any objects.

The highest level of measurement is the *ratio scale*. It possesses the characteristics of the nominal, ordinal, and interval scales, plus it has an absolute or natural zero point that has empirical meaning. If a measurement is zero on a ratio scale, then the object in question has none of the property being measured. All arithmetic operations are possible, such as multiplication and division, and the numbers on the scale indicate the actual amounts of the property being measured. Examples include a person's age or time spent on the Internet.

One can determine one's level of measurement by applying it to the following test: If one can say that one object is different from another, one has a nominal scale; one object is bigger or better or more of anything than another, one has an ordinal scale; one object is so many units (degrees, inches) more than another, one has an interval scale; one object is so many times as big or bright or tall or heavy as another, one has a ratio scale.

See also: ▶ OBSERVATION ▶ OPERATIONALIZATION ▶ QUALITATIVE METHODOLOGY ▶ QUANTITATIVE METHODOLOGY ▶ RELIABILITY

REFERENCES AND SUGGESTED READINGS

Babbie, E. (2013). *The practice of social research*, 13th edn. Belmont, CA: Wadsworth Cengage Learning.
Katzer, J., Cook, K. H., & Crouch, W. W. (1998). *Evaluating information: A guide for users of social science research*, 4th edn. Boston, MA: McGraw-Hill.
Kerlinger, F. N. & Lee, H. B. (1999). *Foundations of behavioral research*, 4th edn. Boston: Wadsworth.
Leedy, P. D. & Ormrod, J. E. (2014). *Practical research: Planning and design*, 10th edn. Harlow: Pearson Education.
Stevens, S. S. (1946). On the theory of scales of measurement. *Science*, 103, 677–680.
Wimmer, R. D. & Dominick, J. R. (2014). *Mass media research: An introduction*, 10th edn. Boston: Wadsworth Cengage Learning.

Media

KLAUS BRUHN JENSEN
University of Copenhagen

Media refers to the tools that humans have used throughout history to communicate about a shared reality. The most common reference is to the modern technologies that facilitate communication across space, time, and collectives.

Three *main concepts of media* inform communication research. The first is Harold D. Lasswell's paradigm – "who says what, in which channel, to whom, with what effect" – which approaches media as neutral conduits of information. The second conception is the mathematical theory of communication by Claude Shannon that emphasizes technical aspects of communication systems. The third concept represents humanistic perspectives on media as cultural carriers of → meaning. In this last respect, Roman Jakobson has made an important distinction between channels or contacts (concrete entities such as → books, newspapers, or the internet) and → codes (forms of expression such as speech, writing, music, or images).

Much media and communication research is characterized by efforts at integrating these concepts theoretically as well as analytically. Studies commonly identify three *aspects of any medium*: Media are physical materials in a particular social shape that enable communication. Such materials are the vehicles of modalities – language, music, moving images, etc. Finally, media are institutions through which individuals and collectives can reflect upon themselves and the rest of society.

Digital media have stimulated renewed interest in the relationship between technologically mediated communication and face-to-face communication, and in the reshaping – remediation (Bolter & Grusin 1999) – of older media (→Digital Media, History of). One may distinguish between *media of three degrees* (Jensen 2010). Media of the first degree are humans – biologically based and culturally shaped resources of communication. Media of the second degree are mass media – from the printing press to television. Media of the third degree are digital media that recombine all previous media on single platforms.

See also: ▶ CODES ▶ COMMUNICATION AS A FIELD AND DISCIPLINE ▶ COMMUNICATION: HISTORY OF THE IDEA ▶ DIGITAL MEDIA, HISTORY OF ▶ DISCOURSE ▶ INTERMEDIALITY ▶ MEDIUM THEORY ▶ REMEDIATION ▶ TECHNOLOGY AND COMMUNICATION

REFERENCES AND SUGGESTED READINGS

Bolter, J. D. & Grusin, R. (1999). *Remediation: Understanding new media.* Cambridge, MA: MIT Press.

Jensen, K. B. (2010). *Media convergence: The three degrees of network, mass, and interpersonal communication.* London: Routledge.

Meyrowitz, J. (1994). Medium theory. In D. Crowley & D. Mitchell (eds.), *Communication theory today.* Cambridge: Polity.

Media Conglomerates

DANIEL BILTEREYST
Ghent University

The issue of media conglomeration, or the phenomenon of a vast amount of cultural (media) production being controlled by a relatively small number of corporations, has generated heated debates among communication scholars, policymakers, and industry practitioners. In these debates, the concept of media conglomeration primarily refers to ownership structures within media and communications industries, as well as to the nature and organization of this type of cultural production. The phenomenon of media conglomeration, though, touches upon a much broader set of interrelated issues – ranging from questions on diversity, competition, and control in a tightly oligopolistic market, to concerns over the wider societal implications of a situation where huge conglomerates dominate the global communications system (→ Globalization of the Media).

Drawing upon → public sphere theories, scholars working within a critical research tradition have been asking questions about how far and at what price a communication system can be dominated by a handful of corporations, and how this might affect the diversity of information and argument needed for effective and well-informed citizenship (→ Critical Theory). Sharp political economic analyses on how the corporate structure and strategy of media conglomerates tend to homogenize cultural production and restrict critical media content have been opposed by advocates of the free market. Media conglomeration is also an important concept in the academic field of → international communication and in debates on media, internationalization, and globalization. Because much of today's communications industry is under the control of multinational corporations with cross-media activities in most parts of the world and with their headquarters in the USA, western Europe, Australia, or Japan, the issue of media conglomeration is often associated with older arguments about Americanization, Eurocentrism, or cultural imperialism (→ Cultural Imperialism Theories).

Although an unparalleled series of international acquisitions and buy-outs of media and entertainment companies from the 1980s onward fueled the debate, it is clear that the issue of media conglomeration is not a new phenomenon. During the second half of the *nineteenth century*, new technologies such as the telegraph, facilitating the transfer of information over a long distance, created the first modern media corporations with an international scope. In the *twentieth century*, the growth of other new media sectors went hand in hand with vertically integrated and internationally active companies. The film industry, for instance, quickly saw the emergence of oligopolistic structures which tried to control most levels of the industry, increased their interests in the wider leisure industry (music, radio, etc.), and operated in an international environment. In the postwar period, the communications industry saw several waves of mergers and concentration. From the 1980s onwards, the rapidly expanding global entertainment market, the availability of new delivery systems, and the development of new markets and technologies, combined with a deregulation policy, all resulted in a further cycle of mergers. This trend did not stop in the 1990s and during the first decade of the new millennium, with spectacular mergers (→ Time Warner Inc.; Disney; News Corporation; Sony Corporation).

This conglomeration trend *raised many questions*. A first set of questions deals with *how far a market can be controlled* without harming competition in terms of production, dissemination, and consumption of media products or content (→ Markets of the Media). Critical voices in the debate argue that the trend reduces the diversity of cultural goods in circulation. From this perspective, conglomeration might have a restricting effect on media content while it tries to offer more variants of the same basic themes and images. Critics argue that conglomerates seek content that can move fluidly across different media and channels (synergy), while they ignore creative talent and content in favor of commercial viability. This analysis is countered by arguments claiming that a free market has led to a decreasing oligopoly and the emergence of new players, while consumers enjoy more choice. This position refers to the growing amount of television and other media providers and the emergence of the Internet as a source for information and entertainment, as well as the notion of counterculture audiences who do not accept what conglomerates offer. The answer to this position is that a key to understanding conglomeration is that major players in the field continuously try to absorb viable alternatives through mergers in order to extend their scope and consolidate their position.

A second set of questions refers to a higher level of implications, dealing with the role of the *media as a central political and societal institution* in democracy. Inspired by public-sphere theories in relation to the media, conglomeration critics express worries about the conglomerates' power in controlling the flow of information and open debate in society. Opponents claim that the danger to democracy is a myth, given the extension of choice and emergence of new alternative sources of information.

See also: ▶ CRITICAL THEORY ▶ CULTURAL IMPERIALISM THEORIES ▶ DISNEY ▶ GLOBALIZATION OF THE MEDIA ▶ INTERNATIONAL COMMUNICATION ▶ MARKETS OF THE MEDIA ▶ MEDIA ECONOMICS ▶ NEWS CORPORATION ▶ PUBLIC SPHERE ▶ SONY CORPORATION ▶ TIME WARNER INC.

REFERENCES AND SUGGESTED READINGS

Bagdikian, B. (2004). *The new media monopoly*. Boston, MA: Beacon Press.

Baker, C. E. (2007). *Media concentration and democracy*. Cambridge: Cambridge University Press.

Compaine, B. (2005). *The media monopoly myth: How new competition is expanding our sources of information and entertainment*. Washington, DC: New Millennium Research Council.

Thussu, D. K. (2000). *International communication*. London: Edward Arnold.

Wasko, J., Murdoch, G., & Sousa, H. (eds.) (2011). *The handbook of political economy of communications*. Oxford: Wiley Blackwell.

Media Content and Social Networks

DIETRAM A. SCHEUFELE
University of Wisconsin–Madison

In The People's Choice, Paul F. Lazarsfeld and his colleagues offered two key constructs to explain the interplay of mass-mediated information, social networks, and political → attitudes that are still relevant today: opinion leadership and political cross-pressures (→ Opinion Leader).

In subsequent research it has been confirmed that the two-step flow of information in social networks is especially effective since interpersonal channels (rather than mass-mediated ones) can counter and circumvent initial resistance to information, based on *partisan preferences* (→ Selective Exposure). More recent research, however, suggests that the likelihood of exposure to attitude-inconsistent information in modern democracies is much higher in news media than in most interpersonal contexts (→ Cognitive Dissonance Theory).

Mutz (2002) distinguished two interrelated processes that undermine political engagement among citizens who are exposed to *cross-pressures*. First, individuals who are part of social networks that expose them to frequent discussions with non-like-minded others steer clear of politics in order not to threaten the harmony of their social relationships ("social accountability effect"). Second, being exposed to counter-attitudinal political views creates greater ambivalence about political actions ("political ambivalence"). Other scholars have suggested that exposure to attitude-inconsistent information in one's social networks and the resulting cross-pressures are an important and normatively desirable part of opinion formation because it may lead to greater → political knowledge and because discussions with citizens who hold different viewpoints can result in network members having to compromise between different viewpoints, motivating them to re-evaluate those issues where conflict occurs (Scheufele et al. 2006).

Today, ever more citizens rely on *online forms of communication* to supplement or even replace face-to-face interactions in their social networks (→ Exposure to the Internet; Social Media). There are still contradicting results as to whether the proliferation of sources on the internet leads to more 'echo chambers', i.e., networks of like-minded people, or whether receiving messages from homophilic sources makes audiences more likely to attend to belief-inconsistent information (Messing & Westwood 2012). Ultimately, the emerging interplay between geographically defined face-to-face networks, online interactions, and traditional mass-mediated information will require a new paradigm for how we think about social-level influences on opinion formation and political participation.

See also: ▶ ATTITUDES ▶ COGNITIVE DISSONANCE THEORY ▶ ELECTION CAMPAIGN COMMUNICATION ▶ EXPOSURE TO THE INTERNET ▶ INFORMATION SEEKING ▶ INTERPERSONAL COMMUNICATION ▶ SOCIAL MEDIA ▶ OPINION LEADER ▶ POLITICAL KNOWLEDGE ▶ SELECTIVE EXPOSURE ▶ TWO-STEP FLOW OF COMMUNICATION

REFERENCES AND SUGGESTED READINGS

Messing, S. & Westwood, S. J. (2012). Selective exposure in the age of social media: Endorsements trump partisan source affiliation when selecting news online. *Communication Research*, doi: 10.1177/0093650212466406.

Mutz, D. C. (2002). Cross-cutting social networks: Testing democratic theory in practice. *American Political Science Review*, 96(1), 111–126.

Scheufele, D. A., Hardy, B. W., Brossard, D., Waismel-Manor, I. S., & Nisbet, E. (2006). Democracy based on difference: Examining the links between structural heterogeneity, heterogeneity of discussion networks, and democratic citizenship. *Journal of Communication*, 56(4), 728–753.

Media Diplomacy

EYTAN GILBOA
Bar-Ilan University

Media diplomacy has become a major instrument of foreign policy, and journalists are more frequently and more intensively engaged in diplomatic events and processes. Sometimes they even initiate diplomatic processes. The media functions both as an independent actor and as a tool in the hands of policymakers and journalists.

Three interrelated revolutionary changes in *mass communication, politics, and international relations* have transformed the traditional secret diplomacy. All-news global networks broadcast almost every significant development in world events to almost every place on the globe or disseminate information on the Internet, available almost everywhere in the world (Seib 2012) (→ Globalization of the Media; International Television). The revolution in politics has generated growing mass participation in political processes and has transformed many societies from autocracy to democracy. Favourable image and reputation around the world achieved through attraction and persuasion (soft power) became more important than territory, access, and raw materials obtained through military and economic measures (hard power). Together, this created new types of interactions between the media and diplomacy. Several experts have argued that global television news now drives foreign policy (the "CNN effect"; Gilboa 2005).

Cohen (1986) suggested that media diplomacy served three *policymaking tasks*: conducting public diplomacy, sending signals to other governments, and obtaining information about world events. Gilboa (2000) distinguished between three uses of the media in diplomacy: "public diplomacy," where state and nonstate actors use the media and other channels of communication to influence → public opinion in foreign societies; "media diplomacy," where officials use the media to investigate and promote mutual interests, including conflict resolution; and "media-broker diplomacy," where journalists temporarily assume the role of diplomats and serve as mediators in international negotiations.

During grave international crises or when all diplomatic channels are severed, media diplomacy provides the sole unblocked channel for communication and negotiation between rival actors. When one side is unsure how the other side might react to conditions for negotiations or to proposals for conflict resolution, officials use the media to send messages to leaders of rival states. Media events – meetings between protagonist leaders seeking an opening for conflict resolution and even longer-term reconciliation – best represent media diplomacy. They help to break diplomatic deadlocks, create a climate conducive to negotiations, and promote a favorable climate for sealing an accord.

See also: ▶ CNN ▶ GLOBALIZATION OF THE MEDIA ▶ INTERNATIONAL COMMUNICATION ▶ INTERNATIONAL TELEVISION ▶ MEDIA EVENTS AND PSEUDO-EVENTS ▶ PROPAGANDA ▶ PUBLIC OPINION ▶ SATELLITE COMMUNICATION, GLOBAL

REFERENCES AND SUGGESTED READINGS

Cohen, Y. (1986). *Media diplomacy*. London: Frank Cass.
Gilboa, E. (2000). Mass communication and diplomacy: A theoretical framework. *Communication Theory*, 10, 275–309.
Gilboa, E. (2005). The CNN effect: The search for a communication theory of international relations. *Political Communication*, 22, 27–44.
Seib, P. (2012). *Real-time diplomacy: Politics and power in the social media era*. Basingstoke: Palgrave Macmillan.

Media Ecology

JULIANNE H. NEWTON
University of Oregon

Media ecology is a multidisciplinary field that studies the evolution, effects, and forms of environments with a focus on both media as environments and environments as media. Scholars work within expansive definitions of media, ecology, and technology, drawing on systems theory to analyze the co-evolution of the human organism and technologies.

Media ecology as a field distinguishes itself from communication per se, positing an open, dynamic, interdependent, and living system of forces. When studying human communication systems, media ecologists work from an inclusive perspective, exploring the creation, exchange, mediation, and dissemination of information, as well as the reciprocally influential relationship among means/content of communication and communicators/users (→ Language and Social Interaction). Neil Postman is credited with coining the term "media ecology" in 1968. However, the history of this expansive approach to studying meaning-making (→ Meaning) and dissemination is often traced back to ancient times, with particular attention to analyzing contemporary media forms in context with the oral traditions of early humans. A *foundational hypothesis* is that each form of communication simultaneously evolves from and affects the nature of thought itself and therefore affects message content and perception.

A number of major *themes and issues* can be identified: (1) Tension between organisms as technologies and organisms as creators of technologies; (2) co-evolution of organisms and technologies, though scholars such as Mumford emphasize development of brain over development of external tools; (3) influence of a medium on content, users, and cultures; transformation through and because of technological use; (4) multidisciplinarity, in which art/science, literature/journalism, fiction/fact, popular/elite, internal/external, figure/ground, and visible/invisible reciprocally inform and transform; (5) concern about deterministic aspects of potentially out-of-control technology, particularly in relation to humanistic values and global sustainability; (6) tension between understandings of word and image, oral and written, visual and acoustic, organism and machine; (7) holistic, contextualized views of particular occurrences; (8) emphasis on synchronous and complementary, rather than distinctive and oppositional, processes and influences; (9) inclusive topics of study ranging from autism to artificial intelligence; (10) playful exploration balanced with theoretical commitment to relationships among organisms and ideas; (11) openness to creative approaches and intellectual risk-taking in the interest of discovery.

See also: ▶ CODE ▶ COMMUNICATION AS A FIELD AND DISCIPLINE ▶ LANGUAGE AND SOCIAL INTERACTION ▶ MEANING ▶ METAPHOR

REFERENCES AND SUGGESTED READINGS

McLuhan, M. (1964). *Understanding media: The extensions of man.* New York: McGraw-Hill.
Postman, N. (1992). *Technopoly: The surrender of culture to technology.* New York: Alfred A. Knopf.
Strate, L. (2006). *Echoes and reflections: On media ecology as a field of study.* Cresskill, NJ: Hampton Press.

Media Economics
ALAN B. ALBARRAN
University of North Texas

Media economics is the study of economic theories and concepts applied to the media industries. Media economics is diverse and includes such topics as policy and ownership, market concentration, performance of firms, and political economy of the media.

The Development of Media Economics

The origins of media economics began with the study of economics. The classical school of economics centered on the interplay of economic forces, operation of markets, and the cost of production. The classical school would later be challenged by 'marginalist' economics and Marxism. The marginalists introduced demand and supply, and consumer utility. Marxism identified labor as the source of production. Marxism rejected the capitalist system and the exploitation of the working class.

By the beginning of the twentieth century, neo-classical economics was introduced, differed by its use of analytical tools and mathematics to examine market behavior and price. Later the development of macroeconomics shifted the focus to aggregate economics, encompassing the entire range of market activity. Economic theories are constantly changing and evolving. By the 1970s new approaches included monetarist theories, which re-emphasized growth in the money supply; and rational expectations, which argues that the market's ability to anticipate government policy actions limits their effectiveness.

As the study of economics evolved, scholars began to investigate different markets and industries. Media economics emerged during the 1950s. The media industries featured all of the elements necessary for studying the economic process. Content providers represented suppliers, with consumers and advertisers forming the demand side of the market (→ Markets of the Media). Regulatory agencies (e.g., → Federal Communications Commission (FCC)) in the US, the Federal Trade Commission, and other entities) affected macroeconomic market conditions, while the relationship among suppliers in various industries created microeconomic market conditions.

Concentration of ownership emerged as a critical topic as it impacts both regulatory and social policy (→ Concentration in Media Systems; Media Conglomerates). Other studies examined media competition, consumer expenditures, barriers to entry for new firms, advertiser/ownership demand, and consumer utility.

Theoretical Dimensions and Methods

Media economics utilizes many theoretical approaches: microeconomic theories, macroeconomic theories, and → political economy of the media. Microeconomic studies center on specific industry and market conditions. Macroeconomic studies take a broader focus, examining such topics as labor, capital markets, and gross domestic product. Political economy emerged as a critical response to positivist approaches.

The *industrial organization (IO) model* offers a systematic means of analyzing a market. The model consists of market structure, conduct, and performance. The model is also called the SCP model. The model posits that if the structure of a market is known, it helps explain the likely conduct and performance among firms. Each area can be further analyzed by considering specific variables within each part of the SCP model. Critics contend that the IO model does not capture the nuances associated with new technologies. However, the model remains a key theory in microeconomics.

The *theory of the firm* examines the most common types of market structure: monopoly, oligopoly, monopolistic competition, and perfect competition. Defining market structure is complicated due to consolidation across the media industries. *Media concentration* is examined in one of two ways. Researchers gather data on firm/industry revenues to measure concentration by applying tools such as concentration ratios. Another method tracks concentration of ownership among the media industries. Research has shown there are a limited number of firms which control media markets. Globalization has contributed to media concentration (→ Globalization of the Media). *Competition studies* draw upon niche theory, which originated in the field of biology. These studies consider competition within an industry or across industries. Indices are used to measure the breadth, overlap, and superiority of one competitor over another. Finally, macroeconomic analysis in media economics includes policy and regulatory analysis, labor and employment trends, and advertising revenues and expenditures at the national level.

Media economics embraces *different methods*. Many include trend studies, financial analysis, econometrics, and case studies. Trend studies are used to compare data over time for topics such as concentration and performance. Financial analysis utilizes different types of financial statements and ratios to measure performance of firms and industries. Econometric analysis uses statistical models to address its research questions. Case studies embrace different methodologies as well as data. Case studies in media economics research tend to be very targeted examinations.

Critics of media economics research contend research is too descriptive in nature, and that methodological approaches are limited. There are also concerns researchers would study only major companies, and not pay sufficient attention to new media enterprises.

Future Directions for the Study of Media Economics

There are a number of steps researchers need to address to further develop media economics. In terms of research, media economics must address how to define a media market given the convergence and consolidation across the media industries. Most media companies are now multimedia enterprises, generating content across a variety of platforms.

In addition to refining key concepts, media economics research must also expand into new arenas. Among the areas where new understanding and investigation are required are → social media, and mobile markets. Media economics scholars should consider new inquiries that draw upon multiple methods of investigation. The interplay of regulation, technology, and social policy presents new opportunities for scholars to generate new theories. Scholars need to examine variables that describe evolving market structures. Improvements in methodological tools are needed to complement expansion in research and theory. New measures are needed to assess within-industry concentration and competition.

Media economics helps to understand the activities and functions of media companies as economic institutions. Media economics research continues to evolve as it analyzes and evaluates the complex and changing world in which the media industries operate.

See also: ▶ ADVERTISING, ECONOMICS OF ▶ COMMODIFICATION OF THE MEDIA ▶ CONCENTRATION IN MEDIA SYSTEMS ▶ DIVERSIFICATION OF MEDIA MARKETS ▶ FEDERAL COMMUNICATIONS COMMISSION (FCC) ▶ GLOBALIZATION OF THE MEDIA ▶ MARKETS OF THE MEDIA ▶ MEDIA CONGLOMERATES ▶ POLITICAL ECONOMY OF THE MEDIA ▶ SOCIAL MEDIA ▶ TELEVISION BROADCASTING, REGULATION OF

REFERENCES AND SUGGESTED READINGS

Albarran, A. B. (2010a). *The media economy.* London: Routledge.
Albarran, A. B. (2010b). *The transformation of the media and communication industries.* Pamplona: EUNSA.
Albarran, A. B., Chan-Olmsted, S. M., & Wirth, M. O. (2006). *Handbook of media management and economics.* Mahwah, NJ: Lawrence Erlbaum.
Croteau, D. & Hoynes, W. (2006). *The business of media: Corporate media and the public interest,* 2nd edn. Thousand Oaks, CA: Pine Forge.
Dimmick, J. W. (2003). *Media competition and coexistence: The theory of the niche.* Mahwah, NJ: Lawrence Erlbaum.
Gershon, R. A. (2013). *Telecommunications and business strategy,* 2nd edn. London: Routledge.
Napoli, P. M. (2003). *Audience economics.* New York: Columbia University Press.
Noam, E. M. (2009). *Media ownership and concentration in America.* Oxford: Oxford University Press.
Picard, R. G. (2011). *The economics and financing of media firms,* 2nd edn. New York: Fordham University Press.

Media Effects

HANS MATHIAS KEPPLINGER
Johannes Gutenberg University of Mainz

Mass media can produce a broad spectrum of effects – on knowledge, attitudes, emotions, social behavior, reputation of people covered by the media, etc. Effects may be the consequences of media use, but also a result of interactions with people who have used the media. Explanations are usually based on two types of theories. Learning-theory approaches address the correct reproduction of information. Therefore divergences between beliefs and information provided by media are considered learning deficits that may also be interpreted as a lack of media effects. Cognitive-theory approaches address the processing of information triggered by media reports. Beliefs and opinions are not regarded as copies of media presentation but indicate the type of information processing.

Effects on Reality Perception

Media coverage of current affairs has an influence on the public's assessment of the significance of social problems and the urgency for solving those problems (→ *Agenda-Setting Effects*). Comparison of all issues on the media's agenda with the population's agenda over a short period of time, as well as comparison of the development of media coverage on single issues with the development of the population's beliefs over a longer period of time, may indicate media effects.

The media – and above all TV – are *also* an important factor in cultural and political socialization (→ *Cultivation Effects*). Through both information and entertainment TV conveys ideas of the state of society in which people live. The more frequently and intensely people watch TV, the stronger the influence of its presentation of reality.

Individuals generally have good judgment concerning the relative frequency of causes of death, but they typically overestimate the occurrence of rare fatalities and underestimate the occurrence of frequent causes of death. The concept of availability heuristic explains how this is related to media coverage (→ *Risk Communication*).

Effects on Social Perception

People tend to overestimate negative media effects (perceptual hypothesis) on other people and take action (behavioral hypothesis) to prevent these negative effects (→ *Third-Person Effects*). In addition, a general correlation between presumed media effects and behavior is assumed. The perceptional hypothesis has been often tested and confirmed. The behavioral hypothesis has seldom been tested and if so, subjects have been uninvolved bystanders instead of decision makers who are protagonists of media messages (Sun et al. 2009).

As 'social beings' people depend on the society of others. Therefore, they constantly monitor their environment in order to avoid social isolation. They draw on their interactions with other people and personal observation as well as media presentations. Each of these resources can incidentally stimulate correct or incorrect ideas about the distribution of opinions. People who consider themselves in the minority tend to withhold their opinions in public. In the process, the presumed majority opinion is artificially inflated, which in turn increases the pressure on the actual or alleged minority (→ Spiral of Silence).

Cognitive and Emotional Effects

Citizen assessments about politicians and voting intentions are based in part on beliefs about politicians' competence. Repeated coverage of issues sensitizes recipients to some issues and makes solutions to the issues seem especially urgent. Thus, the presumed ability of politicians to deal with the issues becomes more significant, contributing to a positive or negative image of them. Accordingly priming effects are based on agenda-setting effects.

Framing theory is based on the assumption that media recipients do not take up individual pieces of information independently of one another and derive meaning from them, but interpret them consistently according to a predetermined frame (or schema) (→ Framing Effects; Schemas). Frame-induced information processing can be controlled by media reports that present events from a certain perspective (Entman 1991).

In the 1940s it was already known that there was a positive correlation between education and the use of information presented by the media. As consequence, in the course of time existing differences in the distribution of information can increase (→ Knowledge Gap Effects).

Descriptions of events trigger predictable *emotional reactions*. If the damage is attributed to uncontrollable natural forces, the event evokes sadness; if it is attributed to a person acting in a controlled way, it evokes anger. The extent of reactions is enforced or diminished by the interaction of emotions and cognitions. Appraisal theory combines elements of attribution theory and emotional arousal theory (Nerb & Spada 2001; → Appraisal Theory).

Axioms of Media-Effects Research

Most studies in the effects of mass media are based on three, mostly unspoken, axioms. The first is *'events happen, media cover.'* According to this axiom, current events on which the media report happen independently of the media. This is doubtful because a number of events on which the media report are the result of previous coverage. Some events would happen without media coverage, but their character is modified by media coverage (mediated events). Some events happen only in order to generate media coverage (staged or pseudo-events) (→ Media Events and Pseudo-Events).

The second assumption is *'no effect without change.'* The axiom holds true only under two conditions. First, if the media did not support the existing beliefs, opinions, and behaviors of its audience, these characteristics and attributes would still exist. Second, beliefs, opinions, and behaviors have developed independently from previous media use. There is evidence that the mass media have at least partly established the information and opinions which are already held and used to interpret news on current events.

The third axiom is: *'no effect without contact.'* This axiom is only acceptable if at least one of two conditions is fulfilled: first, existing attitudes largely prevent the reception of dissonant information (→ Cognitive Dissonance Theory; Selective Exposure;); second, dissonant information will be reinterpreted according to existing attitudes (→ Selective Perception and Selective Retention). As far as conveyors or opinion leaders pass on information and opinion from the mass media unchanged, their effects have to be attributed to the media. Therefore, opinion leaders and other interlocutors do not necessarily restrain the influence of media reports, but rather extend them to those who lack direct contact with media coverage (→ Media Effects: Direct and Indirect Effects).

See also: ▶ AGENDA-SETTING EFFECTS
▶ APPRAISAL THEORY ▶ COGNITIVE DISSONANCE
THEORY ▶ CONSTRUCTION OF REALITY THROUGH
THE NEWS ▶ CULTIVATION EFFECTS ▶ DIFFUSION
OF INFORMATION AND INNOVATION ▶ FRAMING
EFFECTS ▶ KNOWLEDGE GAP EFFECTS ▶ MEDIA
AND PERCEPTIONS OF REALITY ▶ MEDIA EFFECTS:
DIRECT AND INDIRECT EFFECTS ▶ MEDIA EVENTS
AND PSEUDO-EVENTS ▶ MEDIATIZATION OF
POLITICS ▶ OPINION LEADER ▶ PERSUASION
▶ POLITICAL COGNITIONS ▶ POLITICAL
COMMUNICATION ▶ POLITICAL SOCIALIZATION
THROUGH THE MEDIA ▶ PROPAGANDA ▶ PUBLIC
OPINION ▶ REALITY AND MEDIA REALITY
▶ RECIPROCAL EFFECTS ▶ RISK COMMUNICATION
▶ SCHEMAS ▶ SELECTIVE EXPOSURE
▶ SELECTIVE PERCEPTION AND SELECTIVE
RETENTION ▶ SPIRAL OF SILENCE ▶ STIMULUS–
RESPONSE MODEL ▶ THIRD-PERSON EFFECTS
▶ TWO-STEP FLOW OF COMMUNICATION ▶ USES
AND GRATIFICATIONS ▶ VIOLENCE AS MEDIA
CONTENT, EFFECTS OF

REFERENCES AND SUGGESTED READINGS

Bennett, W. L. & Iyengar, S. (2008). A new era of minimal effects? The changing foundations of political communication. *Journal of Communication*, 58, 707–731.

Bryant, J. & Zillmann, D. (2002). *Media effects: Advances in theory and research*, 2nd edn. Mahwah, NJ: Lawrence Erlbaum.

Entman, R. M. (1991). Framing U.S. coverage of international news: Contrasts in narratives of the KAL and Iran air incidents. *Journal of Communication*, 41(2), 6–27.

Nerb, J. & Spada, H. (2001). Evaluation of environmental problems: A coherence model of cognition and emotion. *Cognition & Emotion*, 15(4) 521–551.

Perloff, R. M. (2003). *The dynamics of persuasion: Communication and attitudes in the twenty-first century*, 2nd edn. Mahwah, NJ: Lawrence Erlbaum.

Sun, Y., Pan, Z., & Shen, L. (2009). Understanding the third-person perception: Evidence from a meta-analysis. *Journal of Communication*, 58, 280–300.

Media Effects: Direct and Indirect Effects

HANS MATHIAS KEPPLINGER
Johannes Gutenberg University of Mainz

The term 'indirect effects' denotes the consequences of direct effects on individuals who are not exposed to media content. The concept extends the effect of the mass media beyond the users and to nonusers (Holbert & Stephenson 2003). As far as users transmit information and opinion from the mass media unchanged, they act as filters. As far as they transmit them partly or totally changed, they act as amplifiers of → media effects.

Quantitative and qualitative studies document a broad *variety of indirect effects*. Intensive coverage of terrorism may stimulate additional violence (direct effect) and cause additional victims (indirect effect; → Mediated Terrorism; Violence as Media Content, Effects of). The dominant tone of media coverage may discourage recipients from speaking out in public (direct effect), which may push others into falling silent (indirect effect; → Spiral of Silence). Media coverage of the availability of pornography or violence might stimulate concern about antisocial effects on others (direct effect I), increase support for censorship (direct effect II); and bring into office politicians planning to change the law (indirect effect). Trial publicity may influence witnesses (direct effect) and thus might help or harm defendants (indirect effect).

See also: ▶ MEDIA EFFECTS ▶ MEDIA EFFECTS,
HISTORY OF ▶ MEDIA EFFECTS, STRENGTH OF
▶ MEDIATED TERRORISM ▶ QUALITATIVE
METHODOLOGY ▶ QUANTITATIVE METHODOLOGY
▶ SPIRAL OF SILENCE ▶ TWO-STEP FLOW
OF COMMUNICATION ▶ VIOLENCE AS MEDIA
CONTENT, EFFECTS OF

REFERENCES AND SUGGESTED READINGS

Holbert, R. L. & Stephenson, M. T. (2003). The importance of indirect effects in media effects research: Testing for mediation in structural equation modeling. *Journal of Broadcasting and Electronic Media*, 47(4), 556–572.

Kepplinger, H. M. & Zerback, T. (2012). Direct and indirect effects of media coverage. Exploring the effects of presumed media influence on judges, prosecutors, and defendants. *Studies in Communication Media*, 1(3–4), 473–492.

Weimann, G. & Winn, C. (1994). *The theater of terror: Mass media and international terrorism*. London: Longman.

Media Effects, History of

FRANK ESSER
University of Zurich

The established history of media-effects research is characterized by a series of phases marked by fundamental paradigm shifts. Each of these phases is associated with particular concepts, researchers, studies, and historical circumstances that influenced the perception of media effects (see McQuail's Mass Communication Theory (2010), or Severin and Tankard's Communication Theories (2001); → Media Effects).

The *first phase*, from World War I to the end of the 1930s, was characterized by the assumption that the effects of the media on the population would be *exceedingly strong*. The media were credited with an almost limitless omnipotence in their ability to shape opinion and belief, to change life habits, and to mold audience behavior more or less according to the will of their controllers. The mass media supposedly fired messages like dangerous bullets, or shot messages into the audience like strong drugs pushed through hypodermic needles. Instinct psychology and the theory of mass society were interpreted to show that people were defenseless against the capricious stimuli of the media.

The *second phase* of the standard history lasted approximately from the end of the 1930s to the end of the 1960s and was distinguished by the assumption that the media were largely not influential. In the election study, The People's Choice (1944), Lazarsfeld and colleagues defined all three key concepts that Joseph T. Klapper (1960) later united and used as the basis of his *limited effects theory*: (1) People use selective exposure and selective perception to protect themselves from media influences (→ Selective Exposure; Selective Perception and Selective Retention); (2) opinion leaders initiate a → two-step flow of communication by absorbing and transforming ideas and arguments from the mass media; and (3) social group formation enhances the role that → interpersonal communication plays in protecting an individual member from a change of opinion.

The *third phase*, from the end of the 1960s through the end of the 1970s, was characterized by the *rediscovery of strong media effects*. According to standard media-effects history, new studies (e.g., on → agenda-setting effects or the → spiral of silence) showed that it was possible for the media to overcome some selectivity processes in a television-saturated environment. Also, more sophisticated methods, more specific hypotheses, and more highly differentiated theoretical approaches were used. In addition, effects research since that time has been less focused on crude changes in attitude or behavior, and more interested in subtle changes in our *perception* of the world.

The *fourth phase* of the standard media-effects history is characterized by *negotiated or transactional effects*. Now the central premise maintains that the media exert their greatest influence when they become involved in the process of constructing sense and → meaning. Typical theories connected with this new approach are social constructivism, cultivation (→ Cultivation Effects), framing (→ Framing Effects), and → information processing. Recipients are assumed to construct for themselves their own view of social reality, in interaction with the symbolic constructions offered by the media.

The oversimplified account of the received view of media-effects history has been criticized as unrealistic paradoxes that feigned contradictions that had never existed. Indeed, re-analyses of research literature from the first phase indicate that "few, if any, reputable social scientists in the pre-World War II era ... worked with what was later described as the hypodermic needle model" (Lang & Lang 1981, 655). Even the empirical findings from the second phase, upon closer inspection, show no justification for an overall verdict of media impotence. Two main factors explain the successful run enjoyed by the 'minimal-effects myth': First, there was an exaggerated concentration of a limited range of effect types; and second, the conclusions from key publications of that time were adopted with little critical review. The apparent change of mind leading to the rediscovery of strong effects was then partially motivated by the rapid spread of television.

Today, a growing number of scholars agree that the established standard history of the field is misleading because it tends to ignore those findings that do not fit neatly into the stage-by-stage scenario. Many authors (Chaffee & Hochheimer 1985; McLeod et al. 1991) have thus concluded that the development of mass media-effects research did not move in pendulum swings from "all-powerful" to "limited" to "rediscovered powerful" to "negotiated" effects. Bryant and Thompson argue in Fundamentals of Media Effects (2002) that the body of media-effects research from the beginning showed overwhelming evidence for significant effects.

See also: ▶ AGENDA-SETTING EFFECTS ▶ CULTIVATION EFFECTS ▶ FRAMING EFFECTS ▶ INFORMATION PROCESSING ▶ INTERPERSONAL COMMUNICATION ▶ MEANING ▶ MEDIA EFFECTS ▶ SELECTIVE EXPOSURE ▶ SELECTIVE PERCEPTION AND SELECTIVE RETENTION ▶ SPIRAL OF SILENCE ▶ TWO-STEP FLOW OF COMMUNICATION

REFERENCES AND SUGGESTED READINGS

Chaffee, S. H. & Hochheimer, J. L. (1985). The beginnings of political communication research in the United States: Origins of the "limited effects" model. In E. M. Rogers & F. Balle (eds.), *The media revolution in America and in Western Europe*. Norwood, NJ: Ablex, pp. 267–296.

Lang, G. E. & Lang, K. (1981). Mass communication and public opinion: Strategies for research. In M. Rosenberg & R. H. Turner (eds.), *Social psychology: Sociological perspectives*. New York: Basic Books, pp. 653–682.

McLeod, J. M., Kosicki, G. M., & Pan, Z. (1991). On understanding and misunderstanding media effects. In J. Curran, M. Gurevitch, & J. Woollacott (eds.), *Mass media and society*. London: Edward Arnold, pp. 235–266.

Neuman, R. W. & Guggenheim, L. (2011). The evolution of media effects theory: A six-stage model of cumulative research. *Communication Theory*, 21(2), 169–196.

Media Effects, Strength of

ELIZABETH M. PERSE
University of Delaware

Research has presented significant and consistent evidence that the mass media have noticeable and meaningful effects. These media effects are modest; small to moderate in size. Conclusions about the strength of media effects, however, must be tempered by considerations of research methodology (→ Media Effects; Media Effects, History of).

While some media effects, such as → agenda-setting effects, are fairly strong, in general, meta-analyses (→ Meta-Analysis) reveal that media effects can best be described as small to moderate. Exposure to television violence (→ Violence as Media Content, Effects of), for example, accounts for over half of a standard deviation in negative effects. The connection between playing video games and aggression is $r = 0.15$. The effects of stereotyped media content and sex-role stereotyping range from $r = 0.11$ to $r = 0.31$. Pro-social messages targeted toward children have a moderate effect: $r = 0.23$.

Effects of media violence are larger in laboratories than in the real world. There is also evidence that effects of pro-social media content are larger than those of antisocial media content and that unusual messages have greater impact. For instance, research on US basketball player Magic Johnson's 1991 announcement that he was HIV-positive, for example, had much greater effects on knowledge and attitudes about HIV and AIDS than more routine messages (→ Exemplification and Exemplars, Effects of).

The effects of mass communication might be modest, but they are meaningful because of the size of the audience and the importance of the outcomes. The small effects found for media health campaigns ($r = 0.09$; → Health Communication) cannot be dismissed, because even small effects mean that large numbers of people have been influenced. Scholars estimate that eliminating television violence could reduce aggression in society by small but significant amounts. Small effects translate into large groups of people being affected.

There are some *areas of disagreement regarding media effects*. The most substantial media effects are found in *laboratory experiments* (→ Experiment, Laboratory). Exposure to media content in a laboratory setting, however, is atypical and cannot account for selective exposure or social influences (→ Media Effects: Direct and Indirect Effects). The dependent measures used in laboratories are often artificial and do not translate to real-life actions. Experiments typically focus on short-term effects, so researchers cannot assess the endurance of effects. Research participants might believe that the content presented or actions encouraged in the laboratory are sanctioned or even encouraged by the researcher. Content selected for experiments is often chosen to magnify differences between experimental and control conditions, extreme selections that are often atypical of media content seen in the real world.

Nevertheless, there are several reasons to believe that research underestimates media effects because of methodological imprecision. *Outside of the laboratory*, measures of media exposure are imprecise and subject to a good deal of measurement error (→ Exposure to Print Media; Exposure to Radio; Exposure to Television; Exposure to the Internet). Media effects might be stronger if researchers could access accurate measures of attentive media use.

For ethical reasons, researchers often limit dependent variables to those that cannot harm research participants. So, studies rarely give participants opportunities to enact behaviours, but instead assess attitudes, perceptions, and reactions to hypothetical situations. These 'diluted' measures might not be the most valid and accurate ways to assess the impact of the mass media.

The main reason that media effects appear limited is that it is impossible to isolate media's impact in most developed societies. It is nearly impossible to find someone who has not been exposed to mass media. And even those people who do not watch much television or read newspapers or surf the Internet interact regularly with others who do. Media's influence can go beyond direct exposure to the media; it is filtered through other social contact.

See also: ▶ AGENDA-SETTING EFFECTS
▶ EXEMPLIFICATION AND EXEMPLARS, EFFECTS OF
▶ EXPERIMENT, LABORATORY ▶ EXPOSURE TO PRINT MEDIA ▶ EXPOSURE TO RADIO ▶ HEALTH COMMUNICATION ▶ MEDIA EFFECTS ▶ MEDIA EFFECTS: DIRECT AND INDIRECT EFFECTS
▶ MEDIA EFFECTS, HISTORY OF ▶ META-ANALYSIS
▶ VIOLENCE AS MEDIA CONTENT, EFFECTS OF

REFERENCES AND SUGGESTED READINGS

Hovland, C. I. (1959). Reconciling conflicting results derived from experimental and survey studies of attitude change. *American Psychologist*, 14, 8–17.

Perse, E. M. (2001). *Media effects and society*. Mahwah, NJ: Lawrence Erlbaum.

Preiss, R. W., Gayle, B. M., Burrell, N., Allen, M., & Bryant, J. (2007). *Mass media effects research: Advances through meta-analysis*. Mahwah, NJ: Lawrence Erlbaum.

Media Equation Theory

KWAN MIN LEE
University of Southern California

The term 'media equation' means that → media equal real life. It implies that people process technology-mediated experiences in the same way as they would do non-mediated experiences, because an "individual's interactions with computers, television, and new media are fundamentally social and natural, just like interaction in real life" (Reeves & Nass 1996, 5). More recently, Reeves and his colleagues have usually worked on the first issue, whereas Nass and his lab members have focused on the latter issue under the research paradigm of 'Computers Are Social Actors (CASA).'

Media equation studies on *audience responses to physical features of traditional media* can be categorized into two parts: *media and emotion*; and media and form. With regard to media and emotion, Reeves and his colleagues provide convincing results that the emotional valence (good vs bad) of media stimuli has the same effect on the brain as real-life stimuli in terms of electroencephalogram (EEG) activities.

Studies on *media and form* have focused on audience responses to five physical characteristics of media forms: size; fidelity; synchrony; motion; and scene changes. With regard to audience responses to image *size*, the studies found that big objects on the screen yield more arousal, better memory (descriptive, not image recognition), and more positive social responses (e.g., social attraction, credibility) than smaller ones even when the content is identical (→ Visual Communication; Cinematography). These results confirm general human attention to and preference for big objects in real life. In contrast to audience responses to image sizes, the visual fidelity of a scene does not bring significant differences in arousal, attitudes, and memory. These results indicate that both virtual and real-life objects are visually processed in the same way in which objects and environments are mainly processed through the peripheral vision field, rather than the foveal vision field.

In the CASA research paradigm, Nass and his colleagues have studied *user responses to social characteristics of computers and software agents* (→ Interactivity, Concept of). This research paradigm is based on the idea that when confronted with a machine that has anthropomorphic cues related to fundamental human characteristics, individuals automatically respond socially, are swayed by the fake human characteristics, and do not process the fact that the machine is not a human. For instance, users evaluate computers positively when the computers behave politely, flatter them, and criticize themselves (as opposed to blaming others), in the same way that people like other people who are polite, flattering, and/or self-criticizing. The second-generation CASA studies expanded the domain of research to e-commerce, voice user interfaces, and human–robot interaction. For instance, researchers found that even with conscious knowledge of the nature of synthetic voice, humans keep responding to the synthetic voice as if it were a real human voice and apply various social rules and long-term artificial cognitive development (Lee et al. 2006).

The main reason for the media equation phenomenon is that human brains evolved in a world in which all perceived objects were real physical objects and only humans possessed human-like shapes and human-like characteristics such as language, rapid interaction, emotion, personality, and so on. Therefore, to human minds, anything that seemed to be real was real and any object that seemed to possess human characteristics such as language was a real human.

See also: ▶ AUDIENCE RESEARCH ▶ CINEMATOGRAPHY ▶ COMPUTER–USER INTERACTION ▶ EMOTIONAL AROUSAL THEORY ▶ EXCITATION AND AROUSAL ▶ INFORMATION PROCESSING ▶ INTERACTIVITY, CONCEPT OF ▶ MEDIA ▶ MEMORY ▶ PRESENCE ▶ VISUAL COMMUNICATION

REFERENCES AND SUGGESTED READINGS

Lee, K. M., Peng, W., Yan, C., & Jin, S. (2006). Can robots manifest personality? An empirical test of personality recognition, social responses, and social presence in human–robot interaction. *Journal of Communication*, 56, 754–772.

Moon, Y. (2000). Intimate exchanges: Using computers to elicit self-disclosure from consumers. *Journal of Consumer Research*, 26, 324–340.

Nass, C. & Brave, S. (2005). *Wired for speech: How voice activates and advances the human–computer relationship.* Cambridge, MA: MIT Press.

Nass, C. & Moon, Y. (2000). Machines and mindlessness: Social responses to computers. *Journal of Social Issues*, 56, 81–103.

Reeves, B. & Nass, C. (1996). *The media equation: How people treat computers, television, and new media like real people and places.* Cambridge: Cambridge University Press.

Media Events and Pseudo-Events

HELMUT SCHERER
Hanover University of Music, Drama, and Media

The terms 'pseudo-event' and 'media event' refer to the phenomenon that in modern societies many events are created or shaped because of the existence of the media and in order to stimulate media coverage. Pseudo-events would not occur without the existence of the media but are planned mainly for the purpose of getting media coverage. Media events occur independently from the existence of the media, but they are shaped in a ceremonious character to cater the needs of the media. They are subject to media-related staging, to a mise-en-scène by the media for the viewers, to the telling of a story.

Most *pseudo-events* are basically strategic communication and public relations exercises (→ Advertising; Marketing; Public Relations; Strategic Communication). A media-friendly design is therefore one of the most important aspects of pseudo-event planning. The pseudo-event basically has to be designed according to the media's selection criteria. As the event itself often lacks newsworthiness, it has to be artificially enhanced to make it more interesting (→ News Values). Pseudo-events serve a purpose. Lobbies try to attract attention to their interests or bring about a certain atmosphere by staging such events. Big sports events, political party conventions, and big trade fairs are examples of media events.

A *media event* in itself has a high social relevance and a festive character. The media intensify this festive character and live coverage makes it available to a wide audience around the world. The events are predictable for the media and are staged to gain the highest possible media interest.

See also: ▶ ADVERTISING ▶ ISSUE MANAGEMENT IN POLITICS ▶ MARKETING ▶ MEDIA DIPLOMACY ▶ MEDIA EFFECTS ▶ MEDIATED TERRORISM ▶ NEWS VALUES ▶ PUBLIC RELATIONS ▶ REALITY AND MEDIA REALITY ▶ RECIPROCAL EFFECTS ▶ STRATEGIC COMMUNICATION

REFERENCES AND SUGGESTED READINGS

Boorstin, D. J. (1961). *The image, or, what happened to the American dream*. London: Weidenfeld and Nicolson.
Dayan, D. & Katz, E. (1996). *Media events: The live broadcasting of history*. Cambridge, MA: Harvard University Press.
Nimmo, D. & Combs, J. E. (1983). *Mediated political realities*. New York: Longman.

Media and Group Representations

DANA MASTRO
University of Arizona

The influence of media exposure on the cognitions we hold about our own and other groups in society is well established (see Mastro 2009; → Social Stereotyping and Communication). Research additionally documents that these cognitions impact a wide variety of behavioral outcomes. Given that Americans spend a staggering 13.6 hours per day interacting with media (Short 2013), understanding the manner in which different groups are represented in the media is of great social consequence. For reasons of space this entry concentrates on findings from the US.

Blacks

When it comes to prime-time television, content analyses (→ Content Analysis, Quantitative) indicate that blacks are presented at a rate that meets or slightly exceeds their proportion of the US population (of approximately 13 percent); comprising between 14 and 17 percent of characters (Mastro 2009). In this programming, blacks are found nearly exclusively in sitcoms and crime dramas (→ Fiction). The typical black character is a middle-class, male law enforcer or professional, in his thirties, discussing topics related to work (Children Now 2004; Mastro & Behm-Morawitz 2005; Mastro & Greenberg 2000). Alongside average levels of job and social authority, black characters are among the least aggressive on prime time. They also are more hot-tempered, more provocatively dressed, and less professionally attired than their white peers.

In the → news, blacks are depicted as perpetrators more frequently than whites and at rates exceeding real-world crime data (Dixon & Linz 2000a). Blacks also are seen as victims on the news less often than whites, but at rates nearly equivalent with real-world levels of victimization (Dixon & Linz 2000b). In terms of depictions as law enforcers, 91 percent of police officers shown on television news are white, whereas only 3 percent are black (Dixon et al. 2003). These figures are discrepant from US Department of Labor statistics, which identify 80 percent of officers in the US to be white and 17 percent to be black.

Other Ethnic Groups in the US

The portrayal of *Latinos* on contemporary prime-time television is inauspicious, at best. Latinos are grossly underrepresented when compared with real-world demographics, representing only 4–6.5 percent of the prime-time population but approximately 16 percent of the US population (Mastro & Behm-Morawitz 2005). Like blacks, Latino characters are confined primarily to sitcoms and crime dramas (Children Now 2004). They appear most often as family members; conversing frequently about crime-related topics (Mastro & Behm-Morawitz 2005). Generally speaking, Latinos are depicted as younger, lower in job authority, more provocatively dressed, lazier, less articulate, and less intelligent than their peers on television. Alongside blacks, Latinos are deemed the most hot-tempered characters in prime time. Moreover, when compared with other female characters on TV, Latinas are rated the lowest in work ethic and highest in verbal aggression.

Asian Americans make up about 3 percent of the characters on TV (and 4.6 percent of the US population), and are depicted primarily in minor and non-recurring roles, often centering on the work environment (see Mastro 2009). Native Americans represent less than 1 percent of the characters seen on primetime (if they appear at all) and approximately 1 percent of the US population. Their infrequent roles often are based in an historical context. A mere 0.2 percent of newspaper articles and 0.2 percent of films portray Native Americans (Fryberg 2003). When they are represented in the media, they are characterized in limited roles as spiritual, as warriors, and as a social problem.

Arabs/Middle Easterners represent 0.05 percent of prime-time television characters (Children Now 2004). Nearly half of these characters (46 percent) are portrayed as criminals. Research on film suggests that images of Arabs/Middle Easterners rarely deviate from a limited range of brutal portrayals, typically pertaining to terrorism or of a generally uncivilized nature (see Shaheen 2003). Indians/Pakistanis make up 0.04 percent of the TV population (Children Now 2004). The nature of these roles has yet to be documented.

Age, Gender, and Disability

Characters between the *ages* of 0 and 9 comprise 1.9 percent of the prime-time population (Harwood & Anderson 2002). Those aged 10–19 constitute 9.7 percent of TV roles. Characters aged 20–34 make up nearly 40 percent of television figures. Those aged 35–44 represent approximately 27 percent of roles. Adults from 45–64 make up 18.7 percent of prime-time characters, with only 2.8 percent of characters over age 65. When these figures are compared with US census data, several discrepancies emerge. Adolescents and children (particularly younger children), as well as seniors, are severely underrepresented. On the other hand, characters ranging in age from 20 through the early 40s are depicted at levels far exceeding that of the US population. In terms of the features associated with these different age groups, more positive images are linked with younger characters – seemingly, a function of diminishing perceptions of attractiveness as the characters age.

Misrepresentation also applies to *gender*. Although women outnumber males in the US population, they comprise only 28 percent of the characters in family films, 39 percent of the characters on prime-time TV, and 31 percent of those in children's programs (Smith et al. 2012). Women are more likely to be depicted as parents in both family films and children's programs, but not prime-time TV (a change from previous decades). When it comes to the manner in which men and women are depicted in the media, women are more likely to be sexualized than their male counterparts and less likely to be employed. When employed, women in the media are rarely shown in prestigious positions or scientific fields.

Lesbian, gay, bisexual and transgender characters comprise 3.3 percent of recurring characters on prime-time TV, and are equally divided between men and women (Glaad 2013). Among these characters, 71 percent are white, 15 percent are black, 8 percent are Latino, 2 percent are Asian/Pacific Islander, and 5 percent are 'multiracial.'

Although 12 percent of the US population reports living with a *disability*, characters with disabilities are exceedingly rare in the media. Only about 1 percent of all recurring prime-time characters are portrayed with some type of disability (Glaad 2013). Among these, the majority are represented by non-disabled actors (at least on broadcast television).

When considering the significance of media representations in designating group status, strength and social standing in society, the disparities in the characterizations of the groups addressed here are indeed consequential, and warrant greater research attention.

See also: ▶ CONTENT ANALYSIS, QUANTITATIVE ▶ FICTION ▶ NEWS ▶ SOCIAL STEREOTYPING AND COMMUNICATION

REFERENCES AND SUGGESTED READINGS

Children Now (2004). *Fall colors, 2003–2004: Prime time diversity report.* Oakland, CA: Children Now.

Dixon, T., Azocar, C., & Casas, M. (2003). The portrayal of race and crime on television network news. *Journal of Broadcasting and Electronic Media*, 47, 498–523.

Dixon, T. & Linz, D. (2000a). Overrepresentation and underrepresentation of African Americans and Latinos as lawbreakers on television news. *Journal of Communication*, 50, 131–154.

Dixon, T. & Linz, D. (2000b). Race and the misrepresentation of victimization on local television news. *Communication Research*, 27, 547–573.

Fryberg, S. (2003). Really? You don't look like an American Indian: Social representations and social group identities. *Dissertation Abstracts International*.

Glaad (2013). *2013: Where are we on TV?* Glaad.org. At http://www.glaad.org/files/whereweareontv12.pdf, accessed August 12, 2014.

Harwood, H. & Anderson, K. (2002). The presence and portrayal of social groups on prime time television. *Communication Reports*, 15, 81–97.

Mastro, D. (2009). Effects of racial and ethnic stereotyping. In J. Bryant & M. B. Oliver (eds.), *Media effects: Advances in theory and research*, 3rd edn. Hillsdale: NJ: Lawrence Erlbaum, pp. 325–341. Assoc.

Mastro, D. & Behm-Morawitz, E. (2005). Latino representation on prime time television. *Journalism and Mass Communication Quarterly*, 82, 110–130.

Mastro, D. & Greenberg, B. (2000). The portrayal of racial minorities on prime time television. *Journal of Broadcasting and Electronic Media*, 44, 690–703.

Shaheen, J. (2003). Reel bad Arabs: How Hollywood vilifies a people. *Annals of the American Academy of Political and Social Science*, 588, 171–193.

Short, (2013, October). *How much media? 2013: Report on American Consumers*. Institute for Communications Technology Management, Marshall School of Business, University of Southern California. At http://classic.marshall.usc.edu/assets/160/25918.pdf, accessed August 12, 2014.

Smith, S., Choueiti, M., Prescott, A., & Pieper, K. (2012). Gender roles & occupations: A look at character attributes and job-related aspirations in film and television. Geena Davis Institute on Gender and Media. At http://www.seejane.org/downloads/FullStudy_GenderRoles.pdf, accessed August 12, 2014.

Media History

STUART ALLAN
Cardiff University, UK

Media history as a concept in its own right possesses a relatively recent lineage. In the early decades of the twentieth century, when references to 'the media' – newspapers, magazines, cinema, radio, and the like – were entering popular parlance, university academics tended to be rather skeptical about whether these institutions were important enough to warrant scholarly attention. Traditional historians, in particular, were inclined to be dismissive. Matters would gradually improve over the course of the century, but even today, media history continues to occupy a contested terrain between the principal disciplines informing its development, namely media studies (broadly inclusive of communication, cultural, and journalism studies) and history (→ Communication as a Field and Discipline).

Early conceptions of media history frequently accorded the commercial press a central role in promoting social change, one especially worthy of close scrutiny (→ Journalism, History of). These days much of this research tends to be criticized for being celebratory, however, even romanticizing the press as the pre-eminent catalyst for advancing the cause of freedom in the face of fierce government opposition. In order to overcome the limitations of this 'Whig interpretation,' as it has been described, media historians have begun to diversify their sources and methods. For some this has entailed looking beyond the views of the powerful and privileged so as to recover and interpret the experiences of those typically marginalized – on the basis of class, gender, ethnicity or sexuality – where the making of media history is concerned.

Serious reservations have been expressed by some historians about the very legitimacy of media history as a proper academic subject when it encompasses ostensibly trivial, ephemeral media items (advertisements, comics, graffiti, soap operas, paperback → fiction, music videos, computer games, and the like) within its purview. Others have challenged this perspective, insisting that such value judgments be avoided so as to engage with the whole spectrum of emergent media in all of their complexity (→ Advertising; Video Games).

Defining Media History

Depending on how one chooses to define 'the media,' a case can be made that media history properly begins in the earliest days of human social life and communication. For researchers interested in the emergence of media in oral or pre-literate communities thousands of years ago, for example, the insights of archaeologists and anthropologists have proven invaluable. The advent of reading and writing is of particular significance, enabling the dissemination of → news or → information at a distance, and thereby helping to sustain a shared sense of social order. Studies have examined the emergence and use of various media facilitating communication, ranging from pictographs written on clay tablets, to papyrus, paper, and eventually the movable type of the printing press (→ Printing, History of; Briggs and Burke 2010).

For many media historians, it is the connection between emergent media of communication and the creation of democratic society that is particularly fascinating. In this context, Anderson's (1983) analysis of the rise of print as commodity in western Europe illuminates the emergence of nationality – "the personal and cultural feeling of belonging to a nation" – toward the end of the eighteenth century. He singles out for attention in this regard the fictional novel and the newspaper, arguing that the corresponding print languages helped to engender national consciousness in important ways.

Complementing this line of inquiry into how print enriched the ability of people to relate to themselves and to others in new ways have been efforts to understand how these media shaped the formation of → public opinion. Here researchers have found the notion of a → public sphere, as theorized by Jürgen Habermas (1989), to be useful, especially when investigating how spaces for public discussion and debate were initiated and sustained. Habermas identifies a range of institutions facilitating this process, with special attention devoted to coffee houses and the newspaper press (→ Newspaper, History of; Mulhmann 2008).

Related studies have elucidated the ways in which various media forms and practices helped to give shape to new kinds of public sociability. Such studies include examinations of advertising, art, music, street literature, exhibitions in museums and galleries, as well as reading and language societies, lending libraries, and the postal system, among other concerns (→ Art as Communication). Historiographies continue to rehearse contrary views on the extent to which the normative ideals of a public sphere have been realized in actual terms, a debate that continues to percolate. Nevertheless, there is general agreement that a consideration of the relative freedoms espoused by these ideals throw into sharp relief many of the factors that have acted to constrain public discussion over time.

Researching Media History

For media historians, the rationale for their craft is often expressed as a commitment to interdisciplinarity so as to situate the evolution of media forms, practices, institutions, and audiences within broader processes of societal change. Compounding this challenge, however, is the recognition that media processes can be ephemeral, and thereby elusive in conceptual and methodological terms. Often their very normality, that is, the extent to which they are simply taken for granted as a part of everyday life, means efforts to de-normalize them require considerable effort.

Media historians, it follows, must strive to be sufficiently self-reflexive about their chosen strategies when gathering source material and interpreting evidence, especially where questions related to 'effects' (→ Media Effects) or causation are being addressed. Pertinent in this regard is the status of electronic media, for example, which may pose particular problems for the historian seeking to establish relations of significance. Not only are the actual texts under scrutiny – e.g., an early radio play or television broadcast – unlikely to be amenable to more traditional, print-based methods, but issues with regard to such logistical considerations as access, physical artifacts (microphones, receiver sets, and the like), and format-compatibility (changes in formats can make playback difficult) may surface.

The advent of digital technologies is already engendering similar types of issues for media historians (→ Digital Media, History of). Scholarship increasingly entails finding alternative ways to manage, interpret, and preserve the extensive array of materials available across different storage systems. The sheer volume and range of these materials, coupled with continuing innovation in hardware and software (the obsolescence of technology rendering some types of data difficult to retrieve), can make for challenging decisions about how to maintain libraries, archives, databases, and other repositories of information (→ Archiving of Internet Content). New questions are being posed in this regard by electronic records, including items such as → electronic mail, voicemail messages, word-processing documents, Internet websites, message boards, blogs, Facebook accounts, Tweets and the like (→ Social Media), all of which are highly perishable.

Precisely how media history research will evolve invites thoughtful consideration. Current efforts to build on the foundations set down by the press histories of the nineteenth century are making progress in enriching these traditions, while also pursuing new directions that recast familiar assumptions – sometimes in unexpected ways. The types of criticisms of 'standard' media history identified by Carey, namely that its arguments were based on "nothing more than speculation, conjecture, anecdotal evidence, and ideological ax grinding" (and where conclusions were not "theoretically or empirically grounded; none was supported by systematic research"), no longer aptly characterize the field (1996, 15–16). Indeed, it is reasonable to suggest that there is every indication media history will continue to develop in ever more methodologically rigorous – and intellectually exciting – directions.

See also: ▶ ADVERTISING ▶ ARCHIVING OF INTERNET CONTENT ▶ ART AS COMMUNICATION ▶ BOOK ▶ CENSORSHIP, HISTORY OF ▶ COMMUNICATION AS A FIELD AND DISCIPLINE ▶ DIGITAL MEDIA, HISTORY OF ▶ ELECTRONIC MAIL ▶ FICTION ▶ FREEDOM OF COMMUNICATION ▶ HISTORIC KEY EVENTS AND THE MEDIA ▶ JOURNALISM, HISTORY OF ▶ MEDIA LITERACY ▶ MEDIA EFFECTS ▶ NEWS ▶ NEWSPAPER, HISTORY OF ▶ PRINTING, HISTORY OF ▶ PROPAGANDA ▶ PUBLIC BROADCASTING, HISTORY OF ▶ PUBLIC OPINION ▶ PUBLIC SPHERE ▶ SOCIAL MEDIA ▶ RADIO: SOCIAL HISTORY ▶ TELEVISION: SOCIAL HISTORY ▶ VIDEO GAMES

REFERENCES AND SUGGESTED READINGS

Anderson, B. (1983). *Imagined communities*. London: Verso.

Briggs, A. & Burke, P. (2010). *A social history of the media*, 3rd edn, Cambridge: Polity.

Carey, J. W. (1996). The Chicago School and the history of mass communication research. Repr. in *James Carey: A critical reader* (eds. E. S. Munson & C. A. Warren). Minneapolis, MN: University of Minnesota Press, pp. 14–33.

Habermas, J. (1989). *The structural transformation of the public sphere*. Cambridge: MIT Press.

Mulhmann, G. (2008). *A political history of journalism*. Cambridge: Polity.

Media Literacy

SONIA LIVINGSTONE
London School of Economics and Political Science

SHENJA VAN DER GRAAF
iMinds-SMIT, Vrije Universiteit Brussel

Media literacy has been defined as "the ability to access, analyze, evaluate and create messages across a variety of contexts" (Christ & Potter 1998, 7). This definition, produced by the USA's 1992 National Leadership Conference on Media Literacy, is widely accepted, although many competing conceptions exist.

Traditionally, media literacy research has focused on audiovisual media, though attention is increasingly turning to emerging digital, online and mobile technologies and contents. The priority now is to develop a subtle and detailed account of how people understand, create, trust, and critically evaluate information and communication contents delivered on new platforms, and disseminated and regulated in ways often unfamiliar or complex ways. Research is also prioritizing the reception and, particularly, the production of diverse kinds of content. The media literacy tradition generally stresses the understanding, comprehension, critique, and creation of media materials, whereas the → information literacy tradition places more emphasis on the access, identification, location, evaluation, and use of information materials. However, as taken forward in research and policy terms by → UNESCO, there are growing efforts to examine the convergence of these forms of media in an increasingly convergent communication landscape.

Research in this field is strongly policy-focused, with policymakers calling for evidence to aid them in meeting some key challenges. These include developing and promoting media educational curricula for school children, reaching a diverse population to develop the media and technological skills and knowledge necessary for a participatory, and competitive society, and ways of measuring and evaluating media literacy initiatives. Researchers more influenced by the arts and humanities see media literacy as a route to enhancing the public's understanding and appreciation of, and ability to contribute creatively to, the best that the cultural and audiovisual arts have to offer. By contrast, the social science approach sees media literacy as a form of defense against the normative messages of the big media corporations, whose commercialized, stereotyped, and parochial worldview dominates mass culture in capitalist societies (Livingstone et al. 2012).

See also: ▶ INFORMATION LITERACY ▶ UNESCO

REFERENCES AND SUGGESTED READINGS

Christ, W. G. & Potter, W. J. (1998). Media literacy, media education, and the academy. *Journal of Communication*, 48(1), 5–15.

Livingstone, S., Papaioannou, T., Mar Grandío Pérez, M., and Wijnen, C. (2012). Critical insights in European media literacy research and policy, *Media Studies*, 3(6): 1–13.

UNESCO. (n.d.). Media and information literacy. At http://www.unesco.org/new/index.php?id=19145, accessed September 3, 2014.

Media Messages and Family Communication

CHRISTINE BACHEN
Santa Clara University

Research on media and family communication has focused on the association of demographic factors – especially income and education – on the number and types of media available in a household, amount of time devoted to media use, context for use (e.g., alone, during mealtime), and patterns of use over the life cycle of the family (Alexander 2008). Media provide opportunities for companionship, discussion, and sharing of values, but increasingly families use media in more individualized ways because of lower cost and more personalized media devices (Livingstone & Das 2010).

Alexander (2008) summarizes several *theoretical approaches* that frame contemporary study of family and media. S*ocial cognitive theory* explains children can learn behaviors and attitudes through observation of media models. According to *family systems theory,* media use becomes an extension of the norms, values, and beliefs that define the family system. The *sociocultural perspective* situates the family as a social institution where interactions of families and media often reproduce the social order in terms of gender relationships or generational relationships, or at times resist them.

Media management is recognized as an important task of contemporary parenting, with a wide-ranging set of practices within and across cultures, and ever adapting to emerging media (Livingstone & Das 2010; → Parental Mediation Strategies). Parents are more likely to engage in 'restrictive mediation' when children are young and when they believe the media content is less important than other activities. Co-use of media is more common with young children as well and can enhance the effects of media on children as it signals an acceptance of the content. Active or instructive mediation can limit unwanted effects and enhance positive effects from media especially up until adolescence, helping children to develop critical media literacy skills.

Emerging research is focusing more extensively on family subsystems (e.g., families that have experienced divorce) or cell phone and Internet use (Livingstone & Das 2010; Coyne et al., 2012).

See also: ▶ EXPOSURE TO COMMUNICATION CONTENT ▶ MEDIA EFFECTS ▶ MEDIA AND PERCEPTIONS OF REALITY ▶ MEDIA USE ACROSS THE LIFE-SPAN ▶ PARENTAL MEDIATION STRATEGIES ▶ VIDEO GAMES ▶ VIOLENCE AS MEDIA CONTENT, EFFECTS ON CHILDREN OF

REFERENCES AND SUGGESTED READINGS

Alexander, A. (2008). Media and the family. In S. L. Calvert & B. J. Wilson (eds.), *The Handbook of Children, Media, and Development*. Oxford: Blackwell, pp. 121–140.

Coyne, S. M., Bushman, B. J., & Nathanson, A. L. (eds.) (2012). *Media and Family*. Special issue of *Family Relations*, 61(3).

Livingstone, S. & Das, R. (2010). Media, Communication and Information Technologies in the European Family. A report on Existential Field 8 for the FP7. At http://eprints.lse.ac.uk/29788/, accessed August 15, 2014.

Strasburger, V. C., Wilson, B. J., Jordan, A. B. (2014). The family and media. In *Children, Adolescents, and the Media*. Thousand Oaks, CA: Sage, pp. 487–506.

Media and Perceptions of Reality

LINDSAY H. HOFFMAN
University of Delaware

CARROLL J. GLYNN
Ohio State University

Perceptions of reality, or social reality, can be conceptualized as an individual's conception of the world (Hawkins & Pingree 1982). What intrigues many social scientists is the exploration of the specifics of these → perceptions and the ways in which they are developed. Social perception has been considered from both individual- and social-level perspectives.

The individual-level conception of social reality – or, as McLeod and Chaffee (1972) refer to it, *social* reality – suggests that others exist in one's mind as imaginations, and it is only in these imaginations that others have an effect on the individual. The perspective of social *reality* defines the social system as the unit of analysis. These scholars focus on understanding commonly held perceptions shared in society. They often base their exploration on individuals' perceptions of what others think, or whether an individual believes that an opinion or attitude is shared by others. Because the media, in particular, provide individuals with indirect representations of reality, communication scholars have been particularly interested in how individuals develop cognitions of social reality based upon their use of and attention to the media.

General Perception Effects

Several phenomena describing perceptions (and misperceptions) of social reality have been outlined in the literature. The term → *pluralistic ignorance* is often used as an umbrella to describe all misperceptions of others' opinions. Research in this area is primarily concerned with the factors that lead to individuals being more or less accurate about reality, focusing on the discrepancy between individual perceptions and actual reality.

Consensus occurs when homogeneous opinions exist across a group of individuals. Some research has suggested that an *overestimate of consensus* occurs when individuals perceive greater consensus on their own opinion than exists in reality. In this way, overestimation of consensus is 'absolute' because it is objectively false. The concept of *false consensus* describes the tendency to see one's own behaviors and opinions as normal and those of others as deviant or inappropriate, which results in exaggerating the prominence of one's own opinions.

Social projection is generally defined as the psychological phenomenon that drives several other inaccurate perceptions, including the *silent majority* or *false idiosyncrasy effect*, which occurs when some individuals support a position on an issue vocally and prominently, while those opposed to the issue – even if they are in the majority – remain silent. The *disowning projection* refers to the tendency toward attributing selfish motives, evil intent, or ignorance to others and denying these characteristics of oneself. The *looking-glass perception* occurs when people see others as holding the same view as they themselves hold.

Media-Specific Perception Effects

Another group of theories focuses on individuals' perceptions about media content or its influence on others. The → *third-person effect* predicts that individuals exposed to a persuasive message will perceive greater effects on others than on themselves (Davison 1981). *Impersonal influence* describes the influence derived from anonymous others' attitudes, experiences, and beliefs. From this perspective, media do not need to be universally consonant or even personally persuasive in order to impact individuals' perceptions of media influence (Mutz 1998).

The *hostile media phenomenon* suggests that partisans see news media coverage of controversial events as portraying a biased slant, even in news coverage that most nonpartisans label as unbiased (Vallone et al. 1985). An underlying assumption of this phenomenon is that media coverage is essentially unbiased (→ Bias in the News). The *persuasive press inference* hypothesis draws from the hostile media phenomenon and third-person effect and places the effects into one process, i.e., people overestimate the impact of news coverage on public opinion and because of this misperception, estimates of public opinion are inaccurate (Gunther 1998).

Causal Mechanisms for Social-Reality Perceptions and Misperceptions

Some research on perceptions of social reality has emphasized mass media as the primary causal mechanism explaining perceptions of social reality. Because few people have direct personal experience with politics, mediated information has the ability to influence individuals' perceptions of social reality at the collective level. That is, media enhance the salience of social-level judgments, in addition to influencing perceptions of public opinion.

First, → *spiral of silence theory* suggests that because the climate of opinion is always vacillating, individuals are "scanning" their social environment for cues of what constitutes majority and minority opinion (Noelle-Neumann 1993). The media are one such source, but often present biased viewpoints. As a result of this individuals perceive a majority perspective, and this perception either promotes or prevents them from speaking out (see Schulz and Roessler 2012).

Second, *cultivation* implies that, over time, people are influenced by the content on television so that their perceptions of reality come to reflect those presented on television (→ Cultivation Effects). This theory also purports that media content displays distorted estimates of social reality, e.g., the rates of crime and violence which in turn lead to the overestimation of personal risks (Shrum & Bischak 2001).

Effects of social reality perceptions can also be attributed to other causal mechanisms in three broader categories: individual, individual–other, and social explanations.

Individual explanations include cognitions and motivations. One possible mechanism in this category of cognitive explanations is the accessibility bias, or the tendency to derive estimates of others' views based upon that information that is most accessible in one's memory. The third-person effect also is explained by cognitive 'errors.' The actor–observer attributional error occurs when individuals underestimate the extent to which others account for situational factors, and overestimate their own attention to these factors. Motivational explanations can also be applied to those theories that claim media as the primary causal mechanism. For instance, Noelle-Neumann cites fear of isolation, or a motivation not to be in the minority, as a driving force behind the spiral of silence.

Social harmony and public expression mechanisms belong in the category of *individual–other explanations*. Because conflict is not palatable to many people, there may exist motivations to see others' positions on issues as more like their own in order to avoid argument or dissonance (social harmony). Misperceptions of social reality at the individual–other level also can arise from either intentional or unintentional misrepresentation of one's opinions in public. The *differential interpretation hypothesis* describes a conscious decision to publicly misrepresent one's opinion, while the *differential encoding hypothesis* suggests that some individuals suffer from an "illusion of transparency," mistakenly believing that their own and others' opinions are accurately expressed publicly (Prentice and Miller 1993).

The *social explanations* are based upon what McLeod and Chaffee (1972) referred to as social *reality*, wherein a context or situation serves as the causal mechanism underlying perceptions of social reality. For instance, if an issue is particularly divisive, individuals are prone to the false consensus effect because they see one side as more similar to themselves and the other side as deviant or uncommon.

See also: ▶ BIAS IN THE NEWS ▶ CLIMATE OF OPINION ▶ CULTIVATION EFFECTS ▶ ENTERTAINMENT CONTENT AND REALITY PERCEPTION ▶ INFORMATION PROCESSING ▶ INTERPERSONAL COMMUNICATION ▶ LANGUAGE AND SOCIAL INTERACTION ▶ MEDIA EFFECTS: DIRECT AND INDIRECT EFFECTS ▶ PERCEPTION

▶ PLURALISTIC IGNORANCE ▶ PUBLIC OPINION
▶ SELECTIVE PERCEPTION AND SELECTIVE RETENTION ▶ SPIRAL OF SILENCE
▶ THIRD-PERSON EFFECTS

REFERENCES AND SUGGESTED READINGS

Davison, W. P. (1981). The third-person effect in communication. *Public Opinion Quarterly*, 47, 1–15.
Eveland, W. P., Jr. (2002). The impact of news and entertainment media on perceptions of social reality. In J. P. Dillard & M. Pfau (eds.), *The persuasion handbook: Developments in theory and practice*. Thousand Oaks, CA: Sage, pp. 691–727.
Glynn, C. J., Ostman, R. E., & McDonald, D. G. (1995). Opinions, perception, and social reality. In T. L. Glasser & C. T. Salmon (eds.), *Public opinion and the communication of consent*. New York: Guilford, pp. 249–277.
Gunther, A. C. (1998). The persuasive press inference: Effects of mass media on perceived public opinion. *Communication Research*, 25(5), 486–504.
Hawkins, R. P. & Pingree, S. (1982). Television's influence on social reality. In L. B. D. Pearl & J. Lazar (eds.), *Television and behavior: Ten years of scientific progress and implications for the eighties*. Washington, DC: US Government Printing Office, pp. 224–247.
McLeod, J. M. & Chaffee, S. R. (1972). The construction of social reality. In J. T. Tedeschi (ed.), *The social influence processes*. Chicago, IL: Aldine-Atherton, pp. 50–99.
Mutz, D. C. (1998). *Impersonal influence: How perceptions of mass collectives affect political attitudes*. Cambridge: Cambridge University Press.
Noelle-Neumann, E. (1993). *The spiral of silence: Public opinion, our social skin*. Chicago, IL: University of Chicago Press.
Prentice, D. A. & Miller, D. T. (1993). Pluralistic ignorance and alcohol use on campus: Some consequences of misperceiving the social norm. *Journal of Personality and Social Psychology*, 64(2), 243–256.
Schulz, A. & Roessler, P. (2012). The spiral of silence and the Internet: Selection of online content and the perception of the public opinion climate in computer-mediated communication environments. *International Journal of Public Opinion Research*, 24(3), 346–367.
Shrum, L. J. & Bischak, V. D. (2001). Mainstreaming, resonance, and impersonal impact: Testing moderators of the cultivation effect for estimates of crime risk. *Human Communication Research*, 27(2), 187–215.
Vallone, R. P., Ross, L., & Lepper, M. R. (1985). The hostile media phenomenon: Biased perceptions and perceptions of media bias in coverage of the Beirut massacre. *Journal of Personality and Social Psychology*, 49(3), 577–585.

Media Performance

DENIS MCQUAIL
University of Amsterdam

The term 'media performance' has a broad reference to the assessment of mass media according to a range of evaluative criteria. In practice, most attention has been given to the product of mass media, its content as sent and received (→ Media Production and Content). The criteria applied are mainly derived either from professional goals and standards or from considerations of the public interest as specified in certain evaluative concepts (→ Standards of News). The methods are mainly those of the social sciences, aiming to be systematic, reliable, and leading to some degree of generalization.

From the late 1960s onwards, media performance research was more influenced by *external social and political criticism* than internal professional criteria, following the rise of radical and anti-war movements in North America and Europe. The rise of television news to a central position in the media system by the 1970s was also a factor, not only because of its reach and believed impact but also because of high public expectations of neutrality, truthfulness, and informative power. Much effort was made on both sides of the Atlantic to assess the balance of attention in news between various competing actors, with strong suspicion of hidden ideological motives and equally strong denials (→ Bias in the News). An important advance in media performance research was the program directed at measuring media quality under the auspices of the Japanese Broadcasting Corporation (NHK) (see Ishikawa 1996). It worked with a framework of three different levels at which problems of media quality can be identified: the whole media system; the channel (or equivalent); the content (e.g., program). It also identified four different perspectives from which media could be viewed and evaluated: of the state, of the society, of the audience, and of media professionals.

One of the main roots of critical research lies in ideas about the social responsibility of media to society (→ Journalists' Role Perception). McQuail's "Media performance" (1992) assembled a number of basic criteria of media performance from theory and practice held to be 'in the public interest' and reviewed relevant methods and examples of performance research. Other perennial topics for media evaluation inspired by → critical theory of one sort or another have included: the representation of women and of gender roles in the media or the portrayal of ethnic and other minorities. The case of terrorism raised rather complex issues, with competing journalistic norms of freedom and responsibility (→ Mediated Terrorism).

Media performance research has at times been *inspired by acute public concern* about its potentially harmful effects (→ Media Effects). For instance, it played a part in inquiries into the causes of crime and violence (→ Violence in the Media, Effects of) and the effects of exposure to pornography (→ Sexual Violence in the Media). An abiding focus of performance research is to be found in the field of → political communication. Besides concerns about 'balance' (see above), performance research has been stimulated by the complaint that the mass media are failing the democratic political system by not providing information of substance, by presenting politics in a negative light, and by diverting citizens from active participation (→ News Values; Tabloidization).

The most commonly encountered *evaluative concepts* to be found in the field include the following: *objectivity*, with its component elements as described above; *diversity*, which is a key value in most pluralistic democracies and underlies expectations that media will pay attention, or give access and expression, to a range of persons, groups, ideas, and events that are broadly reflective of the social, cultural, and political environment in which they operate; *cultural quality*, with reference to accepted aesthetic or ethical standards or the prevailing tastes and interests of the public (→ Ethics in Journalism); *freedom*, which here means mainly the independence of media as reflected in a willingness to speak out, to be critical or original, without deference to the power of government, business interests, or (in some cases) the media's owners.

With the *Internet* the criteria of 'good performance' have not changed greatly and the same research apparatus can still serve, but there are significant new challenges. These arise most obviously from the enormous volume of supply transmitted by the Internet and → social media. Such content is also often multimedia in character and may not conform to established genres and the conventions of presentation of traditional media. It is difficult to sample, to generalize about, and to codify, making the methods developed for mass communication inappropriate. New indicators of performance are called for. Crude forms of assessment of Internet flow are already appearing, but the task of performance assessment has barely begun.

See also: ▶ BIAS IN THE NEWS ▶ COMMUNICATION AND LAW ▶ CONCENTRATION IN MEDIA SYSTEMS ▶ CRITICAL THEORY ▶ CULTIVATION EFFECTS ▶ DISCOURSE ANALYSIS ▶ ETHICS IN JOURNALISM ▶ JOURNALISM ▶ JOURNALISM EDUCATION ▶ JOURNALISTS' ROLE PERCEPTION ▶ MEDIA EFFECTS ▶ MEDIA PRODUCTION AND CONTENT ▶ MEDIATED TERRORISM ▶ NEWS VALUES ▶ OBJECTIVITY IN REPORTING ▶ POLITICAL COMMUNICATION ▶ QUALITY OF THE NEWS ▶ SENSATIONALISM ▶ SEXUAL VIOLENCE IN THE MEDIA ▶ SOCIAL MEDIA ▶ STANDARDS OF NEWS ▶ TABLOIDIZATION ▶ VIOLENCE AS MEDIA CONTENT, EFFECTS OF

REFERENCES AND SUGGESTED READINGS

Dayan, D. (2013). Conquering visibility, conferring visibility: Visibility seekers and media performance. *International Journal of Communication*, 7, 137–153.

Ishikawa, S. (1996). *Quality assessment of television*. Luton: University of Luton Press.

Lemert, J. B. (1989). *Criticizing the media*. Newbury Park, CA: Sage.

McQuail, D. (1992). *Media performance*. Beverley Hills, CA: Sage.

Robinson, P., Goddard, P., Parry, K., & Murray, C. (2009). Testing models of media performance in wartime: U.K. TV news and the 2003 invasion of Iraq. *Journal of Communication*, 59(3), 534–563.

Puppis, M., Kunzler, M., & Jarren, Ottfried, eds., (2013). *Media structures and media performance*. Vienna: Austrian Academy of Sciences Press.

Media Planning

EDITH SMIT
University of Amsterdam

The following questions are essential in deciding how to allocate a campaign budget: (1) How many people of the target group do we want to reach? (2) How many times do we want to reach them? (3) Within what time frame do we want to make contact? (4) Which contexts are most suitable to get our message across? These questions refer to four key topics in media planning: reach, frequency, timing, and context (→ Advertisement Campaign Management; Advertising Strategies).

Reach is a measure of how many different audience members are exposed to a media vehicle (→ Audience Research). For broadcast media, the term ratings is used. Campaign reach indicates the number of *contacts* with all the published (advertising) messages in the campaign. To illustrate this concept: if one person is exposed to three commercials in a row, the campaign has generated three contacts. There is the same number of contacts if three people are exposed to one commercial each. We call the total number of contacts with a campaign *gross reach or gross rating points* (*GRP*). Ten GRPs means that the insertion reaches 10 percent. The *net reach* in a media plan is the number of people that are exposed to the campaign at least once. Reach figures for various media are difficult to compare. Industry data for print media, for example, indicate the number of people reading the various titles, not the number of people who have seen an advertisement in that title. Television data, on the other hand, refer to the number of people watching specific content, such as television commercials. Comparing data for print and for television, therefore, is like comparing apples and oranges. Furthermore, 'reach' figures do not tell how advertisements are processed, and the effect they have on brand attitude and behavior (→ Advertisement Effectiveness).

Decisions with respect to *frequency of exposure* are important because media costs are high and campaigners want to avoid wasting money due to a too-low frequency (no effects reached) or too-high frequency (unnecessary costs). Most theories assume that repeating the message is useful because it adds to the effects of the campaign (wear-in). However, after a certain number of repetitions the effects decline, or can even become negative (wear-out).

The most important decision in answering the question about the *timing of the message* is the choice between 'bursting' (large media exposure over a short period) on the one hand and 'dripping' (spreading small media exposure over time) on the other hand. Timing decisions are based on a number of considerations, including the quality of the commercial, irritation effects, the forget effect, share of voice (how active are competitors), and ad stock.

Advertising context is a multifarious concept, consisting of many elements that may influence advertising effectiveness. (1) Media differ with respect to the number and type of modalities such as text, audio, pictures, and video; (2) we can make a distinction between push media (also called display or delivery media) and pull media (also called search or retrieval media); (3) media also vary to the extent to which the audience can influence the timing and pace of the information flow; (4) media differ in 'interactivity' giving 'users' more or less possibilities for contributing to content; (5) the amount of reach and the speed of reach accumulation differ between media types; (6) commercial context concerns the amount and nature of other commercial messages in the environment of an ad, referred to as clutter and competitive clutter; and (7) editorial context refers to the question whether the same source delivering the same message to the same audience on separate occasions might produce different effects depending on the different programs or editorial contexts in which the message appears. In particular, context-induced psychological responses, such as involvement elicited by a documentary, happiness caused by a sitcom, or sadness generated by a drama series, are considered to have an important impact on advertising processing.

Many campaigns make use of more than one medium. In these cross-media or cross-tools campaigns, campaigners seek to maximize the effectiveness of their budgets by exploiting the unique strengths of each medium and tool and by maximizing cross-media consistency and synergy. Finding an answer to the question of how to do this has always been central in media planning, but has become more complicated because of considerable changes in the media landscape that can be characterized by increased fragmentation, increased user control, mobile media, multitasking, consumer-generated information, possibilities for targeting, customization, and personalization, integration of advertising and transaction, and blurred distinctions between editorial content and advertising.

See also: ▶ ADVERTISEMENT CAMPAIGN MANAGEMENT ▶ ADVERTISING ▶ ADVERTISING EFFECTIVENESS ▶ ADVERTISING STRATEGIES ▶ AUDIENCE RESEARCH ▶ BRANDS ▶ EXPOSURE TO TELEVISION ▶ SEGMENTATION OF THE ADVERTISING AUDIENCE ▶ SURVEY

SUGGESTED READINGS

Kelly, L. D. & Juggenheimer, D.W. (2004). *Advertising media planning: A brand management approach.* New York: M.E. Sharpe.

Krugman, H. E. (1972). Why three exposures may be enough. *Journal of Advertising Research*, 12(6), 11–14.

McDonald, C. (1996). *Advertising reach and frequency: Maximising advertising results through effective frequency*, 2nd ed. Chicago: ANA/NTC.

Moorman, M., Neijens, P. C., & Smit, E. G. (2005). The effects of program responses on the processing of commercials placed at various positions in the program and the block. *Journal of Advertising Research*, 45(1), 49–59.

Naik, P. A. & Raman, K. (2003). Understanding the impact of synergy in multimedia communications. *Journal of Marketing Research*, 40(4), 375–388.

Webster, J.G., Pahlen, P.F., & Lichty, L. W. (2014). *Ratings, analysis: Audience measurement and analytics*, 4th edn. Mahwah, NJ: Lawrence Erlbaum.

Media Production and Content

STEPHEN D. REESE

University of Texas at Austin

Research in the sub-field of media production and content seeks to describe and explain the symbolic world of the media with reference to a variety of contributing societal, institutional, organizational, and normative factors. It draws boundaries around a large and diverse body of research efforts, predominantly social science, but also including more interpretive cultural analysis.

Scope of the Research Area

If much of the communication field has concerned itself with the effects of media, and the process by which they are produced (→ Communication as a Field and Discipline; Exposure to Communication Content; Media Effects), this more recently emerging area has treated the media map of the world itself as problematic, something to be understood and predicted through an awareness of underlying forces. These forces provide the context of 'media production,' which is examined for its systematic ties to 'content' – particularly → news and information. Given the multitude of factors influencing the media, this conceptual framework has led the field of communication to devote the same sustained research to the creation, control, and shape of the mediated environment as it has to the effects on audiences of that environment. The objects of study in this area, however, have undergone profound changes, particularly with communication technology, making it more problematic to identify 'the media,' 'the profession,' and the site of 'production.'

This research area is often broadly referred to as '*media sociology*' (reviewed in Berkowitz 1997). Certainly, many of the participant observation ethnographies of newsrooms and other media are so labeled, particularly given their use of traditional sociological fieldwork methods (e.g., Tuchman 1978; Gans 1979; → Ethnography of Communication). The technology of distributed online production makes identifying the 'sites' where news is produced more difficult now, but the ethnography approach continues to be used. The area also encompasses studies of individual media workers, and how their personal traits affect their decisions (e.g., Weaver & Wilnat 2012; → Journalism). Many media critics lodge the blame for press bias (→ Bias in the News) squarely with individual journalists, or find fault with the entertainment industry because of 'out-of-touch'

Hollywood producers, but important explanations for these communication products lie in structural bias, beyond individual prejudice. Although media organizations – including those supported by the state – employ many creative professionals, the work of those individuals is routinized and structured to yield a predictable product. Even the 'news' must be controlled, anticipated, and packaged to allow the organization to manage its task effectively: in Tuchman's (1978) phrase, "routinizing the unexpected" (→ News Routines).

Beginning in the 1950s Warren Breed (1955) and David Manning White (1950) were among the first scholars to examine the *influences on content* directly, with their examinations of social control in the newsroom and the story selections of an editor, described as the news 'gatekeeper'. Reese and Ballinger (2001) observed that the gatekeepers in these studies were deemed representatives of the larger culture, and news policies were assumed to help identify as news those events of interest to the community – rendering the production and control issues unthreatening to the public interest and, as a result, of less interest to researchers. Eventually, however, these questions returned to the fore.

The *hierarchy of influences model* describes the multiple levels of influences – individual, routines, organizational, extra-media (social institutional), and ideological (socio system) – that impinge on media simultaneously and suggests how influence at one level may interact with that at another (Shoemaker & Reese 2014). Within the realm of newsmaking, for example, the individual-level bias of particular journalists may affect their reporting, but journalists of a particular leaning often self-select an organization because of its pre-existing policies, history, and organizational culture (routines). The news organization and its employees, in turn, must function within other institutional relationships and ideological boundaries set by the larger society. Thus, the individual functions within a web of constraints.

The compelling *point of departure for this subfield* is the idea that media content provides a map of the world that differs from the way that world really is, making the research task one of explaining those discrepancies. Media representations can be tied to objects in the real world, but viewed another way media content is fundamentally a 'construction,' and, as such, can never find its analog in some external benchmark, a 'mirror' of reality. This perspective directs research to understanding the construction process (→ Construction of Reality through the News). Journalists, for example, 'see' things because their 'news net' is set up to allow them to be seen.

Research Findings

Given the wide variation among media round the world, generalizations about production and content must be made with caution. Now that more *comparative research* has begun to emerge, it is easier to distinguish between those practices common across countries and those peculiar to one or the other. Certainly, changes in technology have had widespread cross-national effects, blurring craft distinctions in the convergence of media forms.

Although broad generalizations can be made, there are also important *differences across the various media*. These more organizational issues involve the technological imperatives, audience considerations, economic and other dictates, as well as the regulatory environment that they all face. Each medium, whether radio, television, newspapers, or magazines, has its own unique problems to solve in providing a product to a reader, viewer, or listener. The highest level of the hierarchy of influences model, the ideological or social system, considers how the media function within a society by virtue of there being a certain kind of system – which necessarily binds them to the prevailing social order usually associated with nation-states.

Research Methods

These considerations often require a more interpretive analysis, which considers how the media reinforce the definitions of the powerful and linked to media production practices that support them. A *macro level of analysis* directs attention to cross-national comparisons of media production, where important patterns can be found. Shoemaker and Cohen (2006) find that news has a number of common patterns across nations, even if these are filtered through specific national cultures (→ International News Reporting).

Global changes in media ownership, new ways of carrying out gatekeeping across national boundaries, and emerging shared norms of professionalism all give greater emphasis to this perspective (→ Globalization Theories). So, under the continuing processes of globalization, this area of research faces the challenge of identifying the universal aspects of media and social representation, the enduring particularities of individual national contexts, and the increasing interactions between these levels.

See also: ▶ BIAS IN THE NEWS ▶ COMMUNICATION AS A FIELD AND DISCIPLINE ▶ CONSTRUCTION OF REALITY THROUGH THE NEWS ▶ ETHNOGRAPHY OF COMMUNICATION ▶ EXPOSURE TO COMMUNICATION CONTENT ▶ GLOBALIZATION THEORIES ▶ INFOTAINMENT ▶ INTERNATIONAL NEWS REPORTING ▶ JOURNALISM ▶ MEDIA EFFECTS ▶ NEWS ▶ NEWS ROUTINES ▶ NEWS SOURCES ▶ NEWS VALUES

REFERENCES AND SUGGESTED READINGS

Berkowitz, D. (1997). *Social meanings of news*. Thousand Oaks, CA: Sage.
Breed, W. (1955). Social control in the newsroom: A functional analysis. *Social Forces*, 33, 326–355.
Gans, H. (1979). *Deciding what's news*. New York: Pantheon.
Reese, S. & Ballinger, J. (2001). The roots of a sociology of news: Remembering Mr Gates and social control in the newsroom. *Journalism and Mass Communication Quarterly*, 78(4), 641–658.
Shoemaker, P. & Cohen, A. (2006). *News around the world*. London: Routledge.
Shoemaker, P. & Reese, S. (2014). *Mediating the message in the 21st Century: A media sociology perspective*. London: Routledge.
Tuchman, G. (1978). *Making news*. New York: Free Press.
Weaver, D. & Wilnat, L. (2012). *The global journalist in the 21st century*. London: Routledge.
White, D. (1950). The "gatekeeper": A case study in the selection of news. *Journalism Quarterly*, 27, 383–396.

Media System Dependency Theory

SANDRA J. BALL-ROKEACH
University of Southern California

Media System Dependency (MSD) theory emerged to reframe the effects question to ask: "Under what societal and individual conditions do/don't media have substantial effects?" (Ball-Rokeach 1985; 1998). The theory's basic premise is that media effects flow from the information resources of the media system that are implicated in the everyday life requirements of people (micro), groups or organizations (meso), and other social systems (macro) to act meaningfully in ambiguous or threatening social environments. Thus, the media system is best viewed as an information system whose powers vis-à-vis effects rest on the scarcity or exclusivity of their information resources.

The dependency relation reflects the extent to which resources controlled by one entity (the media) have to be accessed by another party (other social systems, organizations, individuals) to attain fundamental goals. Thus follows the notion that effects are by-products of dependency relations. MSD relations arise when individuals, organizations, or other systems consider media information resources – the gathering/creating, processing, and dissemination of information both in → news and in entertainment genres – to be essential or preferable to alternative modes of achieving their goals.

In MSD the *media–audience (macro-to-micro) relation* is conceived to be asymmetric and invariable in structure; that is, media resources are implicated in individuals' goals of understanding (themselves and their social environs), orientation (acting and interacting), and play (solitary and social) more than the resources of most individuals are implicated in media goal attainment. Another major component of the theory is the view of individuals as embedded not only in interpersonal networks that tend to conserve shared beliefs, but also in a larger context, often marked by ambiguity, threat, conflict, and change, that tends to open the door to media effects. Put briefly, the more problematic people's social environs, the more likely it is that the media information system will be a, if not the, major resource in people's efforts to understand and act meaningfully in those environs (→ Attending to the Mass Media).

There is *substantial variation* in how people respond or adapt to the same social environs. Under conditions of ambiguity, for example, some will actively seek to resolve the ambiguity, while others may seek to escape or withdraw. In this case, the more active are also the more likely to experience media effects, because the media system is usually positioned as the best or most accessible information system through which ambiguity may be addressed. How active an individual is at any one point in time will depend on major sources of individual variation. Most important are variations in goals that implicate media resources, variations in structural location or the degree to which people have access to alternative information systems (e.g., experts), and variation in interpersonal network discursive agendas.

As MSD theory developed the macro-/micro-focus was expanded with increased attention to *intervening meso-level forces*, specifically the interpersonal network (→ Interpersonal Communication; Social Networks). Instead of an effects-buffer, interpersonal discourse on media topics was conceived as a variable that could lessen or intensify media effects. Thus, interpersonal networks also have MSD relations for much the same reasons as had been argued for individuals (see Ball-Rokeach, 1998).

Most *empirical studies* examine the intensity of individual MSD relations, but there are also case studies of macro-level issues, such as the evolution of MSD relations under conditions of social change (see Meshkin 1999). However, major changes in media production resources suggested the need for fundamental elaboration of the theory to take into account the less bounded and more chaotic media landscape of the twenty-first century. Obvious examples include the emergence and blending of the Internet with traditional media, the explosion of ethnic media and the multimedia and increasingly centralized ownership structure (→ Media Conglomerates). MSD theory today conceives of a communication ecology where traditional media, new media, ethnic media, the media of community institutions, and interpersonal discourse operate in the context of each other. The expanded version of MSD theory has been incorporated into Communication Infrastructure Theory (CIT).

See also: ▶ AGENDA-SETTING EFFECTS ▶ ATTENDING TO THE MASS MEDIA ▶ CULTIVATION THEORY ▶ ETHNIC MEDIA AND THEIR INFLUENCE ▶ INTERPERSONAL COMMUNICATION ▶ MEDIA CONGLOMERATES ▶ MEDIA EFFECTS ▶ MEDIA EFFECTS: DIRECT AND INDIRECT EFFECTS ▶ MEDIA EFFECTS, HISTORY OF ▶ MODELS OF COMMUNICATION ▶ NEWS ▶ SELECTIVE EXPOSURE ▶ TWO-STEP FLOW OF COMMUNICATION ▶ SOCIAL NETWORKS ▶ USES AND GRATIFICATIONS

REFERENCES AND SUGGESTED READINGS

Ball-Rokeach, S. J. (1974). The information perspective. Paper presented at the annual meetings of the American Sociological Association, August, Montreal.

Ball-Rokeach, S. J. (1985). The origins of individual media system dependency: A sociological framework. *Communication Research*, 12, 485–510.

Ball-Rokeach, S. J. (1998). A theory of media power and a theory of media use: Different stories, questions, and ways of thinking. *Mass Communication and Society*, 1, 5–40.

Ball-Rokeach, S. J. & Jung, J-Y. (2009). The evolution of media system dependency theory. In R. Nabi & M. B. Oliver (eds.), *The Sage handbook of media processes and effects*. Thousand Oaks, CA: Sage, pp. 531–544.

Kim, Y.-C. & Ball-Rokeach, S. J. (2006). Civic engagement from a communication infrastructure perspective. *Communication Theory*, 16, 173–197.

Meshkin, D. (1999). Media dependency theory: Origins and directions. In D. Demers & K. Viswanath (eds.), *Mass media, social control, and social change*. Ames, IA: Iowa State University Press, pp. 77–98.

Media Use and Child Development

PATTI M. VALKENBURG
University of Amsterdam

The media children use, and in particular their media preferences, are predicted – in large part – by their developmental capabilities. Children typically have a preference for media content that does not diverge too much from their existing cognitive capacities, and they show less preference for extremely simple or extremely complex media content (Valkenburg 2004). This so-called 'moderate-discrepancy hypothesis' offers a viable explanation for why the media preferences of children in various age groups differ so greatly.

After all, the perceived simplicity and complexity of media content changes dramatically as children mature. Media content that is only moderately discrepant and therefore attractive to 2-year-olds may be overly simple and thus unattractive to 6-year-olds (→ Developmental Communication).

Around *18 months of age*, most children use media on a daily basis. At this age, they start to develop a genuine interest in the storyline of media products. However, because of their limited information-processing skills, they need more time than older children to make sense of media content. Therefore, they often respond best to programs with a slow pace and lots of repetition. They also prefer familiar contexts, objects and animals. They like to watch programs that show babies and young children, and they adore nonthreatening real or animated animals, such as friendly dinosaurs, and babyish creatures like the Teletubbies. These young children are not yet able to distinguish fantasy from reality in media content. Therefore, fantasy characters or special effects can have a much greater impact on younger than on older children.

By the time they are *4–6 years old*, children begin to develop a preference for more fast-paced and adventurous programs. By that age, they become more responsive to verbally oriented shows, with more sophisticated forms of humor like The Simpsons. At this time, their fantasies more often entail realistic and plausible themes. And they develop a sincere, sometimes even exaggerated, interest in real-world phenomena. Because most fantasy characters have been demystified, children now tend to become attached to real-life heroes, such as sports heroes, movie stars, and action heroes.

Children's developmental level is one of the strongest predictors of their media use. Because media effects are a result of media use, a true understanding of the effects of media on children can occur only by an understanding of their developmental changes and their developmentally-induced media use and preferences.

See also: ▶ COMPUTER GAMES AND CHILD DEVELOPMENT ▶ DEVELOPMENTAL COMMUNICATION ▶ MEDIA USE ACROSS THE LIFE-SPAN

REFERENCES AND SUGGESTED READINGS

Valkenburg, P. M. (2004). *Children's responses to the screen: A media psychological approach*. Mahwah, NJ: Lawrence Erlbaum.

Valkenburg, P. M. & Peter, J. (2013). The differential susceptibility to media effects model. *Journal of Communication, 63*, 221–243.

Media Use, International Comparison of

PATRICK RÖSSLER
University of Erfurt

As data on media use are systematically collected only in a few (mostly western) countries of the world, the international comparison of media use patterns remains fragmentary. Evidence provided by global research agencies is often difficult to interpret because a standardized definition of *media use* is lacking (→ Audience Research; Exposure to Communication Content).

Individual usage patterns depend on several factors that influence the conditions under which media can be used at all, and apply differently to nations worldwide. Among these is, first, the *system of government*. Constitutions of nations in the western hemisphere enshrine freedom of speech (→ Freedom of Communication; Freedom of Information; Freedom of the Press, Concept of). Other political systems hold a different perception of media regulation, including → censorship or access barriers, while their cultural or religious background may enhance the tendency to self-censorship among communicators (→ Political Communication Systems).

Also, *communication style* in a society affects media use. Cultures (→ Culture: Definitions and Concepts) are characterized by different rules and social conventions regarding how media are used, which media are used, and for what purpose. Media use depends also on access to the media, which have different prerequisites for proper distribution (*infrastructure for distribution*). Newspapers and magazines require physical transport and so roads, boats, airplanes; audiovisual media require technical equipment such as broadcasting stations or satellite transmission (→ Satellite Television).

Beyond technical considerations, access is constrained by individual predispositions, particularly by *individual prosperity*. Print media as well as pay-TV stations and Internet providers charge their customers for media use. The money people are able (and willing) to spend for media varies with individual living conditions (→ Digital Divide). Media use always occurs in a particular situation with its own spatial arrangement. Wireless devices such as mobile phones exploit the digital revolution and provide ubiquitous but expensive access to sources. At the same time, online database technologies allow for individual consumption of content according to one's own schedule.

Despite an increasing media convergence, media use patterns can still be described following a segmentation of media types. Detailed information on nation-specific media use patterns can be found in Johnston's (2003–) Encyclopedia of international media and communications and in "The world factbook" in the category on communications (CIA 2014). Data on the *role of television* in more than 40 countries (based on local surveys) is collected, for instance, by the annual International Key Facts study (IP Network 2013). Unfortunately, no such resource is available for the use of radio which, with its ubiquitous availability and its limited technological requirements, has established its role as an unobtrusive companion in the daily life of a global media audience (WRTH 2013; → Exposure to Television; Exposure to Radio).

The use of daily *newspapers* is related to audience literacy and thus varies heavily among nations. The most comprehensive source for data on newspaper markets worldwide is represented by the World Press Trends Database (WAN-IFRA 2014). Dynamics in *Internet* usage patterns are still notable and permanently monitored by Internet World Stats (→ Exposure to the Internet). With the emergence of smartphones, *Internet and mobile communication* merged to a fast-expanding media market. Current data is available from the International Telecommunication Union statistics, including distribution of mobile devices and usage figures.

Unlike market research agencies, academic institutions have contributed only marginally to the level of knowledge in the field, as cross-national research is costly and national grants are often only allowed if funding from different countries is available. Comparative empirical studies are mostly limited to the audience analysis of one media application in some selected countries.

See also: ▶ AUDIENCE RESEARCH ▶ CABLE TELEVISION ▶ CENSORSHIP ▶ CULTURE: DEFINITIONS AND CONCEPTS ▶ DIGITAL DIVIDE ▶ EXPOSURE TO COMMUNICATION CONTENT ▶ EXPOSURE TO PRINT MEDIA ▶ EXPOSURE TO RADIO ▶ EXPOSURE TO TELEVISION ▶ EXPOSURE TO THE INTERNET ▶ FREEDOM OF COMMUNICATION ▶ FREEDOM OF INFORMATION ▶ FREEDOM OF THE PRESS, CONCEPT OF ▶ GLOBALIZATION OF THE MEDIA ▶ GLOBALIZATION THEORIES ▶ MEDIA LITERACY ▶ MOBILITY, TECHNOLOGY FOR ▶ POLITICAL COMMUNICATION SYSTEMS ▶ SATELLITE TELEVISION ▶ TELEVISION NETWORKS

REFERENCES AND SUGGESTED READINGS

CIA (ed.) (2014). *The world factbook*. At https://www.cia.gov/library/publications/the-world-factbook/index.html, accessed August 16, 2014.

Hasebrink, U. (2012). Comparing Media Use and Reception. In F. Esser & T. Hanitzsch (eds.), *Handbook of comparative communication research*. London: Routledge, pp. 382–399.

International Telecommunications Union Statistics (2013). At http://www.itu.int/en/ITU-D/Statistics/Pages/stat/default.aspx?utm_source=twitterfeed&utm_medium=twitter.co.jp, accessed August 16, 2014.

Internet World Stats (2014). At http://www.internetworldstats.com/, accessed August 16, 2014.

IP Network (2013). International Key Facts. At http://www.ip-network.com/studies-publications/television-international-key-facts/, accessed August 16, 2014.

Jensen, K. B. (ed.) (1998). *News of the world: World cultures look at television news*. London: Routledge.

Johnston, D. H. (ed.) (2003–). *Encyclopedia of international media and communications*. Amsterdam: Academic Press.

Shoemaker, P. J. & Cohen, A. A. (2006). *News around the world: Content, practitioners, and the public*. London: Routledge.

WAN-IFRA (2014). World Press Trends Database. At http://www.wan-ifra.org/microsites/world-press-trends, accessed August 16, 2014.

WRTH Publications (ed.) (2013). *World radio TV handbook*, 67th edn, London: WRTH.

Media Use across the Life-Span

MARGOT VAN DER GOOT
University of Amsterdam

JOHANNES W. J. BEENTJES
University of Amsterdam

Age groups differ in the amount and functions of their media use. Communication scholars have pointed out two possible explanations for such differences. First, there are lifecourse or maturational explanations: media use is supposed to change across the life-span in response to an individual's development. Second, there are generational explanations: people who are born in a certain period are supposed to adopt particular patterns of media use. These effects need to be disentangled. For example, it may be that older people watch more television than when they were younger because their situation and needs have changed. Alternatively, older people may watch more television than younger people because television is more important to their generation than it is to younger generations.

Lifecourse Explanations

Empirical research shows relations between *media use and age*. However, researchers writing on lifecourse explanations have argued that this 'chronological age' has its limitations as a concept, because it is not the factor that explains the changes in media use across the life-span. As an example: older people watch more television than when they were younger not because their age has changed but because their situation and needs have changed.

The basic notion in lifecourse explanations is that media use is related to cognitive, physical, social and emotional development across the life-span. The general idea is that when people pass through the stages of life they experience changes and therefore their media use changes as well. Central to these descriptions is that developmental events and processes create needs as well as resources (such as physical or material resources). Subsequently these needs and resources bring about certain types of media use (van der Goot et al. 2006; → Uses and Gratifications). For example, studies have investigated how emotional development across the lifespan affects people's responses to entertainment (e.g., Bartsch, 2012).

Generational Explanations

Generations distinguish themselves because their socialization takes place in unique societal, political and economic circumstances. Scholars argue that experiences during socialization or during adolescence, the so-called 'formative years,' leave long-lasting impressions on values and attitudes, and continue to influence behavior at later stages of life (Peiser 1999). Regarding media, generations may adopt specific patterns of media use when they are young and remain faithful to those throughout the life span (Mares and Woodard 2006). For example, a recent cohort of people has been labelled 'digital natives' or the 'Net Generation' (Hargittai 2010) because they witnessed the introduction and popularization of the new information technologies (→ Electronic Mail; Mobility, Technology for) in their younger years; this may lead to a continuing strong affection for these media during later stages of their lives.

Empirical Research

It is a theoretical and methodological challenge to disentangle these lifecourse and generational influences on media use. Most empirical research is cross-sectional, which means that it consists of data collected at one point in time. *Cross-sectional research* shows differences between age groups, but the problem is that older age groups represent both people in old age and older cohorts. This problem can be illustrated with the cross-sectional finding introduced at the opening of this article: older age groups watch television more than younger age groups. This may either be because their situation and needs have changed as they grew older, or because their generation is more attached to television than younger generations are. In methodological terms: it is impossible to determine whether the differences are caused by lifecourse (age) effects or cohort effects.

Because cross-sectional research cannot disentangle lifecourse and cohort effects, other methods, such as *cohort analysis*, have been designed. To conduct a cohort analysis, data have to be available for several cohorts at a variety of life stages. It is necessary to have cross-sectional surveys with comparable variables on media use, that have been carried out at different times of measurement. These data are hard to find, and therefore only a few cohort analyses on media use have been conducted. Moreover, scholars will have to wait many more years to be able to witness how media use develops across the life-span for the Net Generation in comparison to the older generations.

The cohort analysis by Mares and Woodard (2006) provides some insight into the development of the amount of television viewing across the life-span. The researchers used six measurement times between 1978 and 1998 from the General Social Survey in which respondents were asked how many hours they watched television on an average day. They found that throughout the life-span there are differences in viewing that are not explained by cohort effects. Even after controlling for cohort, period, sex, and education levels, there appeared to be an effect of age on the amount of viewing. As people grew older, they watched more television.

With the introduction of the Internet many cross-sectional surveys have shown that older people have less access to the Internet and use it for a narrower array of activities than do younger people. The concept of the → digital divide (→ Exposure to the Internet) has been used to indicate the gap between groups that are ahead in using new technologies and groups that lag behind. Within western societies, age is one of the factors associated with this gap. Most scholars lean toward generational explanations: the current generation of younger people will continue to use this technology when they grow older and therefore the age divide will probably disappear with time.

See also: ▶ ADVERTISING: RESPONSES ACROSS THE LIFE-SPAN ▶ AUDIENCE RESEARCH ▶ COMMUNICATION SKILLS ACROSS THE LIFE-SPAN ▶ DEVELOPMENTAL COMMUNICATION ▶ DIGITAL DIVIDE ▶ ELECTRONIC MAIL ▶ EXPOSURE TO THE INTERNET ▶ EXPOSURE TO TELEVISION ▶ LONGITUDINAL ANALYSIS ▶ MEDIA LITERACY ▶ MEDIA USE AND CHILD DEVELOPMENT ▶ MOBILITY, TECHNOLOGY FOR ▶ NEWS PROCESSING ACROSS THE LIFE-SPAN ▶ USES AND GRATIFICATIONS

REFERENCES AND SUGGESTED READINGS

Bartsch, A. (2012). As time goes by: What changes and what remains the same in entertainment experience over the life span? *Journal of Communication*, 62(4), 588–608.

Coyne, S.M., Padilla-Walker, L.M., & Howard, E. (2013). Emerging in a digital world: A decade review of media use, effects, and gratifications in emerging adulthood. *Emerging Adulthood*, 1(2), 125–138.

Hargittai, E. (2010). Digital na(t)ives? Variation in internet skills and uses among members of the "Net generation." *Sociological Inquiry*, 80(1), 92–113.

Hofer, M., Alemand, M., & Martin, M. (2014). Age differences in nonhedonic entertainment experiences. *Journal of Communication*, 64(1), 61–81.

Mares, M. L. & Woodard, E. (2006). In search of the older audience: Adult age differences in television viewing. *Journal of Broadcasting and Electronic Media*, 50(4), 595–614.

Mares, M.L. & Sun, Y. (2010). The multiple meanings of age for television content preferences. *Human Communication Research*, 36(3), 372–396.

Peiser, W. (1999). The television generation's relation to the mass media in Germany: Accounting for the impact of private television. *Journal of Broadcasting and Electronic Media*, 43(3), 364–385.

Valkenburg, P.M. & Peter, J. (2011). Online communication among adolescents: An integrated model of its attraction, opportunities, and risks. *Journal of Adolescent Health*, 48(2), 121–127.

Van der Goot, M., Beentjes, J. W. J., & van Selm, M. (2006). Older adults' television viewing from a life-span perspective: Past research and future challenges. In C. S. Beck (ed.), *Communication yearbook 30*. Mahwah, NJ: Lawrence Erlbaum, pp. 431–469.

Van der Goot, M., Beentjes, J. W. J., & Van Selm, M. (2012). Meanings of television in older adults' lives: An analysis of change and continuity in television viewing. *Ageing and Society*, 32(1), 147–168.

Media Use by Social Variable

HELMUT SCHERER

Hanover University of Music, Drama, and Media

It can be observed in all industrialized societies that media use is connected to demographic factors. A good example of such phenomena is the so-called → digital divide, which means that different demographic groups have different access to the Internet, e.g., older people use the Internet less frequently than younger people.

Socio-demographic variables are indicators for specific social situations. Based on these considerations, we can distinguish some characteristics of social situations relevant to media use: needs, media images, values, expectations related to social roles, resources, competence and skills.

The → *uses and gratifications approach* is based on the assumption that people use the media to satisfy needs which makes the media compete with other sources of gratification. Rosengren (1974) differentiates between the terms 'need' and 'problem.' The term need refers to needs in general as part of human nature, whereas the term problem refers to the different forms of specific individual and situational needs (Rosengren 1974, 270f.). For example, one may assume that older people have less need to relax or seek distraction because they are retired and no longer suffer from work-related stress.

In → *social cognitive theory*, media use is explained by media images especially by the anticipation of the consequences of media use (LaRose & Eastin 2004). These expectations are based on users' own experiences but can also be learned by monitoring media behavior of others. It is plausible that the results of these monitoring processes differ between different social groups. Specific age groups, for example, share specific expectations of the media's qualities. These expectations, that the media will be able to meet certain needs, result from the individual's media biography. It is influenced by key events in the media as well as by dominant media contents during biographically relevant periods of life.

The expected effect of media use has to be looked upon favorably by the user. Therefore, every decision to use the media is a value judgment. Moreover, specific media contents or methods of presentation can clash with the moral values of potential users. It is reasonable to assume that some users may expect some gratification from pornography in the media but reject it on moral grounds. Different social groups may have different sets of values. Social milieus often share homogeneous moral concepts that differ from those of other milieus. Different demographic variables are connected with different social roles. We use the term 'gender' to describe the fact that sex is not merely a biological but more importantly a social fact, as it allocates different roles to men and women. Social roles lead to expectations regarding behavior. Society defines the socially accepted behavior for an older or younger person, a man or a woman.

Resources are *external possibilities to act*. They are not personal characteristics of the individual, but the individual can make use of them. Their influence on media use is twofold. On the one hand, the potential media user must have access to necessary resources to be able to afford media use. With regard to the resource of time, for instance, this can be problematic for many potential users. On the other hand, available resources dictate what other possibilities there are to meet specific needs besides media use. The connection between resources and socio-demographic variables is obvious.

Competence and skills are, as opposed to resources, internal possibilities to act. There is a rather simple connection between competence and skills and media use: A user must be able to read to use a newspaper, or must be an experienced and skilled reader to be able to read more demanding literature. The ability to read, however, is closely linked to age and level of education, i.e., to demographic factors.

See also: ▶ AUDIENCE SEGMENTATION ▶ AUDIENCES, FEMALE ▶ DIGITAL DIVIDE ▶ ESCAPISM ▶ ETHNICITY AND EXPOSURE TO COMMUNICATION ▶ EXPOSURE TO COMMUNICATION CONTENT ▶ EXPOSURE TO PRINT MEDIA ▶ MEDIA USE ACROSS THE LIFE-SPAN ▶ SOCIAL COGNITIVE THEORY ▶ USES AND GRATIFICATIONS ▶ VIDEO GAMES

REFERENCES AND SUGGESTED READINGS

LaRose, R. & Eastin, M. S. (2004). A social cognitive theory of Internet uses and gratifications: Toward a new model of media attendance. *Journal of Broadcasting & Electronic Media*, 48(3), 358–377.

Rosengren, K. E. (1974). Uses and gratifications: A paradigm outlined. In J. G. Blumler & E. Katz (eds.), *The uses of mass communications: Current perspectives on gratifications research*. Beverly Hills, CA: Sage, pp. 269–286.

Mediated Populism

GIANPIETRO MAZZOLENI
University of Milan

Populism, a notoriously ambiguous concept, is a political ideology emphasizing the central role of the 'ordinary people' in the political process. 'Mediated populism' means the outcome of the close connection between media-originated dynamics and the rise of populist sentiments, and eventually of populist movements.

In general, tabloid media – which respond primarily to commercial imperatives – are more keen to lend direct and indirect support to populist sentiments and claims, by engaging in sympathetic coverage of populist leaders, whereas the elite media (with significant exceptions) – which tend to be mouthpieces of the ruling classes and paladins of the status quo – usually display overt antagonism and treat negatively populist (→ Commercialization: Impact on Media Content; Tabloidization). For their part, populist leaders and parties engage in intense relations with the media, resorting to different strategies to court the media and/or to secure their media attention (→ Mediatization of Politics). These strategies comprise playing the underdog, rallying crowds with abrasive speech and staging controversial events.

Research has envisaged a *four-stage life cycle* (Stewart et al. 2003). In the *ground-laying phase*, the media may be engaged in providing a dramatic portrayal of the country's illnesses, denouncing corruption in government, highlighting immigration-linked crime stories, and the like. This media coverage in the long run is likely to diffuse social malaise and to trigger popular anger and political disaffection. This domestic political climate represents the ideal milieu for the rise of political figures voicing social discontent and for the dissemination of the populist message. In the *insurgent phase*, populist movements attempt to enlarge and consolidate their popular and electoral support by exploiting more intensely the communication resources that media make available (unintentionally or not). In the *established phase* the movement obtains full legitimization in the country's political system, with seats in parliament and even in cabinet. This often means loss of newsworthiness for the leaders and their stances, as they take on more ordinary political roles in the political arena. Some movements have experienced also a *decline phase*. The attitude and behavior of the media vary widely in this phase. Their spotlights might be suddenly switched on by the political fall of formerly populist 'media darlings.'

See also: ▶ COMMERCIALIZATION: IMPACT ON MEDIA CONTENT ▶ MEDIATIZATION OF POLITICS ▶ TABLOIDIZATION

REFERENCES AND SUGGESTED READINGS

Albertazzi, D. & McDonnell, D. (eds.) (2008). *Twenty-first century populism: The spectre of Western European democracy.* Basingstoke: Palgrave.

Jagers, J. & Walgrave, S. (2007). Populism as political communication style: An empirical study of political parties' discourse in Belgium. *European Journal of Political Research*, 46, 319–345.

Stewart, J., Mazzoleni, G., & Horsfield, B. (2003). Conclusion: Power to the media managers. In G. Mazzoleni, J. Stewart, & B. Horsfield (eds.), *The media and neo-populism: A contemporary comparative analysis.* Westport, CT: Praeger.

Mediated Social Interaction

EUN-JU LEE
Seoul National University

Mediated social interaction refers to the interaction between two or more individuals enabled by various communication technologies. It may take different forms, depending on how many people are involved in message construction and reception, whether participating individuals are required to be present at the time of message transfer, what kinds of modalities are being used and so forth (→ Interpersonal Communication).

Researchers have identified *three key characteristics of computer-mediated communication* (CMC). First, because, the most common form of CMC is text-based, it typically *lacks social context cues*, such as facial expressions, paraverbal cues and physical appearance; (→ Nonverbal Communication and Culture). As such, people may become less aware of their interaction partners, and reduced social presence renders CMC less effective and appropriate than face-to-face (FtF) interaction for socio-emotional communication. Second, cue deficiency fosters perceived *anonymity*. With their identities hidden, people feel freer from social constraints and become more prone to exhibit uninhibited behaviors. At the same time, anonymity can democratize communication by liberating individuals from power differences manifested through various status cues. Lastly, CMC does *not require* participating individuals to be *co-present* in the immediate environment, with its many variants supporting asynchronous interactions. Freed from geographical and temporal constraints, the boundary of an individual's social network has been substantially expanded.

With respect to relationship building, studies have reported that people engage in greater spontaneous self-disclosure in CMC than in FtF interaction, because (1) anonymity reduces perceived risks in disclosing potentially embarrassing aspects of self; and (2) physical separation and the lack of sensory cues lead people to focus more on their inner feelings and thoughts. Not only do people speak more about themselves, but they also speak better of themselves, as text-based CMC facilitates strategic self-presentation by eliminating a number of distractions. As such, thereby people can concentrate on message construction to project preferred self-image, leading to overly positive perceptions and exaggerated interpersonal ('hyperpersonal') expectations.

Text-only interaction was once thought to nullify *social stereotypes*, often linked to physically salient features, like gender and race. Despite the absence of physical indicators, however, some social category cues may remain in CMC in the form of language style, conversation topic, etc. Once the interaction partner's category membership is inferred, the information restrictions of the medium can amplify, rather than attenuate, the category's influence as people turn to social stereotypes to compensate for the deficiency of interpersonal information (→ Social Stereotyping and Communication).

In *work groups*, CMC has the potential to address problems common to FtF discussions by allowing anonymous and simultaneous input from participating individuals: evaluation apprehension and production blocking. When group decision-making is concerned, however, a → meta-analysis (Baltes et al. 2002) showed that FtF groups generally outperformed CMC groups in terms of decision quality, time to decision and member satisfaction, especially when there was a time limit and the group size was large.

Challenging the notion that *anonymity* weakens normative concerns in CMC, the social identity model of 'deindividuation effects' (SIDE) posits that when there is a common group identity, the lack of individuating information (deindividuation) can reinforce group-oriented behaviors by heightening the salience of group identity (Spears et al. 2001). Thus, people are more likely to conform to the local group norms and exhibit ethnocentrism when anonymous than when their personal identity is known.

Thus far, to understand the effects of CMC, researchers have compared CMC with FtF interaction, assuming that certain features of the communication channel (e.g., anonymity) influence individuals' perceptions and behaviors representing technological determinism. However, as social information processing theory posits, people are capable of *adapting to the restrictions of the medium*, for example, by creating emoticons to express their feelings and employing more interactive uncertainty reduction strategies (→ Uncertainty Reduction Theory), thereby achieving the same or even higher levels of intimacy than in FtF contacts (Walther & Parks 2002). Recent studies also demonstrated that different individuals use the same medium differently to different effects, highlighting the need to incorporate individuals' traits and predispositions in investigating the processes and outcomes of CMC.

See also: ▶ INTERPERSONAL COMMUNICATION
▶ LANGUAGE AND THE INTERNET ▶ META-ANALYSIS
▶ NONVERBAL COMMUNICATION AND CULTURE
▶ PERSONAL COMMUNICATION BY CMC
▶ SOCIAL STEREOTYPING AND COMMUNICATION
▶ UNCERTAINTY REDUCTION THEORY

REFERENCES AND SUGGESTED READINGS

Baltes, B. B., Dickson, M. W., Sherman, M. P., Bauer, C. C., & LaGanke, J. S. (2002). Computer-mediated communication and group decision making: A meta-analysis. *Organizational Behavior and Human Decision Processes*, 87, 156–179.

Bargh, J. A. & McKenna, K. Y. A. (2004). The Internet and social life. *Annual Review of Psychology*, 55, 573–590.

Spears, R., Postmes, T., Lea, M., & Watt, S. E. (2001). A SIDE view of social influence. In J. P. Forgas & K. D. Williams (eds.), *Social influence: Direct and indirect processes*. New York: Psychology Press, pp. 331–350.

Walther, J. B. & Parks, M. R. (2002). Cues filtered out, cues filtered in: Computer-mediated communication and relationships. In M. L. Knapp & J. A. Daly (eds.), *Handbook of interpersonal communication*, 3rd edn. Thousand Oaks, CA: Sage, pp. 529–563.

Mediated Terrorism

GIANPIETRO MAZZOLENI
University of Milan

Terrorism has been closely associated with communication and → propaganda. The primary goal of terrorist organizations is, in fact, to 'send a message,' usually to target governments, the victims being the instruments to pursue the goal.

In the global village, the mass media and the new media play a pivotal role in the terrorist scheme. Due to the new communication technologies, today's terrorists themselves control the entire communication process. The attempts of terrorist groups of securing vast publicity for their actions can be defied only in part by the counteractions of government authorities, which might impose → censorship on printed and broadcast news, but cannot regulate the Internet, which remains the most resourceful communication means of postmodern terrorism.

By means of the Internet, political terrorism succeeds in attaining several *strategic purposes*. The Internet serves the practical purpose of planning and coordination and to ensure networking and circulation of key information. Affiliated, semi-independent cells, scattered around the world are able to maintain contact with one another and to plan common actions. It ensures cheap publicity and diffusion of ideological and motivational messages. It makes fundraising easy and safe. Its worldwide reach provides receptive audiences among which to recruit new followers and activists. It can be used to wage psychological warfare, amplified by the mainstream media. In addition to the Internet, the traditional media may also become instrumental to terrorism in several ways.

One question that has often been debated worldwide is whether there occurs a sort of inevitable 'complicity' between the news media and terrorists, especially in political contexts, such as liberal democracies, where censorship is not tolerated by the media. This raises excruciating dilemmas on the part of the free media, battling between the professional imperative of covering what makes the news and the resolution to defend democratic institutions and social peace.

See also: ▶ CENSORSHIP ▶ NEWS ROUTINES ▶ NEWS VALUES ▶ PROPAGANDA ▶ STRATEGIC COMMUNICATION ▶ TERRORISM AND COMMUNICATION TECHNOLOGIES ▶ VIOLENCE AS MEDIA CONTENT

REFERENCES AND SUGGESTED READINGS

Nacos, B. L. (2002). *Mass-mediated terrorism: The central role of the media in terrorism and counterterrorism*. Lanham, MD: Rowman and Littlefield.

Norris, P., Montague, K., & Marion, J. (eds.) (2003). *Framing terrorism: The news media, the government and the public*. London: Routledge.

Weimann, G. (2006). *Terror on the Internet: The new arena, the new challenges*. Washington, DC: US Institute of Peace Press.

Mediatization of Politics

GIANPIETRO MAZZOLENI
University of Milan

Mediatization of politics is a complex process that is closely linked to the presence of a media logic in society and in the political sphere. It is distinguished from the idea of 'mediation,' a natural, preordained mission of mass media to convey meaning from communicators to their target audiences Politics and the way it is performed and communicated have been widely affected by the rise of mass media. Such media-driven influence in the political environment is the core of the concept of mediatization. The media have become indispensable actors within the political domain. They have gained a central position in most political routines, such as election campaigns, government communication, public diplomacy and image building, and national and international celebrations.

Interdependence Model

The centrality of the media in the political arena is a peculiarity of modern democracies, which are strongly characterized by interconnecting forms of mass communication. The media's rise to a pivotal place in the political process has caused significant changes and developments in politics as a whole, to the extent that politics is often considered by political communication scholars as media-dependent. The concept of dependence, however, is not supported by solid empirical evidence.

The interdependence of media and politics seems to constitute a better pattern to represent the actual nature of the relationships between them. The media are nevertheless frequently credited with exercising overwhelming influence on political events, persons, issues, and opinions, and, at the same time, politicians are aware of the media's attention rules, production routines, and selection criteria, and adapt their communication behavior to media requirements.

Effects of Mediatization

Research has pointed out several effects of mediatization, among which are the capacity of the media to set the agenda of the political debate, the spectacularization and personalization of political communication, and the 'winnowing' effect.

The mass media, especially information outlets, are acknowledged to have significant power to structure and frame political reality by determining what is relevant for public discussion, by raising issues, and by providing criticism (→ Agenda-Setting Effects). By pointing their spotlights on certain political events and by investigative reporting, the news media are in a position to drive the public debate, influence the campaign agenda, and prompt political figures to focus and take stances on the issues raised (→ Election Campaign Communication). This power is exalted or mitigated by the nature of the political milieu in a given national context. For example, in political systems that grant large autonomy to the media, political communicators are less successful in neutralizing the agenda shaping of the media. However, in political milieus where media–politics relations are characterized by close interdependence, the political agenda is more likely to be the joint output of the interaction of both actors (Semetko et al. 1991; → Political Communication Systems).

The *spectacularization of politics* is an effect especially linked to the influential presence of television on the political scene. The 'grammar' of television language has increasingly changed the patterns of political communication. By becoming the target of an incessant dramatization on the part of commercial media, political activity has been driven to adjust its traditional forms of communication to the new canons of a media-centered environment. This fact has entailed a recasting of the symbolic and expressive devices of political representation. In addressing citizens and voters, political communicators no longer rely on the mediation of militants. No politician can communicate successfully without molding his or her message to suit the most preferred and most popular language schemes of the mass media, especially those of entertainment, show-biz, and advertising.

A necessary condition of spectacularization is the tendency of mass media, especially those that are commercially oriented, like the tabloids (→ Tabloidization) and their equivalent in broadcast media, to *personalize political information* by focusing on who and how, rather than on what and why. Political players on the contemporary post-ideology political stage seem to respond enthusiastically to this media-driven tendency. They adjust willingly to media personalization, responding to the demands of visibility, look, and image. Television is the 'deus ex machina' of this adaptation: "Political figures cannot help subjecting themselves to the rules of TV popularity, obliged as they are to be either stars or nullities . . . Television is indeed the medium that resorts more to personalisation and relies a lot on rivalry among politicians" (Mouchon 1989).

A final effect of the mediatization of politics is the *selection* ('winnowing') *of political elites* through the imposition of media-driven requisites and coverage formats upon political communication as a whole (Matthews 1978). There is also some indication of a progressive weakening of party organizations in many western democracies. For example, there has been a transfer of methods for recruiting political personnel (leaders, activists, candidates, mayors, etc.) from party machines to external agents – mostly communication experts, spin doctors, and media professionals – that implement tactics that collide with those of traditional professional politics.

The actual selection of political personnel and candidates is to a certain extent affected by the degree of media attention. Leaders chosen in this manner respond to the media's predilection for telegenic, controversial, and possibly colorful personalities. "Those who eventually succeed in election contests are no more local notables, but 'mediatic personages', individuals who master better than others communication techniques; . . . a new breed of communication specialists takes the place of militants and of apparatchiks" (Manin 1995).

Mediatiation and the Internet

Reflecting on the rapid diffusion of online media, Schulz (2004) questions whether the traditional patterns of mediatization of politics will disappear to leave room for new ways of interdependence between the new media and political players. In fact, the new communication environment created by the Internet and other new media is likely to challenge the media logic that characterized the era of mass communication, and consequently its clutch on political communications. Schulz's argument is that there is not yet an end of mediatization as we have known it to date: "Since the new media do not displace the old media, the mediatization effects of the latter endure in the new media environment."

In addition, the new media bring along *new patterns of mediatization*. Clearly, the new media logic will affect politics and political discourse, but the adaptation process will be mutual, not simply on the part of the political players, thanks to interactivity, a feature that conventional media do not possess.

See also: ▶ AGENDA BUILDING
▶ AGENDA-SETTING EFFECTS ▶ ELECTION
CAMPAIGN COMMUNICATION ▶ MEDIUM THEORY
▶ POLITAINMENT ▶ POLITICAL
COMMUNICATION SYSTEMS ▶ TABLOIDIZATION

REFERENCES AND SUGGESTED READINGS

Bennett, W. L. & Entman, R. M. (eds.) (2001). *Mediated politics: Communication in the future of democracy*. Cambridge: Cambridge University Press.

Blumler, J. G. & Kavanagh, D. (1999). The third age of political communication: Influences and features. *Political Communication*, 16(3), 209–230.

Kepplinger, H. M. (2002). Mediatization of politics: Theory and data. *Journal of Communication*, 52(4), 972–986.

Manin, B. (1995). *Principes du gouvernement representatif* [Principles of representative government]. Paris: Calmann-Levi.

Matthews, D. R. (1978). Winnowing: The news media and the 1976 presidential nominations. In J. D. Barber (ed.), *The race for the presidency*. Englewood Cliffs, NJ: Prentice Hall.

Mazzoleni, G. & Schulz, W. (1999). "Mediatization" of politics: A challenge for democracy? *Political Communication*, 16, 247–261.

Mouchon, J. (1989). Médiatisation de la communication politique et logiques structurantes [Mediatization of political communication and structuring logics]. *Mots*, 20, 43–56.

Schulz, W. (2004). Reconstructing mediatization as an analytical concept. *European Journal of Communication*, 19, 87–101.

Semetko, H. A., Blumler, J. G., Gurevitch, M., & Weaver, D. H. (1991). *The formation of campaign agendas*. Hillsdale, NJ: Lawrence Erlbaum.

Medium Theory

JOSHUA MEYROWITZ
University of New Hampshire

Medium Theory explores the influences of communication technologies in addition to, and distinct from, the specific content (messages) they convey. Medium Theory focuses on the characteristics of each medium (or of each type of media) that make it physically, socially, and psychologically different from other media and from face-to-face interaction (→ Interpersonal Communication). Medium theorists analyze media as distinct settings, or environments, that encourage certain types of interaction and discourage others, foster unique uses for each medium, and often lead to different responses to the same messages (→ Media).

The *term 'medium theory'* was coined in the 1980s (Meyrowitz 1985, 16) to give a unifying label to the work of numerous scholars in a variety of fields who explore how different characteristics of various media encourage unique forms of interaction. The singular 'medium' is used in the name of the theory to highlight the focus on the particular characteristics of each medium.

The *characteristics of media* analyzed include: types of transmittable sensory information (visual, aural, tactile, etc.); the nature and forms of information within each sense (pictures vs words, or Morse Code clicks vs. voice); the speed and degree of immediacy of communication through the medium; whether the medium affords unidirectional vs. bidirectional vs multi-directional communication; whether interaction through the medium is simultaneous or sequential; the physical requirements for using the medium; the degree of control the user has over reception and transmission; the scope and nature of dissemination; and the relative ease or difficulty of learning to use the medium to code, decode, and interpret media messages.

Medium Theory *operates on two levels*: 'micro' (how a medium selected by an individual or group influences particular interactions) and 'macro' (how the addition of a new medium to existing media may foster broad shifts in social interactions, thinking patterns, social roles and identities, etiquette, political styles, institutions, collective memory, and social structure in general).

Rapid changes in communication in the mid-twentieth century encouraged the development of *influential medium theories*, including the work of the most famous and controversial medium theorist, Marshall McLuhan, whose popular, but often misunderstood phrase, "The medium is the message" highlights the focus on the medium's influence. But medium-focused perspectives date back to ancient times, including Socrates' analyses of writing versus live dialogue (→ Media History).

See also: ▶ COMMUNICATION THEORY AND PHILOSOPHY ▶ CRITICAL THEORY ▶ DEVELOPMENTAL COMMUNICATION ▶ INTERPERSONAL COMMUNICATION ▶ MEDIA ▶ MEDIA ECOLOGY ▶ MEDIA HISTORY ▶ MEDIA AND PERCEPTIONS OF REALITY ▶ TELEVISED DEBATES

REFERENCES AND SUGGESTED READINGS

McLuhan, M. (1994) [1964]. *Understanding media: The extensions of man.* Cambridge, MA: MIT Press.
Meyrowitz, J. (1985). *No sense of place: The impact of electronic media on social behavior.* Oxford: Oxford University Press.
Ong, W. (1982). *Orality and literacy: The technologizing of the word.* London: Methuen.

Memory

IAN NEATH
Memorial University of Newfoundland

Many people think of memory as a place in which information is stored until it is needed, much like a library. Unfortunately, this metaphor is misleading because it implies a static process. Nothing really happens to library books while sitting on the shelf: once one has the book, the contents are identical to the last time the book was consulted. In contrast, human memory is a dynamic, reconstructive set of processes that enable previously encoded information to affect current and future performance.

Construction and Reconstruction

Memory works like perceptual and other cognitive processes: people use whatever cues and information are available to achieve a sensible interpretation (→ Information Processing). Consider the case of recalling what happened at the football game last week. The first time a retrieval attempt is made, there are three sources of information: (1) the event itself, (2) similar events, and (3) general knowledge. All three sources are involved in the construction of a memory. The spectator might remember a specific play, which most likely comes from memory of the event itself. But information about the coin toss that starts the game might come from the previous week's game, or might be based on general knowledge. Note that the information from general knowledge or from a different event might be accurate, even though it has been retrieved from a different source.

The second time a retrieval attempt is made there is an additional source of information: memory of the previous recollection. Memory is reconstructive in that each time a particular event is recalled a new version is constructed based on the cues and information available at that particular time. The constructed version is then a potential source of information (and misinformation) for subsequent recollections.

The Encoding–Retrieval Interaction

One of the primary determinants of recollection is the relation between the conditions at encoding and the conditions at retrieval (→ Encoding–Decoding). If a person is happy when studying, more information will be recalled if the person is happy at test than if unhappy. Similar results are found with environmental context and with pharmacological state. People taking scuba-diving lessons need to learn decompression tables that tell them how to ascend to avoid decompression sickness; they will do much better if they learn the information underwater, the same environment in which they will need to recall the information, than if they study only on land. The reason is that items and events are not processed in isolation but rather as part of ongoing mental processes. People who are happy (or underwater or intoxicated) process words and events differently than if they are unhappy (or on land or sober). Thus, when trying to access information originally processed in a different state, people will generally be trying to process the information inappropriately.

This interaction naturally lends itself to helping people improve memory ('mnemonics'). The goal is to anticipate the kind of processing that will be required at test and then organize studying around it. For example, how can memory for people's names be improved? At test, the only constant is typically the person's face. Therefore, the face should be used as the retrieval cue, and studying should be built around that. Second, information can be recalled only if it is encoded. Get into the habit of repeating the person's name as soon as the introduction is made. Third, form a link between the cue (i.e., the face) and the name. Fourth, use the person's name a couple more times before moving on to the next person.

Theoretical Accounts of Memory

There are two *basic theoretical accounts* of memory. One views memory as a set of different memory systems (the systems or structuralist account) whereas the other emphasizes the role of processing (the processing or proceduralist perspective).

Most proponents of the systems view posit five different memory systems. *Working memory* (also known as short-term memory) is used for the temporary storage and manipulation of information. Long-term memory is made up of two systems, *episodic memory* (also called autobiographical memory) and *semantic memory* (also called generic memory and general knowledge). The difference between the two lies in whether the remember recollects just the fact itself or whether there is also awareness of the context in which the information was learned. Episodic memory is sometimes described as having the property of mental time travel: you can project yourself backward into particular episodes.

The last two memory systems – *procedural memory* and *the perceptual representation system* – differ from the preceding three in that they are not part of the declarative group of memory systems. A rule of thumb is that if one can say that one 'knows something' (e.g., one knows that $2 +\text{-}2 = 4$, one knows that the capital of Assyria was Nineveh), it is in a declarative memory system. If one 'knows how to do something,' then it is in a procedural memory system. A mother may know how to ride a bicycle, but this information cannot be usefully communicated to her son. She can say, "Balance, pedal, and steer," but he will most likely fall off. Both of these nondeclarative systems are sometimes referred to as *implicit memory*.

Episodic memory requires conscious awareness of the original learning episode, semantic memory requires awareness of the information, but not of the original learning episode, and nondeclarative memory requires no awareness of the information at all.

The Processing View

According to the *systems view*, the mnemonic properties of an item depend on the memory system in which it resides. According to the *processing view*, the mnemonic properties of an item depend on the relation between the conditions at encoding and the conditions at test. According to the former view, one cannot make generalizations about memory as a whole because each memory system operates according to different rules. According to the latter, there are important principles of memory that apply to all memory regardless of the type of information, the type of processing, the hypothetical system supporting the memory, or the time scale.

A proponent of the processing view would agree with almost everything with one exception: what does the distinction between short- and long-term memory add to our understanding? When words are processed on the basis of how they sound, there will be a very small capacity and the information will not be available for long. When words are processed on the basis of what they mean, however, there will be an enormous capacity, and the information will be available for a long time.

See also: ▶ COGNITION ▶ ENCODING–DECODING ▶ EXPERIMENT, LABORATORY ▶ INFORMATION PROCESSING ▶ SCHEMAS ▶ SCRIPTS

REFERENCES AND SUGGESTED READINGS

Conway, M. A. (ed.) (1997). *Recovered memories and false memories.* Oxford: Oxford University Press.
Foster, J. K. & Jelicic, M. (eds.) (1999). *Memory: Systems, process, or function?* Oxford: Oxford University Press.
Nadel, L. & Sinnott-Armstrong, W. P. (eds.) (2013). *Memory and law.* Oxford: Oxford University Press.
Smith, S. M. & Vela, E. (2001). Environmental context-dependent memory: A review and meta- analysis. *Psychonomic Bulletin and Review,* 8, 203–220.
Stadler, M. A. & Frensch, P. A. (eds.) (1998). *Handbook of implicit learning.* Thousand Oaks, CA: Sage.
Surprenant, A. M. & Neath, I. (2009). *Principles of memory.* New York: Psychology Press.
Tulving, E. & Craik, F. I. M. (2000). *The Oxford handbook of memory.* Oxford: Oxford University Press.
Wagenaar, W. A. & Groeneweg, J. (1990). The memory of concentration camp survivors. *Applied Cognitive Psychology,* 4, 77–87.
Worthen, J. B. & Hunt, R. R. (2010). *Mnemonology: Mnemonics for the 21st Century.* New York: Psychology Press.

Message Discrimination

PETER V. MILLER
Northwestern University

Message discrimination is a self-report measure of media exposure. In survey interviews, respondents are asked to recall → information about a particular topic that they have encountered in various media in the recent past. Responses are recorded verbatim and coded into 'messages.' The message discrimination measure is the sum of messages reported by a respondent for the topic of interest across all of the media (→ Audience Research; Exposure to Communication Content; Information Processing).

The term was coined by Peter Clarke and F. Gerald Kline (1974) in an article introducing the measure and its use in research on → media effects. The rationale offered for the use of open recall of information as a measure of media exposure rests on two claims. First, they asserted that frequently used measures of media exposure, which focus on reported time expenditure or frequency of contact with a medium, are too crude to capture what might be called 'meaningful' exposure to the channel. The second rationale was normative: Clarke and Kline struck a decidedly egalitarian note when they declared that previous media research had relied too much on 'researcher definitions' of media exposure and outcomes.

There is some irony in the observation that the 'respondent-centered' message discrimination measure received its major application in the evaluation of 'researcher-driven' information campaigns (→ Health Campaigns, Communication in). The message discrimination approach has not supplanted the time-based or frequency-of-use media exposure measures in reaction to which Clarke and Kline offered their alternative. One reason may be ambiguity in the measurement of the concept. Message discrimination is supposed to measure media exposure, but it does so by asking respondents to recall information that they have received via the media. This means that exposure is confounded with information gain, which is usually treated as a dependent variable in media effects research (→ Validity). Another, maybe more powerful reason for the lack of widespread adoption of the message discrimination measure is that it is more laborious and expensive to execute than the time-allocation or frequency-of-use measures.

See also: ▶ AUDIENCE RESEARCH ▶ CODING ▶ EXPOSURE TO COMMUNICATION CONTENT ▶ EXPOSURE TO PRINT MEDIA ▶ EXPOSURE TO TELEVISION ▶ HEALTH CAMPAIGNS,

COMMUNICATION IN ▶ INFORMATION
▶ INFORMATION PROCESSING ▶ MEDIA EFFECTS
▶ RELIABILITY ▶ SURVEY ▶ VALIDITY

REFERENCES AND SUGGESTED READINGS

Clarke, P. & Kline, F. G. (1974). Media effects reconsidered: Some new strategies for communication research. *Communication Research*, 1(2), 224–240.
Edelstein, A. S. (1974). *The uses of communication in decision-making*. New York: Praeger.
Salmon, C. T. (1986). Message discrimination and the information environment. *Communication Research*, 13(3), 363–372.

Message Production

DALE HAMPLE
University of Maryland

The object of research on message production is to answer the question, "Why do people say what they do?" The standard answer is that situations cause people to form goals, which lead to plans, which direct the messages. This is the GPA model (goals–plans–actions).

In the original formulation, the GPA model's initial processual focus was on goals. A notable advance was Dillard and Solomon's (2000) conceptualization of situations as '*social densities*.' Just as the universe is mainly vacuum interrupted by densities of gravity and mass, so our social world contains recognizable clumps of social significance. People orient to repetitive kinds of interaction. These social densities are stored in long term memory as nodes, which may well be labeled with a particular goal (e.g., persuade, acquaint, etc.).

Message production is said to be under personal control, and therefore responsive to subjective goals (→ Goals, Social Aspects of; Goals, Cognitive Aspects of). Dillard's initial formulation of the GPA specified that *two sorts of goals* would be activated. The first is what he calls the primary goal, which frames the situation, or defines it as a particular type (e.g., as influencing, comforting, joking, etc.). Secondary goals modify that frame, bringing to bear various other motivational issues, such as anxiety, protection of personal resources, and, most importantly, politeness. The secondary goals may be so immediately important that they overwhelm the primary goal (e.g., a person worried about giving offense might actually decline to try to persuade), but the situation remains subjectively defined by the primary goal (e.g., influence).

Several investigators have explored the *consequences of having multiple goals*. Greene and his associates have shown in several studies that people are less articulate and more hesitant when producing messages that respond to two goals, as compared to single goal instructions. In Greene's (1995) work, the second goal is in some way inconsistent with the first (e.g., to give unwelcome information while ensuring that the other person is not offended). Samp and Solomon (2005) assess goal complexity (the number of activated goals) and goal strain (whether both pro-social and anti-social goals are activated). They find that both complexity and strain increase the number of clauses in messages. Thus, multiplicity of goals increases cognitive load, resulting in both immediate nonfluency and more eventual effort.

A '*plan*' is a projected sequence of actions that is intended to achieve a goal. Messages are held to emerge from plans, which may be conscious but which are much more likely to consist of unconscious assemblies and intentions. The plan is the point in the message production process at which content comes into play. For a message, many of the plan steps consist of things one will (or may) say. Berger explains that one may have a simple sequence in mind, but may also have imagined a more complicated pattern that might even have various branch points at which choices must be made. Berger (1997) has demonstrated that a given plan simultaneously exists at several hierarchically organized levels of abstraction, ranging from general intention down to the physical requirements of pronunciation and performance.

Plans can change during the course of invention and interaction. The planning stage is therefore also the site of message editing (Hample 2005), assuming that any editing takes place. Cognitive stores contain two key *kinds of associations*: those between the situation and the message, and those between messages and their outcomes. The situation-message association system generates an initial draft of a message. Once a potential message is assembled and activated, it may in turn stimulate notice of various likely consequences (e.g., cursing causes social disapproval). These consequences reflect the presence of secondary goals, particularly politeness issues. Should the consequences have sufficient activation levels, they may stimulate message revision or abandonment. Rehearsing a message plan improves the fluidity and quality of the resulting message.

Scholars have explored the fluidity of message production, focusing on onset latencies, pauses, and semantic variety. They relate these matters mainly to plan or goal complexity. Either sort of complexity increases cognitive load, interfering with ease of expression. Samp and Solomon's (2005) research program explores message embellishment, length, and focus (e.g., on self or other), linking these outcomes to goal strain and goal complexity. Both strain and complexity lead to longer and more elaborate messages. The 'obstacle hypothesis' connects message content and phrasing all the way back to situation, so that requests acknowledge the situational feature most likely to impede a favorable reply (e.g., *"If you're not too busy,* could you find me a map?").

See also: ▶ ACTION ASSEMBLY THEORY ▶ COMPLIANCE GAINING ▶ GOALS, SOCIAL ASPECTS OF ▶ GOALS, COGNITIVE ASPECTS OF ▶ INTERPERSONAL COMMUNICATION ▶ MEMORY ▶ POLITENESS THEORY

REFERENCES AND SUGGESTED READINGS

Berger, C. R. (1997). *Planning strategic interaction: Attaining goals through communicative action.* Mahwah, NJ: Lawrence Erlbaum.

Dillard, J. P. (ed.) (1990). *Seeking compliance: The production of interpersonal influence messages.* Scottsdale, AZ: Gorsuch Scarisbrick.

Dillard, J. P. & Solomon, D. H. (2000). Conceptualizing context in message-production research. *Communication Theory,* 10, 167–175.

Greene, J. O. (ed.). (1997). *Message production: Advances in communication theory.* Mahwah, NJ: Lawrence Erlbaum.

Hample, D. (2005). *Arguing: Exchanging reasons face to face.* Mahwah, NJ: Lawrence Erlbaum.

Lindsey, A. E., Greene, J. O., Parker, R. G., & Sassi, M. (1995). Effects of advance message formulation on message encoding: Evidence of cognitively based hesitation in the production of multiple-goal messages. *Communication Quarterly,* 43, 320–331.

Samp, J. A. & Solomon, D. H. (2005). Toward a theoretical account of goal characteristics in micro-level message features. *Communication Monographs,* 72, 22–45.

Meta-Analysis

TIMOTHY R. LEVINE
Michigan State University

CRAIG R. HULLETT
University of Wisconsin–Madison

Meta-analysis is a set of methods and statistical analyses for summarizing the findings of existing empirical literature. As the name implies, it is a study of studies. It provides a way to do a quantitative literature review that involves cumulating effects across studies (→ Quantitative Methodology). The purpose of a meta-analysis is to ascertain if the findings from a collection of studies investigating some specific issue lead to some consistent result and, if so, to estimate the magnitude of that finding. If not, it serves to reconcile findings that appear to offer mixed support for a hypothesis. Meta-analysis is also useful in identifying the reasons why findings are inconsistent from study to study and to identify theoretically important moderators. Meta-analysis will likely play an increasingly important role in making sense out of social science research.

The *value of meta-analysis* is particularly apparent when contrasted with the typical narrative review of sustained research on a topic. Due to the nature of social scientific research, the results of different studies investigating the same question will inevitably vary from study to study. Some of this variability is attributable to sampling error. Results can also vary across studies because of methodological artifacts (→ Validity). Finally, results can vary from study to study for theoretically meaningful reasons, a finding might be stronger in some populations or contexts than in others. Because in meta-analyses results are cumulated across studies, low statistical power is less of an issue. Meta-analysis focuses attention on effect sizes, and relies less on significance testing. The degree to which sampling error explains study-to-study variability is estimated, and corrections for many methodological artifacts are possible. Substantive moderators can also be tentatively identified.

Meta-analysis involves *several steps*. First, the relevant and usable studies investigating a topic are collected. Then, the findings of each study need to be converted to some common metric so that the results can be cumulated. Relevant study features are also coded. Next, an average effect across studies is calculated, and study-to-study variability is examined. Analyses are also done to see if and how coded study features affect results. It is important that all the studies included test the same issue or hypothesis. Studies must also report sufficient information so that an effect size can be calculated. Once the criteria for inclusion are determined, a search method is specified.

The findings from each study then need to be converted to a common metric, usually some unit of 'effect size.' The most common metrics used in meta-analysis are d and r, where d is the standardized mean difference, and r is the correlation coefficient (→ Correlation Analysis). Once a set of effects has been collected reflecting the findings in the literature, the findings are cumulated and tested for homogeneity of effects. Findings are cumulated simply by averaging, although the average is usually weighted by study sample. This produces an across-study average effect, and this average effect can be considered an estimation of the population effect. The across-study average can be tested to see if it is likely different than zero, using confidence intervals calculated around the average. In addition to examining the across-study average effect, meta-analysis considers the dispersion of effects; that is, how much the studies vary from one another. For example, some studies might use students while others might use working adults; some might use self-report measures while others might use open-ended coding. Any identifiable subject, context, or method feature could be coded.

A number of *challenges* face meta-analysis. One major challenge is that the results of meta-analysis are no better than the quality of the studies used. For example, if some common bias was evident in all studies of a given topic, then that bias would be reflected in the meta-analysis results and it would be undetectable. A second challenge is a publication bias favoring supportive (often, statistically significant) results. A third problem arises from having only small numbers of studies within a research domain. Finally, there is the question of what do to with heterogeneous effects. If heterogeneity cannot be resolved with moderator analysis, then it is questionable if average results can be meaningfully interpreted.

See also: ▶ CORRELATION ANALYSIS
▶ QUANTITATIVE METHODOLOGY
▶ RELIABILITY ▶ VALIDITY

REFERENCES AND SUGGESTED READINGS

Cohen, J. (1988). *Statistical power analysis for the behavioral sciences*. Hillsdale, NJ: Lawrence Erlbaum.

Hullett, C. R. & Levine, T. R. (2003). The overestimation of effect sizes from F values in meta-analysis: The cause and a solution. *Communication Monographs*, 70, 52–67.

Hunter, J. E. & Schmidt, F. L. (1990). *Methods of meta-analysis: Correcting error and bias in research findings*. Newbury Park, CA: Sage.

Levine, T. R., Asada, K. J., & Carpenter, C. (2009). Sample size and effect size are negatively correlated in meta-analysis: Evidence and implications of a publication bias against non-significant findings. *Communication Monographs*, 76, 286–302.

Rosenthal, R. (1991). *Meta-analytic procedures for social research*. Newbury Park, CA: Sage.

Metadiscourse

ROBERT T. CRAIG
University of Colorado at Boulder

Metadiscourse is talk about talk, the pragmatic use of language to comment reflexively on → discourse itself. Metadiscourse shifts the focus of attention or 'frame' so as to influence the → meaning and practical conduct of ongoing communication.

The frame shift performed by metadiscourse is most often local and momentary, as when a speaker uses the word "first" to frame an immediate following point as the first in a series of points, or says "I understand completely" to mark another's statement as understood and accepted. Extended episodes of meta-talk also occur, for example, when a couple sits down to talk over a problem in how they have been talking with each other. People trading stories about poorly run business meetings or writing newspaper columns about rules of etiquette for the use of mobile phones in public are also engaged in metadiscourse, as are scholars writing academic books and articles about media, discourse, and communication. With a growing cultural emphasis on the importance of communication in modern societies, explicit talk about talk seems to have become increasingly prevalent. A 'communication culture' has evolved that "generates large quantities of metadiscourse" (Cameron 2000, viii).

Researchers have identified a wide array of *linguistic devices* used in metadiscourse, such as 'discourse markers' ("*because*," "you know," "*I mean*"), linguistic action verbs ("she asked," "don't threaten me"), performative utterances ("*I promise*," "I *tell* you"), and reported speech (direct or indirect quotation). Verschueren (1999, 187–188) described these and many more linguistic devices, including subtle cues such as word choice, vocal emphasis, and facial expressions, as indicators of metapragmatic awareness.

Although there are functional similarities in metadiscourse across languages, metadiscourse also reflects communicative forms, belief systems, and language ideologies specific to particular cultures (→ Ethnography of Communication). Language ideologies are "habitual ways of thinking and speaking about language and language use which are rarely challenged within a given community" (Verschueren 1999, 198; see also Jaworski et al. 2004). Language ideologies often stereotype and devalue the communication of culturally marginalized groups such as women, lower classes, and immigrants (→ Social Stereotyping and Communication).

See also: ▶ CYBERNETICS ▶ DISCOURSE ▶ DISCOURSE ANALYSIS ▶ ETHNOGRAPHY OF COMMUNICATION ▶ STRATEGIC FRAMING ▶ INTERCULTURAL AND INTERGROUP COMMUNICATION; ▶ LANGUAGE AND SOCIAL INTERACTION ▶ LINGUISTIC PRAGMATICS ▶ LINGUISTICS ▶ MEANING ▶ SOCIAL STEREOTYPING AND COMMUNICATION

REFERENCES AND SUGGESTED READINGS

Cameron, D. (2000). *Good to talk? Living and working in a communication culture*. Thousand Oaks, CA: Sage.
Jaworski, A., Coupland, N., & Galasinski, D. (eds.) (2004). *Metalanguage: Social and ideological perspectives*. Berlin: Mouton de Gruyter.
Verschueren, J. (1999). *Understanding pragmatics*. London: Arnold.

Metaphor
STUART JAY KAPLAN
Lewis and Clark College

Metaphor is widely regarded as a basic linguistic form in nearly all types of → discourse (→ Linguistics). In contrast to early thinking about metaphor, which emphasized its role as a stylistic embellishment used for rhetorical effect, modern theories consider metaphor to be an essential feature of thinking itself. George Lakoff and Mark Johnson (1980) identified a variety of metaphor types that interconnect to structure how people conceptualize their experiences with their physical and social environments. This cognitive perspective on metaphor has stimulated scholarship on metaphor phenomena in a great many disciplines, including communication, organizational theory, political science, art, philosophy, computer science, and law. The role of metaphor in → persuasion is of particular interest to communication scholars. Research findings suggest, for example, that → advertising containing metaphors receives greater attention from readers and evokes more positive affect toward the ad.

For a metaphor to accomplish its work, there are two additional conditions that must be met. First, the two terms must share some properties and those common properties need to be at least minimally relevant to the claim made by the metaphor (i.e., A is B). Otherwise, the attempt at creating an analogy will seem implausible to the reader. The second essential condition for a metaphor to work is that the attempt to combine properties of the source and target must seem at least mildly incongruous or initially nonsensical to the reader or viewer. The interplay of simultaneous similarity and incongruity in an effective metaphor stimulates a problem-solving response in the reader or viewer and a higher degree of engagement in the process of decoding the meaning of a message.

The preponderance of metaphor research has been conducted with linguistic expressions. In recent years, however, researchers have turned their attention to nonlinguistic forms of metaphor phenomena. Two primary emphases in the field of visual metaphor studies are metaphors in the visual arts and metaphors in advertising.

See also: ▶ ADVERTISING ▶ ADVERTISING AS PERSUASION ▶ ART AS COMMUNICATION ▶ CINEMA ▶ CODE ▶ DIGITAL IMAGERY ▶ DISCOURSE ▶ FILM THEORY ▶ LINGUISTICS ▶ MEANING ▶ PERSUASION ▶ RHETORIC AND LANGUAGE ▶ SEMIOTICS ▶ VISUAL COMMUNICATION ▶ VISUAL REPRESENTATION

REFERENCES AND SUGGESTED READINGS

Forceville, C. (1998). *Pictorial metaphor in advertising*. London: Routledge.
Lakoff, G. & Johnson, M. (1980). *Metaphors we live by*. Chicago, IL: University of Chicago Press.

Mexico: Media System

FRANK PRIESS
Konrad Adenauer Foundation

Mexico is a federal republic with 31 states and a federal district constituted under specific provisions. It has a presidential system in which the significance of the legislative branch is increasing. It has a population of 120.8 million people – to which should be added around 20 to 30 million people living either legally or illegally in the United States – with a per capita income of US$9,640 per year. Almost 90 percent of Mexicans are Catholics. The presence of indigenous groups is another important factor. Mexico is the only Latin American member country of the OECD and is shaping up as a booming developing nation. However, its development has always been hampered by overwhelming social and economic inequality.

Mexico has a pluralistic *media environment*, particularly in its press. Within this scene, the audiovisual media system – primarily television – is shaped by oligopolistic structures. In Mexico, the rights of journalists and the media lack a modern context because their legal framework dates from 1917 (→ Journalism: Legal Situation). Also, many Articles are not enforced and this leads to arbitrariness. In 2003 a step forward was made by the passage of the Ley de Transparencia (Transparency Act) and the constitution of the Instituto Federal de Acceso a la Información (IFAI). The decriminalization of slander constituted another improvement for the media. Nevertheless, users of the media lack rights such as that of rebuttal.

Mexico is one of the most dangerous countries for representatives of the press, primarily *journalists*. The state has been incapable of protecting and ensuring freedom for the media and their representatives (→ Violence against Journalists). Further, the economic conditions under which many journalists live lead to a decrease in the quality of their work. Many of them need to have several jobs at a time so that they can attain a decent way of life. This is why they are the privileged targets of corruption. The lack of job alternatives, particularly outside the capital, leads to risks to journalistic professionalism and independence.

Printed media continue to be elitist and expensive. In some regions, the high percentage of illiteracy is also an exclusion criterion. The circulation of most of the 340 newspapers is low, with the exception of a few tabloids, and they are concentrated within the biggest cities. Public opinion polls show that more than 40 percent of Mexicans never read a newspaper. In the capital there are 21 newspapers with very pluralist features, the influential Reforma having about a quarter of a million readers per day. Free newspapers are offered on street corners and on buses and the subway. Outside of the biggest cities, many of the printed media only survive by means of advertisement by the government, which assures influence for both federal and state governments. This 'carrot and stick' situation also obstructs objective coverage (→ Political Advertising; Propaganda).

Generally speaking, Mexico's *television market* is shared by the Televisa and TV Azteca networks who hold the majority of the close to 500 concessions. The remaining suppliers are state-directed and provide educational and cultural content (→ Educational Media; Educational Media Content). At the federal level, only two channels enjoy national broadcasting, while inside the states the state-owned channels are opinion generators only because people lack alternatives (→ Communication Law and Policy: North America). Television constitutes the main information and publicity medium on which much political-institutional and party propaganda are concentrated. Around 80 percent of Mexicans are reached daily by television programs, followed by 70 percent reached by radio. The contents of television programming are mainly focused on entertainment, dominated by the popular soap operas ('telenovela'), talk shows, and sports programs. In *radio*, there are 1,164 commercial channels, 306 of which are state-owned and have educational content. The latter are financed by the budget held by the Ministry of Public Education or by universities.

Just as in the rest of Latin America, the noncommercial sector of audiovisual media is both underdeveloped and underfinanced. This sector is made up of channels that, in one way or another, are under the direct influence of the state. An *alternative medium of information* is represented by what is referred to as 'community radio,' the survival of which is made difficult due to legislative conditions (→ Community Media). These radio broadcasters lack state funding and do not have access to the commercial market. Such a situation has resulted in the illegal operation of many stations (→ Television Broadcasting, Regulation of).

Mexican youth in particular began to use the *Internet* as an alternative medium. Based on figures of 2012, around 37 percent of Mexicans have access to the web (Internet World Stats 2014). Social differences are also reflected here (→ Digital Divide). What is more, → cable television offers are pluralist – both the Congress and the Supreme Court have a channel of their own and international suppliers have a presence in several channels – but only a reduced number of Mexicans can afford them. Most of the population has to turn to the above-mentioned channels and thus plurality is restricted.

See also: ▶ ADVERTISING ▶ CABLE TELEVISION ▶ COMMUNICATION LAW AND POLICY: NORTH AMERICA ▶ COMMUNITY MEDIA ▶ CONCENTRATION IN MEDIA SYSTEMS ▶ DIGITAL DIVIDE ▶ EDUCATIONAL MEDIA ▶ EDUCATIONAL MEDIA CONTENT ▶ JOURNALISM: LEGAL SITUATION ▶ OBJECTIVITY IN REPORTING ▶ PROPAGANDA ▶ TELEVISION BROADCASTING, REGULATION OF ▶ VIOLENCE AGAINST JOURNALISTS

REFERENCES AND SUGGESTED READINGS

Calleja, A. & Solís, B. (2005). *Con permiso – La radio comunitaria en México*. Mexico: Fundacion Friedrich Ebert.
Cantú, M. E. (2005). *Medios y poder de la radio y la televisión en la democracia méxicana*. Mexico: Norma.
Gómez García, R. & Sosa Plata, G. (2009). Das Mediensystem Mexikos [The media system of Mexico]. In Hans-Bredow-Institut (ed.), Internationales Handbuch Medien [*International media handbook*]. Baden-Baden: Nomos, 1056–1067
Gordon, J. C., Deines, T., & Havice, J. (2010). Global warming coverage in the media: Trends in a Mexico City newspaper. *Science Communication*, 32(2), 143–170.
Internet World Stats (2014). Usage and population statistics. At: http://www.internetworldstats.com/stats2.htm, accessed August 17, 2014.
Trejo Delabre, R. (2005). Medios: el nuevo poder real ante el Estado mexicano. In A. Aziz Nassif & J. Alonso Sánchez (eds.), *Sociedad Civil y diversidad*. Mexico: CIESAS y Miguel Angel Porrúa, pp. 141–166.

Minority Journalism

REBECCA ANN LIND
University of Illinois at Chicago

Minority status is predicated not on numerical representation but social or cultural difference, based on language, religion, or other practices (→ Ethnic Journalism). When language differences exist, the dominant social group considers the work of minority groups 'foreign-language journalism.'

Minority journalism, especially if in a culture's native tongue, fills a vital function. Foreign-language press provides news of the homeland; preserves language and cultural ties, builds community, and socializes newcomers (→ Advocacy Journalism; Journalists' Role Perception). The minority journalism concept seems United States-specific; other countries tend to subsume this into ethnic, partisan, or political journalism. Minority media usually try to improve audiences' lives, often embracing an activist mission; perhaps advocating the group's civil rights and monitoring its cultural, social, political, religious, and economic development.

The first United States foreign-language newspaper – Philadelphia Zeitung – appeared in 1732 (→ Journalism, History of). The 1800s saw

Norwegian, Chinese, Czech, Ukrainian, Polish, Italian, Yiddish, Hebrew, French, Spanish, German, and other newspapers. The bilingual Cherokee Phoenix and the genesis of the US black press appeared in the mid-1900s.

Activist functions frequently continued in radio and television. Initially, minority programs aired in discrete segments on weak stations, surrounded by content produced by other minority groups (→ Broadcast Journalism). The 1940s saw the first full-time Spanish-language radio station in the United States and the first radio stations fully committed to serving the African-American audience. In 1977 the first Native-American-owned commercial radio station launched.

Studying how minority groups use mass media can help reveal the relationships between minority and dominant social groups, and should examine whether minority groups' use of new communications technologies continues to reflect the activist goals and mission observed in early minority journalism.

See also: ▶ ADVOCACY JOURNALISM ▶ BI- AND MULTILINGUALISM ▶ BROADCAST JOURNALISM ▶ ETHNIC JOURNALISM ▶ JOURNALISM, HISTORY OF ▶ JOURNALISTS' ROLE PERCEPTION

REFERENCES AND SUGGESTED READINGS

Danky, J. P. & Hady, M. E. (eds.) (1998). *African-American newspapers and periodicals: A national bibliography*. Cambridge, MA: Harvard University Press.

Kanellos, N. & Martell, H. (2000). *Hispanic periodicals in the United States, origins to 1960: A brief history and comprehensive bibliography*. Houston, TX: Arte Publico Press.

Soltes, M. (1969) [1925]. *The Yiddish press: An Americanizing agency*. New York: Teachers College, Columbia University.

Mobility, Technology for

RICH LING

IT University of Copenhagen

Mobile communication is the most widely diffused form of electronic mediation on the planet. As of 2013 there were more than 6.6 billion connections to 3.2 billion unique mobile subscribers. It has changed our sense of safety and the way we coordinate everyday life. Smart phones and the mobile internet are becoming the most common way that people access the web. In addition, there has been the rise of tablets and also different types of 'wearable' computing devices.

Mobile, radio-based communication grew from the work of Marconi. This developed first as a 'broadcast' form of communication uses of radio to dispatch various services expanded to include police and fire departments, taxis, and even rural veterinary services (→ Radio: Social History). Cellular or mobile telephony was developed by Ring and Young in 1947 at Bell Labs. Rather than 'broadcasting' calls a conversation was 'handed' from one relatively small radio cell to another allowing for more calls and smaller handsets. Indeed, the handsets have moved from being large bulky devices to small multi-functional communication gadgets.

The diffusion of mobile telephony has *changed several dimensions of quotidian life*. It has given us micro-coordination and changed our sense of safety. It has played into teen emancipation, ushered in texting and had dramatic impacts in developing countries.

Perhaps the most profound impact of mobile communication is the ability to micro-coordinate with one another. Rather than calling to a fixed location on the chance that an individual is there, the mobile phone makes us individually addressable. We can iteratively plan and adjust meetings and 'fine-tune' tasks in real time. If we forget whether it is whole milk or skim milk that is needed from the store, we simply call and ask. We often think of micro-coordination in a positive way. However, use of the mobile telephone while driving is dangerous. In another realm, micro-coordination has been used to organize criminal activities and by terrorists and insurgents to manage their affairs. A special case of individual addressability is use of the mobile phone in emergencies. The mobile telephone gives people the chance to call for assistance when they find themselves in difficult settings. These can be minor daily problems (a breakdown in the car) or extremely dramatic events such as natural disasters.

An unexpected consequence of inexpensive mobile communication is its impact on the *teen emancipation*. The ability to contact peers via their own communication channel allows for immediacy in interactions and peer group integration. There is also a fashion dimension (→ Youth Culture). Teens were quick to adopt 'texting' via SMS and increasingly via social networking services (→ Social Media; Facebook). This truncated form of asynchronous written communication is the most common form of interaction in some groups. In 2012 we sent and received over 8 trillion SMSs on a global basis. This mediation form will continue to be a part of the picture as it is adopted into mobile social networking sites.

Mobile communication has grown quickly in the *developing world*. As of 2013, 75 percent of all subscriptions are in the global south. This access has facilitated entrepreneurship simplified everyday life and it provided for social contact. At a broader level, it has facilitated development (→ Developmental Communication).

In the broadest sense mobile communication is a *technology of the intimate sphere*. We use the mobile phone to interact with our closest social ties. Research has shown that half of all calls and half of all text messages go to a small circle of 3 to 5 persons. It is clear that there is a long tail of other interlocutors. However, the mobile phone gives us easy access to those persons with whom we are closest. In this way it tightens the intimate bond. Further, the mobile phone is becoming structured into our interactions. That is, we expect that our closest friends and family are continually available via the mobile phone. We structure our daily activities based on the assumption that we will be able to interact with one another via this channel. If for some reason they are not available (they forgot their phone or their battery is discharged) it means that we are not able to work out our plans.

Mobile communication is taking on *new dimensions* with the development of the mobile internet, tablets, 'heads-up' displays and other forms of wearable computing such as smart watches, armbands, etc. Traditionally mobile communication has been seen as texting and talking using a mobile phone. Increasingly mobile communication also includes accessing the internet via a smart phone, a tablet or some type of wearable device. These developments provide new functionality and also challenge the way that we think of mediated social interaction.

See also: ▶ DEVELOPMENTAL COMMUNICATION ▶ FACEBOOK ▶ RADIO: SOCIAL HISTORY ▶ SOCIAL MEDIA ▶ TECHNOLOGY AND COMMUNICATION ▶ TEXT AND INTERTEXTUALITY ▶ YOUTH CULTURE

REFERENCES AND SUGGESTED READINGS

Donner, J. (2008). Research approaches to mobile use in the developing world: A review of the literature. *Information Society*, 24(3), 140–159.

Jensen, R. (2007). The digital provide: Information (technology), market performance and welfare in the South Indian fisheries sector. *Quarterly Journal of Economics*, 122(3), 879–924.

Licoppe, C. (2004). Connected presence: The emergence of a new repertoire for managing social relationships in a changing communications technoscape. *Environment and Planning: Society and Space*, 22, 135–156.

Ling, R. (2012). *Taken for grantedness: The embedding of mobile communication into society*. Cambridge, MA: MIT Press.

Ling, R. & Yttri, B. (2002). Hyper-coordination via mobile phones in Norway. In J. E. Katz & M. Aakhus (eds.), *Perpetual contact: Mobile communication, private talk, public performance*. Cambridge: Cambridge University Press, pp. 139–169.

Zainudeen, A. et al. (2007). *Teleuse at the bottom of the pyramid: Findings from a five-country study*. Colombo: LIRNEasia. At www.lirneasia.net/wp-content/uploads/2008/07/tbop-gk3.pdf, accessed August 17, 2014.

Models of Communication

DENIS MCQUAIL
University of Amsterdam

A model of communication shows the main elements of any structure or process of human social action and the relations between these elements, plus any flow or exchange that takes place. The purpose of such models is thus to help in the description and explanation of communication. They are also useful as a source of hypotheses, a guide to research, and a format for ordering the results of research. A model can also be developed as an 'ideal type' to represent a certain concept, accentuating key or typical features.

The search for a unifying concept of communication resulted in the formulation of a simple graphic representation of *communication as a process* linking a sender and a receiver by a channel carrying messages from one to the other. This model needed to be adapted to the special case of mass communication. An early version of such a model was proposed by Westley and MacLean (1957). This posits the mass media as playing a mediating role between communicators and potential receivers. The aim is to balance the motives and interests of senders with those of receivers. This represents the mass media as essentially neutral and without purpose of their own.

A fundamental principle that entered into later theory is that of balance, based on the observation that communicative exchanges are governed by the relationships of like or dislike between participants and by the attitudes of like and dislike toward objects of communication. These ideas were formulated into a simple model, known as the ABX model, with A and B being two persons and X an object of attention. According to this theory, flows of information (amount and content) will be governed by a 'strain to symmetry' between A and B with reference to X. This idea is the basis for → cognitive dissonance theory.

An early development was the *modelling of influence* in persuasive campaign situations, as in elections or advertising. The idea advanced by Katz and Lazarsfeld (1955), that influence does not typically flow directly by way of the mass media but indirectly by way of personal contacts, was very readily captured by a *two-step flow* model of communication (→ Two-Step Flow of Communication), in which the intermediaries were identified as → 'opinion leaders' or 'gatekeepers'.

The process of *diffusion* of knowledge or innovation has also lent itself to modelling and communication plays an essential part at four stages: (1) awareness, (2) → persuasion, (3) decision, (4) confirmation by experiences or the approval of others. Another aspect of diffusion relates to public information and → news. News diffusion is affected by many different factors. However, models have shown that there is an inverse relationship between the proportion eventually knowing of an event and the proportion hearing of that event from a personal rather than a mass media source (→ Diffusion of Information and Innovation).

Latterly, research has emphasized the role and motivation of the receiver in achieving 'successful' communication. The theory of audience → uses and gratifications rests on the view that audience choice of media content is active and purposeful, and that media use is structured according to various perceived needs and gratifications sought, deriving from the social background of the individual. This has led to several models (e.g., Rosengren 1974).

Models seem most suited to representing planned communication efforts, where there is some underlying logic and sequence, with discernible criteria of success or failure. However, there are few areas of communication research that have not produced at least one theory or concept that can be described in terms of a model (McQuail & Windahl 1993), including some of the most current approaches, such as gatekeeping, agenda setting, and 'news framing' (→ Agenda-Setting Effects; Framing Effects), as well as entire areas such as → international communication and → political communication. It is likely that fundamental changes stemming from *technological convergence* and the rise of the Internet will stimulate yet more models (→ Technology and Communication). Already Bordewijk and Van Kaam's (1986) model of information traffic has led to an important typology of modes of communication. This differentiates four modes – allocution (mass communication), consultation (of a database), conversation (exchange), and registration (at a central node).

See also: ▶ AGENDA-SETTING EFFECTS ▶ COGNITIVE DISSONANCE THEORY ▶ COMMUNICATION: DEFINITIONS AND CONCEPTS ▶ DIFFUSION OF INFORMATION AND INNOVATION ▶ FRAMING EFFECTS ▶ INTERNATIONAL COMMUNICATION ▶ MEDIA ▶ MEDIA EFFECTS, HISTORY OF ▶ NEWS ▶ OPINION LEADER ▶ PERSUASION ▶ POLITICAL COMMUNICATION ▶ TECHNOLOGY AND COMMUNICATION ▶ TWO-STEP FLOW OF COMMUNICATION ▶ USES AND GRATIFICATIONS

REFERENCES AND SUGGESTED READINGS

Bordewijk, J. & Van Kaam, B. (1986). Towards a classification of new tele-information services. *Intermedia*, 14(1), 16–21.

Katz, E. & Lazarsfeld, P. F. (1955). *Personal influence.* Glencoe, NY: Free Press.

McQuail, D. & Windahl, S. (eds.) (1993). *Communication models for the study of mass communication.* London: Longman.

Rosengren, K. E. (1974). Uses and gratifications: A paradigm outlined. In J. G. Blumler & E. Katz (eds.), *The uses of mass communications.* Beverly Hills CA: Sage, pp. 269–281.

Westley, B. H. & MacLean, M. (1957). A conceptual model for mass communication research. *Journalism Quarterly*, 34, 31–38.

Modernity

JOSEPH STRAUBHAAR
University of Texas at Austin

Since the 1990s, academic debates have revived modernity as a key concept. Tomlinson (1991) argued that much of what was labeled 'cultural imperialism' (→ Cultural Imperialism Theories) was in fact a broader spread of a globalized pattern of modernity. This discourse argued, in particular, that beneath much of what was seen as Americanization or westernization lay a more general, deeper globalization of capitalism, "the broader discourse of cultural imperialism *as the spread of the culture of modernity itself*" (Tomlinson 1991, 89–90, original italics; → Globalization Theories).

A related question is whether modernity is a singular tendency or one with many possible versions and outcomes. A number of aspects of globalization tend to standardize certain kinds of economic modernity, such as financial institutions, trade rules and regimes, and commercial media models (→ Media Economics). However, Tomlinson (1999) also argued later that a "decentering of capitalism from the west" was taking place. A number of writers, e.g., Iwabuchi (2002), argued for distinct Asian or Japanese versions of both capitalism and media/cultural modernity. China has also steadily emerged as a major site and alternative form of capitalist production in the current neo-liberal system with many features of current global capitalist modernity, but with a distinctly different emphasis. The fact that China has refused western prescriptions for the sort of democracy that is supposed to accompany modern capitalist development presents a long list of contradictions to traditional notions of modernity.

One problem with this new modernity-focused analysis in globalization, which relies on a rather systemic notion of modernity as the key concept, is losing sight of real issues of differential power between different parts of the world in economics, in politics, and in cultural industries such as television. Some forms of cultural production, e.g., commercial television genres such as soap opera, could be analyzed either as forms of capitalist production or as manifestations of modern approaches to media. The two angles offer somewhat different insights. One problem with classic, neo-Marxist approaches, in contrast, is that they tend to reduce too many things to *linear conceptions of political economic power* (→ Political Economy of the Media).

See also: ▶ CULTURAL IMPERIALISM THEORIES ▶ GLOBALIZATION THEORIES ▶ MEDIA CONGLOMERATES ▶ MEDIA ECONOMICS ▶ POLITICAL ECONOMY OF THE MEDIA

REFERENCES AND SUGGESTED READINGS

Iwabuchi, K. (2002). *Recentering globalization: Popular culture and Japanese transnationalism.* Durham, NC: Duke University Press.

Tomlinson, J. (1991). *Cultural imperialism.* Baltimore, MD: Johns Hopkins University Press.

Tomlinson, J. (1999). *Globalization and culture.* Chicago, IL: University of Chicago Press.

Mood Management

SILVIA KNOBLOCH-WESTERWICK
Ohio State University

Mood-management theory (Zillmann 1988) has been proposed by Zillmann and Bryant and was initially called the 'theory of affect-dependent stimulus arrangement.' The core suggestion is that media users' moods have a strong influence on media content choices because the individual aims to manage or, more specifically, optimize his or her feeling state. This motivation then drives what media content is selected, as different messages produce different effects on mood. This proposed pattern pertains to all media channels and genre types such as news, music, movies, or online content like → social media.

Mood-management processes involve *three dimensions* on which the *individual's feeling state* can be described and that are also linked to mood-enhancing media choices. The first dimension relates to regulation of *stress and boredom*. Media messages are excellent means of lowering arousal. For instance, most people will find watching a peaceful wildlife documentary relaxing. On the other hand, many types of media content are designed to heighten arousal; for example, fast-paced rock music typically has this effect and might even be chosen for a workout for that reason (→ Emotional Arousal Theory; Excitation and Arousal). The second dimension, *mood valence*, looks at whether the media user is in a positive or negative mood. Negative feeling states call for improvement through selective media use, for example by watching a movie with a 'guaranteed' happy ending. When in positive moods, media users will try to maintain that state by choosing content that does not disrupt it and reinforces it instead. Finally, pertaining to the *semantic affinity* dimension, when in a negative feeling state, the individual will avoid all media portrayals that remind him or her of the source of the ongoing distress.

Mood-management theory also outlines the *characteristics of media messages* that are relevant for choices. The *excitatory potential* of a message relates to its capacity to either increase or decrease arousal levels. The *absorption potential* may have some overlap with the first aspect, yet does not fully converge with it. For example, a newscast with many display elements in the style of → CNN Headlines is more absorbing than a more traditional newscast with just a news anchor and very few additional elements. The *hedonic valence* of media content (e.g. news about a large-scale disaster vs pleasant news) will obviously affect whether it will be selected or avoided, depending on prevailing feeling state. Lastly, the *semantic affinity* is an aspect of the message that is very much related to the individual's perspective and assessment of his/her situation. When the current mood is positive, semantic affinity might actually be welcome.

Although mood-management theory is applicable to choices of any media content type, it has gained the most prominence in the context of entertainment exposure. In fact, it can be seen as the overarching theory for the entertainment context (Knobloch-Westerwick, 2006) that can explain why we turn to a great variety of different entertainment media, designed to play on our emotions, and furthermore offers specific predictions about actual choices.

Two *classical studies* can indicate the approach of mood management studies. Bryant and Zillmann (1984) induced different levels of stress in their participants by having them perform tedious mechanical tasks or challenging test assignments under time pressure. Then, in a purportedly unrelated situation, participants were free to 'surf' some television channels on which pre-categorized programs, being either high or low in their excitatory potential, were shown. The provided TV set was set up to record the choices unobtrusively. The stressed participants spent more time on soothing programs, whereas the bored individuals allotted more time to the exciting programs. Meadowcroft and Zillmann (1987) examined whether the menstrual cycle influenced women's reported preferences for TV genres. In a survey, female college students indicated their intention to watch various TV programs, presented in a list, on the same evening. At the end of the questionnaire, they were asked to report information regarding their menstrual cycle. Premenstrual and menstrual women showed higher interest for comedy than other females in the midst of their cycle. The authors concluded that women aim to overcome noxious mood states, resulting from hormonal phases, by watching comedy.

See also: ▶ AFFECTS AND MEDIA EXPOSURE ▶ CNN ▶ EMOTIONAL AROUSAL THEORY ▶ EXCITATION AND AROUSAL ▶ EXPERIMENT, LABORATORY ▶ MEDIA EFFECTS ▶ SOCIAL MEDIA

REFERENCES AND SUGGESTED READINGS

Bryant, J. & Zillmann, D. (1984). Using television to alleviate boredom and stress: Selective exposure as a function of induced excitational states. *Journal of Broadcasting*, 28(1), 1–20.

Knobloch-Westerwick, S. (2006). Mood management: Theory, evidence, and advancements. In J. Bryant & P. Vorderer (eds.), *The psychology of entertainment*. Mahwah, NJ: Lawrence Erlbaum, pp. 239–254.

Meadowcroft, J. M. & Zillmann, D. (1987). Women's comedy preferences during the menstrual cycle. *Communication Research*, 14(2), 204–218.

Reinecke, L., Tamborini, R., Grizzard, M., Lewis, R., Eden, A., & Bowman, N. D. (2012). Characterizing mood management as need satisfaction: The effects of intrinsic needs on selective exposure and mood repair. *Journal of Communication*, 62, 437–453.

Tamborini, R., Grizzard, M., Bowman, N. D., Reinecke, L., Lewis, R. J., & Eden, A. (2011). Media enjoyment as need satisfaction: The contribution of hedonic and nonhedonic needs. *Journal of Communication*, 61, 1025–1042.

Zillmann, D. (1988). Mood management through communication choices. *American Behavioral Scientist*, 31(3), 327–340.

Music Industry

C. MICHAEL ELAVSKY

Pennsylvania State University

The music industry is a term most commonly deployed in reference to the activities of the four largest transnational record corporations – often designated as the 'majors' namely Sony, EMI (Electric and Music Industries), the Warner Music Group (WMG), and the Universal Music Group (UMG) – which collectively account for a dominant proportion of all legal commercial music sales globally (→ Sony Corporation; Time Warner Inc.). All of these corporations are umbrella organizations linking smaller music labels, subsidiaries, and supplementary organizations together through complex corporate ties to larger transnational → media conglomerates (→ Globalization of the Media). Emerging from a long series of mergers occurring over the past century, these music corporations wield significant influence over the contemporary global music market.

Consequently, many scholars point to the ways these corporations 'control' global music production, sustaining their position through the technological, political, and economic power they bring to bear on the ways music operates transnationally as culture and commodity. Other scholars, however, suggest that the complexities behind this term are not properly engaged within such arguments. Still others critically point to the ways in which the term 'music industry' has come to stand in for all global music practices, ignoring the significant ways music is produced, consumed, and circulated beyond the immediate logics and power of the majors. While debates on specific aspects of the power, identity, and future of these entities continue, their impact on the historical growth and development of music as a global commodity is not in question.

The switch to digital technologies as the industry standard in the 1980s generated dramatic shifts in the production and dissemination of music, stimulating unprecedented and global growth, with the industry recording an all-time-high profit of $40 billion in 1995. However, by 1998, industry dynamics were changing. Sales began to stagnate as the confluence of organized hard piracy networks, CD-R technology, the Internet, and peer-to-peer file sharing presented a dramatic, extensive, and sustained threat to industry profitability.

In light of virtually unabated *music piracy and file sharing*, the imminent demise of the CD and most specialized retail music stores, and shifts in practices and capabilities related to music production, consumption, and distribution, the majors were forced to aggressively pursue alternative income streams (e.g., commercial and television song placement) as a means to offset their losses.

The majors have struggled to *adapt to the new media landscape*, as real competitors have entered the market (e.g., iTunes and subscription-based offerings like Spotify). Although they have retained their ability to impact developments related to global music culture and commodities in general, scholars have begun to reconsider the complexities related to their contemporary situation and how the global dynamics regarding music are being reconfigured. For some, this means reconceptualizing the complexity of these organizations' networks, procedures, and strategies on multiple levels, so as to ascertain a more intricate understanding of how they actually 'dominate' global music production, and also how the current global crisis for these corporations is related to the nexus of cultural identity, globalization processes, and neo-liberal policies and practices.

Others have begun to focus on how music is produced, used, and circulated transnationally within and beyond the reach and logics of the big four, suggesting that conceptions of the global music industry need to be broadened. Still others are considering how alternative spaces, innovative technologies, new products, and emerging policies are redefining the commercial use and value of music. As these research trajectories suggest, much work remains to be done with regard to understanding the emerging dynamics surrounding music as both symbolic culture and transnational commodity in relation to how the music industry – as a cultural industry – is globally organized.

See also: ▶ COPYRIGHT ▶ CULTURAL IMPERIALISM THEORIES ▶ CULTURE INDUSTRIES ▶ DIGITAL MEDIA, HISTORY OF ▶ GLOBALIZATION OF THE MEDIA ▶ INTERNET LAW AND REGULATION ▶ MEDIA CONGLOMERATES ▶ POPULAR MUSIC ▶ SONY CORPORATION ▶ TIME WARNER INC.

REFERENCES AND SUGGESTED READINGS

Garofalo, R. & Chapple, S. (1977). *Rock 'n' roll is here to pay: The history and politics of the music industry*. Chicago, IL: Nelson-Hall.

Gronow, P. & Saunio, L. (1998). *An international history of the recording industry* (trans. C. Moseley). London: Cassell.

Hesmondhalgh, D. (2007). *The cultural industries*, 2nd edn. London: Sage.

Negus, K. (1999). *Music genres and corporate cultures*. London: Routledge.

Wallis, R. & Malm, K. (1984). *Big sounds from small peoples: The music industry in small countries*. New York: Pendragon.

Wikstrom, P. (2010). *The music industry: Music in the cloud*. London: Polity.

Narrative News Story

JOHN NERONE

University of Illinois at Urbana–Champaign

The term 'narrative news story' refers most broadly to any sort of nonfiction storytelling, but more specifically to a → news story that begins with an anecdote rather than a summary lead and then is organized in temporal sequence rather than either by inverted pyramid style or analytically (→ News). Narrative news has a long history, an interesting connection with literary history, a vibrant present, and a hopeful future.

Many of the earlier formats of news were narrative in form. Ballads and newsbooks dwelled on spectacular events and told their stories from beginning to end. Newspapers also featured items in narrative style. Early newspaper content tended to be composed by printers, and stories appeared in vernacular form (→ Journalism, History of; Newspaper, History of). This form, which takes so long to get to the point, became cumbersome by the mid-nineteenth century. Three developments encouraged a less intuitive style: pictures, popular journalism, and bureaucratic efficiency, which in turn promoted the 'inverted pyramid style.'

The 'story model' of journalism competed with an 'information model' that came to rely on the inverted pyramid style (→ Objectivity in Reporting). Although it became common only in the 1890s, examples of the inverted pyramid style appeared earlier in newspapers in items like the US Civil War dispatches. Designed for efficiency, it became the preferred style of bureaucrats first and then reporters, who increasingly worked in industrialized newsrooms and studied in journalism schools. The inverted pyramid style never fully conquered journalism. It was resisted by a verbose tradition of reporting, by the cross-fertilization of journalism with literature by storytellers like Charles Dickens and Mark Twain, and by magazine journalists, like Lincoln Steffens and Ida Tarbell.

Narrative currently is experiencing a revival in print media. The construction of a storyline out of reporting raises inevitable questions about accuracy and detachment and invites the perception of a blurring of the line between fact and fiction. As a result, the narrative form remains on the margins of hard news reporting

See also: ▶ JOURNALISM, HISTORY OF ▶ NEWS
▶ NEWS STORY ▶ NEWSPAPER, HISTORY OF
▶ OBJECTIVITY IN REPORTING
▶ PROFESSIONALIZATION OF JOURNALISM

The Concise Encyclopedia of Communication, First Edition. Edited by Wolfgang Donsbach.
© 2015 John Wiley & Sons, Inc. Published 2015 by John Wiley & Sons, Inc.

REFERENCES AND SUGGESTED READINGS

Barnhurst, K. G. & Nerone, J. (2001). *The form of news: A history.* New York: Guilford.
Schudson. M. (1978). *Discovering the news: A social history of American newspapers.* New York: Basic Books.
Stephens, M. (1996). *A history of news*, 2nd edn. New York: Wadsworth.

Negotiation and Bargaining

MICHAEL E. ROLOFF
Northwestern University

Negotiation is a process by which at least two parties interact in an attempt to reach an agreement. Negotiation is goal driven (→ Goals, Cognitive Aspects of; Goals, Social Aspects of) and negotiation goals reflect underlying interests such as the desire to enhance one's well-being or establish a particular type of relationship.

Negotiators advance positions that reflect how they frame the issues and they enact strategic behaviors. They bargain by exchanging offers and counteroffers. Arguments are made in support of positions. Information is exchanged about goals and priorities (→ Questions and Questioning). Coercive tactics are sometimes used to force agreement.

Negotiation research has focused on a variety of topics (Roloff 2014). Recent research informs as how to reach *integrative agreements,* which afford high joint benefits and are often creative. The integrativeness of an agreement is evaluated relative to the joint outcomes provided by other possible agreements. There are a variety of types of integrative agreements such as logrolling, cost-cutting, bridging, nonspecific compensation, contingent agreements, and reopener agreements. The dual-concern model has guided a great deal of integrative negotiation research (Pruitt & Rubin 1986). To reach integrative agreements, negotiators must be committed to achieving their goals as well as those of their counterpart. When so motivated, they seek information, disclose priorities, and logroll.

Because of the pervasiveness of electronic media, researchers are studying how *mediated negotiation* differs from face-to-face (→ Mediated Social Interaction; Personal Communication by CMC). Because of increasing globalization, negotiation researchers have also studied both intracultural and intercultural negotiations (→ Intercultural and Intergroup Communication; Intercultural Conflict Styles and Facework), and especially those involving business transactions (→ Globalization of Organizations). Finally, researchers are increasingly interested in how negotiation can *resolve intractable disputes.*

See also: ▶ GLOBALIZATION OF ORGANIZATIONS ▶ GOALS, COGNITIVE ASPECTS OF ▶ GOALS, SOCIAL ASPECTS OF ▶ INTERCULTURAL CONFLICT STYLES AND FACEWORK ▶ INTERCULTURAL AND INTERGROUP COMMUNICATION ▶ MEDIATED SOCIAL INTERACTION ▶ PERSONAL COMMUNICATION BY CMC ▶ QUESTIONS AND QUESTIONING

REFERENCES AND SUGGESTED READINGS

Pruitt, D. G. & Rubin, J. Z. (1986). *Social conflict: Escalation, stalemate and settlement.* New York: Random House.
Roloff, M. E. (2014). Negotiation and communication: Explication and research directions. In C. R. Berger (ed.), *International Encyclopedia of Interpersonal Communication.* Berlin: De Gruyter Mouton, pp. 201–224.

Network Organizations through Communication Technology

LEE SPROULL
New York University

CARYN A. CONLEY
New York University

Network forms of organizations are characterized by reciprocal, lateral communication ties. They are often contrasted with hierarchies, which are vertically organized, and markets, which exhibit an atomistic structure of buyers and sellers. Networked organizations are often viewed as more flexible and 'intelligent' than hierarchies and markets. From the 1990s to the present, computer-mediated communication technology has been increasingly employed to extend the scale and scope of networked organizations in order to "connect multiple organizations and people into new entities that can create products or services" (Contractor et al. 2006, 682).

Key attributes of computer-mediated communication technology for networked organizations are that they: (1) reduce physical, organizational, and social constraints on communication; and (2) create a digital record of communication for processing and preservation. Widespread use of these technologies increases reciprocal, lateral communication within organizations and between an organization and its external constituents – customers, suppliers, and partners. Both internally and externally, networked organizations are characterized by the increasing use of distributed work processes and knowledge-sharing processes (→ Communication Networks; Technology and Communication).

Internally, employees who are separated by geographic or functional distance can use communication technology to contribute to common goals and projects. In distributed or virtual work teams, employees use communication and project management software to coordinate their work on a common project. Distributed work teams can bring employee expertise to bear on a project independent of the employee's geographic location. When employees are located across the globe, distributed work teams can make progress 24 hours a day, 7 days a week. Effective deployment of virtual work teams requires careful attention to their *social psychology and group dynamics*. Many laboratory and field studies have demonstrated that people who work together electronically have a relatively difficult time developing common ground and interpersonal trust.

Networked organizations increasingly use *communication technology* to reach beyond the formal corporate boundary. Whereas a focal organization has always had supply-chain relationships with vendors and suppliers, current communication technologies enable one organization to virtually embed its processes (for delivering and billing goods, for example) within another organization's processes (for sales or manufacturing and inventory management, for example).

See also: ▶ COMMUNICATION NETWORKS
▶ INTERORGANIZATIONAL COMMUNICATION
▶ MOBILITY, TECHNOLOGY FOR ▶ ORGANIZATIONAL COMMUNICATION ▶ PERSONAL COMMUNICATION BY CMC ▶ TECHNOLOGY AND COMMUNICATION

REFERENCES AND SUGGESTED READINGS

Contractor, N., Monge, P., & Leonardi, P. (2011). Multidimensional networks and the dynamics of sociomateriality: Bringing technology inside the network. *International Journal of Communication*, 5, 682–720.

Contractor, N. S., Wasserman, S., & Faust, K. (2006). Testing multitheoretical, multilevel hypotheses about organizational networks: An analytical framework and empirical example. *Academy of Management Review*, 31(3), 681–703.

Murase, T., Doty, D., Wax, A., DeChurch, L. A., & Contractor, N. (2012). Teams are changing: Time to "think networks". *Industrial and Organizational Psychology: Perspectives on Science and Practice* 5(1), 41–44.

Neutrality

HEIKKI HEIKKILÄ
University of Tampere

Since the fourteenth century, the word 'neutrality' has predominantly pertained to nonalignment in the realms of politics, diplomacy, and war. Thus, neutrality depends on the political judgment of others: whether they acknowledge one's neutrality to be sincere or expedient to *their* interests. The history of politics shows that in some cases the neutral political status was accepted (for instance, Switzerland since the Congress of Vienna in 1815) and in others it was not (Laos during the Vietnam War).

Another understanding of neutrality is anchored in the facts of nature, which are independent of the individual investigating them. In natural sciences neutrality can be warranted, insofar as one sticks to the methodological rules set by science and does not allow any value-laden interests to interfere with one's relationship with the object. *Neutrality as allegiance to the set of rules*, too, can be charged methodologically and/or politically.

In communications, the concept of neutrality was first introduced by the commercialization of the press. Neutrality as non-alignment was pursued by publishers, who sought to reach larger audiences and greater advertisement revenues by conveying information, not opinion. Consistent with the frailty of neutrality, the nonalignment of news and journalists had to be acknowledged by 'the modernizing societies,' and this was not a straightforward process.

A natural scientific version of neutrality was introduced to journalism by social changes, the acceptance of positivistic epistemology, and photographic realism in the late nineteenth century. This resulted in the development of objectivity as professional doctrine (→ News Ideologies; Objectivity in Reporting). In this framework, neutrality and words with parallel meanings – 'unbiased,' 'nonpartisan,' and 'disinterested' – referred to a style of journalistic expression in which journalists distance themselves from a subject. While for some this is the core of the journalistic role (→ Journalists' Role Perception), critics see this as 'strategic rituals,' which aim at enhancing the credibility of news, diminishing allegations of bias and avoiding dangers of libel suits (Tuchman 1978, 83).

See also: ▶ JOURNALISM ▶ JOURNALISM, HISTORY OF ▶ JOURNALISTS' ROLE PERCEPTION ▶ NEWS IDEOLOGIES ▶ OBJECTIVITY IN REPORTING

REFERENCES AND SUGGESTED READINGS

Schiller, D. (1981). *Objectivity and the news*. Philadelphia, PA: University of Pennsylvania Press.
Schudson, M. (1978). *Discovering the news*. New York: Basic Books.
Tuchman, G. (1978). *Making news: A study in the construction of reality*. New York: Free Press.

New World Information and Communication Order (NWICO)

CLAUDIA PADOVANI
University of Padua

The New World Information and Communication Order (NWICO) is the result of a political proposal concerning media and communication issues emerging from international debates in the late 1970s. The term originated within the Non-Aligned Movement (NAM), expressing the aspirations of southern countries to democratize the international communication system and rebalance information flows worldwide. UNESCO played a major role in fostering the debate until the early 1980s, especially through the work of a commission chaired by Irish diplomat Sean MacBride (→ UNESCO). The commission's report, Many Voices, One World (MacBride Commission 2004), outlined the main international problems in communication and summarized the NWICO's basic philosophical thrust. It was adopted at the twenty-first general conference of UNESCO in 1980, and remains a milestone in the history of global debates around communication issues (→ International Communication; International Communication Agencies).

Changes in world power relations in the 1950s and 1960s resulting from decolonization processes allowed for a coalition of social forces to put communication issues on the international agenda. The NWICO platform identified a number of problematic trends: imbalances in information flows and the inequitable distribution of communication infrastructures, threats to cultural identities, and the monopolistic positions of transnational communication corporations. As summarized by Nordenstreng (1984), the NWICO invited to 'democratize,' 'decolonize,' and 'demonopolize' the international communication system, and to address the challenges of development (→ Development Communication). Furthermore, the idea of communication as a 'basic human right' was outlined.

UNESCO addressed these matters in its General Conferences from the early 1970s and appointed an International Commission for the Study of Communication Problems. The final report – including data, analyses, and 82 recommendations – was adopted at the twenty-first UNESCO Conference in Belgrade (1980), but Cold War-inspired controversies that had accompanied the debate since the beginning continued. As a result, NWICO was no longer mentioned in the UNESCO 1984–1989 plan, and a technical approach to communication development prevailed.

See also: ▶ COMMUNICATION TECHNOLOGY AND DEVELOPMENT ▶ CONCENTRATION IN MEDIA SYSTEMS ▶ DEVELOPMENT COMMUNICATION ▶ INTERNATIONAL COMMUNICATION ▶ INTERNATIONAL COMMUNICATION AGENCIES ▶ UNESCO

REFERENCES AND SUGGESTED READINGS

Carlsson, U. (2003). The rise and fall of NWICO: From a vision of international regulation to a reality of multilevel governance. *Nordicom Review*, 24(2), 31–67.

MacBride Commission (2004). *Many voices, one world: Towards a new, more just and more efficient world information and communication order*, 25th anniversary edn. Lanham, MD: Rowman and Littlefield.

Nordenstreng, K. (1984). Defining the new international information order. In C. Padovani, C. & A. Calabrese, A. (eds.) (2014). *Communication rights and social justice: Historical accounts of transnational mobilizations*. Basingstoke: Palgrave Macmillan.

News

HILLEL NOSSEK
College of Management, Academic Studies

News is a → genre of mass media content resulting from journalists' information gathering and editors' decisions and following professional practices and norms (→ Ethics in Journalism; News Routines; Standards of News). News is the product of teamwork in media outlets. According to functional-structural social theory, news content is information that seeks to meet social needs by observing the natural and human universe in order to help people survive in their physical and social world. The main critical question regarding news is whether there is a consensus on how news is defined and who creates and controls news production and news content.

News theories stem from sociology, psychology, and social psychology. They examine newsroom decision-making, professional socialization, and news creation and production (→ Journalism Education; News Factors; News Values). Some approaches conceive of news as a product of actions by interested parties, ranging from journalists' independent and regular sources through sources with vested interests that leak scandals to public relations agents who actually 'create events' or 'spin' their meaning (→ Framing of the News). News selection occurs on several levels and journalists function within media organizations, each with its own priorities, in a matrix of other organizations. Media organizations also function in the wider social sphere of the social institution of communication with its reciprocal relations and influence by other social institutions. Shoemaker and Reese (2014) proposed a hierarchy-of-influences model, ranging from individual media workers to larger societal forces affecting the news message (→ Media Production and Content).

The *theoretical approaches to news* vary widely. The *normative professional-functional approach* focuses on news production, and argues that although journalists and editors follow professional norms, the economic, political, and cultural environment for news distorts the end product (→ Political Economy of the Media). *Critical approaches* regard news as a capitalist tool for preserving the social and economic status quo, and ask the question of whether the news helps explain and clarify events in the real world or mystifies and obscures them (→ Critical Theory). A *cultural approach* recognizes the many different ways news can be presented, for example, depending on whether a conflict is internal or external to a nation (→ Cultural Studies).

News as a *professional narrative or routine* involves two important factors: journalistic practices and cultural background. Professional journalism has a professional ideology of objectivity, with norms and procedures to eliminate subjective bias – supposedly presenting only the facts (→ Objectivity in Reporting). Studies of → journalists' role perceptions show a close but distinct relationship between their professional and domestic-cultural attitudes. The second factor in professional narrative is cultural context. As part of their cultural role as storytellers, journalists 'manufacture' news by tapping into cultural narratives.

Although much of news originates from within large media organizations, *alternative forms* are widely available. The underlying premise of 'alternative' news is that media ownership, with its bias toward capital and government, is an impossible barrier to news of public importance (→ Alternative Journalism). In the concept of 'open news' journalists and audiences work together creating, editing, and distributing news, with no commitment to a single truth or to following up items, yet coexisting with professional journalists as the formal gatekeepers of conventional news organizations (→ Citizen Journalism).

Around the beginning of the twenty-first century a new trend in theory and professional thinking suggested abandoning the domestic/foreign dichotomization of news and creating a new definition: global news as a concept and as a research field. There is not yet agreement on the definition. Some define global news as news that is transnational and involves a global audience, and others define it as a type of human-interest story (like issues of human and civil rights) that crosses national and cultural borders, or as stories on issues (like climate change) that literally concern the globe (→ Globalization of the Media).

Current *questions for research* are, among others, whether online journalism is creating new modes of news or whether the product is a replication of the well-established normative-professional practices; and whether news will cease to be a product of professionals and media outlets and become an interactive process produced by audiences with no editors or censors.

See also: ▶ ALTERNATIVE JOURNALISM ▶ BIAS IN THE NEWS ▶ CITIZEN JOURNALISM ▶ CRITICAL THEORY ▶ CULTURAL STUDIES ▶ DEVELOPMENT JOURNALISM ▶ GLOBALIZATION OF THE MEDIA ▶ ETHICS IN JOURNALISM ▶ FRAMING OF THE NEWS ▶ INFOTAINMENT ▶ INTERNATIONAL NEWS REPORTING ▶ JOURNALISM ▶ JOURNALISM EDUCATION ▶ JOURNALISTS' ROLE PERCEPTION ▶ MEDIA EVENTS AND PSEUDO-EVENTS ▶ MEDIA HISTORY ▶ MEDIA PRODUCTION AND CONTENT ▶ NARRATIVE NEWS STORY ▶ NEWS FACTORS ▶ NEWS ROUTINES ▶ NEWS SOURCES ▶ NEWS VALUES ▶ OBJECTIVITY IN REPORTING ▶ POLITICAL ECONOMY OF THE MEDIA ▶ PROFESSIONALIZATION OF JOURNALISM ▶ PUBLIC RELATIONS ▶ STANDARDS OF NEWS ▶ TRUTH AND MEDIA CONTENT

REFERENCES AND SUGGESTED READINGS

Donsbach, W. (2004). Psychology of news decisions: Factors behind journalists' professional behavior. *Journalism*, 5, 131–157.
Nossek, H. (2009) On the future of journalism as a professional practice and the case of journalism in Israel. *Journalism*, 10(3), 358–361.
Nossek, H. & Kunelius, R. (2012). News flows, global journalism and climate summits. In E. Eide and R Kunelius (eds.), *Media meets climate: The Global challenge for journalism*. Gothenburg: Nordicom, pp. 67–85.
Reich, Z. (2012). Different practices, similar logic: Comparing news reporting across political, financial and territorial beats. *International Journal of Press/Politics*, 17, 76–99.
Shoemaker, P. & Cohen, A. A. (2006). *News around the world: Content, practitioners and the public*. London: Routledge.
Shoemaker, P. & Reese, S. (2014). *Mediating the message in the 21st century: A media sociology perspective*. London: Routledge.
Thussu, D. K. (2008). *News as entertainment: The rise of global infotainment*. Thousand Oaks, CA: Sage.

News Agencies, History of

OLIVER BOYD-BARRETT
Bowling Green State University

News agencies are among the oldest electronic media, dating back at least to 1835, the year that the French agency Havas was established. Havas was the first news agency to engage in significant international activity. It was followed by Associated Press (AP) in the USA in 1846, Wolff in Germany in 1849, Tuwora in Austria in 1850, and Reuters in the UK in 1851. Very soon there was a national news agency in almost every European country. Outside Europe the pace of development was slower, but comprehensive. Generalist and specialist news agencies operating at international/global, regional, national, and sub-national levels constitute a networked system of news gathering and news distribution (→ International News Reporting).

There were at least four *phases in the development* of the major news agencies: (1) global domination of international news flow by a European-based formal news cartel dominated by Reuters (UK), Havas (France), and Wolff (Germany), 1870–1917; (2) dissolution of the cartel, 1918–1934, and the rise of the US agencies AP and United Press International (UPI); (3) market domination by the 'Big Four' (AP, Agence France-Presse [AFP], Reuters, and UPI) in the 1980s–1990s, and (4) dissolution of the 'Big Four' domination from the 1980s onward. In the latest phase, AP and Reuters continue to dominate among the older generation of 'wholesale' news agencies. UPI is no longer a major global player. Reuters, transformed by 1980 into a primarily financial news agency serving financial and business markets, and now merged into Thomson Reuters, was significantly challenged by US financial news agency Bloomberg. AP and Reuters have television arms, APTN and Reuters TV, respectively, which dominate the wholesale market in international television news footage. Additionally, a new generation of news media, audiovisual and online, claim global market reach.

Throughout this period there were always strong *national news agencies* engaged in significant international news gathering and distribution, although not on the same scale as the majors, nor, in some cases (e.g., TASS in the Soviet period), operating on a commercial basis. Their number in recent decades has included China's Xinhua, Germany's Deutsche Presse Agentur (DPA), Japan's Kyodo, Russia's TASS, and Spain's EFE. From time to time throughout the history of the global news system, there have emerged *regional agencies*, sometimes in the form of consortia of national news agencies, such as the Pan-African News Agency (PANA) providing news of Africa for Africa and the world since 1979, or involving entirely new formations, such as Inter Press Service (IPS), which started as a cooperative of journalists focusing primarily on news of and for developing countries. Some strong national or regional agencies have claimed to provide news services that are *alternative* or even oppositional to the news services of the major (western and big power-based) agencies. The scope for alternative news services has magnified with the development of the Internet.

News agencies such as AP and Reuters were classically defined as 'wholesale' media, gathering news for the purpose of distributing it to other – 'retail' – media, mainly newspapers and broadcasters, which packaged news agency news for their own distinctive readers and audiences. Until recently, news agencies did not have direct access to individual news consumers; their services were mediated, subject to the selection and rewriting practices of their media subscribers, which repackaged agency news for local audiences.

In addition to their traditional wholesale role, news agencies have become increasingly important as retail sources of information not only for media, but also for individual consumers who access news agency services through the Internet and may pay nothing for the privilege. Though they may go direct to news agency sites, Internet consumers more typically access news agency stories through secondary, or retail, agents consisting of general-interest portals (e.g., Yahoo!), corporate websites, and the websites of newspaper and television stations.

Some media that were once 'retail,' servicing discrete geographical markets, have launched themselves as distributors of news services across major regions of the world or around the entire globe. The best-known examples of this phenomenon included BBC World (headquarters in London, UK) and → CNN (headquarters in Atlanta, US) in the 1990s (→ BBC World Service); Al Jazeera (headquarters in Qatar) joined their ranks a decade later, and others will follow (→ Arab Satellite TV News). With the weakening of semantic boundaries, the term 'news agency' has become more diffuse, sometimes used as indistinguishable from 'news media' in general.

See also: ▶ ARAB SATELLITE TV NEWS
▶ BBC WORLD SERVICE ▶ CNN
▶ INTERNATIONAL COMMUNICATION
▶ INTERNATIONAL COMMUNICATION AGENCIES
▶ INTERNATIONAL NEWS REPORTING

REFERENCES AND SUGGESTED READINGS

Boyd-Barrett, O. (1980). *The international news agencies*. London: Constable.
Boyd-Barrett, O. (ed.) (2010). *News agencies in the turbulent era of the Internet*. Barcelona: Generalitat de Catalunya: Col-lecció Lexikon.

News Corporation

MARA EINSTEIN

Queens College, City University of New York

News Corporation was an international media company owned by Australian media mogul Rupert Murdoch. In 2013 it was split into two publicly traded companies: 21st Century Fox, which consists primarily of media outlets like the Fox Entertainment Group and Twentieth Century Fox, and News Corp, which represents the publishing division of the former News Corporation (e.g., *The Wall Street Journal* in the USA and *The Times* in the UK). Murdoch, however, remained chairman of both companies.

While News Corp began as an Australian newspaper company in the late 1970s, it became an American media company when it was incorporated in the United States in 2004. The company's chairman, Rupert Murdoch, was famous for producing racy newspaper headlines and titillating photographs of women to sell newspapers around the world. He brought that successful marketing strategy with him as he acquired an increasing number of media properties within the United States. Murdoch had considerable success in the satellite television business (→ Satellite Television), both in the United Kingdom with − BSkyB (→ United Kingdom: Media System) and in Asia with STAR. News Corp expanded that international expertise into the US market, acquiring 39 percent of DirecTV in 2003. In 1986, Murdoch launched Fox Broadcasting − the first new broadcast network in almost 40 years. Eight years later, the Fox Broadcast Company forced the realignment of the American television landscape when the company acquired New World Communications, a television station group made up of major network affiliates.

Filmed entertainment included both motion picture and television production and was the largest division, representing 25 percent of the organization's revenues annually. Twentieth Century Fox produced three of the top five best-selling pictures of all time, like Titanic and Star Wars. Other hits included X-Men, the animated feature Ice Age: The Meltdown, Walk the Line, and the 3-D movie Avatar. This division was a major supplier of programming for prime-time broadcast television as well as syndicated television product. The company has expanded considerably into local cable sports and owns a number of online sports outlets including FoxSports.com and whatifsports. Two notable corporate snafus: the purchase of MySpace in 2005 which the company sold in 2011 and the phone-hacking scandal by *News International* in the United Kingdom. Recent acquisitions suggest News Corporation has made a significant commitment to increasing its online presence.

See also ▶ CABLE TELEVISION ▶ CINEMA ▶ MEDIA CONGLOMERATES ▶ SATELLITE TELEVISION ▶ UNITED KINGDOM: MEDIA SYSTEM ▶ UNITED STATES OF AMERICA: MEDIA SYSTEM

REFERENCES AND SUGGESTED READINGS

Folkenflik, D. (2013). Murdoch's world: The last of the old media empires. New York: Public Affairs.
Kellner, D. (2011). The Murdoch media empire, ethics, and democracy: Some critical reflections. Turkish Journal of Business Ethics, 4(8), 61–74.
Sherman, G. (2014). The loudest voice in the room: How the brilliant, bombastic Roger Ailes built Fox News − and divided a country. New York: Random House.

News Cycles

KATHRYN JENSON WHITE
University of Oklahoma

A news cycle is a round of coverage once measured in the number of hours between each issue of a newspaper. The term originated in the United States, and the *Oxford English Dictionary* dates the earliest use to a 1922 Los Angeles Times article. Major metropolitan newspapers back then published multiple editions daily, but smaller local and most international newspapers followed a 24-hour cycle, publishing at about the same time daily, either morning or evening (→ News). Broadcast news initially scheduled programs in daily time slots, although stations did interrupt regular programming for breaking news.

With the introduction of the Today Show on the US ABC network in 1952, the broadcast news cycle added a morning to its existing afternoon arc. The 24-hour news channel → CNN launched in 1980, and in the UK Sky News followed in 1989. The phrase '24-hour news cycle' emerged in the 1980s to express the idea that satellite transmissions (and, later, Internet postings) produce a nonstop flow of news updating events internationally (→ Satellite Television; Online Journalism). The global, continuous, or rolling news cycle possible on Internet news outlets has redefined the traditional daily round of print or broadcast journalists (→ News Routines; Internet News).

Journalism practitioners and scholars have expressed *concerns* about a negative impact on news, because the rush to publish limits how much sourcing, fact checking, and editing news producers can do and allows the dissemination of rumor and speculation (e.g., Merritt 2006). The nonstop cycle may degrade news in other ways. Immediacy favors spectatorship over investigation and creates the feeling of discovery while doing little to enhance understanding (Lewis et al. 2005). 'Breaking news,' the very kind that ongoing cycles would seem best suited to serve, may devolve into firsts only because no other channel finds the stories worth reporting. Thus, ever faster news cycles may not lead to better-informed citizens.

See also: ▶ ARAB SATELLITE TV NEWS ▶ BBC WORLD SERVICE ▶ CNN ▶ CROSS-MEDIA PRODUCTION ▶ INTERNET NEWS ▶ MEDIA PRODUCTION AND CONTENT ▶ NEWS ▶ NEWS ROUTINES ▶ NEWS VALUES ▶ ONLINE JOURNALISM ▶ QUALITY OF THE NEWS ▶ SATELLITE TELEVISION ▶ STANDARDS OF NEWS

REFERENCES AND SUGGESTED READINGS

Gowing, N. (2010). 'Skyful of lies' and black swans: The new tyranny of shifting information power in crises. Oxford: Reuters Institute At https://reutersinstitute.politics.ox.ac.uk/fileadmin/documents/Publications/Skyful_of_Lies.pdf, accessed August 18, 2014.

Hess, S. (2002). The CNN effect: How 24-hour news coverage affects government decisions and public opinion. Brookings/Harvard Forum: Press Coverage and the War on Terrorism, January 23. At http://www.brookings.edu/events/2002/01/23media-journalism, accessed August 18, 2014.

Lewis, J., Cushion, S., & Thomas, J. (2005). Immediacy, convenience or engagement? An analysis of 24-hour news channels in the UK. *Journalism Studies*, (6), 461–477.

Merritt, D. (2006). Heroes in the tough transition to digital news. *Nieman Reports*, 60, 77. At http://www.nieman.harvard.edu/reports/article/100442##, accessed August 18, 2014.

News Factors

HANS MATHIAS KEPPLINGER
Johannes Gutenberg University of Mainz

The term 'news factors' denotes characteristics of news stories about events and topics that contribute to making them newsworthy (→ News Values): the more news factors a news story carries, the more newsworthy it is. Besides the number of news factors, their intensity has an influence on the newsworthiness of news stories.

According to Östgaard (1965), one set of news factors is "foreign to the news process" (influences of publishers, etc.) and another set is "inherent in the news process" (simplification, sensationalism, etc.). According to Galtung and Ruge (1965), culture-free and culture-bound news factors can be distinguished. Schulz (1976) explicitly distinguished news factors from news values and developed scales indicating the intensity of news factors.

Shoemaker (1996) presented a catalog of news factors derived from theories of biological and cultural evolutions. In the course of time, all news factors "foreign to the news process" have been excluded from the catalogs. An example is the news factor "consonance" introduced by Galtung and Ruge (1965) with two sub-categories – consonant to expectations (neutral) and consonant to ideals or wishes (normative). As a consequence, the influence of the individual perspectives of journalists and of the editorial line on the selection of news is neglected. This has proved to be unrealistic (→ Bias in the News; Journalists' Role Perception).

See also: ▶ BIAS IN THE NEWS ▶ CRISIS COMMUNICATION ▶ JOURNALISTS' ROLE PERCEPTION ▶ NEWS ROUTINES ▶ NEWS VALUES

REFERENCES AND SUGGESTED READINGS

Galtung, J. & Ruge, M. H. (1965). The structure of foreign news: The presentation of the Congo, Cuba and Cyprus crises in four Norwegian newspapers. *Journal of Peace Research*, 2, 64–91.

Östgaard, E. (1965). Factors influencing the flow of news. *Journal of Peace Research*, 2, 39–63.

Schulz, W. (1976). *Die Konstruktion von Realität in den Nachrichtenmedien. Analyse der aktuellen Berichterstattung* [The construction of reality in the news media. An analysis of the news coverage]. Freiburg: Alber.

Shoemaker, P. (1996). Hardwired for news: Using biological and cultural evolution to explain the surveillance function. *Journal of Communication*, 46(3), 32–47.

News Ideologies

MARK DEUZE
Indiana University Bloomington

An occupational ideology refers to a system of beliefs characteristic of a particular group of workers, including but not limited to their processes of producing meanings and ideas within the group. Research suggests that news workers around the world have in common an occupational ideology consisting of a generally shared system of ideal-typical values (Deuze 2005).

Journalism scholars see professionalization as a distinctly ideological process (→ Professionalization of Journalism). The emerging ideology continuously refined a consensus about who was a 'real' journalist (→ Journalists' Role Perception) and what (parts of) news media at any time qualify as examples of 'real' journalism. Through such definitional debates, and through the processes of legitimizing or excluding particular participants in these discussions, journalists establish (largely informal) barriers of entry to the profession. Because journalists in all media types, genres, and formats share similar values, it is possible to speak of a dominant occupational ideology of news. Most news workers base their professional perceptions and praxis on that ideology but interpret or apply it differently across media. Reporters and editors use news ideology as a "strategic ritual" (Tuchman 1971; → Objectivity in Reporting) to position themselves in the profession and in relation to media critics and the audience. They also use ideology as an instrument to naturalize the structures of news organizations or media industries.

Through news ideology, journalism continuously reinvents itself. Changes in society and fast-paced developments in technology, as well as the ongoing convergence of companies, genres, and media in the field, translate into anxiety about the state of the profession. Journalists, along with scholars and educators, inevitably explore news ideology whenever they ask themselves: what is journalism?

See also: ▶ ETHICS IN JOURNALISM
▶ JOURNALISTS, CREDIBILITY OF ▶ JOURNALISTS' ROLE PERCEPTION ▶ NEUTRALITY
▶ OBJECTIVITY IN REPORTING
▶ PROFESSIONALIZATION OF JOURNALISM
▶ QUALITY OF THE NEWS ▶ STANDARDS OF NEWS

REFERENCES AND SUGGESTED READINGS

Barnhurst, K. (2005). News ideology in the twentieth century. In S. Høyer & H. Pöttker (eds.), *Diffusion of the news paradigm, 1850–2000*. Gothenburg: Nordicom, pp. 239–262.

Chouliaraki, L. (2013). Re-mediation, inter-mediation, trans-mediation: The cosmopolitan trajectories of convergent journalism. *Journalism Studies*, 14(2), 267–283.

Deuze, M. (2005). What is journalism? Professional identity and ideology of journalists reconsidered. *Journalism: Theory, Practice and Criticism*, 6(4), 443–465.

Deuze, M. (2010). Journalism and convergence culture. In S. Allan (ed.), *The Routledge companion to news and journalism*. London: Routledge, pp. 267–276.

Tuchman, G. (1971). Objectivity as strategic ritual: An examination of newsmen's notions of objectivity. *American Journal of Sociology*, 77(4), 660–679.

News Processing across the Life-Span

BARRIE GUNTER
University of Leicester

The → news is like lifeblood to democratic societies. The information provided daily through the major mass media television, radio, newspapers, and, increasingly, the Internet, keeps citizens up to date with the latest political, economic, and social developments, world events, natural and man-made disasters, lives of famous public figures, scientific breakthroughs, and sports and weather. It serves to keep electorates apprised of the performance of their elected political representatives, helps people to cope with bad news, and also provides a sense of continuity in an increasingly varied media landscape and a sense of security even during times of extreme adversity.

The main sources of news have consistently been identified as television, followed by newspapers, then radio. Since 2000, the Internet has emerged as a key news source that rivals other news media in the extent to which it is endorsed (→ Internet News; Digital Media, History of). Young media consumers have adopted digital news sources fastest, but older consumers are catching them (Sasseen et al. 2013; → Exposure to Communication Content).

The news media potentially bring a wealth of information into people's homes. There have been debates about whether broadcast media are better or worse than print media as news sources. Consumption of news media can shape political and current affairs awareness (Iyengar, 1991; → Political Knowledge; Agenda-Setting Effects). Newsrooms generally offer only selective views of the world because of time and spade constraints (→ Bias in the News). Digital media have opened opportunities for news consumers to become news contributors (→ Citizen Journalism).

People fail to remember much of the news to which they are exposed. Failure to pay proper attention can account in part for this outcome for broadcast news. In addition, the way the news is packaged, with an emphasis on entertainment-oriented techniques, and a poor understanding of the psychology of memory in newsrooms are critical factors (Gunter, 1987).

See also: ▶ AGENDA-SETTING EFFECTS ▶ BIAS IN THE NEWS ▶ CITIZEN JOURNALISM ▶ DIGITAL MEDIA, HISTORY OF ▶ EXPOSURE TO COMMUNICATION CONTENT ▶ INTERNET NEWS ▶ NEWS ▶ POLITICAL KNOWLEDGE

REFERENCES AND SUGGESTED READINGS

Gunter, B. (1987). *Poor reception: Misunderstanding and forgetting broadcast news*. Hillsdale, NJ: Lawrence Erlbaum.

Iyengar, S. (1991) *Is Anyone Responsible? How Television Frames Political Issues*. Chicago, IL: University of Chicago Press.

Sasseen, J., Olmstead, K., & Mitchell, A. (2013) Digital: As mobile grows rapidly, the pressures on news intensify. *The State of the News Media 2013*. Pew Research Center. At www.stateofthemedia.org/2013/digital-as-mobile-grows-rapidly-the-pressures-on-news-intensify, accessed 18 August, 2014.

News Routines

WILSON LOWREY
University of Alabama

News routines are repeated practices and forms that make it easier for journalists to accomplish tasks and ensure immediacy in an uncertain world while working within production constraints. Routines structure the context within which journalists make decisions, but journalists may also employ routines.

News routines emerged when the development of western democratic market societies and the rationalization of economic life in the 1800s led to the pursuit of wide audiences, increased scale of production, and larger news organizations. As news staffs increased and external relationships became more complex, management attempted to control production bureaucratically. Rules and new technologies facilitated control, as did professional routines such as the use of balanced sources and a neutral writing style, which served organizational purposes (→ Journalism, History of).

The routines of *objectivity* and *bureaucratic structure* help journalists accomplish work in the face of uncertainty (Reich, 2012). Objectivity routines require balanced sources and personal detachment. These practices help news organizations gain wide audiences and avoid criticism, but encourage journalists to ignore non-official voices (→ Bias in the News; Objectivity in Reporting). Bureaucratic routines lead journalists to perceive officials as reliable, authoritative supplies of information, decreasing uncertainty but letting officials shape the media agenda (→ News Sources).

Variability in routines across media systems indicates influence at the social-cultural level. For example, the highly differentiated, mechanized structures of large British and US news organizations constrain individual journalists more than do German news organizations of similar size, which tend toward role redundancy and informal processes (Esser 1998).

Routines can have the *function* of protecting journalists by allowing individuals to assign the consequences of routinized decisions to a system. Shared conventions and routines also help journalists establish agreed-upon criteria for evaluating professional status and for assessing job candidates, although encouraging workplace homogeneity. In recent years, new social media technologies, new workspace arrangements, and more varied niches in news production are creating opportunities for journalists to be more intentional and reflexive in their decision-making.

See also: ▶ BIAS IN THE NEWS ▶ JOURNALISM, HISTORY OF ▶ JOURNALISTS' ROLE PERCEPTION ▶ NEWS ▶ NEWS SOURCES ▶ NEWS STORY ▶ OBJECTIVITY IN REPORTING ▶ ORGANIZATIONAL COMMUNICATION ▶ PHENOMENOLOGY ▶ PROFESSIONALIZATION OF JOURNALISM

REFERENCES AND SUGGESTED READINGS

Esser, F. (1998). Editorial structures and work principles in British and German newsrooms. *European Journal of Communication*, 13, 375–405.

Reich, Z. (2012). Different practices, similar logic: Comparing news reporting across political, financial and territorial beats. *International Journal of Press/Politics*, 17, 76–99.

Shoemaker, P. & Reese, S. (2014). *Mediating the message in the 21st century: A media sociology perspective.* London: Routledge.

News Sources

LAWRENCE SOLEY
Marquette University

Sources are the individuals that reporters interview to obtain information. It is on this information that news stories are based. Because no standard definition exists for what constitutes a source, documents such as accident reports, corporate press releases, and even other news media reports sometimes serve as sources, providing information that becomes part of, or the basis of, news stories (→ News). Sources also originate news. They call reporters, send press releases, or provide documents in an attempt to disseminate their views through the mass media. By originating news stories and providing viewpoints to reporters, sources can have a major influence on the framing of news stories (→ Framing of the News).

Different types of news stories use *different sources*. For so-called *breaking news* on television about accidents, crimes, and disasters, sources may include victims, police, relatives, or bystanders, who give the reporter their understanding of the event. Reporters can also turn to so-called expert sources who provide insights not available on the scene. Reporters on specific beats like government branches or industry develop and maintain relationships with sources of information, who usually have an appointment in the organization ('routine sources'; → News Routines).

Journalists usually *identify most sources* by name and official position in news stories, but not always. Reporters may describe such anonymous sources in news stories as a 'high-ranking official' or a 'senior official.' The Associated Press (AP) wire service Statement of News Values and Principles advocates using anonymous sources only when (1) the information provided by the source is fact rather than an opinion; (2) the information would not be available otherwise; and (3) the source is reliable and has direct access to the information. Anonymous sources provide reporters with information in several ways, including 'off the record' and 'on background.' They are generally unavoidable, but must be used cautiously, because the information they provide would simply not be available if they had to identify themselves. One reason for caution is that they cannot be held publicly accountable for what they say (→ Source Protection).

See also: ▶ FRAMING OF THE NEWS ▶ NEWS ▶ NEWS FACTORS ▶ NEWS ROUTINES ▶ NEWS VALUES ▶ SOURCE PROTECTION

REFERENCES AND SUGGESTED READINGS

Associated Press (2014). AP news values and principles. At http://www.ap.org/company/news-values, accessed August 18, 2014.

Berkowitz, D. & Beach, D. W. (1993). News sources and news context: The effect of routine news, conflict and proximity. *Journalism Quarterly*, 70, 4–12.

Manning, P. (2001). *New and news sources.* Thousand Oaks, CA: Sage.

Zeldes, G. A. & Fico, F. (2005). Race and gender: An analysis of sources and reporters in the networks' coverage of the 2000 presidential campaign. *Mass Communication and Society*, 8, 373–385.

News Story

SIEGFRIED WEISCHENBERG
University of Hamburg

THOMAS BIRKNER
University of Münster

A news story is the standard format that journalists employ for producing the texts they publish in the media. In contrast to feature narratives or subjective reviews and editorials, the news story aims to give a direct, succinct, and fact-based account (→ Objectivity in Reporting), but instead the news story does political work and gives orientation in a complex world. This difference causes problems not only for storytellers but also for research on the news.

One *standard for the news story* is to begin with a summary lead sentence. Another standard is to choose the most important facts of a story. Other information then follows in descending order. Journalists display their analytical competence by answering the 'five Ws' (and one H): Who did What, Where, When, and Why (and How)? The standard of presenting facts in priority order produces a form called the 'inverted pyramid.' Journalists adjust the news story to fit the intended medium. Different narrative structures and forms have emerged in print, broadcast, and interactive media. In a multimedia setting the structure of online news may change (Barnhurst 2012). Specific topics of journalism emphasize different aspects of the news story. Journalists consider the resulting stories neutral and professional.

The news story is one of the main *objects of journalism and communication study*. News stories are central to how news workers interact (→ Group Decision-Making, Functional Theory of), how the gatekeepers work, and how newsrooms function (→ News Routines), among other aspects of journalism practice. News stories are the product of news selection decisions (→ News Factors; Bias in the News) and manifest news judgments (→ News Values).

A key issue for producing news stories is truth (→ Truth and Media Content). The objectivity norm of professional journalism is an ideal to encourage journalists to minimize the gap between news and truth (Schudson 2001). They achieve a symbolic objectivity by following such routines as using neutral expressions, presenting opposing positions and actors, and making quotations from others distinct from their own voice or prose. These markers of objectivity lend authority to their output (Zelizer 1990).

See also: ▶ BIAS IN THE NEWS ▶ GROUP DECISION-MAKING, FUNCTIONAL THEORY OF ▶ JOURNALISM ▶ NEWS FACTORS ▶ NEWS ROUTINES ▶ NEWS VALUES ▶ OBJECTIVITY IN REPORTING ▶ TRUTH AND MEDIA CONTENT

REFERENCES AND SUGGESTED READINGS

Barnhurst, K. G. (2012). The form of online news in the mainstream US press, 2001–2010. *Journalism Studies*, 13, 791–800.
Schudson, M. (2001). The objectivity norm in American journalism. *Journalism*, 2, 149–170.
Zelizer, B. (1990). Achieving journalistic authority through narrative. *Critical Studies in Mass Communication*, 7, 366–376.

News Values

HANS MATHIAS KEPPLINGER
Johannes Gutenberg University of Mainz

The term 'news values' denotes the impact of → news factors on the processing of news stories by journalists. The term 'newsworthiness' means the chances of news stories to get published and the prominence of their presentation.

The term "news value" was introduced by Walter Lippmann in 1922. The theory of news values was developed by Scandinavian researchers Östgaard (1965) and Galtung and Ruge (1965). Major theoretical and methodological contributions were made by Schulz, Rosengren, Staab, Shoemaker, and Kepplinger and Ehmig (for an overview see Kepplinger & Ehmig 2006). Nonrandom selection of news stories is based upon at least two conditions: characteristics of news stories (news factors) and selection criteria of journalists (news values of news factors). Some news factors might be more relevant for some media outlets than for others. Therefore, the same news factor can have different news values for different journalists.

Five *research designs* have been applied. (1) content analyses of media coverage: Correlations between prominence of news (space, time) and news factors can indicate the influence of news factors on news decisions, but news stories not published may have even more news factors than news stories published; (2) comparisons of real-world indicators with news stories: It is possible to control the influence of real-world factors on the selection of news stories (Rosengren 1977; → Extra-Media Data), but because of the lack of sufficient data, this methodological design is usually limited to few topics; (3) experiments: Subjects are asked to rank news stories according to their newsworthiness. The relevance of individual news factors in comparison to combinations of news factors can be calculated, but because of the type and number of subjects the results cannot be generalized; (4) input–output–studies: Comparison of news factors in news stories discarded with those in published news stories provides valid results, but the combination of news factors cannot be manipulated and tested; and (5) tests of predictions: There, the newsworthiness of news stories is calculated using information on news factors and news values. Theory-based predictions are compared with empirical data from rankings of news stories according to their newsworthiness. The design provides a hard test of the theory, but is limited to a small number of news factors and topics (Kepplinger & Ehmig 2006).

After several decades of research, some basic *questions are still open*. Do news factors have different news values in different countries (Shoemaker & Cohen 2006)? Do news values change in the course of time (Wilke 1984) and after spectacular events? Are news values independent of the available input of news stories? Are news values independent of the events covered? What is the relationship between events, news stories, and news factors included in news stories?

See also: ▶ EXTRA-MEDIA DATA ▶ MEDIA PRODUCTION AND CONTENT ▶ NEWS FACTORS ▶ OBJECTIVITY IN REPORTING ▶ REALITY AND MEDIA REALITY

REFERENCES AND SUGGESTED READINGS

Galtung, J. & Ruge, M. H. (1965). The structure of foreign news: The presentation of the Congo, Cuba and Cyprus crises in four Norwegian newspapers. *Journal of Peace Research*, 2, 64–91.
Kepplinger, H. M. & Ehmig, S. (2006). Predicting news decisions: An empirical test of the two-component theory of news selection. *Communications*, 31, 25–43.
Östgaard, E. (1965). Factors influencing the flow of news. *Journal of Peace Research*, 2, 39–63.
Rosengren, K. E. (1977). Four types of tables. *Journal of Communication*, 27, 67–75.
Shoemaker, P. & Cohen, A. A. (2006). *News around the world: Practitioners, content, and the public*. London: Routledge.
Wilke, J. (1984). The changing world of media reality. *Gazette*, 34, 175–190.

Newspaper, History of

MARTIN CONBOY
University of Sheffield

The introduction of printing to Europe around 1440 did not immediately prompt the development of anything resembling a modern newspaper (→ Printing, History of). The Gazetta of Venice was arguably the first newssheet of modern times, providing the merchant and political classes of Venice with eagerly awaited → news of the perceived threat from the Turkish empire. They were handwritten from 1536, but from about 1570 they were making the best use of available printing techniques.

Early Periodical Publications

The Relation, published by Johann Carolus in Strasbourg from 1605, is regarded as the first regular newspaper in print. The first newspapers in other countries emerged shortly thereafter: France (1631), Italy (1643), Sweden (1645), Spain (1641), Poland (1661), and Russia (1703). In the nonwestern world, newspapers began to replace earlier types of bulletins in the nineteenth century, such as in Mexico (1805), Brazil (1808), India (1819), Japan (1870), China (1874), and Egypt (1867).

Relatively liberal political conditions made periodic news production a viable activity in England from 1621. The first publication to be able to break the taboo on reporting the proceedings of Parliament was the Heads of Severall Proceedings in this Present Parliament in 1641. The years of the English Civil War were the laboratory for many of the permutations of early journalism (Frank 1961 → Journalism, History of).

The Formation of a Public Sphere

By the Restoration of 1660 in *England*, there was a return to central and licensed control over newspaper journalism. The Licensing Act lapsed in 1695, not because the ruling political classes felt secure about unrestricted printing, but because it could no longer be administered efficiently. From this point we see the emergence of newspapers as central to what Habermas (1989) has called a → "public sphere." Similar developments enabled the newspaper to become established within political constraints through much of western Europe. In 1777 the Journal de Paris became *France*'s first daily newspaper. In the *German-speaking territories*, the Intelligenzblatt was from the early eighteenth century a regular supplier of a wide range of commercial information, together with news about trials and deaths. In *colonial America*, Boston was the birthplace of newspaper production with Benjamin Harris's Publik Occurrences of 1690, John Campbell's Boston News-Letter of 1704, and the New England Courant of John and Benjamin Franklin of 1721. The freedom of the American press from colonial control became one of the founding principles of the Republican cause (→ Freedom of the Press, Concept of).

Newspapers also played a central role in the French revolution of 1789. By the end of the century, three daily London-based newspapers had begun to draw together the strands of the extended experiment in newspaper journalism into a successful format. The Morning Chronicle, edited by James Perry, the Morning Post, edited by Daniel Stuart, and The Times were all combining credibility, probity, and financial success.

The Defeat of a Radical Press in England

The government's fears of the impact of revolutionary ideas led them to raise the stamp duty twice between 1789 and 1797, but this merely encouraged the radicals to publish illegally and, in doing so, raise their oppositional credibility with their readers. The first phase between 1815 and 1819 included the writings of Cobbett, Carlile, Wade, and Wooler. The second phase of radicalism in the 1830s accompanied the push toward parliamentary reform, but expressed a strand of radical thinking that went beyond a mere shift in suffrage. Hetherington and O'Brien, for instance, ran unstamped newspapers to push for political representation from the perspective of a specifically socialist critique of property, but the reduction of stamp duty from 1836 meant that the radical press was drowned in a torrent of cheap publications aimed at the working classes as a market.

Newspapers and Markets

By the early nineteenth century it was to be in the commercialization of newspaper production that their editorial independence would come. In the US, Benjamin H. Day produced the first successful *penny newspaper*, the New York Sun, from 1833. It was the first to target the ordinary people of the growing metropolis of New York in a language they could identify as their own. The removal of taxes and duties on newspapers between 1836 and 1855 in England shifted the onus of control definitively from political to commercial interests. The first entrant into this new order was the Daily Telegraph in 1855. It brought together elements of the human interest of American popular journalism, public campaigning around issues of concern to its readership, and celebrity interviews.

In the US, the private transmission of news via telegraph assumed considerable importance during the Civil War (1861–1865). This had an impact on journalism in the systematization of its language and the development of the inverted pyramid of the news story. In combination with the advanced system of shorthand introduced in 1840 by Pitman, it meant that there was more of a verifiable base to much reporting of news. Improvements in print quality and better incorporation of visual material, including advertisements, forced newspapers to look increasingly to their visual aspect as consumers of journalism became more attuned to a wider range of aesthetic considerations in the layout and illustration of their papers (→ Newspaper, Visual Design of).

Pulitzer launched his New York 'World' in 1883 and developed an invigorated version of popular journalism that was to be as influential in the US as it was in the rest of the world. Hearst, with his New York 'Journal' from 1895, provided the competition that was to drive American newspapers more in the direction of → sensationalism and scandal. The drive for readers led to the labeling of such newspapers as 'yellow journalism.' Harmsworth and Pearson founded the two most influential newspapers of the early twentieth century in the UK, the Daily Mail (1896) and the Daily Express (1900). They built on the tradition of an intimate form of address to their readers, a popular feature of both radical pamphlets, women's magazines, and Sunday newspapers.

The Intensification of Press Competition

Sensationalism, special offers, campaigns, layout, and aspects of the writing style of the 1930s all became defining features of the popular newspapers of the age. The relaunched Daily Mirror, from 1934 under the editorial direction of Bartholomew, triggered the tabloid revolution with its signature heavy black boldface for headlines, pin-ups, youthful style, simplified language, and prominent use of pictures to reach a new readership.

The most sustained and widespread set of *debates* around contemporary journalism emanate from the tabloid newspaper (→Tabloidization). Elite newspapers have also been enmeshed in the clustering of trends characterized as tabloidization. The late twentieth century saw a narrowing of ownership and the incorporation of newspapers into more broadly defined → media conglomerates that have eroded the boundaries between journalism and media entertainment (→ Infotainment).

Global trends such as online journalism and the rise of freesheets and blogs mean that the format and content as well as the social use of newspapers are in the process of intense renegotiation. Newspapers are now at the hub of an increasingly hybrid operation with specializations ranged around the core of a more general news function. Elite newspapers give a glimpse of a radically altered, more open-ended journalism under the influence of the Internet, with its archival potential and more direct reader intervention via emails and blogs.

See also: ▶ ADVERTISING ▶ COMMERCIALIZATION: IMPACT ON MEDIA CONTENT ▶ FREEDOM OF THE PRESS, CONCEPT OF ▶ INFOTAINMENT ▶ INTERNATIONAL NEWS REPORTING ▶ JOURNALISM, HISTORY OF ▶ MEDIA CONGLOMERATES ▶ NEWS ▶ NEWSPAPER, VISUAL DESIGN OF ▶ PRINTING, HISTORY OF ▶ PUBLIC SPHERE ▶ SENSATIONALISM ▶ TABLOIDIZATION

REFERENCES AND SUGGESTED READINGS

Chapman, J. (2005). *Comparative media history. An introduction: 1789 to the present*. Cambridge: Polity.
Conboy, M. (2004). *Journalism: A critical history*. Thousand Oaks, CA: Sage.
Frank, J. (1961). *The beginnings of the English newspaper*. Cambridge, MA: Harvard University Press.
Habermas, J. (1989). *The structural transformation of the public sphere: An inquiry into a category of bourgeois society* (trans. T. Burger). Cambridge, MA: MIT Press.
Smith, A. (1979). *The newspaper: An international history*. London: Thames and Hudson.
Wilke, J. (1987). Foreign news coverage and international news flow over three centuries. *Gazette*, 39, 147–180.

Newspaper, Visual Design of

ROBERT L. CRAIG
University of St. Thomas

Newspaper design is planning, selecting, organizing, and arranging the typography, photographs, illustrations, and graphics of newspapers. It also refers to the 'look' or 'style' of a newspaper (→ Design; Graphic Design). Stylistic periods are closely related to how publishers, editors, and journalists define journalism (→ Journalism, History of; Journalists' Role Perception). Changing technology profoundly influences newspaper design.

The design of early newspapers followed the conventions of → book design; they were dominated by text type with the newspaper title ('nameplate' or 'flag') set in larger type, centered at the top of the page. Following eighteenth-century calligraphy, newspapers designed decorative flags. Nineteenth-century industrialization was accompanied by increased literacy and mass consumption. Advertising drove design innovation. When ads employed more space, larger, decorative type, and illustrations, newspapers followed. Larger headlines allowed readers to scan pages for stories of interest and established a visual syntax that made scale and page position communicate stories' relative importance (→ Visual Communication).

In the 1820s, popular illustrated news magazines pressured newspapers to become more visual. The invention of photography in 1834 enhanced this pressure. By the end of the nineteenth century, all the features of modern newspaper design – display type, photography, illustration, and graphics – were in place. The new visual tools allowed unscrupulous editors to sensationalize news with giant, emotional headlines and attention-getting, misleading images (→ Tabloidization). New ethics codes criticized such practices, but sensationalist tabloids continue them today (→ Standards of News; Ethics in Journalism).

Early twentieth-century newspaper designs were cluttered. A dozen stories might appear on the front page with rules between columns, above and below headlines, and after stories. The late twentieth century saw more functional design. Legibility and readability studies helped editors make typographical decisions based on how readers scan and read pages. Modular design simplified newspaper layout by packaging headlines, stories, photos, and graphics into rectangles and squares. Increased use of maps and infographics facilitated readers' comprehension by clearly presenting numerical information, processes, and procedures. Color added visual interest and emphasis. Computer programs Quark Xpress, InDesign, and Photoshop ushered in the era of editorial designers and visual journalists.

Twenty-first-century innovation has been driven by the web. Newspapers built companion web sites to make more information available through sidebars, links to other sites, slide shows, and video.

See also: ▶ BOOK ▶ CARICATURE ▶ DESIGN ▶ DIGITAL IMAGERY ▶ ETHICS IN JOURNALISM ▶ GRAPHIC DESIGN ▶ INTERNET NEWS ▶ JOURNALISM, HISTORY OF ▶ JOURNALISTS' ROLE PERCEPTION ▶ NEWS VALUES ▶ NEWSPAPER, HISTORY OF ▶ PHOTOGRAPHY ▶ PHOTOJOURNALISM ▶ PRINTING, HISTORY OF ▶ STANDARDS OF NEWS ▶ TABLOIDIZATION ▶ VISUAL COMMUNICATION

REFERENCES AND SUGGESTED READINGS

Barnhurst, K. G. & Nerone, J. (2001). *The form of news: A history.* New York: Guilford.

Garcia, M. R. (1981). *Contemporary newspaper design: A structural approach.* Englewood Cliffs, NJ: Prentice Hall.

Harrower, T. (2002). *The newspaper designer's handbook.* New York: McGraw-Hill.

Nonverbal Communication and Culture

HAN Z. LI
University of Northern British Columbia

Humans communicate verbally through words and nonverbally via facial expressions and body movements. Nonverbal communication refers to any human behavior, other than words, that serves a communicative purpose (→ Interpersonal Communication). Such behavior can occur voluntarily or involuntarily, either simultaneously with words or alone.

Nonverbal cues serve several *purposes in interpersonal interactions*. They can convey → attitudes (e.g., likes and dislikes), express emotions (e.g., being pleased or displeased), provide information about personality (e.g., being outgoing or reserved), provide a context for exerting influence (e.g., using silence to show disagreement), and complement, repeat, contradict, or substitute verbal messages (e.g., using a smile instead of words to show happiness). When nonverbal cues illustrate what is being said, they are called 'illustrators'; when they regulate the flow of the conversation, they are termed 'regulators'; when they have a direct verbal translation (e.g., 'V' for victory), they are termed 'emblems.'

The main conceptual framework under which nonverbal communication has been studied is *cultural relativism and universalism* (CRU). CRU categorizes nonverbal communicative behaviors according to their meaning and function. For example, the North American 'okay' sign (the thumb and the index fingers form a circle, with the other three fingers in an upright position) means 'money' in Japan, 'zero' in France, 'sex' in Mexico, and 'homosexuality' in Ethiopia. The 'thumbs-up' gesture also means 'okay' in North America and Europe. But in China, it means 'you are the best.' In Japan, it means 'boyfriend,' and in Iran, it is an obscene gesture.

One can distinguish two *communication styles*: high-context and low-context. With high-context communication, the verbal message is indirect and restricted, and the listener is expected to infer the full meaning or intention of the speaker by analyzing the words in the specific context (→ Language and Social Interaction). Low-context communication is characterized by direct and elaborated verbal messages, leaving little room for the audience to conjecture. Research indicates that low-context communication is the predominant communication style in North American and European cultures, whereas high-context communication is frequently used in Asian and African cultures (→ Intercultural and Intergroup Communication).

Although both the east and west employ *silence* as a communication strategy, it is viewed and used differently. For example, silence is viewed positively in Japan. Japanese who use few words are trusted more than Japanese who speak a lot. A related concept is *turn-taking*, which refers to who speaks, how often, and for how long. Euro-Canadians tend to take long, monologic turns, and take a high percentage of turns in topics that they initiate. Japanese, however, tend to take short turns, and distribute them evenly regardless of who has introduced the topic (→ Conversation Analysis; International Communication).

Past research indicates that *eye contact* serves an important communicative function, and that cultural upbringing dictates the way we gaze and mutually gaze (Li 2006). Researchers found that among the Chinese, conversational partners do not usually look directly at each other's eyes. In both *gaze and mutual gaze behaviors,* Chinese/Chinese interlocutors look less frequently and for shorter durations than do Canadian/Canadian interlocutors, thus documenting an evident cultural difference. This finding has practical value in today's multicultural world. Suppose a Canadian professor finds her Chinese student not looking at her when he is spoken to. She may interpret the student as being inattentive or disrespectful. Or imagine a Canadian businessman finding that his Chinese negotiator is not engaging in eye contact. He may infer that the Chinese person is insincere or uninterested. Researchers have also found that Asians, Indians, and Africans relate constant gaze with being superior, disrespectful, threatening, or insulting. Southern Europeans, Arabs, and Latin Americans, on the other hand, interpret lack of gaze as insincere, dishonest, or shy.

Because the *facial expression of emotions* was observed across cultural groups, as well as species, Darwin postulated that they are innate and biological in nature. This theory was supported by later researchers, who identified six emotions across cultural groups: anger, fear, happiness, sadness, surprise, and disgust (Ekman et al. 1973). Although humans are equally capable of the six emotions, whether, when, and how they display them are decided by their cultural upbringing. He concluded that culture is dictating certain rules about what feelings one should reveal to whom and under what circumstances.

See also: ▶ ATTITUDES ▶ COMMUNICATION ACCOMMODATION THEORY ▶ CONVERSATION ANALYSIS ▶ INTERCULTURAL AND INTERGROUP COMMUNICATION ▶ INTERNATIONAL COMMUNICATION ▶ INTERPERSONAL COMMUNICATION ▶ LANGUAGE AND SOCIAL INTERACTION

REFERENCES AND SUGGESTED READINGS

Ekman, P., Friesen, W. V., O'Sullivan, M. et al. (1987). Universal and cultural differences in the judgments of facial expressions of emotion. *Journal of Personality and Social Psychology,* 53, 712–717.

Jackob, N., Roessing, T., & Petersen, T. (2011). The effects of verbal and nonverbal elements in persuasive communication: Findings from two multi-method experiments. *European Journal of Communication Research,* 36(2), 245–271.

Li, H. Z. (2006). Backchannel responses as misleading feedback in intercultural discourse. *Journal of Intercultural Communication Research,* 35, 99–116.

Matsumoto, D., Consolacion, T., Yamada, H. et al. (2002). American–Japanese cultural differences in judgments of emotional expressions of different intensities. *Cognition and Emotion,* 16, 721–747.

Park, H. S. (2009). Culture, positive and negative face threats, and apology intentions. *Journal of Language and Social Psychology,* 28(3), 244–262.

Andersen, P. A. (1999). *Nonverbal communication: Forms and functions.* Mountain View, CA: Mayfield Publishing.

Knapp, M., Hall, J., & Horgan, T. (2014). *Nonverbal communication in human interaction.* Boston, MA: Wadsworth.

Objectivity in Reporting

ROBERT A. HACKETT
Simon Fraser University

The concept of 'objectivity' connotes a set of practices and ideas, such as a stance of neutrality or balance in relation to the people and events being reported. It is a central ethos in journalism, especially in the Anglo American liberal democracies (→ Ethics in Journalism). It is also acquiring global significance as journalists seek new roles and institutional supports within non-western 'transition societies.' What objectivity means in practice, however, and whether it is a desirable and achievable goal are contentious questions (Donsbach & Klett 1993; → Journalists' Role Perception).

Hackett and Zhao (1998) suggest that in North American journalism, objectivity has constituted a discursive "regime" with *five general dimensions*: (1) a normative ideal, including such goals as completeness, detachment, neutrality, and independence; (2) epistemological assumptions about knowledge and reality, rooted in positivism's confidence in the possibility of accurate description but with some concessions to conventionalism (→ Construction of Reality through the News); (3) newsgathering and presentational practices, such as 'documentary reporting' by which journalists transmit only facts that they can observe or that 'credible' sources have confirmed (Bennett 2005, 184; → News Sources); (4) an institutional framework, including journalistic professionalism and media independence from the state; (5) an active ingredient in public → discourse.

As an ideal, objectivity has *emerged in specific contexts*. It is more typical of journalism in the US, and UK than in continental Europe, with its stronger tradition of partisanship in the press (→ Journalism, History of), or in authoritarian regimes. Even where it is most entrenched, the objectivity regime is more characteristic of some news media – the 'quality press,' public service broadcasting, or news reports – than others, e.g., tabloid press (→ Tabloidization), entertainment-oriented television, opinion columns. The timing and causes of objectivity's emergence are much debated. Various drivers have been identified, including technology (→ Photojournalism) the decline of the partisan press as advertisers, news wire services and commercial press owners sought broader readerships; journalists' pursuit of professional status; the nineteenth-century cultural reverence for science and facts; and conversely, the twentieth-century loss of confidence in citizen rationality and news factuality, given wartime propaganda, totalitarianism, and the new public relations industry (Maras 2013, 22–57). Less conventional interpretations see roots in the democratic discourse of America's nineteenth-century labor press, or the emergence of capitalist social relations and modernity's self-reflexive gaze.

The *political implications of objectivity* are also debatable. In the US, conservatives and progressives alike attack news media for failing to achieve objectivity in practice. More fundamental critiques attack objectivity's very premises. For some, its practices lead to overemphasis on official sources and observable events rather than processes or structures, and to the simplification of conflicts as zero-sum games between two artificially 'balanced' sides. Others suggest that objectivity is deceptive, because any communication is value-laden; that it systematically generates ideological accounts complicit with dominant power relations and media commercialism; that it produces blindness towards journalists' framing of stories, and ignores journalism's necessary subjectivity (Maras 2013, 58–81). Objectivity's defenders respond that the critiques are incoherent, wrongly see objective journalism as precluding interpretation, overlook the significance of consensually-validated facts, and/or are based on mistaken metaphysical grounds, including the assumption that the subjectivity of observers' standpoints necessarily entails abandoning truth (Maras 2013, 104–121).

The *current status of objectivity in journalism* is complicated. In the US, objectivity was a characteristic of journalism's mid-twentieth-century 'high modernist' period (→ Modernity), one that has arguably been eclipsed since the 1980s by a 'postmodern' paradigm (→ Postmodernism and Communication) characterized by a multichannel mediascape, profit-oriented conglomerate ownership (→ Media Conglomerates), deregulation, the commodification of the → public sphere, the displacement of 'serious' news by → infotainment, the unfolding impacts of the internet, and an epistemological relativism that rejects the possibility of objectivity (Baym 2010). Others see American journalism's perceived retreat from objectivity as a strategic co-optation of alternative media's advocacy and subjectivity (Kperogi 2013). In its Anglo American heartland, objectivity is eroding, but no single alternative has replaced it.

Meanwhile, objectivity may be gaining a new lease of life in non-western countries experiencing media globalization, and as an alternative to government-constrained journalism.

See also: ▶ CONSTRUCTION OF REALITY THROUGH THE NEWS ▶ ETHICS IN JOURNALISM ▶ INFOTAINMENT ▶ JOURNALISM, HISTORY OF ▶ JOURNALISTS' ROLE PERCEPTION ▶ MEDIA CONGLOMERATES ▶ MODERNITY ▶ NEWS SOURCES ▶ PHOTOJOURNALISM ▶ POSTMODERNISM AND COMMUNICATION ▶ PUBLIC SPHERE ▶ TABLOIDIZATION

REFERENCES AND SUGGESTED READINGS

Bennett, W. L. (2005). *News: The politics of illusion*, 6th edn. Harlow: Pearson.

Donsbach, W. & Klett, B. (1993). Subjective objectivity: How journalists in four countries define a key term of their profession. *Gazette*, 51, 53–83.

Hackett, R. & Zhao, Y. (1998). *Sustaining democracy? Journalism and the politics of objectivity*. Toronto: Garamond.

Kperogi, F. (2013). News with views: Postobjectivism and emergent alternative journalistic practices in America's corporate news media. *Review of Communication* 13(1), 48–65.

Maras, S. (2013). *Objectivity in journalism*. Cambridge: Polity.

Observation

THORSTEN QUANDT
Westfälische Wilhelms-University Münster

Observation is a very 'natural' way of gathering data and information – probably everybody can identify situations where humans are scrutinizing their surroundings. In order to become a scientific technique, an observation study has to follow some rules – most notably, it has to be systematic in both its planning and recording phases. In comparison to the other two central ways of data gathering in communication studies – content analysis and interview – observation plays a smaller role in research nowadays (→ Content Analysis, Qualitative; Content Analysis, Quantitative; Interview, Qualitative; Interview, Standardized).

When trying to differentiate between several types of observations, one can discern *three dimensions for discriminating* these types: (1) level of standardization; (2) involvement of the observer; (3) visibility of the observer. First, the level of standardization refers to the use of strict observation rules, which may be defined in code-books and formal observation guidelines, in contrast to open documentation or diary methods. Second, in many cases, access to the field is only possible if the observer becomes part of the observed reality. Third, active participation of an observer in the field does not necessarily mean that the observed persons are aware of being studied – for example, if the observer is working undercover. On the other hand, a completely passive observer can be very visible, for example sitting next to and observing somebody.

Historical roots of the method can be found in anthropology, sociology, and psychology. In media and communication studies, (field) observation studies were a central research tool right from the beginning of the discipline (→ Ethnography of Communication). Both the behavior of audience members in natural home environments (→ Audience Research) and the work routines of journalists in newsrooms (→ News Routines) were the targets of many observation studies. Just lately, the influence of cultural studies in communication and media studies has led to a growing number of observation studies, mostly based in the 'qualitative' paradigm (→ Qualitative Methodology).

See also: ▶ AUDIENCE RESEARCH ▶ CONTENT ANALYSIS, QUALITATIVE ▶ CONTENT ANALYSIS, QUANTITATIVE ▶ ETHNOGRAPHY OF COMMUNICATION ▶ INTERVIEW, QUALITATIVE ▶ INTERVIEW, STANDARDIZED ▶ MEDIA PRODUCTION AND CONTENT ▶ NEWS ROUTINES ▶ QUALITATIVE METHODOLOGY

REFERENCES AND SUGGESTED READINGS

Berger, A. A. (2000). *Media and communication research methods: An introduction to qualitative and quantitative approaches.* Thousand Oaks, CA: Sage.

Quandt, T. (2006). Methods of journalism research: Observation. In M. Löffelholz & D. Weaver (eds.), *Journalism research in an era of globalization.* Oxford: Blackwell.

Online Journalism

JANE B. SINGER
City University London

Online journalism involves the creation and delivery of news content through a networked, digital medium. Although citizen journalists have emerged as important information providers (→ Citizen Journalism), this entry focuses on the work of practitioners of a more traditionally defined occupation. The Internet and world wide web, along with mobile platforms, are primary vehicles for online journalism.

Online journalism predates the Internet as we know it today. Proprietary digital services, which evolved along with personal computers in the 1980s, included news media partners. However, contemporary forms of online journalism gained traction only in the 1990s, after the development of a graphic interface and a structure for 'hyperlinking' Internet documents allowed easy navigation around a rapidly growing network (→ Digital Media, History of). By the mid-2000s, virtually all news outlets in the developed world had an Internet presence, and most now also enable access through mobile devices such as smart phones and tablets.

Turning a profit online proved challenging, however. The two primary *revenue sources* for commercial media, advertisers and consumers, did not transfer online easily. With millions of free information sources available, users were reluctant to pay for content. And advertisers struggled to adapt placement and pricing strategies to fit a digital environment (→ Advertising). Virtually all online journalism sites through much of the 2000s were subsidized by traditional news organizations as vehicles for extending their brand name and geographic reach. Content produced for the parent outlet often was minimally repurposed for digital delivery. By the mid-2000s, many online journalism websites had turned a financial corner. Although online news continued to account for only a small fraction of revenue, enhanced placement, tracking, and targeting tools bolstered advertising, which generated most of the income (→ Media Economics). In addition, particularly after the recession of the late 2000s, some traditional news providers renewed their attention to user fees as a revenue source, for instance by erecting a 'paywall' that enabled users to see a limited amount of content for free before having to pay for additional access.

In the meantime, thousands of journalists were laid off amid widespread industry belt-tightening. Some of the vacancies subsequently were filled by digitally savvy younger journalists, but concerns remained about the *impact on civically significant journalism*, particularly at the local level. The US launch of nonprofit, online-only start-ups, many of which pursued investigative journalism backed by foundations or other private money, attracted considerable interest, although their long-term sustainability remained uncertain. In addition, growing numbers of news entrepreneurs rushed to fill niche online markets left unserved or underserved by traditional journalism outlets. Online information sources outside the newsroom – news aggregators, bloggers, and social media users, among others – created additional pressures, including competition for consumer attention and advertiser revenue. The open, participatory nature of the network introduced new relationships for journalists to negotiate, as well.

News outlets today offer *news content* through mobile and social media, as well as the Internet. By the early 2010s, online journalists were commonly using → Facebook, → Twitter, and other social platforms to publish news updates, as well as to obtain content from far-flung sources. Many also had adopted a 'digital-first' publishing strategy, taking advantage of the Internet's strength in providing multimedia breaking news. Many of the most widely used online news sites remained affiliates of traditional media organizations, and stories produced for print or television also typically were disseminated online. However, journalists also handled material unique to the Internet, including interactive graphics, user-generated content, and information housed in large databases. By the late 2000s, many organizations had created 'platform-agnostic' newsrooms in which journalists generated content for different types of media (→ Cross-Media Production) throughout the day. Such structural transitions were not necessarily smooth, sometimes clashing with longstanding newsroom culture and journalists' comfort with older technologies.

Also open to new challenges was *journalists' self-perception* as information gatekeepers, including broadly shared views of their professional role as a 'watchdog' of those in power (→ Journalists' Role Perception). There were signs of a shifting conceptualization of professional roles from the practical realm to a normative one – less about the job itself and increasingly about the standards applied in doing that job. Rather than keeping an item out of circulation, online journalists may see their role as vetting material for veracity and illuminating its context.

See also: ▶ ADVERTISING ▶ CITIZEN JOURNALISM ▶ CROSS-MEDIA PRODUCTION ▶ DIGITAL MEDIA, HISTORY OF ▶ FACEBOOK ▶ JOURNALISTS' ROLE PERCEPTION ▶ MEDIA ECONOMICS ▶ SOCIAL MEDIA ▶ TWITTER

REFERENCES AND SUGGESTED READINGS

Allan, S. (2006). *Online news: Journalism and the Internet*. Maidenhead: Open University Press.

Briggs, M. (2010). *Journalism next*. Washington, DC: CQ Press.

Siapera, E. & Veglis, A. (eds.) (2012). *The handbook of global online journalism*. Oxford: Wiley Blackwell.

Online Media

WOLFGANG SCHWEIGER
University of Hohenheim

The term 'online media' refers primarily to technical communication media where digital content is transmitted from any kind of server to distant receivers via the → Internet (TCP [transmission control protocol]/IP [Internet protocol]) or other digital networks, for example, mobile services, and presented on a computer or a comparable terminal device (notebook, PDA [personal digital assistant], mobile phone, or tablet). In contrast, multimedia CDs, DVDs, DVD players, mp3 players, or media applications on standalone computers are referred to as 'offline media,' as content is stored at the place where it is presented. In opposition to broadcasting media, where analog or digital content is broadly transmitted to all receptive devices, in online media a client computer requests specific content from a server that, in turn, directly – that is, from point to point – delivers the content. According to this technical definition, online media facilitate a broad variety of different forms of computer-mediated communication.

Basic Aspects of Communication Structure

The first dimension in the distinction of online media is the *direction of communication and number of communication partners*. Online communication can take place between single persons who are mutually exchanging messages (interpersonal or one-to-one communication, e.g., email, chat, or Internet telephony; → Electronic Mail; Interpersonal Communication); between several persons, often organized within issue-based groups, e.g., in MUDs (multi-user dungeons), discussion, or chat forums (group or many-to-many communication) where some members are actively participating while passive 'lurkers' are only reading the others' contributions; and between a sender and an arbitrary number of recipients (one-to-many, e.g., websites or weblogs).

A second basic aspect is *synchronicity*. Here we have to distinguish between interpersonal and mass media. Some interpersonal media enable synchronous communication between communication partners, which means that each side instantaneously receives the other side's messages and can, in turn, immediately react (e.g., chat, Internet telephony, video conferences). Other interpersonal media offer asynchronous communication: the sender's message is stored and can be received and answered whenever the recipient wants, e.g., email, voice mailbox. Referring to one-to-many or mass communication, there are also two basic variants of synchronicity. 'Asynchronous online media' permit recipients to receive content whenever they wish (e.g., archives of online news media). 'Synchronous online media' are the equivalent of broadcasting by streaming video, music, or spoken word in real time.

Third, online media can contain *different forms of digital content* ranging from text, photographs (→ Photography), drawings, sound clips, videos, and animations (multimedia) to any imaginable information service or software application. Thus, online media can display all kinds of content from the traditional media, and the concept of hyperlinks allows interconnection of any form of content. This has major implications for the debate on technical media convergence and the replacement of traditional media by online media: theoretically, online media can substitute for any existing medium.

Aspects of Exposure and User Interaction

Until around 2000, online media were almost exclusively *used* on computers situated in (home) offices and mainly used for informational purposes, so-called 'laid-forward media.' Computers are increasingly used as entertainment media, so-called 'laid-back media,' and have started to displace television and other entertainment media in living rooms, children's rooms, and bedrooms. Today, most online offerings can be used at any kind of media terminal as long as a sufficiently fast data connection is established and the terminal's input and output facilities (display, loudspeaker, keypad) are adequate. This allows not only home use, but also the development of mobile media services for portable devices like notebooks, mobile phones, game paddles, and tablets.

There are two different concepts of *interactive media* (→Interactivity, Concept of). In a sociological sense, interactive media allow individuals or groups of individuals to communicate with each other, in what is known as computer-mediated interpersonal communication. Social interactivity is the base concept of the so-called Social Web, or Web 2.0. Examples are online marketplaces like eBay, private and professional networking platforms (e.g., → Facebook, LinkedIn), online communities where users can discuss specific issues or rate products, share personal photographs (e.g., Flickr), videos (e.g., YouTube), or bookmarks. Other services offer web-based short-message, voice, or video communication (e.g., Skype) or micro-blogging tools (e.g., → Twitter). In the last few years, social communication on the web has gained significant relevance in terms of user numbers, usage frequency, personal relevance, and, thus, scholarly attention (→ Exposure to the Internet; Communication Networks; Personal Communication by CMC; Social Media).

The other meaning of interactivity refers to *human–computer interaction*. Here, media content is stored on a server (the computer, usually a web server). The user can access the desired content by selecting one option (hyperlink) or an array of options (e.g., a restaurant database searchable by location, nationality of cuisine, price category) or by inserting text in a text field (e.g., → search engines or expert systems). The more *options the medium provides* and the more easily users can control the content (range of options), the faster the medium reacts to users' choices (speed), and the more flexibility users obtain to decide when to retrieve content (time flexibility), the more interactive a medium is. Highly interactive media can detect users' needs and interests without user input or even awareness. Besides control, the number of *senses a medium activates* (visual, aural, tactile, olfactory, gustatory; 'media richness'), the ease of control (usability), and the user's situational feeling of being personally, emotionally, and locally connected to the described content (established concepts are playfulness, connectedness, sense of place, presence, immersion; → Media Equation Theory; Presence) affect the degree of a medium's interactivity.

Content modularization is an indispensable prerequisite of human–computer interactivity. In the traditional media, specific media products are produced and presented as one integral piece of content. In hypertext and interactive media, content is broken into singular modules that users can deliberately select or arrange by clicking on hyperlinks or applying other forms of control. Consequently, there is no fixed order of reception. The degree of modularization depends on two dimensions: the universality and the size of content modules. If modules are universal, they fit different contexts and can be understood even without context.

Automated content configuration permits the permanent *personalization of online media*, i.e., the repeated provision of a package of content that is automatically selected and presented according to users' preferences. There are two basic variants of personalization. The user may select his or her preferred topics, departments, genres, actors, and locations and is presented with the content in the future ('customization').

Personalization in a narrower sense means that the user is automatically presented with tailored content, i.e., without selecting it and sometimes without noticing the automatic adaptation. Mobile services, for example, automatically provide locally relevant information, such as the next restaurant, hotel, or gas station. Amazon is another example: customers are accurately profiled according to their past purchases and viewed products. In future visits, they are presented with new offers and other information fitting their personal profile.

Online Media Content

This entry has referred to online media as 'technical' media. In communication studies, two other perspectives dominate that are dealt with in other entries. First, there is the meaning of *institutional media*, including a complex and emerging configuration of companies or institutions offering media products, trying to reach defined communication goals, applying processes and rules of content production under public control and regulation (→ Internet Law and Regulation; Media Production and Content), and producing media-specific types of content for audiences with specific needs, gratifications, and patterns of media exposure. According to this cultural meaning, we can distinguish different types of online media, for example, news sites, television network sites, corporate or product sites, political campaign sites, thematic communities, or search engines (→ Internet News; E-Democracy).

Another meaning refers to online media as *concrete media offerings* or products (e.g., cnn.com, msnbc.com, ft.com), which are produced by journalistically and/or economically oriented institutions, disseminated, and received with the help of a technical infrastructure and devices. Most online media providers strive to reach mass audiences with products in order to finance their costly production by advertising revenues (Pew Research Journalism Project 2014; → Online Journalism).

See also: ▶ COMMUNICATION NETWORKS
▶ E-DEMOCRACY ▶ ELECTRONIC MAIL
▶ ENTERTAINMENT CONTENT AND REALITY

PERCEPTION ▶ EXPOSURE TO THE INTERNET
▶ FACEBOOK ▶ INTERACTIVITY, CONCEPT OF
▶ INTERNET LAW AND REGULATION ▶ INTERNET
NEWS ▶ INTERPERSONAL COMMUNICATION
▶ JOURNALISM ▶ MEDIA ▶ MEDIA EQUATION
THEORY ▶ MEDIA PRODUCTION AND CONTENT
▶ NEWS ▶ ONLINE JOURNALISM ▶ PERSONAL
COMMUNICATION BY CMC ▶ PHOTOGRAPHY
▶ PRESENCE ▶ SEARCH ENGINES ▶ SOCIAL
MEDIA ▶ TWITTER

REFERENCES AND SUGGESTED READINGS

Aslinger, B. & Huntemann, N. B. (2013). Digital media studies futures. *Media, Culture & Society.* 35(1), 9–12.

Berker, T., Hartmann, M., Punie, Y., & Ward, K. (2005). *Domestication of media and technology.* New York: McGraw-Hill.

Kiousis, S. (2002). Interactivity: A concept explication. *New Media and Society,* 4, 355–383.

Lee, A. Y. L. (2012). Online news media in the Web 2.0 era: From boundary dissolution to journalistic transformation. *Chinese Journal of Communication,* 5(2), 210–226.

Lehman-Wilzig, S. & Cohen-Avigdor, N. (2004). The natural life cycle of new media evolution. *New Media and Society,* 6, 707–730.

Lin, C. A. (2003). Interactive communication technology adoption model. *Communication Theory,* 13, 345–365.

Pew Research Journalism Project (2014). State of the media 2014. At http://www.journalism.org/packages/state-of-the-news-media-2014, accessed August 18, 2014.

Quiring, O. & Schweiger, W. (2008). Interactivity: A review of the concept and a framework for analysis. *Communications – the European Journal of Communication Research,* 33 (2), 147–167.

Online Research

WOLFGANG SCHWEIGER

University of Hohenheim

Online research refers to two different concepts: (1) applying online methods in social research; and (2) social research of online phenomena. Many traditional methods in communication studies have been successfully transferred and adapted to the Internet as a research tool. Some online methods are new developments (e.g., *data mining*).

Quantitative online surveys apply self-administered questionnaires (→ Public Opinion Polling; Survey). Two strategies are used to reach participants: hyperlinks or pop-up windows on websites (including → Facebook and other social networks) and invitations via → electronic mail or other push-channels. Web questionnaires have technical, socio-psychological, and economic *advantages*: All kinds of multimedia can be displayed; participants' answers can be dynamically evaluated; the order of questions and items can be rotated; questions and answers can be filtered and modified in relation to prior answers in real time (→ Interview, Standardized). The interview situation is anonymous; thus, online surveys can deal with sensitive issues and the effect of social desirable answers is minimized. As no personal interviewers are involved, there are almost no interviewer effects (e.g., sympathy/antipathy). Online surveys are cheap: no interviewers are needed, and there are no postal or telephone charges or manual data entry.

Disadvantages of web surveys are mostly related to sampling procedure and sample quality. Online surveys cannot yield representative samples of a country's total population. Even the total population of Internet users is unknown. Hence, no valid random sampling technique is available. If a restricted and known population is under analysis (e.g., visitors to a website, a company's employees), appropriate random sampling techniques permit representative samples (e.g., drawing email addresses from a list, presenting a pop-up questionnaire to every nth visitor to a web page; → Sampling, Random). There is no control of the questionnaire completion situation, i.e., participants can collaborate, look up an encyclopedia, or visit other websites during a test. Finally, response rates of many online surveys are very low.

Qualitative personal or group interviews generally demand personal contact between interviewer and interviewee, which allows the registration of paraverbal or nonverbal signals. Nonetheless, high-quality audio and/or video conferencing techniques can be pragmatic and affordable tools for qualitative interviews (→ Interview, Qualitative). In in-depth interviews, tools like IP telephone, video chat and collaborative software can be helpful.

Experimental settings involving the exposure to stimuli and measurements can also be conducted online. Advantages are: no investigator is needed; participants can use their own computer/device; and they can perform the experiment whenever and wherever they want to. Online experiments often exhibit extraordinarily large samples. Disadvantages are that sample quality may be poor and the researcher has almost no control over participants' execution of the experiment (→ Experiment, Field; Experiment, Laboratory).

Online research provides unobtrusive methods of *observing human behavior* concerning the use of websites: Log-file analyses measure which pages or documents website visitors open at what time and in which order; additionally they deliver a client's device and software data (→ Observation). With the help of cookies and other device IDs, an individual's visits to distinct websites can be recognized and connected to other data sources (e.g., online questionnaires). Applying client-based software, most of a person's online activities on a device can be registered.

The Internet is a worldwide network of computers containing all kinds of mass-media, individual, and group communication – interconnected by hyperlinks, archived, and retrievable by search engines. Accordingly, it can be used for data mining as a source of all kinds of contents, utterances and documents, which can be gathered automatically and unobtrusively (web monitoring, social media metrics). The Internet also enhances literature research and facilitates *collaborative work*.

Some examples might give an impression of the *breadth of the field of online research*. Research on → online journalism and → public relations looks at new forms of interactions between journalism, stakeholder groups, and PR. In advertising research, content and effects analyses of Internet and mobile advertising are of relevance (→ Advertising Effectiveness, Measurement of). Research in → political communication addresses citizens' participation on the Internet, e-government as Internet-based organization of policymaking and administration, and the impact of political actors' and institutions' online communication on public opinion. Research in health communication deals with online campaigns and recipients' use of and trust in online medical information (→ Health Communication and the Internet). Audience research discusses the use, acceptance and diffusion of media devices, platforms, and products (→ Audience Research).

See also: ▶ ADVERTISING EFFECTIVENESS, MEASUREMENT OF ▶ AUDIENCE RESEARCH ▶ ELECTRONIC MAIL ▶ EXPERIMENT, FIELD ▶ EXPERIMENT, LABORATORY ▶ FACEBOOK ▶ HEALTH COMMUNICATION AND THE INTERNET ▶ INTERVIEW, QUALITATIVE ▶ INTERVIEW, STANDARDIZED ▶ OBSERVATION ▶ ONLINE JOURNALISM ▶ POLITICAL COMMUNICATION ▶ PUBLIC OPINION POLLING ▶ PUBLIC RELATIONS ▶ SAMPLING, RANDOM ▶ SOCIAL MEDIA ▶ SURVEY

REFERENCES AND SUGGESTED READINGS

Macnamara, J. (2010). *The 21st century media (r)evolution: Emergent communication practices.* New York: Peter Lang.

Poynter, R. (2010). *The handbook of online and social media research: Tools and techniques for market researchers.* Chichester: John Wiley.

Open Source

EVANGELIA BERDOU
Institute of Development Studies

Open source software (OSS) refers to software that can be freely used and modified. It is developed collaboratively over the Internet by teams of globally distributed and predominantly volunteer programmers (→ Network Organizations through Communication Technology). The OSS movement is a continuation of a long tradition of sharing and cooperation that started in the early days of the Internet. OSS is protected under copyright licenses that aim to ensure the availability and free (re)distribution of the source code, the set of instructions written by developers that make up a program.

The term 'open source' is frequently used alternatively or in conjunction with the term 'free software' (as in FLOSS – Free Libre Open Source Software). FLOSS encompasses a wide variety of projects and institutional frameworks, such as community-initiated and -led projects, initiatives introduced and controlled by corporations, and restrictive copyleft licenses, as well as more permissive, noncopyleft licenses. Copyleft licenses ensure that all the freedoms in modifying, using, and distributing the source code, which are protected under their terms, are preserved in any of its subsequent versions, whereas noncopyleft licenses allow for various exceptions.

OSS has been regarded as emblematic of processes associated with the transformative socio-economic capabilities of the Internet and of information and communication technologies. In particular, FLOSS has been examined as a revolutionary software development methodology, the principal characteristics of which are the granularity and modularity of the source code, which allow individuals to become as involved as they wish depending on their time and level of expertise, and the intensive release schedule, which leverages user feedback to implement new features and to quickly detect and solve program errors. FLOSS has also been viewed as an engine of economic development that provides the means to correct the deficiencies of proprietary software, especially in cases where access and interoperability are of great importance, such as in the case of e-government services. The topic that has drawn most attention is the question of incentives. One line of research assumes the economic rationality of individual motives and is premised on the view of open source communities as composed by atomized actors whose behavior is influenced by the aggregate behavior of others. This work tends to reduce the complexity of the relationship between the gift and exchange economies to a distinction between monetary and nonmonetary rewards.

See also: ▶ CODE AS LAW ▶ COMMUNICATION TECHNOLOGY AND DEVELOPMENT ▶ INFORMATION AND COMMUNICATION TECHNOLOGY, ECONOMICS OF ▶ INFORMATION SOCIETY ▶ NETWORK ORGANIZATIONS THROUGH COMMUNICATION TECHNOLOGY

REFERENCES AND SUGGESTED READINGS

Boyle, J. (2008). *The public domain: Enclosing the commons of the mind.* New Haven, CT: Yale University Press.

Crowston, K. & Howison, J. (2005). The social structure of open source software development. *First Monday,* 10(2). At http://firstmonday.org/ojs/index.php/fm/article/view/1207/1127, accessed August 18, 2014.

Nafus, D. (2012). "Patches don't have gender": What is not open in open source software. *New Media & Society,* 14(4), 669–683.

Operationalization

STEPHANIE LEE SARGENT WEAVER
Northrop Grumman/Centers for Disease Control and Prevention

Operationalization is the process of translating abstract things into concrete, measurable variables (→ Measurement Theory). It is how researchers define things by what they do. In other words, the "operations" are the procedures or steps one must go through in order to observe the concept being defined (Babbie 2013).

The *research process* starts off with a *concept* that a researcher is interested in measuring or observing. A concept is a "mental image that summarizes a set of similar observations, feelings, or ideas" (Schutt 2012) or a "term that expresses an abstract idea formed by generalizing from particulars and summarizing related observations" (Wimmer & Dominick 2014). Concepts are important for two reasons: (1) they simplify the research process by combining characteristics, objects, or people into more general categories; and (2) they simplify communication among those who have a shared understanding of them. However, sometimes there are concepts used in everyday conversation where people do not share the same definition. When this occurs, we need to explicitly define the concept so that all readers will share the same definition. This is what is known as conceptualization or the process of specifying what we mean by a term.

After we define the concepts in a theory, we can then *identify variables* corresponding to the concepts. Let us say that we are interested in measuring differences between males and females on binge drinking. Our concept is 'binge drinking' and we conceptualize it as 'heavy episodic drinking.' Once we have defined it so that all readers will share the same definition, we can decide how we can measure this variable. One way we can measure it is by asking both males and females how many drinks they consumed in succession during some period.

Once we have specified the variable we want to measure, we can proceed, deciding on our *measurement procedures.* The goal is to devise operations that actually measure the concepts we intend to measure (→ Validity). During this process, there will probably be several possible operational definitions for a given concept; the researcher must make a choice which one is most suitable for their research study.

The *operational definition* is a specification of the activities of the researcher in measuring or manipulating a variable. Generally, there are two kinds of operational definitions: (1) measured; and (2) experimental. A measured operational definition describes how a variable will be measured. Is achievement measured by a standardized test, a teacher-made test, or grades? The experimental operational definition, however, spells out the details of the researcher's variable manipulation. These definitions are indispensable ingredients of scientific research because they allow researchers to measure variables and because they are bridges between the theory-hypothesis-construct level and the level of observation.

Most researchers try to create definitions that ensure publicness, replicability, and, if possible, fruitfulness. First, when researchers talk about reality, one wants to know specifically what they mean. One must look for *clear, unambiguous definitions* of terms. Second, to generate factually accurate information, researchers must *check what they say against reality*, and this means they must do something to define what they are talking about. If a researcher is studying 'eating,' they should specify whether drinking liquids and taking vitamin pills fall under the definition. The researcher needs to specify the method to actually observe eating – ask participants how many meals a day they eat or record what they eat. However, the major criterion for the evaluation of any definition is its fruitfulness, which can be the most difficult to assess. To be fruitful, the conceptual definition must *build on current theories and prior research*.

In addition, the *operational definition should coincide with the conceptual definition* in a useful way. Since operational definitions usually do not include exactly what is of interest; several operational definitions that, taken together, encompass the conceptual definition completely are usually needed. This goal should be of particular concern to the researcher and to the reader or user of research. Having more than one operational definition increases the chances that at least one will be useful.

See also: ▶ MEASUREMENT THEORY ▶ OBSERVATION ▶ RELIABILITY ▶ VALIDITY

REFERENCES AND SUGGESTED READINGS

Babbie, E. (2013). *The practice of social research*, 13th edn. Belmont, CA: Wadsworth.

Katzer, J., Cook, K. H., & Crouch, W. W. (1998). *Evaluating information: A guide for users of social science research*, 4th edn. Boston, MA: McGraw-Hill.

Kerlinger, F. N. & Lee, H. B. (1999). *Foundations of behavioral research*, 4th edn. Boston: Wadsworth.

Leedy, P. D. & Ormrod, J. E. (2014). *Practical research: Planning and design*, 10th edn. Harlow: Pearson Education.

Schutt, R. K. (2012). *Investigating the social world: The process and practice of research*, 7th edn. Thousand Oaks, CA: Sage.

Wimmer, R. D. & Dominick, J. R. (2014). *Mass media research: An introduction*, 10th edn. Boston: Wadsworth.

Opinion Leader

GABRIEL WEIMANN
University of Haifa

In the classic book Personal Influence, opinion leadership is defined as "the almost invisible, certainly inconspicuous form of leadership at the person-to-person level of ordinary, intimate, informal, everyday contact" (Katz & Lazarsfeld 1955, 138). Such opinion leaders are individuals regarded as having expertise and knowledge on a particular subject and often provide information and advice to 'followers' (→ Group Communication). After early studies in the 1940s and 1950s laid the groundwork for opinion leadership theory, subsequent studies led to a greater understanding of how opinion leaders disseminate information – from the more simplistic → two-step flow of communication to the more elaborate model, the multi-step flow of communication.

Elihu Katz suggested three *criteria that distinguish leaders from non-leaders*: (1) who one is – the personification of certain values in the figure of the opinion leader; (2) what one knows – the competence or knowledge leaders have; and (3) whom one knows – their strategic location in the social network. A more debatable characterization relied on the use of the mass media, or the two-step flow model.

Several *research methods* have been used. In the positional approach, persons in elected or appointed positions in the community are assumed to be opinion leaders. (1) The reputation approach relies upon the nomination of selected individuals as, for example, the ten most influential persons in a community regarding a certain issue; (2) in the self-designating method individuals are asked to identify themselves as being influential; (3) sociometric methods trace communication patterns among members of a group, which allows for the systematic mapping of member interactions; (4) observing social action within the community involves first identifying a limited number of people assumed to be knowledgeable and then asking them to identify influentials in that group; (5) finally, one can apply a 'strength of personality scale' with items related to self-perceived levels of personal influence.

The Internet, with its constituent parts (e.g. forums, → social media, lists) has blurred the classic distinction between interpersonal and mass communication. More and more people turn to the Internet and its virtual communities to seek advice, information, and guidance. Within these communities *online opinion leaders* have emerged, generating millions of personal recommendations sent to their virtual followers.

See also: ▶ AGENDA-SETTING EFFECTS ▶ GROUP COMMUNICATION ▶ INFORMATION SEEKING ▶ MEDIA EFFECTS, HISTORY OF ▶ ONLINE MEDIA ▶ TWO-STEP FLOW OF COMMUNICATION

REFERENCES AND SUGGESTED READINGS

Campus, D. (2012). Political discussion, opinion leadership and trust. *European Journal of Communication*, 21(1), 46–55.

Habel, P. D. (2012). Following the opinion leaders? The dynamics of influence among media opinion, the public, and politicians. *Political Communication*, 29(3), 257–277.

Katz, E. & Lazarsfeld, P. F. (1955). *Personal influence*. New York: Free Press.

Nisbet, M. C. & Kotcher, J. E. (2009). A two-step flow of influence? Opinion-leader campaigns on climate change. *Science Communication*, 30(3), 328–354.

Weimann, G. (1994). *The influentials: People who influence people*. Albany, NY: SUNY Press.

Rose, P. & Yong Han, K. (2011). Self-monitoring, opinion leadership and opinion seeking: A sociomotivational approach. *Current Psychology*, 30, 203–214.

Organization–Public Relationships

ROBERT L. HEATH
University of Houston

Organization–public relationships (OPR) are conceptualized as being one of many keys to effective organizational → public relations. OPR theory reasons that public relations can help organizations to create contextually relevant relationships that result in positive outcomes for organizations and their publics. Academics and practitioners have worked for at least five decades to define public relations by what it accomplishes, the role it plays in society, and its ability to create and maintain mutually beneficial relationships (MBR). This tradition positions the practice, and research about the practice, as the impact communicative practices can have on the quality of the relationship between each organization and its key publics.

MBRs are often proposed to be the outcome goal of public relations, without much attention to how that end is achieved or what it entails. Some think, thereby leading to substantial criticism, that mutually beneficial relationships are the exclusive outcome of → strategic communication rather than responsible and reflective management decisions. The logic of MBR is that when people believe that organizations operate with their interests in mind, they support rather than oppose those organizations.

Relationship theory is heavily derivative from the → interpersonal communication literature. Thus OPR advocates comb that literature looking for variables that can define and predict strong, positive relationships. Such efforts often feature communication styles more than discursive substance and may, if so limited, work better in an integrated marketing context than in one which is contentious and issue driven.

In 1997, Broom, Casey, and Richey *challenged OPR theorists* and researchers to build on a conceptual model that addresses antecedents, variables that enact relationship quality, and definable outcomes. Such challenges call for researchers to do more than merely identify variables that seem reflective of higher-quality relationships and to connect those variables to antecedent conditions, operational challenges, and measurable outcomes. Huang and Zhang (2013) called for a theoretical model of OPR that is multidimensional and multi-indexed to define the measurement criteria as relationship dimensions, relational features, relational outcomes, and relationship quality indicators. Johansen and Nielsen (2011) advocated a discursive approach to stakeholder relations. They reasoned, using critical theory and discourse analysis, that when organizations show their commitment to corporate social responsibility concerns and take appropriate management responses to their stakeholders, then relationships become more positive.

See also: ▶ DISCOURSE ▶ INTERPERSONAL COMMUNICATION ▶ ISSUE MANAGEMENT ▶ ORGANIZATIONAL COMMUNICATION ▶ PUBLIC AFFAIRS ▶ PUBLIC RELATIONS ▶ RHETORICAL STUDIES ▶ SOCIAL EXCHANGE ▶ STRATEGIC COMMUNICATION

REFERENCES AND SUGGESTED READINGS

Broom, G. M., Casey, S., & Richey, J. (1997). Toward a concept and theory of organization-public relationships. *Journal of Public Relations Research*, 9, 83–98.

Huang, Y-H. C. & Zhang, Y. (2013). Revisiting organization-public relations research: over the past decade: Theoretical concepts, measures, methodologies, and concepts. *Public Relations Review*, 39, 85–87.

Johansen, T. S. & Nielsen, A. E. (2011). Strategic stakeholder dialogues: A discursive perspective on relationship building. *Corporate Communications: An International Journal*, 16, 204–217.

Organizational Change Processes

THEODORE E. ZORN
Massey University

A 'change process' in the context of formal organizations may be defined as a sequence of events by which alteration occurs in the structure and/or functioning of an organization. Scholarly attention is typically devoted to large-scale planned changes, such as restructuring, mergers, or implementation of major new management methods or technologies. The study of change-related communication (CRC) considers how planned changes are adopted and implemented and how change-oriented discourse can infuse organizational interactions and messages (→ Change Management and Communication; Organizational Communication).

Organizational change processes have been of interest to organizational communication scholars from the early days of the discipline's formation. However, organizational change has not until recently been a direct and significant focus of study for organizational communication researchers. For example, handbooks of organizational communication have given only brief mention of organizational change. The 1990s brought a focus on organizational change processes by communication scholars, largely stimulated by the increased emphasis on change in the contemporary workplace (Lewis 2011).

The *social context in which organizations operate* has changed substantially in the past 40 years, and as a result of a number of converging factors, an intensified commitment to organizational change on the part of managers and executives. Among these factors are: the emergence of Asian and other emerging economies as serious competitors to western businesses in high-profile industries, creating a heightened sense of threat; revolutionary new technologies such as personal computers and the Internet that enable rapid processing and transmission of information across boundaries; and the political-economic force of neo-liberalism, which has resulted in free-market principles being applied globally and in new domains of society (→ Globalization of Organizations).

Alongside these changes is the *global dissemination of management ideas*. Thus, waves of popular management models and methods have emerged and faded from prominence, such as quality circles, total quality management (TQM), business process re-engineering (BPR), downsizing, outsourcing, lean manufacturing, e-business, knowledge management, enterprise resource planning, corporate social responsibility, and sustainability. The recommended response to these forces by popular management 'gurus' has been to organize for continuous change – to become a flexible organization that can adapt quickly to changes in the environment.

At least two broad meta-theoretical perspectives on organizational change processes can be identified in the literature. *Managerialist perspectives*, including positivist, post-positivist, realist, normative, and behaviorist approaches, are prominent in both communication and organization studies, with scholars attempting to discern more or less effective means of communicating in the process of change (→ Communication as a Field and Discipline). From this perspective, communication is seen as a tool or instrumental means to achieve organizational change, and change agents are seen to be attempting to align or adapt organizations to an objective reality (e.g., Tucker et al. 2013).

A second group of perspectives, which might be referred to as *constructivist*, includes social constructionist, interpretive, critical, discourse, and postmodern approaches. This group tends to be more concerned with understanding and critiquing organizational change processes; and communication is viewed as the means by which change is constructed by organizational members (e.g., Bisel & Barge 2011). Interpretively oriented approaches tend to describe patterns of communication practices and meaning construction, whereas critically oriented constructivist approaches see communication as the arena in which organizational members struggle for preferred constructions of change-related phenomena.

Organizational change is often depicted in *phase models*. Communication is implicated throughout the phases of change. For example, in early phases, organizational members become aware of the need for or possibility of change and decide to act through communication with those external and internal to the organization. These communication processes have been the focus of substantial study, especially the processes by which popular management ideas are communicated and adopted. The middle phases of change, in which changes are implemented, are the most extensively researched in both the change management and communication literature. Communication processes here include announcing changes, exchanging task-related information needed to enact planned changes, persuading stakeholders to accept and commit to changes, and resisting the changes.

Much research on communication in the change process has been atheoretical, for example, focusing on variables that are related to perceptions of success or resistance. However, recent research has begun to address this dearth, with stakeholder theory, structuration theory, and discourse theory, among others, being used by scholars in researching CRC.

See also: ▶ CHANGE MANAGEMENT AND COMMUNICATION ▶ COMMUNICATION AS A FIELD AND DISCIPLINE ▶ FRAMING EFFECTS ▶ GLOBALIZATION OF ORGANIZATIONS ▶ INSTITUTIONAL THEORY ▶ ORGANIZATIONAL COMMUNICATION ▶ ORGANIZATIONAL COMMUNICATION: CRITICAL APPROACHES ▶ ORGANIZATIONAL CULTURE ▶ PERSUASION ▶ TECHNOLOGY AND COMMUNICATION

REFERENCES AND SUGGESTED READINGS

Bisel, R. S. & Barge, J. K. (2011). Discursive positioning and planned change in organizations. *Human Relations*, 64(2), 257–283.

Lewis, L. K. (2011). *Organizational change: Creating change through strategic communication.* Oxford: Wiley Blackwell.

Tucker, D. A., Yeow, P., & Viki, G. T. (2013). Communicating during organizational change using social accounts: The importance of ideological accounts. *Management Communication Quarterly*, 27(2), 184–209.

Organizational Communication

KATHERINE I. MILLER
Arizona State University

Because investigations of organizational communication involve the intersection of two complex concepts – organization and communication – the discipline involves a number of diverse topical interests. The scholarly intersection of these two concepts considers the processes through which organizations are constituted through communication process and the ways in which that constituted organization influences ongoing discourse.

Most historians of the field place the beginning of the modern discipline in the middle of the twentieth century (→ Speech Communication, History of). Redding and Tompkins (1988) provide a typical recounting of this history in discussing *three overlapping formative phases*. The first, from 1900 and 1950, is the "era of preparation." During this period, concerns revolved around skills-based training that would achieve "effective" communication in organizations. The second phase (1940–1970), the "era of identification and consolidation," was marked by an emphasis on the scientific method. with empirical attention focused on supervisor–subordinate relationships, employee satisfaction, and group decision-making. Redding and Tompkins argue that organizational communication reached the third era ("era of maturity and innovation") in the 1970s. At this point, organizational communication was recognized as an established discipline with large divisions in the ICA (→ International Communication Association [ICA]) and the National Communication Association (NCA) in the US, graduate programs across the globe, and scholarship represented in disciplinary and interdisciplinary outlets, as well as specialized journals such as *Management Communication Quarterly*.

Theoretical and Methodological Approaches

In recent decades, the discipline has been marked by several major intellectual shifts and conceptual debates. Thus, organizational communication is now an eclectic discipline in terms of theory and method. Three important metatheoretical strands are now prevalent in organizational communication. Following Corman and Poole (2000), these strands are labeled 'post-positivist,' 'interpretive,' and 'critical.'

The *post-positivist approach* was dominant as organizational communication reached maturity in the 1970s. The ontological focus was a realist conception of both 'organization' and 'communication' – organizations were seen as 'containers' within which people worked and communication followed prescribed routes and included defined content. Early examples of post-positivist research included topics such as supervisor–subordinate communication, information flow, feedback, communication climate, and communication networks. Post-positivist scholars today consider crucial questions of organizing in the late modern and postmodern world, including communication and decision-making technologies, globalization, nonprofit organizations, and self-organizing systems.

During the 1970s and 1980s, many organizational communication scholars began to reject realist conceptions of organizations and communication and turn away from positivistic epistemological assumptions and scientific research methods.Within organizational communication, the *interpretive turn* (Putnam and Pacanowsky 1983). The intellectual roots of the interpretive turn in organizational communication can be found in movements such as symbolic interactionism, → hermeneutics, → phenomenology, and ethnomethodology. This approach is marked by a social constructionist ontology and epistemologies that emphasize the relationship between the knower and the known and the value of emergent forms of knowledge (→ Qualitative Methodology). Instead of following the 'container' metaphor, interpretive scholars considered the role of communication in processes of organizing and sense-making (Weick 1979); scholars shifted from a mechanistic view to a constitutive view of oganizing and communicating (Putnam & Nicotera 2009).

During the same time period as the interpretive turn, many scholars were also moving toward a *critical approach* in which organizations were viewed as systems of power and control (→ Organizational Communication: Critical Approaches). In organizational communication, critical scholarship can be traced to formative influences including Karl Marx, Frankfurt School critics, Louis Althusser, Antonio Gramsci, Jürgen Habermas, Michel Foucault, and Anthony Giddens. The turn to critical scholarship involved analyzing organizations as 'sites of oppression,' considering the discursive construction of managerial interests, examining how workers are complicit in processes of alienation, and highlighting processes of resistance. Critical organizational communication scholars' concern with praxis has led to the scholarship considering alternative organizational forms, participatory practices, and opportunities for employee dissent.

With the critical turn also came a move to *feminist scholarship* (Ashcraft & Mumby 2004; → Feminist and Gender Studies). This research has roots in both the critical theory and the political activism at the heart of feminism. Feminist scholarship did not gain a foothold in the discipline until the 1990s, though there had been earlier studies of gender and biological sex in organizational communication processes. In recent decades, feminist scholarship has included the public/private divide, feminist ways of organizing, emotionality in the workplace, feminist approaches to conflict, and embodied organizational experience.with the late twentieth century also marked the emergence of *postmodern theorizing* (→ Postmodernism and Communication) that differentiates organizations and communication in the modern epoch (e.g., centralized authority, rationality, standardization) from the postmodern epoch (e.g., lateral relationships, consensus-based control, interactivity, and change; → Cultural Studies).

Contemporary Frames and Research Topics

Putnam et al. (1996) provide a helpful framework that considers the *metaphors of communication and organization*. In the 'conduit metaphor' communication is seen as transmission that occurs within the container of the organization. Research in this tradition considers formal and informal communication flow, adoption of communication technology, and information load.In the 'lens metaphor' approach, communication is a filtering process and the organization is the eye. This metaphor highlights the possibility of distortion and the importance of message reception. The 'linkage metaphor' shifts emphasis to the connections among individuals and organizations including-communication networks, patterns, and structures. The 'performance metaphor' considers organizations as emerging from coordinated actions (processes including storytelling and organizational image). The 'symbol metaphor' sees communication as a process of representation through which the organizational world is made meaningful and includes scholarship in organizational culture and socialization. The 'voice metaphor' considers how organizational voices are expressed or suppressed through processes including ideology, hegemony, democratization, and cultural difference. Finally, 'discourse metaphor' sees communication as a conversation, as collective action, and as dialogue (→ Discourse; Discourse Analysis).

See also: ▶ CULTURAL STUDIES ▶ DISCOURSE ▶ DISCOURSE ANALYSIS ▶ FEMINIST AND GENDER STUDIES ▶ HERMENEUTICS ▶ INTERNATIONAL COMMUNICATION ASSOCIATION [ICA] ▶ ORGANIZATIONAL COMMUNICATION: CRITICAL APPROACHES ▶ PHENOMENOLOGY ▶ POSTMODERNISM AND COMMUNICATION ▶ QUALITATIVE METHODOLOGY ▶ SPEECH COMMUNICATION, HISTORY OF

REFERENCES AND SUGGESTED READINGS

Ashcraft, K. L. & Mumby, D. K. (2004). *Reworking gender: A feminist communicology of organization*. Thousand Oaks, CA: Sage.

Corman, S. R. & Poole, M. S. (2000). Perspectives on organizational communication: Finding common ground. New York: Guilford.

May, S. & Mumby, D. K. (2005). *Engaging organizational communication theory and research: Multiple perspectives*. Thousand Oaks, CA: Sage.

Mumby, D. K. & Stohl, C. (1996). Disciplining organizational communication studies. *Management Communication Quarterly*, 10, 50–72.

Putnam, L. L. & Mumby, D. K. (eds.) (2013). *The Sage handbook of organizational communication*, 3rd edn. Thousand Oaks, CA: Sage.

Putnam, L. L. & Nicotera, A. (eds.) (2009). Building theories of organization: The constitutive role of communication. London: Routledge.

Putnam, L. L. & Pacanowsky, M. E. (eds.) (1983). *Communication in organizations: An interpretive approach*. Beverly Hills, CA: Sage.

Putnam, L. L., Phillips, N., & Chapman, P. (1996). Metaphors of communication and organization. In S. R. Clegg, C. Hardy, & W. R. Nord (eds.), *Handbook of organization studies*. Thousand Oaks, CA: Sage, pp. 375–408.

Redding, W. C. & Tompkins, P. K. (1988). Organizational communication: Past and present tenses. In G. Goldhaber & G. Barnett (eds.), *Handbook of organizational communication*. Norwood, NJ: Ablex, pp. 5–34.

Weick, K. E. (1979). *The social psychology of organizing*, 2nd edn. Reading, MA: Addison-Wesley.

Organizational Communication: Critical Approaches

DENNIS K. MUMBY
University of North Carolina at Chapel Hill

'Critical' studies examine the relationships among communication, power, and resistance in the process of organizing. Traditions in this research include neo-Marxism, → critical theory, postmodernism, and feminism (→ Postmodernism and Communication; Feminist and Gender Studies), each of which views language and → discourse as constituting → meaning and reality. Communication and organization are seen as co-constitutive (Ashcraft et al. 2009), although such co-constitutive processes are not arbitrary, occurring through complex relations of power. Thus, organizing is a fundamentally political process played out in the dynamics of various competing interests. Critical studies also adopt a praxis orientation toward research, assuming possibilities for more democratic organizational forms (Deetz 1992).

Central to critical efforts to address issues of power and resistance have been the *concepts* of 'ideology' and 'hegemony.' Ideology refers to everyday discourses, practices and meanings that constitute the lived reality of social actors. Hegemony refers to the creation of a 'collective will' among classes and interest groups with competing interests. A group or class is hegemonic when it can articulate the interests of other groups and classes with its own. Much critical research conducted in the last 30 years has taken the form of extended 'ideology critique,' focusing on the discursive mechanisms through which organizations construct social realities that produce and reproduce the interests of 'managerialism' (Deetz 1992).

In the last 20 years the *conceptual terrain of critical organization studies* has broadened with the influence of postmodern and feminist research. Postmodern studies explicate the discursive mechanisms through which power and truth are articulated together, examining discourse as a constellation of intertextual practices that construct subject positions in complex ways (→ Text and Intertextuality). Identities are conceived as the decentered, fragmented effect of discourses. Feminist organization studies have taken up Acker's (1990) idea that organizations are "gendered" structures, constituted around meaning- and materially-based systems of difference. This research examines the communicative and political construction of masculine and feminine identities in the process of organizing.

There are several other *important research trends*. One is the *discursive construction of employee identities* (→ Identities and Discourse) in the increasingly insecure work environments of the neo-liberal, post-Fordist economy. Researchers focus both on corporate efforts to regulate employee identity (often through a discourse of enterprise), and employee efforts to articulate accommodative and/or resistant identities in the face of control strategies. Research on *knowledge work and knowledge-intensive organizations* examines the implications of the shift from production-based to 'cognitive' or 'informational' capitalism, in which workers not only produce information and symbolic forms of capital but are also identified as 'no-collar' workers whose subjectivities are tied into alternative, 'bohemian' relationships to work (Ross 2003). The advent of the post-Fordist organization and phenomena such as corporate campuses, telecommuting, flex-time, and so forth, has produced increased critical focus on the ways in which such structural shifts have changed *employees' relationships to work*. Research has drawn increased attention to the impact of these shifts on the construction of subject positions and the ability of social actors to even contemplate identities separate from work (Gregg 2011).

Research on *sexuality, the body, and emotion* reflects increased critical attention to both the gendered and material character of organizing (→ Emotion and Communication in Organizations). In the latter case, this shift perhaps reflects the recognition that, in privileging the discursive/symbolic character of organizing, critical scholars have sometimes overlooked the flesh-and-blood social actors who people organizations. Studies of the body and sexuality focus on how these issues are read through, and coded into, organizational discourses and practices. Finally, there is greater sensitivity to the *control– resistance* dialectic in everyday organizing (Mumby 2005). It represents a greater recognition that critical research is less about identifying and critiquing specific control (or resistance) practices, and more about explicating the – gendered, classed, raced, etc. – dialectical struggle between multiple interest groups over organizational meaning and identity.

See also: ▶ CRITICAL THEORY ▶ DISCOURSE ▶ EMOTION AND COMMUNICATION IN ORGANIZATIONS ▶ FEMINIST AND GENDER STUDIES ▶ GENDER AND DISCOURSE ▶ IDENTITIES AND DISCOURSE ▶ ORGANIZATIONAL COMMUNICATION ▶ ORGANIZATIONAL COMMUNICATION: POSTMODERN APPROACHES ▶ ORGANIZATIONAL CULTURE ▶ POSTMODERNISM AND COMMUNICATION ▶ TEXT AND INTERTEXTUALITY

REFERENCES AND SUGGESTED READINGS

Acker, J. (1990). Hierarchies, jobs, bodies: A theory of gendered organizations. *Gender and Society*, 4, 139–158.

Ashcraft, K. L., Kuhn, T., & Cooren, F. (2009). Constitutional amendments: "Materializing" organizational communication. *Academy of Management Annals*, 3, 1–64.

Deetz, S. (1992). *Democracy in an age of corporate colonization: Developments in communication and the politics of everyday life*. Albany, NY: SUNY Press.

Gregg, M. (2011). *Work's intimacy*. Cambridge: Polity.

Mumby, D. K. (2005). Theorizing resistance in organization studies: A dialectical approach. *Management Communication Quarterly*, 19, 1–26.

Ross, A. (2003). *No-collar: The humane workplace and its hidden costs*. New York: Basic Books.

Organizational Communication, Postmodern Approaches

SHIV GANESH
Massey University

Postmodern approaches to → organizational communication are diverse forms of inquiry that challenge and reconstruct systems of power, identity, and representation Since the 1980s, postmodern approaches, situated with reference to a larger critical tradition, have burgeoned in organizational communication studies. Scholars working in this tradition sometimes eschew the label 'postmodern' and its attendant baggage, adopting other terms such as 'dialogic' or 'discursive' (→ Discourse).

As in most disciplines that are engaged in investigations of 'the social,' postmodern and critical approaches to organizational communication have wrestled with the *central problematic of modernity*. While both approaches theorize issues of domination, control, and resistance, a crucial difference lies in their respective critiques of modernity. While critical approaches tend to offer an internal critique of modernity, endorsing some central enlightenment ideals such as emancipation, transformation, or progress, postmodern thought tends to take an external critique of modernity, sometimes rejecting it wholesale. Yet, the relationship between postmodern thought and modernity is complex. While some variants affirm the possibility of resistance to modernity, albeit fragmented and partial, others eschew that possibility altogether. However, all postmodern scholars tend to examine postmodern organizational phenomena that arise from modernity itself. These include the replacement of structure with flux, the increasing fragmentation of labor, the emergence of bewildering arrays of difference and identity, the dominance of information and postcolonial economies, and so forth.

Five *tenets of postmodern thought* tend to prevail in organizational communication studies. (1) Drawing from Foucault, scholars consider power in terms of diffuse and disciplinary networks, operating normatively and unobtrusively. (2) Embodied individual identities are seen as fragmented. (3) Issues of representation are examined discursively: reality, for postmodern approaches, is a suspect category, never fully represented in discourse. (4) Postmodern thought attempts to move beyond the examinations of distinct economic, social, political, or cultural foundations for explaining or understanding organizational life. (5) Postmodern scholars theorize issues of resistance to disciplinary practices. These five tenets have shaped work on diverse subjects, including concertive control, identity, resistance, technology, globalization, gender, and sexuality. In recent years, organizational communication scholarship has become concerned with issues of voice and otherness, emphasizing the study of difference. This is especially true of feminist work in organizational communication and also of an emerging body of work on postcolonial theories of organizational communication.

See also: ▶ CRITICAL THEORY
▶ DISCOURSE ▶ ORGANIZATIONAL COMMUNICATION ▶ ORGANIZATIONAL COMMUNICATION: CRITICAL APPROACHES

REFERENCES AND SUGGESTED READINGS

Cheney, G., Zorn, T., Christensen, L., & Ganesh, S. (2003). *Organizational communication in an age of globalization: Issues, reflections, practices.* Prospect Heights, IL: Waveland Press.

Fairhurst, G. & Putnam, L. (2004). Organizations as discursive constructions. *Communication Theory*, 14(1), 5–26.

Ganesh, S., Zoller, H. M., & Cheney, G. (2005). Transforming resistance, broadening our boundaries: Critical organizational communication studies meets globalization from below. *Communication Monographs*, 72(2), 169–191.

Organizational Conflict

LINDA L. PUTNAM
University of California, Santa Barbara

Conflict refers to incompatibilities or diametrically opposed goals and values that occur in organizations. It includes disagreements about ideas, negotiations to obtain scarce resources, informal complaints about work issues, objections to corporate policies, and formal grievances filed against an organization (→ Organizational Communication).

Organizational *conflict develops* through social interactions between two or more people who adjust to each other's language use and interpretations of messages. As conflict develops, it moves in either a constructive or a destructive direction. Constructive approaches to conflict management promote change and enable adaptability while destructive ones become inflexible over time and lead to uncontrolled escalation.

To study conflict, scholars adopt *different perspectives*. When communication surfaces as *a variable,* researchers treat it as a kind of media, a strategy or tactic, or a conflict style. As a process, scholars focus on participants' interactions that unfold over time. Treating communication as → meaning highlights the language that participants use, the stories that they tell, and the ways that they make sense of situations. Finally, a dialectical perspective focuses on the tensions that arise through the simultaneous connection of opposites, such as cooperating and competing or withholding and sharing information.

These perspectives for studying communication and organizational conflict surface in *five areas of research*. First, the area of *conflict styles* refers to a person's predisposition or dominant way of managing a dispute. Researchers have identified five common styles used to manage conflict: (1) problem-solving, (2) competing, (3) smoothing over the situation, (4) avoiding, and (5) compromising. Research suggests that individuals who develop a repertoire of approaches are typically more effective at managing organizational conflicts than are those who rely on only one or two styles. If both parties regard their relationship and their respective goals as important, disputants should use problem-solving or compromise. However, if organizational members need to reach a decision quickly or if only one party's goals are critical, competing, smoothing over, or avoiding are appropriate styles.

The second research area, *communication media,* refers to telephones, memos, computers, or face-to-face interactions that individuals use to manage conflicts. Research reveals that disputants are more likely to cooperate when conflicts are managed through face-to-face interactions than when individuals use telephones, computers, or written messages. However, if parties know each other well, interact regularly, or use multiple media to manage a conflict, cooperative approaches are more likely to occur.

Thirdly, *negotiation* is a form of conflict management in which parties exchange offers and counteroffers in search of a settlement. Research in this area focuses on what bargainers say and how they respond to each other while searching for mutually satisfactory agreements (→ Negotiation and Bargaining). These studies reveal that negotiators typically reciprocate both cooperative and competitive tactics; that is, they match each other's tactics, such as arguments, threats, and demands, and they reciprocate offers and trade problem-solving tactics.

Work/life conflict, also known as incompatibilities between work/family or home/work, is the fourth research area and refers to the tensions that occur from attending to both domains. Organizations often compete with family and personal life for their employees' time and energy. Research reveals that effective management of work/life conflict occurs through having supervisors who are supportive of both domains, enacting and administering fair work/family policies, developing an organizational culture that fosters flexibility, and having co-workers who value personal lives as well as organizational agendas.

Finally, *dispute systems* are formal and informal norms and procedures for preventing, managing, and resolving conflicts. These systems provide steps for processing conflicts, ways to appeal decisions, and procedures for managing conflict in daily organizational routines. Such steps include hiring a neutral facilitator to lead discussions, voting on issues, assigning employees to serve as neutral third parties, or arranging for a mock trial with a jury of peers. Research reveals that the most effective dispute systems are responsive, encourage employees to address conflicts at the lowest organizational level, and develop an organizational culture that supports dissent. Thus, employees feel able to voice complaints without fear of retaliation.

See also: ▶ INTERCULTURAL CONFLICT STYLES AND FACEWORK ▶ INTERGROUP CONTACT AND COMMUNICATION ▶ LANGUAGE AND SOCIAL INTERACTION ▶ MEANING ▶ NEGOTIATION AND BARGAINING ▶ ORGANIZATIONAL COMMUNICATION ▶ RELATIONAL DIALECTICS

SUGGESTED READINGS

Folger, J. P., Poole, M. S., & Stutman, R. K. (2005). *Working through conflict: Strategies for relationships, groups, and organizations*, 5th edn. Boston, MA: Pearson.

Kirby, E. L., Wieland, S. M., & McBride, M. C. (2006). Work/life conflict. In J. G. Lipsky, D. B., & Seeber, R. L. Managing organizational conflicts. In J. G. Oetzel & S. Ting-Toomey (eds.), *The Sage handbook of conflict communication: Integrating theory, research, and practice*. Thousand Oaks, CA: Sage, pp. 359–390.

Oetzel, J. G. & S. Ting-Toomey (eds.) (2006). *The Sage handbook of conflict communication: Integrating theory, research, and practice*. Thousand Oaks, CA: Sage.

Putnam, L. L. (2006). Definitions and approaches to conflict and communication. In J. G. Oetzel & S. Ting-Toomey (eds.), *The Sage handbook of conflict communication: Integrating theory, research, and practice*. Thousand Oaks, CA: Sage, pp. 1–32.

Wilson, S. R., Paulson, G. D., & Putnam, L. L. (2001). Negotiating. In W. P. Robinson & H. Giles (eds.), *Handbook of language and social psychology*, 2nd edn. New York: John Wiley, pp. 303–315.

Organizational Culture

JOANN KEYTON
North Carolina State University

Organizational culture is the "set(s) of artifacts, values, and assumptions that emerge from the interactions of organizational members" (Keyton 2011, 1). These interactions create a social order or a communication construction of the organization. Thus, symbols, messages, and meaning create a continuous communication performance at work (→ Culture: Definitions and Concepts; Meaning). This is why it is frequently stated that an organization is culture rather than an organization has a culture (Smircich 1983). Communication scholars have demonstrated that multiple shared patterns of organizational artifacts, values, and assumptions exist and are constantly being created and re-created through member interactions (→ Organizational Communication).

Artifacts are visible or tangible in themselves or in their manifestations, such as norms about politeness or dress, organizational customs such as new employee orientation, or physical representations such as organizational logos. Artifacts are easy to observe, but can be difficult to decipher. Because an analysis of an organization's artifacts is only partial, a valid interpretation of an organization's culture cannot be constructed from artifacts alone (Schein 1992).

Values shared by organizational members and manifested in their behavior are also a component of organizational culture. Values are strategies, goals, principles, or qualities that are considered ideal or desirable, and, as a result, create guidelines for organizational behavior. Values that are shared inevitably become transformed into assumptions, taken-for-granted beliefs that are so deeply entrenched that organizational members no longer discuss them. Organizational members seldom talk directly about artifacts, values, and assumptions. Rather, organizational culture emerges from the complex interplay of these elements in the organizational communication of all members, all at levels, in all job functions. As a result, culture is nearly impossible to see in its totality.

Characteristics of Organizational Culture

Using a communicative perspective, organizational culture has five important characteristics (Keyton 2011). First, organizational culture is inextricably linked to organizational members, who participate in the organization symbolically and socially construct and sustain the culture. Second, organizational culture is dynamic, not static. Third, organizational culture consists of competing assumptions and values, as organizational members create sub-cultures. Fourth, organizational culture is emotionally charged. Finally, organizational members make sense of their current interactions on the basis of their understanding of the existing culture.

Viewing organizations through a cultural lens reveals the rich symbolism that exists in all aspects of organizational life. A cultural lens also shifts the focus from managers, leaders, and executives to all organizational members. Through a cultural perspective, researchers can explore an organization's way of life, how that reality is created and interpreted by various organizational stakeholders, and the influence of those interpretations on organizational activities. Communication scholars have contributed to the growth and development of the study of organizational culture in five ways (Eisenberg & Riley 2001).

A communication perspective has (1) demonstrated the symbolic nature of day-to-day conversations and routine practices; (2) emphasized the way in which both interpretation and action exist within communication practice; (3) recognized how societal patterns and norms facilitate or constrain the practices of individuals within an organizational culture; (4) acknowledged a variety of researcher–organization relationships; and (5) acknowledged many motives as legitimate for the study of organizational culture. These contributions have helped to move the broader study of organizational communication from a rational and objective perspective to one that produces deep, rich, and realistic understandings of organizations and the experiences of people within them.

Relationships of Sub-Cultures to Culture

A consensus view of organizational culture is based on the congruence of assumptions, values, and artifacts jointly held or shared by organizational members. The more unity there is among members, the more consensual the view of organizational culture. Often referred to as integration, mutually consistent interpretations are abundant and so deeply held that little variation occurs.

An alternate view is that organizations comprise subcultures that are distinguished by clear and systematic differences. This type of segmentation, known as differentiation, reveals oppositional thinking. Within each sub-culture, there is consistency and clarity that makes it distinct from others. In contrast, fragmentation of organizational culture occurs when ambiguity is prevalent. Here, organizational members are part of shifting coalitions, forming and re-forming on the basis of shared identities, issues, and circumstances. Fragmentation tensions are often described as ironies, paradoxes, or contradictions, as employees may belong to sub-cultures that are in agreement on some issues and simultaneously belong to other sub-cultures that are not. The broadest view of cultural consensus and division is that integration, differentiation, and fragmentation coexist. One perspective is not more correct than another, as each offers an incomplete view of an organization's culture, and all three are needed to offer a multifocal view.

Approaches for Organizational Culture Research

Communication scholars have taken several approaches to the study of organizational culture. The symbolic performance perspective examines the way in which a set of artifacts, values, and assumptions reveals cultural meaning as well as how the performance itself is developed, maintained, and changed. Organizational performances have four characteristics (Pacanowsky & O'Donnell-Trujillo 1982). They are (1) interactive and contextual, situated within a larger set of organizational events; (2) episodic with a beginning and ending; and (3) improvisational. While an organization's culture can provide some structure for a performance, a performance is never fully scripted.

A second approach sees organizational culture as a narrative reproduction. A narrative is a story, and a common way for people to make sense of their organizational experiences (→ Storytelling and Narration). The telling and retelling of a narrative reproduces the culture and provides insight culture values. Stories also reveal logics or rationales for understanding the complexity of organizational life, and create bonds that hold organizational members together. Most important, stories are never neutral, and often represent the interests of dominant groups.

A third approach conceptualizes organizational culture as textual reproduction. Written texts, such as formal communication (e.g., newsletters, mission statements, procedures) provide a fixed view of organizational culture (→ Text and Intertextuality). Textual reproductions of organizational culture are especially useful for exploring espoused (revealed through formal texts) versus enacted elements of culture (revealed through informal texts).

In a fourth view, power and politics are manifested in many ways in organizations. Power can exist in an organizational member's ability or others' perceptions of that ability; in interactions among organizational members; from the design of the organization (most commonly based on a job title or job function); or as racism, sexism, and classism. This critical perspective views the communication of an organization as an index of its ideology.

See also: ▶ CULTURE: DEFINITIONS AND CONCEPTS ▶ ETHNOGRAPHY OF COMMUNICATION ▶ MEANING ▶ ORGANIZATIONAL CHANGE PROCESSES ▶ ORGANIZATIONAL COMMUNICATION ▶ ORGANIZATIONAL COMMUNICATION: CRITICAL APPROACHES ▶ STORYTELLING AND NARRATION ▶ TEXT AND INTERTEXTUALITY

REFERENCES AND SUGGESTED READINGS

Deetz, S. A. (1988). Cultural studies: Studying meaning and action in organizations. In J. A. Anderson (ed.), *Communication yearbook 11*. Newbury Park, CA: Sage, pp. 335–345.

Eisenberg, E. M. & Riley, P. (2001). Organizational culture. In F. M. Jablin & L. L. Putnam (eds.), *The new handbook of organizational communication: Advances in theory, research, and methods*. Thousand Oaks, CA: Sage, pp. 291–322.

Keyton, J. (2011). *Communication and organizational culture*, 2nd edn. Thousand Oaks, CA: Sage.

Martin, J. (2002). *Organizational culture: Mapping the terrain*. Thousand Oaks, CA: Sage.

Pacanowsky, M. E. & O'Donnell-Trujillo, N. (1982). Communication and organizational cultures. *Western Journal of Speech Communication*, 46, 115–130.

Schein, E. H. (1992). *Organizational culture and leadership*, 2nd edn. San Francisco, CA: Jossey-Bass.

Smircich, L. (1983). Concepts of culture and organizational analysis. *Administrative Science Quarterly*, 28, 339–358.

Taylor, B. C., Irvin, L. R., & Wieland, S. M. (2006). Checking the map: Critiquing Joanne Martins' metatheory of organizational culture and its uses in communication research. *Communication Theory*, 16, 304–332.

Organizational Image

CRAIG E. CARROLL

New York University

Organizational image is a useful concept for encapsulating the likeness of an organization. There are *six general types of organizational images*: The image as 'impression' conveys affect, sentiment, or status, such as when it is said that an organization has a positive or negative image. In a more cynical view, image is a 'façade' or a public face that contrasts with reality. The 'projected image' refers to the image emitted by the organization. The 'perceived image' emphasizes one's general impressions or perceptions. It includes the organization's public image, perceived organizational identity, construed external image, and corporate reputation. The 'refracted image' comes from information intermediaries, such as the news media, who add their own interpretations. They gain an air of objectivity (→ Objectivity in Reporting) because they are widely distributed, publicly available, and seen as authoritative. The 'defining image' refers to root metaphors used as heuristic devices to capture the general nature, definition, or worldviews of organizations.

These viewpoints can be combined to help organizations and their stakeholders engage in dialogue about the degree of accuracy, agreement, and perceived agreement between them to see where policy changes may need to occur. A tool for engaging in this process is the *Organizational Image, Identity, and Issues Audit* (Carroll 2012). Organizational images have been methodologically assessed in a variety of ways, including participant → observation, in-depth interviews, focus groups, Q methodology, and content analysis (→ Content Analysis, Qualitative; Content Analysis, Quantitative). No standardized questionnaires for assessing organizational images exist (→ Interview, Standardized).

See also: ▶ CONTENT ANALYSIS, QUALITATIVE ▶ CONTENT ANALYSIS, QUANTITATIVE ▶ INTERVIEW, STANDARDIZED ▶ PUBLIC RELATIONS ▶ OBJECTIVITY IN REPORTING ▶ OBSERVATION ▶ STRATEGIC COMMUNICATION

REFERENCES AND SUGGESTED READINGS

Carroll, C. E. (2012). The OTRI-I Audit and the detection and expression of hidden and blind organizational identities: Implications for managing reputational intelligence, authenticity and alignment. *Corporate Reputation Review*, 15(3), 179–197, doi: 10.1057/crr.2012.11.

Harris, L. & Cronen, V. E. (1979). A rules-based model for the analysis and evaluation of organizational communication. *Communication Quarterly*, 27(1), 12–28, doi: 10.1080/01463377909369320.

Treadwell, D. F. & Harrison, T. M. (1994). Conceptualizing and assessing organizational image: Model images, commitment and communication. *Communication Monographs*, (61)(1), 63–85.

Organizations, Cultural Diversity in

MARY M. MEARES
University of Alabama

Cultural diversity is the presence of members with different systems of understanding based on cultural or group affiliation (Cox 1993) – an increasingly salient issue for organizations due to greater geographic mobility among potential members and decreases in barriers to participation in many countries (→ Globalization of Organizations). Cultural diversity includes gender, age, race, ethnicity, socio-economic status, sexual orientation, religion, educational background, or other identity groups (→ Culture: Definitions and Concepts).

Although demographic differences often reflect differences in experiences and patterns of behavior, it is the differences in worldview, values, and ways of understanding that often prove challenging in interacting and understanding diversity in organizations. Cultural diversity leads to both increased potential for conflict *and* the potential for greater creativity and productivity (→ Intercultural Conflict Styles and Facework; Organizational Conflict).

Research on cultural diversity in organizations has been approached from a variety of *meta-theoretical perspectives*. From a *functional perspective*, researchers (e.g., Hofstede & Hofstede 2005) have examined cultural-level factors that influence organizational behavior and affective outcomes (e.g., satisfaction), focusing on the influence of national culture and other easily measured factors (sex, ethnicity, age, etc.). These studies aim to predict behavior, but may essentialize cultural identity, minimizing the influence of multiple cultures and individual differences. *Interpretive* research on cultural diversity in organizations has examined organizations via ethnographic case studies (e.g., Ely & Thomas 2001; → Ethnography of Communication) and in-depth interviews (→ Interview, Qualitative), for example, asking minorities in organizations about their experiences and perceptions. While they examine members' lives more complexly, they rarely suggest ways to improve cultural relations beyond increasing understanding. Research that takes a *critical approach* examines issues of dominant cultural power and privilege in organizations (→ Organizational Communication: Critical Approaches). The critical goal is to critique organizations as sites of power and control. While critical research highlights the changes that are necessary for equality of members, critics note that opportunities for radical change are rarely accessible to organizational members.

Methodological concerns in studying cultural diversity in organizations center on the complexity of cultural identity and identity development, as well as power issues in the research process. Cultural influences are difficult to conceptualize and measure, as much of culture is based on tacit understanding that may be difficult to articulate. Different aspects of identity are salient depending on the organizational context, and personality and life experiences may influence the individual's level of cultural self-awareness. Dominant culture members and those assimilated into the dominant culture may not consider culture to be important, but those who are exploring their nondominant identity and resisting assimilation may be more cognizant of their own cultural group's norms and expectations. Cultures are also in constant change, increasing the complexity of cultural dynamics.

New and continuing directions for research on cultural diversity in organizations includes studying diversity 'competence' at multiple organizational levels, dimensions of culture that have been overlooked or underexamined (e.g., religion, age, language), evolving contexts (e.g., virtual groups), and organizational processes from the perspective of nondominant cultural groups (e.g., emotional labor, leadership, change).

See also: ▶ CULTURE: DEFINITIONS AND CONCEPTS ▶ ETHNOGRAPHY OF COMMUNICATION ▶ GLOBALIZATION OF ORGANIZATIONS ▶ INTERCULTURAL CONFLICT STYLES AND FACEWORK ▶ INTERCULTURAL AND INTERGROUP COMMUNICATION ▶ INTERVIEW, QUALITATIVE ▶ ORGANIZATIONAL COMMUNICATION: CRITICAL APPROACHES ▶ ORGANIZATIONAL CONFLICT

REFERENCES AND SUGGESTED READINGS

Cox, T. H. (1993). *Cultural diversity in organizations: Theory, research, and practice*. San Francisco, CA: Berrett-Koehler.

Ely, R. J. & Thomas, D. A. (2001). Cultural diversity at work: The effects of diversity perspectives on work group processes and outcomes. *Administrative Science Quarterly*, 46(2), 229–273.

Hofstede, G. & Hofstede, G. J. (2005). *Cultures and organizations: Software of the mind*, 2nd edn. New York: McGraw-Hill.

Mor Barak, M. E. (2011). *Managing diversity: Toward a globally inclusive workplace*, 2nd edn. Thousand Oaks, CA: Sage.

Munshi, D. (2005). Through the subject's eye: Situating the other in discourses of diversity. In G. Cheney & G. A. Barnett (eds.), *International and multicultural organizational communication*. Cresskill, NJ: Hampton Press, pp. 45–70.

Oetzel, J. G., Burtis, T., Chew, M. I., & Perez, F. G. (2001). Investigating the role of communication in culturally diverse work groups: A review and synthesis. In W. Gudykunst (ed.), *Communication yearbook 25*. Mahwah, NJ: Lawrence Erlbaum, pp. 237–269.

P

Parasocial Interactions and Relationships

HOLGER SCHRAMM
University of Würzburg

The term 'parasocial interaction' (PSI) was first used by Horton and Wohl (1956) to describe viewers' responses to media characters (called 'personae' in PSI research; singular: 'persona') during media consumption. The authors considered the illusion of interaction and interactivity between media users and personae as one of the most central attributes of mass media consumption.

Television as an audiovisual medium ought to be especially able to constitute an illusion of face-to-face interaction (Hartmann & Goldhoorn 2011). Nevertheless, this mediated form of communication and social interaction is one-sided because the persona's action can reach the media user, while the media user's reaction cannot reach the persona. A notable characteristic of PSI is that in spite of the missing feedback, channel viewers often feel addressed by the personae.

Referring to this, PSI research has shown that the same *key impulses* that play an important role in social interactions are relevant for the constitution of PSI. Key impulses are, for example, the mediated spatial distance between the personae and the viewers (obtrusiveness), the duration of exposure to these personae (persistence), the personae's attractiveness, and especially their nonverbal and verbal addressing performance. By responding to these addressing cues, media users give up their passive roles of being observers and become 'actors.' This activity manifests itself in different cognitive, emotional, and/or behavioral processes, like rising interest, intensive thoughts and deliberations, tense body movements, agile facial expressions and gestures, and/or speaking to the TV screen.

Most research conducted since the early 1990s argues for a clear *distinction between PSI and parasocial relationships* (PSR). PSI, in this sense, specifically means the one-sided process of perception of the media person during media exposure. In contrast, PSR stands for a cross-situational relationship that a viewer or user holds with a media person, which includes specific cognitive and affective components. While PSI is restricted to the duration of media exposure, PSR can endure beyond the single exposure sequence – like a friendship that exists between two persons beyond their face-to-face communication sequences. As a consequence, a first PSI sequence between a viewer and a persona is able to constitute a PSR after media exposure, while this PSR in turn is able to influence future motivations and selection processes as well as PSI processes in subsequent media exposure sequences.

PSI and PSR have been investigated in relation to *diverse personae* such as politicians, news anchormen, soap opera and film characters, TV talk show characters (→ Broadcast Talk), comedians, radio hosts, virtual avatars in computer games (→ Video Games) or on the Internet, comic figures, and characters in audio stories.

In spite of the heterogeneity in the evolution of PSI and PSR research and the focus on positively evaluated PSI/PSR, the existing empirical findings provide some fundamental insight into the phenomenon (Klimmt et al. 2006). The main problem with these findings is the nonstandardized measurement used across the studies (→ Measurement Theory). Most PSI/PSR research is based on the *parasocial-interaction scale* (Rubin et al. 1985) or variations and adaptations of that scale. Schramm and Hartmann (2008) developed a PSI questionnaire that measures positive as well as negative and neutral PSI, is suitable for all TV personae and genres without modifying the items, and allows for comparisons of findings across different studies. The challenge for future research is to provide measurement standards and to build up standards of PSI/PSR findings that are generated, confirmed, and validated across several studies using the same measurements.

See also: ▶ BROADCAST TALK ▶ INTERACTION ▶ INTERPERSONAL COMMUNICATION ▶ MEASUREMENT THEORY ▶ PERCEPTION ▶ PERSONALITY AND EXPOSURE TO COMMUNICATION ▶ SELECTIVE EXPOSURE ▶ SOCIAL COMPARISON THEORY ▶ USES AND GRATIFICATIONS ▶ VIDEO GAMES

REFERENCES AND SUGGESTED READINGS

Hartmann, T. & Goldhoorn, C. (2011). Horton and Wohl revisited: Exploring viewers' experience of parasocial interaction. *Journal of Communication*, 61, 1104–1121.

Horton, D. & Wohl, R. (1956). Mass communication and para-social interaction: Observation on intimacy at a distance. *Psychiatry*, 19, 215–229.

Klimmt, C., Hartmann, T., & Schramm, H. (2006). Parasocial interactions and relationships. In J. Bryant & P. Vorderer (eds.), *Psychology of entertainment*. Mahwah, NJ: Lawrence Erlbaum, pp. 291–313.

Rubin, A. M., Perse, E. M., & Powell, R. A. (1985). Loneliness, parasocial interaction, and local television news viewing. *Human Communication Research*, 12, 155–180.

Schramm, H. & Hartmann, T. (2008). The PSI-Process Scales: A new measure to assess the intensity and breadth of parasocial processes. *Communications: The European Journal of Communication Research*, 33, 385–401.

Parental Mediation Strategies

AMY I. NATHANSON

Ohio State University

'Parental mediation' refers to the interactions that parents have with children about their media use. Parental mediation is comprised of *three dimensions*. The first dimension refers to parent–child *communication about media* (→ Media Messages and Family Communication). Parents might express negative attitudes, encourage children to view the material more critically, provide supplemental information, or endorse the material. The second dimension refers to the *rules* that parents impose on their children's media use. Parents may vary in how they negotiate rules and how strict they are in enforcing rules. The third dimension is called *co-viewing* and refers to parents and children using media together. Parents might co-view because they wish to protect their children from harmful content or help them benefit from positive content.

Each type of parental mediation is related to a variety of *effects among children* (→ Educational Television, Children's Responses to; Violence as Media Content, Effects on Children of). Parent–child discussion is related to less aggression, fewer sex-role stereotypes, better television plot comprehension, more critical viewing, and enhanced learning from educational material. The effects of parent–child communication may be strongest for younger children.

Restrictive mediation is associated with less aggression and better comprehension of television plots. However, restrictive mediation also is prone to backfiring effects, especially among adolescents. Co-viewing enhances the effects of the co-viewed material. In the case of educational material, this effect is desirable. Co-viewing also has been associated with aggression and sex-role stereotypes among children (→ Sex Role Stereotypes in the Media). The presence of parents may lead children to pay greater attention to the co-viewed content and attach more importance to it.

See also: ▶ EDUCATIONAL TELEVISION, CHILDREN'S RESPONSES TO ▶ MEDIA MESSAGES AND FAMILY COMMUNICATION ▶ MEDIA USE AND CHILD DEVELOPMENT ▶ SEX ROLE STEREOTYPES IN THE MEDIA ▶ VIOLENCE AS MEDIA CONTENT, EFFECTS ON CHILDREN OF

REFERENCES AND SUGGESTED READINGS

Clark, L. S. (2011). Parental mediation theory for the digital age. *Communication Theory, 21*, 323–343.
Nathanson, A. I. (2001). Mediation of children's television viewing: Working toward conceptual clarity and common understanding. In W. B. Gudykunst (ed.), *Communication yearbook 25*. Mahwah, NJ: Lawrence Erlbaum, pp. 115–151.
Valkenburg, P. M., Krcmar, M., Peeters, A. L., & Marseille, N. M. (1999). Developing a scale to assess three styles of television mediation: "Instructive mediation," "restrictive mediation," and "social co-iewing." *Journal of Broadcasting and Electronic Media, 43*, 52–66.

Participatory Action Research

THOMAS JACOBSON
Temple University

Participatory action research (PAR) is a methodological approach to research that breaks with science's customary commitment to objectivity by engaging social groups in research while focusing on the primary aim of social change. Given this aim PAR is often conducted in developing countries (→ Development Communication). However, action research approaches have been found useful worldwide in a broad range of contexts including education, urban planning, and environmental conservation.

PAR is not a single method, but rather one of a family of research approaches (→ Communication and Social Change: Research Methods). One approach derives from John Dewey through Kurt Lewin, who is often considered the father of American-styled *action research*. Lewin proposed a kind of action research employing comparative methods into the forms of social action, and including research contributing to social action. Chris Argyris's *action science* is dedicated to improving community and organizational conditions, working largely in industrial and corporate settings. This research includes the study of defensive routines, dispositional attributions, and theories of causal responsibility using field experimental methods that meet the standards of scientific testing.

Another approach to action research has a praxiological, or critical, orientation deriving from Karl Marx and Frederick Engels through Antonio Gramsci. Fals Borda's promotion of *participatory action research* aims to foster community awareness within the perspective of historical materialism, addressing sociopolitical barriers to third world development efforts. William Foote Whyte's influential work focuses on community participation with local members of a community or organization undertaking research in association with a professional researcher.

See also: ▶ APPLIED COMMUNICATION RESEARCH ▶ COMMUNICATION AND SOCIAL CHANGE: RESEARCH METHODS ▶ DEVELOPMENT COMMUNICATION ▶ PARTICIPATORY COMMUNICATION ▶ PLANNED SOCIAL CHANGE THROUGH COMMUNICATION

REFERENCES AND SUGGESTED READINGS

Argyris, C., Putnam, R., & Smith, D. M. (1985). *Action science: Concepts, methods and skills for research and intervention*. San Francisco: Jossey-Bass.
Lewin, K. (1946). Action research and minority problems. *Journal of Social Issues, 2*(4), 34–46.
Whyte, W. F. (ed.) (1991). *Participatory action research*. Beverly Hills, CA: Sage.

Participatory Communication

JAN SERVAES
City University of Hong Kong

Participatory communication stresses the importance of cultural identity of local communities and of democratization and participation at all levels – international, national, local, and individual. However, the point of departure must be the community. It is at the community level that the problems of living conditions are discussed, and interactions with other communities are elicited (Servaes 1999; 2013). It points to a strategy, not merely inclusive of, but largely emanating from, the traditional 'receivers' (→ Models of Communication). Paulo Freire (1983, 76) refers to this as the right of all people to individually and collectively speak their word: "This is not the privilege of some few men, but the right of every (wo)man. Consequently, no one can say a true word alone – nor can he say it for another, in a prescriptive act which robs others of their words" (→ Freedom of Communication).

In order to share information, knowledge, trust, commitment, and a positive attitude, participatory communication is very important. The International Commission for the Study of Communication Problems, chaired by Sean MacBride, argued that "this calls for a new attitude for overcoming stereotyped thinking and to promote more understanding of diversity and plurality, with full respect for the dignity and equality of peoples living in different conditions and acting in different ways" (MacBride 1980, 254).

There are two major *approaches to participatory communication*. The first is the dialogical pedagogy of Paulo Freire (1983), and the second involves the ideas of access, participation, and self-management articulated in the → UNESCO debates of the 1970s (Berrigan 1979; → New World Information and Communication Order [NWICO]). In spite of wide acceptance of these principles of democratic communication in participatory communication projects, there exist today a wide variety of practical experiences and intentions.

The most developed form of participation is *self-management of communication* media. This principle implies the right to participation in the planning and production of media content (→ Media Production and Content). However, not everyone wants to or must be involved in its practical implementation. More important is that participation is made possible in the decision-making regarding the subjects treated in the messages and regarding the selection procedures.

One of the fundamental *hindrances* to the decision to adopt the participation strategy is that it threatens existing hierarchies. Nevertheless, participation does not imply that there is no longer a role for specialists, planners, and institutional leaders. It only means that the viewpoint of the local groups of the public is considered before the resources for projects are allocated and distributed, and that suggestions for changes in the policy are taken into consideration.

These ideas are important and widely accepted as a normative theory of participatory communication: it must involve access and participation. The UNESCO discourse includes the idea of a gradual progression: Some amount of access may be allowed, but self-management may be postponed until some time in the future. Freire's theory allows for no such compromise. We either respect the culture of the other or we fall back into domination and the 'banking' mode of imposed education. The UNESCO discourse talks in neutral terms about 'the public' while Freire talked about 'the oppressed.' Finally, the UNESCO discourse puts the main focus on the institution, for which participatory or community radio means a radio station that is self-managed by those participating in it (→ Community Media).

The freedom and right to communicate (Dakroury et al. 2009) must be approached from a *threefold perspective*: first, it is necessary for the public to participate effectively in the communication field; second, there is the design of a framework in which this can take place; and, third, the media must enjoy professional autonomy, free of economic, political, or any other pressure.

In sum, participatory communication for social change sees people as the nucleus of development (Jacobson & Servaes 1998; Servaes 2013). Development means lifting the spirit of a local community to take pride in its own culture, intellect, and environment. Development aims to educate and stimulate people to be active in self- and communal improvements while maintaining a balanced ecology. Authentic participation, though widely espoused in the literature, is not in everyone's interest.

See also: ▶ CITIZEN JOURNALISM ▶ COMMUNITY MEDIA ▶ FREEDOM OF COMMUNICATION ▶ FREEDOM OF INFORMATION ▶ MEDIA PRODUCTION AND CONTENT ▶ MODELS OF COMMUNICATION ▶ NEW WORLD INFORMATION AND COMMUNICATION ORDER (NWICO) ▶ UNESCO

REFERENCES AND SUGGESTED READINGS

Berrigan, F. J. (1979). *Community communications: The role of community media in development*. Paris: UNESCO.
Dakroury, A., Eid, M., & Kamalipour, Y. (eds.) (2009). *The right to communicate: Historical hopes, global debates, and future premises*. Dubuque: Kendall Hunt.
Freire, P. (1983). *Pedagogy of the oppressed*. New York: Continuum.
Jacobson, T. & Servaes, J. (eds.) (1998). *Theoretical approaches to participatory communication*. Cresskill, NJ: Hampton Press.
MacBride, S. (ed.) (1980). *Many voices, one world: Communication and society, today and tomorrow*. Paris: UNESCO.
Servaes, J. (1999). *Communication for development: One world, multiple cultures*. Cresskill, NJ: Hampton Press.
Servaes, J. (ed.) (2013). *Sustainability, participation and culture in communication*. Chicago, IL: University of Chicago Press.

Pedagogy, Communication in

PHILIP M. BACKLUND
Central Washington University

Pedagogy is defined as the principles and methods of instruction, and it is mediated through the communication process. Successful pedagogy is dependent on successful communication. A teacher's knowledge of content does not mean that she or he can communicate it to students.

Student learning success and teacher satisfaction are based on student–teacher relationship quality. When the communication process works well, learning takes place and relationships are developed. But the process does not always work.

Teachers who also focus on effective communication increase learning, student liking for learning, and teacher satisfaction (→ Classroom Student–Teacher Interaction). Student talk is designed to provide opportunities for student engagement in content. An effective focus on communication can improve student ability to relate effectively to others, build confidence in the social system, and build content confidence.

If one decides to focus on communication in pedagogy, the question becomes one of *implementation*. The choice of pedagogy depends on the teacher's style, the students, the lesson's objective, and the context. The *lecture method* is a common strategy for communicating ideas to others. It is efficient, familiar, and necessary. A key factor in lecturing success is explicitly stating learning outcome(s) for the content and asking the students for their opinions on how course lectures can be bettered. A second method is *classroom discussions*, which is one of the most efficacious strategies for accomplishing student engagement in content, to participate actively, to ask more questions, and to find out how well the students can verbalize the content. Finally, students need *evaluative feedback* on their communication efforts. Evaluation can increase skill, develop confidence, and promote effectiveness. An effective evaluation system includes establishing patterns for effective communication, developing communication guidelines, then using these items to provide formative feedback and evaluation.

Communication in pedagogy is frequently overlooked by content area instructors. A concentrated focus on communication in the classroom can improve learning, increase student participation, and develop a more satisfying learning environment.

See also: ▶ CLASSROOM STUDENT–TEACHER INTERACTION ▶ QUESTIONS AND QUESTIONING ▶ STUDENT COMMUNICATION COMPETENCE ▶ TEACHER COMMUNICATION STYLE ▶ TEACHER INFLUENCE AND PERSUASION

REFERENCES AND SUGGESTED READINGS

Cooper, P. J. & Simonds, C. J. (2003). *Communication for the classroom teacher*, 7th edn. Boston: Allyn and Bacon.

Moffet, T. P., Richmond, V. P., & McCroskey, J. C. (eds.) (2006). *Handbook of instructional communication: Rhetorical and relational perspectives.* Boston: Allyn and Bacon.

Vangelisti, A. L., Daly, J. A., & Friedrich, G. W. (1999). *Teaching communication: Theory, research, and methods,* 2nd edn. Hillsdale, NJ: Lawrence Erlbaum.

Perceived Reality as a Social Process

LYN VAN SWOL
University of Wisconsin-Madison

Research on group communication examines how participation in groups affects perceived reality. Groups create a 'shared reality' in which to work, interact, and complete their tasks. There are three major approaches that address how the perception of reality is a social process within groups: social comparison theory, social proof, and shared mental models (→ Social Perception).

Research on *social comparison* examines how people check their perceptions of reality against similar others in order to establish a social consensus of the correct interpretation of an event or opinion (→ Social Comparison Theory). Many issues people face do not have an objective, correct answer. Perceptions of the correct view often will be based on communicating with others to learn their positions. Lack of validation from the group often leads people to abandon their view and conform to the majority opinion.

Research on *social proof* explores how others' behaviors shape a person's social reality through informational social influence because one assumes that what most people are doing or believing must be true and correct. With social proof, people rely on the behavior of others to form opinions or gain information, and fail to rely on their own internal collection of knowledge or information.

Research on *shared mental models* and 'sense-making' examines how group members create a shared view of group processes, norms, and roles that helps coordination and performance. Through a process of sense-making, group members come to share subjective meaning of ambiguous stimuli and uncertain environments. Through communication of opinions, information, and perceptions, group members can discuss their view of the situation or learn about norms or roles that others hold. This helps them influence one another and build and maintain a shared mental model of the situation and group processes (Cannon-Bowers et al. 1993).

See also: ▶ GROUP COMMUNICATION ▶ INFORMATION PROCESSING ▶ KNOWLEDGE MANAGEMENT ▶ SOCIAL COMPARISON THEORY ▶ SOCIAL PERCEPTION

REFERENCES AND SUGGESTED READINGS

Cannon-Bowers, J. A., Salas, E., & Converse, S. (1993). Shared mental models in expert team decision making. In N. J. Castellan (ed.), *Individual and group decision making.* Hillsdale, NJ: Lawrence Erlbaum, pp. 221–246.

Festinger, L. (1954). A theory of social comparison processes. *Human Relations,* 7, 117–140.

Perception

L. J. SHRUM
HEC Paris

Perception is essentially a process of categorization. In order to initially comprehend something, we take the surface features of the stimulus we encounter (e.g., color, shape, sound) and use them to place the stimulus into some semantic category. These categories can vary in their level of abstractness, from broader categories such as 'plant' to more specific categories such as 'fruit' or 'apple.'

For many years, research on perception took a *positivist perspective* that held that there was an objective reality, or 'pure precept,' that could be perceived, comprehended, and stored in memory. Moreover, these precepts by definition were thought to be influenced by external factors such as intensity or novelty, but for the most part uninfluenced by internal factors of the perceiver. In other words, the mind of the perceiver was considered to be a 'tabula rasa,' or blank slate, that came to the perception situation with no preconceived notions.

The research by Bruner and colleagues, the so-called *NewLook* in perception, challenged these assumptions. In a series of experiments, Bruner and colleagues showed that perception could in fact be influenced by internal constructs such as the expectancies and motivations of the perceiver. These expectancies and motivations can affect "perceptual readiness" (Bruner 1957), that is, the readiness with which individuals are prepared to categorize things as they are encountered. In any particular situation, many concepts may be used to categorize an object. Which one is used is a function of the accessibility of that concept (i.e., the ease with which it comes to mind): the more easily that concept comes to mind, the more likely it is to be used to categorize an object. Hence, the concepts that we think about often (e.g., the personal values we hold in high regard) are more likely to be used to categorize an ambiguous stimulus than are those that we do not think about as often. Indeed, Bruner and colleagues showed that the simple speed with which people could recognize words denoting particular concepts was related to their personal values and to their experiences. What the research by Bruner and colleagues shows is that the probability of categorizing a concept is a function of how frequently certain categorization concepts are activated. When we frequently encounter certain things or frequently think about certain things, we are more likely to think of them first (and thus more likely to use them first) when we attempt to categorize an ambiguous stimulus.

This kind of laboratory research translates very obviously to *real-world perception*. Thus, we might expect that people would categorize the reasons for a person of a certain race sitting on a park bench (lazy, tired) based on their → attitudes toward and stereotypes of people of that race, even though there are many possible reasons for the very innocuous behavior (→ Information Processing). This general line of reasoning can also be extended to the construction of → social perceptions, or attitudes and beliefs about others (→ Climate of Opinion; Pluralistic Ignorance; Third-Person Effects), and the implications are straightforward.

The research on the effects of construct accessibility on social perceptions has important implications for the influence of various types of communication on social perception. One in particular is the *effect of mass media on construct accessibility*, and its consequent influence on social perceptions. Results by Busselle and Shrum (2003) showed that ease of recall of exemplars (e.g., murder, courtroom trial) was positively correlated with the frequency with which examples were portrayed in television programs (but only when direct experience with the examples was low).

See also: ▶ ATTITUDES ▶ CLIMATE OF OPINION ▶ INFORMATION PROCESSING ▶ MEDIA AND PERCEPTIONS OF REALITY ▶ MEMORY ▶ PLURALISTIC IGNORANCE ▶ PRIMING THEORY ▶ SELECTIVE PERCEPTION AND SELECTIVE RETENTION ▶ SOCIAL PERCEPTION ▶ THIRD-PERSON EFFECTS

REFERENCES AND SUGGESTED READINGS

Baumeister, R. F. & Bargh, J. A. (2014). Conscious and unconscious: Toward an integrative understanding of human mental life and action. In J. W. Sherman, B. Gawronski, & Y. Trope (eds.), *Dual process theories of the social mind*. New York: Guilford, pp. 35–49.
Bruner, J. S. (1957). On perceptual readiness. *Psychological Review*, 64, 123–152.
Busselle, R. W. & Shrum, L. J. (2003). Media exposure and the accessibility of social information. *Media Psychology*, 5, 255–282.
Erdelyi, M. H. (1974). A new look at the New Look: Perceptual defense and vigilance. *Psychological Review*, 81, 1–25.
Higgins, E. T. (1996). Knowledge activation: Accessibility, applicability, and salience. In E. T. Higgins & A. W. Kruglanski (eds.), *Social psychology: Handbook of basic principles*. New York: Guilford, pp. 133–168.
Shrum, L. J. & Lee, J. (2012). Television's persuasive narratives: How television influences values, attitudes, and beliefs. In L. J. Shrum (ed.), *The psychology of entertainment media: Blurring the lines between entertainment and persuasion*, 2nd edn. London: Routledge, pp. 147–167.

Personal Communication by CMC

JOSEPH B. WALTHER
Michigan State University

Computer-mediated communication (CMC) includes → electronic mail, group discussion systems, real-time chat, personal blogs, micro-blogs, conversational components of online games and date-finding sites, and interactive aspects of web-based participatory platforms such as social network sites (→ Intergroup Contact and Communication; Media Content and Social Networks; Network Organizations through Communication Technology).

Through these platforms people send messages either to a defined individual or set of recipients, or to a space where many people may read and reply to others' messages. A great deal of CMC is used specifically for personal goals and activities. In some ways CMC is a simple alternative to other forms of communication (→ Online Media), with some socio-technical features that alter communication dynamics. In other ways CMC offers significant opportunities that enhance communication in personal settings by allowing users to contact a large field of potential communication partners, reducing aspects of human interaction that impede communication effectiveness in conventional interaction. CMC can enhance personal communication by allowing users to enhance messaging in ways that conventional interaction does not as readily afford, facilitating new relationships and relational maintenance.

As it became clear that CMC was being used effectively for personal as well as task communication, *new theories* were developed that accounted for such use. For instance, social influence theory argued that the expressive potential of a medium like email was not a deterministic result of specific technological attributes alone. Rather, people use media in accordance with their perception of the media's capabilities, which is shaped, in turn, through the media perceptions and uses of the individuals in one's communication network. Social information-processing theory held that CMC users may have the same relational goals as those who communicate offline, but must adapt to the characteristics of CMC in order to affect the level of impressions and interpersonal relations. As the Internet became more pervasive, news media, → advertising, schools, and word of mouth led to great diffusion and public awareness of the commercial and personal uses to which it was being put.

Online relationships became the object of particular research interest. Anecdotal accounts of people making friends online, or having closer friends online than in offline contexts, were met with skepticism. More disconcerting were accounts of romantic relationships that began as meetings in CMC chatrooms. Research followed such trends and found that relationships quite simply began in online venues that facilitated the meeting of and conversation between individuals who held common interests, as often or more than in chatting venues specifically oriented toward partner seeking per se. Toward the start of the twenty-first century, deliberate online dating and matchmaking systems provided another CMC venue for initiating relationships.

The following distinction offers contingencies with which to understand how each *type of interaction* could be fostered by CMC. Impersonal CMC seemed to be most likely when interaction time and/or interpersonal familiarity were restricted, either by the demands of an experiment, by the organic short-term context in which some (but not all) CMC exchanges take place, or by the imposition of software such as group decision support systems that are designed to enhance anonymity and minimize interpersonal effects in online interaction. Interpersonal CMC is facilitated by sufficient time for ongoing exchanges and by conditions such as anticipated relational longevity that prompt interpersonal interest, with users then deploying CMC in ways described by social information-processing theory to effect these goals. Hyperpersonal communication represents more intimate, satisfying communication and interpersonal evaluations than are typical in comparable offline settings, and was hypothesized to arise as a result of systematic variations in basic communication processes that are facilitated by CMC (see Walther 2007).

Online *social support networks* have arisen spontaneously and purposefully in a variety of Internet venues where individuals exchange information, emotional support, sympathy, and coping strategies with members experiencing various illnesses, psychological issues, or other personal problems (→ Social Support in Interpersonal Communication). However, individuals with skill deficits affecting face-to-face communication appear to find particular gratification (→ Uses and Gratifications) or further deterioration in conducting personal relationships online. Depression, loneliness, shyness, or other similar syndromes (→ Communication Apprehension and Social Anxiety) lead some individuals to withdraw from face-to-face social interaction, preferring instead the message management and distance that CMC interaction allows in the conduct of meeting and chatting online.

See also: ▶ ADVERTISING ▶ COMMUNICATION APPREHENSION AND SOCIAL ANXIETY ▶ ELECTRONIC MAIL ▶ INTERGROUP CONTACT AND COMMUNICATION ▶ INTERPERSONAL COMMUNICATION ▶ LANGUAGE AND THE INTERNET ▶ MEDIA CONTENT AND SOCIAL NETWORKS ▶ NETWORK ORGANIZATIONS THROUGH COMMUNICATION TECHNOLOGY ▶ ONLINE MEDIA ▶ SOCIAL MEDIA ▶ SOCIAL SUPPORT IN INTERPERSONAL COMMUNICATION ▶ TECHNOLOGY AND COMMUNICATION ▶ USES AND GRATIFICATIONS

REFERENCES AND SUGGESTED READINGS

DeAndrea, D. C. (2012). Participatory social media and the evaluation of online behavior. *Human Communication Research* 38(4), 510–528.

Gibbs, J. L., Ellison, N. B., & Heino, R. D. (2006). Self-presentation in online personals: The role of anticipated future interaction, self-disclosure, and perceived success in Internet dating. *Communication Research*, 33, 152–177.

Utz, S. (2010). Show me your friends and I will tell you what type of person you are: How one's profile, number of friends, and type of friends influence impression formation on social network sites. *Journal of Computer-Mediated Communication*, 15(2), 314–335.

Walther, J. B. (2007). Selective self-presentation in computer-mediated communication: Hyperpersonal dimensions of technology, language, and cognition. *Computers in Human Behavior*, 23, 2538–2557.

Walther, J. B. & Jang, J. (2012). Communication processes in participatory websites. *Journal of Computer-Mediated Communication*, 18, 2–15.

Wright, K. B. & Webb, L. M. (eds.) (2011). *Computer-mediated communication in personal relationships*. Cresskill, NJ: Hampton Press.

Personality and Exposure to Communication

MARY BETH OLIVER
Pennsylvania State University

The term 'personality' typically refers to traits, outlooks, and behavioral tendencies that are relatively enduring within individuals. Research in communication has studied the role of personality as a predictor of preference and enjoyment of content, as a predictor of selective exposure, and as an important moderator in explaining differential effects of media content on viewers.

Media use is not uniform across populations. For example, some people have an affinity for action films and horror; others prefer romance, tearjerkers, and melodrama (→ film genres). These sorts of variations may reflect a host of audience characteristics, including gender, social context, or mood, though the viewer's personality undoubtedly plays an important role as well, as personality is thought to be relatively stable across time.

Scholarship from a *uses-and-gratifications perspective* conceptualizes media use as goal-directed, purposive, and effective at fulfilling individuals' needs (Rubin 2008; → Uses and Gratifications). Research generally supports the proposition that personality predicts using media for the fulfilment of various goals, such as information gain, passing time, or habit, among other goals. Research also shows that personality variables predict many preferences for different types of content or portrayals. For example, personality variables indicating greater hostility are predictive of greater enjoyment of media violence (for a review, see Oliver et al. 2006).

Personality and related attitudes also play important roles in individuals' *selective exposure, avoidance, and perception* (→ Selective Exposure; Selective Perception and Selective Retention). For example, research in audience selectivity influenced by theories of cognitive dissonance (Festinger 1957; → Cognitive Dissonance Theory) generally argues that individuals tend to expose themselves to and interpret media messages that are consistent with existing attitudes and to avoid inconsistent messages. Consistent with these basic propositions, research on social and political media content generally shows that individuals tend to select messages that are ultimately supportive of their opinions (Sunstein 2001).

In addition to predicting media enjoyment and selection, personality variables can also serve as important *moderators of the strength and direction of media effects*. For example, personality may play an important role in individuals' processing of media messages that ultimately affects attitude change. To illustrate, higher levels of need for cognition (NFC) generally predict a greater likelihood of careful scrutiny of message arguments. As a result, message quality should play a more important role in persuasion than should peripheral cues such as source attractiveness for individuals scoring high on this trait (Petty & Wegener 1998; → Elaboration Likelihood Model).

Personality can also serve to moderate how media can *prime thoughts, emotions, or action tendencies* that, in turn, affect subsequent behaviour (→ Priming Theory). Priming research implies that for a concept to be primed, the concept must be present in an individual's cognitive structure. Given that personality traits may signify the presence of different cognitive structures, some personalities (e.g., trait hostility) may indicate greater susceptibility to priming effects from different types of media content (e.g., media violence; Bushman 1998; → Violence as Media Content, Effects of).

Because personality is understood to be stable and enduring, research that treats *personality as a dependent variable* is relatively rare. However, given that media consumption (and its accompanying messages and portrayals) begins at a very early age and comprises the bulk of individuals' leisure activities, future researchers may profitably examine how long-term and cumulative media use may play important roles in the formation of personality traits and dispositions.

See also: ▶ COGNITIVE DISSONANCE THEORY ▶ ELABORATION LIKELIHOOD MODEL ▶ FILM GENRES ▶ MEDIA EFFECTS ▶ PRIMING THEORY ▶ SELECTIVE EXPOSURE ▶ SELECTIVE PERCEPTION AND SELECTIVE RETENTION ▶ USES AND GRATIFICATIONS ▶ VIOLENCE AS MEDIA CONTENT, EFFECTS OF

REFERENCES AND SUGGESTED READINGS

Bushman, B. J. (1998). Priming effects of media violence on the accessibility of aggressive constructs in memory. *Personality and Social Psychology Bulletin*, 24(5), 537–545.

Festinger, L. (1957). *A theory of cognitive dissonance.* Evanston, IL: Row, Peterson.

Oliver, M. B., Kim, J., & Sanders, M. S. (2006). Personality. In J. Bryant & P. Vorderer (eds.), *Psychology of entertainment.* Mahwah, NJ: Lawrence Erlbaum, pp. 329–341.

Petty, R. E. & Wegener, D. T. (1998). Attitude change: Multiple roles for persuasion variables. In D. Gilbert, S. T. Fiske, & G. Lindzey (eds.), *Handbook of social psychology*, 4th edn. Boston: McGraw-Hill, pp. 323–390.

Rubin, A. M. (2008). Uses-and-gratifications perspective on media effects. In J. Bryant & M. B. Oliver (eds.), *Media effects: Advances in theory and research*, 3rd edn. London: Routledge, pp. 165–184.

Sunstein, C. R. (2001). *Republic.com.* Princeton, NJ: Princeton University Press.

Persuasion

DANIEL O'KEEFE
Northwestern University

Persuasion is a communicative function that can be pursued in many different settings, ranging from face-to-face interaction to mass communication. Mass media persuasion takes three primary overt forms: commercial advertising (of consumer products and services), pro-social advertising, and political advertising. On each of these subjects, there is extensive empirical research and theorizing (→ Strategic Communication).

Studies of consumer advertising have examined such questions as the effectiveness of different advertising strategies, the role of endorsements in consumer → advertising, effects of varying the frequency and timing of advertisements, and the role of visual elements (→ Advertising as Persuasion). Pro-social communication campaigns aim to forward environmental or charitable causes or to advance health-related ends such as encouraging people to exercise, quit smoking (→ Environmental Communication; Health Campaigns, Communication in; Planned Social Change through Communication; Social Marketing). Studies of political persuasion (especially, but not exclusively, in the context of election campaign advertising) have examined such subjects as the effects of negative advertising and the role of televised political debates in elections (→ Political Advertising; Political Persuasion; Televised Debates). Beyond these three overt forms of mass media persuasion, advocates can also pursue persuasion through two other kinds of media content: news (by means of media advocacy) and entertainment (especially through entertainment education).

A number of more general theoretical perspectives on persuasion have been developed. Among the more prominent and promising are the → elaboration likelihood model (ELM), social judgment theory, and transportation theory. And persuasion has also been illuminated by the application of general models of psychological processes such as → cognitive dissonance theory (often invoked to explain selective exposure to messages) and the theories of planned behavior and reasoned action (two related approaches to understanding the bases of voluntary action; → Planned Behavior, Theory of; Reasoned Action, Theory of).

See also: ▶ ADVERTISING ▶ ADVERTISING AS PERSUASION ▶ COGNITIVE DISSONANCE THEORY ▶ ELABORATION LIKELIHOOD MODEL ▶ ENVIRONMENTAL COMMUNICATION ▶ EXTENDED PARALLEL PROCESS MODEL ▶ HEALTH CAMPAIGNS, COMMUNICATION IN ▶ HEALTH COMMUNICATION ▶ MARKETING ▶ PLANNED BEHAVIOR, THEORY OF ▶ PLANNED SOCIAL CHANGE THROUGH COMMUNICATION ▶ POLITICAL ADVERTISING ▶ POLITICAL PERSUASION ▶ PROPAGANDA ▶ PUBLIC RELATIONS ▶ REASONED ACTION, THEORY OF ▶ SOCIAL MARKETING ▶ STRATEGIC COMMUNICATION ▶ TELEVISED DEBATES

REFERENCES AND SUGGESTED READINGS

Dillard, J. P. & Shen, L. (eds.) (2013). *The Sage handbook of persuasion: Developments in theory and practice*, 2nd edn. Thousand Oaks, CA: Sage.

O'Keefe, D. J. (in press). *Persuasion: Theory and research*, 3rd edn. Thousand Oaks, CA: Sage.

Perloff, R. M. (2014). *The dynamics of persuasion*, 5th edn. London: Routledge.

Phenomenology

RICHARD LEO LANIGAN, JR.
Southern Illinois University

Phenomenology is a movement in philosophy associated with the human sciences as a qualitative approach to the study of human conscious experience. Research → validity and → reliability are assessed as functions of logic, not mathematics or statistics (→ Qualitative Methodology).

Consciousness refers to the unique human ability: (1) to have an awareness of self, others, and the world, i.e., iconic codes of awareness; (2) to be aware of that awareness, i.e., indexical codes of signification; and (3) to displace that awareness of awareness in space and time, i.e., symbolic codes of meaning. The conjunction of these codes is the function of discourse (→ Code). Following Merleau-Ponty, the three stages of defining human communication (→ Semiotics) are known as the phenomenological method of: (1) 'description,' entailing the iconic principle of reversibility of expression and perception; (2) 'reduction,' entailing the indexical principle of reflexivity, where expression structures perception; and (3) 'interpretation,' entailing the symbolic principle of reflection, in which expression and perception represent one another.

There is both a European and a USA tradition in phenomenology, beginning in eighteenth-century Europe with Lambert, Kant, and Hegel. By the nineteenth century, the forerunner of phenomenology was Franz Brentano. He divided consciousness into (1) representations, (2) judgments, and (3) emotive acts. He had several famous students: First the psychoanalyst Sigmund Freud, who stressed the relationship of representation and emotive acts in his famous "talking cure" for neurosis. Second, the logician Edmund Husserl who focused on representation and judgment in consciousness, i.e., 'intentionality.' In his 1922 London lectures, Husserl defined his methodology as centered on the "manifest multiplicity of conscious subjects communicating with one another."

The central personality in American phenomenology is Charles Sanders Peirce, known for his combination of semiotics and phenomenology with an existential focus: "man is a sign … my language is the sum total of myself; for the man is the thought" (5.314). Like Husserl, Peirce (1931–1958) defined his phenomenology by "communication: the recognition by one person of another's personality takes place by means to some extent identical with the means by which he is conscious of his own personality" (6.159).

See also: ▶ CODE ▶ COMMUNICOLOGY ▶ CRITICAL THEORY ▶ DISCOURSE ▶ MEANING ▶ QUALITATIVE METHODOLOGY ▶ RELIABILITY ▶ RESEARCH METHODS ▶ SEMIOTICS ▶ STRUCTURALISM ▶ VALIDITY

REFERENCES AND SUGGESTED READINGS

Kritzman, L. (2006). *The Columbia history of twentieth-century French thought*. New York: Columbia University Press.

Lanigan, R. L. (1988). *Phenomenology of communication: Merleau-Ponty's thematics in communicology and semiology*. Pittsburgh, PA: Duquesne University Press.

Moran, D. (2000). *Introduction to phenomenology*. London: Routledge.

Peirce, C. S. (1931–1958). *Collected papers of Charles Sanders Peirce*, 8 vols; vols. 1–6, ed. C. Hartshorne & P. Weiss; vols. 7 & 8, ed. A. Burks. Cambridge, MA: Harvard University Press.

Photography

JAN-CHRISTOPHER HORAK
University of California, Los Angeles

From its invention in the early 1800s to the beginning of the twenty-first century, photography referred to a photo-chemically based system of analog and indexical still image production that resulted in an optical reproduction of the space in front of the lens. For most of the nineteenth century, photographs were produced only by specialists, using a variety of chemical formulae to make and develop light-sensitive surfaces. By the early twentieth century, photographic processes had become standardized and their production industrialized, allowing a growing number of amateurs, as well as professionals, to document various aspects of everyday life, and create photographic art in all kinds of genres and styles. In the first five years of the new millennium, analog photography was almost completely supplanted by electronically based digital systems that calibrate light intensities in terms of logarithms.

Photography has been *applied in a variety of fields*. With the invention of half-tone printing in the 1880s, photography became all-pervasive in → journalism (→ Photojournalism) and other forms of publishing. With the rise of illustrated news magazines, e.g., the *Berliner Illustrierte Zeitung*, *Picture Post*, and *Life*, as well as the development of the 35 mm Leica camera, modern photojournalism was born. Capturing news events of the day, whether diplomatic conferences or images from a war front, photographers such as Erich Solomon, Alfred Eisenstedt, Umbo (Otto Umbehr), and Margaret Bourke-White traveled the globe to get their scoops.

A major impetus for photography was the *documentation of architecture*, especially historic buildings. In the early twentieth century, photographers became fascinated by cityscapes with skyscrapers as the epitome of modernity. In the 1920s European modernist artists began experimenting with exposing photographic paper to light without a camera, resulting in *purely abstract images*, parallel to painting's evolution toward abstraction (abstract or camera-less photography; → Art as Communication; Visual Communication). With the expansion of mass print media, photography also evolved into the most important tool for → *advertising* consumer goods. Given the huge popularity of fashion magazines, it is not surprising that fashion photography soon became big business.

One of photography's foremost *goals* was to document real-world conditions. Utilizing the camera as a tool for social criticism, Lewis Hine's images of children in New York sweatshops helped pass child labor laws in many states. August Sander's frontal portraits of farmers, workers, and tradesmen created a complex social portrait of Weimar Germany. An important subject from classical art is nude photography. Helmut Newton and H. F. Heinecken have trodden a narrow line between pornography and fashion photography, while Robert Mapplethorpe's large-format homoerotic images of male nudes caused intense political controversy in the 1980s.

In the early years of the twenty-first century, photography has become both more prevalent, retaining its status as a mass medium through Internet distribution, and also subject to the critical and aesthetic winds of postmodernism (→ Postmodernism and Communication). Photographers, such as Marco Breuer, Carl Carienza, Rimma Gerlovina, Richard Misrach, Julie Moos, Sebastiao Salgado, Gary Schneider, and Krizystof Wodiczko, are as diverse as the genres they work in.

In the new millennium, photography has morphed from a chemical-based medium to *digital forms*, with images stored digitally on hard discs in cameras or computers (→ Digital Imagery). While it is still too early to tell what aesthetic consequences the digital revolution will have for photography, it is already clear that both amateurs and professionals have embraced the medium almost instantaneously. Furthermore, distribution of digital images has been revolutionized, allowing consumers to take pictures with their phones and send them to their computers, while professionals can email extremely large image files from almost anywhere on the planet to their editors. However, digitality has also entailed convergence, meaning that film, photography, and other forms of image production have lost much of their media specificity.

See also: ▶ ADVERTISING ▶ ART AS COMMUNICATION ▶ DIGITAL IMAGERY ▶ JOURNALISM ▶ JOURNALISM, HISTORY OF ▶ OBJECTIVITY IN REPORTING ▶ PHOTOJOURNALISM ▶ POSTMODERNISM AND COMMUNICATION ▶ VISUAL COMMUNICATION ▶ VISUAL REPRESENTATION

REFERENCES AND SUGGESTED READINGS

Gernsheim, H. (1988). *The history of photography*. New York: Thames and Hudson.
Newhall, B. (1988). *The history of photography: From 1839 to the present*. Boston: Little, Brown.
Tausk, P. (1980). *Photography in the 20th century*. London: Focal Press.
Van Dijk, J. (2008). Digital photography: Communication, identity, memory. *Visual Communication*, 7(1), 57–76.
Warren, L. (ed.) (2006). *Encyclopedia of twentieth-century photography*. London: Routledge.

Photojournalism

JULIANNE H. NEWTON
University of Oregon

Photojournalism, which means reporting visually, seeks to show the world what it needs to see in spite of the ever-shifting challenges of technology, culture, and perception. The defining characteristic of photojournalism is visual portrayal of an event – a moment as fleeting as a child's smile or as long as a country's struggle to rebuild after war. Images of photojournalism, itself a major genre of the medium of photography, fall into *five sub-genres*: (1) spot news, (2) general news, (3) features, (4) illustrations, and (5) documentary. Content can be expressed as single images with contextualizing verbal captions, as word/picture packages, or as multimedia presentations.

Discussions of *photojournalism's origins* underlie scholarship about visual ways of knowing: the role of the seer versus the role of the seeing technology (→ Photography). Historians date the beginning of photographic reportage to 1826, when the first light-written image was recorded by means other than the action of a human hand and tool. The oldest extant light recording of a human figure is Jacques Louis Daguerre's 1838 image of a man having his shoes shined on a Paris street.

Scholars cite the critical *roles of technological advances* such as the half-tone, and aesthetic, cultural, political, and economic forces in photojournalism's development: artistic and scientific drives toward realistic portrayal or interpretations of the material world, surveillance and → propaganda functions of governments and institutions, economic imperatives of mass distribution systems, public fascination with visual media, experimentation in advertising media, the rise of modernism (→ Propaganda, Visual Communication of), and the contemporary rise of participatory media practices.

Institutional forces played a key role in *professionalizing photojournalism*: cooperative news agencies, international picture agencies, the great picture magazines, and journalism pedagogy. Development of video journalism, information graphics, and digital media led to the inclusive term 'visual journalism,' which can also include editorial cartoons and packages using still and moving images, graphics, and audio. This relatively new form, sometimes called 'new media' or 'multimedia storytelling,' is often disseminated via Internet sites, mobile publications, and → social media applications.

Contemporary analysis of the appropriate role of photography in news reporting founders on issues of truth, accuracy, objectivity, and privacy, under the general term 'photojournalism ethics.'

See also: ▶ DIGITAL IMAGERY ▶ ETHICS IN JOURNALISM ▶ INTERNET NEWS ▶ JOURNALISM ▶ JOURNALISM, HISTORY OF ▶ MEDIA AND PERCEPTIONS OF REALITY ▶ MOBILITY, TECHNOLOGY FOR ▶ NEWSPAPER, VISUAL DESIGN OF

▶ PHOTOGRAPHY ▶ PRINTING, HISTORY OF
▶ PRIVACY ▶ PROPAGANDA ▶ PROPAGANDA, VISUAL
COMMUNICATION OF ▶ REALISM IN FILM AND
PHOTOGRAPHY ▶ SOCIAL MEDIA ▶ TELEVISION,
VISUAL CHARACTERISTICS OF ▶ VISUAL
COMMUNICATION ▶ VISUAL REPRESENTATION

REFERENCES AND SUGGESTED READINGS

Edom, C. C. (1976). *Photojournalism: Principles and practices.* Dubuque, IA: William C. Brown.

Hicks, W. (1952). *Words and pictures: An introduction to photojournalism.* New York: Harper.

Newton, J. H. (2001). *The burden of visual truth: The role of photojournalism in mediating reality.* Mahwah, NJ: Lawrence Erlbaum.

Physiological Measurement

ANDREAS FAHR
University of Fribourg

Psychophysiology is concerned with the link between physiological processes of the human body and brain and the human mind (consciousness, perception, thinking, experiencing, judgement, and memory). For example, where psychologists are interested in why we like a certain TV show, physiologists are interested in the precursory, accompanying, and following processes occurring in the human body and brain. Physiological processes designate physical precursors, accompanying symptoms or reactions of human behaviour, such as cardiovascular activity (e.g., heart rate, blood pressure respiration), electrodermal activity (e.g., skin conductance), brain activity (such as brain waves, blood flow), muscle activity (facial expressions, gestures, eye movements, pupillary reflexes), reaction times, and similar processes.

The focus is primarily on the description, explanation, and prognosis of → information processing (cognitive aspect), experience (affective aspect), and behavior dispositions (conative aspect) of individuals (→ Affects and Media Exposure) by means of physiological phenomena. Therefore, activation concepts, habituation models, perception and decision processes, and emotion theories are of especial significance in communication research. In communication studies these concepts are applied to media attention and information processing, learning, emotional experience, media choice, attitude (change) and persuasion, adaptation research, social cognition, or sleep research.

In contrast to data collection techniques such as interviews or → surveys, psychophysiological data collection is considered to have several *methodological advantages*. While other measuring procedures that accompany exposure – such as real-time response measurement or think-aloud techniques – influence the experience and information processing itself, physiological measures are considered to be less reactive. Besides reaction time measurement they do not require mental resources and/or the verbal abilities of the subjects. At the same time, the reactions are scarcely controllable by the observed person. Moreover, the isochronism between occurrence and measurement allows for the investigation of phenomena which are elusive, hard to remember or susceptible to social desirability. Finally physiological measures produce very scattered time-series data that allow the reproduction of the process of media reception and not only its consolidated result.

See also: ▶ AFFECTS AND MEDIA EXPOSURE
▶ COGNITIVE DISSONANCE THEORY ▶ EXCITATION
AND AROUSAL ▶ EXPOSURE TO COMMUNICATION
CONTENT ▶ INFORMATION PROCESSING ▶ MOOD
MANAGEMENT ▶ OBSERVATION ▶ PERSUASION
▶ SELECTIVE EXPOSURE ▶ SELECTIVE PERCEPTION
AND SELECTIVE RETENTION ▶ SOCIAL COGNITIVE
THEORY ▶ SURVEY

REFERENCES AND SUGGESTED READINGS

Cacioppo, J. T., Tassinary, L. G., & Berntson, G. G. (2013). *The handbook of psychophysiology.* Cambridge: Cambridge University Press.

Potter, R. F. & Bolls, P. D. (2012). *Psychophysiological measurement and meaning: Cognitive and emotional processing of media.* London: Routledge.

Ravaja, N. (2004). Contributions of psychophysiology to media research: Review and recommendations. *Media Psychology*, 6, 193–235.

Planned Behavior, Theory of

JOSEPH N. CAPPELLA
University of Pennsylvania

The theory of planned behavior (TPB) is one of a class of theories of behavior change. The theory was developed by Icek Ajzen (1991) as an extension of the theory of reasoned action (TRA; Fishbein & Ajzen 1975; → Reasoned Action, Theory of). The TRA originated as a solution to the problem of attitude–behavior correspondence (→ Attitude–Behavior Consistency).

To solve the problem of attitude–behavior correspondence, Martin Fishbein and Icek Ajzen introduced the concept of intention mediating attitudes and behavior. When a behavior is one that a person can readily enact or not then the intention to carry out such an action will lead to that behavior under certain circumstances.

To insure correspondence among attitudes, behavioral intention, and behavior requires careful definition and correspondence across the three. For example, losing weight is not a behavior – it is a goal. The goal of losing weight might be achieved in many different ways, such as "my exercising vigorously at the gym for 30 minutes three times per week starting this week." Correspondence requires matching in time, action, context, and target. The action is exercising vigorously for 30 minutes three times per week; the time is this week; the context is "at the gym"; the target is my behavior, not people exercising more generally. By defining behaviors precisely and not confusing behaviors with general goals, intentions can be defined precisely. When matched in level of specificity, behavior and intention will tend to correlate strongly.

The core of the TPB is the TRA. The TRA assumes that behavior is the result of the information people have – correct or incorrect – about good and bad consequences of the behavior for themselves and what others think they should do. The TRA focuses on behaviors that are under the control of actors. For example, exercising at the gym tonight is generally under a person's control and so is volitional. However, if the person requires transportation to the gym and their car is in the mechanic's shop, then going to the gym depends on factors outside of the person's control.

The TPB holds to the core of the TRA but extends it to include *perceived behavioral control* parallel to the attitudinal and social normative routes. Perceived behavioral control is how easy or difficult the performance of the behavior is perceived to be. Perceived behavioral control is related to the concept of self-efficacy introduced by Bandura (1977) and is also a measure of the available resources, opportunities, and skills necessary to undertake a behavior. Perceived behavioral control is itself a function of control beliefs and the power of those beliefs to affect the outcome. So, even if I believe that going to the gym regularly and exercising will improve my physical appearance and believe that my significant others want me to go to the gym regularly, perceived difficulties with transportation may lead me to avoid the gym, marking this behavior as less under volitional control (Ajzen & Albarracin 2007).

The TPB and its variants – including the TRA and the integrated model of behavior change (Fishbein & Ajzen 2010) – have generated thousands of published studies focusing on topics as diverse as politics, consumer behavior, exercise, safe sex, smoking, → video games, among many others (Fishbein & Ajzen 2010). The TPB has wide applicability. For instance, the TPB suggests that specific beliefs or particular routes to persuasion can be made more salient by communication campaigns that target those beliefs (Fishbein & Cappella 2006).

The three routes to persuasion may not be equally strong. Communication campaigns can emphasize one route to intention rather than another or one behavioral belief rather than another in order to make it more salient. If a campaign primes a route or belief, then that component could play a stronger role during decision-making. Thus, the TPB guides communication campaigns and persuasion in two important but complementary ways – persuasion that changes a belief and priming, which makes a belief more cognitively salient (→ Priming Theory).

Criticism of the theory includes the role of affect, causality, sufficiency, habit and past behavior, the nature of the routes to intention, and rationality. Even if one acknowledges criticisms, the TPB and its cousins have had profound effects on the study of human behavior and on the design of communication campaigns and interventions. Few theories have had the staying power, influence, and predictive success of the TPB.

See also: ▶ ATTITUDE–BEHAVIOR CONSISTENCY ▶ COGNITIVE SCIENCE ▶ ELABORATION LIKELIHOOD MODEL ▶ ELECTION CAMPAIGN COMMUNICATION ▶ HEALTH CAMPAIGNS, COMMUNICATION IN ▶ INFORMATION PROCESSING ▶ PERSUASION ▶ PRIMING THEORY ▶ REASONED ACTION, THEORY OF ▶ RISK COMMUNICATION ▶ SOCIAL COGNITIVE THEORY

REFERENCES AND SUGGESTED READINGS

Ajzen, I. (1991). The theory of planned behavior. Organizational behavior and human decision processes, 50, 179–211.
Ajzen, I. & Albarracin, D. (2007). Predicting and changing behavior: A reasoned action approach. In I. Ajzen, D. Albarracin, & R. Hornik (eds.), Prediction and change of health behavior. Mahwah, NJ: Lawrence Erlbaum, pp. 3–21.
Bandura, A. (1977). Self-efficacy: The exercise of control. New York: W. H. Freeman.
Fishbein, M. & Ajzen, I. (1975). Belief, attitude, intention and behavior: An introduction to theory and research. Boston: Addison-Wesley.
Fishbein, M. & Ajzen, I. (2010). Predicting and changing behavior: The reasoned action approach. New York: Psychology Press.
Fishbein, M. & Cappella, J. N. (2006). The role of theory in developing effective health communications. Journal of Communication, 56, S1–S17.

Planned Social Change through Communication

DOUGLAS M. MCLEOD
University of Wisconsin–Madison

Planned social change is intervention to transform human communities, such as campaigns to improve health (→ Health Communication; Prevention and Communication), manage crises (→ Crisis Communication), spread technology (→ Diffusion of Information and Innovation), and promote economic development.

Elements of Campaigns

Campaigns have *three basic phases*: (1) planning, (2) implementation, and (3) evaluation. Significant long-term change is influenced by available resources, quality of strategic planning, and degree of community acceptance (→ Health Campaigns, Communication in; Development Communication Campaigns). Zaltman and Duncan (1977) organize four *strategic approaches* to planned social change: (1) power strategies changing policies and incentives; (2) persuasion strategies utilizing mediated and/or interpersonal communication; (3) normative re-educational strategies spreading information; and (4) facilitation strategies providing resources and opportunities. Most campaigns mix these strategies based on campaign goals and available resources.

Assessing campaign effectiveness blends basic and → applied communication research, putting such theoretical concerns as motivation, learning, and → persuasion to the test in real-world settings. Different disciplines have contributed to theories of planned social change. Psychologists have explored motivation, persuasion, and media in changing knowledge, attitudes, and behaviors (→ Stimulus–Response Model). Sociologists and economists from the 'modernization perspective' investigated the media's 'magic multiplier' role in promoting national development. Political scientists introduced the concepts of → propaganda and social engineering as large-scale attempts to influence mass opinions, attitudes, and behaviors. Communication researchers launched research on the 'diffusion of innovations,' examining the processes that influence the adoption of new technologies and practices in a given society.

Major Principles

Planned social change campaigns are driven by the principles of → strategic communication. As mass media are crucial tools for informing, persuading, and mobilizing the public, strategic campaign principles can be organized according to Lasswell's (1948) communication model: "Who says what to whom through what channel with what effect" (→ Models of Communication). The individuals and organizations that initiate planned social change campaigns (the 'who') are known as change agents. Since campaign effectiveness diminishes when targets perceive sources as being outsiders, most campaigns engage local change agents for points of contact with target audiences.

Successful messages (the 'what') are strategically designed (→ Advertisement Campaign Management) to be attention-grabbing, memorable, and to resonate with intended audiences. An 'entertainment-education strategy' may be used to embed messages in entertainment programs, such as Mexican soap operas with messages about family planning, responsible parenting, and literacy.

Most campaigns target individuals (the 'to whom') who are likely to change, avoiding change-resistant individuals. Targets are more likely to be motivated to receive, process, and yield to campaign messages. Targeting → opinion leaders takes advantage of the → two-step flow of communication, though campaigns must identify context-specific opinion leaders as they differ by context.

Most campaigns use a media mix of channels to carry campaign messages (the 'through what channel') according to campaign goals, target audiences, and resources. For example, the goal of spreading information typically requires textual media (e.g., print media), whereas conveying emotional appeals requires a more vivid modality (e.g., television). Media goals specify the relative emphasis of widecasting (reaching as many people as possible using newspapers and television) or narrowcasting (targeting specific audiences using magazines and radio). Media selection is dictated by the target audience (i.e., media vehicles with high target audience concentrations) and available resources (e.g., radio is inexpensive and magazines are expensive). Campaigns may also use low cost alternatives, such as public service announcements, the Internet, and → social media; however, such low cost media involves risks because the change agent can't control message content nor guarantee message delivery.

Finally, campaign outcomes (the 'with what effect') range from shifts in individual knowledge, attitudes, and behaviors to changes in social norms. Researchers from Yale University laid out the most influential program for studying → persuasion (Hovland et al. 1953), which explores the source, message (i.e., one-sided vs two-sided messages), and channel factors shaping persuasion effectiveness. Research also suggests the importance of targeting social norms (i.e., opinions, attitudes, and behaviors that are considered widely shared), which requires the ability to invoke incentives (e.g., tax incentives) and sanctions (e.g., anti-smoking laws). Campaigns may capitalize on existing norms, or seek to create or change them (e.g., the '5 a Day' campaign to increase fruit and vegetable consumption in the UK). Many campaigns have used Fishbein and Ajzen's (1975) Theory of Reasoned Action, which blends the individual and social norms approach (→ Reasoned Action, Theory of).

Measuring Effects

Planned social change campaigns are often *pilot campaigns* testing the viability of a given campaign approach and rarely achieve lasting system-wide change. Estimating a campaign's impact is complicated by the difficulty of establishing cause and effect. Manipulating and/or measuring campaign exposure and establishing viable control groups is difficult. Some researchers have set up experimental and control communities to assess campaign effects, but it is hard to make the communities comparable and to maintain their purity as experimental and control groups (see Hornik 2002).

The most promising avenues for the *future of research and practice* deal with how to effectively harness the Internet and social media. As planned social change campaigns move forward, there are a few important lessons to bear in mind: (1) it is easier to spread knowledge than to change attitudes and behaviors; (2) mass-mediated messages are more effective when supported by interpersonal communication networks and opinion leaders; and (3) change is most likely to occur when individuals are motivated to process information and when it is consistent with personal values and social norms.

See also: ▶ ADVERTISEMENT CAMPAIGN MANAGEMENT ▶ APPLIED COMMUNICATION RESEARCH ▶ COMMUNICATION AND SOCIAL CHANGE: RESEARCH METHODS ▶ CRISIS COMMUNICATION ▶ DEVELOPMENT COMMUNICATION CAMPAIGNS ▶ DIFFUSION OF INFORMATION AND INNOVATION ▶ HEALTH

CAMPAIGNS, COMMUNICATION IN ▶ HEALTH COMMUNICATION ▶ HEALTH COMMUNICATION AND THE INTERNET ▶ INTERPERSONAL COMMUNICATION ▶ MODELS OF COMMUNICATION ▶ NEWS ▶ NEWS ROUTINES ▶ NEWS VALUES ▶ OPINION LEADER ▶ PARTICIPATORY ACTION RESEARCH ▶ PERSUASION ▶ PROPAGANDA ▶ PUBLIC RELATIONS ▶ REASONED ACTION, THEORY OF ▶ SOCIAL MEDIA ▶ STIMULUS–RESPONSE MODEL ▶ STRATEGIC COMMUNICATION ▶ TWO-STEP FLOW OF COMMUNICATION

REFERENCES AND SUGGESTED READINGS

Demers, D. & Viswanath, K., (eds.) (1999). *Mass media, social control and social change*. Ames: Iowa State University Press, pp. 263–280.

Fishbein, M. & Ajzen, I. (1975). *Belief, attitude, intention, and behavior: An introduction to theory and research*. Reading, MA: Addison-Wesley.

Hornik, R. C., (ed.) (2002). *Public health communication: Evidence for behavior change*. Mahwah, NJ: Lawrence Erlbaum.

Hovland, C., Janis, I., & Kelley, H. H. (1953). *Communication and persuasion*. New Haven, CT: Yale University Press.

Lasswell, H. (1948). The structure and function of communication in society. In L. Bryson (ed.), *The communication of ideas*. New York: Institute for Religious and Social Studies, pp. 37–51.

Rice, R. E. & Paisley, W. J., (eds.) (1981). *Public communication campaigns*. Beverly Hills, CA: Sage.

Salmon, C. T. (ed.) (1989). *Information campaigns: Balancing social values and social change*. Newbury Park, CA: Sage.

Zaltman, G. & Duncan, R. (1977). *Strategies for planned social change*. New York: John Wiley.

Pluralistic Ignorance

GREGOR DASCHMANN
Johannes Gutenberg University of Mainz

Pluralistic ignorance means the inaccuracy with which most people perceive or judge → public opinion or at least the distribution of opinions in social groups (→ Social Perception). If this perception is wrong, this may lead to the paradox that a social group may follow some norms that most group members actually do not accept. The concrete phenomenon of a majority believing itself to be in the minority is what Allport (1933) originally termed 'pluralistic ignorance.'

Research has broadened the definition and understood pluralistic ignorance as an inaccuracy in estimates of public opinion, as the situation when the majority is wrong about the majority, as false social knowledge of other people, or as – especially in the context of the → spiral of silence – "social optical delusion of the public about the public." Taylor's definition as a "situation when a minority position in public opinion is incorrectly perceived to be the majority position and vice versa" (Taylor 1982, 312) is the most accepted. The salience of the concept is due to its behavioral consequences. Each individual's subjective perception of public opinion defines his or her individual social circumstances of behavior.

False consensus can serve as an *explanation* when minorities perceive themselves erroneously to be in the majority, considering their own opinions as common and appropriate (similar: 'looking glass perception,' 'egocentric bias,' or 'social projection'). In contrast, the 'false idiosyncrasy' or 'silent majority' effect describes situations where a majority perceives itself as in the minority.

There are a few approaches in → media effects research that can be usefully linked to the phenomenon: The 'hostile media phenomenon' postulates that those with a strong partisan view on an issue tend to misperceive relatively neutral news content as biased against their own position. This effect may be amplified by the → 'third-person effect,' which postulates that most people believe that the media have a greater impact on others than on themselves. This may lead to changing estimations of public opinion. The → spiral of silence postulates that most people fear isolation and therefore tend to express their opinion only if it is in line with the perceived → climate of opinion. These perceptions can be distorted by media coverage. The cultivation approach suggests that television is shaping viewers' conceptions of social reality ('mainstreaming'), which may result in pluralistic ignorance.

See also: ▶ CLIMATE OF OPINION ▶ CULTIVATION EFFECTS ▶ MEDIA EFFECTS ▶ PUBLIC OPINION ▶ SOCIAL PERCEPTION ▶ SPIRAL OF SILENCE ▶ THIRD-PERSON EFFECTS

REFERENCES AND SUGGESTED READINGS

Allport, F. H. (1933). *Institutional behavior*. Chapel Hill: University of North Carolina Press.

Taylor, D. G. (1982). Pluralistic ignorance and the spiral of silence: A formal analysis. *Public Opinion Quarterly*, 46(3), 311–335.

Pluralistic Ignorance and Ideological Biases

S. ROBERT LICHTER
George Mason University

An ideology is a consistent set of related ideas about the nature and goals of society. Such global perspectives can produce skewed or biased thoughts and perceptions. One such bias is → pluralistic ignorance, an inaccurate perception of how one's own opinions relate to those of a larger group. The communications media are widely believed to produce biases in → public opinion.

Pluralistic ignorance may lead an individual whose views are shared by the majority to inaccurately believe she is in the minority, or vice versa. If such individuals become afraid to speak out, their opponents may dominate public debate and form a new majority. This process is known as the → 'spiral of silence' (Donsbach et al. 2014; → Climate of Opinion).

The *results of pluralistic ignorance* may benefit either side of the political spectrum. For example, global warming skeptics overestimate public support for their views, while white college students overestimate on-campus support for affirmative action. In both cases, a 'false consensus' favors vocal minorities over silent majorities.

The most controversial issue is whether news media favor one side of the *political spectrum*. Leftists indict media for reinforcing and legitimizing the perspectives of ruling elites, while conservatives criticize liberal journalists for undermining traditional social values and institutions (→ Bias in the News). Both sides receive partial support from the scholarly literature (Lichter 2014). Ironically, the debate over media bias is itself colored by pluralistic ignorance. For example, partisans regard neutral news content as favoring their opponents ('hostile media phenomenon'; → Selective Perception and Selective Retention), and there is a widespread belief that the media influence other people more than ourselves (the → third-person effect).

See also: ▶ BIAS IN THE NEWS ▶ CLIMATE OF OPINION ▶ PLURALISTIC IGNORANCE ▶ PUBLIC OPINION ▶ SELECTIVE PERCEPTION AND SELECTIVE RETENTION ▶ SPIRAL OF SILENCE ▶ THIRD-PERSON EFFECTS

REFERENCES AND SUGGESTED READINGS

Comstock, G. & Scharrer, E. (2005). *The psychology of media and politics*. New York: Academic Press.

Donsbach, W., Salmon, C. T., & Tsfati, Y., (eds.) (2014). *The spiral of silence. New perspectives on communication and public opinion*. New York: Routledge.

Lichter, S. (2014). Theories of media bias. In K. Kenski & K. H. Jamieson (eds.), *The Oxford handbook of political communication*. New York: Oxford University Press.

Politainment

JÖRG-UWE NIELAND
German Sport University Cologne / University of Duisburg

Politainment refers to the blending of politics and entertainment into a new type of → political communication. As well as → infotainment, which is used as a label for a specific television program type, the term denotes the entangling of political actors, topics, and processes with the entertainment culture. Politainment may be seen as resulting from an increasing mediatization and professionalization of politics that characterize modern democracies (→ Mediatization of Politics).

According to Dörner (2001), two different *forms of politainment* may be distinguished. *Entertaining politics* serves political actors to get media access in order to enhance their public images and to promote political issues. This is quite obvious during election campaigns (→ Election Campaign Communication), when, for example, party conventions are staged by movie directors mimicking the dramaturgy of pop concerts. Politicians presenting themselves in an entertainment setting, exposing their personal characteristics and private lives, are catering especially to voters with little interest in politics (→ Media Events and Pseudo-Events).

Political entertainment refers to political topics in various entertainment formats of popular music, film, and television (→ Television as Popular Culture). The entertainment industry tends to exploit the world of politics with its sometimes-interesting personalities, prestigious figures, and exciting scandals. Movies and television plays take up political matters as raw material for drama or satire plots, as illustrated by movies such as *Wag the Dog* and *Primary Colors*, and by serials like *West Wing* and *Yes, Prime Minister*.

Politainment offers political actors effective means for reaching the public and pursuing political goals and, in exchange, provides the entertainment industry with celebrity figures and exciting stories. However, it is criticized for downgrading civic culture and for contributing to political cynicism.

See also: ▶ ELECTION CAMPAIGN COMMUNICATION ▶ INFOTAINMENT ▶ MEDIA EVENTS AND PSEUDO-EVENTS ▶ MEDIATED POPULISM ▶ MEDIATIZATION OF POLITICS ▶ POLITICAL COMMUNICATION ▶ TELEVISION AS POPULAR CULTURE ▶ TELEVISION, VISUAL CHARACTERISTICS OF

REFERENCES AND SUGGESTED READINGS

Carpini, M. X. & Williams, B. A. (2001). Let us infotain you: Politics in the new media environment. In L. W. Bennett & R. M. Entman (eds.), *Mediated politics: Communication in the future of democracy*. Cambridge. Cambridge University Press, pp. 160–181.

Dörner, A. (2001). *Politainment: Politik in der medialen Erlebnisgesellschaft* [Politainment: Politics as part of the mediated event society]. Frankfurt: Suhrkamp.

Van Zoonen, L. (2005). *Entertaining the citizen: When politics and popular culture converge*. Lanham, MD: Rowman and Littlefield.

Politeness Theory

SUSANNE M. JONES
University of Minnesota

Politeness theory is a sociolinguistic theory developed by Erving Goffman, who examined how people manage their public identities, which he labeled 'face.' When in the presence of others, one's face is always on display (→ Self-Presentation). The process by which people maintain face is called 'facework,' which is a social ritual that provides the cooperative mechanism for interaction order: to have one's face invalidated by others means to 'lose face,' to have it sanctioned is to 'have face.'

Brown and Levinson refined the concept of face in terms of *two opposing human needs*: 'negative face' (the need for autonomy) and 'positive face' (the need for validation). The struggle to balance positive and negative face points to a conflict of human interaction: people strive to cooperatively manage each other's face, yet also tend to unintentionally commit acts that are face threatening.

Brown and Levinson proposed *five politeness strategies* people use to manage 'face-threatening acts' (FTAs). The most polite strategy is to avoid the FTA, which maximizes face saving at the expense of communicating content. The least polite strategy is to relinquish all efforts at face saving and to go bald-on-record without redress, a strategy that prioritizes the content of the message at the expense of face. In between are three strategies that vary in degree of politeness. People might choose to do an FTA off record through innuendos. When speakers use positive politeness FTAs, they show regard for the recipient's positive attributes (e.g., claiming common ground), whereas negative politeness FTAs minimize imposition on the listener's autonomy (e.g., incurring a debt). According to Brown and Levinson (1987), negative politeness strategies are more polite than positive politeness strategies, because they mark the speaker's self-effacement.

Politeness theory and facework have been *tested* in various face-threatening social contexts (MacMartin et al. 2001; Metts & Grohskopf 2003). Face, faceloss, and facework have entered the common vernacular in a relatively short period of time, indicating their immense relevance and heuristic value.

See also: ▶ INTERPERSONAL COMMUNICATION ▶ SELF-PRESENTATION

REFERENCES AND SUGGESTED READINGS

Brown, P. & Levinson, S. C. (1987). *Politeness: Some universals of language usage*. Cambridge: Cambridge University Press.

Cupach, W. R. & Metts, S. (2004). *Facework*. Thousand Oaks, CA: Sage.

MacMartin, C., Wood, L. A., & Kroger, R. O. (2001). Facework. In W. P. Robinson & H. Giles (eds.), *The new handbook of language and social psychology*. Chichester: John Wiley, pp. 221–237.

Metts, S. & Grohskopf, E. (2003). Impression management: Goals, strategies, and skills. In J. O. Greene & B. R. Burleson (eds.), *Handbook of communication and social interaction skills*. Mahwah, NJ: Lawrence Erlbaum, pp. 357–399.

Political Advertising

LYNDA LEE KAID
University of Florida

CHRISTINA HOLTZ-BACHA
University of Erlangen-Nuremberg

Political advertising is a form of → political communication that uses the mass media to promote political candidates, parties, policy issues, and/or ideas. Advertising messages are generally controlled messages allowing for direct communication with the public and voters without interpretation or filtering by news media or other sources (→ Advertising).

In the United States, where political advertising is the dominant form of communication between political candidates and voters, political advertising is a paid media form, and candidates and parties purchase airtime or space for their advertising messages directly from commercial media outlets. Since political advertising enjoys strong protection as a form of free speech/free expression under the US Constitution, there are very few restrictions (→ Freedom of Communication). In other countries political advertising, particularly on radio and television, is often prohibited and, if at all, allowed only during election campaigns. Switzerland and Denmark are examples of countries where electoral advertising on TV is not allowed. If purchase of broadcast advertising is prohibited, candidates or parties may be given free time for their promotional messages (e.g., UK and France). Other countries (e.g., Germany) have a dual system, providing free time on public broadcasting outlets and allowing purchase of time on commercial stations (→ Political Communication Systems). The significance of televised political advertising varies with the differences in political systems, in the organization of the media, and political culture. In many countries printed forms of political advertising, such as posters and newspaper advertising, remain important forms of electoral communication.

There is a large body of research that provides convincing evidence that political television advertising can be effective in changing a candidate's image and/or in affecting voting decisions about the candidate (→ Media Effects; Advertising Effectiveness). Political advertising is particularly effective in communicating issue information to voters. Exposure to political advertising often leads to increased voter knowledge (→ Political Knowledge). Some campaigners fear a backlash from *negative advertising* that might harm, instead of help, the sponsoring candidate. While a few researchers have observed such effects, the overwhelming evidence suggests that negative advertising is quite effective, with limited backlash potential. One of the reasons for this effectiveness is that the public tends to remember negative information more than positive information. Negative ads also tend to be more effective when they criticize the issue positions of the opposing candidate, rather than the personal qualities or image of the opponent. In order to offset the effects of negative advertising it is helpful to inoculate voters against possible negative attacks by providing counterevidence or positive candidate information first. Once an attack has been made in a negative advertisement, the target must provide a rebuttal to prevent the public believing the attack is true. Concern that increased negative advertising may decrease election turnout by turning voters off and making them cynical about politics have been countered by research suggesting that heightened negativity may increase political interest and stimulate turnout.

Political advertising has taken new directions with the increased importance of the Internet. Candidates are using websites as a form of direct political advertising, and they are also using them to host copies of their political television ads. In addition, some candidates and third-party interest groups are using their own websites to distribute unique video ads produced only for distribution on the web. While the 2008 presidential election campaign in the United States incorporated social networking websites, the 2012 race experienced the breakthrough of targeting and tailored advertising: campaign messages shaped for particular voters on the basis of a targeting process that uses information about individuals' habits and interests (Turow et al. 2012; → Social Media; Facebook; Twitter). While voters reject political advertising tailored to their interests and exploiting their personal data, these strategies raise new questions about their effects and effectiveness.

See also: ▶ ADVERTISING ▶ ADVERTISING EFFECTIVENESS ▶ FACEBOOK ▶ FREEDOM OF COMMUNICATION ▶ MEDIA EFFECTS ▶ POLITICAL COMMUNICATION SYSTEMS ▶ POLITICAL KNOWLEDGE ▶ POLITICAL MARKETING ▶ POLITICAL PERSUASION ▶ PROPAGANDA ▶ SOCIAL MEDIA ▶ TWITTER

REFERENCES AND SUGGESTED READINGS

Kaid, L. L. & Holtz-Bacha, C. (eds.) (2006). *The Sage handbook of political advertising.* Thousand Oaks, CA: Sage.

Kaid, L. L. & Johnston, A. (2001). *Videostyle in presidential campaigns: Style and content of televised political advertising.* Westport, CT: Praeger/Greenwood.

Mark, D. (2006). *Going dirty: The art of negative campaigning.* Lanham, MD: Rowman and Littlefield.

Ridout, T. N. & Franz, M. M. (2011). *The persuasive power of campaign advertising.* Philadelphia, PA: Temple University Press.

Turow, J., Delli Carpini, M. X., Draper, N., & Howard-Williams, H. (2012). *Americans roundly reject tailored political advertising at a time when political campaigns are embracing it.* Philadelphia, PA: University of Pennsylvania, Annenberg School of Communication.

Political Cognitions

DORIS A. GRABER
University of Illinois at Chicago

GREGORY G. HOLYK
Langer Research Associates

'Political cognitions' refers to the ability of human beings to acquire and possess → political knowledge through perception, reasoning, or intuition. Citizens' cognitions about politics come mainly from information supplied by the mass media – television, newspapers, magazines, or the Internet – because most political happenings are beyond the day-to-day experiences of citizens. Dependence on mass media has consequences for peoples' cognitions about politics and makes it important to investigate what kinds of information mass media produce.

Despite news professionals' claims of balanced reporting, information provided by the mass media is often *biased* (→ Bias in the News). By highlighting certain issues, people, and details, and framing them to reflect particular perspectives, the media affect how people interpret information and use it for political decisions (→ Framing Effects). The media deserve blame for often failing to present political information in ways that citizens can easily process and remember. Political events are frequently presented as discrete happenings, unconnected to any political history and narrative. Political stories rarely focus on the aspects that the majority of citizens find most interesting and memorable. That makes it difficult for people to commit these stories to long-term memory, and exacerbates the already considerable negative effects of inattention and apathy.

Although cognitive political processing is an individual activity and a major part of human identity, it also has *social components*. For instance, people monitor their social environment and alter their political communication to conform to the political norms of their society. People also alter their search of political information and their own political communication based on what they believe to be the majority or consensus political opinion (Mutz 1998; → Pluralistic Ignorance; Social Perception; Third-Person Effects).

Distinguishing media impact on citizens' attitudes from the impact of multiple other information sources is difficult. Experiments have been useful in isolating mass media effects but raise questions about the validity of the findings in real-world settings. Though political messages in the media unquestionably affect the political → attitudes of citizens, the process involves more than a simple transfer of information. People combine their own experiences, biases, motivations, and stereotypes with the political information they consume (→ Information Processing).

Political scientists have different conceptions of how much breadth and depth of *political knowledge* average citizens need in a democracy to perform their civic duties. While most deem a well-informed and active public essential, they disagree about the standards that should be applied. Judged by idealistic standards about citizens' roles in a democracy (the 'ideal' citizen), average citizens are woefully uninformed about current and historical political facts. They know too little about their current government officials and political institutions, current domestic and international political issues, political geography, and political history.

Political realists concede that citizens have neither the cognitive capabilities nor the motivation to process the vast amounts of political data necessary to fully understand the major political issues requiring attention at various times. Citizens use cognitive shortcuts in order to simplify and efficiently process political information. They are also unsystematic cognitive processors who do not search their entire memory for relevant political information when expressing political opinions; instead, they tend to use information that is readily available from memory and made salient by the media. For instance, when the media routinely frame politics in terms of politicians' personalities instead of political issues, personality factors become paramount in people's thinking and behavior (i.e., voting).

Despite the pervasiveness of emotion-arousing appeals, *emotional influences on thinking* have been condemned in the past as irrational and harmful, and contrary to the prized canons of rationality. Advances in neuroscience demonstrate that emotional arousal releases hormones that enhance human perceptions, speed reactions, and deepen and sharpen memories. In fact, emotional arousal provides the spark that sets off human thinking processes. The emotional arousal produced by many political messages therefore has a major impact on rational political thinking and on the conduct of politics (→ Emotional Arousal Theory). This is especially true during stirring political events like fiercely contested elections, revolutions, or civil and international wars.

See also: ▶ AGENDA-SETTING EFFECTS ▶ ATTITUDES ▶ BIAS IN THE NEWS ▶ COGNITIVE DISSONANCE THEORY ▶ EMOTIONAL AROUSAL THEORY ▶ FRAMING EFFECTS ▶ INFORMATION PROCESSING ▶ MEDIA EFFECTS ▶ NEUTRALITY ▶ PLURALISTIC IGNORANCE ▶ POLITICAL KNOWLEDGE ▶ POLITICAL PERSUASION ▶ SOCIAL PERCEPTION

REFERENCES AND SUGGESTED READINGS

Graber, D. A. (2001). *Processing politics: Learning from television in the Internet age*. Chicago, IL: University of Chicago Press.

Liu, Y. (2012). The influence of communication context on political cognition in presidential campaigns: A geospatial analysis. *Mass Communication and Society*, 15(1), 46–73.

Moy, P. & Gastil, J. (2006). Predicting deliberative conversation: The impact of discussion networks, media use, and political cognitions. *Political Communication*, 23(4), 443–460.

Mutz, D. C. (1998). *Impersonal influence: How perceptions of mass collectives affect political attitudes*. Cambridge: Cambridge University Press.

Petersen, M. B. & Aarøe, L. (2013). Politics in the mind's eye: Imagination as a link between social and political cognition. *American Political Science Review*, 107(2), 275–293.

Political Communication

WINFRIED SCHULZ

University of Erlangen-Nuremberg

Communication is considered to be 'political' if it relates to the exchange of messages among political actors. For example, most of what politicians do is political communication. Likewise, citizens communicate politics when they discuss political issues with friends or family members, phone in to political radio talk shows, or participate in political chats on the Internet. Demonstrations and other forms of protest are more expressive, sometimes even violent, forms of political communication. Also, the consumption of political media content is a form of political communication too. While politics is becoming more dependent, in its central functions, on mass media, questions relating to the → 'mediatization of politics' are assuming higher ranks on the research agenda (Mazzoleni & Schulz 1999). Politics is adapting to 'media logic' and is thus continuously shaped by interactions with mass media. The redistribution of power that comes along with these processes is affecting the orientations and the communication behavior of political actors and journalists.

The Communication of Politics

In spite of impressive modernization trends, including, for example, the growing importance of → visual communication, most of the discourse among political actors is still language based. Political elites use language for strategic purposes such as building a positive image, winning public support, or establishing specific perspectives for evaluation (→ Political Language; Strategic Communication). On the other hand, language serves citizens to make sense of politics, form opinions, and take political decisions.

The mass media play a pivotal role in making the political discourse open to the public. Mass media select, process, and transmit political news and current affairs content. For ordinary citizens and even for political decision-makers, media coverage of politics is the most relevant and quite often the only *source of information* about current events.

By providing a platform for the public debate of political issues, the media construct a → *public sphere*, that is, an open realm for the exchange of information and opinions among diverse political actors. However, according to Habermas (2006), the dynamics of public communication may be impaired by dominating powerful actors of the political center and by deficiencies of the media system, namely commercialization tendencies and connections with special interest groups.

Rather than confining their role to functioning as intermediaries, i.e., serving the information and publication needs of all groups in society, the *media* themselves have become *powerful political actors*, sometimes referred to as the fourth estate. Media organizations pursue policy objectives, for example, by expressing specific partisan opinions, by endorsing the interests of certain societal groups, or by legitimizing the views of those in power. This may have consequences for the balance of power among the classical political estates – legislative, executive, and judiciary – and thus raises questions concerning the definition of media freedom and mechanisms of media control.

Political Media Use and Effects

The evolution of mass media has brought about contradictory results as to citizens' exposure to political information. On the one hand, due to a number of 24-hour news networks on radio and television and, in addition, a plethora of Internet news pages, the sheer volume of *available political information* has proliferated immensely (→ Internet News). On the other hand, many mainstream broadcasters and newspapers have reduced their hard news coverage, especially foreign affairs reporting, and have instead extended the supply of entertaining content, soft news, and → infotainment formats. This goes along with shrinking audiences for serious newspapers and public affairs programs in many countries. While politically attentive citizens benefit enormously from the enriched political media menu, particularly of the Internet, the majority audience seems to be content with being informed just about the most salient issues.

Television is still the main *source of information about politics* for the average citizen, though digital media are continuously gaining ground, particularly among the younger generation (→ Political Media Use). A high correlation of political media use with certain demographic factors is responsible for large differences in the reach of political news and in citizens' acquisition of political information (→ Knowledge Gap Effects). In all countries those who have a higher income, who are better educated, and who are more strongly interested in politics are the most attentive to political information. However, due to blurring lines between hard news, soft news, and light entertainment in some mass media, there is also a chance that politically inattentive citizens are unwittingly exposed to mediated politics (→ Politainment).

As the study of mass communication is generally based on the premise of → media effects, it is also a central presumption of political communication research that the media have a significant *impact on politics* (Graber 2005). A broad field of communication research is devoted to examining the influence of news and information on cognitions and attitudes. Another strand of research looks at influence processes in campaign contexts, for example in health campaigns, in political information campaigns, in → social marketing campaigns, and most often in election campaigns (→ Election Campaign Communication).

As distinct from such rather pragmatic approaches to media effectiveness, there is a broad field of political communication research with a critical or pessimistic orientation that starts from the more or less explicit assumption that mass communication may have negative implications for democratic citizenship and for the political system as a whole. Among the harmful media effects that have been hypothesized are eroding trust in political institutions and political cynicisms.

Political Communication and Research in Flux

The advent of the Internet and other new media (→ Social Media) has removed some of the constraints that traditional media have imposed on communication processes. Because of the enormous increase in content diversity, citizens can choose according to their individual political preferences among an excessive variety of channels and media products. Bennett and Iyengar (2008) envisage a "new era of minimal effects" resulting from eroding media influences as audiences dissolve into increasingly self-selected segments. On the other hand, while audience members can select more freely, the traditional mass media are losing some of their gatekeeping and filtering functions. Thanks to the new communication technologies, citizens can easily bypass the mass media and disseminate messages via weblogs or Internet platforms such as YouTube, or in direct person-to-person networking. The new media enhance both mediated expressions of political opinion and personal political interaction.

Considerable political communication research attention is directed toward *civic engagement*. The label refers to research that tests the presumed (mal)functioning of mass media for political participation. Research on civic engagement includes studies with an explicit orientation to normative criteria, especially to standards derived from theories of democracy. A continuing theme in this field of research is the relationship between entertainment media and political engagement (see, e.g., Delli Carpini 2012).

See also: ▶ AGENDA BUILDING ▶ AGENDA-SETTING EFFECTS ▶ DELIBERATIVENESS IN POLITICAL COMMUNICATION ▶ E-DEMOCRACY ▶ ELECTION CAMPAIGN COMMUNICATION ▶ ELECTION SURVEYS ▶ INFOTAINMENT ▶ INTERNET NEWS ▶ ISSUE MANAGEMENT IN POLITICS ▶ KNOWLEDGE GAP EFFECTS ▶ MEDIA DIPLOMACY ▶ MEDIA EFFECTS ▶ MEDIA EVENTS AND PSEUDO-EVENTS ▶ MEDIATED POPULISM ▶ MEDIATED TERRORISM ▶ MEDIATIZATION OF POLITICS ▶ OPINION LEADER ▶ PERSUASION ▶ POLITAINMENT ▶ POLITICAL ADVERTISING ▶ POLITICAL COGNITIONS ▶ POLITICAL COMMUNICATION SYSTEMS ▶ POLITICAL EFFICACY ▶ POLITICAL KNOWLEDGE ▶ POLITICAL LANGUAGE ▶ POLITICAL MARKETING ▶ POLITICAL MEDIA USE ▶ POLITICAL PERSUASION ▶ POLITICAL SOCIALIZATION THROUGH THE MEDIA ▶ PROPAGANDA ▶ PUBLIC OPINION ▶ PUBLIC RELATIONS ▶ PUBLIC SPHERE ▶ RHETORIC AND POLITICS ▶ SOCIAL MARKETING ▶ SOCIAL MEDIA ▶ STRATEGIC COMMUNICATION ▶ TELEVISED DEBATES ▶ VISUAL COMMUNICATION

REFERENCES AND SUGGESTED READINGS

Bennett, W. L. & Iyengar, S. (2008). A new era of minimal effects? The changing foundations of political communication. *Journal of Communication*, 58, 707–731.

Delli Carpini, M. X. (2012). Entertainment media and the political engagement of citizens. In H. A. Semetko & M. Scammell (eds.), *The Sage handbook of political communication*. Thousand Oaks, CA: Sage, pp. 9–21.

Gerstlé, J. (2008). *La communication politique*, 2nd edn. Paris: Armand Colin.

Graber, D. A. (2004). Mediated politics and citizenship in the twenty-first century. *Annual Review of Psychology*, 55, 545–571.

Graber, D. A. (2005). Political communication faces the 21st century. *Journal of Communication*, 55, 479–507.

Habermas, J. (2006). Political communication in media society: Does democracy still enjoy an epistemic dimension? The impact of normative theory on empirical research. *Communication Theory*, 16, 411–426.

Kaid, L. L., & Holtz-Bacha, C. (eds.) (2008). *Encyclopedia of political communication*. Thousand Oaks, CA: Sage.

Mazzoleni, G. (2004). *La comunicazione politica*. Bologna: Il Mulino.

Mazzoleni, G. & Schulz, W. (1999). "Mediatization" of politics: A challenge for democracy? *Political Communication*, 16, 247–261.

McNair, B. (2011). *An introduction to political communication*, 5th edn. London: Routledge.

Schulz, W. (2011). *Politische Kommunikation: Theoretische Ansätze und Ergebnisse empirischer Forschung [Political communication: Theoretical approaches and empirical findings]*, 3rd edn. Wiesbaden: VS Verlag für Sozialwissenschaften.

Semetko, H. A. & Scammell, M. (2012). *The Sage handbook of political communication*. Thousand Oaks, CA: Sage.

Political Communication Systems

BARBARA PFETSCH

Free University of Berlin

Looking at political communication phenomena in a systems framework is a common approach in comparative communication analysis. The term 'system,' in its general meaning, denotes a multitude of component parts that depend on each other and function as a whole. The nature of the political communication system is thought of as a multi-component structure of producing, processing, and communicating political messages (→ Political Communication).

Elements of a Political Communication System

A political communication system, by analogy with the earlier political systems research (Almond 1956; Almond & Verba 1963), can be mapped along *four dimensions*. First, this system implies an *institutional structure* – a space within media and politics – in which political actors and media actors relate to each other in order to produce messages (→ Message Production). This structure is directly influenced by the way the media and political system has been designed.

Second, the political communication system implies an *input dimension* of → public opinion that reflects the public's voices. Third, it involves an *output dimension* that refers to the messages produced at the interface between media and politics with regard to the public. The fourth dimension comprises the *role perceptions and norms of the actors* in political communication such as politicians and journalists. Political actors may also include professional communicators in political organizations such as spokespersons or pundits, and new types of media actors may involve communicators in the Internet such as bloggers. Their interactions are subject to behavioral norms and other system constraints (→ Journalists' Role Perception).

The political communication system evolves through continuous exchange between two other social systems: politics and the mass media. It carries and regulates the ongoing cross-border communication between the two systems and eventually through frequent exchange it develops its own language and identity.

Intellectual Roots

Among the first scholars in communication studies promoting the idea of political communication as a system were Jay Blumler and Michael Gurevitch (1995). They called for overcoming the limitations of short-term, issue-related studies in areas such as election campaigns, political → public relations, or newsmaking. In their view, the systems perspective reflects a broader and abstract formulation of the political aspects of the media and the communication aspects of politics. Through this framework political communication processes can be related to each other and their environment systematically.

The conception of political communication as a system is inspired by the idea that a system can be stable only if the fundamental values and orientations of its members are compatible with its socio-political and institutional structure. If this notion is applied to political communication, then it refers to both the institutional setting of the political and the media systems *and* the subjective orientations of political communication actors. Blumler and Gurevitch (1995) argue that interaction in the political communication system and the flow of messages are guided by the actors' professional norms or values. The fit of the actors' attitudes, on the one hand, and the structures of message production, on the other, is a decisive criterion for the stability of the political communication system of a given country (Pfetsch 2004).

The essential value of the concept of political communication systems lies in its potential as a framework that allows categories to be developed for the comparative study of political communication. This approach thus enables us to determine which structural conditions correspond to specific constellations of attitudes and behaviors. Moreover, only comparative research can reveal the variety of political communication systems as well as the systematic link between the political system and the media system (Pfetsch & Esser 2012).

Challenges of Future Research

The interplay between structural conditions and attitudinal and behavioral aspects has not yet been researched systematically. To date, we lack encompassing studies that reveal the variety of national political communication systems and their internal and external conditions. Current research on the interface of media and politics largely follows the path of neo-institutionalism, which has its precursor in formulations such as Siebert and Schramm's *Four Theories of the Press* (1956).

While this study became outdated after the Cold War, Hallin and Mancini's *Comparing Media Systems* (2004) provided a new impetus for analyzing the political aspects of western media systems. Moreover, this work has offered a meaningful framework for the comparative analysis of political communication systems through their typology of three ideal types of media systems: the 'liberal model,' the 'democratic corporatist model,' and the 'polarized pluralist model.' Hallin and Mancini describe these types of media systems as a set of categories that reflect the structural conditions in the media and the political system. However, their framework tends to neglect the subjective dimension of political communication systems which relates to actors' attitudes. Moreover, the framework has been criticized for shortcomings and methodological problems that emerge if the framework is applied to the analysis of cases outside of the western world.

The latter point inspired an update study (Hallin & Mancini 2012) that discussed the political communication systems of countries in Africa, Asia, South America, eastern Europe, and the Israeli and Arab World. In this update, it became clear that the typology applies primarily to western European and US media systems (→ United States of America: Media System). Moreover, one can conclude from the more recent study that media systems are strongly influenced by the larger cultural and historical developments of the societies in which they operate. Thus, scholars will have to develop culture-sensitive models of political communication systems that consider these aspects much more than they did before. Current research has only begun to do so (→ Culture: Definitions and Concepts).

See also: ▶ CULTURE: DEFINITIONS AND CONCEPTS ▶ JOURNALISTS' ROLE PERCEPTION ▶ MESSAGE PRODUCTION ▶ PERCEPTION ▶ POLITICAL COMMUNICATION ▶ PUBLIC OPINION ▶ PUBLIC RELATIONS ▶ UNITED STATES OF AMERICA: MEDIA SYSTEM

REFERENCES AND SUGGESTED READINGS

Almond, G. A. (1956). Comparative political systems. *Journal of Politics*, 18, 391–409.

Almond, G. A. & Verba, S. (1963). *The civic culture: Political attitudes and democracy in five nations*. Princeton, NJ: Princeton University Press.

Blumler, J. & Gurevitch, M. (1977). Linkages between the mass media and politics. In J. Curran, M. Gurevitch, & J. Woollacott (eds.), *Mass communication and society*. London: Edward Arnold, pp. 270–290.

Blumler, J. & Gurevitch, M. (1995). *The crisis of public communication*. London: Routledge.

Hallin, D. C. & Mancini, P. (2004). *Comparing media systems: Three models of media and politics*. Cambridge: Cambridge University Press.

Hallin, D. C. & Mancini, P. (eds.) (2012). *Comparing media systems beyond the western world*. Cambridge: Cambridge University Press.

Norris, P. (2001). Political communication. In N. J. Smelser & P. B. Baltes (eds.), *International encyclopedia of the social and behavioral sciences*. Amsterdam: Elsevier, pp. 11631–11640.

Pfetsch, B. (2004). From political culture to political communications culture: A theoretical approach to comparative analysis. In F. Esser & B. Pfetsch (eds.), *Comparing political communication: Theories, cases, and challenges*. Cambridge: Cambridge University Press, pp. 344–366.

Pfetsch, B. & Esser, F. (2012). Comparing political communication. In F. Esser & T. Hanitzsch (eds.), *The handbook of comparative communication research*. London: Routledge, pp. 25–47.

Siebert, F. S. & Schramm, W. (1956). *Four theories of the press: The authoritarian, libertarian, social responsibility, and Soviet communist concepts of what the press should be*. Urbana, IL: University of Illinois Press.

Political Economy of the Media

VINCENT MOSCO
Queen's University, Ontario

Political economy is the study of the social relations, particularly the power relations, that mutually constitute the production, distribution, and consumption of resources, including communication resources (→ Media Economics).

Political economy has consistently placed in the foreground the goal of understanding social change and historical transformation. It is also characterized by an interest in examining the social whole or the totality of social relations that make up the economic, political, social, and cultural areas of life. It is also noted for a commitment to moral philosophy, understood as both an interest in the values that help to create social behavior and in the moral principles that ought to guide efforts to change it. Following from this view, 'social praxis,' or the fundamental unity of thinking and doing, also occupies a central place in political economy (Wasko et al. 2011).

Research on the Political Economy of the Media

North American research has been extensively influenced by the contributions of two founding figures, Dallas Smythe and Herbert Schiller. Partly owing to their influence, North American research has produced a large volume of literature on industry and class-specific manifestations of transnational corporate and state power, distinguished by its concern to participate in social movements and oppositional struggles to change the dominant media and to create alternatives (McChesney 2013; Mosco 2009; Schiller 2014). A major objective of this work is to advance public interest concerns before government regulatory and policy organs. This includes support for movements that have taken an active role before international organizations, in defense of a new international economic, information, and communication order.

European research is less clearly linked to specific founding figures and, although it is also connected to movements for social change, particularly in defense of public service media systems, the leading work in this region has been more concerned to integrate communication research within various neo-Marxian and institutional theoretical traditions. Of the two principal directions this research has taken, one, most prominent in the work of Murdock and Golding (2000), has emphasized 'class power.' A second stream of research foregrounds 'class struggle' and is most prominent in the work of Armand Mattelart (2000). Mattelart has drawn from a range of traditions including dependency theories, western Marxism, and the worldwide experience of national liberation movements to understand communication as one among the principal sources of *resistance* to power (→ Development Communication).

Research on the political economy of communication from *outside the western core* has covered a wide area of interests, although a major stream has grown in response to the modernization or developmentalist theory that originated in western, particularly US, attempts to incorporate communication into an explanatory perspective on development congenial to mainstream academic and political interests. Drawing on several streams of international neo-Marxian political economy, including world systems and dependency theory, these political economists challenged the fundamental premises of the developmentalist model, particularly its technological determinism and the omission of practically any interest in the power relations that shape the terms of relationships between first and third world nations and the multilayered class relations between and within them (Pendakur 2003; Zhao 2008).

Commodification, Spatialization, Structuration

One can map the political economy of communication through key coordinates or the three social processes that are central to the field: commodification, spatialization, and structuration.

(1) *Commodification* has long been understood as the process of taking goods and services that are valued for their use, e.g., food to satisfy hunger or stories for communication, and transforming them into commodities that are valued for what they can earn in the marketplace, e.g., farming to sell food, producing drama for commercial television (→ Commodification of the Media).

The process of commodification holds a dual significance for communication research. First, communication practices and technologies contribute to the *general commodification process throughout society*. For example, the introduction of computer communication gives all companies, not just communication companies, greater control over the entire process of production, distribution, and exchange, enabling retailers to monitor sales and inventory levels with precision. This enables companies to produce and ship only what they know is likely to sell quickly, thereby reducing inventory requirements and unnecessary merchandise. Similarly, social media companies can more precisely deliver its users to advertisers based on the precise analysis of their postings.

Second, commodification is an entry point to *understanding specific communication institutions and practices*. For example, the general, worldwide expansion of commodification in the 1980s, responding in part to global declines in economic growth, led to the increased commercialization of media programming (→ Commercialization: Impact on Media Content), the privatization of once public media and telecommunications institutions, and the liberalization of communication markets.

(2) *Spatialization* is the process of overcoming the constraints of space and time in social life. Communication is central to spatialization because communication and information processes and technologies promote flexibility and control throughout industry, but particularly within the communication and information sectors. Spatialization encompasses the process of globalization, the worldwide restructuring of industries and firms (Winseck and Jin 2011; → Globalization Theories).

(3) *Structuration* addresses the relationship between human agency and social structure. When political economy has given attention to agency, process, and social practice, it tends to focus on social class. Political economy has also made important strides in addressing the intersection of feminist studies and the political economy of the media (Meehan & Riordan 2002). In the context of structuration, communication studies has addressed 'imperialism' extensively, principally by examining the role of the media and information technology in the maintenance of control by richer over poorer societies (→ Cultural Imperialism Theories). Race figures significantly in this analysis and more generally in the social process of structuration.

See also: ▶ COMMERCIALIZATION: IMPACT ON MEDIA CONTENT ▶ COMMODIFICATION OF THE MEDIA ▶ CONCENTRATION IN MEDIA SYSTEMS ▶ CONSUMERS IN MEDIA MARKETS ▶ CULTURAL IMPERIALISM THEORIES ▶ CULTURAL STUDIES ▶ DEVELOPMENT COMMUNICATION ▶ GLOBALIZATION OF THE MEDIA ▶ GLOBALIZATION THEORIES ▶ MARKETS OF THE MEDIA ▶ MEDIA CONGLOMERATES ▶ MEDIA ECONOMICS

REFERENCES AND SUGGESTED READINGS

Mattelart, A. (2000). *Networking the world, 1794–2000* (trans. L. Carey-Libbrecht & J. A. Cohen). Minneapolis: University of Minnesota Press.

McChesney, R. W. (2013). *Digital disconnect: How capitalism is turning the Internet against democracy.* New York: New Press.

Meehan, E. & Riordan, E. (eds.) (2002). *Sex and money: Feminism and political economy in the media.* Minneapolis: University of Minnesota Press.

Mosco, V. (2009). *The political economy of communication.* 2nd edn. London: Sage.

Murdock, G. & Golding, P. (2000). Culture, communications and political economy. In J. Curran & M. Gurevitch (eds.), *Mass media and society*, 3rd edn. London: Arnold, pp. 70–92.

Pendakur, M. (2003). *Indian popular cinema: Industry, ideology, and consciousness.* Cresskill, NJ: Hampton Press.

Schiller, D. (2014). *Digital depression.* Urbana, IL: University of Illinois Press.

Wasko, J., Murdock, G., & Sousa, H. (eds.) (2011). *The handbook of political economy of communications.* New York: John Wiley.

Winseck, D. & Jin, D. Y. (eds.) (2011). *Political economies of the media: The transformation of the global media.* London: Bloomsbury Academic.

Zhao, Y. (2008). *Communication in China: Political economy, power, and conflict.* Lanham, MD: Rowman and Littlefield.

Political Efficacy

PATRICIA MOY
University of Washington

A multidimensional concept that links political cognitions, → attitudes, and behaviors, 'political efficacy' refers generally to citizens' beliefs in their ability to influence the political system. Early perspectives on the concept saw it not only as a psychological disposition, but also as a norm and as a behavior. In other words, if citizens are politically efficacious, they will be more likely to support a given political regime, be more trusting of that system, and be less likely to engage in activities that challenge the system. If political efficacy is a disposition and a norm, then politically efficacious citizens believe that they can and should participate in politics.

Contemporary views have reverted to the original emphasis on feelings, and conceptualize political efficacy as having *two dimensions*: internal efficacy, which reflects a personal sense of political competence, and external efficacy, the belief that the political system is democratic and will respond to actions taken by its citizens. Operationalizations of *internal efficacy* include survey items such as "I consider myself to be well qualified to participate in politics." *External efficacy*, on the other hand, tends to be measured by items that include, for instance "People like me do not have any say about what the government does." Although internal efficacy and external efficacy have been shown to be empirically related, this relationship is not always constant.

Various studies have investigated the *relationship between media use and political efficacy* caused by the media's different ability to convey political knowledge. For instance, it has been shown that newspaper reading increases knowledge more than television viewing, and with increased knowledge, enhances feelings of self-efficacy. However, the view that newspapers are more effective than television news at imparting political knowledge has come under attack as researchers have begun to scrutinize the conceptualization and measurement of political knowledge and media use (→ Political Knowledge; Political Socialization through the Media).

A second area of research is the *effects of negative media content* on feelings of efficacy. Numerous studies have drawn the same conclusion: media negativity undermines political trust, a very close correlate of external efficacy. Negatively valenced stories of political actors and democratic institutions and certain television production practices – e.g., close-ups of individuals engaged in politically contentious discussions – have been seen as conveying an uncivil image of politics and thus reducing trust in government, which in turn can decrease levels of external efficacy.

With the → Internet a third area of research on communication and political efficacy has emerged. Optimists believe new media technology can lower the costs of communicating with elected officials, expressing their views with others, and participating in public affairs. In addition, the wealth of information available on the Internet has the potential to increase knowledge about political issues. Pessimists contend that the Internet helps only to erode political efficacy. Specifically, the same wealth of political information online that would generate political knowledge could overwhelm a user and reduce his or her sense of self-efficacy. Also, increased levels of communication (e.g., on → social media) with elected officials may not necessarily mean increased responses from these individuals. Empirically, the data linking Internet use to political efficacy have generated inconsistent results. A fourth area of research has been the relationship between *interpersonal communication* and political efficacy (→ Two-Step Flow of Communication).

Most studies in communication research see political efficacy as causally subsequent to communication, not surprisingly given communication scholars' focus on effects research (→ Media Effects). A smaller corpus of literature provides evidence for arguing causality in the other direction, i.e., that efficacy (particularly internal efficacy) influences communication. In sum, it is clear that mass and interpersonal communication can shape one's feelings of efficacy. However, as media outlets and genres proliferate, and as they attempt to attract different segments of the population, each with different orientations and motivations and dispositions, the relationships between communication and efficacy will need to be analyzed more closely.

See also: ▶ ATTITUDE–BEHAVIOR CONSISTENCY ▶ ATTITUDES ▶ INFOTAINMENT ▶ INTERNET ▶ MEDIA EFFECTS ▶ OPERATIONALIZATION ▶ POLITAINMENT ▶ POLITICAL ADVERTISING ▶ POLITICAL KNOWLEDGE ▶ POLITICAL SOCIALIZATION THROUGH THE MEDIA ▶ SOCIAL MEDIA ▶ TWO-STEP FLOW OF COMMUNICATION ▶ USES AND GRATIFICATIONS

REFERENCES AND SUGGESTED READINGS

Hoffman, L. H. & Thomson, T. L. (2009). The effect of television viewing on adolescents' civic participation: Political efficacy as a mediating mechanism. *Journal of Broadcasting and Electronic Media*, 53(1), 3–21.

Kenski, K. & Stroud, N. J. (2006). Connections between Internet use and political efficacy, knowledge, and participation. *Journal of Broadcasting and Electronic Media*, 50(2), 173–192.

Morrell, M. E. (2003). Survey and experimental evidence for a reliable and valid measure of internal political efficacy. *Public Opinion Quarterly*, 67, 589–602.

Moy, P. & Pfau, M. (2000). *With malice toward all? The media and public confidence in democratic institutions*. Westport, CT: Praeger.

Zhou, Y. & Pinkleton, B. E. (2012). Modeling the effects of political information source use and online expression on young adults' political efficacy. *Mass Communication and Society*, 15(6), 813–830.

Political Journalists

THOMAS HANITZSCH
Ludwig Maximilian University of Munich

Political journalists, viewed through the lens of the newsroom, are those who report on political affairs or work on the 'political desk.'

In an era of → mediatization of politics, political journalists play a vital role in informing the electorate. They are expected to act in the public interest, as gatekeepers who provide the citizenry with relevant information, and as watchdogs to safeguard democracy (→ Journalists' Role Perception). However, as media organizations have become subject to marketing, commercializing, and commodifying processes, political journalism has tended to highlight the popular and spectacular over the relevant (→ Infotainment). This tendency, along with a decline in voter participation, has helped give rise to a reform movement that endeavors to reconstruct public life by reconnecting journalists with the communities they cover. Other efforts attempt to furnish political journalists with a more assertive role in national development and nonviolent conflict resolution (→ Development Journalism), especially in poor and war-torn societies of Asia and Africa.

Journalists are also *political actors*. The normative ideal of objectivity notwithstanding, contentious and interventionist practices prevail in some areas of political reporting. Politically active journalists perceive themselves as participants in the debate, as advocates of and missionaries for a particular political cause (→ Advocacy Journalism). Politically assertive journalism has a rich tradition in Latin America and also in parts of Europe, where the media tend to have distinct political orientations. Contentious and interventionist political journalism is generally more common in developing and transitional societies.

See also: ▶ ADVOCACY JOURNALISM ▶ BIAS IN THE NEWS ▶ DEVELOPMENT JOURNALISM ▶ INFOTAINMENT ▶ JOURNALISTS' ROLE PERCEPTION ▶ MEDIATIZATION OF POLITICS ▶ NEWS SOURCES ▶ NEWS ROUTINES

REFERENCES AND SUGGESTED READINGS

Donsbach, W. & Patterson, T. E. (2004). Political news journalists: Partisanship, professionalism, and political roles in five countries. In F. Esser & B. Pfetsch (eds.), *Comparing political communication: Theories, cases, and challenges*. Cambridge: Cambridge University Press, pp. 251–270.

Hanitzsch, T., Hanusch, F., Mellado, C. et al. (2011). Mapping journalism cultures across nations: A comparative study of 18 countries. *Journalism Studies*, 12(3), 273–293.

McNair, B. (2000). *Journalism and democracy: An evaluation of the political public sphere*. London: Routledge.

Weaver, D. H. (ed.) (1998). *The global journalist: News people around the world*. Cresskill, NJ: Hampton Press.

Political Knowledge

WILLIAM P. EVELAND, JR.
Ohio State University

MYIAH J. HUTCHENS
University of Arizona

The centrality of an informed public to democratic theory has made the concept of political knowledge integral to the study of political communication. Various terms have been used to address the concept of political knowledge, such as political sophistication and political expertise.

Political knowledge is often divided into *two components*. Factual political knowledge refers to the ability to remember bits of information that can be determined to be objectively true or false. Factual political knowledge includes knowledge of officials and their roles in the political system, political process, and candidate characteristics. *Structural knowledge* is the way in which factual information is mentally organized. Various terms have been employed to refer to political knowledge structures, including → schemas and political ideologies. A different approach considers knowledge across various political domains such as health care policy, fiscal policy, or international affairs. Individuals who have high levels of knowledge in one domain ('issue publics') do not necessarily have high levels of knowledge in other domains.

There is considerable debate regarding the level of political knowledge of the public, and what level is necessary for the effective practice of democracy. Levels of political knowledge in the US have been low and stable since the mid-twentieth century. Levels of foreign affairs knowledge differ by country, with North Americans being relatively less informed than their European counterparts. Some argue that the lack of political knowledge raises serious questions about the ability of democracy to work effectively in the interests of its citizens. Others counter that citizens with minimal knowledge can use simple heuristics – based on party identification or even visual characteristics of candidates – to make satisfactory choices (→ Information Processing; Elaboration Likelihood Model). Scholars have recently argued that the concept of misinformation – knowledge or belief that is demonstrably inaccurate but widely believed nonetheless – should be given more attention.

Communication is related to political knowledge (→ Exposure to Communication Content; Political Media Use). The positive 'newspaper use–knowledge relationship' has been demonstrated repeatedly, although political learning is typically less from tabloid newspapers than from broadsheets. Television news use is also positively related to knowledge, especially among those with less education (→ Knowledge Gap Effects). In countries, such as the US, where most individuals watch commercial network news, the relationship between television news use and knowledge is not as strong or consistent as the relationship between newspaper use and knowledge, or between television news use and knowledge in countries with more prominent public service broadcasting.

The Internet (→ Internet News) and political comedy programs such as The Daily Show (→ Broadcast Talk) can also be sources for political knowledge. Using the Internet for leisure activities, such as playing games, is negatively related to political knowledge; however, using the Internet to search for political information is positively related to knowledge.

Discussing politics with others in *interpersonal communication* has also been tied to an increase in political knowledge (→ Two-Step Flow of Communication). Frequency of political discussion has one of the most consistent positive relationships with political knowledge. The size of an individual's political discussion network is also positively related to political knowledge.

Regardless of the form of communication, an individual's motivation plays a role in what information is selected and how it is processed (→ Information Seeking; Uses and Gratifications). This will have a large impact on political knowledge. When processing communication, elaboration – making connections between new information and prior knowledge and experience – is associated with increased knowledge.

See also: ▶ BROADCAST TALK ▶ ELABORATION LIKELIHOOD MODEL ▶ EXPOSURE TO COMMUNICATION

CONTENT ▶ INFORMATION PROCESSING
▶ INFORMATION SEEKING ▶ INTERNET NEWS
▶ INTERPERSONAL COMMUNICATION
▶ KNOWLEDGE GAP EFFECTS ▶ POLITICAL
MEDIA USE ▶ SCHEMAS ▶ TWO-STEP FLOW OF
COMMUNICATION ▶ USES AND GRATIFICATIONS

REFERENCES AND SUGGESTED READINGS

Delli Carpini, M. X. & Keeter, S. (1996). *What Americans know about politics and why it matters.* New Haven, CT: Yale University Press.

Eveland, W. P., Jr. (2004). The effect of political discussion in producing informed citizens: The roles of information, motivation, and elaboration. *Political Communication*, 21, 177–193.

Graber, D. A. (2001). *Processing politics: Learning from television in the Internet age.* Chicago, IL: University of Chicago Press.

Price, V. (1999). Political information. In J. P. Robinson, P. R. Shaver, & L. S. Wrightsman (eds.), *Measures of political attitudes.* San Diego, CA: Academic Press, pp. 591–639.

Sotirovic, M. & McLeod, J. M. (2004). Knowledge as understanding: The information processing approach to political learning. In L. L. Kaid (ed.), *The handbook of political communication research.* Mahwah, NJ: Lawrence Erlbaum, pp. 357–394.

Political Language

SHARON E. JARVIS
University of Texas at Austin

Political language has been studied by sociolinguists, communication scholars, political scientists, historians, sociologists, anthropologists, psychologists, and marketing professionals (→ Language and Social Interaction; Political Communication). Shared assumptions are that people come to know their political worlds through messages and political words do not have meaning in themselves (rather their meanings are a function of speakers, contexts, and audiences).

Widely accepted *claims across these fields* include how (1) political language helps people to understand situations (as the structure of any language provides perceptual discriminations to individuals); (2) political names and labels are critical to public life (for only entities that are named can be shared); and (3) political language is not static (as the meanings of words can expand, contract, or shift from their original meanings).

Classic works address how word use shapes culture, ideology, and political life. British theorist Williams (1976) took a longitudinal approach to show how social and historical processes occur within language. Working from a Marxist perspective, Williams examined how certain meanings emerged (e.g., capitalism), older meanings became reversed (e.g., society, individual), and still others were extended (e.g., interest) over time in language. Rhetorician Burke (1966) discussed the capacity of language to shape people's thoughts, particularly subconscious thoughts (→ Rhetorics: New Rhetorics).

Political scholar Murray Edelman (1977) focused on how language is used to classify people, to define groups, and to justify actions. He asserted that individuals are far more likely to experience the language surrounding politics than actual political events themselves. He also described how labeling can cast individuals as deserving of support and signal that issues are appropriate for political discussion. To politicize a person, a group, or an issue, in his mind, is to define it as appropriate for decision-making; in contrast, to ignore an individual, to define a group as an enemy, or to regard an issue as non-political often serves to win general acceptance for elite values.

See also: ▶ DISCOURSE ▶ LANGUAGE AND SOCIAL INTERACTION ▶ MEANING ▶ POLITICAL COMMUNICATION ▶ RHETORICAL STUDIES ▶ RHETORICS: NEW RHETORICS

REFERENCES AND SUGGESTED READINGS

Burke, K. (1966). *Language as symbolic action.* Berkeley, CA: University of California Press.

Edelman, M. E. (1977). *Political language: Words that succeed and policies that fail.* New York: Academic Press.

Williams, R. (1976). *Keywords: A vocabulary of culture and society.* Oxford: Oxford University Press.

Political Marketing

PHILIPPE J. MAAREK
University of East Paris

Political marketing arose when, in the middle of the twentieth century, the methods developed by commercial marketing specialists were adopted for political campaigning. Political marketing replaced unilateral propaganda exactly as commercial advertising has become a plain subsidiary of commercial marketing (Maarek 2011).

While political marketing initially emerged in the United States, it has progressed very quickly to most of the countries where free elections are held (→ Election Campaign Communication). Sometimes considered as an 'Americanization' of political communication processes, this penetration by modern political marketing techniques is now understood as being a sign of plain professionalized modernization, and a reaction to similar media environments and similar electoral circumstances (Negrine et al. 2007). Initially positioned within electoral campaigns, political marketing was quickly applied to government public communication. It has become the counterpart of new media developments, especially of the Internet, then the → social media of 'Web 2.0.' Any announcement in policymaking has now to face the new liberty given to citizens to denounce it instantly and efficiently, thus leading to more carefully planned communication campaigns by marketing specialists.

Two *consequences of an increasing political marketing* influence are discussed quite often in the scholarly literature. *Depolitization of politics* is a paradoxical result of targeting swing voters in election campaigns, who have little interest in politics, parties, and candidates. This has toned down the political core of the campaigns and often resorted to plain populism. In order to reach a wide audience, and particularly citizens with little political interest, politicians are even appearing on media entertainment programs and present themselves like show-business celebrities, hence the depolitization of political communication (→ Politainment).

The marketing strategy of reaching undecided voters by nonpolitical arguments also contributes to *personalization* as does the predominance of television in election campaigning. In addition, negative advertising attacking the opponent directs voters' attention to the personal characteristics of the top candidates (Ansolabehere & Iyengar 1995). Therefore, the personalities of the front runners become the main reason for casting votes, rather than their political programs or their campaigning themes, with a rather dubious side-effect, the celebritization of politics (or 'peopolization').

See also: ▶ ELECTION CAMPAIGN COMMUNICATION ▶ POLITAINMENT ▶ POLITICAL COMMUNICATION ▶ SOCIAL MEDIA

REFERENCES AND SUGGESTED READINGS

Ansolabehere, S. & Iyengar, S. (1995). *Going negative: How political advertisements shrink and polarize the electorate*. New York: Free Press.

Maarek, P. J. (2011). *Campaign Communication and Political Marketing*. Oxford: Wiley Blackwell

Negrine, R., Mancini, P., Holz-Bacha, C., & Papathanassopoulos, S. (2007). *The professionalisation of political communication*. Bristol: Intellect.

Political Media Use

WOLFRAM PEISER
Ludwig Maximilian University of Munich

Political media use refers to peoples usage of both political media (such as newspapers, news magazines, or news sites on the Internet) and political content in all kinds of media. 'Political content' normally means nonfictional content dealing with political events, issues, institutions, etc., but can also mean the conveyance of politically relevant values or perceptions in fictional programs such as the US series *House of Cards*.

Recipients' contact with politics in the media can take very different forms, varying in terms of motivation, attention, and regularity. Hence, just measuring quantitative exposure seems of limited utility, at least if research interest is in news processing and learning (→ Information Processing). Self-reported exposure apparently overestimates political media use (Prior 2009), probably not only because of inaccuracies but also due to social desirability. More concrete measures of actual news use usually find a rather limited portion of the audience who is aware of important news of the day (Donsbach 2014).

Compared to entertainment media, use of political information seems relatively unimportant to most of the audience. Television continues to be the most important source of current affairs information for the general population but in some countries the Internet has already passed television as a source of political news (at least among younger people). However, in terms of percentages such measures have to distinguish between the overall proportion of the population who generally follows the news and the proportion using different media. Data from western democracies indicate that regular followers of the news decrease while among those who follow the news the Internet sources are increasing.

A variety of factors can explain why exposure to political media content can be functional for the recipient, among them the need for surveillance structuring the day, the provision of themes and arguments for discussions (→ Uses and Gratifications). In general, citizens tend to prefer sources that reflect and confirm their own political views. Political media use is shaped by socialization influences, specifically parental information habits (→ Political Socialization Through the Media). Political media use increases markedly during youth and adolescence, along with political interest. However, cohort analyses (comparing the same age groups in different generations) show that the overall interest in political information is on the decline. The severe loss of newspaper readership seems to be only partially compensated by the use of political news in Internet sources. Research still has to investigate how much of this loss can be traced back to a decreasing interest in the → public sphere, and how much to a declining proportion of political content among the ever-increasing content offer in todays media environment.

See also: ▶ ATTENDING TO THE MASS MEDIA ▶ EXPOSURE TO COMMUNICATION CONTENT ▶ EXPOSURE TO THE INTERNET ▶ EXPOSURE TO PRINT MEDIA ▶ EXPOSURE TO RADIO ▶ EXPOSURE TO TELEVISION ▶ INFORMATION PROCESSING ▶ INFORMATION SEEKING ▶ LEARNING AND COMMUNICATION ▶ MEDIA EFFECTS ▶ MEDIA USE ACROSS THE LIFE-SPAN ▶ MEDIA USE BY SOCIAL VARIABLE ▶ NEWS ▶ ONLINE JOURNALISM ▶ POLITICAL COMMUNICATION ▶ POLITICAL SOCIALIZATION THROUGH THE MEDIA ▶ PUBLIC SPHERE ▶ SELECTIVE EXPOSURE ▶ SOCIAL MEDIA ▶ USES AND GRATIFICATIONS

REFERENCES AND SUGGESTED READINGS

Bakker, T. P. & de Vreese, C. H. (2011). Good news for the future? Young people, Internet use, and political participation. *Communication Research*, 38(4), 451–451)

Donsbach, W. (2014). Journalism as the new knowledge profession and consequences for journalism education. *Journalism*, 15, 661u677.

Lee, A. M. (2013). News audiences revisited: Theorizing the link between audience motivations and news consumption. *Journal of Broadcasting and Electronic Media*, 57(3), 300–317.

Prior, M. (2009). The immensely inflated news audience: Assessing bias in self-reported news exposure. *Public Opinion Quarterly*, 73(1), 130–143.

Political Persuasion

RICHARD M. PERLOFF
Cleveland State University

EDWARD HOROWITZ
Cleveland State University

GARY PETTEY
Cleveland State University

Political → persuasion is a process in which communicators try to convince other people to change their attitudes or behavior regarding a political issue through messages, in an atmosphere of free choice (Perloff 2014). It involves the application of persuasion principles to a context in which most individuals possess the seemingly incompatible characteristics of harboring strong feelings about a host of issues, yet caring precious little about the context in which these issues are played out.

If a democratic system is to function efficiently, political persuasion occurs in *both directions*, bottom-up and top-down. The public must be able to persuade politicians to enact public policies that reflect the will of the people. This persuasion can be expressed by the will of the majority, such as by a mandate in a winning election, but it can also be expressed by the minority, such as in the influence of special interests and lobbyists. Alternatively, the direction of influence can go from political leaders to the public. Politicians must be able to persuade the public to support their agenda of foreign policy, domestic policy, and legislative initiatives. For example, the government uses various means of political persuasion to persuade the people to support foreign military action, or support new domestic initiatives. Ultimately, it is the media that are the critical links in this process – regardless of direction – as they transmit carefully crafted messages by government agencies, convey the strength of public support of policies by reporting public opinion polls (Mutz & Soss 1997), and act as gatekeepers and framers of the daily flow of political news.

Along with direction of influence, we must understand the practice of *political persuasion across levels*. At the interpersonal level there is ongoing political persuasion occurring within the halls of legislative bodies, where law-makers engage in endless arm-twisting of their colleagues while seeking support and votes for legislation. Political persuasion at the interpersonal level also occurs among individuals, dyads, and groups within the public. This is most apparent during political campaigns as supporters attempt to convert the undecided as well as rally the faithful. The persuasiveness of interpersonal political communication has become more apparent in recent elections as the use of the Internet, including → electronic mails and blogs, has been found to be an important means of rallying political support and fundraising (→ Election Campaign Communication). Internet campaigns by special interest groups have also been found to be effective in spurring letter-writing, phone calls, and emails to members of parliaments to persuade them to vote for particular legislation. In addition, at the intergroup level members of the public participate in political rallies, marches, and protests that can often be effective means of persuading politicians to pay greater attention to specific social causes or legislative issues.

Most research in the area of political persuasion occurs within the context of elections. At the societal level, political advertising has been found to influence the voting decisions and affect the political knowledge of voters in the US (→ Advertising as Persuasion). Although derided by critics, negative political ads have been shown to be effective.

Converging across levels, attempts at political persuasion by interest groups must continually battle for legitimization from the greater public at large, public officials, and the media. Even as some interest groups find great success in persuading both public and politicians of their message, many other 'fringe' groups may never find their message well received, despite their persuasive attempts.

Thus, the *mediated campaign environment* represents the battleground in the fight for the 'hearts and minds' of public and elites. Legitimation of message is a crucial aspect of persuasion, and the media are primary sources of political information, whether about candidates or about issues (→ Political Cognitions). Media framing provides the audience with a workable model to interpret complex and often confusing information (→ Framing Effects). In this sense, framing is an extension of → agenda-setting effects.

See also: ▶ ADVERTISING AS PERSUASION ▶ AGENDA-SETTING EFFECTS ▶ BROADCAST TALK ▶ ELABORATION LIKELIHOOD MODEL ▶ ELECTION CAMPAIGN COMMUNICATION ▶ ELECTRONIC MAIL ▶ FRAMING EFFECTS ▶ INFORMATION PROCESSING ▶ MEDIA EFFECTS ▶ MEDIA AND PERCEPTIONS OF REALITY ▶ NEWS ROUTINES ▶ PERSUASION ▶ POLITICAL ADVERTISING ▶ POLITICAL COGNITIONS ▶ RHETORIC, ARGUMENT, AND PERSUASION ▶ SCHEMAS ▶ STRATEGIC FRAMING

REFERENCES AND SUGGESTED READINGS

Bishop, G. W. (2005). *The illusion of public opinion: Fact and artifact in American public opinion polls*. Lanham, MD: Rowman and Littlefield.

Kellner, D. (2004). Media propaganda and spectacle in the war on Iraq: A critique of U.S. broadcasting networks. *Cultural Studies/Critical Methodologies*, 4, 329–338.

Lakoff, G. (2004). *Don't think of an elephant! Know your values and frame the debate*. White River Junction, VT: Chelsea Green.

Lees-Marshment, J. (2010). Global political marketing. In J. Lees-Marshment, J. Stromback, & C. Rudd (Eds.), *Global political marketing*. London: Routledge, pp. 1–15.

Mutz, D. C. & Soss, J. (1997). Reading public opinion: The influence of news coverage on perceptions of public sentiment. *Public Opinion Quarterly*, 61, 431–451.

Perloff, R. M. (2014). *The dynamics of political persuasion: Mass media and politics in a digital age*. London: Routledge.

Perloff, R. M. (2014). *The dynamics of persuasion: Communication and attitudes in the 21st century*, 5th edn. London: Routledge.

Political Socialization through the Media

DHAVAN V. SHAH
University of Wisconsin–Madison

Political socialization can be understood as the processes through which democratic societies instill the proper norms among their members to maintain social institutions and practices. Most research on this topic focuses on how individuals engage in political development and learn basic civic skills, with family, schooling, peer groups, and media serving as the major factors involved in this dynamic.

The *general trends* show that the gap in civic engagement between younger and older adults has grown over the past decades in most western democracies. Young people have less → political knowledge and pay less attention to the news than their parents did at the same age. They also are less trusting of their fellow citizens, and even when they do vote, their action is not as likely to be accompanied by other civic actions. Heavy television viewing as measured by hours of use is associated with lower political activity among both adolescents and younger adults, seemingly confirming this suspicion. However, this finding should be interpreted tentatively. First, it only holds for formal political activity and discussion. Second, there might be differences in the effects of various forms of television content. Indeed, the decade's long decline in participation is more likely a direct result of the erosion of print news readership rather than an effect of the rise of television. On the other side, the Internet, especially when used as a source of public affairs information and a sphere for political expression, shows signs of salutary effects rivaling TV and newspapers (Shah et al. 2005).

To understand the effect of media use and political talk on *adolescent socialization*, we must consider both the level of activity and strength of effect. Adolescent news consumption from traditional print and broadcast media is small in comparison to their consumption of entertainment content in the form of television programs, films, and video games. Still, there is a significant rise in news consumption, political talk with peers, and civic engagement from early to late adolescence. Family communication patterns also change during the adolescent years, with parents reducing demands for conformity and instead favoring greater openness to the expression of controversial positions. These changes contribute to adolescent political learning and activity.

Concerning *differential potency of the media*, newspaper hard news reading has the strongest media effect on indicators of youth socialization, after demographic and other controls, in conveying knowledge, stimulating discussion, and shaping attitudes among adolescents. Attentive television news viewing has a positive though weaker impact, while television entertainment viewing has both positive and negative effects. Mental elaboration or 'reflection' – reflecting on issues seen in the news and connecting them with existing beliefs – has a strong effect on engagement beyond exposure to the news. Reflection and issue discussion are both conduits and consequences of news consumption. That is, news consumption encourages these outcomes, but also has its effects on participation channeled through these internal and external forms of deliberation (Yoon et al. 2005). Research on young adults, which focuses on *online news consumption*, political messaging over email, and other online communication tools, suggests even more optimistic outcomes for adolescents (Lee et al. 2013).

Early adulthood is a period of rapid identity change. Although younger adults are generally less active than older adults, the extent of difference varies across indices of civic engagement. Differences are largest for voting, political/public affairs interest, and knowledge. More moderate differences are shown for trust in people and efficacy (→ Political Efficacy). Prior to the rise of the Internet, news reached young adults mainly through television, with young people consuming at lower rates than older citizens during election campaign periods. Internet use, writ large, displays an opposite pattern. Younger adults are the heaviest users, with amount of use declining across increasingly older adults

The prospects for civic renewal and future civic socialization through the media clearly deserve more attention. With the rise of the Internet, patterns of news consumption are shifting, especially among adolescents, with some recent studies suggesting that young people are mainly encountering conventional hard news content through online channels such as customized home pages, social media, and mobile devices. Thus, use of the Internet by the most recent cohorts may partly offset the loss in conventional news consumption via other media.

See also: ▶ EXPOSURE TO COMMUNICATION CONTENT ▶ EXPOSURE TO THE INTERNET ▶ EXPOSURE TO TELEVISION ▶ MEDIA EFFECTS ▶ MEDIA USE ACROSS THE LIFE-SPAN ▶ NEWS ▶ POLITICAL ADVERTISING ▶ POLITICAL COGNITIONS ▶ POLITICAL COMMUNICATION ▶ POLITICAL EFFICACY ▶ POLITICAL KNOWLEDGE ▶ POLITICAL MEDIA USE

REFERENCES AND SUGGESTED READINGS

Bakker, T. P. & de Vreese, C. H. (2011). Good news for the future? Young people, Internet use, and political participation. *Communication Research*, 38(4), 451–470.

Lee, N., Shah, D., & McLeod, J. M. (2013). Processes of political socialization: A communication mediation approach to youth civic engagement. *Communication Research*, 40(5), 669–697.

Moeller, J. & de Vreese, C. (2013). The differential role of the media as an agent of political socialization in Europe. *European Journal of Communication*, 28(3), 309–325.

Shah, D., Cho, J., Eveland, W. P., Jr., & Kwak, N. (2005). Information and expression in a digital age: Modeling Internet effects on civic participation. *Communication Research*, 32, 531–565.

Yoon, S.-H., McLeod, J. M., & Shah, D. V. (2005). Communication and youth socialization. In L. Sherrod, C. Flanagan, & R. Kassimir (eds.), *Youth activism: An international encyclopedia*. Westport, CT: Greenwood Press, pp. 160–167.

Vraga, E. K., Bode, L., Yang, J., Edgerly, S., Thorson, K., Wells, C., & Shah, D. V. (2014). Political influence across generations: Partisanship and candidate evaluations in the 2008 election. *Information, Communication and Society*, 17(2), 184–202.

Popular Communication

DEBRA MERSKIN
University of Oregon

Popular communication is an interdisciplinary, multi-theoretical, multi-methodological philosophy of media and audiences. It has evolved as a nonhierarchical perspective that emphasizes the value of objects, behaviors, attitudes, and beliefs associated with everyday life. In many ways, the term defies definition because of the resistance to categorization inherent in a postmodern vision, which values all products of human endeavor (→ Postmodernism and Communication). Traditionally the term 'popular' was used to express favorability, high regard, and appreciation by the general public (as opposed to small, elite segments). Popular 'culture' is culture of the people by the people and for the people (→ Culture: Definitions and Concepts).

What is Popular Communication Research?

Popular communication research, a product of merger between sciences and the humanities, is critical of systems of power holding that the media are ideological tools with which dominant society maintains power and controls resources by presenting assumed mainstream attitudes, beliefs, and behaviors. One approach to studying popular communication is examination of messages and their potential impact on audiences (→ Media Effects). Another interest of the field is the way(s) people make → meaning from the media (visual and verbal) texts they consume.

The popular communication perspective recognizes that people make their own meaning from content, resisting and transgressing messages of expected behaviors and roles. There are *three primary lenses through which the audience decodes messages*: preferred (as the sender intended with little to no critical evaluation of content), negotiated (audience is aware of the intent of the message, but goes along with it anyway), and resistant (audience awareness is high regarding the persuasive intent of the message and the audience actively works to decode the denotative and connotative meanings within and behind the text). Audiences often participate in the creation of content as well, such as on Internet fan sites.

As a product, mass (simultaneously, widely available) media contain the symbolic products of human communication – language, music, images, signs, and symbols – as well as the technologies that send them. Thus, communication is the transmission of these products by way of books, television, film, the Internet, newspapers, magazines, and radio.

Some popular communication scholars examine the context within which dominant social, political, and economic institutions use the media to retain power. Others focus on structures that contribute to the maintenance of boundaries between those with and without power and resources.

The humanities further influence the trajectory of popular communication research through *four interdisciplinary theoretical traditions* that, in particular, inform philosophy and method in the field: hermeneutics, phenomenology, rhetoric (→ Rhetoric and Media Studies), and semiotics. These ways of knowing about the production, consumption, and content of communication are the foundation on which popular communication research is built. *Hermeneutics*, a reading of texts and/or understanding a culture from the perspective of that culture in order to understand how meaning is made and changes, is considered by many to be a philosophy, theory, and method of analysis. A *phenomenological approach* considers and values everyday life and ways of being in the world, i.e., lived experiences. A *rhetorical analysis* examines the power of language to describe and persuade, including nonverbal forms of communication such as symbols. It is a philosophy, a skill, a method, and a technique that recognizes the power of communication. *Discourse (language) analysis* (→ Discourse) adds the dimension of questioning taken-for-granted meanings and deconstructing them in ways that reveal sources of power by revealing hidden motivations. Associated theorists who have looked at the power of language, metaphor, and the relationship with power include Michael Foucault, George Lakoff, and Mark Turner.

Semiotics, another tool for examining visual and verbal representations in media content, is the study of signs and symbols and the way meaning is constructed and understood. Semiotics is also used in architecture and art. Associated scholars include Charles Sanders Peirce, Ferdinand de Saussure, Roland Barthes, Jean Baudrillard, and Umberto Eco.

Areas of Research

Scholarship is organized according to *three broad areas*: (1) the content of communication, (2) control of distribution, and (3) consumers/audience members who view or read the content. Examples of content-focused research include studies of television programs, Internet sites, and music lyrics, and visual analyses of news photography, portrayals of women and girls in advertising, and the male body in popular culture (→ Sex Role Stereotypes in the Media). Examples of studies that examine corporations and control of the production and distribution of media products, and thereby construct meaning for society, include the related area of political economy. Associated scholars include Karl Marx, Oliver Boyd-Barrett, and Dallas Smythe.

The theories, methods, and objects of study contained within the domain of popular communication include critical studies, → cultural studies, media criticism, and feminist, queer, and game theories (→ Feminist and Gender Studies). Critical studies, genre studies, image and characterization research, cultural studies, cultural history, and audience-focused consumption research are examples of theoretically driven areas. Topics include analyses of postmodernism, blackness and art, telenovelas, television makeover programs, hip-hop culture, television shopping, boys' and girls' responses to and interactions with the *X-Files*, or popular culture in specific countries. Scholars also used a variety of *methods*, such as historical, textual analysis, critical analysis, and semiotics.

Not only has there been a coming together of humanities and social sciences evident in popular communication research in the past few years, but also cross-pollination of media studies areas. Challenges to the field have come from postmodernism, cognitivism, and feminism in particular. While many popular communication scholars study artifacts from popular communication, journalistic media also fall under this purview.

See also: ▶ CONSUMER CULTURE ▶ CRITICAL THEORY ▶ CULTURAL STUDIES ▶ CULTURE: DEFINITIONS AND CONCEPTS ▶ CULTURE INDUSTRIES ▶ DISCOURSE ▶ DISCOURSE ANALYSIS ▶ FEMINIST AND GENDER STUDIES ▶ HOLLYWOOD ▶ INTERNET AND POPULAR CULTURE ▶ INTERPERSONAL COMMUNICATION ▶ MEANING ▶ MEDIA ECOLOGY ▶ MEDIA EFFECTS ▶ PHENOMENOLOGY ▶ POPULAR MUSIC ▶ POSTMODERNISM AND COMMUNICATION ▶ RHETORIC AND MEDIA STUDIES ▶ SEMIOTICS ▶ SEX ROLE STEREOTYPES IN THE MEDIA ▶ TASTE CULTURE ▶ VIDEO GAMES

REFERENCES AND SUGGESTED READINGS

Carey, J. (1989). *Communication as culture: Essays on media and society*. London: Routledge.
Fiske, J. (1987). *Television culture*. London: Routledge.
Gans, H. (1975). *Popular culture and high culture: An analysis and evaluation of taste*. New York: Basic Books.
Grossberg, L. (1994). Can cultural studies find true happiness in communication? In M. R. Levy & M. Gurevitch (eds.), *Defining media studies: Reflections on the future of the field*. Oxford: Oxford University Press, pp. 331–339.
Gunn, J. & Brummett, B. (2004). Popular communication after globalization. *Journal of Communication*, 54(4), 705–721.
Hall, S. (1981). Encoding and decoding in television discourse. In S. Hall, D. Hobson, A. Lowe, & P. Willis (eds.), *Culture, media, language*. London: Hutchinson, pp. 128–138.
Mazzarella, S. (2007). The "fundamental characteristics" of popular communication. *Popular Communication*, 5(2), 85–87.
McAllister, M. (2003). Is commercial culture popular culture? A question for popular communication scholars. *Popular Communication*, 1(1), 41–49.
Williams, R. (1976). *Keywords: A vocabulary of culture and society*. Oxford: Oxford University Press.
Zelizer, B. (2000). Popular communication in the contemporary age. In W. B. Gudykunst (ed.), *Communication yearbook 24*. Thousand Oaks, CA: Sage, pp. 297–316.

Popular Communication and Social Class

ROB DREW
Saginaw Valley State University

Over the past three centuries, the study of popular culture or → popular communication has evolved in ways that reflect not only changing definitions of 'popular' but a growing consciousness of social class and of the interplay between culture and class.

Several perspectives mark the *history of popular communication and social class*. In the eighteenth century, J. G. Herder celebrated the putatively classless culture of the 'folk' as a truer representation of the nation than the Enlightenment's learned culture. By the nineteenth century, Matthew Arnold promoted education in canonical culture as a civilizing bastion against the anarchic tendencies of populism. The twentieth century brought more explicit debates regarding the role of class in popular communication. The Marxist intellectuals of the Frankfurt School (→ Critical Theory) blamed the 'culture industry' for forestalling revolutionary social change by lulling the masses into mindless consumerism. More pluralist US scholars celebrated popular culture as a dialogue of diverse 'class cultures' and viewed social class as only one among many influences on individuals' lifestyle choices (→ Media Effects; Media Effects, History of).

A rapprochement of sorts between Marxist and pluralist perspectives took form within the Birmingham School, which saw popular culture as a potential site for class consciousness and progressive social change. Birmingham scholars decoded the sign systems of youth subcultural styles (→ Youth Culture), locating within them lines of social resistance (Hall 1980).

Another approach, pioneered by sociologist Pierre Bourdieu (1984), views personal affinities and tastes as markers of 'cultural capital' that function to reproduce class membership. The interpenetration of culture and class occurs through the mediation of 'habitus,' an unconscious system of dispositions ingrained through socialization. Bourdieu's field theory forms a counterpoint to mainstream ideologies of social mobility and pluralism, pointing to the symbolic boundaries cultivated by differences in taste and conduct.

See also: ▶ AUDIENCE RESEARCH ▶ CONSUMER CULTURE ▶ CRITICAL THEORY ▶ CULTURAL STUDIES ▶ CULTURE: DEFINITIONS AND CONCEPTS ▶ CULTURE INDUSTRIES ▶ ETHNOGRAPHY OF COMMUNICATION ▶ MEDIA EFFECTS ▶ MEDIA EFFECTS, HISTORY OF ▶ POPULAR COMMUNICATION ▶ SEMIOTICS ▶ TASTE CULTURE ▶ YOUTH CULTURE

REFERENCES AND SUGGESTED READINGS

Bourdieu, P. (1984). *Distinction: A social critique of the judgment of taste.* Cambridge, MA: Harvard University Press.
Hall, S. (1980). Encoding/decoding. In S. Hall, D. Hobson, A. Lowe, & P. Willis (eds.), *Culture, media, language: Working papers in cultural studies, 1972–79.* London: Hutchinson, pp. 123–138.

Popular Music

ROBERT BURNETT
Karlstad University

Music in various functions plays an increasingly important role both as an indicator of and as a medium for changes in society. Popular music is with us constantly; it is part of our everyday environment, and increasingly part of the aural or sonic soundscape that surrounds us. Our brains are constantly registering, monitoring, and decoding popular music. Popular music is one of the more powerful expressions of the → 'culture industries' worldwide. Some would claim that popular music is the only truly universal 'mass medium.' Certainly most people would agree that music speaks a universal language of emotions. Popular music is now the lingua franca for a large segment of the world's youth population (→ Popular Communication).

There is no precise, straightforward *definition of popular music* but rather a common-sense understanding placing an emphasis on 'popular' and based on the commercial nature of music, and embracing genres perceived as commercially oriented. As soon as there were media technically able to transmit sound, and communities economically able to use these media, there was mass communication of music. This occurred first with the development of the record industry, and was later followed by the development of radio, sound film, television, music videos, and the Internet.

The study of *transnational music production* should be able to tell us something about the ways in which international capital works in the field of popular culture and specifically in the entertainment industry. Are we experiencing the rise of a global homogeneous world culture, and if so, will this process still allow for smaller heterogeneous local cultural traditions? One effect of media globalization and commercialization is the almost instantaneous dissemination of popular music developed by the major transnationals to an increasingly global audience spread to the far corners of the world. One can argue that the universal acceptance of popular music indicates that a widely felt need and demand are being met, and its global reach enables greater understanding and the emergence of some sort of global music culture. A controversial effect of the globalization of the music industry is the spread of music and the carrying across borders of some of the *values of the west*, such as human rights, individualism, and questioning of authority. These values embedded in popular music lyrics and music videos, whether explicit or implicit, can lead to controversy in nonwestern cultures.

The few transnational companies that dominate today's world market see themselves as players on a world scale. Advances in communications technology have weakened the nature of traditional national boundaries. The *ownership of major entertainment enterprises* has become increasingly internationalized, reflecting the economic interdependence among nations. In the entertainment industries it goes beyond internationalization of ownership. American film, television, video, record, and music publishing companies now derive at least 50 percent of their revenues from foreign markets, and must therefore consider the tastes of consumers in other countries as well as those of American consumers. One of the reasons why music companies pay million-dollar fees to stars such as Madonna, Britney Spears, and Justin Bieber is the simple fact that with a big selling album, enormous financial returns can be derived outside the United States.

The agent of change in the world of music in recent years is the Internet and the capabilities that it provides. What it has provided is a mechanism and a technology with the capability to bring the artist and the fans together so closely, in every possible way, that it is going to change the mechanics and the dynamics of the business. The *future of the music industry* in many ways coincides with developments in digital media. We are witnessing an important transition period. Historically, intellectual property has been defined by physical boundaries, like the movie, video cassette, CD, or book. Now, because of advances in information technology, this physical boundary has been broken. The best example of this transformation is the music industry, where the music, which is the purest digital format, has left the CD, left the physical product, and spread rapidly across new technologies and networks and in different ways found its way back to consumers.

See also: ▶ COMMODIFICATION OF THE MEDIA ▶ CONCENTRATION IN MEDIA SYSTEMS ▶ CULTURAL IMPERIALISM THEORIES ▶ CULTURE INDUSTRIES ▶ DIGITAL MEDIA, HISTORY OF ▶ EMOTION AND COMMUNICATION IN ORGANIZATIONS ▶ GLOBALIZATION OF THE MEDIA ▶ GLOBALIZATION THEORIES ▶ HOLLYWOOD ▶ INFORMATION SOCIETY ▶ INTERNET AND POPULAR CULTURE ▶ MARKETING ▶ MARKETS OF THE MEDIA ▶ MEDIA CONGLOMERATES ▶ MUSIC INDUSTRY ▶ POPULAR COMMUNICATION ▶ SONY CORPORATION ▶ TIME WARNER INC.

REFERENCES AND SUGGESTED READINGS

Burnett, R. (1996). *The global jukebox: The international music industry.* London: Routledge.
Burnett, R. & Marshall, P. D. (2003). *Web theory: An introduction.* London: Routledge.
Hesmondhalgh, D. (2002). *The cultural industries.* Thousand Oaks, CA: Sage.
Shuker, R. (2001). *Understanding popular music.* London: Routledge.

Pornography, Feminist Debates on

GAIL DINES
Wheelock College, Boston

ROBERT JENSEN
University of Texas at Austin

There have been three *major philosophical/ political positions* within feminism during these debates: (1) anti-pornography feminists, typically identified as 'radical feminists'; (2) anti-censorship feminists who are critical of misogynistic pornography but reject the legal approach radical feminists proposed; and (3) a pro-pornography group valorizing pornography as a → discourse that subverts traditional gender norms and has liberatory potential for women's sexuality. Since the 1980s, these debates have caused major divisions in the global feminist movement and continue to split feminists into anti- and pro-pornography camps.

These camps are also divided on the *nature of the pornography industry*. For radical feminists, the production of pornography in patriarchy exploits women (Dines 2010). While not denying the ability of women in the industry to make choices, the feminist anti-pornography movement focuses on the economic, social, and cultural factors that influence women's choices to perform in pornography, such as histories of sexual abuse in childhood, the violence of pimps, and control by boyfriends and other men. Pro-pornography feminists counter this argument by insisting that women are making rational choices given the reality of employment opportunities and that some women prosper in the industry (Attwood 2009).

This is part of a much larger debate regarding the *nature of work in the sex industry*. Pro-pornography feminists describe prostitutes, strippers, and women in pornography as sex workers who sell their labor, much like other workers, and argue that any problems should be addressed through union organizing and/or health regulations. Radical feminists reject the term 'sex worker,' arguing that women in the sex industry do not perform work as it is typically understood (Jensen 2007). Pro-pornography feminists tend to concentrate more on writing for an academic audience and radical feminists focus on activism outside the academy.

See also: ▶ DISCOURSE ▶ FEMINIST AND GENDER STUDIES ▶ GENDER: REPRESENTATION IN THE MEDIA ▶ PORNOGRAPHY USE ACROSS THE LIFE-SPAN ▶ POSTMODERNISM AND COMMUNICATION ▶ SEXUAL VIOLENCE IN THE MEDIA ▶ WOMEN IN THE MEDIA, IMAGES OF

REFERENCES AND SUGGESTED READINGS

Attwood, F. (ed.) (2009). *Mainstreaming sex: The sexualization of western culture.* London: I. B. Tauris.

Dines, G. (2010). *Pornland: How porn has hijacked our sexuality.* Boston: Beacon Press.

Jensen, R. (2007). *Getting off: Pornography and the end of masculinity.* Boston: South End Press.

Pornography Use across the Life-Span

JOCHEN PETER
University of Amsterdam

The easy availability of pornographic material for basically all age groups has raised questions about the extent to which pornography use differs across the life span. Research suggests that younger people use pornography more often than older people (e.g., Traeen et al. 2004). This particularly applies to males – males generally use pornography more often than females do. Young male adults seem to be the most frequent users of pornography. Exposure to pornography declines somewhat among people older than 30 years. People who are older than 60 are the least frequent users of pornographic materials. This age gap also shows in the fact that people older than 60 years are less likely than young adults to have ever been exposed to pornographic material (Traeen et al. 2004; → Media Use by Social Variable).

The easy availability of pornography on the Internet has also enabled *adolescents* to use pornography. Studies from two culturally diverse countries suggest that 35–70 percent of male adolescents and 10–20 percent of female adolescents have accessed different types of pornography on the Internet (Lo & Wei 2005; Peter & Valkenburg 2011). The respective figures are higher for male adults, but comparable for female adults (Peter & Valkenburg 2011).

Generally, the comparability of research on pornography use is impeded by *conceptual and methodological differences* in the studies. The conceptual and operational definition of pornography use (→ Operationalization) often differs across the studies, as does the sampling technique, target sample, and survey mode. Moreover, research on sexual issues is affected by cultural contexts and technological change. For an encompassing understanding of the implications of exposure to pornography, cross-culturally comparative research is needed, preferably also with a longitudinal component.

See also: ▶ AUDIENCE RESEARCH ▶ EXPOSURE TO THE INTERNET ▶ MEDIA USE BY SOCIAL VARIABLE ▶ OPERATIONALIZATION ▶ PERSONALITY AND EXPOSURE TO COMMUNICATION

REFERENCES AND SUGGESTED READINGS

Lo, V.-H. & Wei, R. (2005). Exposure to Internet pornography and Taiwanese adolescents' sexual attitudes and behavior. *Journal of Broadcasting and Electronic Media*, 49(2), 221–237.

Peter, J. & Valkenburg, P. M. (2011). The use of sexually explicit Internet material and its antecedents: A longitudinal comparison of adolescents and adults. *Archives of Sexual Behavior*, 40, 1015–1025.

Traeen, B., Spitznogle, K. & Beverfjord, A. (2004). Attitudes and use of pornography in the Norwegian population 2002. *Journal of Sex Research*, 41(2), 193–200.

Postfeminism

ROSALIND GILL
City University, London

Postfeminism is one of the most important and contested terms in the lexicon of feminist cultural critique. It was first used in the 1920s to describe the reaction against women's activism in the early part of the twentieth century, but it is only since the early 1990s that it has come to prominence as a central term in the field of gender and media.

The term is *used in four main ways* by researchers in media and communications. First it may be used to signal a historical shift, and to periodize postfeminism as a distinct moment after the height of second wave feminism. Second it is sometimes used to point to a theoretical break with earlier feminisms, and is connected to other 'post' movements such as poststructuralism or postmodernism (→ Postmodernism and Communication). Third, the word postfeminist is sometimes used as a shorthand for a backlash against feminism, indexing media content that attacks feminists and suggests that 'all the battles have been won' or, conversely, that 'you can't have it all.' Finally, the term has been understood as capturing a sensibility that is a complex and contradictory entanglement of feminist and anti-feminist values, in which feminism is simultaneously 'taken into account' and 'repudiated' (McRobbie 2009).

From this latter perspective, now widely used in feminist media studies, the content of postfeminism cannot be definitively specified, but hinges around some recurring elements, offering vocabularies of choice, empowerment, responsibility, and failure – all understood in individualistic terms. It resonates strongly with neoliberalism, downplaying structural accounts of inequality, and presenting actions as freely chosen and self-pleasing. Postfeminism is seen to create 'new femininities,' novel modes of gendered cultural intelligibility (Gill & Scharff 2011).

Key areas of debate about postfeminism include its inclusiveness in class and race terms; its relationship to masculinities; and the extent to which it might be understood as global or transnational. Jess Butler (2013) challenges the putative whiteness of postfeminism and argues for an intersectional approach that considers the ways in which it includes and excludes black western women.

See also: ▶ FEMINIST AND GENDER STUDIES ▶ FEMINIST MEDIA ▶ FEMINIST MEDIA STUDIES, TRANSNATIONAL ▶ FEMINIZATION OF MEDIA CONTENT ▶ POSTMODERNISM AND COMMUNICATION

REFERENCES AND SUGGESTED READINGS

Butler, J. (2013). For white girls only? Postfeminism and the politics of inclusion. *Feminist Formations*, 25(1), 35–58.

Gill, R. & Scharff, C. (2011). *New feminities: Postfeminism, neoliberalism and subjectivity*. London: Palgrave Macmillan.

McRobbie, A. (2009). *The Aftermath of Feminism*. London: Sage.

Postmodernism and Communication

JAY DAVID BOLTER
Georgia Institute of Technology

Postmodernism is one of a series of terms, including postmodernity and poststructuralism, that is applied to cultural production in western Europe and North America in the period from the 1960s to the present. Postmodernity is sometimes used to refer to the cultural history of this period. Poststructuralism was a critical practice directed toward literary, linguistic, and philosophical movements that flourished around this time. The term 'postmodernism' itself is defined in opposition to 'modernism' in order to describe contemporary forms of art and architecture and their aesthetics. Poststructuralism specifically critiques the structuralist analysis of language, literature, and culture. The most influential poststructuralists included Jacques Derrida, Roland Barthes, Michel Foucault, and Paul de Man (→ Structuralism).

Critical theorists developed postmodernism into a general theoretical category – a development exemplified by two very different works: Jean-Francois Lyotard's *The Postmodern Condition* (1984) and Fredric Jameson's *Postmodernism* (1991; → Critical Theory). Lyotard's work offered a critique of the so-called master narratives, which he identified in the ideologies and communicative practices of the modern period. Jameson (1991) took art and aesthetics as its starting point, but argued that postmodernism's aesthetic characteristics could not be separated from postindustrial economic conditions.

Jameson's case for the inseparability of cultural forms and political ideologies seemed particularly relevant for mass communication and entertainment industries, which were at this time becoming 'global' to a degree not previously acknowledged (→ Globalization of the Media). If there is a common element in all of the 'post-'

terms and the work they represent, it might be that all of them are critical reactions to what are perceived as totalizing practices and rhetoric of the modern era. In each case, the reaction was an attempt to subvert claims to unity, simplicity, or universality. Those gestures of subversion constitute a legacy that remains influential today in the fields of art, art theory, and critical theory.

See also: ▶ ART AS COMMUNICATION ▶ COMMERCIALIZATION OF THE MEDIA ▶ CRITICAL THEORY ▶ FICTION ▶ GLOBALIZATION OF THE MEDIA ▶ POPULAR CULTURE ▶ STRUCTURALISM

REFERENCES AND SUGGESTED READINGS

Jameson, F. (1991). *Postmodernism, or the cultural logic of late capitalism*. Durham, NC: Duke University Press.
Lyotard, J.-F. (1984). *The postmodern condition: A report on knowledge*. Minneapolis, MN: University of Minneapolis Press. (Original work published 1979).

Power in Intergroup Settings

SIK HUNG NG
City University of Hong Kong

Exercising power over others is a common human experience. Even in seemingly equal relationships, such as that between spouses, people nonetheless influence or cajole their peers to have their own way. The exercise of power relies partly on → strategic communication, and even apparently powerless individuals may triumph over the more powerful. Just as individuals exercise power over others, they also have the experience of being overpowered by others. Philosopher Bertrand Russell (1938, 35) defines power as "the production of intended effects." According to psychologist Fritz Heider (1958), power is what a person can cause. He differentiates between personal and social power, referring respectively to personal capabilities and social positions.

There are occasions where we think, feel, and act in terms of our unique personal self and treat others as individuals rather than as representatives of particular groups. There are other occasions where group membership and identification take control of our consciousness and induce us to treat others as either 'one of us' or 'one of them,' rather than as unique individuals in their own right. The more the social context shifts toward intergroup, the less interpersonal relations and interaction occur between groups.

An insight from intergroup research is that seemingly interpersonal encounters are in fact intergroup. For example, when we greet a woman in a wheelchair, the one who is in our minds is not a person but a member of a disability group, a disabled 'other,' and we show this by addressing not her, but the person pushing the wheelchair. Another insight is the ease with which discrimination against 'them' (the outgroup) can be triggered in the absence of historical rivalry and even at personal cost to the discriminator, simply by dividing people into (cognitive) groups. World history of peace and war is a constant reminder of this fundamental asymmetry. A third insight is that intergroup interactions are generally more competitive than interpersonal interactions, suggesting greater 'fear and greed' in the former than in the latter situation (→ Social Stereotyping and Communication).

Collectively the three interrelated insights summarized above serve to establish the prevalence of intergroup contexts and their powerful effects on practical issues such as stereotyping, discrimination, competition, and conflict. These insights and other advances in intergroup research provide a basis for understanding power in intergroup settings.

See also: ▶ CONVERSATION ANALYSIS ▶ INTERGROUP CONTACT AND COMMUNICATION ▶ LANGUAGE AND SOCIAL INTERACTION ▶ SOCIAL CONFLICT AND COMMUNICATION ▶ SOCIAL EXCHANGE ▶ SOCIAL STEREOTYPING AND COMMUNICATION ▶ STRATEGIC COMMUNICATION ▶ STRATEGIC FRAMING ▶ UNCERTAINTY REDUCTION THEORY

REFERENCES AND SUGGESTED READINGS

Heider, F. (1958). *The psychology of interpersonal relations*. New York: John Wiley.

Ng, S. H. (1980). *The social psychology of power*. London: Academic Press.

Reid, S. A. & Ng, S. H. (2006). The dynamics of intragroup differentiation in an intergroup social context. *Human Communication Research*, 32, 504–525.

Russell, B. (1938). *Power: A new social analysis*. London: Allen and Unwin.

Prejudiced and Discriminatory Communication

JANET B. RUSCHER
Tulane University

DEVIN WALLACE-WILLIAMS
Washington Hospitality Public Charter High School

Prejudiced and discriminatory communication is studied in a wide range of social science disciplines, including communication, sociology, anthropology, and social psychology (Ruscher 2001). Explicitly prejudiced language may easily be recognized as reflecting prejudiced viewpoints (e.g., hate speech). Implicitly prejudiced language, in contrast, presents bias that may not consciously be recognized. Prejudiced language can reflect stereotypic beliefs (e.g., "They are all alike"), facilitate detachment (e.g., "There is unrest in Sudan"), or dehumanize groups to legitimize extreme behaviours (e.g., "They are parasites who must be exterminated"; Bar-Tal 1989; → Social Stereotyping and Communication).

Explicitly prejudiced communication often involves *derogatory comments*. Comments may comprise brief group epithets or lengthy narratives about alleged negative behavior. In recent years, digital media (e.g., twitter, blogs) has allowed widespread transmission of explicitly prejudiced comments, which presents a striking contrast to some mainstream perceptions that explicit prejudice is largely a thing of the past. *Derogatory labels* allow a shorthand reference for outgroups. Historical examples include "iron maidens" for professional women and "limeys" for British nationals. Derogatory labels imply that the speaker views the target primarily as an outgroup member, and encourages particular emotional and behavioral responses. In wartime or during periods of 'ethnic cleansing,' for example, characterizing outgroups as "savages" and "parasites" helps justify atrocities such as slavery, internment, and extermination. Prejudiced and discriminatory communication also can assume more *subtle implicit forms*; speakers of these communication patterns may not recognize that they are betraying their own prejudices and listeners also may not realize that the language is discriminatory.

From a *legal standpoint*, derogatory labels may not meet stringent criteria for hate speech. In the United States, for example, the first constitutional amendment protects freedom of speech; hate speech is an exception, but is not simply hateful language. The criteria include an immediate threat to the peace, intention to hurt, and that exposure to these words is inescapable to their target (i.e., 'fighting words'). Scrawling derogatory labels in public (e.g., graffiti) or anonymous Internet posting is unlikely to meet these stringent criteria, but it may be harmful notwithstanding.

The *linguistic intergroup bias* (LIB) is an ideal example of implicitly prejudiced communication. Initially investigated by Maass (1999) and her colleagues, the LIB reflects a communication pattern in which the behaviors of the ingroup are portrayed more favorably than the behaviors of an outgroup. When an ingroup member performs a positive behavior, the speaker characterizes the behavior abstractly. For example, if an ingroup member donates money to charity, the speaker might say, "she is generous," implying that the actor performs similar actions across time and different situations. The converse pattern emerges for the outgroup, whereby abstract generalizations are made for negative behaviors (e.g., "He is dishonest"). Because so many outgroup stereotypes are often negative, abstract characterizations bolster and preserve existing stereotypes. The robustness of the LIB is evident in its considerable generalizability across languages and countries (e.g., China, Italy), communication mediums (oral, written, forced choice), and type of intergroup relationship (e.g., political, ethnic; → Intercultural and Intergroup Communication).

Implicitly prejudiced communication also emerges in *how speakers characterize events*. For example, in their delineation of how powerful people camouflage the control that they wield, Ng and Bradac (1993) proposed how speakers rely upon a number of linguistic masking devices, such as generalization. Generalizations include the use of adjectives to characterize behaviors (i.e., as in the LIB), and also generalized references to entire groups (e.g., "People on welfare don't want to work") or unspecified events (e.g., "Immigrants cause a lot of problems"). As with the LIB, these subtle linguistic devices often escape conscious recognition as being discriminatory (→ Power in Intergroup Settings).

See also: ▶ INTERCULTURAL AND INTERGROUP COMMUNICATION ▶ POWER IN INTERGROUP SETTINGS ▶ SOCIAL STEREOTYPING AND COMMUNICATION

REFERENCES AND SUGGESTED READINGS

Bar-Tal, D. (1989). Delegitimization: The extreme case of stereotyping and prejudice. In D. Bar-Tal, C. F. Graumann, A. Kruglanski, & W. Stroebe (eds.), *Stereotyping and prejudice: Changing conceptions*. New York: Springer, pp. 169–182.

Maass, A. (1999). Linguistic intergroup bias: Stereotype perpetuation through language. In M. P. Zanna (ed.), *Advances in experimental social psychology*, vol. 31. San Diego, CA: Academic Press, pp. 79–121.

Ng, S. H. & Bradac, J. J. (1993). *Power in language*. Newbury Park, CA: Sage.

Ruscher, J. B. (2001). *Prejudiced communication: A social psychological perspective*. New York: Guilford.

Presence

TILO HARTMANN
VU University Amsterdam

Presence, in its broadest sense, is a media user's state that is characterized by the illusion of nonmediation. If present, media users are temporarily unaware of the mediated origin of their experience. Their thoughts, feelings, and behavior tend to react to the media content as if the portrayed scenery, persons, or objects were real, because the general artificiality of media imitation produced by human-made technology is not recognized (→ Media Equation Theory).

As a psychological state, presence is determined by the interplay of both situational or enduring individual factors and environmental factors, which include qualities of the media technology and aspects of the content. The potential of the media technology to evoke illusions of nonmediation is addressed as its 'immersive quality.' The greater the likelihood that technological aspects or content factors foster the formation of presence, the more immersive is a medium. Any kind of media experience builds on subjective → perceptions, however, low-immersive media might also initiate a state of presence if users tend to forget that their experiences are triggered by a medium.

A review by Lombard and Ditton (1997) lists six different meanings of presence, ranging from 'presence as social richness' to 'presence as transportation' to 'presence as medium as social actor.' In general, a state of presence can occur in two distinct ways (Lombard & Ditton 1997): "the medium can appear to be ... transparent ... as a large open window, with the user and the medium content (objects and entities) sharing the same physical environment" (invisible medium) or "the medium can appear to be transformed into something other than a medium" (transformed medium). In the context of presence that builds on an invisible medium, a popular classification is to distinguish 'spatial presence' (sometimes addressed as physical presence or telepresence) from 'social presence.'

See also: ▶ COMPUTER–USER INTERACTION ▶ ESCAPISM ▶ EXCITATION AND AROUSAL ▶ EXPOSURE TO COMMUNICATION CONTENT ▶ INVOLVEMENT WITH MEDIA CONTENT ▶ MEDIA EFFECTS ▶ MEDIA EQUATION THEORY ▶ MEDIA AND PERCEPTIONS OF REALITY ▶ PARASOCIAL INTERACTIONS AND RELATIONSHIPS ▶ PERCEPTION ▶ SELECTIVE EXPOSURE ▶ VIDEO GAMES

REFERENCES AND SUGGESTED READINGS

Biocca, F., Ijsselsteijn, W., & Freeman, J. (eds.) (2014). *Handbook of presence research: Cognition, measurement, and interface design*. Heidelberg: Springer.

Lombard, M. & Ditton, T. (1997). At the heart of it all: The concept of presence. *Journal of Computer-Mediated Communication*, 3(2), 0. Available at http://onlinelibrary.wiley.com/doi/10.1111/j.1083-6101.1997.tb00072.x/full, accessed August 21, 2014.

Wirth, W., Hartmann, T., Boecking, S. et al. (2007). A process model of the formation of spatial presence experiences. *Media Psychology*, 9, 493–525.

Prevention and Communication

CLAUDIA LAMPERT
Hans-Bredow-Institut, Hamburg

The main objective of prevention is to avoid diseases by reducing risks that may negatively affect health (→ Health Communication) and to modify attitudes and behavior (e.g., quit smoking) by specific communication strategies such as mass media campaigns.

Different *typologies of prevention* can be classified: one distinction is made between behavioral and/or environmental prevention. While behavioral prevention concentrates on personal factors that influence health-related behaviors of an individual, environmental prevention focuses on external factors, such as living conditions, legislation, or economic and ecological preconditions for healthy living. Another popular typology is the trichotomy of primary, secondary, and tertiary prevention, which considers different stages of health and/or illness. Primary prevention aims at people who are not yet affected by a disease and encompasses broad population-wide communication strategies. Secondary prevention strategies address people in a very early stage of a disease to minimize and/or avoid health risks and tertiary prevention measures are targeted at those who already have established diseases to avoid aggravation and complications.

Media are an important source of information on health, and casual or incidental use of media is associated with people's knowledge, attitudes, and behavior (Finnegan & Viswanath 2002; Wakefield et al. 2010; → Health Campaigns, Communication in). A major aim and challenge of prevention is to reach individuals with health-related information before a disease has developed. The problem is that health information is often not sought until a health-related problem has occurred (→ Information Seeking). Consequently, 'push media' (mass media like radio and televsion) are more appropriate than 'pull media' (like the Internet) to draw attention and arouse interest for preventive topics.

Information campaigns encompass different communicative activities to influence individual knowledge, attitude, → meaning, and/or behavior. Typical vehicles are posters at public places, public service announcements in different media, as well as hotlines and events. A related strategy is 'media advocacy,' which addresses not individuals but decision-makers such as legislators, policy-makers, and media personnel, among others.

Health journalism has an important role with regard to the communication of health-related or preventive messages (→ Health Communication). Journalists 'translate' relevant scientific information for a broad audience and can influence the agenda concerning health-related and preventive topics (→ Agenda-Setting Effects). Media coverage often suffers from the disadvantage of reaching only the educated and those who are already interested in the topic (→ Communication Inequalities). Entertainment education uses entertainment media (e.g., films, serials) to promote pro-social messages, drawing from such theories as → social cognitive theory.

Success in prevention requires several considerations. First, the access to valid health information for different social groups has to be assured. There still exist both health and information disparities with regard to socio-economic status (→ Knowledge Gap Effects). Therefore, special communication strategies are needed to reach the different groups and to close the gap between them (Viswanath 2005). Second, the perception of the message as the most important precondition for following cognitive processes has to be considered: age, gender, socio-economic status, educational background, and health conditions are relevant factors which have influence on media use, and access to and perception of health-related messages. Third, communication strategies have to be seen in a context of a varied media landscape, which consists of different and sometimes inconsistent, contradictory, and competing messages. The success of a strategy might increase if the program is embedded in a media environment that is hospitable to the communicated message. Unconditionally, communication strategies have to be flanked by the allocation of services, products, and activites, which enable and support the communicated preventive behavior (Wakefield et al. 2010).

See also: ▶ AGENDA-SETTING EFFECTS ▶ COMMUNICATION INEQUALITIES ▶ COMPUTER GAMES AND CHILD DEVELOPMENT ▶ HEALTH CAMPAIGNS, COMMUNICATION IN ▶ HEALTH

COMMUNICATION ▶ HEALTH COMMUNICATION AND THE INTERNET ▶ INFORMATION SEEKING ▶ KNOWLEDGE GAP EFFECTS ▶ MEANING ▶ SOCIAL COGNITIVE THEORY ▶ SOCIAL MARKETING ▶ VIDEO GAMES ▶ VIOLENCE AS MEDIA CONTENT, EFFECTS ON CHILDREN OF

REFERENCES AND SUGGESTED READINGS

Finnegan, J. R. & Viswanath, K. (2002). Communication theory and health behavior change. In K. Glanz, B. K. Rimer, & F. M. Lewis (eds.), *Health behavior and health education: Theory, research, and practice*, 3rd edn. San Francisco, CA: Jossey-Bass, pp. 313–341.

Greenberg, B. S., Salmon, C. T., Patel, D., Beck, V., & Cole, G. (2004). Evolution in an E-E research agenda. In A. Singhal, M. Cody, E. Rogers, & M. Sabido (eds.), *Entertainment-education and social change: History, research, and practice*. Mahwah, NJ: Lawrence Erlbaum, pp. 191–206.

Sherry, J. L. (2002). Media saturation and entertainment-education. *Communication Theory*, 12(2), 206–224.

Singhal, A., Cody, M., Rogers, E., & Sabido, M. (eds.) (2004). *Entertainment-education and social change: History, research, and practice*. Mahwah, NJ: Lawrence Erlbaum.

Thomson, T. L., Dorsey, A. M., Miller, K. I., & Parrott, R. (eds.) (2003). *Handbook of health communication*. Mahwah, NJ: Lawrence Erlbaum.

Viswanath, K. (2005). The communications revolution and cancer control. *Nature Reviews Cancer*, 5(10), 828–835.

Wakefield, M. A., Loken, B., & Hornik, R. C. (2010). Use of mass media campaigns to change health behaviour. *Lancet*, 376, 1261–1271.

Priming Theory

SHANTO IYENGAR
Stanford University

The priming effect refers to media-induced changes in voters' reliance on particular issues as criteria for evaluating government officials. Beyond merely affecting the salience of issues, i.e. → agenda-setting effects, news coverage influences the criteria the public uses to evaluate political candidates and institutions. A simple extension of agenda setting, priming describes a process by which individuals assign weights to their opinions on particular issues when they make summary political evaluations. In general, the evidence indicates that when asked to appraise politicians and public figures, voters weight opinions on particular policy issues in proportion to the perceived salience of these issues: the more salient the issue, the greater the impact of opinions about that issue on the appraisal (for reviews of priming research, see Miller & Krosnick 2000; Druckman & Holmes 2004; Iyengar 2011).

Their dynamic nature makes priming effects especially important during election campaigns. A more recent instance of priming comes from the economic crisis of 2008. Prior to the collapse of the banking industry and the spectacular fall in stock markets across the world, Americans were concerned about a variety of issue including illegal immigration, the war on terror, and corruption in government. Post-crisis, however, these issues disappeared from the public agenda as people were preoccupied with the state of the economy. Thus, evaluations of President Obama in early 2009 were significantly more dependent on evaluations of his performance on the economy than illegal immigration (Iyengar 2011).

How can *priming effects be explained*? Priming assumes that the enhanced salience of particular issues is what produces their strengthened effect on evaluations of incumbent officials. But there are alternative explanations for the phenomenon. One possibility is that news coverage enables voters to develop opinions on issues in the news and it is opinion change rather than issue salience that mediates the effects of news coverage on evaluations (see Lenz 2009). A second possibility is that instead of issue opinions driving evaluations of public figures, voters might make their positions on the issues consistent with their evaluations, a phenomenon known as projection.

Media priming effects have been *measured* in a series of experiments (→ Experiment, Laboratory) and → surveys, with respect to evaluations of presidents, legislators, and lesser officials, and with respect to a variety of attitudes ranging from voting preferences, assessments of incumbents' performance in office, and ratings of candidates' personal attributes to racial and gender identities.

The *ability of the news media to prime* political evaluations depends on both media content and the predispositions of the audience. Unsurprisingly, priming effects peak when news reports explicitly suggest that politicians are responsible for the state of national affairs, or when they clearly link politicians' actions with national problems.

In a further parallel with agenda-setting research, *individuals differ in their susceptibility* to media priming effects. Miller and Krosnick (2000) found that priming effects occurred only among people who were highly knowledgeable about political affairs and had high levels of trust in the media. Iyengar and Kinder (1987) found that partisanship affected the issues on which people could be primed: Democrats tended to be most susceptible to priming when the news focused on issues that favor Democrats, such as unemployment and civil rights, while Republicans were influenced most when the news focused on traditional Republican issues like national defense (→ Selective Perception and Selective Retention).

In sum, issues and events in the news are deemed important and weigh heavily in evaluations of incumbent officials and political candidates. As is clear from the way in which President George H. Bush benefited from media coverage of the 1991 Gulf War and then suffered from coverage of the economy in 1992, priming can be triggered by news of political successes and news of political failures. Priming is a double-edged sword.

See also: ▶ AGENDA-SETTING EFFECTS ▶ ELECTION CAMPAIGN COMMUNICATION ▶ EXPERIMENT, LABORATORY ▶ MEDIA EFFECTS ▶ MEDIA EFFECTS: DIRECT AND INDIRECT EFFECTS ▶ PUBLIC OPINION ▶ SELECTIVE PERCEPTION AND SELECTIVE RETENTION ▶ SURVEY ▶ TELEVISED DEBATES

REFERENCES AND SUGGESTED READINGS

Druckman, J. N. & Holmes, J. W. (2004). Does presidential rhetoric matter? Priming and presidential approval. *Presidential Studies Quarterly*, 34, 755–778.

Iyengar, S. & Kinder, D. R. (1987). *News that matters: Television and American opinion*. Chicago: University of Chicago Press.

Iyengar, S. (2011). *Media politics: A citizen's guide*. New York: W. W. Norton.

Lenz, G. S. (2009). Learning and opinion change, not priming: Reconsidering the priming hypothesis. *American Journal of Political Science*, 53(2), 421–437.

Middleton, J. & Hart, A. (forthcoming). Priming, projection, or both? Reevaluating the classic priming hypothesis. *Journal of Politics*.

Miller, J. M. & Krosnick, J. A. (2000). News media impact on the ingredients of presidential evaluations: Politically knowledgeable citizens are guided by a trusted source. *American Journal of Political Science*, 44, 295–309.

Printing, History of

PAUL ARBLASTER

Zuyd University, Maastricht

In the broadest sense, printing is any means by which a pattern, text, or image is impressed on another surface. The creation of an impression in clay or wax with a seal, or in metal with a punch, and the printing of patterns on textiles are all ancient arts that bear some similarity to printing proper.

By the ninth century, printing texts in ink on paper by means of relief-carved wooden blocks was a widespread practice in China. The paper to be printed on was laid face down upon the inked block and rubbed over with a hand-held implement to transfer the ink. The earliest use of printing was for the reproduction of texts from the Buddhist scriptures, a ritualized pious deed not necessarily implying that such texts would be read. China was not only the place where woodblock printing (xylography) was invented, but also the first place where movable type was cast in clay or carved as individual hardwood blocks. The first recorded use of movable metal type, probably cast in bronze, took place in Korea in 1234. The number of characters needed even for simple printing jobs entailed far more complicated systems of storage and retrieval than were required for movable type with alphabetic scripts.

Woodblock printing, primarily of religious images and playing cards, began in Europe around 1400. The 'forme,' a locked frame of metal type ready to be inked and printed from, was known to thirteenth-century Korea. One of Gutenberg's innovations was the press itself, probably based on a wine press. What resulted was a device by which a printer, working a screw-mounted platen by means of a hand-operated bar, evenly pressed the paper against an inked forme. This method of textual reproduction provided greater standardization and considerable savings in time when compared to scribal copying, and for reproducibility of long runs or large texts also offered distinct advantages over woodblock printing. As a result, Gutenberg's technology spread rapidly, and within a century of its invention was in use throughout western Europe and in European settlements in Mexico and Goa.

Eisenstein (1979) views the invention so revolutionary as to mark a clear break with pre-typographical culture, but Chartier (1989) views it more more simply as an important stimulus to the dissemination of cultural practices already inherent in alphabetic script and the codex book. The cultural impact of the shift from scribal publication to print may have been only an acceleration of existing trends, certainly in the first decades when printing was simply a mechanical means of producing books otherwise identical to those already being produced by scribes or stationers. But the impact of printing on the technical and economic organization of book production and the book trade was without doubt revolutionary.

The rapid dissemination of the technology, and the imperative to produce books in previously unheard of numbers, and then sell them as quickly as possible, led to new *commercial interactions and marketing strategies*. The very first products of the Gutenberg press were Latin Bibles, printed indulgences, and calendars, all of which required standardized reproduction in relatively large numbers. These were soon followed by Latin grammars, the works of Cicero, and then those of other classical authors, major works of medieval scholarship in theology, canon and civil law, natural philosophy, medicine, and other subjects. The controversies of the Reformation greatly stimulated the growth of the press, which presented a new means of disseminating religious → propaganda, but also led to stricter regulation, on confessional grounds, of what could be published (→ Censorship; Censorship, History of).

For 350 years the Gutenberg press in use in Europe, and increasingly throughout lands of European settlement overseas, saw constant minor improvements but no major modifications. The last improvement of the handpress era, and the first that considerably increased press output, was Charles Stanhope's press, built entirely of iron. In 1812 the first steam-powered printing machine was built in London by Frederick König. Within two years König had developed a double-cylinder machine, first taken into use by The Times, that could produce over 1,000 impressions per hour. In 1844, in New York, Richard Hoe built the first practical rotary printing press – abandoning the flat bed just as König had abandoned the flat platen, so that the paper ran between an impression cylinder and a type cylinder. His machine could produce 8,000 impressions per hour. The Bullock press of 1865 added a *continuous roll of paper*, boosting the speed of production still further. These developments were of particular interest to newspaper publishers, who throughout the nineteenth century faced the need to print ever-larger runs at ever-greater speeds (→ Newspaper, History of).

Nineteenth-century mechanization was followed in the twentieth century by a profusion of chemical printing processes, electrification, and most recently computerization. Offset filmsetting, or photocomposition, and now computer-to-plate offset printing, have made cast-metal type itself, like the woodblock, obsolete for all but bibliophile editions and quality bespoke printing.

See also: ▶ CENSORSHIP ▶ CENSORSHIP, HISTORY OF ▶ NEWSPAPER, HISTORY OF ▶ PROPAGANDA

REFERENCES AND SUGGESTED READINGS

Chartier, R. (ed.) (1989). *The culture of print: Power and the uses of print in early modern Europe* (trans. L. G. Cochrane). Cambridge: Polity.

Chow, K. (2004). *Publishing, culture, and power in early modern China*. Stanford, CA: Stanford University Press.

Darnton, R. (1979). *The business of enlightenment: A publishing history of the Encyclopédie 1775–1800*. Cambridge, MA: Belknap Press.

Eisenstein, E. L. (1979). *The printing press as an agent of change: Communications and cultural transformations in early-modern Europe*. 2 vols. Cambridge: Cambridge University Press.

Gaskell, P. (1985). *A new introduction to bibliography*. Oxford: Clarendon.

McKenzie, D. F. (1986). *Bibliography and the sociology of texts: The Panizzi Lectures 1985*. London: British Library.

Privacy

FRED H. CATE
Indiana University

BROOKE BARNETT
Elon University

'Privacy' is widely recognized as a legal right, but with a range of different meanings including restraints on intrusion into the home, confidentiality of correspondence, freedom to make certain fundamental decisions, control of personal data, anonymity, and many others.

A number of countries recognize privacy in their constitutions. For example, the South Korean Constitution states: "The privacy of no citizen shall be infringed." Similarly, the Basic Law of Germany protects privacy as part of "human dignity," "inviolability of the home," and the "privacy of correspondence, posts and telecommunications." Other countries in which privacy emanates from constitutions include Brazil, Ireland, India, Japan, the Netherlands, Russia, and the United States. The US Supreme Court has found three privacy rights implicit in the US Constitution based in the Fourth Amendment, a more general constitutional right against government-compelled "disclosure of personal matters," and an amorphous, but controversial right of individuals to make certain fundamental decisions concerning themselves or their families.

In addition to the constitutional guarantee of privacy, many nations regulate privacy as a *civil or criminal offense* through statutes, including the member countries of the European Union, which are required by the 1995 EU Data Protection Directive to adopt omnibus data protection laws applicable to both the government and the private sector (→ European Union: Communication Law). Although many European nations had adopted privacy laws prior to the Directive taking effect in 1998, the Directive significantly increased the scope and burden of privacy law throughout Europe. Argentina, Australia, Canada, Hong Kong, Japan, Singapore, South Korea, Switzerland, Taiwan, and other nations have also adopted broad data protection statutes. Common law has also played a significant role in evolving privacy requirements, especially in the United States and New Zealand.

Privacy concerns almost always respond to new technologies. The latter third of the twentieth century witnessed the creation of a new and different form of privacy protection – data protection – in response to the development of computers since the 1960s. These data protection laws have evolved over the past three decades, and they have taken widely varying forms in different countries. Data protection laws generally focus on investing individuals with control over the collection and use of information about themselves. Earlier data protection laws tended to lay less stress on individual control. Later data protection laws have become almost wholly preoccupied with this goal.

See also: ▶ COMMUNICATION AND LAW ▶ EUROPEAN UNION: COMMUNICATION LAW ▶ FREEDOM OF INFORMATION ▶ FREEDOM OF THE PRESS, CONCEPT OF ▶ INTERNET LAW AND REGULATION ▶ JOURNALISM: LEGAL SITUATION

REFERENCES AND SUGGESTED READINGS

Barnett, B. (2001). Use of public record databases in newspaper and television newsrooms. *Federal Communications Law Journal*, 53, 557–572.

Cate, F. (1997). *Privacy in the information age.* Washington, DC: Brookings Institution Press.

Rosen, J. (2000). *The unwanted gaze: The destruction of privacy in America.* New York: Random House.

Privatization of the Media

ANDREW CALABRESE
University of Colorado at Boulder

The term 'privatization' refers to the transfer of property and/or operations from state or public ownership and control into private hands. Among the principal reasons given to justify privatization is that private ownership and operation make a company perform more efficiently because its managers will be financially obligated to make the company accountable to shareholders. By contrast, government operations are often criticized for being inefficient, corrupt, and insufficiently responsive to the interests of the taxpayers who fund them. Advocates of privatization argue that the competitive environment of private industry fosters greater technological innovation, and that it pressures companies to introduce more stringent cost-cutting measures.

Because media industries and related policies are widely considered vital to sustaining public life, there is strong and widespread opposition to regulating them, as in any other industry, such as steel, coffee, or coal. However, the governments of most countries in the world view media and culture as exceptional because of the role they play in sustaining public life and culture (→ Culture: Definitions and Concepts). Although media privatization is on the rise worldwide, many governments tend to intervene by attempting to sustain the viability of their national media industries through import quotas and subsidies. Such policies are generally opposed by economists, and by governments and intergovernmental organizations that actively promote privatization and market liberalization.

Media industries have been privatized in many countries throughout the world for the past several decades, but the pace accelerated significantly in the 1980s and 1990s, particularly in post-socialist central and eastern Europe, throughout Latin America and much of Africa, and in India and selected East Asian economies. As well, liberal democratic welfare states in western Europe and other parts of the world have embraced media privatization. In the United States, the radio and television broadcasting system as a whole is overwhelmingly commercial, and the US system of public broadcasting, especially television, generally lacks stable and sufficient funding, or influence and importance as a vital stage for American culture and politics.

In many other countries, public service broadcasting has been articulated through government interventions, with reference to liberal democratic ideals, affirming a role for public leaders to develop and sustain political and cultural discourse through the media (→ Public Broadcasting Systems). However, due to pressures from global competition and the rapid increase in the availability of new media sources, even where they are well established and relatively successful, public service broadcasters have found themselves having to compete for audiences in an unfamiliar commercial and multichannel media landscape.

Perhaps even more dramatic than the changes to broadcasting have been the trends in privatization of telecommunications infrastructures and the convergence of mass media and telecommunications infrastructure ownership. In the past 25 years, many governments around the world have privatized their postal, telegraph, and telephone companies (PTTs), resulting in numerous subsequent mergers with and acquisitions by larger foreign companies. As well, foreign telecommunications firms have entered new markets in which privatizations and market liberalization occurred. For example, foreign direct investment poured into post-socialist central and eastern Europe to construct new landline and wireless infrastructures, sometimes in partnership with PTTs and also through new, private companies.

Telecommunications infrastructures are viewed widely as vital tools for developing the economies of the global south, which is why key intergovernmental organizations, such as the Organization for Economic Cooperation and Development (OECD), the International Telecommunications Union (ITU), and the World Bank have been active in promoting this sector. The World Bank in particular has been an advocate of telecommunications privatization, which it has advanced through a "toolkit" developed expressly for this industry sector.

In the twenty-first century, distinctions between ownership of media content and infrastructure are completely blurred, and a new wave of privatization has emerged. While in the 1980s and 1990s, privatization was typically undertaken by public trading in the stock market, a new pattern of private equity investment in media and telecommunications has emerged. Through speculative forms of investment, private equity firms and majority shareholders have managed to take some of the world's leading media and telecommunications companies off the publicly traded stock market, resulting in the removal of these companies from regulatory reach or public scrutiny. This new airtight form of privatization has raised concerns about the lack of transparency in how companies operate, and the weakening of any form of public interest regulatory oversight (Noam 2007).

See also: ▶ BBC ▶ CABLE TELEVISION
▶ COMMUNICATION LAW AND POLICY: NORTH
AMERICA ▶ CULTURE: DEFINITIONS AND CONCEPTS
▶ GLOBALIZATION OF THE MEDIA ▶ MEDIA
CONGLOMERATES ▶ POLITICAL ECONOMY OF
THE MEDIA ▶ PUBLIC BROADCASTING SYSTEMS
▶ UNITED STATES OF AMERICA: MEDIA SYSTEM

REFERENCES AND SUGGESTED READINGS

Bortolotti, B. & Siniscalco, D. (2004). *The challenges of privatization: An international analysis*. Oxford: Oxford University Press.

Kessides, I. N. (2006). *Reforming infrastructure: Privatization, regulation and competition*. Washington, DC: World Bank.

Noam, E. (2007). Private equity is a problem for public media. *Financial Times Online*, February 19, 2007. At http://www.ft.com/cms/s/2/50ca3cb0-c01e-11db-995a-000b5df10621.html#axzz3B0dFz3jp, accessed August 21, 2014.

Petrazzini, B. A. (1995). *The political economy of telecommunications reform in developing countries: Privatization and liberalization in comparative perspective*. Westport, CT: Praeger.

Rhodes, S. (2006). *Social movements and free-market capitalism in Latin America: Telecommunications privatization and the rise of consumer protest*. Albany, NY: SUNY Press.

Professionalization of Journalism

C. W. ANDERSON

College of Staten Island (CUNY)

The professionalization of journalism refers to the process by which a category of workers engaged in reporting and commentary in the public media on current events and ideas achieves the status of the occupational professional. Key issues in understanding the professionalization of journalism center on: the difficulties in defining 'professionalization' itself; the historical differences between US and non-American trajectories of professionalization; the relationship between journalistic objectivity (→ Objectivity in Reporting) and professionalism, especially in the American case; and the dramatic economic, technological, and cultural challenges to the professional status of → journalism since the early 2000s.

Based on sociological research, studies on journalists' professionalization have investigated the means and methods that the journalist has employed to seize control of both the abstract knowledge base (→ Journalism Education) and the occupational autonomy needed to establish professional dominance (→ Freedom of the Press, Concept of). For instance, cross-national empirical evidence demonstrates that journalists see themselves as a professional 'ingroup' (Donsbach 1981). Rather than attempting to shoehorn journalists into traditional professional classifications, a more interesting approach is to determine categories of professional journalistic competence and analyze how much the practice of actual journalists reflects these categories.

Most sociologists and historians of journalism point to the emergence of paid, full-time reporters (coinciding with the birth of the inexpensive popular newspapers in major American urban areas, especially New York City; → Journalism, History of) as marking the first step toward journalistic professionalization (Schudson 1978). Today, several social trends threaten the weak status of journalism as a profession, among them a growing corporatization and politicization as well as the diffusion of digital tools for both many-to-many communication and measuring audience preferences (Anderson 2011; → Commercialization: Impact on Media Content). Overall, trends in the US and elsewhere seem to point toward the de-differentiation of the journalism profession.

See also: ▶ ALTERNATIVE JOURNALISM ▶ CITIZEN
JOURNALISM ▶ COMMERCIALIZATION: IMPACT ON
MEDIA CONTENT ▶ FREEDOM OF THE PRESS,
CONCEPT OF ▶ JOURNALISM ▶ JOURNALISM
EDUCATION ▶ JOURNALISM, HISTORY OF
▶ JOURNALISTS' ROLE PERCEPTIONS ▶ OBJECTIVITY
IN REPORTING ▶ UNITED STATES OF AMERICA:
MEDIA SYSTEM

REFERENCES AND SUGGESTED READINGS

Anderson, C. W. (2011). Between creative and quantified audiences: Web metrics and changing patterns of newswork in local US newsrooms. *Journalism: Theory, Practice, and Criticism*, 12(5), 550–566.

Donsbach, W. (1981). Legitimacy through competence rather than value judgments: The concept of professionalization re-considered. *Gazette, 27*, 47–67.

Schudson, M. (1978). *Discovering the news: A social history of American newspapers.* New York: Basic Books.

Propaganda

JÜRGEN WILKE

Johannes Gutenberg University of Mainz

The term 'propaganda' is of Latin origin, meaning spreading, extending, or propagating with the help of the laity. It was first used by the Catholic Church to denominate its mission: In 1622, the Sacra Congregatio de Propaganda Fide, a council of cardinals responsible for the spread of the Catholic faith, was established in Rome under Pope Gregory XV. In the course of the French Revolution 'propaganda' lost its ecclesiastic meaning in favor of a political one. The term also gained ground in commerce and became partly a synonym for → advertising. Because of its (mis-)use in totalitarian states, the term aroused highly negative associations in western democracies and was replaced there by the term → public relations.

There are numerous definitions of the term propaganda in the literature. One of the earliest scientific definitions was introduced by Harold D. Lasswell, who wrote: "Propaganda is the management of collective attitudes by the manipulation of significant symbols" (1927a, 627). Edward L. Bernays, one of the fathers of public relations, wrote at around the same time: "Modern propaganda is a consistent, enduring effort to create or shape events to influence the relations of the public to the enterprise, idea or group" (1928, 25).

Although the term propaganda was only shaped ideologically and institutionally in the early seventeenth century, the phenomena it refers to are historically much older and may be traced back to antiquity and the Middle Ages. World War I (1914–1918) led to a hitherto unprecedented expansion especially of military propaganda. All parties were convinced that the fight by psychological means was as important as the one with military weapons. In the twentieth century, totalitarian movements drew upon massive propaganda to enforce their ideologies and claims to power. This was first the case in the Soviet Union and then in Nazi Germany and Fascist Italy. National and international propaganda reached a climax in World War II (1939–1945; → Propaganda in World War II). The means of propaganda ruled again during the Cold War. Even after the end of the east/west conflict, propaganda has been revived in *recent conflicts* such as the Gulf War, Afghanistan, the Balkans, and Iraq (→ War Propaganda). Propagandists, such as groups of Islamic terrorists, now even use the Internet (→ Mediated Terrorism).

There are three different *forms of propaganda*: (1) white propaganda, i.e., the open distribution of information regarded as truth; (2) gray propaganda, consisting of statements of doubtful quality, which systematically avoid identification of the source of the information; and (3) black propaganda, consisting of lies whose source is concealed, with the aim of embarking upon deception. Propaganda may be directed inwards (national propaganda) or outwards (foreign propaganda).

All sorts of *communication means* may be employed for propaganda. In the time before modern mass media were available, symbols, coins, heraldic signs, architecture, sculptures, and paintings were used. Later on printing, graphic techniques and all modern media were adopted for purposes of propaganda, particularly film and radio. In Asia, specific means were developed (Ginsberg 2013). During recent years, terrorist groups have been trying to conduct propaganda to promote their aims with the help of videotapes; for this purpose the same groups make use of the Internet (→ Mediated Terrorism).

The effect of the massive impact of propaganda during World War I stimulated an intensive preoccupation with the subject. The beginning of *scientific research* about propaganda in the field of communication was marked by Harold D. Lasswell's study *Propaganda Technique in the World War* (1927b). Lasswell not only described the organization of propaganda, but also distinguished *four major aims*: "(1) To mobilize hatred against the enemy; (2) To preserve the friendship of allies; (3) To preserve the friendship and, if possible, to procure the co-operation of neutrals; (4) To demoralize the enemy" (1927b, 195).

In 1937 the Institute for Propaganda Analysis was founded, with the communication scientist Hadley Cantril as the first president. Harold D. Lasswell's project on National Socialist and allied propaganda became a laboratory of method development, where Lasswell systematically refined the process of quantitative content analysis (→ Content Analysis, Quantitative).

See also: ▶ ADVERTISING ▶ INTERNATIONAL COMMUNICATION ▶ MEDIA EFFECTS ▶ MEDIA EFFECTS, HISTORY OF ▶ MEDIATED TERRORISM ▶ PROPAGANDA, VISUAL COMMUNICATION OF ▶ PROPAGANDA IN WORLD WAR II ▶ PUBLIC RELATIONS ▶ WAR PROPAGANDA

REFERENCES AND SUGGESTED READINGS

Bernays, E. L. (1928). *Propaganda*. New York: Horace Liveright.
Culbert, D., Cull, N. J., & Welch, D. (eds.) (2003). *Propaganda and mass persuasion. A historical encyclopedia from 1500 to the present*. Santa Barbara, CA: ABC Clio-Inc.
Ginsberg, M. (2013). *The art of influence. Asian Propaganda*. London: British Museum.
Jowett, G. S. & O'Donnell, V. (2012). *Propaganda and persuasion*, 5th edn. Thousand Oaks, CA: Sage.
Lasswell, H. D. (1927a). The theory of political propaganda. *American Political Science Review*, 21, 627–631.
Lasswell, H. D. (1927b). *Propaganda technique in the world war*. London: Routledge Kegan Paul.
Welch, D. A. (2013). *Propaganda, power and persuasion*. London: The British Library.

Propaganda, Visual Communication of

GARTH JOWETT
University of Houston

The development of visual → propaganda throughout history moves along two basic trajectories. The first is the desire to disseminate the message to an ever-wider public; the second is to disseminate this message as quickly and effectively as possible. In the ancient world, where communications were severely limited by distance, visual propaganda was initially confined to monumental displays associated with official sites of power such as palaces and temples, where large architectural structures, statues, obelisks, wall engravings, and other visual devices were used as a means of establishing a sense of power, social order, and hierarchy.

As transportation and communications improved in the ancient world, new methods of visual propaganda emerged as a means of creating and maintaining a sense of unity and stability across far-flung regions. In particular, the *use of coins* circulated widely and embossed with the visual images of rulers and symbols of state, were extremely effective as a means of conveying the importance and centrality of the state in the lives of people.

The eventual development of woodblock prints, and later engravings on metal, was a significant breakthrough in the development of visual propaganda. Now the visceral power of the image, often accompanied by written text, could be widely disseminated in the form of broadsheets or pamphlets. These *visual prints* were intended to elucidate current events for the common man, and were focused to a large extent on religious or political themes. For instance, the work of engraver-artist Lucas Cranach (1472–1553) was of enormous assistance to Martin Luther's propaganda campaign against the Roman Catholic Church.

The emergence of *printed propaganda* signaled a major shift away from the feudal power structure of the Middle Ages into a modern 'bourgeois' mentality. It was at this point that propaganda as a deliberate, systematic strategy to alter perceptions, beliefs, and actions of publics begins to emerge, fueled by new forms of communication. Propaganda enters the structure of the modern political state as a powerful weapon both of groups opposed to authority and those in power, and prints, flags, heraldry, medals, regalia, and all manner of art and architecture were used to legitimize authority and symbolize the inherent power of the state. Later, in both of the great wars of the twentieth century the *poster* became a major propaganda weapon, especially in creating morale and civic motivation on the home front with slogans like "Loose lips sink ships" and "Is your journey really necessary?"

The emergence of → *photography* in the 1830s created an entirely new possibility for increasing the effectiveness and emotional impact of visual propaganda. By the 1860s the use of photography as a dramatic illustration of the horrors of war or the plight of the poor in slum living conditions had become a major weapon for the propagandist, despite the fact that such photographs were often deliberately staged by the propagandist as a means of influencing → public opinion (→ Photojournalism). Photography proved to be a particularly powerful propaganda tool in the hands of skilled photographers such as Robert Capra, with his famous 'Moment of death' picture from the Spanish Civil War.

Even as early as the 1890s, *films* taken of the Boer War (many of these were faked) were shown in British and American cinemas for propaganda purposes. By the time of World War I, the cinema was so popular with the international public that motion pictures became an integral part of the 'official' propaganda activities of most governments. Individual films, such as director Leni Riefenstahl's Triumph of the Will (1935), a brilliant cinematic paean to Hitler's 1934 Nazi Party rally in Nuremberg, or controversial documentaries, such as Michael Moore's Fahrenheit 9/11 (2005) can be seen as successfully communicating their propaganda objectives.

Because of the technological barriers to broadcasting *television* signals across oceans and borders, it has only been in the past 30 years that the development of → satellite television has created the potential for global television propaganda (→ Global Media, History of; Globalization of the Media). Particularly with growing international conflicts in the former Soviet Union, the Balkans, and the Middle East, satellite television news channels such as Fox News, → CNN, and Al Jazeera have begun to emerge as significant sources for delivering – often unconsciously – propaganda messages (→ Arab Satellite TV News). The continuous broadcasting of images of conflict, many 'live' as they are unfolding, has made international television among the most powerful propaganda tools now in existence (→ International Television).

New communication technologies, including hand-held mobile phone devices, digital cameras, and palm-sized computer interfaces, all linked to the Internet, promise to facilitate the dissemination of imagery which could be used for a wide variety of propaganda purposes. Government attempts to regulate such widespread use of visual devices have proven to be rather futile, and there is little doubt that in the future the free flow of imagery will only increase, providing an even greater potential for diverse expression, but also for manipulation and the creation of more powerful visual propaganda.

See also: ▶ ADVERTISING ▶ ADVERTISING AS PERSUASION ▶ ARAB SATELLITE TV NEWS ▶ CINEMA ▶ CNN ▶ EDUCATIONAL COMMUNICATION ▶ GLOBAL MEDIA, HISTORY OF ▶ GLOBALIZATION OF THE MEDIA ▶ ICONOGRAPHY ▶ INTERNATIONAL COMMUNICATION ▶ INTERNATIONAL TELEVISION ▶ PERSUASION ▶ PHOTOGRAPHY ▶ PHOTOJOURNALISM ▶ PRINTING, HISTORY OF ▶ PROPAGANDA ▶ PUBLIC OPINION ▶ SATELLITE TELEVISION ▶ TELEVISION AS POPULAR CULTURE ▶ TELEVISION: SOCIAL HISTORY ▶ VISUAL COMMUNICATION

REFERENCES AND SUGGESTED READINGS

Atkinson, N. S. (2011). Newsreels as domestic propaganda: Visual rhetoric at the dawn of the cold war. *Rhetoric and Public Affairs*, 14(1), 69–100.

Bolt, N. (2012). *The violent image: Insurgent propaganda and the new revolutionaries*. New York: Columbia University Press.

Clark, T. (1997). *Art and propaganda in the twentieth century: The political image in the age of mass culture*. New York: Harry N. Abrams.

Jowett, G. S. & O'Donnell, V. (2014). *Propaganda and persuasion*, 6th edn. Thousand Oaks, CA: Sage.

Taylor, P. M. (2003). *Munitions of the mind: A history of propaganda from the ancient world to the present day*. Manchester: Manchester University Press.

Propaganda in World War II

PHILIP M. TAYLOR
University of Leeds

World War II witnessed the greatest propaganda campaigns in history. Often referred to as the "Fourth Arm" after the army, navy, and air force, → propaganda was conducted by all belligerents and was essentially designed to sustain domestic civilian morale during a long war at home while undermining enemy civilian *and* military confidence in the ability to achieve victory. Although propaganda was becoming a characteristic of peacetime politics in the first half of the twentieth century, it was still seen largely as a weapon of war, especially in democracies.

Dictatorships in the Soviet Union, Fascist Italy, and Nazi Germany more readily embraced its peacetime use as a form of coercion of mass populations instead of the individualistic democratic predisposition toward → persuasion and consensus-building. These different ideologies eventually went to war against each other in 1939. Ultimately World War II was won by military power – which prompts the question of what role propaganda actually played in determining the final outcome (→ War Propaganda).

Propaganda was highly organized from the outset, although most sides found it difficult to centralize its various functions. The Nazi Propaganda Ministry had several rival voices from within the 'divide and rule' bureaucracy created by Adolf Hitler (Welch 1994). The British set up a Ministry of Information that stumbled its way through the early wartime years (including the 'Phony War' or 'Bore War') fighting other Whitehall departments like the Foreign Office and Service Ministries. (Taylor 1999). Once the Americans entered the war in late 1941, sufficient lessons had been learned to separate out domestic and overseas propaganda functions through the Office of War Information and the Office of Special Services. For all sides, fighting the war was the major priority, but who was responsible for publicly chronicling or interpreting its progress – image rather than reality – was also important.

The idea of a 'home front' or of a 'nation at arms,' of mobilizing entire populations for sustained conflict, first emerged during the 1914–1918 war. It came into sharper focus in the 1930s with the arrival of the bombing aircraft and its indiscriminate impact on the civilian populations of cities, first witnessed during the Sino–Japanese War (1931–1933 and from 1937 onward) and especially the Spanish Civil War (1936–1939) through newsreel footage of the bombing of Guernica. The mass bombing of cities between 1939 and 1945 was to substantially narrow the gap between soldier and civilian both physically and psychologically. In such an environment, morale became a critical factor and one that might determine the eventual outcome. That environment was also media-rich compared to wars of the past – traditional print media were now supplemented by the arrival of broadcast radio and sound → cinema. Propaganda was also a weapon that could be deployed against the enemy when no other means of attacking them were available, especially in the form of electronic broadcasting.

Propaganda took *many forms*. Movies were so thoroughly infused with wartime propaganda themes that it was difficult for audiences to stand back and say, "That is just a propaganda film." So all-pervading was propaganda that the experience of being propagandized could almost be defined as having lived at the time. Propaganda not only manifested itself in films and radio broadcasts, it also took the form of posters, picture postcards, china plates and ornaments, biscuit tins, cigarette cards, songs, and music. It proved capable of almost infinite applications, as with the British (and later American) 'V for victory' campaign.

The effectiveness of much propaganda depended not only upon events at the fighting fronts but also upon *media access* to them. It took the British more than a year for the military authorities to appreciate the need for war reporters and cameramen to be allowed to accompany the troops. For the Nazis, it was the reverse. Their front line propaganda company units were able to capture spectacular images of the German army's initial successes in Belgium and France, which were duly incorporated into the official newsreels. Once the Americans entered the war, they allowed camera crews to accompany bombing raids over Germany, and William Wyler's documentary *The Memphis Belle* (1943) was testimony to the success of such decisions. One of the tragedies of World War II was that when stories began to emerge from 1943 onward of the death camps built for the 'final solution' they were dismissed by many people as being 'atrocity propaganda' such as that used to demonize the Germans during World War I.

See also: ▶ BBC ▶ CENSORSHIP ▶ CENSORSHIP, HISTORY OF ▶ CINEMA ▶ FILM PRODUCTION ▶ HOLLYWOOD ▶ NEWS ▶ PERSUASION ▶ PROPAGANDA ▶ RADIO ▶ WAR PROPAGANDA

REFERENCES AND SUGGESTED READINGS

Balfour, M. (1979). *Propaganda in war 1939–45*. London: Routledge and Kegan Paul.
Collier, R. (1989). *The warcos: The war correspondent in World War II*. London: Weidenfeld and Nicholson.
Cull, N. J. (1995). *Selling war: The British propaganda campaign against American "neutrality" in World War II*. Oxford: Oxford University Press.
Taylor, P. M. (1999). *British propaganda in the twentieth century: Selling democracy*. Edinburgh: Edinburgh University Press.
Welch, D. (1994). *The Third Reich: Politics and propaganda*. London: Routledge.

Public Affairs

ROBERT L. HEATH
University of Houston

Public affairs is both a generic term used to define socio-economic and socio-political trends and the executive management function that works to position each organization appropriately in its political economy.

Madden (2005, 665) defined it as "the management function responsible for interpreting an organization's external environment, or in the case of a corporation, its noncommercial environment, and managing an effective and appropriate response to that environment." It focuses on the public policy (non-marketplace) arena in which government influences (support or oppose) management decisions and organizational operations and policies. In the United Kingdom, the "emphasis on managing potentially complex relationships and issues that may ultimately affect the destiny of organisations ... led many organisations to recognize the strategic importance of the public affairs function" (Harris & Moss 2001, 6; → Strategic Communication). Different from the US model, public affairs in the United Kingdom is shaped by government policymakers; government is presumed to set the tone and standard for the business and government affairs that affect people's daily lives.

The *concept began* in the 1950s when President Dwight D. Eisenhower brought a group of leading business executives together to encourage a bipartisan forum for Democrats and Republicans. While corporations were praised for their role in the war, questions were being raised about the need to regulate corporations' size and impact and to solve social problems such as workplace safety, racial and gender discrimination and environmentalism. Eisenhower was keenly aware of international socio-economic collisions that would define the political and commercial arrangements and norms in the United States. In a spirit of organizational citizenship participation, he wanted to name the group the Effective Citizens Organization. In 1965, it adopted the name Public Affairs Council.

In many large organizations, public affairs as a management function subsumes → public relations and other communication functions. In such organizations, public relations serves a marketing, product promotion, publicity, and reputation management function. However, in companies with a primary emphasis on consumer marketing, the public relations function is likely to subordinate public affairs as government relations.

See also: ▶ CORPORATE COMMUNICATION ▶ ISSUE MANAGEMENT ▶ ORGANIZATIONAL COMMUNICATION ▶ ORGANIZATIONAL IMAGE ▶ PUBLIC RELATIONS ▶ STRATEGIC COMMUNICATION

REFERENCES AND SUGGESTED READINGS

Harris, P. & Moss, D. (2001). Editorial: Understanding public affairs. *Journal of Public Affairs*, 1, 6–8.
Lerbinger, O. (2006). *Corporate public affairs: Interacting with interest groups, media, and government*. Mahwah, NJ: Lawrence Erblaum.
Madden, W. (2005). Public affairs. In Robert L. Heath (ed.), *Encyclopedia of public relations*. Thousand Oaks, CA: Sage, pp. 665–666.

Public Broadcasting, History of

JAMIE MEDHURST
Aberystwyth University

Public broadcasting can be defined in economic terms (funding from the state or public taxation), cultural terms (maintaining and supporting a minority culture), social terms (broadcasting for the 'public good,' audience terms (the listener/viewer as citizen), and, finally, as 'that which is not commercial broadcasting.'

Scannell (2000) has argued that a historical understanding of public broadcasting needs to take into account two factors: public broadcasting as defined by the state and public broadcasting as interpreted by the broadcaster. In the UK, for instance, broadcasting was viewed as a public utility, and the mandate to develop it as a national service in the public interest came from the state (→ United Kingdom: Media System; BBC). This was in contrast to the model in the United States where broadcasting development took the commercial as opposed to the state-controlled, public service path (→ United States of America: Media System).

Sir John Reith, first managing director (then director-general) of the British Broadcasting Company (which became a Corporation in 1927) interpreted public broadcasting by developing a set of principles which were to dominate British broadcasting for decades. Broadcasting had a duty to bring the 'best' of British culture to every household in the UK, and this reflected the director-general's almost missionary zeal for the task in hand. Reith's concept of public broadcasting influenced the development of radio and television services in many European countries after the end of World War II and formed a key part of the → political economy of the media in these countries.

The period of the Weimar Republic (1918–1933) in Germany witnessed an emergent public broadcasting system, one which was state governed and controlled. As Humphreys (1996) has argued, "the state's grip on the medium had become almost absolute by the time Hitler came to power." By the mid-1930s the Nazis had turned their attention to the new medium of television, and they soon established the world's first high-definition television service, distributed to public spaces (→ Propaganda in World War II).

The world's first regular domestic television service began on November 2, 1936, when the BBC broadcast from Alexandra Palace in north London. However, the outbreak of World War II brought the service to an abrupt halt in September 1939. However, as television services emerged in postwar Europe, some variation in the 'degree' of public service appeared. In France, for example, the state had a closer hold on broadcasters than in Spain, where the television service was funded by advertising but controlled by the state (→ France: Media System). The overwhelming influence on German broadcasting up until the 1980s was a public broadcasting ethos (→ Germany: Media System), whilst further afield, Japan's NHK television service drew closely on the BBC's public service model and was funded by a license fee (→ Japan: Media System). Despite the dominance of the public broadcasting model in Europe, the postwar years saw a gradual shift towards commercialism (→ Commercialization of the Media). In the UK, the debate over a rival television service to compete with the BBC began in the years immediately after the war and the 1954 Television Act introduced a television service funded by advertising revenue to the UK for the first time. The 1960s and 1970s saw the continued abandonment of the Reithian model of public broadcasting across Europe.

In the US, however, there was a concerted attempt to 'ring-fence' public broadcasting by the establishment of the Public Broadcasting Service (PBS) in 1969. After initial success, however, the service soon declined in the face of stiff commercial competition. The 1960s saw an increasingly liberal approach to broadcasting and a further shift took place during the 1980s when citizens were being increasingly defined as consumers. The neo-liberalist stance of the Peacock Report in the United Kingdom, published in 1986, referred to the now-famous notion of 'consumer sovereignty,' a sign for many that the death knell for public broadcasting had been rung.

See also: ▶ BBC ▶ COMMERCIALIZATION OF THE MEDIA ▶ FRANCE: MEDIA SYSTEM ▶ GERMANY: MEDIA SYSTEM ▶ JAPAN: MEDIA SYSTEM ▶ MEDIA ECONOMICS ▶ MEDIA POLICY ▶ POLITICAL ECONOMY OF THE MEDIA ▶ PRIVATIZATION OF THE MEDIA ▶ PROPAGANDA ▶ PROPAGANDA IN WORLD WAR II ▶ PUBLIC BROADCASTING SYSTEMS ▶ RADIO: SOCIAL HISTORY ▶ UNITED KINGDOM: MEDIA SYSTEM ▶ UNITED STATES OF AMERICA: MEDIA SYSTEM

REFERENCES AND SUGGESTED READINGS

Barnouw, E. (1966–1970). *A history of broadcasting in the United States*. Oxford: Oxford University Press.

Briggs, A. (1961–1995). *The history of British broadcasting in the United Kingdom*, vols. 1–5. Oxford: Oxford University Press.

Humphreys, P. (1996). *Mass media and media policy in western Europe*. Manchester: Manchester University Press.

McDonnell, J. (1991). *Public service broadcasting: A reader*. London: Routledge.

Scannell, P. (2000). Public service broadcasting: The history of a concept. In E. Buscombe (ed.), *British television: A reader*. Oxford: Oxford University Press, pp. 45–61.

Public Broadcasting Systems

JO BARDOEL

University of Amsterdam and Radboud University Nijmegen

Public service broadcasting (PSB) refers to "a system that is set up by law and generally financed by public funds (often a compulsory license fee paid by households) and given a large degree of editorial and operating independence" (McQuail 2010, 178). Public service broadcasting is supposed to function independently of both the market and the state, and therefore differs from the alternative systems of commercial broadcasting on the one hand and authoritarian or state-operated broadcasting on the other.

Origins and Philosophical Traces

There is no clear *definition or coherent theory* of public broadcasting. When radio and television were introduced, national governments had to regulate the access to these media – unlike the situation with the press – because of the scarcity of frequencies and a widespread concern about the impact of these new, electronic media on people and society. In this context, public, noncommercial corporations were set up that presented a comprehensive program, consisting of information, education, culture, and entertainment that would raise the level of political awareness and cultural taste of citizens.

The *philosophical traces* of the concept of PSB lie in humanistic Enlightenment ideals and in normative notions on the social responsibility and public interest of media in modern societies. As such this is a negotiated concept that results from a process of political struggle, social debate, and academic reflection and differs from country to country and from period to period, reflecting national media policies and research traditions (→ Public Broadcasting, History of).

Goals and Distribution

In spite of all the differences mentioned, the goals of public broadcasting across cultures show a striking resemblance (McQuail 2010): (1) universality of geographic coverage and audience reach, and a common reference point and forum for all members of the public; (2) pluralistic, innovative, and varied programming, independent of both government and market forces; (3) concern for national culture, language, and identity as well as a reflection of ideas and beliefs in a multiethnic and multicultural society; (4) accountability towards society and the audience.

At present public broadcasting systems exist *all over the world*, but are most frequently found in European countries and in countries that have historical or colonial ties with these European countries. The prime example and model of PSB worldwide is the → BBC, but in fact the position and organization of PSBs as national institutions reflect the history of the respective nation-states.

The American public broadcasting system, PBS, has quite a different tradition and position (Avery 1993). The United States Radio Act of 1927 enabled the commercial, advertiser-funded broadcasting system for which the US is known. In 1945 the → Federal Communications Commission (FCC) created licenses for noncommercial educational radio stations with a public service ideal. Educational television officially began by 1952, but it was only with the Public Broadcasting Act of 1967, following the report of the Carnegie Commission on Educational Television, that more (although limited) funding for both educational radio and television became available. Since then public radio and television gained a fixed but, compared to public broadcasters in Europe and elsewhere in the world, rather marginal position in the media landscape (→ Educational Media).

Public Broadcasting in Question

The changing context of PSB has raised criticism on almost every aspect of its operations: its mission, programming, organization, and funding (Bardoel & d'Haenens 2008). Concerning the *mission* of PSB, the political function of PSB in relation to democracy, pluralism, and public debate is crucial. More recently, socio-cultural goals, such as serving social integration and cohesion, have also become more prominent. However, Hallin and Mancini's seminal book *Comparing Media Systems* (2004) demonstrates that the relation between politics and the media and media freedom across western countries varies greatly according to their political history and culture and the room it leaves for a vivid → public sphere, including public broadcasting. In this respect, the countries of North America and western Europe are ahead of the new democracies of the south and the east.

The debate on the program assignment of public broadcasting can be summarized by the catchwords 'comprehensive or complementary': should PSB still present a full-scale program offering or should it just supplement programs that its commercial counterparts do not offer (Jakubowicz 2007)? Despite accusations of copycat strategies and a convergence between public and commercial broadcasters, research shows that most public broadcasters have chosen the middle way of compensation. Public broadcasters try to stress their distinctiveness more than ever. The alternative option of de-institutionalizing PSB by introducing public program funds comparable with policies vis-à-vis culture and the arts ('distributed public service') has been proposed in countries that reconsidered their public broadcasting system, but no country has dared to take that far-reaching step, with the notable exception of New Zealand, where a drastic reorganization of PSB took place in 1988. Open competition via an 'arts council of the air' model was meant to lead to greater value for money and add to the quality of PSB programming, but in practice it did not work out that way.

Looking further into the organizational aspects, the rapid rise of commercial television has also changed the structure and culture of public broadcasting institutions. From the 1980s on, quasi-commercial elements were introduced within public broadcasting, such as the popularization of programming, the introduction of scheduling techniques, an increasing cost-consciousness by outsourcing activities, and the adaptation of management practices from the commercial sector. PSB institutions are increasingly showing accountability on their overall efficiency and effectiveness.

The main source of finance for most PSBs remains the license fee, but most countries have mixed systems. Despite the criticism on advertising as an additional source of income for public broadcasters, mixed funding has been defended as a proper tool to minimize unilateral dependence on politics. In addition, the overall financial position of public broadcasters differs considerably from country to country and is closely related to the size of the population and territory to be served.

Public Service Broadcasting in a Network Society

After a tradition of paternalism inherent in the pedagogical imperative of the past, public broadcasters now have to redefine their relation with the public and society anew. National identities and collective communities are eroding in favor of individualized and hybrid consumer sovereignty. Digitization further facilitates the fragmentation of audiences (→ Audience Segmentation), personalized media consumption and the dominance of the market logic (→ Markets of the Media). At the same time, many still believe that basic PSB functions, such as a low-cost and universally available reliable provision of information, education, and culture, and the catering for minority tastes and interests, cannot or will not be sufficiently served by the commercial market ('market failure').

In this rapidly changing context the core challenge lies in transforming supply-oriented public service broadcasters (PSB) into demand-oriented public service media (PSM). PSM wants to remain a trusted brand, but also open up to the networked society, building new partnerships with both civil society and the creative industry (European Broadcasting Union 2013). This transformation raises the question of whether the present PSB-institution will survive, will be reduced to a public service publisher, or even integrated into a digital commons model. Also, in the future, the raison d'être of PSB/PSMs will lie in setting the standard by offering quality content, thus providing public value to society and serving as an anchor for citizens amidst the new deluge of information.

See also: ▶ AUDIENCE SEGMENTATION ▶ BBC
▶ EDUCATIONAL MEDIA ▶ FEDERAL COMMUNICATIONS COMMISSION (FCC) ▶ MARKETS OF THE MEDIA
▶ PUBLIC BROADCASTING, HISTORY OF
▶ PUBLIC SPHERE

REFERENCES AND SUGGESTED READINGS

Avery, R. K. (ed.) (1993). *Public service broadcasting in a multichannel environment: The history and survival of an ideal.* White Plains, NY: Longman.

Bardoel, J. & d'Haenens, L. (2008). Reinventing public service broadcasting in Europe: Prospects, promises and problems. *Media Culture Society*, 30(3), 337–355.

European Broadcasting Union (2013). *Vision 2020: Connecting to a Networked Society.* Geneva: EBU.

Hallin, D. C. & Mancini, P. (2004). *Comparing media systems: Three models of media and politics.* Cambridge: Cambridge University Press.

Jakubowicz, K. (2007). Public Service Broadcasting in the 21st Century. What Chance for a New Beginning? In G. F. Lowe and J. Bardoel (eds.), *From public service broadcasting to public service media.* Gothenburg: Nordicom, pp. 29–50.

McQuail, D. (2010). *McQuail's mass communication theory.* Thousand Oaks, CA: Sage.

Public Opinion

CARROLL J. GLYNN
Ohio State University

MICHAEL E. HUGE
Ohio State University

Bearing the dubious distinction of being one of the oldest, yet least understood, concepts in social science, public opinion continues to inspire and perplex scholars from communication and other fields. The term can be adequately defined as a general measure of the directionality and strength of issue-specific views and sentiments held by a relevant group. Public opinion bears a sort of syntactical internal contradiction: While 'public' denotes the group and the universal, 'opinion' on its own is typically associated with the individual and considered a somewhat internal, subjective formulation. The rise of survey research during the early twentieth century further complicated matters with a trend toward quantifying public opinion as a simple aggregation of individual survey responses (→ Survey; Public Opinion Polling). The rejection of such mathematical reductions – along with the suggestion that public opinion was in fact a group-level social force iteratively constructed through interpersonal interaction and media use (→ Interpersonal Communication; Political Media Use) – set the stage for a social science debate that has continued for well over 50 years.

Historical Approaches

The French term *'l'opinion publique,'* originally attributed to sixteenth-century French Renaissance writer Montaigne, was adopted in European thinking as political power and decision-making shifted away from the monarchy and toward the citizenry during the Enlightenment. With the advent of the printing press (→ Printing, History of), knowledge became more distributed within societies, and this led to a realization that it might be possible to arrive at better decisional outcomes if more affected parties (i.e., the citizenry) were consulted. Until recent times, however, the citizenry considered to have a voice consisted primarily of land-owning, wealthy white males.

One of the earliest problems to arise in conceptualizing what constituted public opinion was the difficulty of coming to some type of *decisional outcome* at the end of a public opinion process in which many different viewpoints were voiced. When parties disagreed, it was difficult to discern (1) whose views should be most prominently considered and (2) how other ideas could be eliminated. Additional debate centered on how 'rational' a group could be considered in arriving at a public viewpoint rather than being subject to the manipulation of opinions.

With these challenges in mind, Enlightenment-era thinkers set out to incorporate the views of the public into governmental decisions, while at the same time balancing this democratic input with the presumed knowledge and experience of government officials. In this way, a democratic government could consider the will of the people while maintaining stability against abrupt shifts in sentiment that could overrun the long-term authority of the state. Divergent views of the role of public opinion in a democracy (i.e., a mandate from the people or merely the views of those affected by decisions) were typified by the 1920s debate between Walter Lippmann and John Dewey (Splichal 1999). Dewey believed that the more people included in arriving at a public opinion outcome, the better off the entire society would be. From Lippmann's point of view, governmental decisions were best left to elected and appointed officials who were free to use public opinion as a guide to varying degrees. The trend toward scientific methods to measure people's opinions created another debate, with one side seeing public opinion as an aggregation of survey responses, while others were more interested in public opinion as a socially constructed force that developed through media use and interpersonal conversation.

Public Opinion Processes: Information or Social Control?

From a societal perspective, public opinion can function in a number of different ways. Some scholars (Habermas 1989 [1st pub. 1962]) argue for the merits of thinking about public opinion as a rational, information-based phenomenon in which the best ideas will percolate to the top of the public agenda. Within the confines of the → public sphere, citizens are exposed to a number of different ideas and opinions that they can hold or improve upon. In a manner akin to free market systems, the ideas that hold the most value are in the highest demand, while less popular ideas are pushed aside.

Scholars like Noelle-Neumann (1993) saw public opinion as a *method of social control*. Acknowledging that societies must be held together by some level of group-wide cohesion, this view posits a heavy influence of the mass media upon the general public. Instead of debating within a rational and unbiased opinion climate, most citizens are instead limited to considering the views put forth in newspapers or on television. Noelle-Neumann's → 'spiral of silence' theory predicts that those who believe that their viewpoint is in the minority will be less likely to express that viewpoint (→ Climate of Opinion).

Public Opinion and the Media

Over the past few decades, media effects research has shifted from investigating the direct effects of messages to a more information-based cognitive approach (→ Media Effects; Media Effects, History of). The information-processing approach seeks to identify how new, outside information – most of which is received by individuals via media outlets – is integrated with already-existing information. One example of this shift can be seen in agenda-setting research, which initially focused on matching prominent news stories with lists of what the public perceived to be important issues (→ Agenda-Setting Effects). More recently, agenda-setting research has explored possible mechanisms (e.g., priming) through which this media effect might take place. Other research has focused on how the agenda-setting function can cause shifts in public opinion that go beyond a simple listing of what is important (→ Priming Theory). In other words, agenda-setting research could be a much stronger theoretical framework if differently 'set' agendas were shown to impact individual opinions as well as perceptions of macro-level opinion in a significantly different manner.

Technology and Democratic Outcomes

The recent popularity of websites of many different origins and the role of → social media indicates that many individuals are willing and able to put forth their own views and content for mass consumption. Yet, it remains to be seen whether the increasing availability of political information will have a marked impact on public opinion processes. It is possible that the people who were interested in politics before the Internet revolution will be the same people who make use of new technology (Roessler & Schulz 2014).

Perhaps the tallest hurdle remaining for public opinion scholars is specifying and modeling key contextual factors of public opinion climates.

Spiral of silence research gained much attention by noting that the perception of majority pressure can impact the likelihood of individual opinion expression. However, scholars have more recently recognized that perceptions of majority and minority pressures can vary according to the perceived strength of opinions as well as perceptions of how much agreement there is among a group or community.

See also: ▶ AGENDA-SETTING EFFECTS ▶ ATTITUDES ▶ CLIMATE OF OPINION ▶ COMMUNICATION TECHNOLOGY AND DEMOCRACY ▶ DIGITAL DIVIDE ▶ ELECTION SURVEYS ▶ EXPOSURE TO COMMUNICATION CONTENT ▶ INTERPERSONAL COMMUNICATION ▶ MEDIA EFFECTS ▶ MEDIA EFFECTS, HISTORY OF ▶ MEDIA AND PERCEPTIONS OF REALITY ▶ MEDIA PRODUCTION AND CONTENT ▶ MEDIA USE BY SOCIAL VARIABLE ▶ POLITICAL COGNITIONS ▶ POLITICAL KNOWLEDGE ▶ POLITICAL MEDIA USE ▶ PRIMING THEORY ▶ PRINTING, HISTORY OF ▶ PUBLIC OPINION POLLING ▶ PUBLIC SPHERE ▶ SOCIAL PERCEPTION ▶ SOCIAL MEDIA ▶ SPIRAL OF SILENCE ▶ SURVEY ▶ TWO-STEP FLOW OF COMMUNICATION

REFERENCES AND SUGGESTED READINGS

Binkley, R. C. (1928). The concept of public opinion in the social sciences. *Social Forces*, 6, 389–396.

Blumer, H. (1948). Public opinion and public opinion polling. *American Sociological Review*, 13, 542–549.

Cooley, C. H. (1962). *Social organization*. Brunswick, NJ: Transaction.

Donsbach, W., Salmon, C. T., & Tsfati, Y. (eds.) (2014). *The spiral of silence. New perspectives on communication and public opinion*. London: Routledge.

Fishkin, J. S. (1991). *Democracy and deliberation*. New Haven, CT: Yale University Press.

Habermas, J. (1989). *The structural transformation of the public sphere: An inquiry into a category of bourgeois society*. Cambridge, MA: MIT Press.

Noelle-Neumann, E. (1993). *The spiral of silence: Public opinion – our social skin*. Chicago: University of Chicago Press.

Roessler, P. & Schulz, A. (2014): Public opinion expression in online environments. In W. Donsbach, C. T. Salmon, & Y. Tsfati (eds.), *The spiral of silence: New perspectives on communication and public opinion*. London: Routledge, pp. 101–118.

Splichal, S. (1999). *Public opinion: Developments and controversies in the twentieth century*. Lanham, MD: Rowman and Littlefield.

Zaller, J. R. (1992). *The nature and origins of mass opinion*. Cambridge: Cambridge University Press.

Public Opinion Polling

THOMAS PETERSEN
Allensbach Institute

The term 'public opinion polling' generally refers collectively to both the representative → survey method and to the institutes that specialize in employing this method, particularly to commercial survey institutes. Other terms commonly employed in this context are: 'public opinion research,' 'survey research,' or simply, if somewhat confusingly, → 'public opinion.' The term 'demoscopy' (Greek: 'observation of the public'), originally suggested by American scientist Stuart Dodd (Dodd 1946), is also commonly used in some European countries, particularly in connection with political debate, although it has not gained a foothold in English-speaking countries.

The three *cornerstones of survey research* are: the standardization of the investigative technique, i.e., completing interviews using a firmly worded questionnaire (→ Interview, Standardized); analyzing the findings in aggregate, in other words, observing respondents as a group, not as individuals; and the random selection of respondents to form a group representative of the total population in question. These three core elements of opinion research were first combined systematically in the early twentieth century, although they had already been employed previously in a number of statistical surveys and research projects. The goal of survey research, often misunderstood, is not to ascertain the opinions and behaviors of each single person in all their complexity, but to describe society as a whole.

In completing surveys, strict methodological rules regarding standardization and structuring must be adhered to: as far as possible, all respondents receive the same question wordings and response alternatives regardless of their education or social background. This technique is not meant to provide information about the special characteristics and motives of individual respondents but enables the researcher to determine what respondents think about a certain issue on average (cf. Noelle-Neumann & Petersen 2005, 65–79).

In public opinion polls the respondents are not selected arbitrarily, but in accordance with strict rules that insure that the group of people interviewed is representative of the total population, thus enabling researchers to generalize the responses obtained during the interview. Random samples follow the lottery principle, with samples being selected at random from the total universe. Because of their fundamental principle that every member of the population or group of people under investigation must have an equal chance of being included in the sample, random samples have a mathematical-statistical foundation (→ Sampling, Random). Another technique for drawing representative samples is the 'quota method' where interviewers select respondents according to certain predetermined attributes, such as sex, age group, occupational group, size of place of residence, etc. Taken as a whole, these attributes represent a scaled-down model of the total population. Today, public opinion surveys are conducted either in-person of via the telephone. In addition to that, online surveys are gaining importance despite serious sampling problems (Vehovar et al. 2008).

Survey research has become an integral part of many areas of life. It is the most important research tool in the empirical social sciences, for example in communication research, political science, and sociology. It also plays a central role in the business world. Today, representative surveys are naturally conducted in conjunction with product launches, advertising campaigns, and new design concepts of all kinds. Survey research plays a particularly vital role in the political process and the mass media, especially during election campaigns (→ Election Surveys). Right from the start, election forecasts have been particularly important for survey institutes since they provide a rare opportunity to test the reliability of the survey method against external criteria.

For decades, election surveys have also been the target of critical remarks from politicians and journalists, due to the alleged influence of published election forecasts on voting behavior. However, research to date indicates that the effect of such forecasts on voting behavior is actually only slight. At any rate, the influence exerted by polls on voting behavior is certainly far less significant than the effect of other forms of media reporting. Yet, even if election forecasts did exert a major influence on voting behavior, it is fair to ask whether this would necessarily have a negative influence on the democratic process, as many people assume. Representative surveys are not the only source of information on the relative strength of the political parties prior to an election, but they are certainly the most reliable source.

See also: ▶ ELECTION SURVEYS ▶ INTERVIEW, STANDARDIZED ▶ QUANTITATIVE } METHODOLOGY ▶ PUBLIC OPINION ▶ SAMPLING, RANDOM ▶ SURVEY

REFERENCES AND SUGGESTED READINGS

Dodd, S. (1946). Toward world surveying. *Public Opinion Quarterly*, 10, 470–483.
Donsbach, W., & Traugott, M. W. (eds.) (2008). *The Sage handbook of public opinion research*. Thousand Oaks, CA: Sage.
Noelle-Neumann, E. & Petersen, T. (2005). *Alle, nicht jeder: Einführung in die Methoden der Demoskopie [All but not each: Introduction to the methods of survey research]*, 4th edn. Berlin: Springer.
Taylor, H. (1995). Horses for courses: How different countries measure public opinion in very different ways. *The Public Perspective*, (February/March), 3–7.
Vehovar, V., Lozar Manfreda, K., & Koren, G. (2008). Internet surveys. In W. Donsbach & M. W. Traugott (eds.), *The Sage handbook of public opinion research*. Thousand Oaks, CA: Sage, pp. 271–283.

Public Relations

BETTEKE VAN RULER
University of Amsterdam

ROBERT L. HEATH
University of Houston

Public relations (PR) is a professional practice and academic discipline dedicated to spreading rational and trustworthy information, evaluative judgment supporting enlightened choices, policy recommendations, and appeals for co-created identifications. PR is also seen as a professional practice and academic discipline dedicated to fostering communication, building relationships, and managing change under opinion conditions that can hamper or help the success of the sponsor.

Although 'modern' PR was born in the USA in the nineteenth century, world history in general and European history in particular offer sound evidence of tensions between enlightened choice and engineered consent. In Europe, PR in practice has a long history (see van Ruler & Verčič 2004). The period of the Enlightenment, as developed in the eighteenth century in France and Germany, profoundly influenced the evaluation and practice of PR (even if not by name) in many European countries. Addressing the history of PR in the USA, Scott Cutlip (1994) staked the beginnings of PR in the American Revolution era. The rise of modern PR later paralleled mass media's growth, which allowed mass-produced publicity and promotion, as well as the sort of → issue management that resulted from the efforts of the robber barons to craft the public policy that was needed to support a mass production/consumption society. Similarly, in other parts of the world PR, a timeless craft, is now a growing field.

Public Relations Research

Scholarly literature on PR features one generic principle: PR is the function that helps an organization to communicate well and helps its management to favorably position the organization to earn the favor of targeted markets, audiences, publics, and society at large. This, however, is accomplished in different ways and guided by different theories (Heath 2013).

The *information model* is rooted in classical information, systems, and mass communication theories, such as the → two-step flow of communication (and the multistep flow) theory, the → diffusion of information and innovation theory, the knowledge gap theory (→ Knowledge Gap Effects), the → uses and gratifications approach, and → information processing theories. Viewed this way, successful PR informs the right people at the right time about the plans and decisions of the organization.

The *persuasion model* of PR focuses narrowly on influencing target groups to accept the organization's view on relevant issues (→ Persuasion). One basis for this approach stems from famous pioneer Edward Bernays's theory of PR as consent engineering, and the expanded introduction of a psychological approach to mass communication instead of a sociological one. The key aspect of these theories is seeking to control stakeholders' decision-making through message design featuring the interests of the organization and aligning them with audiences' interests and opinions. Successful PR, by this logic, means 'convincing publics.' Since it is difficult to efficiently convince people, research is thought to be important for discovering the most efficient means to know and communicate what messages the public will accept. Persuasive PR can therefore be primarily impression management.

German sociologist Habermas claimed that the development of PR and advertising changed open democratic → discourse into a non-critical force of acclamation of some powerful elite. In light of this view, critical models of PR have developed, with a main tradition in the United Kingdom, Australia, and New Zealand. Grunig et al. (2002) offered an alternate critical view, but not so much from a societal perspective as from a strategic management perspective based on the logics of systems and institutional theories. They call "scientific persuasion" an asymmetrical approach to PR that presumes that to solve a relationship problem an organization has only to alter key public's view to conform to that preferred by the organization. The authors prefer a *two-way-symmetrical model*, in which relationships are built and maintained through → interaction defined by an organization willing to change and publics who believe they comfortably share control with that organization which behaviorally adjusts to them. Theoretically this approach is rooted in balance theories of communication, e.g., co-orientation models (→ Co-Orientation Model of Public Relations). Another typical interpersonal approach to PR is the *interpersonal influence model*, developed in Asia (Sriramesh 2004).

The *reflective model of PR* strives to integrate many leading perspectives on PR. Dialogue is an important strategy to develop trust, but only the naïve believe that it is an answer to all mistrust (van Ruler & Verčič 2005). That is why managers use all kinds of strategies, including manipulation of frames (→ Framing Effects), in order to curry the favor of publics and achieve favorable outcomes. The constraint on such manipulation is public legitimacy, which, because of increased public counteraction, has become increasingly necessary for business to survive. The basic question in this approach lies in the functional definition of what is seen as legitimate based on outside-in awareness of the organization, its role in society, and how that reflection supports rather than frustrates its need to achieve legitimacy.

The essence of the *rhetorical model* is to know the meaning-making strategies (social construction) and process forces that lead to co-created meaning, collaborative decision-making, and identification. The paradigm of rhetoric is statement and counter-statement. It is advisory, invitational, and propositional, based on attentive, thoughtful, and open contest between choices. At its best, it can lead to enlightenment and wise choice. At its worst, it obscures, obfuscates, and centers on ad hominem dispute that ultimately is damaging to collaborative decision making. The model presumes that society is created for the collective management of risks. Each individual and organization is conjoined in this arrangement. Dialogue is the rationale for bringing information to bear on risks, but the evaluation of such information is not centered in one body, but institutionalized for the collective good of all members of the society. In these ways, PR can help society to be more fully functioning.

The Future of Public Relations

The work of Sriramesh and Verčič (2009), *The Global Public Relations Handbook*, shows that the democratization of the world, especially in the latter half of the twentieth century, goes hand in hand with the growth of PR all over the world, giving the discipline a global scale. Major works by Heath (2010) and Botan and Hazleton (2006) show how robust the discourse on PR theory and practice has become. The discipline is steadily becoming less derivative and more original in its theory building. It continues to make critical and practical advances that have pedagogical and real-world application. The question is how PR can mature into a professional and academic discipline by realizing its potential for making society more fully functional.

See also: ▶ CONSENSUS-ORIENTED PUBLIC RELATIONS ▶ CO-ORIENTATION MODEL OF PUBLIC RELATIONS ▶ CORPORATE COMMUNICATION ▶ CRISIS COMMUNICATION ▶ DIFFUSION OF INFORMATION AND INNOVATION ▶ DISCOURSE ▶ FRAMING EFFECTS ▶ INFORMATION PROCESSING ▶ INTERACTION ▶ ISSUE MANAGEMENT ▶ KNOWLEDGE GAP EFFECTS ▶ PERSUASION ▶ PROPAGANDA ▶ PUBLIC OPINION ▶ RHETORICAL STUDIES ▶ TWO-STEP FLOW OF COMMUNICATION ▶ USES AND GRATIFICATIONS

REFERENCES AND SUGGESTED READINGS

Botan, C. H. & Hazleton, V. (eds.) (2006). *Public relations theory II*. Mahwah, NJ: Lawrence Erlbaum.

Cutlip, S. C. (1994). *The unseen power: Public relations – a history*. Hillsdale, NJ: Lawrence Erlbaum.

Grunig, L. A., Grunig, J. E., & Dozier, D. M. (2002). *Excellent public relations and effective organizations: A study of communication management in three countries*. Mahwah, NJ: Lawrence Erlbaum.

Heath, R. L. (ed.) (2010). *The Sage handbook of public relations*. Thousand Oaks, CA: Sage.

Heath, R. L. (ed.) (2013). *Encyclopedia of public relations,* 2nd edn. Thousand Oaks, CA: Sage.

Sriramesh, K. (ed.) (2004). *Public relations in Asia: An anthology*. Singapore: Thompson Learning.

Sriramesh, K. & Verčič, D. (eds.) (2009). *The global public relations handbook: Theory, research, and practice* (rev. ed.). Mahwah, NJ: Lawrence Erlbaum.

van Ruler, B. & Verčič, D. (eds.) (2004). *Public relations and communication management in Europe*. Berlin: Mouton de Gruyter.

van Ruler, B. & Verčič, D. (2005). Reflective communication management: Future ways for public relations research. In P. J. Kalbfleisch (ed.), *Communication yearbook 29*. Mahwah, NJ: Lawrence Erlbaum, pp. 239–274.

Public Relations Evaluation

DON W. STACKS
University of Miami

'Public relations evaluation' is a management tool that allows the user to establish whether a project or campaign has had its intended effect. Effective evaluation is at the center of any public relations effort and should be a basic element of any planned public relations action. In reality, however, evaluation is often overlooked or not undertaken for a variety of reasons, including costs, lack of resources, or simply a failure to understand how to conduct basic evaluation. Basic evaluation provides the user not only with information on how well the project worked, but also with an indication during the project as to whether it is 'on target,' or 'on phase' (→ Public Relations).

Public relations objectives fall into three areas: informational (was the message sent out, received, and understood?), motivational (did it change or reinforce attitudes and behavioral intentions?), and behavioral (did the targeted audience do what the message asked?). All evaluation is *phase-oriented*. The first phase develops the project and its evaluation. The second phase occurs once the project has begun and, based on periodic evaluation, refines the strategy and tactics employed to meet specified objectives. The third phase occurs post-project as a final evaluation and establishes whether the objectives have been met and the goal achieved. Final evaluation reviews the entire project, from benchmarking to final outcome and provides evaluation of strategy and tactics, as well as a cost–benefit analysis.

Evaluation methods differ in terms of both → reliability and → validity of the 'data' collected and analyzed. The terms 'qualitative' and 'humanistic' are applied to data gathered with the intent of a deep understanding of specific individuals or cases but not meant to be extended to a larger population or public. The difference is to be found in use. Quantitative data establish norms (or parameters) against which groups can be compared, but in establishing a norm any individual differences are lost. Prior to actually beginning data acquisition, evaluation metrics need to be established. A metric is a way to provide both focused and continuous project evaluation.

Developmental phase evaluation focuses primarily on gathering data against which to compare project results over the life of the project. During the *refinement phase* evaluations are undertaken to see if the project is on target and schedule. Data gathered during the refinement phase is evaluated against set objectives. This evaluation allows for alterations in strategy and tactics once the project has begun. Finally, refinement phase evaluation seeks to make better predictions about actual behavior – that which drives the return on investment and project goals in most cases. Final phase methodology is typically divided into three areas. First, was the goal met? Did the project move the needle? Did it meet or surpass expectations and how did it contribute to the client or company bottom line? Second, each objective is examined to evaluate both the strategy and tactics employed. Were objectives met? Were they on target? Were they on schedule? All the data gathered during the development and refinement stages are evaluated against final outcome(s). Finally, a cost–product evaluation is undertaken. Here the evaluation focuses on whether the project was cost effective, that the goal(s) and objective(s) were on target.

Evaluation is an important factor in any public relations project. It should be planned across three phases and take into account both the project goal(s) and the objective(s). Objectives must be actionable and measurable and the methods selected to gather data should be triangulated to gain the best insight into project effectiveness.

See also: ▶ MEASUREMENT THEORY ▶ PUBLIC OPINION POLLING ▶ PUBLIC RELATIONS ▶ QUALITATIVE METHODOLOGY ▶ QUANTITATIVE METHODOLOGY ▶ RELIABILITY ▶ VALIDITY

REFERENCES AND SUGGESTED READINGS

Brody, E. W. & Stone, G. C. (1989). *Public relations research*. New York: Praeger.

Broom, G. M. & Dozier, D. M. (1990). *Using research in public relations: Applications to program management*. Englewood Cliffs, NJ: Prentice Hall.

Carroll, T. & Stacks, D. W. (2004). *Bibliography of public relations measurement*. Gainesville, FL: Institute for Public Relations.

Hocking, J. E., Stacks, D. W., & McDermott, S. T. (2003). *Communication research*, 3rd edn. Boston: Allyn and Bacon.

Michaelson, D. & Stacks, D. W. (2011). Standardization in public relations measurement and evaluation. *Public Relations Journal*, 5, 1–25.

Michaelson, D., Wright, D. K., & Stacks, D. W. (2012). Evaluating efficacy in public relations/corporate communication programming: Towards establishing standards of campaign performance. *Public Relations Journal*, 6, 1–25.

Stacks, D. W. (2011). *Primer of public relations research*, 2nd edn. New York: Guilford.

Stacks, D. W. & Bowen, S. A. (2013). *Dictionary of public relations measurement and research*, 3rd edn. Gainesville, FL: Institute for Public Relations.

Public Relations: Media Influence

JAN KLEINNIJENHUIS
Free University Amsterdam

Earning public understanding and acceptance through reports in the press is a major aim of → public relations (PR). Firms, governments, NGOs, and interest groups alike use the media to convey their message to their publics. Media influence is a two-step process. Whether PR efforts lead to news items depends on the relations of the company with the media and on the newsworthiness of its publicity efforts (→ News Values). Once PR-based news is published, PR media influence can be understood through theories about media effects (→ Media Effects).

PR efforts connect markets with media. News about worldwide markets explained the sales success of the newspapers that were printed during the seventeenth century in the Netherlands. During the last forty years business news came to flourish once more, as a result, first, of the increased speed of financial news and global trading (fax, financial news wires, → satellite television) and, next, of new PR tools to attract stakeholder attention through mass media and → social media. Firms increasingly present market competition as popular drama with their CEO's in a new role as media personalities. Business news relies heavily on PR sources, but may occasionally build up a momentum of its own, especially in market panics and organizational crises in which failing firms and failing banks loose their reputation as trustworthy news sources.

PR media influence is a special field of media effects because of the involvement of stakeholders. Typical stakeholders are competitors, investors, financial analysts, interest groups, employees, and consumers. Stakeholders are active players in the publicity arena themselves. They may take sides, and attract media publicity through social media, websites, and classic PR means. Business reporters rely routinely on PR, but stakeholders may serve as alternative sources for journalists who want to verify stories about market competition and business performance. Stakeholders may also be located within the organization itself.

Employees and stakeholders alike often learn from the press about takeover negotiations, organizational scandals, or the relative performance of their firm as compared to competitors, especially in global firms. Issues in the news typically shape the criteria by which audiences and stakeholders evaluate orgnanizational performance (→ Framing Effects).

See also: ▶ COMMUNICATION MANAGEMENT ▶ CRISIS COMMUNICATION ▶ EXPOSURE TO COMMUNICATION CONTENT ▶ FRAMING EFFECTS ▶ INTERORGANIZATIONAL COMMUNICATION ▶ ISSUE MANAGEMENT ▶ MEDIA EFFECTS ▶ NEWS VALUES ▶ PUBLIC AFFAIRS ▶ PUBLIC RELATIONS ▶ SATELLITE TELEVISION ▶ SOCIAL MEDIA ▶ TRUST OF PUBLICS

REFERENCES AND SUGGESTED READINGS

Carroll, C. E. (ed.) (2011). *Corporate reputation and the news media: Agenda-setting within business news coverage in developed, emerging, and frontier markets.* London: Routledge.

Kiousis, S., Popescu, C., & Mitrook, M. (2007). Understanding influence on corporate reputation: An examination of public relations efforts, media coverage, public opinion, and financial performance from an agenda-building and agenda-setting perspective. *Journal of Public Relations Research*, 19(2), 147–165.

Kleinnijenhuis, J., Schultz, F., Oegema, D., & van Atteveldt, W. (2013). Financial news and market panics in the age of high-frequency sentiment trading algorithms. *Journalism*, 14(2), 271–291.

Public Relations Planning

SHERRY DEVEREAUX FERGUSON
University of Ottawa

Public relations planning appears as the second of a four-stage process model (fact-finding, planning, communicating, evaluation) in the pioneering work of Cutlip and Center (1958) and in

Marston's (1963) RACE (research, action, communication, and evaluation) model (→ Public Relations). The term 'strategic planning' refers to future-oriented, long-term, and goal-oriented planning, which is tied to the mission, mandate, vision, and broad goals or objectives of the organization (→ Strategic Communication).

Strategic planning takes place at the corporate, business, and program levels. Before engaging in high-level planning, the organization conducts a situation audit, clarifies its mandate, and writes or updates its mission and vision statements. Next the planners create a multi-year communication plan, identifying the opinion environment, issues, communication objectives, messages, priorities, strategic considerations, desired outcomes, and global budget. The plan links to the multi-year corporate plan.

Operational planning involves making concrete choices about how to reach the strategic goals. It transforms communication priorities for the immediate planning period (usually one year) into products and services, assigns priorities to these activities and services and identifies key target audiences, methods for carrying out the activities, performance indicators, evaluation methods and tools, milestones and timelines, and resources required to deliver the products and services.

Support planning brings activities identified in the operational plan to life. They include not only operational elements such as timelines, budgets, and responsibilities, but also strategic (e.g., communication objectives and messages) and tactical (e.g., timing and vehicles for carrying the message) elements. Single-use support plans address non-recurring events such as policy announcements, special events, campaigns, press conferences, publications, and capital expenditures. Standing plans (e.g., websites and annual recurring events) have no set time frame.

Different from other planning exercises, *crisis communication plans* anticipate negative events that could potentially occur, e.g. industrial accidents, environmental problems, massive restructuring, union–management conflicts, product recalls, hostile takeovers, terrorist acts, or major economic and technological changes (→ Organizational Conflict). Planners assess both the probability of occurrence and potential impact, and they look for advance indicators. Crisis management teams include PR personnel, and crisis management plans have communication components: parties responsible for managing the crisis, required support systems, information strategies, response and control mechanisms, guidelines for dealing with the media, and evaluation plans. Simulations prepare organizations for crises (→ Crisis Communication). *Risk management* involves assessing and developing strategies to manage potential risks such as losses, injuries, or threats to the organization's image (→ Risk Communication).

Since 1952, three major themes have emerged in the PR planning literature: a focus on research as the foundation for planning, a stress on linking PR plans to business and corporate plans, and an emphasis on evaluation (→ Public Relations Evaluation). A focus on linking communication to corporate and business planning emerged in the late 1980s with a large-scale experiment by the Canadian government to require long-term, research-based communication planning by all departments, agencies, and regions. In 1988, the Privy Council Office (PCO) asked every federal entity to submit annual strategic and operational communication plans. After reviewing the plans for conformity to the corporate objectives of the government, they provided feedback to strategic planners. Once approved, all subsequent planning efforts were tied to these plans (Ferguson 1999; 2000).

By 2000, a spate of articles on strategic communication planning had appeared, and every professional conference hosted sessions on planning. Led by an editorial board from the Netherlands, Singapore, Slovenia, and the US, *The International Journal of Strategic Communication* published its first issue in January 2006. In Great Britain, the National School of Government established training in strategic communication planning. In the late 1980s, practitioners identified accountability as a critical concern, and accountability implies the need to evaluate. By the 1990s, professional associations and academics (e.g., Institute for Public Relations Research and Education, International Public Relations Association, International Association of Business Communicators, and Public Relations Society of America) called for greater investment in evaluation.

See also: ▶ CRISIS COMMUNICATION
▶ ORGANIZATIONAL CONFLICT ▶ PUBLIC
RELATIONS ▶ PUBLIC RELATIONS EVALUATION
▶ RISK COMMUNICATION ▶ STRATEGIC
COMMUNICATION

REFERENCES AND SUGGESTED READINGS

Broom, G. & Dozier, D. M. (1990). *Using research in public relations: Applications to program management.* Englewood Cliffs, NJ: Prentice Hall.
Cutlip, S. M. & Center, A. H. (1952, 1958). *Effective public relations: Pathway to public favor.* New York: Prentice Hall.
Ferguson, S. D. (1999). *Communication planning: An integrated approach.* Thousand Oaks, CA: Sage.
Ferguson, S. D. (2000). *Researching the public opinion environment: Theories and methods.* Thousand Oaks, CA: Sage.
Marston, J. E. (1963). *The nature of public relations.* New York: McGraw-Hill.

Public Sphere

FRANK MARCINKOWSKI
University of Münster

The public sphere is defined as a network of all the communicative spaces within which → public affairs are debated and a → public opinion is formed. The concept is closely connected to the idea of a deliberative democracy pointing out that such an infrastructure of political communication is crucial for democratic self-governance and the social integration of modern society.

Every form of citizens' participation in collectively binding decisions presupposes that political actors explain their intentions, while citizens can catch up on the issues at stake, articulate their interests and opinions openly, listen and evaluate the arguments of others to make up their mind. The public sphere establishes an arena of discussion on current affairs in order to achieve a rational decision (Chambers 2003). In modern democracy the public sphere not only encompasses the public domain but also the *news media arena*. Nowadays public communication is mainly mediated and, therefore, lacks defining features of deliberation, although it can still function as an arena for perception, identification, and definition of problems related to society as a whole (→ Mediatization of Politics). The task of the media is to make public and to confront selected issues, arguments, and opinions of the political elites and actors in civil society.

Empirical research related to public sphere focuses, for example, on the fragmentation of national mediated public spheres in many segmented publics due to more media channels, content, and individualized media usage (Dahlgren 2005). Opposed tendencies are yielded through a transnationalization of the public sphere and its consequences, for example in the European Union. It is also discussed if the deficits of an ideal political discourse in the public sphere can be solved by the diffusion of the Internet with its open access, transparent way of discussion, and desired broadening of political participation (→ E-Democracy). The ambitious expectations regarding a revitalization of public discourses in the online world have not been fulfilled yet.

See also: ▶ E-DEMOCRACY ▶ MEDIATIZATION OF POLITICS ▶ PUBLIC AFFAIRS ▶ PUBLIC OPINION

REFERENCES AND SUGGESTED READINGS

Chambers, S. (2003). Deliberative democratic theory. *Annual Review of Political Science*, 6, 307–326.
Dahlgren, P. (2005). The Internet, public spheres, and political communication: Dispersion and deliberation. *Political Communication*, 22, 147–162.
Habermas, J. (2006). Political communication in media society: Does democracy still enjoy an epistemic dimension? *Communication Theory*, 16, 411–426.

Qualitative Methodology

ARMIN SCHOLL
University of Münster

Qualitative methodology is basically characterized by its openness towards the research object in order to reconstruct its attributes authentically and to gain a deeper insight into these attributes. As a consequence, the research process includes an interactive and close relationship between the researcher and the researched persons or material rather than an objective, detached, or neutral relationship.

Principal Aim of Qualitative Methodology

Insofar as methods are not considered neutral tools to describe and explain reality as objects, researchers are part of the social reality under study. In action research, e.g., researched persons are even considered participants of a common research aim, which should be cooperatively and commonly developed (→ Participatory Action Research). The researcher's subjectivity does not impede the quality of the research results; it is clearly visible within the research process and guarantees a successful collection of information about the researched phenomenon and an in-depth understanding of it. The results of qualitative research processes are context-bound ('thick') descriptions, which can be enriched by choosing varying perspectives and tools.

Therefore qualitative research approaches often include a combination of methods, e.g., ethnography (→ Ethnography of Communication), which combines participant → observation and in-depth interviews (→ Interview, Qualitative). Such combinations do not only provide a more detailed and comprehensive understanding of the researched phenomena but also stabilize the results of a research process and make the descriptions and information more reliable and more valid than by using only single-method strategies.

Characteristics of Qualitative Methodology

There are some further features characterizing qualitative methodology, which are relevant and helpful for a better comprehension but which are not necessarily exclusive characteristics of qualitative methodology. In most of the cases qualitative methodology tries to *discover new hypotheses* in an explorative rather than confirmative manner. The procedure of qualitative research often starts with open research questions and eventually results in hypotheses or theory building. However, it is possible to test previously raised hypotheses qualitatively, too.

Gathering and analyzing information are not strictly separated but sometimes are interconnected. The *Grounded Theory approach*, for example, includes alternate steps of collecting information and of preliminary analysis of them in order to collect further information of the research object until the researcher considers the knowledge gained is saturated (→ Grounded Theory). In contrast to this kind of spiral-like research process, for example, in-depth interviewing is separated from its analysis whether analysis of the interviewee's answers is a hermeneutic interpretation or a qualitative content analysis. It is even possible to combine qualitative data collection with standardized methods of coding and statistical methods.

Although, in the main, the *understanding of → meaning* characterizes the aim of qualitative research, it would be a mistake to attribute this aim to qualitative research exclusively, because all kinds of social or cultural research share this characteristic to a greater or lesser degree. Even the strictest hypothesis-testing approach within → quantitative methodology does not work mechanically by simple statistical decisions. Instead, data and statistical results need further interpretation and a deeper understanding than mere counting.

The research process involves a more intensive and more specific *relationship between the researcher and the researched persons* or material. This applies especially to ethnography or action research. Although the degree of intensity distinguishes all qualitative approaches from quantitative and standardized methodology, it varies within qualitative approaches, too.

The most relevant criteria of *evaluating qualitative research* are considered the step-by-step transparency of the research procedures. This is again common to all scientific research, even if it has a special connotation within qualitative methodology. So-called communicative → validity is a more specific criterion, which implies that the researcher does not only rely on their own analysis and interpretation but confirms it with the help of the researched persons.

Finally, *generalizing the results* does not include a quantitative aspect, such as representativeness, but is achieved if the conclusions of the results are transferrable to other settings or contexts than those under study. Again, this is not specific to qualitative methodology, as the abstractions of results are characteristic of all kinds of scientific research. However, the strategy of generalization in qualitative methodology is different from quantitative methodology, as it tries to conclude generalizability from the intensively elaborated context even of single or individual cases.

All in all, qualitative research can be regarded as an effort to develop a methodology which matches particular phenomena under study rather than applying general methods and tools to any phenomena. Therefore, it is not its aim to contribute to a universal methodological framework but it is limited to the study of psychical, social, or cultural fields of research and the disciplines involved.

Methods and Tools in Qualitative Methodology

Some prominent methods in qualitative methodology will be described briefly. With the help of *observation*, events and actions can be investigated. There is a preference for participant observation in qualitative research in order to develop a closer relationship to the people observed. *Interviewing* can be very open, such as narrative interviewing (storytelling), or structured (although flexible), such as guided interviews. Unlike individual interviews, *focus groups* consist of moderated discussions among a group of respondents (discussants). *Qualitative content analysis* is a method for developing categories from texts or visual material, including media content as well as transcribed interview texts, documents, or video-taped observations (→ Content Analysis, Qualitative). The most open and less rule-based kind of interpretation are (social scientific) → *hermeneutics*, which are particularly used in analyzing narratives or stories. *Conversation analysis* serves as a tool to analyze dialogues (→ Conversation Analysis) while → discourse analysis is applied to discursive and argumentative communication. *Qualitative experiments* use a particular stimulus to explore the range of subjects' reactions.

As research instruments are open and flexible, so are *sampling procedures*. In qualitative research they are mostly deliberative or purposive and not random (→ Sampling, Random). The sample should either be homogeneous, in order to find the small distinction among the sample units, or heterogeneous, in order to cover maximum variation and find the commonalities (and differences) among the sample units. Very often sampling procedures are driven by convenience if access to the field or population investigated is hard to gain. However, sampling procedures are far from being arbitrary; instead they are coherent and consistent with the research questions and the theoretical aim of the study.

See also: ▶ CONTENT ANALYSIS, QUALITATIVE ▶ CONVERSATION ANALYSIS ▶ DISCOURSE ANALYSIS ▶ ETHNOGRAPHY OF COMMUNICATION ▶ FIELD RESEARCH ▶ GROUNDED THEORY ▶ HERMENEUTICS ▶ INTERVIEW, QUALITATIVE ▶ LANGUAGE AND SOCIAL INTERACTION ▶ MEANING ▶ OBSERVATION ▶ OPERATIONALIZATION ▶ PARTICIPATORY ACTION RESEARCH ▶ PHENOMENOLOGY ▶ QUANTITATIVE METHODOLOGY ▶ RELIABILITY ▶ VALIDITY ▶ SAMPLING, RANDOM

REFERENCES AND SUGGESTED READINGS

Cresswell, J. W. (2013). *Qualitative inquiry and research design: Choosing among five approaches*. 3rd edn. Thousand Oaks, CA: Sage.

Denzin, N. K. & Lincoln, Y. S. (eds.) (2011). *The Sage handbook of qualitative research*, 4th edn. Thousand Oaks, CA: Sage.

Punch, K. F. (2005). *Introduction to social research: Quantitative and qualitative approaches*, 2nd edn. Thousand Oaks, CA: Sage.

Ragin, C. C. (1994). *Constructing social research: The unity and diversity of method*. Thousand Oaks, CA: Pine Forge.

Seale, C., Gobo, G., Gubrium, J. F., & Silverman, D. (eds.) (2004). *Qualitative research practice*. Thousand Oaks, CA: Sage.

Silverman, D. (2006). *Doing qualitative research: A practical handbook*, 2nd edn. Thousand Oaks, CA: Sage.

Somekh, B. & Lewin, C. (eds.) (2005). *Research methods in the social sciences*. Thousand Oaks, CA: Sage.

Quality of the News

ADAM JACOBSSON
Stockholm University

EVA-MARIA JACOBSSON
KTH Royal Institute of Technology

Quality of the news is a difficult and complex concept to define. Quality depends in part on what uses and gratifications are demanded from the media and by whom.

From a normative viewpoint a high-quality news service is expected to help citizens make informed decisions that in turn will help develop society. This view has support from disciplines other than journalism and mass communication studies, such as economics. Here, a high-quality news service is perceived to help economic development, as it reduces uncertainty by providing accurate and reliable information. In political science the media is seen as the fourth estate, informing citizens, maintaining checks and balances on the political process, and thereby increasing the efficiency of government and helping to resolve social conflict by giving a multifaceted description of events, among other things. The above functions are largely supported by what the journalism and mass communication literature describes as commonly shared professional standards of → journalism (→ Standards of News). Sometimes, however, there is tension between these standards and a demand for a lighter kind of news reporting, geared toward entertaining → sensationalism that pits professionalism against commercialism (→ Commercialization: Impact on Media Content).

Generally, research divides the definitions of news media quality into *three sub-categories:* content, organizational, and financial commitment (Hollifield 2006). Some measures for content are balance (→ Bias in the News), fairness, or lack of sensationalism. Organizational aspects of quality can be divided into two major categories: 'Editorial quality' includes editorial independence and courage, while 'financial commitment' again comprises sub-categories like the advertising: editorial copy ratio, the size of the news staff, or the number of news agencies subscribed to.

See also: ▶ ADVERTISING, ECONOMICS OF ▶ BIAS IN THE NEWS ▶ COMMERCIALIZATION: IMPACT ON MEDIA CONTENT ▶ ETHICS IN JOURNALISM ▶ FREEDOM OF THE PRESS, CONCEPT OF ▶ JOURNALISM ▶ NEWS SOURCES ▶ SENSATIONALISM ▶ STANDARDS OF NEWS ▶ USES AND GRATIFICATIONS

REFERENCES AND SUGGESTED READINGS

Becker, L. B., Hollifield, C. A., Jacobsson, A., Jacobsson, E.-M., & Vlad, T. (2009). Is more always better? Examining the adverse effects of competition on media performance. *Journalism Studies*, 10(3), 368–385.

Bogart, L. (2004). Reflections on content quality in newspapers. *Newspaper Research Journal*, 25(1), 40–53.

Hollifield, C. A. (2006). News media performance in hypercompetitive markets: An extended model. *International Journal on Media Management*, 8(2), 60–69.

Kim, K.-H. & Meyer, P. (2005). Survey yields five factors of newspaper quality. *Newspaper Research Journal*, 26(1), 6–15.

Quantitative Methodology

ARMIN SCHOLL
University of Münster

The results of polls tell us how many people intend to vote for a certain political party, watch TV more than four hours a day, or favor a certain TV program. We call methods of collecting and analyzing such data 'quantitative methodology' because individuals' attributes are counted in large numbers.

Aims of Quantitative Methodology

The main aim of quantitative methodology is comparison and measurement (→ Measurement Theory). To compare individuals, text units, or behavior it is necessary to have a common basis as a starting point for comparison. The logic of quantitative methodology is basically the *logic of standardization*, which implies reducing context complexity around the research object in question. With the help of standardization it is possible to measure the attributes of research units that can be analyzed as 'variables.'

One can standardize either different features of the research process or the research process as a whole. *Standardizing* the entire research process means proceeding systematically and in a certain order of procedures. If hypotheses, which can be deduced from abstract theories, are available, a confirmative research strategy will be preferred to test whether the hypotheses are right or false. Starting with research questions without hypotheses implies an explorative research strategy. Theoretical concepts used in hypotheses must then be translated into empirical indicators (→ Operationalization). Furthermore, a sample of research units needs to be selected. The following process of data collection demands a direct contact and interaction between researcher and the research field explored. After collection, the data will be analyzed with quantitative (statistical) tools and interpreted in the context of the research questions or hypotheses.

Methods, Instruments and Research Designs

The most relevant objects of standardization are the research instrument and the research situation. In *polls and surveys* people are questioned about their opinion toward certain social phenomena (→ Public Opinion Polling; Survey; Election Surveys). The respondent's opinion is treated as a variable that can be separated from other (measurable) attributes. The wording and the order of the questions are laid down in a questionnaire. The interviewer is admonished to follow the interviewing rules strictly. The respondent has to fit the answers to preformed categories of answers, such as 'strongly agree,' 'somewhat agree,' 'don't know,' 'somewhat disagree,' and 'strongly disagree.'

The research instrument of *content analysis* is called a 'codebook.' It includes a set of standardized semantic categories of attributes that are relevant for the research questions, and which the coder searches for within the documents (text, proposition, photograph, film, etc.). Coding categories can be formal elements (such as the length of an article or the position of an article within a newspaper), semantic variables (such as the theme of an article or actor-related categories), or pragmatic variables (such as the assessments of actors, organizations, or arguments,). A coding manual or commentary contains the coding rules the coder has to apply to the material to be coded.

With regard to *observational methods*, the observer pays attention to overt behavior or apparent attributes of observed people, which are recorded on a code sheet or a list with given categories (→ Observation). Other concomitants spontaneously observed are not of interest in the context of the standardized schedule. The coding process works analogously to the coding process of content analysis.

As well as the research instrument and the research situation, the complete research design and the process of data collection can also be standardized. Within *experimental research designs* (→ Experiment, Laboratory) independent variables are controlled with the help of manipulated stimulus material or the treatment of experimental subjects. In order to test causal effects (dependent variables), subjects are randomly allocated to experimental groups and/or a control group. This experimental design proves the causal effect hypothesized if the experimental group and the control group clearly differ with respect to a dependent variable. Alternatively, experimental designs compare several measurements of the same subjects: Between the points of measurement subjects are exposed to a stimulus. If measurements of the dependent variable differ clearly between the measurements the stimulus has caused the effect.

Longitudinal research uses trend or panel designs. In *trend studies* the same research instrument is used for different samples at different points of time. The collected data can be analyzed with the help of time-series statistics (→ Longitudinal Analysis). In *panel designs*, standardized measurements can be repeated several times for the same sample.

Sampling Procedure and Data Analysis

Quantitative methodology requires sufficiently large samples (of respondents or text units) for data analysis, which aims at generalizing the results and representing a population to which the study refers. A *random sampling* technique tries to maintain the chance of getting into the sample (approximately) equal for every unit (→ Sampling, Random). If some relevant parameters of the total population are known, a *quota-sampling* is also possible. The distributions of these variables in the total population serve as quota instructions for the sampling procedure, which makes sure that the distributions in the sample represent the distributions in the total population. Other sampling procedures and techniques vary according to the research question or the data-collection method applied.

Data can be analyzed with the help of *statistical procedures and tools*. They are used to describe the collected variables (univariate statistics) or to correlate variables (bivariate statistics; → Correlation Analysis). Information about the sample distribution is expressed as means and standard deviation of variables; information about the correlation of variables can be documented in cross-tabulations or mean comparisons between group variables. It is also possible to test complex theoretical models with many variables (multivariate statistics).

Evaluative Criteria for Quantitative Research

Quantitative methodology is based on certain criteria to assess its quality. These criteria are objectivity, → validity, and → reliability. The notion of *objectivity* is somewhat misleading because it neither implies truth in an epistemological sense nor does it neglect the researcher's subjectivity. Instead, objectivity is related to the research process and procedures. Research procedures have to be systematically planned and carried out. In that sense, objectivity has been replaced by the notion of 'intersubjectivity.'

The same is true for *validity*: a research instrument is valid if it measures what it claims to measure. Validity is a criterion to assess the relationship between theoretical concept and empirical indicator. To measure the relevance of media coverage on a certain theme with the help of the position of articles in a newspaper makes sense because front-page news is considered more relevant than articles placed at the back of the newspaper. *Reliability* is a more formal criterion, which can be mathematically calculated as a coefficient of agreement and of stability: In content analysis, for example, the coding scheme is reliable if different coders use it in the same way with the same coding results (inter-coder-reliability) or if the same coder uses it the same way at the beginning of the coding procedure as at its end (intra-coder-reliability).

In sum, quantitative methodology is characterized by a relationship between (1) standardization of research instruments, research situations, and research designs; (2) quantification of analysis; (3) generalization of results gained from samples; and (4) systematizing research procedures. Research is a technical and rule-based process. The underlying premise says that standardizing method and research procedure create a common basis of preconditions, which allows for comparison across different research objects.

See also: ▶ CONTENT ANALYSIS, QUANTITATIVE ▶ CORRELATION ANALYSIS ▶ ELECTION SURVEYS ▶ EXPERIMENT, LABORATORY ▶ LONGITUDINAL ANALYSIS ▶ MEASUREMENT THEORY ▶ OBSERVATION ▶ OPERATIONALIZATION ▶ PUBLIC OPINION POLLING ▶ QUALITATIVE METHODOLOGY ▶ REGRESSION ANALYSIS ▶ RELIABILITY ▶ SAMPLING, RANDOM ▶ SURVEY ▶ VALIDITY

REFERENCES AND SUGGESTED READINGS

Adèr, H. J. (ed.) (1999). *Research methodology in the life, behavioural and social sciences*. Thousand Oaks, CA: Sage.
Babbie, E. R. (2007). *The practice of social research*. Belmont, CA: Wadsworth Thomson Learning.
Kaplan, D. (ed.) (2004). *Handbook of quantitative methodology for the social sciences*. Thousand Oaks, CA: Sage.
Punch, K. F. (2005). *Introduction to social research: Quantitative and qualitative approaches*, 2nd edn. Thousand Oaks, CA: Sage.
Somekh, B. & Lewin, C. (eds.) (2005). *Research methods in the social sciences*. Thousand Oaks, CA: Sage.

Questions and Questioning

IRENE KOSHIK
University of Illinois at Urbana–Champaign

Any discussion of questions and questioning needs to distinguish between questions as a linguistic form and the social actions accomplished through this form. Questions can be formed in a variety of ways. Wh-questions use question words such as 'which,' or 'how.' Polar (yes/no) questions are formed in English by inversion of subject and auxiliary (or do-auxiliary) or by using rising instead of falling intonation on declarative statements (Quirk et al. 1985). In other languages they can be formed using phrases or particles. Even declarative statements with falling intonation can, in some contexts, be heard as questions (Heritage 2012).

Questions are used for a variety of functions other than asking for information. They are used to initiate repair on prior talk (e.g., "Huh?"), for invitations ("Wanna have lunch with me?"), offers ("Would you like some coffee?"), and requests ("Can I borrow your pen?"). Some questions, commonly known as 'rhetorical questions,' can be used as accusations, challenges, or complaints, e.g., "Why is it that we have to go there?" (Koshik 2005). Questions are used in culture-specific ways to perform these actions.

According to conversation analysts, questions are *first pair parts* (→ Conversation Analysis), initiating courses of action and making certain kinds of responses relevant. The question form can put constraints on the form of answers , e.g., polar questions make relevant 'yes' or 'no' answers. However, when participants disagree with a presupposition embedded in a polar question, they can give a "non-type-conforming answer" that displays that the question is problematic (Raymond 2003).

With some exceptions (e.g., self-deprecations), responses that forward the action initiated by the question and promote social solidarity are called 'preferred responses,' and those that block the action are 'dispreferred responses.' For example, accepting an invitation is preferred and rejecting it is dispreferred. These are not personal, psychological preferences but structural and social preferences. *Preferred and dispreferred responses* are generally formed differently. Preferred responses are given quickly and simply. Dispreferred responses are often delayed by silence and discourse markers such as 'well,' mitigated, and often include accounts.

The *design of the question* itself can also convey a preference for a certain type of answer. Linguistics call these questions "conducive" (Quirk et al. 1985). For example, the questions

"Didn't he arrive yet?" and "Do you really want to leave now?" seem to expect negative answers because of the negative polarity item 'yet' and the intensifier 'really.' The questions "Did someone call?" and "Hasn't the boat left already?" seem to expect affirmative answers because of the *positive polarity* items 'someone' and 'already.' The design of an information-seeking question can also display the *epistemic stance*, or knowledge state, of the questioner relative to the recipient (Heritage 2012). Questions like "Are you married?" and "You're married, aren't you?" both display the questioner's 'unknowing' state and the recipient's 'knowing state,' but the latter question displays more knowledge.

Questions play an important role in *institutional talk*. According to Drew and Heritage (1992), question–answer sequences are the dominant form of interaction in institutional talk such as counseling interviews, medical interactions, broadcast news interviews (→ Broadcast Talk), survey interviews (→ Survey; Interview, Standardized), employment interviews, emergency calls, courtroom interactions, and pedagogical interactions (→ Educational Communication). Questions are used to enact institutional roles, with the professional often leading the layperson through a series of question-initiated sequences, creating interactional asymmetry. Questions are central to accomplishing institutional goals and are designed in special ways to meet those goals. Doctors use questions to elicit the patient's history in medical examinations and to maintain control over the interaction (Drew & Heritage 1992). Broadcast news interviewers and courtroom attorneys ask questions to which they know the answer, designed for an overhearing audience, often containing propositions that support their views (Drew & Heritage 1992). Certain types of 'known-information questions' are identified with teaching. They initiate a sequence that ends with a third-turn evaluation of the student's answer.

See also: ▶ BROADCAST TALK ▶ CONVERSATION ANALYSIS ▶ EDUCATIONAL COMMUNICATION ▶ INTERVIEW, STANDARDIZED ▶ LINGUISTIC PRAGMATICS ▶ SURVEY

REFERENCES AND SUGGESTED READINGS

Drew, P. & Heritage, J. (1992). Analyzing talk at work: An introduction. In P. Drew & J. Heritage (eds.), *Talk at work*. Cambridge: Cambridge University Press, pp. 3–65.

Freed, A. F. & Ehrlich, S. (2010). *"Why do you ask?": The function of questions in institutional discourse*. Oxford: Oxford University Press.

Heritage, J. (2012). The epistemic engine: Sequence organization and territories of knowledge. *Research on Language and Social Interaction*, 45, 30–52.

Koshik, I. (2005). *Beyond rhetorical questions: Assertive questions in everyday interaction*. Amsterdam: John Benjamins.

Quirk, R., Greenbaum, S., Leech, G., & Svartvik, J. (1985). *A comprehensive grammar of the English language*. Harlow: Longman.

Raymond, G. (2003). Grammar and social organization: Yes/no interrogatives and the structure of responding. *American Sociological Review*, 68, 939–967.

Radio for Development

ROBERT HUESCA
Trinity University

Radio for development is the strategic use of this medium to effect social changes beneficial to a community, nation, or region. Within the study and practice of communication for national development and social change, radio has claimed a prominent place as it obviates the need for a literate audience, is inexpensive and widely accessible in poor, rural areas, and is cost-effective for donor agencies to produce and distribute.

'Modernization' theory constituted the dominant paradigm of *early development communication efforts* and focused on the mere exposure to radio and on the diffusion of 'good information' as 'magic multipliers' of development and as the gateways to 'empathy' and social mobility (→ Diffusion of Information and Innovation). For modernization theorists, radio, along with other mass media, was considered an 'index of development' measurable by such things as → UNESCO-issued standards for media sufficiency of the 1960s of five radios per 100 inhabitants as a measure of minimal development.

The dominant paradigm was *challenged* in the 1970s by a confluence of intellectual and social factors, including: (1) the work of Paolo Freire on dialogic pedagogy; (2) dependency theory's critique of capitalism; and (3) liberation theology's option for the poor. All of these movements reacted against the top-down, modernization model of development and called for participatory, grassroots communication approaches (→ Participatory Communication). This shift was reinforced by global movements such as the call for a → New World Information and Communication Order (NWICO) and the publication of UNESCO's Belgrade Document, which had a strong impact on radio for development.

In a move stemming from these theoretical debates, some clear descendants of the dominant paradigm approach to radio for development have undergone rigorous *reformulation since the 1990s*. These approaches include development journalism, → social marketing, and entertainment education. Development journalism is a somewhat ambiguous and contradictory model of producing radio functioning as an auxiliary to bigger development projects (→ Development Journalism). Social marketing draws on research and methods from consumer behavior and attaches pro-social messages to radio advertising, announcements, and programs. Finally, entertainment education borrows formulas from commercial media, such as soap operas, both to entertain and to educate audiences with the aim of changing attitudes and behavior.

See also: ▶ DEVELOPMENT JOURNALISM ▶ DIFFUSION OF INFORMATION AND INNOVATION ▶ NEW WORLD INFORMATION AND COMMUNICATION ORDER (NWICO) ▶ PARTICIPATORY COMMUNICATION ▶ SOCIAL MARKETING ▶ UNESCO

REFERENCES AND SUGGESTED READINGS

Gumucio Dagron, A. (2001). *Making waves: Stories of participatory communication for social change: A report to the Rockefeller Foundation*. New York: Rockefeller Foundation.

Manyozo, L. (2010). Researching developmental uses and formats of rural radio: A development broadcasting approach. *The Radio Journal: International Studies in Broadcast and Audio Media*, 8, 141–159.

Mody, B. (1991). *Designing messages for development communication: An audience participatory-based approach*. Thousand Oaks, CA: Sage.

Radio: Social History

CHRIS PRIESTMAN
Staffordshire University

The introduction of radio broadcasting during the 1920s released a tide of profound social changes, which have subsequently been amplified by television and information and communication technology (→ Television: Social History). The defining characteristic of these electronic, public media is that they provide systems for communicating simultaneously with large, geographically dispersed audiences via pathways that are immediate and capable of delivering messages live: they abolish the delay between production and reception inherent in all earlier public media. Their combined effect has been greatly to accelerate the formation and shaping of cultural consciousness within societies. They provide mechanisms of continuous reference and comparison by which individuals perceive their relationships beyond their immediate private sphere.

Since its first construction as a public medium the history of radio has been remarkable for the variety of uses and listening locations to which the radio receiver has become adapted in response to successive technological shifts. Most adaptations have made listening more mobile and independent of established infrastructures, as illustrated by recent worldwide use of mobile phones as radio receivers. Many authors have observed that the source of the medium's adaptability and enduring social role lies in its paradoxical offer to the listener of both a highly personal choice of aural accompaniment to private life and, simultaneously, a means of participation in the shared experience of a tangible public community of concurrent listeners (→ Technology and Communication).

Early Political and Economic Shaping

The social significance of the pre-1920s era of radio lay less with either its content or the numbers of listeners, but in the *ideas* it created in the popular imagination of what it might make possible. Early electronics manufactures envisaged new business opportunities; newspaper owners and organizers of live entertainments saw their livelihoods threatened and responded defensively; governments realized the need for new systems of regulation to decide who would be allowed to communicate what and to whom.

The first decision to fundamentally shape radio for the twentieth century was that, for the general public, it would be a *one-way medium* with government agencies licensing operators to transmit on given frequencies. The second was to determine *how it was to be funded*. Most governments favored a public service model in which a national broadcast network would be paid for from the public purse, while America opted for a commercial model of privately owned local broadcasters funding their competing services through on-air advertising (→ Public Broadcasting Systems; Public Broadcasting, History of). Thus, between the two world wars the fundamental markers of radio's position in the → public sphere were established: the imperatives of winning advertising inclining the commercial model toward entertainment while the underpinning ideology of the public service model attached higher importance to radio's educational role.

During the lead-up to World War II radio's importance as a potent → *propaganda tool* became sharply evident. The imperial nations of the day invested in increasingly powerful transmission technologies in order to reach their colonies and allies overseas (→ BBC World Service). Significantly, radio was then the only mass medium able to reach pre-literate audiences, a fact that clearly framed the spread of state-sponsored 'external' radio services from the 1930s onwards and, more recently, → UNESCO's many local radio development projects (→ Radio for Development).

Radio broadcasting proved to be of critical importance during World War II and of greater pervasive and persuasive influence on → public opinion than the press. Trust in the medium grew as home audiences listened daily to familiar voices reporting the news, as their political leaders spoke directly to them through the wireless, and as musical, comic and dramatic entertainment built morale and identification with shared cultural values.

The Changing Roles of Radio Post-War

During the 1950s two technological innovations combined to force a shift in radio's position in listeners' lives: television began rapidly to supplant the wireless as the centerpiece of the domestic living space (→ Television: Social History of); and the mass manufacture of transistors made new radio receivers both portable and cheap to buy (→ Mobility, Technology for). Also the increasingly *consumerist societies* to which radio stations were integral were being transformed by the postwar boom. With portability the choice of station became a personal matter: radio could now accompany the individual listener almost anywhere, including – importantly – in the car; as a direct consequence demand for ever more culturally and demographically differentiated stations grew.

A significant outcome of this shift was that the fortunes of the radio industry become ever more closely entwined with those of the record industry, such that today the overwhelming majority of total radio output around the world is of *recorded popular music* (→ Music Industry). For rural and less developed societies with little or no access to mains electricity the availability of affordable battery-powered radios created a surge in radio listening, and in many such parts of the world it remains the dominant mass medium. Radio's ability to reach across cultural boundaries (→ International Radio) has been largely responsible for the mixing of musical traditions that have given rise to the proliferation of popular music genres and cultures, from the evolution of rock 'n' roll in the southern USA to the internationalization of local indigenous musical forms.

Listener Relationship

The closeness of the radio station's relationship to its listeners, however, has been built through talk. The words and voices of presenters and contributors define the appeal to audiences both according to social grouping (by class, age, language, etc.) and identification with the locality (→ Broadcast Talk). The voices of 'ordinary people,' expressing opinion and giving glimpses directly into their ways of life, started to appear on the radio from the 1940s onwards. In the late 1960s the radio phone-in emerged, paving the way for the *talk radio* format – typically as deliberately contentious as regulation allowed.

Toward the end of the twentieth century claims of both music and speech-oriented stations to significant *interactivity* between presenter and listener became key markers in their social raison d'être: for stations funded by government or license fee, interactivity has become emblematic of their public service; for commercial stations it is key to nurturing the listener loyalties they sell to advertisers; for 'third sector,' not-for-profit stations it evidences their appeal to volunteers and donors (→ Interactivity, Concept of). How these twentieth-century constructs of collective allegiances as listening publics will fare in the face of the present proliferation of digital media platforms and the accompanying deregulation of radio institutions around the world is widely debated (→ Audience Segmentation).

See also: ▶ AUDIENCE SEGMENTATION ▶ BBC ▶ BBC WORLD SERVICE ▶ BROADCAST TALK ▶ INTERACTIVITY, CONCEPT OF ▶ INTERNATIONAL RADIO ▶ MEDIA HISTORY ▶ MOBILITY, TECHNOLOGY FOR ▶ MUSIC INDUSTRY ▶ PROPAGANDA ▶ PUBLIC BROADCASTING, HISTORY OF ▶ PUBLIC BROADCASTING SYSTEMS ▶ PUBLIC OPINION ▶ PUBLIC SPHERE ▶ RADIO FOR DEVELOPMENT ▶ TECHNOLOGY AND COMMUNICATION ▶ TELEVISION: SOCIAL HISTORY OF ▶ UNESCO

REFERENCES AND SUGGESTED READINGS

Briggs, A. & Burke, P. (2002). *A social history of the media: From Gutenberg to the Internet.* Cambridge: Polity, pp. 152–163, 216–233.

Douglas, S. J. (1999). The zen of listening. In *Listening in: Radio and the American imagination.* New York: Times Books, pp. 22–39.

Dubber, A. (2013). Radio in society. In *Radio in the digital age.* Cambridge: Polity, pp. 150–174.

Habermas, J. (1989). *The structural transformation of the public sphere.* Cambridge: Polity.

Hendy, D. (2000). Culture. In *Radio in the global age.* Cambridge: Polity, pp. 194–240.

Hilmes, M. (1997). Radiating culture. In *Radio voices: American broadcasting 1922–1952.* Minneapolis, MN: University of Minnesota Press, pp. 1–33.

Lacey, K. (2013). The privatization of the listening public. In *Listening publics.* Cambridge: Polity, pp. 113–131.

Scannell, P. (1996). *Radio, television and modern life.* Oxford: Blackwell, pp. 22–25.

Winston, B. (1998). Wireless and radio. In *Media technology and society: A history: From the printing press to the superhighway.* London: Routledge, pp. 67–87.

Rapport

AMANDA R. HEMMESCH
St. Cloud State University

LINDA TICKLE-DEGNEN
Tufts University

Rapport is interpersonal harmony, or being 'in sync' with another person. Rapport can be a goal, or contribute to the achievement of interpersonal goals (→ Goals, Social Aspects of). It is important for personal relationships and has applications in effective clinician–patient relationships, teaching, negotiation, online communication, and business (→ Interpersonal Communication; Classroom Student–Teacher Interaction).

The *components of rapport* convey interest and caring for the social partner and the → interaction. Verbal components include self-disclosure, politeness, and expressions of empathy and understanding. Nonverbal components include mutual attentiveness (shared focus), positivity (warm or friendly behavior), and coordination (behavioral synchrony), as well as eye contact, smiling, forward lean, and postural mimicry.

Rapport is a quality of a dyad or group, and can vary over time and with social roles. Cultural background may also influence expressions of rapport, although rapport is felt similarly across cultures (→ Nonverbal Communication and Culture; Intercultural and Intergroup Communication).

Rapport binds people together by marking group membership, promoting adaptive outcomes, fostering feelings of connectedness, and facilitating supportive or reciprocal exchanges. In difficult situations, rapport promotes smooth interaction between individuals with conflicting goals. Recent advances in artificial intelligence and human–computer interaction suggest that incorporating rapport cues into computer programs can improve interactions with non-human entities. Other recent research has investigated the neural correlates of rapport: mirror neurons may help people understand behavior and experience empathy and social coordination (→ Information Processing). Rapport may be jeopardized by health conditions that threaten self-expression, which could compromise interactions and relationships.

See also: ▶ CLASSROOM STUDENT–TEACHER INTERACTION ▶ COMMUNICATION SKILLS ACROSS THE LIFE-SPAN ▶ GOALS, SOCIAL ASPECTS OF ▶ INFORMATION PROCESSING ▶ INTERACTION ▶ INTERCULTURAL AND INTERGROUP COMMUNICATION ▶ INTERPERSONAL COMMUNICATION ▶ INTERPERSONAL COMMUNICATION COMPETENCE AND SOCIAL SKILLS ▶ NONVERBAL COMMUNICATION AND CULTURE

REFERENCES AND SUGGESTED READINGS

Grahe, J. E. & Bernieri, F. J. (1999). The importance of nonverbal cues in judging rapport. *Journal of Nonverbal Behavior,* 23, 253–269.

Tickle-Degnen, L. (2006). Nonverbal behavior and its function in the ecosystem of rapport. In V. Manusov & M. L. Patterson (eds.), *The Sage handbook of nonverbal communication.* Thousand Oaks, CA: Sage, pp. 381–399.

Tickle-Degnen, L. & Rosenthal, R. (1990). The nature of rapport and its nonverbal correlates. *Psychological Inquiry,* 1, 285–293.

Realism in Film and Photography

THEO VAN LEEUWEN
University of Technology, Sydney

Photography has always been a medium for recording reality as well as an art form (→ Photography; Art as Communication). The same can be said of the → cinema. But until the 1960s the former dominated the way the medium was conceived of. Critics such as André Bazin and Siegfried Kracauer praised its ability to create an "impersonal, completely artless camera record" (Kracauer 1960, 12), even though Russian constructivists had argued for its ability to 'construct' reality, through editing.

In the 1960s, this view was challenged by a combination of → semiotics and Marxism. Writing about The Family of Man, a 1950s photography exhibition, Roland Barthes (1977) denounced its aim to celebrate the universality of human experience as a "bourgeois myth." Brecht's "alienation effect" became an important reference point for filmmakers such as Jean-Luc Godard, and theorists like Colin MacCabe critiqued the "classic realist text" as presenting the dominant discourse not as discourse, but as objective fact.

As these *anti-realist views* were taught to generations of media students, photography and film were themselves overtaken by the new digital media with their much greater potential for 'construction' (→ Digital Media, History of). The market for photojournalism contracted as editors increasingly relied on the stock photography provided by image banks such as Getty Images and Corbis. Ambitious young photographers began to focus on art photography. In Hollywood the disaster movies of the early 1970s had inaugurated a return to the studio and 'special effects.' 'Dramatized documentaries' became increasingly indistinguishable from fiction films, and today's 'reality television' differs from the *cinéma vérité* of the 1960s and early 1970s in that it no longer pretends that what it shows would also have occurred if no cameras had been present.

Yet at the level of technology, realism still dominates. Computer games, even when representing fantasy worlds, strive for ever greater photorealism (→ Video Games). As a result the focus is no longer on the reality of what is represented by photography, but on the surface realism of today's entertainment media. Society needs clues as to whether the information in images can be relied upon as a guide for judgment and action. The 'guarantee' which photography and film, as 'mechanical duplicates of reality', traditionally provided, is of course still used, for instance in surveillance. But in other areas, for example in the media, it is retreating and new guarantees have perhaps not yet developed to the point that we can again judge the reliability of images with confidence.

See also: ▶ ART AS COMMUNICATION ▶ CINEMA ▶ DIGITAL MEDIA, HISTORY OF ▶ FILM THEORY ▶ PHOTOGRAPHY ▶ SEMIOTICS ▶ VIDEO GAMES

REFERENCES AND SUGGESTED READINGS

Barthes, R. (1977[1957]) *Mythologies*. London. Paladin.
Kracauer, S. (1960) *Theory of Film: The redemption of physical reality*. Oxford: Oxford University Press.
Van Leeuwen, T. (2001). *The handbook of visual analysis*. Thousand Oaks, CA: Sage.

Reality and Media Reality

MICHAEL MORGAN
University of Massachusetts Amherst

For decades, research and public concern have focused on how media representations compare to the real world (→ Media and Perceptions of Reality). Many theorists note that 'reality' is merely something that humans construct through social and cultural processes. Nevertheless, many scholars have compared the world represented in media to 'facts' about life and society. The task is to determine the most useful and reliable indicators of how the media world deviates from observable parameters, or to compare mediated and unmediated versions of the 'same' event or phenomenon. Studies in this vein often show sharp disjunctures between 'reality' and media coverage.

Theoretical Background of the Concept

Although many scholars concerned with the correspondence of media to reality focus on news, distinctions among news, scripted programs, and → 'reality TV' are not relevant here; media themselves constitute a way of knowing (Chesebro 1984). Media representations are 'real' as dreams, legends, and rumors are real – they exist as phenomenological narratives (→ Narrative News Story; Storytelling and Narration). A statement about an event is not 'the' event, but it is nonetheless an event. Moreover, the 'unreality' of media can shape our sense of reality. Mexicans are fond of saying "Life is like a telenovela" (Pearson 2005, 406).

Comparisons of media and reality reveal whether media stories reflect the facts, providing a basis for further studies of different media, or other societies, or over time. The goal is to illuminate any discrepancies in order to better understand media institutions and investigate how media images inform social beliefs. Much of what we 'know' is based not on first-hand experience, but on media representations of life and society. Researchers in the cultivation tradition note that most people have limited experience of courtrooms, police stations, or hospitals, yet we have vivid images of them and those who work in them (→ Cultivation Effects). Media offer us representations of things about which we have no direct knowledge, contributing to many of our intersubjective beliefs.

Analyses of Media Content

Content analysis reveals how media construct reality (→ Content Analysis, Quantitative) across immensely diverse topics. The *number of areas* in which the real and media worlds can be compared is virtually boundless. Studies comparing reality and media reality have examined such issues as the portrayal of older people in commercials; alcohol and tobacco use in soap operas; news coverage of infectious diseases; women scientists in popular magazines; sex and contraception in prime-time programs; art and artists on television news; television's environmental messages; and images of journalists on television (→ Media Production and Content). Researchers have studied images of girls and women (→ Women in the Media, Images of; Sex Role Stereotypes in the Media), ethnic minorities, weight loss surgery, bipolar disorder, terrorism, hate crimes, workplace sex, sports, suicide, poverty, and more. In the 1930s and 1940s, content analyses were conducted on burgeoning forms of *popular culture* (movies, radio, magazines); later, the technique was applied to television (→ Television as Popular Culture). Smythe (1954) and Head (1954) established parameters for examining television's representations of gender, age, class, race, occupations, and violence that other studies have emulated.

Both found that the *demography of the television world* diverged from the real world. Television portrayed twice as many males as females, and males tended to be older. Adults were vastly over-represented, and most characters were white Americans. Violence occurred at a rate of 6.2 acts per hour (Smythe 1954), and was far more frequent on children's programs (→ Violence as Media Content). Upper- and upper-middle-class occupations were greatly over-represented. Dozens of subsequent studies have confirmed and replicated these early findings, especially with regard to gender, class, and violence. The most sustained investigation of media reality has been the *Cultural Indicators Project*, started by George Gerbner in 1967, which systematically analyzes annual week-long samples of US television. The project has accumulated data on thousands of programs and tens of thousands of characters over more than 45 years.

Although the percentage of women in the TV world has increased, males continue to outnumber females. Women tend to be defined by family/marital status and to age faster than men. Older people are far fewer on television than in reality. Poor and working-class people remain nearly invisible on television, while middle-class characters and professionals are over-represented, as are white males. Villains and 'bad guys' are disproportionately shown as lower class, or as people of color, or as mentally ill.

Media reality remains violent. Between 60 and 70 percent of network programs contain *violence*, with 4 to 6 acts of violence per hour. The National Television Violence Study in the US examined 10,000 hours of programming in the 1990s, finding many parallel patterns.

Beyond its frequency, media violence bears little resemblance to reality; most mediated violent incidents depict no pain, and almost 90 percent show no blood or gore. These patterns are highly consistent over decades. Stories of crime and violence dominate US news coverage as well as fictional programs, and coverage does not match real-world crime. Murder suspects represent 0.13 percent of those arrested, but 25 percent of suspects in the news. Editorial decisions and judgments of → news value, not actual crime rates, determine coverage. Television news over-represents white (and under-represents African-American) victims. Perpetrators are apprehended and convicted far more often on television. Women are more likely than men to be victims of homicide (the reverse is true in reality). Researchers have observed many other discrepancies between the reality of crime statistics and television's depictions.

Accounting for Media Reality

These patterns stem from commercial and cultural factors. Early content analysts pointed to the *commercial context of programming* to explain the media reality they found (→ Commercialization: Impact on Media Content). Commercial media thrive on imitating the successful and reproduce formulas to gratify audience expectations; straying too far from the mold would be jarring. Fear of losing the audience drives programming decisions.

Patterns of media reality have deep cultural and historical roots that predate modern media; media are not the source of these images, but television in particular has mass-produced and mass-distributed them to an unprecedented degree (→ Television: Social History). All cultures use stories to express and reproduce reality and ideology, but no earlier society has produced and consumed as many as ours. These stories reflect persistent *ideological and commercial values*, including glorification of youth culture, consumption, intersections of race, class and gender, and the struggle of good vs. evil.

See also: ▶ BIAS IN THE NEWS
▶ COMMERCIALIZATION: IMPACT ON MEDIA

CONTENT ▶ CONSTRUCTION OF REALITY THROUGH THE NEWS ▶ CONTENT ANALYSIS, QUANTITATIVE ▶ CULTIVATION EFFECTS ▶ ENTERTAINMENT CONTENT AND REALITY PERCEPTION ▶ MEDIA AND PERCEPTIONS OF REALITY ▶ MEDIA PRODUCTION AND CONTENT ▶ NARRATIVE NEWS STORY ▶ NEWS VALUES ▶ OBJECTIVITY IN REPORTING ▶ REALITY TV ▶ SEX ROLE STEREOTYPES IN THE MEDIA ▶ STORYTELLING AND NARRATION ▶ TELEVISION AS POPULAR CULTURE ▶ TELEVISION: SOCIAL HISTORY ▶ TRUTH AND MEDIA CONTENT ▶ VIOLENCE AS MEDIA CONTENT ▶ WOMEN IN THE MEDIA, IMAGES OF

REFERENCES AND SUGGESTED READINGS

Berger, P. L. & Luckmann, T. (1966). *The social construction of reality: A treatise in the sociology of knowledge.* Garden City, NY: Doubleday.

Center for Communication and Social Policy (1998). *National television violence study,* Vol. III. Thousand Oaks, CA: Sage.

Chesebro, J. W. (1984). The media reality: Epistemological functions of media in cultural systems. *Critical Studies in Mass Communication,* 1, 111–130.

Gerbner, G. (1994). Women and minorities on TV: A study in casting and fate. *Media Development,* 41(2), 38–44.

Head, S. W. (1954). Content analysis of television drama programs. *Quarterly of Film, Radio, and Television,* 9(2), 175–194.

Pearson, R. C. (2005). Fact or fiction? Narrative and reality in the Mexican telenovela. *Television and New Media,* 6(4), 400–406.

Smythe, D. W. (1954). Reality as presented by television. *Public Opinion Quarterly,* 18, 143–156.

Reality TV

MARC ANDREJEVIC

University of Iowa

Reality TV became an increasingly prevalent global entertainment → genre in the 1990s and early 2000s. The popularity of reality shows with producers is due in large part to the fact that they represent a cheap, flexible form of programming that is easily customizable to different audiences and lends itself to forms of interaction and participation associated with new communication technologies (→ Interactivity, Concept of). As an entertainment genre that relies on the unscripted interactions of people who are not professional actors, reality TV develops and discards formats at a rapid rate, parasitizing the permutations available in everyday life – including everything from romance to warfare – for raw material. Their focus is not on bringing the public realm of politics into the private sphere, but on publicizing the private and intimate (→ Tabloidization). The emphasis is on therapy and social experimentation for the purpose of diversion. Reality formats make their claim to reality on the basis of their lack of scriptwriters and professional actors, but they are, for the most part, highly edited portrayals of patently contrived situations.

Successful formats rapidly replicate themselves from region to region, drawing cast members from local populations. Thus, for example, the Big Brother format, which isolates a group of strangers in a house where they compete to be the last one voted out by viewers, was pioneered in the Netherlands but became successful in local versions across Europe and in the Americas, Australia, and Asia, as well as in regional versions in Africa and the Middle East (→ Globalization of the Media; International Television). The reality TV boom in the early twenty-first century was built around successful blockbuster formats like Survivor and Big Brother, but reality TV, broadly construed, has been around since the dawn of television. The development of lightweight cameras and recording equipment facilitated the migration of reality-based formats from the soundstage to the home, the street, the school, the workplace, and beyond

Murray and Ouellette (2004) list several *subgenres* including, the 'gamedoc' (in which cast members compete for prizes as their daily lives are recorded), the dating show, the makeover show, the 'docusoap', the talent contest, court and police shows, and celebrity formats that feature behind-the-scenes glimpses of the real lives of the rich and famous.

See also: ▶ GENRE ▶ GLOBALIZATION OF THE MEDIA ▶ INTERACTIVITY, CONCEPT OF ▶ INTERNATIONAL TELEVISION ▶ MEDIA ECONOMICS ▶ TABLOIDIZATION

REFERENCES AND SUGGESTED READINGS

Andrejevic, M. (2004). *Reality TV: The work of being watched*. Lanham, MD: Rowman and Littlefield.
Hill, A. (2005). *Reality TV: Audiences and popular factual television*. London: Routledge.
Kjus, Y. (2009). Idolizing and monetizing the public: The production of celebrities and fans, representatives and citizens in reality TV. *International Journal of Communication*, 3, 277–300.
Murray, S. & Ouellette, L. (eds.) (2004). *Reality TV: Remaking television culture*. New York: New York University Press.
Ouellette, L. (ed.). (2013). *A companion to reality television*. Chichester: John Wiley.

Reasoned Action, Theory of

MARTIN FISHBEIN
University of Pennsylvania

The theory of reasoned action (TRA) is a general theory of behavior that was first introduced in 1967 by Martin Fishbein, and was extended by Fishbein and Icek Ajzen (e.g., Ajzen & Fishbein 1980). Developed largely in response to the repeated failure of traditional → attitude measures to predict specific behaviors, the theory began with the premise that the simplest and most efficient way to predict a given behavior was to ask a person whether he or she was or was not going to perform that behavior. Thus, according to the theory, performance or non-performance of a given behavior is primarily determined by the strength of a person's intention to perform (or to not perform) that behavior, where intention is defined as the subjective likelihood that one will perform (or try to perform) the behavior in question (→ Attitude-Behavior Consistency).

Although the theory focuses upon behavioral intentions (e.g., to jog 20 minutes every day), it can also *predict and explain intentions* to engage in categories of behavior (e.g., to exercise) or to reach certain goals (e.g., to lose weight). According to the theory, however, unlike the strong relation between intentions to engage in a given behavior and behavioral performance, there is no necessary relation between intentions to engage in a behavioral category and whether one does (or does not) perform any single behavior in that category or between intentions to reach a specific goal and goal attainment. Thus, although the theory can predict and explain any intention, the TRA recognizes that only intentions to engage in volitionally controlled behaviors will consistently lead to accurate behavioral predictions.

The intention (I) to perform a given behavior (B) is, in turn, viewed as a *function of two basic factors*: the person's attitude toward performing the behavior (i.e., one's overall positive or negative feeling about personally performing the behavior – Ab) and/or the person's subjective norm concerning his or her performance of the behavior (i.e., the person's perception that his or her important others think that he or she should [or should not] perform the behavior in question – SN). Algebraically, this can be expressed as: $B \sim I = w_1 Ab + w_2 SN$, where w_1 and w_2 are weights indicating the relative importance of attitudes and subjective norms as determinants of intention. It is important to recognize that the relative importance of these two psychosocial variables as determinants of intention will depend upon both the behavior and the population being considered. Thus, for example, one behavior may be primarily determined by attitudinal considerations while another may be primarily influenced by perceived norms. Similarly, a behavior that is attitudinally driven in one population or culture may be normatively driven in another. While some behaviors may be entirely under attitudinal control (i.e., w_2 may be zero), others may be entirely under normative control (i.e., w_1 may be zero).

The theory also considers the *determinants of attitudes and subjective norms*. On the basis of Fishbein's earlier expectancy value model, attitudes are viewed as a function of behavioral beliefs and their evaluative aspects. Algebraically: $Ab = f(\Sigma b_i e_i)$, where Ab = the attitude toward performing the behavior, b_i = belief that performing the behavior will lead to outcome 'I' and e_i = the evaluation of outcome 'i.' Somewhat similarly, subjective norms are viewed as a function of normative beliefs and motivations to comply. Algebraically: $SN = f(\Sigma Nb_i Mc_i)$, where SN = the subjective norm, Nb_i = the normative belief that referent 'i' thinks one should (or should not) perform the behavior and Mc_i = the motivation to comply, in general, with referent 'i.' Finally, the TRA also considers the role played by more traditional demographic, economic, personality, attitudinal, and other individual difference variables, such as perceived risk (→ Risk Perceptions) or → sensation seeking.

In 1991, Ajzen introduced the theory of planned behavior, which extended the TRA by adding the concept of perceived behavioral control as a predictor of both intention and behaviour (→ Planned Behavior, Theory of). And in 2000, Fishbein introduced the *integrative model*, which extended the theory of planned behavior by expanding the normative component to include descriptive as well as injunctive norms, and by explicitly acknowledging the role of skills and abilities and facilitating factors as moderators of the intention–behavior relationship. The reasoned action approach has been used successfully to predict and/or explain a wide variety of behaviors, including such things as wearing safety helmets, smoking marijuana, voting, or drinking alcohol (see, e.g., Ajzen et al. 2007).

See also: ▶ ATTITUDE-BEHAVIOR CONSISTENCY ▶ ATTITUDES ▶ PLANNED BEHAVIOR, THEORY OF ▶ RISK PERCEPTIONS ▶ SENSATION SEEKING

REFERENCES AND SUGGESTED READINGS

Ajzen, I. (1991). The theory of planned behavior. *Organizational Behavior and Human Decision Processes,* 50(2), 179–211.

Ajzen, I. & Fishbein, M. (1980). *Understanding attitudes and predicting social behavior.* Englewood Cliffs, NJ: Prentice Hall.

Ajzen, I., Albarracin, D., & Hornik, R. (eds.) (2007). *Prediction and change of health behavior: Applying the reasoned action approach.* Mawah, NJ: Lawrence Erlbaum.

Fishbein, M. (1967). Attitude and the prediction of behavior. In M. Fishbein (ed.), *Readings in attitude theory and measurement.* New York: John Wiley, pp. 477–492.

Fishbein, M. (2000). The role of theory in HIV prevention. *AIDS Care,* 12(3), 273–278.

Reciprocal Effects

HANS MATHIAS KEPPLINGER
Johannes Gutenberg University of Mainz

The term 'reciprocal effects' denotes the effects of the mass media on actual and potential protagonists of media coverage. Protagonists are distinguished from bystanders who are not addressed by media coverage. *Anticipatory (re) actions* are intended to avoid or seek to bring about media coverage (e.g., Cohen et al. 2008) (→ Agenda Building; Mediatization of Politics). *Immediate reactions* are instantaneous consequences of interactions with journalists. *Corrective reactions* are stimulated by existing news coverage.

With respect to reciprocal effects, linear models of media effects have to be supplemented by feedback models: protagonists stimulate media reports that, in turn, influence their behavior which causes subsequent media coverage (Fishman 1980; → Media Effects; Media Effects, Direct and Indirect Effects).

Six types of effects can be distinguished: (1) *awareness*: protagonists are highly involved in the issue at hand and motivated to follow more reports than bystanders; (2) *appraisals*: protagonists tend to see themselves as victims of circumstances and believe they would be misrepresented if reported as independent actors; (3) *assumptions*: most people attribute stronger negative effects of media messages to others than to themselves (→ Third-Person Effects); (4) *observations*: protagonists observe behavioral changes and correctly or incorrectly attribute them to media coverage; (5) *emotions*: protagonists of negative reports develop feelings like anger; protagonists of positive reports feelings like pride; and (6) *interactions of emotions and observations*: emotions and perceived behavioral changes reinforce each other (Kepplinger & Glaab 2007).

See also: ▶ AGENDA BUILDING ▶ MEDIA EFFECTS
▶ MEDIA EFFECTS: DIRECT AND INDIRECT EFFECTS
▶ MEDIA EVENTS AND PSEUDO-EVENTS
▶ MEDIATIZATION OF POLITICS
▶ THIRD-PERSON EFFECTS

REFERENCES AND SUGGESTED READINGS

Cohen, J., Tsfati, Y., & Sheafer, T. (2008). The influence of presumed media influence in politics. *Public Opinion Quarterly*, 72, 331–344.

Fishman, M. (1980). *Manufacturing the news*. Austin, TX: University of Texas Press.

Kepplinger, H. M. & Glaab, S. (2007). Reciprocal effects of negative press reports. *European Journal of Communication*, 22(3), 337–354.

Regression Analysis

ALAN M. RUBIN
Kent State University

As scientists seek to explain phenomena, they use empirical measures such as correlation to express the relationships among variables. Correlations can range from 0.0 (no relationship) to 1.0 (a perfect relationship between the variables' values) with coefficients being either positive or negative (→ Correlation Analysis). Regression moves beyond correlation by analyzing the variability of the dependent variable based on the information from one or more independent variables, seeking to explain which independent variables best predict the dependent variable.

The *regression equation* indicates how well we can predict values of the dependent variable by knowing the values of the independent variable or variables. The equation is represented by the regression line, which depicts the relationship between the variables. The sum of squares, which is fundamental to regression analysis, refers to the deviation or variance of a score from the average score of a distribution. The least-squares line depicts the best-fitting regression line or lowest sum of squared distances of all data points.

Simple regression analysis seeks to learn how much one continuous independent variable explains or predicts the dependent variable. Its equation refers to how the dependent variable scores rely on the independent variable scores. *Multiple regression analysis* estimates the separate and collective contributions of two or more independent variables to explaining the dependent variable (Kerlinger & Pedhazur 1973).

Based on the size of each regression coefficient, researchers can compare the contribution of each independent variable to predicting the dependent variable. Multiple R indicates the strength of relationship. R^2 depicts the proportion of explained variance for the predictors, and F is the test of significance. If the predictor variables are intercorrelated, it becomes difficult to assess individual contributions to the equation. Depending on the objective, a researcher might choose to enter all predictors simultaneously. Or, if the researcher's goal is to test a communication model, he or she might enter the predictor variables in blocks, hierarchically, according to the sequential steps in the model.

Examples from communication research: Ohr and Schrott (2001) found campaign information seeking can be explained in a local German election mainly by social expectations to be politically informed, but also by a personal duty to stay politically informed, a desire to vote, and the entertainment aspect of politics. Slater (2003) found gender, → sensation seeking, aggression, and frequency of Internet use contributed to explaining the use of violent media content and violent website content.

See also: ▶ CORRELATION ANALYSIS ▶ MEASUREMENT THEORY ▶ SENSATION SEEKING

REFERENCES AND SUGGESTED READINGS

Kerlinger, F. N. & Pedhazur, E. J. (1973). *Multiple regression in behavioral research*. New York: Holt, Rinehart and Winston.

Ohr, D. & Schrott, P. R. (2001). Campaigns and information seeking: Evidence from a German state election. *European Journal of Communication*, 16, 419–449.

Slater, M. D. (2003). Alienation, aggression, and sensation seeking as predictors of adolescent use of violent film, computer, and website content. *Journal of Communication*, 53(1), 105–121.

Relational Control

FRANK E. MILLAR
University of Wyoming

Relational control is the most dynamic of the three dimensions of social relationships proposed by Millar and Rogers (1987) – the other two are trust and intimacy. Control represents the vertical "distance" between the persons in an ongoing interaction; it refers to the pattern of rights and obligations to define or direct and to defer or accept the other's assertions while constructing the continually re-produced form of any interpersonal relationship. The temporal relevance of control is the present, since the right to direct and the obligation to accept the dyad's form varies by topics, social roles, and social settings.

Functionally, control structures serve to regulate how each person acts toward and with the other and the dyad's ability to accomplish interdependent and individual goals subjective judgments about the vertical distance between persons are encapsulated in the notions of freedom and equity. Freedom concerns the possibility of one's own actions affecting the forms and outcomes of the relationship, while equity judgments concern the fairness of one's own rewards in comparison to the other's, considering the amount and type of one's contributions to the relationship.

Relational control has been most frequently *measured* with the Relational Communication Control Coding System (RCCCS), or some modification of it (Rogers and Escudero 2004). Briefly, the RCCCS uses a three-digit code to categorize any speech turn; the first digit codes the speaker, the second codes the verbalization's format, and the third classifies the turn's response mode relative to the prior statement from the previous speaker.

Two measures of the relational control dimension have received a fair amount of empirical attention. *Dominance* is operationally defined as the number of one-up moves responded to with a one-down maneuver. Dominance is a momentary outcome in an ongoing conversation where one person asserts a definition of the relationship and the other accepts that assertion. *Redundancy* is operationally defined as the sum of the absolute deviation from random use of the nine transactional configurations indexed by the RCCCS. Either highly redundant or highly chaotic patterns are problematic for the relationship.

See also: ▶ INTERPERSONAL COMMUNICATION

REFERENCES AND SUGGESTED READINGS

Millar, F. E. & Rogers, L. E. (1987). Relational dimensions of interpersonal dynamics. In M. E. Roloff & G. R. Miller (eds.), *Interpersonal processes: New* directions in communication research. Newbury Park, CA: Sage, pp. 117–139.

Rogers, L. E. & Escudero, V. (eds.) (2004). *Relational communication: An interactional perspective to the study of process and form.* Mahwah, NJ: Lawrence Erlbaum.

Relational Dialectics

LESLIE A. BAXTER
University of Iowa

Relational dialectics is a theory of meaning-making in relationships (→ Meaning). Formally articulated in 1996 by Leslie Baxter and Barbara Montgomery, and revised by Baxter in 2011, Relational Dialectics Theory (RDT) is grounded in the philosophy of dialogism articulated by Russian language philosopher Mikhail Bakhtin in its emphasis on the fragmented and contested nature of meaning-making. It relies primarily on qualitative methods, with a goal of rendering a rich understanding of the meaning-making process (→ Qualitative Methodology).

Relational dialectics RDT consists of three *core propositions*. The first proposition is that meanings emerge from the struggle of different, often opposing discourses (→ Text and Intertextuality). Following Bakhtin, all of meaning-making can be understood metaphorically and literally as a dialogue. Everyday dialogue presupposes difference in the unique perspectives of the interlocutors. Bakhtin's lifelong intellectual project was critical of monologues of all kinds – authoritative discourses that foreclose the struggle of competing discourses by centering a single discursive point of view. RDT thus seeks to reclaim discursive conflict in relating.

The *second proposition* is that the interpenetration of discourses is both synchronic and diasynchronic (→ Linguistics; Semiotics). Meanings emerge in any given interaction moment, and in this sense, they are, at least momentarily, synchronically fixed. But meanings are also fluid; in subsequent interactions, relational parties might construct meanings that reproduce existing meanings, or they could produce new meanings. The *third proposition* is that the interpenetration of competing discourses constitutes social reality. In this third proposition, RDT joins a growing number of theories committed to a constitutive view in which communication is positioned to construct the social world, not merely to represent an objective world that precedes communication. What is unique about RDT is its articulation of the mechanism by which such construction takes place: the tensionality of difference.

See also: ▶ DISCOURSE ▶ LINGUISTICS ▶ MEANING ▶ QUALITATIVE METHODOLOGY ▶ SEMIOTICS ▶ TEXT AND INTERTEXTUALITY

REFERENCES AND SUGGESTED READINGS

Baxter, L. A. (2011). *Voicing relationships: A dialogic perspective.* Thousand Oaks, CA: Sage.

Baxter, L. A. & Montgomery, B. M. (1996). *Relating: Dialogues and dialectics.* New York: Guilford.

Relational Uncertainty

LEANNE K. KNOBLOCH
University of Illinois

'Relational uncertainty' is the degree of confidence (or lack of confidence) that individuals have in their perceptions of involvement within interpersonal relationships (Knobloch, 2010). It arises from self, partner, and relationship sources. 'Self uncertainty' indexes questions about people's own participation in the relationship. 'Partner uncertainty' encompasses questions about their partner's participation in the relationship, and 'relationship uncertainty' involves questions about the state of the relationship itself. The three sources of relational uncertainty tend to co-occur but are conceptually and empirically distinct.

Relational uncertainty can be further *distinguished by content areas*. In courtship, self and partner uncertainty involve the questions people have about their desire for the relationship, their evaluation of its value, and their goals for its progression. Relationship uncertainty includes the ambiguity individuals experience about the norms for appropriate behavior, the mutuality of feelings between partners, the definition of the association, and the future of the relationship. Nuanced issues of relational uncertainty are experienced by spouses within marriage; by romantic couples grappling with breast cancer, infertility, or depression; and by military couples reunited after deployment (Knobloch & Theiss 2012).

Relational uncertainty can have important *consequences for communication* (Knobloch et al. 2011). With respect to message production, relational uncertainty can provoke face threats because individuals lack information about how their partner will respond. Consequently, people experiencing relational uncertainty are less willing to discuss sensitive topics with their partner (Knobloch 2010). Relational uncertainty can also complicate message processing. Under conditions of relational uncertainty, individuals are prone to information-processing biases that hinder them from drawing accurate conclusions about their own behavior and their partner's behavior in conversation.

See also: ▶ EXPECTANCY VIOLATION ▶ INFORMATION SEEKING ▶ UNCERTAINTY AND COMMUNICATION ▶ UNCERTAINTY MANAGEMENT ▶ UNCERTAINTY REDUCTION THEORY

REFERENCES AND SUGGESTED READINGS

Knobloch, L. K. (2010). Relational uncertainty and interpersonal communication. In S. W. Smith & S. R. Wilson (eds.), *New directions in interpersonal communication research*. Thousand Oaks, CA: Sage, pp. 69–93.

Knobloch, L. K., Knobloch-Fedders, L. M., & Durbin, C. E. (2011). Depressive symptoms and relational uncertainty as predictors of reassurance-seeking and negative feedback-seeking in conversation. *Communication Monographs*, 78, 437–462.

Knobloch, L. K. & Theiss, J. A. (2012). Experiences of U.S. military couples during the post-deployment transition: Applying the relational turbulence model. *Journal of Social and Personal Relationships*, 29, 423–450.

Reliability

KLAUS KRIPPENDORFF
University of Pennsylvania

'Reliability' is the ability to rely on something, a tool, a service, or data. In empirical research, unreliable data limit their use as evidence for theories or scientific arguments. Here, reliability is inferred from the degree of agreement observed among data generated by several independent methods.

There are many *sources of unreliability*. Measuring instruments may malfunction or be affected by spurious causes. Scientific observers may be influenced by the theory they are pursuing. Eyewitnesses' accounts of events could be biased by selective recall, self-interests, or information obtained subsequent to the event. Coders employed by content analysts may disagree on their reading of given texts.

The use of data faces two *epistemological limitations* that motivate reliability assessments: (1) when the phenomena of interest are transitory, it is empirically impossible to verify whether the data about these phenomena are accurate. This is so for earthquakes, historical events, and conversations. Some leave traces behind. Most are known through records kept for a variety of often institutional reasons; (2) even persisting phenomena may not be unambiguously analyzable, in which case the act of observing and recording constitutes the phenomena studied. For example, measuring time presupposes a clock. The meanings of texts arise in processes of reading. Attitudes do not exist in someone's head; they are created by psychological measurements. Relying on data as unquestionable givens may lead to invalid conclusions.

Unable to refer to the phenomena in place of which data are examined, all one can observe is the agreement among several methods of generating data from the same phenomena. Reliability assumes that above chance agreement among methods can happen only if they respond to something real, not what the phenomena are (→ Validity).

Three concepts of reliability can be distinguished: (1) in theories of measurement, reliability provides assurances that the process of generating data is not influenced by circumstances that are extraneous to observation, description, or measurement. For example, when observers or coders generate records, one needs to assure that their coding instructions yield the same data no matter who is employed (→ Content Analysis, Quantitative); (2) interpretation theory acknowledges that researchers may have different backgrounds, interests, and theoretical orientations which can lead them to different interpretations of the same data. Accordingly, interpretations are reliable when, after accounting for explainable discrepancies, three or more interpretations come to the same conclusion about what is (triangulation); (3) in pursuit of psychometric tests, researchers consider a measure to be reliable when it correlates with other not necessarily identical measures across time, individuals, and situation.

Further, *three kinds of reliability* can be distinguished: stability (test-retest reliability), reproducibility (test-test reliability), and accuracy (test-standard reliability). Accuracy is the strongest reliability measure, but rarely obtainable for the frequent lack of available standards. Data for measuring reproducibility require two or more independently obtained sets of data describing the same set of phenomena. The cut-off point below which the data need to be rejected as too unreliable to precede with their analysis should be determined by the probability and costs of leading to wrong conclusions.

See also: ▶ CONTENT ANALYSIS, QUANTITATIVE ▶ EXPERIMENT, LABORATORY ▶ EXPERIMENT, FIELD ▶ MEASUREMENT THEORY ▶ RESPONSE RATES ▶ SURVEY ▶ VALIDITY

REFERENCES AND SUGGESTED READINGS

Krippendorff, K. (2013). *Content analysis: An introduction to its methodology*, 3rd edn. Thousand Oaks, CA: Sage.

Merrigan, G. & Huston, C. L. (2009). *Communication research methods*, 2nd edn. Oxford: Oxford University Press.

Remediation

JAY DAVID BOLTER

Georgia Institute of Technology

Remediation (Bolter & Grusin 1999) refers to a historical process through which newer media forms interact with earlier ones. On the first page of *Understanding Media* (1964), Marshall McLuhan noted that the "'content' of any medium is always another medium: the content of writing is speech, just as the written word is the content of print." Remediation proceeds from this insight, but understands the process as more complex and historically nuanced.

The relationship between media is not a linear process of replacement or incorporation, as McLuhan suggested; instead, the media of a given culture enter into a *configuration of relationships* involving cooperation as well as competition. When a new medium is introduced (e.g., film at the beginning of the twentieth century, television in the middle, or the computer at the end), the whole configuration may shift. Designers and producers working in the new medium may seek to take over the roles previously played by the established media, and their counterparts in the established media may respond either by yielding easily or by reasserting their own roles. This dual 'process of appropriation and reappropriation' will remain ongoing as long as the various media remain vigorous. A claim to greater authenticity (or sometimes even 'reality') is a defining aspect of remediation. The producers of the new form borrow representational elements from the older one, but, in refashioning those elements, they further make an implicit or explicit claim that their new form is in some way better, i.e., more authentic or more realistic.

Bolter and Grusin (1999) identified *two main representational strategies* of remediation. *Transparency* is a strategy that dates back at least to Renaissance painting, in which the artist or producer tries to make the medium disappear so that viewers feel as if they were in the presence of the object or scene represented (→ Art as Communication). *Hypermediacy* is the opposite strategy, in which the producer acknowledges and even celebrates the process of mediation. As approaches to remediation, a focus on either transparency or hypermediacy indicates whether the producer is inclined to cover up or to acknowledge a dependence on earlier media forms.

See also: ▶ ART AS COMMUNICATION ▶ MEDIUM THEORY ▶ TEXT AND INTERTEXTUALITY

REFERENCES AND SUGGESTED READINGS

Bolter, J. D. & Grusin, R. (1999). *Remediation: Understanding new media*. Cambridge, MA: MIT Press.

Manovich, L. (2001). *The language of new media*. Cambridge, MA: MIT Press.

McLuhan, M. (1964). *Understanding media*. New York: McGraw-Hill.

Response Rates

MICHAEL W. TRAUGOTT
University of Michigan

The term 'response rates' refers to the level of cooperation of respondents in a → survey. 'Unit nonresponse' refers to the difficulty that a researcher has in contacting the individuals in the study's sample. 'Item nonresponse' is based upon a refusal to give answers to specific questions within the survey (→ Election Surveys; Interview, Standardized; Public Opinion Polling). There has been a *decline in response rates* across a wide range of survey types and across countries for the last several decades, raising basic questions about the general quality of data collected through surveys. In a political survey, for example, people who are less interested in politics may be less likely to agree to be interviewed. As a consequence, the results of the survey may underestimate levels of interest in the population. The item nonresponse rate can vary for different questions in the survey, creating bias in some measures but not others.

The *highest unit response rates* are achieved by government agencies, followed by academic survey research centers and then commercial firms. The trend over time is present in all three kinds of surveys. Generally, response rates are highest in face-to-face surveys conducted in people's homes by well-trained interviewers. As contacts become less personal, such as through the telephone, individuals are less likely to agree to spend time speaking with an interviewer. With changing living patterns, the number of single-person households has increased significantly. Single persons are much more difficult to locate for an interview. Also, people are more concerned about issues of privacy and confidentiality. Research on the shifts in willingness to participate in surveys is complicated because of the lack of data from those who were not interviewed.

The impact of lowered response rates on data quality is not well understood; existing research suggests that there are some instances in which they do not have any effect (Keeter et al. 2006). There is no clear set of actions that researchers can take to sustain or increase response rates with an understanding of their relative cost–benefit tradeoffs.

See also: ▶ ELECTION SURVEYS ▶ INTERVIEW, STANDARDIZED ▶ PUBLIC OPINION POLLING ▶ SURVEY

REFERENCES AND SUGGESTED READINGS

Curtin, R., Presser, S., & Singer. E. (2005). Changes in telephone survey nonresponse over the past quarter century. *Public Opinion Quarterly*, 69, 87–98.

de Leeuw, E. & de Heer, W. (2002). Trends in household survey nonresponse: A longitudinal and international comparison. In R. M. Groves, D. A. Dillman, & J. L. Eltinge (eds.), *Survey nonresponse*. Chichester: John Wiley, pp. 41–54.

Keeter, S., Kennedy, C., Dimock, M., Best, J., & Craighill, P. (2006). Gauging the impact of growing nonresponse on estimates from a national RDD telephone survey. *Public Opinion Quarterly*, 70, 759–779.

Rhetoric, Argument, and Persuasion

FRANS H. VAN EEMEREN
University of Amsterdam and Leiden University

Rhetoric, argument, and persuasion come together in the study of argumentation (van Eemeren et al. 2014). Argumentation is advanced to defend a standpoint to people who (are assumed to) doubt its acceptability. They are to be convinced by making an appeal to reasonableness (→ Discourse).

The *study of argumentation* includes not only philosophical and theoretical investigations of the concepts of reasonableness inspiring the various models of argumentation, but also empirical and analytic research aimed at explaining argumentative reality and reconstructing it from the perspective of these models, and practical research aimed at tackling argumentative practices. The research program serves the analysis, evaluation, and production of argumentative discourse. The state of the art is characterized by the coexistence of a *variety of approaches*. Some, especially those having a background in discourse analysis and rhetoric, have a descriptive goal. They are aimed at making clear how speakers and writers use argumentation to convince or persuade others. Other approaches, inspired by logic and philosophy, study argumentation for normative purposes. They are aimed at developing soundness criteria for reasonable argumentation. Most argumentation theorists agree that the study of argumentation has a normative as well as a descriptive dimension.

All modern approaches are strongly affected by the perspectives on argumentation developed in antiquity. *Dialectically* oriented approaches put an emphasis on maintaining reasonableness and focus on the quality of argumentation in regulated critical dialogues. *Rhetorically* oriented approaches put an emphasis on the effectiveness of argumentation, viewing effectiveness as a matter of 'entitlement.' Effectiveness in the sense of actual persuasiveness is at issue in empirical *persuasion research* (→ Persuasion).

Reacting against the logical approach, Toulmin (1958) presented a *model of the steps* that can be distinguished in the *defense of a standpoint*. In his view, the soundness of argumentation is determined by the degree to which the warrant, which connects the data adduced with the claim defended, is acceptable or made acceptable by a backing. This 'procedural form' of argumentation is field-independent, but the evaluation criteria are field-dependent, because what kind of backing is required depends on the field to which the claim belongs.

In their *new rhetoric* Perelman and Olbrechts-Tyteca (1958) regard argumentation as sound if it adduces (more) assent with the standpoint among the target group: a "particular audience" or the "universal audience" that embodies reasonableness. Apart from the elements serving as point of departure of argumentation, such as facts and values, they discuss the argument schemes that can be used. Since the 1970s in Canada a movement called *informal logic* has been promoted that covers a collection of normative approaches which remain closer to argumentation in ordinary language than formal logic (see Tindale 2004, for a rhetorical approach). The norms proposed for interpreting, assessing, and construing argumentation include premise acceptability, relevance, and sufficiency (→ Rhetoric and Logic).

Formal dialecticians develop procedures for resolving differences about the tenability of standpoints. According to Barth and Krabbe (1982), the dialectical rules must be "problem-valid" in the sense of optimally serving the purpose for which they are designed and "conventionally valid" in the sense of being intersubjectively acceptable. Building on dialogue logic, they present a regimented dialogue game between a proponent and an opponent of a thesis who try to establish whether the thesis can be defended.

Van Eemeren and Grootendorst's *pragma-dialectical theory of argumentation* combines a dialectical approach with a 'pragmatic' approach inspired by speech act theory, Grice's logic of conversation and discourse analysis. In their model of a critical discussion four stages are distinguished in resolving a difference of opinion on the merits, the speech acts that can play a constructive role are identified, and the discussion rules for non-fallacious testing of the acceptability of standpoints are formulated.

In the past decades the sharp division between rhetoric and dialectic is weakened. Van Eemeren (2010) argues that the reconstruction of argumentative discourse can be made more precise if allowance is made for the arguers' strategic maneuvering to keep their dialectical and rhetorical pursuits in balance. For this purpose he integrates insight from rhetoric into the pragma-dialectical theory.

See also: ▶ DISCOURSE ▶ LINGUISTIC PRAGMATICS ▶ PERSUASION ▶ RHETORIC AND DIALECTIC ▶ RHETORIC AND LOGIC ▶ RHETORICAL STUDIES

REFERENCES AND SUGGESTED READINGS

Barth, E. M. & Krabbe, E. C. W. (1982). *From axiom to dialogue: A philosophical study of logics and argumentation*. Berlin: De Gruyter.

Perelman, C. & Olbrechts-Tyteca, L. (1958). *Traité de l'argumentation: La nouvelle rhétorique* [Treatise on argumentation: the new rhetoric]. Paris: Presses Universitaires de France.

Tindale, Chr. W. (2004). *Rhetorical argumentation.* Thousand Oaks, CA: Sage.

Toulmin, S. E. (1958). *The uses of argument.* Cambridge: Cambridge University Press.

van Eemeren, F. H. (2010). *Strategic maneuvering in argumentative discourse.* Amsterdam: John Benjamins.

van Eemeren, F. H., Garssen, B., Krabbe, E. C. W., Snoeck Henkemans, A. F., Verheij, B., & Wagemans, J. H. M. (2014). *Handbook of argumentation theory.* Dordrecht: Springer.

Rhetoric and Dialectic

PETER MACK
Warburg Institute, University of London

Rhetoric and dialectic are closely related theories of (and trainings in) → persuasion. They have some distinct bodies of doctrine (e.g., the topics of invention belong to dialectic; the figures of speech to rhetoric). For Plato dialectic meant the training in philosophy acquired through dialogue and argument (→ Rhetorical Studies).

Aristotle says that rhetoric and dialectic are counterparts because they are both concerned with questions that cannot be resolved scientifically. For much of late antiquity and the early Middle Ages it was usual to study rhetoric and dialectic together in the cycle of seven liberal arts. Rudolph Agricola's De Inventione Dialectica (1479) treats dialectical invention as the key element in the composition of texts. Agricola rewrites the topics of invention so as to put more emphasis on the nature of the argumentative relationship defined and, on its use in practical arguing.

In effect Agricola's work proclaimed the new technique of dialectical invention to be the core of the composition of literary, technical, and persuasive works. Erasmus combined techniques from both subjects under the umbrella of variation and rhetorical amplification of an existing text in his highly successful De Copia (1512). Philipp Melanchthon emphasizes the close relationship between rhetoric and dialectic.

Peter Ramus adopted a different approach to the problem of combining rhetoric and dialectic. He always expected that rhetoric and dialectic would be taught together and that the theoretical training offered by manuals of the two subjects would be complemented by readings in classical literature and oratory.

Reactions against the abstractness and lack of application of formal logic have caused some recent philosophers to attempt to formulate rules for practical arguing. Toulmin's The Uses of Argument (1958) develops a theory that allows people to assess the strength of arguments in practical life. Perelman and Olbrechts-Tyteca (1958) incorporated theories of argumentation, topics of invention, and persuasive principles taken from rhetoric.

See also: ▶ PERSUASION ▶ RHETORIC AND LOGIC
▶ RHETORIC, ARGUMENT, AND PERSUASION
▶ RHETORIC, GREEK ▶ RHETORIC, ROMAN
▶ RHETORICAL STUDIES

REFERENCES AND SUGGESTED READINGS

Mack, P. (2011). *A history of Renaissance rhetoric 1380–1620.* Oxford: Oxford University Press.

Perelman, C. & Olbrechts-Tyteca, L. (1958). *Traité de l'argumentation: La nouvelle rhétorique.* Paris: Presses Universitaires de France. [*The new rhetoric: A treatise on argumentation*, trans. J. Wilkinson & P. Weaver. (Notre Dame, IN: University of Notre Dame Press, 1969).]

Toulmin, S. E. (1958). *The uses of argument.* Cambridge: Cambridge University Press.

Rhetoric and Ethics

RONALD C. ARNETT
Duquesne University

Communication ethics in a postmodern context recognizes that differing 'goods' shaped from biased ground necessitate rhetoric of rival traditions. Bias assumes the reality of situated, tainted ground that links communication ethics to learning about different 'goods' that are protected and promoted by those dissimilar to us. Dissimilarity nurtures alterity, radical Otherness, and tainted/biased ground, requiring rhetorical action bearing witness to a communication ethic that houses goods that matter (Arnett et al. 2008).

Tainted ground is the home of radical otherness, represented in a philosophical turn of Heidegger and Nietzsche marking a disputed end to the reign of virtue ethics and marking the entrance of a hermeneutic of suspicion (→ Hermeneutics). Communication ethics unmasks a multiplicity of perspectives, akin to the Sophists, who argued that virtues are polis dependent, not universal (MacIntyre 2007). We dwell in a moment defined by the metaphor of standpoint, which rejects conventional individualistic thinking that assumes a flight above human history in an effort to proclaim and tell, enveloped in a mythic, arrogant assumption that untainted perception guides communication ethics.

Concepts such as standpoint, ground, embeddedness, situatedness, social–cultural limits, and the unavoidable bias of tradition explicate the necessity of provincial soil that generates authentic communication ethics differences while requiring a cosmopolitan recognition of multiplicity and learning from differences. This unity of contraries perspective neither stands above our historicity nor languishes in solipsism. Communication ethics as responsiveness in this historical moment acknowledges biased ground and moves rhetoric to the forefront. Assuming a given communication ethic is a persuasive task that necessitates expression of a public map about the 'why' and 'how' of a given communication ethics position. Communication ethics assumes a pragmatic rhetorical turn, pivoting on tainted ground, forming a public map of the 'for,' the 'by,' and the 'about' of communication ethics, Schrag's (1986) articulation of communicative praxis. Communication ethics in such an era begins with attentiveness to alterity in order to learn and understand, followed by a rhetorical turn that is responsive to otherness—the socio-cultural context, communicators, and communicative content.

See also: ▶ ETHICS IN JOURNALISM ▶ HERMENEUTICS ▶ POSTMODERNISM AND COMMUNICATION ▶ RHETORICAL STUDIES

REFERENCES AND SUGGESTED READINGS

Arnett, R. C., Harden Fritz, J., & Bell, L. M. (2008). *Communication ethics literacy: Dialogue and difference.* Thousand Oaks, CA: Sage.
MacIntyre, A. (2007). *After virtue: A study in moral theory,* 3rd edn. Notre Dame, IN: University of Notre Dame Press.

Schrag, C. O. (1986). *Communicative praxis and the space of subjectivity.* Bloomington, IN: Indiana University Press.

Rhetoric and Gender

KAREN A. FOSS
University of New Mexico

Rhetoric began in ancient Greece as the art of persuasion, applied principally to political, legal, and judicial contexts (→ Rhetoric, Greek). Gender is the assignment of meaning to bodies – what is constructed as masculine and feminine by culture (Foss et al. 2012).

To begin, gender was conceptualized as 'irrelevant' to rhetoric. The assertion of authority and expertise, the use of logical argument, and the manipulation of → discourse to affect an audience's beliefs and actions were seen as masculine prerogatives (→ Rhetoric and Logic), unsuitable for women (Campbell 1981). The first recognition of a relationship between rhetoric and gender was an examination of difference. Women speakers, the obstacles they faced because of their gender, and their effectiveness when compared with men began to be studied. Also investigated were communicative differences between women and men in type, topic, and amount of talk.

The next development, gender as *rhetorical standpoint,* recognized the distinctive circumstances of a woman's body, life, and culture that produce a different way of making sense of experience (Wood 1992). Standpoint epistemology enabled rhetorical scholars to consider the practices of marginalized rhetors and rhetorical systems that would not have been visible in traditional rhetorical paradigms (→ Rhetoric and Race).

A final relationship between rhetoric and gender is the *capacity of gender to transform rhetorical theory* itself. Some scholars suggest that gender cannot help but alter rhetoric; others believe the incorporation of gender into rhetoric necessarily will transform rhetoric itself.

Gender is now a fully acknowledged dimension in rhetorical theory, with the capacity to influence if not transform the rhetorical terrain. Gender intersects with rhetoric to expand what counts as rhetoric.

See also: ▶ DISCOURSE ▶ RHETORIC, GREEK
▶ RHETORIC AND LOGIC ▶ RHETORIC AND RACE
▶ RHETORIC AND SOCIAL PROTEST ▶ WOMEN'S
COMMUNICATION AND LANGUAGE

REFERENCES AND SUGGESTED READINGS

Campbell, K. K. (1981). *Man cannot speak for her: A critical study of early feminist rhetoric*, Vol. I. Westport, CT: Greenwood Press.

Foss, S. K., Domenico, M. E., & Foss, K. A. (2013). *Gender stories: Negotiating identity in a binary world*. Long Grove, IL: Waveland.

Wood, J. T. (1992). Gender and moral voice: Moving from woman's nature to standpoint epistemology. *Women's Studies in Communication*, 15, 1–24.

Rhetoric, Greek

LAURENT PERNOT
University of Strasbourg

The word rhetoric comes from the Greek rhêtorikê, which means the art of speaking. In its full sense, the word rhetoric covers both the theory and the practice of speech. It is defined as the art of persuasion (→ Persuasion).

Rhetoric was developed in Greece, at Athens above all, during the classical era (fifth and fourth centuries BCE). Subsequently, the elements put in place were never forgotten. They constituted a platform for the later history of rhetoric, not only during antiquity but right up until the modern era of European and American history (→ Rhetorical Studies).

The Athenian *oratorical practice* spread within a democratic context. By law, parties were obliged to plead their cause personally, without being represented by a lawyer. In politics, the main organ was the Assembly of people, who exercised the executive power. Added to that were the ceremonial speeches made on occasions such as national funerals and religious feast days, as well as ambassadorial speeches and all sorts of private conferences. Such a system supposed an effective commitment from the citizens. It was a question of making oneself heard in large crowds, in acoustically uncomfortable conditions, and with a view to real and immediate consequences.

Oratorical practice relied on a vigorous *teaching*, which included theoretical lessons, case studies, the learning of exemplar speeches assigned by the master, practical composition exercises on real or fictional subjects, and verbal sparring matches between students, as well as gesture and voice training. The most important *theoretical treatise* is the Rhetoric by Aristotle (around 360–325 BCE), which draws a distinction between two main forms of persuasion: logical persuasion through intellectual demonstration and moral persuasion through psychological means.

See also: ▶ METAPHOR ▶ PERSUASION
▶ RHETORIC, ARGUMENT, AND PERSUASION
▶ RHETORIC, PRE-SOCRATIC ▶ RHETORICAL STUDIES

REFERENCES AND SUGGESTED READINGS

Pernot, L. (2005). *Rhetoric in antiquity*, trans. W. E. Higgins. Washington, DC: Catholic University of America Press.

Vickers, B. (1988). *In defence of rhetoric*. Oxford: Clarendon Press.

Rhetoric and History

KATHLEEN J. TURNER
Davidson College

The conjoining of the terms 'rhetoric' and 'history' suggests at least three related but distinct areas of study. One, the history of rhetoric, focuses on rhetorical theory and practice during particular time periods (e.g., → Rhetoric, Pre-Socratic). The focus here is on rhetorical processes in history and the rhetoric of history.

The first, the *study of rhetorical processes in history* focuses on the ways in which rhetoric functions in historical contexts. The scholarship of the first decades of 'speech' focused on specific speeches and speakers in historical contexts using 'historical-critical research,' exemplified by the classic three-volume anthology, A History and Criticism of American Public Address (Hochmuth 1955; → Speech Communication, History of). Criticized in the 1960s as producing 'cookie cutter' studies lacking theoretical value (→ Rhetorical

Criticism), many scholars shifted from rhetorical texts as historically situated products to explorations of historical developments as captured in, and created by, rhetorical processes.

A move toward book-length studies created venues in which to make significant arguments and interpretations. The renewed use of primary resources stressed the invaluable insights from examining such archival materials as correspondence, oral histories, and photographs. Increasing digital access to archival holdings facilitates meticulous historiographical research in the face of accelerated scholarly schedules.

Studies of rhetorical processes in history still attend to *individual rhetors*, with particular attention to the speeches of American presidents (e.g., Stuckey 2013). Other examinations broaden the scope of 'public address' to incorporate differing forms of communication, such as the wide-reaching exploration in which Condit and Lucaites (1993) delineate the evolution of the term 'equality' from the mid-eighteenth to the end of the twentieth centuries. Rhetorical historians do debate certain aspects. Should rhetorical history be defined as seeking "to understand the context through messages that reflect and construct that context" (Turner 1998, 2), or as any study of rhetoric of the past? Are rhetorical history and criticism distinct approaches or indistinguishable? Must historical studies be explicitly based on and constructed as contributions to theoretical inquiry? Is rhetorical history thriving or marginalized?

More recently, the second area *rhetoric of history* focuses on how the construction of history constitutes an essentially rhetorical process. Such studies argue that the standard of 'objectivity' masks the choices that not only can but must be made in constructing stories of the past, such as developing narrative frameworks and creating arguments of causality and relationship. Such choices constitute essential epistemological decisions: one's very way of knowing about what and who have gone before is created through the writing of history, perhaps even to the point that there *is* no 'history' – at least, none that is humanly knowable – beyond what is rhetorically constructed. From this perspective, such cherished criteria as 'accuracy' and 'facts' depend on not only the individual but also the social and cultural context in which the histories are created and received. As Carpenter (1995) contends, historians serve as opinion leaders because they create stories that resonate with their audiences and the social truths of their times.

Some scholars extend this investigation to explore the *rhetorical purposes to which historical arguments are put*. Precisely because historical accounts are rhetorically constructed, the 'lessons of history' drawn from the same events are often diametrically opposed. 'The lessons of Vietnam' suggest to some that the United States and its allies should have been more aggressive in their military intervention in Iraq, and to others that they should not have undertaken the venture in the first place.

An additional rhetorical use of history celebrates *the past as embodying the essence of the society*. Blair (2007) examines how civil rights memorials use historical concepts to inspire and symbolize public memory. Whether rhetorical processes in history or the rhetoric of history, the connection between these two key terms reveals both the interdisciplinary significance of communication as a central liberal art, and the valuable insights to be generated through the interdisciplinary turn in academia.

See also: ▶ RHETORIC, PRE-SOCRATIC ▶ RHETORICAL CRITICISM ▶ SPEECH COMMUNICATION, HISTORY OF

REFERENCES AND SUGGESTED READINGS

Blair, C. (2007). *Civil rights/civil sites: … Until justice rolls down like waters …* National Communication Association Carroll C. Arnold Distinguished Lecture. Boston, MA: Allyn and Bacon.

Carpenter, R. H. (1995). *History as rhetoric: Style, narrative, and persuasion*. Columbia, SC: University of South Carolina Press.

Condit, C. & Lucaites, J. L. (1993). *Crafting equality: America's Anglo-African word*. Chicago, IL: University of Chicago Press.

Hochmuth, M. (ed.) (1955). *A history and criticism of American public address*, Vol. 3. New York: McGraw-Hill.

Stuckey, M. (2013). *The good neighbor: Franklin D. Roosevelt and the rhetoric of American power*. East Lansing, MI: Michigan State University Press.

Turner, K. J. (ed.) (1998). *Doing rhetorical history: Concepts and cases*. Tuscaloosa, AL: University of Alabama Press.

Rhetoric and Language

CORNELIA ILIE
Zayed University, Abu Dhabi

When exploring rhetoric in relation to language we need to examine the diverse ways in which people use language to reach their goals, by shaping, reflecting, and changing societal practices, and thereby making an impact on our commonly shared perceptions, values, and beliefs. Some of the most influential ideas about the rhetorical use of language were effectively expressed by famous philosophers in ancient Greece and Rome, and later updated in the modern age (Perelman and Olbrechts-Tyteca 1969; Groupe μ 1976). The Greek philosopher Aristotle is frequently quoted for his definition of rhetoric as "the faculty of discovering in any particular case all of the available means of persuasion." This is a basic rhetorical use of language meant to achieve far-reaching effects like changing reality by changing our perceptions through the intermediary of discourses that affect our modes of thinking and acting (Bitzer 1968; → Rhetorical Studies).

In ancient times rhetoric was a vast and influential branch of learning, closely tied to grammar and to logic within the famous medieval trivium. As a field of linguistic studies, grammar examines the nature, structure, functions, and evolution of language (→ Linguistics). Although linguistics is a much later development than rhetoric, scholarly evidence shows that the study of language and rhetoric has been intertwined (→ Rhetoric, Greek; Rhetoric, Roman). The earliest linguistic debate is found in Plato (4th century BCE), whereas the study of the persuasive functions of language was situated by Aristotle alongside the study of philosophy and science as a vital scholarly endeavor (→ Persuasion).

The complex relation between rhetoric and language can be explored from three perspectives: (1) semiotic-evolutionary, i.e., the role of language in thinking and communicating effectively; (2) structural-comparative, i.e., the role of specific language codes in shaping thought; and (3) functional-discursive, i.e., the role of linguistic conventions, discursive practices, and ideologies in cultivating specialized forms of thought for various situations and purposes). From a semiotic-evolutionary perspective, there is a strong interdependence between language systems and thinking patterns. Since language serves as both an instrument of thought and a means of expression, it reflects and shapes socially and culturally generated → meaning (→ Semiotics).

The rhetorical dimension of language use is always present when we communicate a message since we need to capture and maintain our interlocutors' attention. The much-debated distinction made by structuralists between 'langue' and 'parole' (Saussure 1916), as well as the distinction between the 'competence' and 'performance' of language users (Chomsky 1965) acquire a new significance in rhetorical theory through a change of focus. Whereas linguistics examines the way in which language is used by human beings, rhetoric examines the active role of human beings when using language. Consequently, the two approaches are regarded as complementary in the context-based, goal-oriented, and audience-targeted process of communication.

From a structural-comparative perspective, the situation-adjusted language use involves understanding its persuasive potential as well as the speaker's ability to influence beliefs and behaviors through the power of symbolic action. Rhetoricians argue that the manner and form of → discourse play a central role in shaping and motivating collective identity and action. Modern rhetoric follows classical rhetorical theory in treating the relationship between language and meaning as contextual, i.e., the meaning of a particular linguistic usage derived from a particular speaker's understanding of a particular audience addressed at a specific moment in time (→ Linguistic Pragmatics). From a *functional-discursive perspective*, language acquires meaning and value in actual use, depending on socio-cultural contexts and historical conditions.

By emphasizing the functioning of public discourse, scholars of rhetoric have drawn attention to communicative acts that affect the entire community and are typically performed in law courts, legislative assemblies, and occasional gatherings of citizens.

See also: ▶ DISCOURSE ▶ LINGUISTIC PRAGMATICS ▶ LINGUISTICS ▶ MEANING ▶ PERSUASION ▶ RHETORIC, GREEK ▶ RHETORIC AND POLITICS ▶ RHETORIC, ROMAN ▶ RHETORICAL STUDIES ▶ SEMIOTICS

REFERENCES AND SUGGESTED READINGS

Bitzer, L. F. (1968). The rhetorical situation. *Philosophy and Rhetoric*, 1, 1–14.
Bizzell, P. & Herzberg, B. (2000). *The rhetorical tradition: Readings from classical times to the present*. New York: St. Martin's Press.
Chomsky, N. (1965). *Aspects of the theory of syntax*. Cambridge, MA: MIT Press.
Fahnestock, J. (2011). *Rhetorical style: The uses of language in persuasion*. Oxford: Oxford University Press.
Groupe μ [Dubois, J., Edeline, F., Klinkenberg, J. M., Minguet, Ph., Pire, F., & Trinon, H.] (1976). *Rhétorique générale [General rhetoric]*. Paris: Larousse.
Perelman, C. & Olbrechts-Tyteca, L. (1969). *The new rhetoric: A treatise on argumentation*, trans. J. Wilkinson & P. Weaver. Notre Dame, IN: University of Notre Dame Press.
Saussure, F. de (1916). *Cours de linguistique generale [Course in general linguistics]*, ed. C. Bally & A. Sechehaye, with A. Reidlinger. Paris: Payot.
Warnick, B. (2007). *Rhetoric online: Persuasion and politics on the world wide web*. Berne: Peter Lang.

Rhetoric and Logic

HANS V. HANSEN
University of Windsor

Considered narrowly, logic is concerned with the analysis and evaluation of the 'following from' relationship between premises and conclusions of arguments whereas, considered widely, it is about the overall goodness of arguments from an evidential perspective.

The wide sense of logic, therefore, takes an interest in the evidentiary acceptability of premises. 'Rhetoric,' in its broadest meaning, is about affecting audiences through the use of symbols (not just linguistic symbols). All kinds of discourse, as diverse as poetry, narratives, and instruction manuals, as well as visual art objects and music, may be said to have rhetorical aspects (→ Rhetorical Studies). 'Rhetoric' also has a narrower meaning in which it is associated with appropriateness of arguments used in persuasion. Thus, logic in the wide sense and rhetoric in the narrow sense (hereafter 'logic' and 'rhetoric') have arguments as their overlapping subject matter.

Logical analysis focuses on clarifying premises and conclusions, identifying unstated premises, and discerning patterns of reasoning. Logical evaluation depends on criteria built on the concepts of acceptability, plausibility, probability and necessity. Rhetorical analysis is concerned with identifying a speaker, an exigency, and an audience (see Bitzer 1968)). Evaluation from a rhetorical perspective is concerned with how well speakers fit their discourse dealing with the exigency facing an audience. Accordingly, rhetoric takes into account the historical situation of a discourse as well as the psychological disposition of the target audience.

Arguments need to be evaluated from both logical and rhetorical perspectives. One way to bridge the gap is for each subject to borrow principles from its counterpart. Thus, many *elementary logic books* include rhetorical principles, and many rhetoric primers include a chapter on the elements of logic. Another possibility is to nest both rhetorical and logical components in an encompassing theory of argumentation. One attempt at this is the pragma-dialectical theory of argumentation developed by van Eemeren and Grootendorst (see van Eemeren 2010), and another is Tindale's (2004) comprehensive rhetoric-based theory of argumentation.

See also: ▶ RHETORIC, ARGUMENT, AND PERSUASION ▶ RHETORIC AND DIALECTIC ▶ RHETORIC, GREEK ▶ RHETORICAL STUDIES ▶ RHETORICS: NEW RHETORICS

REFERENCES AND SUGGESTED READINGS

Bitzer, L. F. (1968). The rhetorical situation. *Philosophy and Rhetoric*, 1, 1–14.
Tindale, C. (2004). *Rhetorical argumentation*. Thousand Oaks, CA: Sage.
van Eemeren, F. H. van (2010). *Strategic maneuvering in argumentative discourse*. Amsterdam: John Benjamins.

Rhetoric and Media Studies

JAY P. CHILDERS
University of Kansas

As a discipline, media studies focuses on the history, production, and effects of mediated communication, such as television, film, and video games (→ Communication as a Field and

Discipline). Rhetorical studies is concerned with the ways in which humans influence and persuade one another (→ Rhetorical Studies). Together, rhetoric and media studies explores how mediated communication influences and persuades people, often in subtle, unconscious ways. Given the pervasiveness of media in people's lives today, such matters are central to understanding the ways in which media play a vital role in shaping people's lives.

The Role of Media

Although rhetoric's purview was traditionally understood as speech and writing, the field has expanded its attention to include both visual and aural aspects of persuasion (→ Speech Communication, History of). For some, this shift has meant employing key concepts in traditional rhetorical studies onto new types of texts (→ Text and Intertextuality). For others, the inclusion of the visual and aural has required new ways of doing → rhetorical criticism.

This latter view is supported by those, like the German philosopher Walter Benjamin, who argue that technology changes the very nature of communicative messages. In his landmark essay, The Work of Art in the Age of Mechanical Reproduction (1968), Benjamin argues that traditional forms of art are unique because of the sense of awe that the individual feels when he or she directly engages them, something he refers to as its aura. The use of mechanical reproduction, Benjamin suggests, destroys the aura as the mass audience takes the place of the individual. The recording of Mozart heard on the radio by millions of listeners is altogether different from the Vienna Philharmonic's live performance. Rhetorical studies have struggled to deal with these feelings created by media.

Approaches to Mediated Rhetoric

Kenneth Burke understood rhetoric to be the study of symbols and their many functions, and many rhetorical critics have found it useful to adapt his critical concepts to modern media. One such adaptation has been based on Burke's belief that the languages people use allow them to do and think certain things and, conversely, to hide alternatives, what he called "terministic screens." Through these screens, identifications with others are both created and stifled. David Blakesly argues that "film rhetoric – the visual and verbal signs and strategies that shape film experience – directs our attention in countless ways, but always with the aim of fostering identification and all that that complex phenomenon implies" (2003, 3; → Film Theory; Cinema). In addition, Burke's rhetorical pentad (act, agent, agency, scene, and purpose) as a way of critically engaging mediated texts, particularly those that are narrative in nature, has also proved invaluable to the study of media.

Although primarily empirically based, Cappella and Jamieson's study (1997) has shown how *underlying metaphors* used by news media create what the title of their book makes clear, a "spiral of cynicism" for the American electorate. Using the classical notion of mimesis, Parry-Giles and Parry-Giles have turned to the popular television drama *The West Wing* to suggest that it teaches the American public about the presidency and the nation ("a reality of the presidency that is persuasive and credible", 2006, 4). Mimesis, as first explored by Plato and Aristotle, is rooted in the notion that through imitation or representation rhetorical work is being done.

In addition to these more traditional forms of rhetorical criticism of media, scholars have also begun to explore newer territory assuming that technologically mediated communication's reliance on the *image* requires new rhetorical approaches. The first of these approaches is rooted in ideological criticism, which explores and uncovers the media's reinforcement of hegemonic forces in society writ large (→ Critical Theory). Feminist scholar Bonnie Dow (1996) has, for instance, turned a rhetorical eye on the images of female identity created by media. Dow uncovers a number of symbolic representations of women in popular media that offer mixed portrayals of feminist ideals (→ Women in the Media, Images of).

Another, newer approach that applies rhetorical methods to media emphasizes the fact that visual media do *affect audiences at an emotional level*. Rhetorical critic Roderick Hart made just this argument when he turned to television. Taking a broad view of television – its role as a medium and its content – Hart argues that television reaches audiences at the level of consciousness. To make sense of this aesthetic response, he uses a phenomenological approach. Focusing on the level of emotional consciousness, → phenomenology acknowledges that media reach the individual at an unconscious level. In the end, such a rhetorical inquiry leads Hart to argue that "television makes us feel good about feeling bad about politics" (Hart 1999, 10).

Relatedly, one recent dominant approach to understanding media rhetorically has been to dig deeply into a text to understand how its symbolic images impact audiences at the unconscious level. Such *psychoanalytic criticism* opens up possible understandings of how media influence the way people live with and through technologically reproduced communication. Incorporating the work of Sigmund Freud, Jacques Lacan, and others, rhetorical theorist Joshua Gunn has begun advancing new ways of using a psychoanalytic approach to mediated communication. In one such instance, Gunn (2004) argues that a psychoanalytic understanding of fantasy offers a way to mediate the disjointed relationship between fragmented texts and de-centered subjects. Gunn's assertion is, put simply, that the media offers dominant portrayals of fantasy that causes one to desire and, ultimately, to repress such a desire. Psychoanalytic criticism, while not an uncontested rhetorical approach, continues to offer new ways of engaging media studies.

Rhetorical and media scholar Barry Brummett (2004) has recently suggested that *homologous patterns* of → discourse exist across communicative texts that work to structure lives through formal patterns. Brummett explores how films can present audiences with stories and images that are homologous to lived experience, additional mediated texts, and other, larger narratives. A rhetorical criticism built from an understanding of homologies offers the possibility of bringing media more directly into connection with other human communication.

Future Directions

While the Internet incorporates many modes of communication (discussed above) with more traditional print-based media, how rhetorical scholarship might engage it theoretically or critically remains to be seen. This is not to suggest that it cannot. But to begin to understand how communities of individuals on Facebook 'live' together or how virtual communities (e.g., Second Life) influence the way individuals see themselves and the physical world around them will require even newer ways of understanding the use of symbols through mediated channels toward further identifications.

See also: ▶ CINEMA ▶ COMMUNICATION AS A FIELD AND DISCIPLINE ▶ CRITICAL THEORY ▶ CULTIVATION EFFECTS ▶ DISCOURSE ▶ FILM THEORY ▶ ICONOGRAPHY ▶ MEDIA EFFECTS ▶ MEDIA AND PERCEPTIONS OF REALITY ▶ PHENOMENOLOGY ▶ PHOTOGRAPHY ▶ RHETORIC AND LANGUAGE ▶ RHETORICAL CRITICISM ▶ RHETORICAL STUDIES ▶ SPEECH COMMUNICATION, HISTORY OF ▶ TEXT AND INTERTEXTUALITY ▶ VISUAL COMMUNICATION ▶ VISUAL REPRESENTATION ▶ WOMEN IN THE MEDIA, IMAGES OF

REFERENCES AND SUGGESTED READINGS

Benjamin, W. (1968). The work of art in the age of mechanical reproduction. In *Illuminations* [1936], ed. H. Arendt, trans. H. Zohn. New York: Harcourt Brace Jovanovich, pp. 217–252.

Blakesly, D. (2003). *The terministic screen: Rhetorical perspectives on film*. Carbondale, IL: Southern Illinois University Press.

Brummett, B. (2004). *Rhetorical homologies: Form, culture, experience*. Tuscaloosa, AL: University of Alabama Press.

Burke, K. (1966). *Language as symbolic action: Essays on life, literature, and method*. Berkeley, CA: University of California Press.

Burke, K. (1969). *A grammar of motives*. Berkeley, CA: University of California Press.

Cappella, J. N. & Jamieson, K. H. (1997). *Spiral of cynicism: The press and the public good*. Oxford: Oxford University Press.

Dow, B. J. (1996). *Prime-time feminism: Television, media culture, and the women's movement since 1970*. Philadelphia, PA: University of Pennsylvania Press.

Gunn, J. G. (2004). Refitting fantasy: Psychoanalysis, subjectivity, and talking to the dead. *Quarterly Journal of Speech*, 90, 1–23.

Hart, R. P. (1999). *Seducing America: How television charms the modern voter*. Beverley Hills, CA: Sage.

Parry-Giles, T. & Parry-Giles, S. J. (2006). *The prime-time presidency: The West Wing and U.S. nationalism*. Urbana, IL: University of Illinois Press.

Rhetoric and Politics

ALYSSA A. SAMEK
Drake University

SHAWN J. PARRY-GILES
University of Maryland

The study of rhetoric and politics examines the role of → persuasion in the political process. Classical scholars conceived of rhetoric as a practical art involving the performance of public oratory in the contexts of politics, law, and ceremonial occasions, separated from the philosophy of knowledge.

While twentieth-century rhetorical scholars continued to address the role of persuasion in the → public sphere, its study has more recently expanded beyond public oratory to include other persuasive texts, including advertisements, films, photographs, television, or digital news (→ Advertising; Cinema; Photography). Rhetoricians of today also recognize the epistemological contributions of rhetoric, which accentuate its role in creating knowledge and constituting perceptions of political reality (→ Media and Perceptions of Reality).

Scholarship that intersects *rhetoric and politics includes* not only the study of electoral politics, but other forms of political persuasion involving institutions (e.g., governments, corporations) and individuals and/or groups working to disrupt such institutional power (e.g., activist leaders and social movements). Such scholarship often relies on humanistic methodologies yet also utilizes social scientific measurements. The study of rhetoric and politics often focuses on two broad areas of examination: the consideration of history in the study of rhetoric and politics and the examination of how political messages make meaning.

The study of rhetoric is often attuned to the *history of ideas* and how public texts contribute to the evolutionary understanding of political and cultural conflicts and norms. A public text, thus, functions as a historical artifact, which reflects the political and cultural ideas of the moment in which it was created. For some, an understanding of the historical and political context represents a necessary component in the comprehension of textual → meaning. Rhetoricians also are mindful of rhetoric's role in creating historical narratives, which are likewise dependent on arguments and evidence.

Regardless of its rhetorical dimensions, *history* serves as a *key component* in the study of rhetoric and politics. Rhetorical analyses cognizant of history demonstrate how rhetoric helps enact, empower, and constrain human behavior over time, excavating the "rhetorical climate of an age" (Zarefsky 1998, 31; → Rhetoric and History). For some, understanding the relationship among history, rhetoric, and politics necessitates an examination of archival resources that inform the meanings of the public discourse.

Rhetorical scholars attending to *political messages* often rely on social scientific and critical-historical perspectives in their scholarship (→ Political Persuasion). Utilizing social scientific methods, Hart, for example, demonstrates his theoretical conclusions about political messages with his creation of a computer program (DICTION), which examines the "unconscious language choices people use when talking to one another" (Hart 2000, 4). Analyzing over 20,000 public texts into DICTION, Hart contends that political campaigns ideally reinvigorate the country, involving a "conversation" among candidates, the media, and the public. In the end, he offers an optimistic assessment of campaigning and its democratizing tendencies.

Other scholars of rhetoric and politics interrogate the nuances of meanings, utilizing, among others, rhetorical, political, and media theories as critical lenses by which to analyze public discourse. With such *critical perspectives*, objectivity is often shunned in favor of a rhetorical critic's insights that offer new ways to understand discursive meaning. Questions of ideology and thus power are often foundational to rhetorical studies focused on political meaning.

In the end, attention to issues of civic engagement represents for many the foremost outcome of scholarship associated with the study of rhetoric and politics. Scholars often return to rhetoric's roots when detailing notions of civic engagement, recognizing the contributions of Aristotle and Cicero, in particular, to notions of citizenship and rhetorical practice. The scholarship is designed to help promote civic engagement among citizens, particularly students in the earliest stages of civic consciousness, strengthening the relationship between democratic practice and rhetorical principles.

See also: ▶ ADVERTISING ▶ CINEMA
▶ DISCOURSE ▶ ELECTION CAMPAIGN
COMMUNICATION ▶ FICTION ▶ FRAMING EFFECTS
▶ FRAMING OF THE NEWS ▶ JOURNALISM
▶ MEANING ▶ MEDIA AND PERCEPTIONS OF REALITY
▶ NEWS ▶ PERSUASION ▶ PHOTOGRAPHY
▶ POLITICAL COMMUNICATION ▶ POLITICAL
PERSUASION ▶ POSTMODERNISM AND
COMMUNICATION ▶ PUBLIC OPINION POLLING
▶ PUBLIC SPHERE ▶ RHETORIC AND GENDER
▶ RHETORIC, GREEK ▶ RHETORIC AND HISTORY
▶ RHETORIC AND MEDIA STUDIES ▶ RHETORIC
AND RACE ▶ RHETORIC, ROMAN ▶ RHETORICAL
CRITICISM

REFERENCES AND SUGGESTED READINGS

Dow, B. J. (2010). Feminism and public address research: Television news and the constitution of women's liberation. In S. J. Parry-Giles and J. M. Hogan (eds.), *The handbook of rhetoric and public address*. Oxford: Wiley Blackwell, pp. 345–372.

Hart, R. P. (2000). *Campaign talk: Why elections are good for us*. Princeton, NJ: Princeton University Press.

Kennedy, G. (trans.) (1991). *Aristotle, On Rhetoric*. Oxford: Oxford University Press.

Parry-Giles, S. J. & Hogan J. M. (eds.) (2010). Introduction: The study of rhetoric and public address. In *The handbook of rhetoric and public address*. Oxford: Wiley Blackwell, pp. 1–15.

Zarefsky, D. (1998). Four senses of rhetorical history. In K. J. Turner (ed.), *Doing rhetorical history: Concepts and cases*. Tuscaloosa, AL: University of Alabama Press, pp. 19–32.

Rhetoric, Pre-Socratic

RICHARD LEO ENOS
Texas Christian University

Pre-Socratic Rhetoric is an overarching concept capturing both the traits of Hellenic rhetoric that were demonstrated by the sophists who immediately preceded Socrates, and the antecedent forces that shaped sophistic thought and its relationship to expression. Four primary forces shaped pre-Socratic rhetoric.

First, *Homeric antecedents*: Now recognized as inscribed oral → discourse, Homerica reveal emerging notions of rhetoric in two dimensions. The compositional patterns of the Iliad and the Odyssey reveal systemic formulae that served as both an aid to memory for early bards (aoidoi) and later for the more formal guild of rhapsodes (Homeridae). In addition, the characters themselves – such as Odysseus' wily exploits used to trick the cyclops Polyphemus in Book 9 of the Odyssey – demonstrate techniques of persuasion that would one day be formalized by sophists and theorized by rhetoricians.

Second, the *rise of logography*: Greece's evolution in writing from Bronze Age ideograms and syllabaries to an alphabet provided a technology for preserving the spoken word while facilitating abstract thought and prose composition. As literacy grew in popularity and importance logographers, or composers of discourse, evolved from chroniclers and narrative storytellers to specialized writers who composed discourse for such civic functions as forensic and deliberative rhetoric. Third, the *emergence of pre-Socratic philosophy*: Empedocles and other pre-Socratic philosophers – such as Parmenides and Zeno— reflected not only on the nature and function of the universe, but also on human understanding and expression. They maintained that knowledge was constrained by the limitations of our own sense-perceptions, arguing that knowledge is therefore probable and interpretative. The insights of pre-Socratic philosophy provided a foundation for sophistic rhetoric that would be based on oppositional thought (dissoi logoi', sense-perception, relativism and opinion (doxa)).

Finally the *rise of the Greek city* (polis) also played an important role in the emergence of pre-Socratic rhetoric. The archaic and classical periods of Greece witnessed the emergence of powerful political city-states, who aggressively promoted their hegemony through kinship ties and military conquest. In all such cities, even those that were not democratic, rhetoric in some form was a social activity as an art, an ambassadorial function, a topic for advanced education, and a process for civic deliberation.

See also: ▶ DISCOURSE ▶ RHETORICAL STUDIES

REFERENCES AND SUGGESTED READINGS

Enos, R. L. (2012). *Greek rhetoric before Aristotle*, revised and expanded edn. Anderson, SC: Parlor Press.

Schiappa, E. (1999). *The beginnings of rhetorical theory in classical Greece*. New Haven, CT: Yale University Press.

Rhetoric and Race

MARK LAWRENCE MCPHAIL
University of Wisconsin–Whitewater

Before the 1960s, few studies in either composition or communication addressed issues of race either directly or indirectly. In the 1960s, researchers began to focus their research efforts on the relationship between rhetoric and race, and by the 1970s, scholars began to question the efficacy of rhetoric for addressing racial issues, and theorized the need to reconceptualize and redefine rhetoric's traditional preoccupation with persuasion and argumentation (→ Rhetorical Studies).

In the US in the 1980s studies of rhetoric and race began to evolve toward descriptive studies of the language of oppression as well as more theoretically complex explorations of the language of white racism. The focus on white identity and privilege continued to increase in the 1990s, as research began to attend to *issues of power, ideology*, and *domination* in areas such as critical legal studies, critical race studies, and media studies. In the 1980s and 1990s, researchers continued to offer theoretically driven examinations of the *social and symbolic construction of whiteness and racial privilege*, and a rethinking of rhetoric informed by emerging ideological and epistemological concerns invigorated thinking about rhetoric and race as the twenty-first century began.

Since 2000, studies of Native American conquest and disenfranchisement, black nationalism and identity, the aesthetics of whiteness and anti-racism, visual rhetoric, racial reconciliation, and explorations of race in composition and pedagogy have defined current research on rhetoric and race. The election of Barack Obama to the White House has had a predictably strong impact on rhetorical considerations of race.

Rethinking the relationship between rhetoric and race has returned researchers to one of the earliest questions raised by scholars: whether or not racial conflict and division are, in fact, problems that can be remedied by rhetoric. In addition to studies of reparations and reconciliation, research on the rhetorical dimensions of the African-American public sphere also raise the question of whether or not America's white majority can 'hear the hurt' that has consistently been expressed in the rhetoric, aesthetics, and politics of black voices.

See also: ▶ RHETORIC AND HISTORY ▶ RHETORIC AND SOCIAL PROTEST ▶ RHETORICAL CRITICISM ▶ RHETORICAL STUDIES

REFERENCES AND SUGGESTED READINGS

Daniel, G. R. & Williams, H. (2014). *Race and the Obama phenomenon: The vision of a more perfect multiracial union*. Jackson, MI: University of Mississippi Press.

Lacy, M. & Ono, K. (2011). *Critical rhetorics of race*. New York: New York University Press.

Watts, E. (2012). *Hearing the hurt: Rhetoric, aesthetics, and politics of the new negro movement*. Tuscaloosa: University of Alabama Press.

Rhetoric, Roman

JON HALL
University of Otago

Roman rhetoric aimed to present theoretical and practical guidelines for effective verbal → persuasion. Its main principles derived from earlier Greek rhetorical theory, which achieved impressive levels of sophistication during the fourth century BCE (→ Rhetoric, Greek). As Greek-speaking communities were incorporated into the Roman Empire from the second century BCE onwards, the value of rhetorical training gradually came to be appreciated by members of the elite, and, by the end of the first century BCE, formal instruction in the subject had become an established feature of upper-class Roman education.

The two *best examples* of Roman rhetoric are Rhetorica ad Herennium (Rhetorical precepts addressed to Herennius, author unknown) and Quintilian's Institutio Oratoria (The education of the orator). The first takes the form of an instructional handbook (c.88–82 BCE), and is closely modeled on contemporary Greek works. Its extensive use of categorization and taxonomy illustrates well the main methodological hallmark of ancient rhetoric. Quintilian's treatise operates on a much larger scale, and its twelve books (c.93–95 CE) present the most comprehensive discussion of rhetoric to come down to us from the ancient world. The work addresses every facet of the discipline, frequently summarizing the contrasting views expressed on specific topics over the centuries by various rhetoricians, and displays sound judgment in its handling of them.

Several other discussions of Roman rhetoric survive from the classical period: Cicero's De Inventione, De Oratore, Brutus, Orator, De Partitione Oratoria, De Optimo Genere Oratorum and Topica (between 91 and 44 BCE); Tacitus' Dialogus de Oratoribus (c.96–102 CE); and Iulius Victor's Ars Rhetorica (probably fourth century CE). During the Renaissance, rhetorical handbooks such as Rhetorica ad Herennium enjoyed a renewed prominence as they came to form the basic educational texts of the ruling classes learning Latin for both administrative and broader cultural purposes.

See also: ▶ PERSUASION ▶ RHETORIC, GREEK

REFERENCES AND SUGGESTED READINGS

Clarke, M. L. (1996). *Rhetoric at Rome: A historical survey* (rev. D. H. Berry), 3rd edn. London: Routledge.
Dominik, W. & Hall, J. (eds.) (2007). *Blackwell companion to Roman rhetoric*. Oxford: Blackwell.
Kennedy, G. (1972). *The art of rhetoric in the Roman world 300 bc–ad 300*. Princeton, NJ: Princeton University Press.

Rhetoric and Social Protest

CHARLES J. STEWART
Purdue University

Research in rhetoric and social protest strives to discover how organized, uninstitutional forces use symbols and symbolic actions to promote or resist change in societal norms and values. Its focus ranges from interpersonal to mass communication, the colonial period to the present, moderate to radical elements, and formal → discourses to the rhetoric of the streets (→ Rhetorical Studies).

Rhetorical scholars view protestors as facing nearly impossible rhetorical situations in which they are viewed as illegitimate, systematically denied access to normal channels and procedures, and have severely limited powers of reward and punishment. Confrontation is inevitable because clashes between protestors and institutions and their supporters occur in zero-sum situations in which one party's relative gain is the other's relative loss. Rhetorical struggles become moral battles for power and legitimacy to define and control the social order. Institutions are loath to share powers with forces they see an uninformed at best and evil at worst, and protestors provoke confrontations and violent reactions to reveal how ugly institutions really are.

Those studying rhetoric and social protest claim that confrontational strategies in social protests are not only inevitable but essential for successful outcomes of protestors and the development and improvement of society. Protestors resort to coercive rhetoric to persuade target audiences that dire consequences are likely, if not certain, to make these audiences feel forced to comply and convinced of the protestor's probable capacity and intent to follow through with threatened action. The focus is to understand them as opportunities for social growth and progress, adaptation, and evolution.

A functional approach sees rhetoric as the agency through which protestors perform necessary functions that enable organized efforts to come into existence, to meet oppositions, and perhaps to succeed in bringing about or resisting change. Studies focus on the channels protestors use to transmit their messages to believers, nonbelievers, and the opposition and to sustain their efforts. Social protestors have always sought access to 'new media,' starting with the printing press and moving on to the telegraph, telephone, radio, television, Internet, and now → social media.

See also: ▶ DISCOURSE ▶ RHETORICAL STUDIES ▶ RHETORIC AND POLITICS ▶ SOCIAL MEDIA

REFERENCES AND SUGGESTED READINGS

Morris, C. & Browne, S. (eds.) (2006). *Readings on the rhetoric of social protest*. State College, PA: Strata.

Stewart, C. (1980). A functional approach to the rhetoric of social movements. *Central States Speech Journal*, (31), 298–305.

Stewart, C., Smith, C. A., & Denton, R. (2007). *Persuasion and social movements*, 5th edn. Long Grove, IL: Waveland.

Rhetorical Criticism

KARLYN KOHRS CAMPBELL
University of Minnesota

Rhetorical criticism analyzes → discourse to assess its persuasive power (→ Persuasion; Political Persuasion). Criticism began in ancient Greece and Rome as teachers developed their curricula by identifying what made some rhetorical acts successful and some not. Analyzing discourse became part of disciplinary scholarship in communication only in the modern period, but drew on the works of Aristotle, Isocrates, Cicero, Quintilian, and Augustine (→ Rhetoric, Greek; Rhetoric, Roman).

Rhetorical criticism as literary analysis *developed as field* in the 1940s in English departments. 'New critics' treated literary works as existing for their own sake. They warned against the intentional fallacy, interpreting a work in relation to its author, and the affective fallacy, evaluating a work by its effects. Instead, they held that "explication *is* criticism; it *is* the evaluative account of the poem" (Wimsatt 1963, ix).

In *The Philosophy of Rhetoric* (1776), George Campbell defined rhetoric as "that art or talent by which discourse is adapted to its end," identifying the critic's primary concern as the relationship between form – the choices made in rhetorical works – and function – what an act is designed to achieve. Accordingly, rhetorical criticism can be applied to literary, political, commercial, or philosophical discourse. Rhetorical criticism in communication studies focused on the discourse of the marketplace and developed methods to explicate the power of political speech to influence public behaviors and attitudes.

Public address criticism emerged in the 1940s. Ernest Wrage claimed that "from the speeches given by many men [*sic*], it is possible to observe the reflections of prevailing social ideas and attitudes. … A speech is an agency of its time,… a repository of themes and their elaborations from which we may gain insight into the life of an era as well as into the mind of a man [*sic*]" (1947, 455–456). Public speaking was seen as a distinctively democratic practice with special relevance during the Cold War. That studying public address was a means to promote patriotism focused scholarship on addresses by major figures as historical-cultural documents central to the nation's mythic heritage and historical experience. Accordingly, critics studied the rhetoric of US presidents, leaders of national movements, and eminent churchmen, and ignored protestors and dissidents, including trade unionists, socialists, and anarchists and outsiders, such as women and minorities.

The *evaluative standards of critics* were the arguments, emotional power, and character of the speaker, the structure, style, and delivery, echoing the Greco-Roman modes of proof – logos, pathos, and ethos – and the classical canons of invention, disposition, style, and delivery.

The civil rights, antiwar, New Left, countercultural and feminist movements transformed the rhetorical landscape and demanded that communication scholars respond to rhetoric that challenged conventional assumptions about public deliberation. *The civil rights movement* grew after World War II with picketing, sit-ins, freedom rides, and powerful speakers such as Martin Luther King, Jr., John Lewis, and Fannie Lou Hamer. Struggles over how best to achieve civil rights sparked the Black Power movement, which echoed the discourse of Black Muslims heard in the rhetoric of Malcolm X. Eloquent African-Americans such as Barbara Jordan and Shirley Chisholm spoke as members of Congress. The civil rights movement challenged rhetorical critics because it questioned the relationship of public speaking to democracy as activists challenged Americans to live up to the values praised in public discourse while pointing to the history of American racism as a national disgrace. In addition, almost exclusively white critics needed to analyze rhetoric that challenged their beliefs and values, their stereotypes about race, ethnicity, and norms of public deliberation. In the 1960s and 1970s, anthologies of civil rights rhetoric appeared, as did critical studies in journals that explored alternative approaches to analysis and evaluation.

In the 1960s, *countercultural, antiwar, New Left, and feminist rhetoric* demanded fresh approaches to nontraditional social movement texts, and critics responded guided in part by the theoretical and critical works of Northrop Frye and Kenneth Burke. European theorists were influential, particularly Jürgen Habermas, Mikhail Bakhtin, Jacques Derrida, and Michel Foucault.

See also: ▶ DISCOURSE ▶ RHETORIC, GREEK ▶ RHETORIC, ROMAN ▶ RHETORICAL STUDIES ▶ POLITICAL COMMUNICATION

REFERENCES AND SUGGESTED READINGS

Smith, A. L. [Asante, M.]. (1969). *The rhetoric of black revolution*. Boston, MA: Allyn and Bacon.
Wimsatt, W. K. (1963). *Explication as criticism: Selected papers from the English Institute, 1941–1952*. New York: Columbia University Press.
Wrage, E (1947). Public address. *Quarterly Journal of Speech*, 33, 455–456.

Rhetorical Studies

ROBERT N. GAINES
University of Maryland

BRUCE E. GRONBECK
University of Iowa

The rhetorical impulse may be conceived as the desire to express one's thoughts in a way that affects the thoughts of others. Such an impulse is universal among humans, and historical evidence exists for its cultivation in ancient civilizations of Africa, Asia, Europe, and the Americas. Early instances of theoretical inquiry concerning rhetorical communication have been documented in China (*c*. eighth century BCE), Egypt (*c*. eleventh century BCE), India (*c*. fourth century BCE), and Greece (including Magna Graecia, *c*. fifth century BCE). Arguably, each of these regional developments gave rise to a different tradition and trajectory of indigenous rhetorical studies. However, as a historical matter, the European tradition was most closely related to the emergent discipline of communication; accordingly, it receives emphasis here.

Ancient Rhetorical Studies

Within the European tradition of rhetorical studies, self-conscious attempts to theorize persuasive speaking were initially concerned with speech organization and elaboration of subject matter. Theoretical studies of rhetoric soon became abstract, with a focus on functions of speakers and types of speeches (→ Rhetoric, Greek). By the second century BCE, both of these theoretical categories became more or less crystallized; the functions of speakers were conceived as invention, arrangement, style, memory, and delivery; likewise, the kinds of speaking were conceived as deliberative, judicial, and demonstrative (or occasional) (→ Rhetoric, Roman).

The development of *rhetorical theory* was accompanied by the rise of pedagogical, critical, and historical studies. Pedagogical inquiry was concerned with effective means of inculcating rhetorical expertise in practitioners. Early materials for rhetorical instruction included rudimentary treatises, model speeches, and specimens of eloquence. Educational theory became a deliberate part of rhetorical education in the school of Isocrates, who stressed preceptive instruction, practice, and moral as well as literary imitation of political discourse. In Hellenistic times, rhetoric was adopted as the centerpiece of an ancient literary educational program. During the Roman imperial era, the rhetorical program of education was codified in Quintilian's Institutio oratoria (*c*.95 CE).

Rhetorical criticism was pursued as an independent form of literary production. Cicero may be credited with historicizing rhetorical criticism in Brutus (43 BCE), which provided a chronology and critique of Roman speakers up to his own day. History of rhetorical theory was invented by Aristotle when he gathered early rhetoric books in his Collection of arts (mid-fourth century BCE).

Medieval Rhetorical Studies

The Middle Ages were marked by both tradition and innovation in the theory and practice of rhetorical arts. The ancient tradition of rhetoric was represented initially within new encyclopedic treatments of rhetoric as part of the liberal arts Later on, traditional rhetoric found a place in rhetorical compendia as well as in commentaries and translations of 'classical' authors.

Rhetorical criticism frequently takes on a historical outlook. Partly this is because much of such criticism is designed to explain, assess, or defend the composition of ancient authors in the Bible. Innovation in medieval rhetoric came chiefly in development of discourse types that achieved new significance in the Middle Ages, specifically preaching, letter writing, and poetry writing. By the thirteenth century, preaching theory reached a new level of advancement; the result was the thematic sermon, a rhetorical discourse of religious worship built around the elements of theme, division, and development (of divisions).

Renaissance Rhetorical Studies

Early Renaissance thought was dominated by the humanist objective to re-create the culture of classical antiquity, not least through the studia humanitatis, a program of education designed to inculcate eloquence through instruction in grammar, rhetoric, poetic, history, and moral philosophy. Consistent with the humanist objective, Renaissance rhetoricians turned to ancient materials – many newly found – for inspiration in their development of rhetorical works.

Given the admiration of ancient culture that motivated many Renaissance humanists, the rhetorics they produced were inevitably connected with historical concerns. At least in part, the same was true of rhetorical criticism in this period. Renaissance humanists extended rhetorical criticism to the problem of interpreting Biblical texts (e.g., Philipp Melanchthon). Of course, not all rhetorical criticism in the Renaissance addressed ancient works.

Modern Rhetorical Studies

Faculty psychology was perhaps first applied to the uses of rhetorical theory at the beginning of the seventeenth century, when Francis Bacon explained the function of rhetoric with reference to four mental capacities – reason, imagination, emotions, and will. Blaise Pascal's idea, that auditors possessed multiple mental faculties, each of which was subject to rhetorical appeal, was quickly seized on by rhetorical theorists as the basis for new approaches to the discipline. Early belletrists offered rhetorical theory (and criticism) emphasizing aesthetic reception of discourse. Likewise, preaching theorists placed new stress on appeals to emotions as well as reason in the composition of sermons.

In the eighteenth century Thomas Sheridan characterized "elocution" as an unexplored language of imagination and passions, and he argued that this language shed as much light on human nature as the language of understanding. Certainly, in this era, the work most obviously influenced by faculty psychology is George Campbell's The philosophy of rhetoric (1776); here the definition and types of eloquence are both tied to mental faculties: eloquence is the "art or talent by which discourse is adapted to its end."

Contemporary Rhetorical Studies

The focus of this new rhetorical outlook was upon → meaning (→ Rhetoric and Language). Meaning-making became understood as a textual struggle, requiring both rhetors and audiences to be sensitive to linguistic constructions and psychological processing to overcome multiple obstacles to clear communication. Misunderstanding could be avoided or sidestepped through analytic processes that students of general semantics turned into laws of language use.

By around mid-century, rhetoric's search for 'informed opinion' separated it from the exploitation of advertising and propaganda, the indirection of poetry, the facticity of science. Its central function of 'adjusting ideas to people and people to ideas' operated by leveraging emotions at play in specific situations and rationally assembling ideas in bundles compatible with auditors' capabilities and circumstances (→ Rhetoric, Argument, and Persuasion). Developing simultaneously were new rhetorics fostering basic understandings of language-in-use, pedagogical approaches to teaching composition and criticism, and tools for pursuing historical-comparative studies of rhetorical style, broadly conceived (→ Linguistics).

These approaches encouraged a reconsideration of rhetorical criticism, particularly its sources of evidence, standards of evaluation, and relation to the critic. Further, popular reform and protest movements, antiwar and race riots, and a growing feminist consciousness began to put stress on traditional, civic, and civilized conceptions of the rhetorical arts (→ Rhetoric and Social Protest). The scope of rhetoric enlarged and its functions multiplied (Gronbeck 2004).

Three *dilations of rhetoric's scope* in the last third of the twentieth century are especially noteworthy. First, identity, self, subjectivity, and consciousness are concepts deployed across the communication arts generally, and the rhetorical arts specifically, when speculating about the person-centered dimensions of discoursing (→ Identities and Discourse). Second, many relational activities, e.g., parent–child interactions or manager–worker interactions, occur outside of formally constituted 'places.' Third, we have come to understand that human beings relate to each other through multiple symbol systems like films or television (→ Rhetoric and Media Studies; Semiotics).

Among the *new functions of rhetoric* is the call for more engagement with the psychoanalytic and the psychotherapeutic dimensions of shared culture. Erving Goffman's (1959) conception of human interactions as negotiative and transactional suggested that rhetorical encounters could become instrumental in self-development and the fostering of healthful relationships. Further, following the revolutionary temper of mid-century politics, it was but a short step for rhetoricians to critique institutions and seek empowerment (→ Critical Theory; Cultural Studies). Finally, coming forward from Claude Lévi-Strauss's conception of 'making something,' including ideas, out of found materials, came an expanded function of rhetoric: articulation, i.e., "the production of identity on top of differences, of unities out of fragments, of structures across practices" (Grossberg 1992, 54).

See also: ▶ CRITICAL THEORY ▶ CULTURAL STUDIES ▶ DISCOURSE ▶ DISCOURSE ANALYSIS ▶ HERMENEUTICS ▶ IDENTITIES AND DISCOURSE ▶ LINGUISTICS ▶ MEANING ▶ PROPAGANDA ▶ PUBLIC SPHERE ▶ RHETORIC AND DIALECTIC ▶ RHETORIC AND GENDER ▶ RHETORIC AND HISTORY ▶ RHETORIC AND LANGUAGE ▶ RHETORIC AND MEDIA STUDIES ▶ RHETORIC AND POLITICS ▶ RHETORIC AND RACE ▶ RHETORIC AND SOCIAL PROTEST ▶ RHETORIC, ARGUMENT, AND PERSUASION ▶ RHETORIC, GREEK ▶ RHETORIC, ROMAN ▶ RHETORICAL CRITICISM ▶ RHETORICS: NEW RHETORICS ▶ SEMIOTICS ▶ SPEECH COMMUNICATION, HISTORY OF ▶ WAR PROPAGANDA

REFERENCES AND SUGGESTED READINGS

Connors, R. J., Ede, L. S., & Lunsford, A. A. (eds.) (1984). *Essays on classical rhetoric and modern discourse*. Carbondale, IL: Southern Illinois University Press.
Goffman, E. (1959). *The presentation of self in everyday life*. Garden City, NY: Doubleday.
Green, L. D. & Murphy, J. J. (2006). *Renaissance rhetoric: Short-title catalogue 1460–1700*. Burlington, VT: Ashgate.
Gronbeck, B. E. (2004). The functions and scope of rhetoric *redivida*. In R. N. Gaines (ed.), *Advances in the history of rhetoric*, vol. 7. College Park, MD: American Society for the History of Rhetoric, pp. 152–177.
Grossberg, L. (1992). *We gotta get out of this place: Popular conservatism and postmodern culture*. London: Routledge.
Lipson, C. S. & Binkley, R. A. (eds.) (2004). *Rhetoric before and beyond the Greeks*. Albany, NY: SUNY Press.
Lundberg, C. O. (2013). Letting rhetoric be: On rhetoric and rhetoricity. *Philosophy & Rhetoric*, 46(2), 247–255.
Lunsford, A. A., Wilson, K. H., & Eberly, R. A. (eds.) (2008). *The Sage handbook of rhetorical studies*. Thousand Oaks, CA: Sage.
Smith, C. R. (2013). *Rhetoric and human consciousness: A history*, 4th edn. Long Grove, IL: Waveland.
Wander, P. (1983). The ideological turn in modern criticism. *Communication Studies*, 34, 1–18.

Rhetorics: New Rhetorics

ANDREEA DECIU RITIVOI
Carnegie Mellon University

New rhetorics are the product of postmodern conceptions of truth, which challenge the distinction between certain and probable knowledge. The classical tradition relegated rhetorical discourse to the province of probable knowledge, because such discourse rests on beliefs, customs, and values shared by a given community under specific circumstances (doxa; → Rhetoric, Greek; Rhetoric, Roman). With the gradual rise of scientific discourse in the western world, which reached a climax in the seventeenth century, ideals of truth and epistemic certainty came to define the worthiness of an intellectual discipline, and thus made rhetoric seem deficient (→ Rhetorical Studies).

New rhetorics have *arisen* in response to challenges from emerging fields and to pressures from the political and social sphere. They are profoundly interdisciplinary and live in tense relationship with the classical tradition, especially in how they define their epistemic status of rhetoric, and how they establish the disciplinary parameters of rhetorical theory. One of the major 'new rhetorics' of the twentieth century, that of Perelman and Olbrechts-Tyteca (1958), identifies as one of its premises the departure from a Cartesian notion of certainty as epistemic ideal, and takes on instead the goal of examining the formation of convictions as facilitated by the adherence to particular sets of values and beliefs, rather than correspondence to a universal notion of truth or validity.

This *understanding of truth* signals a new, postmodernist rhetoric, predicated on a relativist and contingent epistemology, which no longer privileges universal and formalized criteria for inquiry. New rhetorics are grounded in a post-Nietzschean sensibility that views certainty as an illusion made possible by cultural and social conventions. This is a sensibility that enables a view of rhetoric as a social force that can organize communities, structuring their beliefs and values in ways that allow them to pursue ethical goals and to live a common good life. By contrast, this new rhetoric deems dialectic socially subversive, inasmuch as dialectic taunts the very idea of consensus by trying to replace it with universal standards for truth that are not dependent on the values or beliefs of a particular community (Weaver 1994). Thus re-articulated, the new rhetoric is not only departing from the original core, but also re-evaluating classical terms and their meaning, rewriting the tradition in a way that allows it to legitimize its own enterprise (→ Rhetoric and Dialectic).

Despite enthusiastic celebrations of interdisciplinarity, knowing what defines uniquely the discipline of rhetoric in modernity (and postmodernity), comprising a recognizable set of concepts and questions, as well as likely to be associated with particular figures, has been a contentious issue. New rhetorics are defined less by schools or theorists unique to the field, and more by a critical approach to the past, such as the one proposed by Blair, who argues that a theoretical vocabulary changes meaning and significance over time but believes that we can to identify coherent conceptual trajectories, focusing on the explanatory value of a pedigree concept in response to culturally situated problems. Similarly, Gross offers a conception of the new rhetorics that sees theorists from other fields as potential participants in an intellectual conversation centered on "a set of problems, initiated by an exemplar, and subsequently addressed, directly and indirectly, by various thinkers" (2005, 42; → Rhetorical Criticism).

This opening of new rhetorics to other disciplines, and the simultaneous loosening of ties to a particular tradition, has led to a proliferation of *novel research endeavours*, among them, some well established already, such as feminist rhetoric and composition studies, or more recent ones, such as environmental rhetoric and rhetoric of science. The proponents of these agendas depart in significant ways from a traditional understanding of rhetoric: they focus on writing and not oratory (composition), insist on bringing to the fore the discourse of previously marginal or delegitimized rhetors, and disavow any distinction that would relegate certain discursive genres outside the purview of persuasion.

At the same time, this scholarship draws not only on Aristotle or the Sophists, but also – if not even more so – on theories from fields like philosophy, sociology, psychology, or anthropology. Such new rhetorics represent an attempt, successful by many accounts, to keep up with a broader trend that favors interdisciplinarity as a source of intellectual richness.

See also: ▶ RHETORIC, GREEK ▶ RHETORIC, ROMAN ▶ RHETORIC AND DIALECTIC ▶ RHETORICAL CRITICISM ▶ RHETORICAL STUDIES

REFERENCES AND SUGGESTED READINGS

Blair, C. (1992). Contested histories of rhetoric: The politics of preservation, progress, and change. *Quarterly Journal of Speech*, 78, 403–428.
Gross, A. G. (2005). The rhetorical tradition. In R. Graff, A. Walzer, & J. Atwill (eds.), *The viability of the rhetorical tradition*. Albany, NY: SUNY Press, pp. 31–45.
Perelman, C. & Olbrechts-Tyteca, L. (1958). *Traité de l'argumentation: La nouvelle rhétorique* [Treatise on argumentation: the new rhetoric]. Paris: Presses Universitaires de France.
Weaver, R. M. (1994). The cultural role of rhetoric. In T. Enos & S. C. Brown (eds.), *Professing the new rhetorics: A sourcebook*. Englewood Cliffs, NJ: Prentice Hall, pp. 75–89.

Risk Communication

GEORG RUHRMANN
University of Jena

Risk communication can be defined as a process that increases the selectivity of the → perception and communication of decision consequences. It is used by a variety of professionals, including → public relations involved in purposive communications in government and the private sector (→ Strategic Communication). These consequences experienced by the decision-maker often are based on calculated uncertainty under conditions of incomplete information (Luhmann 2005).

Risk communication is contingent upon the actual *issue that is assessed and perceived as being risky* (Althaus 2005). A 'risk' (R) is the product of the probability (P) of damage and the seriousness of this damage (S), that is $R = P \times S$. The → audience may pay attention to the → news, may understand it, and may accept it → Selective Exposure; Selective Perception and Selective Retention). Risk perception is influenced considerably by attitudes about science, technology, and culture (→ Risk Perceptions).

Conflicts can be seen as a cause and a consequence of risk communication (→ Social Conflict and Communication). On a *factual level*, arguments about the accuracy of statements and facts are relevant. On the *social level*, conflicts become apparent when 'winners' and 'losers' are identified and the actions and decisions of both groups become based on this construct.

More research is called for in some areas. The basic conditions under which journalists and editors work still need to be analyzed in detail (→ Journalists' Role Perception). Adequate methods are necessary to measure cognitive *and* affective reception modalities of the audience (→ Audience Research). Such analyses are most successful if they employ multi-methods.

See also: ▶ AUDIENCE ▶ AUDIENCE RESEARCH ▶ CRISIS COMMUNICATION ▶ ETHICS IN JOURNALISM ▶ HEALTH COMMUNICATION ▶ JOURNALISTS' ROLE PERCEPTION ▶ MARKETING ▶ NEWS ▶ PERCEPTION ▶ PUBLIC RELATIONS ▶ RISK PERCEPTIONS ▶ SELECTIVE EXPOSURE ▶ SELECTIVE PERCEPTION AND SELECTIVE RETENTION ▶ SOCIAL CONFLICT AND COMMUNICATION ▶ STRATEGIC COMMUNICATION

REFERENCES AND SUGGESTED READINGS

Althaus, C. (2005). A disciplinary perspective on the epistemological status of risk. *Risk Analysis*, 27, 567–588.
Luhmann, N. (2005). *Risk: A sociological theory*. Piscataway, NJ: Aldine/Transaction.
Lundgren, R. A. & A. H. McMakin (2013). *Risk communication. A handbook for communicating environmental, safety, and health risks*. New York: John Wiley.

Risk Perceptions

ISAAC M. LIPKUS
Duke University School of Nursing

One definition of → risk communication is "communication with individuals ... that addresses knowledge, perceptions, attitudes, and behavior related to risk" (Edwards & Bastian 2001, 147). We often hear about the dangers of poor lifestyle habits (e.g., smoking, drinking, not exercising, failure to vaccinate or screen for cancer) or how to engage in preventive health behaviors (e.g., taking aspirin to prevent heart disease; → Health Communication). The basic idea behind these messages is that increasing a person's perceived risk will motivate behavior change to prevent or diminish the threat. A comprehensive understanding of risk entails that patients/public know the antecedents (e.g., risk factors), likelihoods (probabilities), and consequences and preventive actions (pros and cons) necessary to control/avert harm. Not all communications will review each of these components. Rather, risk communication is focused usually on conveying probabilistic information, often numerically.

Numbers (e.g., percentages, frequencies) are used to *convey risk magnitudes* because of their appealing qualities. For example, they: (1) are precise; (2) convey an aura of 'scientific credibility'; (3) can be converted from one metric to another (e.g., 10 percent = 1 out of 10); (4) can be verified for accuracy; (5) can be computed using algorithms (e.g., Gail Score for breast cancer; Windschitl & Wells 1996); and (6) are appreciated due to people's mathematical training in school and/or occupation. A marker of understanding risk is whether the public or patients reflect back a numerical probability estimate. Yet, after receipt of a numerical risk, many provide a risk estimate that deviates from that received (e.g., Braithwaite et al. 2004).

The following are the most frequent *reasons for such deviations*: *Format of information*: individuals may receive their estimate in a poorly understood format. Wide variability in use of formats and a tendency to convey too much information may cause confusion. Of import, no single format is best in all situations. *Low message engagement*: individuals may not fully engage with the information for various reasons (e.g., relying on experts; poor math skills, topic not viewed as relevant). *Biased processing*: individuals may not believe or distort the risk magnitude to reduce threat or interpret it favorably (e.g., optimistic bias; Klein & Weinstein 1997). *Incorporated behavior change*: individuals have taken into account future actions in their estimate, thus diminishing or increasing the perceived risk. *Mood states*: positive and negative moods can affect processing of (risk) information (Slovic et al. 2005). *Use of heuristics*: individuals use mental shortcuts (i.e., heuristics) to make risk judgments. They may feel that they resemble the person at higher/lower risk (i.e., representative heuristic), recall instances that make the event less/more likely (i.e., availability heuristic), or be influenced by numbers they encountered (i.e., anchoring; → Elaboration Likelihood Model). *Assessments of risks*: assessment (e.g., numerical vs. verbal scales), may not be valid and reliable (Windschitl & Wells 1996).

How do we *judge risk communication as effective*? There exist very few guidelines on this issue (Weinstein & Sandman 1993). Below are ways efficacy of risk communication might be judged. *Engagement in recommended behavior(s)*: a risk communication leads to the recommended behavior. *Paying attention to the message*: risk messages are attended to (e.g., information recalled, use, and dissemination to others). *Acquisition of factual knowledge*: communication results in greater understanding of the phenomenon (e.g., knowing the risk factors, what to do, knowing how to balance the pros and cons of action. *Judging the direction of risk magnitude*: an individual judges the risk as objectively higher or lower as intended by the source. *Conflict/trust*: presentation of risk results in greater trust/less conflict. *Evocation of extreme negative/positive affect*: communication does not result in undue anxiety, stress, anger, or unexpectedly high levels of positive affect in light of high probabilistic negative outcome(s).

In addition to specifying the goal(s) of the communication, accessibility and channel of dissemination, understanding the target audience (e.g., needs, values, prior experiences with health issue), context (e.g., socio-political environment), and resources (e.g., staffing, costs), *attention should be given* to the following questions: (1) What dimensions of a comprehensive understanding of risk will be covered? (2) Does one want to communicate information numerically, verbally, and/or graphically? (3) Will the audience bias/distort the processing of the messages (e.g., give selective attention to information (→ Selective Perception and Selective Retention), react optimistically or pessimistically, superficially, with counterarguments)? If so, one has to examine ways to curb the potential effects of biases (e.g., increase self-efficacy). (4) How will one judge whether the communication was effective (e.g, actions taken, better informed decisions)? In sum, effective risk communication involves the consideration of a multitude of factors, some of which have been highlighted here.

See also: ▶ ELABORATION LIKELIHOOD MODEL ▶ HEALTH COMMUNICATION ▶ RISK COMMUNICATION ▶ SELECTIVE PERCEPTION AND SELECTIVE RETENTION ▶ STRATEGIC COMMUNICATION

REFERENCES AND SUGGESTED READINGS

Braithwaite, D., Emery, J., Walter, F., Prevost, A. T., & Sutton, S. (2004). Psychological impact of genetic counseling for familial cancer: A systematic review and meta-analysis. *Journal of the National Cancer Institute*, 96, 122–133.
Edwards, A. & Bastian, H. (2001). Risk communication: Making evidence part of patient choices. In A. Edwards & G. Elwyn (eds.), *Evidence-based patient choice: Inevitable or impossible?* Oxford: Oxford University Press, pp. 144–160.
Klein, W. M. & Weinstein, N. D. (1997). Social comparison and unrealistic optimism about personal risk. In B. P. Buunk & F. Gibbons (eds.), *Health, coping, and well-being: Perspectives from social comparison theory*. Mahwah, NJ: Lawrence Erlbaum, pp. 25–61.
Slovic, P., Peters, E., Finucane, M. L., & MacGregor, D. G. (2005). Affect, risk, and decision making. *Health Psychology*, 24(4, suppl.), S35–S40.
Windschitl, P. D. & Wells, G. I. (1996). Measuring psychological uncertainty: Verbal versus numerical methods. *Journal of Experimental Psychology, Applied*, 2, 343–364.
Weinstein, N. D. & Sandman, P. M. (1993). Some criteria for evaluating risk messages. *Risk Analysis*, 13, 103–114.
Witte, K., Meyer, G., & Martell, D. P. (2001). *Effective health risk messages: Step-by-step guide*. Thousand Oaks, CA: Sage.

Russia: Media System

ELENA VARTANOVA
Lomonosov Moscow State University

The Russian Federation covers an area of 17.1 million square kilometers, has a population of 143.5 million, and borders 16 countries in Europe and Asia. The official language is Russian, but more than 100 languages are spoken. The economic situation remains uneven despite the country's rich natural resources.

The *development of the Russian media* has been traditionally controlled by the political elite. Censorship in the eighteenth and nineteenth centuries hindered the progress of the press. Until the reforms of 1865, literary magazines dominated, and private newspapers operated only in St-Petersburg and Moscow. In 1880 the number of newspapers outnumbered that of magazines. After the revolution in 1905, political parties and their newspapers began to operate legally, although formal censorship still existed. Press freedom (→ Freedom of the Press, Concept of) was legally introduced in April 1917, in the course of the bourgeois revolution.

After the socialist revolution (1917) the media were used to promote the dominant communist ideology and social unanimity (→ Propaganda). The Soviet media were organized in a pyramidical hierarchy, which subordinated all media to Moscow and was controlled by the Communist Party to safeguard political accuracy. Changes began to be made after Mikhail Gorbachev came to power in 1985. Although it resulted in revolutionary changes, glasnost was a variation of the late Soviet media policy with a clear instrumental character. The dichotomy between etatism and the market-driven economy became the crucial characteristic of the Russian media system (Nordenstreng et al. 2002).

The Russian media are *regulated* by the Russian Law on Mass Media (1991), which guaranteed the inadmissibility of censorship and → freedom of information. After this several attempts were made to introduce limiting amendments (e.g., restrictions on violence and pornography on television), but the Law has undergone no significant changes. Self-regulation exists in the form of the Professional Code of the Union of Journalists and codes of professional associations. In 2005, the Public Collegium for Press Complaints was established by the Russian Union of Journalists.

Newspapers have lost their central position in the national media system, but play an important role regionally and locally. The most widely distributed dailies are *Komsomolskaya Pravda* (circulation 655,000), *Rossijskaya Gazeta* (166,675), and *Sport-Express* (650,000). The press market is divided between quality dailies, mostly business-oriented, and popular newspapers that follow the trends of tabloidization. Among *popular magazines* the publications most in demand are illustrated TV guides.

Key players in the *radio market* are 31 Moscow-based commercial radio networks with affiliations all over Russia, but the national radio landscape is shaped by the two state-owned stations – Radio Rossiyi and Mayak, received by the majority of Russians. The most popular media is *television* (91 percent of Russians watch it daily). The national TV market comprises 20 broadcasters, with the first 'Big Three' channels (public-private Pervyi kanal, the state channel Rossiya 1, and the commercial channel NTV) available to almost everyone. Russian television is financed primarily by advertising and sponsorship, but its ownership and programming is a mixture of two models: state-owned and commercial. The state retains an important role in broadcasting through its operation of VGTRK (comprising 5 national TV and 2 radio channels, 80 regional television companies, and 100 transmission centers). Although the leading private channels are financially independent from the state, they provide few program alternatives to state-controlled channels and follow commercial programming strategies based on entertainment.

The Internet began to develop rapidly after 1993. In 2012, the average daily number of Russian Internet users stood close to 52.2 million (about 45 percent of the adult population). Its progress is steadily decreasing the inequality of geographical regions. The Internet in Russia has become the most open medium closely corresponding to the concept of the public sphere, regardless of some recent attempts by Russian legislators to introduce restrictions in this area.

The Russian media have a contradictory nature which has been shaped by many factors: globalization (→ Globalization of the Media), the introduction of market relations (→ Markets of the Media), digitalization, nationally determined political culture (→ Political Communication Systems), and professional traditions of Russian/Soviet journalism. There still exists a strong belief in the crucial regulatory role of the state shared by players on the media scene. The introduction of advertising made the Russian media openly commercial, minimizing ideas of social responsibility and public service obligations of media companies (Vartanova 2012). In addition, the Russian media are affected by conflicting multiethnic, multiconfessional, and multicultural interests, where contemporary lifestyle values confront paternalistic traditions. Their complexity is also reinforced by the lack of commonly shared professional values and the dangers that still exist for journalists.

See also: ▶ FREEDOM OF INFORMATION ▶ FREEDOM OF THE PRESS, CONCEPT OF ▶ GLOBALIZATION OF THE MEDIA ▶ MARKETS OF THE MEDIA ▶ POLITICAL COMMUNICATION SYSTEMS ▶ PROPAGANDA

REFERENCES AND SUGGESTED READINGS

Nordenstreng, K., Vartanova, E., & Zassoursky, Y. (eds.) (2002). *Russian media challenge*, 2nd edn. Helsinki: Kikimora.

Vartanova, E. (2012). The Russian media model in the context of post-soviet dynamics. In D. C. Hallin & P. Mancini (eds.), *Comparing media systems beyond the western world*. Cambridge: Cambridge University Press, 119–142.

Sampling, Random

ANDREW F. HAYES
Ohio State University

Researchers are usually interested in making some kind of an inference from the data obtained from the sample – a 'generalization' of some sort. However, practical considerations typically require the researcher to limit his or her data collection to a sample drawn from a larger population of interest. The ability to make a population inference is going to depend in large part on how the sample was obtained, for the method chosen influences how similar the sample is to the population on all dimensions, characteristics, or features that are likely to influence or be related to the measurement of the variables in the study. When population inference is the goal the researcher is well advised to employ some kind of random sampling method.

Random sampling (also called 'probability' or 'probabilistic' sampling) requires that the process through which members of the population end up in the sample be determined by chance. Furthermore, for each member of the population, it must be possible to derive the probability of inclusion in the sample (even if you never actually calculate that probability). Random sampling is extremely important when the goal of the research is population inference, for it is the random sampling process that will, over the long haul, produce a sample that represents the population. Although it is possible that, just by chance, a specific sample will be unrepresentative of the population as a whole on one or more relevant dimensions, random sampling ensures that no conscious or unconscious biases will influence who ends up included in the sample.

The most basic form of random sampling is *simple random sampling*. Here, every unit of the population must have an equal probability of being included in the sample. In order to conduct a simple random sample, the researcher must have some means of identifying who (→ survey) or what (→ Content Analysis, Quantitative) is in the population in order to implement a method for making sure that each member has an equal chance of being included. Thus, simple random sampling requires that the investigator have some kind of list of the population prior to sampling – the 'sampling frame.' However, for many populations that communication researchers would be interested in sampling from, such lists do not exist.

There are reasons not to use simple random sampling even when it is possible. When conducting a *stratified random sample*, the population is first split into groups (strata) that are homogeneous on the stratification variable. Then a simple random sample of each stratum is taken. The sample will contain as many members of population in each stratum as you desire, with that number being a function of whether the stratified sampling is done proportionally or non-proportionally.

A related method easily confused with stratified sampling is *cluster sampling*. To conduct a cluster sample, it must be possible for members of the population to be classified into groups (clusters) in some fashion. When you cluster sample, all you need to have available is the universe of clusters. You randomly sample clusters from the universe of clusters, and for those clusters that are randomly selected, you include each and every cluster member in the sample.

The penetration of the telephone into most households has made sampling of people much easier than in the past. By *randomly dialing telephone numbers*, it is possible to collect random samples of large populations of people who are geographically dispersed. This approach does not require an enumeration of the members of the population in advance of sampling because it relies on the assumption that most people are attached to at least one phone number.

In practice, random sampling plans are often *multistage, mixing sampling methods* of different types that are conducted at different stages during the sampling process. For example, a researcher who wanted to collect data by doing face-to-face interviews of a random sample of urban city dwellers of an entire country would find it very difficult to collect a simple random or stratified sample of that population. Even if it were possible to enumerate the population, it might be cost-prohibitive to travel to the residences of, say, 1,000 different people dispersed across an entire country.

It is important to acknowledge that even if the selection of members of the population for inclusion in a sample is governed by a random process, nonrandom processes can adulterate random samples. For instance, an investigator might select a sample of people randomly from a population of interest, but certain people who are approached for inclusion in the study are likely to choose not to participate. The process that drives that choice may not be a random one ('nonresponse bias').

See also: ▶ CONTENT ANALYSIS, QUANTITATIVE ▶ EXPERIMENT, LABORATORY ▶ INTERVIEW ▶ PUBLIC OPINION POLLING ▶ SURVEY

REFERENCES AND SUGGESTED READINGS

Frick, R. W. (1998). Interpreting statistical testing: Process and propensity, not population and random sampling. *Behavior Research Methods, Instruments, and Computers*, 30, 527–535.

Hayes, A. F. (2005). *Statistical methods for communication science*. Mahwah, NJ: Lawrence Erlbaum.

Lacy, S., Riffe, D., Stoddard, S., Martin, H., & Chang, K.-K. (2001). Sample size for newspaper content analysis multi-year studies. *Journalism and Mass Communication Quarterly*, 78, 836–845.

Satellite Communication, Global

HEATHER E. HUDSON
University of Alaska Anchorage

In a 1945 article in Wireless World, Arthur C. Clarke described a system of "extraterrestrial relays" or repeaters in space. He noted that three such repeaters located 36,000 km above the equator, 120 degrees apart would cover the entire globe. Only 12 years later, the Soviets launched Sputnik, a satellite that simply beeped, but spurred US scientists and engineers to develop more sophisticated satellites for commercial use. In 1965, the first commercial international satellite, known as Early Bird or Intelsat I, was launched to link North America and Europe. Today, there are numerous satellites that provide global, regional, or national coverage. Satellites serve nations including Australia, Brazil, Canada, China, India, Indonesia, Russia, and the US, and regions such as North America, Africa, East Asia, Southeast Asia, and South Asia.

Satellite technology has evolved dramatically since the early 1960s. Early Bird had only 240 telephone circuits, while today's geostationary satellites have 24–72 transponders, each capable of carrying a high-definition TV channel, or multiple television channels, or thousands of telephone calls, text, and data messages. Satellites offer *several advantages*. They can serve rural and remote areas because earth stations can be installed virtually anywhere. Satellite networks are highly reliable; a problem with an earth station affects only that location. Satellite capacity is also flexible; for example, a community can begin with a few voice circuits, and then add more capacity for Internet access and television reception. The cost of communication via satellite is independent of distance. A *disadvantage* of geostationary (GEO) satellites for interactive services (such as telephony) is latency or delay from transmitting to and from the satellite. Low earth orbiting (LEO) satellites have no noticeable delay because they are located only about 1000 km above the earth. At this altitude, numerous satellites in various orbits must be used to provide continuous coverage.

The most common *use of satellites* is for television transmission such as news feeds and major sporting events such as the Olympic Games and the World Cup (→ Satellite Television). Satellites transmit television signals to local television stations for terrestrial rebroadcast or to distribution through cable networks. High-powered GEO systems transmit satellite signals to satellite dishes on houses or apartments. Satellites can also be used for global telephone service. Internet access including broadband can also be provided by satellite, either directly to end users or through satellite gateways.

In developing regions, satellites can help to close the → digital divide by providing access to the Internet and broadband. Very small aperture terminals (VSATs) operating with GEO satellites can be used for interactive voice and data, as well as for broadcast reception. VSATs are also used for telephony and Internet access in Alaska and the Australian Outback. Banks in remote areas of Brazil are linked via VSATs; microfinance offices in African villages linked via satellite allow people to transfer or withdraw funds. Satellites can also be used for telemedicine and distance education. In Alaska, village health aides communicate daily via satellite with physicians at the regional hospitals (→Health Communication). The University of the South Pacific uses a satellite-based network to provide tutorials to correspondence students scattered in 12 island nations of the South Pacific from its main campus in Fiji. The University of the West Indies links its campuses in Jamaica, Barbados, and Trinidad with extension centers throughout the Caribbean (→ Educational Communication; Educational Media; Educational Media Content). The Inuit Broadcasting Corporation (IBC) in the Canadian Arctic was the first indigenous media project in the world to broadcast by satellite.

Satellite communications have had dramatic *impacts* in ending isolation and creating a truly global village. But will satellites survive, as companies install more optical fiber, and terrestrial wireless networks link computers and mobile phones? Satellites will still have roles to play, particularly for broadcasting and in developing regions. Satellites will remain an important means of transmitting video and between continents. They will also serve as a backup for submarine cables if cables are cut or circuits are overloaded. In the developing world, satellites will deliver television and radio signals and provide broadband Internet access.

See also: ▶ DIGITAL DIVIDE ▶ EDUCATIONAL COMMUNICATION ▶ EDUCATIONAL MEDIA ▶ EDUCATIONAL MEDIA CONTENT ▶ HEALTH COMMUNICATION ▶ MOBILITY, TECHNOLOGY FOR ▶ SATELLITE TELEVISION

REFERENCES AND SUGGESTED READINGS

Clarke, A. C. (1945). Extra-terrestrial relays: Can rocket stations give world-wide radio coverage? *Wireless World*, 51, 305–308.

Elbert, B. R. (2006). *Introduction to satellite communication*. Norwood, MA: Artech.

Hudson, H. E. (ed.) (1985). *New directions in satellite communications: Challenges for north and south*. Norwood, MA: Artech.

Hudson, H. E. (1990). *Communication satellites: Their development and impact*. New York: Free Press.

Hudson, H. E. (2006). *From rural village to global village: Telecommunications for development in the information age*. Mahwah, NJ: Lawrence Erlbaum.

Pelton, J. N., Oslund, R. J., & Marshall, P. (eds.) (2006). *Communications satellites: Global change agents*. Mahwah, NJ: Lawrence Erlbaum.

Pelton, J. (2011). *Satellite communications*. Berlin: Springer.

Satellite Communication, Regulation of

DONG HEE SHIN
Sungkyunkwan University

In the past, national satellite regulations in most countries were dictated by their domestic communication policies. National satellite regulations focused on who could provide services and in what markets. Since the 1990s, governments have liberalized satellite communication regulation, opening up the market to new players and promoting universal services. Such governmental liberalization of satellite regulation has two goals.

The blanket licensing policy, which was proposed by the US → Federal Communications Commission (FCC) in the 1990s, facilitates licensing of the maximum number of systems, with minimal interference. This regulation has streamlined licensing procedures and provided a wide variety of business opportunities for the telecommunications industry. The open skies policy provides licensees maximum flexibility in operating their systems to meet market demands with minimal regulation. In the past, governments developed policies to protect their own satellite systems. These '*closed skies*' policies required service-providers to use only locally owned satellites when providing satellite services. National regulators realized that the massive demand for data, voice, video, and other convergence services is best addressed by permitting open access to all satellite resources.

The changes in international satellite communications have been driven by competitive global markets and technological capabilities (→ Globalization of the Media). The major goal of the two largest international satellite organizations – Intelsat and Inmarsat – has been to eliminate unnecessary regulatory barriers that tend to inhibit the use of satellite services. Intelsat and Inmarsat have consistently applied competition as a policy to increase efficiency in the global market. As the key objective of communication reform is increased efficiency, competition and cooperation are two tools available to policymakers to achieve this goal.

Meanwhile, a series of international efforts have been launched to improve satellite regulation in *developing countries* (→ Communication Technology and Development; Television for Development).

Despite several open border initiatives by European and American countries, the Asia Pacific nations show little concrete effort to harmonize the use of spectrum and licensing policies and regulations. In Korea and Japan, for example, satellite communications have been hindered because of separate licensing (or sometimes duplicate licensing) requirements for satellite service-providers, space segment operators, end-users, and radio spectrum. Many regulations in these countries focus mainly on technical issues, such as technical coordination and avoidance of system interference, and few regulations focus on international satellite interoperability or interconnection (→ Communication Law and Policy: Asia). In Africa and Latin America, satellite communication regulations entail a multiplicity of authorities and application forms. Besides, lack of transparency, requirement for bilateral and interconnection agreements, and security and trade issues remain challenges to satellite policy and regulations (→ Communication Law and Policy: Africa; Communication Law and Policy: South America).

With the proliferation of satellite communications, *content regulation* has emerged as a major concern. Internationally, the degree of content regulation varies from country to country; however, the majority of industrialized nations regulate obscene and/or objectionable content. In Europe, indecency regulations are now extended to satellite communications, which did not previously have as many restrictions. Interestingly, the content regulation of satellite broadcasting in Europe is related to the structural questions of how much market share satellite communications have, how much of a threat the satellite industry is to broadcasters, and what impact the satellite industry will have on the media market.

In the matter of 'satellite spillover' (when the signal falls outside the beam pattern's defined border of coverage) the world is dividing into two opposing camps. The US and the EU nations, which support free flow of information, base their argument on the Universal Declaration of Human Rights, the United Nations Charter, customary law, and the International Telecommunication Convention (→ United Nations, Communication Policies of; Communication Law and Policy: Europe; Communication Law and Policy: North America; European Union: Communication Law). Less liberal countries (mostly in Asia,

Africa, and Latin America) support national sovereignty and turn to customary law, the United Nations Charter and UN Resolution 110, and Resolution 37/92. To protect their interests, these countries prefer strict regulation of content and sanctions for nonconforming communications. The free-speech countries like the US and the UK view this state intervention as little more than government-sponsored censorship.

See also: ▶ CABLE TELEVISION ▶ CENSORSHIP ▶ COMMUNICATION AND LAW ▶ COMMUNICATION LAW AND POLICY: AFRICA ▶ COMMUNICATION LAW AND POLICY: ASIA ▶ COMMUNICATION LAW AND POLICY: EUROPE ▶ COMMUNICATION LAW AND POLICY: NORTH AMERICA ▶ COMMUNICATION LAW AND POLICY: SOUTH AMERICA ▶ COMMUNICATION TECHNOLOGY AND DEVELOPMENT ▶ COPYRIGHT ▶ EUROPEAN UNION: COMMUNICATION LAW ▶ FEDERAL COMMUNICATIONS COMMISSION (FCC) ▶ FREEDOM OF THE PRESS, CONCEPT OF ▶ GLOBALIZATION OF THE MEDIA ▶ SATELLITE COMMUNICATION, GLOBAL ▶ SATELLITE TELEVISION ▶ TELEVISION FOR DEVELOPMENT ▶ UNITED NATIONS, COMMUNICATION POLICIES OF

REFERENCES AND SUGGESTED READINGS

Frieden, R. M. (2000). Satellite technology and regulation. In K. Terplan (ed.), *The telecommunications handbook*. Boca Raton, FL: CRC Press.

Hachten, W. & Scotton, J. (2007). *The world news prism: Global information in a satellite age*, 7th edn. Oxford: Blackwell.

Nuttall, C. (2005). Defining international satellite communications as weapons of mass destruction: The first step in a compromise between national sovereignty and the free flow of ideas. *Houston Journal of International Law*, 27, 389.

Shin, D. (2011). A policy analysis of Korean smart grid project. *International Journal of Mobile Communications*, 9(4), 383–400.

Satellite Television

STYLIANOS PAPATHANASSOPOULOS

National and Kapodistrian University of Athens

In 1945, Arthur C. Clarke pointed out that an orbiting satellite at an altitude of 22,000 miles would revolve around the earth with the same period as the earth rotates on its axis, thereby remaining above a fixed point on the earth's surface, and so could be used as a transmitting TV station. Since then there have been marvelous developments and there are many different uses for satellite technology (→ Satellite Communication, Global). In television, satellite is the easiest way to transmit a large number of services and thus a wide range of choices across a wide region, thereby overcoming the need for the complex infrastructure of transmitters that a terrestrial network needs to broadcast its signals throughout a country.

By and large, the *technological principles* of satellite television offer instant and almost total coverage within its footprint, giving it an advantage over both terrestrial and cable television. A coded ('scrambled') signal carrying the television programs is beamed from an earth station via a large dish (9 to 12 meters in diameter) up to the satellite, where it is amplified and retransmitted toward the earth to individual consumers. At the earth reception level, satellite television requires the installation of a dish and a 'set-box' to decode the incoming signal.

Satellite television is affected by the *convergence and digitalization* of the media communication technologies since it can be connected by various types of new television services such as Internet Protocol Television (IPTV) as well as to provide access to basic broadband around the world (Informa Telecoms & Media 2012). According to the Satellite Industry Association (2012), overall worldwide satellite industry revenue growth was 5 percent in 2011, equaling the 5 percent growth rate in 2010. More precisely, satellite services revenues grew by 6 percent, led by a steady increase in Direct-to-Home Television (DTH) subscribers, particularly in emerging markets (Satellite Industry Association 2012).

See also: ▶ COMMUNICATION TECHNOLOGY STANDARDS ▶ SATELLITE COMMUNICATION, GLOBAL ▶ SATELLITE COMMUNICATION, REGULATION OF ▶ TECHNOLOGY AND COMMUNICATION

REFERENCES AND SUGGESTED READINGS

Informa Telecoms & Media (2012). *The future of TV: Strategies for becoming connected, social and in the cloud*. London: Informa Telecoms & Media.

Papathanassopoulos, S. (2002). *European television in the digital age: Trends, realities and issues*. Cambridge: Polity.

Satellite Industry Association (2012). *State of the satellite industry report. Futron analysis; All data current as of May 2012.* Washington, DC: Futron Corporation. At www.futron.com/upload/wysiwyg/Resources/Reports/SSIR_2012.pdf, accessed August 18, 2014.

Schemas

DAGMAR C. UNZ
University of Applied Sciences Würzburg-Schweinfurt

Our mental architecture is shaped in a way that helps us to deal with our complex environment. Since much of our everyday behavior and many experiences are repetitive and routine, our knowledge of the world can be organized in a highly structured way. Schemas are networks of interconnected concepts that organize past experiences in long-term → memory. By representing general knowledge about concepts, objects, events, etc. in a certain area of reality, schemas give a framework to interpret current experiences (→ Information Processing).

Schemas consist of *different components*, including specification about the relationships among the components and slots for all components that can assume different values, as well as default values. Normally, new information is processed according to how it fits into existing schemas, but schemas may also be reorganized when new information makes it necessary to restructure the concept. Schemas are thought to have an activation level that spreads among related schemas. The current level of activation influences how easily a schema comes to mind (accessibility). The more a schema is used, the higher its level of activation.

The *function of schemas* is to simplify the world around us. They reduce the need to remember huge amounts of information and influence perception, memory, and recall. In most everyday situations information processing can be done without effort, people can quickly organize new perceptions into existing schemas, predict new situations, and act effectively. But schemas may bias the encoding of information (→ Encoding–Decoding). Information that does not fit into existing schemas may not be comprehended and remembered, or may not be comprehended correctly and may be re-interpreted so that it makes sense. Prejudices are typical schema-based errors. Schema theory stresses the role that culture and experience play in processing information.

Schema theory has numerous *implications* for designing communication processes. Meaningful titles or visuals in texts, the use of familiar scenarios or examples, the use of analogies, or the use of multiple perspectives are among those tools that help to make connections between existing schemas and new information. 'Media schemas' may substantially influence the acquisition of knowledge from the media and attitudes toward media.

See also: ▶ ENCODING–DECODING ▶ INFORMATION PROCESSING ▶ MEMORY

REFERENCES AND SUGGESTED READINGS

Howard, S. C. (2012). Intercultural (mis)communication. Why would you "out" me in class? *Sexuality & Culture*, 16, 118–133.

Mandler, J. (1984). *Stories, scripts, and scenes: Aspects of schema theory*. Hillsdale, NJ: Lawrence Erlbaum.

Saito, A. (ed.) (2000). *Bartlett, culture, and cognition*. New York: Psychology Press.

Science Journalism

HOLGER WORMER
Dortmund University of Technology

Science journalism deals mainly with results and events in science, technology, and medicine. Its main sources are publications in scientific journals and conference papers, but science reporting may also be prompted by interesting phenomena in daily life or from general → news (such as natural disasters or political debates).

Compared to other forms, science journalism is a relatively new addition to the news (Friedman et al. 1986). It *emerged* especially during the second half of the twentieth century while certain incidents can be identified to influence intensity and the dominant nature of reporting. Whereas the Sputnik shock in 1957 was a trigger for increasing as well as mostly optimistic science reporting, the environmental debates after Rachel Carsons "Silent Spring" and the nuclear accidents at Harrisburg and Chernobyl began to strenghten *critical science journalism* (→ Journalists' Role Perception). Bioethical debates (concerning cloning, genome projects, and stem cells) have underlined the political role of science journalism in society. Debates about risks (climate change, flu epidemics, and the like) and about special technologies (such as nuclear energy, once more after the Fukushima accident) are an essential element of science journalism, too (→ Risk Communication).

Scientists often see science journalism as an educational tool and instrument to improve public acceptance of research. From this perspective, science journalism is *part of the Public Understanding of Science movement* and its successors. Functionally, journalists are seen here as translators and advocates of science. Critics of a 'gee-whiz' reporting claim journalists should resist an assigned function of only popularizing science (Kohring 2005). This modern role of science journalism is similar to political journalism as critical observer and watchdog, also supporting the scientific system in safeguarding its own standards (e.g., in cases of fraud).

In many newly industrialized countries, the growing interest in research and development enhances broader science reporting, whereas, especially in the US and many European countries, science journalism is seen as rather in a crisis (Bauer et al. 2013). One reason (in addition to the general trends in the media) may be also the increased competing efforts of scientific institutions to communicate to a broader audience via internet, blogs and social media (cf. Allan 2011). However, from a normative point of view it does not seem reasonable that a 'direct-to-consumer' science communication could replace critical science journalism.

See also: ▶ JOURNALISTS' ROLE PERCEPTION ▶ NEWS ▶ RISK COMMUNICATION

REFERENCES AND SUGGESTED READINGS

Allan, S. (ed.) (2011). Special issue: Science journalism in a digital age. *Journalism*, 12(7), 771–919.
Bauer, M. W., Howard, S., Romo Ramos, Y. J., Massarani, L., & Amorim, L. (2013). *Global science journalism report: Working conditions and practices, professional ethos and future expectations*. Science and Development Network, London. At www.scidev.net/global/evaluation/learning-series/global-science-journalism-report.html, accessed August 18, 2014.
Friedman, S., Dunwoody, S., & Rogers, C. L. (1986). *Scientists and journalists: Reporting science as news*. New York: Free Press.

Scripts

KATHY KELLERMANN
ComCon Kathy Kellermann Communication Consulting

TAE-SEOP LIM
University of Wisconsin–Milwaukee

Understanding and production of messages and social behaviors are based on communicators' prior knowledge, which is organized and structured by → schemas. Scripts are event schemas, that is, they structure common and ritualized activities that involve a sequence of actions. A script is a sequential list of characteristic actions of events or activities, such as eating at a restaurant or attending a birthday party. Scripts guide one's actions, expectations, and understandings during the enactment of the script-based activities.

Schank and Abelson (1977) introduced the concept, which consists of the name of the script, roles, props, entry conditions, results, and scenes. The concept generated many *predictions* related to the structure, nature, and use of → memory. The 'typicality effect' occurs when people encounter the information that fits the activated script well. The 'atypicality effect' takes place when people encounter information that does not fit the script. Comparing the two types of effects, the typicality effect lasts longer: while recognition and recall memory is initially better for atypical than typical actions, the rate of forgetting is greater for the tagged atypical actions than for tagged typical actions. Schank (1982) developed a more flexible theory, called 'dynamic memory theory,' and a less rigid concept, called a 'memory organization packet' or MOP.

Schank's (1982) reformulated theory differentiated *four levels of memory*: (1) event memory (EM), (2) generalized event memory (GEM), (3)

situational memory (SM), and (4) intentional memory (IM). EM contains specific remembrances of particular situations. GEM is a collection of events whose common features have been abstracted. SM contains relevant contexts, and the rules and standard experiences associated with a given situation in general. While information about dentists resides in GEM, SM contains more general information like 'going to a health professional's office.' IM, the highest level of memory, includes the rules for getting people to do things for oneself and other plan-like information. A MOP, a memory structure at the level of situational memory, keeps information about how memories are linked in frequently occurring combinations. The basic building blocks of MOPs are scenes, which are groupings of generalized actions with a shared instrumental goal. What a MOP does is to prescribe how scenes are linked together in order to accomplish a higher-order goal. The number of scenes is limited, and any given scene can be used by many different MOPs. For example, the waiting room scene can be organized by most MOPs that seek help from a professional.

A MOP, a *memory structure* at the level of situational memory, keeps information about how memories are linked in frequently occurring combinations. The basic building blocks of MOPs are scenes, which are groupings of generalized actions with a shared instrumental goal. What a MOP does is to prescribe how scenes are linked together in order to accomplish a higher-order goal. The number of scenes is limited, and any given scene can be used by many different MOPs. For example, the waiting room scene can be organized by most MOPs that seek help from a professional.

Scripts have been investigated *in communication research* in two primary ways. First, a group of researchers have examined the role of scripts in social relationships. For instance, Honeycutt et al. (1989) reported that a prototypical relational escalation memory structure contained 13 typical behaviors. Sexual scripts (see La France 2010), informal, initial conversation MOPs, and initial interaction scripts describe other roles of scripts in interpersonal communication. A second use of MOPs in communication research is in the domain of small group communication.

See also: ▶ DISCOURSE COMPREHENSION ▶ INFORMATION PROCESSING ▶ INTERACTION ▶ INTERPERSONAL COMMUNICATION ▶ MEMORY ▶ SCHEMAS ▶ STEREOTYPES

REFERENCES AND SUGGESTED READINGS

Honeycutt, J. M., Cantrill, J. G., & Greene, R. W. (1989). Memory structures for relational escalation: A cognitive test of the sequencing of relational actions and stages. *Human Communication Research*, 16, 62–90.

Kellermann, K. & Lim, T. (1990). The conversational MOP III: Timing of scenes in discourse. *Journal of Personality and Social Psychology*, 59, 1163–1179.

La France, B. H. (2010). What verbal and nonverbal communication cues lead to sex? An analysis of the traditional sexual script. *Communication Quarterly*, 58(3), 297–318

Pavitt, C. & Johnson, K. K. (2001). The association between group procedural MOPs and group discussion procedure. *Small Group Research*, 32, 595–624.

Schank, R. C. (1982). *Dynamic memory: A theory of reminding and learning in computers and people.* Cambridge: Cambridge University Press.

Schank, R. C. & Abelson, R. P. (1977). *Scripts, plans, goals, and understanding: An inquiry into human knowledge structures.* Hillsdale, NJ: Lawrence Erlbaum.

Search Engines

ELIZABETH VAN COUVERING
London School of Economics and Political Science

A search engine is a computer program that allows the Internet user to enter a series of keywords, usually called a 'query,' and that responds with a list of results from a database that match the query. Major search engines, such as Google, Yahoo Search, and Bing (previously Microsoft Live Search), provide the most widely used method of finding information on the world wide web. Search engine websites are the most visited in the world. Google is the dominant leader with above 70 percent market share worldwide, around 60 percent in the US and up to around 90 percent in countries like Germany. The second biggest search engine, with 16 percent, is Baidu in China, introduced by the government to control Internet traffic. In 2013 Google worldwide received close to 6 billion searches per day (!), a figure that had doubled in only four years (→ Exposure to the Internet).

There are at least four different *dimensions in research on search engines*. On the dimension of information-retrieval the search engine is studied as a complex programming problem. On the dimension of information literacy, the interactions between search engines and user skills are of paramount concern. Research on online marketing investigates the search engine's effectiveness as a marketing tool. Finally, media law and policy scholars debate regulations relating to search engines.

A search engine has *three core technological elements*: the index, the crawler, and the search algorithm. The index contains references and pointers to the information on the web, much as the word and page numbers in a printed index refer to text in a book. In order to obtain the references for the index, search engines on the web use another computer program, called a 'crawler' or a 'spider,' to automatically browse pages by traversing hyperlinks between and within websites. The search algorithm has the complex task of matching the terms the user types into the search box with the references in the index and displaying them in ranked order. Problems revolve around the *search algorithm* and how to ensure that its results have sufficient precision related to the query.

With the world wide web, *new challenges* have been introduced. Among them are that the web demands search engines on a *scale* never seen before (web search indices contain references to billions of documents), that hundreds of thousands of queries must be processed per second, or that today the web contains many types of non-textual multimedia files, such as audio files, videos, and pictures.

Search engines are valuable sources of customers for *online businesses*. Search engines fund themselves primarily through advertising (→ Advertising, Economics of). Advertising does not appear typically in the main search engine listings, but instead the search engine operates a separate index of advertisements that are returned along with the main results when a user types in a query. These paid-for results are indicated as 'sponsored links' or 'recommendations' on the main search engine results page and are often set off in a separate area, for example in a column on the right-hand side of the page or in a box at the top.

Another element of marketing on search engines is *search-engine optimization* (SEO). In SEO, the marketer tries to achieve a good placement in the main index (rather than purchasing results in the advertising index) by 'optimizing' their web pages so that they match the criteria used by the search engine's ranking algorithm. In addition to legitimate SEO, the value of search engine traffic means that some marketers try to boost their traffic by artificially inflating some indicators. Google has been criticized for displaying search results not according to their fit for the user's needs but as a result of advertising contracts with the respective companies or because of Google's own commercial stakes in the respective business area.

Search engine companies are also increasingly involved in a series of *legal controversies*. A major focus of concern is a debate over censorship and free speech (→ Censorship, History of; Freedom of the Press, Concept of). Search engine owners have been criticized for censoring results in other countries, notably China, in accordance with government wishes. A second issue is user → privacy because search engines routinely collect data on their users, including their queries and usage patterns. A third legal controversy concerns intellectual property rights online (→ Intellectual Property Law) as search engines offer videos or news produced by others. A fourth area of legal discussions is the above mentioned fact that Google favors its own search results (for certain products) over those of specialist competitors. This legal conflict is currently under negotiation between Google and the European Commission.

See also: ▶ ADVERTISING, ECONOMICS OF ▶ CENSORSHIP, HISTORY OF ▶ CONCENTRATION IN MEDIA SYSTEMS ▶ EXPOSURE TO THE INTERNET ▶ FREEDOM OF THE PRESS, CONCEPT OF ▶ INFORMATION LITERACY ▶ INFORMATION SEEKING ▶ INTELLECTUAL PROPERTY LAW ▶ INTERNET LAW AND REGULATION ▶ ONLINE RESEARCH ▶ PRIVACY

REFERENCES AND SUGGESTED READINGS

Berman, R. & Katona, Z. (2013). The role of search engine optimization in search marketing. *Marketing Science*, 32(4), 644–651.

Halavais, A. (2009). *Search engine society*. Cambridge: Polity.

Levy, S. (2011). *In the plex: How Google thinks, works, and shapes our lives*. New York: Simon and Schuster.

Mowshowitz, A. & Kawaguchi, A. (2005). Measuring search engine bias. *Information Processing and Management*, 41(5), 1193–1205.

Scharkow, M. & Vogelgesang, J. (2011). Measuring the public agenda using search engine queries. *International Journal of Public Opinion Research*, 23(1), 104–113.

Segmentation of the Advertising Audience

PATRICK DE PELSMACKER
University of Antwerp and Ghent University

Organizations communicate core messages to different types of audiences (target groups) that they select out of a list of possible audience segments or profiles, defined according to a number of segmentation criteria (→ Audience Segmentation). On the basis of this segmentation, audience profile selection, and positioning decision, organizations will define communication objectives and messages and build a communication plan.

Communication by organizations is targeted at different types of audiences. Marketing communication is all commercially relevant communication directed at customers and potential customers with the intention of selling products in the short or long term (→ Integrated Marketing Communications; Marketing). Corporate communication is all communication by organizations the objective of which is to establish and/or maintain a good corporate identity, corporate image, and reputation, and build good will with various stakeholders or publics (→ Corporate Communication).

Markets can be divided into *geographical segments* such as continents, countries, regions, neighborhoods or cultures (→ Culture: Definitions and Concepts). Consumer needs, wants, and reactions to marketing efforts often differ between these geographical or cultural segments, and therefore may require a different communication approach. *Demographic segmentation* divides the market on the basis of sex, age, income, race, education, and profession. Consumer markets can also be targeted on the basis of *household life-cycle criteria* such as marital and occupational status and the age of children. *Social stratification* is a permanent and ordered division of society based on criteria such as education, profession, income, and status.

Lifestyle measurement is based on the activities, interests, and opinions of consumers (→ Taste Culture). Activities include how people spend their money and time, i.e., work, leisure, product use, shopping behavior, etc. Interests can be in fashion, housing, food, cars, culture, and so on. *Personality traits* are relatively stable characteristics of individuals that guide their specific behavior. For instance, a person can be extravert or introvert, sensation-seeking or not, high or low affect-intense, or have a low or high need for knowledge.

Organizations can divide their consumers with reference to *product- or brand-related aspects*. Consumers can be segmented on the basis of the occasion on which they use a product or brand or on the basis of their usage status: nonuser, potential user, first-time user, regular user, or ex-user. Especially for direct marketing purposes (direct mailing, telemarketing, etc.), customers can also be divided on the basis of their *buying history*, i.e., the recency and frequency of their purchases and the amounts they have spent buying products from the company. Markets can often be segmented on the basis of specific *benefits that consumers prefer* or are looking for.

On the basis of individual and relevant segmentation variables, *segmentation profiles* are defined that are combinations of these criteria. For instance, a segment may be defined as 'all middle-class men between 20 and 30 years old that are heavy users of our product and price-sensitive.' Companies will define several of these profiles and select a number of them as target groups for their marketing communication campaigns.

Organizations do not only sell to individual end consumers. Often, marketing communication is directed at organizations or companies (*business-to-business marketing*). Target segments can be based on the type of organization, organizational characteristics, buying roles of individuals within that organization, and the purchase situation. Corporate communication is aimed at correctly communicating the corporate identity and strategy and at developing and maintaining a good image, reputation, and good will with various stakeholders or publics. Most organizations have multiple *stakeholders*, such as shareholders, employees, labor unions, governments, suppliers, distributors, banks, pressure groups, competitors, media, and so forth. Corporate communication campaigns aimed at these stakeholders use various tools, such as → public relations, corporate advertising, annual reports, press releases, and internal communication tools (e.g., newsletters, presentations, mailings, bulletin boards) to convey the appropriate message to these various publics.

See also: ▶ AUDIENCE SEGMENTATION ▶ CORPORATE COMMUNICATION ▶ CULTURE: DEFINITIONS AND CONCEPTS ▶ INTEGRATED MARKETING COMMUNICATIONS ▶ MARKETING ▶ PUBLIC RELATIONS ▶ TASTE CULTURE

REFERENCES AND SUGGESTED READINGS

Coe, J. M. (2003). *The fundamentals of business-to-business sales and marketing*. New York: McGraw Hill.
De Pelsmacker, P., Geuens, M., & Van den Bergh, J. (2007). *Marketing communications: A European perspective*. Harlow: Financial Times and Prentice Hall.
Dibb, S. & Simkin, L. (2008). *Market segmentation success*. Binghamton, NY: Haworth Press.
Kitchen, P. & De Pelsmacker, P. (2005). *Integrated marketing communication: A primer*. London: Routledge.
McDonald, M. & Dunbar, I. (2004). *Market segmentation: How to do it, how to profit from it*. Oxford: Elsevier Butterworth-Heinemann.
Nelson-Field, K. & Riebe, E. (2011). The impact of media fragmentation on audience targeting: An empirical generalisation approach. *Journal of Marketing Communications*, 17(1), 51–67.

Selective Exposure

JENNINGS BRYANT
University of Alabama

JOHN DAVIES
Brigham Young University

The study of selective exposure seeks to understand how and why people consume particular communication content when faced with a constellation of choices. Broadly defined, selective exposure refers to behaviors that are deliberately performed in an effort to bring communication content within reach of one's sensory apparatus (Zillmann & Bryant 1985; → Exposure to Communication Content).

Cognitive Dissonance

By the conclusion of World War II, → propaganda researchers had long noted that people avoided messages that conflicted with their opinions, and even interpreted those messages differently (→ Propaganda in World War II; Selective Perception and Selective Retention). The idea that media functions to reinforce existing beliefs and conditions is formalized in Festinger's (1957) influential → cognitive dissonance theory. Festinger proposed that selectivity is motivated by dissonance reduction and characterized by avoidance of information inconsistent with one's beliefs and attitudes, and pursuit of messages that are consistent with those cognitions. Field studies generally supported the theory, but laboratory experiments were inconclusive because of methodological shortcomings of early experiments (→ Media Effects, History of).

In recent years, psychologists have introduced *new explanations* for why dissonance occurs, including threats to positive self-image, and personal behavior that is inconsistent with normative standards. Although scholars are still divided on this issue, it is clear that the inclusion of such moderating variables in experimental designs has confirmed the viability of cognitive dissonance theory as an explanation for selective exposure. Indeed, a recent meta-analysis along with current studies that account for the moderating effect of self-esteem, attitude strength, information quantity, and other such variables have revealed relatively strong support for the theory's assumptions.

Communication research in consumer behavior, journalism, and health communication centers on the demonstration of selectivity as a result of dissonance reduction. Communication scholars, however, have generally failed to consider whether individuals in a state of consonance will display selective avoidance. Donsbach (2009) argues that this is an important issue, given that media exposure often occurs under conditions of consonance.

Emotion, Mood, and Selective Exposure

A large body of literature has accumulated that confirms that emotion and mood play an integral role in media choices (→ Mood Management). Much of this research is based on the affect-dependent theory of stimulus arrangement (Zillmann & Bryant 1985). Founded on the premise that individuals are motivated to seek pleasure and avoid pain, this theory recognizes that individuals often use media as a means to achieve this goal even though they may not always be aware of the motivating role of their own moods. Rather, through classical and operant conditioning, individuals learn which types of stimuli are best suited to alleviate or maintain particular moods.

Particularly strong, supportive evidence for the theory originated in studies that investigated correlations between mood shifts associated with pregnancy and menstrual cycles and preferences for certain media content (e.g., Meadowcroft & Zillmann 1987). Experimental and survey research has shown that media may be used to alleviate boredom, stress, apprehension, annoyance, and depression (→ Experiment, Laboratory). Research also supports the prediction that good moods can be maintained or enhanced by consumption of media messages that are minimally involving, have a high behavioral affinity to positive mood, or are highly pleasant (e.g., Knobloch & Zillmann 2002). However, recent scholarship suggests that positive moods result in selection of media that matches, rather than enhances a positive affective state.

Selective exposure theory makes predictions about mood and media preferences based on the combination of *four key variables*: excitatory homeostasis, intervention potential, message-behavioral affinity, and hedonic valence. Although theoretically distinct, overlap exists between these four variables in practice. (1) *Excitatory homeostasis* refers to the human tendency to seek out states of psychological arousal that are neither over- nor under-stimulating (Bryant & Zillmann 1984; → Excitation and Arousal). (2) *Message-behavioral affinity* refers to the degree of similarity between communication content and affective state. (3) The ability of media content to engage cognitive processing resources and disrupt mental rehearsal of thoughts related to specific moods is referred to as its '*intervention potential*' (or 'absorption potential/capacity'). (4) *Hedonic valence* refers to the negative or positive quality of a message.

Zillmann (2000) introduced the notions of *spontaneous and telic hedonism* to account for selection of counter-hedonistic media fare. He argued that at times it may be emotionally functional to engage in spontaneous hedonism by selecting media that immediately relieves one of negative feelings. However, individuals may also postpone the immediate gratification of altering their mood state, in favor of loftier goals, or more pressing needs. In such cases media use may be counter-hedonistic in the short run, but conform to theoretical assumptions in the long run.

Seemingly *counter-hedonistic media preferences*, such as viewing a sad film, reflect so-called eudaimonic, or 'truth-seeking,' concerns (e.g., Oliver & Raney 2011). This line of inquiry shows how hedonic and eudaimonic motivations vary according to their interaction with message characteristics, one's stage in the life span, or gender. Recent studies have begun to apply the theory to *new interactive media*, such as the Internet and → video games. Scholars in this area have observed that mood repair through the satisfaction of intrinsic needs is an additional mechanism of mood management (Reinecke et al. 2012).

Informational Utility

The concept of → informational utility refers to situations where information is sought out to reduce uncertainty. Whereas the hedonistic assumptions of mood management are particularly suited for explaining consumption of entertainment media, these assumptions may have less application in cases where media use is motivated by a need or desire for information. Selective exposure to communication that is motivated by informational utility is conceptually distinct from selective exposure behavior designed to reinforce pre-existing beliefs or conditions (as in cognitive dissonance theory).

In recent years, informational utility has been studied in the context of a model developed by Knobloch-Westerwick and colleagues. This model assumes that information has utility to the degree individuals perceive that it represents a threat or opportunity, the likelihood such threats or opportunities will materialize, the immediacy of materialization, and one's perceived self-efficacy to influence them. Tests of this model have produced supportive evidence of selective exposure to online news and political information.

See also: ▶ AFFECTS AND MEDIA EXPOSURE
▶ COGNITIVE DISSONANCE THEORY
▶ EXCITATION AND AROUSAL ▶ EXPERIMENT, LABORATORY ▶ EXPOSURE TO COMMUNICATION CONTENT ▶ EXPOSURE TO THE INTERNET
▶ INFORMATION SEEKING ▶ INFORMATIONAL UTILITY ▶ MEDIA EFFECTS ▶ MEDIA EFFECTS, HISTORY OF ▶ MOOD MANAGEMENT
▶ PROPAGANDA ▶ PROPAGANDA IN WORLD WAR II ▶ SELECTIVE PERCEPTION AND SELECTIVE RETENTION ▶ SURVEY ▶ UNCERTAINTY AND COMMUNICATION ▶ UNCERTAINTY REDUCTION THEORY ▶ USES AND GRATIFICATIONS

REFERENCES AND SUGGESTED READINGS

Bryant, J. & Zillmann, D. (1984). Using television to alleviate boredom and stress: Selective exposure as a function of induced excitational states. *Journal of Broadcasting*, 28, 1–20.

Donsbach, W. (2009). Cognitive dissonance theory – a roller coaster career. How communication research adapted the theory of cognitive dissonance. In T. Hartmann (ed.), *Media choice: A theoretical and empirical overview*. London: Routledge, pp. 128–149.

Festinger, L. (1957). *A theory of cognitive dissonance*. Evanston, IL: Row and Peterson.

Knobloch, S. & Zillmann, D. (2002). Mood management via the digital jukebox. *Journal of Communication*, 52, 351–366.

Knobloch-Westerwick, S., Carpentier, F. D., Blumhoff, A., & Nickel, N. (2005). Selective exposure effects for positive and negative news: Testing the robustness of the informational utility model. *Journalism & Mass Communication Quarterly*, 82(1), 181–195.

Knobloch-Westerwick, S. & Johnson, B. (2014). Selective exposure for better or worse: Its mediating role for online news' impact on political participation. *Journal of Computer-Mediated Communication*, 19(2), 184–196.

Meadowcroft, J. M. & Zillmann, D. (1987). Women's comedy preferences during the menstrual cycle. *Communication Research*, 14, 204–218.

Oliver, M. B. & Raney, A. A. (2011). Entertainment as pleasurable and meaningful: Identifying hedonic and eudaimonic motivations for entertainment consumption. *Journal of Communication*, 61(5), 984–1004.

Reinecke, L., Tamborini, R., Grizzard, M., Lewis, R., Eden, A., & David Bowman, N. (2012). Characterizing mood management as need satisfaction: The effects of intrinsic needs on selective exposure and mood repair. *Journal of Communication*, 62(3), 437–453.

Zillmann, D. (2000). Mood management in the context of selective exposure theory. In M. E. Roloff (ed.), *Communication yearbook 23*. Thousand Oaks, CA: Sage, pp. 103–123.

Zillmann, D. & Bryant, J. (eds.) (1985). *Selective exposure to communication*. Hillsdale, NJ: Lawrence Erlbaum.

Selective Perception and Selective Retention

L. J. SHRUM
HEC Paris

Perception refers to the process of categorizing and interpreting information that is attended to (→ Perception). *Selective perception* refers to the process of categorizing and interpreting information in a way that favors one category or interpretation over another. Thus, selective perception is generally considered to represent a bias in → information processing. More specifically, information tends to be selectively perceived in ways that are congruent with existing individual needs, goals, values, → attitudes, and beliefs. This process generally occurs automatically, outside the conscious awareness of the perceiver. The process of selective perception can occur at various stages of perception, including the initial recognition and categorization of stimuli, attention to competing stimuli, and the interpretation of these stimuli.

Selective retention (also known as selective memory) is a similar process by which some information is retained and stored in → memory (and is thus available for retrieving) and other information is not (and is thus forgotten). Like selective perception, selective retention is biased in terms of what information gets retained, with information that is more congruent with existing belief structures more likely to be retained in memory (and thus more likely to be recalled at a later time) than information that is less congruent with existing belief structures.

The processes of selective perception and retention can best be *explained* by the concept of construct accessibility. Construct accessibility refers to the extent to which any particular concept can be recalled from memory. Constructs can be very specific (for example, attitudes) or very general (for example, → schemas). When information is processed in the course of everyday experiences, the information is integrated into existing concepts stored in memory. Those concepts that are at the 'top of mind,' are the most likely to be retrieved in everyday experiences, and thus are most likely to be used in interpreting everyday experiences. This bias toward the most accessible constructs in memory for interpreting situations defines the concept of selective perception. Similarly, when interpreting new situations in terms of existing constructs in memory, the information that fits within that accessible construct is integrated into existing memory structures. However, the information that may not fit with that accessible construct (e.g., disconfirming information), is not well integrated into existing memory structures, and thus is not as easily recalled. This exemplifies the notion of selective perception.

There are several class studies in selective perception and retention. Hastorf and Cantril (1954) investigated the perceptions of student spectators at a football game between Princeton and Dartmouth that produced many injuries. The researchers interviewed spectators a week after the game and found that Princeton students thought the Dartmouth team committed many more infractions than did the Dartmouth students, and vice versa. Vallone et al. (1985) conducted a study in which pro-Arab, pro-Israel, and neutral students were shown a videotape of television news coverage of the Beirut massacre in which civilian refugees in Lebanon were killed. The results showed that prior attitudes influenced both the interpretation of and memory for the events, and both pro-Arab and pro-Israeli groups perceived that the coverage was biased against them, with neutral viewers falling in the middle. This effect of differing perceptions of biased media coverage against one's own group has been termed the 'hostile media effect.'

The results of such studies can be interpreted in terms of both selective perception and selective retention. Across the studies the results provide strong evidence that individuals' perceptions are biased toward pre-existing attitudes and beliefs.

See also: ▶ ATTITUDES ▶ COGNITIVE DISSONANCE THEORY ▶ INFORMATION PROCESSING ▶ MEMORY ▶ PERCEPTION ▶ SELECTIVE EXPOSURE

REFERENCES AND SUGGESTED READINGS

Cooper, E. & Jahoda, M. (1947). The evasion of propaganda: How prejudiced people respond to anti-prejudice propaganda. *Journal of Psychology*, 23, 15–25.

Hastorf, A. H. & Cantril, H. (1954). They saw a game: A case study. *Journal of Abnormal and Social Psychology*, 49, 129–134.

Vallone, R. P., Ross, L., & Lepper, M. R. (1985). The hostile media phenomenon: Biased perception and perceptions of media bias coverage of the Beirut massacre. *Journal of Personality and Social Psychology*, 49, 577–585.

Vidmar, N. & Rokeach, M. (1974). Archie Bunker's bigotry: A study in selective perception and exposure. *Journal of Communication*, 24, 36–47.

Zanna, M. P., Klosson, E. C., & Darley, J. M. (1976). How television news viewers deal with facts that contradict their beliefs: A consistency and attribution analysis. *Journal of Applied Social Psychology*, 6, 159–176.

Self-Presentation

SANDI W. SMITH
Michigan State University

JINA H. YOO
University of Missouri–St. Louis

JOSEPH B. WALTHER
Michigan State University

In 1959, Erving Goffman published The Presentation of Self in Everyday Life. The heuristic value of its concepts has been wide-ranging, particularly in the field of communication. The driving force behind self-presentation, accomplished by exchanging verbal and nonverbal messages during ongoing interactions, is to present and gather information that will help ascertain what can be expected in particular social situations, as people present or infer the ostensible character of the self or of others (→ Interpersonal Communication).

The following are some *basic self-presentation concepts*. (1) 'Self-presentation': individuals project an image of themselves and thereby make explicit or implicit claims to be a particular type of person within that situation. This projected image demands that others treat him or her in the way that this type of person has a right to expect. (2) 'Interaction': reciprocal influence individuals have on one another when in face-to-face and mediated communication contexts (→ Mediated Social Interaction; Interaction). (3) 'Performance': activities of a participant in a particular situation that influence other participants' impressions. The sincerity of the performance ranges on a continuum from completely authentic to a dishonest portrayal of self. (4) 'Social role': enactment of rights and duties associated with a particular status when performances are enacted in similar situations or with the same audience on different occasions.(5) 'Defensive practices': strategies and tactics to protect a self-presentation. (6) 'Protective practices': strategies and tactics to protect self-presentations of others, or tact. (7) 'Preventive practices': practices to avoid damaging a self-presentation before a mistake. (8) 'Corrective practices': strategies or tactics to repair self-presentations after they have been questioned. (9) 'Team': a set of individuals who cooperate in a performance. (10) 'Frontstage': the place where the performance is given and decorum is maintained. (11) 'Backstage': a place where the impression fostered by the performance is contradicted as a matter of course. (12) 'Information control': a team or individual's withholding of certain information from the audience that would contradict the definition of the situation they are presenting (13) 'Discrepant roles': unexpected and unapparent relations between feigned role, information possessed, and regions of access. (14) 'Face': the line that a participant takes when presenting the self.

Brown and Levinson's (1987) → *politeness theory* also addresses cooperative performances that preserve self-presentation. It includes 'positive face,' or the need to be connected to and positively regarded by others, and 'negative face,' or the need to be independent and autonomous.

Lim and Bowers (1991) added 'competence face,' or the need to appear capable. Research in interpersonal communication includes 'self-disclosure', the revelation of information that cannot be ascertained by other means that might result in loss of face if known by others. There is also a rich tradition of work on face, politeness, mitigating face threats, and the identity implications of social influence goals in different contexts.

The formal organization was the original context in which Goffman explicated the concept of self-presentation. Organizational communication involving self-presentation includes employment interviews, negotiation, gender diversity, job loss, public relations, and social responsibility (→ Organizational Communication).

Computer-mediated communication (CMC) is one of the most fertile venues for the dynamics of self-presentation and discerning the veracity of others' performances. Communication may take place online with no offline anchors to one's physical or non-conscious characteristics, rendering CMC entirely comprised of cues that are 'given' rather than 'given off.' The most detailed theoretical treatments of self-presentation appear in two of the four elements of the 'hyperpersonal model of CMC' (Walther 1996). (1) Selective self-presentation explains how CMC users employ writing to reveal desirable information about the self in ways that are more intentional and discretionary than face-to-face communication allows (→ Social Media). (2) They exploit characteristics of the channel to rehearse, edit, and rewrite messages, with interaction suspended or retarded, in ways that favor themselves and target their recipients; CMC messages are composed 'backstage.' Goffman's influence is reflected in analyses of self-presentation through personal websites (Miller 1995) and, recently, in online match-making services.

Health communication is more recent focus of scholars in communication. Some work has been done on self-presentation in this context, such as on support groups, and the area is one that should produce substantial future self-presentation research.

See also: ▶ INFORMATION PROCESSING: SELF-CONCEPT ▶ INTERACTION ▶ INTERPERSONAL COMMUNICATION ▶ MEDIATED SOCIAL INTERACTION ▶ ORGANIZATIONAL COMMUNICATION ▶ POLITENESS THEORY ▶ SOCIAL MEDIA

REFERENCES AND SUGGESTED READINGS

Brown, P. & Levinson, S. (1987). *Politeness: Some universals in language use.* Cambridge: Cambridge University Press.

Cupach, W. R. & Metts, S. (1994). *Facework.* Thousand Oaks, CA: Sage.

Goffman, E. (1959). *The presentation of self in everyday life.* Garden City, NY: Doubleday.

Goffman, E. (1967). *Interaction ritual.* New York: Pantheon.

Rosenfeld, P. (2002). *Impression management in organizations.* London: Thomson Learning.

Walther, J. B. (1996). Computer-mediated communication: Impersonal, interpersonal, and hyperpersonal interaction. *Communication Research*, 23, 3–43.

Self-Regulation of the Media

DAMIAN TAMBINI

London School of Economics and Political Science

Media self-regulation is the setting of rules for the media and oversight of compliance with those rules by media organizations or by users. Self-regulation should be distinguished from state or statutory regulation by law or by a statutory regulatory authority. Means of self-regulation include dispute resolution procedures, rating boards, codes of conduct, and at the level of the user, technical measures such as filtering, encryption, and pin numbers that regulate children's and others' behavior.

Self-regulation is often seen as more attractive than state regulation because it has legitimacy with the industry, is more flexible in responding to change, and can offer an alternative to state and political interference with media content. On the other hand, self-regulation is often criticized because it is overly flexible and too close to the industry to offer genuine protection of the public interest. Usually, exclusion from the trade association or self-regulatory scheme is the ultimate sanction. Forms of self-regulation are in some cases linked to statutory schemes. For example, the self-regulatory ratings provided by the Motion Picture Association of America and the British Board of Film Classification are adopted in the statutory framework for video rental or film exhibition. Such hybrids between state and self-regulation are referred to as 'co-regulation' or 'regulated self-regulation.'

The *aims and justifications* of self-regulation of the media vary sector by sector. For example, a study of self-regulatory codes for Internet service providers (ISPs) found that codes had articles relating to illegal content, → privacy, hate speech, spam, or protection of minors. By contrast, press codes focus on the practice of ethical journalism, in matters such as intrusion into privacy and accuracy of information provided (→ Ethics in Journalism). Codes for the electronic gaming sector focus narrowly on protection of minors and content standards. In the context of convergence these sectoral differences will be increasingly significant as codes and self-regulatory schemes overlap and potentially conflict.

Newspapers generally feature one or more of three forms of self-regulation: press councils, news ombudsman, or *codes of conduct*. For internet content ISP codes set out the procedures for dealing with illegal content (Tambini et al. 2008; → Internet Law and Regulation). News provision by new entrants such as bloggers, and by broadcasters, who have their own codes, have illustrated the complexity and overlap that result in the new environment.

See also ▶ CINEMA ▶ ETHICS IN JOURNALISM ▶ INTERNET LAW AND REGULATION ▶ PRIVACY ▶ VIDEO GAMES

REFERENCES AND SUGGESTED READINGS

Beard, F. & Nye, C. (2011). A history of the media industry's self-regulation of comparative advertising. *Journalism History*, 37(2), 113–121.

Bertrand, C.-J. (2002). *Arsenal of democracy: Media accountability systems.* London: Hampton Press.

Tambini, D., Marsden, C., & Leonardi, D. (2008). *Codifying cyberspace: Communications self-regulation in the age of Internet convergence.* London: Routledge.

Semiotics

KLAUS BRUHN JENSEN

University of Copenhagen

Semiotics is an interdisciplinary field that studies "the life of signs within society" (Saussure 1959, 16). While 'signs' most commonly refer to language and other symbolic communication, it may denote any means of knowing about or representing an aspect of reality (→ Sign).

The American pragmatist philosopher Charles Sanders Peirce was the first thinker to develop a *general semiotic* (Peirce 1992–1998). He understood his theory of signs as a form of logic, which informed a comprehensive system addressing the nature of being and knowledge. The key to the system is Peirce's definition of the sign as having *three aspects*: a 'sign' (or representamen), an 'object' that the sign refers to, and an 'interpretant,' which is somebody's understanding of the object via the sign. The *key implication* is that the relationship between objects in the world, including social facts, and concepts in the mind is always mediated by signs. A further implication is that human understanding is not a singular internalization of reality, but a continuous process, what Peirce called "semiosis."

One influential element of Peirce's semiotics has been his categorization of *different* types of signs, especially icon, index, and symbol. 'Icons' relate to their objects through resemblance (a realistic painting of a landscape); 'indices' have a causal relation (a photograph registers a segment of that landscape); and 'symbols' have an arbitrary relation to their object (a novelist puts aspects of the landscape into words).

Compared with Peirce, the *other main founder* of semiotics, the Swiss linguist Ferdinand de Saussure, focused on verbal language (and used the term 'semiology'). The main achievement of Saussure was to outline a framework for contemporary → linguistics. In contrast to the 'diachronic' emphasis of earlier philology, Saussure proposed to study language as a system in a 'synchronic perspective.' Language as an abstract system ('langue') could be distinguished from the actual uses of language ('parole'). The language system has two dimensions. Along the 'syntagmatic dimension,' letters, words, phrases, etc. are the units that combine to make up meaningful wholes. Each of these units is chosen as one of several possibilities along a 'paradigmatic dimension;' for example, one verb in preference to another. An important legacy of Saussure has been his account of the 'arbitrariness' of the linguistic sign. A sign is said to have two sides, a 'signified' (concept) and a 'signifier' (the acoustic image associated with it). The point is that the interrelations within the linguistic system of representation are arbitrary, but fixed by social convention, and hence open to critique and change.

It was the application to wider social and cultural issues that consolidated *semiotics as an interdisciplinary field* from the 1960s. The influential work of Claude Lévi-Strauss (1963) on structural anthropology examined cultures as systems of interpretation, and inspired critical analyses of culture, society, and the human unconscious as "languages" (→ Structuralism). Roland Barthes (1973) suggested that the combined signifier and signified (expressive form and conceptual content) of one sign (e.g., a magazine picture of a young black man in a French uniform saluting the flag) may become the expressive form of a further, ideological content (e.g., that French imperialism was not a discriminatory or oppressive system). This semiotic mechanism serves to naturalize particular worldviews, while obscuring others, and can be exposed analytically (→ Critical Theory).

In *current research*, semiotics is applied to the study of texts and as part of 'social semiotics,' integrating semiotic methodology with other social and communication theory (e.g., Jensen 1995). Semiotics has also influenced theory of science by emphasizing the role of signs as evidence of necessary or probable relations, as in logical inferences. As such, semiotics offers means of reflexivity regarding the life of signs both in society at large and in scientific disciplines and fields.

See also: ▶ CRITICAL THEORY ▶ FILM THEORY ▶ LINGUISTICS ▶ MEDIA ▶ POSTMODERNISM AND COMMUNICATION ▶ PRAGMATISM ▶ SIGN ▶ STRUCTURALISM ▶ VISUAL REPRESENTATION

REFERENCES AND SUGGESTED READINGS

Barthes, R. (1973). *Mythologies*. London: Paladin.
Bignell, J. (2002). *Media semiotics: An introduction*, 2nd edn. Manchester: Manchester University Press.
Jensen, K. B. (1995). *The social semiotics of mass communication*. Thousand Oaks, CA: Sage.
Lévi-Strauss, C. (1968). *Structural anthropology*. Harmondsworth: Penguin.
Peirce, C. S. (1992–1998). *The essential Peirce*. Bloomington, Indiana University Press.
Saussure, F. de (1959). *Course in general linguistics*. London: Peter Owen.

Sensation Seeking

MARVIN ZUCKERMAN
University of Delaware

Sensation seeking is a basic personality trait that has been defined as "the seeking of varied, novel, complex, and intense sensations and experiences, and the willingness to take physical, social, legal, and financial risks for the sake of such experience" (Zuckerman 1994, 27).

The *test used to measure the construct*, the Sensation Seeking Scale (SSS), contains four subscales: (1) *thrill and adventure seeking* (TAS), an expressed desire to engage in risky physical activities or sports that provide unusual sensations of speed or defiance of gravity; (2) *experience seeking* (ES): seeking of sensations and experiences through the mind and the senses, as through music, art, and travel, and social nonconformity and unconventionality; (3) *disinhibition* (Dis), i.e., seeking sensation through social activities, sex, and drinking, and associating with people who share these hedonistic preferences; and (4) *boredom susceptibility* (BS), which represents an intolerance for repetitious experience or predictable and unexciting people. A fifth may be added as part of a five-factor personality test (Zuckerman 2002): (5) *impulsive sensation seeking* (ImpSS). A *biological basis* for sensation seeking has been found in physiological characteristics like evoked cortical potentials, hormones, including testosterone and cortisol, enzymes that regulate neurotransmitters, and specific neurotransmitters, including noradrenaline, serotonin, and dopamine.

High-sensation seekers are particularly attentive to novel stimuli. The *orienting reflex* (OR) is a measure of this characteristic. When a novel stimulus is presented in the visual or auditory fields, a measurable arousal response occurs in the form of a transient increase in skin conductance or deceleration in heart rate. On subsequent presentations of the stimulus these physiological reactions diminish in amplitude and disappear. The high sensation seeker shows a stronger OR to the first presentation of a stimulus.

Researchers have been particularly interested in relating sensation seeking theory to the prevention of unhealthy and risky behaviors. High-sensation seekers are over-represented among those who engage in risky behaviors, so it makes sense to design communications that will engage the attention of such people and imprint their message in memory. Another area of application has been the relationship between sensation seeking and exposure to media content.

See also: ▶ ADVERTISING EFFECTIVENESS ▶ EXPOSURE TO COMMUNICATION CONTENT ▶ PERSONALITY AND EXPOSURE TO COMMUNICATION ▶ PREVENTION AND COMMUNICATION

REFERENCES AND SUGGESTED READINGS

Donohew, L., Bardo, M. T., & Zimmerman, R. S. (2004). Personality and risky behavior: Communication and prevention. In R. M. Stelmack (ed.), *On the psychobiology of personality: Essays in honor of Marvin Zuckerman*. New York: Elsevier, pp. 223–245.

Zuckerman, M. (2007). *Sensation seeking and risky behavior*. Washington, DC: American Psychological Association.

Zuckerman, M. (1994). *Behavioral expressions and biosocial bases of sensation seeking*. Cambridge: Cambridge University Press.

Sensationalism

PAUL HENDRIKS VETTEHEN
Radboud University Nijmegen

Sensationalism may be defined as a concept that encompasses those features of news stories that journalists use to attract the attention of the audience. In the literature, a number of *sensationalist news categories* have been distinguished.

The oldest and most heavily investigated category includes audio, visual, and verbal news *content* that may be considered as attention-grabbing because of its reference to basic human needs; e.g., stories about sex, violence, or disasters. A second category includes *formal features* that represent unexpected or changing information, and that consequently elicit attention responses (e.g., Grabe et al. 2003). In television news, transitions between scenes or camera perspectives are the most obvious examples, but also sudden camera movements and uncommon editing techniques. In newspapers and newssites

(→ Internet News), extraordinarily large headlines or pictures are examples. Finally, some studies have included a category of sensationalist *storytelling features*, which because of their vividness are expected to be attention grabbing (e.g., Hendriks Vettehen et al. 2012; → Narrative News Stories). Examples of vivid storytelling are the insertion of soundbites by lay persons in news reports, or the insertion of an individual case history (→ Exemplification and Exemplars, Effects of).

Although sensationalist news has been defended as an appropriate response to the evolutionarily developed human habit of attending to information that increases the chances of survival and reproduction, it has also raised many *criticisms*. First, it has been considered as a product of market-driven journalism (→ Commercialization: Impact on Media Content). This view has received support in both longitudinal and cross-sectional studies, although the evidence so far cannot completely rule out alternative influences, such as technological innovations, or trends in → journalists' role perceptions. Second, sensationalism has been accused of being at odds with the informative function of news. Studies on this issue show that sensationalist features increases attentiveness during the viewing process, but an unrestricted use of sensationalist devices induces cognitive overload. Moreover, sensational features may draw attention to the sensational parts of the story, thus evoking distorted comprehension and judgments.

See also: ▶ COMMERCIALIZATION: IMPACT ON MEDIA CONTENT ▶ EXEMPLIFICATION AND EXEMPLARS, EFFECTS OF ▶ INTERNET NEWS ▶ JOURNALISTS' ROLE PERCEPTION ▶ NARRATIVE NEWS STORY ▶ POLITAINMENT ▶ TABLOIDIZATION

REFERENCES AND SUGGESTED READINGS

Grabe, M. E., Lang, A., & Zhao, X. (2003). News content and form: Implications for memory and audience evaluations. *Communication Research*, 30(4), 387–413.

Hendriks Vettehen, P. G. J., Zhou, S., Kleemans, M., d'Haenens, L., & Lin, T. C. (2012). Competitive pressure and arousing television news: A cross-cultural study. *Asian Journal of Communication*, 22(2), 179–196.

Sex Role Stereotypes in the Media

JOY L. HART
University of Louisville

Sex role stereotypes represent women and men in highly generalized, unrealistic ways. Media stereotypes are important because representation plays a key role in shaping social reality (→ Media and Perceptions of Reality; Social Stereotyping and Communication). Mediated messages influence knowledge and what is deemed significant (Brooks & Hébert 2006). Repeated media images shape attitudes, beliefs, and values. Media communicate current social reality while simultaneously shaping it. Considerable research addresses the media's role in perpetuating stereotypes. Scholars have examined a variety of media types – e.g., movies (→ Cinema), television, radio, advertisements (→ Advertising), newspapers, Internet – and highlighted the negative social influence of repeated exposure to stereotypes. Sex role stereotypes convey messages about expected appearance and behavior of women and men, shaping our ideas and expectations. Moreover, such stereotyping perpetuates a reality that oppresses less powerful social groups.

Findings show, despite some more realistic portrayals, stereotyping continues. For example, *women* are underrepresented on television in relation to men and to their actual numbers in society. Most women who appear are young (Eschholz et al. 2002). Older male characters tend to be depicted as wise and independent, whereas older women are often represented as irrational and dependent. Women are more often presented as emotional and sensitive; men as serious, dominant, and prone to violence. Men act as workforce and women as domestic role models. A number of common sex role stereotypes have been discussed. These include general depictions of women and men as well as specific stereotypes based on factors such as race and sexual orientation. Griffin (1998) highlighted common images of women that *reinforce ideas of sex difference*, including hetero-sexy beauty queens, wholesome girls next door, cute pixies, and wives and mothers. Contemporary media often show women wearing sexy clothes posing in decorative ways (Lavine et al. 1999). *Stereotypical images of men* are also commonly presented by the media (→ Masculinity and Media). For example, male heroes abound, often demonstrating aggression in ways that receive validation.

Several studies have examined how *women and men of different races* are portrayed. There has been considerable criticism of the mediated sex role stereotypes of African American women. Brooks and Hébert (2006) discuss several common stereotypes, including 'mammies,' 'matriarchs,' 'jezebels,' and 'welfare mothers.' African American men are also stereotyped in the media. According to Brooks and Hébert (2006), common stereotypes include 'the shuffling Uncle Tom,' 'the savage,' and the 'childlike Sambo.' Some studies cite frequent depictions of anger and aggression, reinforcing fear of black men.

Women from the *Far East* tend to be stereotyped as lotus blossoms or dragon ladies (Brooks & Hébert 2006). *Latinas* tend to be depicted as highly emotive, possessing hypersexual toughness, and exotic temptresses. According to Brooks and Hébert (2006), Far Eastern men are often depicted as menacing foreigners, laborers, corrupt businessmen, and martial artists. Latinos tend to be represented in problematic work roles (e.g., drug dealers, criminals) and as prone to violence. The repetition of mediated stereotypes counteracts strides made by women and minorities. Through their subtle unity, sex role stereotypes reinforce patriarchy and hegemonic masculinity (Eschholz et al. 2002; → Sexism in the Media) and heterosexual relationships (Wade & Sharp 2011).

Overall, results are mixed – suggesting some, little, or no progress in ending sex role stereotypes in the media. Much work remains to achieve fairness and equality. Sex role stereotyping continues – as do admonitions from scholars, researchers, and activists that it perpetuates sexism and makes it less likely for equality between women and men to be imagined and made real.

See also: ▶ ADVERTISING ▶ CINEMA ▶ CULTIVATION EFFECTS ▶ MASCULINITY AND THE MEDIA ▶ MEDIA AND PERCEPTIONS OF REALITY ▶ SEXISM IN THE MEDIA ▶ SOCIAL PERCEPTION ▶ SOCIAL STEREOTYPING AND COMMUNICATION ▶ WOMEN IN THE MEDIA, IMAGES OF

REFERENCES AND SUGGESTED READINGS

Brooks, D. E. & Hébert, L. P. (2006). Gender, race, and media representation. In B. J. Dow & J. T. Wood (eds.), *Handbook of gender and communication*. Thousand Oaks, CA: Sage, pp. 297–317.

Eschholz, S., Bufkin, J., & Long, J. (2002). Symbolic reality bites: Women and racial/ethnic minorities in modern film. *Sociological Spectrum*, 22(2), 299–334.

Griffin, P. (1998). *Strong women, deep closets*. Champaign, IL: Human Kinetics.

Lavine, H., Sweeney, D., & Wagner, S. (1999). Depicting women as sex objects in advertising: Effects on body dissatisfaction. *Personality and Social Psychology Bulletin*, 25(8), 1049–1058.

Wade, L. & Sharp, G. (2011). Selling sex. In S. D. Ross & P. M. Lester (eds.), *Images that injure: Pictorial stereotypes in the media*. Santa Barbara, CA: Praeger, pp. 163–172.

Sexism in the Media

CAROLYN M. BYERLY
Howard University

KAITLYNN MENDES
De Montfort University

Sexism in the media relates to concerns about a range of gender inequalities – in content, employment, policy, decision-making, and ownership – that have been a major focus of global women's liberation movements since the 1970s. Mass media matter to women everywhere and play a central role in the formulation and dissemination of ideas and the shaping of → public opinion and → social perception (→ Feminist and Gender Studies). Popular media such as film television, newspapers, and magazines (→ Popular Communication) have universally tended to frame women within a narrow repertoire of types which bear little or no relation to how real women live their real lives (Byerly & Ross 2006; → Framing Effects). Starting in the 1960s and 1970s, with the rise of women's liberation movements around the world, women began to recognize and analyze these problems. Women also understood that having respectful, accurate, and progressive images and messages about themselves in the media was essential if they were to have a louder public voice and participate more fully in public life.

Feminists have *critiqued the media* for the 'symbolic annihilation' of women, which comments upon women's absence, trivialization and misrepresentation in the news and other 'serious' media forms. Although women's presence in mass media has improved over the years, women remain underrepresented, marginalized, and trivialized in ways that men are not (Collins 2011; → Sex Role Stereotypes in the Media; Social Stereotyping and Communication). All across media forms, women are consistently hypersexualized and exploited. These are often manifested through undue emphasis on women's sexual attributes over other qualities (e.g., intelligence, competence, achievement), through patriarchal (i.e., male superior) messages, or through overt use of male violence against women, and depicting women in humiliating positions. Feminists have also focused on the structural marginalization of women in the media industries, particularly women's exclusion from ownership and decision-making positions (Byerly 2013). Having more senior women within the media industries is necessary to encourage egalitarian content and increase women's visibility across all sectors. While women have had some important successes in overcoming sexism in the media, they remain vigilant of the persistent sexist patterns described above. Although new technologies and social media have enabled many women to engage in multiple forms of networking, information sharing, political analysis, collaboration, and agenda building, they are also potent spaces for (re)producing sexism and misogyny (Jane 2014).

In the traditional media, there are some *signs of change*. There are stronger and more plentiful roles for women today in both movie and television programming in many nations, and women of varied races and of lesbian identity have found roles in movies and television dramas. In terms of news coverage, many of the issues that women have agitated for (e.g., rape law reform, an end to domestic violence, AIDS prevention) are being covered with greater regularity and sensitivity by many news organizations (Byerly & Ross 2006).

Nevertheless, women are still at the periphery of most news (Global Media Monitoring Project 2010). Three-fourths of the people heard or read about in the world's news are male, and women account for less than half of the news sources (44 percent) and even fewer (37 percent) of the reporters covering the news. Some of women's progress in overcoming sexism in the media can be seen in the creation of large-scale strategies with long-range goals. Central here are the more than two dozen media monitoring and advocacy groups functioning in nearly as many nations. Monitoring produces data that can be used to advocate for changes within the news media.

Overall, feminist-led efforts to end sexism in the media occur at national, international and grassroots levels. The optimistic view of these efforts, taken together, is that change is coming and will continue to come, and that an important role for communication researchers is to follow and evaluate their results.

See also: ▶ CYBERFEMINISM ▶ FEMINIST AND GENDER STUDIES ▶ FEMINIST MEDIA ▶ FEMINIST MEDIA STUDIES, TRANSNATIONAL ▶ FRAMING EFFECTS ▶ GENDER: REPRESENTATION IN THE MEDIA ▶ POLITICAL ECONOMY OF THE MEDIA ▶ POPULAR COMMUNICATION ▶ PUBLIC OPINION ▶ SEX ROLE STEREOTYPES IN THE MEDIA ▶ SEXUAL VIOLENCE IN THE MEDIA ▶ SOCIAL PERCEPTION ▶ SOCIAL STEREOTYPING AND COMMUNICATION ▶ WOMEN IN THE MEDIA, IMAGES OF

REFERENCES AND SUGGESTED READINGS

Byerly, C. M. (2013). *The Palgrave international handbook of women and journalism.* Basingstoke: Palgrave MacMillan.

Byerly, C. M. & Ross, K. (2006). *Women and media: A critical introduction.* Oxford: Blackwell.

Collins, R. L. (2011). Content analysis of gender roles in media: Where are we now and where should we go? *Sex Roles,* 64(3–4), 290–298.

Global Media Monitoring Project (2010). *Who makes the news? The Global Media Monitoring Project Report 2010.* Toronto: World Association of Christian Communication (WACC).

Jane, E. A. (2014). "Your a ugly, whorish, slut": Understanding e-bile. *Feminist Media Studies,* 14(4), 531–546.

Sexual Violence in the Media

JENNY KITZINGER
Cardiff University

The media are key players in both the promotion of, and efforts to combat, sexual violence and have been subject to *critical inquiry in two main ways*. One strand of research explores whether scenes of sexual violence (e.g. in films or computer games; → Cinema; Video Games) might trigger sexual aggression; this sort of research is often pursued under the umbrella of psychology (→ Violence as Media Content, Effects of). A second strand, more often pursued by communication scholars, focuses on exploring how the media represent the causes of, and solutions to, such violence, and how this might help to shape public and policy responses. This approach also includes an interest in the everyday representations of sexuality that infuse popular culture and how these might romanticize sexual aggression.

Research into sexual violence blossomed from the 1970s onwards alongside the emergence of the women's liberation movement. Feminist activists highlighted a continuum of abuses, including rape, sexual harassment and the sexual exploitation of children by men in positions of trust and authority and challenged the salacious reporting of attacks as titillation and the promotion of the idea that women enjoy rape or victims provoke abuse (→ Gender: Representation in the Media; Pornography, Feminist Debates on).

Although there have been major changes in media representation since the 1970s, some problems remain including trivialization and a disproportionate focus on stranger-danger (Kitzinger 2004) alongside victim blaming and the promotion of (often racist) stereotypes about abusers (Moorti 2002; → Sexual Stereotypes in the Media; Sex Role Stereotypes in the Media). Journalists sometimes seem to prefer to sensationalize the details of an individual attack than reflect on the patterns of sexual violence, orchestrating outrage about sentencing, or the release of individual convicted sex offenders, rather than looking at the social changes within the dominant culture that are needed to make rape and sexual abuse a thing of the past There is a failure to confront the widespread nature of 'mundane,' everyday, sexual violence and the cultural attitudes that support it and when journalists *do* connect sexual violence to endemic cultural attitudes, it is usually in considering 'sub-' or 'foreign' cultures.

Some of the most interesting *critical work in this field* is emerging from parts of the world such as Asia. Issues such as the use of sexual violence in ethnic cleansing and genocide have increasingly gained recognition, as has military sexual slavery and the growing trade in sex trafficking. Commentators stress the importance of including a gender-sensitive perspective in thinking about disarmament and reintegration, and the importance of linking issues such as trafficking to the breakdown in social structure. The connection between academic analysis and activism in much of this work is often very strong. Media monitoring groups challenge bad reporting, as well as providing support and advice to journalists to improve their practices (Lloyd & Howard 2005).

Technological changes also present new sites of research. The ways in which sexual violence can be facilitated by the Internet (including 'Internet pedophilia' and trafficking) are gaining attention (→ Internet: International Regulation) and key questions are being raised by the routinization of sexual objectification, bullying and harassment on platforms such as → Facebook and → Twitter (→ Social Media). At the same time questions are being raised about how the Internet might help to challenge sexual violence, creating an avenue for alternative discourses and challenges to the status quo, and supporting international dialogue – a dialogue. Such areas can provide productive new directions for research in a field of inquiry that is constantly evolving in response to social, political, and technological changes.

See also: ▶ AUDIENCES, FEMALE ▶ CINEMA ▶ FACEBOOK ▶ FEMINIST MEDIA STUDIES, TRANSNATIONAL ▶ FRAMING EFFECTS ▶ GAY, LESBIAN, BISEXUAL, AND TRANSGENDER MEDIA STUDIES ▶ GENDER: REPRESENTATION IN THE MEDIA ▶ INTERNET: INTERNATIONAL REGULATION ▶ PORNOGRAPHY, FEMINIST DEBATES ON ▶ SEX ROLE STEREOTYPES IN THE MEDIA ▶ SEXISM IN THE MEDIA ▶ SEXUAL STEREOTYPES IN THE MEDIA ▶ TWITTER ▶ VIDEO GAMES ▶ VIOLENCE AS MEDIA CONTENT, EFFECTS OF ▶ VIOLENCE AS MEDIA CONTENT, EFFECTS ON CHILDREN OF

REFERENCES AND SUGGESTED READINGS

Kitzinger, J. (2004). *Framing abuse: Media influence and public understandings of sexual violence against children.* London: Pluto Press.

Lloyd, F. & Howard, R. (2005). *Gender, conflict and journalism: A handbook for South Asia.* Paris: UNESCO.

Moorti, S. (2002). *Color of rape: Gender and race in television's public spheres.* Albany, NY: SUNY Press.

Sign

CLAY STEINMAN
Macalester College

The sign, in terms first articulated by Ferdinand de Saussure (1857–1913), the Swiss linguist, has come to serve as the basic unit of approaches to communication that focus on meaning-making relations rather than on the effectiveness of senders' communication of intended messages to designated receivers (→ Linguistics; Meaning). For Saussure communication involves not messages but signs, i.e. material forms that when articulated and then encountered engender meanings bounded by cultural schemata (→ Culture: Definitions and Concepts). The study of signs, then, is at its core social: What conventions determine how signs are made? What conventions determine their readings?

We communicate about the world indirectly through mediating sign languages – gestures, images, sounds, and words but also through such vehicles as decor, design, and dress (→ Code). Signs may be studied as a matter of dispassionate interest, as instruments of persuasion, or as objects of social criticism. In the latter case researchers would ask: if communication is mediated by signification, what forms of economic, political, and social power determine the mediations? Because it does not privilege the intentions of senders as does the sender–receiver model, semiotics finds interest in whatever meanings a communication happens to produce.

Saussure saw each sign as embedded in a complex chain of differentiations, its meanings comparative and multiple, depending upon its semiotic surroundings. "Morphologically there are neither *signs* nor *meanings*, but *differences in signs* and *differences in meanings*, (1) each of which exist solely in their relations to others, hence inseparable, but (2) never come into direct contact with each other" (2006, 46; emphasis in original). For Saussure's theory, "context is everything" (Jameson 1972, 17; → Text and Intertextuality). The relationship between concept and sound pattern, between the idea of a cat, for example, and the understood articulation of the spoken or written word 'cat,' is "conventional, and thus arbitrary, wholly lacking in any natural link with the object, completely free of and unregulated by it" (Saussure 2006, 140). The object need not exist; 'unicorn' can be a sign no less than 'cat.' Herein lies the axiomatic ground for communication and cultural studies oriented toward change.

Roland Barthes (1915–1980) parted from Saussure over the arbitrariness of signification, preferring 'unmotivated' to 'arbitrary' for the Sd/Sr relation. He maintained that lack of motivation in signs may be complete or be partial, as in fire/smoke or footprints/past presence, a semiotic category of effect/cause. Barthes also questioned the description 'arbitrary' because no individual is "free to modify it" (Barthes 1970, 50), at least under ordinary circumstances of language use. For a semiology without guarantees, without fixed meanings, denotation might most usefully be conceptualized as the most common connotation, rather than as a foundational meaning on which connotation trades. Thinking of connotation as a location for changeable flickers of meaning highlights its ideological quality.

This can be seen in Stuart Hall's (2006) discussion of encoding/decoding television. Hall offers three general categories to describe the movement from Sr to Sd in this second, connotative system: 'dominant-hegemonic,' 'negotiated,' and 'oppositional.' In the first category, the sign is decoded "in terms of the reference code in which it has been encoded," and meaning is made "within the dominant code" (Hall 2006, 171). In cases in which the movement from Sr to Sd has been 'negotiated,' general meaning-making along dominant-hegemonic lines is supplemented by 'particular or situated logics.' Oppositional readings see the Sr in terms hostile to the dominant code, and so understand the sign in terms of a Sd that objects to the dominant project with which it is associated.

Louis Althusser (1971) argued that whenever we make sense of our contemporary world according to dominant codes, our very construction as subjects of that world occurs yet again. For him, ideology was not an organized body of ideas but the way the world is 'lived' in meaningful terms (Althusser 1971, 217). Yet the sense that, yes, this is the world, is not a recognition of reality – here Althusser followed Jacques Lacan – but a "misrecognition" (1971, 219) that forgets that signs are always maps, always representational, and never territories themselves (→ Realism in Film and Photography).

See also: ▶ ADVERTISING ▶ BRANDING ▶ CARICATURE ▶ CODE ▶ CRITICAL THEORY ▶ CULTURAL STUDIES ▶ CULTURE: DEFINITIONS AND CONCEPTS ▶ DISCOURSE ▶ GENDER AND DISCOURSE ▶ GENDER: REPRESENTATION IN THE MEDIA ▶ ICONOGRAPHY ▶ LINGUISTICS ▶ MASCULINITY AND THE MEDIA ▶ MEANING ▶ MEDIA EFFECTS ▶ PERSUASION ▶ REALISM IN FILM AND PHOTOGRAPHY ▶ SEMIOTICS ▶ STRUCTURALISM ▶ TEXT AND INTERTEXTUALITY ▶ VISUAL COMMUNICATION ▶ VISUAL REPRESENTATION

REFERENCES AND SUGGESTED READINGS

Althusser, L. (1971). *'Lenin and philosophy' and other essays* (trans. B. Brewster). New York: Monthly Review. (Original work published 1964).

Barthes, R. (1970). *'Writing degree zero' and 'Elements of semiology'* (trans. A. Lavers & C. Smith). Boston: Beacon Press. (Original work published 1964).

Hall, S. (2006). Encoding/decoding. In M. G. Durham & D. M. Kellner (eds.), *Media and cultural studies: Key works*, 2nd edn. Oxford: Blackwell, pp. 163–173. (Original work published 1973).

Jameson, F. (1972). *The prison-house of language: A critical account of structuralism and Russian formalism*. Princeton: Princeton University Press.

Sanders, C. (ed.) (2004). *The Cambridge companion to Saussure*. Cambridge: Cambridge University Press.

Saussure, F. (2006). *Writings in general linguistics* (ed. S. Bouquet & R. Engler with A. Weil; trans. C. Sanders & M. Pires with P. Figueroa). Oxford: Oxford University Press.

Situation Comedies

RICHARD F. TAFLINGER
Washington State University

The situation comedy, or 'sitcom,' has been a staple of entertainment media for decades. Starting on radio, it quickly became popular with audiences. With the advent of television (in the US) in the late 1940s, sitcoms migrated to the small screen, and it is these sitcoms with which most people today around the world are familiar. A definition of situation comedy should look at each word of the name, starting with *situation*. There is a continuation from episode to episode of the same elements: (1) a regular group of characters who appear in all or almost all episodes and who maintain a continuing relationship to each other; (2) a group of settings used in all or almost all episodes in which most of the actions take place and in which (3) the premise of the show is established.

Six *criteria are required for comedy*, for an event to elicit laughter from a person. First, it must be mechanical (Bergson 1956). In this criterion, the laughable element consists of a mechanical inelasticity, just where one would expect adaptability and flexibility. Second, it must be inherently human, or with the capability of reminding us of humanity. Something is funny only insofar as it is or reminds the audience of humanity. Third, there must be a set of established societal or human norms with which the observer is familiar; and fourth, the situation and its component parts (the actions performed and the dialogue spoken) must be inconsistent or unsuitable to the surrounding or associations (i.e., the societal or human norms). Fifth, it must appeal to the intellect rather than the emotions. Finally, it must be perceived by the observer as harmless or painless to the participants. The comic action is perceived by the audience as causing the participants no actual harm: their physical, mental, psychological, and/or emotional well-being may be stretched, distorted, or crushed, but they recover quickly and by the end of the performance they are once again in their original state. When all these criteria have been met, people will usually laugh.

Dramatic stories (both dramas and comedies) are constructed following some basic rules: there is a universe in which the stories take place (e.g., unmarried friends looking for love, a war zone, an office); a problem arises in that universe; the characters do things to solve that problem, making the problem worse; and finally, they do the right thing and the problem is solved. Because of the way stories are constructed, there are *three basic types of situation comedies*: the action comedy, the character comedy, and the dramatic comedy (Taflinger 1996). In an *action comedy*, the characters simply do things, they perform actions, until they finally do the right thing to solve the problem. The *character comedy* requires that in order to solve the problem a character undergoes a fundamental change in who he or she is. The problem arises because a character is doing or believing something wrong: that looks are everything, that social status is more important than being true to oneself, that selfishness is the way to behave. In the early part of the story the character seems to be right, but then the negative consequences start to impact the character's life, and they come to the realization that they were wrong and need to change what they believe. This change solves the problem. The character sitcom is rare because it is more difficult to do than just have the characters perform actions to solve the problem, and it requires a greater effort on the part of and concentration by the audience to understand the characters' personal problems and solutions. The third and rarest type of sitcom is the *dramatic comedy*, or 'dramedy.' In this type of sitcom, the solution to the problem presented in the show is often unsatisfactory or poor, leaving it up to the audience to think about the problem and decide how they would solve it. For example, two characters may hold diametrically opposed extreme points of view.

From its inception as a form of episodic entertainment, the situation comedy has been a major element of mass media. Reflecting the mores of its audience and the times in which they live, and poking fun at them, it has provided amusement, and occasionally edification, for its viewers. Although it has had its ups and downs, and even had its obituary published more than once, it has always been and will continue to be a favorite with audiences looking for a laugh.

See also: ▶ EXPOSURE TO TELEVISION ▶ GENRE ▶ TELEVISION: SOCIAL HISTORY OF

REFERENCES AND SUGGESTED READINGS

Bergson, H. (1956). Laughter. In W. Sypher (ed.), *Comedy*. Garden City, NY: Doubleday, pp. 61–190.
Brooks, T. & Marsh, E. (1999). *The complete directory to prime time network and cable TV shows: 1946–present*. New York: Ballantine.
Seylor, A. & Haggard, S. (1957). *The craft of comedy*. New York: Theatre Arts Books.
Taflinger, R. (1996). Sitcom: What it is, how it works. At www.wsu.edu/~taflinge/sitcom.html, accessed August 28, 2014.

Social Cognitive Theory

ALBERT BANDURA
Stanford University

Social cognitive theory is rooted in an agentic perspective of human behavior (Bandura 1986, 2006). To be an agent is to influence one's own functioning and events that affect one's life. In this view people are contributors to their life circumstances, not just products of them.

Human behavior has often been explained in terms of unidirectional causation. In the environmental deterministic view, behavior is shaped and controlled by environmental forces. In the dispositional deterministic view, behavior is driven by internal drives and dispositions. Social cognitive theory explains human functioning in terms of triadic reciprocal determination. In this transactional view of self and society, personal factors in the form of cognitive, emotional, and biological processes, the way one behaves, and environmental forces all operate as interacting determinants that influence each other.

Humans are endowed with an extraordinary *capacity for symbolization* that provides them with a powerful tool for comprehending their environment and altering it in ways that touch virtually every aspect of their lives. Most environmental influences operate through cognitive processes. Cognitive factors partly determine which environmental events will be observed, what meaning will be conferred on them, whether they leave any lasting effects, what emotional impact and motivating power they will have, and how the information they convey will be organized for future use. The remarkable flexibility of symbolization enables people to create ideas that transcend their sensory experiences. Through the medium of symbols they can communicate with others at any distance in time and space. With the aid of symbols, people give structure, meaning, and continuity to their lives.

There are *two basic modes of learning*. Learning by experiencing the effects of one's actions is not only an exceedingly tedious process, but a hazardous one when mistakes have costly or injurious consequences. Fortunately, this process can be cut short by the second mode, 'social modeling.' Humans have an advanced capacity for observational learning that enables them to expand their knowledge and competencies rapidly through the information conveyed by a rich variety of models (Rosenthal & Zimmerman 1978). The models upon whom people pattern their behavior involve behavioral modeling in informal everyday activities. With the revolutionary advances in communications technology, lifestyles are now being modeled and rapidly diffused worldwide by symbolic modeling.

See also: ▶ GOALS, COGNITIVE ASPECTS OF ▶ POLITICAL EFFICACY

REFERENCES AND SUGGESTED READINGS

Bandura, A. (1986). *Social foundations of thought and action: A social cognitive theory*. Englewood Cliffs, NJ: Prentice Hall.

Bandura, A. (2006). Toward a psychology of human agency. *Perspectives on Psychological Science*, 1, 164–180.

Bandura, A. (2011). Social cognitive theory. In P. A. M. van Lange, A. W. Kruglanski, & E. T. Higgins (eds.), *Handbook of social psychological theories*. Thousand Oaks, CA: Sage, pp. 349–373.

Rosenthal, T. L. & Zimmerman, B. J. (1978). *Social learning and cognition*. New York: Academic Press.

Social Comparison Theory

MARIE-LOUISE MARES
University of Wisconsin–Madison

The central idea of social comparison theory is that individuals often judge how well they are doing by comparing themselves with others around them. When Festinger (1954) originally developed the theory, he argued that individuals want an accurate assessment of their opinions and performance, and that in the absence of objective standards, they look to others (preferably those who are similar in a relevant dimension) for information about their relative standing.

The theory has subsequently expanded to include *additional motives and targets for comparison*. Those seeking self-enhancement may choose downward comparison (i.e., contrast themselves to those doing less well on a relevant dimension) in order to feel relatively successful and may avoid ego-threatening upward comparisons with those doing better than them. However, those desiring self-improvement or inspiration may choose upward comparison with those performing brilliantly, to provide hope for the possible future, information about how to perform similarly, and motivation to work hard.

More recently, researchers have argued that comparison choices and outcomes may be even more complicated. For example, individuals seeking reassurance and self-enhancement may avoid downward comparisons if such comparisons raise the possibility of similar bad outcomes occurring to them. Instead, these individuals may look for successful role models to provide the needed reassurance ("If they can do it, so can I"). Conversely, individuals seeking self-improvement may sometimes look to unsuccessful others to provide information about what to avoid or to create fear as motivation to work hard. In a critique of the theory, Kruglanski and Mayseless (1990) noted the difficulty of predicting who would be a relevant or similar target for comparison, even when an individual's motives are given.

Although much social comparison research has examined the above contrast effects, other work has focused on assimilation. At times, individuals may focus on, and overestimate, the similarities between themselves and the target, rather than focusing on the differences. *Assimilation* has been observed when individuals share common attributes or group membership with the comparison target, and when they are very confident and so do not tend to engage in explicit self-evaluations. *Contrast effects* have been observed when individuals are less confident of their self-image and more interested in self-evaluation. For example, studies of media use and eating disorders find both assimilation (thin women feeling good after exposure to thin, attractive models) and contrast (e.g., other women feeling worse after seeing images of thin, attractive models).

See also: ▶ INTERPERSONAL COMMUNICATION ▶ INTERACTION ▶ LANGUAGE AND SOCIAL

INTERACTION ▶ SOCIAL COGNITIVE THEORY
▶ SOCIAL PERCEPTION

REFERENCES AND SUGGESTED READINGS

Festinger, L. (1954). A theory of social comparison processes. *Human Relations*, 7, 117–140.
Kruglanski, A. W. & Mayseless, O. (1990). Classic and current social comparison research: Expanding the perspective. *Psychological Bulletin*, 108, 195–208.

Social Conflict and Communication

DOUGLAS BLANKS HINDMAN
Washington State University

Communication is crucial to social conflict because through it social conflict can escalate into violence or de-escalate into resolution and reconciliation, and can lead to clearer definitions of opposing positions (Gilboa 2006). Conflict is a ubiquitous form of social interaction that can have positive or negative consequences for the groups involved, can have implications for both social change and social stability, and can be understood as both a product of the social setting and a purely symbolic act that has no relationship to what are imagined as real conditions.

Social conflicts, as intense forms of human → interaction, tend to draw crowds of bystanders wherever they occur. News media, perhaps relying on the idea of 'what the public wants,' include a disproportionate amount of social conflict, occasionally framing as conflict situations that are not viewed that way by the participants (→ Framing of the News). In most cases, however, the parties involved in conflict are often quite eager to make their position known to a wider audience. Hence, social conflict is a frequent theme of news coverage, particularly television news about international politics.

The emphasis among conflict scholars has *changed in tandem with broader social changes*. In the nineteenth and early twentieth centuries, social conflict was understood in the context of industrialization, urbanization, and bureaucratization. The failure of socialist revolts and the rise of fascist regimes in the early middle of the twentieth century coincided with scholarship that critiqued scientific approaches to communication research and that focused on the role of ideology and coercion in stemming revolution. The relatively stable social environment in the US during the late middle of the twentieth century was paralleled by studies of the integrative aspects of social conflict like the civil rights protests focusing attention on communication and social conflict as symbolic struggles over ideology, with potential for individual emancipation and radical social change.

Just as the communication and social conflict research of the previous generation was responsive to the social and cultural climate of the day, *current and future research* acknowledges significant trends in the nature of conflict itself. As communities become more diverse, with more potential centers for organized social power, contentious politics have replaced a previous generation's bowling leagues and fraternal clubs as the primary method of social participation. In the US, for instance, the partisan and ideologically based divisions among elected officials are dutifully reflected in press reports which give equal play to Republicans and Democrats, regardless of the veracity of each side's arguments. Whereas community conflict has been shown to reduce knowledge gaps, media coverage of ideologically based conflict over issues such as global warming and health care reform instead tends to contribute to 'belief gaps' in the distribution of knowledge and beliefs among ideologically sympathetic groups (Hindman 2012).

Scholars and community organizers are developing *new methods of conflict mediation* to manage racial, ethnic, and environmental disputes. The idea is that conflict is primarily a communication-based act that can be channeled, via communication, into positive outcomes (Gilboa 2006). Through this process, social conflict and communication can activate citizens to participate in their community's civic life, even as more benign forms of social participation such as bowling leagues and civic club membership continue to decline (Hindman & Yamamoto 2011; → Community Media).

Mass media do not create social conflict or social movements, yet media coverage is one of the key resources that conflict groups seek to mobilize to achieve political goals. New information technologies are also proving to be valuable tools for coalition formation and message dissemination, both among protest groups and between protest groups and the public. Arab Spring protests leading to regime change in Egypt, Yemen, and Libya were coordinated with mobile phones and social media after repressive governments shut down mainstream media channels. Social conflict theorists tend to view all of history as a result of various groups' struggles to control scarce resources. As long as humans continue to interact, communication, as the primary expression of social conflict, will continue to be an important field of study.

See also: ▶ COMMUNITY MEDIA ▶ FRAMING OF THE NEWS ▶ INTERACTION ▶ PLANNED SOCIAL CHANGE THROUGH COMMUNICATION

REFERENCES AND SUGGESTED READINGS

Gilboa, E. (2006). Media and international conflict. In J. G. Oetzel & S. Ting-Toomey (eds.), *The Sage handbook of conflict communication: Integrating theory, research, and practice*. Thousand Oaks, CA: Sage, pp. 595–626.
Hindman, D. (2009). Mass media flow and the differential distribution of politically disputed beliefs: The belief gap hypothesis. *Journalism and Mass Communication Quarterly*, 86, 790–808.
Hindman, D. (2012). Knowledge gaps, belief gaps, and public opinion about health care reform. *Journalism and Mass Communication Quarterly*, 89, 585–605.
Hindman, D. & Yamamoto, M. (2011). Social capital in a community context: A multilevel analysis of individual- and community-level predictors of social trust. *Mass Communication and Society*, 14, 838–856.

Social Exchange

MICHAEL E. ROLOFF
Northwestern University

Acquiring needed resources is critical for survival, and social exchange is one means of doing so. Communication is a tool by which exchanges are negotiated (→ Negotiation and Bargaining) as well as a means for providing resources. Researchers have used social exchange frameworks to study communication in close relationships (see Roloff 1981), organizations (see Cropanzano & Mitchell 2005) and social networks (see Cook & Rice 2003).

A *social exchange occurs* when individuals provide each other with resources. Tangible resources, such as money, goods, and services, involve transfers by which one person gains a resource while another loses it. Symbolic resources, such as love, status, and information, can be exchanged without loss. In contrast to purely economic exchanges, social exchanges are guided by informal expectations and social norms which can make social exchanges more difficult to negotiate and enforce. Restricted social exchanges are those in which members of a dyad provide each other with resources. In contrast, generalized exchanges involve several partners, none of whom returns resources to those from whom they received resources. In some cases, social exchanges involve distributions in which resources from a common pool are provided to members of a social system.

Several *social exchange theories* exist that differ in their academic origins and assumptions. Regardless, a set of shared ideas embodies a social exchange perspective. First, people are self-interested and pursue actions that have allowed them to gain needed resources and/or they anticipate will do so. Second, to prevent exploitation, groups develop and enforce norms that guide social exchanges. Restricted exchanges follow the norm of reciprocity that dictates that individuals should return resources and are obligated to treat their benefactors with respect until they have done so. Generalized exchanges are guided by group norms aimed at helping members of a social system and often create feelings of social solidarity. Resource distribution is often guided by norms of distributive justice such as equity, equality, need, and status. The negative outcomes of violations of distributive justice may be offset by following rules of procedural justices, such as letting those affected by the distribution have voice into it or achieving interaction justice by providing a full and sensitive accounting of how a decision was made. Third, social exchanges influence relationships. Individuals form and maintain relationships with others who are available and dependable resource providers. There are also emotional byproducts of stable relational exchanges such as trust, gratitude, caring, and affection. Another relational consequence of social exchange is dependency. In some cases, individuals possess valuable resources and many people want to enter into exchanges with them. Consequently, they could form exchange relationships that afford benefits that are superior to those received from their current partners. If their partners lack such opportunities, individuals gain power from their partners' relative dependency.

Given the inherent link between social exchange and relationships, social exchange theories have been used to study *communication in close relationships*. For example, the Investment Model posits that investments, satisfaction with current outcomes, and alternative sources for rewards determine the degree to which partners are committed to remaining in a relationship. Commitment, in turn, increases the likelihood that individuals will try to maintain their relationship. Maintenance includes devaluing alternatives and responding to a partner's provocative actions in a constructive fashion. Social exchange frameworks have also been used to study → organizational communication, some of which are tied to the exchange relationship between employees and the organizations. For example, Organizational Support Theory assumes that employees are willing to expend effort at work if they perceive that their organization supports them by providing favorable work conditions, fair treatment, and supervisor support. Finally, social exchange theories have been used to study social networks. Exchange perspectives inform as to how position within a social network influences a person's power and pattern of exchanges with others in the network.

Although contributing to many bodies of research, social exchange perspectives have been criticized for their roots in operant psychology and/or economics, portraying an overly strategic view of human behavior, inadequate explication of constructs, and providing little insight into the fundamental mechanisms that produce communication.

See also: ▶ INTERPERSONAL COMMUNICATION ▶ INTERPERSONAL CONFLICT ▶ NEGOTIATION AND BARGAINING ▶ ORGANIZATIONAL COMMUNICATION

REFERENCES AND SUGGESTED READINGS

Chadwick-Jones, J. K. (1976). *Social exchange theory: Its structure and influence in social psychology.* New York: Academic Press.

Cook, K. S. & Rice, E. (2003). Social exchange theory. In J. Delamater (ed.), *Handbook of social psychology.* New York: Plenum, pp. 53–76.

Cropanzano, R. & Mitchell, M. S. (2005). Social exchange theory: An interdisciplinary review. *Journal of Management*, 31, 874–900.

Roloff, M. E. (1981). *Interpersonal communication: The social exchange approach.* Thousand Oaks, CA: Sage.

Social Marketing

TIMOTHY EDGAR
Emerson College

Social marketing is a framework that aims to change human behavior within a population. Although social marketing has been used to address many problems, it has been used primarily in health promotion and disease prevention (for examples, see Edgar et al. 2011; Lee & Kotler 2011; → Health Communication; Health Campaigns, Communication in; Planned Social Change through Communication).

Social marketing is characterized by *six defining criteria* (Andreasen 2002): (1) behavior change is the end goal; (2) audience research drives strategy (→ Audience Research); (3) audiences are segmented to insure maximum efficiency; (4) social marketers create attractive motivational exchanges with target audiences; (5) interventionists assess the competition faced by the desired behavior; and (6) strategy relies on all four Ps of the marketing mix, as described below.

The last criterion is the central element of social marketing. The first of the four Ps is *product*. The product can be a physical object such as a condom that facilitates one's ability to engage in a desired action, but most commonly social marketers attempt to 'sell' a change of behavior (e.g., using seatbelts). *Price* refers to the barriers that an individual must overcome to adopt the proposed action. Price, however, also involves identifying the incentives one can enjoy from adopting a new behavior (e.g., increased self-esteem after losing weight). *Place* refers to the strategy for making the desired behavior as convenient as possible such as placing hand sanitizer dispensers in front of elevators.

Promotion is the social marketing element most directly linked to communication. The communication options available to a social marketer can include, for instance, promoting a product through → advertising, → public relations, consumer promotions, education, interpersonal networks (→ Communication Networks), direct mail, signage, printed materials, → social media, and the Internet. For an initiative to be labeled accurately as social marketing, the process should include the entire mix.

See also: ▶ ADVERTISING ▶ AUDIENCE RESEARCH ▶ COMMUNICATION AND SOCIAL CHANGE: RESEARCH METHODS ▶ COMMUNICATION NETWORKS ▶ HEALTH CAMPAIGNS, COMMUNICATION IN ▶ HEALTH COMMUNICATION ▶ PLANNED SOCIAL CHANGE THROUGH COMMUNICATION ▶ PUBLIC RELATIONS

REFERENCES AND SUGGESTED READINGS

Andreasen, A. R. (2002). Marketing social marketing in the social change marketplace. *Journal of Public Policy and Marketing,* 21, 3–13.

Edgar, T., Volkman, J., & Logan, A. (2011). Social marketing: Its meaning, use, and application for health communication. In T. Thompson, R. Parrott, & J. Nussbaum (eds.), *Handbook of health communication,* 2nd edn. London: Routledge, pp. 235–251.

Lee, N. R. & Kotler, P. (2011). *Social marketing: Influencing behaviors for good,* 4th edn. Thousand Oaks, CA: Sage.

Social Media

NINA HAFERKAMP
Independent Scholar

In its core meaning, 'social media' is closely allied to the terms 'Web 2.0' and 'social web.' However, while these describe the novelty of the Internet's second generation, the term 'social media' covers the specific types of participatory digital media.

Key Characteristics of Social Media

Two *key characteristics* are 'user-generated content' (UGC) and 'produsage' (Bruns 2013). Both terms connote the idea that people are actively participating in social media; they are generating and sharing content themselves. UGC emphasizes that it is not only professionals who are creating content, but mainly ordinary people, who need only access to the Internet. All types of media – including social media – have a specific audience, but only social media allow sharing, copying, and generating content without having specific professional qualifications or expertise. Thus, social media cannot perpetuate the traditional roles of recipients on the one hand and producers on the other.

Another feature of social media is → interpersonal communication. Obviously social networks facilitate communication among users, by offering comment functions, email accounts, or chat capabilities (→ Electronic Mail; Personal Communication by CMC). As research has already shown for social networks, communication partners frequently know their counterparts from everyday life, but this is not always the case. Particularly when dealing with wikis, people with different backgrounds collaborate on a subject of common interest, although they have never met in person. *Linking* also comes into play in various contexts. It means adding someone to one's 'friends' list; linking hypertexts in wikis; placing web links in personal weblogs; or simply having a URL for connecting content to external networks. Also, tagging can be understood as linking. The opportunity to connect content has significantly changed people's use of media, as extensive searching is abandoned in favor of spontaneous and interest-based use.

Sub Genres

Due to the rapidly developing character of *social media sub-genres*, new forms of media that meet the qualifications for being 'social' media emerge within very short periods of time. The main purpose of publishing tools is the publication of content that can be related to specific authors. Some researchers have called this social media sub-genre *personal publishing*, thereby indicating that publishing tools are not used mainly by professionals, but rather by lay persons (DeAndrea 2012).

Social networks like → Facebook are mainly concerned with interpersonal communication. Each user hosts a public or semi-public online profile to which various dynamic and static features can be uploaded. This profile offers a platform for various communication tools, such as chat or news feeds or sending private messages by using a specific mail function. The profile owner shares a connection with other users by inviting them to join his or her 'friends' list (Good 2013). More and more social networks are emerging that focus on specific target groups. One prominent example is XING, used for occupational networking. *Wikis* (for collaboration) and → *search engines* are further sub-genres. The latter are designed to search for information on the Internet but, like Google, offer advertisers the opportunity to present information based on the user's location or his or her personal interests disclosed in previous activities on the Internet.

Areas of Research

There are five main *research questions* concerning social media. First, researchers have been interested in the *influence of social media on social relations*. They have demonstrated that social networks are primarily used to maintain pre-existing relationships, and less often for meeting new people. From a sociological perspective, the particular benefit of using different social media devices can be related to the concept of social capital (Ellison et al. 2014). Results indicate further that social media use impacts networks among socially heterogeneous groups ('bridging') and among homogeneous groups ('bonding'), as well as enabling users to keep in touch with a group after physically disconnecting from it (maintaining social capital).

Second, there is an ongoing debate about negative effects of self-disclosure in social media with respect to → *privacy*. Several studies found that, while users have concerns about privacy issues this does not very much affect their behavior in social networks (Taddicken 2012). A third issue is the use of social networks for → *self-presentation* – i.e., control of the impressions that other people form of a person online. Surprisingly the majority of studies revealed that most users aimed at leaving an authentic impression.

Strategic communication through social media is a fourth area of research. Using social media for strategic purposes is meaningful for various fields such as politics, → advertising, or → public relations (→ Strategic Communication). For these activities social media can be of great use because of the possibility of addressing a large audience. Regarding political communication, social media are used not only for circulating personal opinions but also for professional political campaigning (Bode et al. 2013). With regard to public relations, research has analyzed how nonprofit organizations use social media for free and effective image building (Kent 2013).

Finally, communication researchers have investigated the role of social media for *political upheavals* such as the 'Arab Spring.' Although the role of the social media for causing social unrest cannot be fully assessed (mainly because of methodological reasons), it is evident that social media provided information the regime could not control, shaped the → climate of opinion, and thus had an impact on citizens' decisions to get engaged. According to a study by Tufekci and Wilson (2012), social media use increased the probability that Egyptians attended protests.

See also: ▶ ADVERTISING ▶ ELECTION CAMPAIGN COMMUNICATION ▶ ELECTRONIC MAIL ▶ FACEBOOK ▶ INTERPERSONAL COMMUNICATION ▶ ON-LINE JOURNALISM ▶ ONLINE MEDIA ▶ ONLINE RESEARCH ▶ PERSONAL COMMUNICATION BY CMC ▶ POLITICAL COMMUNICATION ▶ PRIVACY ▶ PUBLIC RELATIONS ▶ SEARCH ENGINES ▶ SELF-PRESENTATION ▶ STRATEGIC COMMUNICATION ▶ TWITTER ▶ WEB 2.0 AND THE NEWS

REFERENCES AND SUGGESTED READINGS

Bode, L., Vrada, E. K., Borah, P., & Shah, D. V. (2013). A new space for political behavior: Political social networking and its democratic consequences. *Journal of Computer-Mediated Communication*, 19(3), 414–429.

Bruns, A. (2013). From prosumption to produsage. In R. Towse & C. Handke (eds.), *Handbook on the digital creative economy*. Cheltenham, UK: Edward Elgar, pp. 67–78.

DeAndrea, D. C. (2012). Participatory social media and the evaluation of online behavior. *Human Communication Research*, 38(4), 510–528.

Ellison, N., Vitak, J., Gray, R., & Lampe, C. (2014). Cultivating social resources on social network sites: Facebook relationship maintenance behaviors and their role in social capital processes. *Journal of Computer-Mediated Communication*, 19(4), 855–870.

Good, K. D. (2013). From scrapbook to Facebook: A history of personal media assemblage and archives. *New Media and Society*, 15(4), 557–573.

Kent, M. (2013). Using social media dialogically: Public relations role in reviving democracy. *Public Relations Review*, 39(4), 337–345.

Taddicken, M. (2012). Privacy, surveillance and self-disclosure in the social web: Exploring the user's perspective via focus groups. In C. Fuchs, K. Boersma, A. Albrechtslund, & M. Sandoval (eds.), *Internet and surveillance. The challenges of web 2.0 and social media*. London: Routledge, pp. 255–272.

Trepte, S. & Reinecke, L. (2011). *Privacy online: Perspectives on privacy and self-disclosure in the social web*. New York: Springer.

Trepte, S. & Reinecke, L. (2013). The reciprocal effects of social network site use and the disposition for self-disclosure: A longitudinal study. *Computers in Human Behavior*, 29, 1102–1112.

Tufekci, Z. & Wilson, C. (2012). Social media and the decision to participate in political protest: Observations from Tahrir Square. *Journal of Communication*, 62(2), 363–379.

Social Perception

JAKUB SAMOCHOWIEC
University of Basel

MICHAELA WÄNKE
University of Basel

The term 'social perception' might seem a misnomer, as it refers less to how people perceive their social environment through their senses (→ Pluralistic Ignorance; Climate of Opinion) than to how they make a judgment. Unlike the color of a car or the loudness of a piece of music, both of which can be more or less directly perceived by the respective sensory systems, the trustworthiness of a person or the aggressiveness of a social exchange can only be inferred or construed from various indirect cues. People have to go beyond the information given in order to arrive at a social judgment. In this sense, social perception is an active and constructive process of the perceiver. Not surprisingly, then, the same social situation or the same person may be 'perceived' quite differently by different perceivers, or by the same perceiver in different situational contexts.

A theoretical framework that was originally suggested for visual perception (→ Visual Communication), Brunswick's 'lens model' (1947), provides a quite suitable approach to social perception. This model suggests that objects have certain 'real' properties (distal stimuli; e.g., shyness), which translate into certain *cues* (proximal stimuli; e.g., little eye contact). Only the cues, not the 'real' thing, can be directly perceived by an observer. Cues are retranslated and inferences from different cues are then put together to form a picture. Proximal cues can differ dramatically in their abstractness and in the information they imply. A cue might be simple and concrete, such as a behavior (e.g., avoiding eye contact) or the physical appearance of a person. Cues also may be abstract, such as biographical data or group membership. The cue as such is meaningless. It is only meaningful to a particular perceiver, who has stored an association of the cue with the concept to be judged (e.g., shyness).

One *source of cue significance* is that people have learned over time and over many observations that the proximal stimulus co-varies with a particular distal stimulus (eye contact and shyness). Other associations may have originated from single observations. Whether on the basis of multiple or single observations, people form individual and subjective lay theories about the associations of particular behaviors, appearance, biographical data, etc. with personality traits. Yet, other associations may not be based on individual theories about the significance of cues but on shared cultural knowledge.

The lens model offers a nice framework for understanding where *errors* may happen. First, perceivers – or, better, judges – can never fully observe all possible cues but only a subset. Moreover, some distal stimuli have clearer cues than others. Heider (1958) proposed that what people need to do in order to find out what a person is like (e.g., whether aggressive or not) is to correct for the situational influence in the observed behavior. For Heider a person's trait is a stable concept, which can be extracted despite steadily changing observations in different situations. Although there is no act without both an actor and a situation, one can at least attempt to disentangle the two factors and determine which influence is a stronger cause, by using the 'principle of covariance': in order to be attributed as a cause of an effect, the factor should be present when the effect occurs but be absent when the effect does not occur. By this logic Heider (1958) and other authors proposed one can identify dispositions by comparing the behavior of a person over many situations and also comparing the behavior of other persons in such situations.

What the social perceiver *should* do is assess the situation to determine whether it allows a broad range of behaviors. However, what the social perceiver really *does* instead is often something very different. Initially, people automatically infer personality traits from observed behavior. This tendency to think that people are the way they act and to explain behavior with underlying personality traits is often called the 'correspondence bias' or 'fundamental attribution error.' Even in those cases where people are motivated to find out about the real causes of a behavior, they may not succeed. The problem for social situations is that it is not always possible to compare different people and different situations.

Several factors make social perception a more *complex and difficult task* than simply perceiving the color of a car or the size of a building (see Bless et al. 2004). First, people may try to influence the impression others have of them. Second, people may change and perceivers may need to update their impressions accordingly. And third, social perception is being constructed in our brains. Even if we do not always realize it, the construction site of social reality is a very busy place.

See also: ▶ CLIMATE OF OPINION ▶ INTERPERSONAL COMMUNICATION ▶ NONVERBAL COMMUNICATION AND CULTURE ▶ PLURALISTIC IGNORANCE ▶ SOCIAL STEREOTYPING AND COMMUNICATION ▶ VISUAL COMMUNICATION

REFERENCES AND SUGGESTED READINGS

Bless, H., Fiedler, K., & Strack, F. (2004). *Social cognition: How individuals construct reality*. Hove: Psychology Press.

Brunswick, E. (1947). *Systematic and representative design of psychological experiments: With results in physical and social perception*. Berkeley, CA: University of California Press.

Gilbert, D. T. (1998). Ordinary personology. In D. T. Gilbert, S. T. Fiske, & G. Lindzey (eds.), *Handbook of social psychology*, 4th edn. New York: McGraw-Hill, vol. 2, pp. 89–150.

Heider, F. (1958). *The psychology of interpersonal relations*. New York: John Wiley.

Social Stereotyping and Communication

MARY LEE HUMMERT
University of Kansas

Psychological theory conceptualizes 'stereotypes' as cognitive structures or → schemas that represent widely shared beliefs about the defining characteristics of social groups. Any group might be subject to stereotypes, but the most commonly studied stereotypes are those based on race or ethnicity, nationality, religion, sex, and age. The beliefs that compose stereotypes may include physical characteristics, personality traits, behavioral tendencies, etc. According to the Stereotype Content Model (SCM; Fiske 2012), warmth (or its lack) and competence (or its lack) are the fundamental dimensions that define stereotypes of all groups. As cognitive structures, stereotypes serve as resources that help individuals to organize and respond to new people and situations. Social stereotyping refers to this use or application of stereotypes in person perception and social interaction. Because stereotypes are often applied without conscious awareness of their influence, they have the potential to lead to bias and prejudiced behaviors (→ Information Processing).

Giles' → Communication Accommodation Theory (CAT; Giles et al. 1991) showed how group identity processes can influence communication behavior, outlining the conditions under which an individual might choose to converge with or diverge from the linguistic style or accent of an outgroup member, as well as the consequences of that convergence or divergence. CAT later expanded its focus to incorporate stereotypes of outgroups into its model of the communication process, considering how individuals accommodate or not to group stereotypes in their communication with outgroup members (→ Intercultural and Intergroup Communication). As CAT has continued to evolve, its models have incorporated the individual characteristics of communicators as predictors of both their reliance on negative as opposed to positive stereotypes of outgroup members, and their proclivity to approach the interaction as intergroup rather than interpersonal.

Social stereotyping can also be reflected in the *language used* to describe the behaviors of those in stereotyped groups in comparison to that used to describe the behaviors of members of ingroups. These characteristics of language in the context of social stereotyping are reflected in the linguistic intergroup bias. That is, individuals tend to use more abstract language in describing negative characteristics of outgroups and positive characteristics of their ingroups, whereas they tend to use more concrete language to describe positive behaviors of outgroups and negative behaviors of ingroups (Biernat 2009).

Recently interest has developed in the phenomenon of *self-stereotyping*, i.e., behaving in ways consistent with negative stereotypes of one's group (Hummert 2011). Some self-stereotyping behavior may result from situational factors that call forth negative group stereotypes, such as the over-accommodative or biased communication behaviors of others or requests to perform tasks on which one's group is stereotyped negatively (e.g., a memory test for older people, a math test for women). Other self-stereotyping can occur as individuals describe their own actions in stereotypic terms (Hummert et al. 2004).

The interrelationship of communication and social stereotyping creates a challenge for reducing social stereotyping in the communication process. First, from a cognitive perspective, stereotypes are useful heuristics that enable communicators to reduce their uncertainty when they encounter new people. Second, from a CAT perspective, communicators rely on stereotypes not because they wish to engage in prejudiced communication, but to be effective communicators by adapting their communication to the needs of the other person. Third, stereotyping in communication occurs most often at an implicit or unconscious level, so that communicators are unaware that they are basing their communication choices on stereotypes. Fourth, the ways in which stereotyping emerges in communication can be very subtle, occurring even at the level of word choice, and serve to reinforce the underlying stereotypical beliefs. Communication is thus inextricably linked to the creation and maintenance of social stereotyping, but as a result also offers the route to its reduction (Yzerbyt & Carnaghi 2008).

See also: ▶ COMMUNICATION ACCOMMODATION THEORY ▶ INFORMATION PROCESSING ▶ INTERCULTURAL AND INTERGROUP COMMUNICATION ▶ INTERGENERATIONAL COMMUNICATION ▶ INTERGROUP ACCOMMODATIVE PROCESSES ▶ INTERGROUP CONTACT AND COMMUNICATION ▶ POWER IN INTERGROUP SETTINGS ▶ PREJUDICED AND DISCRIMINATORY COMMUNICATION ▶ SCHEMAS ▶ SOCIAL IDENTITY THEORY ▶ SOCIAL PERCEPTION

REFERENCES AND SUGGESTED READINGS

Biernat, M. (2009). Stereotypes and shifting standards. In T. D. Nelson (ed.), *Handbook of prejudice, stereotyping, and discrimination*. New York: Psychology Press, pp. 137–152.

Fiske, S. T. (2012). The continuum model and the stereotype content model. In P. A. Lange, A. W. Kruglanski, & E. T. Higgins (eds.), *Handbook of theories of social psychology: vol 1*. Thousand Oaks, CA: Sage, pp. 267–288.

Giles, H., Coupland, N., & Coupland, J. (1991). Accommodation theory: Communication, context, and consequence. In H. Giles, J. Coupland, & N. Coupland (eds.), *Contexts of accommodation: Developments in applied linguistics*. Cambridge: Cambridge University Press, pp. 1–68.

Hummert, M. L. (2011). Age stereotypes and aging. In K. W. Schaie & S. L. Willis (eds.), *Handbook of the psychology of aging*, 7th edn. San Diego, CA: Elsevier Academic Press, pp. 249–262.

Hummert, M. L., Garstka, T. A., Ryan, E. B., & Bonnesen, J. L. (2004). The role of age stereotypes in interpersonal communication. In J. F. Nussbaum & J. Coupland (eds.), *The handbook of communication and aging research*, 2nd edn. Mahwah, NJ: Lawrence Erlbaum, pp. 91–114.

Yzerbyt, V. & Carnaghi, A. (2008). Stereotype change in the social context. In Y. Kashima, K. Fiedler, & P. Freytag (eds.), *Stereotype dynamics: Language-based approaches to the formation, maintenance, and transformation of stereotypes*. Mahwah, NJ: Lawrence Erlbaum, pp. 29–57.

Social Support in Interpersonal Communication

DAENA J. GOLDSMITH
Lewis & Clark College

Social support is a multidisciplinary field that asks: Why are people who are involved in relationships mentally and physically healthier than those who are not? It includes enacted support/supportive communication (what people say and do to help one another cope with stress), perceived available support (beliefs about relationships that influence coping and outlook on life), and social network/integration (structures of interconnection that affect opportunities, information, immunity, and resources). Because relationships are sometimes harmful, support research identifies when and how relationships produce positive outcomes (→ Language and Social Interaction).

Interpersonal communication researchers most often study the messages and conversations that constitute *enacted support*. Theories explain why some interactions are more effective than others by specifying processes (e.g., uncertainty management or emotional re-appraisal; → Uncertainty Reduction Theory) that connect message features to beneficial outcomes. Well-intended support attempts can threaten a recipient's autonomy, imply criticism, and convey status or solidarity. Consequently, person-centeredness, face-saving, and → relational control are important message features. Partners also must coordinate whether problem-solving, emotional support, or avoidance is desired.

Perceived available support is one's perception of being valued by others who will provide support if needed. This belief enhances coping and contributes to relational satisfaction. Perceptions of available support are not strongly correlated with reports of enacted support; instead, perceptions arise from individual cognitive structures for relationships (e.g., attachment models) and ongoing global properties of relationships such as responsiveness, trustworthiness, and care.

Densely connected *social networks* validate social identities and coordinate provision of aid, whereas loose interconnections facilitate new identities, information, and resources. Network size is a poor predictor of outcomes, perhaps because conflictual ties can offset the benefits of supportive ties. *Social integration* entails a diverse range of relationships, including family, friends, neighbors, co-workers, and community and religious organizations. Those who are well integrated live longer and healthier lives than those who are isolated. Integration enhances personal control, meaning, affect, and healthful behaviors.

Social support research provides a basis for interventions, including providing new supportive relationships and making existing relationships more supportive. Support groups and self-help groups, both face-to-face and electronically mediated, are a popular form of social support intervention.

See also: ▶ IDENTITIES AND DISCOURSE ▶ INTERPERSONAL COMMUNICATION COMPETENCE AND SOCIAL SKILLS ▶ LANGUAGE AND SOCIAL INTERACTION ▶ POLITENESS THEORY ▶ RELATIONAL CONTROL ▶ RELATIONAL DIALECTICS ▶ UNCERTAINTY MANAGEMENT

REFERENCES AND SUGGESTED READINGS

Goldsmith, D. J. (2004). *Communicating social support*. Cambridge: Cambridge University Press.
Goldsmith, D. J. & Albrecht, T. L. (2011). Social support, social networks, and health. In T. L. Thompson, R. Parrott, & J. Nussbaum (eds.), *Handbook of health communication*, 2nd edn. London: Routledge, pp. 335–348.
MacGeorge, E. L., Feng, B., & Burleson, B. (2011). Supportive communication. In M. L. Knapp & J. A. Daly (eds.), *The Sage handbook of interpersonal communication*. Thousand Oaks, CA: Sage, pp. 317–354.

Sony Corporation

MARA EINSTEIN
Queens College, City University of New York

Sony is a leading global producer of consumer electronic equipment. Principal products include, among many others, home and portable audio, video cameras, digital cameras, Aiwa products, and home and portable gaming systems. Sony is also a producer of media content including recorded music and motion pictures. Sony had revenues of approximately US$72 billion in 2013 and operations in 200 countries worldwide. Sony business divisions include electronics, games, pictures, and financial services.

Sony was established in Tokyo, Japan, in May 1946 as an electronics company, making its reputation for innovation starting with the first all-transistor radio in 1954. Over the decades, Sony became an international company, establishing divisions around the world including in the United States, Britain, and Germany. The company continued to innovate, with the Trinitron television introduced in 1968 and the Betamax VCR in 1975, the Sony Walkman in 1979, the first CD player in 1982, and the first consumer camcorder in 1983.

Moving beyond its machine-based roots, the company began acquiring content providers in the late 1980s. The first acquisition was CBS Records, which was purchased in 1988. The following year, Sony acquired the long-running → Hollywood film studio Columbia Pictures Entertainment. In 1991, these two companies were renamed Sony Music Entertainment Inc. and Sony Pictures Entertainment Inc., respectively. In the 1990s, Sony made its entry into the → video game industry through collaboration with Nintendo. That partnership was unsuccessful, however, and Sony began developing its own gaming system, which would become the first PlayStation, launched in 1995.

Sony Corporation develops, designs, manufactures, and sells electronic equipment and consumer entertainment in seven main areas: electronics, video and online games, music, movies, television, robots, and internet services and applications. Product names produced by Sony include Vaio, Trinitron, Bravia, and Handicam. Sony also offers financial services such as insurance.

See also: ▶ CINEMA ▶ HOLLYWOOD ▶ MEDIA CONGLOMERATES ▶ VIDEO GAMES

REFERENCES AND SUGGESTED READINGS

Sony (2013). Consolidated financial statements for the fiscal year ended March 31, 2013. At http://www.sony.net/SonyInfo/IR/financial/fr/FY13_Consolidated_Financial_Statement.pdf, accessed August 27, 2014.

Wikinvest (2014). http://www.wikinvest.com/stock/Sony_(SNE)/Data/Revenue/2013/Q1, accessed August 27, 2014.

Source Protection

ANTHONY L. FARGO
Indiana University

Confidential sources have helped journalists uncover government and corporate wrongdoing, but journalists can face jail or fines if they disobey court orders to reveal sources. They can also be sued by sources if they voluntarily publish their names (→ Journalism: Legal Situation). Reporters say that their sources will not speak out if journalists do not have a privilege to shield their identities. Critics say journalists should obey the same laws as other citizens. Professional ethics codes (→ Ethics in Journalism) generally urge journalists to promise confidentiality cautiously but keep all promises (→ Professionalization of Journalism).

Journalists in many nations enjoy *qualified legal protection* from forced disclosure of sources, but some authorities are reluctant to give privileges to unlicensed professionals. Constitutions in Argentina, Mozambique, and Sweden specifically protect journalists' rights to keep sources confidential. General evidence or procedure codes provide protection in Australia, Austria, El Salvador, France, Germany, Japan, and Norway. Russia and several former Soviet republics have specific mass media laws that protect source confidentiality.

In Canada, New Zealand, Nigeria, the United Kingdom, and the United States, journalists' rights to conceal source identities mostly rely on judicial interpretations of constitutional or statutory free press guarantees. The European Court of Human Rights and the International Criminal Tribunal for the Former Yugoslavia also have recognized qualified privileges for journalists (→ European Union: Communication Law).

One unresolved issue is whether nontraditional journalists, such as bloggers, are protected under laws designed to protect mainstream media employees. The debate focuses on whether legal protection should be defined by function or employment status.

See also: ▶ COMMUNICATION AND LAW ▶ ETHICS IN JOURNALISM ▶ EUROPEAN UNION: COMMUNICATION LAW ▶ FREEDOM OF COMMUNICATION ▶ FREEDOM OF THE PRESS, CONCEPT OF ▶ INTERNET LAW AND REGULATION ▶ JOURNALISM: LEGAL SITUATION ▶ NEWS SOURCES ▶ PROFESSIONALIZATION OF JOURNALISM

REFERENCES AND SUGGESTED READINGS

Martin, J. A., Caramanica, M. R, & Fargo, A. L. (2011). Anonymous speakers and confidential sources: Using shield laws when they overlap online. *Communication Law and Policy*, 16, 89–125.

Weaver, D. (1998). Journalists around the world: Commonalities and differences. In D. H. Weaver (ed.), *The global journalist: News people around the world*. Cresskill, NJ: Hampton Press, pp. 455–480.

Youm, K. H. (2006). International and comparative law on the journalist's privilege: The Randal case as a lesson for the American press. *Journal of International Media and Entertainment Law*, 1, 1–56.

Special Effects

SEAN CUBITT
Goldsmiths, University of London

Special effects are those techniques employed in moving image technologies to provide images other than those recorded by simply opening the camera's shutter and recording. In some cases the entire image may be produced using non-camera techniques, as in both cel (for 'celluloid') and digital animation. Alternatively, events may be staged or images altered to produce special effects (→ Cinema).

Some effects are as old as cinema itself, including stunts, sets, make-up, props, rear-projection and mattes (paintings on glass placed between camera and physical objects to provide extensions of sets and locations), pyrotechnics, and miniatures. In-camera effects like stop-motion have also been used since the earliest times, and effects of over- and under-cranking (exposing frames at higher or lower speeds) were common throughout the studio era, for example to give extra dynamism to chase sequences. Extreme forms include the bullet-time technique best known from The Matrix (1999). In post-production, printing and editing of film has offered such techniques as boosting colour since the 1920s, but the arrival of digital tools passed control over these processes from technical to creative staff.

Among the most significant changes in recent years are: Steadicam stabilisation of mobile cameras, allowing extreme perspectives on action; motion-capture, which allows actors to be replaced with CGI (computer-generated imagery); and compositing, in which elements derived from photographic and digital sources are combined, and camera movement records matched with the design, lighting, and recording of 3D vector graphic into seamless wholes (→ Digital Imagery).

Metz (1977, 657) once declared, "all cinema is a special effect." Klein (2004) is among those who assert continuity between special effects and the spectacular expression of power in the baroque. Pierson (2002) emphasises, on the contrary, the assimilation of effects to realist aesthetics. Rodowick (2007) argues the loss of both realism and humanism in digital cinema and its discontinuity with previous visual regimes. Realism remains popular even in digital television's documentaries, reality TV, and adult drama; but the alliance of spectacle with anti- or post-humanism remains deeply problematic in effects-based media.

See also: ▶ CINEMA ▶ CINEMATOGRAPHY ▶ DIGITAL IMAGERY ▶ FILM GENRES ▶ FILM PRODUCTION

REFERENCES AND SUGGESTED READINGS

Klein, N. M. (2004). *The Vatican to Vegas: A history of special effects*. New York: New Press.

Metz, C. (1977). Trucage and the film. *Critical Inquiry*, 3(4), 657–675.

Pierson, M. (2002). *Special effects: Still in search of wonder*. New York: Columbia University Press.

Rodowick, D. N. (2007). *The Virtual life of film*. Cambridge, MA: Harvard University Press.

Speech Anxiety

CHIA-FANG (SANDY) HSU
University of Wyoming

Speech anxiety, also known as 'stage fright,' refers to the feeling of anxiousness or fear associated with delivering a speech. The symptoms of speech anxiety involve physiological arousal (e.g., elevated heart rate), negative thoughts (e.g., being negatively evaluated), and behavioral disruptions (e.g., verbal disfluency; Ayres & Hopf 1993).

The *causes of speech anxiety* can be attributed to trait (enduring) or state (situational) factors (→ Communication Apprehension). The trait explanations include learned helplessness, modeling, and genetic predisposition. From the 'learned helplessness' perspective, people develop speech anxiety because they learn to associate negative outcomes with speaking, such as being ridiculed by peers. According to the 'modeling' explanation, people develop speech anxiety when they cannot learn proper speaking skills from others. More recently, some scholars have argued that communication fear, such as speech anxiety, is mostly genetically determined. Despite these different explanations, many scholars hold the → 'interaction' view, i.e., that the interaction between genes and environment results in speech anxiety (Daly et al. 2009).

Regarding state anxiety, there are *eight situational factors*: novelty (new experience), formality (formal situation), conspicuousness (too noticeable), subordinate status (inferior to audience), unfamiliarity (unfamiliar audience), dissimilarity (different from audience), degree of attention (too little or too much), and degree of evaluation. Many scholars believe that trait anxiety predisposes speakers to experience these situational factors in certain ways, which in turn affects their state anxiety level (Daly et al. 2009).

Ayres' *component theory* further argued that state anxiety can be predicted by the interaction of the speaker's nervous system sensitivity, and self-perceptions of motivation, negative evaluation, and communication competence (Daly et al. 2009). Speakers experience high levels of state anxiety when they are very sensitive to environmental changes, are motivated to accomplish a goal via speech, anticipate being negatively evaluated by others, and perceive themselves as having low speaking ability.

The three primary approaches to *measuring* trait and state public speaking anxiety are self-report scales (e.g., Personal Report of Public Speaking Anxiety), physiological instruments (e.g., measure of heart rate), and observers' ratings (e.g., tense bodily movement).

See also: ▶ COMMUNICATION AND APPREHENSION ▶ INTERACTION

REFERENCES AND SUGGESTED READINGS

Ayres, J. & Hopf, T. S. (1993). *Coping with speech anxiety*. Norwood, NJ: Ablex.
Daly, J., McCroskey, J. C., Ayres, J., Hopf, T., Ayres, D. M., & Wongprasert, T. K. (eds.) (2009). *Avoiding communication: Shyness, reticence, and communication apprehension*, 3rd edn. Cresskill, NJ: Hampton Press.

Speech Communication, History of

WILLIAM KEITH
University of Wisconsin–Milwaukee

The field of Speech emerged out of changing teaching practices in US higher education in the early twentieth century. Before 1900, speech instruction had traditionally been integrated into the general, liberal education of the private colleges. The relationship between speech teachers and English departments was generally unstable. At the 1914 meeting of the public speaking section of the National Council of Teachers of English (NCTE) speech teachers decided to create a new association, the National Association of Academic Teachers of Public Speaking (NAATPS), along with a journal, the *Quarterly Journal of Public Speaking*. The first years of the NAATPS saw the widespread change in universities from departments of 'Oratory' and 'Elocution' to departments of 'Speech.'

The new field was more than public speaking. The most *common pattern* for Speech departments and courses included public speaking, debate, persuasion, physiology of the voice, diction and vocal expression, theater, and interpretation (of literature), the new name for what had been called 'reading.' The early field did not view these as separate areas simply thrown into a department (as had been the case with speech in English departments) but as a unified course of study, beginning with the voice mechanism and proceeding to the various uses of human speech.

The curriculum also included some *novel areas*. Rhetoric became a standard part of the curriculum due to the many PhDs produced by the program at Cornell University; sometimes the focus was classical, sometimes on the emerging idea of 'rhetorical criticism,' but most often it involved a study of British and American public address of the last two hundred years (→ Rhetorical Studies). Speech pathology became a staple of the field. Consistent with the unified vision of the field, improvement of speech by addressing lisping or stuttering was of a piece with improving speech by 'normalizing' students' accents, and improving his or her interpersonal skills. This last function was often glossed as 'speech hygiene.' Teachers by the late 1920s assumed that there was a normal, 'healthy' function of individuals in social groups. Rather than conformity, they posited a kind of civic humanism inspired by John Dewey, where the democratic functioning of groups (large or small) required individuals who possessed the skills of both contributing their individual points of view and helping the group to function overall.

The NAATPS changed its name in 1920 to the National Association of Teachers of Speech (NATS), which conserved the pedagogic focus that defined the early field while accommodating the move to teaching the full range of courses involving speech. In 1947, they changed the name to the Speech Association of America, recognizing the growing research component of the field, demonstrated in the *Quarterly Journal of Speech* and *Speech Monographs* (now *Communication Monographs*), established in 1934. *The Speech Teacher* (now *Communication Education*) began in 1952 as a forum for teaching methods, and later published mainly social scientific work on communication pedagogy.

In the post-World-War II era, the Speech discipline began, slowly but steadily, to lose the integrated structure that had characterized its early years, in several ways. In departments with components of mass media, radio, television, or film, the level of student interest and increasing scholarly and professional profile for media scholars and practitioners, led in many cases to the formation of a separate department in cases where there wasn't already one.

On the social science side of the field, the quickly growing body of research on persuasion and influence in psychology and sociology stimulated parallel lines of research for Speech Communication scholars. Expanding on the Yale studies of persuasion, communication research, both in Speech and media departments, began to take a variable-centered approach to studying interpersonal and public influence. As more and diverse topics were included in the curriculum, the term 'speech' began to seem restrictive, and the more general term 'communication' seemed more appropriate. In 1968, a conference sponsored by the US Office of Education and the Speech Association of America resulted in a paper, Conceptual Frontiers in Speech-Communication, which recommended changing the name of the field, resulting in the Speech Communication Association (SCA).

Speech Communication as a field of undergraduate instruction underwent explosive growth in the 1970s (Craig & Carlone 1998). Students wanted to study in the many 'new' areas of communication: interpersonal, organizational, group, and others. In fact, the diversity began, gradually, to outgrow the bounds of the term 'speech' as → cultural studies and media studies became integrated into the field's teaching and research (→ Communication as a Field and Discipline). So, despite being shared by other departments, including media and speech pathology, 'communication' seemed increasingly a better fit. Another name change, based on the results of a vote by the membership, created the current National Communication Association in 1997.

See also: ▶ APPLIED COMMUNICATION RESEARCH ▶ COMMUNICATION AS A FIELD AND DISCIPLINE ▶ COMMUNICATION AND MEDIA STUDIES, HISTORY OF ▶ COMMUNICATION: DEFINITIONS AND CONCEPTS ▶ CULTURAL STUDIES ▶ CONVERSATION ANALYSIS ▶ DISCOURSE ▶ INTERPERSONAL COMMUNICATION ▶ RHETORICAL STUDIES

REFERENCES AND SUGGESTED READINGS

Bitzer, L. & Black, E. (eds.) (1971). *The prospect of rhetoric: Report of the National Developmental Project, sponsored by the Speech Communication Association.* Englewood-Cliffs, NJ: Prentice-Hall.

Cohen, H. (1994). *The history of speech communication: The emergence of a discipline, 1914–1945.* Annandale, VA: Speech Communication Association.

Corbett, E. P. J. (1985). The Cornell School of Rhetoric. *Rhetoric Review*, 4, 4–14.

Keith, W. M. (2007). *Democracy as discussion: Civic education and the American forum movement*. Lanham, MD: Lexington.

Oliver, R. T. & M. G. Bauer. (1959). *Re-establishing the speech profession: The first fifty years*. University Park, PA: Speech Association of the Eastern States.

Wallace, K. (ed.) (1953). *The history of speech education in America: Background studies*. New York: Appleton-Century-Crofts.

Speech Fluency and Speech Errors

KYLE JAMES TUSING
University of Arizona

Speech fluency refers to clear oral communication. A speaker who is able to deliver a message that features a continuous flow of information at an appropriate rate, unmarred by speech errors, is said to possess speech fluency, an area of communication mastery. Speech fluency is the product of mental skills, such as recall of procedural and declarative knowledge, and physical motor skills involving correct functioning and use of the vocal cords, tongue, mouth, and lips to produce speech (→ Message Production).

Situational factors that facilitate speech fluency include an attentive audience, an absence of distraction, the speaker being able to prepare and practice the message ahead of time, and a monologue rather than a dialogue communication format, where there are fewer opportunities for interruptions and no requirement to manage turn-taking. *Individual difference factors dictate that* some speakers are naturally fluent, whereas others are burdened by anxiety with regard to communication (→ Speech Anxiety). Nearly all speakers have the ability through training and practice to become communication masters whose speech is fluent. There are treatments available to improve speakers' speech fluency. Treatments include physical therapy, coaching, and confidence training.

There are many different *types of speech errors*, which are most often, though not universally, a nonverbal part of speech. Among the most common types of speech errors are stuttering, audible pauses such as 'uh' or 'ah,' excessively long, frequent, or misplaced silent pauses, an unusually slow or accelerated speech rate, and counterfactual utterances.

Some of the *causes of speech errors* include a heavy cognitive load, → communication apprehension and social anxiety, physical deformity, Broca's aphasia (a brain disorder that affects the user's ability to produce fluent speech), mental illness, advancing age (→ Aging and Message Production and Processing), message complexity (→ Information Processing), and a dialogue rather than a monologue communication format, where turn-taking is an additional communication obstacle speakers must successfully negotiate.

See also: ▶ AGING AND MESSAGE PRODUCTION AND PROCESSING ▶ COMMUNICATION APPREHENSION AND SOCIAL ANXIETY ▶ INFORMATION PROCESSING ▶ LISTENING ▶ MESSAGE PRODUCTION ▶ NONVERBAL COMMUNICATION AND CULTURE ▶ SPEECH ANXIETY

REFERENCES AND SUGGESTED READINGS

Greene, J. O. (1984). Speech preparation processes and verbal fluency. *Human Communication Research*, 11, 61–84.

Subramanian, A. & Yairi, E. (2006). Identification of traits associated with stuttering. *Communication Disorders*, 39, 200–216.

Spiral of Silence

THOMAS PETERSEN
Allensbach Institute

Developed by German survey and communication researcher Elisabeth Noelle-Neumann (1916–2010), the spiral of silence theory describes collective opinion formation and societal decision-making in situations where the issue being debated is controversial and morally loaded. The theory is one of the most frequently cited and debated to emerge from the field of communication studies during the latter half of the twentieth century (Donsbach et al. 2014).

With the spiral of silence theory, Noelle-Neumann attempts to describe how public opinion functions. The term 'public opinion' refers to opinions or behavior that can be displayed or expressed in public without running the risk of social isolation, or, in some cases, that even must be displayed to avoid the danger of isolation. Noelle-Neumann views public opinion as a form of social control that ultimately applies to everyone, regardless of social class. She states that this control is apparent in many areas of life, ranging from controversial political issues to fashion, morals, and values. Noelle-Neumann's understanding of public opinion stands in contrast to another conception that views public opinion as the result of rational debate among an educated elite that is of crucial importance for the state.

The theory comprises the following *key elements*: People experience *fear of isolation*. For this reason, people constantly monitor the behavior of others in their surroundings, attentively noting which opinions and modes of behavior meet with public approval or disapproval (→ Pluralistic Ignorance; Social Perception). But people do not only observe their environment. They also issue their own *threats of isolation* via what they say and do, via behavior such as knitting their brow, laughing at someone, etc. These are signals that individuals perceive, and that show people which of their opinions meet with their fellow humans' approval and which do not. Since most people fear isolation, they tend to *refrain from publicly stating their position* when they perceive that this would attract such threats of isolation. Conversely, those who sense that their opinion meets with approval tend to voice their convictions fearlessly. Speaking out loud enhances the threat of isolation directed at those who think differently. It reinforces their sense of standing alone with their opinion and thus augments their tendency to conceal their opinion in public. A *spiraling process* begins, whereby the dominant camp becomes ever louder and more self-confident, while the other camp falls increasingly silent.

This process does not occur at all times and in all situations, but only in connection with issues that have a strong moral component. The process is not set in motion if there is no underlying moral foundation implying that those who think differently are not merely stupid, but bad. This moral element is what gives public opinion power, allowing it to raise the threat of isolation that sets the spiral of silence in motion. Only controversial issues can trigger a spiral of silence. The *news media* can significantly influence the spiral-of-silence process. If the majority of the media take the same side in a morally charged controversy, they exert a substantial, presumably even decisive influence on the direction that the spiral of silence takes.

Public opinion serves as an instrument of social control, indirectly insuring *social cohesion*. Whenever there is especially strong integrative pressure in a society, as found in connection with the spiral of silence, this generally indicates that the issue or controversy that triggered the spiral of silence poses a particularly great threat to social cohesion. In extreme cases, the spiral of silence culminates in a situation where certain topics can either only be broached using a specific vocabulary (political correctness) or cannot be mentioned at all (taboo), lest people wish to be the target of extremely harsh signals of social isolation (Noelle-Neumann 1993).

See also: ▶ IMAGINED INTERACTIONS ▶ INTERACTION ▶ PLURALISTIC IGNORANCE ▶ PLURALISTIC IGNORANCE AND IDEOLOGICAL BIASES ▶ PUBLIC OPINION ▶ SOCIAL PERCEPTION ▶ SOCIAL COMPARISON THEORY

REFERENCES AND SUGGESTED READINGS

Bodor, T. (2012). The issue of timing and opinion congruity in spiral of silence research: Why does research suggest limited support for the theory? *International Journal of Public Opinion Research*, 24, 269–286.

Donsbach, W., Salmon, C. T., & Tsfati, Y. (eds.) (2014). *The spiral of silence. New perspectives on communication and public opinion*. New York: Routledge.

Noelle-Neumann, E. (1974). The spiral of silence: A theory of public opinion. *Journal of Communication*, 24, 43–51.

Noelle-Neumann, E. (1993). *The spiral of silence: Public opinion – our social skin*, 2nd edn. Chicago: University of Chicago Press.

Scheufele, D. A. & Moy, P. (2000). Twenty-five years of the spiral of silence: A conceptual review and empirical outlook. *International Journal of Public Opinion Research*, 12, 3–28.

Sports and the Media, History of

DAVID ROWE
University of Western Sydney

Sports and the media are often regarded as a 'match made in heaven,' but their relationship is prone to some disharmony over their mutual power. As products of modernity, these institutions have developed a close interdependence since the mid-nineteenth century, with sport providing popular content for the media, which in return gave sport high visibility and substantial income, especially after television (→ Television as Popular Culture) supplanted first print and then radio as the principal medium of sport communication.

Television helped make sport into a key component of many national cultures, a process which first took shape in Britain and in turn became the major global phenomenon that is most dramatically evident during events like the Olympic Games and FIFA World Cup (→ Globalization of the Media; Cultural Products as Tradable Services). Broadcast television remains powerful, but networked digital media sport via the Internet now offers enhanced flexibility and interactivity that, through → social media platforms and Internet Protocol Television (IPTV), promises to transform the mediated experience of sports.

There is continuing concern over the corporate media's capacity to dominate sports culture, with the rising commercial value of premium sports progressively reducing the role of public service broadcasters (→ Public Broadcasting Systems) and commercial free-to-air networks as subscription ('pay') television has acquired broadcast rights and required audiences to pay to watch. For some critics, 'cultural citizenship' rights of free TV sport viewing are the subject of contention over audience exploitation (→ Political Economy of the Media).

Others raise concerns over possible impacts of economic factors on media sports texts (→ Text and Intertextuality). Sports are shaped as spectacles by the media to engage audiences, becoming increasingly 'telegenic' as rules and event timing change to accommodate the media, and with greater emphasis on entertainment gossip and celebrity. The qualities, → meanings, and uses of these media sports texts and audience interaction with them are of crucial interest to critical media sports scholars, who analyze the ways in which these seemingly innocent, pleasurable texts have embedded within them damaging ideologies, including sexism, homophobia, racism, ethnocentrism, class prejudice, excessive nationalism, and xenophobia.

See also: ▶ ADVERTISING ▶ CONCENTRATION IN MEDIA SYSTEMS ▶ GLOBALIZATION OF THE MEDIA ▶ MEANING ▶ POLITICAL ECONOMY OF THE MEDIA ▶ POPULAR CULTURE ▶ PUBLIC BROADCASTING SYSTEMS ▶ SATELLITE TELEVISION ▶ SOCIAL MEDIA ▶ TELEVISION AS POPULAR CULTURE ▶ TEXT AND INTERTEXTUALITY

REFERENCES AND SUGGESTED READINGS

Hutchins, B. & Rowe, D. (2012). *Sport beyond television: The Internet, digital media and the rise of networked media sport.* London: Routledge.
Pedersen, P. M. (ed.) (2013). *Handbook of sport communication.* London: Routledge.
Rowe, D. (2011). *Global media sport: Flows, forms and futures.* London: Bloomsbury Academic.

Standards of News

HAZEL DICKEN-GARCIA
University of Minnesota

News standards connote normative qualities, such as accuracy and decency (→ Ethics in Journalism), but the term specifically means the way information is gathered, made into news reports, and presented (Dicken-Garcia 1989). For example, objectivity encompasses six standards: verified facts, fairness, non-bias, independence, non-interpretation, and neutrality (Ward 2004; → Objectivity in Reporting). Journalists develop standards to gain credibility in society, and standards change across space and time. In the US news, for instance, standards changed as the press shifted from partisan to event-centered to commercial during nineteenth-century industrialization. Accuracy and balance, of little concern to partisan journalists, became more important with the shift from producer to consumer society (→ Professionalization of Journalism).

Western hegemony spread news standards, which developed with the rise of capitalism and the middle class. The need to sell news profitably required qualities the public would buy, and investments shaped standards as ties to political parties weakened. Around 1900, western journalism also became more about structuring than recording reality, resulting in image politics and an emphasis on objectivity.

Whether the press serves primarily the government or the public affects standards. History shows more concern with printing itself than with news standards, especially in authoritarian societies, because rulers feared its permanence and reach (→ Freedom of the Press, Concept of). France executed printers for criticizing religion or government as late as 1760. England shaped colonial news standards through libel laws and press licensing, controlled reporting on Parliament until at least 1845, and monitored journalism thereafter. In open societies, norms and the market shape standards, although laws prohibit libel, obscenity, and breach of security (→ Media History).

News standards under conditions of *convergence of media systems* remain underdeveloped. Old issues re-emerge with new urgency when fact-checking is non-existent and news-gatherers unknown. If Daniel Defoe was not a journalist because he wrote about events he never saw, then determining who is a journalist on the Internet has even greater implications for news standards.

See also: ▶ ETHICS IN JOURNALISM ▶ FREEDOM OF THE PRESS, CONCEPT OF ▶ GLOBALIZATION THEORIES ▶ MEDIA HISTORY ▶ OBJECTIVITY IN REPORTING ▶ PROFESSIONALIZATION OF JOURNALISM ▶ TABLOIDIZATION

REFERENCES AND SUGGESTED READINGS

Dicken-Garcia, H. (1989). *Journalistic standards in nineteenth-century America*. Madison: University of Wisconsin Press.

Dunaway, J. (2011). Institutional effects on the information quality of campaigns news. *Journalism Studies*, 12(1), 27–44

Ward, S. J. A. (2004). *The invention of journalism ethics*. Montreal: McGill Queen's University Press.

Stimulus–Response Model

FRANK ESSER
University of Zurich

The stimulus–response model is associated with the assumption that the mass media has powerful effects (→ Media Effects). Also referred to as the 'hypodermic needle' or 'transmission belt theory,' it can be considered one of the first general conceptions describing mass media effects. The basic assumption is that because people's actions in anonymous mass societies are not so much influenced by social ties but are still evolutionarily guided by a uniform set of instincts, individuals attend to media messages similarly and interpret them in a uniform way. In this model, media messages are seen as 'magic bullets,' striking every eye and ear, resulting in effects on thought and behavior that are direct, immediate, uniform, and, therefore, powerful. According to the generally accepted history of media effects research, the stimulus–response model was the guiding perspective in the media effects field during the early days of communication study (→ Media Effects, History of).

Today, however, this received view is disputed. Most probably the stimulus–response model was never explicitly endorsed by any early mass communication scholar but instead invented by Katz and Lazarsfeld (1955) as a straw man against which their own *limited effects model* could be contrasted and presented as an impressive paradigm shift. Other scholars later dismissed the standard history and provided evidence demonstrating how advocates of an early stimulus–response era were patently relying on a mistaken interpretation of the early effects literature. Bineham (1988) explains the differing interpretations of these early studies with the idea that advocates and critics of the received view had a very different understanding of what the hypodermic needle model meant. Advocates see the recognition of intervening variables as mere elaborations upon the hypodermic model if the studies still assume that mass communication is a one-directional and linear process; critics of the received view see the recognition of differences among media audiences and the inclusion of mediating variables as a break from the established tradition.

See also: ▶ MEDIA EFFECTS ▶ MEDIA EFFECTS, HISTORY OF

REFERENCES AND SUGGESTED READINGS

Bineham, J. (1988). A historical account of the hypodermic model in mass communication. *Communication Monographs*, 55, 230–246.

Katz, E. & Lazarsfeld, P. F. (1955). *Personal influence.* Glencoe, IL: Free Press.

Lang, G. E. & Lang, K. (1981). Mass communication and public opinion. In M. Rosenberg & R. H. Turner (eds.), *Social psychology: Sociological perspectives.* New York: Basic Books, pp. 653–682.

Storytelling and Narration

TAMAR KATRIEL
University of Haifa

Storytelling as a discursive activity is central to the construction of identities, relationships, and groups (Fisher 1987). Narration creates a sense of order and meaning by interweaving events, circumstantial elements, and emotions in such a way as to signal temporal coherence, causal links, and value orientations. Narrative research addresses the poetics and politics of high-profile public narratives as well as the dynamics of everyday storytelling – both face-to-face and technologically mediated.

Research into storytelling has involved: (1) Studying the discursive organization of narratives as *structural units*, including cultural myths, folktales, and personal experience stories (Labov & Waletzky 1967), as well as exploring the interactional structure of storytelling performances that are embedded in conversational exchanges (in terms of the distribution of speaking rights). (2) Exploring the socio-cultural *functions* of storytelling activities as meaning-making discursive strategies that serve personal, interpersonal, and collective ends (such as self-presentation, status negotiation, or the production of group solidarity, respectively). (3) Tracing the *dynamic construction of storytelling* as a situated performance that involves negotiation over narrative entitlement, narrative authority, and the modifications introduced by story recipients, who may elaborate upon or challenge the teller's storyline (Ochs & Capps 2001).

The power of narrative to inscribe particular versions of reality, and to endow protagonists and their actions with a particular valence, makes them effective tools in both interpersonal and collective struggles over → meanings, values, privilege, and control. Narratives construct competing collective memories in national conflicts, and new storytelling platforms – such as truth and reconciliation commissions in post-traumatic societies or digital media in global culture – open up new social possibilities.

Studies of storytelling rights – rights to the floor, access to knowledge, or recognition of one's point of view – have been central to communication scholarship about the social and interactional life of narrative. The patterns of obligation associated with storytelling in such contexts as therapy, informal settings of sociability, children's socialization into storytelling, legal proceedings, news reporting, or national commemorations deserve more research attention.

See also: ▶ CONVERSATION ANALYSIS ▶ IDENTITIES AND DISCOURSE ▶ MEANING ▶ NARRATIVE NEWS STORY

REFERENCES AND SUGGESTED READINGS

Fisher, W. (1987). *Human communication as narration.* Columbia, SC: University of South Carolina Press.

Labov, W. & Waletzky, J. (1967). Narrative analysis: Oral versions of personal experience. In J. Helm (ed.), *Essays on the verbal and visual arts.* Seattle: University of Washington Press, pp. 12–44.

Ochs, E. & Capps, L. (2001). *Living narrative: Creating lives in everyday storytelling.* Cambridge, MA: Harvard University Press.

Strategic Communication

DERINA HOLTZHAUSEN
Oklahoma State University

Strategic communication can be defined as "the practice of deliberate and purposive communication a communication agent enacts in the public sphere on behalf of a communicative entity to reach set goals" (Holtzhausen & Zerfass 2013, 74). This definition emphasizes purposiveness, the role of communication agents and thus practice, and the importance of the → public sphere, which sets the field apart from interpersonal or small group communication.

At a professional level the field faces challenges in coordinating and integrating the communication activities of organizations (→ Organizational Communication). Theoretically it is challenged to create a multidisciplinary, but unified, body of knowledge that better serves communicative entities in a society consisting of fragmented audiences and message delivery platforms. Strategic communication also has a significant impact on society at large.

The Meaning of Strategic

While the term 'strategic' originated in warfare, organizations originally used it to describe how they competed in the marketplace to gain competitive advantage and market share (Hatch 1997). Supporters of this view see strategic planning as a rational process that starts with an analysis of the organization's internal strengths and weaknesses and external opportunities and threats (SWOT analysis). The role of the practitioner is to replicate this process with the focus on how communication can be used strategically to support the organization's overall goals.

New perspectives on strategy formulation in organizations provide several alternative, and more inclusive, interpretations. *Emergent strategy* holds that strategy is based on prior experience and actions, which values the contribution of employees at every level of the organization. In learning organizations, strategy formulation is viewed as more short-term and agile, which allows organizations to react quickly to developments in their environments. Emergent strategy also implies that there is not necessarily a beginning and end to the strategic process, that it can emerge at any point during strategy formulation, and that it can be immediate and spontaneous. One of the most important emerging perspectives in strategic communication is the rejection of linearity. Meanings and messages are now viewed as negotiated and subjective, where the outcome of the communication process depends more on the receiver than on the sender. Thus dialogic communication and how it shapes strategy has now become one of the major focus areas for strategic communication research.

Strategic Communication and Society

The environment in which the communicative entity operates affects the way strategic communication is practiced. Systems, chaos, and complexity theory perspectives also often explain communication behavior, particularly to the study of → crisis communication (Gilpin & Murphy 2008). From theories of the environment comes the concept of strategic communicators as boundary spanners who help organizations adapt to their environment by in turn representing the viewpoints of constituents and the organization.

Although Habermas has somewhat softened his stance on strategic communication, he views it as a form of communication that is "pseudoconsensual," meant to help organizations, politicians, and lobbyists to get access to the media and so gain political influence (Habermas 2006). Postmodernists in turn argue that all discourse is political and therefore strategic (Lyotard 1988). What these philosophers have in common is that strategic communication is a real and influential feature of the public sphere.

Strategic Communication in the Organizational Context

Factors that affect strategic communication at organizational level are, among others, organizational structure, decision-making processes, leadership styles, and worldviews of organizational leaders and professional communicators. Strategic communication requires a holistic approach to communication; therefore, the communication function should be integrated into a single organizational function. This is difficult in complex organizations where communication functions are often scattered across divisions and departments. This fragmentation is further exacerbated by the strict definition of roles within each of these disciplines. In a strategic communication approach it is important that all these communicators work in a team, which is difficult when they have different reporting structures and strictly defined roles.

This fragmentation is further facilitated by the overly specialized approach to communication education, where marketing, public relations, advertising, and speech communication are seldom integrated into a single educational unit. Power relations within an organization are another stumbling block. The marketing function is typically included in the "strategic apex" of the organization (Mintzberg 1996, 237), while communication functions are viewed as support staff.

This access to power gives marketing departments a decision-making advantage over other communication functions, which overemphasizes consumers at the cost of other, often more important, audiences.

Organizations that are able to integrate their communication activities into a single, integrated unit that has influence at the highest level of the organization and represents all strategic audiences can use the skills of all communicators while addressing every audience in the communication process in a coordinated way, ensuring consistency of strategic messages and message delivery platforms (Grunig et al. 2002).

Strategic Communication at the Micro-Level

The outcome of strategic communication at this level is aimed at reaching the goals set out in the strategic planning phase. Strategic communication goals vary according to the situation at hand, such as brand building (→ Brands) and improving sales and reputation management through increasing awareness, maintaining positive attitudes and relationships, or changing negative behavior and poor relationships.

New communication technologies help to integrate strategic communication at this level. New media platforms such as the Internet and different → social media outlets now allow strategic communicators to bypass traditional media and overcome these divisions among audiences through a holistic approach. New communication platforms make it possible for strategic communicators to reach broad but specific targeted audiences outside of the traditional media. New analytics and the ability to micro-segment an audience, or even target individuals directly, also allow for shaping messages tailored to individual needs (→ Audience Segmentation). These technologies support networks, which Barney (2004, 2) describes as "a structural condition," that bring many people together in multiple, decentralized matrices. Strategic communicators need to identify their target audiences through micro-segmentation and they also have to assume that an audience member's multiple identities are reached through different media and different platforms. This is known as media fragmentation.

Measurement of Outcomes

Traditionally the success of marketing communication has been measured in terms of return on investment (ROI). Return on communication investment, be it financial or time, in activist groups, non-profit organizations, or political campaigns is measured in social change or election outcomes that require benchmark research to measure progress against.

Online and social media metrics provide new methods for measuring strategic communication outcomes. Baym (2013, 1) argues, "Metric and big data analysis generally serves economic values, while other approaches … may be more appropriate for assessing social and personal values."

See also: ▶ AUDIENCE SEGMENTATION ▶ BRANDS ▶ CRISIS COMMUNICATION ▶ ORGANIZATIONAL COMMUNICATION ▶ PUBLIC RELATIONS ▶ PUBLIC SPHERE ▶ SOCIAL MEDIA

REFERENCES AND SUGGESTED READINGS

Barney, D. (2004). *The network society*. Cambridge: Polity.

Baym, N. K. (2013). Data not seen: The uses and shortcoming of social media metrics. *First Monday*, 18(10), 1–16.

Bentele, G. & Nothhaft, H. (2010). Strategic communication in the public sphere from a European perspective. *International Journal of Strategic Communication*, 4(2), 93–116.

Gilpin, D. R. & Murphy, P. J. (2008). *Crisis management in a complex world*. Oxford: Oxford University Press.

Grunig, L. A., Grunig, J. E., & Dozier, D. M. (2002). *Excellent public relations ands effective organizations. A study of communication management in three countries*. Mahwah, NJ: Lawrence Erlbaum.

Habermas, J. (2006). Political communication in media society – Does democracy still enjoy an epistemic deminsion? The impact of normative theory on empirical research, *Annual Convention of the International Communication Association*. Dresden: International Communication Association.

Hatch, M. J. (1997). *Organisation theory. Modern, symbolic, and postmodern perspectives*. Oxford: Oxford University Press.

Holtzhausen, D. R. & Zerfass, A. (2013). Strategic communication – Pillars and perspectives of an alternative paradigm. In A. Zerfass, L. Rademacher, & S. Wehmeier (eds.), *Organisationskommunikation und public relations*. Wiesbaden: Springer, pp. 72–94.

Lyotard, J. F. (1988). *The differend: Phrases in dispute. Theory and history of literature* (Vol. 46). Minneapolis: University of Minnesota Press.

Mintzberg, H. (1996). The five basic parts of the organization. In J. M. Shafritz & J. S. Ott (eds.), *Classics of organization theory.* Fort Worth, TX: Harcourt Brace College, pp. 232–244.

Strategic Framing

KIRK HALLAHAN
Colorado State University

Framing is a rhetorical tool used by communicators to delimit the scope of a situation or argument and is a critical element in constructing social reality because it helps shape perceptions and provides a context for processing information (→ Information Processing). As a surrounding picture frame delimits a landscape painting, so frames add salience to certain elements of a topic by including and focusing attention on them while excluding other aspects.

Anthropologist Gregory Bateson (1972, 191) first defined a *psychological frame* as a "spatial and temporary bounding of a set of interactive messages" that operates as a form of meta-communication. Erving Goffman later used 'frame' to describe social scenes as "schemata of interpretation" (→ Schemas). *Framing of attributes* is a fundamental strategy in promotional communication (→ Advertising; Public Relations; Strategic Communication). Marketers, for example, have a choice of promoting ground beef as either '75 percent lean' or '25 percent fat.' Evidence suggests that positive framing of attributes such as these almost leads to more favorable responses (→ Framing Effects).

In the arena of → news, attribute framing forms the basis for 'second-order agenda setting,' which claims that media can tell people *how* to think about a topic, not merely *what* topics to think about (traditional or first-order agenda-setting; → Agenda-Setting Effects).

Framing of risk or potentially risky choices is grounded in prospect theory, which posits that people tend to avoid risks when a choice is stated in terms of gains but will take greater risks when choices are stated in terms of losses (Kahneman & Tversky 1979; → Risk Perceptions; Risk Communication). In the health arena, for example, patients are willing to select greater risks if their decision means saving a life or reducing suffering.

Framing of actions in terms of negative consequences similarly appears to be more effective than posing positive outcomes. *Framing of issues* or *social problems* is used by social movement activists who build their agenda for change by engaging in diagnostic, prognostic, and motivational framing processes and mobilize support through frame enterprise, sponsorship, alignment, bridging, amplification, extension, and contests (→ Agenda Building). *Framing of responsibility* draws from attribution theory and suggests the cause of events can be alternatively ascribed to different causes – such as a social actor, the object upon which the action is taken, or the environment or circumstances in which the event occurs.

See also: ▶ ADVERTISING ▶ AGENDA BUILDING ▶ AGENDA-SETTING EFFECTS ▶ CONSTRUCTION OF REALITY THROUGH THE NEWS ▶ EXEMPLIFICATION AND EXEMPLARS, EFFECTS OF ▶ FRAMING EFFECTS ▶ FRAMING OF THE NEWS ▶ HEALTH COMMUNICATION ▶ INFORMATION PROCESSING ▶ MEANING ▶ NEWS ▶ NEWS ROUTINES ▶ NEWS VALUES ▶ PRIMING THEORY ▶ PUBLIC RELATIONS ▶ RISK COMMUNICATION ▶ RISK PERCEPTIONS ▶ SCHEMAS ▶ STRATEGIC COMMUNICATION

REFERENCES AND SUGGESTED READINGS

Bateson, G. (1972). *Steps to an ecology of mind: Collected essays in anthropology, psychology, evolution and epistemology.* San Francisco: Chandler.

Gamson, W. A. & Modigliani, A. (1989). Media discourse and public opinion on nuclear power: A constructionist approach. *American Journal of Sociology*, 95(3), 1–37.

Hallahan, K. (1999). Seven models of framing: Implications for public relations. *Public Relations Review*, 11(3), 205–242.

Iyengar, S. (1991). *Is anyone responsible?* Chicago: University of Chicago Press.

Kahneman, D. & Tversky, A. (1979). Prospect theory: An analysis of decision under risk. *Econometrica*, 47, 263–291.

Structuralism

KLAUS BRUHN JENSEN
University of Copenhagen

Structuralism suggests that → interactions, → discourses, and social formations can be understood as self-contained systems. Jean Piaget

(1971, 5) identified *three distinctive assumptions*: the wholeness of a structure of elements; that structures are subject to transformations; and that these structures are self-regulating.

Piaget further distinguished between a weak or 'global' form of structuralism and a strong or 'analytic' structuralism. Whereas the sociologist Émile Durkheim's structuralism is weak, speaking of the social whole as a union of components, the anthropologist Claude Lévi-Strauss's structuralism is strong because it refers to specific rules of composition that account for particular cultural practices. Most important, structuralism proper assumes that the diverse observable aspects of social life bear witness to generative deep structures.

The linguist Ferdinand de Saussure originated the prototypical formulation of structuralism, describing language as a combinatorial system of concrete expressions ('parole') and an underlying system ('langue'; → Semiotics). The transformational-generative grammar of Noam Chomsky has been an influential variant of a strong, analytic structuralism in → linguistics. But the most elaborate application of structuralism to social life occurred in anthropology, where Lévi-Strauss (1963) accounted for myths in terms of their constituent units by analogy to sentences. Structuralist approaches have been especially manifest in critical traditions of the social sciences (→ Critical Theory).

In its strong sense, structuralism became a major *influence on two interrelated forms of media and communication research* – qualitative textual analysis and → cultural studies. Textual media analyses draw on formalist models to indicate how form carries content (→ Text and Intertextuality), further exploring the interrelations between textual and cognitive structures (→ Film Theory). In cultural studies, structuralism is one of two constitutive paradigms, the other being culturalism (Hall 1980).

Structuralism provides a conceptual matrix to account for the combined dynamism and stability of contemporary culture and society. As a prototype of interdisciplinary scholarship, structuralism has developed alongside and in dialogue with media and communication research.

See also: ▶ CRITICAL THEORY ▶ CULTURAL STUDIES ▶ DISCOURSE ▶ FILM THEORY ▶ INTERACTION ▶ LINGUISTICS ▶ POSTMODERNISM AND COMMUNICATION ▶ SEMIOTICS ▶ TEXT AND INTERTEXTUALITY

REFERENCES AND SUGGESTED READINGS

Hall, S. (1980). Cultural studies: Two paradigms. *Media, Culture and Society*, 2, 57–72.
Lévi-Strauss, C. (1963). *Structural anthropology*. Harmondsworth: Penguin.
Piaget, J. (1971). *Structuralism*. London: Routledge and Kegan Paul.

Student Communication Competence

SHERWYN P. MORREALE
University of Colorado at Colorado Springs

Communication researchers have defined communication competence as the extent to which people achieve their desired goals through communication acceptable in the situation (Morreale et al. 2013). This conceptualization suggests that students' communication is competent when it is perceived as both effective and appropriate. Effective communication means using communication to achieve the most desirable goals or outcomes in the context and situation. Appropriate communication means acting in ways suitable to the norms and expectations of the context and situation.

This model of communication competence also identifies three *components of effective and appropriate communication*. First, students must be motivated to communicate competently. Second, they must be knowledgeable about the communication situation and the kinds of messages expected, permitted, or prohibited in the situation. Third, they must be skilled at actually communicating messages in that situation. This description suggests that motivation, knowledge, and skills are fundamental to competent communication for students whether in interpersonal, group, public, or technologically mediated communication situations, and whether in or outside the US.

In addition to models, scholars and teachers also have explicated student communication competence by outlining *lists of communication skills* for students. These listings include basic speech skills, like developing messages for speeches and communicating interpersonally and in small groups, as well as advanced skills related to persuading, informing, and relating. Others, including governmental and testing agencies, have examined how to assess communication competence (Morreale et al. 2011). While these efforts were mainly carried out in the US, scholars also have a keen interest in intercultural communication competence (Chen & Starosta 1996).

Two international scholars state that, "Communicative competence is fundamental for a successful life in our society … it is of great importance for all areas of life" (Rickheit & Strohner 2010). For example, national reports provide evidence of the importance of students' competent communication to personal development, psychologically and socially, succeeding in school and at work, and becoming responsible world citizens.

Given this importance of communication to students, several governmental and testing agencies are working to describe the communication competencies necessary for students to succeed in college or to be effective at work, in society, and in their private lives. In the US, the College Board, a primary agency for college-entrance testing, collaborated with communication experts to develop and publish twelfth-grade *performance expectations* for reading, writing, speaking, listening, and media literacy. These 'Standards for College Success' are available in their entirety from the College Board (see www.collegeboard.com). Another national effort of governors and state education chiefs in the US produced a set of 'Common Core State Standards for English Language Arts.' These standards, adopted in 45 states in the US, were derived from national and international models for progressive learning. The standards identify what students should learn and be able to do, progressively from kindergarten through to grade 12, in the areas of speaking and listening.

Teachers and administrators should be aware of how their perceptions of students' communication competence may vary based on the students' cultural background, communication propensities, and ability to communicate competently using the mediated-communication technologies now ubiquitous in the US and other countries. Researchers in and outside the US are considering the impact of these changing communication technologies on communication competence. As in all contexts, perceptions of communication competence in a world of changing communication technologies is dependent on students' motivation to use technology to communicate, their knowledge of how to use it, the communication context and the message, and the students' skills in sending and receiving messages using technology (Spitzberg 2006).

See also: ▶ CLASSROOM STUDENT–TEACHER INTERACTION ▶ INTERPERSONAL COMMUNICATION COMPETENCE AND SOCIAL SKILLS ▶ LANGUAGE AND SOCIAL INTERACTION

REFERENCES AND FURTHER READINGS

Chen, G. M. & Starosta, W. J. (1996). Intercultural communication competence: A synthesis. *Communication Yearbook*, 19, 353–384.

Morreale, S., Backlund, P., Hay, E., & Moore, M. (2011). A major review of the assessment of oral communication. *Communication Education*, 60(2), 255–278.

Morreale, S. P., Spitzberg, B. H., & Barge, J. K. (2013). *Human communication: Motivation, knowledge, and skills*, 3rd edn. New York: Peter Lang.

Rickheit, G. & Strohner, H. (2010). *Handbook of communication competence*. Berlin: Mouton de Gruyter.

Spitzberg, B. H. (2006). Preliminary development of a model and measure of computer-mediated communication (CMC) competence. *Journal of Computer-Mediated Communication*, 11(2), 629–666.

Survey

MICHAEL W. TRAUGOTT
University of Michigan

Surveys are uniquely suited to the collection of knowledge, attitudes, and opinions. In political research, for example, there are many ways to obtain information about voter turnout, including official government statistics. But governments do not collect information on candidate or party preferences, and surveys are required to obtain such information, as well as on attitudes about issues of the day (→ Election Surveys). In economic research, sales data indicate the preferences of consumers for products or their relative market share. But the only way to obtain systematic data on the nature of preferences underlying these purchases is through surveys (→ Marketing).

Surveys represent a system for data collection that involves *several steps*. These include selection of a mode of interviewing, sampling, questionnaire design and pre-testing, training of interviewers, preparation of the final questionnaire, fieldwork for data collection, and data analysis (→ Interview, Standardized; Interview, Qualitative; Sampling, Random).

The *mode of data collection* comes first because so many other issues follow as a result. Data can be collected through face-to-face interviews where the interviewer and the respondent meet. This is expensive because of travel costs. Data can also be collected on the telephone, which is generally less expensive. Telephone interviews are usually shorter and consist primarily of closed-end questions, and they can usually be done in a shorter period of time. Pencil-and-paper surveys can be administered in person or by mail and are often employed because they are inexpensive and are sometimes preferred for asking about sensitive topics. Surveys on the Internet permit rapid data collection and are very amenable to the use of examples and illustrations, including embedded video and audio segments.

Mode of data collection is a primary concern because so many additional choices are affected by it. *Sampling* is a prime example. Face-to-face interviews employ multi-stage area probability samples based on geography in order to reduce travel costs. For telephone surveys, a list of phone numbers can be developed or purchased from a commercial vendor, often on the same day a decision is made to field a study. Thus they have true random dispersion across a nation. Procedures have to be followed to ensure that unlisted numbers are incorporated into the sample, as well as mobile phones for those who don't have landlines. In mail surveys, lists of addresses sometimes have to be located and checked independently for currency. Specific procedures have been developed for pursuing mail surveys to maximize response rates.

Seeing a survey as a process provides the basis for reviewing and controlling potential data quality through a *total survey error (TSE) perspective*. The TSE approach acknowledges that errors derive from any stage of the process. This approach permits available resources to be invested effectively at different stages in order to reduce likely errors. As the preceding discussion suggests, the organization and management of surveys is a complex and expensive process. A researcher can construct a general design of all the elements of a survey and then put the study out for bids, eventually contracting with a firm that offers the best quality within the constraints of the available budget.

See also: ▶ AUDIENCE RESEARCH ▶ ELECTION SURVEYS ▶ INTERVIEW, QUALITATIVE ▶ INTERVIEW, STANDARDIZED ▶ MARKETING ▶ PUBLIC OPINION ▶ PUBLIC OPINION POLLING ▶ SAMPLING, RANDOM

REFERENCES AND SUGGESTED READINGS

Biemer, P. B. & Lyberg, L. E. (2003). *Introduction to survey quality*. New York: John Wiley.
Groves, R. M., Fowler Jr., F. J., Couper, M. P., Lepkowski, J. M., Singer, E., & Tourangeau, R. (2004). *Survey methodology*. New York: John Wiley.
Weisberg, H. (2005). *The new science of survey research: The total survey error approach*. Chicago: University of Chicago Press.

Tabloidization

S. ELIZABETH BIRD
University of South Florida

Since the 1980s, 'tabloidization' has been used to describe changes in journalism perceived to represent a decline in traditional journalistic standards. The term *'tabloid'* strictly refers only to certain newspapers' half-broadsheet size, but it has come to define a kind of formulaic, colorful narrative distinct from standard, 'objective' styles of journalism (→ Objectivity in Reporting), and appealing to base instincts and public demand for → sensationalism. British and US tabloids emerged in the early twentieth century, written in the idioms of the people, as William Randolph Hearst declared. The tension between a perception of tabloid style as representing either the legitimate voice of the people, or as a vulgarization of public → discourse, has undergirded the debate about tabloidization since.

'Tabloidization' is a fairly recent term developed to describe *a process* of journalism's decline. In the nineteenth and early twentieth centuries, critics bemoaned the cheapening of public discourse represented by popularization of the news, and this lament gathered momentum over the next 100 years. However, neither journalists nor critics agree precisely what tabloidization is, or whether it is invariably a negative force. Empirical attempts to demonstrate the process have been inconclusive, but the phenomenon is seen to have distinctive characteristics of style and content. Stylistically, tabloid writing avoids complex analysis in favor of short, narrative sentences with a central emphasis on the personal, and dependence on visual images (→ Narrative News Story; New Factors; News Values).

Tabloidization of content is usually framed as trivialization, with celebrity gossip and human-interest stories crowding out serious news. Tabloidization is primarily audience- and advertiser-driven, in an increasingly competitive news environment (→ Commercialization: Impact on Media Content). News outlets have proliferated across the digital world, with non-serious 'chatter' dominating. Recent fears about tabloidization are now less focused on print media, and more on a general decline toward 'tabloid culture.' Tabloidization may mean different things depending on context, and so the term lacks a single, clear definition.

See also: ▶ COMMERCIALIZATION: IMPACT ON MEDIA CONTENT ▶ DISCOURSE ▶ ETHICS IN JOURNALISM ▶ INFOTAINMENT ▶ INTERNET NEWS ▶ JOURNALISM, HISTORY OF ▶ NARRATIVE NEWS STORY ▶ NEWS FACTORS ▶ NEWSPAPER, HISTORY OF

The Concise Encyclopedia of Communication, First Edition. Edited by Wolfgang Donsbach.
© 2015 John Wiley & Sons, Inc. Published 2015 by John Wiley & Sons, Inc.

▶ NEWS VALUES ▶ OBJECTIVITY IN REPORTING
▶ QUALITY OF THE NEWS ▶ SENSATIONALISM

REFERENCES AND SUGGESTED READINGS

Bird, S. E. (1992). *For enquiring minds: A cultural study of supermarket tabloids*. Knoxville: University of Tennessee Press.
Sparks, C. & Tulloch, J. (eds.) (2000). *Tabloid tales*. New York: Rowman & Littlefield.
Zelizer, B. (eds) (2009). *The changing faces of journalism: Tabloidization, technology and truthiness*. New York: Routledge.

Taste Culture

DIANA CRANE-HEVRE
University of Pennsylvania

The idea that popular culture consists of distinct 'taste cultures' was developed by Herbert Gans (1974) as an alternative to the then dominant theory of mass culture (Horkheimer & Adorno 2001) which viewed popular culture as a commercial enterprise that represented a debased form of high culture. Gans argued that popular culture exists in various forms that appeal to audiences with different educational backgrounds and tastes. Gans developed a *typology of "taste publics"* that consume taste cultures appropriate for their educational level and social background.

A taste culture consists of values and aesthetic standards for culture, cultural forms that express those values, and the media in which they are expressed. *Five principal taste cultures*, stratified by social class, represented American culture in the 1970s. *High culture* comprised both classic and contemporary styles in literature and the arts. Its taste public included creators and highly educated upper- and upper-middle-class people. *Upper-middle culture* was associated with an upper-middle-class taste public, who were uninterested in the relatively esoteric aspects of high culture, preferring forms of culture that spoke to issues that were relevant to their personal lives. *Lower-middle culture* was America's dominant taste culture. Its taste public provided the major audience for mass media and sought content that confirmed its worldview, particularly its moral values. The taste public for *low culture* consisted of older, lower-middle-class people who preferred entertainment that dealt with traditional working-class values. *Quasi-folk low culture* was a simpler version of low culture. Its taste public consisted of unskilled blue-collar and service workers with little education.

Bourdieu (1984) developed a theory to explain how social class and education influence cultural choices. Recent research reveals that many people do not restrict their attention to a particular type of culture, because of the enormous variety of cultural choices now available. Differences among lifestyles within the same social class as well as across social classes are anticipated.

See also: ▶ AUDIENCE RESEARCH ▶ CONSUMER CULTURE ▶ CRITICAL THEORY ▶ CULTURE: DEFINITIONS AND CONCEPTS ▶ MEDIA USE BY SOCIAL VARIABLE

REFERENCES AND SUGGESTED READINGS

Bourdieu, P. (1984). *Distinction: A social critique of the judgment of taste*. Cambridge, MA: Harvard University Press.
Gans, H. (1974). *Popular culture and high culture: An analysis and evaluation of taste*. New York: Basic Books.
Horkheimer, M. & Adorno, T. W. (2001). The culture industry: Enlightenment as mass deception. In M. G. Durham & D. M. Kellner (eds.), *Media and cultural studies*. Oxford: Blackwell, pp. 71–101.

Teacher Communication Style

JON F. NUSSBAUM
Pennsylvania State University

Norton (1977) utilized his conceptualization of communicator style to investigate teacher effectiveness as a function of the way a teacher communicates within the classroom. Anderson et al. (1981) found that perceptions of teacher effectiveness and perceptions of student cognitive, affective, and behavioral learning were related to perceptions of active and open stylistic communication dimensions. In addition, these particular studies located teacher communication style within a much larger teacher–student relational context (→ Classroom Student–Teacher Interaction).

Kearney and McCroskey (1980) pointed out that the concept of communicator style utilized by Norton and others in their investigations of classroom communication was not solidly grounded within instructional communication theory. They grounded their notion of teacher communication style (TCS) within instructional communication theory, and defined TCS as "the collective perceptions of a teacher's relational image in the classroom" (Kearney & McCroskey 1980, 533).

Norton and Nussbaum (1980) investigated the link between dramatic style and found that *two dramatic style behaviors* related strongly to effective teaching: the teacher is entertaining and the teacher performs double takes. In addition, several other teacher dramatic behaviors were shown to be utilized by highly effective teachers: storytelling; gets others to laugh; catches others up in stories; pokes fun; and is sarcastic.

A series of *investigations* were conducted by Scott Myers and several colleagues to investigate the relationship between teacher argumentativeness, teacher verbal aggressiveness, and positive student outcomes. The results of these investigations support the notion that perceived instructor argumentativeness in the classroom is positively related to student outcomes while teacher aggressiveness is negatively related to positive classroom outcomes. Numerous additional variables related to teacher communication style have been investigated and related to positive student and teacher outcomes within the classroom. For instance, teacher self-disclosure, teacher humor, and positive facework by teachers have all been shown to produce positive student and teacher outcomes (→ Teacher Influence and Persuasion).

See also: ▶ CLASSROOM STUDENT–TEACHER INTERACTION ▶ EDUCATIONAL COMMUNICATION ▶ INTERPERSONAL COMMUNICATION COMPETENCE AND SOCIAL SKILLS ▶ TEACHER INFLUENCE AND PERSUASION

REFERENCES AND SUGGESTED READINGS

Anderson, J., Norton, R., & Nussbaum, J. F. (1981). Three investigations exploring the relationship among perceived communicator style, perceived teacher immediacy, perceived teacher–student solidarity, teacher effectiveness and student learning. *Communication Education*, 30, 377–392.

Kearney, P. & McCroskey, J. C. (1980). Relationship among teacher communication style, trait and state communication apprehension, and teacher effectiveness. *Communication Yearbook*, 4, 533–552.

Myers, S. A. & Rocca, K. A. (2001). Perceived instructor argumentativeness and verbal aggressiveness in the college classroom: Effects on student perceptions of climate, apprehension, and state motivation. *Western Journal of Communication*, 65, 113–137.

Norton, R. W. (1977). Teacher effectiveness as a function of communicator style. *Communication Yearbook*, 1, 525–542.

Norton, R. & Nussbaum, J. F. (1980). Dramatic behaviors of the effective teacher. *Communication Yearbook*, 4, 565–574.

Teacher Influence and Persuasion

JENNIFER H. WALDECK
Chapman University

PATRICIA KEARNEY
California State University, Long Beach

The purpose of teacher influence messages is to change, modify, or shape student thoughts and behaviors in ways that promote engagement with course material and maximize learning.

Researchers have examined *four primary strategies* for influencing student cooperation and engagement. (1) Classroom management, or the use of policies and structure, is one of the most-studied ways to influence students to spend time on tasks that will enhance learning; however, an overemphasis on rules and structure may demotivate some learners. (2) Mentoring influences students to stay in school, persist in their learning, seek assistance, come to class prepared, and enjoy the learning process. (3) Teachers who make content relevant influence students' willingness to focus on and retain important information. For example, teachers must ensure the relevance of their disclosures and personal examples to course material to maximize student influence. (4) Power-based strategies are conceptualized and operationalized as specific behavioral alteration techniques and messages teachers use to influence and manage students' behavior and misbehavior.

Teacher persuasiveness is a function of *several antecedents*. First, nonverbal immediacy signals perceptions of friendliness, warmth, and interpersonal closeness and can be demonstrated with head nods, smiling, eye contact, vocal expressiveness, gestures, and other nonverbal messages. Research on teacher immediacy has established a consistent, substantial, and positive association with students' affect toward the teacher, school, and course content, and to a lesser extent, with students' cognitive learning. Credibility encompasses student perceptions of teachers' competence, character or trust, and caring. Credible teachers have the potential to positively influence student motivation, evaluations, enjoyment, and willingness to recommend the teacher to others. Another influence strategy is teacher confirmation, or messages designed to recognize learners as valuable and significant. Teachers who engage in confirming behaviors promote motivation to learn, reduced apprehension to communicate in class, increased affective and cognitive learning, and consequently have enhanced power to influence.

REFERENCES AND SUGGESTED READINGS

Finn, A. N. & Ledbetter, A. M. (2013). Teacher power mediates the effects of technology policies on teacher credibility. *Communication Education*, 62, 26–47.

Waldeck, J. H. (2007). Answering the question: Student perceptions of personalized education and the construct's relationship to learning outcomes. *Communication Education*, 56, 409–432.

Woolfolk, A. (2001). Educational psychology, 5th edn. Boston, MA: Allyn and Bacon.

Technology and Communication

ROBIN MANSELL
London School of Economics and Political Science

The relationship between technology and communication can be studied analytically at any time in human history (→ Media History; Digital Media, History of). With the Internet, personal computers, the world wide web, mobile communications (→ Mobility, Technology for), and smart phones and tablets, digitization has been seen as contributing to the blurring of boundaries between segments of the media and communication industry. No single disciplinary approach encompasses all facets of the complex relationship between technology and communication. With the spread of these technologies, the term → 'information society' has gained currency across the disciplines of the social sciences and the humanities and the terms 'knowledge society' and 'network society' are also used (Castells 2009). Some refer to information, knowledge, or network 'societies' to signal the diverse ways in which ICTs are appropriated around the world by their users.

Endogenous and Exogenous Perspective

ICT innovation can be treated conceptually as either exogenous or endogenous to a social system. The *exogenous perspective* treats ICTs as if they are objects isolated from the social, political, and economic environment in which they are produced and consumed. If it is technology that is the determining factor in social organization, then what is left for the researcher is an observer role. The exogenous perspective emphasizes the efficiency and rationality of an autonomous technological system where there is little room for human agency.

In contrast, from an *endogenous perspective*, research focuses on the way ICTs become woven into the fabric of life – in terms of morality, the economy, culture, or the political world and on the specific, material conditions under which technology is produced and consumed. Technology is regarded as part of the social fabric where actors sanction certain forms of change and not others. Power is understood to be located in the interwoven alignment of state (administrative and military), private capital, and civil society interests. In this view, the emphasis is on the way technology mediates human relationships and on the constraints that distort benefits that might otherwise accrue to those who are not at the center of economic and political power (Curran et al. 2012; Mansell 2012; Silverstone 2007).

Among the many strands of research in this context are studies of the *political implications* of the information society for democracy and participation in public debate (→ Communication

Technology and Democracy) and in electoral processes and whether a right to communicate should be enshrined in international law (Jørgensen 2013). Within sociology, research on the → domestication of technologies (Hartmann 2013) has helped to reveal that ICT artifacts are not prefigured by technology designers for their users, and that older and newer media and ICTs are appropriated in unpredictable ways depending on the cultural specificities of their use. Economic analysis tends to focus on the diffusion of ICTs and the implications for productivity in the economy since these technologies are classed as general-purpose technologies and associated with major transformations when they become widely dispersed across all ICT-using sectors of the economy (Freeman 2007; → Information and Communication Technology, Economics of).

Research Topics

The disruptive characteristics of innovations in ICTs have given rise to many debates about their positive or negative implications for the *global order*, with research emphasizing links between local and distant places and the sometimes unifying, and at other times fragmenting, consequences. There is no stable definition but the term virtual community generally applies to online interactions that give rise to new forms of relationships and new organizational forms. Research focuses on the network relations among activists, bloggers, scientists and many other communities of users of social media. The digital platforms that support these communicative activities are increasingly being used by researchers to map the architecture of networks and social relations with a focus on the directionality of communication, synchronicity, content modularity, interactivity (→ Interactivity, Concepts of), personalization, and → meaning construction. Research on issues of information control, → privacy, and security raised by user-generated content, the co-creation of content, and interactive Web 2.0 applications is beginning to tackle the implications of 'big data' analytics which uses web-harvesting, ratings systems, and identity profiling to support corporate and state information collection and processing activities (Mayer-Schönberger & Cukier 2013). Digital means of interacting online support the networking activities of individuals and of networked organizations (→ Network Organizations through Communication Technology) which enable virtual teamworking and outsourcing, raising questions about the ownership of creative capabilities, privacy, and trust, whether the public can have confidence in the digital services provided by governments, and whether new forms of interaction are consistent with democratic practice.

When the diffusion of ICTs is uneven, or where the distribution of the gains as a result of investing in them is uneven, this is referred to as a → *digital divide*. For some it is an article of faith that ICTs hold the solutions to economic, political, and cultural problems, while others argue that digital divides mean that it is unlikely that these technologies will alleviate deeply rooted social and economic problems. This concept has been criticized for its oversimplification of the factors that give rise to inequality and research focusing on digital literacies (including → information literacy or → media literacy) and cultural differences have yielded insight into the many forms and consequences of digital exclusion (Livingstone and Helsper 2010). Differences in views about the relationship between technology and communication and the persistence of digital divides are reflected in research on whether a global media and communication policy environment is feasible and the roles of the nation state and multi-stakeholder groups in governing digital media.

Different framings of the relationship between *globalization and communication* are echoed in research on the governance regimes that enable the production and consumption of ICTs and media content, locally and globally (→ Globalization Theories). The governance of Internet has become a hotly contested area of research drawing on legal expertise and examining the values embedded in the architecture of the Internet and other digital applications. Brown and Marsden (2013) provide comprehensive examinations of the proliferation of policies, regulations, and legislation in response to the global spread of digital networks and their applications, especially the Internet (→ Communication and Law; Internet: Law and Regulation). In addition, there is research on specific online behaviors and whether there should be sanctions for 'bad' behavior in the case of hacktivism or crime and terrorism (→ Crime and Communication Technology; Terrorism and Communication Technologies; Mediated Terrorism).

Finally, the relationship between technology and communication raises many issues with respect to *ethical conduct* within the humanities and the social sciences. Guidelines with respect to Internet-related research have been developed nationally and by organizations such as the Association of Internet Researchers (AoIR). Different methods raise concerns about the risks involved to researchers and to those they study.

See also: ▶ ARCHIVING OF INTERNET CONTENT ▶ COMMUNICATION AND LAW ▶ COMMUNICATION INEQUALITIES ▶ COMMUNICATION TECHNOLOGY AND DEMOCRACY ▶ COMMUNICATION TECHNOLOGY STANDARDS ▶ COPYRIGHT ▶ CRIME AND COMMUNICATION TECHNOLOGY ▶ DIGITAL DIVIDE ▶ DIGITAL MEDIA, HISTORY OF ▶ DOMESTICATION OF TECHNOLOGY ▶ GLOBALIZATION OF THE MEDIA ▶ GLOBALIZATION THEORIES ▶ INFORMATION AND COMMUNICATION TECHNOLOGY, ECONOMICS OF ▶ INFORMATION LITERACY ▶ INFORMATION SOCIETY ▶ INTERACTIVITY, CONCEPT OF ▶ INTERNET LAW AND REGULATION ▶ LANGUAGE AND THE INTERNET ▶ MEANING ▶ MEDIA ECONOMICS ▶ MEDIA HISTORY ▶ MEDIA LITERACY ▶ MEDIATED TERRORISM ▶ MOBILITY, TECHNOLOGY FOR ▶ NETWORK ORGANIZATIONS THROUGH COMMUNICATION TECHNOLOGY ▶ NEWSPAPER, HISTORY OF ▶ ONLINE MEDIA ▶ ONLINE RESEARCH ▶ OPEN SOURCE ▶ PERSONAL COMMUNICATION BY CMC ▶ PRINTING, HISTORY OF ▶ PRIVACY ▶ TERRORISM AND COMMUNICATION TECHNOLOGIES

REFERENCES AND SUGGESTED READINGS

Brown, I. & Marsden, C. (2013). *Regulating code: good governance and better regulation in the information age.* Cambridge, MA: MIT Press.

Castells, M. (2009). *Communication* Power. Oxford: Oxford University Press.

Curran, J., Fenton, N., & Freedman, D. (2012). *Misunderstanding the internet.* London: Routledge.

Freeman, C. (2007). The ICT paradigm. In R. Mansell, C. Avgerou, D. Quah, & R. Silverstone (eds.), *The Oxford handbook of information and communication technologies.* Oxford: Oxford University Press, pp. 34–54.

Hartmann, M. (2013). From domestication to mediated mobilism. *Mobile Media and Communication,* 1(1), 42–49.

Jørgensen, R. F. (2013). *Framing the net: The Internet and human rights.* Cheltenham: Edward Elgar.

Livingstone, S. & Helsper, E. (2010). Balancing opportunities and risks in teenagers' use of the Internet: The role of online skills and Internet self-efficacy. *New Media & Society,* 12(2), 309–329.

Mansell, R. (2012). *Imagining the Internet: Communication, innovation and governance.* Oxford: Oxford University Press.

Mayer-Schönberger, V. & Cukier, K. (2013). *Big data: a revolution that will transform how we live, work and think.* London: John Murray.

Silverstone, R. (2007). *Media and morality: On the rise of the mediapolis.* Cambridge: Polity.

Televised Debates

CARSTEN REINEMANN
Ludwig Maximilian University of Munich

MARCUS MAURER
Johannes Gutenberg University of Mainz

Televised debates have become a key feature of election campaigns in many countries around the world although their format differs between and within countries. Unlike regular campaign media coverage, they provide voters with the chance to directly listen to the candidates and learn about their stands on the issues and their personalities without the filter of the media's news selection (→ Election Campaign Communication). In many countries, televised debates reach a larger audience, generate more media coverage, and stimulate more discussion among citizens than any other single campaign event. However, due to differences in political systems, electoral procedures, the role of the candidates, political cultures, and the debates themselves, these findings should not be uncritically transferred to other countries (→ Political Communication Systems). The first televised election debate took place in 1956 in the US when Adlai Stevenson and Estes Kefauver ran for the nomination as presidential candidate for the Democratic Party. In 1960, the four debates between John F. Kennedy and Richard Nixon were the first US presidential debates broadcast on television.

Numerous studies have dealt with various aspects of what happens during a debate using both social science content analysis and classical rhetoric. Studies on *verbal content*, for example, have examined the use of arguments, evidence, and humor, the number of attacks, acclaims, and defenses, language styles, and the degree of clash. Most of these studies show that debates are rather issue-oriented and contain fewer character discussions or attacks on opponents than other forms of campaign communication. In contrast to that, studies on *visual content* have been rather rare. This is quite surprising, bearing in mind the widespread notion that the visual appearance of candidates is able to decide a debate.

The largest amount of debate research investigates their *effects*. Most studies focus on immediate effects on perceptions of who won the debate, knowledge about candidates' issue stands, candidate images, and voting behavior (→ Political Cognitions). A limited number of studies deal with more latent effects on, for example, voters' civic engagement and political alienation. Most effect studies use pre-test/post-test design with (representative) → surveys or focus groups. In addition, there are an increasing number of experimental studies and studies using real-time response measurements of viewers' reactions during debates (→ Quantitative Methodology; Experiment, Laboratory). Generally, debates seem to differ in their impact on voters because of differences in the specific campaign contexts, formats, candidates involved, their performances, etc. This means that some debates seem to have strong effects whereas others remain of marginal influence. Post-debate surveys of viewers and large portions of post-debate media coverage focus on the question of who won the debate. Generally, those *verdicts* are affected by political predispositions, expectations, and the perception of the debate itself. The likelihood of positive verdicts can be increased by candidates when they use acclaims and commonplaces in the debate. These often result in positive reactions from viewers. On the other hand, attacks and factual evidence tend to polarize supporters and opponents of the candidates (Reinemann & Maurer 2005).

Numerous studies have shown that televised debates can enhance viewers' *knowledge of candidates' issue stands* (→ Political Knowledge).

Effects on the *candidates' images* can be differentiated: whereas perceptions of political traits like issue competences or effectiveness seem to be more strongly affected by verbal message components, perceptions of personal traits like trustworthiness or likeability are more strongly affected by visual elements. Studies on priming effects of televised debates (→ Priming Theory) have found that debates can (1) increase the importance of some personality traits in comparison to others, (2) enhance the importance of personality traits in comparison to personal issue competences, and (3) enhance the importance of candidates in comparison to party identification and issue positions, changing voting intentions. Usually, debates tend to reinforce the *voting intentions* of those already committed more than they change them (→ Political Persuasion).

See also: ▶ AGENDA-SETTING EFFECTS ▶ ELECTION CAMPAIGN COMMUNICATION ▶ EXPERIMENT, LABORATORY ▶ MEDIA AND PERCEPTIONS OF REALITY ▶ POLITICAL COGNITIONS ▶ POLITICAL COMMUNICATION SYSTEMS ▶ POLITICAL KNOWLEDGE ▶ POLITICAL PERSUASION ▶ PRIMING THEORY ▶ QUANTITATIVE METHODOLOGY ▶ SURVEY

REFERENCES AND SUGGESTED READINGS

Blais, A. & Perrella, A. M. L. (2008). Systemic effects of televised candidates' debates. *International Journal of Press/Politics*, 13, 445–464.

Coleman, S. (2013). Debate on television: The spectacle of deliberation. *Television and New Media*, 14(1), 20–30.

Fridkin, K. L., Kenney, P. J., Gershon, S. A., & Woodall, G. S. (2008). Spinning debates: The impact of the news media's coverage of the final 2004 presidential debate. *International Journal of Press/Politics*, 13, 29–51.

McKinney, M. S. & Carlin, D. B. (2004). Political campaign debates. In L. L. Kaid (ed.), *Handbook of political communication research*. Mahwah, NJ: Lawrence Erlbaum, pp. 203–234.

Reinemann, C. & Maurer, M. (2005). Unifying or polarizing: Short-term effects and post-debate consequences of different rhetorical strategies in televised debates. *Journal of Communication*, 55, 775–794.

Rhea, D. M. (2012). There they go again – the use of humor in presidential debates 1960–2008. *Argumentation and Advocacy*, 49(2), 115–131.

Television Broadcasting, Regulation of

ROGER L. SADLER
Western Illinois University

Historically, TV regulation in various countries has fallen into one of *four broad categories*. (1) Authoritarian: The government strictly controls the information that is broadcast. (2) Paternalistic: TV programming content is to be determined by a combination of free-market forces and government regulations. (3) Permissive: The marketplace plays a dominant role, with limited regulation from the government. Advertising is the dominant funding source. (4) Pluralistic: This is a blend of paternalistic and permissive frameworks, where the government carefully balances the marketplace and the public interest.

The US is the world's model for permissive broadcasting regulation. Regulatory authority is given to the → Federal Communications Commission (FCC). The FCC also oversees telecommunications such as the telephone. However, in the paternalistic UK, the Department for Culture, Media and Sport oversees broadcasting while a separate entity, Ofcom, regulates telecommunications. Communist China tends to be authoritarian in its television regulation, and the central government controls all telecommunications.

The FCC requires stations to serve the 'public interest.' The US government applies the scarcity rationale, which says the public airwaves are a 'scarce' resource and need to be regulated. However, courts in recent years have argued the scarcity rationale may no longer be valid because of the proliferation of other media such as satellite, the Internet, and cable (→ Satellite Communication, Regulation of). The UK government has a paternalistic approach and has traditionally seen TV broadcasting as a public service. Therefore, a main mission of the British Broadcasting Corporation (→ BBC) has been to provide the citizenry with news, information, and education programs. In authoritarian systems such as those of Saudi Arabia or the People's Republic of China, the airwaves are considered a government entity, and programming critical of the government is prohibited.

Regulatory bodies in most countries are given the power to grant *licenses* to broadcasters. In the US, the FCC uses a variety of ownership rules to limit how many media outlets may be owned by one person or company.

The FCC in the US is prohibited from "censorship," but courts have upheld certain *content regulations* such as political broadcasting rules. These rules ensure that broadcasters do not use the power of the airwaves to favor one candidate over another, especially in regard to political ads. In some countries, politicians are granted free airtime before elections. The FCC more directly regulates content through "indecency rules," handing out fines to broadcasters that air "patently offensive" material relating to "sexual or excretory activities or organs at a time of day when children are likely to be in the audience." Over the years, most FCC fines have been issued to radio stations in instances where on-air hosts have used graphic sexual language. The FCC has also fined TV stations for indecency, often for sexual content involving sexual situations and nudity. Such standards are more liberal in countries such as Japan, Brazil, and Germany, where nudity or coarse language is considered less objectionable than in the US. At the opposite end of the spectrum are authoritarian systems like that of China, where indecent or offensive material is prohibited.

The US regulates cable and satellite with more of a 'hands-off' approach because these media do not operate on the 'public airwaves.' Many countries have separate government agencies that oversee *advertising on television*. In Denmark, the Radio and Television Advertising Commission reviews citizen complaints about ads. In the US, the Federal Trade Commission (FTC) punishes false and misleading advertising. Otherwise, most governments avoid content regulation of commercials. One major exception is advertising for tobacco. The UK bans all TV ads for cigarettes, cigars, and other tobacco products. The US bans broadcast ads for cigarettes, smokeless tobacco, and little cigars. The EU bans cigarette advertising on TV, radio, the Internet, and print media (→ Advertising Law and Regulation).

The International Telecommunication Union (ITU), founded in 1865, is an international body comprised of roughly 200 countries. The ITU's constitution says the organization's mission is to "promote the extension of the benefits of the new telecommunication technologies to all the world's inhabitants." The ITU is a United Nations organization. There are also agencies that deal with telecommunications issues on a regional basis including the Asia-Pacific Broadcasting Union (ABU) and the European Broadcasting Union (EBU). Such regional groups provide technical advice and support to members (→ International Communication Agencies).

See also: ▶ ADVERTISING LAW AND REGULATION ▶ BBC ▶ COMMUNICATION AND LAW ▶ FEDERAL COMMUNICATIONS COMMISSION (FCC) ▶ INTERNATIONAL COMMUNICATION AGENCIES ▶ POLITICAL COMMUNICATION SYSTEMS ▶ PUBLIC BROADCASTING SYSTEMS ▶ SATELLITE COMMUNICATION, REGULATION OF ▶ TELEVISION: SOCIAL HISTORY

REFERENCES AND SUGGESTED READINGS

Aster, H. (ed.) (1992). *Challenges for international broadcasting*. New York: Mosaic.
Jacobs, G. (ed.) (2005). *World radio TV handbook: The directory of global broadcasting*. Oxford: WRTH.
Sadler, R. (2005). *Electronic media law*. Thousand Oaks, CA: Sage.
Smith, A. & Paterson, R. (eds.) (1998). *Television: An international history*. New York: Oxford University Press.

Television for Development

BELLA MODY
University of Colorado at Boulder

During their colonial occupation, many parts of Asia, Africa, Latin America, and the Caribbean were underdeveloped; forced labor was used in mines, fields, and plantations to supply the factories of Europe. Television has been part of state-led reconstruction attempts for national development since the 1970s, albeit with no explicit policies.

After the Second North Atlantic War of 1939–1945, the Soviet bloc, the US, and the Bretton Woods institutions (the UN, the World Bank, and the IMF) initiated *modernization and development projects* in Europe's former colonies. By the 1960s, this 'social-engineering-of-change project' began to be called "economic development." A communication medium like television with audio and visual capability and two sound tracks was considered an extremely promising educational tool for low-literacy populations and a channel for their modernization (→ Educational Communication).

The introduction of television began in the 1950s and was much more complex than radio. The capital and operating costs of television production, costs to the consumer of receiver purchase, and for electricity were high. The modes of different nations' entry to television varied according to the nature of the state, audience/market size, domestic capital, and national cultural characteristics. These *modes of television entry* were initiated by domestic private capital for urban entertainment, grants by foreign governments to help market expansion, sales promotion by their manufacturers, and UN- and foreign-aided demonstrations of television's educational potential.

Competing foreign equipment manufacturers used 'aid-for-trade offers' from their home governments. Local television set distributors or ad agencies took the initiative for the introduction of television in countries where there was domestic capital and openness to financing by advertising. UNESCO, the Ford Foundation, and bilateral foreign aid agencies promoted demonstrations of the audiovisual capability of the medium as an educational solution for low-literacy countries (→ UNESCO). In many cases, once the short-term financing ended, the donated equipment and facilities were transformed into a sports and entertainment channel for the middle and upper classes.

With the introduction of *direct-broadcast satellites* pioneered by NASA in the early 1970s, development pilot projects of varying lengths were conducted to demonstrate the capability of TV, radio, and telecommunication (→ Satellite Television). The mid-1970s saw a more advanced NASA satellite demonstrate educational applications in Alaska, the Pacific, Appalachia, and India. India's year-long (1975–1976) "Satellite Instructional TV Experiment (SITE)" was investigated by national and international scholars whose findings elaborated on the results of projects elsewhere: more attention should have been paid to the design of educational programs. The total SITE effort involved 3,300 person years of which 2,050 were spent on technology, hardware, or equipment: only 9 percent was dedicated to program development (Mody 1987). Nevertheless, some *effects* materialized. Children exposed to TV in the classroom showed significant gains in language development; programs led to enquiries for more knowledge, as measured by the greater utilization of libraries in schools, and the adult education evening transmissions resulted in statistically significant gains in the knowledge of preventive health.

In the 1980s, US foreign aid (USAID) and the then satellite cooperative INTELSAT conducted educational demonstrations of satellite capability. INTELSAT enabled the Chinese Open University to experiment with one-way video and audio applications; Ireland and Jordan to exchange university courses; and hospitals in Latin America and Miami, and Uganda, Kenya, and Canada, to do telemedicine.

Until the 1980s, TV was owned and operated in Asia, Africa, and the Caribbean by the state. TV in Latin America had fallen under US commercial influence after its independence from European colonizers. The few applications of television for development were expensive and state-financed, and hence constituted additional demands on already overstretched state budgets. As developing countries struggled with their economy, the US, western Europe, and Japan pushed them to open up national firms (including state broadcasting monopolies) to *private and foreign investment*. Simultaneously, domestic lobbies were advocating the US model of advertising-based radio and TV ownership so coverage could expand beyond the capital city.

The instructional design model of the 1960s and 1970s for specific educational audiences, which was so expensive to implement and was infrequently used outside short-lived, aid-financed projects, has given way to another educational model initiated by foreign aid that is more suited to the large-audience needs of an advertiser-financed media system. Entertainment education has actually been credited with helping the state broadcaster to move from state public service ownership to a commercially competitive operator in India. Television for development in the early twenty-first century is promoting *modernization via the marketplace*. Audience-specific educational media interventions are limited to community radio initiatives, where they exist.

See also: ▶ BBC WORLD SERVICE ▶ DEVELOPMENT COMMUNICATION ▶ EDUCATIONAL COMMUNICATION ▶ INSTRUCTIONAL TELEVISION ▶ MEDIA EFFECTS ▶ RADIO FOR DEVELOPMENT ▶ SATELLITE TELEVISION ▶ UNESCO

REFERENCES AND SUGGESTED READINGS

Enghel, F. & Wilkins, K. (eds.) (2012). Communication, media and development: Problems and perspectives. *Nordicom*. Special Issue. Vol. 31.

Hornik, R. C. (1988). *Development communication: Information, agriculture and nutrition in the third world*. New York: Longman.

McAnany, E. (2012). *Saving the world: A brief history of communication for development and social change*. Urbana: University of Illinois Press.

Mody, B. (1987). Contextual analysis of the adoption of a communication technology: The case of satellites in India. *Telematics and Informatics*, 4(2), 151–158.

Singhal, A. (ed.) (2004). *Entertainment, education and social change*. Mahwah, NJ: Lawrence Erlbaum.

Wilkins, K., Tufte, T., & Obregon, R. (eds.) (2014). *Handbook of development communication and social change*. Oxford: Wiley Blackwell.

Television as Popular Culture

TOBY MILLER
University of Cardiff/Murdoch

'Television' describes a physical device, a cultural system, and a labor process that brings the two together and embeds them in the daily experience of half the world's population. 'Popular' signifies of, by, and for the people, offering transcendence through pleasure (→ Popular Communication). 'Culture' signifies everyday customs and tastes (→ Culture: Definitions and Concepts). In the humanities, popular television texts are evaluated by criteria of quality and politics, understood through criticism and history. The social sciences focus on television viewers ethnographically, experimentally, and statistically. 'Popular culture' relates to markets. Neo-classical economics assumes that expressions of the desire and capacity to pay for services animate entertainment and hence determine what is 'popular.'

People had long fantasized about transmitting images and sounds. TV has its own patron saint, Clare of Assisi, a teen runaway from the thirteenth century who was canonized in 1958 for imagining a midnight mass broadcast on her wall. In 1935, Rudolf Arnheim predicted that television would bring global peace, but also warned that "television is a new, hard test of our wisdom." The emergent medium's easy access to knowledge would either enrich or impoverish its viewers, manufacturing an informed public, vibrant and active – or an indolent audience, domesticated and passive (Arnheim 1969, 160–163; → Television: Social History).

Ever since the Industrial Revolution, anxieties have existed about urbanized populations vulnerable to manipulation by images and demagogues through the popular. This is spectacularly the case with television. The notion of the suddenly enfranchised being bamboozled by the unscrupulously fluent has recurred throughout the modern period. It leads to an emphasis on the number and conduct of television audiences: where they came from, how many there were, and what they did after being there. These audiences are conceived as empirically knowable, via research instruments derived from sociology, demography, psychology, communications, and marketing. Such concerns are coupled with a concentration on content. Texts are also conceived as empirically knowable, via research instruments derived from communications, sociology, psychology, and literary criticism.

TV has given rise to three *key topics in research*: (1) ownership and control, (2) texts, and (3) audiences, with the question of the audience, and the knowledge that it has or that it lacks, as the governing discourse. Approaches to *ownership and control* vary between neo-liberal endorsements of limited regulation by the state, in the interests of guaranteeing market entry for new competitors, and Marxist critiques of the bourgeois media's control of the agenda for discussing society. Approaches to *textuality* either unearth the meaning of individual programs and link them to broader social formations and problems or establish patterns across significant numbers of similar texts (→ Text and Intertextuality). Approaches to *audiences* vary between social-psychological attempts to validate correlations between watching TV and social conduct, and culturalist critiques of imported television threatening national culture (→ Audience Research; Exposure to Television).

There are several *models of the impact of* television on popular culture. Most reception studies assume that audience members risk abjuring either interpersonal responsibility (in the US) or national culture (in the rest of the world). The *domestic effects model* (DEM), dominant in the US and increasingly exported around the world, is typically applied without consideration of place and is psychological. Entering young minds hypodermically, TV can both enable and imperil learning and drive viewers to violence (→ Violence as Media Content, Effects of).

The other key formation is a *global effects model* (GEM), primarily utilized in non-US discourse. Whereas the DEM focuses on individual human subjects, via observation and experimentation, the GEM looks to customs and patriotism (→ Globalization Theories). Instead of measuring audience responses to TV electronically or behaviorally, the GEM interrogates the geopolitical origin of televisual texts and the themes and styles they embody.

A third tendency endorses *the audience as active rather than passive*: consumers who use TV like an appliance, choosing what they want from its programming, and interpreters who use it to bring pleasure and sense to their lives. The television audience supposedly makes its own → meanings, outwitting institutions of the state, academia, and capital that seek to measure and control it (→ Uses and Gratifications).

See also: ▶ AUDIENCE RESEARCH ▶ CULTURE: DEFINITIONS AND CONCEPTS ▶ EXPOSURE TO TELEVISION ▶ GLOBALIZATION THEORIES ▶ MEANING ▶ MEDIA ECONOMICS ▶ MEDIA EFFECTS ▶ MEDIA HISTORY ▶ POPULAR COMMUNICATION ▶ TELEVISION: SOCIAL HISTORY ▶ TEXT AND INTERTEXTUALITY ▶ USES AND GRATIFICATIONS ▶ VIOLENCE AS MEDIA CONTENT, EFFECTS OF

REFERENCES AND SUGGESTED READINGS

Arnheim, R. (1969). *Film as art*. London: Faber and Faber.
Miller, T. (2010). *Television: The basics*. London: Routledge.

Television, Social History of

JÉRÔME BOURDON

Tel Aviv University

Television history has developed relatively recently. After pioneering work in the UK and the US (Barnouw 1990), national histories of television have been written, mostly in Europe. Historians have started from political and institutional history. Gaining access to television archives (open only in very few countries), globalizing mostly national efforts and digging into past viewing remain the major challenges facing them.

Television started in the 1930s, mostly in the UK and the US, but really took off after the war in these two countries, and in the 1960s in western Europe and the Soviet bloc. From the start, the medium was entrusted with national missions: fostering national identity and culture, representing the nation to itself, notably through major media events (e.g., the UK Coronation 1953). Everywhere, including in poor countries which made tremendous efforts to set up networks of transmitters, a television station was considered part of the outfit of a 'full fledged' nation. In strong nations the willingness to export one's culture, in weak nations the real or imagined threat of transmissions spilling, encouraged the development of television. Early television was also appropriated by a hybrid class of creators who tried to use it to promote a new art form, notably with live drama, a now extinct genre.

Public Versus Commercial

Beyond these common features, television developed according to two models: public and commercial models. *Public television* applies to stations controlled or supervised by the state. It is financed by the state budget or a specific tax, the license fee on receivers ('invented' for radio by the UK), although some advertising is sometimes added. Television is not only a question of national sovereignty and identity, but also of national education. In authoritarian, dictatorial systems, and some Southern European countries, it is or has been attached to a ministry of information. It addresses its viewers as part of a political community. In the western European public service variation, the official aims were those that were first set for radio in the → BBC royal charter of 1927, to "inform, educate, and entertain." Public service is public television with loftier, democratic ideals, addressing its viewers mostly as citizens (→ Public Broadcasting Systems).

Commercial television is financed by advertisements only, and state control is relatively weaker. It addresses its viewers mostly as consumers, and only the middle classes in unequal countries. In typologies of media models, commercial television has often been associated with liberal, democratic regimes. However, just like public television, it has democratic and undemocratic variants. Brazil's commercial network, Globo, did well during the dictatorship; and witness commercial stations in China or Russia today.

Public Television, Dominant but Weak

In the beginning, at a world level, the public model was dominant. Commercial television reigned mainly in the United States. It spread into the Latin American 'backyard,' where educational attempts yielded to the ambition of media entrepreneurs supported by US networks. Commercial television coexisted with public television from the start in Japan (1953) and Australia (1956). It was launched in 1955 in the UK.

US stations might have been relatively independent vis-à-vis governments and political parties. They could affect the agenda and formats of political life (Kennedy–Nixon debates in 1960). US television was also a tool of imperial policy, aggressively exporting programs and technologies and also controlling foreign stations. Produced by a very effective system, able to attract variegated audiences quickly, US programs were attractive and sold at a low price.

By the early 1960s, *I Love Lucy* was popular in parts of South America, Africa, and Japan. In addition, game show formats were adapted in many places, eagerly by British and Australian commercial TV, more discreetly by public European stations which 'domesticated' them. In the 1970s, many public television countries talked of promoting a → "New World Information and Communication Order" (NWICO) to counteract US influence (→ International Communication). At the same time, the success of American series (such as *Dallas*) revealed the weakness of European public television, affected by financial crises, increased criticism, and pressures from capitalist groups eager to use the medium.

The Global Rise of Commercial Television

In the 1980s, the *deregulation of television* started in western Europe, but spilled to the south, and later to the former communist world (→ Television Broadcasting, Regulation of). New commercial stations were born everywhere. Media barons became key figures, both globally – for example, → News Corporation's Rupert Murdoch – and nationally – for example, Mediaset's Silvio Berlusconi.

The rise of commercial television has been accompanied by increased format circulation. Format circulation was given much publicity by the rise of European 'reality games' such as *Big Brother* (→ Reality TV). But it started earlier (Oren & Shahaf 2011) and affected other genres, mostly game and variety shows and later sitcoms. Television has been increasingly 'formatted' in many other ways, through professional norms, ways of scheduling, and audience measurement methods (Bourdon & Méadel 2014; → Advertising, History of).

The End of Television?

Despite much writing on its end (Katz & Scannell 2009), television is dying more slowly than predicted. Analogue television passed the bar of the majority of world households only in the late 1980s, but there is still much room for expansion in Africa and Asia. In most countries, general-interest channels with traditional schedules still garner the majority of viewers. Public television has resisted better than predicted, at least in Europe. It still schedules more news and current affairs. In rich countries in the 2000s, the rise of digital terrestrial television has led to the creation of more general-interest channels, with high penetration. Older genres are the basis for much cable programming: such as cinema, TV fiction (e.g., Home Box Office) or news (→ CNN).

Purportedly global channels (e.g., MTV, started 1981) have been split into continental, national, or diasporic versions. For immigrants, cable channels "deterritorialize" but perpetuate national cultures (→ Ethnicity and Exposure to Communication). 'Old' channels have also combined with new media. The relations between television and the Internet are the best example of this, be it for traditional genres like news, or for reality TV, with high viewer involvement. In short, television has become a different, weaker, much more commercial and entertainment oriented medium, but is still structured nationally around major genres, with reality television as an important addition.

See also: ▶ ADVERTISING, HISTORY OF ▶ AUDIENCE SEGMENTATION ▶ BBC ▶ CABLE TELEVISION ▶ COMMERCIALIZATION OF THE MEDIA ▶ DEVELOPMENT COMMUNICATION ▶ ETHNICITY AND EXPOSURE TO COMMUNICATION ▶ FREEDOM OF COMMUNICATION ▶ GLOBALIZATION OF THE MEDIA ▶ HISTORIC KEY EVENTS AND THE MEDIA ▶ INTERNATIONAL COMMUNICATION ▶ MEDIA CONGLOMERATES ▶ MEDIA HISTORY ▶ NEWS CORPORATION ▶ REALITY TV ▶ SATELLITE TELEVISION ▶ TECHNOLOGY AND COMMUNICATION ▶ TELEVISION BROADCASTING, REGULATION OF ▶ TELEVISION FOR DEVELOPMENT

REFERENCES AND SUGGESTED READINGS

Barnouw, E. (1990[1976]). *Tube of plenty: The evolution of American television*, 2nd edn. Oxford: Oxford University Press.
Bignell, J. & Fickers, A. (eds.) (2008). *A European television history*. London: Blackwell.
Bourdon, J. & Méadel, C. (eds.) (2014). *Television audiences across the world. Deconstructing the ratings machine*. London: Palgrave.
Oren, T. & Shahaf, S. (eds.) (2011). *Global television formats*. London: Routledge.
Hallin, D. & Mancini, P. (eds.) (2012). *Comparing media systems across the world*. Cambridge: Cambridge University Press.
Katz, E. & Scannell, P. (eds.) (2009). The end of television? Its impact on the world (so far). *The Annals of the American Academy of Political and Social Science*, 625.

Television, Visual Characteristics of

JOHN T. CALDWELL
University of California, Los Angeles

Television – which literally means 'seeing from a distance' – has seldom been researched as a visual medium, in part because television from the start was deemed 'the small screen,' clearly inferior to cinema's widescreen quality. Yet, television does not have one look, but involves many different imaging practices. Reality TV, for example, looks very different than Home Box Office's filmed dramas (→ Reality TV). 'The' audience, far from monolithic, is now splintered and diverse, consuming everything from high-resolution HD 'home theatre' to grainy videos on smart phones. Additionally, many humanities and social science researchers presupposed that TV's 'media specificity' reduced it to nonvisual traits: effects (→ Media Effects), → propaganda, → agenda setting effects, content analysis, or psychological gratifications. Television's visual characteristics, therefore, depend upon which historical genres, end uses, and modes of production one analyses.

TV's *early prototypes* produced ghostly, amorphous, black-and-white imagery. Subsequent critics praised live drama and method acting as defining 1950s television's 'golden age,' arguing that artifice and visual quality obstructed naturalistic, psychological authenticity. In live anthology dramas, jostled stage flats, sweating actors, and lighting hot spots didn't lessen television art. They challenged sensitive, nonvisual writers, directors, and actors to 'operate without a net' and without elaborate artifice for the camera's existential gaze. This 'three-camera,' live, studio production mode – offering few visual complexities – spread internationally, partly because real-time 'editing' (switching), fewer lighting set-ups, and a singular production spaces were more economic.

A related production mode, electronic news gathering (ENG), used smaller crews and portable equipment to gather late-breaking reality images for the three-camera studio. ENG, while rapidly cut and catastrophe-focused, works visually, not because of its high resolution, illusionism, or formal beauty, but because of its fragmentary → sensationalism. Today, 24/7 cable news (→ Cable Television) has embellished the three-camera mode with digital graphics (→ Digital Imagery), text crawls, and multi-screens.

A competing production mode – single-camera, film-style, location production popularized in → Hollywood telefilms – displaced live drama in the mid-1950s, and has served as a workhorse mode since then. Golden-age critics resisted Hollywood's inroads by denigrating telefilms as mindless, lowest-common-denominator factory products from studio assembly lines. These critics made the writer – not the image-maker – the key creative force during this period. Yet, despite this critical anti-film posture, all of the studios (including Paramount, RKO, Disney, and Selznick) systematically made television central to their business plans. As a result, Hollywood's one-camera stylishness infiltrated television. In Europe and the US, many series opted for film style, given prime-time drama's higher budgets and stylistic expectations. For years, shows shot on film negative offered higher resolution, richer contrast and tonality, and more subtle colors than shows shot on video. The emergence of HDTV and '4 K' (or 'ultra-HD') now means that the actual capture device (film or chip) is less important than the cinematic look achieved. Today, contemporary series like *Madmen* or *Game of Thrones* are as stylistically sophisticated as high-budget studio films.

Dramatic television has offered high-level cinematic experiences throughout its history. A-list film directors that pushed network television boundaries in the US include John Cassavettes, John Frankenheimer, Paddy Cheyevsky, Michael Mann, Steven Spielberg, Oliver Stone, Spike Lee, and Robert Altman. Cassavettes' 1960s cinéma vérité-based improvisational TV dramas, for example, prefigure contemporary 'improvisational' genres, from reality TV to the faux-documentary quality of frantic 'real-time' dramas. By contrast, stylistically excessive commercial production and music videos taught television how to standardize cinematic and videographic looks across channels. After 1990, new digital production *and* viewing technologies spurred a diverse range of television forms and genres, each with distinctive aesthetic implications.

For McLuhan (1964), television's 'cool,' low-resolution appearance evoked a common all-at-once viewing experience, shared globally. This networked simultaneity eclipsed both television content and style. Researching live broadcasts of 'liminal' media events, in turn, underscored not TV's formal dimensions, but rather vast shared rituals of watching in real time through a national TV window. Later theorists (Negroponte 1995) celebrated the 'revolution of new media networking' precipitated by the wired global Internet rather than TV's local visual screen. Raymond Williams (1974) proposed examining not just communication technology's history, but the history of the technology's social uses as well.

Subsequently, critical scholars began engaging television aesthetics (Newcomb 2006), yet still favored narrative and ideological analysis over visual research. Growing interest in postmodernism – characterized by intertextuality, visual simulation, and pastiche – drove this aesthetic turn (→ Postmodernism and Communication; Text and Intertextuality). While some ideological theorists defined → cultural studies in direct opposition to aesthetics (Fiske 1987), others researched industry's multichannel programming changes, new technology instabilities, and the economic volatility spurring sophisticated new televisual advancements (Caldwell 1995).

See also: ▶ AGENDA-SETTING EFFECTS ▶ AUDIENCE RESEARCH ▶ CABLE TELEVISION ▶ CINEMA ▶ CRITICAL THEORY ▶ CULTURAL STUDIES ▶ DIGITAL IMAGERY ▶ HOLLYWOOD ▶ MEDIA EFFECTS ▶ MEDIUM THEORY ▶ MOBILITY, TECHNOLOGY FOR ▶ POSTMODERNISM AND COMMUNICATION ▶ PROPAGANDA ▶ REALITY TV ▶ TELEVISION: SOCIAL HISTORY ▶ VISUAL COMMUNICATION ▶ VISUAL REPRESENTATION

REFERENCES AND SUGGESTED READINGS

Caldwell, J. (1995). *Televisuality*. New Brunswick, NJ: Rutgers University Press.
Caldwell, J. (2004). Convergence television. In L. Spigel & J. Olsson (eds.), *Television after TV: Essays on a medium in transition*. Durham, NC: Duke University Press, pp. 41–74.
Fiske, J. (1987). *Television culture*. London: Methuen.
McLuhan, M. (1964). *Understanding media: The extensions of man*. New York: McGraw-Hill.
Negroponte, N. (1995). *Being digital*. New York: Knopf.
Newcomb, H. (ed.) (2006). *Television: The critical view*, 7th edn. Oxford: Oxford University Press.
Williams, R. (1974). *Television: Technology and cultural form*. New York: Schocken.

Terrorism and Communication Technologies

PRASUN SONWALKAR
University of the West of England

Communication and communication technologies are intrinsic to the idea of terrorism as formulated and understood from the nineteenth century onwards (→ Technology and Communication). The discourse of terrorism has come to be symbiotically linked to communication technologies as state and nonstate actors across the globe use and exploit technological advances to further their causes. However, there is no universally accepted definition of the term, mainly because it is vulnerable to vastly different interpretation by state and nonstate actors (→ Political Communication).

Groups and individuals branded by states as 'terrorists' use communication technologies at two levels: to orchestrate events and insure that news about them is communicated through the news media for maximum effect on governments and the public; and to coordinate, plan, and execute acts of political violence (→ Electronic Mail). The success of a terrorist operation depends on its publicity, which stresses the importance of communication technologies in the process of communicating acts of violence. The technologies constitute the cornerstone that links the *three elements of a terrorist strategy*: the terrorist, the target of the terrorist (victims), and the actual target of the acts of violence (the government or the public). The idea is often to evoke reactions from the government and instill apprehension or fear in the public.

Terrorist activity is immensely newsworthy as it satisfies several → news factors such as negativity, timeliness, and scale. Both state and nonstate actors use communication technologies to achieve contending propaganda objectives. Al-Qaeda using video tapes to communicate messages by Osama bin Laden through the Al Jazeera television channel (and many others) is a visible example of the ways in which terrorist groups deploy communication technologies effectively to propagate their perspectives (→ Arab Satellite TV News).

Before communication technologies such as the press became key elements of everyday life, the maximum audience that could be reached was limited to the range of the human voice. Nineteenth-century European anarchists faced the problem that their pamphlets had limited distribution. The anarchists turned to the 'propaganda of the deed,' which meant using acts of violence to secure coverage from the national and international press as well as encourage word-of-mouth communication. Nineteenth-century Italian anarchists Malatesta and Cafiero are said to be among the first to understand and exploit the symbiotic relationship between the news media and acts of terror. Around the same time in Russia, Peter Kroptokin stated, "By actions which compel general attention, the new idea seeps into people's minds and wins converts. One such act may, in a few days, make more propaganda than a thousand pamphlets" (in Weimann & Winn 1994, 53).

Every new communication technology invented increased the potential for effective propaganda as well as better coordination and execution of acts of violence. The assassination of Abraham Lincoln in 1865 via the national press took weeks to be known widely, but when John F. Kennedy was shot in 1963, more than 70 percent of Americans had heard about it within half an hour through television. The potential for propaganda further increased exponentially with the invention of and advances in radio, film, television, and the world wide web and its many networks of communication. Particularly *television* not only insured that acts of violence could be covered live, but that the leading nonstate actors could also counter official versions in the cut and thrust of politics in the aftermath. Bin Laden's selective video appearances made as much news in the western media as outside the west, insuring that western perspectives in international communications did not go unchallenged.

The *new ICTs* allow the diffusion of command and to control as well as targeting the information stores, processes, and communications of their rivals. The developments in communication technologies facilitate what has been called *netwar*, which refers to offensive acts carried out by often geographically separate, diverse, interconnected nonstate actors. Called 'cyberterrorism,' the latest convergence between nonstate actors and communication technologies involves hackers (cyberterrorists) who cripple websites, data systems, and networks of rival groups and/or governments. A new phenomenon are also the so-called 'lone wolves,' like the Unabomber or the Norwegian mass mudererer Anders Breivik. They seemingly act alone but behind them is a virtual supportive network via the Internet.

See also: ▶ ARAB SATELLITE TV NEWS ▶ BROADCAST JOURNALISM ▶ ELECTRONIC MAIL ▶ MEDIA EFFECTS ▶ NEWS FACTORS ▶ POLITICAL COMMUNICATION ▶ PRINTING, HISTORY OF ▶ PROPAGANDA ▶ SATELLITE TELEVISION ▶ TECHNOLOGY AND COMMUNICATION ▶ VIOLENCE AS MEDIA CONTENT ▶ WAR PROPAGANDA

REFERENCES AND SUGGESTED READINGS

Amble, J. C. (2012). Combating terrorism in the new media environment. *Studies in Conflict and Terrorism*, 35(5), 339–353.

Nacos, B. (2008). Mass-mediated terrorism. *Terrorism and Political Violence*, 20(4), 621–624.

Weimann, G. & Winn, C. (1994). *The theatre of terror: Mass media and international terrorism*. London: Longman.

Weimann, G. (2012). The role of the media in propagating terrorism. In U. Kumar & M. Mandal (eds.), *Countering terrorism: Psycho-social strategies*. New Delhi: Sage, pp. 182–202.

Winseck, D. (2008). Information operations "blowback": Communication, propaganda and surveillance in the global war on terrorism. *International Communication Gazette*, 70(6), 419–423.

Text and Intertextuality

KLAUS BRUHN JENSEN
University of Copenhagen

Texts are vehicles of communication. While traditionally reserved for written and other verbal messages, the term refers to any meaningful entity, including images, everyday interaction, and cultural artifacts. Deriving from classical Latin 'texo' (to weave, to construct), *texts* emphasize the complex process in which ideas are articulated and communicated. Texts lend themselves to content and → discourse analysis (→ Content Analysis, Qualitative), feeding into qualitative approaches to the study of media reception, culture, and society.

The inclusive notion of texts has been elaborated with reference to intertextuality. The seminal contribution was made by the Russian literary scholar Mikhail Bakhtin in the early twentieth century (Bakhtin 1981). Bakhtin's basic concept – dialogism – was translated by Kristeva (1984) as intertextuality. Fiske (1987) distinguished *two dimensions of intertextuality*. 'Horizontal intertextuality' covers the transfer of meanings over historical time, as preserved in the metaphors, characters, and styles of traditional arts as well as popular media. 'Vertical intertextuality' operates during a delimited time period but extends across media and social contexts.

To specify this synchronic perspective, Fiske identified *three categories of texts*. Primary texts are carriers of significant insight in their own right. In the horizontal perspective, the primary texts are the center of attention. If the primary text is a new feature movie, the secondary texts consist of studio publicity, reviews, and criticism. And the tertiary texts are produced by audiences before, during, and after attending the movie.

In combination, the two axes of intertextuality amount to a model of how → meaning is produced and circulated in society. The rise of digital media and networked communication has given the concept of intertextuality renewed importance (Bolter 1991). Hyperlinks may be understood as operationalized forms of intertextuality.

See also: ▶ CONTENT ANALYSIS, QUALITATIVE ▶ CULTURAL STUDIES ▶ DISCOURSE ▶ DISCOURSE ANALYSIS ▶ FILM THEORY ▶ HERMENEUTICS ▶ INTERACTIVITY, CONCEPT OF ▶ MEANING ▶ STRUCTURALISM

REFERENCES AND SUGGESTED READINGS

Bakhtin, M. M. (1981). *The dialogic imagination*. Austin, TX: University of Texas Press.
Bolter, J. D. (1991). *Writing space: The computer, hypertext, and the history of writing*. Hillsdale, NJ: Lawrence Erlbaum.
Fiske, J. (1987). *Television culture*. London: Methuen.
Kristeva, J. (1984). *Revolution in Poetic Language*. New York: Columbia University Press.

Third-Person Effects

HANS-BERND BROSIUS
Ludwig Maximilian University of Munich

CHRISTINA PETER
Ludwig Maximilian University of Munich

The third-person effect (TPE) was introduced into communication research by W. Phillips Davison in 1983 and states that people overestimate the impact that mass media content has on others – so-called 'third persons' – while they underestimate the influence that media has on themselves (→ Media Effects).

This does not mean that media are actually influential at all; the TPE is a purely *perceptual phenomenon* (→ Media and Perceptions of Reality; Social Perception). In addition, it includes a behavioral component, meaning that people might take action on the basis of the presumed media influence on others, e.g., argue for regulation or censorship of apparent negative media content. Davison's basic assumption has already been confirmed by a series of more than 100 empirical studies with different topics (e.g., → advertising effectiveness and violent or pornographic media content (→ Violence as Media Content, Effects of).

One of the most important *moderators for the effect* turns out to be the so-called distance corollary: The more distant or different others are from oneself, the larger the third-person effect becomes. The third-person effect is also influenced by the perceived intensity of the third person's exposure to the related media message. When media effects are described as positive and personally or socially desirable, the third-person effect not only decreases in size, but it can also develop into a reverse third-person effect (first-person effect). Besides, perceived knowledge, age, high education, and low media usage lead to a greater third-person effect.

'Optimistic bias' has been seen as one of the *causes* for TPE. As people have a more positive picture of themselves than of others and because media impact in general is perceived to be negative, people might ascribe such effects more to others than to themselves. Another explanation for TPE is the concept of self-enhancement. However, these psychological causes are still not fully investigated (Quiring et al. 2007).

See also: ▶ ADVERTISING EFFECTIVENESS ▶ MEDIA EFFECTS ▶ MEDIA EFFECTS, STRENGTH OF ▶ MEDIA AND PERCEPTIONS OF REALITY ▶ POLITICAL ADVERTISING ▶ SOCIAL PERCEPTION ▶ VIOLENCE AS MEDIA CONTENT, EFFECTS OF

REFERENCES AND SUGGESTED READINGS

Davison, W. P. (1983). The third-person effect in communication. Public Opinion Quarterly, 47, 1–15.

Quiring, O., Huck, I., & Brosius, H.-B. (2007). On the causes of third-person perception: Empirical tests of previous speculations. Paper presented at the 57th Annual Conference of the ICA, San Francisco, CA, May 24–28.

Sun, Y., Pan, Z., & Shen, L. (2008). Understanding the third-person perception: Evidence from a meta-analysis. *Journal of Communication*, 58, 280–300.

Time Warner Inc.

MARA EINSTEIN

Queens College, City University of New York

Time Warner is the world-leading multimedia conglomerate (→ Media Conglomerates), with operations in filmed entertainment, broadcast and → cable television, Internet services, and print media. The company generated more than US$30 billion in revenues in 2013. Time Warner was built through a series of mergers over more than 80 years.

Time Inc. began in 1922 as a publishing company for *Time* magazine. Over the years, the company created additional titles such as *Fortune, Life, Sports Illustrated*, and *Money* magazines. In 1965, Time entered the cable distribution business; it launched Home Box Office (HBO), a premium cable program network, in 1972 (→ United States of America: Media System).

Warner Brothers, a producer of filmed entertainment, was founded in 1923. It was home to the first talking picture, *The Jazz Singer*, and the production home for the animation studio Looney Tunes. Warner Bros also became a major producer of recorded music, with Atlantic Records, Elektra Records, and Reprise Records among its many labels (→ Music Industry). As television became popular in American homes, Warner Bros began producing programming for this medium. It entered the cable television business in 1973.

In 1989, Time merged with Warner Communications and the combined company was renamed Time Warner in 1990. This merger created the first vertically integrated media behemoth, mixing the publishing and cable system expertise of Time with the filmed entertainment cords, and Repriseure and television ted the first vertically integrated media behemoth, mixing thntinued to create new magazines and cable networks after the merger, but achieved its most significant growth in 1996 when it acquired the Turner Broadcasting System, home of several major cable networks, including → CNN.

Time Warner s operations today span across the three business divisions: Internet networks; film and TV entertainment; and publishing. Originally created as a purveyor of commercial-free movies, HBO became a leader in prime-time television programming, with shows such as *Sex and the City* or *The Sopranos*. Time Warner Cable was the second largest US cable provider in the United States behind Comcast. At the end of 2012, Time Inc. published 21 magazines in print in the US and over 70 magazines outside the US.

See also: ▶ CABLE TELEVISION ▶ CINEMA ▶ CNN ▶ MEDIA CONGLOMERATES ▶ MUSIC INDUSTRY ▶ UNITED STATES OF AMERICA: MEDIA SYSTEM

REFERENCES AND SUGGESTED READINGS

Time Warner (2014). Fourth Quarter and Full Year 2013 Results. At http://ir.timewarner.com/phoenix.zhtml?c=70972&p=irol-IRHome, accessed September 1, 2014.

Wasko, J., Murdoch, G., & Sousa, H. (eds.) (2011). *The handbook of political economy of communications*. Malden, MA: Wiley Blackwell.

Transnational Civil Society

JOHN D. H. DOWNING

Southern Illinois University

'Civil society' has been through a series of definitions since the eighteenth century. In Soviet bloc countries in the final years of the bloc's disintegration, and in Latin America as military dictatorships declined, the term denoted the hopeful shoots of democratic process emerging. By 2000 the term came to denote projects undertaken by grassroots political interests, in particular, citizens' actions against globalized neo-liberal economic policies (→ Globalization Theories), i.e. ongoing movements from below.

However, the term remains vague. One major response is to define nongovernmental organizations (NGOs) as civil society's tangible expression. Yet, NGOs across the planet held very diverse agendas, even diametrically at odds (e.g., over abortion). What then is the effect of using 'global' or 'transnational' to define it? Keck and Sikkink (1998) wish to retain a strong sense of agency, indeterminacy, and conflict, so prefer 'transnational' civil society over 'global' civil society. They read 'globalization' as inexorable economic, transport, and communication change. Kaldor (2003) attacks the 'NGO definition' of civil society. She proposes that there is a long-term process underway toward "multi-lateralist law-making states," where global meetings offer increasing participation at global levels (→ International Communication Agencies; Internet: International Regulation; UNESCO).

While these definitions may convey the scope, fluidity, and contradictoriness of global/transnational civil society, they never or only briefly engage with the media communication process as central to these activities. In particular, little or no attention is given to social movement media. Juris's (2008) ethnography of the global social justice movement's communication activities in the early 2000s offers one contribution to fill this gap. He brings together a series of dimensions: face-to-face practices in largely consensus-based planning meetings, Internet uses, performative tactics in marches, as well as the communicative terror induced by harsh policing tactics.

See also: ▶ COMMUNITY MEDIA ▶ GLOBALIZATION THEORIES ▶ INTERNATIONAL COMMUNICATION AGENCIES ▶ INTERNET: INTERNATIONAL REGULATION ▶ UNESCO

REFERENCES AND SUGGESTED READINGS

Cammaerts, B., Mattoni, A., & McCurdy, P. (eds.) (2013). *Mediation and protest movements*. London: Intellect.
Juris, J. (2008). *Networking futures*. Durham, NC: Duke University Press.
Kaldor, M. (2003). *Global civil society: An answer to war*. Cambridge: Polity.
Keck, M. E. & Sikkink, K. (1998). *Activists beyond borders: Advocacy networks in international politics*. Ithaca, NY: Cornell University Press.

Trust of Publics

GÜNTER BENTELE
University of Leipzig

Public trust can be defined as a process and outcome of a publicly generated, communicative mechanism within which publicly perceptible individuals, organizations, and other social systems act as 'trust objects.' Public trust is generated within the public communication process in which 'trust subjects' attribute more or less trust to trust objects (see Bentele 1994; Bentele & Seidenglanz 2008).

On the one hand, the term public trust refers to the attribution of different degrees of trust or distrust. On the other hand, the possibility of observing publicly perceptible agents and organizations is produced and controlled by actively organized communication (journalism, media, → public relations). Thus, in that sense, public trust refers to the social mechanisms of public communication by which the attitude of agents' trust is generated.

Bentele's (1994) *theory of public trust* differentiates between trust subjects, trust objects, trust mediators, facts, and events, as well as texts and messages (→ Message Production). Usually, trust subjects (trustors) are individuals, while trust objects (trustees) can be individuals, organizations (→ Corporate Communication), and even more extensive social systems (e.g., the health system of a society, the political system, etc.). Those agents that intentionally or unintentionally mediate trust to the trust subjects within the public communication process are called 'trust mediators.' Journalists and PR professionals, as well as organizations, act as intermediaries of trust. The relationships between PR and → journalism itself depend on mutual attributions of trust. The theory distinguishes *four types of trust* (basic, 'public personal,' organizational, and system trust) and various *trust factors* (e.g., problem-solving competencies, adequacy of communication, communicative consistency, etc.). The latter are responsible for creating higher or lower, empirically measurable levels of trust.

See also: ▶ CONSENSUS-ORIENTED PUBLIC RELATIONS ▶ CORPORATE COMMUNICATION ▶ JOURNALISM ▶ MEDIATIZATION OF POLITICS ▶ PUBLIC RELATIONS ▶ STRATEGIC COMMUNICATION

REFERENCES AND SUGGESTED READINGS

Bentele, G. (1994). Öffentliches Vertrauen: Normative und soziale Grundlage für Public Relations [Public trust: A normative and social foundation for public relations]. In W. Armbrecht & U. Zabel (eds.), *Normative Aspekte der Public Relations: Grundlagen und Perspektiven. Eine Einführung* [Normative aspects of public relations: Foundations and perspectives. An introduction]. Opladen: Westdeutscher, pp. 131–158.

Bentele, G. & Seidenglanz, R. (2008). Trust and credibility – prerequisites for communication management. In A. Zerfass, B. van Ruler, & K. Sriramesh (eds.), *Public relations research. European and international perspectives and innovations*. Wiesbaden: VS Verlag für Sozialwissenschaften, pp. 49–62.

Seiffert, J., Bentele, G., & Mende, L. (2011). An explorative study on discrepancies in communication and action of German companies. *Journal of Communication Management*, 15(4), 349–367.

Truth and Media Content

KARIN WAHL-JORGENSEN
Cardiff University

Truth is a slippery concept, and philosophers since Aristotle have battled over its meaning. The most intuitive understanding of truth is that of correspondence theory – the idea that "for a proposition to be true is for it to correspond to the facts" (Blackburn & Simmons 1999, 1).

As several observers have suggested, the cultural authority of → journalism derives from its discursive status as truth. This status, in turn, is underpinned by the belief that it is possible to separate facts from values and the observer from the observed; that journalism can capture the world in its entirety. It provides media producers with a set of readymade justifications for their practices, but also grants them the privilege of being the masters of our collective truths (→ Objectivity in Reporting; Reality and Media Reality).

Scholars in media studies and beyond have nudged at journalism's commitment to a correspondence theory. In particular, proponents of a *constructivist perspective* question the idea of a direct denotative relationship between language and reality. Instead, such an approach starts from the presumption that all truths are contingent because reality is ultimately socially constructed. For James Carey, communication is "a symbolic process whereby reality is produced, maintained, repaired, and transformed" (1992, 23). Carey proposes that we actively make the world through the stories we tell about it.

In today's mass societies, most of our store of knowledge about the world comes from mass media, rather than from personal experience (→ Media and Perceptions of Reality; Media Effects). Media content therefore plays a key role in shaping our notion of truth – an insight which has been central to work ranging from Marxist critiques of hegemonic power relations in the media to the approaches of cultivation theory and framing.

Finally, communication scholarship has shown that consumers of media are often concerned with the truth of texts in a rather different sense: audiences judge whether content is authentic, or whether it is thought to be true to the essence of the object considered. Notions of truth as authenticity have been particularly influential in research on audience participation genres, including → reality TV, → broadcast talk, and user-generated content.

See also: ▶ BROADCAST TALK ▶ JOURNALISM ▶ MEDIA EFFECTS ▶ MEDIA AND PERCEPTIONS OF REALITY ▶ OBJECTIVITY IN REPORTING ▶ REALITY AND MEDIA REALITY ▶ REALITY TV

REFERENCES AND SUGGESTED READINGS

Blackburn, S. & Simmons, K. (1999). Introduction. In S. Blackburn & K. Simmons (eds.), *Truth*. Oxford: Oxford University Press, pp. 1–28.

Carey, J. (1992). *Communication as culture: Essays on media and society*. Boston: Unwin Hyman.

Twitter

ALFRED HERMIDA
University of British Columbia

Twitter is a free service that combines elements of blogging and social networking (→ Facebook; Social Networks) and is considered as a form of → social media. Commonly described as a microblogging service, it is one of a class of communication and information platforms defined as social awareness streams that allow for the rapid and immediate sharing of content.

Launched in August 2006 by San Francisco start-up Odeo, Twitter rose to prominence during key news events in 2008 and 2009. By October 2013, it had more than 215 million monthly active users and 500 million messages daily, describing itself as "a real-time information network that connects you to the latest stories, ideas, opinions and news about what you find interesting." Users can send instant messages, called tweets, of 140 characters or under to people who have subscribed to the messages. The tweets are usually accessible to a wider audience, as most accounts are public. The retweet is generally used to resend messages and the @ symbol is used to reply to or to mention another user. The hashtag (#) is used to associate messages with specific topics, which can be tracked and ranked to indicate popularity.

Status updating and the sharing of news and information have become the dominant uses of Twitter (van Dijck 2012). News organizations have used Twitter to gather, report, and distribute news, with journalists largely transferring existing norms and practices, and concerns over the professional and personal boundaries (Hermida 2013; → Ethics in Journalism). Twitter and other participatory platforms gain prominence as news channels when mainstream media access is limited or restricted and/or a story is rapidly unfolding, compressing → news cycles. Tweets provide an ambient mix of news, information, and comment, usually connected to current reality, but without an established order based on journalistic vnorms (Hermida 2013; → News Story). The convergence of news, fact, rumor, speculation, and opinion has prompted news outlets to issue social media guidelines and the development of practices for real-time live reporting using Twitter (Hermida 2013).

Studies suggest Twitter can function as a mechanism for collaborative storytelling and filtering, with narratives constructed organically from the aggregate behaviour of a crowd (Meraz and Papacharissi 2013). There is debate about the role of Twitter and associated social media platforms in social movements, with studies indicating it may have helped to amplify messages and mobilize resistance in cases such as the Egyptian uprising.

See also: ▶ ETHICS IN JOURNALISM ▶ FACEBOOK ▶ NEWS CYCLES ▶ NEWS STORY ▶ SOCIAL MEDIA

REFERENCES AND SUGGESTED READINGS

Hermida, A. (2013). #Journalism: Reconfiguring journalism research about Twitter, one tweet at a time. *Digital Journalism*, 1(3), 295–313.

Meraz, S. & Papacharissi, Z., (2013). Networked gatekeeping and networked framing on #Egypt. *International Journal of the Press and Politics*, 18(2), 1–29.

van Dijck, J. (2012). Tracing Twitter: The rise of a microblogging platform. *International Journal of Media and Cultural Politics*, 7(3), 333–348.

Two-Step Flow of Communication

MARCUS MAURER
Johannes Gutenberg University of Mainz

The two-step flow of communication hypothesis was first formulated by Paul F. Lazarsfeld and his colleagues (1944) in their classic study on the 1940 American presidential election. It states that there is usually no direct influence of the mass media on the general public. Rather, "ideas often flow from radio and print to the → opinion leaders and from them to the less active sections of the population" (Lazarsfeld et al. 1944, 151). This assumption, challenging the then popular idea of strong direct media effects on the public (→ Media Effects, History of), turned out to be one of the most influential ideas in communication research from the 1940s until at least the 1960s.

The two-step flow of communication model consists of at least *five* more or less explicitly stated *hypotheses*. (1) Most people are not directly exposed to the mass media. They are rather informed via interpersonal communication by so-called opinion leaders. (2) Opinion leaders are much more exposed to mass media and much more engaged in active communication than the general public is. (3) Opinion leaders not only inform the followers, but also transmit the content of the mass media to them. (4) The general public is not only informed but also influenced by opinion leaders. (5) Opinion leaders are not passive gatekeepers of media information. They transmit media content biased through their own opinions.

In recent research these hypotheses have often been disentangled and studied separately. Generally, *three types of studies* can be distinguished. First, studies on the *diffusion of news* show that nowadays in western democracies about 80–90 percent of adults are exposed to any kind of media news on an average weekday while less than 5 percent say that they are primarily informed by interpersonal communication. Second, studies on *opinion leaders* suggest that the concept of a two-step flow of communication is oversimplified (e.g., opinion leaders engage in interpersonal communication with followers as well as with other opinion leaders). Third, studies on the *sources of* → *public opinion* show that people frequently talk about media content, but it remains unclear whether they convey it neutrally or in a manner that is biased by their own opinions.

See also: ▶ INTERPERSONAL COMMUNICATION ▶ MEDIA CONTENT AND SOCIAL NETWORKS ▶ MEDIA EFFECTS ▶ MEDIA EFFECTS, HISTORY OF ▶ OPINION LEADER ▶ PUBLIC OPINION

REFERENCES AND SUGGESTED READINGS

Brosius, H.-B. & Weimann, G. (1996). Who sets the agenda? Agenda-setting as a two-step flow. *Communication Research*, 23, 561–580.

Lazarsfeld, P. F., Berelson, B., & Gaudet, H. (1944). *The people's choice: How the voter makes up his mind in a presidential campaign.* New York: Duell, Sloan, and Pearce.

Weimann, G. (1994). *The influentials: People who influence people.* New York: State University of New York Press.

U

Uncertainty and Communication

DALE BRASHERS

University of Illinois at Urbana-Champaign

Uncertainty has been an important concept in communication theory for many decades (→ Uncertainty Reduction Theory). Understanding how people respond to uncertainty in developing relationships (→ Relational Uncertainty) and in intercultural encounters has been the foundation of a large body of interpersonal communication research. This work has demonstrated complex relationships between communication, → information seeking, and the management of uncertainty (→ Uncertainty Management). "Uncertainty exists when details of situations are ambiguous, complex, unpredictable, or probabilistic; when information is unavailable or inconsistent; and when people feel insecure in their own state of knowledge or the state of knowledge in general" (Brashers 2001, 478).

Recent theory-building and theory-testing have extended the concept into the domains of social influence and behavioral change, primarily through → health communication research. Theories of communication and uncertainty management, motivated information management, problematic integration, and the risk-perception attitude are recent theoretical directions that recognize the complexity of uncertainty and information management in the area of health. Social influence researchers have used theories of → information processing and uncertainty management in recent research on health behavior change. Other related areas of research have included tests of messages promoting HIV testing (Hullett 2006) and organ donation.

One complexity that has received attention is the *collaborative nature* of uncertainty management. Researchers need to account for the motivations, outcome assessments, and efficacy beliefs of both information seekers and information providers. Support from others can assist with uncertainty management by helping achieve information goals, but also by means such as facilitating skill development, providing acceptance or validation, or encouraging reappraisal or perspective shifts (→ Social Support in Interpersonal Communication).

See also: ▶ EXTENDED PARALLEL PROCESS MODEL ▶ HEALTH COMMUNICATION ▶ INFORMATION PROCESSING ▶ INFORMATION

The Concise Encyclopedia of Communication, First Edition. Edited by Wolfgang Donsbach.
© 2015 John Wiley & Sons, Inc. Published 2015 by John Wiley & Sons, Inc.

SEEKING ▶ PERSUASION ▶ RELATIONAL UNCERTAINTY ▶ SELECTIVE PERCEPTION AND SELECTIVE RETENTION ▶ SOCIAL SUPPORT IN INTERPERSONAL COMMUNICATION
▶ UNCERTAINTY MANAGEMENT
▶ UNCERTAINTY REDUCTION THEORY

REFERENCES AND SUGGESTED READINGS

Antheunis, M. L., Schouten, A. P., Valkenburg, P. M., & Peter, J. (2012). Interactive uncertainty reduction strategies and verbal affection in computer-mediated communication. *Communication Research*, 39(6), 757–780.

Babrow, A. S., Kasch, C. R., & Ford, L. A. (1998). The many meanings of uncertainty in illness: Toward a systematic accounting. *Health Communication*, 10, 1–23.

Brashers, D. E. (2001). Communication and uncertainty management. *Journal of Communication*, 51, 477–497.

Hullett, C. R. (2006). Using functional theory to promote HIV testing: The impact of value-expressive messages, uncertainty, and fear. *Health Communication*, 20, 57–67.

Uncertainty Management

WALID A. AFIFI
University of Iowa

Uncertainty reflects a perceived inability to predict or explain a person, interaction outcome, or issue with confidence. The theoretical debates about uncertainty have revolved around why and how people experience and manage uncertainty (→ Relational Dialectics; Uncertainty and Communication; Uncertainty Reduction Theory).

The predominant position is that individuals have an innate motivation to predict and explain lived experience, making uncertainty inherently distressing. Some, however, have argued that people's experience of uncertainty differs according to context and culture, with evidence that uncertainty is sometimes the preferred state. For example, studies have shown that people diagnosed with chronic illness view uncertainty as hope (Brashers 2001). Still, most experiences of uncertainty involve some potential threat that encourages uncertainty management. So, how is that done?

Scholars initially proposed that individuals manage uncertainty by seeking information through observation, third parties, or direct communication with the target (Berger & Kellermann 1994). However, more recent scholarship recognizes that individuals might respond to their uncertainty experiences by avoiding information altogether, cognitively re-assessing the state of uncertainty, or even basking in its presence.

Afifi and Weiner (2004) advanced the Theory of Motivated Information Management (TMIM) as a way to address some of the inconsistencies in the literature and more fully capture the complexity of uncertainty management decisions within interpersonal encounters. The theory proposes that process starts with awareness of a discrepancy between the amount of uncertainty one has and the amount one wants about an important issue. That discrepancy is then appraised and experienced emotionally in some manner (most commonly, as anxiety). In response, people consider two general questions: "What are the costs and benefits of information seeking?" (labeled 'outcome expectancy'), and "Am I able to seek and cope with the information received?" (labeled '*efficacy*').

The *theory predicts* that individuals are increasingly likely to seek information directly to the extent that outcome expectancies are positive and the efficacy assessments are high. Afifi and Weiner (2004) argue that information providers go through similar assessments in determining what information to give and how to do it. The end result of this process depends on the seeker's strategy and the provider's response. Most recently, scholars have turned their attention to the neurological and physiological implications of uncertainty management, with considerable promise for linking uncertainty and its management to well-being.

See also: ▶ INFORMATION SEEKING ▶ RELATIONAL DIALECTICS ▶ RELATIONAL UNCERTAINTY
▶ UNCERTAINTY AND COMMUNICATION
▶ UNCERTAINTY REDUCTION THEORY

REFERENCES AND SUGGESTED READINGS

Afifi, W. A. & Weiner, J. L. (2004). Toward a theory of motivated information management. *Communication Theory*, 14(2), 167–190.

Berger, C. R. & Kellermann, K. (1994). Acquiring social information. In J. A. Daly & J. M. Wiemann (eds.), *Strategic interpersonal communication*. Hillsdale, NJ: Lawrence Erlbaum, pp. 1–30.

Brashers, D. E. (2001). Communication and uncertainty management. *Journal of Communication*, 51(3), 477–497.

Uncertainty Reduction Theory

DENISE HAUNANI SOLOMON
Pennsylvania State University

Uncertainty reduction theory (URT) explains how → interpersonal communication is affected by a lack of knowledge and how people use communication to gather information (→ Uncertainty and Communication). This theory was founded on the observation that initial interactions between strangers routinely involve an exchange of demographic and public information, and these interactions change in predictable ways as they progress (Berger 1997). Interpersonal communication plays two roles within URT: (1) communication is among the behaviors that people seek to predict or explain; and (2) communication is a tool people use to gather information or form predictions and explanations (→ Information Seeking).

URT assumes that people are driven to increase the predictability of their own and their communication partner's behavior. Uncertainty reduction can be 'proactive,' focused on predicting future behaviors, or 'retroactive,' focused on explaining past experiences. The theory also distinguishes between 'behavioral uncertainty,' which is a lack of knowledge about the behaviors that are appropriate or expected, and 'cognitive uncertainty,' which involves questions about a communication partner's personal qualities.

Berger and Calabrese (1975) advanced URT *as seven axioms* concerning the association between uncertainty and facets of interpersonal communication within initial interaction between strangers: (1) as the amount of verbal communication between strangers increases, uncertainty decreases; as uncertainty is reduced, verbal communication increases; (2) as the amount of nonverbal warmth expressed between strangers increases, uncertainty decreases; as uncertainty is reduced, nonverbal expressions of warmth increase; (3) when uncertainty is high, information-seeking behavior is frequent; as uncertainty decreases, information-seeking behavior decreases; (4) when uncertainty is high, the intimacy level of communication content is low; as uncertainty decreases, the intimacy level of communication content increases; (5) when uncertainty is high, partners are more likely to reciprocate each other's communication behaviors; as uncertainty decreases, the rate of reciprocity decreases; (6) similarities between communication partners decrease uncertainty; dissimilarities between communication partners increase uncertainty; and (7) when uncertainty is high, liking for a communication partner is low; as uncertainty decreases, liking increases.

By considering all possible pairwise combinations of these seven axioms, Berger and Calabrese (1975) offered *21 specific theorems* linking uncertainty to interpersonal communication variables and outcomes. For example, considering the first two axioms in tandem generates the prediction that amount of verbal communication and expressions of nonverbal warmth are positively correlated.

Berger and Bradac (1982) elaborated on the methods people use to gather information about a target person. "Passive strategies" involve observing a person. "Active strategies" involve altering the physical or social context and observing a person's responses to that environment or asking third parties for information. "Interactive strategies" involve communicating directly with the target person.

Tests of uncertainty reduction theory have addressed three general issues: (1) how uncertainty reduction changes over the course of developing relationships; (2) the factors that prompt uncertainty reduction; and (3) the communication behaviors that people use to gather information during face-to-face interactions (→ Questions and Questioning).

Uncertainty reduction theory has been *applied to various communication situations*, such as the experiences of new employees, doctors and patients, students in a classroom setting, television viewers (→ Parasocial Interactions and Relationships), computer-mediated communication partners, intercultural communication experiences, and romantic relationship transitions (→ Relational Uncertainty).

The theory's claim that uncertainty reduction is a motivating force in interpersonal interactions is debated. Alternative views suggest that (1) communication in initial interactions is motivated by a desire to predict the rewards and costs of continued interaction; (2) people may prefer to maintain uncertainty if the information they might gain is threatening (→ Uncertainty Management); and (3) uncertainty is both desirable and undesirable in the context of ongoing personal relationships (→ Relational Dialectics).

See also ▶ INFORMATION SEEKING ▶ PARASOCIAL INTERACTIONS AND RELATIONSHIPS ▶ INTERPERSONAL COMMUNICATION ▶ QUESTIONS AND QUESTIONING ▶ RELATIONAL DIALECTICS ▶ RELATIONAL UNCERTAINTY ▶ UNCERTAINTY AND COMMUNICATION ▶ UNCERTAINTY MANAGEMENT

REFERENCES AND SUGGESTED READINGS

Berger, C. R. (1987). Communicating under uncertainty. In M. E. Roloff & G. R. Miller (eds.), *Interpersonal processes*. Newbury Park, CA: Sage, pp. 39–62.

Berger, C. R. (1997). Message production under uncertainty. In G. Philipsen & T. L. Albrecht (eds.), *Developing communication theories*. Albany, NY: SUNY Press, pp. 29–55.

Berger, C. R. & Bradac, J. J. (1982). *Language and social knowledge: Uncertainty in interpersonal relations*. London: Edward Arnold.

Berger, C. R. & Calabrese, R. J. (1975). Some explorations in initial interaction and beyond: Toward a developmental theory of interpersonal communication. *Human Communication Research*, 1, 99–112.

Berger, C. R. & Kellermann, K. (1994). Acquiring social information. In J. A. Daly & J. M. Wiemann (eds.), *Strategic interpersonal communication*. Hillsdale, NJ: Lawrence Erlbaum, pp. 1–31.

UNESCO

ANDREW CALABRESE
University of Colorado at Boulder

UNESCO – the United Nations Educational, Scientific, and Cultural Organization – is a specialized UN agency, founded in 1945, and composed of 196 member states. Its headquarters are in Paris. UNESCO also has more than 50 field offices around the world. The preamble to the UNESCO constitution emphasizes the importance of the organization's mission of peace through intellectual and cultural development and exchange, stating that "since wars begin in the minds of men, it is in the minds of men that the defences of peace must be constructed." For the 2012–2013 biennium, UNESCO had a budget appropriation of US$653 million, with an additional US$541 million in "extra-budgetary resources" (additional funds from sources other than member states' assessed contributions), for a total budget of US$1.19 billion for the two-year period.

In 2005, under the leadership of the Culture sector, the organization adopted a "Convention on the Protection and Promotion of the Diversity of Cultural Expressions." The convention aims "to protect and promote the diversity of cultural expressions," and it emphasizes the unique nature of cultural goods and services as "vehicles of identity, values and meaning" (UNESCO 2005; → Culture: Definitions and Concepts). The culture sector also works to promote cultural exchange through modern → 'culture industries,' including publishing, music, or the Internet, focusing particularly on freedom of expression (→ Freedom of Communication), cultural diversity, and economic development. For pursuing its goals UNESCO runs five program areas: education, natural sciences, social and human sciences, culture, and communication and information. In monitoring its activities in the communication sector UNESCO created a 'Observatory on the Information Society,' established in 1997. Today, reports, statistical data and many other resources are available on the sub-website Communication and Information of the UNESCO Institute for Statistics (UNESCO 2014).

In the 1970s and 1980s there was significant criticism by several countries about the majority call by UNESCO members for a → 'new world information and communication order' (NWICO), which was articulated in Belgrade in 1980 at the 21st UNESCO General Conference. The report Many Voices, One World (see MacBride Commission 2004) highlighted many controversial issues that continue to define the north–south divide related to communication and information.

See also: ▶ COMMUNICATION TECHNOLOGY AND DEMOCRACY ▶ CULTURAL PRODUCTS AS TRADABLE SERVICES ▶ CULTURE: DEFINITIONS AND CONCEPTS ▶ CULTURE INDUSTRIES ▶ FREEDOM OF COMMUNICATION ▶ FREEDOM OF INFORMATION ▶ GLOBALIZATION OF THE MEDIA ▶ NEW WORLD INFORMATION AND COMMUNICATION ORDER (NWICO)

REFERENCES AND SUGGESTED READINGS

MacBride Commission (2004). *Many voices, one world: Towards a new, more just and more efficient world information and communication order*, 25th anniversary edn. Lanham, MD: Rowman and Littlefield.
UNESCO (2005). Convention on the Protection and Promotion of the Diversity of Cultural Expressions. At http://unesdoc.unesco.org/images/0014/001429/142919e.pdf, accessed August 31, 2014.
UNESCO (2014). UNESCO Institute for Statistics – Communication and Information. At: http://www.uis.unesco.org/Communication/Pages/default.aspx, accessed August 31, 2014.

United Kingdom: Media System

DOMINIC WRING
Loughborough University

The modern *newspaper industry* developed during the mid-nineteenth century (Curran & Seaton 2010). The growth of literacy enabled proprietors to use their newspapers' burgeoning popularity to assert their influence. These 'press barons' promoted a largely center-right agenda through titles like the Mail and Express that became hostile towards the growing Labour Party, whose only reliable media support came from the Daily Herald. Despite its large readership the Herald lacked advertising revenues and was rebranded as the Sun before its purchase by Rupert Murdoch in 1969. The proprietor turned the daily and its Sunday sister, the News of the World, into the UK's bestselling titles and consolidated his influence by acquiring The Times and Sunday Times and forging relationships with successive governments (→ Media Conglomerates; News Corporation).

The seeming omnipotence of the Murdoch operation helped his News of the World initially rebut allegations made by the Guardian over alleged phone hacking involving numerous victims. However, when the full scale of this was revealed in 2011 it led to the immediate closure of the paper. The scandal led the government to set up an inquiry which recommended the abolition of the Press Complaints Commission (→ Ethics in Journalism). The PCC, originally set up in 1991, was the latest in a line of self-regulatory bodies consisting of industry figures adjudicating on cases brought to it by aggrieved parties (→ Accountability of the Media). A perceived reluctance by the Commission to censure newspapers had previously led to calls for new statutory regulated system to protect the public from invasions of their → privacy. The scandal gave major impetus to those seeking such reforms. Newspaper sales were in decline before the hacking controversy and fierce competition for advertising only further curtailed revenues (→ Media Economics). Local newspapers have been affected, although the London Evening Standard has seen a revival in its circulation following its 2009 relaunch as a free newspaper. Similarly Metro, another advertising-reliant giveaway, is widely circulated throughout the country.

Historically, whereas politicians have been reluctant to regulate the so-called 'free press' they have been keener to supervise the electronic media in the guise of *radio* and then *television*. The → BBC, founded as a private company in 1922, was brought under government supervision as a public corporation in 1927 (→ Public Broadcasting, History of; Public Broadcasting Systems). Granted a license to operate courtesy of a periodically renewable Charter, the BBC was overseen by a government-appointed Board of Governors and adhered to a so-called "public service model" that sought "to inform, educate and entertain" (Curran & Seaton 2010). Though television began in 1936 it was not until the 1950s that television superseded radio as the most popular medium following the coronation of Elizabeth II and arrival of commercially funded Independent

Television (ITV) network of regionally based channels (→ Privatization of the Media).

Like ITV, the BBC developed a regional identity through its television programming, an effort supplemented by local radio. The BBC also sought to cater for different age groups through the launch of popular music stations in 1967. Initially the commercial response came with new local radio in the 1970s and later, national services. The latter tendency encouraged the merging of the once independent ITV network of regional franchisees in 2004 into a single company following a decline in advertising revenue (→ Television Broadcasting, Regulation of). This was partly in response to new non-terrestrial broadcasters created during the 1980s, notably Rupert Murdoch's BSkyB, which became the dominant force in the market (→ Satellite Television). Take-up of digital television reached 93 percent of households by 2011 (Ofcom 2011).

There was also a rapid increase in *Internet usage*. In 1998, less than 10 percent of households had online access; by 2014, this had risen to 87 percent. Traditional news media have been particularly proactive in developing their online presence with the BBC, Mail Online and theguardian.com boasting some of the most visited news sites in the world, attracting significant traffic from outside as well as within the UK. This may in part explain why some of the most established media brands look set to continue to shape national debates as well as those beyond the nation's borders.

See also: ▶ ACCOUNTABILITY OF THE MEDIA ▶ BBC ▶ ETHICS IN JOURNALISM ▶ FREEDOM OF COMMUNICATION ▶ FREEDOM OF THE PRESS, CONCEPT OF ▶ MEDIA CONGLOMERATES ▶ MEDIA ECONOMICS ▶ NEWS CORPORATION ▶ PRIVACY ▶ PRIVATIZATION OF THE MEDIA ▶ PUBLIC BROADCASTING, HISTORY OF ▶ PUBLIC BROADCASTING SYSTEMS ▶ SATELLITE TELEVISION ▶ TELEVISION BROADCASTING, REGULATION OF

REFERENCES AND SUGGESTED READINGS

Curran, J. & Seaton, J. (2010). *Power without responsibility: The press and broadcasting in Britain*. London: Routledge.
Ofcom (2011). Statistics. At www.ofcom.org.uk.
Williams, K. (2009). *Get me a murder a day! A history of mass communication in Britain*. London: Bloomsbury Academic.

United Nations, Communication Policies of

EMMANUEL DERIEUX
University of Paris II

The general principles of the United Nations (UN) communication policies are found in the Charter of the United Nations, although the Charter does not explicitly refer to them. They are enumerated in the Universal Declaration of Human Rights (UDHR) and in the International Covenants on Civil and Political Rights and on Economic, Social, and Cultural Rights. UDHR was adopted on December 10, 1948, as a 'resolution' by the UN General Assembly. It recognizes the classic idea of freedom of expression, with both its necessary limits and, in a positive and concrete manner, certain rights including the possibility of demanding those rights, which constitutes, as it were, the basis or inspiration of national communication laws.

Freedom of expression is set forth in Article 19 of the UDHR: "Everyone has the right to freedom of opinion and expression; this right includes freedom to hold opinions without interference and to seek, receive and impart information and ideas through any media, regardless of frontiers" (→ Freedom of Communication; Freedom of Information). The limitations on free expression are in Article 12, which states "No one shall be subjected to arbitrary interference with his privacy, family, home or correspondence, nor to attacks upon his honour and reputation. Everyone has the right to the protection of the law against such interference or attacks."

The differences between western Europe's individualistic idea of freedom, based on the idea of the state's abstention, and the more collective and interventionist approach to human rights of the eastern block led, in December 1966, to the establishment of two international covenants in order to strengthen the UDRH principles: one on civil and political rights (ICCPR), and the other on economic, social, and cultural rights. The latter, called *International Covenant on Economic, Social, and Cultural Rights (ICESCR)* stands in sharp contrast to the ICCPR in that it provides for a more positive and collective framework of human rights to communication.

Several specialized UN institutions determine and implement a wide range of international communication policies. Among the most important institutions relating to communication law and policy are the UN Educational, Scientific, and Cultural Organization (→ UNESCO) and the World Intellectual Property Organization (WIPO). WIPO is primarily concerned with intellectual property issues, especially copyright and related rights.

See also: ▶ COMMUNICATION AND LAW ▶ COPYRIGHT ▶ FREEDOM OF COMMUNICATION ▶ FREEDOM OF INFORMATION ▶ INTELLECTUAL PROPERTY LAW ▶ INTERNATIONAL COMMUNICATION ▶ NEW WORLD INFORMATION AND COMMUNICATION ORDER (NWICO) ▶ UNESCO

REFERENCES AND SUGGESTED READINGS

Derieux, E. & Granchet, A. (2011). *Droit de la communication. Lois et règlements. Recueil de textes*, 9th edn. Paris: Victoires.
Derieux, E. (2003). *Droit européen et international des médias* [European and international media law]. Paris: LGDJ.
United Nations (2014). The Universal Declaration of Human Rights. At: http://www.un.org/en/documents/udhr/index.shtml, accessed August 31, 2014.
World Intellectual Property (2012). International survey on private copying. Geneva: WIPO At: http://www.wipo.int/export/sites/www/freepublications/en/copyright/1037/wipo_pub_1037_2012.pdf, accessed August 31, 2014.

United States of America: Media System

ROBERT L. STEVENSON
University of North Carolina at Chapel Hill

GLENN SCOTT
Elon University

DONALD L. SHAW
University of North Carolina at Chapel Hill

LARS WILLNAT
Indiana University

The first newspaper published in the British North American colonies was *Publick Occurrences, Both Forreign and Domestick*. One issue appeared in 1690 in Boston. It was soon closed down by the colonial government. The first continuously published newspaper was the *Boston News-Letter*, which began publication in 1704 and continued for several decades. The oldest daily paper still publishing is the *Hartford Courant*, which was founded in 1764. Newspapers and especially pamphlets such as Thomas Paine's *Common Sense* played an active role in the movement for independence (→ Newspaper, History of).

Partisan journalism remained the standard for most of the nineteenth century. The latter years of the century introduced two trends that are still visible in newspapers in many countries. Excessive competition between William Randolph Hearst and Joseph Pulitzer for dominance of the New York market led to 'yellow journalism'. In contrast was the sober, non-partisan coverage pioneered by the *New York Times*. Adolph Ochs took over the financially ailing *Times* in 1896 and declared that it would publish "All the News That's Fit to Print," a slogan that still appears on the nameplate on page one.

Legal Framework

The simple statement guaranteeing press freedom in the First Amendment to the US Constitution is one of the oldest and surely the most famous legal formulation of what is now considered a universal right (→ Freedom of the Press, Concept of; Freedom of Communication). The American approach to press freedom is minimalist. It is mostly a set of restraints on government, as the First Amendment specifies. At its core is the principle that government cannot prevent publication of information but can hold journalists responsible after publication.

The Freedom House Report 2013 ranked the United States eighteenth among 63 'free press' countries. The Obama administration has promised, for example, that it will improve public access to official information. A memo from US Attorney-General Eric Holder said that "an agency should not withhold information simply because it may do so legally." In early 2009, however, the US government opposed the publication of photos that showed prisoners tortured by US troops in Afghanistan and Iraq. The administration argued that these photos could undermine military morale and encourage anti-American feeling.

Printed Press

Daily newspaper *circulation* reached a peak in 1985 when 1,676 daily newspapers produced 62.8 million copies. Since then, circulation – along with the number of daily newspapers – has declined steadily. This loss in circulation has led to a huge decline in advertising revenue. Overall newspaper revenue declined 52 percent from 2003 to 2012 to $22 billion. While digital advertising grew almost three times in the same period to $3.4 billion, the increase was still a long way off compensating for the huge losses on the print side (Pew Research Journalism Project 2014).

The United States has three *daily newspapers* that circulate nationally: the popular *USA Today*, which was founded in 1982 as a national newspaper (circulation, print only, in 2013 was 1.4 million), the business-oriented *Wall Street Journal* (circulation 1.5 million), and the general news-oriented *New York Times* (circulation 731,395). Most daily papers are small and oriented toward local communities. Circulation figures mask the full impact of newspaper decline because they omit reference to the rapid population growth of the United States.

The percentage of Americans who had read a newspaper 'yesterday' dropped from 40 percent in 2006 to 29 percent in 2012, with most of the loss in readership coming from those who read print newspapers (Pew Research Journalism Project 2013). However, this loss is somewhat balanced by the growing number of people who read newspapers online. US newspaper websites in late 2012 drew an average of 113.7 million unique visitors per month, generating more than 4.17 billion page views (Newspaper Association of America 2012).

Radio and Television

Terrestrial broadcasting in the United States is regulated by the → Federal Communications Commission (FCC), which grants broadcast licenses and maintains limited oversight under a 'trusteeship' model of broadcasting represented by the phrase "public interest, convenience, and necessity." As of June 2009, the FCC had granted active licenses to 11,249 commercial *radio* stations and 3,106 educational or public radio stations, and to 1,395 commercial TV stations and 390 public TV stations. Additional licenses, mostly for translators and boosters and for low-power licenses operated by universities and a few communities, brought the number of terrestrial broadcasters licensed in the United States to 30,473.

Most commercial *television stations* are affiliated to one of the three traditional networks – CBS, ABC, or NBC – that provide news and prime-time entertainment programming, or to one of the limited networks, such as Fox or the CW network aimed at young adults.

Cable television is the standard delivery system, providing, in some cases, more than 300 programs as well as high-speed Internet access and a telephone service (→ Cable Television). In 2012, 90 percent of all TV households were cable subscribers. There are close to 8,000 cable systems, although most are owned by a handful of large corporations such as Comcast, Time-Warner, and Cox. Federal regulations require cable providers to carry all local terrestrial stations. Since the federal government's authority to regulate content does not apply to cable or satellite broadcasting, cable content on pay services such as Home Box Office (HBO) often includes nudity, rough language, and graphic violence that are prohibited on traditional channels.

Direct broadcast satellite (DBS) is available in the United States but relatively limited (→ Satellite Television). Terrestrial digital radio is slowly gaining in popularity in the United States, although only about 14 percent of all radio stations broadcast a digital-signal version of their traditional terrestrial programs. Satellite radio reaching from coast to coast is available through the sole operator, SiriusXM.

Role of the Internet

Almost three-quarters of all US adults enjoyed a connection to the Internet in 2013 (Smith 2014). The recent growth has occurred in the accelerating adoption of high-speed Internet service. Over time, media groups have increased their reliance on the web, building more sophisticated sites to exploit its interactive features and to combine traditional forms of video, audio, print, → photography, and graphics in multimedia offerings.

News organizations moved warily onto the web as some journalists cautioned against a loss of control, and perhaps function, in a more fluid, interactive environment (→ Online Media; Online Journalism). The surge of independent publishing on the web, popularly labeled → citizen journalism, has awakened the established media to the revolutionary possibilities of digital networking through blogs, podcasts, video sites, and popular social networking sites. Scholars and professionals continue to explore the implications of the new digital landscape, debating issues such as whether news and advertising will continue to be presented in bundled forms via branded websites, or more commonly delivered through personalized channels and services via feeds to PCs and other, more portable devices such as mobile telephones.

See also: ▶ CABLE TELEVISION ▶ CITIZEN JOURNALISM ▶ CNN ▶ COMMUNICATION LAW AND POLICY: NORTH AMERICA ▶ FEDERAL COMMUNICATIONS COMMISSION (FCC) ▶ FREEDOM OF COMMUNICATION ▶ FREEDOM OF THE PRESS, CONCEPT OF ▶ JOURNALISM ▶ NEWSPAPER, HISTORY OF ▶ ONLINE JOURNALISM ▶ ONLINE MEDIA ▶ PHOTOGRAPHY ▶ SATELLITE TELEVISION

REFERENCES AND SUGGESTED READINGS

de Beer, A. S. & Merrill, J. C. (eds.) (2009). *Global journalism: Topical issues and media systems*, 5th edn. Harlow: Pearson.

Gillmor, D. (2006). *We the media: Grassroots journalism by the people, for the people*. Sebastopol, CA: O'Reilly Media. At www.oreilly.com/catalog/wemedia/book/index.csp, accessed August 28, 2014.

Meyer, P. (2009). *The vanishing newspaper: Saving journalism in the information age*, 2nd edn. Columbia, MO: University of Missouri Press.

Newspaper Association of America (2012). Trends and Numbers. At http://www.naa.org/Trends-and-Numbers/Newspaper-Websites/Newspaper-Web-Audience.aspx, accessed August 28, 2014.

Pew Research Journalism Project (2013). State-of-the Media 2013. At http://stateofthemedia.org/2013/newspapers-stabilizing-but-still-threatened/#fn-12990-2, accessed August 28, 2014.

Pew Research Journalism Project (2014). State of the media. At http://www.journalism.org/2014/03/26/state-of-the-news-media-2014-key-indicators-in-media-and-news/, accessed August 28, 2014.

Schudson, M. (1999). *The good citizen: A history of American civic life*. Cambridge, MA: Harvard University Press.

Smith, A. (2014). *Older adults and technology use*. At www.pewinternet.org/files/2014/04/PIP_Seniors-and-Tech-Use_040314.pdf, accessed August 28, 2014.

Tunstall, J. (2007). *The media were American: U.S. mass media in decline*. Oxford: Oxford University Press.

Uses and Gratifications

JOHN L. SHERRY
Michigan State University

ANDY BOYAN
Michigan State University

Media uses and gratifications (U&G) research represents one of the oldest and largest continuous programs of research in the field of communication. The tradition investigates the reasons why people use mass media. The product of this massive research effort has been a large set of taxonomies of media use motives; research linking those motives to antecedent variables (e.g., social factors, personality) and media use, along with some consequences (effects) of that use; and an extensive theoretical discussion and critique.

Major Dimensions of Uses and Gratifications

Katz et al. (1974) provided the germinal theoretical description of the U&G paradigm, stating that U&G research is concerned with "the social and psychological origins of needs, which generate expectations of the mass media or other sources, which lead to differential patterns of media exposure (or engagement in other activities), resulting in need gratifications and other consequences, perhaps mostly unintended ones" (Katz et al. 1974, 20). In contrast to → media effects theories, U&G posits an active audience that uses media to satisfy felt needs, rather than a passive media audience that is affected by media messages (→ Media Effects, History of).

Rubin specified *five a priori assumptions* embodied in U&G research: 1) media use is motivated, goal-directed, and purposive behavior; 2) individuals initiate media use in response to felt needs; 3) a variety of individual differences and social factors guide and filter media use behavior; 4) media use is just one of many alternatives people have; and 5) U&G research assumes that people are a more powerful influence than media in most cases. Schramm et al. (1961) specified three motives for television use among children: entertainment, social interaction, and learning. As other taxonomies were specified with the emergence of new media and genres, these three core motives expanded, but remained fairly consistent with the original formulation.

Changes Over Time in the Topic and its Treatment

According to Rosengren et al. (1985), U&G research proceeded in *three major phases* up until 1985. The first phase from 1940s until the late 1950s was characterized by descriptive research focusing on the reasons individuals use media. The second phase focused on developing typologies of media use during the 1960s. The second era efforts culminated in the early paradigm models proffered by Katz et al. and by Rosengren in Blumler & Katz's classic 1974 collection. Of these perspectives, the model advanced by Rosengren (1974) best encapsulates the core concepts and theoretical linkages of U&G, stating that basic needs, individual differences, and social pressures combine to result in a variety of perceived problems and motivations to which gratifications are sought from the media and elsewhere, leading to differential patterns of media effects on both the individual and societal levels.

From the mid-1970s on, researchers continued to expand empirical data in support of the Rosengren model. This effort resulted in the emergence of *several core concepts and debates*. Some scholars attempted to reduce existing taxonomies into clearer theoretical distinctions, specifying 'instrumental use motives' (seeking exciting or entertaining information) and 'ritualistic use motives' (habitual). Another focus emerged from the debate as to whether media audiences were 'active' or 'passive.' Though the paradigm had always posited an active audience, this notion was difficult to sustain as research into habitual or ritualistic motives continued to emerge.

Researchers also began to investigate the differences between *media gratifications sought and media gratifications obtained*. Recently research has shown that unconscious selection of media and → genres may be driven by biological states that are either transitory or relatively stabile across the life-span (Sherry 2001). Thus, media use is likely both active and passive; conscious and unconscious.

Criticism of the Uses and Gratifications Approach

Several scholars have criticized U&G as *non-theoretical* and lacking in conceptual clarity and explanatory mechanisms. In particular, critics claim that many of the key concepts, particularly motives, needs, gratifications, and uses, are not conceptually distinct from one another. Recently, however, scholars have begun to clarify the concepts implicated in reasons for media use by borrowing concepts from psychology like intrinsic, implicit, and explicit motives, as well as intrinsic motivations.

Another problem is that the taxonomic tendencies in the literature are too compartmentalized to support the *notion of a unified theory* of media use. Careful consideration of the guiding model suggests that this conclusion is more due to the research that has been undertaken than to any deficit in the potential explanatory power of the U&G model.

Finally, critics have complained that U&G research is *narrowly focused on individuals* and does not acknowledge the impact of societal factors and societal-level changes. While this has certainly been the case with the empirical research, scholars have begun to call for cross-level theorizing in media research. U&G is a good candidate for cross-level thinking; Rosengren's (1974) model clearly articulates the importance of both individual- and societal-level variables as a part of the media selection process.

Future Directions in Research, Theory, and Methodology

One of the advantages of the U&G approach is the ease with which it applies to new media. In fact, interactive technologies such as the Internet and video games have breathed new life into U&G research and its emphasis on active audiences. Online users and games must make frequent content or response choices while engaged with these new media. Taxonomies of Internet usage motivations parallel earlier media in some ways (e.g., interpersonal utility, pastime, information seeking, convenience, and entertainment) but also provide a place to communicate with family and friends. This difference marks one of the major distinctions in this new medium (→ Exposure to the Internet).

Recent work on new media highlight two broad types of gratifications users can expect: process gratifications (activities such as surfing the net or playing games) and content gratifications (information such as → news stories, product information). In addition, new media offers a new social aspect that traditional media lack (e.g., instant messaging, talking over the Internet while gaming), putting more information in the hands of users more quickly than any other medium.

For now, growing numbers of young scholars are focusing attention in *two directions*. First, they are creating taxonomies of use of emerging media as scholars did in the past. More importantly, they are more closely examining the experience of media use through an array of entertainment media theories and concepts. Like the U&G scholars that preceded them, they are addressing the weaknesses of the paradigm through continuing empirical and theoretical advances.

See also: ▶ AUDIENCE RESEARCH ▶ EXPOSURE TO COMMUNICATION CONTENT ▶ EXPOSURE TO THE INTERNET ▶ GENRE ▶ MEDIA EFFECTS ▶ MEDIA EFFECTS, HISTORY OF ▶ MOOD MANAGEMENT ▶ NEWS STORY

REFERENCES AND SUGGESTED READINGS

Katz, E., Blumler, J. G., & Gurevitch, M. (1974). Utilization of mass communication by the individual. In J. G. Blumler & E. Katz (eds.), *The uses of mass communications: Current perspectives of gratifications research*. Beverly Hills, CA: Sage, pp. 19–32.

Palmgreen, P. C., Wenner, L. A., & Rosengren, K. E. (1974). Uses and gratifications research: The past ten years. In K. E. Rosengren, L. A. Wenner, & P. C. Palmgreen (eds.), *Media and gratifications research: Current perspectives*. Beverly Hills, CA: Sage, pp. 11–37.

Rosengren, K. E. (1974). Uses and gratifications: A paradigm outlined. In J. G. Blumler & E. Katz (eds.), *The uses of mass communications: Current perspectives of gratifications research*. Beverly Hills, CA: Sage, pp. 269–286.

Rosengren, K. E., Wenner, L. A., & Palmgreen, P. C. (eds.) (1985). *Media and gratifications research: Current perspectives*. Beverly Hills, CA: Sage.

Rubin, A. M. (1994). The uses-and-gratifications perspective of media effects. In J. Bryant & D. Zillmann (eds.), *Media effects: Advances in theory and research*, 2nd edn. Hillsdale, NJ: Lawrence Erlbaum, pp. 525–548.

Ruggiero, T. E. (2000). Uses and gratifications theory in the 21st century. *Mass Communication and Society*, 3, 3–37.

Sherry, J. (2001). Toward an etiology of media use motivations: The role of temperament in media use. *Communication Monographs*, 68(3), 274–288.

V

Validity

KLAUS KRIPPENDORFF
University of Pennsylvania

In *mathematics*, an argument is valid if its conclusion is logically entailed by its premises. In the *social sciences*, empirical research proceeds analogously from data to the scientific theories or answers research questions. However, social researchers tackle many more uncertainties than mathematicians do. For once, the social sciences are inductive and theorize statistical phenomena, hence social theories need to embrace probabilistic notions of validity. Moreover, if data are of questionable validity, their methodologically conclusive analysis is not likely to yield valid conclusions.

Validity should not be confused with → Reliability. Data are reliable to the extent to which the process of generating them is replicable. Replicability says nothing about what data are about. By contrast, data are valid to the extent to which they accurately represent the phenomena of analytical interest. A theory is valid to the extent to which it is corroborated by independently obtained evidence. In → Measurement Theory, a test is valid to the extent it measures what it claims it measure.

Four major kinds of validity can be distinguished. *Logical validity* concerns the conclusiveness of propositions derived from known premises. Logic has little to do with what resides outside its discourse but informs scientific argumentation and writing. *Face validity* is obvious or common truth. Researchers invoke face validity when they accept data, methods, and conclusions because they make sense to them without feeling the need to give reasons for their assessments. The use of face validity in research is more common than seen. *Social validity*, also called "pragmatic validity," is the quality of research results to speak to current public concerns or contribute to prevailing social issues (Riffe et al. 1998). Justifications of research projects to funding agencies almost always rely on claims of their potential value and social impacts. *Empirical validity* is the primary concern of all sciences. It is the degree to which independently available evidence supports various stages of the research process and withstands the challenges of additional data, competing theories, and alternative experiments or measurements.

Several methods have been used to assess empirical validity. Based on a recommendation by the American Psychological Association (1999), we can distinguish the following: (1) *content validity* refers to phenomena that must be read or interpreted in order to become data. Most theories in social research are based on written documents, communications, and representations, including assertions by interviewees. To capture their meanings in the form of analyzable data requires culturally competent observers or readers. The results obtained from such data need to be interpreted as well – unlike meter readings; (2) *sampling validity* responds to media biases, and institutional reasons for selectively preserving records of analytical interests; (3) *semantic validity* responds to whether the categories of an analysis are commensurate with the categories of the object of inquiry; (4) *construction and use* is concerned with how a research process – its algorithms and networks of analytical steps – relates to or models structures in the object of an analysis. Simulation studies, for example, define a dynamics that takes off from how variables in its object of attention are related; (5) *structural validity* relies on demonstrating the structural correspondence of the research methods and the way the phenomena represented by the data relate to claims made by research results; (6) *functional validity* is the degree to which a method of analysis is vindicated by repeated successes rather than validated by structural correspondences (Janis 1965).

Correlative validity is established by correlating the research results with variables concurrent with but extraneous to the way these results were obtained. Its purpose is to confer validity to the research results from measures known to be valid. An important systematization of correlative validity is the multitrait-multimethod technique (Campbell & Fiske 1959). It distinguishes: (1) *convergent validity*, the degree to which research results correlate with other variables known to measure the same or closely related phenomena; (2) *discriminant validity*, the degree to which research results are distinct from or unresponsive to unrelated phenomena and hence do not correlate with the research results; and (3) *predictive validity*, the degree to which research results pertain to anticipated but not yet observed phenomena, whether at a future point in time or elsewhere.

See also: ▶ CONTENT ANALYSIS, QUALITATIVE
▶ CONTENT ANALYSIS, QUANTITATIVE
▶ MEASUREMENT THEORY ▶ RELIABILITY
▶ RESEARCH METHODS ▶ SAMPLING, RANDOM

REFERENCES AND SUGGESTED READINGS

American Educational Research Association, American Psychological Association, and National Council on Measurement in Education (1999). *Standards for educational and psychological testing*. Washington, DC: American Psychological Association.

Campbell, D. T. & Fiske, D. W. (1959). Convergent and discriminant validation by the multitrait-multimethod matrix. *Psychological Bulletin*, 56(2), 81–105.

Headland, T. N., Pike, K. L., & Harris, M. (eds.) (1990). *Emics and etics: The insider/outsider debate*. Newbury Park, CA: Sage.

Janis, I. L. (1965). The problem of validating content analysis. In H. D. Lasswell, N. Leites et al. (eds.), *Language of politics*. Cambridge, MA: MIT Press, pp. 55–82.

Krippendorff, K. (2013). *Content analysis: An introduction to its methodology*, 3rd edn. Thousand Oaks, CA: Sage.

Riffe, D., Lacy, S. & Fico, F. G. (1998). *Analysing media messages: Using quantitative content analysis in research*. Mahwah, NJ: Lawrence Erlbaum.

Video Games

KIMBERLY GREGSON
Ithaca College

A game is a voluntary activity with rules and some sought-after outcome. A video game is a game played on some electronic device. Computer or video games have been around since at least 1962, when MIT student Steve Russell programmed Spacewar! There was no keyboard, no joystick, and no sound; instead users toggled built-in switches to move the rocket ships. Ten years later, Nolan Bushnell, Atari founder, successfully introduced a version of Pong (electronic Ping-Pong). The first home console units were introduced in the 1970s and the well-known arcade game PacMan was introduced in 1980, followed by Donkey Kong in 1981 (→ Digital Media, History of).

A 2013 Entertainment Software Association report shows that in 2012, the video game industry in the US saw about US$23 billion in sales. Video games are often classified into casual, serious, and educational games with casual ones being by far in the lead. Puzzle, board, card, trivia games or game shows are the most often online games played. Players use consoles, computers, and mobile devices for playing video games. The increased capacity in data transfer on the Internet increased the market share of online games where players in distant places compete or cooperate in games of all kinds (e.g. Minecraft). People wo have increased their time spent with video games report that they reduced the time spent with (non-digital) board games, watching TV, and going to the movies. In 2013, the average age of video game players in the US was 30 years and, almost half were women. Gamers are not anymore sitting in a dark room at home: 36 percent are playing on their smartphone and 25 percent on a wireless device (Entertainment Software Association 2013).

Video games have influenced movies, too (→ Cinema). One of the earliest movies based on a video game was Super Mario Brothers. No less than 16 Pokemon movies, based on Nintendo's video game have been released in the United States. The most successful movie on the international market was Prince of Persia – The Sands of Time, based on a game by Ubisoft, that grossed more than US$300 million.

The amount of attention paid to video games as a part of → popular culture is mirrored by the attention paid by academics to video games and the effects they have on the people who play games (→ Youth Culture; Violence as Media Content, Effects of). Research on the effects of playing video games has either concentrated on the production of aggression and hostility, or on positive effects like cognitive, social, emotional and motivational benefits (Granic et al. 2014).

See also: ▶ CABLE TELEVISION ▶ CINEMA ▶ COMPUTER GAMES AND CHILD DEVELOPMENT ▶ DIGITAL MEDIA, HISTORY OF ▶ INTERNET AND POPULAR CULTURE ▶ MEDIA EFFECTS ▶ VIOLENCE AS MEDIA CONTENT, EFFECTS OF ▶ YOUTH CULTURE

REFERENCES AND SUGGESTED READINGS

Entertainment Software Association (2013). 2013 sales, demographic and usage data. Essential facts about the computer and video game industry. At www.theesa.com/facts/pdfs/esa_ef_2013.pdf, accessed August 28, 2014.

Granic, I., Lobel, A., & Engels, R. C. M. E. (2014). The benefits of playing video games. *American Psychologist*, 69(1), 66–78.

Shafer, D. M. (2012). Causes of state hostility and enjoyment in player versus player and player versus environment video games. *Journal of Communication*, 62, 719–737.

Shaw, A. (2013). Rethinking game studies: A case study approach to video game play and identification. *Critical Studies in Media Communication*, 30(5), 347–361.

Violence against Journalists

JOHN NERONE

University of Illinois at Urbana-Champaign

Violence against journalists is universal, found everywhere there is journalism. But the level and type of violence vary according to a series of factors, involving the general level of violence in a society or political system, the level of professionalism in the news media, and the extent to which violent action is useful in representing public opinion. Violence against journalists almost always includes a symbolic dimension; in some cases, the violence is primarily symbolic.

Several organizations *track violence* against journalists worldwide. These organizations note that, especially in conflict zones, journalists are increasingly subject to violent attack. Wartime and social upheaval have always produced violence against journalists. Autocracies use violence to stifle criticism (→ Freedom of the Press, Concept of), and crime reporting can also be glamorously dangerous. In China, for instance, a rapidly expanding media system at the beginning of the twenty-first century produced a wave of exposés of local corruption, and the targets of the exposés frequently became violent.

Violence operates at the boundaries of the → public sphere and can be a form of policing. In any political system, the media are involved in the representation of → public opinion. Historically, political forces attempt to capture the representation of public opinion through various means: making news, exerting political or economic pressure, winning elections. When peaceful means fail, violence becomes useful (→ Freedom of Communication). Violence has been used to try to exclude ideas and groups from public discussion. Such exclusionary violence often appears to be a surrogate for government censorship (→ Censorship, History of).

Violence against the press is a common feature in many countries with diverse populations. Communal media in India, for instance, have experienced violence similar to that visited upon African-Americans in the US south at the end of the nineteenth century. Such actions often look like spontaneous popular outbursts (→ Mediated Populism); they are usually carefully scripted to do so. The line between public and private has also been a site of violence (→ Privacy). The subjects of personal criticism in the press, whether private or public figures, have often struck back. Also, the publicists for labor movements have been targets of violence as labor activists have targeted anti-labor newspapers. Further, movements that feel themselves neglected by the news media will sometimes commit acts of spectacular violence to claim coverage for themselves.

See also: ▶ CENSORSHIP, HISTORY OF ▶ CHINA: MEDIA SYSTEM ▶ ETHNIC JOURNALISM ▶ FREEDOM OF COMMUNICATION ▶ FREEDOM OF THE PRESS, CONCEPT OF ▶ JOURNALISM, HISTORY OF ▶ JOURNALISTS' ROLE PERCEPTION ▶ MEDIATED POPULISM ▶ MINORITY JOURNALISM ▶ PHOTOJOURNALISM ▶ PRIVACY ▶ PROFESSIONALIZATION OF JOURNALISM ▶ PUBLIC OPINION ▶ PUBLIC SPHERE

REFERENCES AND SUGGESTED READINGS

Committee to Protect Journalists (2006). *Attacks on the press in 2006*. Washington, DC: Brookings Institution.

Nerone, J. (1994). *Violence against the press: Policing the public sphere in U.S. history*. Oxford: Oxford University Press.

Reporters without Borders (2011). *Annual reports*. At http://en.rsf.org/safety-of-journalists.html, accessed August 28, 2014.

Violence as Media Content

NANCY SIGNORIELLI
University of Delaware

Most of what we know about violence in the media comes from studies of violence on television. While some studies of television violence were conducted during the 1950s and 1960s, most of the information about the amount of violence on television in the US comes from the long-term research conducted as part of the Cultural Indicators (CI) Project's analysis of samples of prime-time network programs (1967–2013; → Cultivation Effects) and the National Television Violence Study's (NTVS) short-term analysis of a larger sample of network and cable channels from the mid-1990s (→ Cable Television). In the UK, information about television violence comes from an analysis of samples of programs from the mid-1990s. Knowledge about television violence in other countries (e.g., Japan or the Netherlands) comes from studies looking at violence in samples of programs taken at one point in time. Most of these studies, whether conducted in the US or in other countries, focus on physical violence (hurting or killing) because emotional violence is extremely difficult to define and isolate in a consistent way.

Amount of Violence in Television Programming

The CI studies show that the levels of violence on television are quite high and have been relatively stable for the past 45 years. Signorielli (2003) found in samples of prime-time programs broadcast between 1993 and 2002 that violence appeared in 6 out of 10 programs at an average rate of 4.5 acts of violence per program. Current ongoing research by Signorielli finds similar levels of violence in the most recent samples of prime-time network programs. In the UK, Gunter et al. (2003) sampled programming for 20 days in both 1994–1995 and 1995–1996. In both samples, the percentage of programs with violence was considerably smaller than in the US studies (37 and 45 percent of the programs were violent).

Japanese television programs are considerably more violent than programs in most other countries, but quite similar to US programming (Iwao et al. 1981). Japanese television violence, however, tends to be more graphic than violence seen in other countries. Violence in the programming seen in the Netherlands is similar in level to that seen in the US. Canadian, Finnish, and Korean programming is considerably less violent than US programming.

Overall, the US studies, particularly those conducted in the 1990s, show *stability in the amount of violence* on television: violence appears in roughly 6 out of 10 programs. Consequently, whether viewers watch network broadcast channels or cable channels, it is relatively difficult to avoid violence. From an international perspective, countries that import considerable amounts of programming from the US have levels of violence on television similar to those seen in the US, whereas those that do not import many programs have lower levels of violence. One of the reasons for the high level of violence in imported (typically US) programs is that violence transcends language barriers – it is relatively easy to translate, because pictures are self-explanatory.

The Context of Violence

The NTVS study with data from 1994–1995 found that the context in which violence is presented poses risks for viewers. In particular, three-quarters of the violent scenes were committed by characters who were not punished, *negative consequences of violence* were rarely presented, one-quarter of the violent incidents involved the use of a handgun, and fewer than 1 in 20 programs emphasized anti-violence themes.

Similarly, CI research also found that violence tends to *lack context* and that most programs do not show any long-term consequences of violence, such as remorse, regret, or sanctions. The lack of contextual elements is not limited to US programming. The UK study found that programming does not show violence that is particularly harmful and that there was little evidence of blood, gore, and pain. Most of the motives for violence in UK television were related to evil and destruction. The major situations in which violence occurred were interpersonal disputes and crime, followed by scenes focusing on power and self-preservation.

Who is Involved?

CI studies show that television violence illustrates and provides *lessons about power*. Violence illustrates who is on top and who is at the bottom, who gets hurt and who does the hurting, and who wins and who loses. These studies consistently find a power structure related to character demographics, with earlier studies finding women and minorities more likely to be hurt than to hurt others. Recent studies, however, find that during prime time, men are now more likely than women to be hurt (victimized) and/or hurt others (commit violence).

In the programs of the 1980s, *men* were slightly less likely to be involved in violence than in the programs of the 1970s. During the 1990s, the ratios of hurting to being hurt changed from the patterns seen in the 1970s and 1980s for women but not for men. Today, for every 10 male characters who hurt or kill, 11 are victimized, the same ratio found in the earlier samples. For women, however, instead of 16 women being victimized for each woman who hurts or kills, the odds are even – women are equally likely to hurt or kill and to be hurt or killed. Moreover, although whites are a little more likely to be victimized than to hurt others, the odds for minority characters are even (→ Sex Role Stereotypes in the Media). Overall the research shows that more men than women and more whites than minorities are involved in violence. Similarly, studies conducted in the UK found that women were much less likely to be involved in violence.

Overall, the consensus of findings from studies of media content indicated that contemporary television programs and video games may not adequately support or reinforce the lesson that 'crime does not pay.' Thus, the environment of violent entertainment in which many people, including children, spend most of their free time may be potentially harmful. Finally, the lack of realistic contexts for violence on television may signal that aggression and violence are acceptable modes of behavior (→ Violence as Media Content, Effects of; Violence as Media Content, Effects on Children of).

See also: ▶ CABLE TELEVISION ▶ CULTIVATION EFFECTS ▶ SATELLITE TELEVISION ▶ SEX ROLE STEREOTYPES IN THE MEDIA ▶ SEXUAL VIOLENCE IN THE MEDIA ▶ TELEVISION, VISUAL CHARACTERISTICS OF ▶ VIOLENCE AS MEDIA CONTENT, EFFECTS OF ▶ VIOLENCE AS MEDIA CONTENT, EFFECTS ON CHILDREN OF

REFERENCES AND SUGGESTED READINGS

Gerbner, G., Morgan, M., & Signorielli, N. (1994). *Television violence profile no. 14: The turning point.* Philadelphia: Annenberg School for Communication.

Gunter, G., Harrison, J., & Wykes, M. (2003). *Violence on television: Distribution, form, context, and themes*. Mahwah, NJ: Lawrence Erlbaum.

Hetsroni, A. (2007). Four decades of violent content on prime-time network programming: A longitudinal meta-analytic review. *Journal of Communication*, 57(4), 759–784.

Iwao, S., deSola Pool, I., & Hagiwara, S. (1981). Japanese and U.S. media: Some cross-cultural insights into TV violence. *Journal of Communication*, 31(2), 28–36.

Kapoor, S., Kang, J. G., Kim, W. Y., & Kim, S. K. (1994). Televised violence and viewers' perceptions of social reality: The Korean case. *Communication Research*, 11, 189–200.

Mustonen, A. & Pulkkinen, L. (1993). Aggression in television programs in Finland. *Aggressive Behavior*, 19, 175–183.

Signorielli, N. (2003). Primetime violence, 1993–2002: Has the picture really changed? *Journal of Broadcasting and Electronic Media*, 47(1), 36–57.

Simonds, G. (2012). *The aesthetics of violence in contemporary media*. London: Bloomsbury Academic.

Timmer, J. (2013). Television violence and industry self-regulation: The V-Chip, television program ratings, and the TV Parental Guidelines Oversight Monitoring Board. *Communication Law and Policy*, 18(3), 265–307.

Wilson, C., Robinson, T., & Callister, M. (2012). Surviving Survivor: A content analysis of antisocial behavior and its context in a popular reality television show. *Mass Communication and Society*, 15(2), 261–283.

Violence as Media Content, Effects of

MICHAEL KUNCZIK
Johannes Gutenberg University of Mainz (Emeritus)

ASTRID ZIPFEL
Heinrich Heine University of Düsseldorf

Discussion of the harmful effects of media violence is as old as the media themselves. There is no medium that has not been suspected of stimulating real-world aggression. Apart from television, research has also focused on violent content in music and music videos, the Internet, and especially computer games (→ Video Games). Typically, studies examine media depictions of personal violence (i.e., intended physical and/or psychic damaging of persons, living beings, and inanimate objects by another person).

Theories of Pro-Social and Antisocial Effects

Research on the effects of mediated violence has been conducted within several theoretical frameworks. According to *catharsis theory* the viewing of media violence would lead to an engagement in fantasy aggression that permits the discharge of aggressive tendencies. Catharsis theory could not be confirmed by methodologically sound research. The simple assumption that media violence is imitated directly through a *suggestion process* has also been refuted. There may be special conditions that allow imitation of violent acts as well as suicide – however, media content seems to be only one of many more important causes or the final trigger for a previously planned action.

Habituation theory emphasizes long-term effects in the form of desensitization. Whereas viewing media violence seems actually to reduce physiological and emotional reactions to the respective content, evidence is scarce that it also affects attitudes towards violence in real life, diminishes empathy, and reduces the inhibition threshold for one's own aggressive behavior. *Cultivation theory* assumes that heavy television viewers suffer from a distorted view of social reality. Viewing violence thus may cultivate fear of crime and the belief that the world is a mean and scary place (→ Cultivation Effects). Research is currently concentrating on intervening variables (e.g., experience of victimization).

According to *excitation transfer theory* different types of media content (violence, but also eroticism, humor, sports, etc.) cause a state of unspecific arousal that intensifies any (not necessarily violent) subsequent actions (→ Excitation and Arousal). *Priming theory* assumes that violent media stimuli can activate violent associations (thoughts, emotions, behavior) in the individual's brain, and in the short term (in case of repeated stimulation perhaps even in the long term), unconsciously influence the perception of situations and the choice of behavioral options (→ Priming Theory).

Bandura's *theory of social learning* seems to be the most appropriate approach to explain the heterogeneous results of medium-to-long-term studies on media violence. It postulates that people adopt patterns of behavior by observing other people's actions (in reality or in the media; → Reality and Media Reality). However, these patterns do not necessarily have to be acted out.

Normally, they remain latent. Violent actions usually underlie inhibiting conditions (e.g., social norms, fear of punishment, feelings of guilt). They only transfer into manifest action under adequate conditions, especially if the role model and/or the observer experiences or expects success or rewards (or at least no punishment). Social learning theory also considers attributes of media content (e.g., comprehensibility, justification), attributes of the observer (e.g., character, cognitive abilities, former experiences), and social conditions (e.g., socialization, values).

The *general aggression model* is an *integrative model* that tries to combine different concepts. It suggests that behavior results from personal and situational factors that affect cognitions, emotions, and arousal, thereby influencing the appraisal of a situation and the subsequent choice of behavioral options. Environmental reactions to this behavior lead to reinforcement or inhibition of the chosen behavior in the future. Repeated exposure to violent stimuli helps to develop easily accessible aggression-related knowledge structures that may be reinforced by successful application and that become increasingly complex, automatized, and resistant to change. Together with desensitization effects, this may lead to an aggressive personality.

Effects Strength and Future Research

Most researchers agree that media violence may cause negative effects. However, correlations found in empirical studies on television violence are usually quite small, and no more than 9 percent of a person's total aggression is explained by media violence (Comstock 2004, Ferguson & Kilburn 2009, Anderson et al. 2010). Although it is often assumed that because of interactivity computer games (→ Computer Games and Child Development) should be far more dangerous, particularly strong effects of computer-game violence have not been found (Sherry 2007; Ferguson & Kilburn 2009).

The small effects point to the fact that media violence is *only one factor within a complex set of causes* for real-world aggression. However, the small correlation between media violence and violent behavior that holds true for the average of recipients does not mean that strong effects for particular forms of media contents and for particular recipients cannot be found.

According to the present state of knowledge (Kunczik & Zipfel 2010), the *context of violent depictions* is much more important than their sheer amount. Violent content presents a higher risk if it shows violence in a realistic and/or humorous way, if violent behavior seems justified and is committed by attractive, successful protagonists with whom the recipient can identify, and especially if violence is not punished and does not harm the victim visibly.

Concerning the recipient, negative effects of media violence are most likely to occur to young, male, socially deprived heavy viewers/players who already possess a violent personality, grow up in violent families with high media (violence) usage, experience much violence from their parents and in school, and belong to aggressive and/or delinquent peer groups. As the "downward spiral model" (Slater 2003), supported by longitudinal studies, postulates, there is a mutual interplay between preferences for violent media content and violent behavior. Already aggressive recipients are attracted to media violence, and this content may intensify aggressive tendencies.

If children grow up in a violent social environment aggressive media protagonists are particularly interesting and useful for them. They are exposed to a 'double dose' of violent role models because the behavior of violent media characters is affirmed by real-life experience. That way, violent media content and one's own violent experiences may interact and reinforce each other. To further explore the role of moderating factors and their Interaction remains an important scientific task to be fulfilled.

See also: ▶ COMPUTER GAMES AND CHILD DEVELOPMENT ▶ CULTIVATION EFFECTS ▶ EXCITATION AND AROUSAL ▶ MEDIA EFFECTS ▶ PRIMING THEORY ▶ REALITY AND MEDIA REALITY ▶ VIDEO GAMES ▶ VIOLENCE AS MEDIA CONTENT ▶ VIOLENCE AS MEDIA CONTENT, EFFECTS ON CHILDREN OF

REFERENCES AND SUGGESTED READINGS

Anderson, C. A., Shibuya, A., Ihori, N. et. al (2010). Violent video game effects on aggression, empathy, and prosocial behaviour in eastern and western countries: A meta-analytic review. *Psychological Bulletin*, 136, 151–173.

Comstock, G. A. (2004). Paths from television violence to aggression: Reinterpreting the evidence. In L. J. Shrum (ed.), *The psychology of entertainment media: Blurring the lines between entertainment and persuasion*. Mahwah, NJ: Lawrence Erlbaum, pp. 193–211.

Ferguson, C. J. & Kilburn, J. (2009). The public health risks of media violence: A meta-analytic review. *Journal of Pediatrics*, 154, 759–763.

Huesmann, L. R., Dubow, E. F., & Yang, G. (2013). Why it is hard to believe that media violence causes aggression. In K. E. Dill (ed.), *The Oxford handbook of media psychology*. Oxford: Oxford University Press, pp. 159–171.

Kirsh, S. J. (2012). *Children, adolescents, and media violence: A critical look at the research*, 2nd edn. Thousand Oaks, CA: Sage.

Kunczik, M. & Zipfel, A. (2010). *Medien und Gewalt: Befunde der Forschung 2004–2009* [Mass media and violence: Research findings 2004–2009]. Bonn: Bundesministerium für Familie, Senioren, Frauen und Jugend.

Riddle, K. W., Potter, J., Metzger, M. J., Nabi, R. L., & Linz, D. G. (2011). Beyond cultivation: Exploring the effects of frequency, recency, and vivid autobiographical memories for violent media. *Media Psychology*, 14(2), 168–191.

Sherry, J. L. (2007). Violent video games and aggression: Why can't we find effects? In R. W. Preiss, B. M. Gayle, N. Burrell, M. Allen, & J. Bryant (eds.), *Mass media effects research: Advances through meta-analysis*. Mahwah, NJ: Lawrence Erlbaum, pp. 245–262.

Slater, M. D. (2003). Alienation, aggression, and sensation seeking as predictors of adolescent use of violent film, computer, and website content. *Journal of Communication*, 53, 105–121.

Violence as Media Content, Effects on Children of

BRAD BUSHMAN
Ohio State University

L. ROWELL HUESMANN
University of Michigan

Many children today spend more time consuming media than they spend attending school, or in any other activity except for sleeping. By media we mean any form of mass communication such as television, the Internet, video and computer games (→ Video Games), comic books, and radio. Violence is a dominant theme in most forms of media. For example, content analyses show that about 60 percent of television programs in the USA contain violence, and so do about 70–90 percent of the top-selling video games. By violence we mean an extreme act of physical aggression, such as assaulting another person (→ Violence as Media Content; Violence as Media Content, Effects of).

Types of Violent Media Content

For decades researchers have investigated the short- and long-term effects of media violence (→ Media Effects, History of). These researchers have found evidence for at least two important short-term effects and three important long-term effects. The *short-term effects* are 'priming effect' (→ Priming Theory) and 'mimicry effect.' The *long-term effects* are the 'mean-world effect' (→ Cultivation Effects); the 'observational learning effect,' and a 'desensitization effect.'

Regarding the short-term effects, experimental studies on *priming effects* have shown that exposing participants of any age to violent media for relatively short amounts of time (e.g., 20 minutes) causes increases in their aggressive thoughts, angry feelings, and aggressive behaviors (→ Experiment, Laboratory). For example, exposure to violent media makes people more willing to shock others or blast others with loud noise. The exposure to violent media activates these aggressive ideas and thoughts in the mind (primes them), which in turn makes aggressive behavior more likely. Experiments on *mimicry effects* have shown that even very young children will immediately mimic violent or nonviolent behaviors they see being done in the mass media. Bandura et al. (1963) first showed this for nursery school children hitting Bobo dolls, but others have shown the same effect with nursery school children hitting other children. The propensity to mimic facial expressions and simple observed behaviors seems to be a 'hard-wired' process that emerges in infancy. It is differentiated from 'imitation,' which is a longer-term process requiring encoding of a → script, its retention in memory, and its use at a later time.

In the area of long-term effects research has shown that heavy TV viewers are more fearful about becoming victims of violence, are more distrustful of others, and are more likely to perceive the world as a dangerous, mean, and hostile place (*mean-world syndrome*). This process seems to begin early in childhood, with even 7–11-year-olds displaying this pattern. In general, the mean-world syndrome only seems to apply to appraisals of environments with which people have relatively little experience. More recent theoretical approaches to *imitation* have distinguished immediate copying of observed behaviors (mimicry) from delayed copying (imitation, or observational learning). Often what is acquired in observational learning is not a simple behavior but behavioral scripts, beliefs, → attitudes, and other cognitions that make a class of behaviors (e.g., aggressive behaviors) more likely.

A number of *longitudinal studies* have now shown that exposure to media violence in childhood has a significant impact on children's real-world aggression and violence when they grow up (Anderson et al. 2003; → Longitudinal Analysis). For example, in one study children exposed to violent media were significantly more aggressive 15 years later. Importantly, this study also found that aggression as a child was unrelated to exposure to violent media as a young adult, effectively ruling out the possibility that this relationship is merely a result of more aggressive children consuming more violent media (Huesmann et al. 2003).

The effects of violent *video games* on children's attitudes toward violence are of particular concern. Violent video games encourage players to take the perpetrator's perspective. Exposure to violent TV programs and films increases people's pro-violence attitudes, but exposure to violent video games has the additional consequence of teaching decreased empathy for victims. For instance, in one study, children who saw a violent movie were then less willing to intervene when they saw two younger children fighting (Drabman & Thomas 1974; → Computer Games and Child Development). In part, this impact occurs because exposure to violent media desensitizes people emotionally to violence and makes them more tolerant of their own aggression (see below). However, a more important process is likely that violent media teaches children that violent behavior is an appropriate means of solving problems, the violent scripts they can use to solve social problems, and that good consequences can come from behaving violently. In addition, the more realistic a game is perceived to be, the greater the player's immersion, and the greater the immersion, the more cognitive aggression is generated in the player (McGloin et al. 2013).

Moderators and Size of Violent Media Effects

Not all forms of violence are alike. Media that glamorize violence and feature attractive role models (e.g., 'good guys') may have a particularly strong influence, especially when the model's behaviors are reinforced. Whether someone is more likely to become an aggressor or a victim may also depend on whom they identify with, the perpetrators of violence, or their victims. However, for practical purposes, the sheer amount and variety of violence children are exposed to make it likely that all children are vulnerable to these effects in varying degrees. Both boys and girls, more and less intelligent children, and aggressive and nonaggressive children are affected. The long-term effects are greater for children than for adults (Bushman & Huesmann 2006).

Not everyone who smokes gets lung cancer, but smoking is an important risk factor for the disease. Similarly, not everyone who consumes violent media becomes aggressive, but violent media is an important risk factor for aggression. Research has clearly shown that effects of violent media content are not restricted to people who are genetically or biologically predisposed to be aggressive (and thus also exposing themselves to more violence; see Bushman & Huesmann 2014).

See also: ▶ ATTITUDES ▶ COMPUTER GAMES AND CHILD DEVELOPMENT ▶ CULTIVATION EFFECTS ▶ EXPERIMENT, LABORATORY ▶ LONGITUDINAL ANALYSIS ▶ MEDIA EFFECTS ▶ MEDIA EFFECTS, HISTORY OF ▶ PRIMING THEORY ▶ SCRIPTS ▶ VIDEO GAMES ▶ VIOLENCE AS MEDIA CONTENT ▶ VIOLENCE AS MEDIA CONTENT, EFFECTS OF

REFERENCES AND SUGGESTED READINGS

Anderson, C. A., Berkowitz, L., Donnerstein, E. et al. (2003). The influence of media violence on youth. *Psychological Science in the Public Interest*, 4, 81–110.

Anderson, C. A., Shibuya, A., Ihori, N. et al. (2010). Violent video game effects on aggression, empathy, and prosocial behaviour in eastern and western countries: A meta-analytic review. *Psychological Bulletin*, 136, 151–173.

Bandura, A., Ross, D., & Ross, S. A. (1963). Imitation of film-mediated aggressive models. *Journal of Abnormal and Social Psychology*, 66, 3–11.

Bushman, B. J. & Huesmann, L. R. (2006). Short-term and long-term effects of violent media on aggression in children and adults. *Archives of Pediatrics and Adolescent Medicine*, 160, 348–352.

Bushman, B. J. & Huesmann, L. R. (2014). Twenty-five years of research on violence in digital games and aggression revisited: A reply to Elson and Ferguson. *European Psychologist*, 19(1), 47–55.

Carnagey, N. L., Anderson, C. A., & Bushman, B. J. (2007). The effect of video game violence on physiological desensitization to real life violence. *Journal of Experimental Social Psychology*, 43, 489–496.

Drabman, R. S. & Thomas, M. H. (1974). Does media violence increase children's toleration of real-life aggression? *Developmental Psychology*, 10, 418–421.

Huesmann, L. R., Moise-Titus, J., Podolski, C. L., & Eron, L. D. (2003). Longitudinal relations between children's exposure to TV violence and their aggressive and violent behavior in young adulthood: 1977–1992. *Developmental Psychology*, 39, 201–221.

Huesmann, L. R., Dubow, E. F., & Yang, G. (2013). Why it is hard to believe that media violence causes aggression. In K. E. Dill (ed.), *The Oxford handbook of media psychology*. Oxford: Oxford University Press, pp. 159–171.

Kirsh, S. J. (2012). *Children, adolescents, and media violence: A critical look at the research*, 2nd edn. Thousand Oaks, CA: Sage.

McGloin, R., Farrar, K., & Krcmar, M. (2013). Video games, immersion, and cognitive aggression: Does the controller matter? *Media Psychology*, 16(1), 65–87.

Meirick, P. C., Sims, J. D., Gilchrist, E. S., & Croucher, S. M. (2009). All the children are above average: Parents' perceptions of education and materialism as media effects on their own and other children. *Mass Communication and Society*, 12(2), 217–237.

Visual Communication

MICHAEL GRIFFIN
Macalester College

In communication and media studies the term 'visual communication' did not come into use until after World War II and has been used most often to refer to 'pictures,' still and moving, rather than the broader concept of 'the visual.' Studies of visual communication arose primarily in response to a lack of attention to the pictorial in mass communication research. The study of visual communication comprises such wide-reaching and voluminous literatures as art history; the philosophy of art and aesthetics; → semiotics, cinema studies, television and mass media studies; the history and theory of → photography; the history and theory of → graphic design and typography; the study of word–image relationships in literary, aesthetic, and rhetorical theory (→ Rhetorical Studies); the development and use of charts, diagrams, cartography, and questions of geographic visualization; the physiology and psychology of visual → perception; and the impact of new visual technologies, including → digital imagery.

The Pictorial Turn

The rise of contemporary visual communication studies was preceded by centuries of thought and writing concerning the arts and the visual image. Yet the last decades of the twentieth century saw a renewed philosophical concern with the visual that Mitchell (1994) calls "the pictorial turn." This increased attention to the visual can be seen as an outgrowth of scholarship on photography, which since the middle of the nineteenth century has continually explored and revisited the nature of the photographic image as a reflection of reality. Whether couched in terms of art vs. science, pictorial expression vs. mechanical record, or trace vs. transformation, the practice of photography has been dogged by ongoing contradictions between the craft of picture-making and the status of photographs as technological recording. Similarly, the extensive literature of → film theory has revolved around questions of cinema's proper aesthetic status.

An important foundation for the development of visual communication studies, film theory synthesized a body of concepts and tools borrowed from the study of art, psychology, sociology, language, and literature, and work in visual communication has often returned to these various sources for new applications to photography, design, electronic imaging, or virtual reality. Central issues have included the distinction between formative and realist theories, and the scope and centrality of narrative, issues that have preoccupied the philosophy of representation more generally (→ Realism in Film and Photography; Reality and Media Reality).

Theoretical Approaches

The precise nature of visual images as copies or records continues to be a defining issue for visual communication studies in an era of ubiquitous photo-electronic reproduction, with various technical advances promising ever more convincing images and simulations of the external world. Against the commonsense assumptions so often made that visual media give us a window on reality, from the beginning photography and film studies have interrogated the ways in which such 'windows' are created and structured to shape our view.

British → *cultural studies* also incorporated work on film and photography to analyze the culturally constructed nature of visual representation, what many Anglo scholars increasingly called 'lens theory.' Concurrently, interest in the *psychology of the visual* made its way through art history to visual media studies. For instance, Gombrich makes the case that picture forms of all kinds are conventionally constructed according to learned schemata, not simply copied from nature (→ Art as Communication). Pictures rarely stand alone, and rarely communicate unambiguously when they do. Together with film theory, semiotics, and the social history of art, the psychology of visual representation has contributed to an eclectic body of theory and research on which communications scholars have drawn for conceptualizing approaches to visual communication analysis.

The *social history of art* offers models for investigating relationships between the production of images and the social contexts of their sponsorship, use, and interpretation. Alpers has explored the relation between picture-making and description. Baxandall's (1972) study of painting and experience in fifteenth-century Italy provides a historical ethnography of patronage, contractual obligations, and viewer expectations, mapping a social world of visual communication (→ Ethnography of Communication). Becker's *Art Worlds* (1982) applies a similar approach to twentieth-century social worlds of artistic production, with specific attention paid to photography.

Related to these extra-textual studies of visual communication practice and meaning is a long history of attention to the intertextual *relationships between word and image*. Whether in studies of the relationship between religious painting and scripture, pictures and narrative, or in attempts to pursue the study of iconology (the general field of images and their relation to discourse), the existence of pictures within larger multi-textual contexts has led to several rich traditions of scholarship.

Influenced by these parallel developments, social communication theorists in anthropology and sociology took an interest in the *social and discursive role of visual images*. In the 1960s and 1970s scholars studied the cultural codes and social contexts of image-making within particular communities, sub-cultures, and social groups. This movement was influenced by work in the psychology of art and representation, film theory, symbolic interactionism, semiotics, and the social history of art.

Current and Future Research Topics

The key issues for visual communication in the new millennium are surprisingly similar to those of 30 years ago, although greater attention is being paid to these issues within communications studies itself. A still largely unmet challenge for visual communication scholars is to scan, chart, and interrogate the various *levels at which images seem to operate*: as evidence in visual rhetoric, as simulated reality bolstering and legitimizing the presence and status of media operations themselves, as abstract symbols and textual indices, or as 'stylistic excess' – the self-conscious performance of style. These issues are perhaps more significant than ever for the processes of 'remediation' that characterize new digital media and the emphases on 'transparent immediacy' and 'hypermediacy' that distinguish digital visualization.

There is an issue of particular concern to visual communication researchers as we proceed into an era of increasingly convincing *virtual realism* on the one hand, and an increasingly systemic *textualization of images* in cyberspace on the other. It is not just what we *can* do with new digital technologies of manipulation but to what purposes we seek to use the production of images in a 'post-photographic age.'

Finally, in that emerging condition often referred to as the 'global media environment', visual images have become a new sort of transnational cultural currency. Not the 'universal language' that promoters such as Eastman Kodak claimed for photography earlier in the century, but a currency of media control and power, indices of the predominant cultural visions of predominant media industries.

See also: ▶ ADVERTISING ▶ ART AS COMMUNICATION ▶ CINEMA ▶ CULTURAL STUDIES ▶ DIGITAL IMAGERY ▶ ETHNOGRAPHY OF COMMUNICATION ▶ FILM THEORY ▶ GRAPHIC DESIGN ▶ ICONOGRAPHY ▶ MEDIA EFFECTS ▶ MEDIA PRODUCTION AND CONTENT ▶ NEWSPAPER, VISUAL DESIGN OF ▶ PERCEPTION ▶ PHOTOGRAPHY ▶ REALISM IN FILM AND PHOTOGRAPHY ▶ REALITY AND MEDIA REALITY ▶ RHETORICAL STUDIES ▶ SEMIOTICS ▶ SOCIAL STEREOTYPING AND COMMUNICATION ▶ VISUAL CULTURE ▶ VISUAL REPRESENTATION

REFERENCES AND SUGGESTED READINGS

Alpers, S. (1983). *The art of describing: Dutch art in the seventeenth century*. Chicago, IL: University of Chicago Press.

Baxandall, M. (1972). *Painting and experience in fifteenth-century Italy*. Oxford: Oxford University Press.

Becker, H. S. (1982). *Art worlds*. Berkeley, CA: University of California Press.

Gombrich, E. H. (1972). The visual image. *Scientific American*, 227(3), 82–96.

Griffin, M. (ed.) (1992). Visual communication studies in mass media research, Parts I and II. *Communication* (special double issue), 13(2/3).

Gross, L. (1981). Introduction. In S. Worth, *Studying visual communication*. Philadelphia, PA: University of Pennsylvania Press, pp. 1–35.

Lester, P. (2013). *Visual communication: Images with messages*, 6th edn. Andover: Cengage Learning.

Mitchell, W. J. T. (1994). *Picture theory*. Chicago, IL: University of Chicago Press.

Worth, S. (1981). *Studying visual communication*. Philadelphia, PA: University of Pennsylvania Press.

Visual Culture

LISA CARTWRIGHT
University of California, San Diego

Visual culture is an area of study focused on practices of looking and the role of → visual representations in the arts, popular and alternative media cultures, institutional and professional contexts, and everyday life. Art history, film and media studies, → cultural studies, sociology, and anthropology are some of the fields in which visual culture study is conducted. Forms of visual representation studied include museum display, fine art, film and television, old and new media, computer and → video games, digital culture, medical images such as X-rays and sonograms, and → advertising (→ Art as Communication; Cinema; Digital Imagery; Television, Visual Characteristics of).

The study of visual culture emphasizes the relationship of looking and visual representation to forms of knowledge, power, experience, and ideology in everyday life and culture in different historical periods – within and among social groups including nations, communities, workplaces, audiences, and members of institutions such as schools, churches, and cultural organizations. Research in visual culture tends toward qualitative and interdisciplinary methods informed by poststructural critical theory and cultural studies (→ Structuralism; Qualitative Methodology).

Visual culture emerged as an area of study in the period during which electronic and digital media became pervasive components of industrialized cultures. Individual works of fine art were subject to more pervasive reproduction and circulation with the rise of digital imaging and the world wide web, changing the status of the original work of art. Mechanical forms of reproduction such as → photography and motion-picture film converged with digital media in production and exhibition processes. With the increased and enhanced presence of visual media forms in everyday life, the visual became a more crucial area of research in many fields. Visual culture has achieved recognition as a viable approach in many of the traditional disciplines including literature, history, art history, film and media studies, and communication studies.

See also: ▶ ART AS COMMUNICATION ▶ CINEMA ▶ CULTURAL STUDIES ▶ DIGITAL IMAGERY ▶ ICONOGRAPHY ▶ PHOTOGRAPHY ▶ PHOTOJOURNALISM ▶ POPULAR COMMUNICATION ▶ POPULAR COMMUNICATION AND SOCIAL CLASS ▶ QUALITATIVE METHODOLOGY ▶ SEMIOTICS ▶ STRUCTURALISM ▶ TELEVISION, VISUAL CHARACTERISTICS OF ▶ VIDEO GAMES ▶ VISUAL COMMUNICATION ▶ VISUAL REPRESENTATION

REFERENCES AND SUGGESTED READINGS

Dikovitskaya, M. (2005). *Visual culture: The study of the visual after the cultural turn*. Cambridge, MA: MIT Press.

Fuery, K. & Fuery, P. (2003). *Visual culture and critical theory*. London: Edward Arnold.

Morra, J. & Smith, M. (eds.) (2006). *Visual culture: Critical concepts in media and cultural studies*, 4 vols. London: Routledge.

Sturken, M. & Cartwright, L. (2001). *Practices of looking: An introduction to visual culture*, 2nd edn. Oxford: Oxford University Press.

Visual Representation

CAREY JEWITT
University of London

The study and conceptualization of visual representation were primarily associated with art and art history prior to the twentieth century, and drew on the analytical tools of iconology with a focus on the artist's intention and perception (→ Iconography). With the advent of → semiotics, followed by other theories of the visual, the twentieth century marked a broadening in conceptions of visual representation from the realm of art to the realm of the everyday. This includes studies of images in film, the use of photography, advertising, scientific imagery, learning and development, and the representation of social identities. This expansion of the domain of the visual has influenced how visual representation is theorized and approached, including a shift in focus from the image to contexts of production and viewers. Today a range of theories is applied to understanding the visual, including theories drawn from anthropology, art history, cognitive psychology, cultural studies, linguistics, psychoanalytical theories, and sociology.

The twenty-first century is marked by a plethora of imaging and visual technologies, and in contemporary western society everyday life is saturated with the images that these technologies make available. Studies of late twentieth-century culture have noted a "turn to the visual" (Mirzoeff 1999) in which the modern world has become a visual phenomenon; a world that conflates looking, seeing, and knowing to become a "vision machine" created through new visualizing technologies in which people are all caught (Virilio 1994).

There is a general agreement that the meaning of an image is 'made' at three sites. First, semiotics proposes that there is a wide range of *visual, pictorial, material, and symbolic* → *signs* that are conventional in the way that they simplify, and yet bear some kind of resemblance to, an object or quality in the 'real' world that they signify. What is depicted in an image and how it is represented are an obvious starting point for understanding the process of visual representation. Second, the economics, motives, and intentions of those who *produce and disseminate* visual representations are aspects of the site of production. That is, visual representations need to be understood in context because these social factors and experiences are not separate from the signifying systems of the visual, but structure it. Third, understanding the *agency of the viewer* demands a shift of analytical emphasis away from the image or text to the social identities and experiences of the viewer. From this perspective, meaning is understood as constituted in the articulation between the viewer and the viewed, between the power of the image to signify, and the viewer's capacity to interpret meaning.

Signification and how to theorize the relationship between referent, signifier, and signified are central to the way visual representation is conceptualized. Current theories of → perception, structuralism, poststructuralism, and postmodernism theorize their relationship in different ways (→ Postmodernism and Communication). This influences how the power of visual representation is understood to shape people's experience of the world, what the world is, and what it can be.

The visual produces as well as represents culture, constituting (and constituted by) its *relations of power and difference*, so that cultures of everyday life are entwined with practices of representation.

In the ways that people are depicted, vision is complicit with power and discipline through surveillance (→ Propaganda, Visual Communication of). Understanding visual representation as embodying and constituting ideologies shows how ways of investing meaning in the world are realized in visual representations. Looking at how representations attempt to fix difference offers a way of conceptualizing the complex relationship of power and representation. Visual representations are, then, a discursive means by which a dominant group works to establish and maintain hegemonic power within a culture in which meaning is constantly reproduced and remade as signs are articulated and rearticulated. Images are thus a site of *struggle for meaning*, a site of power, and constitutive of society.

See also: ▶ CODE ▶ CULTURAL STUDIES ▶ CULTURE: DEFINITIONS AND CONCEPTS ▶ ICONOGRAPHY ▶ MEANING ▶ PERCEPTION ▶ POSTMODERNISM AND COMMUNICATION ▶ PROPAGANDA, VISUAL COMMUNICATION OF ▶ SEMIOTICS ▶ SIGN ▶ STRUCTURALISM ▶ TECHNOLOGY AND COMMUNICATION ▶ VISUAL COMMUNICATION

REFERENCES AND SUGGESTED READINGS

Hall, S. (1997). *Representation: Cultural representations and signifying practices*. Thousand Oaks, CA: Sage.

Kress, G. & van Leeuwen, T. (2006). *Reading images: A grammar of visual design*. London: Routledge.

Lester, P. (2013). *Visual communication: Images with messages*, 6th edn. Andover: Cengage Learning.

Mirzoeff, N. (1999). *An introduction to visual culture*. London: Routledge.

Mitchell, W. J. T. (1995). *Picture theory: Essays on verbal and visual representation*. Chicago, IL: University of Chicago Press.

Virilio, P. (1994). *The vision machine*. Indianapolis, IN: Indiana University Press.

War Propaganda

ROBIN ANDERSEN
Fordham University

War propaganda fuses international and domestic processes in communicating one or more nations as the 'Other,' as worthy en masse of death and mutilation. During the twentieth century, as examples from Britain, Germany, and the US indicate, domestic as well as international media propaganda became essential for planning and engaging effectively in combat against other countries. In World War I, governments employed verbal and visual strategies that effectively influenced mass public opinion in favor of war. Since then, technological media developments and advances in communication design have been employed to promote positive attitudes toward war, albeit with varying effectiveness. Terms such as 'public diplomacy,' media campaign, information management, 'stagecraft,' spin, and even 'militainment' have also been deployed to characterize ever-evolving propaganda strategies.

Wartime rhetoric includes linguistic and visual strategies that either obscure the human costs or present the loss of human life as acceptable (→ Linguistics; Propaganda, Visual Communication of). Phrases such as 'smart bombs' assure that only military targets will be destroyed; the identification of images of dead and wounded civilians as 'enemy propaganda' denies their reality; and 'collateral damage' presents human destruction as a legitimate and inevitable by-product.

When *historical frameworks* are used to shape news of war, certain war events may be turned, very questionably, into transferable reference points, yet others may stay untouched, almost untouchable. Many US news media equated the 9/11 terrorist attacks with the 1941 Pearl Harbor attack that drove the US into World War II. Historical references to the danger of appeasing Hitler (in the infamous 1938 Munich summit) placed Afghanistan, Iraq, even Iran, within the context of the 'Good Fight' of World War II. Yet during the build-up to the Afghanistan and Iraq wars, no mention was made in US news media of the standard brutalities of actual military interventions, to well-documented massacres by US troops such as No Gun Ri in the Korean War and My Lai in the Vietnam War, or to the fact the US was forced to withdraw from Vietnam.

War rhetoric *nurtures fear and hatred*, rendering reasoned discussion less compelling. Society generally punishes unlawful violent behavior, so that mobilizing collective hatred of an enemy requires blocking out peacetime inhibitions. In promoting state-sanctioned violence the enemy's actions must be defined as so far outside the bounds of tolerance that negotiation is absurd. War must appear to be the only defense against a menacing, murderous aggressor. The demonized enemy is no longer recognizably human, and can be killed with impunity. Such narratives of exclusion provide the necessary psycho-political context for war.

The cognitive, linguistic, and visual communication strategies that fueled *World War I* were designed in a variety of ways. In conjunction with → censorship, the repetition of carefully designed messages helped fuel the public's fear and hatred, and to drag out the conflict over four years, with many millions of dead and maimed. The linguistic and conceptual devices used almost a century ago are still recognizable today. Ambiguity must be eliminated, replaced by definitive assertions. The world is divided between 'our civilized way of life' and 'their barbarism.' A simple 'binary of good and evil' facilitates mass consensus. War propaganda asserts that conflict is caused by the inherent evil of the enemy, not by historical injustices, failed diplomacy, competition for economic resources, or global inequities. The Third Reich, emerged from the ashes of World War I, brought new and even more effective forms of war propaganda to live (→ Propaganda in World War II).

New hybrid formats blur the boundaries between fiction and nonfiction; the latter, referred to as 'militainment,' being employed by the US media and military to represent war. Militainment and 'stagecraft' are attempts to control the meanings of war through fictional formatting, information management, and media choreography. After 9/11, Pentagon officials met with Hollywood producers and directors and requested they join the fight against terrorism. They collaborated on such films as Behind Enemy Lines, a story validating unilateral US military action, and ABC's Profiles from the Front Lines, a 'reality show' about the Afghanistan war (→ Reality TV).

See also: ▶ CENSORSHIP ▶ LINGUISTICS ▶ PROPAGANDA ▶ PROPAGANDA IN WORLD WAR II ▶ PROPAGANDA, VISUAL COMMUNICATION OF ▶ REALITY TV

REFERENCES AND SUGGESTED READINGS

Andersen, R. (2006). *A century of media, a century of war*. New York: Peter Lang.
Brewer, S. (2011). *Why America fights: Patriotism and war propaganda from the Philippines to Iraq*. Oxford: Oxford University Press.
Knightly, P. (2002). *The first casualty: The war correspondent as hero and myth-maker from the Crimea to Kosovo*. Baltimore, MD: Johns Hopkins University Press.
Lasswell, H. D. (1927). *Propaganda techniques in the World War*. London: Keagan, Paul, Trench.
Rampton, S. & Stauber, J. (2006). *The best war ever: Lies, damned lies, and the mess in Iraq*. Harmondsworth: Penguin.
Welch, D. & Fox, J. (eds.) (2012). *Justifying war: Propaganda, politics and the modern age*. Basingstoke: Palgrave Macmillan.

Watergate Scandal

RUSS WITCHER
Tennessee Tech University

The press played a major role in the beginnings of Watergate. In June 1971 the *New York Times* began publishing a series of articles that chronicled American involvement in the Vietnam War. The documents, leaked by former Pentagon employee Daniel Ellsberg, were basically a historical account of American participation in the conflict. President Richard Nixon's National Security Advisor Henry Kissinger convinced the president that to allow the leakage of such classified information without retaliation on his part would be harmful to ongoing secret negotiations with the North Vietnamese, the Chinese, and the Soviet Union. The Nixon Justice Department sought and obtained an injunction against the *New York Times* and other papers that were running the series of articles. The US Supreme Court ruled that the government had not met the heavy burden of proof that continued publication of these Pentagon Papers would cause a direct and immediate threat to national security (→ Freedom of the Press, Concept of; Freedom of Information).

Nixon then ordered the creation of a White House investigative unit that would search for and stop further damaging leaks by government employees to the press. This unit eventually broke into Ellsberg's psychiatrist's office in California

(Ambrose 1989). Another intelligence-gathering operation was the break-in at the Democratic national headquarters in the Watergate complex in Washington, DC, in June 1972, where five burglars were arrested by the police. The incident eventually led to the exposure of White House complicity in the break-in and Nixon's own involvement in the cover-up (Aitken 1993). The early reporting of Bob Woodward and Carl Bernstein of the Washington Post was an important factor in keeping the Watergate story alive.

The issue of whistleblowers is still alive in America, with the recent leaks of US wartime activity by Specialist Bradley Manning concerning the Iraq and Afghanistan conflicts, and the release of classified information of domestic spying by the National Security Agency by a government-contracted employee, Edward Snowden. To what extent can secrets in wartime be maintained in a democratic society? That question has to be resolved ultimately, with the help of an independent press, by the judicial branch.

See also: ▶ CENSORSHIP ▶ FREEDOM OF INFORMATION ▶ FREEDOM OF THE PRESS, CONCEPT OF ▶ JOURNALISM, HISTORY OF ▶ JOURNALISTS' ROLE PERCEPTION ▶ UNITED STATES OF AMERICA: MEDIA SYSTEM

REFERENCES AND SUGGESTED READINGS

Aitken, J. (1993). *Nixon: A life*. Washington, DC: Regnery.
Ambrose, S. E. (1989). *Nixon: The triumph of a politician, 1962–1972*. New York: Simon and Schuster.
Nixon, R. N. (1978). *RN: The memoirs of Richard Nixon*. New York: Grosset and Dunlap.

Web 2.0 and the News

ALFRED HERMIDA
University of British Columbia

Web 2.0 is a term Internet entrepreneur Tim O'Reilly popularized to describe a stage in the development of the world wide web as a platform. It refers to a set of technical changes that facilitate the creation, dissemination, and sharing of digital content. Web 2.0 frames users as collaborating in the production, shaping, and distribution of → news and → information, rather than passively consuming content that others create (→ Computer-User Interaction; Interactivity, Concept of). Web 2.0 provides the infrastructure for potentially geographically dispersed individuals with common interests to connect and collaborate via the Internet without any central coordination. The new generation of Internet services and devices, often called → 'social media,' includes blogs, wikis, social networking sites, web applications, mashups, and folksonomies. Web 2.0 is a relatively new and underdeveloped concept in communication and journalism research. Studies to date indicate it has *affected the news media in three broad ways*.

First, Web 2.0 extends the notion of a *participatory media culture*. During major news events, users have taken on roles once reserved for professional journalists (Newman 2009). The terms used, often interchangeably, to refer to the activity of users who gather, report, analyze, and share news and information include 'participatory journalism,' 'user-generated content,' and → 'citizen journalism.' Participatory media reduce the hierarchy of owners, producers, and audiences and undermine the journalists' control of gatekeeping. In the first decade of Web 2.0, news organizations strictly circumscribed opportunities for users to participate in news production. The mechanism most often adopted was audience comments on stories (Singer et al. 2011). Users may contribute raw news material and comment on finished journalistic products, but journalists retain editorial control. The online mechanisms reproduce past practices, such as letters to the editor or radio call-in programming.

Second, the news media are incorporating the ethos of Web 2.0 into journalistic practices on an ad hoc basis (Singer et al. 2011). In *collaborative initiatives*, or 'pro-am' journalism, professional journalists work with users to cover stories or topics, supplementing existing news gathering and enhancing output ('social news'). Networked, distributed, and real-time services such as → Twitter are influencing the dissemination of news. New social media allow immediate sharing of short fragments of data. First reports routinely come from those on the scene rather than from professional journalists. Immediate services such as Twitter may compress → news cycles, particularly in countries with high levels of Internet connectivity and mobile telephony. Social media may also potentially speed up the spread of rumors or wrong information. Newsrooms face pressures over what to report and when, shifting from being first to instead curating and verifying content (Newman 2009).

Third, Web 2.0 blogs and other social media *focus on openness, connection, and sharing*. The news media have widely adopted blogging by journalists, who see the conversational, informal, and often personal format as a way to connect with audiences and demonstrate transparency. Journalists have similarly incorporated Twitter into their daily routines as a way to share content, develop relationships, and build community. The use of social media has led to a debate over journalism ethics, particularly over how these media blur the professional and personal (→ Ethics in Journalism). Newsrooms have set editorial policies for social media due to concerns about trust and credibility (→ Journalists, Credibility of). Research so far indicates that journalists are adding social media tools to fit their existing norms and practices.

For the audience, sharing and discussing news can now take place online through social networks. In some settings, exchanging links and recommendations is a form of cultural currency in social networks (Purcell et al. 2010). A large segment of the audience then relies on their electronic social network to alert them to news of interest. But social networks may limit the breadth of information people receive. On Web 2.0, audiences appear to consult multiple sources on multiple platforms (Purcell et al. 2010). Social recommendation may extend the reach of news content and drive traffic to it. Websites of large, mainstream news organizations include social networking functionality to let users share links (Singer et al. 2011), impacting business models based on delivering large, aggregate audiences to advertisers (→ Media Economics).

See also: ▶ CITIZEN JOURNALISM ▶ COMPUTER–USER INTERACTION ▶ ETHICS IN JOURNALISM ▶ INFORMATION ▶ INTERACTIVITY, CONCEPT OF ▶ INTERNET NEWS ▶ JOURNALISM ▶ JOURNALISTS, CREDIBILITY OF ▶ MEDIA ECONOMICS ▶ NEWS ▶ NEWS CYCLES ▶ NEWS STORY ▶ PROFESSIONALIZATION OF JOURNALISM ▶ SOCIAL MEDIA ▶ TWITTER

REFERENCES AND SUGGESTED READINGS

Gillmor, D. (2004). *We the media: Grassroots journalism by the people, for the people.* Sebastopol, CA: O'Reilly.

Newman, N. (2009). The rise of social media and its impact on mainstream journalism. Working Paper, Reuters Institute for the Study of Journalism. At https://reutersinstitute.politics.ox.ac.uk/fileadmin/documents/Publications/The_rise_of_social_media_and_its_impact_on_mainstream_journalism.pdf, accessed August 28, 2014.

O'Reilly, T. (2005). What is Web 2.0: Design patterns and business models for the next generation of software. At http://oreilly.com/web2/archive/what-is-web-20.html, accessed August 28, 2014.

Purcell, K., Rainie, L., Mitchell, A., Rosenstiel, T., & Olmstead, K. (2010). Understanding the participatory news consumer. At www.pewinternet.org/Reports/2010/Online-News.aspx, accessed August 28, 2014.

Singer, J. B., Hermida, A., Domingo, D. et al. (2011). *Participatory journalism in online newspapers: Guarding the Internet's open gates.* Oxford: Wiley Blackwell.

Women in the Media, Images of

LANA F. RAKOW
University of North Dakota

Images of women in the media have presented a serious problem and challenge to feminist activists and scholars concerned about women's status in societies. In the US in particular, but also in other parts of the world, the type, quality, and number of images of women in various fictional and nonfictional → genres (in film, television, → advertising, and magazines especially) have been well documented since the 1970s.

Research History

Consistently, such research documents women's subordinate status to men, demonstrated by their key absences (such as in the → news) and attention to physical appearance or domesticity (such as in commercial advertising; → Sex Role Stereotypes in the Media).

However, other feminist approaches to media have raised challenges about the *theoretical and political shortcomings* of a focus on 'images.' Consequently, more sophisticated understandings of the relationship between mass media, reality, and racial, global, political, and economic structures have taken hold in feminist communication scholarship (→ Reality and Media Reality; Media and Perceptions of Reality). Nonetheless, analysis of women's media images in countries around the world has been important in efforts to make changes for women (→ Feminist and Gender Studies).

In the US, the scholarly and *systematic documentation of women's media images* was among the first concerted efforts on behalf of women by women media scholars. The approach got its impetus from the dominant approach of the field concerned about the effect of messages on audiences, as well as from liberal feminism. Researchers accumulated empirical evidence that women were absent, denigrated, and devalued throughout much of the mass media, supported by the theoretical work in Tuchman et al. (1978). Tuchman's concept of "symbolic annihilation" in the book's introduction is still used today, although in at least one case appropriated to dissect racial and gender power axes. Molina-Guzmán (2010) uses "symbolic colonization" to analyse white mainstream media's use of the Latina body.

Early research, which typically focused on white women, consistently demonstrated that in programming aimed at women, domestic responsibilities were shown as the natural fulfilment of women. On the one hand, media content directed at men often displayed women as sexual enhancements of male power. The 'sexualization of women's images' began in the mainstream mass media in the 1960s, in what many feminists considered a co-optation of the women's movement. Contemporary manifestations of the problem are suggested by the alarming rise of eating disorders in girls and young women, signaling that men's surveillance of women in media content may result in women's self-surveillance to achieve a particular shape and look. A recent study of Israeli women revealed, however, that at least some women consider themselves discerning enough not to be affected by images in media content, although they think other women are not (Barak-Brandes 2011).

New Orientations in Research

Early images research has been criticized for undertheorizing both gender and media in their economic and cultural contexts. The approach has been wedded to a liberal social theory that accepts the current commercial media system while arguing for only limited reforms (i.e., making representations of women 'more realistic'). *Socialist feminists* pointed out that the economic system and the power of ownership and production must be accounted for to produce a sufficient critique of the media. Other feminists have pushed for changes that would give women access to the means of production and representation (→ Commercialization: Impact on Media Content).

Further, the images approach undertheorized the *relationship between media and reality*. The mirror-image relationship between reality and media texts assumed by the approach is based on the premise that reality exists outside of human meaning. Postmodern feminists challenged the position with a constructivist rendering of both social reality and gender (→ Media and Perceptions of Reality).

Undertheorizing gender and media also had the consequence of ignoring key relationships among women along *ethnic and racial lines*. While white women often were portrayed as madonnas or whores, Native American women were shown as beautiful Indian princesses or unattractive squaws (Bird 1999), African-American women as mammies or matriarchs (Collins 1990), Chicana/Latina women as Spanish noblewomen or beautiful cantina girls (Fellner 2002), and Asian/Asian-American women as sexually servile geishas or powerful dragon ladies (Kim 1986; → Feminist Media Studies, Transnational).

International Comparisons

While research on images of women has been primarily a US liberal feminist project, women around the world have found political and theoretical value in examining and challenging women's images in media systems. The United Nations Fourth World Conference on Women, held in Beijing in 1995, identified a strategic objective in its platform for action to promote non-stereotyped portrayals of women in the media. A number of media-monitoring projects developed to document problems and changes in representation.

While there are notable similarities in women's images in many countries, there also are important differences, as demonstrated in a study of sexual advertising content (Nelson and Paek 2005). These differences dispel the assumption there is a universal image and meaning of 'woman' across countries as well as within them. Barbara Sato's interpretation of *the new woman* that emerged in Japan between the two world wars, confronting previous notions of women as gentle and meek with a new urban femininity, shows how images of women can be used to explain and manage periods of social change (Sato 2003).

By attending to larger political, economic, and ideological meaning systems, more sophisticated notions of both 'images' and 'women' have extended and enriched the important work begun by liberal feminist scholars. An edited volume by Carille and Campbell (2012) captures a range of approaches now embraced under the images research rubric. Contributions tackle women's representations in various parts of the globe (Pakistan, India, China, Bulgaria), of racial and sexual minority identifiers (Black women and lesbian women), and of different genres (film, advertising, news, and new media).

See also: ▶ ADVERTISING ▶ COMMERCIALIZATION: IMPACT ON MEDIA CONTENT ▶ FEMINIST MEDIA STUDIES, TRANSNATIONAL ▶ GENDER: REPRESENTATION IN THE MEDIA ▶ GENRE ▶ MASCULINITY AND THE MEDIA ▶ MEDIA AND PERCEPTIONS OF REALITY ▶ NEWS ▶ POLITICAL ECONOMY OF THE MEDIA ▶ REALITY AND MEDIA REALITY ▶ SEX ROLE STEREOTYPES IN THE MEDIA ▶ SEXISM IN THE MEDIA ▶ SEXUAL VIOLENCE IN THE MEDIA

REFERENCES AND SUGGESTED READINGS

Barak-Brandes, S. (2011). 'I'm not influenced by ads, but not everyone's like me': The third-person effect in Israeli women's attitude toward TV commercials and their images. *Communication Review* 14(4), 300–320.
Bird, E. S. (1999). Gendered representation of American Indians in popular media. *Journal of Communication*, 49(3), 61–83.
Carille, T. & Campbell, J. (eds.) (2012). *Challenging images of women in the media: Reinventing women's lives*. Lanham, MD: Lexington.
Collins, P. H. (1990). *Black feminist thought: Knowledge, consciousness, and the politics of empowerment*. Boston, MA: Unwin Hyman.
Fellner, A. M. (2002). *Articulating selves: Contemporary Chicana self-representation*. Vienna: Braumuller.
Kim, E. (1986). Asian Americans and American popular culture. In H.-C. Kim (ed.), *Dictionary of Asian American history*. New York: Greenwood, pp. 91–114.
Molina-Guzmán, M. (2010). *Dangerous curves: Latina bodies in the media*. New York: New York University Press.
Nelson, M. R. & Paek, H.-J. (2005). Cross-cultural differences in sexual advertising content in a transnational women's magazine. *Sex Roles*, 53(5/6), 371–383.
Sato, B. H. (2003). *The new Japanese woman*. Durham, NC: Duke University Press.
Tuchman, G., Daniels, A. K., & Benet, J. (eds.) (1978). *Hearth and home: Images of women in the mass media*. Oxford: Oxford University Press.

Women's Communication and Language

KANDI L. WALKER
University of Louisville

Women's language and communication research can be traced back to a 1664 report that cited differences in speech forms of 'Carib' women and men. This research was the beginning of a fruitful area of study looking at language use, speech styles, and communication strategies associated with women.

Early research on women's language and communication focused on linguistic aspects of language, mainly concentrating on sounds (e.g., phonetics) and syntax (→ Linguistics). The more systematic interest and dichotomy of sex role- and gender-related aspects of language and communication came much later (→ Rhetoric and Gender). With the influence of the feminist movement in some parts of the world, a serious interest in women's language and communication research materialized. Thus, in these countries research concerning women's language and communication became apparent from the 1970s.

Robin Lakoff's publications have often been deemed the foundational work of describing feminine speech style, illustrating the significant relationship between language and gender. Lakoff identified a number of characteristics in women's speech patterns (hedges, super-polite speech, tag questions, speaking with intonation emphasis, empty adjectives, hypercorrect grammar and pronunciation, lack of sense of humor, direct quotations, a special lexicon, rising intonation in declarative statements). Although criticized for labeling women's language as varying from the norm, Lakoff's research has had great heuristic value in current communication, linguistic, and gender studies.

From Lakoff's work, *three influential perspectives* emerged with regard to women's language and communication. Researchers from a "sex-role perspective" believe there are innate similarities and differences between women's and men's language and communication. For "feminist researchers," women's language and communication are analyzed in relation to issues of power (or lack thereof; → Gender and Discourse). Researchers from the "gender-as-culture perspective" argue that similarities and/or differences found between women's and men's language are a creation of performing gender.

See also: ▶ GENDER AND DISCOURSE
▶ INTERPERSONAL COMMUNICATION, SEX AND GENDER DIFFERENCES IN ▶ LINGUISTICS
▶ RHETORIC AND GENDER

REFERENCES AND SUGGESTED READINGS

Bonvillain, N. (2006). *Women and men: Cultural constructs of gender*, 4th edn. Englewood Cliffs, NJ: Prentice Hall.

Lakoff, R. (2004). *Language and woman's place: Text and commentaries*, rev. edn., ed. M. Bucholtz. Oxford: Oxford University Press.

Wood, J. (2005). *Gendered lives: Communication, gender, and culture*. Belmont, CA: Wadsworth.

Y

Youth Culture

RICHARD KAHN
University of North Dakota

DOUGLAS KELLNER
University of California, Los Angeles

'Childhood' and 'youth' are socially constructed conceptions of age and not biological givens (Ariès 1962). The idea that a transitional period of youth occurs between childhood and adulthood is a relatively recent invention, beginning with Rousseau's novel Émile in mid-eighteenth-century Europe, which celebrated childhood and delineated stages of youth. Generational terms referring to the 'lost generation' of the 1920s, or the 'silent generation' post-World War II (1950s), began emerging in the twentieth century. During the post-World War II period, 'youth culture' was widely used to describe the growing music and rock culture and consumer and fashion styles of the era that quickly mutated into the counterculture of the 1960s.

Since then there has been a flourishing industry in sociology, → cultural studies, and popular media (→ Popular Communication) designing terms like '*baby-boomers*' – those who were born in the mid-1940s and the postwar period and came of age during the affluence of the 1950s and 1960s (Gillon 2004).This generation were the beneficiaries of an unprecedented economic expansion and a highly self-conscious sense of generation, having gone through the turbulent 1960s together and emerged in many cases to prosperity and success in corporate, academic, and political life in the 1970s and beyond.

Theorists in the Centre for Contemporary Cultural Studies in Britain emphasized youth culture's counter-hegemonic and 'generational' qualities and examined the ways in which *working-class youth sub-cultures* resisted subordination through the production of their own culturally subversive styles (Hall & Jefferson 1976). From this perspective, youth of the 1950s celebrated beatniks, teddy boys, and the styles associated with American rhythm and blues music. A decade later, when these became appropriated by the mainstream, 1960s youth turned to the mods on the one hand, and hippy and countercultural styles of sex, drugs, and rock and roll on the other. After the commercialization and appropriation of the counterculture in the 1970s, youth turned to new movements like punk and, with the rise in global popularity of hip-hop culture from the 1980s onward, youth have turned increasingly to more urban and underprivileged "gangsta" styles of violent rap sub-culture (Kellner 1995).

The Concise Encyclopedia of Communication, First Edition. Edited by Wolfgang Donsbach.
© 2015 John Wiley & Sons, Inc. Published 2015 by John Wiley & Sons, Inc.

While there have been attempts to present baby-boomers and 'post-boomers' as coherent generations (Howe & Strauss 1993; 2000), in fact *contemporary youth* embrace a wide array of young people and its youth culture is equally heterogeneous. Post-boomers include those who helped create the Internet and the culture of video-gaming; the latchkey kids who are home alone and the mallrats quaffing fast food in the palaces of consumption; the young activists who helped generate the anti-globalization and emerging peace and antiwar movements; the café slackers, klub kidz, computer nerds, and sales clerks; a generation committed to health, exercise, sustainability, ethical dietary practices, and animal rights, as well as anorexics and bulimics in thrall to the ideals of the beauty and fashion industries. Today's youth also include creators of exciting zines and diverse multimedia such as can be found on sites like MySpace, Facebook, and YouTube; the bike ponies, valley girls, and skinheads; skaters, gangstas, low-riders, riot grrrls, and hip-hoppers; all accompanied by a diverse and heterogeneous grouping of multicultural, racial, and hybridized individuals seeking a viable identity.

Youth sub-cultures can comprise an entire way of life, involving clothes, styles, attitudes, and practices. Youth sub-cultures contain potential spaces of resistance, though these can take various forms ranging from narcissistic and apolitical to anarchist and punk cultures, from environmental and social justice activist cultures promoting progressive vegan lifestyles to right-wing skinheads and Islamic jihadists promoting startlingly reactionary ideas and values.

Today, youth culture is *increasingly global* with the Internet, new media, and social networking transmitting global forms of culture through proliferating channels and media of communication (→ Social Media). Yet one should distinguish between a youth culture produced by youth themselves that articulates their own visions, passions, and anxieties, and media culture produced by adults to be consumed by youth. One also needs to distinguish between youth cultures that are lived and involve immediate, participatory experience as opposed to mediated cultural experience and consumption, and to be aware that youth cultures involve both poles. Moreover, one should resist both reducing youth culture merely to a culture of consumption, or glorifying it as a force of resistance.

See also: ▶ CULTURAL STUDIES ▶ POPULAR COMMUNICATION ▶ SOCIAL MEDIA

REFERENCES AND SUGGESTED READINGS

Ariès, P. (1962). *Centuries of childhood: A social history of family life*. New York: Alfred A. Knopf.

Gillon, S. (2004). *Boomer nation: The largest and richest generation ever, and how it changed America*. New York: Free Press.

Hall, S. & Jefferson, T. (eds.) (1976). *Resistance through rituals: Youth subcultures in post-war Britain*. London: Hutchinson.

Howe, N. & Strauss, W. (1993). *Thirteenth generation: America's thirteenth generation, born 1961–1981*. New York: Vintage.

Howe, N. & Strauss, W. (2000). *Millennials rising: America's next great generation*. New York: Vintage.

Kellner, D. (1995). *Media culture: Cultural studies, identity and politics between the modern and the postmodern*. London: Routledge.

Index

Note: Page numbers in **bold** indicate main articles. A single page range may include more than one article.

accommodation processes **70–71**, 148–149, 274, **275–276**, 586–587
accountability of the media **1–2**, 630
accounting research **2**
acculturation processes **2–3**
action assembly theory **3–4**
addiction to media use 191
advertising 4, **5–7**, **15**, 38, 53, 109, 336, 387, 562
  see also commercialization: impact on media content; marketing
advertising, cross-cultural **7–8**
advertising, economics of **8–9**, 12, 13
advertising, history of 5, **13–14**, 109
advertising, political **458–459**, 471, 473
advertising agencies 5, 13
advertising campaigns **4–5**, 366–367, 392
advertising context 366
advertising effectiveness 5–6, 7–8, **9–12**, 19–20, 49–50, 366, 458
advertising: global industry **12–13**
advertising law and regulations 6, **14–15**, 69, 184, 611
advertising literacy 16
advertising: representation of women 41
advertising: responses across the life-span **15–16**
advertising strategies **16–18**, **124**, 366–367
advocacy journalism **18**, 26, 204
affective disposition theories **18–19**, 191
affects and media exposure **19–20**, 451 see also mood management

affinity seeking **264–265**, 328
Africa **20–22**, 45, **82–83**, 92, 100, 103, 301, 557, 558
age and communication **22–23**, **25–26**, 148–149, 274
age and media use 194, 361, 370–371, **373–374**, 375, 406–407, 472, 474–475, **480**
agenda building **23–24**, 141, 222, 305–306, 600
agenda-setting effects **24–25**, 170, 214, 305–306, 349, 350, 379, 501, 600
age representation in the media 357
Al Jazeera 30, 50, 65, 228, 282
alternative journalism **26–27**, 62, 291, 401
animals 75
anime **27**
anonymity 377, 421
apologia 122
apologising 278
applied communication research **27–29**, 77
appraisal theory **29**
apprehension, communication **71–73**, 329, 445–446, **590–591**
Arab nations **29–31**, 50, **86–87**, 196, 290
Arab satellite TV news **29–31**, 50
archiving of Internet content **31**, 359–360
argument (conflict) see entries beginning conflict
argumentation (debate) 139, **531–533**, 538
arousal **173–174**, **185–186**, 187, 354–355, 394, 460, 565, 571, 642
art as communication **31–33**, 123, 249, 647, 648

Asia **33–35**, 50, 59–60, **83–85**, 91, 228, 290, 557–558
  see also China; India; Japan
attention **35–36**, 110, 166, 186
attitude–behavior consistency **36–37**, 452–453,
  524–525
attitudes **37–38**, 277–278, **326–327**, 345
audience frames 213
audience polarization 40
audience research **38–39**, 109–111, 194, 208, 238, 354,
  373–374, 614
audiences, ethnicity of 41, 181
audiences, female **40–41**, 227
audiences, in communication theory 74–75
audiences as commodities 8–9, 69
audience segmentation **39–40**, 181, 191, 194, 238–239,
  563–564, 599
Australia **41–42**, 315

bad news in medicine, communicating **43–44**
bargaining **398**, 432
BBC **44**, 45, 165, 497, 611, 630–631
BBC World Service **44–45**
behavioral alteration techniques 328–329
behavioral norms: perception through the media **45–46**
bias, researcher 189
bias in the news **47**, 197–198, 301, 362–363, 367–368,
  456, 459 *see also* hostile media phenomenon
Bible, King James 78
bilingualism **46**, 278
blasphemy 84
blogging 292, 624, 654
Bollywood **47–48**, 228
books **48–49**
branding **49**, 109, 124
brands 5, 9, 10, 12, **49–50**, 334–335
broadband services, development and 100
broadcast journalism **50–51**, 314
broadcast talk 30, **51**, 139, 519
bullying 173

cable television **52–53**, 286, 389, 633
campaigns 392, 452, **453–455** *see also* social protest
campaigns, advertising **4–5**, **366–367**
campaigns, development communication 143, **144–145**
campaigns, election **169–171**, 379, 456–457, 458–459,
  471, 473, **609–610**
campaigns, health 97, 100, 145, 197, **238–240**, 241,
  353, 485
Canada 52, **53–54**, 87–88, 91
caricature **54–55**
cartoons 27, 55
CATV (community antenna television) 52
censorship **55–56**, 60, 220–221, 378, 562 *see also*
  freedom of expression; freedom of the press;
  television broadcasting, regulation of

censorship, history of **56–57**, 247, 312–313, 596
change, organizational **57–58**, 293, **426–427**
change, social **97–98**, **142–143**, **144–145**, 440,
  453–455
child pornography 289
children, advertising and 16
children, attention strategies of 36
children, computer games and **104–105**
children, educational media and 163–164, 165–166,
  166–167, 613
children, family communication and 361, 439–440
children, media-induced fear in 200
children, media violence and 105, 353, 643, **644–646**
children: friendship 96
children: media use and child development **104–105**,
  163–164, 165–166, 361, **370–371**, 613
children's television 27, 163–164, 165, 166
China 33, 34, 50, 57, **58–60**, 84–85, 92, 218, 314, 393,
  611, 639
church: censorship 56
cinema 40–41, **60–61**, 220–221, 494, 495, **590**, 639
  see also Bollywood; Hollywood; *and entries*
  beginning film
cinematography **61–62**
citizen journalism 26, **62–63**, 309, 317, 401, 634, 653
civil society, transnational **621–622**
classroom student–teacher interaction **63–64**, 163,
  328–329, 442, **605–606**
class (social), popular communication and **477–478**
climate of opinion **64–65**
CNN **65**, 228, 286
code as law **66–67**, 288–289
code(s) **65–66**, 210, 235 *see also* encoding–decoding
coffee houses 13, 74
cognitive dissonance theory 37, 38, **67**, 191, 392,
  446, 564
cognitive restructuring 72
cognitive science 35–36, **67–68**, 164, 232, 258–259, 349
coherence 156
comedy **577–578** *see also* humor
commercialization: impact on media content 6, 8,
  34–35, **68–69**, 376, 411–412, 523, 571–572, 604
commodification of the media **69–70**, **128–129**, 281,
  283, 466
communication accommodation theory **70–71**,
  148–149, 274, **275–276**, 586–587
communication apprehension **71–73**, 329, 445–446,
  590–591
communication campaigns **4–5**, 143, **144–145**,
  366–367, 392, 452, **453–455** *see also* election
  campaigns; health campaigns; social protest
communication competence 25–26, **95–97**, 162,
  297–298, 375, **601–602**
communication: definitions and concepts **73–75**,
  78–79

communication design (graphic design) 140, **233–234**
communication ethics 1, **179–180**, 316, 365, **533–534**, 589
communication: history of the idea **78–79**, 90–91
communication inequalities **79–80**, 98, 130, **151–152**, 243, **244**, 256, 372, 374–375, 608
communication law **80–82**, **314–316**, 489, 589 *see also entries beginning* regulation of ...
communication law: Africa **82–83**, 557, 558
communication law: Asia 34, 59–60, **83–85**, 557–558
communication law: Europe **85–86**, **183–185**, **215–216**, 289–290, 314–315, 489, 552, 557
communication law: international 282–283
communication law: Middle East **86–87**, 196
communication law: North America 14, **87–88**, **201–202**, 315, 611, 632–633 *see also* Federal Communications Commission (FCC)
communication law: South America **88–89**, 557, 558
communication management **89–90**
communication networks **92–95**, 135, 199–200, 230, 262
communication skills 25–26, **95–97**, 162, 297–298, 375, **601–602**
communication studies 27–28, 74, **76–78**, **90–92**, 182–183, **283–284**, 342–343 *see also* speech communication, history of
communication technology, economics of 101–102, **255–257**
communication technology appropriation 159, 608
communication technology and crime **121–122**
communication technology and democracy **98–99**, **160–161**, 170
communication technology and development **99–101**, 195–196, 290, 391
communication technology and education 162, 163
communication technology standards **101–102**
communication technology and terrorism **618–619**
communication theory 74, 76, 391–392
communicology **102–103**
community media **103**, 253, 389
compensation, in interpersonal communication 187–188, 295
compliance gaining **103–104**, 328–329
computer games 40, **104–105**, 176, 353, 521, 569, 589, **638–639**, 643, 645
computer-mediated communication (CMC) 105–106, 176, 296, **376–377**, 419–420, **444–446**, 568, 583 *see also* digital media; online media
computer technology in education 162, 163, 165–166
computer–user interaction **105–106**, 355, 420, 520
concentration in media systems 86, **106–107**, 348
conflict, intercultural **270–271**
conflict, intergenerational 274
conflict, interpersonal 96, 232, 252, **299–301**, 333–334

conflict, organizational **432–433**
conflict, social **278–279**, **544–545**, 550, **580–581**
conflict: intergroup reconciliation processes **278–279**
conflict: media diplomacy 346
consensus-oriented public relations **107–108**
construction of reality 23–24, **108–109**, **125–126**, 175–176, 197–198, 368, **521–523**
consumer culture **109**
consumer health informatics 242
consumer markets, segmentation of **563–564**, 599
consumers in media markets **109–111**
content analysis, qualitative **111–112**, 112–113, 302, 511
content analysis, quantitative 111–112, **112–113**, 513–514
convergence, media (cross-media production) **124–125**, 170, 279, 418, 596
conversational implicatures 330
conversational skills, aging and 25–26
conversation analysis **113–114**, 157, 323, 515
co-orientation model of public relations **114–115**
copyright **115–116**, **267–268**, 289, 338–339 *see also* open source
corporate communication **116–118**, 122–123, 211–212, 496, 563–564 *see also* organizational communication; public relations
corporate identity 117–118, **118–119**, 230
corporate reputation 117–118, **119–120**, 122, **251**
correlation analysis **120–121**
credibility of journalists 316
crime and communication technology **121–122**
crime: representation in the media 523
crisis communication **122–123**, 251, 346, 508
critical theory **123–124**, 229, 230, 250, 430–431, 436, 481
cross-cultural adaptation 2–3
cross-cultural advertising 7–8
cross-media marketing **124**, 366–367
cross-media production **124–125**, 170, 279, 418, 596
cultivation effects **125–126**, 349, 363, 455, 522, 642
cultural hybridity 133, 229, 231, 281
cultural imperialism **126–128**, 133, 281, 286, 393
cultural products as tradable services 69–70, **128–129**, 281, 283, 466
cultural studies **129–131**, 268, 477–478
cultural voyeurism 181
culture, consumer **109**
culture, nonverbal communication and **413–414**
culture, organizational 173, 222, **433–435**
culture, popular 292, 457, 595–596, 605, **613–614**
culture, taste **605**
culture, visual **648–649**
culture, youth 227, 390–391, 477, **658–659**
culture and communication **128**, **131–132**, 141, **413–414**

culture and media use 371
culture: definitions and concepts 128, 130, **132–133**, 262–263
culture industries 123, **133–134**, 477
cyberfeminism **134–135**, 204
cybernetics **135–136**
cyberterrorism 619

danger control responses 197
data protection 489
deception 75, **137–138**, 296 *see also* propaganda
decision-making **138–139**, 140, 235, **237**, 377, 500–501
defamation 81, 87, 88
deliberative communication **139–140**, 279
delphi studies 140
dementia 26
democracy, communication technology and **98–99**, **160–161**, 170
demoscopy *see* public opinion polling
derogatory speech 483
desacato laws 86, 88, 89
design **140–141**, 233–234, 411, **412–413**
design theory (discourse analysis) 323
determination theory in public relations **141–142**
development, communication technology and 99–101, 195–196, 290, 391
developmental communication **148–150**, 273–274
development communication 99–101, **142–144**, **441–442**, 490
development communication campaigns 143, **144–145**
development communication: journalism **147–148**, 517
development communication: radio 21, 100, 103, **517–518**
development communication: television 21, **612–613**
development discourse **145–146**
development institutions 142, **146–147**
development journalism **147–148**, 517
dialect 324
dialectic 532, **533**, 549
diffusion of information and innovation **150–151**, 195–196, 392, 625
digital divide **151–152**, 243, 256, 372, 374–375, 608
digital imagery 62, **152–153**, 449–450, 590, 648
digital literacy 257
digital media **153–154**, 165, 343, 359–360, 395, 417, 479, 638 *see also* online media
digitizing of communication 75, 339
disability: intergroup relations 482
disability: representation in the media 357
discourse 102, **154–155**
discourse, development **145–146**
discourse, gender and **221–222**, 275
discourse, identities and 23, **250–251**, 324, 430, 470
discourse analysis 111–112, **155–156**, 250, 323, 476, **545–546**

discourse comprehension **156–157**
discursive psychology **157**, **276–277**, 323
discursive turn 222
Disney 127, **157–158**
diversification of media markets **158–159**
domestication of technology **159**, 608

economics, media 109–111, 115, 128–129, 180, 208, **347–349**, 417–418
economics of advertising **8–9**, 12, 13
economics of information and communication technology 101–102, **255–257**
e-democracy **160–161**, 170
educational communication **63–64**, **161–163**, **328–329**, **442**, 578–579, **605–607**
educational media 100, 103, 162, **163–167**, **266–267**, 326, 439–440, 498, 556, **612–613**
e-government 160–161, **167–168**, 170
e-health 106, **242–243**
elaboration likelihood model 15, 37, **168–169**, 447
elderspeak 22–23, 25, 26
election campaigns **169–171**, 379, 456–457, 458–459, 471, 473, **609–610**
election surveys 170, **171–172**, 503
electronic mail **172–173**, 292, 337
electronic news gathering 617
email **172–173**, 292, 337
emoticons 172, 377
emotional arousal theory **173–174**, 185–186, 354–355, 394, 460
emotions 19–20, **173**, 185, 350, 354, 414, 430, 539–540 *see also* mood management
emotions: appraisal theory 29, 185, 350
encoding–decoding 65–66, 75, **174–175**, 382, 475–476, 576 *see also* code(s)
engaged communication scholarship 28
England 54–55, 56–57, 410–411, 596 *see also* UK
entertainment education 517–518
entertainment media **175–176**, 178–179, 191, **264**, 394, 419, 577–578
environmental communication **177–178**
environment and social interaction **176–177**
escapism **178–179**
ethics, rhetoric and **533–534**
ethics in journalism 1, **179–180**, 316, 365, 589
ethics: Internet-related research 609
ethnicity and exposure to communication 181, **182**
ethnicity: representation in the media **356–357**, 655
ethnic media and journalism **180–181**
ethnography of communication 131–132, 175, **182–183**, 250, 323, 367
Europe 85–86, 90–91, 92, 411, 616 *see also* European Union; *and individual countires*
European Union **85–86**, **183–185**, 215–216, 289–290, 489, 557

excitation and arousal 173–174, **185–186**, 187, 354–355, 394, 460, 565, 571, 642
exemplification effects **186–187**, 353
expectancy violation **187–188**, 295, 300
experiments, field **188**, **207**
experiments, laboratory **189–190**, 353–354, 514
experiments, online 421–422
explaining 2
exposure to … *see also entries beginning* media use
exposure to advertising 11, 12, 366
exposure to electronic educational media 165–166
exposure to media 110, 126–127, **190–192**, 354, 361, **371–372**, **383**, 406–407, 474–475 *see also entries beginning* media use
exposure to media, ethnicity and 181, **182**
exposure to online media 419 *see also* exposure to the Internet
exposure to political communication 461, 469, **471–472**, 474–475
exposure to print media **192–193**, 474
exposure to radio **193–194**
exposure to television **125–126**, 182, **194–195**, 372, 373, 374, 390, 474–475, 614
exposure to the Internet across the life-span 374
exposure to the Internet: international variation 54, 59, 87, 88, 89, **195–197**, 216, 226, 253, 290, 326, 372, 389, 553, 631, 633–634
exposure to the Internet: social networks 345 *see also* social media
extended parallel process model **197**
extra-media data **197–198**
eye contact 414

face and facework **270–271**, 457, 568
Facebook **199–200**
face-to-face communication 176–177, 296
facial expression 414
family communication **361–362**, 391, **439–440**, 474
fear, media-induced **200–201**, 239
Federal Communications Commission (FCC) 52, **201–202**, 266, 557, 611, 633
feminist media **204–205**, 655–656
feminist studies 134, **202–204**, 429, 430, **479–480**, 573–574 *see also entries beginning* women; *and entries beginning* gender
feminization of media content **205–206**
fiction **206–207**
field research **188**, **207**
film, fear induced by 200
film, realism in 61, **521**
film, women and 40–41
film genres **207–208**
film industry 344, 404 *see also* Bollywood; cinema; cinematography; Hollywood

film production 60, 61–62, 158–159, **208–210** *see also* Hollywood
film theory **210–211**, 539
financial communication **211–212**
flow theory **212**
fluency, speech 3, 25–26, **593**
focus groups 302
foreign-language journalism **389–390**
framing 170, 177, **212–214**, **215**, 239, 350, 580, **600**
France 13, 50, 54, 56, 81, **215–216**, 281, 289, 596
freedom of expression (freedom of communication) 14, 80–81, 116, **217–218**, 315, 441–442, 557–558, 631 *see also* censorship; freedom of the press; political advertising
freedom of expression: Africa 45, 83
freedom of expression: Asia 34, 254
freedom of expression: Europe 85–86, 215, 217
freedom of expression: North America 14, 80, 87, 88, 217, 247
freedom of expression: South America 89
freedom of information 84, 86, 87, 88–89, **218**
freedom of the press 1, 80–81, 179, 217, **219** *see also* censorship; freedom of expression
freedom of the press: Africa 82, 83
freedom of the press: Asia 84, 254
freedom of the press: Europe 215, 226, 552
freedom of the press: North America 81, 87, 179, 217, 219, 632–633, 652–653
freedom of the press: South America 89
free software **422–423**
free speech *see* freedom of expression
friendship 95–97, 277
functional theory of decision-making 235, **237**

gay, lesbian, bisexual, and transgender media studies **220–221**, 340, 357
gaze behavior 414
gender and discourse **221–222**, 275
gender and journalism 203, 205–206, **222**
gender and rhetoric **534–535**
gender differences in interpersonal communication **298–299**
gender: representation in the media 7, 62, 126, 203, 205–206, 222, **223–225**, **340–341**, 357, 522, 539, **572–574**, **654–656**
gender studies **40–41**, **104–105**, 134, **202–204**, 227, 324, 375 *see also* masculinity and the media; postfeminism; *entries beginning* women; *and entries beginning* feminist
genre(s) 155, **207–208**, **225**
Germany **225–227**, 489, 495, 497
girl culture **227**
GLBT media studies **220–221**, 340, 357
global civil society **621–622**
globality 231

globalization 230, **231–232**, 281, 393, 466
globalization of communication and media studies 92
globalization of the media 109, 158–159, **227–229**, 339, 343–344, 346, 368–369, 395–396, 478, **555–556** *see also* international communication; international television
globalization of organizations **229–231**
global news 402
goals **232–233**, 295–296, 300, 384–385, 398
government *see* democracy, communication technology and; e-government; *and entries beginning* political
graphic design 140, **233–234**
gratifications *see* uses and gratifications
Greek rhetoric 533, **535**, 537, **542–543**
grounded theory **234–235**, 302, 511
group communication **235–237**, 377, 399, **443**, 592
group decision-making **138–139**, 140, 235, **237**, 377, 500–501
group interviews 302
group representations in the media **356–358**, 522, 572–573

hate speech 81, 88, 483
health campaigns 97, 100, 145, 197, **238–240**, 241, 353, 485
health communication 23, 79–80, 97, 100, 188, 197, **240–242**, 568, 626
health communication and the Internet 106, **242–244**
health communication: bad news **43–44**
health communication: prevention **485–486**
health literacy **244**
hermeneutics **245**, 476, 511
heuristic systematic processing model 15
high-context communication 7, 413
historic key events and the media **245–246**
Hogarth, William 55
Hollywood 60, 61, 207–208, 228, **246–248**, 617, 652
homosexuality **220–221**, 340, 357
hostile media phenomenon 47, 362–363, 455, 567
human–computer interaction **105–106**, 355, 420, 520
humor 7–8, 63, 96, 162, 173, 329 *see also* comedy
Hutchins report 179
hypermediacy 530
hypodermic needle theory **596–597**

iconography **249–250**
icons 234, 570
identities and discourse 23, **250–251**, 324, 430, 470
identity, age **22–23**
identity, organizational 117–118, **118–119**, 230
identity (self-concept) **260–261**, 437
image restoration theory **251**
images *see* photography; visual communication; visual representation

imagined interactions **251–253**, 278
immediacy, teacher 63, 328, 607
impression management *see* public relations; self-presentation
India 34–35, **47–48**, 84, 92, 228, **253–254**
inequalities, communication **79–80**, 98, 130, **151–152**, 243, **244**, 256, 372, 374–375, 608
information **254–255**
information, diffusion of **150–151**, 195–196, 392, 625
information, freedom of 84, 86, 87, 88–89, **218**
informational utility 261, **263–264**, 565–566
information and communication technology (ICT) 101–102, **255–257**, 262, 320, **607–609** *see also entries beginning* communication technology
information bureaus 13
information literacy **257–258**, 360
information processing 20, 164, 213, 257, **258–261**, 501, 559
information seeking 241, 243, **261–262**, 627, 628
information society **262–263**, 607
infotainment 175, **264**
ingratiation **264–265**
institutional interactions 114, 324, 516
institutional theory **265–266**
instructional communication **63–64**, **161–163**, **328–329**, **442**, 578–579, **605–607**
instructional television **266–267**, 612–613 *see also* educational media
insult laws 86, 88, 89
integrated marketing communications 5–6, 124, **267**, 335
intellectual property law **115–116**, **267–268**, 289, 338–339
interaction **268–269**
interactivity 75, 239, **269–270**, 291, 355, 419–420, 519
intercultural communication 2–3, 156, 230, **271–273**, 295
intercultural conflict styles **270–271**
intergenerational communication 22–23, 25–26, 148–149, **273–275**
intergroup accommodative processes 274, **275–276**, 586–587
intergroup communication **271–273**, 274, **276–278**, **482–483**
intergroup reconciliation processes **278–279**
intermediality **279–280**
International Association for Media and Communication Research (IAMCR) 91, 92, **280**
International Chamber of Commerce (ICC) 14
international communication **280–282**, 343–344, 345–346, 400 *see also* globalization of the media
international communication agencies **282–283**, 611–612
International Communication Association (ICA) 77, **283–284**

international communication law 282–283
international news reporting 65, 282, **284–285**, 368, 402–403
international radio 44–45, **285**
International Telecommunication Union (ITU) 611–612
international television 228, 254, **285–287**, 346, 494
Internet, citizen journalism and 62
Internet, commodification of 69
Internet, government and 161, **167–168**
Internet, health communication and 106, **242–244**
Internet, history of 154
Internet, language and the **322–323**
Internet, political efficacy and 467
Internet, political knowledge and 469
Internet, political socializing and 474–475
Internet, terrorism and 378
Internet and popular culture **292**
Internet: audience segmentation 40
Internet campaigns (marketing) 337
Internet content, analysis of 113
Internet content, archiving of **31**, 359–360
Internet Corporation for Assigned Names and Numbers (ICANN) 283, 287–288
Internet: digital divide 151–152
Internet exposure: international variation 54, 59, 87, 88, 89, **195–197**, 216, 226, 253, 290, 326, 372, 389, 553, 631, 633–634
Internet exposure: life-span variation 374
Internet exposure: social networks 345
Internet: gendered usage 41
Internet Governance Forum (IGF) 288
Internet law and regulation 59, 66–67, 84–85, 88, 116, 201–202, 281, **287–290**, 569, 608–609
Internet news **290–292**, 301, 474–475
Internet performance (evaluation) 365
Internet protocol television (IPTV) 53
Internet regulation *see* Internet law and regulation
Internet search engines **561–563**, 584
Internet: social media 26, 121, 187, **199–200**, 231, 292, 337, 418, 419–420, **583–585**, **624**, 653–654
Internet use *see* Internet exposure; Internet: gendered usage
interorganizational communication **293–294**
interpersonal attraction 187, **294–295**
interpersonal communication 70–71, 176–177, 187–188, 233, 241, 261, 264–265, **295–297**, 370, 469, **520**, 561 *see also* imagined interactions; listening; nonverbal communication; personal communication by CMC
interpersonal communication, environment and **176–177**
interpersonal communication, uncertainty and 294, 295, **528–529**, **626–629**
interpersonal communication competence 25–26, **95–97**, 162, **297–298**, 375, **601–602**
interpersonal communication: friendship 95–97, 277

interpersonal communication: gender differences **298–299**
interpersonal communication: social support 299, 324, 445–446, **588**, 626
interpersonal conflict 96, 232, 252, **299–301**, **333–334**
interpretation 213–214, **245**, 529–530 *see also* meaning
interpretive journalism **301**
interspecies communication 75
intertextuality **619–620**
interviews, qualitative 111–112, 250, **301–302**, 421, 511
interviews, standardized **303–304** *see also* surveys
intimacy 96, 187–188, 298, 391
investor relations **211–212**
involvement with media content 212, **304–305**, 484
ISOTYPE (International System of Typographic Picture Education) 234
Israel 86, 87
issue management **305–306**
ITERA (Intuitive Thinking in Environmental Risk Appraisal) 29

Japan 27, 50, 234, **307–308**, 315, 557, 640, 656
Johnson, Samuel 13
journalism **308–311** *see also* Internet news; media diplomacy; news
journalism, advocacy **18**, 26, 204
journalism, alternative **26–27**, 62, 291, 401
journalism, broadcast **50–51**, 314
journalism, citizen 26, **62–63**, 309, 317, 401, 634, 653
journalism, development **147–148**, 517
journalism, ethics in 1, **179–180**, 316, 365, 589
journalism, ethnic **180–181**
journalism, foreign-language **389–390**
journalism, gender and 203, 205–206, **222**
journalism, history of 309, **312–314**, 389–390, 397, 407, 604
journalism, interpretive **301**
journalism, minority 180–181, **389–390**
journalism, online 291, 317, **417–418**
journalism, parachute 284
journalism, photo- 449, **450–451**
journalism, political **468**
journalism, political control of 312
journalism, professionalization of 309, 311–312, 313–314, 316, 388, 406, 407, 450, **491–492**
journalism, rooftop 284
journalism, science 177–178, **559–560**
journalism education 309–310, **311–312**
journalism: legal situation **314–316**, 589
journalists, credibility of **316**
journalists, violence against 34, 89, 284, 314–315, 388, **639–640**
journalists' role perception 18, 26, 179–180, **316–318**, 401, 406, 418, 468, 560

knowledge gap 80, 98, **319**, 350, 461, 485
knowledge management **320–321**

language, gender and 221–222
language, rhetoric and **537–538**
language ideologies 387
language and the Internet **322–323**
language and social interaction 25–26, 113–114, **323–325**, 413–414
language learning 46
Latin America **88–89**, 92, 127, **325–326**, 557, 558
 see also Mexico
latitude of acceptance **326–327**
law *see* advertising law and regulations; communication law; intellectual property law; Internet law and regulation; journalism: legal situation; regulation of radio broadcasting; regulation of television broadcasting; regulation of the press
LC4MP (Limited Capacity Model of Motivated Mediated Message Processing) 35–36
leadership in organizations **327–328**
learning 95, **328–329**, **442**, 578–579, 607 *see also* educational communication; educational media
lesbian, gay, bisexual, and transgender media studies **220–221**, 340, 357
libel 81, 88
life-span communication 25–26, **148–149**, 273–274
life-span variations: communication skills 25–26, **95–97**
life-span variations: media use 104–105, 194, 361, 370–371, **373–374**, 375, 406–407, 472, 474–475, **480**
life-span variations: news processing **406–407**
life-span variations: pornography use **480**
life-span variations: response to advertising **15–16**
linguistic intergroup bias 483
linguistic pragmatics **329–330**, 387
linguistics **330–331**, 387, 537, 570
listening **331–332**
local radio 103
logic, rhetoric and **538**
logos (plural of logo) 49
longitudinal analysis **332**, 374, 514
low-context communication 7, 413–414
lying 75, 137, **137–138**, 296 *see also* propaganda

MacBride report 179, 282, 400, 441, 628–629
magazines 53, 59, 192–193, 216, 552
mainstreaming 125–126, 175
manga 27
marital communication 252, 299–300, **333–334**
marketing 49, **334–337**, 562 *see also* advertising
marketing, cross-media 124, 366–367
marketing, political **471**
marketing, social 517, **582–583**
marketing: audience segmentation **563–564**, 599

marketing communications, integrated 5–6, 124, **267**, 335
markets of the media *see* media markets
masculinity and the media 223, 224, **340–341**, 572–573
meaning 104, 245, **341**, 528, 541, 547, 576–577
mean-world syndrome 644–645
measurement theory 36, **341–342**, 529
media **342–343**
media, accountability of the 1–2
media appropriation 159, 608
media characters, relating to 18–19, 278, **438–439**
media conglomerates 59–60, 124, **158–159**, 247, 286, **343–344**, 395 *see also* Disney; News Corporation; Sony Corporation; Time Warner Inc.
media content, quality of 197–198, 243, **364–365**
media content and social networks 345
media convergence (cross-media production) **124–125**, 170, 279, 418, 596
media diplomacy **345–346**
media ecology 182, **346–347**
media economics 109–111, 115, 128–129, 180, 208, **347–349**, 417–418
media effects 29, 139, 170, 174, 191, **200–201**, 304, 316, **349–351**, 365, 501, 539–540, 572, 614
 see also agenda-setting effects; cultivation effects; exemplification effects; framing; media system dependency theory; mood management; reciprocal effects; third-person effects; violence in the media, effects of; public relations: media influence 507
media effects, direct and indirect **351** *see also* two-step flow of communication
media effects, history of 60, 67, 200, **352–353**, **596–597**
media effects, strength of 352, **353–354**, 446–447, 643
media effects: politics 458, 461–462, 467, 610
media effects: stimulus–response model **596–597**
media effects on children *see entries beginning* children
media equation theory **354–355**, 484
media events 350, **355–356**
media and family communication **361–362**, **439–440**
media and group representations **356–358**, 522, 572–573
media and reality perception 45, **125–126**, **175–176**, 349, **362–364**, 623, 655
media fragmentation 599
media functions, in health communication 241
media history **358–360**, 596, 614 *see also* newspapers, history of; printing, history of; public broadcasting, history of; radio: social history; television, social history of
media literacy 162, 225, **360–361**
media markets 34–35, **338–340**, 344, 346–347
media markets, consumers in **109–111**

media markets, diversification of **158–159**
media neutral planning 5–6
media performance **364–366**
media planning **366–367**
media production and content (media sociology) 68–69, 222, **367–369**
media reality 23–24, **108–109, 125–126**, 175–176, 197–198, **521–523**
media studies, history of 74, **90–92**
media studies, rhetoric and **538–540**
media system dependency theory **369–370**
mediated populism 376
mediated rhetoric **538–540**
mediated social interaction 105–106, 296, **376–378**, 419–420, 583
mediated terrorism 246, 351, **378**
mediatization of politics 376, **378–380**, 456–457
media use ... *see also entries beginning* exposure to ...
media use, international comparison of **371–372**
media use, motives for *see* uses and gratifications
media use, personality and 168–169, **446–447**
media use across the life-span 104–105, 194, 361, 370–371, **373–374**, 375, 406–407, 472, 474–475, **480**
media use and child development **104–105**, 163–164, 165–166, 361, **370–371**, 613
media use by social variable 104–105, 192, 194, **374–375**, 474–475, 480
medium theory 74, **380–381**
meeting procedures 236
memory 37, 95, 164, 260, **381–383**, 559, 560–561, 566–567
message discrimination **383–384**
message production 3–4, **25–26**, 232, 295–296, **384–385**, 593
meta-analysis **385–386**
metadiscourse 324, **386–387**
metaphor **387–388**
Mexico 52, **388–389**
microblogging 624
Middle East **29–31**, 50, **86–87**, 196, 290
minority journalism 180–181, **389–390**
mirror neurons 297, 520
miscommunication 75
mobile communication 21–22, 100, 216, **390–391**, 519
models of communication 102, **391–393**
modernity **393**
mood management 19, 174, 178–179, 186, 189, 190, **393–395**, 565
moods 19–20
movies *see* Bollywood; cinema; cinematography; Hollywood; *and entries beginning* film
multilingualism **46**
multitasking 26
MUM effect 43

Murdoch, Rupert 158, 286, 403–404, 630
music industry 193, 285, 289, **395–396, 478–479**, 519

narration and storytelling 2, 138–139, 206, 239, 302, 324, **397–398**, 435, 572, **597**
narrative news story **397–398**
National Communication Association 28
negotiation **398**, 432
netwar 619
network organizations 199–200, 292, **398–399**
networks, communication **92–95**, 135, 199–200, 230, 262
networks, social 241, 292, **345**, 370, 582, 583–584, 588, 654
networks and knowledge management 320
networks of human discourse 102
neutrality 18, 179–180, **399–400**
news 23–24, **124–125**, 127, 141, 170, 177, **215**, 290–292, 356, 367–369, **401–402**, 624, **653–654** *see also* journalism
news, Arab satellite TV **29–31**, 50
news, Internet **290–292**, 301, 474–475
news agencies 59, 284, **402–403**
news and entertainment 175, 264
news and reality **108–109**, 175, 368
news bias **47**, 197–198, 301, 362–363, 367–368, 456, 459 *see also* hostile media phenomenon
News Corporation 42, 158, 286, **403–404**
news cycles **404–405**
news factors **405**, 409–410
news ideologies **406**
newspapers, exposure to 192, 372, 474
newspapers, history of 13, 26, 59, 62, 82, 83, 226, 253, 312–313, 389–390, 397, **410–412**, 488, 552, **604**, 630, 632
newspapers, tabloidization of 376, 412, **604**
newspapers, visual design of 411, **412–413**
newspapers: Asia 59, 253, 307
newspapers: Australia 41–42
newspapers: Europe 216, 226, 552
newspapers: Latin America 325, 388
newspapers: North America 53, 632–633
newspapers: self-regulation 569
newspapers: UK 630
news processing across the life-span **406–407**
news quality 23–24, 68–69, 141, 179–180, 197–198, 291, 316, 364, 404–405, **512–513** *see also* newspapers, tabloidization of
news reporting, international 65, 282, **284–285**, 368, 402–403
news routines 309, **407–408**
news sources 315, 407, **408**
news standards **595–596**
news story **397–398, 408–409**, 409–410, 571–572
news values 23–24, **409–410**, 523

New World Information and Communication Order (NWICO) 80, 127, **400–401**, 628–629
noncommunication 75
nonverbal communication 75, 137, 296, 299, 329, **413–414**, 520, 607
North America **87–88**, 91 *see also* Canada; USA

objectivity (in quantitative research) 514
objectivity (in reporting) 18, 177, 179–180, 301, 313, 317, 400, 401, 407, 409, **415–416**, 595
observation **416–417**, 422, 451, 511, 514
online communities 94, 105–106, 199–200
online games 40, **104–105**, 176, 353, 521, 569, 589, **638–639**, 643, 645
online journalism 291, 317, **417–418**
online media **418–421**, 636
online relationships 96, 445
online research 113, **421–422**
open source **422–423**
operationalization 303, **423–424**
opinion leaders 350, 352, **424–425**, 624–625
oral communication 73, 542
organizational change processes 57–58, 293, **426–427**
organizational communication 57–58, 89–90, **116–118**, 122–123, 172, 229–230, 295, 327–328, 398–399, **427–429**, 496, 568, 582, 598–599 *see also* financial communication; interorganizational communication; public relations
organizational communication, postmodern approaches **431–432**
organizational communication: critical approaches 428–429, **430–431**
organizational communication: emotion 173
organizational conflict **432–433**
organizational culture 173, 222, **433–435**
organizational identity 117–118, **118–119**, 230
organizational image 117–119, 122, **251**, **435–436**
organization–public relationships **425–426**
organizations, cultural diversity in **436–437**
organizations, leadership in **327–328**
organizations, globalization of **229–231**
organizations: issue management 305

parasocial interactions and relationships 18–19, 278, **438–439**
parental mediation strategies 361, **439–440**, 474
participation 63, 98–99, **160–161**
participatory action research **440**, 510
participatory communication 103, 142, 291, **441–442**, 653 *see also* citizen journalism
participatory research 97, **440**, 510
pedagogy 63–64, **161–163**, 328–329, **442–443**, 605–607
perceived reality: effect of group participation 443
perceived reality: effect of media 45, **125–126**, 175–176, 349, 362–364, 623, 655

perceived reality: effect of rhetoric 537
perception 45, 47, 352, **443–444**, 446, **566–567**
perception, social 349–350, 443, 444, 455, **585–586**
personal communication by CMC 105–106, 296, **376–377**, 419–420, **444–446**, 583
personality 168–169, **446–447**, 563, **571**, 586
persuasion 103–104, 181, 387, **447–448**, 452 *see also* campaigns; *and entries beginning* rhetoric
persuasion, advertising as 15
persuasion, political **472–474**
persuasion, teacher 63–64, **606–607**
persuasion: elaboration likelihood model 15, 37, **168–169**, 447
persuasion model: public relations 504
phenomenology **448–449**, 476, 540
photography 61, 66, 152–153, 206, **449–450**, 493–494, **521**, 646
photojournalism 449, **450–451**
physiological measurement 451
place, effect on social interaction **176–177**
planned behavior, theory of **452–453**, 525
planned social change 143, 144–145, **453–455**
pluralistic ignorance 362, **455–456**
politainment **456–457**
politeness theories 323, **457–458**, 568
political advertising **458–459**, 471, 473
political cognitions **459–460**, 610
political communication 139, **160–161**, **169–170**, 264, 345, 365, **378–380**, 456–457, **460–463**, 541, 545, 584
political communication systems 379, **463–465**
political debates, televised **609–610**
political economy of the media **465–466**
political efficacy **467–468**
political journalists 468
political knowledge 345, 459–460, 467, **469–470**
political language 470
political marketing 471
political media use 461, 469, **471–472**, 474–475
political persuasion **472–474**
political socialization **474–475**
politics, rhetoric and **541–542**
politics: issue management **305–306**
popular communication **475–478**, 573, 613–614
popular culture 292, 457, 595–596, 605, **613–614**
popular music 193, 285, 289, **395–396**, **478–479**, 519
populism, mediated 376
pornography 289, 351, 375, **479–480**
postfeminism 224, **480–481**
postmodernism 208, 310, 429, 430, **431–432**, **481–482**
power in intergroup settings 70, 272, **482–483**
PRCA-24 (Personal Report of Communication Apprehension) 73
preaching 547
prejudiced communication 22–23, **483–484**

presence **484**
press freedom *see* freedom of the press
press regulation 84, **569**, 630 *see also* freedom of the press
prevention and communication **485–486**, 571
priming theory 447, 452, **486–487**, 610, 642, 644
printing, history of 56, 74, 82, 115, 217, 309, **487–488**, 596
print media 165, 215, 216, 359, 493 *see also* books; magazines; *entries beginning* newspapers
print media, exposure to **192–193**, 474
privacy 81, **489**, 584, 631
privatization of the media **489–491**
professionalization of journalism 309, 311–312, 313–314, 316, 388, 406, 407, 450, **491–492**
propaganda 91, 280, **492–493**, 518–519, 619
propaganda, visual communication of **493–494**
propaganda, war 492, 493, **494–496**, **651–652**
protests **544–545**, 581, 584
pseudo events 350, **355–356**
psychoanalytic criticism 540
psychophysiology **451**
public affairs **496**
public broadcasting, history of 50, **496–498**, 518
public broadcasting systems 44, 53–54, 165, 184, 226, 308, 490, **498–500**, 615–616, 630–631
public opinion 64, 302, 313, 359, 363, 455, **500–502**, 593–594, 625
public opinion polling 170, **171–172**, **502–503**
public relations 116, 211, 251, 336, 355, **425–426**, 496, **503–505**, 584 *see also* strategic communication
public relations, consensus-oriented **107–108**
public relations, co-orientation model of **114–115**
public relations, determination theory in **141–142**
public relations: crisis communication **122–123**, 251, 346, 508
public relations evaluation **505–507**
public relations: media influence 507
public relations planning **507–509**
public service broadcasting *see* public broadcasting, history of; public broadcasting systems
public speaking 72, 73, 535–536, 545, 546, 591
public sphere 26, 123, 313, 343, 344, 359, 410–411, 461, **509**
public trust 316, **622–623**
publishing, book 48

qualitative methodology 111–112, **155–156**, **234–235**, 506, **510–512**
quality of the news 23–24, 68–69, 141, 179–180, 197–198, 291, 316, 364, 404–405, **512–513** *see also* tabloidization
quantitative methodology 120–121, 506, **513–515**
queer media 220–221
questionnaires *see* surveys
questions and questioning 303–304, **515–516**

race, representations of 573, 655
race, rhetoric and **543**, 545–546
racism 276
radio, educational 165
radio, exposure to **193–194**
radio, international 44–45, **285**
radio, local 103
radio broadcasting, regulation of 201, 283, 633
radio broadcasting: Africa 21, 83
radio broadcasting: Asia 59, 253
radio broadcasting: Australia 42
radio broadcasting: Europe 216, 552
radio broadcasting: Latin America 325, 389
radio broadcasting: North America 53, 54, 633
radio broadcasting: UK 630–631
radio for development 21, 100, 103, **517–518**
radio: minority journalism 390
radio music 193, 519
radio: social history 390, **518–520**
rapport **520**
reading 192
realism in film and photography 61, **521**
reality, media 23–24, **108–109**, **125–126**, 175–176, 197–198, **521–523**
reality, relational dialectics and 528
reality perception: effect of group participation **443**
reality perception: effect of media 45, **125–126**, 175–176, 349, **362–364**, 623, 655
reality perception: effect of rhetoric 537
reality TV 521, **523–524**
reasoned action, theory of 452, **524–525**
reciprocal effects 198, **525–526**
reciprocity, in interpersonal communication 187, 295
reconciliation, intergroup **278–279**
regression analysis **526–527**
regulation of advertising 6, **14–15**, 69, 184, 611
regulation of the Internet 59, 66–67, 84–85, 87, 88, 116, 201–202, 281, **287–290**, 569, 608–609
regulation of the media, self- 1, **569**
regulation of the press 84, **569**, 630 *see also* freedom of the press
regulation of radio broadcasting 201, 283, 633
regulation of satellite communication **557–558**
regulation of television broadcasting 42, 52–53, 59, 184, 201–202, 215–216, 253, 552, **611–612**, 630–631, 633
relational communication 252, 299–300, **333–334**, **361–362**, 391, 527, 529, 582 *see also* family communication; interpersonal communication
relational communication in groups 236
relational control **527–528**
relational dialectics 296, **528**
relational maintenance behaviors 299
relational perspective in teaching 63, 162
relational uncertainty **528–529**

relationship development 296
reliability (research) 303, 514–515, **529–530**
religion and the media 325–326
religion: blasphemy laws 84
religious communication 493, 547
religious hatred 81
religious texts 74
remediation 279, **530–531**
reputation 117–118, **119–120**, 122, **251**
research methods for social change **97–98**
resonance (cultivation theory) 125–126
response rates **531**
rhetoric, argument, and persuasion **531–533**
rhetoric, Greek 533, **535**, 537
rhetoric, pre-Socratic **542–543**
rhetoric, Roman **543–544**, 546
rhetorical analysis 476
rhetorical criticism **545–546**
rhetorical model of public relations 505
rhetorical perspective in teaching 63, 162
rhetorical questions 515
rhetorical studies **546–548**, 591–592
rhetoric and dialectic **533**, 549
rhetoric and ethics **533–534**
rhetoric and gender **534–535**
rhetoric and history **535–536**, 541
rhetoric and language **537–538**
rhetoric and logic **538**
rhetoric and media studies **538–540**
rhetoric and politics **541–542**
rhetoric and race **543**, 545–546
rhetoric and social protest **544–545**
rhetorics, new **548–550**
right of reply 86–87
right to information 84, 86, 87, 88–89, **218**
risk communication 177–178, 349, **550**, 600
risk perceptions 197, 363, **550–552**
Roman rhetoric **543–544**, 546
Russia 57, **552–553**

sampling procedures 235, 421, 503, 512, 514, **554–555**, 603
satellite communication, global **555–556**
satellite communication, regulation of **557–558**
satellite television 29–30, 52, 285–286, 404, 494, 556, **558–559**, 612–613, 633
schemas **559**, 560–561 *see also* stereotyping
science journalism 177–178, **559–560**
scripts 295–296, **560–561**
search engines **561–563**, 584
secrecy 56
segmentation, audience **39–40**, 181, 191, 194, 238–239, **563–564**, 599
selective exposure 67, 190, 194, 263, 352, 446, **564–566**

selective perception and retention 47, 352, 446, **566–567**
self-concept **260–261**, 271–272
self-disclosure 96, 162, 274, 277, 298, 377, 584
self-presentation **22–23**, 264–265, 324, 328, 377, **567–569**, 584
self-regulation of advertising 6, 14
self-regulation of the media 1, **569**
self-stereotyping 587
Semantic Structure and Content Analysis 113
semiotics 65–66, 102, 476, 537, **569–570**, 649
sensationalism **571–572**
sensation seeking 194, **571**
September 11 terrorist attacks 246
Sesame Street TV series 163–164
sexism in the media 205–206, 224, **573–574**
sex roles, cross-cultural differences 7
sex role stereotypes in the media 7, 126, 203, 205–206, 222, 223–224, 340, 353, 357, 439, 440, 522, **572–574**, 641, **654–656**
sexual minorities **220–221**, 340, 357
sexual violence in the media **575–576**
shield laws (source protection) 88, 315, **589–590**
sign(s) 65, 66, **576–577** *see also* semiotics
silence 414
singing 71
situation comedies **577–578**
soap operas 40
social anxiety **71–73**, 329, 445–446, **590–591**
social change **97–98**, **142–143**, **144–145**, 440, **453–455**
social class, popular communication and **477–478**
social cognitive theory 191, 375, **578–579**
social-communicative anxiety **71–73**, 329, 445–446, **590–591**
social comparison theory 443, **579–580**
social conflict **278–279**, **544–545**, 550, **580–581**
social exchange 294, 296, **581–582**
social interaction 70–71, 176–177, 187–188, 233, 241, 261, 264–265, **295–297**, 370, 469, **520**, 561
 see also imagined interactions; listening; nonverbal communication
social interaction, environment and **176–177**
social interaction, language and 25–26, 113–114, **323–325**, 413–414
social interaction, mediated 105–106, 296, **376–378**, 419–420, 583
social interaction, uncertainty and 294, 295, **528–529**, **626–629**
social interaction: communication competence 25–26, **95–97**, 162, **297–298**, 375, **601–602**
social interaction: friendship 95–97, 277
social interaction: gender differences **298–299**
social learning theory 642–643
social marketing 517, **582–583**

social media 26, 121, 187, **199–200**, 231, 292, 337, 418, 419–420, **583–585**, **624**, 653–654
social perception 349–350, 443, 444, 455, **585–586**
social protest **544–545**, 581, 584
social responsibility (of the media) 1
social role theory 299
social skills **297–298**
social stereotyping and communication 22–23, 25, 148–149, 274, 276, 377, 482, **483–484**, **586–587**
social stereotyping in the media **356–358**, 522, 572–573
social support in interpersonal communication 299, 324, 445–446, **588**, 626
socio-emotional selectivity theory 274
Sony Corporation 286, 395, **588–589**
source protection 88, 315, **589–590**
South America **88–89**, 92, 127, **325–326**, 557, 558 *see also* Mexico
special effects **590**
spectacularization of politics 379
speech accommodation theory *see* communication accommodation theory
speech acts 156
speech act theory 323, 329–330
speech analysis **113–114**, 157, 323, 515
speech anxiety 71–73, **590–591**
speech communication, history of 161–162, 535–536, 542, **591–593**
speech complementarity 70
speech fluency and speech errors 3, 25–26, **593**
speech maintenance 70
spiral of silence 64, 350, 351, 363, 455, 456, 502, **593–594**
sports and the media **594–595**
stage fright (speech anxiety) 71–73, **590–591**
standards, communication technology **101–102**
standards, news **595–596**
stereotypes in the media: sex roles 7, 126, 203, 205–206, 222, 223–224, 340, 353, 357, 439, 440, 522, **572–574**, 641, **654–656**
stereotypes in the media: social **356–358**, 522, 572–573
stereotyping, self- 587
stereotyping and communication, social 22–23, 25, 148–149, 274, 276, 377, 482, **483–484**, **586–587**
stimulus–response model **596–597**
storytelling and narration 2, 138–139, 206, 239, 302, 324, **397–398**, 435, 572, **597**
strategic communication 57–58, 355, 378, 453–454, 508, 584, **597–600** *see also* election campaigns; health campaigns; public relations
strategic framing 212–214, 215, **600**
structuralism **600–601**
student communication competence **601–602**
student–teacher interaction **63–64**, 163, 328–329, 442, **605–606**
subcultures 133

supportive communication 299, 324, 445–446, **588**, 626
surveys 140, 239, 303–304, 421, **502–503**, 513, **602–603**
surveys, election 170, **171–172**, 503
surveys: response rates 531
symbols and symbolization 235–236, 578–579
syndicated audience research 39

tabloidization 376, 412, **604–605**
talk shows 30, **51**, 139, 519
taste culture **605**
teaching **63–64**, **161–163**, **328–329**, **442**, **605–607**
technology and communication 184, 398–399, **607–609** *see also entries beginning* communication technology
televised debates **609–610**
television, children's 27, 163–164, 165, 166
television, effects of **125–126**, 166, 200–201, 379, 439–440, 474, 539–540, **642–643**
television, exposure to **125–126**, 182, **194–195**, 372, 373, 374, 390, 474–475, 614
television, instructional **266–267**, 612–613 *see also* educational media
television, international 228, 254, **285–287**, 346, 494
television, masculinity and **340–341**
television, reality 521, **523–524**
television, satellite 29–30, 52, 285–286, 404, 494, 556, **558–559**, 612–613, 633
television, social history of **615–616**
television, visual characteristics of **617–618**
television and politics 379, 474, **609–610**
television as popular culture 457, 595–596, **613–614**
television broadcasting, regulation of 42, 52–53, 59, 184, 201–202, 215–216, 253, 552, **611–612**, 630–631, 633
television broadcasting: Africa 21, 22
television broadcasting: Asia 58, 59, 253, 308
television broadcasting: Australia 42
television broadcasting: Europe 552–553
television broadcasting: France 215–216
television broadcasting: Latin America 325–326, 388–389
television broadcasting: North America 53–54, 633
television broadcasting: UK 630–631
television characters, relating to 18–19, 278, **438–439**
television for development 21, **612–613**
television: minority journalism 390
television violence **640–642**, 643
terrorism 246, 351, **378**, 492, **618–619**, 652
texts 155, 541, **619–620**
textual analysis **111–113**, 302, 511, 513–514
textual reproduction, organizational culture as 435
Theory of Motivated Information Management (TMIM) 627
theory of planned behavior **452–453**, 525

theory of reasoned action 452, **524–525**
third-person effects 349–350, 362, 363, 455, **620–621**
Time Warner Inc. 395, **621**
transmission belt theory **596–597**
transnational civil society **621–622**
transnational media *see* globalization of the media; international communication
transparency (corporate communication) 117–118
transparency (remediation strategy) 530
trust 121, 316, **622–623**
truth 179–180, 251, 316, 409, **623**
turn-taking 414
Twitter **624**, 653, 654
two-step flow of communication 74, 345, 352, 392, **624–625**

UK: caricature 54–55
UK: history of censorship 56–57
UK: history of communication and media studies 91–92
ukiyo-e movement 234
UK: media system 44, 50, 313, 410–411, 412, 497, 611, **630–631**
UK: television violence 640, 641
uncertainty, relational **528–529**
uncertainty and communication **626–627**
uncertainty management 626, **627–628**
uncertainty reduction theory 294, 295, **628–629**
UNESCO 80, 91, 127, 280, 400, 441, 612, **629–630**
United Nations 288, 289, **631–632** *see also* UNESCO
United Nations communication agencies 283
USA: cultural imperialism 127
USA: economics of ICTs 256
USA: ethnic media 181
USA: freedom of the press 81, 87, 179, 217, **219**, 632–633, 652–653
USA: free speech 14, 80, 81, 87, 88, **217**, 219, 247
USA: history of communication and media studies 91
USA: Hollywood 60, 61, 207–208, 228, **246–248**, 617, 652
USA: journalism 50, 313, 315, 317, 415–416
USA: law and regulation 14, **87–88**, **201–202**, 315, 611, 632–633 *see also* Federal Communications Commission (FCC)
USA: media and group representations **356–358**
USA: media system 52–53, 497, 498, 615, **632–634**
USA: newspapers 411–412, 632–633
USA: privacy rights 489
USA: privatization of the media 490

USA: television violence 640–641
USA: video games 104
USA: Watergate scandal **652–653**
uses and gratifications 75, 105, 175, 178–179, 190, 191, 193, 194–195, 247, 263, 286, 304, **373–374**, 375, 392, 445–446, 614, **634–636** *see also* mood management; selective exposure

validity (research) 303, 511, 514, **637–638**
video games 40, **104–105**, 176, 353, 521, 569, 589, **638–639**, 643, 645
violence against journalists 34, 89, 284, 314–315, 388, **639–640**
violence in the media 126, 522–523, 527, **640–642**
violence in the media, effects of 105, 126, 185, 259, 351, 353, 447, **642–644**
violence in the media, effects on children 105, 353, 643, **644–646**
violence in the media, sexual **575–576**
visual communication 113, 140, 152–153, 249, 354–355, 388, **493–494**, 539–540, 610, **617–618**, **646–648** *see also* photography
visual culture **648–649**
visual design of newspapers 411, 412–413
visual representation **617–618**, 647, 648, **649–650**
VNS Matrix 134

Walt Disney Company 127, **157–158**
Warner Brothers *see* Time Warner Inc.
war propaganda 492, 493, **494–496**, **651–652**
Watergate scandal **652–653**
Web 2.0 239, 291, 419, **653–654**
web archiving **31**, 359–360
weblogging (blogging, microblogging) 292, 624, 654
WikiLeaks 315
women and language **221–222**, 275, **534–535**, **656–657**
women and media use **40–41**, 100–101, 196, 394
women in media organizations 222, 574
women in the media, images of 7, 62, 126, 203, 205–206, 222, **223–225**, 357, 522, 539, **572–574**, **654–656**
written communication 73–74

Xinhua 59

youth culture 227, 390–391, 477, **658–659**

zone of indifference 327